A Dictionary of
SPORTING ARTISTS
1650-1990

A Dictionary of
SPORTING ARTISTS
1650-1990

Mary Ann Wingfield

Antique Collectors' Club

Published for the Antique Collectors' Club
by the Antique Collectors' Club Ltd.

British Library CIP Data
A catalogue record for this book is
available from the Brtitish Library.

Printed in England by the Antique Collectors' Club Ltd.,
Woodbridge, Suffolk, England

THE ANTIQUE COLLECTORS' CLUB

The Antique Collectors' Club was formed in 1966 and now has a five figure membership spread throughout the world. It publishes the only independently run monthly antiques magazine *Antique Collecting* which caters for those collectors who are interested in widening their knowledge of antiques, both by greater awareness of quality and by discussion of the factors which influence the price that is likely to be asked. The Antique Collectors' Club pioneered the provision of information on prices for collectors and the magazine still leads in the provision of detailed articles on a variety of subjects.

It was in response to the enormous demand for information on ''what to pay'' that the price guide series was introduced in 1968 with the first edition of *The Price Guide to Antique Furniture* (completely revised, 1978 and 1989), a book which broke new ground by illustrating the more common types of antique furniture, the sort that collectors could buy in shops and at auctions rather than the rare museum pieces which had previously been used (and still to a large extent are used) to make up the limited amount of illustrations in books published by commercial publishers. Many other price guides have followed, all copiously illustrated, and greatly appreciated by collectors for the valuable information they contain, quite apart from prices. The Antique Collectors' Club also publishes other books on antiques, including horology and art reference works, and a full book list is available.

Club membership, which is open to all collectors, costs £17.50 per annum. Members receive free of charge *Antique Collecting*, the Club's magazine (published ten times a year), which contains well-illustrated articles dealing with the practical aspects of collecting not normally dealt with by magazines. Prices, features of value, investment potential, fakes and forgeries are all given prominence in the magazine.

Among other facilities available to members are private buying and selling facilities, the longest list of ''For Sales'' of any antiques magazine, an annual ceramics conference and the opportunity to meet other collectors at their local antique collectors' clubs. There are over eighty in Britain and more than a dozen overseas. Members may also buy the Club's publications at special pre-publication prices.

As its motto implies, the Club is an amateur organisation designed to help collectors get the most out of their hobby: it is informal and friendly and gives enormous enjoyment to all concerned.

For Collectors — By Collectors — About Collecting

The Antique Collectors' Club, 5 Church Street, Woodbridge, Suffolk

SPORTING ART SERIES

This *Dictionary* is part of a series of major reference books by Mary Ann
Wingfield in which the depiction of sports and games by contemporary
artists, starting in the seventeenth century, is brilliantly recorded.
7,000 artists, both celebrated and obscure, are detailed.

To appreciate the art illustrating a particular sport, its historical background
is important. The *Dictionary of Sporting Artists* therefore
is best used in conjunction with its companion volumes
describing and illustrating the sport itself.

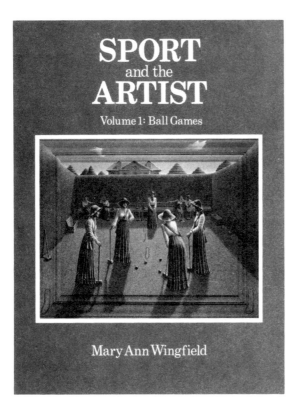

Volume I: Ball Games

Published in 1988, this book was the first in the
series. The 360 pages contain a wealth of
information on the origins and histories of
individual ball games, including cricket, tennis,
golf, bowls, croquet, badminton, football, polo,
snooker, etc. The social attitudes to particular
sports are also discussed, thus providing the
context in which artists work, while the art
associated with each sport is described and
illustrated in 274 black and white and 75 colour
illustrations.

Volume 2: Horse Racing

To be published in 1993, this depicts the story of the sport of kings, the racecourses and the
characters who organised and frequented them. This readable, accurate history of horse racing is
comprehensively illustrated with paintings and drawings, many of which can be dated by studying
the dress and equipment portrayed. It will be approximately 250 pages and contain 190 black and
white and 32 colour illustrations.

This series of art reference books will be enjoyed by sportsmen and sporting art collectors alike.

Contents

INTRODUCTION

A Dictionary of Sporting Artists is meant in this instance to give the collector some idea of those artists who have painted at least one good painting of a sport during their career. There are a few artists who devoted their life's work to the subject. There are many more who painted one or two sporting examples and would not consider themselves, nor wish others to think of them, as sporting artists.

The subject is confining and yet paradoxically wide with over two hundred actively played sports throughout its history. What is sometimes referred to by traditionalists as the British School of Sporting Painters is also misleading since there is not and never was a School of sporting painters. A School implies a style of painting, as in Cubism, and it has never been a defined style that unites these artists, but the subject. The most successful paintings of sport were, and still are, undertaken by artists who thoroughly understand their sport. In the majority of cases the artist is, or has been, an active participator. Occasionally a successful sports painting has been achieved by an artist with an apparently minimal interest in the subject - but as often as not the sport has been implied rather than stated, as in W.P. Frith's "Derby Day" or William Holyoake's "Keen Spectators at the Boat Race".

There have been four grey areas to contend with in compiling this Dictionary. Firstly, were paintings of what were clearly fringe subjects - dead game, grouse, pheasants, etc. - to be included? Were indeed painters of game birds, game dogs, poachers and gamekeepers to be included? Secondly, were foreign artists to be included if their contribution to English sports paintings had been considerable? Thirdly, did a human speck in an extensive landscape really constitute a fishing or shooting painting? Fourthly, should artists of wildly inaccurate and absurdly romantic paintings of sport be included or would the problem that beset the organisers of the Football Exhibition in 1953 occur? "It [the exhibition] irritated those that knew about the sport and failed to please those that knew about art."

In order to resolve these grey areas I have used the best guidelines possible, namely my own. I have not, in general, included "specks" in the Dictionary, nor have I included the numerous Victorian dead and live game artists unless of course their work included at least one active sporting scene. Artists who confined their work to studies of game dogs, although loosely connected with sport, I have again in general omitted since I felt they might be more accurately classified under the heading of animal painters which is not necessarily the same thing as sport. As to foreign artists, I have again used my discretion. If the artist worked in Britain in a sporting capacity at any time during his or her career then he or she is automatically included. If he or she did not, but his or her work is represented in this country or if, as in the case of skiing, the sport for the most part takes place abroad, then the artists who best depicted that subject are included, whatever their nationality. It is obviously logical that as sports are now international then so too are the artists. I have included all painters of sport whether their paintings are wildly inaccurate and absurdly romantic conceptions or not. To have left them out would have been to tell only one part of the story. Where appropriate, though, I have gently exposed the inaccuracies, hopefully to both the credit of the sport and its art.

Undoubtedly in a book of this size there will be errors and some omissions, especially amongst contemporary sporting artists who feel that they should have been included. I hope that I may be allowed to rectify any errors in the next edition, if they are pointed out, and include omissions, bearing in mind that this is not a Dictionary confined to contemporary sporting painters. It is, I hope, a balanced, historical and alphabetical record of painters of sports throughout the last three hundred years which includes some contemporary artists who specialise in the newer sports.

If you have as much fun using the dictionary as I have had in compiling it, then my work will have been rewarded.

Acknowledgements

A book of this complexity could never have been undertaken without the unstinting help and encouragement of a great number of people. In particular I should like to thank all art galleries and auction houses who have kindly contributed material. I should also like to extend a special word of thanks to my tireless secretary, Lois Glass, to Greg Way for his help with reference books, to Margie Christian of Christie's and to John Biggs of J. Collins, Bideford, Malcolm Fare of *The Sword* magazine and Richard Wheatland of The Guild of Motoring Artists for their patient help with research.

I should also like to thank Diana Steel of the Antique Collectors' Club who commissioned the *Dictionary*.

I compiled a great deal of this *Dictionary* in spare moments while travelling around Britain selling our sporting pictures and, besides the conventional thanks to museums and art galleries, I must also thank the great number of long-suffering husbands (my own included), lovers or landlords who toiled up and down the stairs of numerous bed and breakfast establishments all over Britain carrying back-breaking boxes of reference books which accompanied me everywhere for over two years. They willingly and patiently undertook this onerous task for the sake of the *Dictionary*. Even when I successfully fused the whole of one dairy farmer's electrical circuit in the middle of the night – when my bedside lamp, perched precariously on a pile of books, inevitably fell to the ground and plunged us into darkness – nobody ever complained. It's all in a good cause, they said. Well, I hope it is, for their sakes as much as for everybody else's.

A

A.T.
"Girl with Shuttlecock" signed with mono. and dated 1902. Watercolour 15in.x10¼in. Chris Beetles Ltd., St. James, London W1.

Abbott, Lemuel Francis, RA (1760-1803)
Distinguished portrait painter included in this Dictionary for his portraits of the golfers William Innes and Henry Callender and for the fact that the sporting artist Ben Marshall (q.v.) studied under him for three years from 1791. "A Portrait of William Innes" (1719-1795), Captain of the Society of Golfers at Blackheath Golf Club in 1778 (Royal Blackheath Golf Club Collection). The uncoloured mezzotint by Valentine Green (1739-1813) after Abbott's work 25¼in.x16¾in. (cut impression) pub. by the artist 1790 is in the British Museum, London. The original oil painting is thought to have been destroyed by Indian Mutineers in Lucknow on 30 May 1857. William Innes was a previous Captain of the Royal Blackheath Golf Club and a friend of Henry Callender, whose portrait by Abbott is in the Club's collection, inscr. "To the Society of Golfers at Blackheath". The mezzotint by William Ward (1762-1826) 25½in.x16¾in. pub. by the engraver (1812), British Museum, London. Henry Callender was secretary, then Captain of the Royal Blackheath Golf Club in 1790, 1801 and 1807. The medal and epaulette are badges of office gained when he became the Club's first Captain General in 1808.

Abbott, Richmond (op.1861-1924)
Liverpool painter of animal subjects who exh. BI and SS (1861-1866).

Absolon, John, RI, ROI (1815-1895)
Fine watercolour artist, included in this Dictionary for his illustrations to the 1844 edn. of "The Compleat Angler" (Walton) and for his exhibited work at the BI in 1836 "The Wild Boar Hunter".

Adam, Albrecht Friedrich Christopher (1786-1862)
Military, battle and equestrian painter whose work includes a number of hunting scenes.

Adam, Benno (1873-1936)
Member of a famous German family of equestrian painters whose work includes a number of hunting and racing scenes painted in England at the turn of the century.

Adam, Benno Rafael (1812-1892)
Son of Albrecht Adam (q.v.) and member of a famous German family of equestrian painters. Known as "the German Landseer", Adam's work includes a higher percentage of domestic animals than it does horses, but he painted a few hunting scenes and was father of the better known equestrian artist Emil Adam (q.v.).

Adam, Emil (1843-1924)
Member of a famous German family of equestrian painters who settled in England in 1885 and became the leading racehorse painter of his day. His patrons included the Prince of Wales, the Dukes of Westminster and Portland and the Empress of Austria, an outstanding horsewoman of the 1870s who hunted in England and Ireland. English racehorses painted by Adam include "Persimmon", "La Flèche", "Ormonde", "Diamond Jubilee", "Spearmint", "Isinglass", "St. Amant", "Lonely", "Flying Fox", "Roxanne", "Cherry Lass" (see also Fernandez), "Mulberry" and "Ladas". Adam is also responsible for one cartoon of the steeplechase horse "Luttuer III" contributed to "Vanity Fair" in 1909. A number of his racehorse portraits are in the collection of the Jockey Club, Newmarket.

Adam, Victor (1801-1866)
Paris-born equestrian artist, the son of the engraver Jean Adam. Victor Adam studied at the Ecole des Beaux Arts (1814-1818) and under Charles Meynier (1768-1832) and Jean Baptiste Regnault (1754-1829). Although Adam is probably better known for his battle scenes he also painted a large number of sporting and English racing scenes including "The Derby" in 1838 featuring the winner "Amato".

Adams, Harry William, RBA (1868-1947)
Worcester landscape, fishing and equestrian painter. Worked for eight years as a decorative artist at the Royal Worcester Porcelain Factory before studying art at Julians, Paris (1895/6). Exh. at the RA from 1896. Elected RBA (1912). This artist, who operated from the same address in Surrey as the landscape painter John Clayton Adams (1840-1906), became President of the Birmingham Art Circle and examples of his work are in the Tate Gallery Collection.

Adams, Henry Clayton (exh.1906-1908)
This artist operated from the same address in Surrey as the landscape painter John Clayton Adams (1840-1906). His work includes a number of equestrian portraits of hunters.

Adams, W. Douglas (1853-1920)
Landscape and wildfowl painter who also included

fishing, shooting, golf and hare-coursing scenes amongst his work. Illus. A.E. Gathorne Hardy's "The Salmon" (pub. 1898). Exh. eight paintings at the RA including "Return of the Stalker" (1900) and "Straight for the Guns", and six at SS including "Sport in the Highlands" (1882). His three known coursing scenes include "The Slip", "The Turn" and "The Kill" s.&d. 1894. His golfing scenes "The Drive" and "The Putting Green" were engraved and pub. by Henry Graves, 15 May 1894. He is almost certainly an underrated artist and deserves to be better known.

Adamson, Dorothy, RI, ROI (1893-1934)
Animal painter who studied under Lucy Kemp Welch (q.v.) (1913-1915), becoming one of her most promising pupils. She specialised in game dog studies exhibiting widely from 1915 until her early death at the age of forty-one. Elected RI and ROI (1929).

Addenbrooke, Miss Rosa (op.1891-1892)
Salisbury painter of freshwater fish subjects. Exh. one picture at the RA (1891) and one at SS (1892).

Addison, V.S. (op. late 19th century)
Amateur artist of several golfing watercolours. Possibly a relation of R.W.M. Addison whose large library and collection of golfing watercolours and prints was sold by Christie's (Edinburgh) in 1987 and in whose collection several works by V.S. Addison were found.

Ader, W.
Unrecorded artist of a painting entitled "Partridge Shooting" indistinctly signed and inscr. on reverse, 27in.x35½in., but sold for £1,650 Sotheby's (Sussex) 1983.

Adrion, Lucien (1889-1953)
French artist of urban scenes who painted his impression of the XI Olympic Games in Berlin in 1936. He also painted "A Day at the Races, Longchamp", a very fine impression of pre-2nd World War racing in France.

Africano, Nicholas (b.1948)
American painter of baseball scenes whose portrait of Ernie Banks, acrylic on canvas, 13in.x32½in. was painted in 1979.

Agasse, Jacques Laurent (1767-1849)
Swiss-born animal and equestrian artist who trained under the great French painter, Jacques Louis David (q.v.). He settled in England in 1800 after an earlier visit in 1790 to Stratfield Saye, the home of his patron the Hon. George Pitt (1751-1828) who succeeded as 2nd Lord Rivers in 1803. His sporting scenes include "Lord Rivers Hare Coursing at Newmarket Heath" in 1818. His portrait of the stallion "Bay Aschem" led through a gate to a mare, painted 1802/4, is in The Paul Mellon Collection, Upperville, Va, USA.

Aikman, George W., RSW, ARSA (1830-1905)
Edinburgh landscape artist and engraver who painted a number of sporting scenes including "Shooting the Braids" (1869) and "The Lost Fish" (1881). He also exh. a golf painting entitled "Playing a Stymie" at the RSA in 1894 (the stymie was finally abolished in 1951).

He engraved several etchings of golfing greens after the watercolours by John Smart, RSA (q.v.) (1893). Elected RSW (1878) ARSA (1880).

Aikman, William (1682-1731)
Portrait painter who was encouraged to study art by his uncle, Sir John Penicuik. Aikman studied under Medina in Edinburgh and then in London and Italy. He returned to Scotland in 1711 where he established himself as a fashionable portraitist. He moved to London in 1723 to widen his reputation. His fine self-portrait is in the Scottish National Portrait Gallery. Portrait of William Somerville (1675-1742) holding a flintlock fowling piece in a landscape with his dog beside him, painted c.1727, 85in.x50in. William Somerville of Warwickshire, a large landowner, was better known as the author of "The Chase", the most comprehensive and important work of its kind, compiling every aspect of field sport throughout its history. Pub. in 1735, it was followed in 1742 with a poem on hawking called "Field Sports". Aikman's greatest patron was John, the 2nd Duke of Argyll (1680-1743) and many portraits by Aikman of the Duke exist.

Ainslie, Miss (op.1823-1835)
Painted game and sporting subjects. Exh. eleven paintings at the RA (1823-1831). Titles include "Grouse" (1835), "Hare and Pheasant" (1829), "The Thief" (1826).

Aitkin, R. Sinclair (fl. early 20th century)
Painter of dogs and hounds including a portrait entitled "The Hound Left Behind", s.&d. 1911, 20in.x12in.

Alderson, Dorothy Margaret (b.1900); Elizabeth Mary (1900-1988)
Identical twins born Girsby, Yorks., part of a family of twelve. Their mother was Mary Etty, a descendant of the Yorkshire artist William Etty (1789-1849). The twins were largely self-taught and painted from a very early age. They usually painted together and such paintings carry joint signatures. Most of their work is in watercolours but they occasionally painted in oils. Dorothy Margaret married Robert Caine in 1934 and lived in Sawley, nr. Ripon. They exh. regularly locally and at the RA (1984). Their sporting work includes hunting and steeplechasing scenes and portraits of hunters.

Aldin, Cecil Charles Windsor, RBA (1870-1935)
Best known for his dog subjects but his work includes hunting, coaching, racing, ice hockey, lawn tennis and hawking scenes. His first set of hunting prints, "The Fallow Field Hunt", was pub. in 1899 and followed by many others. Aldin worked mainly in pastel or watercolour and produced a number of fine etchings in limited edns. A keen sportsman, he hunted with the West Surrey Staghounds during the early 1900s, keeping his horse in a shed in Chiswick. Later he hunted with the South Berkshire and also founded a pack of beagles for the RAF. Aldin, who studied as a pupil of Albert Moore in Kensington (1885), the National Art Training School and under Frank Calderon (q.v.) made a successful career as an illustrator. He sold his first

drawing in 1890 and there were few periodicals during the 1890s to which he did not contribute. He became a close friend of Lance Thackeray (q.v.) who also lived in Chiswick, and together they explored Kent in a donkey cart.

Aldridge, Denis (1890-1985)

Leicestershire sporting artist in both oil and watercolour who was strongly influenced by Lionel Edwards (q.v.). A great rider to hounds, Aldridge hunted mainly with the Atherstone and Pytchley Hunts, and later with the Devon and Somerset Staghounds and the Quorn for which he was Secretary for eleven seasons. Much of his equestrian work went to the USA where it was introduced by Neil Ayer, Aldridge's close friend and Master of the Myopia Hunt, Mass.

Aldworth, Ernest W. (op.1959)

Painted several hunting scenes in watercolour.

Alexander, Lady (op.1843)

An engraving by John Harris of the Grand Military Steeplechase at London, Canadian West, 9 May 1843, after the work by this artist was pub. by R.Ackermann on 21 February 1845.

Alexander, Carolyn (b.1948)

Contemporary equestrian artist whose portraits of racehorses are well known both in England and abroad. Her mother is the sculptor Peggy Alexander, famous for her bronze studies of horses.

Alexander, Edwin John, RSA (1870-1926)

Animal and bird painter the son of Robert L. Alexander (q.v.). Visited Tangier in 1887 with his father and Joseph Crawhall (q.v.) whose influence can be seen in his work. Studied at the Royal Institution, Edinburgh (1887/8) and in Paris (1891). Lived in Egypt (1892-1896) but settled in Midlothian, Scotland in 1904. Elected RSA (1913).

Alexander, George Edward (1865-after 1926)

Animal painter who exh. at the RA and elsewhere. His painting "Guarding the Day's Bag" s.&d. 1894, 31in.x42in. was illus. and repro. in "Country Life" (3.10.85). This interesting painting shows six Dandie Dinmont terriers grouped defensively in front of a game bag. Lovers of this grand little game dog might remember that an early reference to them occurs in "Guy Mannering" by Sir Walter Scott (1815).

Alexander, R.M. (op.1880-1906)

Sporting artist and author who worked for "Fores Sporting Publications" and illus. many articles (mostly on sailing) for their "Sporting Notes and Sketches" (1886-1906). A keen fisherman, he also included a number of angling scenes amongst his work.

Alexander, Robert L., RSA, RSW (1840-1923)

Scottish painter who was considered by many to be the finest horse painter of his time and certainly influenced the young G.D. Armour (q.v.) whom he took with his family to Tangier in 1887. His patrons included the Duke of Portland. Elected RSA in 1888, but resigned in 1907. His exh. work at the RSA included "Hunting Friends" in 1881.

Alfred, Henry Jervis (op.1855-1883)

Very little is known, unfortunately, about this fine painter of freshwater fish. Records show that in 1864 he wrote "The Modern Angler" under the pen name "Otter". He also wrote for "Fishing Tackle Market". He exh. at the Great Fisheries Exhibition in 1883. Between 1847 and 1898 his family ran a tackle shop in Moorgate Street, London. His jewel-like effect of painting puts him in the top class of 19th century British angling artists. Exh. two paintings of fish at SS in 1855.

Alken, George (c.1794-1837)

Third son of Samuel Alken, Snr. and brother of Henry Thomas Alken, Snr. (qq.v.). Member of a large family of sporting artists who is best known for his book of forty-seven rather indifferent sporting and animal lithographs which was pub. after his work by Rowney and Foster of Rathbone Place, London in 1823. In 1827 he drew an aquatinted set of St. Leger winners and in May 1826 a print of Epsom races apparently drawn and engraved by George Alken was pub. by S. Knights of London.

Alken, George (1812-1862)

Sporting painter of no great ability. Second son of Henry Thomas Alken, Snr. (q.v.). He worked mostly in watercolours although the example here is painted in oil. "Paddy", a chestnut hunter, the favourite horse of Stephen Peet, in a loose box s.&d. 1854, Christie's London. Considerable confusion has arisen over the three George Alkens.

Alken, George (1846-1883)

The elder son of Sefferien John Alken (q.v.). He became a butcher but threw himself into the Thames from London Bridge (the Southwark side, as Lady Bracknell might have said) on 13 April 1883 and drowned. The Deputy Coroner for Southwark, Samuel G. Langham, held an inquest, the verdict, temporary insanity. Much misunderstanding has occurred as a result of this complex family but so far as is known this George Alken never painted.

Alken, Henry Thomas (1785-1851)

Danish ancestry. The son and pupil of Samuel Alken, Snr. (q.v.) but also studied art under J.T. Barber Beaumont (1774-1841). Prolific painter of many sporting works including hunting, coaching, racing, and steeple-chasing scenes. Best known perhaps for one of the most famous sets of sporting prints of all time, "The Midnight Steeplechase or the First Steeplechase on Record" but correctly entitled "The Night Riders of Nacton" (engraved by J. Harris, pub. by R. Ackermann 1839). Alken worked in both oil and watercolour and was a skilled etcher. His book, "A Treatise on Etching", consolidates his experience of forty years of engraving. He also wrote the "National Sports of Great Britain", pub. Thomas Maclean, London 1821. His work was copied frequently by his son, Henry, Jnr. (see Alken, Samuel Henry), and many of his pictures were produced in pairs or sets.

Alken, Samuel, Snr. (1756-1815)

Painter of shooting, hunting and racing scenes and an

aquatint engraver. Father of Sefferien John Alken, a carver and gilder, and of Henry Thomas Alken (qq.v.). Studied at the RA Schools.

Alken, Samuel, Jnr. (1784-1824)
The eldest son of Samuel Snr. and brother of Henry Thomas Alken (q.v.). The same confusion over the two Samuel Alkens exists as it does for the three Georges. Samuel Alken is known to have included otter and fox-hunting, racing, shooting and fishing scenes amongst his work.

Alken, Samuel Henry (Gordon) (1810-1894)
Known as Henry Alken, Jnr. Eldest son of Henry Thomas Alken (q.v.), he worked in both oil and watercolour in his father's style. Tended to paint small pictures in sets. He also painted several minority sports such as prize-fighting, bear-baiting, cock-fighting, dog-fighting, bull-baiting, cat-baiting and ratting as well as the more popular sports of boxing and cricket. Much of Alken's work was engraved by professionals but he did engrave a few plates himself after presumably his own work, including "Herne Bay Grand Steeplechase" 1834, and "The Sporting Exploits of the Late Henry Hunt" c.1840.

Alken, Sefferien, Jnr. (1821-1873)
Second son of Henry Thomas Alken (see Alken, Samuel Henry) who is known to have painted sporting pictures. He also signed his work S. Alken which has added to the confusion of attribution.

Alken, Sefferien John (1796-1857)
Son of Samuel Alken, Snr., and brother therefore of Henry Thomas, Samuel Jnr. and George (qq.v.). Believed to have painted some equestrian scenes and shared lodgings with his brother George for some time.

"Allan-a-Dale"
Bonham Carter Evelegh (1847-1910), croquet champion 1877, 1879, 1899 and contributor to "The Field" magazine under that pen name.

Allan, David (1744-1796)
Scottish portrait and history painter. Best known in sporting circles for his portrait group of the Cathcart family at Schawpark House near Alloa with a cricket match being played on 3 September 1785 in the background. The cricket match is of secondary importance to the sitters although Lord Cathcart holds a cricket bat in the family group. Allan's golf portrait of William Inglis on Leath Links painted in 1787 is also well known. The portrait hangs in the Scottish National Portrait Gallery and has been engraved, since the 2nd World War, by Lawrence Josset. Inglis was Captain of the Honourable Company of Edinburgh Golfers from 1782-1784. Allan's painting of "Curlers at Canonmills Loch, Edinburgh", a very fine watercolour painted before 1796, is the earliest picture known so far of curling. Whether Allan was a player himself is not known, but if not his knowledge of the game was most carefully researched.

Allan, W (op.1789)
This artist exh. a single picture at the RSBA which is in the collection of the Birmingham AG: "A Birmingham Prize Fight between Tom Johnson, Champion of England, and Isaac Perrins of Birmingham", s.&d. 1789.

Allen, Henry (Harry) Epworth (1894-1958)
Sheffield-born artist who painted for the Royal Doulton Porcelain Company c.1920. His work includes beautiful scenes of horses and domestic animals. He also painted hunting scenes on canvas including his portrait of a huntsman, painted in 1917 and sold Thos. Watson 1986. Allen, who lost a leg fighting in the 1st World War, became private secretary to Arthur Balfour (created Lord Riverdale 1935) who had originally employed Allen in his steelworks as a school leaver. It was not, therefore, until the 1930s that Allen became a full-time professional painter.

Allen, J. (op.1954)
Painted for the Royal Worcester Porcelain Company c.1954; he includes many animals amongst his work.

Allen, Joseph (1769-1839)
Birmingham-born portrait painter, sometimes of sporting personalities and subjects. Studied at the RA Schools (1787). Exh. fifty works at the RA (1792-1822). Titles include "Portrait of a Horse" (1792), "Mr. Johnson's Children with Favourite Pony Brown George aged 40" (1808), "Mr. Cockburn and Dog" (1803). Became a founder member of the Liverpool Academy (1810).

Allen, R.
Contemporary American portrait painter included in this Dictionary for his portrait of Dr. James Naismith (1861-1939), the inventor of basketball (1891). Charcoal drawing 1978, 18in.x28½in., Naismith Memorial Basketball Hall of Fame, Springfield, Mass., USA.

Alleyne, Francis (op.1774-1790)
Portrait painter who exh. two works at the RA and FS in 1774 and one at SA in 1790. Little is known of his life but he presumably went from family to family painting their portraits as he went. His portrait of John Call at the age of six years old with a cricket bat and ball painted in 1784 was sold Christie's 1981. He also painted the portrait of William Wheatley at the age of fourteen with a cricket bat over his shoulder, oil on panel (oval), 14in.x11in., 1786. MCC Collection.

Allingham, Charles (op.1802-1820)
London portrait painter who exh. at the RA (1802-1812). His fine portrait of Edward Oates and his friend John McKerrell seen out shooting in Malta with their dogs "Baron" and "Ponto", painted in Malta c.1820, 25½in.x36in., was auctioned Sotheby's 1970. Allingham also painted the portrait of James Belcher, the pugilist, which was engraved by George Clint (q.v.).

Allinson, Adrian Paul, ROI, RBA, LG, PS (1890-1959)
Painter of several sporting scenes including football and cricket. "At the Goal Mouth", a picture of football at Stamford Bridge, Chelsea, exh. at the FE. Allinson, who studied at the Slade School (1910-1912) contributed

caricatures to "The Daily Express" and "Daily Graphic". He exh. widely at the leading London galleries and elsewhere. Elected RBA (1933), ROI (1936).

Allinson, Garlies W. (op.1935-1936)
Equestrian artist whose hunting scenes were often painted in gouache. His picture of "Hippos" and "Cattistock Rusticus" at play was repro. in "The Field" 17 October 1936. Exh. at the RA 1935-1936.

Allsop (Alsop), William (op.1775-1780)
This artist exh. nine paintings at FS (1775-1780) from a Wandsworth address including "A Portrait of a Gentleman Going a'Shooting" in 1780.

Alma Tadema, Laura Theresa (1852-1909)
A picture of "A Game of Battledore and Shuttlecock" after a painting by this artist was repro. in "The Art Journal", 1929 (two young girls are playing watched by a woman with a baby on her knee). Laura Theresa Epps studied art under (Sir) Lawrence Alma-Tadema, RA, and married him as his second wife in 1871. She exh. regularly at the RA from 1873 and was one of only two English women artists to contribute to the International Exhibition in Paris in 1878. She specialised in painting interior scenes, modelling her style on that of the 17th century Dutch masters.

Almond (op. c.1783)
Apparently an itinerant artist who painted a number of small portraits of the servants of the 3rd Duke of Dorset at Knowle, Kent, which he visited in 1783. These include a portrait of the cricket playing Edward "Lumpy" Stevens, which is probably the first portrait of a cricketer identified solely in that capacity. 11½in.x9½in. (oval). Lord Sackville Collection.

Alonso, Anthony M.
Contemporary American painter of horse racing scenes who lives in New York.

Alpenny, Joseph Samuel (1787-1858)
London portrait painter who lived in Dublin from 1812 to 1824. Recorded as J.S. Halfpenny between 1805/8 for reasons best known to himself. The Piscatorial Society have a number of fine fishing watercolours, all signed J.S. Alpenny, in their collection including an interesting scene entitled "Fishing on Wandsworth Common" s.&d. 1851.

Alstrop, E. (op. late 19th century)
Animal painter who included a number of rabbiting scenes with terriers and several of otter hounds amongst his work.

Ambrose, Charles (op. c.1905-1911)
A magazine illustrator who drew a long series of golf and tennis personalities for Edwardian publications including "Country Life" 1909/1910/1911. Golf players featured include Harry Vardon, James Braid, Ted Ray and J.H. Taylor.

"Amicus RF"
Pseudonym used by the artist Sir Robert Frankland (q.v.) on a print of the racehorse "Rosette" pub. by J. Masham, Bedale, Yorks., 1811.

Amiel, Louis Felix (1802-1864)
French equestrian artist, included in this Dictionary for his fine painting of "Le Prix de l'Arc de Triomphe au Champ de Mars" painted in 1840, 28in.x46in., now in a private collection New York.

Amoore, E.J. (op.1902-1910)
This artist is said to have worked for a famous porcelain company painting game birds and landscape scenes. His painting of "Ring Necked Pheasants" dated 1902 is repro. "Game and the English Landscape" by Vandervell and Coles, pub. Debrett's Peerage Ltd. (1980).

Anderson, Arthur (1861-1904)
See Fraser, Arthur Anderson.

Anderson, John (op.1844-1849)
Scottish painter who included a number of Highland sporting scenes amongst his work. His study of a horse drawn carriage and groom s.&d. 1844 and inscr. "Paisley", 8in.x23in., was auctioned Christie's (Sth. Ken.) 1985, and his portrait of a "Highland Sportsman with his Pony and Dog", s.&d. 1849, was auctioned Sotheby's 1984.

Anderson, John Corbet (1827-1907)
Draughtsman and lithographer mainly of cricket portraits which he produced both singly and in groups. His portrait of "Thomas Barker of Nottingham", 21in.x 16½in., c.1845, umpire and groundsman of the MCC standing in black coat and brown trousers on a cricket field, is typical of his cricket work.

Anderson, Martin (1854-1932)
Landscape painter from Fife who worked as the cartoonist "Cynicus" (q.v.).

Anderson, Robert, ARSA, RSW (op.1842-1885)
Scottish painter, etcher and engraver of landscapes who lived in Edinburgh. "Curling on Duddingston Loch", 26½in.x40in., 1846, Caledonian Club, London.

Anderton, S.J. (op.1905)
This artist produced a set of four flat racing scenes in pen, black ink and watercolour each 11in.x15in. "The Cesarewitch" 1905, signed and inscr., and three other flat racing scenes in the same year, including the July Handicap, Newmarket and the Duke of York Stakes.

Andrews, Henry (1804-1868)
A very prolific painter of genre who exh. at the RA, BI and SS (1830-1868). Painted in a very Watteau-like style and included hawking, archery and hunting subjects amongst his work, very often depicting them in romantic settings of an earlier date, a style which continued to be much favoured by the later Edwardians.

Andrews, Sybil (b.1898)
Suffolk-born colour lino cut artist of figure subjects in a futuristic style such as "The Race" (1930). Studied art at Heatherleys and then shared a studio in Hammersmith with Cyril L. Power (q.v.). Together they helped set up the New Grosvenor School of Modern Art in 1925 with Iain McNab who became Principal.

Angellis (Angillis), Pieter (1685-1734)
French-born artist who lived in London for some years. According to Pilkington's "Dictionary of Painters", 1824, Angellis "profited little by the popularity he acquired - owing to his modesty". Also, "his style is good and his execution neat and graceful but the colouring feeble". His painting of "A Game of Skittles", s.&d. 1727, 25in.x29¼in. might seem to bear Pilkington out. The Paul Mellon Collection in the Virginia Museum of Fine Arts.

Angus, William (op. late 18th century)
Painter, etcher and line engraver who contributed one plate to T. Baldwin's "Airopaedia Containing the Narrative of a Balloon Excursion from Chester, the eighth of September, 1785".

Annison, Edward, RSMA (op.1910-1948)
Painted predominantly marine subjects in oils, very often of sailing and yachting scenes. Exhibitor at inaugural RSMA exhibition in 1946. Also an exhibitor at the RA and the Walker AG, Liverpool. His painting of the Chester/London Stagecoach leaving the Greyhound Inn, 9¼in.x12¼in., is an unusual subject for him.

Anquetin, Louis (1861-1932)
French artist of equestrian scenes including "Over the Water Jump - a Steeplechase", 8¼in.x13½in. Christie's (Tattersalls) 1990.

Anscombe, R. (op.1950s)
The Jockey Club, Newmarket, has a collection of racehorse portraits by this artist painted during the 1950s. These include "Hard Ridden" Charlie Smirke up, "St. Paddy" Lester Piggott up, "Crepello" Lester Piggott up. Portraits of "Honey Light" and "Pinza" appeared on the front covers of the "British Racehorse", March 1954 and Spring 1957 respectively.

Ansdell, Richard, RA (1815-1886)
Liverpool-born sporting, animal and historical painter who sometimes collaborated with the artists W.P. Frith (q.v.), John Philip, Thomas Creswick (q.v.) and Samuel Sidley (q.v.). Best known for the "Waterloo Cup Coursing Meeting" painted in 1840 for the Earl of Sefton, the first of three large sporting groups which made his name. In 1844 he painted the 5ft.x10ft. "Caledonian Coursing Meeting at Ardross, Ayrshire, Scotland" held on 26, 27 and 28 March which was sold for 34,000 guineas in 1969, a then record price for a work by the artist. Ansdell's patrons included the Earls of Sefton, Derby, Spencer and the Marquess of Bute. His paintings of stalking, shooting and fishing illustrate his fine technique and show more than a working knowledge of these sports. A number of his works are in the collection of the Town Hall, Lytham St. Annes. His painting "Gaffing a Salmon" was engraved by William Simmons in 1857, and his portrait of "Mr. Harrison Blair with his Ghillie landing a Salmon on the River Spean", 31in.x53in., is dated 1858. Ansdell trained as a portrait painter under W.C. Smith, and later studied at Liverpool Academy where he became President (1845/6). He exh. there at the BI and at the RA (1840-1885). Elected RA (1870).

Ansell, Charles (op.1780-1789)
A little-known animal painter who exhibited four paintings at the RA (1780-1781), including a self-portrait. Is said to have been born in London in 1752 (from the Students Register L'Académie Royal de Paris of 30 March 1778) who lists a Charles Ansell from London as a pupil of Vincent. The following engravings are known after paintings by Ansell, "Life of a Racehorse" (six) engraved by Dukes in 1784, "Hunting" scenes (ten) engraved by Sutherland 1789, "Shooting" engraved by Sutherland 1789.

Ansted, William Alexander (op.1883-1892)
Exh. four works at the RA (1883-1892) including "Woodcock Shooting" (1892). Graves lists him as an etcher operating from a Chiswick address.

"AO"/"Armadillo" alias Ronald L'Estrange
Produced nine cartoons (all after 1900) for "Vanity Fair".

"Ape"
Pseudonym used by the Italian caricaturist Carlo Pellegrini (q.v.).

Appart, A.
A painting inscribed "Group of Sportsmen watching Cocks Fighting in a Barn", 19¼in.x23½in. was sold at Christie's 1962. The artist's surname is more likely to be Appert, a 20th century French painter of bird subjects.

Apperley, Charles James (1778-1843)
See "Nimrod"

Applebee, Leonard, ARCA (b.1914)
Born in London, studied at the Goldsmith's School of Art (1931-1935) under Clive Gardner and at the RCA (1935-1938) under Barnett Freedman. Exh. at the RA from 1947. Created ARCA (1938). Is known to have painted angling subjects (Pavière). Exh. at the RA from 1937. Fishy titles include "Salmon" (1960), "The Catch" (1957), "Pike" (1964), and "The Salmon Pool" (1956).

Appleyard, Frederick, RWA (1874-1963)
Landscape and figure painter born in Middlesbrough. Studied at Scarborough School of Art, under Albert Strange, and at the RCA and the RA schools where he won the Creswick Prize for landscape painting. Exh. at the RA from 1900 and at the RWA from 1918 of which Society he was elected a Member in 1926. Worked in South Africa (1910-1912). Died Alresford, Hants., where he had lived for many years. He features in this Dictionary for his motor racing/rally painting of a "Hill Climb" - a study of a 1½ litre ERA negotiating a steep hill at speed, watercolour, 6¾in.x9½in. Appleyard shared a studio at 18 Kensington Court Place, London, with his brother-in-law Christopher Williams (q.v.).

Appleyard, John
Contemporary motor racing artist, well known for his paintings of vintage cars.

Appleyard, Joseph (1908-1960)
A leading Yorkshire sporting painter in both oil and

watercolour whose subjects include racing, hunting and polo scenes. "The Finish of the St. Leger 1959" (won by "Cantello") is in the collection of Doncaster Museum and AG. Other racehorses known to have been painted by Appleyard include "Airborne", "Sayajirao", "Ridgewood", "Chamossaire", "Ballymoss" and "Black Tarquin". His painting of the Fourth Test Match at Headingley, March/July 1953 was exh. at the Yorkshire Artists 1953, no. 64A.

Archer, Alexander (op.1810-1848)
This equestrian artist operated at the same time as J.S. Archer and Archibald Archer (qq.v.). His painting of "The Emperor", a prize stallion belonging to Samuel Clark held by a groom in a landscape, s.&d. 1848 and inscr., 22in.x24¼in. is a very fine work indeed.

Archer, Archibald (op.1810-1845)
Included in this Dictionary for his painting entitled "The Young Archer" exh. at the RA in 1836. The title is tenuous, however, since this could have been a self-portrait.

Archer, J.S (op.1850)
Exh. a painting of "Zuleika" a mare belonging to J.L. Gaskin, Esq. at the RA (1850).

Archer, James, RSA (1824-1904)
Scottish animal painter whose study of a brindle Staffordshire bull-terrier, 24in.x20in., is a fine example of his work. Archer studied at the Trustees Academy under Sir William Allan and Thomas Duncan. He settled in London in 1864, painting portraits and historical subjects.

Archer, John Wykeham, ARWS (1808-1864)
Watercolour artist, etcher and line engraver from Newcastle upon Tyne who worked as an animal illustrator for "The Illustrated London News" (1847-1849). He trained under the animal painter and engraver John Scott (q.v.) (who made illustrations for "The Sporting Magazine") and then in W. & E. Finden's studio in London. Elected ARWS (1842). Brother-in-law of George Lance (q.v.).

Archer, M.B.
Nothing known about this artist except that he or she produced a very fine pencil drawing, 17¾in.x24¾in., of the London-Brighton coach near Burgess Hill, Sussex, auctioned Sotheby's (Sussex) 1987.

Arden, Edward
The pseudonym used by Edward Tucker (q.v.).

Arman, Armand
Contemporary French painter whose study of twenty-six American football helmets cut cleanly in half to expose the guts of the headgear, like so many split chickens, was exh. at NAMOS, Indianapolis, 1991.

Armfield, Edward (op.c.1864-1875)
A very prolific painter of terriers, often depicted ratting, some gun dogs and shooting scenes. His "Waiting for the Guns" and "The First of October" a pair each signed and inscr., 21in.x17in., was auctioned Bonhams 1984. His work is very rarely dated, an oil painting

s.&d. 1864 and two spaniels seated by a table, s.&d. 1873, 5½in.x7½in., being exceptions. Many people think that Edward Armfield was the son of George Armfield and this is certainly borne out by W. Shaw Sparrow, ("Connoisseur Magazine", April 1931) who recorded that George Armfield resorted to the law to stop a son marketing his signature. I can find no evidence of this since none of George Armfield's children was called Edward and the only son that made adulthood was William (b.1858).

Armfield, George (Smith) (1810-1893)
London sporting artist who until 1839 used his real surname Smith to sign his paintings, abandoning this in favour of his second christian name Armfield, in 1840. His brother, the artist, W. Armfield Smith (op.1832-1861) did not change his name. According to the 1871 census return Armfield gave his place of birth as Bristol, but in the 1881 census it is stated that he was born in Monmouth. He may have been closely related to C.N. Smith, the engraver, for whom Armfield painted "The Young Warrener". A prolific artist, Armfield exh. thirty-two paintings at RA, thirty at BI, forty-two at SS and nine elsewhere (1840-1875). His sporting work includes "The Burst Gun" s.&d. 1853, "Waiting for Master" s.&d. 1890, and several paintings of otter hounds and hunting. Armfield is recorded as being a dedicated sportsman and an excellent horseman. He married three times and had seven children which illustrates that his prolificacy was not confined to his paintings. He died at the age of eighty-three and was buried in a public grave in Lambeth Cemetery on 16 August 1893. See also George Smith for additional biography.

Armitage, Joshua Charles (b.1913)
See "Ionicus"

Armour, George Denholm (Lt. Col), OBE (1864-1949)
Scottish sporting artist and a brilliant draughtsman whose drawing of a horse could seldom be faulted. The sporting subjects he painted include salmon fishing, polo, bull-fighting, hunting and racing. Armour studied at Edinburgh School of Art and the RSA Schools from 1880, after his return from Tangier with Robert Alexander (q.v.). He shared a studio in London with Phil May (q.v.) and contributed illustrations - many of them sporting - to "The Graphic", "Punch" and "Country Life". Armour also illus. many books including "Reynard the Fox" by John Masefield, "The Story of a Red Deer" by John W. Fortescue, "Hunts with Jorrocks" and "Jorrocks Lectures" (1908), and "Humour in the Hunting Field" with comments by "Crascredo" pub. "Country Life" (1928).

Armstead, Henry Hugh, RA (1828-1905)
Better known for his sculpture which he turned to completely after 1862. Studied at the RA schools. His early painting work includes a number of racing scenes. His canvas entitled "Taking a Fence", a steeplechasing scene, was exh. at Ackermanns in London, and his work after J.F. Herring, Snr. (q.v.) of the racehorses

"Charles XII" and "Euclid" with jockeys up, s.&d. 22 December 1859, 13in.x17in., shows his great interest in this sport. His interest in racing came as a result of the racing trophies he made in silver, having originally trained as a silversmith.

Armstrong, James (op.1886-1893)

Carlisle artist and engraver who also ran a print business. Specialised in the sport of hare-coursing and his pair of paintings of the celebrated greyhounds "Lobelia", "Master McGrath" and "Bab" at the Bowster and "Cerito", "Mocking Bird" and "Hughie Graham" painted in 1886, 20in.x27in., are fine studies. The paintings were engraved by W. Brookes & J. McGabey of Liverpool in 1870. "Cerito" was also painted by Richard Ansdell (q.v.).

Armstrong, John, ARA (1893-1973)

Imaginative painter in oil and tempera of classical compositions and later a designer of stage and film sets. His rowing picture entitled "Regatta", 15in.x23½in., was auctioned by Christie's in 1986.

Armstrong, Robin

Contemporary wildlife artist and writer especially of fishing subjects. River warden in south-west of England. Wrote and illus. "The Painted Stream" pub. by J.M. Dent & Sons Ltd. London 1985. A TV programme on his work entitled "Water Colours" was shown by the BBC1 in 1986.

Armstrong, W. (op1909)

A portrait of a chestnut hunter in a stable, s.&d. 1909, 18in.x22in., was auctioned Tennants 1990.

Arnald, George, ARA (1763-1841)

A landscape painter who studied under William Pether and exh. at the RA (1788-1841). His exhibit in 1800 was of "Spider", an Irish horse. His painting of two young anglers was sold at the Gilbey sale of sporting pictures at Christie's April 1940. Apart from that Arnald painted "a steady stream of dull landscapes" (Waterhouse).

Arnesby-Brown, Sir John Alfred R.A. (1866-1955)

Norwich landscape artist whose fine oil painting "Waiting to Hear the Results of the Great Notts. v Surrey Match, August 1892", signed, 9½in.x10½in. was auctioned Sotheby's 1987. Brown exh. at the RA until 1945 and was elected a member in 1915. His many landscapes, often featuring estuary scenes, also include a number of yachts racing.

Arnold, George (1753-1806)

Oxford artist who exh. at the SA 1770-1776. His subject matter included dead game, game birds, sporting dogs, hounds and horses.

Arnold, George (op.1887-1891)

Variously recorded under Arnold, Arnald and Arnull but clearly operating at a later date. Equestrian artist whose painting of the Derby, 1887 (won by "Merry Hampton") 43in.x66in., is a fine work. He also painted the portrait of a bay racehorse with Sam Basden in red silks up galloping (the wrong way) down a racecourse, s.&d. 1891, 18¼in.x24in., and "The Brighton to London Stage on the Road", 12¼in.x18¼in. signed but undated.

Arnold, Jane (b.1821)

Amateur artist, daughter of the famous headmaster of Rugby School, Dr. Thomas Arnold. Sketch of the "Game at Rugby School", repro. "Dr Arnold of Rugby", by Norman Wymer, pub. by Robert Hales, depicts the dowager Queen Adelaide, widow of William IV, watching the boys playing football at Rugby School in 1839, with Dr Arnold and his son Matthew. Collection Mrs. Mary Moorman.

Arnold, Reginald Ernest, RBA (1853-1938)

Decorative painter who is included in this Dictionary for his painting of the 1887 Derby (won by "Merry Hampton") s.&d. 1887, 43in.x63in., Christie's, 1984. Arnold, who was also a sculptor, studied art under Legros at the Slade School and Carolus Duran in Paris. He exh. at the RA and SS from 1876. Elected RBA 1909.

Arnst, A. (op.c.1863)

"A Croquet Game" c.1863, signed, watercolour, 13¾in.x29¼in. Sotheby's London.

Arnull, George (op.1820)

Three paintings are recorded by this artist in the Witt Library. They are a pair of racing scenes painted c.1820, "Going Out" and "The Finish", and a picture of a tram car pulled by coloured horses. These were repro. in "Country Life" (21.12.67).

William Arnull was the jockey who rode "Augustus" in the great match against "Priam" (who won) at Newmarket in 1831. He was the son of Sam Arnull (c.1760-1800) who was the jockey of "Diomed" and "Sir Peter Teazle" (1784). It is possible that George Arnull was part of this great racing family.

Arsenius, John (Johann Georg) (1818-1903)

Swedish equestrian artist who painted horse portraits and fox-hunting scenes.

Arsenius, Karl Georg (1855-1908)

Swedish equestrian artist who is known to have painted English racecourse scenes. Examples of his work are seen to best advantage in the plates made after his paintings to illustrate the "History of Celebrated English and French Thorough-Bred Stallions" (S.F. Touchstone 1890).

"Arundel" alias William Charles Arlington Blew

Author of "A History of Steeplechasing" (1901) and "The Quorn and its Masters".

Ashford, William, PRHA (1746-1824)

Born in Birmingham but lived most of his life in Ireland. Painter of landscapes and some sporting subjects including several with a shooting or an angling interest. His portrait of a dapple grey hunter standing in a landscape with a spaniel (25in.x29½in.) auctioned Sotheby's 1987. Ashford, who was elected President of the Irish Society of Artists in 1813, played a major role in establishing the RHA, becoming its first President in 1823.

Ashland, J. (op.1819)
"The Bristol-London Royal Mail Coach" s.&d. 1819, 17½in.x35⅛in., auctioned Christie's 1983.

Ashley, Frank N. (b.1920)
American equestrian artist who exh. at the Tryon Gallery in London 1975. Specialises in racing scenes. Best illustrated by his watercolour painting, 30in.x22in., of the 200th (1980) running of the Derby at Epsom entitled "Pulling Up".

Ashton, George Rossi (b.1857) (op.1874-1901)
Cornish-born animal and sporting painter mostly in watercolour who worked on "The Sydney Bulletin" with Phil May (q.v.). He contributed a number of black and white illustrations to "The Graphic" and "Pall Mall" magazines. Exh. at SS from 1874. Lived in Melbourne, Australia from 1879-1901 where he followed his elder brother, the artist Julian Rossi Ashton, who emigrated there in 1878. His painting "Coursing in Victoria" is in the Sydney Art Gallery Collection, Australia.

Askew, Miss Felicity Katherine Sarah (b.1894)
Painter and sculptor of horses. Studied art under Max Kruse, Frank Calderon (q.v.) and Ernesto Bazzaro. Exh. at the Paris Salon, in Germany, USA and at Liverpool. Lived and worked at Newmarket and at Berwick on Tweed.

Astley, P.H. (op.1840)
Portrait of the racehorse "Deception" in a stable s.&d. 1840 and inscr., 16in.x20in. Recorded Lyle Arts Review 1975. Auctioned Phillips

"Astz"
Pseudonym of unidentified caricaturist who contributed to "Vanity Fair" 1913.

Atkins, Burnaby C. (op.1903)
Indifferent amateur watercolour artist. Included in this Dictionary for his painting of "A Ness Salmon" caught by J.B.A. at Ballindalloch, 9 October 1903. Watercolour signed and inscr., 17in.x45in..

Atkinson, Charles (op.early 19th century)
Lithographer, seemingly after his own work. "A Match at Lord's Cricket Ground", 8in.x10in..

Atkinson, Christopher (Revd.) (1754-1795)
Talented bird artist in watercolour who included hawks and game birds amongst his work. Son of the Vicar of Thorpe-Arch, Yorks., he was based at Trinity College, Cambridge from 1773 to 1785, firstly as Pensioner and Fellow, then as Vicar of St. Edwards and Fellow of Trinity Hall. From 1785 until his death he was Vicar of Wethersfield, Essex, where he is buried.

Atkinson, E. (op.1790s)
London painter of game subjects. Exh. three paintings at the RA, "Snipe" (1793), "Woodcock" (1794) and "Fish" (1797), from a Long Acre address.

Atkinson, Herbert D. (c.1863-d.1936)
Sportsman, writer and an artist who specialised almost entirely in poultry scenes including the portraits of a great number of fighting cocks. Atkinson, who was born at Wallingford where his father Dr. William Atkinson

had practised for many years, was one of the great world authorities on cock-fighting and one of the original founders of the Oxford Old English Game Club in 1885. He was also Honorary Vice President of the Game Fowl Club of America as well as Honorary Vice President of the Game Fowl Club of South Africa. He came from a great cocking family since his father, grandfather and great grandfather were all cockers. Atkinson, who was a fine rider and a great judge of horses, hunted regularly with the Devon and Somerset and was a keen follower of the Dulverton. He painted several racehorses for the Duke of Sutherland and for Lord Londonderry and was commissioned by King Edward VII to paint "Minoru" after he won the Derby in 1909. This painting was amongst his most successful works. Atkinson was also a sculptor and modelled in silver a fine portrait of "St. Simon" for the Duke of Portland. Under the pseudonym "HA", Atkinson contributed widely to both "The Field" and "The Feathered World". He travelled widely and remained a bachelor. Exh. at the RBA, ROI and the Walker AG, Liverpool (1882-1890).

Atkinson, J. (op.1796-1807)
Exh. one painting only of a horse and a dog at RA in 1796, but several other portraits of hunters in landscapes are recorded by him.

Atkinson, John (1863-1924)
A Newcastle painter in both oils and watercolours and an etcher of animals, horses and sporting scenes. Painted a number of greyhound studies and hare-coursing scenes as well as hunting and racing. An exhibition of his work was held posthumously at Armstrong College in 1925.

Atkinson, John Augustus, OWS (1775?-1833)
London-born artist, aquatint engraver and soft line etcher who spent fifteen years of his youth in Russia (until 1801) producing "Four Panoramic Views of St. Petersburg" and "Manners, Costumes and Amusements of the Russians". Included in this Dictionary for his coloured aquatint, 8¾in.x13⅜in., of "Skating" showing the scene at the edge of a frozen pond with skaters having their skates put on and others skating around, pub. W. Miller 1807, British Museum. His watercolour drawing "The Dover-London Stage Coach", 8¾in.x12⅝in., and inscr. is in the Paul Mellon Collection, Upperville, Va, USA.

Attwood, Thomas (op.1857)
A painting of the Southdown Steeplechase at Ringmer, s.&d. 1857, was exh. Ackermanns London.

"Audax"
Pseudonym used by John Lawrence, since 1959, for his racing reports in "Horse and Hound".

Audubon, John James (1785-1851)
Famous bird artist, best known for his fine colour plates for the "Birds of America 1827-1838". Born at Les Quay, St. Dominique, Audubon arrived in England in 1826 where he proceeded to give a staggering number of one-man exhibitions throughout the provinces. His sporting paintings include the "Entrapped Otter" and

"Spaniels flushing Pheasants" - a large oil painted in 1827 for King George IV which was sold to the Macbeth Gallery by Parke Bernet. An unfinished replica is in the Museum of Natural History in New York.

Audy, Jonny (op.1844-1882)
French-born equestrian artist who specialised in racing scenes, very often painted in watercolour. He always signed but only occasionally dated his work. "The Sporting Life", a set of four watercolours, each signed and one dated 1844, were auctioned Sotheby's (NY) 1990, and a racehorse and trainer in a landscape, s.&d. '82, were auctioned Bonhams 1988.

Aumonier, James, RI (1832-1911)
Camberwell-born artist. Trained as a calico print designer. Exh. at the RA from 1870, bravely exhibiting a painting of football there in 1888. Elected RI (1879). A memorial exhibition of his work was held at the Goupil Gallery in 1912.

Ausiter, T. (op.1783-1786)
Exh. six paintings at the RA (1783-1786) including studies of dead game and young hare.

Austen, Alexander (op.1880s)
Specialised in paintings of shooting and fishing.

Austen, Winifred Marie Louise, SWA, RI, RE (Mrs. Oliver Frick) (1876-1964)
Talented painter and etcher of birds and animals whose sporting work included East Anglian wildfowlers and a number of equestrian paintings, studies of horses in stables. Exh. thirteen paintings at the RA (1899-1903). Elected SWA (1905), RE (1922) and RI (1933).

Austin, Robert Sargent, RA, RWS, RE (1895-1973)
Leicestershire animal and figure painter, watercolourist and engraver. Studied at the Leicester School of Art (1914-1916) and at the RCA (1919-1922). Rome scholar (1922). Elected RE (1928), RWS (1934) and RA (1949). Tutor of engraving at RCA (1927-1944) and Professor in the Department of Graphic Design (1948-1955). A fine craftsman, his work reflects his interest in Dürer. Engraved his own work "The Fisherman" and made the plates at Bures, Suffolk, in August 1927. British Museum.

Austin, William Frederick (1833-1899)
Norfolk based artist of topographical scenes in pencil and watercolour who worked with his father as J. Austin & Son, initially in Oxford (1866). "The Fishing Match at Reedham", watercolour, 8in.x14½in.

Aveling, H.J. (op.1839-1882)
London portrait and figure painter who exh. five pictures at SS (1839-1842) including one of a cricket match played by members of the Royal Amateur Society at Hampton Court Green on Wednesday 3 August 1836.

Avercamp, Hendrick (1585-1663)
Dutch painter included in this Dictionary for "Golf on Ice on the River Ijssel Near Kampen", watercolour, Christie's 1976, repro. "Country Life" (8.9.77).

Avery, Milton (1893-1965)
American equestrian artist. Largely self-taught, his early work was influenced by Matisse. His watercolour "A Female Gamester", s.&d. 1944, 22in.x30in., was a departure from his usual equestrian studies and with such a sporting title merits its own place in this Dictionary. His dramatic painting "Fencers" (1944) depicting two fencers, one dressed in white, one in contrasting black, was exh. at NAMOS, Indianapolis (1991).

Ayers, R. (op.1823)
London animal painter who exh. one animal painting at the RA (1823).

Ayrton, Michael, RBA (1921-1975)
Imaginative figure artist who contributed a football painting "Arsenal v. Aston Villa 1952", 26½in.x41in., to the FE. Ayrton, who had studied spasmodically at several art schools including Heatherleys and St. John's Wood, had an equally varied career as an art historian, novelist, broadcaster, film director, art critic and theatrical director.

Azars, Imegal de
French 19th century watercolour painter who painted a portrait of a Falconer of the Club de Champagne in the uniform of that Club. Founded by M. Amedee, the Club de Champagne was instrumental in reviving falconry in France in 1865. Musée d'Histoire Naturelle, Paris.

B

"B.B"
Pseudonym used occasionally by the sporting author and illustrator, Denys Watkins Pitchford (q.v.).

Babbage, F. (op.1858-1916)
Animal painter and wood engraver whose sporting works include fox-hunting and racing. His advertisement in "Bailys" magazine 1895 (back page) reads "Artist and engraver (horses and cattle) 9 Robert Street, Hampstead Road, London NW." Best known for his small wood engraving of the famous Master of foxhounds, John Warde, seated on "Blue Ruin" with his favourite foxhound "Betsy" in the background. This was taken from the painting by William Barraud (q.v.) and appears in "Animal Painters of England" by Gilbey, pub. 1900.

Bache, Otto (1839-1927)
Danish artist of equestrian and some domestic scenes including "The Game of Croquet" signed (with inits.) 11¾in.x15¾in., auctioned Christie's 1988.

Backshell, W. (op.1848-1858)
Genre painter and line engraver who exh. two watercolour paintings at SS in 1848 from a Kentish Town address. Is known to have engraved a sporting painting for Henry Barraud (q.v.) in 1858.

Bacon, D'Arcy (op.1855-1874)
Painter of animals and sporting subjects. Exh. at the RA, BI and SS. Titles include "The Twelfth of August" "Setter with Ptarmigan", "Setters with Grouse", "Setters with Black Game".

Bacon, Frederick W. (1803-1887)
Painter, line and mezzotint engraver of portraits, historical and some sporting subjects. "A Horse and Gig" signed twice and dated 1883, 8in.x5½in., was auctioned Sotheby's 1978.

Bacon, H.D. (op.1861)
Exh. one sporting painting at the Portland Gallery in 1861 from a London address.

Bacon, H. L.
An illustration entitled "A Sibyl of the Racecourse" appeared in "The Graphic" in 1903 depicting high society at Epsom learning their destiny from a fortune teller - or perhaps the winner of the 2.30.

Badcock, Kathleen S. (op.1889-1890)
Yorkshire animal artist, daughter of the Dean of Ripon, who exh. two paintings at SS in 1889 and 1890. Her painting "A Cleveland Bay Carriage Horse", s.&d. 1890 is a competent study.

Badmin, Stanley Roy, ARCA, RWS, RE (1906-1989)
Interesting landscape etcher and watercolourist of several football scenes including "Here they come - the Valley" 15½in.x9½in., watercolour, exh. at the FE in 1953. Studied at Camberwell School of Art and at the RCA under Schwabe, Millard and Tristram. Exh. at the RA, RWS, RE and the provinces. Elected RE (1935) and RWS (1939) and is represented in many public collections. Lived in Sussex.

Bagnall, R.H. (op. early 20th century)
"Eight Metre Yacht Racing off the Clyde", signed, 16in.x20in., Bonhams 1986.

Bagshaw, William (op.1846)
Listed as Bagshaw, William (painter) in "Pigot's Commercial Directory for Rugby" under section headed "Plumbers and Glaziers". Oil paintings of a white ram and a white ewe (Dishley Leicesters) painted in 1846 are so far the only identified works of this semi-professional artist.

Bailey, George (b.1796) (op.1810-1822)
Bailey was born at Bawtrey, near Doncaster where he was described in a local Directory of 1822 as a house, animal and sign painter living in the High Street. He painted animals including "The Ox Prince" (1824) (University of Reading), "Lavinia" a shorthorn cow, s.&d. 1822 (Collection Doncaster Museum and Art Gallery). His sporting works include a racing caricature of "A Tipster and Jockey", s.&d. 1810 and a portrait of Colonel Harry Mellish and Frank Buckle, s.&d. 1810, 16in.x20in. Colonel Harry Mellish (1780-1827) was a reckless gambler on horses, cards and dice. He was also a prize-fighter and a racehorse owner with forty horses in training. He was known as an intelligent, likeable and, oddly enough, totally honest fellow but left racing after crashing in the 1806 St. Leger, having won the 1804 St. Leger with "Sancho" (National Horse Racing Museum).

Bailey, Henry (op.1879-1907)
Landscape painter who exh. at the principal London galleries from 1879. Included in this Dictionary for his watercolour "Fly Fishing", 11in.x9in., s.&d. '80, Bonhams 1991.

Bailey, John (1750-1819)
Yorkshire-born agricultural and animal painter who worked at Barnard Castle before becoming land agent for Lord Tankerville at Chillingham. He was also his own and other people's engraver for illustrating books.

Bailey, Wilfred (op.c.1900)
Painter of equestrian and sporting scenes including "Pendle Forest and Craven Harriers - The start of the Hunt Cup", signed, 20in.x29in., Sotheby's (Sussex) and "Scenes from the Grand National", signed, 19in.x30in., Henry Spencer.

Baily, R.M. (op.1846)
Game bird artist. His known paintings include those of "Black Grouse", "Ptarmigan", and "Red Grouse".

Baird, Nathaniel Hughes John, ROI (1865-1936)
Portrait and landscape painter. Born in Roxburghshire and studied art in Edinburgh, London and in Paris under Bouguereau and Carolus Duran and at the Herkomer School at Bushey. Also well known for his paintings of horses. His equestrian scenes were mostly portraits of heavy horses but he did paint a few hunting scenes. He illus. the memoirs of the Rev. John Russell the fox-hunting parson and originator of the Jack Russell terrier, by E.W.S. Davies (pub.1902). Elected ROI (1897).

Baird, William Baptiste (op.1872-1899)
Born in Chicago but lived in London. Domestic and genre painter who exh. in Paris and at the RA (1877-1899). He specialised in poultry and cock-fighting scenes, often painting the latter in pairs or sets of four.

Baker, Arthur (op.1864-1911)
Painted sporting and numerous cattle subjects in oil and watercolour. Exh. at the RA, SS and BI. Titles include "Breaking Cover" (1866) and "Otter Hounds" (1874/5). Exh. from addresses in London and Tunbridge Wells. Said to be a friend of the animal painter Alfred Strutt (q.v.). Baker painted the Duke of Hamilton's hounds in kennels (1897), 35in.x60in., in which each hound is depicted as a portrait in itself.

Baker, Frances (Mrs. Kennedy Cahill) (op.1897-1921)
Irish painter who exh. at the NEAC a painting of "The Races in Sligo" and "The Turf Road" in 1913 from a County Sligo address.

Baker, George Arnald (op.1861-1867)
"The Armchair Angler", 15in.x21in., Sotheby's 1990.

Baker, John, RA (1736-1771)
London artist who originally trained as a coach painter. His painting "A Difficult Fence" which shows stout riders dragging their reluctant horses through fences was exh. at the Rutland Gallery, London, 15in.x29½in., painted c.1770, private collection, London. Baker was one of the first members of the RA where he exh. four paintings (1769-1771).

Baker, John, S.Equ.A.
Contemporary painter and illustrator of equestrian scenes, particularly racing. A founder member of the Society of Equestrian Artists. Studied Birmingham School of Art. Teaching Diploma Slade School, under Professor Schwabe, Slade prize winner, Diploma Fine Art. A Judge at horse shows - Concourse D'Elegance at Smith's Lawn, Windsor, etc. Exh. at the leading London galleries and elsewhere. One-man shows Birmingham and Guildford.

Baker, Wilfred Carmichael (1815-1891)
Born in Norfolk, the son of an innkeeper. A self-taught artist who specialised in sporting subjects. He possessed a natural talent but had little opportunity of enlarging it and died in poverty. His painting "The Norfolk Foxhounds" was engraved by Thomas Fairland and published by Day & Haghe, lithographers to Queen Victoria. He specialised in portraits and studies of hunters standing in a landscape. His portrait of the cob "Confidence" was engraved and produced in Vol. 133 of "The Sporting Magazine".

Baldock, Charles Edwin (1876-1941)
Nottingham sporting painter who exh. "Hard Pressed - South Notts Hounds" at the RA in 1900. Orphaned when he was very young and bought up by his grandfather, James Walsham Baldock (q.v.).

Baldock, James Walsham (1822-1898)
Nottingham animal and sporting painter who lived in Worksop. He was born J.W. Markham but took his maternal grandfather's name who adopted him after the death of his parents. He started his career working on a farm whose owner sent him to have art lessons. Said to have painted in a similar style to J.F. Herring Snr. (q.v.) and painted in both oil and watercolour. He in turn brought up his own orphaned grandson Charles Edwin Markland who took the name Baldock (q.v.). James Baldock painted several members of the Meath Hunt including a large equestrian portrait of "Samuel Reynell with Hounds and Huntsmen" which was presented to him on his retirement from the Mastership in 1871. Reynell's house, Archerstown, is in the background and in the foreground the hounds bear the brandmark "M" to identify their pack. Baldock's distinguished clients included Viscount Galwey and the 5th Duke of Portland. His portrait of "Mountain Dew", a hunter, 19in.x26in., s.&d. 1873 which he painted for Caroline Foljambe, daughter of Viscount Milton, is in the collection of the Nottingham AG. Between 1867-1887 Baldock exh. sixteen oils at SS and six watercolours at the NWS, all landscapes and rural scenes. He also exh. at the Sheffield Society of Artists of which he was a founder member in 1875 and at the Nottingham Society of Artists from 1881, when it was formed, until his death in 1898. Baldock was elected VP of the Sheffield Society of Artists in 1881, 1883, 1889, 1890 and 1893.

Baldry, G.W. (op.1882)
"Lady Rose and Lady Violet Nevill dressed for skating on the lake at Eridge Park, Sussex", 5ft.4in.x4ft.7in., private collection, exh. Colnaghi "Pastimes, Pleasures & Pursuits" June 1986. The subjects of the painting were the twin daughters of William, 1st Marquess of Abergavenny. Both ran away and remarried at a time when divorce was considered to be taboo. Lady Rose married firstly John Blundell Leigh, then the 4th Earl of Cottenham. Lady Violet married the 3rd Earl of Cowley, and subsequently Robert Edward Myddelton, of Chirk Castle.

Bale, Charles Thomas (op.1868-1886)
Still life painter who occasionally included equestrian scenes amongst his work. He exh. fifteen paintings at SS (1868-1875).

Balfour-Browne, Vincent Robert Stewart Ramsey (1880-1963)
Scottish sporting painter who specialised in Highland stalking and golfing scenes, painted mostly in watercolour. Said to have been a pupil of the wildlife artist, George Lodge (q.v.) and exh. much of his work at the Tryon Gallery London. He wrote and illus. many books on stalking and the red deer.

Ballantyne, John, RSA (1815-1897)
Scottish portrait painter who studied in Edinburgh and taught at the Trustees Academy. Included in this Dictionary for the painting of George Glennie, the amateur golfer, captain of both Royal Blackheath (which he joined in 1853) and the R & A. Ballantyne collaborated with Heywood Hardy (q.v.) on this painting. Elected RSA 1860.

Ballantyne, R.M. (op. 1865-1887)
Landscape painter who exh. sporting works at the RSA.

Ballingall, Alexander (1880-1910)
Edinburgh painter of marine subjects who was supposed, according to Sir John Caw ("Scottish Paintings 1620-1908" pub. 1908) to have had very little technical ability. He nevertheless included a number of attractive fly fishing scenes amongst his work.

Bancroft, Shelley (b.1955)
Portrait of "Chris Ronaldson, World Champion (Real Tennis), 1981-86" painted in 1984, 9¾in.x18in., collection Chris Ronaldson.

Banks, A. (op.c.1909-1917)
Equestrian artist operating in the first quarter of the 20th century about whom very little is known. "A Black Hunter in a Loose Box", s.&d. 1917, 12in.x16in., was auctioned Bonhams 1986.

Banner, Alfred (op.1878-1914)
Birmingham artist, brother of Joseph Banner (q.v.) Painted a number of sporting scenes in the traditional manner.

Banner, Joseph (op.1860-1887)
Birmingham artist, brother of Alfred Banner (q.v.). This artist's sporting work includes "After the Shoot" and "Resting by a Gate", a pair, 6in.x9in., s.&d. 1887. Sotheby's.

Bannister, Graham
Contemporary artist of golfing subjects whose work includes "A View of Wentworth Golf Club", acrylic, s.&d. 1985, 40in.x61in., Sotheby's (Glasgow) and "View of Sunningdale from the 5th Tee" 30in.x40in., Sotheby's (Glasgow) 1989.

Barber, Charles Burton (1845-1894)
London sporting and animal painter, particularly of dogs, who studied at the RA Schools. His chief patron was Queen Victoria for whom he painted the portrait of the revolting "Florrie". His portrait of the celebrated greyhound "Snowflight" winner of the Waterloo Cup (1882) is masterly, as are his Highland sporting scenes.

Barclay, James (op.1888-1899)
Little known Scottish artist whose sporting work includes Highland shooting scenes in watercolour and an occasional hunting scene.

Barclay, John Rankine (1884-1962)
Painter and etcher of ice skating scenes who also included golf etchings amongst his work. He won the Carnegie Travelling Scholarship and the Guthrie Award and worked in Edinburgh and St. Ives (1937).

Barclay, William (op.1881-1898)
Equestrian artist who specialised in hunting scenes and portraits of hunters.

Barenger, James, Jnr. (1780-1831)
London-born sporting artist. The son of James Barenger, Snr. (a glazier and an amateur painter from Kentish Town who exh. eight of his paintings at the RA (1793-1799) and who specialised in insect painting). James Barenger was also the nephew of W. Woollett, the engraver. Barenger's best hunting painting is probably the portrait of Jonathan Griffin, huntsman to the Earl of Derby's Staghounds seated on "Spanker", s.&d. 1819, 36in.x48in., the Paul Mellon Collection, Upperville, Va, USA. He also painted "The Earl of Derby's Staghounds", a painting which was later engraved by R. Woodman and pub. in 1823. He is famous for his life-size canvas of "A Cockfight" measuring 30in.x25in., a grey cock having just killed a red cock. His sporting scenes include coursing, hunting, shooting, racing and his many patrons included the Earl of Derby, the Duke of Grafton, the Marquis of Londonderry and Mr. Richard Tattersall with whom he formed a life-long friendship in 1815 and from then on exh. all his pictures at Hyde Park Corner. An engraving by Thomas Prattent of 'Phenomena' the Celebrated Trotting Mare" after the work by Barenger was pub. in 1813, 20¼in.x25¼in.

Barker, A. (op.1834)
Exh. one sporting work at SS (1834) and a study of a dog's head at BI in the same year.

Barker, Benjamin, Snr. (c.1739-1793)
Nottingham-born artist whose main claim to fame is generally recognised as being the sire of the Barker of Bath artists. Started life as a decorator in japanned ware and later became the owner of a livery stables which led him to paint horses. His painting of "Babraham", a bay racehorse in a landscape being led by a groom, signed and inscr. with the identity of the horse, 26in.x31¼in., is a nice example of the work of this rare artist, Sotheby's, 1980.

Barker, John Joseph (op. 1835-1866)
Landscape and figure painter. A member of the Bath family of artists. His painting entitled "Croquet in the time of Charles II" was exh. at the BI in 1866.

Barker, Kathleen ("Kay") Frances (b.1901-c.1969)
This sporting writer and illustrator was the daughter of the animal and sporting painter Wright Barker, RBA (q.v.). She was born at the Beeches, Ollerton, Newark, was a keen sportswoman and lived at Harrogate. She was an illustrator of horses and dogs, mostly pencil sketches, and illus. "Black Beauty" by Anna Sewell

(1936). Wrote and illus. "Bellman the Beagle" pub. A.C. Black (1933) and sequels, "Bellman carries On", etc. (1934). Produced a book of pencil sketches entitled "Just Dogs" which was pub. by Country Life Ltd. (1933) and illus. "The Silver Horn" by Gordon Graham pub. "Country Life" (1934). Contributor to "The Field".

Barker, T. (of Thirsk) (op.1855)

Painter of the racehorse "Refraction", s.&d. 1855, 10¼in.x14⅛in. and inscr. "Thirsk" (formerly purchased at Puttick & Simpson, Lot 150 22 July 1913 for £1.10s.).

Barker, Thomas (1769-1847)

Bath landscape and sporting painter, also a lithographer. His brother was Benjamin Barker, his son was Thomas Jones Barker (q.v.) and his father was Benjamin Barker Snr. (q.v.). Exh. at the RA, SS and BI including "Lansdown Fair with men playing Ninepins" (1813). Collaborated on at least one painting with his son.

Barker, Thomas Jones (1815-1882)

Born in Bath, the eldest son of Thomas Barker (q.v.). Painted sporting and military scenes, including cricket and equestrian studies. Exh. at the RA, BI and SS (1844-1876) from a London address including "The Horse Race at Rome" at the RA (1860). In 1834 Barker went to Paris to study under Horace Vernet. While there he exh. at the Salon and received three gold and twenty silver medals. Amongst his patrons were Louis Philippe and Benjamin Disraeli. Barker collaborated on at least one sporting painting with his father and "The Young Sportsman" painted in 1834, 35½in.x50¾in., is signed by both artists.

Barker, W. Bligh (op.1835-1850)

London artist who exh. ten paintings at SS (1833-1845). Titles include "Shot Wood Pigeons", "Ferreting", "Rabbits" and "A Field Day" - all watercolours.

Barker, Wright, RBA (1864-1941)

A talented but no-nonsense Nottingham painter of large hunting and sporting scenes, including polo, who became a picture dealer towards the end of his life. His daughter was Miss Kathleen F. Barker (q.v.).

Barland, Adam (op.1843-1875)

London landscape painter who painted a number of fishing scenes. Exh. at the RA (1843-1875) and at the BI and SS. "Fly Fishing - North Wales" signed with mono. and dated '64, 10in.x8in., Phillips (Bath).

Barlow, Francis (c.1626-1704)

Lincolnshire sporting artist, often known as the "Father" of sporting art since he was the first British-born artist in this subject. Barlow turned to book publishing and illus. and pub. "Several Ways of Hunting, Hawking and Fishing according to the English Manner" in 1671. His vast canvas of the old "Southern Mouthed Hounds" 35in.x140in. is well known at Clandon Park, Surrey (National Trust). Barlow, who was one of the first etchers of merit that this country produced, also etched "The Last Horse Race Run Before Charles II of Blessed Memory by Dorsett Ferry near Windsor Castle, August 24 1684", the first English racing print of any quality.

Barlow, Gordon Clifford (b.1913)

Yorkshire landscape artist who studied at the Bradford Regional College of Art and under Herbert Royle as a private pupil for many years. Barlow, in his turn, became a part-time art teacher and a visiting lecturer to Bradford College of Art (1946-1976). He has exh. at the ROI, RI and the Paris Salon. Included in this Dictionary for his series of nine famous golf courses, painted c.1975, each 29½in.x39½in. oil on canvas.

Barnard, Edward (1785-1861)

Founder member of the Houghton Fishing Club in 1822. Wrote and illus. "Angling Memories and Maxims" pub. after his death through the Chronicles of the Houghton Fishing Club by Sir Herbert Maxwell, repro. "Angling in British Art" by W. Shaw Sparrow (pub.1923).

Barnard, George (op.1832-1890)

London landscape painter, lithographer and water-colourist. Pupil of J.D. Harding. Exh. at the RA, RI and SS (1837-1873). His sporting work includes "A Rugby Match" at the school of that name, painted in 1852, 24in.x36in., which perhaps contributed to his appointment as Professor of Drawing at Rugby in 1870.

Barnard, Mary B. (Mrs. McGregor Whyte) (1870-1946)

Flower painter who exh. her work widely (1894-1913). Not known as a sporting artist but her charming painting of "The Cyclist" earns her a place in this Dictionary.

Baron, Henri C.A. (1816-1885)

French figure artist who painted "Les Joueurs de Boules", depicting bowlers playing on a stretch of dry clay or sand. National Art Gallery Coll., Sydney, Australia.

Barrable, George Hamilton (op.1873-1887)

London painter of genre subjects who painted "England v Australia at Lords", 58in.x117in., in 1886, in collaboration with Sir Robert Ponsonby Staples (q.v.) to commemorate the Jubilee of Queen Victoria and the centenary of the Marylebone Cricket Club. The view of Lords is seen from the "A" enclosure and depicts an imaginary match between the two countries. All the portraits are however of real people, including the Prince and Princess of Wales, and the cricketers portrayed all represented their country at some time. A photogravure with a key was pub. by Boussod Valadon. Barrable exh. at the RA and RBA.

Barratt, Thomas of Stockbridge (op.1852-1899)

Sporting artist from Stockbridge (near Liverpool) who exh. seventeen works at the RA including his portrait of "Sultan", winner of the 1855 Cambridgeshire, which he exh. in 1856. His sporting work includes portraits of "Andover", winner of the Derby in 1854, "Breaking Cover" 1858, "Virago", winner of the Goodwood Gold Cup in 1854 with his trainer Mr. John Day, the stable lad W.S. Cooper and Wells, the jockey, up.

Barraud, Francis Philip (1824-1900)

This watercolour painter of topographical scenes was the younger brother of Henry and William Barraud (qq.v.). He produced a series of drawings and paintings of the cathedrals and public schools of England in which sports like cricket and hockey are being played in the foreground. Barraud was a partner in the family firm Lavers & Barraud, the well-known Victorian stained glass makers at 22 Endell Street, London WC where he worked as a designer. "Rossall School, a View from the Cricket Field". An etching 13¾in.x19in. by W.A. Allingham after this painting was pub. by Dickinson & Foster, 2 April 1891.

Barraud, Henry (1811-1874)
Fine sporting artist who studied art under J.J. Middleton (the portrait and topographical painter). Henry was the younger brother of William Barraud (q.v.) with whom he often collaborated on sporting pictures. Henry specialised in portraits and William in painting horses. Henry's portrait group of about ninety of the MCC members painted just before his death in 1874 is in the Museum of London. He was one of the first English artists to use photography in his work and became a keen photographer. Exh. at the RA (1833-1859). His son, Francis James (1856-1924), is known for his painting of "Nipper" the terrier who belonged to his brother Mark, a scenic artist, which was used for years as the symbol of "His Master's Voice".

Barraud, William (1810-1850)
Fine sporting artist, particularly of equestrian scenes, which include a portrait of John Warde on "Blue Ruin" with his favourite foxhound "Betsy" beside him. This subject was engraved on woodcut by F. Babbage (q.v.) and repro. in the first number of "The New Sporting Magazine" (1831). William Barraud often collaborated on sporting paintings with his brother Henry (q.v.). A pupil of Abraham Cooper, RA, (q.v.) he was probably the better painter of animals of the two brothers, but an early death limited his output. Exh. at the RA (1826-1850).

Barret, George, Snr., RA (1728-1784)
Dublin-born landscape and portrait painter who became one of the founder members of the RA. A pupil of Robert West, Barret became a drawing master at the Society of Artists School, Dublin. He came to London in 1763 and did not return to Ireland. Barret included several sporting scenes amongst his work. These were largely, I suspect, as a result of commissions from his many distinguished clients, rather than any natural inclinations, but he may have been encouraged by the sporting artist Sawrey Gilpin (q.v.) with whom he often painted during the last ten years of his life. A large canvas painted by both artists, showing horses and dogs waiting to cross the bay in a ferry which is already full of horses and carts, was exh. by Messrs. Spink in 1976 and repro. in "Country Life". His patrons included Edmund Burke, the 4th Viscount Powerscourt and the sportsman Lord Edward Bentinck.

Barret, George, Jnr. (1767-1842)
The son of the artist George Barret RA (q.v.). Many people believe that he far surpassed his father in technical skill. He first exh. at the RA in 1800 but he sent the bulk of his drawings (581) to the exhibitions of the Watercolour Society. He painted several pictures between 1834 and 1836 with John Frederick Tayler (q.v.) including a watercolour entitled "Young Anglers by a River". George Barret Jnr.'s sister was Mary, a

pupil of both George Romney and Mrs. Mee. Mary Barret was a good watercolourist whose subjects were mainly birds, fish and still life. She lived with her brother in Paddington until her death in 1836.

Barrington, E.Z. (op.c.1949)
Included in this Dictionary for his, or her, painting of the show jumping Colonel Harry Llewellyn and "Foxhunter", signed, 9½in.x13½in. The artist is unknown to the subject, Sir Harry Llewellyn, who did not sit for the portrait.

Barrington Browne, William Ellis (1908-1985)
Painter of sporting subjects, but in particular fishing scenes, "Coming to the Gaff", "Fishing the Test", "A Grilse from the Dee" etc. A keen fisherman and sportsman who lived in Gloucestershire. Illus. "The Immortal Trout" (1955) by Eric Taverner and "The Running of the Salmon". Son of the artist H. Needham-Browne. Studied art in Venice and at the Académie Julian in Paris. Taught art at Cheltenham College for ten years.

Barron, Hugh (1747-1791)
Portrait painter and pupil of Sir Joshua Reynolds (q.v.). Painted the children of George Bond of Ditchleys, South Weald Essex, 41¾in.x55in., about to play cricket which he exh. at the RA in 1768 (4) as "Young Gentlemen at Play". Barron exh. at the RA in 1782, 1783 and 1786 and at the SA in 1766 and 1778.

Barrow, Julian (b.1939)
Cumberland-born contemporary artist whose golfing scenes, painted in oil, include "The European Open Championship (1987)" with Severiano Ballesteros playing his tee shot at the 9th hole on the Old Course at Walton Heath, 20in.x30in.

Barry, Frederick (op.1826-1849)
London painter of sporting subjects and dead and live game, painted mostly in watercolours. Exh. at SS (1826-1849). Titles include "Shooting" (1833) and watercolours of snipe, pheasants, teal, partridge, game, pigeons and ducks and hares, both dead and alive.

Barry, James (op.1813-1839)
Equestrian artist whose small output seems to have been centred around hunting and includes a very fine example entitled "A Fox", s.&d. 1830, as well as "A bay Hunter in a Landscape" s.&d. 1831. Barry's work also includes a study of "The Andover to London Stage passing a Sportsman on an Open Road", 1834 ,and "A Bay Racehorse in a Stable", s.&d. 1839.

Barry, M.
Unknown painter of "The Polo Match". Signed pastel and dated (indis.), 11½in.x17¾in., Christie's (Sth. Ken.).

Bartell, George (American)
Contemporary painter of American football scenes.

Bartlett, Charles William, RWA (1860-c.1930)
Landscape and figure artist whose painting "Before the Match" shows a small girl with racket and shuttlecock seated on a garden chair, s.&d. '91, 17in.x14½in., Phillips. Bartlett exh. at the RA, RI, RBA, ROI and elsewhere (1885-1928).

Bartlett, John
Fishing and shooting scenes by this artist have come up at auction, usually painted in pairs, each 17in.x13in.

Bartlett, William H., ROI, RBA (1858-1932)
London painter of sporting and domestic pictures who studied at the Ecole des Beaux-Arts under Gérome and then with Bouguereau and Fleury. He exh. at Paris (1889) and at the RA and SS from 1880 and painted several angling scenes including "Salmon Spearing" and "Fishing on the Greg" (1880).

Barwick, John (op.1837-1876)
Yorkshire-born equestrian artist who included hunting and hare-coursing scenes amongst his sporting work. He also contributed illustrations to "The Sporting Magazine". He was patronised by Lords Fitzwilliam and Willoughby D'Eresby, exh. a painting of one of the latter's horses at the RA in 1844.

Basebe, Charles J. (op.1849-1865)
Sussex portrait painter, based in Brighton who included a number of cricket portraits and sketches amongst his work, some of which are in the collection of the MCC at Lords and were repro. "The Pictures of Cricket" by John Arlott (1955). A number of coloured aquatints by C. Hunt, all 5¾in.x7½in., were pub. by W.H. Mason c.1850 after the work by Basebe including portraits of George Leopold Langdon, Esq., Alfred Mynn, Esq., Roger Kynaston, Esq. and Charles George Taylor, Esq.

Bastin, A.D. (op.1871-1900)
A pencil study of the boxer "Peter Jackson", 23in.x15¾in., was sold Sotheby's (Sussex) 1988.

Bateman, G. (op.c.1898)
"After the Shoot" and "Waiting for the Squire" a pair of sporting paintings, both signed, 16in.x24in., were auctioned at Sotheby's (Glen.) 1989.

Bateman, Henry Mayo (1887-1970)
Australian-born artist, caricaturist and illustrator who included many sporting subjects amongst his work. Studied at Westminster and New Cross Art Schools and then under Charles van Havenmaet. Bateman contributed a numbered series of sporting cartoons to "The Field" (1935-1937). These included hunting incidents and adverts. for Gibbs shaving cream. Famous for his series of sporting situations captioned as "The Man Who .....". Illus. many books including "Adventures at Golf" (1923), "Fly Fishing for Duffers" (1934), "Spinning for Duffers" (1939) and "The Evening Rise" (1960).

Bateman, James (1814-1849)
London sporting painter who included fishing and shooting scenes amongst his work. Bateman shared a studio with E.H. Landseer (q.v.) and contributed to "The Sporting Review" (1842-1846). He also had forty-five plates pub. in "The Sporting Magazine" (1842-1846).

Bateman, James, RA, RWS, RE (1893-1959)
Cumbrian-born painter of landscapes and a distinguished wood engraver. Studied art at the Slade School (1919-1921). Prix de Rome finalist 1920. Although Bateman painted occasional horse portraits he is included in this Dictionary for his portrait of Freddie Mills, the boxer, a pastel which he executed in 1951, 9½in.x15¼in. Bateman had the previous year (1950) produced a pastel, 9½in.x15¼in., entitled "The Bruce Woodcock - Freddie Mills Fight at the Local" which he exh. at Frost and Reed in 1950.

Bates, David (1840-1921)
Father of the animal, sporting and landscape artist John Bates Noel (q.v.). David Bates was a Midland landscape painter in both oil and watercolour who worked in Birmingham and Worcester and who painted a number of gamekeeper scenes. Bates, father and son, both painted the "Gamekeeper's Gibbet", David Bates exh. his version at the RA in 1873.

Bath, W. (op.1840-1872)
London landscape painter who exh. at the RA, SS and BI (1840-1851). His portrait "A Gentleman seated on a bay Hunter standing in a Landscape with Huntsman and Hounds Beyond", s.&d. 1872, 9½in.x23½in., was auctioned Bonhams (1984).

Bathgate, Miss Hattie E. (op.1909-1914)
Member of an Edinburgh family of painters, she exhibited at the Walker AG, Liverpool (1911-1914). Painter of several equestrian portraits.

Batiss, Walter (op.1948)
South African artist who won an Hon. Mention with his painting "The Quagga Race" and third prize with his etching "Sea Side Sport" in the Olympics Art Competition, July/August 1948.

Batsford, Sir Brian (see also Cook, Brian) (1910-1991)
Distinguished publisher, painter, illustrator and conservationist who, as the artist Brian Cook (q.v.), painted and illus. many sporting subjects. Amongst his work is the dust jacket he designed for "Hunting England" written by Sir William Beech Thomas (pub. 1936) and "Racing England", featuring Ascot race-course, written by Patrick R. Chalmers and pub. (of course) by Batsford in 1937.

Batson, Frank (op 1892-1926)
Landscape painter who exh. at the RA (1892-1904) including his fine cricket match "Playing out Time in an Awkward Light", 48in.x72in. (1901), Nottinghamshire County Cricket Club Collection (presented by the artist's daughter in 1904). The bowler in this picture is seen through the eyes of the batsman. The painting was exh. at the RA in 1901 (571).

Batt, Arthur J. (op.1867-1898)
Hampshire animal artist who painted small studies of donkeys and "feathered friends" popular at the time. His equestrian and dog paintings are good.

Bauer, Carl Ferdinand (1879-1954)
Austrian equestrian artist who specialised in racing scenes and studies of racehorses.

Baumeister, Willi (1889-1955)
German figure artist who included a number of ball game paintings amongst his work, particularly of football.

Baumer, Lewis Christopher Edward, RI, PS, (1870-1963)
London-born portrait painter and illustrator. Studied at St. John's Wood Art School, the South Kensington Schools and the RA Schools. "Punch" artist of football and other sporting scenes. Exh. at the RA, RI, SS and elsewhere from 1892. Elected RI (1921). Illus. "Winter Sportings" (1929), "Ski Fever" (1936) and "The Complete Sportsman" (1914).

Bawden, Edward, CBE, RA (1903-1989)
Painter, designer and illustrator, also an etcher and a linocut print maker. Born in Braintree, Essex. Studied at the RCA (1922-1925) where he was influenced by his tutor, Paul Nash (q.v.). He later returned to the RCA to teach on a part-time basis. Included in this Dictionary for the poster of "York Races" designed for British Rail (1961). Chalk collage and lino printing ink, 31in.x47¾in. Exh. Fine Arts Society, London 1991.

Baxter, Graeme William
Born 1958. Contemporary artist of golfing scenes and famous courses including "Ailsa Course Turnberry" and his painting of Christy O'Connor's shot to the 18th at the Ryder Cup 1989. Exh. at the Centre Gallery, Sth. Methuen St., Perth (1988). Studied at the Glasgow School of Art and began his career as a realist painter.

Baxter, Thomas (1782-1821)
Porcelain painter at Worcester and Swansea who ran an art school in London (1814-1816). He exh. sixteen works at the R.A (1802-1821). A portrait of "Honest" Baxter of the Surrey Cricket Club as a young cricketer holding his bat on Richmond Green is presumably a self-portrait. Pencil, brown wash, signed, 20½in.x 15½in., Sotheby's 1964.

Baxter, William Giles (1856-1888)
Brilliant caricaturist in b/w. Originator of "Ally Sloper" the lovable character created for Charles Ross's "Ally Sloper's Half Holiday" who became a Victorian legend. The V & A Museum has a print by this artist of a scene at an outdoor "Roller Skating Rink" c.1885.

Bayes, Alfred Walter, RE, RWS (1832-1909)
Yorkshire-born painter of landscapes, portraits and fishing subjects. His exhibit to the RA for 1876 was entitled "Anglers of the Wye". Father of the sculptor Gilbert Bayes (q.v.).

Bayes, Gilbert, PRBS, HRI (1872-1953)
The architectural sculptor whose 1934 relief panel is set into the wall surrounding Lord's Cricket Ground and shows sportsmen and women in stylish contemporary dress. The carved inscription reads "Play up, play up, play the game". Bayes studied at the City and Guilds Schools and the RA Schools (1896-1899).

Bayley, Chapman (op.1818-1832)
London painter of landscapes and shooting subjects in oil and watercolour. His RA exhibit in 1825 was entitled "Pheasant Shooting at Didlington, Norfolk" He also painted "Out Shooting", s.&d. 1832, 11½in.x15½in., auctioned Sotheby's 1985.

Beach, Thomas, ARA (1738-1806)
Dorset-born portrait painter, a pupil of Sir Joshua Reynolds (q.v.) (1760) as were James Northcote (q.v.) and Hugh Barron (q.v.). Painted the portraits of several distinguished sportsmen including that of Richard Tattersall (1724-1795) with his famous racehorse "Highflyer" (1774) in the background, which Beach exh. at the RA in 1787 (No. 101). The painting of Tattersall was engraved by John Jones in the same year (1787). "Mr. & Mrs. Thomas Tyndall of the Fort, Bristol and their Children", 104in.x74in. "The Three Children of Sir John William de la Pole" (6th Baronet) painted in front of the gate house at Shute, the two boys holding cricket bats, the girl the ball, s.&d. 1793, 79½in.x55½in., exh. at the RA (British Art) 1934, collection of Sir John Carew Pole, Bt.

Beale, Shell (op.c.1898)
Late 19th century watercolour artist of a number of equestrian scenes, including "A Two Horse Gig on a Country Road" and "A Study of a Gentleman on his Chestnut Hunter", Bonhams 1984.

Beard, James Henry (1814-1893)
American sporting artist of hare-coursing scenes and greyhound portraits.

Bearman, P.J.
"Setting off in the Yare Navigation Race", signed and inscr. 13in.x24in., auctioned Taylors Honiton 1990.

Beaton, Sir Cecil, CBE (1904-1980)
Distinguished painter, designer, illustrator, photographer and writer. Included in this Dictionary for his portrait of "Joe Louis, the Boxer", whom he painted in 1965, 22in.x14in.

Beaton, F.V.
Marine artist and painter of yacht racing scenes.

Beatty (Beattie), J. Lucas (op.1832-1846)
This equestrian and animal artist's rare work includes portraits of the racehorses "Moonraker" (1833), "Elis" with jockey up on a racecourse, and "A Dark Bay Hunter" (1846). An engraving of "The Chillington Oxon" after the work by Beatty (Beattie) was engraved by John Porter and pub. (1838).

Beaty, Allan C. (op.1875)
Landscape and equestrian artist whose portrait of "A Bay Hunter in a Stable", s.&d. 1875, 7½in.x9½in., was auctioned Sotheby's (Sussex) 1985.

Beauchamp, W.K.A. (op.1850)
A double portrait of two bay hunters held by a groom standing before a house, s.&d. 1850 and inscr. "'Burton-y-Sprig' The property of Edward Bowley Esq., Siddington House, Gloucestershire" on the reverse, 21in.x26½in., was auctioned Bonhams 1984.

Beaufort, C. (op.1831)
A pair of "Hunting Scenes", s.&d. 1831, each 17½in.x21½in., and a "Shooting Scene" 17½in.x 21½in. were auctioned at Christie's in 1969. These were previously in the possession of Major R.E.H. Finch and are referred to by Sydney Pavière in his "Dictionary of British Sporting Painters" (pub. 1965).

Beauvais, Walter John (b.1942)
Studied art under his father, Arnold Beauvais (1886-1982) who became President of the London Sketch Club (1936). W.J. Beauvais, who was influenced by the French Impressionists and also the British Post Impressionists, paints in a highly impressionistic style and his small, Ascot racing scenes are really impressions in soft pastel colours. Beauvais is an enthusiastic golfer and a keen sportsman, having taught boxing at a boys' boarding school.

Beavis, Richard, RWS (1824-1896)
Born at Exmouth, Devon. Studied at the Government School of Design, Somerset House before joining Trollope, a decorating firm, as an artistic designer (1850-1867). Predominantly a landscape painter but also a painter of animals and horses. Included hunting scenes amongst his work and "A portrait of a Huntsman" was auctioned at Sotheby's (Chester) 1980.

Beddington, Roy (b.1910)
Landscape painter and illustrator of angling subjects. Born in London, the son of a barrister. Studied at the Slade School (under Schwabe) and in Florence. Exh. at the RA, NEAC and in the provinces. Has illus. several books on angling including: "The Floating Line for Salmon and Sea Trout" (1938), "The Adventures of Thomas Trout" (1939) and "To Be a Fisherman" (1955).

Beddows, Michael
Contemporary marine artist who has included a number of yacht racing scenes amongst his work. "The America" racing in the Solent and the schooner "Westward" racing in Torbay, 24in.x36in.

Bede, Cuthbert
Alias the Revd. Edward Bradley (1827-1889), Vicar of Lenton with Harby (1883-1889) and the father of the sporting painter Cuthbert Bradley (q.v.). Included in this Dictionary for his sporting illustrations to his own publication "The Adventures of Mr. Verdant Green", an Oxford Freshman (1853-1856), particularly under the chapter "Mr. Verdant Green's Sports and Pastimes". He may, or may not be, the same Edward Bradley (q.v.) who painted a cricket scene showing the University side, the All England Eleven and the Durham Club taking part in a cricket match in 1849. The odds are that he is since he was educated at University College, Durham, and ordained deacon in 1850.

Beecham, W.R. (op.1846)
"A Study of a bay Hunter in a Landscape", s.&d. 1846, was auctioned Bonhams 1981.

Beechey, Richard Brydges (Admiral) (1808-1895)
Marine painter, son of Sir William Beechey RA (q.v.). His painting of the America's Cup on the New York Club Course, "'The Galatea' v. 'The Mayflower' crossing the line at the Start", s.&d. 1888 is in the Collection Royal Northern & Clyde Yacht Club. The painting depicts the sixth defence of the America's Cup in September 1886. The race was held in the Sandy Hook area on the outskirts of New York Harbour between New York Yacht Club's "Mayflower" and the Royal Northern Yacht Club's challenger "Galatea". The first race of the series of three took place on 7 September over a course of 32.6 miles and the "Mayflower" won by 12 minutes 2 seconds. The second race on 11 September was again won by the "Mayflower" this time by a margin of 29 minutes 9 seconds over a course of 40 miles. Among the crew of the "Galatea" was Mrs. Heun, the wife of the yacht's owner and probably the first female contender for the cup since she paid for the boat's construction and continued to cruise aboard it after her husband's death some time later.

Beechey, Sir William, RA (1753-1839)
Oxfordshire-born portrait painter who studied at the RA schools in 1772. He exh. a great number of portraits at the RA (1776-1839). Elected portrait painter to the court of Queen Charlotte (1793) and an RA (1798). His sporting portraiture includes studies of "Thomas Assherton Smith (1796-1858), the well known MFH of Tedworth", "The Meredith Children Fishing" and "The Cricketer, the Revd. Lord Frederick Beauclerk", painted at Bowhill c.1789, which the MCC have in their collection, 28¾in.x23¼in.

Beedlemaker, Adriaaen Cornelise (1625-1701)
Dutch artist of sporting scenes and hunting parties.

Beer, John (op.1885-1915)
London sporting artist who specialised in racing scenes, particularly featuring the finish. A very competent equestrian painter with a prolific output. Illus. Boyles "Sport in Borneo" in 1896 and "Tales for Sportsmen" with Georgina Bowers (q.v.) in 1885. He worked for Messrs. Fores, meeting the punishing deadlines demanded by the sporting illus. journals. The Walker AG, Liverpool have over one hundred of his racing scenes (prov. Lord Wavertree). His painting "The Finish - Henley", watercolour 9¾in.x13½in. showing an eight just passing the finishing post was exh. (No. 342) at the Parker Gallery for their bicentenary in 1950.

Beer, John Axel Richard (1853-1906)
An illustrator, very often of sporting scenes. An excellent figure and equestrian artist, at his best in free pen and wash sketches. Born in Stockholm he went to America as a young man in 1869 where he stayed for five years. He travelled to Russia and worked as an artist at the Imperial Court, eventually settling in London, where he worked for the principal illus. magazines of the time. He contributed sketches of horses to "The Graphic" in 1886 and to "The Sporting and Dramatic News" in 1894.

Beer, W. Andrew (op.1904-1944)
Interesting sporting artist who worked almost exclusively on portraits of racing pigeons, all of which were inscr. and very often dated. His paintings of hunting are rare and usually painted in grisaille. His painting in watercolour of "St. Amant" winning the Derby in 1904 is a fine example of his equestrian work. It is also very similar to the work of John Beer (q.v.) who may have been closely related.

Beerbohm, Sir Max (1872-1956)

Brilliant caricaturist and novelist whose cartoon portrait of the cricketer Dr. W.G. Grace receiving a cheque for £10,000 bearing the signature of the editor of "The Daily Telegraph", pen and ink, 8in.x12¾in. is in MCC Collection. Beerbohm, who was an admirer of Carlo Pellegrini (q.v.), the "Vanity Fair" caricaturist, sketched his subjects in a very similar style and under the sobriquet "Ruth", "Max" or "Bulbo" drew nine cartoons for "Vanity Fair" which appeared between 1896-1905.

Begg, Samuel (op.1886-1916)

A prolific illustrator who drew sporting sketches for "The Sporting & Dramatic News" in 1896 with almost photographic precision. He exh. at the RA (1886- 1891) including his painting of "The Grand Stand - Melbourne Cup". Begg was one of the first illustrators to show the dangers of mixing motor cars with horses. His "Worse than Wire - a Motor in the Hunting Field" appeared in "The Illustrated London News", 21 December 1901.

"Beggarstaff, J & W"

Pseudonym used by the artists William Nicholson and James Pryde (qq.v.) for their poster work, to distinguish it from their serious painting.

Belcher, George Frederick Arthur, RA (1875-1948)

Black and white artist, illustrator and a leading comic draughtsman of the 1920s and 1930s. Studied at Gloucester School of Art and exh. at the RA from 1909. Elected RA in 1945, a highly unusual distinction for an illustrator. Belcher was a keen sportsman who enjoyed hunting and fishing. His illus. sporting work includes portraits of members and boxers of the National Sporting Club entitled "Odd Fish" 1923 while the British Museum have a hand coloured etching dated 1918 of a portrait of Pat O'Keefe, the wild Irishman, an outstanding middleweight boxer of the 1920s. Belcher contributed humorous sketches to "The Tatler", "Punch" and "The Graphic" and exh. at the RA from 1909. He usually drew in charcoal and it is for his brilliance as a comic draughtsman that his name will endure and his work remain a valuable contribution to social historians.

Bell, A.D. (op.1929-1967)

Decorative sporting artist of small, undistinguished hunting and sailing scenes in both oil and watercolour. A.D. Bell is said to have been an alias for the marine artist, Wilfred Knox (q.v.) though for what reason is obscure. "The Meet at the Inn", 6⅝in.x10⅞in., auctioned Phillips (Cheshire) 1992.

Bell, Arthur George, RI, ROI (1848-1916)

London-born landscape and genre painter who included some coaching scenes amongst his work. Studied at the Slade School and under Gérome at the Ecole des Beaux Arts in Paris. Exh. at the RA from 1879 and at SS.

Bell, Edward (op.1811-1847)

Worcester painter of game, fish, still lifes and landscapes. According to Grant, Bell was "a well known painter of fish and game". His RA exhibits include "Fish Peculiar to the River Severn" (1815) and "A Wounded Pheasant" (1821). Of the twenty-four paintings he exh. at BI (1814-1847) titles include "Fisherman Landing a Fish" (1831) and "The Shot Mallard" (1842).

Bell, James Torrington (1898-1970)

Scottish landscape painter who exh. at the RA, RCA and the RSA (1934-1940). Bell's painting "The 1st Green at Carnoustie", s.&d. 1952, 20in.x24in., shows his own golf club at Carnoustie, Angus, close to his home. Christie's (Chester) July 1991.

Bell, John Christopher (op.1841-1869)

Scarborough painter of sporting and equestrian subjects, game, animals and genre. He painted a number of portraits of hunters, standing in their loose boxes, between 1841 and 1860. His portrait of "Sheldrake", s.&d. 1857, 8in.x12in., was exh. "British Sporting Paintings", Harris Museum and AG Preston 1943.

Bell, Thomas Blakemore (op.1933-1939)

Yorkshire painter whose portrait of "A Golfer" is larger than his normal paintings, which are usually of miniature size. Exh. one painting at the RA and two at RMS in 1933 and 1938. "A Golfer", s.&d. 1939, 32¾in x24¼in., Sotheby's.

Bellany, John (b.1942)

Contemporary Scottish painter of portraits and figurative compositions, often symbolic, always strongly painted with a fine sense of colour. His portrait of the cricketer, "Ian Botham", is in the National Portrait Gallery, London. Bellany studied at Edinburgh College of Art (1960-1965) under Sir Robin Philipson. Awarded Andrew Grant Scholarship (1962). Travelled to Paris. Awarded post graduate (1965). Attended Royal College of Art, London. Studied under Carel Weight (q.v.) and Peter de Francia (1965-1968). Lecturer in painting Brighton College of Art (1968).

Bellard, I.B.G. (op.1838-1839)

Equestrian artist whose paintings of "Bessy Bedland" a bay racehorse on a course, s.&d. 1838, and "Miss" inscr. "A chestnut hunter aged four years, the property of Mark Milner of Anley Hall", s.&d. 1839, were auctioned at Sotheby's in 1972 and 1979 respectively.

Bellinger (op.1803)

Exh. three paintings at the RA in 1803, "Bear Hunting", "Hay Making" and "Mare with a Spaniel", from a Kentish Town address.

Bellows, George (1882-1925)

American portrait painter, illustrator and engraver. Better known, perhaps, as one of the finest boxing artists of all time. Studied art under Robert Henri (1865-1929) from 1904-1906. Although not a founding member of the Ash Can School, Bellows became one of its leading representatives. Most late 19th century American artists in common with many British artists had deliberately ignored urban life in favour of Arcadian landscapes, and compared with these the paintings of the Ash Can School appeared brash and raw. The National Gallery of Washington has examples of Bellows' boxing paintings. In the early days Bellows was a passionate baseball player and indeed was so good at the game that the Cincinnati Reds offered him a contract, which he declined, solely because he wanted to be an artist. His baseball drawings were never exh. but were executed in crayon using the vivid colours that identify his work. He also made a number of tennis engravings and his painting "Tennis Tournament" 1920, 59in.x66in., is in the National Gallery of Art, Washington DC.

Belon, J. (op.1899)
"Les Jeux Scolaires au Bois de Boulogne - Les jeu de la crosse". March 1899.

Belshaw, Frank (c.1850-1910)
Exh. one painting of river fish at the RA and two at SS (1881-1882) from a Nottingham address.

Beltyukov, Boris (b.1926)
Contemporary Russian painter, born in Kirov in the Urals. Beltyukov studied at the Serov School of Painting in Leningrad before entering the city's famous Repin Institute. His painting "The Race", 1989, 39in.x24in., Roy Miles Gallery, London, shows the Russian love of trotting races, the only sport upon which gambling is permitted.

Ben, I. (b.1935)
Contemporary artist of sporting scenes whose work includes a painting of "HRH the Prince of Wales Shooting Pheasants at Sandringham" (1987), 12in.x15in., "Tattersalls Yearling Sales at Newmarket" and "In the Paddock at Newmarket" both s.&d. '88, 9¼in.x7¼in.

Benger, Berenger, RBA, RCA (1868-1935)
Landscape painter, the son of the artist W. Edmund Benger. Studied at Antwerp under Verlat and exh. widely from 1884. His watercolour portrait of a female golfer on a Scottish fairway, 10in.x14in., was auctioned Christie's (Chester) July 1991.

Benham, Thomas C.S. (op.1878-1922)
London painter of undistinguished landscapes, portraits, sporting figures and flower subjects. Exh. a poaching picture at the RA (1883) and twenty-three other works (1878-1893).

Bennett, Frank Moss (1874-1953)
Liverpool-born sporting painter. Studied art at the Slade School, St. John's Wood School of Art and the RA Schools where he won a gold medal and a travelling scholarship. Like many distinguished early 20th century artists, he tended to paint his subjects in romantic 18th century settings. The sporting subjects he painted include hunting, fishing and lawn bowls. Exh. at the RA (1898-1928). Titles include "The Greek Runner, Ladas Falling Dead as he goes to Receive his Crown at Olympia" (1900).

Bennett, Godwin
Marine artist who included yachting races amongst his work. "Rounding the Buoy", 19½in.x23½in., Sotheby's (Sussex) 1985.

Bennett, Miss Isabel (op.1870-1889)
London painter of river scenes and angling subjects who exh. several at SS (1870-1877) including "On the River Mole - an Angling Party" in 1871.

Bennett, S. (op.1898)
His painting of "A Shooting Pony with Game and a Dog", s.&d. '98, 9½in.x13½in., was auctioned at Bearnes in 1988.

Bennett (or Bennet), Thomas (op.1796-1821)
A sporting painter from Woodstock who exh. seven sporting paintings at the RA (1796-1799), and six animal watercolours at OWS (1816-1819). Whessel engraved a plate from his painting "William Phelps on his Pony with Hounds" in 1812. William Phelps was kennel huntsman to William Lowndes Stone of Brightwell near Oxford. A painting of "Nineteen Couple of Harriers, their Master and Huntsman", 4ft.6in.x6ft.9in., was repro. and illus. in "Country Life" (10.6.76). An engraving of "A Fox and Cubs" by Charles Turner after the work by Bennett was pub. in 1821, 18½in.x20¼in.

Bennett, William (1811-1871)
Landscape painter who included a number of fishing scenes amongst his work.

Bensing, Frank C. (1893-1983)
Chicago-born magazine illustrator who became increasingly a portrait painter and whose subjects include Herbert Hoover and Joseph P. Kennedy. Bensing's portrait of "Walter Hagen" (1892-1969), 39in.x29¾in., painted in the 1950s and based on photographs, hangs in the museum of the USGA to whom it was presented in 1958 by Robert A. Stranahan. Hagen won the U.S. Open Golf Championship twice (1914 and 1919) and the Open in Britain four times (1922, 1924, 1928 and 1929), the USPGA Championship five times (1921, 1924, 1925, 1926 and 1927) and he captained the American Ryder Cup team several times well into the thirties.

Benson, E. (op.1846-1847)
Equestrian and sporting artist whose portrait "A Squire with his Dog and Horse in a Landscape", painted in 1847, was auctioned at Christie's 1988. Very little is known about this artist except that he exh. at the Liverpool Academy in 1846 and a portrait by him of John Bramley-More was exh. at Liverpool in "A Taste of Yesterday" (1970).

Benson, Frank Weston (1862-1951)
American angling and wildfowl artist whose work was exh. at Maxwell Galleries Ltd., San Francisco, California.

Benson, J. (op.1805-1811)
Animal, sporting and landscape artist originally from Lancashire. He exh. "A Hare Coursing Scene" at the RA (1807), a portrait of "A Pointer" (1809) and "Warrior" a favourite hunter (1811) from a London address in Soho.

Benson, J. (op.1870-1890)
Later artist of several game shooting paintings, s.&d. between 1870 and 1890. Possibly American as all have been auctioned in New York in recent years.

Benstead (or Bensted), Joseph of Maidstone (op.1828-1849)

Kent sporting and landscape painter who exh. at the RA (1828-1847). Subjects include dead game, snipe, heron and shot mallard. Two paintings by him, "The Maidstone Steeplechase" (1839) and "Tally Ho", were lithographed by J.W. Giles. He also exh. at SS (1830-1846), including a painting in 1834 entitled "Firstling" the property of J. Hickham, Esq. His painting of the horse "Batchelor" with his owner John Roper of Hollingbourne, Kent, s.&d. 1814, was exh. at Messrs. Ackermanns Gallery, June 1930, as reported in "The Connoisseur" of that date. This painting was lithographed by T. Fairland (1804-1852).

Bentley, Joseph Clayton (1809-1851)

Bradford-born landscape artist in watercolour who is known to have made copies of the sporting works of Henry Alken Snr. (q.v.) He was also an engraver and studied under Robert Brandard (1805-1862). His portrait "A Gentleman on a bay Hunter with his Dogs and a Country House beyond", s.&d. February 1829, 27in.x28in., was auctioned at Sotheby's (1987).

Bentley, Nicolas Clerihew, FSIA, FRSA (1907-1978)

London journalist, author and humorous illustrator who studied art at Heatherleys. Illus. the daily pocket cartoons for "The Daily Mail" (1958-1962). His illustrations, many of them sporting, often depict figures without background or setting. Bentley's method is typically and superbly illustrated by the quintessentially, tough, middle-aged Englishwoman, pole-vaulting a ditch whilst otter hunting. A prolific book illustrator, including his own "Le Sport" (1937), Bentley became a director of André Deutsch (1950).

Béraud, Jean (1849-1936)

French figure and café scene painter whose fine painting of a café interior with a billiard scene "La Partie de Billiard", 13in.x19in., was exh. Richard Green, London. Although a close friend of the Impressionist painter Gustave Caillebotte (1848-1894) Béraud was never part of the Impressionist group. The son of a French sculptor, Béraud studied art at Leon Bonnat's school for two years. Exh. at the Paris Salon (1873-1889). He was also a member of the French Pastel Society and in 1885 was noticed by the French critic, Roger Portalis, who admired his work. Founder of the Salon de la Société Nationale des Beaux Arts in 1890, where he exh. until 1929. Béraud's fine painting of horse racing at Longchamp in 1886 is a thrilling crowd scene of fashionable race-goers cheering the horses past the post. Béraud has wisely featured the horses in a secondary role since his talents clearly do not lie in horse portraiture.

Beresford, Frank Ernest (1881-1967)

Derby-born equestrian artist who studied at Derby School of Art (1895-1900), St. John's Wood Art School (1900-1901) and later at the RA Schools (1901-1906).

Bergandi, Hector Luis (b.1950)

Argentinian painter and illustrator of motor racing scenes who has received international recognition through the publication of his automotive subjects in "Road and Track" magazine. His work includes thirty-two World Championship winning Grand Prix cars and their drivers, since the inception of the championship in 1950, which appeared in "Road and Track" (June 1982) in their 35th Anniversary issue.

Berkeley, Stanley, RE (1855-1909)

London etcher, animal and sporting painter who also included a number of historical and battle scenes, as well as landscapes, amongst his work. Exh. at the RA (1884-1891) including his painting entitled "Full Cry", and at SS, NW, GG and elsewhere (1878-1902). He illus. the "Wild Red Deer" in "A Year of Sport and Natural History" (1895) and contributed to "The Sporting and Dramatic News" (1896), "The Graphic" and "The Sketch". Lived in Esher and Surbiton. Berkeley also illus. the "Athletics and Football" edn. of the "Badminton Library" series, pub. in 1888, of which "The Association Game" is the frontispiece. Contributed to "The Sporting and Dramatic News" (1896). His painting "The Eclipse Stakes, Sandown Park" was repro. as a hand-coloured lithograph.

Bernasconi A. (op.1893)

Portrait of the cyclist "F.J. Osmond on his Bicycle", s.&d. 1893, and inscr., was auctioned Phillips (Edinburgh) 1987.

Berridge, John, FSA (1740-1804)

Lincolnshire portrait painter, pupil of Sir Joshua Reynolds (1766-1768). Studied at the RA Schools (1769). Exh. nine works at the RA and twenty-eight at SS (1766-1792) from a London address. His half-length portrait of "Jim Belcher, Champion Boxer of England", in a dark coat, yellow waistcoat and white stock, 30in.x25in., was auctioned Bonhams 1984.

Berrie, John Archibald Alexander, RCA, FRSA, (1887-1964?)

Manchester-born portrait painter, who studied at Liverpool School of Art and in Paris. Exh. five works at the RA from 1924 and at the Paris Salon (1935) a portrait of the flat race jockey, Gordon Richards, in racing silks. His portrait of the American amateur golf champion Robert "Bobby" Tyre Jones, Jnr. (1902-1972) hangs in the Royal Liverpool Golf Club at Hoylake. Berrie, who was himself a club golfer, probably painted the portrait to mark Jones' "Grand Slam". His other sporting portraits include those of the champion golfers Sir Henry Cotton, MBE, Bobby Locke and Dai Rees. Berrie was apparently living in Johannesburg in 1964 (Pavière).

Berry, John (b.1920)

Painter and illustrator, sometimes of equestrian scenes. Studied at Hammersmith School of Art (1934-1939) and won a scholarship to the RA Schools (not taken up due to the war). Has illus. books for the publishers Ladybird, Pan and Corgi.

Berthoud, Henry (1790-1864)

Born London, died Paris. Exh. two game paintings in 1846 at SS. Two poaching pictures engraved by R.G. Reeves, after the work by this artist, were sold at Sotheby's (Bel.) 1979.

Bertrand, Guillaume (op.1764-1800)
A French portraitist of this name exh. four paintings at FS in 1764 of which one was "A Gentleman Going A'Shooting". Bertrand was a pupil of Carl Van Loo, at the same time as R. West of Dublin which may explain Bertrand's move to Dublin in 1765 where he opened a drawing school. Exh. Dublin (1765-1770) after which he returned to Paris and exh. Paris Salon (1791 and 1800).

Best, John (op.1750-1801)
London semi-primitive sporting artist about whom very little is known. He exh. two works at the RA and seven at SA (1772-1780). His sporting work includes portraits of game and fighting cocks and several portraits of racehorses including Lord Claremont's racehorse "Imperator" (1780), "Eager" (the 1791 Derby winner), and "Marcia", owned and bred by Sir William Aston, for whom she won over twenty matches (1789-1791).

Best, Thomas (op.1730-1798)
Author of "A Concise Treaty on the Art of Angling" (1798). Walter Shaw Sparrow had seen two good equestrian paintings by him, one an oil of a horse, boy, groom and dog. Unfortunately he did not record where he had seen them. Several paintings of racehorses have been seen signed "Thos. Best".

Bestosmith, W. (op.1836-1837)
Suffolk artist who painted fish in a similar manner to Stephen Elmer (q.v.) Exh. two fish paintings at the RA in 1836 and 1837.

Bettesworth, Walter Ambrose (op.1878-1906)
Cricket correspondent to "The Field" from 1904 who illus. his articles. To an expert knowledge of cricket he added a thorough appreciation of art and was a capable landscape artist. Educated at Ardingley College, Sussex where he was a promising bat, he later played for Sussex, representing that county against the Australians in 1878 and 1882. Exh. one painting at the Walker AG, Liverpool (1906).

Beuttler, E.G.O. (op.1938)
"The Navy takes on the Royal Horse Artillery at Olympia in a Race", watercolour, 13¼in.x21¼in., s.&d. 1938, repro. "The Field" 1986.

Bevan, Robert Polhill, NEAC, LG (1865-1925)
Landscape and equestrian artist. Studied at Westminster School of Art in 1888, under Fred Brown (q.v.) and then at the Académie Julian in Paris (1891-1893). Bevan developed a highly individualistic style and produced a number of lithographs depicting fox-hunting which appeared at the end of the 19th century. These include "Huntsman and Hounds" c.1896, "Hounds at Work" c.1896/7, "Forrard On" c.1898. Bevan was a fine horseman and hunted with a number of packs including the Crawley and Horsham, the Southdown, the Dulverton, the Devon and Somerset and the Tangier Hunt.

Bewick, Robert Elliot (1788-1849)
Newcastle-born engraver and illustrator. The only son of Thomas Bewick (q.v.). In 1812 he assisted his father with the illustrations for "Aesops Fables" (1818) and on the uncompleted "History of British Fishes". Sketches by this artist for the latter book as well as some of the illustrations for "British Birds" (1826) are in the British Museum.

Bewick, Thomas (1753-1828)
Newcastle engraver who was apprenticed to Ralph Beilby and became proficient in wood cutting. It was Beilby who wrote the text to Bewick's "General History of Quadrupeds" pub. in 1790. One of the many facets of their work together were beautiful engraved hunt cards. Deservedly famous for his book of "British Birds" (1797 and 1804), Bewick also painted birds in watercolour. Both the British Museum and V & A have collections of his work, but very few of his exquisite drawings remain. Bewick had a number of pupils including the sporting artist Luke Clennell (q.v.).

Bickerdyke, John
Nom de plume of Charles Henry Cook, English novelist, journalist and writer on angling and other sports. Born in London (1858). Pub. "Angling in Salt Water" (1887), "Days on Thule with Rod, Gun and Camera" (1894), "Wild Sports in Ireland" (1897, "Sea Fishing" (Badminton Library) (1895) and "The Book of the All Round Angler" (1900).

Biddulph, S. (Colonel) (op.c.1890)
This artist from Kings County in Ireland spent over thirty years in the army in India where he was President of the Indian Falconry Society. He specialised in paintings of hawking and falconry and portraits of peregrine falcons. He may well have been closely related to General Sir Michael A. Biddulph, who exh. an Indian scene at SS in 1890.

Biegel, Peter (1913-1987)
One of the finest sporting artists of his generation. A pupil of Lucy Kemp-Welch (q.v.) at her school of animal painting at Bushey until the outbreak of war (1939-1945). An admirer of the sporting artist Lionel Edwards (q.v.) he became the only pupil that Edwards ever had, joining him after his studies at Bournemouth School of Art. Biegel held his first one-man shows at the Rowland Ward Gallery in Piccadilly and then at the Tryon Gallery, London. His work became widely known through several extremely successful Christmas card designs for the Injured Jockeys Fund in the 1960s, one of which showing four great chasers, "Pas Seul", "Arkle", "Mill House" and "King's Nephew" sold over 85,000 copies in 1964. Biegel's sporting and equestrian work includes point-to-points, steeplechasing, flat racing, show jumping and hunting scenes and ranges from a portrait of Pat Smythe over the waterjump at Hickstead to the Cambridgeshire (1949). A number of his works have been repro. as prints.

Bielfield, H. (op.1826-1847)
This artist from Exeter, Devon painted several equestrian scenes which he exh. at the SS (1826-1847) all featuring children and ponies, "Children Riding", "Boys and Pony" etc.

Bigg, William Redmore, RA (1755-1828)
Painter of portraits and rustic genre. Pupil of Edward Penny (q.v.). Entered the RA Schools (1778). Prolific exhibitor at the RA (1780-1827), FS and BI (1806-1828). His exh. sporting work at the RA includes a portrait of "A Gentleman and his Son Returning from Coursing" (1787). His painting "The Angler" was engraved in 1787 by John Ogborne (1755-1837). His portrait of "John Charles Rheade with Cricket Bat and Ball" is in the Lords Collection, MCC.

Biggs, Thomas (op.1893-1903)
Indifferent equestrian artist of a number of portraits of hunters in stables.

Bihan, Peter Le (op.1860-1870)
French painter of "Longchamp" (14 July 1862) showing a detailed but distant view of the fashionable race crowd and the new grandstand at Longchamp racecourse opened in 1857, in the smart setting of the Bois de Boulogne, 20in.x35in., Sotheby's (NY) 1986.

Bindley, Charles (1795-1859)
Better known as the first class rider, sporting writer and illustrator "Harry Hieover" (q.v.) who wrote "Practical Hints on the Management of the Stable", first pub. by Longmans in 1848, and "The Pocket and The Stud". Born at Enfield Chase he died at Brighton whilst staying with Sir Thomas Barratt-Lennard. The self-portrait of Charles Bindley on his favourite horse "Harlequin" was painted by Bindley, engraved by E. Hacker and repro. "The British Racehorse" in August 1953.

Binks, Ruben Ward (op.1924-1930s)
Lancashire-born sporting artist of gundogs and hounds, who went to live in America in the 1930s. He was commissioned to paint the dogs at Girelda Farms by Mrs. Geraldine Rockefeller Dodge in 1929. Illus. "Gundogs" by Patrick Chalmers and "About Our Dogs" by A. Croxton Smith. Exh. Preston HM and AG 1943 "British Sporting Paintings".

Binnie, William, DA (b.1941)
Scottish landscape artist who won the Stewart Prize in the painting competition held by the RSA in 1963. "The 17th", a watercolour, 26in.x19¼in., painted in 1985, features the 461 yard par 4 hole at St. Andrews, one of the most difficult in championship golf and known as the "Road" hole. Collection Royal Liverpool Golf Club, Hoylake.

Binns, David (op.1874-1884)
Sporting artist who included a number of fox and fox-hunting studies amongst his work.

Birch, Samuel John Lamorna, RA, RWS, RWA (1869-1955)
Cheshire-born landscape and angling painter and a very keen fly fisherman. From 1889 he regularly visited Cornwall where he adopted the name Lamorna to distinguish himself from another artist living in Newlyn, Lionel Birch. Birch's river and fishing scenes are usually of a very high quality although his later work became loose and the quality somewhat uneven. He painted a fly fishing study at Lamorna in 1923 especially for W. Shaw Sparrow's book "Angling in British Art" (1923). Birch occasionally painted skiing scenes which are interesting examples of the talent that this artist showed for water subjects.

Bird, Cyril Kenneth (1887-1965)
Black and white, humorous and poster artist who often signed his work "Fougasse" (q.v.). Art editor of "Punch" (1937) and editor (1949-1952). Son of the England cricketer, Arthur Bird. Illus. "So This is Golf" (1923) and "A Gallery of Games" (1920).

Bird, John Alexander Harrington (1846-1936)
London sporting, equestrian and animal painter in both oil and watercolour. Studied at the RA Schools and exh. at the RA from 1870. Went to Montreal, Canada (1875), becoming Director of Art at the Board of School Commissioners. Elected an Associate of the Royal Canadian Academy (1880). Returned to England (1885). Painted a great number of equestrian scenes, some for the Royal Family, and many Arab horse scenes. The sports he covered include fox-hunting, coaching, dressage, pig-sticking, coursing - the Waterloo Cup, and racing, including his portrait of "Signorina" a filly by St. Simon who won all nine of her races as a two year old in 1889.

Bird, W.
The pseudonym used by the artist Jack Butler Yeats (q.v.) for his work contributed to "Punch" (1896-1914).

Birley, Sir Oswald Hornby Joseph, RP, ROI, NPS, IS (1880-1952)
Distinguished portrait painter whose fine study of Benjamin and Oliver Jones, the Liverpool banking twins, hangs at the Walker AG. Benjamin was President of the Royal Falconry Club at Marlborough and has a hooded falcon on his fist. His brother is shown, seated under a tree, with his favourite grey fighting cock beside him, trimmed and spurred. Birley, who was born in New Zealand, studied in Dresden and Florence and at the Académie Julian in Paris. In 1902 he entered as O.H. Birley as a young competitor in the Champion Cup for Croquet. He did not win and does not seem to have painted the game. Birley's famous portrait of the falconer, Mr. G. Blackhall-Simmonds, was painted in 1927.

Bischoff, C. Frederick (1819-1873)
German artist who exh. a painting of "The Secret" winning the Challenge Cup of the RTYC for the second time (value 130 guineas) 8 June 1847, at SS in 1848 from a London address.

Bishop, Alfred S. (op.1861-1889)
Sporting and equestrian artist who painted a portrait of the 4th Marquess of Salisbury on horseback, s.&d. 1874, which is at Hatfield, a bearded gentleman on a bay hunter, s.&d. 1878, 18in.x14in., which was auctioned Bonhams 1985 and a portrait of "John Watson, MFH to the Carlow Hunt", s.&d. 1861, 14in.x11in., which was exh. by Messrs. Ackermanns. Bishop painted a fine coaching scene featuring "John Selby's Brighton coach outside the New White Horse

Cellar, Piccadilly", s.&d. 1889, which is in the collection of the London Museum. This famous record which is known as the "Selby Run" was also painted by John Alexander Harrington Bird (q.v.). The run took place on 13 July 1888 in 7 hours 50 minutes - a total of 108 miles in a coach called "The Old Times".

Bishop, Evelyn
Pseudonym used by the marine artist Frank Dobson (q.v.) RA, ARBS (1883-1963) with which name he often signed his work.

Bispham, Henry Collins (1841-1882)
American artist from Philadelphia who specialised in animal painting. Studied art under William T. Richards and later, under Otto Weber in Paris. Exh. one work of a "Lion" at the RA in 1880. He also painted "Colonel Kane's coach on the open road", s.&d. 1876, 30in.x48in., auctioned Christie's (NY) 1982.

Blackburn, Jemima (Mrs., née Wedderburn)
See Wedderburn

Blackburn, Joseph (op.1752-1778)
Itinerant portrait painter who came to London in 1764. "Furley", a chestnut gelding standing in a stable, signed and inscr. "Coxshill", 27½in.x35in.

Blackburne, E.R. Ireland (op.1891-1901)
Landscape artist who exh. three paintings at the RA (1891-1901) from a Newlyn address. His RA exhibit for 1897 was "Rough Shooting - a Right and a Left".

Blair, Andrew (op.1847-1885)
Scottish landscape painter who exh. "The Quoit Players" at the BI in 1847 from a Dunfermline address.

Blake, Benjamin, RBA (op.1807-1830)
London painter of countless game studies but also some sporting scenes. Elected RBA in 1824. "Coursing at May Hill, Gloucestershire" signed but not dated, 24½in.x29½in.. was auctioned at Sotheby's in 1973.

Blake, Geraldine B. (Mrs. Thomas) (op.1906-1919)
Sculptor and artist who exh. at the RA (1906-1919). Her portrait "A Hunter in a Stable", painted in 1906, was exh. Astley House Fine Art, Moreton-in-Marsh, Glos.

Blake, J. (op.1796)
A watercolour, 8¼in.x13in., showing hounds emerging from a covert, hot on the scent, s.&d. "J. Blake, Winchester, August 29th 1796" was exh. at the Parker Gallery, London (1950).

Blake, Peter (b.1932)
Born Dartford. Studied at Gravesend School of Art and the RCA. Became a wrestling enthusiast and has painted wrestlers in many guises, including Kendo Nagasaki.

Blake, T. (op.1818-1831)
Little is known about this artist except that he possessed considerable ability when he painted "The Fives Court, James Street, Haymarket with Jack Randall and Ned Turner sparring", 23¼in.x28½in. This is a portrait of prize-fighters and others at one of the principal London meeting places. The Prince Regent was patron and the boxers Randall, with Tom Cribb and others, attended his coronation as "bouncers". This oil painting was exh. by Richard Green in 1984 at his London Gallery. An etching and an uncoloured aquatint by Charles Turner, 20in.x26in., after this painting but with a number of differences, pub. 1821 and printed by McQueen & Co. was lent by the British Museum for the Exhibition of British Sporting Paintings at the Haywood Gallery in 1974. Blake also painted a watercolour of the same subject, 18¼in.x26in. which was lent from a private collection for the same exhibition and it is of course possible that Turner took his etchings from the watercolour. A coloured aquatint by Turner after Blake (1818) is in The Paul Mellon Collection, Upperville, Va, USA. Blake exh. one portrait of - Westcar, Esq. at SS in 1831 from a London address, 22 Clarence Gardens, Regents Park. In 1821 Turner engraved a singerie subject after Blake entitled "The Duellists" showing monkeys duelling with pistols. Blake also painted eight illustrations of a Poacher's Progress which were engraved and pub. again by Turner, in 1826. Interestingly in 1825/6 Charles Turner also engraved a work entitled "Poachers" which was after the work by C. Blake and I.L. Turner, indicating again the Turner and Blake link.

Blake, William (1757-1827)
"The Echoing Green" I and II from "Songs of Innocence" showing a pencil sketch of a cricketer. First pub. in 1789 and re-issued in 1794 when Blake revised the illustrations to "The Echoing Green", substituting a straight bat for the older type curved bat. Blake was a poet and a painter who studied at the RA Schools and studied engraving under James Basire (1730-1802). He was influenced by the neo-classicists and violently opposed to the ideals of Reynolds (q.v.).

Blake, William of Newhouse (op.1794-1798)
This artist is said to have been a pupil of J.M.W. Turner (q.v.). He lived in Glamorgan and was active between 1794 and 1798. He is eligible in this Dictionary for his painting of a "Hunter on a Path in a Landscape" which was auctioned at Bonhams in 1983.

Blaker, Hugh, RBA (d.1936)
Sussex landscape and figure painter who exh. a painting entitled "Regatta Day" at the NEAC in 1897. Also exh. "The Brawl" in 1909. Elected RBA 1913. Became curator of the Holbourne Art Museum, Bath in 1909. Elected RBA (1913).

Blampied, Edmund, RBA, RE (1886-1966)
Landscape and equestrian painter in oil and watercolour. Born in Jersey. Studied art under P. Connard and J. McKeggie (1903-4) and at the L.C.C Art School (Bolt Court) (1905-13). Exh. at the R.A. and the Paris Salon. He was also a fine etcher which he took up in 1913. Elected RE (1921) and RBA (1938). Won a gold medal for lithography at the Paris International Exhibition in 1925. He included several polo studies amongst the sporting work he covered often accompanied by a witty caption.

Blanche, Jacques Emil, NEAC, RP (1861-1942)
French equestrian artist of several fox-hunting scenes in England including "The Cattistock Hunt" (Retour de Chasse) s.&d. 1913, 13in.x18in. and one inscr. "Fleet House, Weymouth, Devonshire" 1931. Blanche, who studied in Paris and London, had dual French/English nationality. Member NEAC 1887, RP 1905.

Bland, Miss Emily Beatrice, NEAC (1864-1951)
Lincolnshire-born landscape painter in oil who studied at Lincoln School of Art and at the Slade School (1892-1894) under Fred Brown (q.v.) and Henry Tonks (q.v.). Exh. at the NEAC from 1897. Elected member (1926). Bland's painting "The Game of Croquet" was exh. at the NEAC in 1913 (No.232).

Bland, John H. (op.1860-1890)
Landscape painter whose charming watercolour 11¼in.x8¼in. "Off to the Shoot" is signed but indis. dated. Christie's (Sth. Ken.) 1987.

Blazeby (Blaseby), James (op.1854-1880)
Animal and equestrian painter whose work includes portraits of prize winning cattle and several paintings of saddled hunters and ponies in harness.

Blinks, Thomas (1853-1910)
London sporting and animal painter who was born at Maidstone, Kent. A very fine horseman who specialised in painting hunting scenes. He collaborated on more than one occasion with Fred Roe (q.v.), Roe painting the portraits and Blinks the horses. Blinks exh. at the RA from 1883. Titles include "Portrait of a Gentleman on Horseback with Hounds" in 1898 and "The Hunter's Funeral" in 1886. Blinks was one of the few artists to portray George V in the hunting field. His studio sale "the remaining works of the late Thomas Blinks" took place on 25 March 1911, auctioned by Christie's.

Blood, Gerry, RSA
Contemporary painter from Nottingham whose watercolour of a man playing bowls with other figures in the background, 12in.x18in., was contributed to the Art Exhibition held at the V & A Museum during the Olympic Games in London (1948). He became the official artist to the Olympic Games at Seoul in Korea in 1988.

Blunt, Sir Charles William, Bt. (1810-1890)
Talented amateur artist who painted a number of sporting scenes including a portrait of his cousin "Sir Walter Blunt Bt." (1826-1847), "Chamois Shooting" and a painting of "A Point to Point" in 1846.

Blyth, E. (op.1836-1838)
Equestrian artist of several hunting portraits.

Blythe, David Gilmour (1815-1865)
American painter of pessimistic urban scenes which epitomised life's darker side. Included in this Dictionary for his watercolour still life of baseball equipment entitled "Youth", 8in.x12in., private collection USA. "Youth" and its companion "Old Age" were commissioned by a Pittsburgh merchant and collector, Christian H. Wolffe, for 25 dollars, including frames.

Board, John Arthur (Major) (1895-1965)
Illustrator, author, sportsman and sports correspondent. Member of "The Times" sporting staff for thirty years covering hunting, polo, horse shows, real tennis, rackets and, on occasions, golf tournaments when Bernard Darwin was unavailable. His natural talent for drawing horses was outstanding. He was a fine sportsman, reaching the last eight players of the amateur golf championship to play in two Walker Cup Trials, and he was a keen cricketer. As "The Times" obituary to Board said (26 June 1965) "As an illustrator to his own books and notably in 'From Point to Point' (1953) he had a remarkable gift for depicting the polo pony in action and catching the finer points of the game at high speed." Author and illustrator of "Polo" pub. Faber (1956).

Boardman S.R., (op. 1940s)
"The Sergeant Major Playing Snooker", pen/black ink and blue wash, Christie's (Sth. Ken.).

Boddington, Edwin Henry (c.1836-1905)
London landscape painter, often of river scenes with an angling interest. Son of Henry John Boddington (q.v.), the landscapist, who changed his name from Williams.

Boddington, Henry John (1811-1865)
London landscape painter, second son of Edward Williams, who took his wife's maiden name so as not to be confused with the rest of the Williams family of artists. He specialised like his son in river scenes with a strong angling interest. Exh. the main bulk of his work (244 pictures) at SS including two of "Rabbit Shooting" in 1847 and 1850.

Bodger, John (op.1770-1821)
An engraver of sporting subjects who exh. "A View of Newmarket - Racehorses in Exercise" at the RA in 1821 after the work by E.F. Burney (q.v.). He is recorded as engraving a "Chart of the Fishery at Little Wittlesea Mere, Huntingdonshire" (1786) and James Seymour's "Carriage Match at Newmarket" pub. 23 April 1789.

Boetticher, Otto (c.1816-d. after 1864)
American painter and draughtsman whose drawing of a baseball game entitled "Union Prisoners at Salisbury", made while the artist was a prisoner himself in the Confederate Prison in 1862, was later adapted as a lithograph and distributed by the printing firm of Sarony, Major and Knapp in 1863.

Boilly, Louis Leopold (1761-1845)
French portraitist whose fine painting "The Interior of the Jeu de Paume, Versaille", with a game of real tennis in progress, is in a private collection. His painting "The Billiard Players", 22in.x32in., was auctioned Sotheby's (NY) 1989.

Boin, Rene (b.1953)
Interesting Dutch graduate of the Academy of Art in Arnhem who specialises in paintings of golf, tennis and cricket showing the irony of the games. "The Wedge" is a good example of Boin's work. It shows an impossible shot, even with the use of "the wedge", the golf club invented by Gene Sarazene after he lost the British Open in 1928. With his newly invented club he won it in 1932.

Boitard, Louis Philippe (op.1738-1763)
French draughtsman and engraver who worked in London and is best known for his "Exact Representation of the Game of Cricket" (engraved by H. Roberts in 1743) and the design for "The Match Ticket for 18th June 1744" which was derived from it. Boitard was a pupil of La Farge and came to England with his father c.1738.

Boldini, G. (op.1878)
This competent amateur portrait painter and caricaturist was a friend of Monsieur Perelli Rocco, who had a restaurant in Greek Street, Soho. He painted a famous watercolour in 1878 of nineteen members of the Piscatorial Society, including the angling artist H.L. Rolfe (q.v.), seated at a "T" shaped table which hung in their London club room for many years. He also did a number of drawings of other members of the Society. Sydney Pavière has mistakenly entered this artist in his Dictionary under "Boulding". Neither is he the Italian artist, Giovanni Boldini (1842-1913), who was operating at the same time.

Bolton, D.C. (op.1910-1920)
"Skiing at Gstaad", s.&d. 1914, pen, ink and watercolour. This sporting artist also painted "The Tennis Pro" (Madam Joan Carthesy) 9in.x7½in. which was auctioned at Christie's (Sth. Ken.) 1989.

Bomberg, David, LG, NS (1890-1957)
Figure painter, in both oil and watercolour, a draughtsman and a lithographer who studied at the City and Guilds School, the Westminster School of Art (1908-1910) under Sickert and the Slade School (1911-1913). "The Wrestlers", Indian ink, 10½in.x8in. drawn in 1919, auctioned Sotheby's 1988.

Bombled, Louis Charles (1862-1927)
French artist of many equestrian subjects including racing.

Bond, Arthur J.F., RSMA. (1888-1958)
Marine painter in oils and watercolours. Exhibits at RSMA include "Racing at St. Mawes - Cornwall".

Bond, John Lloyd (op.1868-1872)
London landscape painter who exh. at SS (1868-1872). His sporting watercolour "Golfing on the Common", s.&d. 1870, 7½in.x12¼in., was auctioned Christie's (Glasgow) 1984.

Bond, William Joseph J.C. (1833-1928)
Liverpool landscape and sporting artist who painted in both oils and watercolours. Apprenticed to Thomas Griffiths, a picture dealer and restorer. Lived in Caernarvon, then in Liverpool. Worked mainly for northern patrons. Exh. at SS but only twice at the RA (1871 and 1874). Included in this Dictionary for his portrait of a chestnut hunter held by a stable boy, s.&d. 1887, 11¾in.x15¼in., Sotheby's (Bel.) 1973.

Bone, Sir David Muirhead, NEAC, HRWS (1876-1953)
Glasgow-born painter who studied at Glasgow School of Art and came to London in 1901. Exh. at the RA from 1900 and NEAC from 1901. Elected member (1902).

Knighted (1937). Served as official artist during both World Wars. His painting "The Old Racecourse at Ayr" was purchased by the Scottish Modern Arts Association in 1922. He also painted "Eight Weeks at Oxford", signed and inscr. "to Mrs. Mabbott with best wishes", 5½in.x8¼in. Christie's (Sth. Ken.) 1988.

Bonnar, John A.T. (op.1885-1889)
This artist who exh. twelve works at the RSA (1885-1889) painted a portrait of "William Park Snr.", the first Open Golf Championship winner, in 1860, 107in.x70in., Royal and Ancient Golf Club of St. Andrews, Fife, Scotland. Bonnar probably painted the champion after he moved to Musselburgh from Edinburgh in 1887.

Bonnard, Pierre (1867-1947)
French painter whose interesting interpretation of "The Races" was inspired by a visit to the racetrack in 1894. The watercolour shows the starter, flag behind his back, waiting for the jockeys and their horses to sort themselves out. "The Races" is in the collection of the Virginia Museum of Fine Arts, Richmond, USA.

Bonnemer?, Thomas H. (op.1878)
"A Boat Race, Bumping Races at Oxford", signed (indis.) and dated 1878, 14in.x30in., pencil. Bonhams 1986.

Bonner, Albert E. (op.1887-1905)
London painter who exh. five pictures at the London Salon in 1905. "A Shooting Party" and "By the Stile", s.&d. 1887, 6¼in.x9½in., a pair, Bonhams 1985.

Boodle, Walter (ex.1891-1908)
Landscape painter who included hunting scenes amongst his work. His fine canvas, 20in.x36in., showing hounds hot on the scent, with the field spread out over the countryside in the background, was exh. at the Parker Gallery, London, in 1950 for their bicentenary.

Booth, J.L.C. (op.1901-1908)
Black and white artist of hunting scenes who contributed to "Punch" (1896-1906). He sometimes signed his work J.C. Booth and worked in watercolour. He was also a political cartoonist.

Booth, James William (Wilson), RCA (1867-1953)
Manchester-born landscape painter, in both oil and watercolour who included a few paintings of horses amongst his work, mostly hunter portraits.

"Borderer"
Alias Sir Richard Green-Price who wrote, amongst other topics, about racing crime which was very bad in 1898 (Bailys p.251, 1898).

Borein, Edward (1872-1945)
American etcher, artist and illustrator whose work includes several polo sketches in pencil, black ink and pen, 14in.x18½in., Christie's (NY). Borein who studied at Hopkins' Art School, San Francisco was a member of the Print Makers Society of California and the Art Students League of NY City.

Boroughs, J.
No details discovered about this artist but listed in this Dictionary for his painting entitled "Rough Shooting", signed, 23¼in.x34in., Sotheby's 1987.

Bostock, James Edward, RE, SWE, ARCA (Lond.) (b.1917)
Painter, etcher and illustrator who studied at the Medway School of Art, Rochester (1933-1936) and at the RCA (1936-1939). He contributed a football scene in woodcut entitled "Sport on the Common" to the XIVth Olympiad Sport in Art exhibition held at the V & A Museum, London (1948). Elected RE (1961).

Boswell, James E., ARCA (1906-1971)
Painter and illustrator. Studied at the Elam School of Art, Auckland, New Zealand and at the RCA (1925-1929). Exh. at the RA, LG and abroad. Represented in several public collections. Contributed a lithograph of football to School Prints, an organisation started by Derek Rawnsley (1911-1934) whose object was to hire out sets of reproductions to schools so that pupils could become familiar with great works of art. Boswell also contributed a watercolour entitled "Chelsea Football Ground", s.&d. 1952, 31¾in.x24½in., to the exhibition held by the Football Association in 1953 - see "Sport and the Artist - Vol. I: Ball Games" (pub. ACC 1988). The V & A Museum has a drawing (1937) entitled "The Swimmer".

Bothams, Walter (op.1882-1925)
Landscape painter of rural subjects who contributed fishing sketches to "The Illustrated London News" in 1883, 1884 and again in 1894. Exh. at the RA and RBA (1882-1891).

Botheras, B.B. (op.1873-1890)
Liverpool sporting artist of a competent but provincial talent who tended, presumably through ignorance, to prepare his canvases insufficiently, if at all, for paint, with the result that while the composition remains good, the paint is often fragile and the canvas thin. The landscape backgrounds, like those of many third rate artists, tend to be weak. His portrait of "Fly", a greyhound coursing winner, s.&d. '73 and inscr., 20in.x27in., was auctioned Sotheby's (Glasgow) 1985.

Bott, R.T (op.1824-1862)
Listed as a London portrait and figure painter who exh. at the RA (1847-1862). He was also an equestrian artist who specialised in portraits of racehorses, including those of "Jerry" (by "Smolenska") winner of the 1824 St. Leger with his groom and jockey and "Birmingham" winner of the 1830 St. Leger. (Both horses were also painted by J.F. Herring Snr. (q.v.)). His portrait of Sir Robert Peel, the reformer who was incidentally a very keen racing man, is in the Birmingham AG and his competent portrait of a mounted Hussar was painted in 1839. It is more likely that Bott came from the Birmingham area and not London.

Bouché, Louis (1896-1969)
Painter of American baseball scenes whose work spanned the Depression years. His painting of 1939, a "Baseball Game, Long Island" shows a match taking place in a relaxed, leisure setting, more reminiscent of pre-Depression times, 20in.x25in. The Metropolitan Museum of Art.

Boudin, Eugène (1824-1898)
French landscape painter who was a close friend of Monet (1840-1926). Included in this Dictionary for "The Race Track at Deauville", 1866, The Paul Mellon Collection, Upperville, Va, USA. In 1850 Deauville was a dying fishing village until Dr. Joseph Olliffe and the great sportsman, the duc de Morny, transformed it between 1855-1866, opening a new race track in 1864. 250 villas were built in three years and the permanent population of Deauville increased from 113 in 1850 to 1,150 in 1866, augmented by summer visitors. Boudin, who specialised in beach scenes and was an advocate of "direct painting from nature", exh. at the first Impressionist exhibition in 1874.

Bough, Samuel, RSA, RSW (1822-1878)
Scottish landscape painter in both oil and watercolour who included amongst his sporting work paintings of otter hunting, shooting, golf, skittles, cricket, fishing etc. He collaborated with Robert Harrington (q.v.) to paint "The Carlisle Steeplechase at Broadfield" (1844), 24½in.x35½in., a work on which Sidney Gilpin, later Bough's biographer (1905) commented in "The Carlisle Journal", 22 June 1844: "We have just seen on the easel of Mr. S. Bough, a most promising young artist of this City, a view of the steeplechase on Broadfield. Some excellent likenesses have been introduced and the picture is one of interest and beauty and will when finished materially advance Mr. Bough's reputation as an artist". Bough's painting "Cricket at Edenside, Carlisle", 24in.x35in., was commissioned by Mr. William Howe, one of the umpires at the match. Carlisle City AG. Elected RSA (1875), RSW (1878).

Boughton, George Henry, RA, RI, ROI (1833-1905)
Painted very decorative landscapes and some sporting scenes. Born near Norwich but went with his family to live in America in 1839. Came to London in 1853 to study art and then returned to the States to practise as a landscape painter until 1859 when he went to Paris to study under Edouard Frère. He finally settled in London in 1862. A prolific exhibitor at the RA where his work included "A Sportswoman on a Highland River" (1896) and another fishing painting in 1898. An attractive painting entitled "The Skater", a subject that he painted several times, was auctioned Sotheby's (Sussex) 1986. Elected RI (1879), ROI (1887) and RA (1896).

Boughton, H. (op.1827-1872)
London portrait painter whose painting of "The Defiance Coach at Hyde Park Corner", s.&d. 1828, was exh. at the Christie's Art Treasures Exhibition of 1932. He exh. at the RA, BI, and SS (1830-1872), including several biblical and literary subjects.

Boult, Augustus S. (op.1813-1853)
London painter of sporting, game and landscape subjects who exh. at the RA, BI and at SS (1815-1853). His sporting work includes a number of shooting scenes,

including an interesting painting entitled "Pheasant Shooting" where the sportsman shooting pheasants is bravely doing so from the back of his pony.

Boult, Francis Cecil (op.1877-1895)

London painter of sporting subjects, mostly hunting, who exh. one painting at SS in 1885 entitled "Gone Away". He also painted "Point to Point Racing" in 1895, Bonhams (1979), which extends his recorded operating dates.

Boultbee, John, Snr. (1753-1812)

Sporting painter, chiefly of equestrian subjects, who is said to have entered the RA Schools in 1775 but unlike his twin brother Thomas (q.v.) there is no record of his enrolment amongst the students there. The Boultbee family records record that he was a pupil of Sir Joshua Reynolds (q.v.). Boultbee's patrons included the Lords Stamford and Egremont, the pioneering stock breeder Robert Bakewell (1726-1795), Richard Tattersall who commissioned John Boultbee to paint a portrait of his famous horse "High Flyer"(1774) and Thomas William Coke, later 1st Earl of Leicester. His fine study of "Charles, James Packe, the younger, Shooting at Prestwold, Leicestershire", 60in.x46½in., was repro. "The Connoisseur", March 1933.

Boultbee, John, Jnr. (op.c.1815)

Walter Shaw Sparrow said he had seen one painting signed "John Boultbee, Jnr.". This may have been by one of the five sons of John Boultbee (q.v.).

Boultbee, Thomas (1753-1808)

Twin brother of John Boultbee, Snr. (q.v.) with whom he lived and often worked. Entered the RA Schools in 1775. He also painted for Thomas William Coke, 1st Earl of Leicester, and exh. the same year as his brother John, a hunting and a shooting horse belonging to this gentleman. He must have been a very close twin for he echoed every move that his brother John made. He seems to have abandoned his professional painting career after a very fortunate marriage to Mary Kempson and he died in Shropshire in 1808. Exh. at SA, FS, and at the RA (1775-1783).

Boultbee, Thomas Joseph (1787-?)

The second son of John Boultbee, Snr. (q.v.). A Loughborough-born artist who exh. three paintings of game at the Liverpool Academy in 1812 and in 1813 he exh. a study of "A Wounded Stag taking to the Water". Boultbee remained a bachelor.

Boulton, P. (op.1898-1904)

Competent animal and equestrian artist who specialised in paintings of hunters and terriers at the turn of the century.

Bourgain, Gustave (d.1921)

French artist included in this Dictionary for his fine watercolour painting entitled "A Wrestling Match at Brest", 13in.x19¾in. Sotheby's 1989.

Bourgeois, Sir Peter Francis, RA (1756-1811)

Landscape, sporting, animal and historical painter. A pupil of De Loutherbourg (q.v.) (1774-1776) but never achieved his master's talent. Exh. 103 works at the RA (1779-1810) including "Hunting the Royal Tiger" (1787), "Hunting the Wild Boar (1787), "Horses Watering" (1793) and "Bathing Horses" (1796). Elected RA (1793). Bequeathed a collection of pictures and funds to build and maintain a gallery in Dulwich College. His portrait of a horse, signed with mono. and dated 1781, was exh. at British Sporting Paintings, Harris Museum and AG, Preston, 1943. Bourgeois died from a fall from his horse in 1811, inappropriately, as he was an excellent horseman. Knighted by the King of Poland but allowed by George III (16 April 1791) to use the title in England.

Bourhill, James E. (op.1884-1892)

This artist's sporting work includes a number of fishing scenes and studies of foxhounds. He also painted a portrait of a horse, s.&d. 1887, and head studies of foxhounds in 1880.

Boutelle, De Witt Clinton (1820-1886)

American painter of coastal and river scenes who painted a number of good fly fishing scenes, usually of trout fishing.

Bouvier, Joseph (op.1839-1889)

Anglo French artist who painted sugary subjects in pretty settings - such as "Fairies by Moonlight". His painting "Ready to Play" s.&d. 1889, 40in.x31in., (Sotheby's) shows a young boy (dressed as a girl in pink and white frills) armed with a shuttlecock racket in his right hand and a bunch of flowers in his left. This is Bouvier at his most typical and the scene, whilst decorative for those that like that sort of thing, bears little relation to a sporting contest.

Bowden, W. (op.c.1899)

The painter of a horse and rider, in an extensive landscape, s.&d. 1899, 25in.x30in., auctioned Christie's (NY) 1987.

Bowditch, Sarah (Mrs.) (1791-1856)

A talented fish painter who used a very mixed media, including gold and silver. She was the wife (and editor) of T. Bowditch, the African traveller. She illus. "Freshwater Fishes of Great Britain" pub. for the authoress in 1828. There are forty-seven plates, all exquisitely painted by hand. Example Ashmolean Museum, Oxford.

Bowen, Ralph (ex.1884-1915)

Figure painter, included in this Dictionary for his painting of a chestnut hunter in an extensive landscape 25in.x30in., Sotheby's (Chester) 1986.

Bowers, Georgina (Mrs. Bowers Edwards) (c.1830-1900)

A caricaturist and cartoonist, very often of sporting subjects, who copied John Leech's style and was indeed encouraged to draw by him. She worked for "Punch" (1866-1876) and exh. in London (1878-1880) including the Society of Female Artists in 1862. She illus. a number of sporting and country books (1862-1889) including "Canters in Crampshire" (c.1880) and "Mr. Crop's Harriers" (c.1880). She worked with John Beer (q.v.) illustrating "Tales for Sportsmen" (1885) by

"Wanderer" (W.S. Dixon) under the pseudonym of "Dragon" and "Loose Rein".

Bowkett, Jane Maria (Mrs. Charles Stuart) (op.1860-1891)
London painter of family life scenes and portraits. These include a charming study of a lady croquet player, painted c.1881, 24in.x18in. The girl, for she is hardly older, is seated, while her croquet mallet and red ball lie at her feet. Jane Bowkett exh. at the RA, BI, SS and elsewhere (1861-1891) and appears to have belonged to a large family of spinster Bowketts, all of whom painted domestic scenes and landscapes.

Bowles, Ian (b.1946)
Wildlife artist who studied ceramics at the Sir John Cass College of Art for five years. Started his own ceramics and painting studio specialising in fine watercolour paintings and glazed studies of birds. Game birds and birds of prey in landscapes are his favourite subjects.

Bowman, Jean (20th century)
Contemporary American artist who has painted horses in England and signs her name with a picture of a hunting crop.

Bowyer, William, RA (b.1926)
Staffordshire-born portrait painter who studied at Burslem School of Art, Stoke-on-Trent and at the RCA, graduating in 1949. Taught at Gravesend School of Art, Maidstone College of Art, the Central School of Art and Walthamstow School of Art, becoming Head of Fine Art at Maidstone (1971-1981) A keen cricketer himself, Bowyer's cricket portraits include Viv Richards and "Richard Hadlee in the Act of Batting". Exh. at the R.A. Summer Exhibition 1988. (No. 49). He also exh. "The Marksman" at the RA 1964 (No. 77), a painting of competitive rifle shooting at a target. His fine painting "The Bicentenary Match between the MCC XI and the Rest of the World XI", s.&d. 1987, 39in.x59in., is in the MCC Coll. Bowyer has exhib. widely and was elected RA (1981). He is a member of the RWS and RP. He is also Honorary Secretary of the NEAC.

Boyle, Cerise, The Hon. Mrs. Robert (née de Crespigny) (b.1875- op.1916)
Watercolour painter of horses from a great sporting family. Daughter of Sir Claude Champion de Crespigny. Studied art at Westminster under Sir Arthur Cope RA (1857-1940) and at the Frank Calderon School of Animal Painting for three years. Exh. two paintings at the RA and several at the Alpine Club Gallery. She also signed her equestrian work C.C. de Crespigny (q.v.).

Boyne, John (c.1750-1810)
Equestrian artist specialising in racing scenes including "A Close Finish", 16in.x28in., watercolour, pen, grey ink, auctioned Sotheby's 1988.

"Boz"
Alias the novelist Charles Dickens, writing "The Pickwick Papers".

Brabbins, Oliver
20th century illustrator whose original cricket drawings were used for the paperback covers of "England Their England" by A.G. Macdonell, pub. by Pan Books in 1949.

Brackett, W.M. (op.1869/1905)
Sporting artist and illustrator of fishing scenes who contributed much of his work to Messrs. Fores in 1905 including a series entitled "Salmon Fishing" and a number of coaching scenes. Exh. at the Great Fisheries Exhibition (1883) "The Rise", "The Leap", "The Struggle" and "Landed". Some of his early work was inscribed "Bolton".

Bradburne, Miss L. (op.1872)
A watercolour painter who exh. a portrait of "Ned Gillet, the Fisherman" at SS in 1872 from a Northwich address and one of dead game.

Bradley, Basil, RWS (1842-1904)
Landscape, sporting and animal painter. Born in London, the son of William Bradley (q.v.) Exh. at the RA from 1873 but mainly at the RWS where he was elected a full member in 1881. Became chief equestrian artist to "The Graphic" in 1869 and his lively sketches did much to help its early and best years. He included fox-hunting, otter-hunting and fly fishing amongst his work as well as a number of paintings of shooting and game dogs. Occasionally he collaborated with Francis Trappes (q.v.).

Bradley, Cuthbert (1861-1943)
Sporting artist, journalist, author and illustrator. Born in Lincolnshire, the son of the Revd. Edward Bradley (1827-1889), Vicar of Lenton with Harby (1883-1889), better known as the successful writer "Cuthbert Bede" and a keen follower of hounds, although he never hunted. Cuthbert Bradley became an architect but his great love lay in hunting and art in which he was entirely self-taught. Bradley became a highly successful sporting journalist, sometimes using the pseudonym "Whipster", and an extremely talented portrayer of hounds. He became a close friend of Frank Gillard, the famous huntsman of the Belvoir (1860-1895) with which pack Bradley hunted for many seasons. Through this friendship Bradley was able to use many hounds from this famous pack as models and it also enabled him to write "The Reminiscences of Frank Gillard, Huntsman with the Belvoir Hounds 1860-1895". As a reporter he covered many of the leading hound shows of the day including Peterborough where it is said he never missed a year. His famous watercolour work "The Peterborough Hound Show" was shown at the Bond Street galleries of Messrs. Dickinson & Foster (qq.v.) in 1900 and a report noted "the scheme of colour is pleasing in the quietness of its tones, but it is rather as a series of portraits that it claims attention - these are excellent". He regularly contributed articles to Fores "Sporting Notes and Sketches", at one time sharing the entire workload of the journal with George Finch Mason (q.v.) and R.M. Alexander (q.v.). Bradley also contributed six cartoons

to "Vanity Fair" (1899, 1901 and 1902) under his initials "C.B.". He painted "The Quorn at Kirby Gate with Tom Firr, the Huntsman" in retirement in 1899 and he worked for "Horse and Hound" during the 1930s as an illustrator. Amongst the books he wrote and illus. were "Foxhunting from Shire to Shire with many Noted Packs", "Good Sport seen with some Famous Packs" and "The Foxhound of the 20th Century" (1914).

Bradley, Edward (op.1824-1866)
"Durham", a cricket match in a field with Durham Cathedral and Castle to the right, pen and some body-colour on white paper, 14½in.x11½in., s.&d. 1849, MCC Coll. On the cricket ground the highly decorated tents represent the Gentlemen of the University, the All England Eleven and the Durham Club. The sketch is taken from the small hill in Pellaw Wood. The odds are that the cricket match was drawn by Cuthbert Bradley's father - Edward Bradley - see Cuthbert Bede. Bradley was a London painter of landscapes and still lifes who exh. at the RA, BI and RBA.

Bradley, Edward (Revd.) (1827-1889)
See "Cuthbert Bede"

Bradley, Helen, MBE (1900-1979)
Painter of naïve scenes from Wilmslow who usually inscribed her work at length and trade-marked it with a fly. She was born in the village of Lees near Oldham and attended Oldham School of Art. She married a textile designer and had two children. At the age of sixty-five she began to paint pictures to show her grandchildren what life was like when she was a child. "The Cricket Match at Blackpool in 1908", signed and inscr., 17½in.x23in., Christie's.

Bradley, V.F.
Amateur equestrian artist of hunting scenes.

Bradley, William (1801-1857)
Talented Manchester portrait and sporting painter, although largely self-taught. He set himself up as animal painter and teacher of drawing in a Manchester warehouse. A great friend of another young, self-taught Mancunian artist, Henry Liverseege. He married the daughter of the artist, Charles Calvert, (q.v.) and became the parent of Basil (q.v.) and William Bradley, Jnr. He painted "Old Billy", the oldest horse perhaps in authentic history at sixty-three years old and recorded also by Charles Towne (q.v.) in four of his paintings. Bradley's painting was engraved by T. Sutherland and is inscr. "Old Billy" was employed as a gin horse until May 1819 by the proprietors of the Mersey & Irwell Navigation Company. He first belonged to Mr. Henry Harrison of Manchester, who trained him for the plough, and who knew him for fifty-nine years, "Billy" having been about two years old when he came to him first. Bradley also painted the portrait of "George Fraser, First Captain of the Manchester Golf Club", 44in.x36in., s.&d. 1818, Manchester City Art Galleries.

Bradshaw, Stanley Orton (op.1930s)
Artist and book illustrator whose particular sporting subject was aviation which he painted in watercolour.

Bragg, Aston (op.1861)
Draughtsman and lithographer whose portrait of the American boxing champion John C. Heenan (1835-1873) was engraved in 1861, presumably to commemorate his forty-two round draw with Sayers. Heenan came to England in 1860.

Brakespeare, William A. (1855-1914)
London genre painter, some sporting subjects. Studied art at Birmingham School of Art and in Paris. Member of the Newlyn School in Cornwall. Exh. at the RA (1891-1903). His sporting contribution includes hawking and fox-hunting.

Bramatti, G. (17th century?)
"Ice Yachting", colour aquatint after the work by this artist, showing a 17th century scene of skaters with a boat fitted with an ice runner and sails, and another on the ice with wheels and sails, pub. 1805 by V.Raineri, exhib. Parker Gallery, No. 476, 1950.

Bramley, Frank, RA (1857-1915)
Distinguished Royal Academician who included a number of paintings of hunt terriers amongst his early work. Bramley, who was a member of the Newlyn School, exh. at the RA from 1884 and was elected RA (1911). He was a founder member of the NEAC and turned increasingly to portrait painting after 1897.

Brandt, William (op.1893-1895)
Four watercolours by this artist depicting "The Oaks 1893", "Mrs. Butterwick" beats "Treasure" and "Cypria" with vignette figures in each corner, signed and inscr. 13½in.x20½in., and three others in the same year, "The Derby", "The Ascot Gold Cup" and "The Hardwicke Stakes" were sold at Phillips (the Pilkington Collection) in 1989. Brandt's pen/watercolour painting "Racing at Epsom - the City and Suburban", s.&d. '95, 12½in.x9¾in., Bonhams 1990.

Branscombe, Charles H. (op.1880-1920)
Dorset landscape painter who included a fine hunting scene (1892) amongst his work. Exh. one painting at ROI 1891.

Branscombe, C. J. (op.1785-1840)
Nottingham provincial sporting painter who did not apparently exhibit in London. His work shows more than a primitive talent and includes coursing, coaching, and game dog scenes. Branscombe was another artist (see also Botheras) who either through ignorance or poverty never sized his canvases so that they have not stood the test of time.

Bransom, Paul (b.1885)
American animal painter and illustrator of Methuen's 1913 edn. of "The Wind in the Willows" which came in for some adverse criticism at the time, depicting the animals too faithfully to nature and thereby losing the spirit of the story.

Breach, Edward R. (op.1868-1887)
London painter of sporting subjects particularly gundogs in Highland settings. Exh. one work at the RA in 1875 entitled "A Brace, Steady at the Point" and thirty-three at SS (1868-1886) including "12th August - on the Moors" in 1878.

Breakell, Mary Louise (op.1880-1912)
This artist from Prestwick, Manchester exh. eight paintings at SS (1880-1893), one of which was entitled "Hunting Styles - Westmorland".

Breeden, W.L. (op.1882-1920)
Birmingham landscape painter. "A Rugby Match", s.&d. 1893, The Harry Langton Collection.

Bremy, J.R. (op.1807)
An interesting portrait of "A Gentleman standing by his saddled Hunter in a Landscape", s.&d. 1807, 20in.x 23½in., auctioned Christie's 1990.

Brereton, Robert (op.1831-1847)
Portrait painter who lived in London and Melton Mowbray where he painted a few sporting and equestrian subjects.

Bressin, J.
A portrait of the racehorse "Prestige" with J. Ransch up, 21½in.x25½in., was exh. at the McConnell Mason Gallery, London, December 1984.

Bretherick, Clarence F. (op.1890-1897)
Lancashire artist who exh. between 1890 and 1891. "The Football Match", s.&d. 1897, 20⅞in.x29⅞in., monotone, Phillips (West 2) 1989.

Bretland, Thomas Walker (1802-1874)
Nottingham sporting and animal painter who worked for private patrons including the Dukes of Buccleuch and Montrose, Lord Chesterfield and Baron Rothschild. Sporting subjects include fox-hunting, racing, coursing, shooting and gundogs, painted in oils.

Breun (Brown), John Ernest, RBA (1862-1921)
London portrait painter, second son of John Needham Breun, Duc de Vitrie. Educated in London, studied art at South Kensington and at the RA Schools (1881-1884) where he won a number of medals and prizes. Exh. nine works at the RA including a portrait of Henry F. Compton, Esq., Master of the New Forest Hounds in 1904. His sporting work also includes coursing as well as fox-hunting. Elected RBA (1896).

Brewster, J. (op.1890s)
"Adam Bede" and "Fred Archer" greyhounds in a landscape, the property of Mr. Fred Calvert of Hartlepool, s.&d. 1893 and 1894, a pair, auctioned Bonhams 1986. Little known of this artist who was probably a local painter.

Brewtnall, Edward Frederick, RWS, RBA, (1846-1902)
London landscape and figure painter, in both oil and watercolour, who exh. from 1868 at the RA, SS, GG and elsewhere. He is included in this Dictionary for his fine painting "The Wimbledon Tennis Party", s.&d. 1891, watercolour, 16½in.x24in. Wimbledon Lawn Tennis Museum.

Bridgehouse, Robert (op.1844-1846)
A fine equestrian portrait artist about whom little has so far been traced. Included in this Dictionary for his equestrian portrait of the four sons of John Owell of Arden House, Cheshire, painted in 1846, 39½in.x 49½in., Christie's 1980.

Bridgeman, G. (op.1880-1882)
Little known painter of hunting scenes who exh. one black and white landscape at the DG 1880 from a London address.

Bridges, John (op.1812-1878)
Oxford portrait painter, included in this Dictionary for his painting of "The Rev. J.W. Pears, Vicar of Tetsworth and family, his son holding a cricket bat", s.&d. 1854 and for his fine portrait of "The Oxford Oarsman" standing half-length, with a view of Oxford behind him, 20¼in.x16¼in., Sotheby's.

Bridgman, Frederick Arthur (1847-1928)
American landscape and historical painter who studied under Gérome in Paris. His painting of "Tennis at Vechiville", 21¼in.x31¾in., may therefore date from this period.

Bridie, James (op.1907)
An interesting angling painting by this artist, signed, inscr. and dated November 1907, 5¾in.x3¾in., shows Professor Paton carrying out investigations on salmon.

Briggs, Ernest Edward RI, RSW (1866-1913)
Angling artist who probably did more for the subject than any previous painter. Born at Broughty Ferry, near Dundee. After training as a mining engineer, he studied art at both the Slade and Heatherley Schools and then in Italy. First exh. at the RA in 1889. He illus. his book "Angling and Art in Scotland" with thirty-two colour plates, pub. in 1908 just five years before his untimely death from a heart attack. His great friend and companion was Norman Wilkinson (q.v.) whose own fine work in angling art did much to continue the interest in the subject started by Briggs. Elected RI (1906) and RSW (1913).

Briggs, G. (op.1816-1831)
London equestrian artist operating at approximately the same date as H. Briggs (q.v.).

Briggs, H. (op.1816-1831)
London landscape and equestrian painter who exh. twenty-one works at the RA. Titles include "Portrait of a Mare, the property of Mr. J. Reeve" (1818) and "Portrait of a Favourite Horse" (1828) (as an honorary exhibitor). Of the latter "The Sporting Magazine" had to say "This painting has no great claims to commendation".

Bright, Alfred (op.1880-1929)
Equestrian artist who painted several watercolour portraits of racehorses (in grisaille) from a Fairfield address between 1880 and 1893. These include the stallion "Crowberry", "The Rowan", "Minting", "Stoneclink" (with foal by "Minting"), "Esterling", "Albert Victor", "Chippendale" and "Mint Sauce". Bright also painted the Grand Nationals of 1910, 1911 and 1912. Much of his work was painted in grisaille which may have been intended for reproduction in sporting journals. Exh. in 1929 at the Liver(pool) Sketching Club and lived in Oxfordshire.

Bright, Harry (op.1867-1897)
A watercolour artist, more widely known for his bird paintings and illustrations than for his sporting scenes.

His watercolour of "The Royal Hunt Cup, Ascot, 1895", 12½in.x18¼in., signed and inscr., was exh. at Messrs. Colnaghi, Bond Street, London. June 1986.

Bright, Henry (1810-1873)
Norwich landscape painter. Exh. at SS (1836-1876) (presumably posthumously). Sentimental titles popular at the time include "Won't you tell me why, Robin?" or "Where can my little brother be?". Painted with John Frederick Herring Snr. (q.v.) "A Meeting of the Deer Stalkers" in 1858. This subject was engraved but the original painting is 41in.x71in. It shows two Highlanders with ponies, one with a dead stag and a large herd of cows in a landscape and is signed by both artists. Bright also painted with Sir Edwin Henry Landseer RA (q.v.) "The Sentinel", a portrait of a dog on the eve of the battle of Edgehill, which was exh. at the RA in 1845, No. 275. The dog painted by Edwin Landseer was part of the picture but was later cut out and the background, a castle wall, was added by Henry Bright.

Bright J. (op.1858)
Little known artist who painted a dog fighting scene at Westminster Pit, s.&d. 1858 and inscr., 15¼in.x19¾in.

Bright, J. (op.1883-1920)
This interesting equestrian artist specialised in portraits of racehorses and racing scenes painted in both oil and watercolour. His portraits include studies of the racehorses "St. Simon" (s.&d. 1897), "Shotover" (s.&d. 1888), "Glendale" and "Lily Agnes" with her foal (s.&d. 1888). "Horses Exercising on Middleham Moor", s.&d. 1920 and inscr. "Middleham Moor, Penhill and Spigot Lodge in the distance, Peacocks String", 8½in.x17¼in.

Brightwell, Leonard Robert (1889-1983)
Animal painter and etcher who studied at the Lambeth School of Art and who contributed sketches, some sporting, to "Punch" in 1914. He exh. 1926 and 1938 mostly at the Connel Gallery. Served in the 1st World War and made animal studies at the Zoological Gardens.

Bril, Paul (1554-1626)
Flemish landscape artist, brother of Matthew who was probably his tutor. Included in this Dictionary of sporting artists for his "Landscape with Golfers" 1624, Minneapolis Institute of Arts.

Brill, Frederick (1920-1984)
Painter of many subjects including football. His watercolour "Chelsea Football Ground", 31¾in.x 24½in., s.&d. 1952 was exh. at FA exhibition in 1953. Brill studied at Hammersmith Art School, the Slade and the RCA whilst it was evacuated to Ambleside during the war. His sketches there unearthed a passion for the Yorkshire Dales which he painted with great feeling and talent. He became Head of Painting at Chelsea Polytechnic and eventually Principal of Chelsea School of Art. Exh. regularly at the RA and other leading London galleries.

Briscoe, Arthur John Trevor RI, RE (1873-1943)
Marine artist, illustrator and etcher who contributed many sporting sketches to Fores "Sporting Notes and Sketches", sometimes of clever and often amusing yachting scenes but sometimes of hunting and shooting including "A Tragedy, shot a Beater? No, far worse than that, he shot a fox!" pub. Messrs. Fores 1906. The sporting subjects that Briscoe painted include wildfowling, shooting, fishing and "le sport nautique". Briscoe who studied at the Slade School of Art and at Julians in Paris was a fine draughtsman and a keen sailor with seafaring experience. He played a leading part in arranging a series of pre-war marine exhibitions which eventually led to the formation of the RSMA. A fine work entitled "Yachts at Sea" inscr. "J Class" and dated '32, watercolour 10in.x13¾in., was shown at the Fine Art Society. He painted mostly in watercolour and both these and his etchings are much sought after by sailing collectors. Served in the 1st World War as a lieutenant in the RNVR.

Briscoe, Michael J. (b.1960)
Studied Wrexham College of Art (1978-1979) and Sheffield City Polytechnic (1979-1982). Contemporary painter of ballooning scenes.

Bristow, Edmund (1787-1876)
Sporting and equestrian artist who was born at Windsor, the son of an heraldic painter from whom he received his early training. His chief patron was the Duke of Clarence, later William IV. Painted small scale pictures in the manner of Dutch 17th century cabinet pictures and was much influenced by the work of Charles Turner (q.v.), thirteen years his senior, who was also the son of an heraldic painter.

Brittan, Charles Edward, Snr. (1837-1888)
West Country landscape and sporting artist who lived in Truro. Father of the landscape painter of the same name. Amongst the sports he painted are otter hunting scenes and racehorse studies. Exh. one animal painting "The Antlered Monarch of the Waste" at SS in 1858.

Broadhead, W. Smithson (1888-1960)
Born at Barrow in Furness and educated at the Central School, Sheffield and then at the Sheffield School of Art. Portrait and horse painter who exh. (1923-1937) at the RA before moving to the United States in 1934. Broadhead painted the portraits of many famous racehorses including the hurdler and flat race stayer "Brown Jack". He also painted "Battleship" a son of "Man O'War" who won every distance from 5 furlongs on the flat to 4½ miles over jumps and became not only the first American owned and bred horse to win the Aintree Grand National in 1938, but one of the very few entire colts to carry off the prize. National Museum of Racing, Saratoga Springs, NY.

Brocas, William, RHA (c.1794-1868)
Irish landscape and equestrian painter, the third son of Henry Brocas, Snr. President of the Society of Irish Artists. Elected RHA (1860). He painted the portrait of the racehorse "Freney" with her trainer, jockey and groom (Sotheby's 1964).

Brock, Charles Edmund, RI (1870-1938)
Illustrator, cartoonist and sporting artist in black and white and watercolour. Born London (Holloway) and

went to school in Cambridge where he lived for the whole of his working life, sharing a studio with his two artist brothers H.M.Brock (q.v.) and R.H. Brock (q.v.). Studied art under Henry Wiles, the sculptor, specialising in the illustration of period books. His work depicting golf is of the highest ranking and includes a series of sepia prints of golfers in action on the links, reproduced by Leggatt Bros of London in 1894.

Brock, Henry Matthew, RI (1875-1960)
Brother of R.H. and C.E. Brock (qq.v.). Book illustrator and landscape painter, very often of sporting subjects including his painting of a boxing contest at a fair inscr. "Sportsmen, Try Your Skill", watercolour, 14in.x20¾in., Pilkington Coll.

Brock, Richard Henry (op.1890-1925)
Brother of C.E. and H.M. Brock (qq.v.). Landscape artist and illustrator, very often of equestrian subjects, in particular fox-hunting scenes.

Brockbank, Russell P. (1913-1979)
Motor racing draughtsman, illustrator and cartoonist who worked for "Speed" magazine (1935-1939) and then "Motor" magazine. Became art editor to "Punch" (1953-1960). Brockbank, who was born in Canada, studied at Ridley College, Ontario and at Chelsea School of Art, London. He served in the RNVR throughout the 2nd World War.

Brockhurst, Gerald Leslie, ARA (1890-1978)
Painter and etcher who studied at Birmingham School of Art and the RA Schools. Exh. at the RA (1923-1953). Elected ARA (1937). "A Young Lady at Archery Practice" (attrib.), 12in.x9in., was auctioned Bonhams 1988.

Broders, Roger (op.1920s)
French graphic artist who worked in the art nouveau style. His poster, advertising the sporting facilities at Chantilly, shows a '20s style. "Girl with a Tennis Racket", 31½in.x22in., Sotheby's (Bel.).

Brodie, Howard (b.California 1916)
Illustrator for "Yank" magazine during the 2nd World War. Has included American Football in his work.

Brodie, John Lamont (op.1841-1889)
London portrait and landscape painter whose golfing picture "A Close Putt", 17½in.x23in., s.&d. 1889 was auctioned Sotheby's 1977.

Bromley, Clough W. (op.1870-1904)
Landscape painter who lived at Lavender Hill and exh. several watercolour views of Clapham and Wandsworth. Mitchell has recorded him for his painting "The Oxford - Bristol Mail Coach", s.&d. 1892.

Bromley, Valentine Walter, RBA (1848-1877)
London portrait painter, watercolourist and illustrator whose engraving "At the Eton and Harrow Match" c.1877/8 shows a fielder retrieving the ball from the spectators on the boundary but shows nothing of the game of cricket. Bromley also painted a fine fencing scene entitled "Early Lessons" (1874) which was repro. in "The Illustrated London News", the journal which

employed him between 1873-1875 when he went to America. A son of William Bromley, the Victorian genre painter, Bromley exh. at the RA, NWS and RBA (1867-1874). Elected RBA (1871).

Brompton, Richard (c.1734-1783)
See also David Morier (q.v.). Portrait painter of a number of equestrian groups in which the horses were painted by Morier. Pupil of Benjamin West (q.v.). Exh. SA (1767-1780) (elected President 1780), FS and the RA where he exh. portraits of the Duke of York and the Prince of Wales (1772). He and Morier shared the patronage of the Earl of Pembroke and both shared financial problems towards the later years of their lives.

Brook, David
Contemporary painter of naïve scenes whose oil on board "The Tennis Match", 12in.x13in., s.&d. 1966, was exh. at Portal Gallery, London.

Brook, Maria Burnham (op.1872-1885)
London portrait and figure painter who exh. at the RA and RHA (1880-1889). Her hunting painting entitled "Going to the Meet" a portrait of Sarah Ebben, signed with mono., 20½in.x15in., was exh. at the RA 1876 (No. 759). (Note: the buttons on this equestrienne's habit and the feathered hat are unusual for this date but it may depict an earlier date. Alternatively it may illustrate a non-hunting lady looking decorative for the meet - who was Sarah Ebben anyway?)

Brooke, C. (op.1815)
"Knutsford Racecourse, Cheshire", pen/ink, 8½in.x 13in., The Paul Mellon Collection, Upperville, Va, USA. Possibly copied from the aquatint "Knutsford Racecourse" engraved by R.G. Reeve after H. Hazlehurst (q.v.) and pub. 1815.

Brooke, E. Adveno (op.1844-1878)
London landscape painter of hunting, shooting and fishing scenes. Exh. at the RA, BI, SS (1844-1864) many paintings with sporting titles. He illus. the "Book of South Wales" by Mr. and Mrs. S.C. Hall (1861). A fine pair of hunting paintings, s.&d. 1878, were auctioned at Austin Wyatt (Winchester) 1886.

Brooke, John William (c.1854-1919)
Portrait and figure painter who collaborated with George Wright (q.v.) on an equestrian painting of "Lily", daughter of J. Wallace, on "Countess" (exh. RA 1899). Brooke studied art at the Herkomer School at Bushey and in Paris where he exh. frequently at the Paris Salon.

Brooke(s), William (exh.1779-1801)
Cattle and landscape painter who exhibited at the RA (1779-1801). "A Hunt in Full Cry - Breaking Cover", s.&d. 1792, 26⅛in.x40⅛in. was auctioned Christie's 1988 after an engraved painting by Francis Sartorius (q.v.).

Brooker, Harry (op 1876-1918)
Painter of domestic scenes often involving children playing games. "The Game of Cricket", s.&d. 1904, 27½in.x35½in., The Royal Exchange Art Gallery, London.

Brookes, Lionel, ARCA (b.1915)
Portrait, landscape and equestrian artist of "The Morning Ride" painted 1954. Studied art at the RCA under Gilbert Spencer (1937-1940). Exh. at the RA, RP and RBA.

Brooks, Henry Jamyn (op.1884-1908)
London portrait painter who exh. at the RA from 1890. His work covers a number of sporting scenes and personalities including "The Eton Boat House with Boat Crews and a View of Windsor Castle in the Background", "An Association Football Match between Oxford and Cambridge Universities in 1905", s.&d. 1908 (Queens Club, London), "Rugby School - New Big Side Cricket" (an engraving after this work by F.G. Stevenson dated 1890, 21in.x14in.), "The Hurlingham Polo Team mounted in front of the Pavilion 1890", 42in.x90in. (with key identifying the spectators and the team). The Hurlingham Club, London and the polo match between the 9th Lancers and the 10th Hussars at Hurlingham, pub. as a lithograph in 1892 by Dickinson and Foster.

Brooks, Peter (20th cent.)
Cricket illustrator of the book "England their England" by A.G. Macdonell pub. in 1986 by the Folio Society. This book was previously pub. by Pan Books in 1949 and the illustrations were by Oliver Brabbins (q.v.).

Brooks, Thomas (1749-after1791)
London landscape and equestrian painter who exh. nine paintings at FS (1782-1783).

"Brooksby"
Alias Captain Pennell Elmhirst who wrote for "The Field" on hunting subjects at the end of the 19th and turn of the 20th century.

Broomfield, Frances (b.1951)
Painter in a bold, naïve style of several sporting scenes in oil and tempera on wood panels. Born in Warrington, Frances Broomfield studied at Warrington College of Art (1967-1969) and Newport College of Art (1969-1972) where she gained a diploma in Art and Design - Fine Art (Painting). She has exh. almost exclusively since 1977 with Portal Gallery, London and occasionally with the Wingfield Sporting Gallery, London. Her sporting work includes a portrait of the Rugby League player Jackie Fish, exh. at her one-woman show at "The Story and The Fable", Warrington Museum AG, 1989. (When Warrington won the Challenge Cup for the first time in 1905, they beat Hull Kingston Rovers, 6-0, in the final after a tough strugle. Warrington's match winner was the legendary right winger, Jack Fish, who scored two tries. "We've got a Fish to Plaice a try", the cry rang out. Fish's fans used to make cardboard fish to wave when he was playing. His son "Young Jackie" still lives in Warrington.) Her work includes several paintings of lawn tennis and "A Golden Duck", a portrait of George Duckworth, the famous wicket keeper who came from Warrington and took part in cricket matches in many countries before retiring to own a pub back in his home town. Frances Broomfield's paintings are in public and private collections all over the world.

Broughton, H. or T. (op.1814-1840)
Interesting painter of coaching scenes. His fine painting "The Defiance Coach", s.&d. 1828, 71in.x91½in., was lent from a private collection for the exhibition of British Sporting Paintings at the Haywood Gallery, London in 1974. His "Glasgow to London Royal Mail Coach", an oil painting on panel showing the coach travelling at speed between Shap and Penrith, a lady the only apparent passenger seated beside the coachman, 27¼in.x35¾in., s.&d. 1840, was originally exh. by the Parker Gallery for their bicentenary in 1950.

Brown, Cecil (Major), RA, RBS (1868-1926)
Equestrian artist and sculptor who studied art in London and Paris. Taught art at Charterhouse (1907-1910). He became an authority on horses and horsemanship contributing several articles and illustrating "The Horse in Art and Nature". A fine rider and sportsman, he painted several hunting and polo scenes and died on the hunting field when he suffered a heart attack out with the Oakley. "A Game of Polo", signed and inscr. (silk laid on board), 11½in.x8½in., Sotheby's.

Brown, Dexter (b.1942)
London-born painter of motor racing scenes who studied at Harrow College of Art where he graduated in 1960. Recognition for his work began in 1967 with his one-man exhibition at the Monte Carlo Galleries in Alexandria, Va (USA) and subsequently through exhibitions at the Thackeray Gallery, London. He also exh. at the RI and the RBA.

Brown, E.M. (op.1891-1899)
Edinburgh artist who exh. at the RSA (1899). He included several equestrian scenes amongst his work.

Brown, Edward (1823-1877)
Midland sporting artist who worked in Warwickshire and Coventry. Prolific provincial artist who painted with great competence for local patrons including the Warners of Bulkington. Did not, so far as is known, exhibit in London. Confined his work for the most part to portraits of hunters, prize cattle and greyhounds, although his painting "The 1st of September" shows a primitive but pleasing composition of a sportsman holding a shotgun and waiting for his dog to flush a partridge out of a covert, 24¼in.x29½in., auctioned Christie's 1990.

Brown, Elmore J. (b.1899)
American painter who was educated with the American novelist Ernest Hemingway (1898-1961) at Oak Park, Illinois, and subsequently illustrated Hemingway's first pub. short story "In our Time" (1924). Brown's painting "Oklahoma" shows the training track across the road from the Saratoga racecourse and depicts the "behind the scenes" activities of this world famous race track. The painting is in the collection of the National Museum of Racing and Hall of Fame, Saratoga, NY.

Brown, Ford Madox (1821-1893)
Victorian romantic painter. Included in this Dictionary for his mural of children playing stoolball (an early form of cricket) entitled "Humphrey Chetham's Life Dreams"

which was one of twelve murals that Brown painted in 1886 for Manchester Town Hall, showing the history of Manchester.

Brown, Frederick (Fred) (Professor) (1851-1941)
Landscape, genre and portrait painter. Studied at the Royal College of Art (1868-1877) and in Paris. Taught at the Westminster School of Art (1877-1892). Distinguished Professor of the Slade School (1892-1918). Founder member of the NEAC (1886), where he exh. a number of paintings (1886-1916) including "An Amateur of Fencing" (1907). Since his subjects were mostly rural this might have been a farm fence?

Brown, G. (1830-)
Painter of game and shooting subjects. His pencil and watercolour study "Grouse Shooting" 5½in.x8⅜in., signed and inscr., is in The Paul Mellon Collection, Upperville, Va, USA

Brown, Hugh Boycott, RSMA (1909-1990)
Norfolk landscape and marine artist who has included a number of sailing barge matches in his work. A keen dinghy racer. Boycott Brown was educated at Trent College and studied at Heatherleys School of Art. He began teaching at the Royal Masonic School at Bushey and returned to teaching after the 2nd World War. Exh. at the leading London galleries and elsewhere and was a member of the RSMA, and the Wapping Group. He is represented in the National Maritime Museum.

Brown, J. (op.1866-1888)
The painter of several equestrian and sporting pictures including "The Boating Party, the River Swale, Richmond Castle", s.&d. 1886, 26in.x36in., auctioned Sotheby's (Chester) 1986 and "A Portrait of a Horse", s.&d. 1866, 14in.x18in., Glennies (Norfolk) 1989.

Brown, James Michael (1854-1957)
Edinburgh painter of golfing scenes who studied at Edinburgh College of Art and Dundee. Member of the Pen and Pencil Club and the Scottish Arts Club. Exh. at the RA (1885-1900) including "On Leven Links, Fifeshire" (1890). "Championship on the Course at Carnoustie", dated 1891, watercolour 8in.x15¾in., was auctioned Sotheby's (Glen.) 1973. Brown's fine watercolour "A Match at Duddingston, March 25 1898" between two amateur champions, Freddie Tait and Leslie M. Balfour-Melville, and two professionals, Willie Auchterlonie, the 1893 Open winner, and Ben Sayers from North Berwick, appeared in a calendar produced by the Life Association of Scotland, some of whose executives were enthusiastic players themselves.

Brown, John (op.1824-1830)
This artist exh. two sporting paintings at BI, one of "Bull Baiting" in 1824 and the other "The Sayers v. Heenan Boxing Match" which took place on 17 April 1860 and which Brown painted with J. Rowbotham (q.v.). "Cricket Match at Stonehenge", watercolour, 12in.x17in., s.&d. 1830, Salisbury & South Wiltshire Museum. "The Horsemarket - Smithfield", painted for Lord Stirling (1783-1859), 28½in.x38¼in., was auctioned Sotheby's 1982 (sold previously at Leeds & Miners sale, May 1879 Lot 2010).

Brown, John George (1831-1913)
Influential American genre painter whose prolific output includes his sentimental portrayal of the game of baseball in his painting "Put it There" showing a young street urchin pounding his gloved hand in an invitation to action. The Carnegie Museum of Art, Pittsburg, Pa.

Brown, John Lewis (1829-1890)
Little known equestrian artist of Irish origin who was born and lived all his life in France. He exh. "La Halte en Foret" at the RA in 1875 from a Paris address. His sporting work includes fox-hunting and a number of riding scenes. He also painted a formal portrait of Queen Victoria and Prince Albert driving in a carriage and four.

Brown, K.C. (op.1938)
A pen and watercolour portrait of "Nearco", winner of the Italian Derby (1938), is recorded by Mitchell.

Brown, Mather (c.1761-1831)
American portrait painter who studied art in London, under Benjamin West (q.v.) and who produced work of a very uneven quality. The British Museum has a colour mezzotint by William Ward (1766-1826) pub. by Bradshaw (1788) after a work by Mather Brown of a portrait of the fencer Monsieur de St. George (1745-1799). Born at Guadeloupe, St. George was a notable violinist as well as a fencer. It is possible that Monsieur de St. George may have been an adopted name based on the "St. George", a term for a defensive parry - see also Robineau. The original painting by Brown was owned by the famous fencer Henry Angelo (1756-1835) and it remained in Angelo's School of Arms for about a hundred years until 1890, when it disappeared. Its whereabouts today are unknown - at least to me - but the painting is the first to show a foil with the figure of eight guard that was to become the predominant shape for the next 130 years. A portrait by Brown of Henry Angelo is in the National Portrait Gallery, London.

Brown, Nathaniel (op.1753-1779)
This artist painted a wide range of subject matter including some equestrian and game shooting scenes. Exh. fifty-four paintings at FS (1765-1779) including "A Hunter and Sportsman with Dogs" (1753) (exh. by Frank T. Sabin, London).

Brown, Paul (b.1893)
American equestrian painter, sporting writer and illustrator who was born at Mapleton, Minnesota, USA. Educated New York City and served in both World Wars. His book, which was illus. by himself, "Aintree - Grand Nationals Past and Present", was pub. by the Derrydale Press (founded by Eugene V. Counett, III, in 1927) in New York in 1930. The sporting subjects he covered include shooting, trout fishing, racing and polo. Much of his work was in pen, brush and black ink, sometimes coloured chalks and occasionally watercolour. Author and illustrator of "Hits and Misses" pub. by Derrydale Press (1935) and "Polo" pub. Charles Scribners and Sons New York (1949)

Brown, R.G.

Brown, R.G. (op.1844-1859)
Lancashire sporting painter of mediocre talent who exh. one painting of dead game at the RA in 1844. Wood also records "Three Hunters at a Paddock Gate" - no date - and "A Grey Pony with a Spaniel and Two Pointers at Work". His other sporting work includes a number of game and shooting paintings. Also a painting of coursing entitled "In the Slips" with the slipper holding a pair of greyhounds in a landscape, s.&d. 1849, 25in.x36in., auctioned Christie's (Glasgow) 1984.

Brown, R.W.
Unknown artist of a hunting watercolour entitled "Mutton Fist - A Follower of Our Hunt" signed and inscr. 11½in.x8½in.

Brown, Rick
Contemporary American football painter.

Brown, Robert (ex.1792-1834)
London landscape painter "of modest powers" (Waterhouse) who exhibited a painting of "A Sportsman Discovering a Poacher" in 1809 at BI.

Brown, A.E.D.G. Stirling (op.1900-1929)
Equestrian portrait painter - see also Stirling.

Brown, W.M. (op.1849-1856)
Painter of animals and equestrian studies. Exh. four works at SS (1849-1856). Titles include "The Doctor's Horse" and "The Parson's Horse" (1851).

Brown, William, Jnr. (op.1798-1808)
London landscape and sporting painter who exh. a painting of a sportsman with setters at the RA (1808). His portrait of the sportsman Charles Lorraine Smith on a horse was exh. at Leicester 1951 (Leicestershire Hunting Pictures) lent from a private collection.

Brown, William (op.1886-1936)
Interesting sporting artist who included studies of racehorses and salmon fishing amongst his sporting works. Appears to have come from Carlisle since most of his work is so inscr. This artist may well have been the William Brown who exh. one painting at the Glasgow Institute of the Fine Arts in 1893. His salmon fishing painting certainly dates from then and his portraits of racehorses are dated 1926 and 1936. His portrait of Fred Archer on "Ormonde" is undated but "Ormonde" won the Triple Crown in 1886.

Browne Balfour, Vincent R. (1880-1963)
See Balfour

Browne Blair, Nassau, RHA (op.1880s-d.1940)
Irish painter of landscapes and animals including horses and hounds. Exh. 122 works at the RHA. Elected a member (1902). Painted "The Hounds of the Kilkenny Hunt" and "Glencairn with 'Boss' Croker's Horses". These include the very successful "Orby", the first Irish-trained horse to win the English Derby (1907) from the unlucky "Wool Winder" whose portrait was painted in the same year by Percy Earl (q.v.). "Orby" also won the Irish Derby with ease but broke down before the St. Leger and was retired to stud.

Browne, Ethel C. Robertson (op.1930s - d.1975)
A fine portrait by this artist of the 2000 Guineas winner "Big Game" (1939) leased for racing to King George VI appeared on the front cover of the "British Racehorse" in 1961. Her portrait of "Pebble Ridge" winner of the Welsh Grand National in 1933 and owned by Lord Glanely is signed C.R. Browne as she signed most of her work.

Browne, Gordon Frederick, RBA, RI (1858-1932)
Painter and illustrator, the son of Hablot Knight Browne (Phiz) (q.v.) . His tennis illustration for the Story of "Mazurka" featured in "The English Illustrated Magazine" 1893 - Victoria & Albert Museum, London. Browne, who was born at Banstead, Surrey, studied art at Heatherleys. In 1886 he first exh. at the RA. Elected RBA (1894) and RI (1897). A competent artist but he suffered from the handicap of an illustrious father and many of his contemporaries knew him as his father's son rather than for his own artistic ability. He died suddenly on 27 May 1932 at his home in the Upper Richmond Road, London.

Browne, Hablot Knight ("Phiz") (1815-1882)
Humorous illustrator and watercolour painter who specialised in hunting, shooting and fishing scenes. See also "Phiz". Browne was first apprenticed to Finden, the engraver. He continued to attend the Life School in St. Martin's Lane, where he won the Silver Isis Medal in 1832, even after he had set up in watercolour practice on his own. In 1836 Browne started his long association with Charles Dickens (until they fell out in 1864) as the illustrator for many of Dickens' works including "The Pickwick Papers" under the pseudonym "Phiz" (1836). Browne also contributed work to "The Sporting Times", "The New Sporting Magazine" (1839) and "Punch" (1842-1844). Browne lived in Croydon for much of his life. He worked in a style similar to that of John Leech (q.v.) but was the better equestrian draughtsman of the two. Leech was known to have said on one occasion "I wish I could draw horses as well as Browne". Browne was an accomplished horseman and is known to have stayed with the 3rd Earl Fortescue at Castle Hill in Devon and hunted on Exmoor. He also hunted in the Home Counties. In 1867 Browne became partially paralysed and, being desperately poor, was granted financial help from the Turner Fund set up by the RA to help deserving artists in need.

Browne, J. (op.1912-1936)
Competent painter of prize racing pigeons whose prolific work was extremely detailed. He usually printed with a fine paint brush all the details of the prize winner's pedigree and the races won on the canvas under the portrait. He was probably based in Derby although he travelled the length and breadth of the country to visit his subjects. He appears only to have painted racing pigeons and carefully s.&d. his work in every case.

Browne, Philip (op.1804-1868)
Shrewsbury landscape, sporting and still life painter who exh. seventy works at the RA and thirteen at SS

(1824-1868). His RA exhibit for 1855 was "A Stray Shot". He worked in both oil and watercolour but was an unsuccessful candidate for the NWS in 1841. His oil painting "A Horse with Two Hounds in a Stable", s.&d. 1804, 8½in.x10¼in. was auctioned 1989.

Browne, Thomas (Tom) Arthur, RI (1872-1910)
Illustrator, black and white artist, often of sporting subjects, including golf. He was a keen horseman like his contemporaries Phil May (q.v.) and Cecil Aldin (q.v.). Famous for the character he created for the Johnny Walker Whisky Company, "The Regency Buck", beaver-hatted and top-booted appraising everyone through his quizzing glass as he strides purposefully forward. "Johnny Walker" was depicted playing a series of sports including golf, skating, curling, cricket, coaching and shooting. Browne was an original member of the London Sketch Club and a close friend of Lawson Wood (q.v.). Elected RBA (1898), RI (1901), RMS (1900), Member London Sketch Club (President 1907-1908).

Browne, William Ellis Barrington (1908-1985)
See Barrington

Browning, Robert Barrett (1846-1912)
Painter and sculptor, the son of Robert and Elizabeth Barrett Browning. Browning was another artist helped by Sir John Millais (q.v.) early in his career - see also Wortley. After Millais' help, Browning studied in Antwerp and Paris where he won the Bronze Medal in 1889. Exh. at the RA (1878-1884) including "Watching the Skittle Players" (1880).

Brownlow, Charles S. (op.1903-1937)
Sporting and equestrian painter who exh. 141 pictures at the Arlington Gallery in 1937. His portrait "Pitch Dark", a painting of a greyhound in a landscape, s.&d. 1903 and inscr., 14in.x18in., was auctioned Bonhams 1987.

Brownwood Potts, Robert (op.c.1889)
Thought to be a Sussex artist, the son of George Brownwood Potts, the landscape painter, His watercolour "The Croquet Tournament, Wimbledon", 10½in.x15in., was auctioned Sotheby's (Sussex).

Bruce, J. (op.1826)
"A Coaching Scene at the Devil's Dyke, near Brighton in the County of Sussex" was pub. from 84 St. James's Street, Brighton in 1826, after the painting by this artist.

Bruce, Matt, RI (b.1915)
Landscape painter in oil and watercolour who has painted a number of flat racing scenes including the 1979 Derby. Studied at Edinburgh College of Art (1932-1939) Taught art in Brighton until ill health forced him to retire from teaching in 1977.

Bruce, Ralph (op.c.1954)
Contemporary painter whose contribution to football art lies in his painting "Tourists Opening Match at Worcester", c.1954. The Wiggins Teape Group.

Brueghel, Pieter (the Younger 1564-1637)
Flemish painter of "The Bird Trap" (where a curling match is being played in the foreground but is incidental

to the winter scene portrayed in the painting), s.&d. 1603. At one time in the collection of Lady Price Thomas. Repro. Antique Dealer & Collectors Guide February 1980 p.71.

Bruhl, Louis Burleigh, RBA (1861-1942)
Landscape painter whose golfing view of "Old Cassiobury from the 8th Tee", signed and inscr., 10in.x18in., was auctioned Taylors of Honiton.

Brunery, François (op.1901-1913)
Italian artist who worked from a Paris studio. His fine portrait in oils of Baptiste Bertrand (1811-1898), founder of the famous salle of the same name, dates from the 1890s and hangs at the de Beaumont Centre, London. Baptiste Bertrand was a supporter of fencing for women and taught the three daughters of the Prince of Wales (later Edward VII) which encouraged many other women to take up the sport.

"Brush and Feather"
The pseudonym used by the artist John Shirley-Fox, RBA (q.v.) for his articles in "The Field".

Bryan, Alfred (Charles Grineau) (1852-1899)
Caricaturist, illustrator and equestrian artist who worked mainly for "The Sporting and Dramatic News" where he did weekly cartoons as "Our Captious Critic". He is best remembered as chief cartoonist of "Moonshine". His real name was Charles Grineau but for professional reasons he worked under the name of Alfred Bryan, which he adapted from an old family name. His fine drawing of "Sandown Park Racecourse" with portraits of the leading turf personalities of the day c.1883, 15½in.x24in., signed (mono.), pen, black ink and grey wash now belongs to United Racecourses Ltd. It may have been used originally as an illustration in "The Sporting and Dramatic News" where a scribe in the '83 October issue claimed that it (Sandown Park) is "one of the most select, pleasantest and therefore the most aristocratic of meetings, happily combining the 4 and 5 o'clock tea business and a charming spot for a picnic".

Bryan, John (op.1814-1832)
His portrait of "Birmingham", a bay racehorse with his jockey Patrick Conolly up, seen with his owner John Beardsworth at Newmarket, was painted in 1832 ("Birmingham" won the 1830 St. Leger, his only Classic win). An engraving by J.W. Giles, pub. by J. Graffe (1841), after a painting by John Bryan dated 1826 shows John Twemlow of Hatherton, Cheshire, with his favourite horse "Sultan", his groom, and his Scottish terrier. An earlier painting by this artist of a horse and groom, dated 1814, was auctioned in 1986.

Bryan, John A. (1882-1957)
Brilliant motor racing artist, son of Alfred Bryan (q.v.). See also de Grineau and Grineau. Christened Charles William Grineau, he became famous as Bryan de Grineau but used the name John A. Bryan for all his early work. Later at his wife's suggestion he "married" his real and professional names, added a "de" and became known as Bryan de Grineau.

Bryant, Alfred Moginie (op.1879-1907)
London equestrian artist who painted several portraits of hunters, usually s.&d. and posed in a stable interior.

Bryant, Alice Maud (op.1875-1910)
Australian artist who specialised in equestrian works including "The Racecourse" from "The Old Curiosity Shop" by Charles Dickens - Little Nell and her grandfather escaping from Codlin and Short, 18½in.x28in., J. Collins Bideford. A portrait of the racehorse "Bachelor's Button" with D. Mather up, s.&d. '06, 12in.x21in. was auctioned 1985.

Bryant, Joshua (op.1798-1810)
Draughtsman and etcher of landscapes and sporting subjects who drew most, and engraved three, of the fifty-five plates used to illustrate "Colonel Thornton's Sporting Tour Through France" (1806).

Buchanan, Fred (op.1900-1906)
Illustrator of sporting scenes, including golf, for illustrated journals such as "Fun" (1900), "The Graphic" (1906) and "The Strand". Subtle examples include "Aren't you a little off your game this morning Mr. Smythe?", "Punch" 18 May 1904.

Buchanan, P.R.G. (1870-1950)
Alias "The Tout" (q.v.), the well-known illustrator of sporting magazines.

Buchanan-Dunlop, A.H. (Lt. Col.), OBE (1874-1947)
This artist contributed pen and ink portraits of the great golfers of the 1920s including Tolley, Wilson, Darwin, Sarazen, Whitcombe, Hagen, Herd and others. He was himself twice captain of Royal Musselburgh in the 1920s and a member of the R & A and other clubs. Buchanan-Dunlop was commissioned into the Royal Berkshire Regiment, served in South Africa, and later in both World Wars.

Buchel, Charles A. (Carl Auguste) (1872-1950)
Portrait painter and illustrator. Born in Germany and came to London in 1877. Exh. at the RA (1895-1935). Included in this Dictionary for his large boxing painting at the National Sporting Club, painted in the 1930s. It includes portraits of all the members. Buchel also painted the "Young Angler" in 1910 which is now in America.

Buck, Adam (1759-1833)
Irish portrait and miniature painter whose work includes a "portrait of Master Edward Currie holding a cricket bat", s.&d. 1830, watercolour, 10¾in.x8½in., Sotheby's 1986.

Buck, S. (op.1840)
A coloured lithograph, 12in.x10in., after the work by this artist of a "Hansom Cab" inscr. "The Blacker Blacked" c.1840 with shoe blacks, a hansom cab and a policeman was exh. by the Parker Gallery, London 1950 for their bicentenary.

Buckley, John E. (op.1843-1871)
London painter of historical subjects who exh. at SS (1843-1861). Buckley also painted a number of sporting scenes although his figures were almost always dressed

in Carolean costume as his fine watercolour painting "Dorothy Vernon Out Riding", s.&d. 1871, shows. Almost all his work appears to be in watercolour including "Rook Shooting - Penshurst Park" which he painted in 1871.

Buckman, Edwin, ARWS (1841-1930)
London watercolour painter, etcher and engraver who studied at the Birmingham School of Art and later in Paris and Italy. Became one of the original staff at "The Graphic" where his drawing "North Country Wrestling" appeared 30 April 1870. His drawings were mainly concerned with the poor and socially deprived. He is included in this Dictionary for his RA exhibits in 1874 and 1876 entitled "North Country Wrestling, "Skittles" and "Tug of War". "Football" (a scrimmage), etching, 1886, signed in pencil, 8½in.x28½in., auctioned Bonhams (Chelsea). Buckman also contributed three plates to "British Athletic Sports and Games" (1886).

Buckman, Percy RMS (b.1865)
Dorset-born landscape and portrait painter. Studied art at the RA Schools and exh. at the leading London galleries from 1886, chiefly at the RA, RI, RBA. Elected RMS 1920. His fine painting of "Mr. Christopher Hammond Trout Fishing on the Exe", s.&d. 1891, 24½in.x35½in., auctioned Sotheby's 1986, merits his inclusion in this Dictionary.

Bucknall, Ernest Pile (b.1861 op.1919)
Liverpool-born landscape painter who studied art at the Lambeth and South Kensington Schools. Exh. (1885-1919) at the RA, SS and WS and elsewhere. Included in this Dictionary for the fine hunting scene which he painted with Frank P. Freyburg (q.v.) which fetched £8,000 at Phillips 1986.

Budd, C. F.
Equestrian portrait artist. "A Bay Hunter in a Stable Interior", Sotheby's (Sussex) 1982.

Buhler, Robert, RA, NEAC, LG (1916-1989)
London-born landscape and portrait artist who taught at the Royal College of Art with Ruskin Spear, Rodrigo Moynihan and Carel Weight. Originally studied art at St. Martin's School of Art (1934-1936) and at the RCA. Exh. with the NEAC from 1945, becoming a member the following year. Elected RA (1956). Included in this Dictionary for his painting "The Football Match" signed, 25in.x30in., Sotheby's 1989.

Bulham, Henry Robert (op.1917)
Exh. one painting at the NEAC in 1917 entitled "Balloons going up at Hurlingham".

Bull, Rene (op.1892-d.1942)
Irish-born illustrator and cartoonist, often of motoring subjects, who studied engineering in Paris. Studied art in London after meeting the outstanding draughtsman, Caran d'Ache. Contributed to the leading illus. magazines from 1892. Founder member of the London Sketch Club.

Bullen, Anne (b.1914)
Animal painter and illustrator. Studied art at the Académie Julian in Paris and at the Chelsea School of

Art. Her book illustrations are almost exclusively equestrian, drawn in crayon and pen and ink. They include "The Midnight Horse" (1949), "I Wanted a Pony" (1946), "The Horseman's Week End Book", "Showing Ponies" (1964), "A Pony for Jean" (1936) and "Wish for a Pony" (1947).

Bullen, John (op.1850-1860)
A lithograph by C. Moody, after the work by this artist, of Charles Payne, huntsman to the Pytchley with his hounds and whips, John Woodcock and Edward Kingsbury, 20in.x26½in., is dedicated to the Hon. C.H. Cust.

Bulley, Ashburnham H. (op.1841-1851)
London animal and game painter. Exh. three paintings at the RA including a portrait of "Vixen" the property of E. Sherwell, Esq. (1846), thirteen at BI and seven at SS including "Rabbit Terriers" (1848), "Wild Ducks" (1850) and "Scotch Game" (1851).

Bullock, G.G. (d.1859)
London painter who exh. at BI and SS (1828-1859). Subjects include game, both live and dead, a portrait of "Harry Hall, the ratcatcher of Land Guard Fort" (1843) and "Ferreting Rabbits" (1844).

Bullock, Ralph (op.1895-1928)
Portrait painter and teacher who exh. at the RA (1927-1928). Painted some game dog studies.

Bulmer, Thomas (op.1756)
Equestrian artist whose fine portrait of the racehorse "Scope" is inscr. "Scope by Regulus out of XXX taken from the Life. Thomas Bulmer, Pall Mall, London 1756", 22in.x25½in.

Bunbury, Henry William (1750-1811)
See also "Geoffrey Gambado". Gifted amateur artist and caricaturist. The son of Sir William Henry Bunbury, 5th Baronet of Mildenhall, Suffolk. He was also the brother of Sir Charles Bunbury, Bt. (1740-1821) the owner of the famous racehorse "Grey Diomed", painted in watercolour by Samuel Alken (q.v.) and the most successful son of "Diomed" winner of the first Epsom Derby in 1780. Bunbury painted a wide variety of sporting subjects including billiards, fishing, poaching, racing, and hunting. Pub. and illus. "An Academy for Grown Horseman" in 1787 under the pseudonym "Geoffrey Gambado". This included twenty-seven hand coloured plates after his work, pub. by Ackermanns (1825).

Bundy, Edgar, ARA, RI, RBA (1862-1922)
An apparently self-taught artist, although he spent some time in the studio of Alfred Stevens (q.v.). Exh. at the RA from 1881 and at the Paris Salon from 1907. Tended to paint historical subjects, often in Elizabethan costume, a fashion much favoured by Edwardian artists. Included a number of hawking scenes amongst his work.

Bunny, Rupert Charles Wulsten (1864-1947)
Australian artist whose painting of "The Nautilus Race" (swimming), 13½in.x25in., inscr., entitles him to inclusion in this Dictionary.

Burford, Thomas (c.1710-c.1775)
London painter and engraver, mostly of sporting subjects. Exh. seven works at the SA (1762-1774). His fine painting of "Cosmo" beating "Gimcrack" (1760) at Newmarket, 34in.x55in., was exh. at the British Sporting Paintings Exhibition at the Haywood Gallery in 1984. His engraved work includes several fox-hunting pictures after James Seymour (q.v.). Burford was a member of the Incorporated Society of Artists and exh. both sketches and engravings with them (1762-1774). He drew and engraved a portrait of the racehorse "Aaron", the property of a Mr. Rogers, showing him held by his groom in a landscape.

Burgess, F.L. (op.1778)
Exh. one sporting painting at the RA in 1778 from a London address entitled "Return from Shooting".

Burgess, H.G. (op.1898-1907)
American painter, illustrator and etcher. His fine etching "England v. Ireland Rugby Football Match at Richmond" appeared in "The Illustrated London News" (1898) for whom Burgess worked (1896-1898). Examples of his work are in the V & A Museum.

Burgess, William (1805-1861)
Canterbury-born draughtsman and lithographer of topographical subjects in and around the Dover area. These include his painting of a cricket match "Kent v. All England at Canterbury 1845". A coloured lithograph after this work, 13½in.x19½in., was published by Henry Ward, Canterbury, Kent. Burgess, who exh. at the RA and the RBA was a friend of the animal painter Thomas Sydney Cooper, RA (q.v.).

Burnet, Mabel F. (op.1895-1920)
Equestrian artist who specialised in horse portraiture. She lived in Shrewsbury and exh. at the RCA (1920).

Burnett, C. (op.1889)
A coaching scene painted by this artist and inscr. "Tiverton" is recorded by Mitchell.

Burnett, James Walton (b.1874)
Landscape and marine painter and a naval architect. Studied Liverpool School of Art and Liverpool University. He painted several yacht racing scenes including "The Fifth Challenge" a watercolour, signed, 13½in.x16in. The painting shows Sir Richard Sutton's "Genesta" against the New York Yacht Club's "Puritan" 18 September 1885. The "Puritan" passed the "Genesta" near the finish in one of the hardest fought races, winning by one minute and thirty-eight seconds.

Burney, Edward Francis (1760-1848)
Included in this Dictionary for his "View at Chelsea" showing the annual sculling race for Doggett's Coat and Badge, 10⅞in.x16⅝in., watercolour, pen/ink, The Paul Mellon Collection, Upperville, Va, USA. Thomas Doggett (d.1721) was a famous Irish comedian who left money for Thames watermen to perpetuate a rowing race to be held on 1 August every year "for ever". The first race was in 1716 and the contest still takes place today. It is the oldest sculling race in the world. Doggett's

aim, which was to encourage a young apprentice in his first year as a tradesman on the river, has resulted in producing the best known professionals, including nearly all the British champions and some world champions. The original course was from the White Swan, London Bridge, to the Swan Inn in Chelsea. A coloured aquatint, 15½in.x26in., by J. Vollyer, pub. J. Bodger (q.v.) in 1791, after the work by Burney of a "View of the Noblemen's and Gentlemen's Trains of Running Horses Taking their Exercise Up the Warren Hill, East of Newmarket", which was dedicated to HRH the Prince of Wales, was exh. by the Parker Gallery, 1950.

Burney, James (Lt.)

"Students playing cricket at The Royal Naval Academy, Gosport" (now disbanded, Cold Harbour), watercolour, 14in.x21½in., Rutland Gallery, London.

Burnham, Patrick (b.1939)

British sculptor, now living in France, who studied at Guildford Art School and became interested in sport through the medium of textile appliqué. His Formula I motor racing pictures have been exh. at the British Grand Prix in 1982 and 1983 and in Paris (1986). His sporting work includes pictures of skiing, motor cycling and American Football. "American Football" (appliqué), 48in.x28in., The Wingfield Sporting Gallery, London.

Burns, Milton (1853-1933)

American marine artist who painted a number of yacht racing scenes including a fine study of the winner of the America's Cup 1899, the "Columbia" forging ahead of the challenger "Shamrock", 30½in.x24in. The "Columbia", owned by J. Pierpoint Morgan, was the only vessel to defend the America's Cup twice. "Shamrock" was the first of the two challengers of that name owned by Sir Thomas Lipton.

Burns, William, RIBA, FSAI, FRSA (b.1923)

Born Sheffield. Studied (briefly) at the Sheffield College of Art. Formed his own architectural practice in 1962 but studied and painted landscapes as a relief from the rigid discipline of architectural drawing. Was influenced by the East Anglian painters Bernard Priestman, Arnesby Brown, and Edward Seago (q.v.). Included in this Dictionary for his fine painting "The Chatsworth Horse Trials", 16in.x22in., exh. November 1987, 20th Century Gallery, Fulham, London.

Burr, Alexander Hohenlohe, (1835-1899)

Scottish historical painter, pupil of John Ballantyne (q.v.) in Edinburgh and younger brother of the painter John P. Burr, RBA (1831-1893). Fond of painting children very often engaged in some sort of sport as the following examples show:"A Game of Battledore", signed, 10¾in.x17¾in., Bonhams; "A Game of Cricket - Youth and Age", 18in.x26in., painted c.1860-1870, Harvert Consultancy (Holdings) Ltd, Dundee.

Burras, T. (op.1891)

High quality, s.&d. sporting work by this artist, clearly operating at a later date than Thos. Burras (q.v.), is possibly that of a son. For example, "Two Spaniels in a Landscape with the Day's Bag", s.&d. 1891, 23¾in.x19¾in., Christie's 1990.

Burras Thomas, (1790-1870)

Leeds landscape, sporting and animal artist. The sixth of eight boys in a family of fourteen. His father, George, was a shoemaker in Park Lane, Leeds. Young Burras entered the textile industry but by 1822 he had launched himself on a second career as a painter having taken lessons from Joseph Rhodes (1782-1855) along with the artists William Robinson and Thomas Hartley Cromek. His first recorded work was exh. at the Northern Society for the Encouragement of the Fine Arts in Leeds (1822). In 1826 he was listed for the first time in the Directories as a landscape painter and by 1830 as an animal and landscape painter. In 1825 Burras exh. a portrait of a favourite pony in Leeds. He also exh. at the Bradford Exhibition of 1827 where the "Bradfield & Huddersfield Courier" remarked that they admired the colouring of his landscapes which had no "glare" about them. So far as is known he did not exhibit or travel outside his native Yorkshire. His work is competent but not in the first league of animal or landscape artists. Against the competition of artists like Turner who, for instance, exhibited twenty-two watercolours at Leeds in the Exhibition of 1826, local artists like Burras had difficulty in attracting important commissions. His one major work is a spectacular panorama of Leeds which he painted in 1844, apparently for William Binns, a local banker. He died virtually forgotten on 14 July 1870 and is buried in Woodhouse Cemetery. His sporting work includes grouse shooting, donkey racing, salmon netting and a number of equestrian paintings. Collection Leeds AG.

Burrows, Robert (op.1851-1871)

Ipswich landscape painter who exh. two paintings at the RA, "Scene at Sproughton, nr. Ipswich" (1851) and a scene on the banks of the River Orwell (1855), and one at BI. Tended to paint his sportsmen as rather incidental to his landscapes.

Burt, Charles Thomas (1823-1902)

Midlands landscape and sporting painter, pupil of Samuel Lines in Birmingham and also a friend and pupil of David Cox by whom he was much influenced. Specialised in Highland scenes - "Grouse Shooting", "Covert Shooting", "The Shooting Party", "Walking up Partridges in a Turnip Field", etc. Member of the Birmingham Society of Artists 1856. He also painted a number of fly fishing scenes.

Burt, Revell N. (op.1885-1892)

Exh. nine paintings at the Royal Society of Artists Birmingham between these dates and may well have been related to Charles Thomas Burt (q.v.). Revell Burt specialised in hunting and shooting scenes.

Burtenshaw, George R. (op.1842)

Painted a coaching scene, s.&d. 1842, 14½in.x23in., Christie's (Sth. Ken.) 1986.

Burton, Charles (op.1906)

Equestrian paintings by this artist have been seen including "The Royal Mail Coach Outside an Inn" s.&d. 20 October 1906, Bonhams 1987.

Burton, Claire Eva (b.1955)

A leading equestrian artist, particularly of horse racing subjects, who studied at the Medway College of Art

(1971-1975) gaining a diploma in illustration. An enthusiastic horsewoman herself, Burton was commissioned to paint the series of twelve pictures for the Queen Mother's box at Cheltenham, in 1981, by the Directors of Cheltenham Racecourse. Has had one-woman exhibitions at the Court Gallery (1986), Roger Green Fine Art Gallery, Kent (1988) and Oliver Swann Gallery (1989 and 1990). Burton is widely known through her series of limited edn. horse racing prints pub. since 1985 by Felix Rosenstiel's Widow and Son, Fine Art Publishers Ltd., London.

Burton, Miss May (op.1904)
Equestrian artist who painted a portrait of a hunter in a landscape (1904).

Burton, Mungo, ARSA (1799-1882)
Scottish portrait painter who lived in Edinburgh and who exhibited there (1838-1880) showing four or five portraits a year. His portrait of John Logan Campbell (1817-1912) in the Club Dress of the Edinburgh Allcion Archers painted in 1838, 29in.x21in., is in The Paul Mellon Collection, Upperville, Va, USA. No record of the archery club now exists but it is thought to have been a short-lived society organised by and for the students at Edinburgh University.

Burton, Miss Nancy Jane, RSW (op.1920-1950)
Equestrian and animal painter. Born in Invernesshire, studied at the Glasgow School of Art. Exh. at the RSA, RSW, GI, SSA.

Bury, Adrian, HRWS (b.1891)
Portrait and landscape painter sometimes of river and angling scenes. A nephew of the sculptor Sir Alfred Gilbert, RA, he studied art in London, Paris and Rome. Wrote a number of articles on sporting painters and art for "The British Racehorse" during the 1950s. Exh. at the RA, RP, NEAC and held several one-man shows.

Busby, Thomas, Lord (op.1804-1837)
A figure artist who exh. portraits at the RA (1804-1837). The British Museum has an aquatint dated 1851 of Lieutenant Fairman in the act of running, after an original painting by this artist.

Buss, Robert William (1804-1875)
London painter of historical and humorous sporting subjects. Pupil of George Clint ARA (q.v.). His painting "The First of September" depicts a sportsman in a wheelchair, presumably suffering from gout, being pushed by a small black boy in livery. This painting which was repro. in "Country Life" (1968) is in the collection of the Arts Council of Great Britain. Buss exh. at the RA, BI and SS (1826-1859) where his work included the "Enthusiastic Sportsman" and was for some years editor of "The Fine Art Almanack".

Busson, Georges (1859-1933)
French artist who painted the racehorse "Britannic" with jockey A. Gottlieb up, s.&d. 1923, watercolour, 11¾in.x16½in.

Butcher, Laura (op.1905)
This unrecorded animal artist painted a portrait of a foxhound in a panelled room in 1905.

Butler, Bryon T. (op.1889-1904)
Equestrian artist who specialised in horse portraiture, mainly studies of hunters.

Butler, Elizabeth Southerden, Lady (Miss Elizabeth Thompson), RI (1846-1933)
Equestrian artist but largely of military and battle scenes. Studied at South Kensington Art School in 1866 and became a pupil of Giuseppe Belluci in Florence in 1869.

Butler, Mildred Anne, ARWS (1858-1941)
Irish landscape and animal painter who studied at Westminster School of Art and with Frank Calderon (q.v.) at his School of Animal Painting in Kensington. Elected ARWS (1896).

Butler, Thomas (op.1750-1759)
Bookseller and stationer in Pall Mall until 1750 when he employed assistants who would, as his advertisements claimed, tour the country to paint sporting subjects. Equestrian artist who painted in a very similar style to James Seymour (q.v.) and Thomas Burford (q.v.). An outrageous entrepreneur, it is very difficult to know whether he himself ever painted a work entirely unaided. Certainly Butler received no professional training but the Butler style was very impressive and he is said to have worked with James Seymour. An inventory of the Duke of Hamilton's pictures in 1759 (Hamilton MSS) includes a set of eight portraits of horses by Butler with their pedigrees and prizes. In 1754 he pub. a series of engravings entitled "Portraitures of Horses". "The Great Carriage Race" (also painted by Seymour), 57½in.x95in., shows the race between Lord March and Lord Eglington which was run in a time of 53 minutes 27 seconds over a distance of 19 miles.

Butterfield, Kenneth (b.1921)
Artist and sporting writer who has contributed to "The Field" for many years.

Butterfield, Sarah Harriet Anne (b.1953)
Studied at the Ruskin School of Fine Art at Oxford University. Qualified as an architect in 1983. Exhib. RCA 1978, MG 1979, 1980, 1985, 1987, Hamilton Gallery Carlos Place, 1988, Agnew's Gallery, Bond Street, 1988. Was awarded the Edgeton Coghill Landscape Prize in 1977, the Windsor and Newton Award in 1978 and the Hunting Group Competition Finalist in 1987. Specialises in paintings of tennis.

Butterworth, Ninetta (b.1922)
Jersey-born equestrian artist who paints hunting and racing scenes and dog portraits. Influenced by Lionel Edwards (q.v.) but totally self taught. From the late 1950s this artist became interested in coaching and carriage scenes, some of which were pub. by Royle as greeting cards. Exh. with Messrs. Fores Gallery in 1951 and in 1955 her work was published in limited edns. under the pseudonym "Vixen" (q.v.)

Buxton, Dudley (op.1904)
Contributor of half-tone comic sporting subjects to "Punch" in 1904.

Buxton, Robert Hugh (b.1871)

London painter of landscapes and sporting subjects. Studied art at the Herkomer School at Bushey and at the Slade School. Has included a number of hunting watercolours amongst his work, "Find the Scent", "Over the Fence", "Tally Ho" and "The Chase" etc. Exh. at the RA, RI, ROI, IS and at the Paris Salon.

Buxton-Knight, John
See Knight

Byles, William Hounsom, RBA (op.1872-1940)

Painter of landscapes, portraits and some equestrian scenes including his portrait of "Milenko" winning the 1921 Cambridgeshire Stakes. He also painted "The Stewards Cup, Goodwood" in 1940 and a lively scene entitled "Joie de Vivre" showing a lady galloping side-saddle on the sands with two dogs in 1906. Elected RBA (1901). Contributed illustrations to "The Pall Mall Magazine" and "The Sketch" in the 1890s.

Byng, Robert (op.1704-d.1720)

Portrait painter who included an occasional sporting subject in his work. Probably an elder brother of the portrait painter Edward Byng, a pupil and close follower of Godfrey Kneller (q.v.). Sometimes painted equestrian scenes including one dated 1706, "A Master of Hounds with Attendants". Several plates after Byng's work were engraved including "The Deer Hunter" by Charles Ruben Riley (1782), 15in.x12in.

Byron, Frederick George (1764-1792)

This artist exh. five drawings at SA in 1791 as an honorary exhibitor including "Changing horses on the road to Paris". His style was apparently similar to that of the amateur sporting artist H.W. Bunbury (q.v.). His death is recorded in the annual register early in 1792 and in "The Gentleman's Magazine" of the same date it says "at Bristol Hot Wells wither he went for the recovery of his health" (unfortunately unsuccessfully) "Frederick George Byron, Esq. nephew to (5th) Lord Byron and the Countess Dowager of Carlisle."

C

"CJG"

A woodcut of "Mr. Pickwick Skating" by this artist was repro. in "The Connoisseur", December 1925 p.203 from "The Penny Pickwick" edited by "Boz" alias Charles Dickens. "The Penny Pickwick" was first issued in 1837 in penny parts of 8 pages each. E. Lloyd of 62 Broad Street, Bloomsbury (and later of 44 Wych Street, Strand) was the publisher. "The Penny Pickwick" boasted in its complete form more than 300 woodcut illustrations, apart from woodcut title pages and coloured pictorial wrappers. "CJG", the artist, is thought to bear a resemblance to "Phiz" Hablot Knight Browne (q.v.).

Cadell, Francis Campbell Boileau, RSA, RSW (1883-1937)

Edinburgh portrait painter who is represented in several public collections. Studied art at Julians in Paris and Munich and is included in this Dictionary for his painting "The Royal Procession at Ascot", brush/ink, signed and inscr., 2¾in.x19¼in., Calton Gallery, Edinburgh.

Cadmus, Paul (b.1904)

American painter and engraver. Studied at the National Academy of Design, New York, under W.A. Levy. A pupil also of Francis C. Jones and Charles C. Curran.

Included in this Dictionary for his brilliant and socially satirical golf painting "Aspects of Suburban Life" (1936) exh. NAMOS, Indianapolis (1991).

Cadogan, Sidney Russell (op.1877-d.1911)

Landscape painter in oil. Born in England but especially fond of Scotland - painting Scottish scenes, very often sporting, and animal life. Exh. at the RA from 1877 and at the Grosvenor and New Galleries. Lived in Fifeshire.

Caffieri, Hector, RI, RBA (1847-1932)

Landscape and sporting watercolourist. Studied art in Paris under Bonnat and J. Lefebvre. Worked in London and in Boulogne sur Mer. Exh. at the RA (1875-1901), SS, NWS and in Paris. Elected RBA (1876) and RI (1885), retired 1920. Specialised in fishing and boating subjects and is known to have painted a croquet scene in 1877/8 which he exh. at SS in that year. He exh. fishing scenes in 1875 and 1876.

Caffyn, Walter Wallor (op.1876-d.1898)

Surrey landscape and river painter who frequently painted the landscapes in the angling paintings of H.L. Rolfe (q.v.).

"Calamo Currente"

Alias James M'Hardy, author of "Half Hours with an Old Golfer" (1895)

Caldecott, Randolph, RI, ROI (1846-1886)

Watercolour illustrator, very often of sporting scenes and a keen sportsman himself. Known as the "Man in the Round Hat". He contributed to "London Society" from 1871 and from 1872 to "Punch", in which year he settled in London and studied at the Slade School, under the sculptor, Dalou. He also drew for "The Graphic" and illus. many books including the tale of the infamous John Gilpin - a picture book for children. Exh. at the RA (1872-1885) and at the RI. Elected a Member (1882). His studio sale was held by Christie's in 1886.

Calderon, Philip Hermogenes, RA (1833-1898)

An artist more usually associated with historical works than sporting but he did paint "Captain of the Eleven" exh. posthumously at the Fine Art Society in 1907, engraved in mezzotint by R. Josey and pub. by the Fine Art Society Ltd., 1 June 1883 (Coll. Thames County Primary School, Blackpool). Calderon, Spanish by birth, studied art at James Matthews Leigh's art school in Newman Street (1850) and in 1851/2 he studied in Paris under Picot. First exh. at the RA in 1853 and was elected a member in 1867. In the summer of 1866 Philip Calderon and his fellow students from Heatherleys, including G.A. Storey, RA, to whose sister Calderon was married, rented Hever Castle for three months which may have inspired Calderon's croquet scene "Resting in the Shade after a Croquet Match", s.&d. 1867, 25½ in.x18½ in., Sotheby's (Sussex) 1989. Painted a striking portrait of the artist Joseph Mallord Turner (q.v.) working in his studio in 1855.

Calderon, (William) Frank, ROI (1865-1943)

Portrait, landscape and sporting painter, particularly of hunting scenes, the third son of Philip Calderon (q.v.) Frank Calderon founded and became principal of the School of Animal Painting in Kensington (1894-1916). His students included Cecil Aldin, Lionel Edwards and A.J. Munnings (qq.v.). He was a regular contributor to the RA (1881-1921). Sporting titles include "The Jolly Huntsman", "Ran to Earth" (1894) and "Coursing" (1902). He was elected ROI (1891) and pub. "Animal Painting and Anatomy" (1936).

Caldwell, Edmund G. (1852-1930)

London animal and sporting painter who later turned to animal sculpture. Produced many illustrations for "The Gun at Home and Abroad" for Fores (1912-1915). Contributed to "The Sporting and Dramatic News" and exh. at the RA, RBA and RI. Illus. "Jock of the Bushveld", the story of a remarkable dog, by Sir Percy Fitzpatrick, pub. Longmans 1908, and the section on beagling in "The Encyclopaedia of Sport" (1897).

Califano, John (b.1864)

Born in Rome but lived in Chicago USA. Student of Dominico Morelli, Naples. Won the Gold Medal of Milan (1880) and the Read Prize (1908). Exh. at the National Academy of Design and the Art Club of Philadelphia. Painted a number of game dogs and shooting scenes.

Calkin, Lance, ROI, RBA (1859-1936)

London portrait painter who studied art at the RCA, RA and the Slade Schools. A number of his portraits were of famous sportsmen, often posed in sporting settings. Exh. at the RA (1882-1926) including "The Salmon Poachers" (1892).

Callaway, William, Frederick (Revd.) (op.1855-1899)

A Baptist minister at York and a painter of historical and literary subjects who exh. at the RA, BI and the Portland Gallery (1855-1861). He included a number of game and animal subjects amongst his work. Callaway was also by way of being an amateur cartoonist and was a contributor to "Punch" (1855).

Callcott, Sir Augustus Wall, RA (1779-1844)

Sea and landscape painter who included a number of angling scenes amongst his work. Studied at the RA Schools and with the portrait painter John Hoppner (q.v.). Exh. at the RA and BI. Elected RA (1810). He was Keeper of the Royal Collection for many years for which service he was knighted in 1837. He married Maria Graham (1785-1842) the daughter of Rear-Admiral Dundas, a notable seafaring lady herself and an intrepid traveller. She married firstly Captain Thomas Graham RN who inconveniently died off Cape Horn in 1822 and then married Callcott in 1927. Lady Callcott wrote on art and on her travels which she illus. most competently.

Calvert, Charles (1785-1852)

Landscape painter, some sporting scenes. Brother of the sporting artist Henry Calvert (q.v.). Father-in-law of William Bradley (q.v.) Art teacher who numbered Joshua Maiden (q.v.) amongst his pupils, Calvert was a founder member of the Royal Manchester Institution.

Calvert, Henry (1798-c.1869)

Fine sporting and animal painter. Born in Manchester but worked mainly in Wales and the Chester area. Exh. at the RA (1826-1854) including a notable work entitled "The Wynnstay Hunt" (1852). He is best known for his painting "The Cheshire Hunt at Tatton Park" (1839) which depicts Joe Maiden, huntsman to the hunt (1832-1844), mounted on a hunter in the foreground (in the coll. of the National Trust). Joe Maiden was the brother of Joshua Maiden (q.v.), the sporting artist. Calvert was greatly influenced by the work of John Ferneley Snr. (q.v.) with whom he was increasingly in competition. Ferneley also painted a massive picture of "The Cheshire Hunt" for the Grosvenors (later Westminster) of Eaton Hall where it still hangs. Calvert's "The Meet of the Vine Hounds" was engraved by William Simmons in 1844. The Wynnstay hunt was engraved by W.T. Davey in 1855.

Camden, P. (op.1805-1809)

Known by only two paintings, one of a fishing party (a scene at the New Lock, Medenham) which was illus. in the Farington Diary, Vol. I p.50, and the other a large landscape. The artist is said "to have possessed a fine talent of the second class" - Grant, "The Old English Painters", Vol.7, p.518.

Cameron, Angus (op.1870s)
This artist specialised in shooting scenes and his work has been shown at Frost and Reed Ltd., London. Examples include "Out for a Day's Shooting", s.&d. 1870, and "The End of the Day".

Cameron, Sir David Young, RA, RSA, RWS, RE (1865-1945)
Scottish painter, watercolourist and a talented etcher who specialised in majestic Highland scenes later in his life. His enchanting painting "Battledore and Shuttlecock", 14in.x17in. is in the Glasgow AG and Museum and qualifies him for inclusion in this Dictionary but he also painted and etched several works with an angling interest. Illus. (with engraved plates) "The Story of the Tweed" by Sir Herbert Maxwell (1905), and the 1902 edn. of "The Compleat Angler" (Walton). Cameron, who studied at the Glasgow School of Art and at the Royal Institution, Edinburgh (1885) taught at the British School in Rome (1919) was elected RE (1895), RSA (1918), RA (1920) and was knighted (1924).

Cameron, Mary (Mrs. A. Millar) (b.c.1865-d.1921)
Edinburgh painter of equestrian and racing subjects in oil. Exh. at the RSA and exh. a painting entitled "At the Starting Post" at the RA in 1900. This artist had an exhibition in Paris in 1911 at the Galleries des Artistes Modernes. Mary Cameron lived for a period of time in Madrid and Seville and specialised in bull-fighting scenes.

Campbell, George F., RHA (b.1917)
Irish-born figure painter and of urban scenes in both oil and watercolour. His painting "A Lion Rugby Football Player", 13⅜in.x10⅛in., Christie's (Belfast), is unfortunately an unexciting representation of a rare subject.

Campbell-Black, Geoffrey (b.1925)
Game bird and wildfowl painter. Educated at Repton in Derbyshire. Served in the army at the tail end of the 2nd World War and after. Lives in Devon.

Campion, George Bryant, NWS (now RI) (1796-1870)
London landscape and topographical painter in watercolour and an original contributor to the New Watercolour Society in 1834. He was elected a member (1837). A very prolific artist, he occasionally painted sporting scenes and concentrated on these much more after he went to live in Germany publishing "The Adventures of a Chamois Hunter". He often worked on coloured paper. His painting "The Hastings Races", 10¼in.x18in., is a good illustration of his work in this subject as is his watercolour "Sports at the RMA, Woolwich", s.&d. June '62, 16in.x21½in. This was painted whilst Campion was instructor of military drawing at the RMA which was at Woolwich until 1939. It moved to its present home at Sandhurst in January 1947.

Campione, S. (op.1831-1853)
London painter of live and dead game subjects. His painting "Duck Shooting" (1832) was exh. at the BI where he exh. (1831-1853).

Canchois, Henri (op.1883-1890)
This artist exh. nine paintings at SS (1883-1890) including "Fishers" and "A Return from Sport" from a Regents Park address.

Cane, Herbert Collins (op.1883-1891)
London animal painter who exh. at the RA and NWS (1883-1891). His work includes pictures of fighting cocks.

Canfield, Birtley (1866-1912)
American animal sculptor and artist who met an untimely end, bitten by one of his favourite models - a dog.

Cantelo, C. (op.1863-1888)
Equestrian artist who painted steeplechasing, racing and hunting scenes. These include a portrait of the 1863 Oaks winner "Queen Bertha" with her trainer John Scott, a set of four hunting scenes, dated 1864, and a pair of steeplechasing scenes, dated 1888.

Caparn, W.J. (op.1882-1893)
Landscape painter from Oundle who painted several interesting little trout fishing paintings. Exh. one work at SS (1882). Usually inscribed his work "Oundle".

Carey, Joseph William, RUA (1859-1937)
Irish marine and coastal painter. Included in this Dictionary for his watercolour "A Yacht Race in Bangor Bay" showing "Britannia" beating "Vigilant", 11½in.x 9in., Christie's (Belfast) 1991.

Carlaw, John, RSW (1850-1934)
Glasgow painter and etcher of animals, especially dogs and horses. Studied Glasgow School of Art but started his career as a designer in the Saracen Foundry, Glasgow. Exh. at the RA and RSW from 1883. Elected RSW (1885).

Carlile, Joan (1606-1679)
A gifted amateur painter with influential patrons both before, during and after the Civil War. The daughter of William Palmer, an official in the Royal Parks. In 1626 she married Lodowic R. Carlile, Gentleman of the Bows to Charles I and a Keeper at Richmond Park. She included a number of sporting scenes amongst her work and was represented at the exhibition of British Sporting Painters (1650-1850) at the Hayward Gallery in 1974.

Carline, George F., RBA (1855-1920)
Portrait and landscape painter with a particular interest in flowers who also included a number of fishing scenes amongst his work. Studied art at Heatherleys in London and also in Paris and Antwerp. Father of the artist Sydney William Carline (1888-1929).

Carmichael, John Wilson (1800-1868)
Newcastle marine painter and of some sporting scenes; for example "The Gannet Shoot" which he painted in 1843, 17in.x24in., and "Grouse Shooting on the Moors", a watercolour painted in 1835. Friend and pupil of T.M. Richardson, Snr. Carmichael exh. mainly at the Northern Academy of Arts in Blackett Street, Newcastle, close to his studio. The Laing Art Gallery, Newcastle held a most comprehensive exhibition of his work in November/December (1968). His studio sale was held by Christie's 1870.

Carolus-Duran, Charles Emile (1838-1917)
Fashionable French portrait painter. Elected a member of the Institute in 1905 and appointed Director of the French School in Rome. He had many pupils including John Singer Sargent (q.v.).

Carpenter, Percy (op.1841-1860)
London painter of foreign scenes and church interiors. Exh. at the RA and BI. A set of five hog hunting scenes entitled "Pig Sticking in India", "The Meet", "Tally Ho", "First Spear", "The Charge" and "The Hog at Bay" were lithographed by E. Walker, after the work by Carpenter, and pub. by Day & Son in 1861.

Carr, Tom (1909-1977)
Interesting artist who was originally employed as a blacksmith by the Priestman Collieries for the pit ponies who lived underground. Mr. Lewis Priestman was MFH of the Braes of Derwent. Tom was a keen border terrier man and entered his terriers to the fox with the Braes. He was very severely injured in a fall at work underground, and when lying in hospital discovered his talent for painting. Mr. Priestman arranged for Tom to go to the King Edward Art College which was then part of Durham University where he was awarded a Certificate of Fine Art (1950). His first commissions came from local sportsmen and his reputation soon spread among the "posh" packs in the south. His work includes hunting, racing, driving and beagling scenes and his patrons included the Dukes of Beaufort and Northumberland. Carr also illus. a number of books including "A Hunting Man's Rambles" by Stanislaus Lynch.

Carr, William (op.1831-1836)
Norfolk sporting artist who was recorded in the local Directory as an animal and heraldic painter.

"Edward Carrick"
The pseudonym used by the artist Edward Anthony Craig (q.v.).

Carrick, John Mulcaster (op.1854-1878)
Brother of Robert Carrick (q.v.). Scottish landscape painter, often of fishing scenes and an illustrator of books including "The Home Affections" by Charles MacKay (1858). Included in this Dictionary for his paintings "Casting a Fly on the Ogwer, Glamorgan" (1873) and "Fisherman by a Stream" (1870).

Carrick, Robert, RI, ROI (op.1829-1904)
Scottish painter of rather dreary landscapes who included a number of angling scenes amongst his work. Brother of the better known John Mulcaster Carrick (q.v.). Elected RI (1850) and ROI (1883).

Carroll, Larry
Contemporary artist of American football scenes. "Portrait of Joe Theisimann" (1980), acrylic on illustration board.

Carse, Alexander (op. 1800-1843)
Scottish figure and portrait painter in both oils and watercolour. Pupil of David Allan (q.v.) before joining the Trustees Academy in 1806. Included in this Dictionary for his painting of football entitled "The Doonies v. the Croonies on New Years Day". The Robertson Collection, Orkney.

Carstairs, John Paddy (b.1916)
Landscape painter in watercolour, oils and gouache. Studied art at the Slade School and exh. a rugger painting at the RA in 1963 entitled "The School Match". Has had several one-man shows.

Carter
The artist of a fine watercolour painting, 5¾in.x9¾in., of "A Sea Plane competing for the Schneider Trophy", signed with his surname only, Bonhams 1988.

Carter, E. (op.1850-1877)
Included a portrait of "An Arab Pony with Hounds by a Gate", signed and painted in 1850, 15½in.x19½in., amongst his, or her, work.

Carter, Frank William, ROI (1870-1933)
Portrait and landscape painter whose portrait of an early lady motorist, 37in.x29in., was auctioned Christie's (Sth. Ken.) 1990. Carter, who was the son of the artist Hugh Carter (q.v.), studied at the Slade School and exh. widely at the leading London galleries and elsewhere. Elected ROI (1905).

Carter, Henry William (op.1867-1904)
London painter of animals and domestic subjects. Included a number of game scenes amongst his work such as "A Spaniel with a Mallard, "A Spaniel with a Pheasant", "A Lurcher with a Hare", etc. His coursing scene "Catch as Catch Can" is decorative rather than factual, "The Judge" being dressed in historical costume. His paintings are of a very high quality and he also painted a number of fishing scenes. Exh. at the RA and SS (1867-1893).

Carter, Hugh, RI, ROI (1837-1903)
Predominantly a landscape painter but also noted for some distinguished portraits. Studied art at Heatherleys, London and afterwards with J.W. Bottomley (whose daughter, Maria, he married) and Alexander Johnston. He also studied in Dusseldorf, under K.F. von Gebhardt. Exh. at the RA (1859-1902) and at the RI. Elected RI (1875). Carter was a Member of the (Royal) Institute of Oil Painters from its start in 1883. He also exh. at the NEAC (1898-1903) including "Hunting Recollections at the Black Horse Inn" (at Battle, in Sussex). Carter's uncle was Sir Francis Ronalds, the inventor of the first working telegraph (1823) and his portrait by Carter is in the National Portrait Gallery. Father of the artist Frank William Carter (q.v.). A memorial exhibition of Hugh Carter's work was held at Leighton House in 1904 and much of his best work was done in watercolour and pastel.

Carter, R.J. (op.1840)
Painted a portrait of "A Bay Hunter in a Stable" in 1840, Sotheby's 1985.

Carter, Samuel John, Snr., ROI (1835-1892)
Illustrator, sporting and animal painter. Born in Swaffham, Norfolk and studied in Norwich. He was the principal animal illustrator for "The Illustrated London News" for many years contributing marvellous sketches

of horses and agricultural shows all over Britain. Elected ROI (1883). Exh. at SS from 1861. Titles include "A Warm Bath after Hunting", "The First Grouse of the Season", "Hunters - the property of E. Birbeck, Esq." and "At the Stud - 'Marionette' and 'Tamark'" - the property of C. Johnstone, Esq.". His other sporting work includes portraits of deerhounds, carriage horses, hunters and greyhounds.

Carter, Samuel, Jnr. (op.1880-1888)
London landscape and sporting painter, son of Samuel John Carter (q.v.). Painted a fine portrait of "Miss Ethel Buxton of East Anglia, riding sidesaddle" in 1887.

"Cassandre"
The name used by the French poster artist Adolphe Mouron (q.v.) for his famous "Triplex" motor poster in 1931.

Casse, S.B. (op.c.1796)
Irish painter of game subjects whose painting "Wild Duck Shooting" was engraved by James Pearson, c.1796.

Cassie, James, RSW, RSA (1819-1879)
Aberdeen painter of rustic landscapes, sporting and sometimes coastal scenes. Cassie, who was very badly injured in a street accident as a child, studied art with James Giles (q.v.). His fine painting "A Gentleman with three Greyhounds", 1853, was exh. by Arthur Ackermann & Son. Cassie exh. at the RA, BI, SS and elsewhere (1854-1879). Elected RSW (1878) and RSA (1879).

"Castor"
Alias B.F.S. Mulcaster, northern correspondent to "The Field" on coursing matters and Keeper of the Greyhound Stud Book (1914).

Catlin, George (1796-1872)
American artist, best known for his fine paintings of the Indian tribes of the Trans Mississippi West during the 1830s. He also painted hunting scenes. His painting of an early game of lacrosse, as played originally by the Indians, is in the Thomas Gilcrease Institute of American History of Art. Another painting by Catlin on the same subject entitled "Ball Play of the Choctaw - Ball Up", 19½in.x27½in., painted 1834/5 is in the National Museum of American Art - Smithsonian Institute.

Cattermole, Charles, RI, RBA (1832-1900)
London painter and watercolourist, nephew of George Cattermole (q.v.). Included a fine watercolour painting of "A Coach and Four" amongst his work.

Cattermole, George, OWS (1800-1868)
Norfolk-born painter of very often romantic scenes who included a number of hawking and falconry paintings amongst his work. His painting "The Castle - Rook Shooting" is in the collection of Birmingham AG. Elected OWS (1833).

Cattermole, Leonardo F.G. (op.1869-1886)
The son of George Cattermole (q.v.). London painter of historical subjects, often featuring horses. Painted

mostly in watercolour and exh. eight works at SS and eight at GG (1872-1886). His portrait of a racehorse in a landscape, painted in 1869, was sold by Christie's in 1981. His portraits of "Middlesex" and "Peggy" and the hunter "Brunette" with the dog "Coolie" are both s.&d. 1870, Bearnes 1991.

Cattley, George A. (Major, Third Carbineers) (1896-1978)
Very competent although amateur equestrian artist, who, through his profession painted a number of military horses as well as hunters and polo ponies. A fine horseman, Cattley hunted with the Quorn and often rode with the East Essex Hunt. Cattley was a staff instructor at the military riding school of Weedon. He was also a Carbineer, a member of the regiment which won the inter-regimental polo tournament in 1886 and 1887.

Catton, Charles, Snr., RA (1728-1798)
Born in Norwich. Heraldic coach painter to King George III. A founder member of the RA where he exh. (1760-1798). Included hunting portraits amongst his work.

Catton, Charles, Jnr. (1750-1819)
Son of Charles Catton Snr. (q.v.) Studied at the RA Schools and under his father. Exh. a number of works at the RA including a horse racing scene. An engraver of his own and other people's work including that of George Morland (q.v.). Pub. "Animals Drawn from Nature" (1788). Emigrated to America in 1804.

Cauldwell, Leslie Giffen (1861-1941)
American landscape and figure painter who lived mostly in Paris and New York. Cauldwell studied at the Académie Julian in Paris, under Boulanger, Lefebvre and Carolus Duran. He exh. two paintings at the RA, three at RBA and four at the Walker Art Gallery. Included in this Dictionary for his painting "The Boxer", 24½in.x14½in., auctioned Sotheby's 1971.

"Cavendish" alias Henry Jones (Dr.) (1831-1899)
Contributor to "The Field" from 1866 and co-founder of the All England Croquet Club with his cousin Whitmore Jones, and W.H. Walsh (q.v.). Author of the article on croquet for the 1877 edn. of the Encyclopaedia Britannica and "The Science of Croquet" (1868) which was serialised in "The Gentleman's Magazine".

Cawse, John (1779-1862)
London portrait and historical painter who included a number of horse portraits amongst his later work. Exh. at the RA, BI, SS and OWS (1801-1845). Pub. "The Art of Drawing in Oil" (1840).

Cawthorne, Neil (b.1936)
A Leicestershire-born equestrian artist who studied art under the guiding hand of the sporting artist John Kenney (q.v.). He specialises in hunting, racing and polo scenes including "The Last Chukka, 1981" repro. "The World of Polo, Past and Present", by J. N. P. Watson, pub. The Sportsman's Press, 1986.

Cemansky (op.1931)
This artist formed a pastiche in 1931, based on William Frith's "Derby Day" but imposing popular turf socialites

in the foreground including Lords Lonsdale and Derby, Edgar Wallace, the Aga Khan, the actress and film star Greer Garson, Winston Churchill and the Bluebird driver Donald Campbell. Repro. "The Derby" by Michael Wynn Jones, pub. Croome Helm, London (1979).

Ceriez, Theodore (1832-1904)
Belgian artist who painted "A Game of Skittles", signed, 8½in.x14½in., Christie's.

Chalmers, Sir George, Bt. (c.1721-1791)
Edinburgh portrait painter who started his career as an heraldic painter. Studied first with Allan Ramsay (q.v.) then in Rome. His portrait of William St. Clair of Roslin (d.1778) as Captain of the Honourable Company of Edinburgh Golfers, aged seventy-one, in the act of driving off the links, is now in the Hall of the Royal Company of Archers, 88in.x61in. Chalmers, who was a keen golfer, was also a member of the Honourable Company of Edinburgh Golfers.

Chalmers, Hector (c.1849-1943)
Scottish landscape painter who studied at the Trustees Academy and the RSA schools and exh. at the leading Scottish and Irish galleries. His painting "Golfing at Elie", signed and inscr., 11½in.x15in., was auctioned Phillips (Edinburgh) 1987.

Chalon, Alfred Edward, RA (1780-1860)
Prolific portrait and historical painter. Born in Geneva, the younger brother of J.J. Chalon (q.v.). Studied at the RA Schools (1797). Became a member of the Associated Artists) in 1807. Resigned (1808) to found Sketching Society with his brother and F. Stevens. Exh. at the RA and BI (1801-1860). His watercolour of "John Talbot Clifton with Cricket Bat" was painted in 1834, 20in.x 16in. Collection Lytham Hall, Lancs.

Chalon, Francis (1776-1836)
"A sporting painter of repute" according to Sydney Pavière (Dictionary of Sporting Artists) though little is known about either him or his work.

Chalon, Henry Barnard (1771-1849)
London sporting and animal painter in both oil and watercolour. Born in London. Of Dutch extraction, he was no relation of his contemporaries the Swiss-born brothers J.J. Chalon, the landscape painter, and A.E. Chalon (qq.v.) the portrait painter. Chalon's mother was the daughter of Sir John Barnard, a successful London financier and MP. He acquired his mother's maiden name as his second Christian name and through his mother's family he presumably acquired his many distinguished patrons. Chalon studied art at the RA Schools and was appointed animal painter to the Duchess of York (1795) and later to the Prince Regent, and William IV. He dedicated to the Duchess of York, his book "Studies from Nature" which he produced in collaboration with the artist, J.C. Nattes, which shows how much he was influenced by George Stubbs (q.v.). He also pub. Chalon's "Drawing Book of Animals and Birds of every Description" and the "Seven Passions of the Horse" engraved and pub. by Jackson. His other important patrons included the Dukes of Beaufort and

Devonshire, Earl Grosvenor, Lord Raby and Colonel Thornton. His brother-in-law was the sporting artist James Ward (q.v.), whose youngest sister, Sarah, he married. Chalon's sporting work includes portraits of racehorses, greyhounds, foxhounds, hunters and a number of shooting scenes some of which he exh. at SS including "1st October - Pheasant Shooting" and "12th August - Grouse Shooting", painted in 1841, and "Spaniels Flushing a Woodcock" (1834).

Chalon, John James, RA, OWS (1778-1854)
Landscape and animal painter. Studied at the RA Schools (1796) and exh. his first painting at the RA (1800). Became one of the first Associates of the OWS (1805) and was elected a full Member (1807). Elected RA (1841). A friend of the sporting and equestrian artist Jacques Laurent Agasse (q.v.) who painted his portrait (Agasse lived with the two brothers in Church Street, Kensington, for many years). Chalon often painted river and angling scenes, in oil and watercolour, and the Birmingham Art Gallery have a painting entitled "The Angler's Pool" 1809.

Chalon, Kingsley S.
This artist painted a work entitled "Side Saddle with the Hounds", 6in.x12in., Sotheby's 1971.

Chamberlain, Christopher (1918-1984)
Oil painter of figure subjects, also of urban scenes and landscapes. Studied at the Clapham School of Art (1934-1938) and at the RCA (1938-1939) and again after the war (1946-1948). His fine painting of football "Chelsea plays Arsenal", 47½in.x95¾in. was painted for the 90th Anniversary of the FA in 1953, FA Coll. Chamberlain was married to the artist and lecturer, Diana Copley (b.1920) with whom he often collaborated, especially on book illustrations.

Chamberlain, Miss E. (op.1816)
Exh. a painting of fish at the RA (1816).

Chamberlain, Joseph (op.1920s)
Wiltshire landscape painter in oil who studied art at Heatherleys. Exh. at the RA, RI and the Paris Salon. Painted his own version of "Mr. Francis Bennoch of the Blackheath Golf Club" which was repro. in "The Home Lovers' Book of Fine Prints" (1966), pub. Frost and Reed Ltd. The print has close similarities to the work by L.F. Abbott (q.v.) of William Innes known as the "Blackpool Golfer".

Chamberlain, Julian Ingersoll (b.1873)
American portrait painter whose fine study of Mr. A. Henry Higginson (b.1876-d.c.1957), MFH of the Cattistock Hunt on his horse "The Prophet", was illus. and repro. in "British Sports & Sportsmen". A. Henry Higginson is also known for his book "British and American Sporting Authors" and for the fact that after his death he left his complete library of sporting books to the London Library in St. James's. He was Master of the Cattistock Hunt for nine seasons. Chamberlain was a writer and painter of sporting subjects, born in Columbia, South Carolina, the son of Major D.H. Chamberlain, a veteran of the American Civil War.

Educated Phillips Academy, Andover, Mass. and Yale University (1891-1895). Qualified as an architect and had his own successful practice in Boston. A keen horseman, he hunted with the Middlesex Hounds in 1900. In 1928 he wrote with A. Henry Higginson "Hunting in the United States and Canada" pub. 1929. Came to England (1932) to hunt and to paint commissioned work of hunting and hounds for various patrons. Thereafter he lived in Dorset.

Chamberlain, William (1771-1807)
London animal, sporting and equestrian painter. Studied at the RA Schools (1790) and became a pupil of John Opie (q.v.) in 1794. His small output includes portraits of a number of racehorses including "Pantagruel" by "Driver" s.&d. 1801 and inscr. "Patroclus" by Mr. Vernon's "Pantaloon" out of a dam by "Florizel", the property of Sir Charles Burrell, Baronet. Both paintings auctioned by Tennants 1985.

Chambers, Alfred (op.c.1859-1862)
"The Meet", two pictures of hounds meeting outside country houses, one signed and indistinctly dated, 17½in.x25in., a pair, were auctioned Christie's 1969. This artist could be Alfred P. Chambers who exh. two paintings at the BI and three at SS (1859-1862).

Chandler, John Westbrooke (1764-1805)
Portrait and miniature painter who exh. a portrait of an English boxer at the RA in 1788 from a London address. The subject may well be canine and not human - were boxer dogs around in the 18th century? Chandler studied at the RA Schools (1784) and exh. at the RA (1787-1791). His father was the 2nd Earl of Warwick, though not legitimately. Chandler's artistic merit does not seem to have been considerable and he died insane c.1804/5.

Chantrey, Sir Francis Legatt, RA (1781-1842)
Distinguished sculptor and sportsman included in this book for his feat of shooting two woodcock with one shot at Holkham Hall, Norfolk, on 20 November 1829, and two days before that he shot a rabbit and a hare with one shot. Both amazing events are recorded in the Holkham Game Book (1826-1831). Chantrey, who was elected RA in 1816, is also the subject of a pen and ink drawing by George Jones, RA, (q.v.) s.&d. 1832 showing him "dapping" or "blowing" as it was then called, a method of fishing by "dancing" a fly on the surface of the water using a long rod, held so that the breezes blew out a special floss silk line. The drawing is the property of the Houghton Fishing Club. Chantrey is probably best remembered nowadays for the reversionary interest in his estate that he left to the RA to be spent annually on works of art to form a national collection known as the Chantrey Bequest.

Chantry, N. (op.1797-1838)
London sporting and still life painter who exh. at the RA (1797-1836) and SS (1824-1838). Titles include "A Hawk painted from Nature" (1819) and at the RA "The Poacher Alarmed" (1826), "The Young Sportsman" (1828) and "Pheasant" etc. (1832).

Chapeau, E.C. (op.1887)
Painted a fox-hunting scene entitled "Drawing a Covert" in 1887.

Chapin, James (1887-1975)
American painter of baseball scenes who studied art in Antwerp and Paris. He was profoundly influenced by Cézanne and the modernists, a style that was to remain with him after his return to New York. His fine painting of a baseball game entitled "Man on First" painted in 1948 shows two figures, the first baseman tense with anticipation waiting the outcome of the toss and the runner, waiting his opportunity on the way to second base, 28in.x24in., The Gladstone Collection of Baseball Art.

Chapman, Miss A.M. (op.1902)
Animal painter who exh. one painting at the Bailie Galleries in 1902.

Chapman, Abel (1851-1929)
Natural history writer and illustrator. Born in Sunderland and a cousin of Joseph E. Crawhall (q.v.) the sporting artist. Chapman pub. a number of bird books including "Retrospect Reminiscences of a Hunter Naturalist" with illustrations by Crawhall (1928) and he illus. others on game hunting. Contributor to "The Field" during the 1920s, including an article entitled "Sixty Years of Grouse Shooting" (1925).

Chapman, John Watkins (1853-1903)
London painter and etcher who exh. at the RA (1853-1903). Chapman painted a steady stream of Victorian genre including countless studies of dead game. His painting "A Game of Bowls on the Lawn of Haddon Hall" is therefore a delightful interlude from a somewhat monotonous output.

Chapman, W.J. (op.1835-1864)
This primitive, provincial artist painted a number of horse, dog and cattle portraits. (He may be the same artist as W.P. Chapman (q.v.) but the date span ranges from 1835 to 1871.) Pavière refers to a painting by W.J. Chapman, s.&d. 1864, and repro. "Country Life" (13.6.68) by Chichester Antiques.

Chapman, W.P. (op.1869-1871)
Gloucester provincial sporting artist who painted portraits of cattle and hunters between these dates.

Chappell, R. (op.1842)
This equestrian artist painted a pair of horse portraits, "Hunters in Stables", s.&d. 1842, 22¾in.x29¼in., Sotheby's, 1990. These paintings are interesting since they are clearly not by Ruben Chappell (1870-1940) nor by William (q.v.). They are pleasing and accomplished works of art.

Chappell, William (op.1858-1882)
London painter of figure subjects and some sporting, although the latter are not very good. Exh. at the RA, BI and SS and elsewhere (1858-1882). A pair of hunting scenes was auctioned Bonhams 1984.

Chardin, Jean Baptiste Simeon (1699-1779)
French artist whose painting "The Girl with a Shuttlecock" was shown at the exhibition of French 18th

century paintings at Hertford House in 1932. Described by "The Connoisseur" (March 1932) as having "all the charm of solemn childhood".

Charles, James, NEAC (1851-1906)
Portrait and landscape painter. Studied at Heatherleys School and the RA Schools (from 1872) and in Paris at the Académie Julian where he was influenced by the plein-air movement. Painted "Shooting over a Wheat Field", 19½in.x23½in., auctioned Sotheby's 1987. Exh. at the RA from 1875, at the Paris Salon, and at the NEAC, becoming a member in 1886.

Charles-Jones, Alexander (b.1959)
Gloucestershire based sporting and equestrian artist. Encouraged to paint by Raoul Millais (q.v.), he is official artist to the Racehorse Owners Association. Sports painted include racing, hunting, polo, shooting and a number of sporting cartoons.

Charlton, Evan (1904-1984)
London figure painter whose fine oil on board of a "Fencing Match", dated 1932, 36in.x48in. was auctioned Christie's 1989. Charlton studied at University College London (1923-1927) and at the Slade School (1930-1933). Taught at the West of England College of Art (1935-1938), Head of Cardiff School of Art (1938-1945), war artist (1939-1945), HM Inspector of Art for Wales (1945-1966). Exh. NEAC and elsewhere.

Charlton, George, NEAC (b.1899)
Landscape painter and book illustrator. Studied art at the Slade School (1914) and later became a member of the staff (1919-1962). Exh. at the NEAC from 1916. Elected Member (1926) and became Hon. Treasurer (1958). Taught at Willesden School of Art (1949-1959). Worked in oil, watercolour and pastel. His painting "The Greasy Pole" shows figures participating in maritime water sports, signed, 39in.x59in., W.H. Lane 1988.

Charlton, John, RBA, RI, ROI (1849-1917)
Primarily a sporting artist and an illustrator who also painted portraits, battle scenes and landscapes. Studied at the Newcastle School of Art, under W. Bell, at the suggestion of the sporting artist Joseph E. Crawhall (q.v.), and at South Ken., London. Exh. at the RA (1870-1904), SS and the NWS. Elected RBA (1882). Charlton moved to London in 1870 and worked for some years in the studio of J.D.Watson, RWS. He contributed illustration work to "The Graphic". Charlton had few rivals in portraying hounds and was a first rate illustrator but surprisingly, since he was a competent horseman and a keen rider to hounds, he seems to have been less happy with horse portraiture. He collaborated occasionally with Richard Ansdell's collaborator, Samuel Sidley (q.v.). Charlton had many distinguished patrons including Earl Spencer for whom he painted at least three pictures, and Queen Victoria who commissioned him to paint the "Jubilee Procession" in 1897. Pub. "Twelve Packs of Hounds" (1891) and illus. H.A. MacPherson's "Red Deer" (1896). His biography is reported in "Cassells Magazine" (1906).

Chase, Frank M. (op.1874-1898)
London painter, in both oil and watercolour, of fishing and river scenes who exh. at SS and RI (1874-1889). Titles include "Eel Bucks at Hurley" in 1875 and "The First of June - Fishing Commences" in 1881. Also exh. at the RA, NWS and elsewhere. He was the son of John Chase RI (1810-1879) and brother of Miss Marion Chase RI (d.1905).

Chaulms, T. (op.1889)
"The Links with Players of the Royal Liverpool Golf Club" s.&d. 1889, collection of the Royal Liverpool Golf Club, repro. in "British Golf" by Bernard Darwin, pub. by Collins (1946).

Chepik, Sergei (b.1953)
Contemporary Russian painter who has already received France's highest award, the Gold Medal, at the Salon d'Automne in 1989. His work embraces sporting subjects including boxing and racing. His first one-man exhibition in London was held at the Roy Miles Gallery. His painting "The Boxers" 1991, 47in.x47in., is a reflection of human life - fighting, winning and losing. "Afternoon at the Races" 55in.x86in. Exh. Roy Miles Gallery, London, 1991.

Chevalier, Sulpice Guillaume (op.1874)
See Gavarni

"Cheviot"
Alias Eric Parker, the sporting journalist, who wrote for "The Field" on topical shooting matters and became its editor (1931-1937). Pub. "Elements of Shooting" (1924).

Cheviot, Lilian (op.1910-1920s)
Animal and equestrian painter in oil. Studied at Frank Calderon's School of Animal Painting, South Ken. and at Walter Donne's Life School. Exh. at the RA and in the provinces. The Earl of Lonsdale was her chief patron and several of her equestrian paintings were auctioned at the Lowther Castle sale in 1947.

Chialiva, Luigi (1842-1914)
Swiss painter who lived in France and who exh. in England (1880-1911). He is included in this Dictionary for his angling painting "The Fishing Lesson", a delightful study, 9½in.x15½in., which sold for £21,000 in 1984.

Chichester, N. (op.1859-1895)
Intriguing equestrian artist whose fine work ranges between his operating dates. An inscription on his painting (1878) of "Rosebud" and "Lady Jane" reads "Bay mare "Rosebud" a wonderful fencer. Grey mare "Lady Jane" given to us by Lord Portsmouth - for driving. She dropped down dead going at a fast pace. Joe Chichester with "Rosebud", Painted from Life (1878), retouched (1895)."

Childe, Elias, RBA (op.1798-1848)
London landscape painter, brother of James Warren Childe, the miniaturist. A very prolific exhibitor of nearly five hundred works at the RA, BI and SS (1798-1848). His best loved and recurring subjects were river scenes and stable and blacksmiths' interiors, also

several examples of that favourite Victorian subject, the farmyard. A painting entitled "To Teach the Young Idea how to Shoot" was exh. at SS in 1843.

Childe, James Warren (1778-1862)
Portrait painter and miniaturist who is recorded in the sporting Colonel Hawker's diary of September 1827 as follows: "September 15th Mr. Childe, the artist, arrived at Long Parish and Mr. Joseph Manton, the famous gun maker perative to a painting being made of our partie de chasse". "September 16th Assembled my .... for one more grand field day in order to have some of their likenesses - Mr. Childe attended as a strict observer and Mr. Joseph Manton shot with me." "September 18th Stayed at home with Mr. Childe to arrange for the disposition of the picture while a friend and Joe Manton went off shooting." Mr Childe's sketch was engraved by H. Adlard and pub. by Longman & Co. in 1830. Colonel Hawker is the centre figure on horseback with Joseph Manton on foot to his left talking to him. Siney, the ratcatcher, is on the donkey and the double mounted markers are coming up on the left of the picture. Mounted behind Colonel Hawker is his boy who took charge of the horse whenever Colonel Hawker dismounted to shoot on the dogs pointing. Long Parish House stands in the background and the game is spread out before them. James Childe is also known to have painted a portrait of two young cricketers in 1817 which was auctioned at Christie's in 1977 and "A Cricket Match" 19¼in.x23¼in. c.1740-5 is in the Tate Gallery Collection, London.

Childs, J.M. (op.1804-1828)
This artist exh. one painting of fish at SS (1828), from a Dudley address, and one at the RA of "Pike and Trout" (1827). He may also have exh. a fish painting in 1827 at SS as J.M. Child from Mr. Brown's establishment in High Holborn and another of a butterfly, a watercolour of a Purple Emperor. A still life of seven fish including trout, pike, barbel and greyling with a lignum vitae reel on a river bank "painted on stone by himself" c.1827 is an interesting work (Charles Hullmandel's book "The Art of Drawing on Stone" had been pub. in 1824 hence this form of painting was currently very popular). An engraving of this painting by Engelmann Graf Coindet & Co. of 66 St. Martins Lane is in the collection of the Piscatorial Society. Mr. Child(s) must have been an extremely accomplished artist for the foliage plants and flowers on the river bank are quite beautifully executed, as indeed are the fish.

Chinnery, George, RHA (1774-1852)
There are, surprisingly for an artist more usually connected with Mid to Far Eastern landscapes and portraits, a small number of enchanting animal and equestrian paintings by this London-born artist who studied at the RA Schools. He exh. at the RA from 1791, mostly miniatures, until 1846. He moved to Madras in 1802, and from there to Calcutta in 1807. A portrait of Lady Louisa Duncombe out riding, pen/ink, 7in.x9¾in., is in the Paul Mellon Collection, Upperville, Va, USA.

Choquet, René (op.1896-1939)
French equestrian painter of fox-hunting scenes, including "The Meet" s.&d. 1903, 19½in/x29½in., Sotheby's 1986.

Christmas, Thomas C. (op.1819-1825)
London sporting painter who exh. at the RA, BI, SS and OWS including portraits of horses and dogs.

Christopher, Tom
Contemporary painter of American Footballers. "Portrait of Randy Gradishar, Denver Bronco's middle line backer", oil, 1979.

Church, C. (op.1821-1823)
Interesting equestrian artist of several racehorse portraits including "Soothsayer" held by his trainer, s.&d. 1821, and "Burleigh" with Sam Chifney, Jnr. up, s.&d. 1823. Since "Soothsayer" won the St. Leger in 1811 and the Doncaster Stakes the following day, he was clearly not still racing in 1821, when Church appears to have dated his painting. Besides which, "Soothsayer" had already sired the 1819 Derby winner "Tiresias", so had presumably gone to stud by 1815/16. Either Church finished earlier sketches made of the horses during their racing days or they were copies of portraits painted by other artist(s).

Churchyard, Thomas (1798-1865)
A solicitor by profession, this amateur artist had a freshness and lightness of touch in his painting which often made professionals look heavy handed. He painted in both oil and watercolour, mostly landscapes, of his beloved Suffolk. A great admirer of John Crome (1768-1821), with twenty of the latter's works in his collection, and an even greater admirer of Constable (1776-1837) whom he may have met on his visit to Woodbridge in 1815. His watercolour painting of three men in a gig c.1850 entitled "The Wits of Woodbridge" is in the collection of the British Museum. "The Wits of Woodbridge" include the artist, the poet Edward Fitzgerald (the translator of Omar Khayyam, 1859), Bernard Barton, a banker, poet and friend of the artist and shows them bowling along in a gig drawn by an enthusiastic if somewhat odd-gaited horse.

Clampitt, W. J. (op.1883)
An artist of this name painted a hunting scene entitled "On the Scent" s.&d. 1883, 31in.x25in., auctioned Sotheby's (Chester) 1987.

Clark, Albert, Snr. (op.1860-1910)
Senior member of a large provincial family of sporting artists who all appear to operate at the identical time, c.1860-1910. Often signed his work "Albert Clark & Son" so was presumably the father of Albert Clark, Jnr. (q.v.).

Clark, Albert, Jnr. (op.1880-1910)
London animal painter in oil, especially of horses, who exh. at the RA (1900-1910). He obtained many commissions in Essex and was presumably a son of Albert Clark Snr. (q.v.) with whom he collaborated on a number of paintings. In 1909 Clark painted the portrait of "Cicero" the third and last Derby winner

(1905) owned and bred at Mentmore by the 5th Earl of Rosebery and trained by Percy Pack at Exning. Clark's very fine portrait shows "Cicero" ridden by Danny Maher. The painting, 18¾in.x23¾in., made £1,400 at auction which hardly reflects this artist's talents.

Clark, Albert James (op.1890s-c.1943)
Presumably part of the large Clark clan of animal and equestrian painters.

Clark, Benton (1895-1964)
American artist of equestrian scenes, particularly fox-hunting.

Clark, Christopher RI (1875-1942)
Painter and illustrator of military and historical subjects and an equestrian artist of some skill. Included hunting scenes amongst his work. Elected RI (1905). He was said to have been a self-taught artist and he was also a poster painter. Illus. many books including R.D. Blackmore's "Lorna Doone" (1912).

Clark(e), Frederick Albert (op.1886-1909)
Provincial sporting artist who specialised in painting harness and trotting horses. Said to have been a son of Albert Clark, Snr. (q.v.). He painted for Mr. Reeves who had a number of trotters and Lady Batt who had hackneys. A study of the racehorse "Ormonde" winner of the 2000 Guineas, the Derby and St. Leger was signed F.A. Clarke and dated 1886. Clark's tiny portrait of the trotting mare "School Girl" is 2¾in.x 4¾in., Christie's (Tattersalls) 1989.

Clark(e), James, Snr. (1860-1902)
Provincial, but surprisingly competent equestrian artist who also painted portraits of prize pigs and cattle. Sometimes signed himself James Clark, Snr. so presumably there was a James Clark, Jnr. amongst this complicated family, especially as many paintings of this date are signed James Clark and Son. None, however, is signed James Clark Jnr. so presumably the latter was destined to play a purely supporting role. "The Call of the Hunt" was a subject much used amongst the Clark(e) family. W.A. Clark (q.v.) painted a similar scene with the same title in 1927 and James Clark used the subject again and again in almost identical paintings of an old hunter breaking harness to follow the hunt. The artist referred to above should not be confused with the biblical painter and illustrator, James Clark (1858-1943). Dated works by Clark(e) Snr. exist before the younger Clark was old enough to paint.

Clark, Jean (Mrs.) (b.1902)
Oxfordshire artist who exh. at the RA (1945-1969) including a painting of "The Royal Tennis Court at Hampton Court" (1950) and "In The Dedans, Queens Club" (1951). Married to the artist, John Cosmo Clark (q.v.).

Clark, John (op.1805-1824)
London painter, draughtsman and aquatint engraver of many sporting scenes after his own and other artists' work. He also described himself as "animal painter to the Queen". This artist was responsible for the fifty plates in Henry Thomas Alken's (q.v.) book "The

National Sports of Great Britain" pub. Thomas Maclean, London, 1821. Clark's painting of "The Royal Ratcatcher" shows that gentleman with pint pot, top hat and sash of office.

Clark, John Cosmo, CBE, RA, RWS, NEAC (1897-1967)
London sporting painter whose subjects include rowing, skating, boxing, hurdling, fishing and sailing. The son of James Clark, RI. Studied at Goldsmiths College of Art (1912-1914), Julians in Paris (1918-1919) and the RA Schools (1919-1921). Exh. at the RA (1931-1964). Elected RA (1958) and made a CBE (1955). Married to Jean Clark (q.v.), painter of real tennis pictures. John Cosmo Clark's interesting series of sporting panels for "The Peacock", Islington in 1931 depicting boxing, rugger, hockey, fencing, rowing and steeplechasing was referred to in the June issue of "The Connoisseur" 1932 and illus. The Peacock was unfortunately bombed and the sporting panels destroyed during the 2nd World War. Clark's painting "Skullers Practising on the Thames" s.&d. 1946 and inscr., gained an honourable mention in the Olympic Arts Competition held at the V & A Museum, London, in July/August 1948. The painting, 32in.x52in., will have been seen by thousands of diners at Langan's Brasserie, London.

Clark, Joseph, ROI (1834-1926)
Born at Cerne Abbas in Dorset. Studied art at J.M. Leighs in Newman Street and later at the RA Schools. Exh. at the RA (1857-1916). Painter of domestic genre and scriptural scenes. His painting of a bull in a field tossing a dog over his back with another running beside him entitled "Bull Baiting" indis. dated 184?, must be a very early work.

Clark, Samuel Joseph (op.1868-1918)
Sporting and animal painter of whom very little is known, but presumably he belonged to the large equestrian Clark clan based in Essex.

Clark, W. (op.1850)
Draughtsman and lithographer of four fox-hunting plates each 11½in.x15¼in., presumably after his own work.

Clark, William (of Greenock) (1803-1883)
Scottish marine painter whose work includes a number of colourful yacht racing scenes, many of which were engraved by Edward Duncan (q.v.) including "Regatta of the Royal Northern Yacht Club". Clark's best known work is probably "The Queen's Visit to the Clyde, 17th August, 1847".

Clark, William Albert (op.1906-1937)
Equestrian painter, presumably part of the large Clark family of artists. A business card clamped to the reverse of one of his paintings reads "W.A. Clark - animal and portrait painter. Studio - 51 Hanover Road, South Tottenham, London N. Gentlemen waited upon in any part of the country".

Clarke, Miss Maud Umfreville (op.1887-1899)
Illustrator, particularly of horses and fox-hunting scenes, who contributed to "The Illustrated London

Clarke, Richard E.

News", "The Sporting and Dramatic News", "The English Illustrated Magazine" and "The Badminton Magazine of Sports and Pastimes" (1899).

Clarke, Richard E.
"The Football Match", pencil and colour washes, signed, 20¾ in.x14¼ in., Phillips (Leeds).

Clater, Thomas (1789-1867)
Prolific figure and domestic painter who exh. extensively at SS and the RA (1819-1862). Titles include "The Gamesters Last Hit - not a Miss", "The Game of Put, or the Cheat Detected".

Claude, Jean Maxime (1824-1904)
French equestrian artist of many sporting scenes in watercolour.

Cleaver, Dudley (op. 1890-1908)
Illustrator and contributor to "The Penny Illustrated Paper" c.1890, pen/black ink portraits of lawn tennis personalities including Mr Rhodes, (presumably the American Champion, D.P. Rhodes); Miss Gladys Eastlake Smith (Covered Courts Champion 1907); Mr A. W. Cole; Miss Coles; Mr Garcia; and Mr. A. F. Wilding (later the winner of the Men's Singles Championship at Wimbledon in four successive years, 1910-1914. (Wilding was killed in action at Neuve Chapelle, France in 1915.) Underneath the portrait of a miserable looking umpire is inscr. "The Office of Umpire is not a matter of much competition among Club members", s.&d. 1907. Queens Club, London.

Cleaver, Ralph (op. 1893-1932)
Black and white artist who contributed regularly to "The Graphic" and "The Daily Graphic" from 1906. His drawing of a university hockey match "Varsity Match at Surbiton, March 1905" was clearly contributed as an illustration, as was his lively version of the 1901 Oxford and Cambridge Boat Race. Brother of Reginald Cleaver (q.v.). Illus. "Here's Horse Sense" by Reginald Summerhays (1932).

Cleaver, Reginald Thomas (op.1893-d.1954)
Black and white artist and illustrator to "The Graphic" and "Punch" (Mr. "Punch" with Horse and Hound - New "Punch" Library c.1930 p.115). Brother of Ralph Cleaver (q.v.) and illustrator "A Winter Book of Sport" (1911).

Cleaver, Roland (op.1890s)
Fox-hunting scenes in watercolour were auctioned Bonhams 1983. He is possibly F.R. Cleaver who contributed to "The Illustrated London News" (1889) and probably related to both Ralph and Reginald Cleaver (qq.v.)

Clements, James (op.1820s-1830s)
"Bowling", south-east view of the Saracen's Head Bowling Green, Worcester, an aquatint engraving by Joseph Gleadah (op.1815-1830) after a work by this artist was pub. by James Clements, Worcester c.1830, 10in.x17¾ in. "The Great Boxing Contest between Spring and Langan" was also aquatinted by Gleadah, after Clements' work with J. Pitman (q.v.) (1824).

Cleminson, Robert (op.1865-1903)
London based sporting painter who specialised in Highland scenes. Exh. at SS (1865-1868) two works depicting red deer. His painting "A Chamoise Cocker Spaniel with a Pheasant" dated 1868 is signed R. Cleminson Morris which makes one wonder whether this artist should also be listed under M for Morris. Auctioned Christie's 1991.

Clennell, Luke, ARWS (1781-1840)
Northumberland-born artist who was apprenticed to Thomas Bewick (q.v.) at the age of sixteen. Came to London (1804). Practised as an engraver until 1812 when he was elected an Associate of the Watercolour Society. Exh. at the RA (1810). Titles include "Foxhunters Regaling after the Chase" (the day's sport being over) (1812), "The Old Fisherman" (1813), and "The Gamekeeper" (1814). He also exh. in the provinces, mainly in the Midlands and his painting "Sportsmen taking Refreshment at a Country Inn" was shown at the Liverpool Academy in 1813. He painted a variety of sporting subjects including fox-hunting and fishing and in 1814 collaborated with the sporting artist Ben Marshall (q.v.) on a portrait of the famous sportsman and bookbinder, Thomas Godstone.

Cleveley, Robert (1747-1809)
Marine painter and draughtsman to HRH the Duke of Clarence and his brother HRH the Prince of Wales. Twin brother of the painter John Cleveley. Cleveley exh. "The Rowing Match at Richmond" at the RA in 1793.

Cleyn, Francis (1582?-1658)
This artist was principal designer to the Mortlake Tapestry Factory for the greater part of his life in England (1625-1658). His figure in hunting dress, holding a spear, standing in a wooded landscape, pen, brown ink and wash, 11⅜ in.x7⅞ in., is in the Paul Mellon Collection, Upperville, Va, USA.

Clifford, H.J. (op.1863)
This unrecorded artist painted a racing scene in watercolour entitled "At Full Stretch" (1863). Phillips 1987.

Clifton, Frances (op.1871-1899)
Very capable equestrian artist who included portraits of both racehorses and hunters amongst her work which is clearly signed Frances and not Francis and dated, spanning her operating dates.

Clint, Alfred, PRBA (1807-1883)
Prolific landscape and coastal scene painter who exh. a great number of works (406) at the SS (1831-1881). His 1864 exhibit was entitled "The Royal Regatta at Henley on Thames". This was obviously one of his more important works since it was priced for the sale at that date at £200 against many of his run of the mill paintings at £8-£10. He was elected RBA (1843) and President (1879). Son of George Clint, ARA (q.v.).

Clint, George ARA (1770-1854)
Portrait painter and engraver who included a few equestrian portraits in his work, namely the portrait of

"Lord and Lady Suffield out Riding with the Honourable Miss Harbord in Gunton Park with their Gamekeepers". He also engraved the portrait of James Belcher, the pugilist, after the original painting by Charles Allingham (q.v.). Clint exh. at the RA (1802-1845) and was elected ARA (1821) but resigned (1836). He was said to have become disappointed in not being elected an RA.

Clostermann, Johann Baptist (c.1660-d.1711)
Portrait painter whose sitters included some sporting personalities and a picture dealer. Born in Osnabrück, the son of a painter. Studied under his father, and then in Paris under François de Troy. Arrived in London (1681) and joined John Riley, the portrait painter, as a partner. Clostermann visited Spain (1696) and Rome (1699). Vertue considered Clostermann to be "a very moderate performer, his colouring strong but heavy and his pictures without any idea of grace". Nevertheless his portrait of a gentleman with his racehorse, jockey and trophies, 25½in.x30in., auctioned Christie's (NY) 1983 does not qualify him for Vertue's scathing statement.

Clowes, Daniel (1774-1829)
Chester sporting artist who worked for many patrons including Lord Robert Grosvenor who became the 1st Marquis of Westminster, Sir John Grey Egerton of Oulton Park, Sir Charles Knightley for whom Clowes painted the Pytchley Hunt in Northamptonshire, Earl Fitzwilliam of Wentworth Woodhouse in Yorkshire for whom he painted a similar canvas and the Vaughans of Nannan in Merionethshire. Chester races are the oldest English races still in existence, dating from at least 1540 and Daniel Clowes in his last years painted some of his most notable paintings of the Chester races and race-winners. He was the son of another Daniel Clowes (1743-1829) described in the Church Register as a "gentleman's servant". There is no record that Daniel Clowes Snr. ever painted but he may well have been influential in bringing his son's work to the notice of the local gentry.

Clowes, Frederick (1801-op.1840)
Artist brother of Henry Clowes Snr.(q.v.) and son of Daniel (q.v.). He worked in the same Chester studio as his brother Henry for a long time but seems to have been a less dedicated painter. The brothers are known to have collaborated on at least two canvases. One of three hunting dogs in a landscape signed by both artists and dated 1830, 18in.x24in., was in the collection of Iona Antiques, London.

Clowes, Henry, Snr. (1799-1871)
Sporting and animal painter, son of Daniel Clowes (q.v.) He worked from a studio in Watergate Street, Chester and produced attractive, if somewhat naïve, paintings of horses and views of Chester. His portrait of "Touchstone", winner of the St. Leger (1834) was painted for his owner, Lord Westminster in 1853. By 1853 he had been joined by his son, Henry Clowes, Jnr. (q.v.) who worked on after his father's death in 1871 as a genre animal painter.

Clowes, Henry, Jnr. (op.1834-1891)
Animal and genre painter, son of Henry Clowes (q.v.) who worked with his father in Chester from 1853. His painting of "A Carthorse in a Stable" was painted in 1871, the year that his father died.

Clowes, J. (op.1770-1849)
A painting of "Dodger Vernon" with jockey up, 34in.x44in., signed J. Clowes, pinxit 1824, was exh. at the Exhibition of Sporting Pictures at Harris Museum and Art Gallery, Preston (1943).

Coates, Michael, RI (b.1937)
Contemporary painter of equestrian scenes particularly hunting and racing. "The Leicestershire Hunt" etc. Painter also of cricket and golf scenes. Exh. at the Mall Galleries, London. Elected RI (1973). His works are in private collections in the British Isles, Canada, America and Spain.

Coates, Thomas J. (Tom), PRBA, ROI, NEAC, PS (b.1941)
Talented contemporary artist who includes a number of equestrian scenes amongst his work. Studied at the Bournville School of Art (1955-1959), Birmingham College of Art (1959-1961) and the RA Schools (1961-1964). Taught art at Reading College of Technology, High Wycombe College of Technology and School of Art, South East Essex School of Technology and School of Art and Maidenhead School of Art. Exh. at most major exhibitions and is a member of the Society of Equestrian Artists. Elected PRBA (1988).

Coates, W.R. (op.1740-1745)
An oil on canvas painting of a cricket match (19¼in.x 23¼in.) from "An Exact Representation of the Game of Cricket" by L.P. Boitard (q.v.) is attributed by the Tate Gallery to this obscure artist.

Cobb, David, ROI, PRSMA (b.1921)
Marine artist of several yacht racing scenes. Naval cadet at Pangbourne Nautical College (1935-1937). Served in the Royal Navy. Started painting professionally in 1946 at Newlyn and in that year exh. at the RSMA. President RSMA from 1979.

Cobb, Henry Ives (b.1883)
American painter during the depressive 1930s. His urban scenes of the American backstreet poor include games of backyard baseball played by the neighbourhood kids and painted in the bright cheerful colours of gouache paint.

Cockburn, R.D. (op.1833-1848)
Sporting artist with a limited, but well-painted output although his commissions clearly came from influential patrons who included the Earl of Stradbroke. His sporting work includes portraits of "Minerva" a celebrated greyhound, painted in 1848 and a grey hunter in a horse box, painted in 1833, Phillips 1986.

Cocking, Edward (op.1830-1848)
Exh. eight paintings at SS (1830-1848), three of them of dead game, from a London address.

Cocking, W. (op.1830s)
It seems likely that this artist, his equestrian work the subject of a series of plates engraved by R. Lloyd of Gibson Street, Lambeth in the 1830s entitled "Mr.

Ducrow in the Viscissitude of a Tar", was a close kinsman of Edward Cocking (q.v.).

Cocks, E.W.
A ballooning scene entitled "The Ascent of the Balloon, the 'Royal Vauxhall'" signed and inscr. "Vauxhall", 24½in.x18in., was auctioned Christie's 1882.

Codner, John
See J. Whitlock

Coghill, Sarah (b.1948)
Contemporary figure painter in oil, pastel and charcoal who specialises in cricket subjects. Studied at the Byam Shaw School of Drawing and Painting (1964-1968) and the RA Schools, London (1968-1971). Won the Special Prize for Life Drawing, RA Schools (1969). Exhibitions include The Knap Gallery, London (1987) and "Art '91", Wingfield Sporting Gallery, London.

Cohen, Isaac Michael, RP, ROI, PS, SGA (1884-1951)
Australian portrait painter who studied art at the National Gallery of Victoria, where he won a travelling scholarship (1905), and in Paris. Exh. at the principal London galleries and at the Paris Salon where he won gold and silver medals. Represented in many public collections. His painting entitled "The Fencer" shows an unknown lady foilist of the 1930s and hangs in the de Beaumont Centre, London.

Cole, Miss A. (op.1843-1856)
The artist thought to be responsible for a pair of paintings of a dark bay horse and two terriers, s.&d. 1843. She also exh. two portraits at the RA (1855/6).

Cole, George, RBA (1810-1883)
Painted sporting and animal subjects early in his career but turned to landscape painting after the mid-1840s. Self-taught artist who started his career by painting advertisements for Wombwells Travelling Circus. Father of George Vicat Cole (q.v.). Exh. SS, BI, and the RA (1838-1882). Elected RBA (1851). It is interesting that his best sporting works were painted after the mid-1840s including the many paintings commissioned by J.S.W. Sawbridge-Erle-Drax. His other sporting work includes several shooting pictures and portraits of hunters.

Cole, George Vicat, RA (1833-1893)
Landscape painter, very often of fishing subjects. Born in Portsmouth, the eldest son of George Cole (q.v.) and father of the artist Rex Vicat Cole (1870-1940). Exh. at the RA (1853-1892). Elected RA (1880). His work includes several angling scenes including "Fishing on the Test" painted on a terracotta plaque, 6½in.x10in., Christie's 1973.

Cole, James William (op.1849-1889)
London animal and equestrian painter. Exh. at the RA, BI and SS (1849-1882) including "Meet of the Limerick Hunt - A Bye Day", "Foxhounds at Croome Castle with Mr. and Mrs. Green of Green Mount, Mr. Henry, the Rev. Mr. Coker and Mr. Foster", s.&d. 1853 and inscr. with the principal figures, 38½in.x59in., exh. at the RA 1853 (No. 377).

Coleman, Charles (op.1839-1869)
A fine painting by this artist "A White Terrier attacking a Fox with a Cock Pheasant", painted in 1845, 32¾in.x41¾in., was auctioned Christie's 1969.

Coleman, Edward, RBSA (op.1813-1848, d.1867)
Birmingham painter of dead game and fish still lifes who exh. at the RA (1813-1848). He was the son of James Coleman the portrait painter. He was also a contributor to the Royal Birmingham Society of Arts from 1827. Elected Member of RBSA (1836). Is known to have painted shooting subjects.

Coleman, John (op.1828-1846)
Angling artist with a prolific output of dead fish displayed on the river bank, along with the tackle by which they were caught. Many of them were entitled "The Day's Catch" or "Still Life of Fish on a River Bank". Many of them are inscr. "Birmingham" so it is reasonable to suppose that John Coleman was related to James and Edward Coleman (q.v.).

Coleman, Roger (op.1973)
Prints of "Brigadier Gerard" and "Mill Reef" after the work by this artist were pub. in 1973. Coleman's portrait of "Nijinsky" hangs in the Jockey Club.

Coleridge, Francis George (op.1865-1870)
Berkshire landscape painter in watercolour. Exh. at the SS, RA, NWS and elsewhere and his work is represented in the Laing AG Newcastle. His watercolour "Rowing at Eton" with Windsor Castle in the background, was painted in 1870, and qualifies him for this Dictionary.

Collet, John (c.1725-1780)
London animal and bird painter, also of caricature subjects, who worked in both oil and watercolour. Studied art at the St. Martin's Lane Academy and became a pupil of George Lambert (1700-1765). Collet exh. works on a wide selection of subjects, including sport. His satirical subjects were engraved in mezzotint and pub. by Carrington Bowles and Robert Sayer. An early supporter of "women's lib" he painted a sporting series showing ladies' recreations, "The Female Foxhunter", "The Ladies Shooting Party", "Miss Wicket and Miss Trigger Playing Cricket" and "Shooting". Many of his original paintings have been engraved including that of "Miss Wicket" and "Miss Trigger", British Museum. His portrait of "A Lady Shooting over her Pony's Withers" while the pony grazes, was repro. in "Country Life" (5.7.84).

Collie, George RHA (c.1925-1950)
Irish sporting artist who lived in Dublin and exh. mostly at the RHA including a "Study of a Jockey in red and green silks", Bonhams 1983.

Collier, F.S. (op.1937)
Irish animal painter who exh. two works at the RSA in 1937.

Collier, H.H. (op.c.1900)
Unknown painter of a group of schoolboys c.1900 watching a hunt cross the road entitled "Schoolday Memories", Bonhams 1985.

Collier, Imogen (op.1899-1904)
Landscape and equestrian painter of hunters who lived at Horrabridge, Devon. Exh. at the RA.

Collier, J.H. (c.1899)
An angling still life showing pike, brown trout, perch and minnow, with tackle box and reel, 20in.x27in., signed by this artist was auctioned Bonhams 1983.

Collier, The Hon. John, ROI, RP (1850-1934)
Portrait and history painter, second son of the distinguished judge, Sir Robert Porrett Collier (1817-1886), later Lord Monkswell (1885). Studied art under Sir Edward Poynter PRA at the Slade School and continued his studies in Paris (under Laurens) and Munich. Exh. at the RA from 1874 including the full-length portrait of the great batsman "A.N. Hornby, Esq. (1847-1925) Captain of the Lancashire XI", which he exh. at the RA in 1893 (No. 921). (Collection of the Blackburn Museum and AG.) His portrait of the golf enthusiast Dr. W. Laidlaw Purves (1843-1918), 71¼in.x 437½in., founder of the Royal St. George's Club, Sandwich, Kent (founded in 1887) is in that Club's collection. Collier also collaborated with Heywood Hardy (q.v.) on the portrait of "Gerald H. Hardy, Master of the Meynell Hunt", painted in 1913, which was sold to the USA in 1990 for £17,000 (Sotheby's, 21 March). John Collier wrote three books on painting including "A Manual of Oil Painting" (1886) and "The Art of Portrait Painting" (1905). He married twice, both daughters of the Rt. Hon. T.H. Huxley, and he is best known for his domestic scenes of upper class life.

Collingwood-Smith (op.c.1910)
A fisherman with his fish and creel in a river landscape was auctioned Christie's (Sth.Ken.) 1985.

Collins, Charles, RBA (op.1867-1894-d.1921)
Surrey painter of rustic genre and Surrey angling scenes including "Fishing from the Bank", s.&d. 1874, and inscr. "Study from Nature", Sotheby's 1987. Elected RBA (1895).

Collins, Miss Elizabeth, (op.1866-1869)
London painter in both oil and watercolour who exh. "The First Shot" at SS (1866). This was the first and most expensive of her five exhibits there (1866-1869).

Collins, John (op.1838-1866)
Equestrian artist of a number of hunter portraits, posed in stable or landscape backgrounds and painted in oils.

Collinson, James (1825-1881)
A fine painting entitled "Before the Race", 20in.x27in., was auctioned Sotheby's (NY), 1989. Collinson, an original Pre-Raphaelite Brother, studied at the RA Schools with Holman Hunt and D.G. Rossetti to whose sister, Christina, Collinson was briefly engaged (1849-1850). Collinson, a staunch Roman Catholic, retired from the Brotherhood after his broken engagement and became a monk at Stoneyhurst until 1854 when he re-emerged to become a painter again. In view of his background "Before the Race" would seem to be an untypical subject for Collinson to paint but his work of whatever subject is always very attractive.

Collyer, Margaret (op.1892-1910)
London painter of equestrian, animal and figure subjects who exh. at the RA (1897-1903). Painted a portrait of the racehorse "Tedworth Shadow" (1901) and "Black Prince", winner of the Portman point-to-point (1893) and the York and Ainsty point-to-point (1892). The painting is s.&d. 1897 and inscr., J.Collins, Bideford.

Colmore, Nina (Mrs., née Murray), MBE (1889-1973)
Equestrian and animal painter and a dedicated sportswoman. Studied art at Heatherleys and at the Académie Julian in Paris. Exh. NEAC and at the Paris Salon where she won a diploma. Much of her work was painted for private commissions and her patrons included H.H. The Maharaja of Jaipur, H.H. The Prince Aly Khan, H.R.H. The Duke of Windsor, Lord Rosebery and the Duchess of Westminster.

Colquhoun, Ithell (b.1906)
Born in India. Studied art at the Slade School and won the Slade summer competition in 1929. She also studied in Paris and Athens. She exh. widely at the leading London galleries and in Paris and Athens (1930-1935). Her painting of football entitled "The Game of the Year", inscr. with the title, c.1953, may have been inspired by England's great match with Hungary in 1953. The Harry Langton Football Coll.

Colville, Alex
Contemporary Canadian figure painter. Included in this Dictionary for his striking painting "The Skater", exh. NAMOS, Indianapolis (1991).

Comber, Miss Mary E. (op.1886-1910)
Painter of still lifes of fresh water fish. Her portrait entitled "The Day's Catch", 8½in.x6½in., was exh. J. Collins, Bideford, September 1990.

Compard, Emile (b.1900)
French equestrian artist of many racing scenes.

Conder, Charles Edward, NEAC (1868-1909)
Landscape and portrait painter, very often of sporting subjects, who was also a lithographer. He spent his early years in India and Australia where he studied art in Melbourne and Sydney gaining a post on "The Illustrated Sydney News". In 1890 he went to Paris to study art at the Académie Julian where he also exh. He exh. at the NEAC (1893-1906) where his sporting titles include "The Golfers", "The Players" and "The Bathers". He was elected a member (1893).

Condy, Nicholas Matthew (1816-1851)
Marine artist who included a number of yacht racing scenes amongst his work. His painting of James Hare's appropriately named vessel "'The Leveret' BWYC Racing Offshore" is dated 1840, Sotheby's 1979.

Congreve, Miss Frances Dora, SSA (b.1869)
Landscape and marine artist with a particular interest in sailing scenes. Born in Scotland, studied art in Edinburgh, Rome and Naples. Exh. at the RSA and other Scottish galleries. Elected SSA (1909). Examples of her work include "Racing Yachts" and "Start of the Race".

Conner, Angela (Mrs. John Bulmer) (20th century)
Sculptor and painter, very often of equestrian subjects who was apprenticed to Barbara Hepworth, the sculptor. Has exh. at the Lincoln Centre, New York (1971), at Gimpel Fils, New York, Friends of the Tate Gallery Studio Show, RA and at the Horse Artists of the World Exhibition, Tryon Gallery, London.

Conor, William, OBE, RHA, PRUA (1884-1968)
Irish figure painter whose work includes a number of equestrian scenes. "Racing at Punchestown" painted in wax crayons, 15½ in.x18in., was auctioned Christie's (Belfast) 1990. "The Farmer's Race", 20¼ in.x24¼ in., showing the exciting finish of a point-to-point, was exh. at the RHA in 1954 (No.4).

Cook (op.1793)
An artist and engraver whose line engraving "The Grand Cricket Match at Lords", 1793, signed without a Christian name, 4¼ in.x6in., was presumably engraved after his own work. He was possibly Thomas Cook (1744-1818), the line engraver.

Cook, Beryl (b.1926)
Popular painter of everyday scenes in a naïve and often humorous style. Born Beryl Lansley in Egham, Surrey. Married John Cook in 1956. Together they managed a pub in Essex before moving to Rhodesia where Cook decided to become a painter. Author of "Private View" (1980) which became a best seller. "Bar Billiards", s.&d. 1978, 26in.x30in., Bonhams.

Cook, Brian (see also Batsford) (1910-1991)
Brilliant illustrator and painter, quite often of sporting subjects, who operated in the 1930s under this pseudonym. Became famous for the book jackets which he designed and illus. for the Batsford Heritage Books.

Cook, E. (1843-1926)
Painted "A Fishing Fantasy" in watercolour with grasshoppers angling, nine vignettes on one sheet, 11in.x9in., which was auctioned Christie's 1986. This artist might have been Ebenezer Wake Cook (1843-1926) who also painted in watercolour.

Cook, Joshua (op.1838-1848)
Exh. at the RA. Titles include "Return from Hawking" (1838), "Study of a Hawk" (1838). His exhibits at SS include "The Gidding Hall Tournament given by the Earl of Eglington" (1839) and "Coursing" (1844)

Cook, S.J. (op.1843)
Exh. one equestrian painting entitled "'The Duke' the property of Mrs. Pearl" at the RA in 1843 from a London address.

Cooke, Edward William, RA (1811-1880)
Painter of river and coastal scenes in oil and watercolour and included in this Dictionary for his sketch entitled "The Boat Race" and his painting of "The Balloon Trials at Blois, France" (1856).

Cooper, Abraham, RA (1787-1868)
London sporting painter, also of battle and historical scenes. Started his career at the age of thirteen in Astley's Circus. Became a pupil of Ben Marshall (q.v.)

(1807). In 1809 the old "Sporting Magazine" pub. the first of 189 plates from his work and he quickly made his reputation as a painter of dogs and horses. He set up a studio and took pupils amongst whom were John Frederick Herring Snr. (q.v.) who always painted in a very similar style and William Barraud (q.v.) who didn't. Another of his pupils was Harry Hall (q.v.). Cooper was a very keen fly fisherman and painted many pictures of his favourite sport including "Shury's Fishing House at Chingford", engraved by Webb, which was repro. for "The Sporting Magazine", May 1828. Cooper also contributed many plates to the "New Sporting Magazine" including a magnificent fly fishing illustration engraved by W. Smith, pub. June 1832 but repro. Vol. III May 1832. Ironically it was Cooper who in later life opposed Marshall's election to the RA. Exh. 332 paintings at the RA. Titles include "Gig" a favourite greyhound, the property of Lord G. Bentinck (1813), "A Celebrated Fly Fisher" (1819), "Shooters on the Hills" (1864). Elected RA (1820).

Cooper, Alexander Davis (ex.1837-1880)
Portrait and sporting painter, son of Abraham Cooper (q.v.) whose portrait he exh. at the RA where he exh. (1837-1888), also at the BI, SS and elsewhere. Titles of his SS exhibits include "The Young Sportsman" (1843) and "The First of October" (1880). His delightful portrait of a cheeky terrier entitled "Up To No Good" shows that this artist was a talented animal painter and almost certainly overshadowed by the popularity of his father's work.

Cooper, Alfred (ex.1854-1864)
Exh. at the RA, BI, and SS (1854-1864) including still life studies of fish.

Cooper, Alfred Egerton, RBA, ARCA (Lond.) (1883-1974)
Portrait, landscape and figure artist in both oil and watercolour. Studied at Bilston School of Art and at the RCA where he won his Diploma in 1911. Exh. at the RA. Titles include "Derby Day - 77 Years after Frith" (1934) and "Paddock at the Pony Races" which was also the title of the watercolour he contributed to the XIVth Olympiad Sport in Art exhibition at the V & A Museum, London (1948). Elected RBA (1914). His best known sporting works include "A Cricket Match at Lords" (1938), "The Prize Catch at Strathtay" (1945) "Fly Fishing", "The Paddock at Ascot", "Racing in London" and "The University Boat Race" (1935). Member of the Brighton Arts Club until he died.

Cooper, Alfred W. (op.1850-1901)
London painter in both oil and watercolour of domestic and figure scenes, including several sporting subjects. Exh. at the BI and SS (1850-1901). Titles include "A Good Morning's Sport" (1853), a watercolour of "Trout Fishing" (1879/80) and "After the Shoot". Cooper was a close friend and neighbour of the angling editor of "The Field", Francis Francis (1822-1886) whose classic "A Book on Angling" was pub. 1867. The artist painted Francis Francis several times in watercolour, fishing the river Crane from his garden at Twickenham. His delightful study entitled "Hampshire Trout" was painted in watercolour in 1855.

Cooper, Claude (op.1870)

Exh. a fish painting at the Dudley Gallery (1870) from a Berkshire address. His painting "Anglers with a Trout beside a Stream" was auctioned Christie's 24.4.1940.

Cooper, Edwin, of Beccles (1785-1833)

Suffolk-born animal and sporting painter who could produce work of outstanding merit in both oil and watercolour. A prolific artist, his patrons included the Dukes of Grafton and York, Lord Grosvenor, Sir Thomas Gooch, and Sir Jacob Astley. He exh. with the Norwich Society (1806-1832) and became an honorary life member in 1817. Cooper exh. one equestrian painting at the RA (1803) and then not again until 1831 following a row with the Hanging Committee over a work they alleged was a copy of George Stubbs (q.v.). Cooper painted cock-fighting scenes including "The Set To" and "The Death" dated 1816, each 10½in.x14½in. and several horseracing scenes including "Brightelmstone Races" (1804) and the match between "Gullwer" and "Sir John" which took place in 1803.

Cooper, George (op.1875-1901)

Equestrian and sporting painter. His watercolour "An Afternoon with the Batcombe Beagles at Firth Farm", was painted in March 1879, and auctioned Christie's (NY) 1987.

Cooper, S. (op.1826)

"A chestnut hunter standing by a fence in an open landscape", s.&d. 1826, auctioned Christie's 1970.

Cooper, T. C. (op.1811-1816)

Painter of mail coaches and a number of decorative scenes, including "The Brighton to London Mail passing the ruins of an Abbey" (1811) and "The Bath-London Mail at Hyde Park" (1816).

Cooper, Thomas George (op.1857-1895)

Son of Thomas Sydney Cooper (q.v.). He painted a few hunting scenes which are of no great merit. Cooper exh. at the main London galleries from 1861.

Cooper, Thomas Sydney, RA (1803-1902)

Better known as a landscape artist featuring cattle and sheep although he did paint a few horse studies including a portrait of a chestnut hunter inscr. "From Nature" in 1875. The Paul Mellon Collection, Upperville, Va, USA, have several pencil sketches of harness horses ascribed to Cooper.

Cooper, W. P (op.1831-1832)

This artist painted two or three portraits of hunters and one of huntsmen and hounds, which have appeared at auction, painted between these dates.

Copley, John PRBA, RE (1875-1950)

Painter, but primarily an etcher and a lithographer of great and imaginative talent. Studied at the Manchester School of Art, in the studios of John Watson Nicol and Arthur Cope, and at the RA Schools. Copley was deeply interested in sport, producing lithographs of "Lacrosse" (1910), "Athletes Dressing" (1912), "Tennis Players" (1917), and "The Polo Players" (Copley won 2nd prize with this etching in the Olympic Arts Competition in July/August 1946), and "Hurlingham Polo", drypoint, 14¾in.x11in. (1947), British Museum. Copley hardly ever dated his work and his printed impressions were always of a very small size, rarely exceeding twenty-five in an edn. Founder of the Senefelder Club and Hon. Secretary (1910-1916). Won the major award at the First International Exhibition of Lithographs at the Chicago Art Institute (1930). Exh. at the RA, RBA, RSA and NEAC. Elected RBA (1933). A major retrospective exhibition of his work took place at the Yale Center for British Art in April 1990.

Copley, John Singleton, RA (1738-1815)

American portrait and history painter who was born in Boston and was largely self-taught in art. Influenced by Reynolds (q.v.) Copley became the stepson of the English portrait painter and mezzotint engraver, Peter Pelham who died in Boston in 1751 and who is responsible for a sketch of Copley. He is also thought to have given some painting and etching instruction to Copley as witnessed by a small mezzotint plate of the Revd. Mr. William Welsted of Boston (d.1753). Copley came to England in 1775 after a successful career as a portrait painter in Boston. His cricket portrait of Richard Heber (1773-1833) as a boy of about ten years old, 65¼in.x51¾in., is in the Yale Center for British Art, The Paul Mellon Collection, New Haven, Connecticut, USA.

Copper, D.E. (op.1880s)

A pair of watercolours, "Fishing" and "Snipe Shooting", each 6¾in.x9½in., s.&d. 1880, were painted by this artist and auctioned Dreweatt Neate.

Corbet, Edward (Edouard) (b.1815 -op.1850-1878)

Prolific French artist who painted a large number of horse portraits, racehorses and fox-hunting scenes. Contributed many illustrations to "The Farmers Magazine" and his works were also engraved and pub. in "The Sporting Magazine". He exh. one painting at the RA (1854). His charming portrait of a "Hunt Terrier" painted in 1860 was auctioned Phillips (1986).

Corbould, Alfred (op.1831-1875)

London based sporting painter who also collaborated with H.L. Rolfe (q.v.) on a superb painting entitled "Fishermen with their Catch by a River" (1862). He also painted a charming portrait group of Frances and Blanche Maynard with their pony and two dogs set in a Scottish coastal scene. The painting was commissioned by the Earl and Countess of Rosslyn and exh. at the RA 1871 (No. 510). Corbould exh. at the RA (1835-1875), BI and SS. Paintings mainly of shooting scenes and game dogs. He was presumably related to the other artist Corboulds.

Corbould, Alfred Chantrey, RBA (1852-1920)

Suffolk-born sporting artist and caricaturist, son of the artist Alfred Hitchens Corbould (q.v.). Named after Sir Francis Chantrey, RA (q.v.) who was godfather to his uncle. Alfred Corbould was war correspondent for "The Graphic" in the Russo-Turkish War, illustrator for "Punch" and also for "Harpers Magazine" (1885). Nephew of Charles Keene (q.v.) under whom he studied. Exh. at the RA and SS including "The Wrong

Side of the Post" (1893-4) and "Over". Elected RBA (1893). In 1901 Messrs. Bradbury Agnew & Company Ltd. pub. a book of hunting pictures entitled "The Corbould Sporting Alphabet" to which the artist also wrote the letterpress.

Corbould, Alfred Hitchens (op.1842-1864)
London portrait and animal painter in both oil and watercolour who exh. at the RA (1844-1864) and SS (1842-1853). Son of Henry Corbould FSA (1787-1844), brother of Edward Henry Corbould (q.v.) and father of Aster Chantrey Corbould (q.v.). Alfred Hitchens Corbould married a sister of Charles Keene (q.v.), the illustrator. His painting of a groom with a lady's saddled hunter and an attendant dog, painted in 1859, was auctioned Sotheby's 1985.

Corbould, Arthur (op.1853-1864)
This member of the Corbould family of artists appears to have specialised in painting carriage horses including the Fitzwilliam carriage horses (1864) and presumably the Royal carriage horses entitled "Returning From Her Majesty's Drawing Room" (1853).

Corbould, Aster Richard Chantrey, RBA (op.1841-1892)
Sporting painter and illustrator, son of Alfred Hitchens Corbould (q.v.) and brother of Alfred Chantrey Corbould (q.v.). Studied art with his uncle Charles Keene (q.v.) who introduced him to "Punch" in which magazine much of his work was pub. Exh. at the RA (1842-1877) including "The Madras Hunt" and "Mrs. Craven on her Favourite Mare". Corbould was at his best when illustrations of horses were involved but his work also included military drawings and cartoons. Elected RBA (1893). Painted several pheasant and partridge shooting scenes.

Corbould, Edward Henry, RI (1815-1905)
This sporting artist who painted a number of angling scenes, was the son of the artist Henry Corbould, FSA, (1787-1844), best known for his design of the young Queen Victoria for Britain's first adhesive postage stamp in 1840. Edward Corbould carried on his father's work and his name is identified with some of the most effective designs repro. for the early Victorian postal emissions of the British Empire, engraved and printed by Perkins Bacon & Co. Edward Corbould worked chiefly in watercolour and his drawings are of exceptional delicacy and detail. He painted a fine portrait of Queen Victoria riding side saddle (repro. "Country Life" 1965). He is included in this Dictionary for his angling painting "The Biter Bit" painted with Henry Leonidas Rolfe (q.v.) and signed by both artists, 17½in.x15in. (oval). Exh. at SS (1835-1842). Became a member of the New Society of Painters in Watercolours in 1853 and was appointed drawing master to the Royal children by Queen Victoria and Prince Albert.

Cordrey, John (c.1765-1825)
Primitive painter of animals and sporting subjects who may have worked as a carriage designer, since he specialised in coaching scenes. His paintings, which are very wooden, have nevertheless a great attention to detail and many of his sporting scenes are charming. As in the coaching paintings of T.C. Cooper (q.v.) the horses move from right to left across the canvas. His coaches include "The Royal Manchester Telegraph", "The Princess Charlotte State Landau, driven by Mr. Mainwaring" (1814), "The Wandsworth London Coach" (painted in 1797) and "The Reading to London Coach" (1803).

Corning, Merv
Contemporary American painter of American football scenes including "The First 50 Years" (1969). Mixed media on illustration board and a portrait of "Carl Eller" (1974) watercolour on Arches paper.

Cornish, John (op.1751-1762)
Very little known about this artist who does not appear to have exh. in London. He was probably a portrait painter working in Oxford in the middle of the 18th century. W. Shaw Sparrow refers to a racing picture of his at Newmarket, "an apprentice copy of Tilleman's" (q.v.) and Waterhouse refers to a portrait, dated 1762, and a portrait of the American, Charles Paxton, in England (1751).

Corson, Richard (1919-1981)
One of America's best-known motor racing artists, who began his artistic career as a commercial illustrator, designing book jackets for Doubleday, Harper and Random House, and jazz album covers for Savoy, Dawn and Jubilee. He began an association with "Road and Track" magazine in 1962 (which was to last until his death in June 1981) and became known as an authority on motor racing. He painted in a fluid impressionistic style but could also be intense and vigorous as illustrated by his series of motor racing subjects, painted in gouache, and completed just before his death. Corson's book "Champions at Speed" (pub. Dodd Mead, 1979) contains some of his best pen/ink work, often accompanied by short commentaries written by himself, and serves as a fitting tribute to his many talents.

Cosomati, Aldo (op.1929-1930)
Painter and commercial artist who contributed sporting work to London Transport including "The Wimbledon Tournament, June 25th 1930". Collection London Transport Museum.

Cotes, Francis, RA (1726-1770)
Portrait painter who studied art under George Knapton (1698-1779). Cotes, who became a founder member of the RA, painted several portraits of young sportsmen, in both oil and pastel, including Lord Lewis Cage of Milgate Park, Maidstone, Kent, aged five and a half years old holding a curved cricket-bat with a two stick wicket and a ball to the left, 66½in.x 43½in., exh. at the RA 1769 (No. 23) (Collection Lord Brocket). A coloured mezzotint by L. Busiere after this work, pub. by Graves 1929, 21½ x 14½in., was exh. by the Parker Gallery London 1950. "The Revd. Charles Collyer as a Boy Cricketer", 35¾in.x27¾in., Yale Center for British Art, The Paul Mellon Collection, New Haven, Connecticut, USA.

Cotlison, V.J. (op.1890)
French painter of equestrian scenes whose work is seen to its best advantage in the plates made to illustrate the "History of Celebrated English and French Thorough-Bred Stallions" (S.F. Touchstone, 1890). He painted many portraits of racehorses, some over prints and several of which have been auctioned under various misspellings of his name.

Cottrell, Edmund (op.1822-1858)
London painter and sculptor who entered the RA Schools (1820) and included sporting and equestrian scenes amongst his work. He exh. at the RA (1822-1858) and SS (1829-1838). Titles include "The Sportsman" and "Hawking" from a model he made in silver for Messrs. Garrards.

Cottrell, Henry S. (1840-1860)
Sporting and equestrian painter about whom unfortunately very little is known although he may have been related to Edmund Cottrell (q.v.). His excellent work includes portraits of racehorses with jockeys up, hare-coursing and portraits of mail coaches including "The Bath to London Royal Mail Coach". His "Brighton to London Mail Coach passing Ardingly Viaduct" is topographically interesting and beautifully painted as is his portrait of "Mr. Gill's Celebrated Trotter 'Confidence'". He rarely seemed to date his work and did not exhibit in London.

Couch, Jonathan (op.1860-1863)
Illus. and wrote "Couch's Fishes of the British Isles" pub.in four volumes in London (1863). 250 of his watercolours of fish were auctioned as one lot, Phillips 1984.

Couder, Louis Charles Auguste (1790-1873)
French historical painter. Said to have been a pupil of Jacques Louis David (q.v.) but unlikely since Couder was only fifteen years old when David was banished to Brussels (1805) by Napoleon Bonaparte. Couder's major work "Le Serment du Jeu de Paume", painted in 1848, and engraved in aquatint by Jazet, records an incident in 1789 concerning the constitutional powers of France when the Real Tennis Court at Versailles, used for the meeting of the Convention on 20 June that year, became an historical monument, preserved by the nation for all time. Musée National du Château de Versailles.

Couldery, Horatio Henry (1832-1893)
Skilful animal painter who exh. at the RA, BI and SS (1861-1892). Sporting titles include "The First Game of the Season" (1886), "Cruel Sports" (1888) and "Rabbiting". His painting of "A Game of Croquet", played between two dogs, 5½in.x8in., was auctioned Sotheby's.

Coulidge, Rosamund (op.1936-1941)
Boston artist whose portrait of "A Tennis Player", painted 1936, 36⅛in.x30¼in., is in a private collection, USA.

Couper, George (Lieutenant, RN) (early 20th century)
Talented amateur artist who depicted sporting scenes wherever he was throughout the world. Polo in Vancouver and the Argentine, bull-fighting in Peru, horse races in Montevideo, Sydney and Hong Kong. He painted many of them in grisaille, or pen and ink with coloured washes.

Courselles-Dumont, Henri (ex.1889-1891)
French artist who exh. a fishing painting at SS (1890/1) from the London address of a Mr. Wright.

Co(u)zens, William (op.1820-1874)
Essex sporting painter who exh. at the RA (1820-1828) and at the BI. Titles at the RA include a portrait of "The Hon John Jocelyn with a favourite Pony and Harriers" (1820), "A Portrait of a Horse" (1828) and "A Favourite Pony with a Groom, the property of W.W. Prescott", painted in 1827 and exh. at the RA (No. 307) in 1828. "The Sporting Magazine" of 1828 (p.171) said this painting "has nothing particular to recommend it". His portrait of "Crib", a Staffordshire bull terrier standing in a wooded landscape, was painted in 1874.

Coverley-Price, Victor, MA (Cantab.), FRGS (b.1901)
Self-taught artist and illustrator in both oil and watercolour. Member of HM Diplomatic Service (1925-1946). Paints, and has painted a number of sporting scenes including polo and cricket. "A Cricket Match at Eton", with Windsor Castle in the background, grey wash, signed, 8in.x12in., repro. "The Sphere" 12.7.1952, and "Cricket Match at Lords between the Wars", grey wash, signed, 9in.x12in., repro. in "The Sphere" 12.7.52. Exh. at the RA, RBA, RI, RP and elsewhere.

Cowen, William (1797-1861)
Landscape and topographical artist who exh. views of Ireland at the BI (1823). His painting "An Archery Contest" from a vista view of Harrow, seen from the east side of the park, was painted in 1845. Cowen was patronised by Earl Fitzwilliam who would also appear to have patronised the artist Arthur Corbould (q.v.).

Cowland, R.M. (op.c.1880)
A painting of a pair of harnessed coach horses standing in stalls was auctioned Bonhams 1981.

Cox, Frank E. (op.1870-1894)
London landscape painter and of pastoral scenes who exh. at the leading London galleries (1870-1894). His painting "Hampton Court in the Olden Times", showing a bowling green at the Palace, with players in Queen Anne costumes is typical of his style of sentimental painting.

Cozzens, Frederic Schiller (1846-1928)
American marine painter and illustrator. Born in New York City. Studied at Reunselaer Polytechnic Institute, Troy, NY (1864-1867). His illustrations appeared in New York's "Daily Graphic" and "Harper's Weekly" (1874-1898). He is best known for his series of watercolours for Kelly's "American Yachts, their Clubs and Races" pub. by Scribners (1884). Illus. many books and magazines on yachting and yacht racing including every match in the America's Cup held off New York harbour.

Crabtree, Percy
A pen and ink sketch entitled "A'Hunting We Will Go" was recorded in the Pilkington Collection.

Craft, Percy Robert, R.Cam.A, RBC (1856-1925)
London painter of landscapes in oil, watercolour and pastel, and an engraver who contributed plates to "English Etchings". Studied at Heatherleys and the Slade School (under Poynter and Legros). Exh. at the major London galleries from 1878. Elected RBC (1888) and R.Cam.A. (1925). In the same year Craft painted "The 1st Tee at Cannes Golf Links" showing players enjoying the winter sun, 9½in.x16½in. Exh. Burlington Gallery, London.

"Crafty"
Alias the French equestrian and figure draughtsman in pen, ink and wash, Victor Gerusez (q.v.).

Craig, David (1888-1961)
Portrait painter whose oil painting (1958) of Charles de Beaumont (1902-1972) hangs in the foyer of the de Beaumont Centre (opened in 1963). The enormous contribution that Charles de Beaumont made to British fencing is described in "Modern British Fencing Vol. IV" by Richard Cohen. Craig represented Great Britain at epée in two Olympic Games, first in 1924, and then again, twenty-four years later, in 1948 when he was sixty, thus becoming the oldest British fencer to represent his country at an Olympics or World Championship.

Craig, David (b.1948)
Irish painter of portraits and sporting activities including horseracing, cricket and polo. Craig was born in County Kildare and studied at Trinity College, Dublin. An active sportsman, his paintings in pastel and watercolour reflect his knowledge. His original polo paintings feature in the Polo Club of "The Edwardian", Heathrow, London.

Craig, Edward Anthony (b.1905)
London born painter, wood engraver and illustrator who worked under the name of "Edward Carrick" to distinguish himself from his early acting career with his grandmother, Ellen Terry. He became a leading art director in the film world from 1939, but his early work consists of some striking pen and ink drawings which occasionally embraced sporting scenes.

Craig, Frank, ROI, NPS (1874-1918)
Kent-born black and white illustrator who studied at the RA Schools, under E.A. Abbey. Worked on "The Graphic" (1895) and was sent by "The Graphic" to the South African War as a special artist. Craig was an accomplished illustrator and included a great number of hunting scenes amongst his work. His fine painting in grisaille entitled "A Meet at the Manor" was auctioned Sotheby's (Sussex) 1989.

Craig, Henry Robertson, RHA (1916-1984)
Irish painter of equestrian scenes including "At the Races - Curragh, Dublin", 25in.x30in., auctioned Sotheby's (NY) 1990.

Craig, James Humbert, RHA, RUA (1878-1944)
Irish landscape artist who painted a number of equestrian scenes including "Jumping the Ditch", a point-to-point scene, 15in.x19¾in., Christie's (Belfast) 1990.

Craig, William Marshall (c.1765-1834)
Manchester drawing master who came to London in 1791. His watercolour painting "A Game of Skittles" was auctioned by Lacy Scott. Craig, who was also an illustrator and an etcher, was one of the first designers of illustrations for wood engraving and many of his drawings were engraved by T. Bewick (q.v.). Craig himself engraved some plates for Orme's "British Field Sports" after the work by Samuel Howitt (1807-1808).

Craig-Wallace, Robert (1886-1969)
Scottish artist of river, sea and coast scenes who exh. at the Glasgow Art Club, the RA and RSA (1929-1940). His fine watercolour "Regatta Day - Tarbert, Loch Fyne" was painted in 1909. Many of his paintings were of rod and line fishing from the rocks or of yachts racing in inshore coastal waters. Craig-Wallace was a keen yachtsman, often painting on the family yacht "The Calmara".

Cranch, John, of Bath (1751-1821)
West country sporting artist who worked firstly as an assistant to a lawyer. Is said to have found painting guidance from Sir Joshua Reynolds (q.v.) and John Constable RA (1776-1837) although a letter from Constable in 1799 refers to Cranch as a rather "eccentric character". Painted a number of shooting and fishing scenes and some equestrian portraits. Author of "Inducements to Promote the Fine Arts in Great Britain" (1811).

Crane, John (op.1880)
An equestrian painting by this artist, s.&d. 1880, was auctioned Christie's 1987.

Crane, R. (op.1832-d.1834)
This sporting artist lived at Newmarket and was obviously employed by the Grosvenor family. He apparently died very young. A lithograph after his painting entitled "A Royal Bowman at Eaton Hall" is dated 18 October 1832. A painting entitled "The Mask" (fox's), 11in.x9in., signed by Crane was exh. at Colnaghi June 1986. An engraving by Parr of the racehorse "Plenipotentiary" after the original painting by this artist is recorded by Mitchell.

Crane, Thomas (1808-1859)
Chester-born portrait and figure painter who studied at the RA Schools and who painted in both oil and watercolour. This artist, who may well have been a close relation of R. Crane (q.v.), also apparently sketched the meeting of the Royal British Bowmen in front of Eaton Hall, 18 October 1832, brown wash over pencil, 15¾in.x20⅝in., auctioned Christie's (NY) 1986.

Crane, William H. (op.1865)
A portrait of the chestnut racehorse "Gladiateur" (1862) with jockey up in an open landscape, s.&d. 1865, 20in.x24½in., was auctioned at Christie's 1969.

"Gladiateur" was the first French horse to win the Derby (1865). He also remains the only horse to win not only the Triple Crown but the Grand Prix de Paris as well.

Cranstoun, James Hall (1821-1907)
Perth born landscape painter whose "Angler on a Salmon River", s.&d. 1856, 40in.x50in., was auctioned Glennie's 1989. Cranstoun, who studied at the Slade School of Art, painted in oil and watercolour.

Craven, Edward (op.1910)
Painter of equestrian subjects which include the portrait of "A Skewbald Horse in a Loosebox" and "The Champagne Stakes", a head-on painting of two horses showing the jockey, Cliff Richards, beating his more famous brother, Gordon Richards, the only time that this apparently happened, 9in.x15in., Dreweatt Neate 1986.

Crawford, Robert Cree, RSW (1842-1924)
Scottish painter of most subjects, including sport. His painting entitled "The Golf Course", s.&d. 1874, 16in.x 27in., was auctioned Sotheby's 1985. Crawford lived in Glasgow and is represented in the Glasgow AG. He exh. at the RA from 1872 and RSW. Elected RSW (1878).

Crawford, Susan (b.1941)
Talented Scottish equestrian artist who has had a number of one-woman shows at the Tryon Gallery and elsewhere. Studied in Florence with Signorina Simi. Several limited edns. have been pub. after her work and her portrait of H.M. The Queen on "Worcran" in Windsor Great Park was painted to celebrate the Jubilee (1977). She painted the portraits of the champion racehorses and sires "Mill Reef", "Ribot" and "Troy".

Crawford, William (1913-1982)
American illustrator and editorial cartoonist for "The Newark Evening News" who drew the "National Pastime" (baseball) as a larger than life figure sitting in a vast chair astride two tiny figures identified as the Mexican League and the New Players Union who are trying to knock the chair legs (baseball bats) out from underneath him. The drawing, entitled appropriately "Termites in the Temple", was executed c.1946 before the Major League Baseball Players Association was formed to settle players' disputes.

Crawhall, Joseph E., RSW, NEAC (1861-1913)
An adopted member of the Glasgow Boys, best remembered for his humorous images of animals. Illustrator, sporting and animal painter mostly in watercolour. Studied art in Paris (1882) in the studio of Aimé Morot and was introduced to "Punch" by his father's friend Charles Keene (q.v.) who encouraged his talent and his passion for horses. Illus. many books including two by his cousin Abel Chapman (q.v.) "Unexplored Spain" (1910) and "Retrospect Reminiscences of a Hunter Naturalist" (1928). Exh. at NEAC (1890-1912). An outstanding horseman, he hunted with the York and Ainsty, the Sinnington and the Middleton. Artist of several polo scenes including "The Polo Player", watercolour, 4in.x5in. Collection Glasgow Hunterian A.G. University of Glasgow. Elected RSW (1887), resigned (1893).

Crawhall, Joseph, Snr. (1821-1896)
Painter in oil and watercolour, writer and illustrator mostly of sporting books. For example "A Collection of Right Merrie Garlands for North Country Anglers" pub. in Newcastle (1864), "Border Notes and Mixtey Maxty" (1880) and probably his best known "The Compleatest Angling Booke that ever was Writ" (1859), with woodcuts and etchings - some hand coloured, "A Jubilee of Thought " (1887), "The Berkshire Lady's Garland" (1883) and "Impresses Quaint" (1889). He also collaborated on Reid and Crawhall's "Chorographia" or "A Survey of Newcastle upon Tyne" (1884). He was the father of Joseph E. Crawhall (q.v.).

Crawshaw, J.T. (op.1850-1855)
Sheffield painter of game dogs whose work, spanning these dates, includes several kennel scenes with hounds.

Crealock, Henry Hope (Lt. Gen.) (1831-1891)
Author, sportsman, amateur painter and illustrator whose work includes hunting scenes and canine studies. Illus. "Wolf Hunting and Wild Sport in Lower Brittany" (1875) and "Sport" (1885). Crealock joined the army (1848) and served in the Crimea (1857-1858), the Indian Mutiny, New Brunswick (1861) and Zululand (1879). He was made Lt. Col. (1861) and Lt. Gen. (1884). Lived in Devon where the family tomb is to be found in Littleham churchyard. Crealock's pen and ink drawing "Tally Ho, Tally Ho, Gone Away, Gone Away", dated 1877, 13in.x15¾in., was auctioned Christie's (Sth. Ken.) 1984.

Crehays, G. (fils) (op.c.1895)
Racing pigeon artist at the end of the 19th century; the son, presumably, of another artist, Crehays (père).

Creswick, Thomas, RA (1811-1869)
Landscape painter and illustrator whose work includes several sporting scenes. Is known to have collaborated with Richard Ansdell RA (q.v.). His SS exhibit in 1829 was entitled "Sportsmen Regaling". Creswick painted several coursing and river scenes and illus. a version of Walton's "Compleat Angler". Elected RA (1851).

Cristall, Joshua, POWS (1768-1847)
Watercolourist of many subjects including figure, marine, some fishing and landscapes. Painted in a style as diverse as his subjects, sometimes like John Cotman and then again very like Cornelius Varley. He moved to Goodrich in the Wye Valley for the sake of his health in about 1822 and was responsible for the hanging of the pictures at the exhibition given by the Ross Society of Artists and Amateurs in 1827 and 1828. He became a founder member of the Society of Watercolour Painters and exhib. work there on a regular basis. He also exhib. at the RA and BI. Elected POWS (1816) and again (1821-1831).

Critchley-Salmonson, Mary Clare (Mrs Henry Scrope)
Contemporary artist and illustrator who studied life drawing under Signorina Simi in Florence and paints outstanding watercolour portraits of falcons. She attended a falconry course in 1974 and kept and flew her own birds. Many of her works are in private collections in the Middle East and in Britain. She illus. "Falconry in Arabia" by Mark Allen, pub. Orbis, London (1980).

Critchlow, M.B. (op.1953)
Contributor of a football painting entitled "Craven Cottage", oil, 23½in.x36in. Exh. at FE (1953).

Crombie, Charles E. (1885-1967)
This artist created the best known series of golf cartoons "The Rules of Golf" pub. by Perrier (the sparkling table water firm) as a book at the beginning of the 20th century. Their titles, pub. in both French and English, showing golfers dressed in medieval costume in impossible situations has been repub. at least once in recent years and prints after his work are numerous. Crombie's work on golf was quite prolific and included several calendars . His work was pub. in the "Bystander" (1904) and "Punch" (1902, 1907, 1908). Also in "The Illustrated News" and "Graphic" Christmas numbers (1911) and (1912). Illus. "The Laws of Cricket" (1906) and "Motoritis" (1906).

Crook, P.J. (b.1945)
Interesting and successful figure painter whose work includes some sporting subjects. "The Ladies Croquet Match" painted in 1986, 45in.x55in. (including painted frame), The Portal Gallery, London, and "The Snooker Hall", 45in.x57in., painted in 1990, Wingfield Sporting Gallery, London. Born Pamela Jane Hagland in Cheltenham, Gloucestershire, P.J. studied at Gloucestershire College of Art, specialising in textiles and print making. Moved to London (1965) and first exh. at the Portal Gallery (1977). Exh. regularly at the RWEA and the Portal. Has exh. in the USA and in Paris and with the Wingfield Sporting Gallery in London, 1990. Uses the distinctly unusual technique of incorporating the frame of the painting into the scene, giving the end product a 3D effect and added depth.

Crooke, Miss Muriel Elise (1901-1975)
Painter of landscapes and animals. Studied art in Paris and exh. there. Also exh. at the RA. Her studies of racehorses and hunters were given high praise by the press at the time and she was also a famous breeder and judge of alsatian dogs.

Croome, C.J. (1840-1848)
Animal, sporting and rustic painter who exh. at SS (1842-1845). Several sketches of hunting and racing are recorded in the Witt Library and a picture of the Duke of Grafton's hounds meeting at Shepley, January 1840 was lithographed by Day and Haghe.

Croome, J.D. (op.1839-1852)
Figure and landscape painter who exh. a portrait of "Two Arabian Horses, presented to Her Majesty", at the RA (1846). He painted another fine hunting scene (1848).

Crosby, Frederick Gordon (1885-1943)
Brilliant motor artist and a mechanical draughtsman. Started life as an engineering draughtsman in Coventry in the Daimler drawing office before the 1st World War, making precise mechanical drawings. Joined "The Autocar" at their Coventry offices in about 1905 and worked for many years as their resident artist and motoring correspondent. Sadly, like many amusing people, he was prone to melancholia and after his son was killed flying in 1943, he took his own life. His work deteriorated at the end of the '30s through too many press deadlines and the birth of the contemporary motor car. Some of his best work was repro. in "The Art of Gordon Crosby" by Peter Garnier, pub. Hamlyn (1979). Crosby's painting of the crash at White House Corner, Le Mans (1927) is perhaps his most famous painting. Repro. in "Country Life" 1984.

Crosby, John (op.1884)
Equestrian artist at the end of the 19th century whose portrait of "A Dapple Grey Hunter in a Stable", s.&d. 1884, 17½in.x23½in., was auctioned Sotheby's (Sussex) 1988.

Cross, Henry H. (1837-1918)
American equestrian artist who specialised in trotting race scenes and portraits. His painting "The Old Union Racecourse", s.&d. 1884 and inscr., 42in.x60½in., includes a key of personalities amongst whom are John Morrissey, who initiated racing at the Saratoga track in New York and opened the Canfield casino where he made his fortune. At one time or another he was a heavyweight boxing champion of the world, a Senator in the New York State Legislature, a politician in Washington, a notorious gambler and a bookie. Cross's work is colourful and action packed. Amongst Cross's patrons was the racehorse trainer and breeder, Marcus Daley, who emigrated to the USA in 1841 from Ireland.

Crossman, F.G. (op.1924)
This artist painted a watercolour portrait of "H.R.H. The Duke of Windsor, as Prince of Wales, riding with the Beaufort Hunt" (1924), Sotheby's (Bearne) 1980.

Crowquill, Alfred
Alias the writer, comic artist, caricaturist and illustrator, Alfred Henry Forrester (1804-1872) who contributed to "The Graphic" (1871) and illus. numerous children's books.

Crowther, Henry (op.1913-1933)
Equestrian and sporting artist whose work includes a portrait of "Woodrow Wilson Out Shooting" (1913). Paintings of game dogs, greyhounds and equestrian portraits by Crowther have been recorded at auction, dated between these dates. Crowther exh. at the RA (1876-1898) and at the Royal Pavilion Gallery, Brighton (1875). He is best known as a topographical painter with a great attention to detail.

Crowther, John (op.1875-1898)
An interesting watercolour picture (because it includes an early motor car) was painted by Crowther in 1894 and shows a "Shooting Party at Lunch", 11½in.x 17½in., Sotheby's 1986.

Crowther, T.S.C. (op 1891-1902)
Painter and illustrator whose work includes a hockey scene entitled "The North V The South at Richmond 1892 - A Corner Hit", pen/black ink. Crowther, who worked with a very fine ink line, contributed to "The Graphic", "The Daily Graphic", "The English Illustrated Magazine" and "The Idler".

Crowther Smith, H.F. (op.1920s)
Sporting caricaturist of golf and rugby subjects often used for advertising purposes. "Portrait of a Gentleman Golfer", s.&d. 1928, pen/black ink and watercolour, Christie's (Sth. Ken.) 1991.

Crozier, Robert, of Manchester (1815-1891)
Apprenticed to Wm. Maskery, a coach painter at the age of twelve, Crozier moved to Manchester in 1836 where he met William Bradley (q.v.). In 1838 he studied under John Zephania Bell at the Manchester School of Design and formed the United Society of Manchester Artists with a group of contemporaries. He became a founder member of the Society (1857), where he regularly exh. until 1891, Literary Secretary (1861), Treasurer (1868) and President (1878). He exh. at the RA and SS (1854-1882). Crozier painted a number of sporting and equestrian pictures including "A Gentleman in a Grey Coat and a Top Hat on a Hunter" (1858), 21½in.x16½in., auctioned Christie's 1978.

Cruikshank, George, Snr. (1792-1878)
London-born illustrator, artist and etcher, often of sporting scenes and a leading caricaturist of his day. He sketched a number of boxing studies and illus. Pierce Egan's "Life In London" pub. (1821). He also illus. W. Harrison Rinsworth's "Jack Shepherd" pub. (1839). Cruikshank's sketch entitled "A Day Out with the Surrey Hounds", dated 1840 and inscr., was contributed to the "Comic Almanack". This monthly periodical was pub. by Charles Till (1835-1854) and was the main vehicle for Cruikshank's prodigious output of caricatures during this period.

Cruikshank, Isaac (1756-1811)
Edinburgh-born watercolourist, caricaturist and etcher of caricatures. He produced a few sporting sketches and "Football", an etching aquatinted by George Hunt c.1825. Father of George, and Isaac Robert Cruikshank (qq.v.).

Cruikshank, Isaac Robert (1789-1856)
Sporting caricaturist and miniature painter who gave up a seaman's life to become an artist. Illustrator of many books, sometimes with his brother George (q.v.). Exh. at the RA (1811-1817). His RA exhibit in 1817 was "Archers Target Shooting at Waring's Archery. Bayswater". A pair of mezzotints after the work by Cruikshank entitled "Archery" were exh. in 1974 at the Hayward Gallery, London, at the Exhibition of British Sporting Paintings 1650-1850. The British Museum Collection has boxing scenes by this artist including "Going to a Fight", a panorama dated 1819, and a drawing of the north-east view of "The Cricket Grounds at Darnall, Near Sheffield, Yorkshire", pen and brown ink, 3½in.x5½in., dated 1827. "A Football Match", c.1825, 9½in.x13½in, drawn and etched by this artist, pub. by George Hunt was exh. by Arthur Ackermann & Son, London.

Cucuel, Edward (1875-1951)
American painter and illustrator. Pupil of Constant, Laurens and Gérome in Paris and Leo Putz in Munich. Painted occasional sporting subjects including "The Polo Set - Palm Beach", signed, 30in.x25in., Sotheby's 1989.

Cuitt, George, Jnr. (1779-1854)
Yorkshire landscape and topographical painter, the only son of the artist George Cuit (1743-1818) who added an extra "t" to his surname to distinguish himself from his father. Taught drawing in Richmond, Yorkshire and Chester (1804-1820). Pub. several books on North Country buildings. A charming pencil sketch of a basket of Talyllyne (Welsh lake) trout, painted 25 May 1852, 7in.x10¼in., secures his entry in this Dictionary.

Cullin, Isaac A. (op.1881-1947)
London equestrian painter about whom extraordinarily little is known considering the number of paintings that come to auction. Oddly enough none of his four RA exhibits (1881-1889) was in the least to do with sport. Perhaps he knew that the RA were not keen to exhibit sporting subjects which may be why he used the pseudonym "Pantaloon" (q.v.) for much of his racing and illustration work. He drew sporting subjects for "The Illustrated London News" (1893-1894). His many racing scenes covered the "Epsom Derby" (1883), the "Cambridgeshire" (1918), the "Thursday Nursery Plate" (1916), the "Lincolnshire Handicap" (1931), the "Finish of 1000 Guineas" (1910) and many more. He collaborated with J.A. Wheeler (q.v.) on the portrait of "Zoedene" the 1883 Grand National winner, and in the late 1890s-1900s painted the portraits of several famous racehorses including "Isinglass", "La Roche" and "Flying Fox".

Cumberland, George (1754-1848)
An enthusiastic amateur painter and collector, famous for his description of the managers of the Bristol Institution as a "sad stuffed set". The Bristol Institution opened with its first exhibition on 18 June 1824. The Paul Mellon Collection, Upperville, Va, USA, have a pen, ink and watercolour painting of the racecourse at Bristol, 6¼in.x8⅞in. inscr., "Raceground, Bristol Races 1825 May 15th". The seven gaming tables to the left were licensed, interestingly, by the Lord of the Manor.

Cuming, Frederick (Fred), RA (b.1930)
Distinguished painter who studied at Sidcup School of Art (1945-1949) and at the RCA (1951-1955). Awarded Abbey Travel Scholarship with which he continued his studies in Italy. Exh. regularly at the RA and elected RA (1974). Won the Sir Brinsley Ford Award, NEAC (1986).

Cumming, R.A. (R.H.) Neville (1883-1908)
Marine artist in oil, watercolour and gouache who included a great number of racing yachts and yacht racing scenes amongst his work.

Cunaeus, Conradyn (1828-1895)
Dutch painter of game dogs and birds and some equestrian portraits.

Cundall, Charles Ernest, RA, RWS, RP, RSMA, NS, NEAC (1890-1971)
Urban and landscape painter in oil and watercolour who included a number of excellent sporting scenes amongst his work. Studied at the Manchester School of

Art obtaining a scholarship to the RCA (1912). After the war (1914-1918) in which he served, Cundall studied at the Slade School (1919-1920) and in Paris. Exh. at the RA from 1918, RHA, RSA, RWS, NEAC and many other galleries. Also exhibited at the RSMA inaugural exhibition (1946). First one-man show at Colnaghi (1927). Elected NEAC (1924), RP (1933), RWS (1941) and RA (1944). Travelled extensively in Europe and Russia. His sporting paintings include "A Hastings Cricket Festival" exh. at the RA (1953), 50in.x30in., and now in the collection of Hastings Borough Council (on loan to the Museum and AG), "Epsom Racecourse" (1933), "Arsenal v. Sheffield United at Wembley" (1936), "The Derby" (1938) and "The St. Leger" (1939), "Chelsea v. Arsenal" at the Stamford Bridge Ground, Chelsea, showing the old 'E' stand, which was knocked down in 1972, "Thurston's Leicester Square Billiard Match Hall" (1938) and "The Test Match", s.&d. 1938, 42in.x60in., MCC Coll. Cundall's watercolour portrait of "Corporal Archibald Sharpe", the top-hatted club maker to the Royal Blackheath Golf Club, hangs in the Club House. The painting, commissioned by the Blackheath golfers as a grateful tribute to their much loved employee, continued the fashion for such pictorial tributes.

Cuneo, Cyrus Cinciunato, ROI (1879-1916)

Painter, illustrator and boxing champion. Born in San Francisco of Italian descent. Fly weight boxing champion of San Francisco in 1898, he used his prize money to travel to Paris to study at Colarossi's studio and became a student of Whistler. In 1899 he set up an afternoon drawing class with Edith Oenone Somerville (q.v.) and gave boxing lessons to supplement his income. He settled in London (1903) and became a regular contributor to "The Illustrated London News". Elected ROI (1908) and became a member of the Langham Sketch Club. Father of the artist Terence Tenison Cuneo (q.v.).

Cuneo, Terence Tenison, OBE, RGI, PIPG (b.1907)

London-born portrait and figure painter (known as the "Mouseman" for the small mouse usually hidden in his paintings). Son of the artist Cyrus Cuneo (q.v.) and named Tenison after his mother's maiden name. Studied art at Chelsea and the Slade Schools. Cuneo is probably one of the most important painters of the 20th century and his work fortunately includes a number of sporting subjects. He was originally known as a motor racing artist with such paintings as "Pitwork" in the 1929 twenty-four hour race at Le Mans and "Pitworks on a Sunbeam", on its way to winning the 1912 Coupe de L'Auto. His work covers a wide range of subject matter including paintings of aeroplanes, equestrian (first President of the Society of Equestrian Painters), and football scenes. For example "The FA Challenge Cup Final", between Tottenham Hotspurs (white shirts) and Burnley (blue/claret shirts), s.&d. August

1962, 4ft.x6ft., painted for the FA Centenary in 1963. His official portraits include that of the Duke of Beaufort as "Master of the Horse" (1976). Exh. at the RA, RP, ROI and held one-man shows at RWS Galleries (1941-1958) and the Sladmore Gallery (1971-1973) where he showed "Pony Lines, Cirencester" (1972).

Cunliffe, David (op.1826-1855)

London equestrian and sporting painter with occasional portrait and figure subjects. His hunting paintings include "The Berkeley Hunt" (1842), "Portrait of a Hunter" (1831) and two portraits of "Philip Booth of the Oakley Hounds, Bedfordshire". His patrons included the Marchioness of Londonderry.

Curling, Peter (b.1955)

Talented Irish-born equestrian artist who studied in Florence, with Signorina Simi (1972-1974) and briefly with John Skeaping (q.v.). His work has been exh. by the Tryon Gallery, London and includes many paintings of racehorses.

Currie, R.W. (Capt.) (op.1835-1840)

London animal and sporting painter who exh. these subjects at the BI and SS (1835-1840).

Curtis, Charles M. (op.1834-1839)

Talented angling artist who painted a number of watercolour illustrations including those to "The Growth of the Salmon in Fresh Water" by William Yarrell, FLS, with six colour illustrations engraved by R. Sands, pub. 1839.

Curtis, John Digby (c.1775-1837)

Landscape and topographical painter in both oil and watercolour, who worked almost exclusively, it appears, in the Newark area. His painting of a "Cricket Match at Newark-on-Trent", 22in.x36in. (1823), is in the MCC Collection.

Cutler, Cecil E.L. (op.1886-d.1934)

London (Putney) based portrait painter, mostly in watercolour, who included a number of sporting scenes amongst his work. Cutler painted a very fine study of the distinguished cricketer "W.G. Grace" (1895), 10in.x8in., a watercolour entitled "Going to the Races" (1893) and in 1900 he painted with Frank Paton (q.v.) the presentation picture to "Lord Willoughby de Broke, Master of the Warwickshire Hunt". His fine watercolour "The Royal Diamond Jubilee Procession", June 1897, 13½in.x19¾in. was auctioned Christie's 1984. Cutler first exh. at the RA (1886).

Cuyp, Aelbert (1620-1691)

Dutch landscape artist of predominantly pastoral scenes who included a portrait of a "Young Dutch Golfer" c.1647 amongst his work.

"Cynicus"

Alias the political and social cartoonist Martin Anderson (op.1890-1893).

D

Dadd, Frank, RI, ROI (1851-1929)
Painter in both oil and watercolour and an illustrator of a number of sporting and equestrian subjects. Studied at the RCA and the RA Schools. Worked for "The Illustrated London News" (1878-1884) and later for "The Graphic". Exh. occasionally at the RA (1878-1912) including a painting entitled "Teaching the Young Idea How to Shoot" (1885). Elected RI (1884) and ROI (1888). Also exh. RBA (1872-1877) including a watercolour entitled "Hard Pressed" (1875). Illus. "Boating" for the Badminton Library series by W.B. Woodgate, pub. 1888 and contributed polo sketches to the Badminton Library issue of "Polo". His sporting work included watercolours of skating, hunting, gun dogs and shooting. "A Game of Bowls Played in the Garden", drawn for "The Graphic" in 1907 (note that the play is from corner to corner).

Dadd, Richard (1819-1887)
Fantasy painter of great, but unbalanced talent. Studied at the RA Schools. Included in this Dictionary for his epic work "Atalanta's Race" painted in 1875 whilst he was in Broadmoor prison, having murdered his father. He portrays the story of Atalanta, daughter of the King of Scyros, running a race with her suitors in order to select a husband.

Dadd, Stephen T. (op.1879-1914)
London figure painter and black and white illustrator of many sporting scenes including the Public School Rackets Championship at Queens Club (1888) and The World Title (rackets), the 1911 match at the Princes Club, London, between Charles Williams, who won, and J. Jamsetje of India, the first overseas player to hold the title (1903-1911). He was peculiarly attracted by hare-coursing which he drew and painted particularly well showing a special talent for movement and an obvious knowledge of the sport. Much of his work went to "The Illustrated London News" including his coursing scene featured on the front page on Saturday 12 February 1887. Dadd contributed to a number of other sporting magazines including "The Graphic" and "The Sporting and Dramatic News" and produced a series of coursing incidents entitled "Recollections of Altcar" for Messrs. Fores Sporting Publications.

Dadelbeek, G. (op.1776)
18th century Dutch painter who included equestrian portraits amongst his work. A fine study of a groom holding a bay horse with a terrier, painted 1776, 13in.x16in. was repro. "Country Life" 1965.

Dafter, William (20th century)
A signed oil painting by this artist entitled "Go Cart Racing" 14in.x24in. was auctioned Sotheby's 1982.

Dagley, Richard (1765-1841)
Best known for his depressing series "Death's A'Doings" in 1826 comprising a set of etchings, one depicting a skeleton (death) bowling at a boy batsman behind whom a winged wicket keeper waits. This gloomy work is appropriately entitled "Death among the Cricketers". He is almost certainly the artist (signed by inits. only) of the portrait of Benjamin Disraeli (1804-1881) the statesman and novelist, at the wicket, c.1824, when Disraeli was staying with his publisher John Murray (Coll. MCC).

Daglish-Fitch, Eric, ARE, SWE (1894-1966)
London-born watercolour painter and illustrator of birds and animals, also a wood engraver. Exh. at the leading London galleries (1921-1937). Represented in many public collections both here and abroad. Pub. and illus. several books including "Wood Cuts of British Birds", "Animals in Black and White", "Game Birds" and "Birds of the British Isles". His illustrations to other people's work include the 1927 edn. of Izaak Walton's "The Compleat Angler" and "Fly Fishing" by Edward Grey (1930). Elected ARE (1931) but resigned in the same year. Elected SWE (1922).

Daintrey, Adrian Maurice, RWA (1902-1988)
Landscape and portrait painter who studied art at the Slade School, under Henry Tonks (q.v.) and in Paris where he lived for some years. Art critic to "Punch" (1953-1961). Pub. his autobiography "I Must Say" (1964). Included in this Dictionary for his cricket sketch entitled "Lords", signed and inscr., pen/brown ink and wash, 12in.x16½in., Sotheby's (Sussex).

Dalby, David, of York (1794-1836)
Yorkshire sporting and topographical painter who did not apparently exh. in London. His work, much of which is to be found in private collections, is of a very good quality and has more than a suggestion of influence from John Ferneley, Snr. (q.v.). Supposedly the brother of John Dalby (q.v.). He painted Lord Harewood's Hunt (the Bramham Moor) 1824.

Dalby, John (op.1826-1853)
Yorkshire sporting painter, supposed to be the brother of David Dalby (q.v.) and he certainly painted similar subjects of a high quality. His portrait of "General Chasse" a bay racehorse with his owner, Sir James

Boswell, and jockey, Holmes, on Aintree racecourse, 31in.x41in., was auctioned Sotheby's 1968. Dalby painted "The Royal Rock Beagles in Full Cry" (1845) 24in.x32in. A further painting of beagles, 14½in.x 19¼in. is in the Paul Mellon Collection, Upperville, Va, USA.

Dalby, Joshua, of York (op.1838)
Sporting painter from Yorkshire, assumed to be closely related to the other members of the Dalby family. Painted for the 7th Dragoon Guards and included hunting and shooting portraits amongst his work which are quite clearly signed "Jos (small "a" above Jos) Dalby, York".

"Dalesman"
Alias C.N. de Courcy Parry. Contributor to "Horse and Hound" during the 1920s. Master of the Wexford (1927/8) with a reputation for hard and fearless riding.

Dallison, Ken (b.1933)
London-born painter of motor and racing subjects, who has worked as a commercial artist in both London and New York, contributing to such publications as "Car and Driver" which has featured his work for over twenty years. He has also completed a series of paintings documenting the 1982 Kentucky Derby for "Sports Illustrated". His work has received numerous awards including a Gold Medal from the New York Society of Illustrators, two Gold Medals from the Detroit Club and a Cleo Award for his work with Mercedes Benz.

Dalton, H. (op.1903-1922)
A portrait of the winner of the November Handicap in 1922, signed and inscr. "Torelore", 15½in.x19¼in., was auctioned Bearnes 1987. The artist is possibly Miss Helen Dalton who exh. at the RI (1903).

Danby, Thomas, RHA, RWS (c.1818-1886)
Bristol-born landscape artist who painted some angling subjects in oil and watercolour. Examples include "Fishing on the Wye" and "Trouting in North Wales". Danby exh. at the RA (1843-1882). His studio sale was held at Christie's, 17 June 1886.

Dance, Nathaniel (Sir Nathaniel Dance-Holland, Bt., MP) (1734-1811)
London-born caricaturist and a painter of some sporting subjects in both oil and watercolour. Elder brother of George Dance, Jnr. RA. Pupil of Francis Hayman (q.v.) c.1749. Exh. at the RA, FS, SA (1761-1800). Became MP for East Grinstead (1790) and was created a baronet (1800). His painting "A Gentleman and His Three Dogs Shooting in a Landscape" (1776) was exh. Arthur Ackermann & Son, London. Nathaniel Dance's portrait of Herbert Newton Jarrett leaning on his cricket bat and holding a cricket ball was sold to the Fine Art Society. The large canvas, 5ft.6in.x3ft.9¼in., was painted before the cricket bat went straight, probably some time between 1750 and 1770.

Dandridge, Bartholomew (1691-c.1755)
Portrait and conversation piece painter who worked from Godfrey Kneller's old studio in London (1731). Recorded in this Dictionary for his portrait of a young

boy standing holding a racket on a terrace by a balustrade, 60in.x40in.

Daniel, T. Llewelyn, ARIBA (b.1891)
Landscape artist of some equestrian scenes in watercolour. Exh. "The Meet at Exmoor" at the RI in 1963.

Daniel, W.B. (op.1805)
A painting of two sportsmen, a horse and various dogs in a landscape is recorded by Mitchell.

Daniell, Thomas, RA (1747-1840)
Distinguished landscape and topographical artist, also of some sporting subjects. His watercolour painting "Beagling in Brimham Crags near Ripon", 15¾in.x 21½in. was auctioned Christie's 1988. In 1778 Daniell exh. a view of part of Brimham Crags near Ripon, Yorks, belonging to the Rt. Hon. Sir Fletcher Norton at the RA (No. 79) which may well be the same painting. Daniell spent two years in Calcutta with his sixteen year old nephew, William (q.v.) (1785-1787) and returned again to Calcutta (1793-1794). His painting "A Calcutta Cricket Match" probably dates from 1792, which would coincide with the formation of the Calcutta Cricket Club and would explain the reason for its existence. Daniell's watercolour wash entitled "Preparing for a Hunt at Selhurst Park" (1796), 7⅞in.x 9¾in. is in the Paul Mellon Collection, Upperville, Va, USA. It is thought to depict Norwood, Surrey.

Daniell, William, RA (1769-1837)
Landscape and brilliant topographical artist. Nephew of Thomas Daniell (q.v.) who went as his uncle's assistant to India in 1785. Daniell exh. at the RA and BI (1795-1838) including his painting entitled "Tiger Hunting in India" (1835). The V & A Museum has a "Hippopotamus Hunt" by Daniell.

Daniels, Alfred, RSW, RBA (b.1926)
Contemporary artist whose painting entitled "Cricket at Kew" was exh. at the RA (Summer Exhibition 1952) and "Spring Regatta at Bradford on Avon" was exh. at the RA (Summer Exhibition 1988 No. 50). Daniels studied at Woolwich Art School and the RCA. Became tutor in drawing at the RCA and Hornsey College of Art. Has had solo exhibitions at John Whibley Gallery, London 1968-1971. Elected RSW (1972) and RBA (1982).

Danloux, Henri Pierre (1753-1809)
Fashionable French portraitist who came to England in 1792, the year he painted "The Masters Foster Holding (fancy) Cricket Bats" (private collection). Exh. at the RA 1793 (No.213).

Danson, R. (op.1862)
Walworth artist (from near the Oval, Kennington) who exh. a painting of "A White Horse" at the BI in 1862.

D'Arcy, Roger (op.1970)
Artist of several racehorse portraits including those of "Arkle", "Nijinsky" and "Brigadier Gerard".

Darley, Matthew (op.1750-1780)
Draughtsman, etcher, engraver and publisher of caricatures who kept an art shop in the Strand. He also

pub. much of the early work of Henry Bunbury (q.v.) "The Head of a Jockey" (1761), 3in.x3in., drawn in pen/ink for Darley's "Book of Caricatures" (1763).

Darlridge, A.A. (op.1884)
Equestrian artist of a hunter portrait dated 1884. Bearnes 1988.

Dartiguenave, Victor (op.1841-1854)
Miniature and watercolour artist who exh. a portrait of an equestrian lady at SS (1864) from a London address.

Darwin, Sir Robin (1910-1974)
Figure and landscape painter who studied at Cambridge University and at the Slade School (1929). His painting entitled "Ice Hockey at the Empress Hall", s.&d. 1949 is in the collection of Hove Museum of Art. Darwin became Principal of the RCA (1948-1971) largely through a report he wrote whilst working for the Council of Industrial Design (1945-1946) proposing curriculum changes at the RCA. This period of change at the RCA under his guiding hand has become known as the Darwin era. He was knighted in 1964.

Daugherty, James (1890-1974)
American painter who was influenced by the Italian Futurist painters and used brilliant colour to clever effect in his paintings of cityscapes. His baseball scene "Three Base Hit" (1914) was repro. in the "New York Herald", 12 April 1914 as a "Futurist picture of the opening game" with the following analysis by the artist: "This is not a picture of a baseball game. It is a representation of the various sensations of the onlooker ...". Painted in gouache and ink on paper, 12¼in.x 17⅛in., Whitney Museum of American Art.

Dav(e)y, A.M. (op.1884)
Animal and sporting artist working at the end of the 19th century. "A Ghillie and his Otterhounds", watercolour, s.&d. 1884, was auctioned Sotheby's 1980.

Davey, Randall (1887-1964)
American sporting artist of uneven talent, although some of his work was very fine. He has a faithful following in America. He painted a number of English steeplechase scenes including "Steeplechasers Leaving the Paddock", 18in.x22in., Sotheby's (NY) 1978.

David, Jacques Louis (1748-1825)
Leading French portrait and historical painter and an ardent revolutionary. A senior member of Robespierre's secret police, David was exiled to Brussels in 1805 by Napoleon for his leading part in the murder of Louis XVI. David is included in this Dictionary for his unfinished version of "The Interior of the Jeu de Paume at Versailles" painted in 1791, a subject also painted by Couder (q.v.) and Leopold Boilly (q.v.), Musée National du Chateau de Versailles. One of David's pupils was the equestrian painter Jacques Laurent Agasse (q.v.).

David, S. (op.1822-1841)
Angling artist. Illustrator of the 1822 edn. of "The Compleat Angler" by Izaak Walton. His painting entitled "Dibbing for Chub" s.&d. 1841 was auctioned Christie's, A.N. Gilbey Collection 25.4.1940.

Davidson, A. Murray (op.1893-1905)
Liverpool artist who exh. three works at the Walker AG (1904-1905). Painted the portraits of "Master Bob Podmore MH" in hunting clothes, s.&d. 1893, 34in.x 18¾in. and a portrait of "Edward Boyce Podmore, Master of the Vine", 92in.x51½in., auctioned Sotheby's (Sussex) 1984.

Davidson Cara (op.1892-1894)
Portrait of a golfer, watercolour, signed with inits. and dated '94, 11½in.x9in., and one smaller golf watercolour inscr. "North Berwick" and dated 1892. Phillips (West Two) 1989.

Davidson, R. (20th century)
"The Cambridge University Eight", a pair, 6½in.x 10¾in., both signed by this artist, were auctioned Sotheby's (Sussex) 1988.

Davidson, Thomas, Jnr. (op.1863-1893)
London artist who exh. (1863-1893) at the RA including "Hawking" (1871), BI, SS, including "Angling" (1885) and "A Carriage Drive" (1889). His charming painting of a game of croquet entitled "The Winning Stroke" was auctioned Sotheby's 1984.

Davies, C.W. (op.1818-1824)
A portrait of "Zinc", the racehorse, s.&d. 1824 is at Euston Hall. Probably the same artist as W. Davies (q.v.).

Davies, Marion (b.1944)
Leading specialist painter of sports subjects, particularly tennis and cricket. Studied at Newport College of Art (1959-1964) where she gained a diploma in design and graphic illustration (NDD). Studied University of Wales (1965-1966) where she gained her art teaching diploma (ARD). Designer and Head of Design at the Cockpit Arts Theatre, London (1978-1990). Solo exh. in New York, London and the Hague, 1972, 1975, 1979, 1984 and 1987. Wingfield Sporting Gallery, London.

Davies, Roland (op.1933)
Contemporary motor racing artist whose watercolour and gouache painting "At Brooklands" was painted in 1933, 14in.x21in. Sotheby's (Sussex) 1989.

Davies, W. (op.1818-1824)
This artist exh. eight paintings at the RA (1818-1824) from a London and a Shrewsbury address. "Severn Fish", 1820.

D'Avigdor, Elim H.
See "Wanderer"

Davinci, L. (op.1839)
London artist who exh. an angling painting at the BI (1839) entitled "Minnow Fishing".

Davis, Arthur Alfred (op.1863-1911)
London based artist who painted sporting scenes in both oil and watercolour but who seems, like C.T. Bale (q.v.), to have known of the Academy's dislike of such subjects for his exh. work included none. Exh. at SS (1877-1894). Davis was very fond of depicting hounds which he painted extremely well. He very often featured

them streaming over a fence and water and usually painted them without much evidence of huntsmen or the rest of the field. Davis included several grisly but fine paintings of otter hunting which are historically interesting but pictorially depressing.

Davis, Charles F. (c.1788-1866)
This artist is better known as the Master of the Royal Buckhounds to George IV, a position to which he was elected in 1822 and held under three successive sovereigns. He was the brother of the sporting artists R.B. Davis (q.v.) and W.H. Davis (q.v.). He painted several portraits of horses in stables and extended his talents to include a fine model of "A Fox Hunt", c.1850, carved in twigs, brushwood and papier mâché which was exh. at the British Sporting Heritage Exhibition at Sotheby's, 1984/5, 34½in.x23in. and 29in. high. He himself was painted on his grey hunter "The Hermit" by the Barraud brothers (q.v.) (1847) and "The Hermit" was painted by Alexander Forbes (q.v.) in 1839.

Davis, G.H., RSMA (op.1947-1959)
Marine illustrator who contributed naval subjects to "The Graphic" (1910) and angling illustrations to "The Illustrated London News" (1952). A Brighton based artist, he exh. at the RSMA (1947-1959).

Davis, Harry (op.1902-1916)
Painted for the Royal Worcester Porcelain Company. His sporting scenes include "Fly Fishing".

Davis, Heather St. Clair (b.1937)
Cotswold-born landscape and equestrian artist who studied at the Cheltenham and Birmingham Colleges of Art and graduated in life drawing, sculpture and three-dimensional design. Davis married and settled in America. She makes regular visits to England to paint in the Cotswolds and has had two one-man exh. at Frost and Reed, London, featuring English hunting scenes and dramatic racing pictures.

Davis, Henry T. (op.1850-1881)
An equestrian artist who painted the portraits of a great number of racehorses between 1850 and 1881 including "Blair Athol" (1864) and "Robert the Devil" (1881). He also painted the 1850 St. Leger, the race between "Voltigeur" and "Russborough" which was engraved by C.N. Smith (op.1848-1855) and pub. by Ackermanns, December 1850.

Davis, Henry William Banks, RA (1833-1914)
London animal, sporting and landscape painter whose output was prolific. Studied art at the RA Schools and exhi. at the RA from 1853. Also exh. BI, SS, NG and elsewhere. Elected RA (1877) and painted in both oil and watercolour. Included fox-hunting, coursing and fishing scenes amongst his work.

Davis, Joseph Lucien, RI (1860-1941)
Liverpool-born artist and illustrator, very often of sporting subjects, who worked for "The Illustrated London News" (from 1885) for over twenty years as their chief artist. He was the son of the Irish landscape painter William Davis (1812-1873) and entered the RA schools in 1877 where he won several prizes. He began his career with "Cassells Publications" in 1878 but had his first important drawings pub. in "The Graphic" (1880-1881). He was particularly skilled in figure drawing and illustrated many of the Badminton Library Series, in particular their books on cricket, lawn tennis and billiards. Davis was elected RI (1893).

Davis, Louis
Unrecorded artist of "The Shuttlecock Player", s.&d. '79, 18in.x14in. Exh. Christopher Wood Gallery, London.

Davis, Richard Barrett, RBA (1782-1854)
Sporting artist, brother of William Henry Davis (q.v.) and Charles Davis (q.v.). Richard Barrett Davis received his art training under Royal Patronage from Sir Francis Bourgeois RA (q.v.) and Sir William Beechey RA (q.v.) and also at the RA Schools. He was appointed animal painter to various members of the Royal Family and as a result received commissions from half the nobility in England. He also painted several portraits of his brother's hunter "The Hermit" - a splendid grey horse by "Grey Skin" out of an Arab mare who had carried a trumpeter in a dragoon regiment in India, and several scenes of the Royal Buckhounds. The Royal Buckhounds hunted over land in Berkshire and Buckinghamshire and had kennels at Ascot. They were finally disbanded in 1901 after the death of Queen Victoria. One of his paintings of his brother Charles on "The Hermit" appeared as the title page to the "Hunters Annual" (1836-1841). The first volume of this famous book of lithographs in four volumes was dedicated to William IV and the other three to Queen Victoria. It included coursing portraits of greyhounds, the property of Sir Harvey Bathurst, Bt. (1835). Davis' contribution to the game of cricket is covered by his painting "Landscape with Children Playing Cricket", 18in.x21in., s.&d. 1827 (whereabouts unknown).

Davis, S.C.H. "Sammy" (op.1920s)
Motor racing artist and driver, sports editor of "The Autocar". He was the Bentley driver involved in the famous White House crash at Le Mans in 1927 (a race which he ultimately won), the incident most frequently depicted by motor sporting artists including Gordon Crosby (q.v.).

Davis, T. (op.1852)
This artist exh. one painting at the RA (1852) entitled "Hounds running into a Fox in a Stone Wall Country". He is possibly Thomas or Tyddesley Davis (see above). The painting was obviously not painted in his native Sussex which is not stone wall country.

Davis, Thomas R. (op.1826)
A mezzotint engraved by Charles Turner after a painting by this artist of Philip Payne, Huntsman to the Duke of Beaufort, on his horse "Cherrington" with the Badminton hounds, was dedicated to the Duke by the artist and pub. by Ackermann, 8 December 1826. The original painting, 27in.x40½in., was auctioned Christie's 1990.

Davis, Tyddesley R.T. (op.1831-1857)
Sporting painter who may have been a student at the RA Schools in 1826 and who lived in Brighton, Sussex

and St. Elbs, Oxford. Exh. seven paintings at the BI (1831-1857). Titles include "Horses at Play" and "The Find - Unkennelling" (1831), "The Blind Hunter in a Plough Team" and "Dejeuner on Dartmoor" (1851) and "Close of the Day on Dartmoor" (1852). His painting of Samuel Beale, Huntsman to the Carew family, mounted on a grey hunter, surrounded by hounds in a landscape, includes the first Jack Russell to be used in hunting in the foreground. It is reasonable to assume that the Carew family, being an old Devon family and keen sportsmen, and the Revd. John Russell (q.v.), were well acquainted with each other.

Davis, William Henry (c.1786-1865)
Sporting and animal painter, brother of R.B. Davis (q.v.) and Charles Davis (q.v.). Studied landscape painting in Rome but turned to animal painting in which he made his name. In 1837 he was appointed animal painter to William IV who died later that year. Typical of W.H.D's luck, for he always lay in the shadow of his brother R.B. Davis who had himself held the royal post nine years earlier. Exh. at the RA and BI including many commissioned portraits of horses. His fine painting entitled "A Coursing Meeting", painted in 1819, 16in.x20.¾in. was exh. Richard Green, London.

Davis, William Steeple (b.1884)
American marine painter whose watercolour and gouache painting entitled "Racing on the Mississippi", 9in.x11in., was sold Christie's (NY) 1988.

Davison, Jeremiah (1695-1745) (Attrib. to)
This artist is said to have painted a portrait of Alexander, 1st Lord Macdonald (1745-1795) holding an adult golf club, 69½in.x58in. The Scottish National Portrait Gallery, Edinburgh. From the dates it must be quite obvious that whoever painted the portrait of Lord Macdonald, it was not Jeremiah Davison. Nevertheless the portrait is well painted and is an historically interesting representation of early golf in Scotland. The artist is, in my opinion, more likely to have been William Mosman (c.1700-1771) who is known to have painted the Macdonald boys.

Daws, Frederick Thomas (b.1878- op.1949)
London-born animal painter. Studied at Lambeth School of Art. Exh. at the RA from 1896, also at the RI, RBA and in the provinces. Principal works include "The Royal Tiger Shoot in Nepal". Specialised in painting prize dogs, especially terriers, during the 1930s and '40s.

Dawson, Frederick (op.1901)
Australian marine painter whose watercolour "The Yacht Race - Port Adelaide" 19in.x26in. was painted in 1901.

Dawson, Henry (1811-1878)
Hull-born marine and landscape artist who painted several angling scenes in the latter half of his life. Studied for a short time with J.B. Pyne (he had twelve days' tuition to be exact). An ardent admirer of Turner whose work greatly influenced his style. Dawson's paintings are famous for their colour. His early work is rich and Turneresque while soft greys and silvery rivers dominate the paintings of the middle period of his life. He tended to paint massive canvases frequently 4-9ft in length. Grandfather of the famous marine painter, Montague Dawson (q.v.). His painting entitled "Duck Shooting" (1863) was auctioned Sotheby's 1985 and his portrait of "A Fisherman with a Creel on his back, Fishing a River", 19in.x22¾in., was sold by Sotheby's, 1975.

Dawson, J. Allan (op.1893-1936)
Edinburgh angling artist who exh. one painting only at the RA in 1897 entitled "Steady Noo!" but whether his entreaties are directed at a horse or a fish, or even a dog, I do not know. He also exh. at the RSA and Royal Glasgow Institute where his painting "Salmon and Trout" was exhibited (No.366).

Dawson, J. Montague, RS, MA (1895-1973)
Distinguished marine painter, Dawson was the son of a sea captain and was born at sea. Dawson's father was in turn son of the marine artist Henry Dawson (q.v.). Montague Dawson was apprenticed to a commercial studio in Bedford Row at the age of fifteen. He became a pupil of Charles Napier Hemy (q.v.) whose influence may be seen in Dawson's work. Exh. at the RA (1917-1936). His many scenes of yachts racing include "'Evain' and 'Sceptre', 12 Metre Yachts Racing in the Solent".

Dawson, Lucy (Mrs.) (d.1958)
Painter and etcher of dog portraits who exh. in London, the provinces and abroad. Published "Dogs as I See Them" (1936), "Dogs Rough and Smooth" (1937) and "Lucy Dawson's Dog Book" (1938).

Dawson, Miss Mabel, RSW, SSA (1887-1965)
Edinburgh-born animal and bird artist, who painted in watercolour and tempera. Studied Edinburgh College of Art, under William Walls (q.v.), also under Frank Calderon (q.v.) at his school of animal painting in Kensington. Exh. at the RA, RSA, RSW, SSA, GI and abroad. Elected SSA (1907), RSW (1917).

Day, G.F. (op.1849-1873)
Leicester painter of game and rustic subjects and some sporting. His portrait of Mr. John Purser of the Cardington Club with his greyhounds "Pansey" and "Pilot" painted in 1849, was engraved for the "Sporting Magazine" (Vol. I, p.116) (1850). Day exh. at the RA and SS (1850-1868), mostly children, ponies and dogs.

Day, T. (op.1783)
A painting entitled "Morning with Hunters Going Out" was exh. at the SA (1783). This was sent from Brakes Place near Romford, Essex.

Dayes, Edward (1763-1804)
Landscape and topographical painter in watercolour, very often of angling scenes. Studied under William Pether, the mezzotinter, and produced prints, miniatures and book illustrations as well as his better known watercolours. He had many pupils and apprentices including Thomas Girtin whom he is supposed to have put in prison. Nevertheless, he had great influence on Girtin's work and indeed on that of the young Turner

(q.v.). He exh. at the RA and SA (1786-1804). He committed suicide in 1804. Pub. "Instructions for Drawing and Colouring Landscapes" (1805), "Professional Sketches of Modern Artists" (1805) and "The Works of the Late ED" (1805). Collections British Museum, V & A Museum, Haworth AG, Accrington, Greenwich, Leeds City AG, etc.

Dayrell, B. (op.1853-1858)
A primitive painter, described in some reference books as "of no great merit". However his work from recent auction results merits high prices. His sporting subjects include cock-fighting and fox-hunting.

Deacon, Augustus Oakley (1819-1899)
London based artist who exh. a watercolour painting entitled "Grouse Shooting on the Derbyshire Moors" at SS (1847).

Deane, Frederick A. (op.1902-1954)
Portrait painter who contributed "A portrait of Frank Swift", oil, 27in.x35in., at the exh. held by the Football Association in conjunction with the Arts Council in 1953.

Deanes, Edward (op.1860-1895)
London painter of figure subjects and portraits, sometimes in watercolour, who included a number of angling scenes amongst his work. Exh. at the RA, BI, SS and elsewhere (1860-1893).

Dearman, John (op.1824-1856)
London painter of cattle, horses and some angling scenes who exh. at the BI (1825-1856). At his obvious best with river scenes and cows.

Dearn, T.D.W. (late 18th-early 19th century)
A coloured aquatint 8⅞in.x12½in. of "Surrey Chapel, Blackfriars Road", dedicated to the Rev. Rowland Still. This building afterwards became known as "The Ring, Blackfriars" and the home of boxing in London. The aquatint after the work by this artist and pub. by Charles Rosenberg 1812 was exh. Parker Gallery, London, 1950 (No.3).

Deas, Charles (1818-1867)
American artist, included in this Dictionary for his painting "The Indian Ball Game" (1843) (Thomas Gilcrease Institute of American History of Art). This ball game is the oldest organised sport played in North America. The French and English watched the Indians play and in 1840 the French settlers revived the rules and adopted the game. They named the game "Lacrosse" because of the long handled hook stick which resembles the bishop's staff or crosier. In 1839 Deas visited the George Catlin (q.v.) Indian Gallery Exhibition and recognised the importance of Catlin's paintings. In 1840 Deas left Philadelphia to work and travel in the west. He joined his brother, an officer in the Fifth Infantry stationed at Fort Crawford and had the opportunity of going on missions with the army to the surrounding forts and Indian territory. In 1841 he established permanent residence in a studio in St. Louis but continued to spend several months a year with the Indians. His melodramatic paintings won high praise at the time for their sense of the terror and violence on the frontier but today most of his paintings have been lost and he is virtually forgotten. Always plagued by severe depression, in 1847 he suffered a major mental breakdown and after many years of confinement died in an asylum.

de Block, Eugène François (1812-1893)
Belgian artist who included a painting entitled "Sportsmen Going Out" at the RA in 1845. Exh. at the RA, GG, and NG (1845-1867).

de Breanski, Alfred, ARCA (1852-1928)
Landscape and river painter. Member of a large family of artists. His brother was Gustave de Breanski and his two sons were Alfred Fontville and A. de Breanski, Jnr. Alfred de Breanski exh. at the RA and SS (1872-1890). His painting "Henley Regatta" was exh. at the RA 1885 (No. 227) and his fine painting "Salmon Fishing on the Flooded Lledr Bettws-y-Coed", painted in 1875, was auctioned Sotheby's 1988.

de Bree, Anthony (op.1876-1917)
London sporting and domestic painter. Another artist who was careful in selecting his exhibition work, knowing the Academy's dislike of sporting subjects. The eight works he exh. at SS (1876-1893) are of Dutch interiors. His sporting work includes "Portraits of Five Hunters belonging to Sir Edward Ridley Colborne of Bradford" (1907), "Sir Ralph Payne Gallway in his gunroom at Thirkleby Hall, Yorkshire" (1914), and "At the End of a Day's Shooting" (1881).

de Courcy Parry, C.N.
See "Dalesman"

de Crespigny C.C. (see Boyle, Cerise)
"A Chestnut Racehorse in a Stable", 12½in.x17in. Painted in 1899, under her married name. Sotheby's (Sussex) 1985.

de Dreux, Alfred (1810-1860)
French equestrian painter of great skill who came to England with the French Royal Family after the Revolution in 1848. De Dreux was influenced by Géricault (q.v.) a friend of his uncle and he was already producing fine drawings by the age of thirteen. In 1831 he exh. "L'Intérieur d'Ecurie" at the Paris Salon which made his name. From 1840 he began a series of horse paintings for the Duke d'Orléans for which he was highly paid. The circumstances of his death are mysterious but he is thought to have died as the result of a duel with the Comte Fleury after a dispute over a commission to paint the portrait of Napoleon III in 1859. De Dreux was very popular in England and included many fox-hunting scenes amongst his work, painted in both oil and watercolour. Often included humorous touches in his paintings, like the small dog in his "Retour de la Course", Virginia Museum of Fine Arts, Richmond, USA.

Degas, Edgar (1834-1917)
Brilliant French Impressionist painter who included a number of horse racing scenes amongst his work, between 1864 and 1872. Degas' companion at the

racetrack was Edward Manet (q.v.) whom Degas depicted in a little sketch "Manet at the Races" which is in the Metropolitan Museum of Art. Unlike Manet, Degas was more concerned with painting the movements before the start of a race and the pencil sketches he made around 1860 served him well when, decades later, he was to work them into his paintings. His "Jockeys in the Rain" is in the Glasgow City AG and Museum and "Before the Start - A Gentlemen's Race" is in the Musée d'Etat. Degas was an admirer of the American action photographer Eadweard Muybridge whose pictures of a horse in motion were first published in an article in 1878 and then in full in Muybridge's book "Animal Locomotion" in 1887. "The Billiard Room at Menil-Hubert" c.1892, 25½in.x31¾in. Staatsgalerie, Stuttgart. Degas painted two versions of the billiard room at Menil-Hubert, the chateau home in Normandy of his childhood friends the Valpinçons.

De Geest, Wybrand Simons (the elder) (1592-1659)
Dutch artist whose "Portrait of a Young Golfer", s.&d. 1613, shows a young boy holding a golf club, 46in.x 26½in. Private collection.

De Glehn, Wilfred Gabriel, RA, NEAC (1870-1951)
Portrait and landscape painter and a stained glass designer. Studied at the RCA and the Ecole des Beaux Arts, Paris. First one-man exhibition at the Carfax Gallery (1908). Included in this Dictionary for his fine painting entitled "Fishing" c.1931/1932, painted as his Diploma work to the RA. Elected NEAC (1900) and RA (1932).

De Grineau, Bryan (John A. Bryan) (1882-1957)
One of the best motor racing artists during the 1920s and '30s. Also an etcher. Born at Stroud Green, London, son of Alfred Bryan (q.v.) (Charles Grineau), the caricaturist. Joined the staff of "The Motor" as John A. Bryan in 1905 (see also Bryan). His work, although brilliant and technically sound, suffered slightly from the tight deadlines to which he had to work. "The Motor" went to press on a Sunday night in order to be on the bookstalls by Tuesday morning. "The Autocar", for example, for which Gordon Crosby (q.v.) worked, was not published until Friday. Bryan joined the Royal Field Artillery in France as Second Lieutenant in 1916 and sent home sketches for "The Illustrated London News" and "Illustrated War News". Studied art in New York, under Joseph Pennell, and became well known in America where several exhibitions of his work were held. See also Grineau for other examples of his sporting work.

de Gryeff, Adriaan (1670-1715)
Flemish painter of hunting and game subjects.

D'Egville, James T. Hervé, NWS (c.1806-1880)
A good watercolour artist, cartoonist and writer who painted landscapes and sporting scenes and is referred to in the Sporting Art section "Fores Sporting Notes and Sketches" (1905). He studied at the RA schools (1823) under A. Pugin. Exh. at the RA, BI and NWS. Elected NWS (1848).

De Hooch, Pieter (1629-1681)
Dutch painter of domestic and garden scenes often featuring courtyards. His painting "The Game of Nine-Pins" is in Waddeston College (near Aylesbury, Bucks.).

Deighan, Peter (b.1941)
Irish portrait painter of well-known sporting personalities including Lester Piggott, John McCririck, Robert Sangster, Steve Davis, Barry McGuigan, etc. "The 100th Hurling Final 1987 - Galway 1-12 Kilkenny 0-9", s.&d. 1987, 30in.x24in., painted for the Gaelic Athletic Association (Ireland). Deighan, who won the highly competitive Moyglare International Painting Competition, was bought up on a farm in Ireland. He studied at Luton College of Art for four years (1966-1970).

De Kooning, Elaine (1920-1989)
Brooklyn-born American artist, included in this Dictionary for "Campy At The Plate", a painting of an American baseball game which she originally sketched in 1953 and finally painted in acrylic in 1980, 30in.x39½in. The painting shows Roy Campanella, Brooklyn's premier catcher and slugger, hitting a home run while Carl Furillo (No. 6), the great right fielder, waits expectantly in the batter's box. De Kooning's work is characterised by bold brush strokes and a great mastery of light best illustrated, perhaps, in "Scrimmage" exhibited at NAMOS, Indianapolis (1991).

De la Bere, Stephen Baghot, RI (1877-1927)
Figure and landscape painter who studied at the Westminster School of Art. Exh. at the RA, RI and elsewhere (1904-1915). His watercolour of a polo scene entitled "On the Boards", 15in.x21in., is a fine example of his work. He was a close friend of both Edmund Dulac (q.v.) and John Hassall (q.v.) who influenced his work. They were all London Sketch Club members. Elected RI (1908).

Delamarre, Henri (1829-1913)
Talented French amateur artist of equestrian scenes, particularly racing, who was also a racehorse owner. His painting of "Potocki", winner of the Prix du Jockey Club in 1857 (the year that the racecourse at Longchamp was opened in the Bois de Boulogne), is in the Société d'Encouragement, Paris.

De la Montagne Cary, William (1840-1922)
American artist, included in this Dictionary for his painting entitled "The Canoe Race", 12in.x30in. (Thomas Gilcrease Institute of American History and Art). The artist made two voyages up the Missouri River in 1860 and 1874 and made on the spot sketches which he used later for his oil paintings. The Indian tribes of both the north-eastern plains and the north-east woodlands enjoyed competitive boat races with members of the neighbouring tribes, travelling great distances to watch, cheering and firing their guns on the shore to encourage their favourites.

Delaney, Joseph (b.1904)
American painter and writer whose charcoal drawing entitled "The Brooklyn Bums Clubhouse", 1955, 24in.x30in., cleverly portrays the influence of this

famous team on the American game of baseball in the '50s. Ewing Gallery of Art and Architecture, University of Tennessee, Knoxville.

De Lattre, Henri (De Latre, Henry) (1801-1876)
French equestrian painter who exh. at the Paris Salon (1824-1875). Exh. a painting "A Mare and Foal" at BI in 1838 under the name of De Latre, his only known exhibition work in this country. De Lattre quite often signed his name with only his surname. Examples of his work include "The Percheron Stallion 'Dilligence' in a Stall" dated 1853, and "Mr. Dickinson Logan's Daughter with her Riding Master", s.&d. 1850, 20¾in.x29¼in. Christie's (NY) 1983.

Delion, Madlle (op.1836)
This lady exh. a portrait of a little Arabian horse at SS in 1836 from Miss Thompson's establishment at Blackheath.

De Loutherbourg, Philip James, RA (1740-1812)
Strasbourg-born landscape, equestrian and sporting painter. Exh. at the RA, FS, and BI (1772-1814). Elected RA (1781). Greenwich Art Gallery has his painting "The Evening Coach" climbing Greenwich Hill, with a view of London in the distance.

De Maistre, Roy L. (1894-1968)
Australian-born painter who won the Artists Travelling Scholarship (1923) and went to study art in Paris. Worked in London from 1938. Exh. at the Paris Salon and at the RA where he exh. "The Rugby Match" in 1964 (No. 358) and "Footballers" (No.204) Exh. at the XIVth Olympiad Sport in Art Exhibition held at the V & A Museum, London 1948.

Demand, Carlo (b.1922)
American painter, writer and illustrator of motor racing subjects who was born of French parents in Frankfurt, Germany. He obtained his American citizenship in 1951. Demand, who studied at the Frankfurt Art Academy for five years, subsequently pub. his first illustration - a drawing of a Mercedes Benz W-154 Grand Prix car. He is probably best known for his charcoal drawings which are remarkable for their expressive vitality and sense of movement, although he used most mediums. In 1956 Demand pub. his first book "The Big Race" with 128 charcoal illustrations of historic motor racing scenes and has since pub. seven others including "The Supercharged Mercedes" (Edita).

De Mejo, Oscar (b.1911)
American folk artist whose imaginative painting entitled "Tagged", 1980, vividly portrays the gutsy side of the game of baseball while the umpire stands declaring "out", 16in.x20in. Aberbach Fine Art.

Deming, Edwin Willard (1860-1943)
American equestrian painter and a sculptor who studied art in Paris, a pupil of Boulanger and Lefebvre. His work includes paintings of racing, fishing and coaching scenes.

Demoline, A. (op.1853-1875)
A French equestrian artist who painted fox-hunting and racing scenes including "Le Départ Pour La Chasse", s.&d. '74, 13⅜in.x21½in., auctioned Sotheby's (NY) 1985.

De Momper, Frans (1603-1660)
Flemish painter from a large family of painters who exercised a significant influence on landscape painting during their time. "Soldiers Playing Skittles - a view of Breda beyond", signed, oil on panel, 16in.x21¾in. Sotheby's.

de Montpezat, H. (op.1853)
London painter who exh. "The Morning Ride" at the BI (1853) and a portrait of a "Young Lady on a Pony".

Denew, Richard (op.1827-1858)
London painter of Italian subjects and equestrian scenes. His portraits of "Stockwell" and of "Lottery" with Jem Mason up (winner of the Grand National 1839) are in private collections. Exh. at the RA, BI and SS (1827-1858) including "A Game of La Mora" as played by the Italians (SS 1845).

Denning, Stephen Poyntz (1795-1864)
London portrait and miniature painter who became a pupil of Joseph Wright (q.v.). Exh. at the RA, SS and BI (1814-1852). Appointed Curator of the Dulwich Gallery (1821). His portrait of "A Sportsman seated with a Shotgun and a Spaniel by his side near a Window", painted in 1832, 24in.x19½in., was auctioned Christie's 1974.

Dennis, William (op.1834-1849)
London still life painter, especially of fish and game subjects.

Dent, Adrian (b.1965)
Born in Griffithstown, the younger brother of the equestrian artist David Dent (q.v.) Specialises in painting horse racing and, in particular, steeplechasing scenes. His ability to paint an accurate equestrian scene makes Adrian's style distinctive and his clever use of the typically harsh, atmospheric conditions associated with the sport of steeplechasing creates a memorable picture.

Dent, David (b.1959)
Born in Solihull. Educated at Bristol Polytechnic where he studied art history and education, graduating with honours. In addition to teaching art in South Wales he travels around the country's racecourses sketching and painting. He is particularly interested in atmospherics and capturing the motion of the horses and has a wide and specialist knowledge of steeplechasing. He is the elder brother of Adrian Dent (q.v.) with whom he shares a studio.

Dent, Rupert Arthur (op.1882-1904)
Animal and sporting painter. Exh. at the RA (1884-1898) including his painting "The Sporting Character" (1889). His work includes portraits of champion greyhounds and foxhounds.

Denton, Charles (op.1853)
A set of four prints entitled "The Abergavenny Steeplechase" (1853), presumably after the work by Denton, were also lithographed and pub. by him.

Denyer, David Anthony (b.1937)
Equestrian artist of horse racing, greyhound racing and hunting scenes. The son of the flower painter Ginnette

Denyer. Studied at Brighton College of Art in 1954/5. Graduated into stage management and then joined R.T.S. with whom he remained for thirty years, retiring as senior announcer to pursue his career as an equestrian painter.

De Penne, Olivier Charles (1831-1897)
French sporting painter who exh. two works at Agnew's in 1880. Specialised in dog paintings and hunting scenes.

De Prades, Alfred P. (op.1844-1889)
French-born equestrian artist who exh. at the BI (1858-1867) and at Crystal Palace (1889) where he was described as "a French artist". He would appear to have been the brother of both Antonio and Frank de Prades (qq.v.). His portrait of HRH The Prince of Wales's bay colt "Fair Play" by "Paganini" out of "Astrea" with Mr. Luke White up at Sandown, Lord Marcus Beresford, Racing Manager to the Prince and John Jones, the trainer, painted in 1882, 18in.x24in., is a very fine work indeed. ("Fair Play" won the Household Brigade Cup at Sandown in 1882.) De Prades painted "Shooting Grouse on Ilkley Moor" in collaboration with Edmund Niemann (q.v.).

De Prades, Antonio F. (op.1844-1886)
French-born portrait painter, presumably the brother of the artists Alfred P. and Frank de Prades (qq.v.), who sometimes painted very accomplished equestrian subjects in both oil and watercolour. His sporting work includes a group painting of past and present Derby winners (1853) entitled "The Derby Stakes at Epsom", a portrait of the race filly "Nancy" which was engraved by C.N. Smith (1851), 17in.x26in., "Members of the London Rowing Club" (1859) which was engraved, and an excellent view of Aldridges, the horse dealers, with horses, carriages and figures. This firm was originally established in Upper St. Martins Lane in 1753 and was considered second only to Tattersalls for horse sales. Exh. two paintings, both portraits, at the RA in 1879 and painted full-length portraits of Lord and Lady Cardigan which can be seen at Dean Park, Northants. (engraved by H. Cousins). Original works by this artist appeared at Messrs. Fores Gallery at 41 Piccadilly in 1886.

De Prades, Frank, (op.1857-1866)
Exh. two paintings at the RA (1857-1861) and a fine portrait of a bay hunter standing in a stable in 1866, 32½in.x33in. was auctioned Christie's 1974.

De Rockstro, J. Sambroke (op.1832-1852)
London based artist who exh. a portrait of an angler at SS (1850) amongst the many landscapes of Northumberland and Scotland which he exh. at the RA and SS between these dates.

De Rose, Gerard, RBA, ARCA (1918-1987)
Lancashire painter of wrestlers and wrestling. One of his oils of the sport is in the Rochdale AG. Rose studied at the RCA, to which academy he won a scholarship, gaining his diploma in 1949. He exh. at the RA and elsewhere. Nowadays probably best known as the painter who left instructions to be buried with a telephone, alcoholic refreshment and a box of cigars.

De Ryck, John (op.1710)
The painter of a portrait of a gentleman in Archers Company uniform c.1710 (Archers Hall, Edinburgh) signed John de Ryck (Fecit.) is a "competent professional work" (Waterhouse).

Des Clayes, Miss Alice, ARCA (b.1891 ex.1905-1927)
Aberdeen-born animal and sporting painter. Studied art at the Herkomer School, Bushey under Rowland Wheelwright (q.v.) and in France under Dudley Hardy (q.v.). Exh. at the RA, the provinces, the Paris Salon and in Canada. Elected an Associate of the Royal Canadian Academy.

Desfontaines (Des Fontaines), Jacques François Swebach (1769-1823)
French military painter during the Napoleonic wars and an equestrian artist of many racing scenes including "Jockeys at the Starting Post with Spectators", pen, grey ink, watercolour, dated 1800 and "At the Finishing Post" s.&d. 1804, 13in.x19in., Sotheby's 1988.

Desportes, Alexandre François (1661-1743)
French court painter to Louis XIV (1638-1715) and to the King of Poland. Initially a portrait painter, he concentrated on sporting subjects from the 1690s and was responsible with Oudry (q.v.) for painting the royal hunting scenes. He also painted shooting subjects including "A Marlborough Spaniel with the Day's Bag and French Flintlock Gun in the Gardens of a Country House", 30in.x39in., auctioned Christie's (Sth. Ken.) 1989. Desportes, who made one highly successful visit to England in 1712, was commissioned by the Gobelins tapestry factory in his later years to design eight large sporting works in which he used the King of France's hounds as models.

De Stael, Nicolas (1914-1955)
French figure painter in an abstract style. Included in this Dictionary for his "Footballeurs", 9in.x13in., dated '52, auctioned Christie's (NY) 1989 and "Soccer Players" exh. NAMOS, Indianapolis (1991).

Desvignes, Herbert Clayton (op.1831-1863)
London based sporting, landscape and cattle painter who included coaching, racing and hunting subjects amongst his work. Exh. at the RA, BI and SS (1833-1863). Titles at SS include "Going to Covert", "Breaking from Covert", "The Poacher Detected", etc. He appears to have painted for the Earls of Stradbroke. His painting of "Sweetmeat", a bay racehorse, with Whitehouse up, being led by his trainer on to a racecourse, s.&d. 1845 and inscr., 17½in.x23½in., was in the collection of Sir Walter Gilbey.

De Swertschkoff, Georges (op.1888-1954)
Russian-born equestrian artist who painted the leading British racehorses of his time including portraits of "Persimmon" (1893) by "St. Simon", "Perdita II" inscr. "Cheveley Park" and dated 1906, "Cyllene" (1895) by "Bona Vista", "Arcadia" inscr. "Enfield", "Common" (1888) by "Isonomy", "Thistle", s.&d. 1906 and inscr. "Newmarket". His work also includes Russian hunting scenes, lurchers racing and "A Horse Race in Paris", 14in.x20in., dated 1954.

Detmold, Henry E. (1854-1924)

Landscape and marine artist who painted several angling scenes. Born at Thames Ditton, studied art in Brussels, Dusseldorf and in Paris under Carolus Duran where he exh. at the Salon in 1882. Exh. at the RA (1882-1898) including "Hooked, Not Landed" (1890). The City Art Gallery Manchester has a painting by Detmold (1892) entitled "Spearing Fish". In a letter to his mother, written 29.5.1887, the artist Stanhope Forbes wrote "Even old Detmold has caught the Jubilee fun and gone up to see the Queen!".

Detti, Cesare Auguste (1847-1914)

Italian genre painter who exh. one painting at the RA (1889), "Departure of the Hawking Party".

Deuchar, David (1745-1808)

This artist is known to have included figures ice-skating amongst his etchings after the most "eminent masters" 1803.

Devis, Arthur (1712-1787)

Preston-born portrait painter, half brother to the artist Anthony Devis (c.1729-1816) and father of Arthur William Devis (q.v.) and Thomas Anthony Devis (1757-1810). Pupil of Peter Tillemans (q.v.). Opened a studio in London in 1745 and specialised in painting conversation pieces of, and for, the well-to-do middle-class families. Although he did not undertake sporting scenes he often painted his sitters in sporting attire to go with their new found status. He was not regarded as the greatest of painters, perhaps unfairly, for he painted the silk of his sitters' dresses quite beautifully. He did not appear of any great consequence until after the 2nd World War when the demand for his work increased. He is probably best known for his painting "The Swaine Family Fishing", painted in 1749, his portrait of "Henry Savage of Bromley, Kent" with a groom leading his horse towards him, painted in 1750, and John Orde and his second wife watching "William Orde's Return from Shooting", 37in.x37⅞in., painted c.1750/1755, The Paul Mellon Collection, Upperville, Va, USA.

Devis, Arthur William (1762-1822)

Nineteenth child and pupil of his father, Arthur Devis (q.v.). Arthur W. Devis also studied at the RA Schools. He visited Canton and India, returning to England in 1795. His portrait of "John Addison, Tiger Shooting in India" is in the collection of the Preston and Harris Museum and A.G.

de von Blaas, Eugène (1843-1932)

Austrian artist who exh. at the RA (1875-1891). Included in this Dictionary for his painting "The Wildfowler".

de von Blaas, Julius (1845-1922)

Austrian artist, the younger brother of Eugène de von Blaas (q.v.). Painter of several equestrian and sporting subjects but he particularly specialised in horse racing scenes and portraits.

De Wint, Peter, RWS (1784-1849)

Staffordshire-born landscape painter, many of his pictures have an angling interest. Apprenticed to John Raphael Smith (q.v.), the engraver, he then studied at the RA Schools. He was a very fine watercolour painter and exh. mainly at the OWS. Elected a member in 1811. His patrons included the Earls of Lonsdale and Powys and his studio sale was held at Christie's on 22-28 May 1850. His sporting work includes "The Cricketers", watercolour 22¼in.x34¾in, painted probably 1815 and exh. as "A Cricket Match" at the OWS in the same year. V & A Museum. His landscape with "Sportsman and Pointers in a Turnip Field" was auctioned Sotheby's 26.10.1932. "A Meet in the Grounds of Raby Castle", black chalk, is in the Paul Mellon Collection, Upperville, Va, USA.

Dews, John Steven (b.1949)

Marine artist whose paintings of the old 12 metre racing yachts are fine works. Dews studied at Hull Regional College of Art and comes from a seafaring family.

Deykin, Henry Cotterill (b.1905)

Portrait and landscape painter in oil. Born at Edgbaston. Studied at the Birmingham School of Art and the Slade School, which school he depicted in his RA exhibition work of 1935. Exh. at the RA until 1956. Art Master at Warwick School (1935-1965). Painted a series of twenty-two sports for Geoffrey Pugh of the Atco Mowing Machine Company (1950-1952) including "The Cup Final at Wembley, 1951", in which Newcastle United beat Blackpool 2-0, inscr. "Milburn Scores Again, April 28th 1951"; "Aston Villa v. W. Bromwich 1950", signed, 19½in.x23½in.; "In Recognition of their Work", a study of the men behind the scene, groundsmen and their equipment (Leamington Cricket Ground) August 1951, 19½in.x23½in.; "Cricket on Frenchay Common, Nr Bristol", Frenchay Cricket Club v. Clifton Cricket Club, 8 August 1950, signed, 17½in.x25½in.; "Lords", England v. West Indies, 2nd Test match of the 1950 series, May 1950, signed, 19½in.x23½in.; "Country House Cricket at Ascot Park, Warwickshire", Coventry Hobos v. Ascot Park, signed, 19¾in.x23¾in.; "Leamington Cricket Club v. Free Foresters at Leamington 1949", canvas mounted on board, signed 20¼in.x24¼in., previously in the collection of the late Geoffrey Pugh, the Club Captain; "Croquet at Hurlingham", The Ladies Field Cup Tournament, 3 August 1950, signed, 19½in.x23½in.; "View of the 9th Hole on the Royal/Ancient Golf Club Links at St Andrews", during the Eden Golf Tournament, G.T. Black beating P.R. Fallon, 12 August 1950, signed, 19½in.x23½in.; "Royal Cinque Ports Golf Club, Deal the 4th hole, Sandy Parlour", Halford-Hewitt Tournament, April 1950, signed, 19½in.x23½in.; "Hockey at Malvern Girls College", Kidderminster Club defeat the School 27 October 1951, signed, 17½in.x25½in.; "Oxford and Cambridge Jubilee Hockey match, Beckenham, 18th February 1950", signed, 19½in.x23½in.; "Presidents Day at the Eastbourne Bowling Club", August 1951, painted with the Clubhouse behind the artist, 19½in.x23½in.; "Bowls at the George Hotel, Solihull", a friendly match on the Ancient Green of the 16th Century Inn, August 1951. Ladies Day, Polo at Cowdray Park, Sussex, "Cowdray Park defeat Henley", 6½ to 9, 27 August 1951, signed, 19¾in.x23¾in. (The Henley team included Major A.David, E.C.Roarke, A.L.Roberts and the Maharajah of Jaipur; The Cowdray Park team included Commander P.Howes, Lord Cowdray, C.Smith Ryland and Lt. Colonel P.W.Dollar); "View from the Competitors' Sun Roof, during the Lawn Tennis Championships at the All England Club, Wimbledon, 1950.", 20in.x24in.; "The Centre Court at Wimbledon", Budge Patty defeating Frank Sedgman in the final, 7 July 1950, 19½in.x 23½in.

Dickinson, H.B.

A portrait of Lord Wavertree (1856-1933) (formerly Colonel William Hall-Walker) on "First", a polo pony, 16in.x20in., Walker A.G. Liverpool. Lord Wavertree is chiefly remembered today for having presented his magnificent stud at Tully, Co. Kildare, to the nation.

Dickinson, Lowes Cato (1819-1908)

London painter and a lithographer of portraits and sporting subjects. The son of Joseph Dickinson, a publisher of lithographs, and the brother of W.R. Dickinson with whom he formed a firm of lithographers, printers and publishers under the name of Dickinson Bros. It subsequently became Dickinson & Foster after Dickinson formed an association with the watercolour artist, Myles Birket Foster (q.v.). Dickinson painted a number of sporting scenes including "The Bird Cage", Newmarket 1885 (repro. BR August 1949), "The Members of the Royal Yacht Squadron" (1895), 62in.x118in., which he painted with Myles Birket Foster, collection Royal Yacht Squadron and "A portrait of Sir Spencer Ponsonby Fane", founder of the I. Zingari Cricket Club with a cricket match in the background, 52in.x38in. Another version of this painting with two other sitters, John Lorraine Baldwin, founder of The Four in Hand Club, and Lord Bessborough, brother of Ponsonby Fane and co-founder of I. Zingari Cricket Club, hangs in the library at Lords. Dickinson also painted a marvellous panoramic view of over 200 notable members of the aristocracy, sportsmen and dignitaries on the lawn at Goodwood, c.1886 and "Tattersalls Sale at Doncaster", which he painted in collaboration again with Birket Foster as a subscription picture, featuring distinguished members of society and notable personalities in the racing world, c.1885. Doncaster Museum and AG.

Diepenbecke (Diepenbeck, Diepenbeeck), Abraham van (1596-1675)

A Belgian glass painter and a one time pupil of Rubens. Included in this Dictionary for his illustrations to William Cavendish, Duke of Newcastle's book on horsemanship "La Methode Nouvelle et Invention Extraordinaire de Dresser les Chevaux" (1658). The Duke founded a school of equitation in Antwerp during his exile from the Commonwealth and Diepenbecke's drawings show early dressage.

Diggelmann, Alex Walter (op.1948)

A Swiss artist who won second and third prizes in the Olympic Arts Competition in July/August 1948 for his two posters depicting the Cycling and Ice Hockey World Championships. He also won an Hon. Mention with his medal designed for the Swiss Roller Skating Championship.

Dighton, Denis (1792-1827)

Son of Robert Dighton (q.v.) and brother of Richard and Joshua Dighton (qq.v.). Studied art at the Royal Academy Schools and became military painter to His Royal Highness the Prince Regent in 1815. His fine watercolour "A Hawking Party", showing a lady and gentleman on horseback with a falconer and his cadger, 14¾in.x20¾in. was auctioned Christie's 1988.

Dighton, Joshua (op.1820-1840)

Sporting artist and caricaturist who produced a number of works (c.1820-c.1840). Son of Robert Dighton and brother of Richard Dighton (qq.v.), he drew small, full-length portraits of sporting celebrities. Exh. one work only at the RA (1832).

Dighton, Joshua (1831-1908)

London sporting painter of many equestrian portraits and the grandson of Robert Dighton (q.v.). His portrait of "Manifesto", winner of the 1899 Grand National, with his jockey up was exh. April 1960 at the Rutland Gallery, London. A watercolour of "Flying Fox", winner of the Triple Crown (1899), with his jockey, Mornington Cannon (1873-1962) up was auctioned Bonhams 1984. Dighton also painted the Grand National winners "Ilex" (1890) and "Old Joe" (1886).

Dighton, Richard (1795-1880)

Etcher, caricaturist and draughtsman, the son of Robert Dighton (q.v.). Included in this Dictionary for his drawings and prints of boxers and billiard players. His portrait of R.W. Selby-Lowndes, JP (1811-1892) of Elmers, Bletchley shows him in a pink hunting coat. Selby-Lowndes' brother William was Master of the Whaddon Chase Foxhounds for over forty years. The Paul Mellon Collection, Upperville, Va, USA.

Dighton, Robert (1752-1814)

London portrait painter and caricaturist who lived and worked as a drawing master. He was also an able etcher. Exh. at the RA and FS (1769-1799). Painted many delightful sporting scenes including a series of water-colours depicting "Football played at the Market Place, Barnet", "Quoits played opposite the Horns at Kennington Common", "Trapball played at the Black Prince, Newington, Bath", "Fives played at the Tennis Court, Leicester Fields", and "Four Corners" played at the Swan, Chelsea. He also drew and etched a portrait of "Richmond" the black boxer in 1810. The discovery that Dighton had stolen (and sold) since May 1795 a number of prints from the Cracherode Collection in the British Museum leaving copies in their place did not enhance his reputation. His pen/ink and watercolour drawing "Cricket played by the Gentleman's Club, White Conduit House" (1784) was one of the pre-liminary drawings for "British Sports" pub. in 1784, engraved by an unknown engraver, etching and aquatint 7½in.x8¾in. and in the British Museum Collection. Thomas Rowlandson (q.v.) also depicted

"Cricket at White Conduit Fields" (White Conduit House was a tea and coffee house in Islington with small pleasure gardens).

Dill, Otto (1884-1957)
German equestrian artist of many hunting, racing and polo scenes.

Dingle, Thomas, Jnr. (op.1880-1890)
Landscape painter who included a painting of a hunt moving through a covert amongst his work. The son of the landscape painter Thomas Dingle (op.1846-1888)

Dingley, Humphrey J. (op.1888-1893)
Landscape painter whose imaginative portrait of Charles I playing his favourite game of lawn bowls, whilst a captive in Carisbrooke Castle, Isle of Wight, was painted in 1893.

Dinhofer, Lisa (b.1952)
American painter whose oil on canvas still life "Spring Street Hard Ball" (1988) shows modern baseballs elegantly set on antique lace and silk, 25in.x40in. The Gladstone Collection of Baseball Art.

Dinkel, Joseph (op.1833-1861)
An architectural and botanical illustrator, born in Munich, who exh. one picture of a "Fossiled Fish" at the RA in 1840. Prints after this artist's work of many species of fish were auctioned Christie's (Sth. Ken) 1988. Chatto records that Dinkel was "a very accurate draughtsman of subjects of natural history, especially of fossil remains, but though he has most practice in this department he also undertakes architectural and engineering drawings" (Chatto and Jackson, "Treatise on Wood Engraving 1861", p.593). Illus. "Poissons Fossiles" (1833-1843).

Dixon, Alec R. (op.1954)
Contemporary marine artist whose painting entitled "Yachts Racing Past Cape Town" s.&d. 1954, 40in.x 82in. was auctioned Sotheby's 1985.

Dixon, Alfred (op.1864-1889)
London painter of domestic scenes who exhibited at SS. Titles include "You're a good hand at fishing, says Kate", etc. Father of Charles Edward Dixon (q.v.).

Dixon, Charles Edward, RI (1872-1934)
Watercolour painter of marine and river subjects, some sporting. The son of Alfred Dixon (q.v.). He contributed to "The Graphic" (1900-1910) and other periodicals and exh. at the RA from 1889. Elected RI (1900). The quality of his work is very fine and he is amongst the best marine painters of this period. He was a keen yachtsman, living for many years at Itchenor on the Sussex coast where he died. His sporting work includes "A Yacht Race", pen and ink, s.&d. 1932, 3½in.x7in. and "Yachts Racing for the America's Cup", s.&d. 1896, a watercolour which was auctioned at John Francis (Carmarthen) 1988.

Dixon, George H. (op.1845-1888)
Painter of many fox-hunting and hare-coursing pictures. Illus. "The Book of the Greyhound", Edward Ash, pub. 1933. His pair of paintings "A Huntsman on a Chestnut Hunter with Hounds passing through a Gate" and "Greyhounds Coursing" are both s.&d. 1845, each 8½in.x10in.

Dixon, Henry Hall (1822-1870)
Sporting writer who used the pseudonym "The Druid" for much of his work. His books on horse-racing include "Post and Paddock" (1856), "Silk and Scarlet" (1858) and "Scotland and Sebright" (1862).

Dixon, Otto Murray (op.1909-1914)
Painter of game and wildfowl often in grisaille, and an animal illustrator who contributed to "The Illustrated London News" (1909).

Doar, Miss M. Wilson (b.1898)
Animal painter in oil and pastel, also a sculptor. Educated at Eastbourne. Studied art at Heatherleys (1936) under Bernard Adams and Frederick Whiting (q.v.). Exh. at the RSA, R.Cam.A, RBA and PS.

Dobbs, John (b.1931)
Painter of an American baseball game entitled "Play At The Plate" (1980). Oil on canvas, 26in.x30in. Collection of the artist.

Dobell, Sir William (1899-1970)
Australian portrait painter. Studied art in Sydney (where he won a Travelling Scholarship, 1929) and at the Slade School (1930). Included in this Dictionary for his pen drawing of a "Jockey mounting a Racehorse". Exh. at the RA, NEAC, LG but chiefly in Australia where he lived. Knighted (1966).

Dobie, Beatrix Charlotte (Madam Rene Vernon) (b.1887)
New Zealand-born animal, equestrian and landscape painter. Studied art at the Frank Calderon School of Animal Painting in South Kensington. Exh. IS, SWA and in the provinces. Principal works include "The White Horse" and "Station Hacks".

Dobson, Elizabeth (op.1851)
Painted William J. Verner's peregrine falcon sitting on his fist, pastel, s.&d. 1851, 26½in.x19¼in. Bonhams 1986.

Dobson, Frank, CBE, RA, PLG (1886-1963)
This marine artist often used the pseudonym "Evelyn Bishop" with which name he usually signed his work. His sporting paintings include "Yachts Racing" and "The Shooting Butt", watercolour, pen, ink, 13¾in.x 17¾in., Sotheby's 1990. Dobson studied at Leyton School of Art (1900-1902). Apprenticed to Sir William Reynolds-Stephens (1902-1904). Won a scholarship to Hospitalfield Art Institute, Arbroath, Scotland (1906-1910). Studied City and Guild School, Kensington (1910-1912). Elected President London Group (1924). Created CBE (1947). Elected RA (1953).

Dobson, Henry John, RSW (1858-1929)
Scottish romantic painter who included a few equestrian scenes amongst his work. Studied at the ECA. Elected RSW (1890).

Dobson, William (1611-1646)
Portrait painter who was probably taught to paint by Francis Cleyn (?1582-1657/8) and apprenticed to William Peake (?1580-1639). Included in this Dictionary for his portrait of Endymion Porter, c.1642, with gun, dog and dead game. Collection Tate Gallery, London.

Docharty, James, ARSA (1829-1878)
Glasgow landscape painter who painted several angling scenes. Docharty exh. at the RA (1865-1877). Titles include "Gaffing a Salmon" (1875) and "A Good Fishing Day, Loch Lomond" (1877). His angling work "A Salmon Stream - the Lochy Water - with an Angler" (1878) is in the collection of the Glasgow AG. Docharty studied at the Glasgow School of Art. Elected ARSA (1877).

Dodd, Arthur Charles (op.1878-1890)
Sporting, rustic and figure artist who lived and worked in Tunbridge Wells, Kent. Probably the son of the artist C.T. Dodd (1815-1878). Dodd's paintings of foxhounds are of a very high quality. He seems to have been less happy painting horses since very few are included in his work. His patrons included the Marquis of Abergavenny whose deerhounds he painted. He exh. at the RA, SS, GG and elsewhere (1878-1890).

Dodd, Joseph Josiah (1809-1880)
"The Cricket Match at Tonbridge School", 20in.x 31¾in. A lithograph by W.L. Walton after the work by Dodd was pub. c.1850. Exh. RA and SS.

Dodd, Robert (1748-1816)
Painter, etcher and aquatint engraver of marine and sporting subjects after his own designs and those of his contemporaries. He also pub. many of his own prints. "Gathering at the Start", s.&d. 1816, 9in.x11¼in., shows the preparation of a race, Tennants 1985.

Dodson, Tom
Contemporary painter of "Swinton Rugby League Match", 19¼in.x23¼in., s.&d. 1975, auctioned Capes Dunn (Manchester) 1990.

Dollman, John Charles, RWS, RI, ROI, RBC (1851-1934)
London painter of highly dramatic animal pictures and historical genre, also of dog portraiture. Studied at the RCA and at the RA Schools where he won prizes for drawing from life. Exh. at the RA (1872-1904) and at SS where his work included several beagling studies, "Beagles Full Cry" (1873), and "Beagles and Rabbits" (1874/5). Dollman is perhaps best remembered for his famous picture "The Sabbath Breakers" painted in 1896. It shows a curious representation of the incident in 1592 when John Henrie and Pat Rogie were prosecuted "for playing golf on the links of Leith every Sabbath during the time of the Sermons". This was pub. as a large black and white engraving by the Fine Art Society in 1896. Dollman was clearly attracted to the game of golf for in 1899 he painted "A Stymie at Musselburgh", golfers and caddies on the green watching a putt. He illus. "In the Days when We went Hog Hunting" by J.M. Brown, pub. 1891. Elected RI (1886), ROI (1887), RWS (1913).

Dollman, Ruth (op.1905-1928)
Landscape painter, daughter of John Charles Dollman (q.v.). Lived in London where for some time father and daughter shared the same house in Bedford Park. Her "The Hunt in Open Country", watercolour, s.&d. 1906,

was auctioned by Phillips 1984. Exh. sixty-nine works at the Fine Art Society, 112 at the Leicester Gallery, eleven at the RA, fourteen at RI and six at RWS.

Donnison, T.E. (op.1880-1899)
Cheshire artist who exh. one painting at the Walker AG in 1882 and whose work includes golfing caricatures drawn in ink and watercolour, 8¾in.x5in. Donnison contributed to "The Boys Own Paper" in the 1890s.

Donnithorne, Peter
Contemporary painter of "The Berkeley Gone to Ground near Bevington" (a hunting scene in Gloucestershire near the River Severn), 24in.x36in., Christie's (NY) 1987.

"Dooker"
The pseudonym sometimes used by J. Moray Brown, author of "In the Days when We Went Hog Hunting" (1891) illus. by John Dollman (q.v.) and many other sporting titles.

Dore, Paul Gustave Louis Christophe (1832-1883)
French artist and one of the most famous book illustrators of Victorian England ("The Adventures of Baron Munchausen" 1866 and "The History of Don Quixote" 1863). He arrived in London in 1868 having already given his first exhibition at the Egyptian Hall, Piccadilly, the previous year. By 1869 he had a gallery named after him at 35 New Bond Street, which operated there until 1892 when the auctioneering firm of Sotheby's took it over. During this period the Dore Gallery attracted over 2½ million visitors. Dore painted a number of racing scenes including "Tattenham Corner", "The Stands at Ascot", "The Start at Ascot" and "Return from the Derby" showing over-exuberant revellers travelling on overladen coaches and carriages pulled by overloaded horses.

Dorrell, Edmund (1778-1857)
London watercolour painter of landscapes whose painting "Cricket near Richmond" was engraved by F.C. Lewis (q.v.). He exh. at SS (1819-1836). Dorrell was elected AOWS in 1809 but resigned in 1812.

d'Orsay, Count Alfred Guillaume Gabriole (1801-1852)
Paris-born soldier, artist and sculptor who painted a number of equestrian subjects, in particular a steeple-chase scene which was pub. in lithograph. D'Orsay, is probably better known for the fashionable society Salon he established with Lady Blessington, his mother-in-law, who became his close companion after she was widowed.

Douglas, Edward Algernon Stuart (op.1860-1918)
A talented sporting painter in both oil and watercolour who operated from Barnes. Exh. ten paintings at the RA including "Foxhounds in Covert" (1880), "After a Long Run" (1883), "The Huntsman's Favourites" (1884), "Listen How the Hounds, etc" (1887) and "Lord Portman's Hounds" (1890). Tended to produce pictures in pairs or sets of four and sometimes worked in miniature. Douglas also painted four superb hare-coursing scenes in 1885/6 which were engraved by C.R. Stock and pub. by Ackermanns in 1887.

Douglas, Edwin (1848-1914)

Edinburgh-born sporting and animal painter and a fine engraver. Studied at the RA Schools and at the RSA in Edinburgh where he first exh. until 1872 when he went to London. Painted in the style of Sir Edwin Landseer (q.v.) with much of the latter's ability. Exhibited forty-one works at the RA including "Mountain Shooting" (1874), "The Bagged Fox" (1876) and "Ferreting" (1882). His RA exhibit (No. 127) 1875 was reported in "Baily's Magazine" Volume 27, June 1875 as follows, "We were almost forgetting a very clever hunting bit of Mr. Douglas's. A fox headed by sheep with the shepherd waving his hat on high to show which way the varmint has gone. The sheep attempting to show a bold face to the intruder and the attitude of the slinking fox are wonderfully well done". This painting was auctioned by Christie's in 1986. Douglas also painted the Triple Crown winner "Persimmon" in a stable interior in 1896.

Douglas, Hope (Mrs., née Smith) RMS (b.1883)

London-born animal painter. Studied at Frank Calderon's School of Animal Painting in Kensington and at Frank Brangwyn's Life School and under Alan Williams. Exh. at the RA, RMS and in the provinces. Elected RMS (1913).

Douglas, James, RSW (1858-1911)

Edinburgh landscape painter whose watercolour painting of a game of golf entitled "Driving from the 2nd Tee at North Berwick" can be dated between 1890-1895 since it shows red jackets still being worn by the players. Phillips (Chester) 1991. Douglas exh. at the RI (1885). Elected RSW (1900), resigned (1907).

Douglas, Keith Sholto, MC (1882-1963)

Equestrian painter, the son of a doctor and an American mother. Studied art in New York under Robert Henri (q.v.). Joined the Royal Engineers in 1914 for the duration of the 1st World War and won the MC in Gallipoli. During the 1920s he became a commercial artist working with and for advertising agents, in particular Howard Bull in Reading. He also collaborated with Lawson Wood (q.v.), whose daughter Phoebe he married, on many humorous sketches under the name of "Hustlebuck". A keen horseman all his life, his horse portraiture, although limited in its output, reflects this knowledge. He exh. at the Royal Institute in Piccadilly. "The Start at Ascot" s.&d. 1950 and inscr. "They're Off", 12in.x18in. Private collection.

Douglas, W. (20th century)

Edinburgh sporting painter who exh. one work at the RSA in 1935. He also painted a portrait of "Atlas", a dark bay hunter tended by a groom with a hound, signed and inscr. "Edinburgh", 20½in.x24¾in. auctioned Bearnes 1981.

Douglas, William (1780-1832)

Edinburgh miniature painter who was commissioned by Charles, the future 4th Duke of Buccleuch (succeeded in 1812) to paint the charming portrait of Thomas Hudson, the Duke's keeper, seated on his pony, his gun in his right hand, his dogs beside him, in 1810. The painting which is in the collection of the Duke of Buccleuch and Queensberry KT, Bowhill, Selkirk was engraved by John Young (1755-1825). Douglas also painted a fine sporting portrait of General Lord Robert Kerr (1780-1843) of New Battle Abbey rough shooting in a mountainous landscape with his pony and two pointers, s.&d. 1816.

Douglas, Sir William Fettes, PRSA (1822-1891)

Scottish landscape artist who took up painting in 1847 after ten years as a bank clerk. Mainly self-taught. His early works are mostly portraits and his watercolour of Tom Beattie, huntsman to Richard Oswald of Auchincruive, on a pony with a pair of grey hounds and a dead hare slung from his saddle, 18in.x16½in., dates from this period. Sotheby's 1990. Elected RSA (1854), PRSA (1882-1891).

Doutreleau, Pierre (op.1970s)

A Parisian who paints American football and equestrian scenes, particularly racing. Large oils.

Dovaston, Miss Margaret, RBA, NBA (b.1884)

Painter of portraits and figure subjects. Studied art under Thomas William Cole at Ealing Art School and under Arthur S. Cope at Kensington and at the RA Schools where she received three silver medals. Exh. at the RA from 1908 and was elected RBA (1910), NBA (1911). Her painting entitled "Cock Fighting", 20½in.x 27¼in., ensures her entry in this Dictionary. She also painted fox-hunting scenes, "The Master of the Hounds" (1918), pencil, watercolour, 13½in.x10¼in., Christie's 1988.

Doveton, J.F. (Revd.) (op.1802)

This talented amateur artist painted a tiny watercolour of "Taunton Races, August 3rd and 4th, 1802" and inscr. his work, 3in.x5in. auctioned Sotheby's 1985.

Dowd, James H. (1884-1956)

Painter, etcher and black and white artist whose tennis cartoon drawn originally for "Punch", s.&d. 22 June 1927, is entitled "The Man who Knew his Place".

Dowling, Tom B.

Contemporary artist of marine subjects. His yacht racing scene "Cowes Week Finish" (1987), signed with init. 12in.x15½in. was auctioned Bonhams 1988.

Downey, Thomas (op.1890-1935)

Figure painter and illustrator, very often of cricket subjects. His sketches of the Surrey bowler, George Lohmann (1865-1901) on the cricket field were contributed to "Moonshine", 11 July 1901. Downey, who was a pupil of Alfred Bryan (q.v.), a leading illustrator of sporting events and chief caricaturist to "Moonshine", worked for numerous magazines during the 1890s.

Downie, Patrick, RSW (1854-1945)

Scottish marine painter who started life as a postman before turning to painting. Studied art in Paris but was largely self-taught and exh. at the RSA from 1885. Elected RSW in 1902 at which Society he exh. 126 paintings. In addition he exh. works at the RA, RI,

RSA and RBA. His watercolour painting "Yacht Racing in the Firth of Clyde", 14½in.x20½in., was auctioned Christie's 1984.

Downing, Charles Palmer (op.1870-1898)
London portrait painter who included a number of sporting paintings amongst his work. Exh. mainly at the RA 1872-1898, also at SS. "The Cruel Spur" s.&d. 1889, 25in.x16in. was auctioned Bonhams 1986.

Downman, George (c.1820)
The Brighton - London Mail passing another coach at speed and a coach and four being sneered at by the owner of a donkey-drawn trap, a pair, 7⅛in.x12in. and 5½in.x7¾in. were auctioned Sotheby's 1972.

Downman, J.T. (Lieut. 83rd Regiment) (op.1810-1840)
Watercolour artist of military and some non-military equestrian scenes. Aquatints after his work depict a curricle, riders and a milestone reading XIII miles to Westminster and a private carriage and riders.

Doyle, Charles Altamont (1832-1893)
London-born caricaturist and illustrator, often of sporting subjects. The son of John Doyle (q.v.). Charles Doyle was a professional civil servant for most of his life so his work is somewhat limited. It includes, none the less, some delightful sporting scenes of curling, racing and several shooting and fishing as befits a member of this talented family. A contributor to "The Illustrated Times" 1859-1860, "London Society" 1863-1864 and "The Graphic" in 1877. He was the father of the detective novelist Sir Arthur Conan Doyle which may explain the rather sinister undertone which accompanies his illustrative sketches to children's books. "The Curling Match on Duddingston Loch", watercolour, 7in.x11in., Edinburgh City AG. "The Winning Shot - Duddingston Loch" a curling match, 9in.x7in., watercolour, from the collection of Sheriff B. Smith.

Doyle, John ("HB") (1797-1868)
Irish lithographer, caricaturist and portrait painter. Better known perhaps as a political illustrator who worked under the pseudonym of "HB". His anonymous political caricatures pub. as lithographs started in 1827 and it was in 1829 that Doyle started to sign them "HB". This series of famous political sketches ran to 1851, an astonishing output of nearly 1,000 plates. Many of John Doyle's pencil sketches are in the British Museum. His sporting paintings include "A saddled Grey Hunter held by a Groom in the yard of Carlton House, London", the residence of the Prince Regent, s.&d. 1822, and "A Gentleman leading a Bay Racehorse, with jockey up, on the Curragh, County Kildare", 27in.x35½in., Christie's 1984.

Doyle, Richard ("Dick Kit Cat") (1824-1883)
London-born humorous artist. Brilliant cartoonist and illustrator. Second son of John Doyle (q.v.). He was probably the most talented artist in a very gifted family. He and his two brothers were "discovered" by Queen Victoria when "Dicky" Doyle was barely nineteen years old. Her Majesty's diary for 1844 records "We looked at some very clever drawings by James Doyle and his two younger brothers - Richard's are beautiful, little pen and ink drawings full of wit and fun. They have not yet been seen by anyone. Albert was quite delighted with them and very anxious to bring these talented young men forward" and indeed six months later Doyle had the honour of finding his name associated with that of the Queen on an etching which clearly bears the inscription "V.R. Dell after R. Doyle (1845)". In 1843 Doyle was introduced to "Punch" and by the mid-1850s had become a household name through his popular series "Manners and Customs of Ye Englishe" and later "Birds Eye View of Society" (1864). In 1881 Doyle designed the frontispiece of the Drumlanrig Game Book in pen and ink (Drumlanrig Castle belongs to the Dukes of Buccleuch and Queensberry).

"Dragon"
The pseudonym used by the artists Georgina Bowers (q.v.) and John Beer (q.v.) for their illustrations to "Tales for Sportsmen" (1885).

Drake, Nathan, FSA (1727-1778)
Lincolnshire-born country painter whose subjects include sporting activities, portraits, animals and topographical views of Lincolnshire. Drake advertised as a limner and landscape painter in 1752. Married (1763) he had two sons and two daughters. William Joliffe Tufnell of Nunmonkton Priory, North Yorks. became an important patron in about 1766 and Drake painted him with his hounds in 1769. Three pictures which Drake painted for him are still in the family collection. Drake is sometimes confused with Nathaniel Drake, a London colour man and artist, possibly a relative, of the White Hart, Long Acre. Nathan Drake exhibited five paintings at SA and one at FS (1771-1783) including a "View of a Gentleman's Seat in Yorkshire with two Gentlemen going a'Hawking". The bulk of Drake's sporting work centres around fox-hunting.

Drake-Brookshaw, P. (op.1920s)
Futurist painter and illustrator who contributed work to London Transport for their posters including "The Boat Race", Saturday 31 March 1928. Collection London Transport Museum.

Draper, George (op.1820s)
A coloured lithograph by J. Scrutton, 14¼in.x21¼in., of a sketch after the work by this artist of "The New Race Stand built at Goodwood for his Grace the Duke of Richmond" was pub. c.1829.

Drew, Mary (op.1880-1901)
London portrait painter whose painting of a girl with a badminton racket and a shuttlecock entitled "I cannot play alone" is in the Southampton Gallery. Her attrib. painting of a "Woolwich Cadet in a cricket cap", oil on board c.1890, is in a private collection.

Drewell, Robert (1844-1860)
Equestrian artist who lived in Beccles, Suffolk and painted portraits of racehorses, often shown with jockeys up.

Dring, William, RA (1904-1990)
Painter who studied at the Slade School of Art. Included in this Dictionary for his RA exhibit "Doctor Marsden Roberts with Gun" (1964). Elected RA (1955).

Driscoll, Barry (op.1960s)
Animal illustrator whose work in this field includes illustrations to Henry Williamson's "Tarka the Otter" (1964) and "The Big Cats" (1965).

"The Druid"
Pseudonym used by the well-known sporting writer Henry Hall Dixon (q.v.).

Drumach, H.B. (op.1826)
"A Chestnut Hunter outside a Stable", dated 1826, 25½in.x29½in., was auctioned Sotheby's 1973.

Drummond, Arthur (1871-1951)
Bristol-born figure and historical artist. Studied art under Alma Tadema and also under Constant and Laurens in Paris. Drummond's work includes a number of equestrian and sporting scenes, often of dogs and game in Highland settings. His painting of "Bretwalda", a bay racehorse in a loose box, s.&d. 1896, was auctioned Bonhams 1986.

Drummond, E. (op.1869)
Black/white artist whose watercolour of a lady with a hunter and hounds, 13in.x12in., probably painted for a magazine or book illustration, was auctioned Sotheby's 1987. Exh. one figure subject at the RA (1869).

Drummond, James (op.1881-1895)
A watercolour by this talented Victorian artist entitled "The Shooting Party", s.&d. '95, 29in.x21¼in., was auctioned Sothebys (1985).

Drummond, Miss Jane (op.1825-1830)
London portrait painter who exh. a watercolour portrait of J. Sadler, Esq. the aeronaut, at SS in 1828.

Drummond, John Murray (1802-1889)
Scottish landscape painter whose watercolours are of a higher quality than his oil paintings. The eldest son of Admiral Sir Adam Drummond of Megginch and Lady Charlotte Murray, he studied art under Alexander Nasmyth (1758-1840), the portrait and landscape painter, in Edinburgh and went to Sandhurst in August 1818. He was a prolific amateur artist and his watercolour painting of "Partridge Shooting" is an extremely good example of his work, 20in.x29in.

Drummond, Miss Norah Hardy (op.1876-1892)
Very competent sporting painter of hunting and shooting scenes, usually in watercolour or gouache, of whom surprisingly little is known. Her fine watercolour entitled "Sportsman's Companions" shows gundogs, shotgun and cartridge bag and is signed N. Hardy Drummond and dated '92, 20½in.x28½in., Lawrence (Crewkerne) 1990.

Drummond, William (op.1830-1865)
Sussex portrait and figure painter who exh. at the RA and BI (1830-1843). He is known to have painted cricket scenes and portraits and collaborated with both Charles Basebe (q.v.) and William Mason (q.v.) on a coloured lithograph after his work entitled "Sussex v Kent at the Sussex Cricket Club Ground, Brighton, s.&d. 1849, 16½in.x24.¾in., exh. Richard Green, London and repro. "Country Life". An engraving by George Henry Phillips after a cricket painting by Drummond was pub. in 1849. "A Young Batsman", pencil and watercolour 18¼in.x12½in., s.&d. 1848. Sotheby's.

Drummond-Fish, George (Captain) (op.1906-1938)
Portrait and landscape painter. Studied Liverpool School of Art. Won a travelling scholarship to Paris, Brussels and Antwerp. Painted a number of golfing scenes at St. Andrews in watercolour including "St. Andrews from the 10th Tee", 12in.x19in., and "St. Andrews, the Fairway to the 12th Green", 12in.x19in.

Dubaut, Pierre (1886-1968)
French artist of polo scenes in watercolour.

Dubois, Simon (1632-1708)
Pupil of C.P. Berchem at Haarlem and P. Wouverman. Dubois came to England in 1685 and painted a number of hunting and equestrian scenes and many portraits.

Dubost, Antoine (1769-1825)
French artist, a pupil of Vincent and C. Vernet in Paris. Came to England in 1813. A series of eleven plates entitled "A View of Newmarket " and "The Life of a Racehorse" were lithographed in 1818. The original works were painted in 1809 when Dubost was on a visit to England. He exh. at the RA "Preparations for a Horse Race" (1806) and is said to have been killed in a duel on 6 September 1825 in Paris.

Dudgeon, James (op.1844-1881)
Several good, solid portraits of hunters in stables painted between these dates have been seen at auction. He is possibly the father of Emelia Dorothea Maria Dudgeon (b.1866) who married the sporting artist Philip Eustace Stretton (q.v.) and who studied at Calderon's School of Animal Painting in Kensington.

Dudley, Charles (op.c.1853-1870)
Victorian painter of hounds and game dogs who painted in a most competent way but rarely dated his work. His paintings include pictures of otter hounds, retrievers, pointers and shooting still lifes. Surprisingly little is known about this quite prolific artist. He may have been the Robert Charles Dudley who exh. one painting at the RA in 1853.

Duer, Douglas (op.1911-1926)
American illustrator and painter of equestrian scenes, particularly racing. His set of four oil paintings "Weighing In", "Going to the Start", "The Finish" and "The Winner", s.&d. 1911 (three are 30in.x20in. and one 20in.x30in.), were auctioned Sotheby's (NY) 1990. Member of the Society of Illustrators. Lived in Brooklyn, NY, in 1926.

Duffield, Frank
Contemporary artist whose equestrian painting "Bertie Hill at Badminton" (1956), 18in.x22¾in., was auctioned Sotheby's 1986.

Duffield, William (1816-1863)
A painter of dead game subjects in oil and watercolour whose fine work "The Poachers" was painted with Sir John Gilbert RA, signed by both artists and dated 1863,

42in.x62in. Duffield died of an infection caught from a dead stag which he was painting in his studio, possibly as a model for "The Poachers" since he was working on this during the year that he died.

Dufy, Jean (1888-1964)

French artist of several racing scenes in watercolour or gouache. "Au Champ de Courses à Longchamp" and "Aux Courses à Auteuil" are just two examples.

Dufy, Raoul (1877-1953)

Prolific French Fauve artist who painted a number of sporting scenes, including racing, rowing and even a baseball game. Dufy designed for the Lyon silk manufacturers, Bianchini-Farier (1912-1928). During this period more than a thousand designs were submitted, many of them of equestrian scenes, for example, "The Paddock", "The Wild Horses", "The Three Horses", "The Man and the Horse" and were carefully preserved by the firm. It was a long time before Dufy was taken seriously as a painter for he continued to take commissions to design for manufacturers, hotels and even the ocean-going liners of the 1930s. He appeared to be quite unaffected by two World Wars and the Nazi occupation and indeed his inventive imagination found wit and amusement in all these situations causing his work to be dismissed as superficial by many of the contemporary art critics. His friend and inspiration was Matisse (1869-1954), his subject an apparent un-ending season of regattas, race meetings and garden parties. "My eyes were made to efface what is ugly" he said. Towards the end of his life he was virtually paralysed by arthritis but even the paintings worked under these increasing difficulties lost little of their freshness and gaiety. In 1950 Dufy travelled to Boston (USA) for treatment for his arthritic condition. Whilst there he painted "Park Ball - Boston" as a result of seeing a Boston Red Sox baseball game, watercolour, 19½in.x25½in., Rose Art Museum, Brandeis University, Waltham, Mass. Dufy's painting of "Ascot" (1935), now in the Paul Mellon Collection, Upperville, Va, USA, was the result of thirty-eight fascinating pencil drawings and notes on colour and clothing that he made at the racecourse.

Du Gravier, A. (op.c.1880)

A "Hunting Scene" and "A Field in Full Cry" painted in the style of the 1880s appeared in a provincial sale room.

Duke, Alfred (op.1893-1905)

An artist of whom little is known except that he lived most of his life in or around Manchester. He painted game dogs - very often foxhounds - most competently and usually in oil. He nearly always signed his work but hardly ever dated it. There is no record of his exhibiting at any of the major London galleries and his exhibition work appears to have been confined to the Midland art galleries of Manchester, Liverpool and Birmingham. He is thought to have died in about 1905.

Duke, Arthur (1850-1920)

A sporting painter who specialised in fox-hunting and shooting scenes. He may well have been a brother of Alfred Duke (q.v.) since he painted in a similar style. Certainly both artists were hound and dog men and both painted otter hounds.

Dulac, Edmund (1882-1953)

French artist and a leading book and magazine illustrator who became a naturalised British subject in 1912. Studied at the Toulouse School of Art and at Julians in Paris (for three weeks). His painting of a figure playing croquet with a black dog looking on, watercolour, s.&d. '18, 10½in.x6½in., was auctioned Gorringes (Sussex).

Du Maurier, George Louis Palmella Busson, RWS (1834-1896)

Very talented black and white artist, illustrator and novelist who studied art in Paris (1856-1857) and Antwerp (1857-1860). In 1864 he became a regular contributor to "Punch", when he succeeded John Leech (q.v.), and where he contributed lively golf drawings showing women playing golf seriously for the first time. "Our Croquet Party", 6½in.x5¾in., a wood engraving by Horace Harral (op.1860s) after the work by Du Maurier, was contributed as an illustration to "London Society" June 1864, British Museum.

Duncan, Edward, RWS (1803-1882)

Landscape artist in watercolour, aquatint engraver and lithographer of marine and sporting subjects after his own work and that of his contemporaries. He was apprenticed to R. Havell (q.v.) from whom he learnt to engrave. Duncan set up his own engraving business working mostly for Messrs. Fores of Piccadilly on sporting subjects (as did John Beer (q.v.) at a later date) and for William Huggins (whose daughter, Bertha, he married) on marine subjects. Duncan was a prolific artist exhibiting over 500 works at the OWS and NWS alone. Most of his good shooting paintings are early works. He exhibited "Grouse Shooting" and "Pheasant Shooting" at SS in 1830 and his pair "Pheasant Shooting" and "Partridge Shooting", each 12in.x16in., are in the Paul Mellon Collection, Upperville, Va, USA.

Duncan (Mr.)

Sketched "The Curling Match at Montreal" in 1855. Repro. in "The Illustrated London News" 17 February 1855 where Duncan was described as "that clever artist from Montreal".

Dunn, Joseph, of Worcester (1806-1860)

This artist of sporting subjects was the son of William Dunn of Birmingham who ran a coaching service to London. He appears to have lived only for painting and hunting though he may have indulged in the former to pay for the latter. Dunn's reputation, no doubt put about by his long suffering family, was that of a no good wastrel who frequently deserted them to hunt, which he appears to have done in Hereford and Warwickshire as well as in his own county of Worcestershire. His paintings reflect his knowledge of sport and the country-side and are both talented and charming. They are also rare. Appropriately he died in the hunting field at the age of fifty-four.

Dunnington, Albert (1920)

Sporting painter from the Midlands who exh. one painting at Manchester City AG (1886). Specialised in shooting scenes, for example "Rough Shooting", "The Pheasant Season near Abber", "On the Moors, Loch Fynn" and "Glen Sannox - Wild Duck Shooting".

Dunsmore, John Ward (op.1884-188?)
This artist from Blackheath is recorded by Mitchell as painting historical figures and sporting subjects.

Dunstan, Bernard, RA, RWEA, NEAC (b.1920)
Painter of figure subjects in oils. Married to the artist Miss Diana Armfield. Studied art at the Byam Shaw School under Ernest Jackson and at the Slade School (1939-1941). Taught at the West of England School of Art, Bristol (1946-1949). Elected NEAC (1946). Elected RWEA (1949). President RWEA (1979-1983). Elected RA (1968). Exh. at the RA and other leading and provincial galleries. Sporting titles include "Cricket at Kew Green" (1953). Pub. several books on how to paint pictures. Represented in many public collections at home and abroad. His painting entitled "A Game of Football", 6½in.x13½in., was auctioned Sotheby's 1987.

Dunthorne, James, Snr. (1730-1815)
Portrait painter who practised in Colchester, Essex. Father of James Dunthorne, Jnr. (c.1758-1792) a portrait painter and caricaturist. James Dunthorne, Snr. exh. two miniatures at the RA in 1784 and 1786. His death at the age of eighty-five was reported in "The Colchester Gazette" and his talents as a painter extolled. The James Dunthornes, père et fils, are not the same artists as John Dunthorne, Snr. (1769-1844) and Jnr. (1798-1832) the friends of the landscape artist John Constable at East Bergholt. The portrait of "John Sidey and his Hounds at a Farmhouse near Hadleigh, Suffolk", painted in 1765 by James Dunthorne, Snr., 35½in.x 54in. is in the Paul Mellon Collection, Upperville, Va, USA.

Dupont, Richard John Munro (1920-1977)
Somerset-born equestrian painter, illustrator and writer. The elder son of a doctor and a direct descendant of the painter Thomas Gainsborough (q.v.). Studied art at the RA Schools. After the 2nd World War he returned to the RA Schools under Sir Philip Connard. During his last year at the Schools he became an associate of Sir Alfred Munnings (q.v.) who helped and encouraged him. Richard Dupont also painted dogs with flair as shown in his study of the champion hound "Pickwick", painted for the Master of the Cambridgeshire Hunt, Mrs. Gingel. His painting of "Hyperion" (1960) was featured on the front cover of "The British Racehorse", July 1963. He also painted the portrait of "Nimbus" ("Nearco" and "Kong") winner of the 1949 2000 Guineas and The Derby.

Duppa, Bryan Edward (1804-1866)
Portrait painter who also painted some animal and sporting scenes. He probably painted as an amateur until the 1830s using the title "Esquire" after his name to sign his work until that time. From 1832 he exh. in London though shortly after this date he seems to have dropped his early flirtation with horse portraiture in favour of human portraiture. He exh. a portrait of the racehorse "Nanine" at the BI (1833) and sketched "The White Horse" from which Robert Roe (q.v.) took his etching. He also painted a mounted portrait group of the various members of the Tickham Hunt, including himself, in 1841. The Tickham, founded in 1831, hunted around the Ashford and Maidstone area in Kent and amalgamated with the West Street in 1990. Duppa turned to portraiture later on in his life and became well known through the engravings after certain of his works for Saunders' "Living Political Reformers".

Duval, John (1815-1892)
This equestrian artist was commissioned to draw and paint a series of illustrations for Voit's "Suffolk Stud Book" which was produced by the first Secretary of the Suffolk Horse Society, Hermann Bidell in 1880. Duval painted many portraits of hunters and racehorses, hunting scenes and Highland scenes with ponies, but he also painted shooting and coursing scenes in a very competent manner.

Dyer, Simon (b.1962)
Watercolour painter of sporting caricatures who showed interest in art at school, winning minor competitions. Commissioned into the army (1984) and painted watercolour caricatures in Northern Ireland in his spare time. His skill and natural talent in this field developed rapidly and he found many painting commissions amongst his fellow officers. Left the army in April 1989 to become a professional artist. Exhibitions: Malcolm Innes Gallery, London (1989/1990).

E

Eakins, Thomas, NA (1844-1916)
One of America's leading painters and portraitists. His range of subject matter was wide and included many fine equestrian and sporting works. Born in Philadelphia, he commenced his art studies at the PAFA (1862) and went to Paris (1866) to continue his studies at the Ecole des Beaux Arts where he was a pupil of Jean Léon Gérome (q.v.) and Augustine Dumont. In about 1880 Eakins began to experiment with photography and his painting "The Fairman Rogers Four-in-Hand" (1879) (Philadelphia Museum) was almost the first painting to show horses trotting accurately. Among his other sporting works is a painting of boxers entitled "Between Rounds (1899) (Philadelphia Museum) and his rowing portraits include those of Max Schmidt in a single scull (1871) (MMA) and "The Biglin Brothers Racing" (1873) National Gallery of Art, Washington DC. He also painted a number of hunting scenes which are less anecdotal than those of his contemporaries including Winslow Homer (q.v.). Eakins' watercolour painting "Baseball Players Practising", 1875, 10⅞ in.x12⅞ in., is in the Museum of Art, Rhode Island School of Design.

Earl, George (1864-1943)
London sporting and animal painter who lived at Banstead, Surrey and had a studio in Newman Street, London which he shared with Thomas Earl (q.v.). He exh. at the RA (1857-1883). Titles include "A Polo Match at Hurlingham" (between the Royal Horse Guards (Blues) and the Monmouthshire Team, 7 July 1877), "Deer Stalkers Returning" and "A Grouse Drive on Bowes Moor, Yorkshire". His daughter was the very competent artist Miss Maud Earl (q.v.).

Earl, Maud (Mrs. West Watson) (op.1884-1943)
London-born animal and sporting artist who was taught to paint by her father, George Earl (q.v.). Specialised in painting dogs and illus. many books including "The Pointer" (Arkwright 1902), "Dogs by Well Known Authorities" (ed. Harding Coggs 1906 and 1908), "The Power of the Dog" (A. Croxton Smith 1911) and "My Dog Friends" (1913). After her marriage Maud Earl signed her work Maud West Watson. Painted both Queen Victoria and Edward VII's dogs and many others for private patrons. Held several one-man shows including "British Hounds and Gun Dogs" (1902) and "Whose Dog Art Thou" (1913). She also became well known through her engraved work. She died in New York where she had emigrated in 1916.

Earl, Percy (op.1896-1930)
A fine equestrian artist who contributed ten cartoons of horse subjects to "Vanity Fair" (1909-1910). He was the son of the painter George Earl (q.v.) and brother of Maud Earl (q.v.). He became well known after Edward VII commissioned him to paint a number of his horses including the racehorse "Persimmon" with his groom, winner of the 1896 Derby, watercolour, 14in.x19¾in. He also painted the portraits of "Wool Winder" with jockey up, s.&d. 1907, and "Asetic Silver", winner of the Grand National 1906, with the Hon. Aubrey Hastings up.

Earl, Thomas (op.1836-1885)
Sporting and animal painter who exh. a total of 238 paintings at the RA, BI, SS and elsewhere (1836-1885) from London addresses including 76 Newman Street, the studio address of George Earl (q.v.) to whom he was presumably related.

Earl, Thomas Percy (op.1900-1940)
This equestrian painter specialised in horse racing scenes and racehorse portraits.

Earle, T.A. (op.1927)
Equestrian artist whose painting "Becher's Brook, the Grand National 1927", 27¼in.x35½in., is a fine work. That year's National was won by "Sprig" with "Bovril III" second and "Brights Boy" third. There were thirty-seven starters and the going was heavy.

Earnshaw, Harold C. (op.1908-d.1937)
Watercolour painter and illustrator. Husband of the children's illustrator Mabel Lucie Attwell (1879-1964) whom he married in 1908. Earnshaw worked extensively for the publisher Blackie, for whom he designed many colour covers. He was a keen golfer, playing regularly with his great friend Harry Rountree (q.v.). Earnshaw lost his right arm in the (1914-1918) war but with great determination taught himself to paint with his left hand. He was also a keen billiards player to which the loss of his arm proved only a minor obstacle. He acquired a hook and gripping his cue with this wicked attachment, gave lovers of the green baize many a nervous moment as he prepared to strike the ball.

Earp, George (op.1833-1874)
A member of a large Brighton based family of landscape artists. Earp painted "The Brighton Hurdle Race, December 20th 1833" and "Coming In", a fine pair of panoramas of a race meeting, which were engraved by C. Hunt and pub. by W.H. Mason.

Earp, Henry, Snr. (1831-1914)

Landscape, animal and sporting painter in both oil and watercolour. A senior member of the large Brighton family of painters whose members include Frederick, Edwin, George (q.v.), Vernon and William Henry Earp (but not Wyatt). George and Henry, Snr. were, so far as I know, the only Earps to have painted sporting scenes. These include several of fox-hunting which Henry Earp discharged in a competent if somewhat uninspired style. He exh. in London (1871-1884) mainly at SS and NW.

East, Adam (op early 19th century)

Draughtsman and lithographer of sporting subjects whose work includes a lithograph entitled "Crack Hounds", presumably after his own work.

East, Sir Alfred, RA, PRBA, RI, RE (1849-1913)

Landscape painter and etcher, very often of sporting subjects, usually shooting. Born in Kettering, Northamptonshire. Studied at the Glasgow School of Art and the Ecole des Beaux Arts in Paris, subsequently joining the Académie Julian where he worked under Bouguereau and Fleury. He painted mostly in watercolour and found his subject matter largely in the Midlands. He was a prolific artist and exh. widely at the major galleries in both Glasgow and London. Sporting titles include "A Salmon Fishing Station on the Scottish Coast and "Fowl Play". He was elected RE (1885), RI (1887), PRBA (1906) and was knighted (1910). He was elected RA just before he died in 1913. His painting "The Cricket Field, Stratford on Avon" was auctioned Christie's.

Easto, A. (op.1819)

Stipple engraver and etcher of portraits after his own designs and those of his contemporaries. An etching of William Eels, the boxer, dated 1819, 10½in.x13½in., is recorded.

Eckersley, Tom (op.c.1930-c.1938)

Painter and illustrator who worked with Eric Lombers (q.v.) during the 1930s until the war broke the partnership up. Contributed work for posters to London Transport during the pre-war period including "The Rugby League Final" (1938).

Eden, Sir William (7th and 5th Bt.) (1849-1915)

Soldier, boxer, MFH and amateur artist, he succeeded to the baronetcies in 1873. In 1875 he became involved in a lawsuit against the painter James Whistler, over the portrait by Whistler of Lady Eden, which became known as the case of the Baronet and the Butterfly and led to Whistler's bankruptcy in 1879.

Edgerton, Daniel Thomas, RBA (op.1823-d.1842)

See Egerton

Edouart, Augustine (op.1815-1835)

Animal painter who exh. five works at the RA, one of a horse and the rest of dogs, between 1815 and 1816 from a London address. Edouart was also well known as a silhouettist and an artist in hair work but the exact medium of his RA exhibits is not recorded in Graves RA Exhibitors. It is likely however that all of his animal portraits were worked in either human or the exhibitor's own hair. Whilst this may seem grisly the effect was stunning and as "The Connoisseur" (1932) recorded "the work has to be seen to be appreciated and no description can really do justice to the skill and ingenuity with which it is accomplished". In his book "Silhouette Likenesses", pub. 1835, Edouart devotes a chapter to hair pictures.

Edridge, Henry, ARA (1769-1821)

A portrait miniaturist who was apprenticed to William Pether (1738-1821) and painted portraits. He worked in black lead and Indian ink to which he added watercolour. Exh. at the RA showing portraits of George III and Queen Charlotte (1803). Elected ARA (1820). His sporting work includes fishing scenes and several portraits of young cricketers. His portrait of Philip Woodhouse at the age of thirteen shows him, cricket bat in hand, with a view of Harrow School in the background. Pencil/grey wash, 13in.x9in., s.&d. 1802, auctioned Sotheby's 16.7.1970.

Edwards, Charles

Late 19th century painter of fox-hunting and fishing scenes (1884)

Edwards, Edward, ARA (1738-1806)

Landscape, topographical and animal portrait painter who included among his RA exhibits two portraits of spaniels in 1796 and 1805.

Edwards, James (op.1846-1868)

Nottingham landscape artist who also painted racehorse and hunter portraits in 1846.

Edwards, John

Contemporary artist and sporting cartoonist who works under the pseudonym "Jedd" (q.v.).

Edwards, Lionel Dalhousie Robertson, RI, RCA (1878-1966)

Painter, chiefly in watercolour of sporting scenes, mainly hunting and horses. Studied art under Sir A.S. Cope, RA at Heatherleys and Frank Calderon (q.v.) at the latter's School of Animal Painting in Kensington. Edwards worked extensively as a reporter and illustrator, firstly for "The Graphic" in about 1910, where he reported the Lisbon Revolution, and then for "Punch", both before and after the 1st World War, in which he served in the army remount service. His great friend was Dennis Aldridge (q.v.) who painted in a very similar style and his work was also echoed by that of Peter Biegel (q.v.). He painted a series of pictures of named hunts entitled "Shires and Provinces" which were produced as limited edn. prints and he wrote and illus. a number of books including "Sketches in Stable and Kennel" and "Reminiscences of a Sporting Artist". Sporting subjects covered by Edwards include, fox-hunting, beagling, racing, steeplechasing and polo. "Ranelagh v Royal Horse Guards Subalterns" playing on Saturday 17 June 1899, inscr. "Result: R H G ' 8 goals, Ranelagh ' 1 goal", s.&d. 1899, 14in.x10in., pen/black ink. Edwards would have been twenty-one years old when he sketched these polo scenes, probably as an illustration for a magazine. This drawing is interesting because it depicts a match at Barn Elms, Barnes after the Ranelagh Club had moved from its old site beside the Hurlingham Club in 1894. The date of this picture, 1899, represented the first season that Ranelagh had its own house team consisting of Captain L.C.D. Jenner, Mr A. Rawlinson, Mr E.A. Gill and Mr Scott Robson, the latter a fine player from South America with the rare gift of being able to play with either left or right hand. The Royal Horse Guards were a splendid team who, to quote from T.F. Dale in his book "Polo Past and Present" (1905), "The last named regiment (R.H.G) has a great polo record and although they have never succeeded in winning the Inter Regimental Cup, they have been very near. Their polo team has produced some notable players... The regiment has a most successful club and magnificent team of ponies and owe a great deal to the efforts of the late Major Ferguson and to Captain Fitzgerald (who often plays No 3 for them) in organising and promoting polo in the regiment". Wingfield Sporting Gallery, London. "Polo at Tidworth", signed (with inits.) and dated 1964, 9¾in.x14in, Woolley & Wallis, Salisbury. This painting is equally interesting for the fact that the artist painted it two years before he died and therefore almost seventy years after his polo sketch at Barn Elms. The unmistakable style is there in the '64 painting but the features are blurred in the medium that Edwards did not work best in.

Edwards, Sydenham Teast (1768-1819)

Monmouth-born animal and sporting artist who exh. at the RA. Titles include "Red Grouse", "A Cocking Spaniel", "Staghounds in Kennel" and a "Portrait of a Hunter with Hounds being Unkennelled". He also painted cattle subjects and contributed illustrations to both "The Botanical Magazine" and "The Sportsman's Magazine". Scott engraved his painting of "Lancashire Longhorns" in 1807. Coll. the V & A Museum and British Museum.

Eerelman, Otto (1839-1926)

Dutch artist who painted a number of equestrian race-horse portraits.

Egerton, Daniel Thomas, RBA (op.1823-d.1842)

An aquatint engraver, lithographer and painter in oil and watercolours of landscapes, topographical, angling and equestrian scenes. A founder member of the RBA, where he exhibited sixty-five works (1824-1840) including a portrait of a favourite hackney "Leicester Bob" owned by Thomas Williams, Esq. and a Durham cow, fed by Mr. W. Goodall of Market Deeping, winner at the Smithfield Show in 1827. Egerton's other exh. work includes a portrait of "Malcolm", an Arabian charger and a Leicester Weatherbred, owned by the Marquis of Exeter, which took the prize at Smithfield in 1827. Presumably the Durham cow also belonged to the Marquis. Egerton's portrait of "A Grey Hunter in a Stable", s.&d. 1827, 25in.x29½in., was auctioned Sothebys (NY). His angling scene "Wiring Pike", s.&d. 1823, drawn and engraved by himself is in the Collection of the Piscatorial Society. Egerton travelled widely and was murdered in Mexico in 1842.

Egerton, M. (op.1824-1828)

Social caricaturist who worked in London in the 1820s in the manner of George Cruikshank (q.v.). His pair of coaching scenes entitled "Stage" and "Wagon" were engraved by George Hunt in 1824. He also produced a set of six coaching and four racing scenes which were engraved by Hunt and pub. by J. Brooker of Southampton Row in 1825. Egerton contributed several social illustrations to publications including "Humorous Designs" (1828).

Eglington, Samuel, PLA (op.1830-1856)

Liverpool artist who exh. thirteen paintings at BI (1841-1855). Titles include "Ptarmigan" (1841), "Grouse" (1846). He became an Associate of the Liverpool Academy (1832), a Member (1837) and President (1845). The Walker AG have his "Trout Fishing in North Wales" in their collection.

Ehlers, Ernest Herman, RWA (1858-1942)

Landscape artist and painter of some game subjects. Born in St. John's, Newfoundland, the son of a salt cod merchant and grandson of the Governor of Newfoundland. Came to England c.1865 and settled in Bristol at which port his father had his fishy dealings. Ehlers studied in Germany at the Carlsruhe School of Art and continued his studies at Edinburgh School of Art. He painted in both oil and watercolour and was elected a member of the Royal West of England Academy in 1896. He was also a founder member of the "Bristol Savages". His recreations were officially listed as bicycling and skating, although to the end of his days he remained puzzled by this, always maintaining that he disliked physical exertion. His fine painting "The Fox and the Pheasant" was painted in 1890. J. Collins, Bideford.

Eichel, G. (op.1768-1771)

18th century painter of sporting subjects including "Partridge and Hare Shooting", s.&d. 1768, each 6½in.x8¾in., Christie's 1990. Eichel exh. small landscapes at the Free Society in 1770 and 1771 and four paintings by him are in the British Museum.

Einsle, J. (op.1788)

The artist of a "Boxing Match Between Humphreys and Mendoza" engraved after this work by Joseph Grozer (op.1785-1799) and pub. in 1788.

Eisenberg, Baron Reis d' (op.18th century)

A renowned horseman and an amateur artist who wrote and illus. "Description du Manège Moderne", pub. in 1747. The fifty-five illustrations of school movements were commissioned by the 10th Earl of Pembroke and now hang at Wilton House.

Elcock, Howard, K. (op.1910-1923)

Figure artist and illustrator who contributed sporting subjects to "Punch" and designed dust jackets, notably for the 1923 edn. of "The Prisoner of Zenda" by Anthony Hope.

"ELF"

Caricaturist of eighteen cartoons for "Vanity Fair" (1908-1910) including some sporting subjects, for example, curling. "Dr. H.S. Lunn (of Travel Agency fame) in the act of Throwing his Stone", pub. "Vanity Fair" "Men of the Day" issue, No. 1193, 6 October 1909.

Elgood, George Samuel, RI, ROI, NWS (1851-1943)
Landscape painter in watercolour who specialised in garden scenes. "The Bowling Green, Berkeley Castle", watercolour, 15¼in.x23¼in., s.&d. 1887, is a charming and typical example of his work, Phillips 1987.

Elim, Frederick (Frank) (op.1920-1947)
Equestrian artist of racing scenes and racehorse portraits of whom, unfortunately, very little is known. "The Finish of the Handicap Race at Newmarket" (1947) shows a competent hand and his "Racing to the Finish" (1924) depicting Deauville Racecourse shows that he was at home in both French and British racing. His racehorse portraits include those of "White Cockade" with W. Payne up, winner of the Pershore Hunter Chase in 1920 and "Le Prodige" with O'Neill up in 1922.

Eliot, Granville (op.1890s)
Sporting artist from Horsham, Sussex, who included fox-hunting and point-to-point scenes amongst his work. He usually painted these in pairs although his RA exhibit in 1891 is a single painting of a fishing scene. His pair of steeplechase scenes, entitled (unimaginatively) "Full Cry" and "Clearing the Hedge", each 9in.x16in., were auctioned Christie's 1989.

Eliott, Harry (op.1900-1925)
An American artist with something of a playboy reputation who settled in Paris at the beginning of the 20th century. Eliott was highly influenced by the poster artist of motoring subjects, Ernest Montaut (q.v.), whom he probably met in New York where Montaut opened his gallery. Eliott's original lithographs of motor racing include "The 1906 Grand Prix de France - Szisz sur Renault" (a lithograph of that year's race was also designed by Montaut) and "The 1907 Automobile Club de France Controle". Eliott was also a good illustrator of golfing scenes - some of his work in this subject was illus. in the catalogue produced by M. Machoir, Hotel des Ventes Rameau, 5 Rue de Rameau, 78000 Versailles, 1989.

Ellenor, Laura K. (op.1893)
Exh. two paintings including "The Angler's Hobby" at SS in 1893 from a Tooting address.

Elliott, Daniel Giraud (1835-1915)
American bird painter and successor, in some degree, to John James Audubon (q.v.).

Ellis, Alfred (op.1885-1903)
Landscape painter whose work includes equestrian scenes and portraits of greyhounds.

Ellis, C. Wynn (op.1880-1904)
Portrait painter who exh. "The Whip" at the RA (No. 1054) in 1895. This was, according to Baily's Magazine (June 1895, p.428) "A really pretty little drawing. The Whip at the end of the covert is calling the hounds out. The position of the man on the horse is good as also are those of the horse and hounds. The picture is evidently painted by a man accustomed to the sport and having an eye for a horse".

Ellis, Clifford and Rosemary (op.1930s)
Husband and wife team of illustrators, in particular book illustrators, and commercial artists. Contributed work to London Transport during the 1930s including "The 3rd Test Match at the Oval", 1939.

Ellis, Edwin, RBA (1841-1895)
London marine and landscape painter, born in Nottingham where he first worked in a lace factory. Exhibited at SS (1868-1892) and elected RBA (1875). Titles include "The Haunt of the Wildfowl" but apart from that a steady stream of Welsh and Cornish land and coastal scapes.

Ellis, J.H. (op.1853)
Equestrian artist who painted portraits of the "Flying Dutchman" and "Voltigeur" in 1853. The two Derby winners (1849) and (1850) raced against each other in 1851 in the most celebrated match in the history of the turf when the "Flying Dutchman" won by a short length.

Ellis, Joseph F. (1783-1848)
Landscape artist and painter of river scenes whose painting "Fishing on a Welsh River" 12in.x20in. was auctioned Sotheby's 1986.

Ellis, Lionel, NS, ARCA (Lond.) (b.1903)
Equestrian artist who also painted portraits and flowers. Born in Plymouth, studied at the Plymouth School of Art (1918-1922) and the Royal College of Art (1922-1925) under Sir William Rothenstein where he won the travelling scholarship to Colarossi in Paris, then to further studies in Florence and Rome. Became a painting master at the Wimbledon School of Art. Exh. three paintings at the NEAC and forty-five at the Redfern Gallery as well as the RA and NS. Elected NS (1930). Became founder member of Society of Animal Painters (1930). His scene of riders exercising their racehorses entitled "Morning Exercise - Six Mile Bottom, Newmarket", painted in 1951, was auctioned Phillips (Wales) 1986.

Ellis, T.J. (op.1872-1877)
London landscape artist who exh. at SS including a watercolour painting entitled "Trout in Danger" and "Highland Cattle in England".

Ellison, Alan (b.1948)
Contemporary equestrian artist, etcher and engraver of in particular, racing, hunting and driving scenes. A keen horseman, Ellison hunts regularly with the Burton and lives in Lincolnshire. His work is shown in a number of American galleries including the Racing Hall of Fame in South Carolina.

Ellison, Thomas, R.Cam.A. (1866-c.1942)
Lancashire-born landscape painter. Elected R.Cam.A (1907), the same year that he painted a fine shooting picture, 14¼in.x20½in., auctioned Sotheby's (Chester) 1985.

Elmer, Stephen, of Farnham ARA (1717-1796)
Painter of game (usually alive) and sporting dogs. Born, lived and died in Farnham, the son of a maltster whose trade he continued. Appears to have been self taught but painted very competently. His son, William Elmer (q.v.) held an exhibition of 148 of his father's works after his death as "Elmer's Sporting Exhibition" although a great deal of Elmer's work was destroyed in a fire in 1801. Stephen Elmer painted a number of fishing and shooting scenes.

Elmer, William (b.1762 -c.1812)
Sporting artist, apparently the son of Stephen Elmer (q.v.). Exh. six paintings at the RA (1783-1799) including "Spaniels pursuing a Wounded Pheasant" (1797). His portrait "The Young Cricketer" 25½ in.x 18¼ in. was painted in 1812.

Elsley, Arthur John (1861-1952)
Landscape, sporting and animal painter who specialised in painting children, whom he used in many of his pictures. Exh. at the RA. Titles include "Portrait of an Old Pony" (1878), "Hard Pressed" (1898), "Hold Up" (1901) and "Golden Hours with a Pony and Dog" (1903). His "First Shot", painted in 1903, was auctioned Sotheby's (Chester) 1986. Many engravings were made of his work and some were used for advertising purposes.

Elsley, J. (op.1845)
This artist exh. a painting of a group of horses at the BI in 1845.

Elvery, James (op.1762-c.1809)
Portrait painter who exh. three portraits at FS in 1762. A portrait of "A Gentleman mounted on a Hunter with a Dog", painted in the style of Francis Sartorius (q.v.), s.&d. 1762 by this artist is recorded (Mitchell).

Elwell, Francis Kenneth (op.1922-d.1944)
Portrait and figure painter and of hunting and racing scenes in oil. Born in Beverley, Yorkshire. Nephew of Frederick William Elwell, RA. Usually signed his paintings by his second name Kenneth. His work rarely appears on the market but a painting entitled "Racehorses at Morning Exercise" was sold at Sotheby's 18 May 1973 and his portrait of "John Harrison, W.H. Broadley (Master of the Holderness) and Arthur Stanley (First Whip) with hounds in an extensive landscape", s.&d. 1922, 38¾ in.x48¼ in., was auctioned Christie's (1978). Francis Elwell was reported missing at sea following the sinking of the transport vessel in which he was travelling en route for Japan on 12 September 1944.

Elwell, Robert Farrington (1874-1962)
Born in Boston, Mass. A self-taught artist, although both his parents were talented amateurs. Colonel William F. Cody, better known as "Buffalo Bill", met young Elwell in the 1890s while he was in Boston with his Wild West Show. Elwell was fascinated by the spirit of the Wild West and spent his spare time sketching the real life cowboys, Indians and their horses. "Buffalo Bill" invited him to his ranch in Wyoming where Elwell's interest was further developed. During the last

fifteen years of his life he took up sculpture and his bronze figures are noticeably influenced by the work of Frederic Remington (q.v.). Apart from horses and Indians, Elwell painted some fine fishing scenes.

Emery, James (1777-1822)
Born in Sunderland. An actor and a painter of equestrian subjects who gave his address as the Covent Garden Theatre. According to Shaw Sparrow he was "One of the first Englishmen to suggest speed at the new Gallop as distinct from the old rocking horse style". Exh. at the RA (1801-1817) including several portraits of horses. A set of watercolours of racehorses featuring Mr. Wilson's "Lurcher" (by "Dungannon"), "Johnny", "King Fergus" (a son of "Eclipse"), "Otho" (by "Moses") and Mr. Wilson's "Creeper" (by "Tandem") at Newmarket, all painted between 1808 and 1809, each 5½ in.x7in., were auctioned Sotheby's 1989. An etching of a print of the "York Highflyer" after his own work is also recorded.

Emery, W.F. (19th century)
Animal painter operating at a slightly later date than James Emery (q.v.).

Emes, John (op.1762-c.1809)
Oil and watercolour painter and a line engraver who was a pupil of W. Woollett. He collaborated with Robert Smirke (q.v.) on "The Meeting of the Society of Royal British Archers in Gwersyllt Park, Denbighshire". The print etched in aquatint by C. Apostool after this work was pub. in 1794 and is in the British Museum. Emes exh. at the RA in 1790 and 1791.

Emmerson, Henry Hetherington (1831-1895)
Northumberland landscape and figure painter who studied art at the Government School of Design in Newcastle under William Bell Scott, the Pre-Raphaelite painter. Between 1851 and 1893 Emmerson exh. fifty-four works at the RA, mainly country life subjects centred around his native Northumberland. His fine picture "The Wildfowler" was painted in 1870.

Emmerson, Percy (op. late 19th century)
"England v Scotland", s.&d. 1892, 45¼ in.x34in., collection the RFU HQ at Twickenham. This painting shows Fredrick Hodgson Rudd Alderson, who captained England on his international debut against Scotland at Raeburn Place, Edinburgh in 1891.

Emms, John (1841-1912)
This artist, like so many of the best sporting painters, was a keen and active sportsman, especially in the hunting field. The son of the artist Henry William Emms, he is said to have studied under the neo-classical painter, Frederick Leighton and as his assistant, helped to execute the "Ten Virgins" fresco at Lyndhurst parish church to which work he added the embellishment of an owl. He lived a bohemian life in London, affecting a long black cloak and a wide brimmed black hat. Through his hunting he found many clients and subjects but he was constantly short of money. Indeed at one time he and his family were virtually destitute until a kind woman lent them a house. Emms was a particularly

skilful painter of hounds many of which he exh. at SS (1867-1885). Titles include "Beagles", "Cub Hunting", "Otter Hounds", "Old Foxhounds Coupled", etc. Emms visited Clumber Park in Nottinghamshire on a number of occasions in the early 1880s where he painted several portraits of the famous Clumber spaniels belonging to the Duke and Duchess of Newcastle. His work is recognised by strong brushwork and generous applications of paint.

Emms, John Victor (b.1912)
Painter in oil and watercolour. Born at Bourdon, near Aldershot. Studied at Woolwich Polytechnic Art School (1930-1934), Hornsey School of Art (1946-1948) and at Goldsmith's College of Art (1948-1949). Exh. at the RA and in the provinces and has painted a number of fox-hunting scenes.

England, E.S. (op.1890-1910)
A prolific and mediocre painter in oils of huntsmen and hounds and country scenes, which he very often painted in pairs or multiple sets. He lived in Halifax.

Erni, Hans (b.1909)
Swiss painter and etcher of many sports who won the Olympic Prize for Art at the games held at Barcelona in 1992. His etching, an illustration from "Pindare Olympiques", was contributed to the Art Competition and subsequent exhibition held at the V & A Museum during the Olympic Games in London in 1948.

Essex, William (op.1821-1858)
This London artist painted sporting and other scenes on enamel. He was appointed "Enamel Inordinary to Her Majesty Queen Victoria and HRH Prince Albert".

Estall, William Hardman (ex.1889-1895)
This Sussex artist exh. a number of paintings at the NEAC (1889-1895) including a pastel study of a horse.

Etty, William, RA (1787-1849)
Yorkshire artist who came to London in 1805 and attended the RA Schools. Exh. at the BI and RA from 1811. Elected RA 1828. He presented his painting of a carthorse to Joseph Rickman, the owner of the horse, in return for the loan of the model for Etty's study of "Pluto carrying off Prosperene", exh. at the RA in 1839. His study "The Bowman" is in the collection of Leicester AG.

Eurich, Richard Ernest, RA, NEAC, RSMA (b.1903)
A distinguished oil painter of predominantly marine subjects and some landscapes. Born at Bradford. Studied at Bradford School of Arts and Crafts under H. Butler (1920-1924) and at the Slade School under Professor Tonks (1924-1926) His first one-man show was at the Goupil Gallery in 1929. Taught at Camberwell School of Art from 1949. Exh. NEAC from 1927. Elected member 1943. Exh. at the RA and elected RA 1953. His painting "Doncaster Races - the St. Leger", 19¾in.x 24in., was auctioned Bonhams 1985. He is represented in many public collections.

Evans, F.S. (op.1887)
An unrecorded painter of a portrait of "Tip Top", a hunter in a loose box, painted in 1887, 15in.x17in., auctioned Sotheby's (Sussex) 1989.

Evans, Frederick, McNamara (op.1886-c.1930)
London-born genre painter in watercolour whose painting "The Fencing Lesson", 24in.x48in., was exh. Priory Gallery, Cheltenham.

Evans, John A. (op.c.1910)
A painting entitled "A Day at the Races" was auctioned Sotheby's (Bearne) September 1980.

Evans, Powys Arthur Lenthall (b.1899)
Portrait and figure painter who studied at the Slade School. Exh. at the NEAC and other leading galleries. His portrait of "Major Hezlett" in plus fours with a golf club, s.&d. 1930, 13in.x9in., drawn for the "Saturday Review" in pen and black ink.

Evans, S.B. Hope (op.1877-1896)
This artist from Kenilworth exh. one picture at the BI in 1896 and two at the RBSA. A portrait of a clipped hunter was sold by Sotheby's, 1989.

Evans, Wilfred (op.1884)
Exh. a watercolour study of fish at SS in 1884.

Evans, William, RWS (1798-1877)
Landscape painter. Born and educated at Eton College, the son of Samuel Evans, the drawing master at Eton whom he followed in the same profession in 1818. Exh. at OWS (1828-1873). Painted in a similar style to that of David Cox. Painted many sporting scenes including "The Wall Game at Eton", repro. in "The Treasures of Eton" ed. by James William-McConnel. "Cricket on College Field - Eton", watercolour, 26in.x37in., collection Eton College and "Curlers on the Loch at Dunkeld", watercolour, repro. "Curling - An Illustrated History" by David Smith. A watercolour painting of "Eton Eyot", showing a gentleman fishing with a companion in a gown beside him and Eton College in the background was in the A.N. Gilbey Collection.

Everett, John (1876-1949)
A very talented but relatively little known marine painter who lived in Dorset. Artist brother of Herbert Everett who exh. one painting in 1900 at NEAC. John Everett exh. at NEAC (1908-1910). A collection of some 1,700 oil paintings and an even larger number of drawings and sketches are in the National Maritime Museum. This represents almost the entire marine output of this artist who rarely sold any of his work, having sufficient private income. He studied at the Slade School of Art and at Julians in Paris. From 1898 onwards he made numerous sea voyages, sometimes as an ordinary seaman, which gave him firsthand knowledge and experience of the sea. His work includes paintings of barges racing, yachts sailing in the Solent and "The Regatta", a painted impression exh. at the NEAC in 1910.

Evergood, Philip (1901-1973)
A founding member and President of the radical Artists' Union (American) and an active participant in the Artists' Congress in 1936. Studied in England at the Slade School of Art where he learned the meticulous drawing techniques practised at that time. Studied at the Art Student's League with George Luks (q.v.)

returning to Paris for further studies. In view of his early and thorough art training his naïve style of painting was presumably deliberately contrived. His baseball painting "Early Youth of Babe Ruth" is a narrative of the "Babe's" life in Baltimore and presents an imaginative interpretation of the American dream of success. Baseball was a game which fascinated Evergood and a subject that he frequently used in his paintings. "Come and Help Grandad", painted in 1944, 28¾in.x 39½in., is a sentimental scene showing the distance that the war put between the young and the old and the emerging importance of sport in the lives of the young.

Ewbank, P. (op.1843)
A painting by this artist of Mr. Hindley's "Rosina" with the owner up on Lincoln Racecourse with the Cathedral beyond, 23½in.x29½in., painted in 1843, was auctioned Christie's 1985. Exh. "Lincoln Comes of Age", April-October 1984.

Ewing, Leckie (op.c.1897)
Amateur but competent artist from a Scottish family who painted "The Old Stone Bridge at the 18th Hole, St. Andrews", watercolour, signed, 7½in.x11in., Sotheby's (Glasgow).

Eyre, Edward (op.1771-1798)
Very little is known about this artist except that he exh. fifteen landscapes at the RA (1771-1786). Eyre's sporting work includes "The Cricket Match" a water-colour painted c.1798, 7¾in.x10½in., auctioned Sotheby's 1970. The match represented is said to be that played between the Kingscote Club and eleven gentle-men of Oxford on 7 August 1798 for 100 gns. at the Kingscote Ground, Sussex. The former team won by six notches (scoring being recorded at this time by notches cut in a stick). Eyre's watercolour "A Sailing Match at Brighton", dated 1788 and inscr., 8½in.x14¼in. was auctioned Sotheby's 1988.

Eyre, John, RI, ARCA (Lond) (op.1877-1910 d.1927)
Staffordshire-born painter and book illustrator. Studied art at the RCA. Exh. at the RA, RI and the Paris Salon. Painted a number of fishing scenes including "The Thrill of the Catch", a watercolour dated 1908, 26in.x 40in., showing two gentlemen in Tyrolean costume, one holding the rod and the other bringing in the net containing the fish.

Eyres, Miss Emily (op.1899-1905)
Portrait painter who exh. six paintings at the RA, one of which may have been a full-length portrait of a gentleman in hunting pink, s.&d. 1900, 79½in.x35in.

F

Fabris, Pietro (op.c.1770)
Italian painter whose fine portrait c.1770 of Lord Fortrose and his friends fencing at his Italian villa is in the Scottish National Portrait Gallery, Edinburgh. Lord Fortrose, an Irish peer, spent two years in Italy practising fencing, one of his many accomplishments.

Faed, John, RSA (1819-1902)
Scottish painter specialising in genre scenes who exh. on a regular basis at the RSA. Elected a member in 1851. Exh. at the RA (1862-1880) and worked in both oil and watercolour. "An Archery Contest at Haddon Hall", s.&d. '68, was auctioned Sotheby's 1964.

Fairbairn, C. (op.c.1909)
Scottish artist of angling scenes and of fish portraits whose oil painting of a large salmon was auctioned Prudential (Manchester) 1988.

Fairbairn, Hilda M. (d.1917)
Genre and domestic painter who studied at the

Herkomer School of Art at Bushey. She exh. three works at the RA (1896-1903). "A Game of Croquet", s.&d. 1908, pastel, 10¾in.x14½in., auctioned Sotheby's (Sussex).

Fairclough, Wilfred, RWS (b.1907)
Painter and printmaker. Studied at the RCA (1931-1934) and the British School in Rome (1934-1937). Became Principal of Kingston School of Art (1962-1972). Included in this Dictionary for his RA exhibit "Henley Regatta" (1954) and "Racing Rudders, Venice" (1964). Elected RWS (1967).

Fairless, Thomas Kerr (1825-1853)
Northumberland-born landscape painter who studied for a time under Thomas Bewick's pupil Nicholson - a wood engraver at Newcastle. Exh. at the RA, BI and SS (1848-1851). Fairless's paintings have great feeling and colour for the beauties of country scenery. His sporting work includes shooting scenes and "A Sportsman and his Dog Shooting in a Valley", painted in 1840, 23½in.x 35¼in., was auctioned Sotheby's (Chester) 1988.

Fairlie, Henry (op.1874-1876)
A watercolour entitled "The Hampton Court - Staines Coach at Full Gallop", painted in 1876, was auctioned Christie's, 24 January 1964. "A Coach on an Open Road" and "A Steeplechase", a pair of watercolours painted in 1874, were auctioned at Bearnes 1986.

Fairman, Miss Frances C., SWA (1836-1923)
London painter of fish and animals, including hounds and beagles. She was a member of the SWA and exh. at the RA (1897-1899) and once at SS in 1893.

Faivre, Jules Abel (1867-1945)
French painter and poster designer, also a leading cartoonist. He was responsible for an early Automobile Club de France poster (1905) known as "Sarah Bernhardt au Volante".

Fanner, Alice (Mrs. Alice Taite) (1865-1930)
A prolific artist in oil and watercolour of river and estuary scenes who exh. at the NEAC (1897-1917). Sporting titles include "Six Metre Yachts Racing on the Crouch" and "Six Metre Yachts manoeuvering for a Start on the Crouch". Alice Fanner lived at Burnham on Crouch, Essex from 1914. She also exh. at the RA, RBA, RCA, RHA, ROI, RSA, SWA, etc.

Fare, G. (op.1870)
"Portrait of a Hound in a Landscape", painted in 1870, was auctioned Bearnes 1989.

Farington, Joseph, RA (1747-1821)
Landscape and topographical painter who included a number of river and estuary scenes amongst his work, often depicting yacht racing. "A View of Cowes" (1794) looking up the river Medina with a Trinity House Regatta in progress, a watercolour, 8½ in.x40in., is the property of the Royal Yacht Squadron, London. Nowadays Farington is probably better known for his diary which carefully recorded current gossip events. These diaries have now been pub. (Yale University Press 1979) and give a fascinating insight into the artistic world of the early 19th century. See William Hamilton, RA.

Farley, William (op.1936-1951)
Equestrian artist from Bury St. Edmunds, Suffolk, who exh. several sporting paintings at the RA (1936-1951). These include "Galloway Races at Buckingham" (1936) and "Barnet Fair" (1937). He also painted "The Water Jump at Towcester" and "The Suffolk Point to Point at Bradfield". Gouache, each 12¼ in.x17¼ in. and 11½ in.x 16½ in., auctioned Christie's 1969.

Farmer, J. (op.1796)
"A Racehorse in an extensive Landscape", s.&d. 1796, 24¼ in.x28¾ in., was auctioned Christie's (NY) 1986.

Farquharson, David, ARSA, RSW, ROI, ARA (1839-1907)
Landscape painter in watercolour whose work includes a number of shooting and fishing scenes, usually set in the Scottish Highlands. He is not the elder brother of Joseph Farquharson (q.v.). Elected ARSA (1882), RSW (1885) ROI (1904), ARA (1905).

Farquharson, Joseph, RA (1846-1935)
Scottish landscape painter, the second son of a well to do landowner in Aberdeenshire. He became 13th Laird of Finzean in 1918. Friend of the artist John Singer Sargent (q.v.). Farquharson studied art under Peter Graham RA and at the Life School at the RSA. A great countryman, Farquharson painted a number of salmon fishing scenes including "Salmon Fishing on the Dee" and other sporting paintings. These include "Highland Raider", 39¾ in.x60in., which was painted in 1900 to support an amendment to the Grouse Game Bill (moved by the artist's brother as MP for West Aberdeenshire) to enable farmers to shoot grouse in fields adjoining the moors. The painting is supposed to show the damage that grouse can do to cornfields. Elected RA (1915).

Farrow, Will (op.1919-1968)
Australian-born artist whose early art training took place in New Zealand. Farrow worked on "The Sydney Bulletin" in Melbourne and later moved to London where he settled. He contributed caricature cartoons and illustrations to most weekly and monthly magazines including "Punch" and "The Tatler". Wrote three books on cartooning as well as illustrating over sixty other books. He has contributed to most daily and evening newspapers since 1919, including comic strips for the "Daily Mail" and "Daily Sketch". A crayon and watercolour drawing "The Duke of Edinburgh on the Polo Field", 21in.x14½ in., was auctioned Bonhams 1988.

Fasanella, Ralph (b.1914)
American folk artist who painted some baseball scenes. "Night Game (Practice Time)", 40in.x50in., was painted in 1979, and shows the game of baseball played as the people's pastime.

Faulkner, Charles (op.1874-1896)
An equestrian painter who was born at Fareham, Hants. There are five paintings by him at the Witt Library, all 6½ in.x12½ in. Faulkner seems to have painted the majority of his work on small canvases although his painting of "The Colonel" by "Polestar", s.&d. 1890, 17in.x22in., is clearly a larger addition, as is his fine painting of "The 1896 Derby" showing "Persimmon" carrying the royal colours first past the post by a neck. His sporting work includes fox-hunting, racing and coach driving scenes.

Faulkner, John, RHA (op.1830-1890)
Dublin painter who exh. one work at the RA entitled "Home of the Red Deer" (1865) and one at BI entitled "The Hawking Party" (1882). He also painted a fine watercolour entitled "Rough Shooting", 30in.x52in., which was auctioned Sotheby's 1984. Collaborated on at least one painting with John Wainwright (q.v.).

Fawkes, Lionel Grimstone (Colonel) (1849-1931)
Amateur portrait painter whose work includes a number of sporting personalities of the Victorian era.

Fawsett, John (b.1939)
See also Steinberg. American photo realist painter and of some baseball art including "My Favourite Artist - Saul Steinberg" 1986. The Gladstone Collection of Baseball Art, USA.

Fearnley, Alan

Contemporary Yorkshire-born artist who paints sporting scenes including motor racing and cricket. Studied at Batley College of Art. Widely known through his many limited edn. prints. "The County Cricket Ground at Taunton", collection Somerset County Cricket Club.

Feininger, Lyonel (1871-1956)

Born in New York of German parents, Feininger studied art at the age of sixteen in Hamburg and Berlin before going on to Paris. He was a member of the Expressionist Blaue Reiter Movement. He practised as an art teacher at the Bauhaus in Dessau. He left Germany for the USA in 1937 but not before he painted "Les Velocepedistes" (figures on bicycles) in Berlin - Zeklendorf in 1910 which sold for £710,000, Sotheby's 1989.

"Felix"

Pseudonym used by the painter of cricket scenes, Nicholas Wanostrocht (q.v.).

Feller, F. (op.1884)

The artist of a sporting work entitled "The Last Eleven at Maiwand" which was engraved by Charles Tompkins in 1884, 25½in.x36½in.

Fellow(e)s, William M. (op.1823-1827)

Sporting and equestrian artist of whom surprisingly little is known considering that his output was quite prolific. His work includes a portrait of "Ratler", a dark bay hunter with a bull terrier in a stable, a painting of "A Phaeton with two Horses and a Groom", "Carlo" and "Juno" portraits of two pointers after grouse and "A figure in a top hat seated in a chair back gig before a thatched stable with a white Staffordshire Bull Terrier in the foreground". He also included paintings of terriers ratting. He is possibly one and the same artist as William Dorset Fellows (q.v.).

Fellows, William Dorset (op.1792-1824)

Draughtsman, etcher and aquatint engraver of sporting subjects after his contemporaries and his own designs. His engraving of "The Celebrated Trotting Mare" (I wish I knew which one) presumably after his own work, was pub. in 1824. He is possibly one and the same artist as William M. Fellow(e)s (q.v.).

Fenn, George (1810-1880)

A provincial painter in both oil and watercolour of sporting scenes and portraits. The son of John Fenn, he was born in Beccles, Suffolk into a well-known local family of auctioneers at Colchester - which firm he later joined. He started his career as an assistant in the studio of Edwin Cooper (q.v.). He exh. in Norwich (1833) and at the Beccles Exhibition (1839) where he was described as an animal and portrait painter. He lectured on painting to the local institute (1842). This talented man of wide and varied interests became Mayor of Beccles (1856) and advocated the drainage of the corporation marshes by steam power which proved highly successful. His sporting work includes a watercolour of "Two Men Fishing" (in the collection of the Piscatorial Society). Studies of racehorses and hunters with their groom/

trainer/jockey and "A One Horse Gig on a country road with a Groom holding another Horse and Gig", painted in 1839. Fenn exh. one painting "Hound Puppies bred by G. Freestone, Esq." at the RA in 1839. His painting "North Walsham Races" was engraved by Thos. Fairland (1804-1852).

Fenton, Samuel, RI (b.1923)

Landscape and figure painter in watercolour who has produced several interesting studies of lawn bowls, winning second prize at the Singer and Friedlander Sunday Times Painting Competition in 1989 with his "Playing Bowls" painted at St. Ann's Well Gardens, Hove. Born in London, Fenton, who is self-taught except for a short period at the Regent Street Polytechnic, London, moved to Brighton in 1948 where he has lived ever since. He has exh. regularly at the RA from 1943 and was elected RI in 1964. He was the subject of an article by Marina Vaizey in "Art Review" 1972, and was a prize winner in the Saunders Watercolour Competition in 1975 and 1981.

Fergusson, William

Watercolour, "Nedderwich Hill Golf Course", 9in.x7in., signed, auctioned Sotheby's (Chester) 1987.

Fernandez, H. (op.1902-1906)

Unrecorded equestrian artist who painted a series of racehorses in watercolour. These are winners of major races on both the flat and over jumps. They include "St. Amant" (won the Derby 1904), "Shannon Lass" (winner of the Grand National 1903), "Cherry Lass", "Trappist", "Flying Peggy", "Scotchman II", "Cherry Derry" and "Pretty Polly". The twelve little watercolours, which are all competent works, show the horses either singly or in pairs. Some are dated and all are signed.

Ferneley, Claude Lorraine (1822-1892)

Sporting and equestrian artist who was born at Melton Mowbray, Leicestershire, the son of John Ferneley, Snr. (q.v.) by his first wife Sarah. Named after his godfather, the sportsman Charles Lorraine Smith (q.v.), the famous squire of Enderby whom John Ferneley Snr. depicted in his painting "The Start of the Billesdon Coplow Run" in 1800 (sold Christie's 22.11.85). Lorraine Smith is said to have been so excited by "The Start of the Billesdon Coplow Run" that he had three versions made of the "Finish". Ferneley exh. only one picture at the RA in 1868. He became a fine watercolourist but his work in this medium is seldom seen on the market. His patrons included Lords Lonsdale and Cardigan and the Gilmore family. He lived all his life at Melton Mowbray and died a bachelor. He specialised particularly in fox-hunting scenes and horse portraiture.

Ferneley, John, Snr. (1782-1860)

Leicestershire-born sporting artist who showed great talent for painting when apprenticed as a wheelwright to his father. His work caught the attention of the Duke of Rutland who arranged for Ferneley to study under Ben Marshall (q.v.). He remained in London with Marshall for three years, this great master remaining a strong influence on his work throughout the rest of his life. Ferneley painted a portrait of Marshall with his dog and his gun, 29¼in.x24¼in., which was exh. at BSH, Sotheby's, 1984/5. Ferneley's great friend was Sir Francis Grant (q.v.) whom he met in about 1824. He painted Grant sitting on a favourite hunter which he exh. at the RA in 1850. Exh. at SS (1824-1841). Sporting titles include a "Portrait of a Greyhound", "The Kennel - Drawing Hounds for Feeding", and "Breaking Cover", portraits of the gentlemen of the Sedgefield Hunt. Ferneley had many patrons including Robert, 2nd Earl of Grosvenor, later 1st Marquis of Westminster for whom he painted a massive picture of the Cheshire Hunt which still hangs at Eaton Hall and Mr. W. Stirling Crawford who married the Duchess of Montrose - widely known in racing circles as "Old 6 Mile Bottom" as much for her place of residence as her figure - in 1876.

Ferneley, John, Jnr. (1815-1862)

Eldest son of John Ferneley Snr. (q.v.). Young Ferneley lived all his life in the north of England working in Manchester and York. His sporting paintings are sometimes confused with those of his father and indeed they probably collaborated on many pictures, but his work is coarser and less competent.

Ferneley, Sarah (Mrs. Johnson) (1812-1903)

Daughter of John Ferneley Snr. (q.v.). She married the artist Henry Johnson in 1838. Her work very seldom comes on the market but she is included in this Dictionary for her painting of "A Fox's Mask", s.&d. 1829 and inscr. "from nature, Melton Mowbray" and an unfinished painting entitled "The Game of Bowls". She appears to have worked in both oil and watercolour and was widowed in 1850 after which she went to look after her twice widowed father until he died in 1860. She then looked after her brother Claude Lorraine Ferneley (q.v.) and was with him when he died in 1892. Is said to have been very beautiful and loved riding. She exh. "A Study of Dead Pheasants" at SS in 1829 when she was seventeen years old. Her painting "A Game of Skittles" 27in.x44½in. was auctioned Sotheby's.

Ferrier, George Straton, RI, RSW, RE (1852-1912)

Scottish landscape and marine painter and an etcher who painted a number of shooting and fly fishing scenes. These include "Landing a Trout" and "Casting", 14in.x9¾in., a pair of watercolours, auctioned Christie's 1986 and "The Twelfth of August", an evocative painting suggesting the pleasures of grouse shooting. A watercolour of a red coated golfer addressing the ball was auctioned Sotheby's 1992. Elected RI (1898) and RSW (1881).

Fidler, Harry, ROI, RBA (op.1890-d.1935)

Painter of rustic and genre scenes in oil who studied art at The Herkomer School at Bushey. Exh. at the RA from 1891 including his painting "Victimised by Golf - Hark! Hark! the Dogs do Bark" (RA 1891).

Fiefield, J. (op.1874)

A hunter in a stable s.&d. 1874, 12in.x10in., was auctioned by Maple and Co. Ltd. by order of the Earl of Lonsdale at the Lowther Castle sale, 29.4.1947.

Field, Henry (1837-1901)

The son of a solicitor who was drowned in a boating accident (1871) but not before he had rendered good service to artists as legal adviser to the Old Watercolour Society. Henry Field painted a number of regatta scenes and two entitled "Henley Regatta" (1880) and (1884).

Fielder, E.H. (op. late 19th century)

This unrecorded artist produced a number of 19th century equestrian caricatures in coloured chalks. Possibly Henry Fielder (op.1872-1885).

Fielding, Newton Smith Limbird (1799-1856)

Youngest son of Nathan Theodore Fielding and brother of Copley, Theodore and Thales Fielding (q.v.). He ran the family engraving business in Paris until the Revolution of 1830 when he returned to London. His work in watercolour is of a fine quality. Examples of his sporting scenes which include a watercolour "Salmon Fishing" and other angling scenes are in the collection of the Piscatorial Society. He would also seem to be the same Fielding who exh. twelve sporting paintings in London in 1851. A print engraved after Fielding's "Eel Fishing near Maintenon", pub. by M.H. Pitman, Warwick Square on 1 October 1834 is also in the collection of the Piscatorial Society. His four cock-fighting scenes entitled "Fight", "Throat", "Recovery", and "Death" were pub. as a set of four coloured aquatints by Newton Fielding after his own work in 1853.

Fielding, Thales Henry Augustus, AOWS (1793-1837)

Brother of Newton Limbird Fielding (q.v.) who also worked in the family engraving business in Paris and shared a house whilst there with Eugène Delacroix. His sporting work includes "Landscape with Hunters" which he exh. at the BI (1817) and "An Offshore Wildfowler", watercolour, 5⅜in.x6in., is in the Paul Mellon Collection, Upperville, Va, USA.

Fildes, Sir Samuel Luke, RA (1843-1927)

Liverpool-born portrait painter and black and white illustrator. Studied at the Warrington School of Art, under J. Christmas Thompson, as a teaching pupil. Won a scholarship to the newly formed South Kensington School of Art and came to London in 1863. Studied at the RA Schools for a short time to become a book illustrator. Fildes was not a noted horseman but he is known to have hunted in Shropshire in 1894 where the Master, A.P. Heywood Lonsdale presented him with the brush. This in itself does not qualify him for inclusion in this Dictionary but his painting "Salmon Fishing in North Wales" (1868) repro. for "Once A Week", October 1868, does. Elected RA (1887). Knighted (1906).

Fillams, R. (op.1871)

A pair of hunters in loose boxes, s.&d. 1871, 17½in.x 21½in., were auctioned Christie's (Tattersalls) 1988.

Finch, Charles (op.1880)

Equestrian artist in watercolour, who painted small pictures, usually signed in mono.

Finnemore, Joseph, RBA, RBSA, RI (1860-1939)

An etcher, illustrator and painter of literary and royal family subjects. These include his portrait of "HRH The Prince of Wales Shooting at Sandringham", a painting which Finnemore exh. at the RA. Finnemore, who studied at the Birmingham Art School and at Antwerp, became special artist to "The Graphic" (1886-1910). Elected RBA (1893), RBSA (1901) and RI (1898).

Finney, Harry (op.c.1895-1905)
The painter of "The Paddock at Longchamp" - a vast panorama which hangs in the clubhouse of America's most elegant racecourse at Keenland, Kentucky. Finney's painting depicts some of the most famous European racing personalities of the time and may well have been a subscription picture.

Fischer, Johann Georg Paul (1786-1875)
This German artist is included in the Dictionary for his fine watercolour "At One with the World" which shows a young man on his horse with his dogs in a country lane, auctioned Sotheby's 1981.

Fischer, Paul (1860-1934)
Danish artist whose sporting work includes "Golf Players at Copenhagen Golf Club, Ermitage" 12in.x 14in. and "Cyclists on a Beach" 16in.x24½in., painted in 1900. He also included a number of beach and bathing scenes.

"Fish Hawk"
Pseudonym used by the wildlife and gamebird artist, Colonel David Wolfe-Murray (q.v.).

Fisher, Alvan (1792-1863)
American equestrian artist from Dedham, Mass., who painted the great racehorse "American Eclipse" in 1823, a horse also painted by Edward Troye (q.v.)

Fisher, Jonathan (d.1809)
Irish? painter and aquatint engraver of landscapes, topographical views and hunting scenes.

Fisher, Rowland, ROI, RSMA (1885-1969)
Landscape and marine artist in oil whose work includes a number of yacht racing scenes. Exh. at the RA, ROI and RSMA. Lived for fifty years at Great Yarmouth in Norfolk and was President of the Yarmouth and District Society of Artists. Son of a master mariner.

Fisher, Vernon
20th century American artist who painted "The President's Golf Lesson 2", 60in.x60in., mixed media, auctioned Sotheby's (NY) 1986.

Fisher, William (op.1938-1948)
London painter who exh. a picture entitled "The Cart Shed" at the RA in 1938. He is also possibly the same artist whose oil painting "Village Cricket" was exh. at the XIVth Olympiad Competition and Sport in Art Exhibition (No.154) London 1948 in the V & A Museum, London.

Fisk, William Henry, Jnr. (1827-1884)
London landscape painter, the son of the artist William Fisk (1796-1872). Fisk, who had been a student at the RA Schools, taught drawing and painting at University College, London and exh. landscapes at SS (1846-1862) including "A Study of Dead Grouse" and "A Scene in the Highlands of Braemar".

Fitch, Fred (op.1880-1925)
The painter of a pair of fox-hunting scenes in watercolour entitled "Setting Out" and "The Meeting Place", each 10¼in.x15in., on Whatman paper, dated 1905, J. Collins, Bideford. Fitch is also known to have painted otter hunting scenes, in watercolour and in pairs, and his "An Angler on a River Bank" was auctioned Lane (Cornwall) 1988.

Fitz, William (op.1880-1910)
London sporting artist of game and equestrian scenes. Exh. at the RA and SS (1880-1891).

Fitzgerald, Claude J. (op.1893-1912)
Painter who exh. a work entitled "The Hunt" at the RA in 1912, his only year to exhibit there.

Fitzgerald, Florence (ex.1884-1900)
Liverpool sculptor and figure and landscape painter in both oil and watercolour who exh. at SS (1884-1894). Exh. at the RA (1887-1900) and included a hunting scene amongst her work, auctioned Eldon Worrall, 1985.

Fitzgerald, Frederick R. (op.1897-1899)
Painter of coastal and marine subjects who included yachting scenes amongst his work. He exh. in Birmingham (1897).

Fitzgerald, John Anster (1819-1906)
Prints after the work by this artist were engraved by Vincent Brooks and T.W. Huffam including "The Start - Just Off" and the "Ass-tocratic Stakes", c.1846.

Fitzhenry, S. (op.1840)
London artist who exh. a study of "A Diligence" at SS in 1840.

Flanders, French (op.1856-1857)
This artist who exh. at the BI in 1857 from an address in Islington painted "A Pipe at Lunch Time", depicting a sportsman in a Highland setting with a pony and dogs.

Flatman, J. (op.1875-1884)
Equestrian artist of racehorse portraits including those of "St. Simon" (1884), "Barcaldine", "Tristan", "Isonomy" (1884) and "Galopin" (1875). The back of this painting bears an inscription "Presented to Mr. Tapper by "Sporting Life" on August 18th 1915".

Flavell, W. (op.1820)
Mitchell records a coaching scene by this artist - with matchstick-like horses.

Fletcher, Geoffrey Scowcroft (b.1923)
Landscape and portrait painter. Studied art at the Slade School, under Schwabe. Exh. at the RA and NEAC. Illus. children's books and contributed a number of club interiors to "The Sphere" (1959-1963). These include "Pratts Club, the Billiard Room", signed and inscr., grey wash pen and black ink, 14in.x2in., repro. "The Sphere" 2.11.63 and the "Interior of the London Fencing Club" s.&d. 1961, pen, black ink, 13½in.x22in., repro. "The Sphere" 4.3.61.

Fletcher, Rosamund M.B., FRBS (b.1914)
This artist won third prize in the Olympic Arts Competition, July/August 1948 with her stone relief entitled "The End of The Covert" showing pheasants after a day's shooting, relieved to be alive. Rosamund Fletcher, a sculptor in bronze and stone who won the Feodora Gleichen Award (1948), studied at the Ruskin School in Oxford (1935-1937) and at the Slade School (1937-1939). She is the daughter of the artist Blandford Fletcher and has exh. widely at the leading London galleries and elsewhere.

Fleury, H., Jnr. (op.1885-1890)
Yorkshire-based landscape painter who exh. Manchester City AG and Walker AG, Liverpool. His work includes some hunting scenes: "Before the Meet" and "After the Kill", 23½in.x35in., auctioned Christie's (Sth. Ken.) 1986. A set of four prints after the work of this artist depicting the sale of a hunter entitled "Good Points", "A Taste of His Bad Points", "More than He Bargained For" and "Dear at any Price" were auctioned Henry Spencer 1985.

Flint, Savile Lumley William (op.1874-1895)
London landscape painter who exh. at SS (1880-1888) and at the RA (1882- 1892). His shooting subject, painted in 1874, and entitled "A Rest from Shooting" was auctioned Sotheby's (Chester) 1986.

Flint, Violet
Pseudonym used by Colonel J.E. Thompson who wrote "A Golfing Idyll' (1898).

Flouest ? (op. 1789)
A small (14in.x5in.) drawing depicting the historic meeting of the Tier Etats in the Jeu de Paume at Versailles on 20 June 1789, sold for £17,800 (January 1992). The drawing in black chalk, pen, brown ink and grey wash is the only known work by this unrecorded French artist. The famous meeting known as the Tennis Court Oath saw the Tiers Etat declare itself a national assembly and the government of France. It is probably better known through the drawing by Jacques Louis David (q.v.) and it is thought likely that David based his drawing on that of Flouest.

Flower, Clement (op.1899-1914)
Hertfordshire-based portrait painter whose fine golfing picture "The Triumvirate, Driving Off" was painted in 1913. This shows the three great professional golf champions Harry Vardon, James Braid and John Henry Taylor who dominated golf from the mid-1890s, 60in.x40in. Collection of the Royal and Ancient Golf Club of St Andrews. Flower, who exh. at the RA, was himself a scratch player at Westward Ho. He was commissioned to paint the 6ft. canvas by "Golf Illustrated" and he directed an engraving of 250 artists' proofs, signed by himself in 1914.

Flowers, F.H.
A watercolour by this equestrian artist "The Horse Show" 9in.x11in. was auctioned Biddle and Webb 1987.

Floyd, Gareth (b.1940)
Illustrator, very often of sporting subjects, who studied at Lowestoft School of Art, Guildford School of Art, and Brighton School of Art. Lecturer in illustration at Leicester College of Art (1964-1967) and a regular contributor to "Cricket" magazine before its demise. Books illus. include "The Great Cup Tie" Laurence Meynell (1974), "The Goalkeeper's Revenge and Other Stories" (1976).

Focardi, Ruggero (1864-1934)
Italian figure painter. "Le Jeu de Boules", Galleria d'Arte Moderna, Florence.

Fogarty, Thomas (1873-1938)
American painter and illustrator whose pen and ink drawing of a game of baseball, "The Town Team" c.1905, 15in.x15in. is in the Marbella Gallery Inc.

Foggie, David, RSW, RSA (1878-1948)
Portrait and figure painter in oil, watercolour and pastel whose pastel portrait of "A Scottish Rugby Player" painted in the late 1930s is in the Harry Langton Football Collection. Foggie who was born in Dundee, studied art in Antwerp, Paris, Florence and Holland. He lived in Edinburgh for many years where he taught drawing at the ECA and exh. at the RA, RSA, GI and in the provinces. Elected RSW (1918) and RSA (1930).

Folkard, R.W. (op.1831-1844)
Provincial sporting painter from Suffolk who was at one time an assistant in the studio of Edwin Cooper (q.v.). Folkard painted pony, hunter and greyhound studies and usually s.&d. his work. His portrait of "Mariner", a black greyhound by "Ambiguity" out of "Mouse", s.&d. 1831, 22½in.x28in., was auctioned Sotheby's 1971.

Fonesca, John Joseph (op.1860s)
An artist, probably of Portugese extraction, who worked in Madras in the mid-19th century. His portrait of the racehorse "Grand Master" with jockey up, signed and inscr. "Madras" was painted in watercolour in 1866, 14in.x18¼in. "Grand Master" born in 1857, was out of "The Gem" by "Voltigeur" and was owned by Mr. Jaf Coulson.

Forain, Jean Louis (1852-1931)
Worked in France and England as a horse draughtsman and illustrator. Brilliant, but sometimes cruel cartoonist, who also painted in watercolour. His horse paintings are few but being a life long friend and admirer of Degas (q.v.) he could not avoid an attempt at equine portraiture. "The Woman in the Stable", a watercolour painted in about 1887, was lent by Lord Kinnaird for an exhibition at Browse and Darby and repro. in "Country Life" (22.6.78). The Virginia Museum of Fine Arts, Richmond, have Forain's fine watercolour painting "Deauville Races".

Forbes, Alexander, ARSA (1802-1839)
Scottish animal painter, particularly of dogs and of some horses. His portrait "The Hermit" a grey hunter in a landscape, painted in 1839, and presumably the same famous hunter as that ridden by Charles Davis (q.v.), was exh. at the RSA in 1839, the year of his death. Exh. sixty-five animal or sporting paintings at

the RSA (1828-1840) (posthumously) including "Portrait of a Horse" (1829), "The Favourite Springer" (1832) and "Prince Charlie", a favourite hunter (1836). Elected ARSA (1830).

Forbes, Bart John (b.1939)
Born in Altus, Ok., USA. Illustrator for such magazines as "Time". Painted American footballers including his portrait of Walter Payton (1980). Artists' dyes on illustration board.

Forbes, Elizabeth Adela (Mrs. Stanhope) ARWS, RE (1859-1912)
Born in Canada, née Armstrong. Came to England and exh. at the RA from 1883. Married Stanhope Forbes in Newlyn (1889) and co-founded (with him) the Newlyn Art School in 1899. She painted a portrait of her son, Alec, holding a tennis racket in about 1910 which she entitled "Alec in Whites", watercolour, 18in.x12½in. Exh. Arthur Ackermann & Son Ltd. April 1989.

Forbes, Vivienne, IS (1891-1937)
London portrait painter of historical and figure subjects in oil. Studied art at the Chelsea Polytechnic, under Glyn Philpot, and in Paris. Exh. at the RA from 1920. Elected IS (1925). Held first one-man show in Chicago (1921). Her boxing painting entitled "Third Round, New York" painted in 1929, 11in.x14½in., was auctioned Sotheby's 1986.

Ford, Ernest L. (op.c.1909-1929)
Motor racing artist, in black and white, who worked for "Motor" before the 1st World War. Became free lance after leaving the magazine's publishers, Temple Press, and opened a studio of his own from where he covered the RAC Tourist Trophy Races for "The Car" magazine, founded by John, Lord Montague of Beaulieu. Ford's painting of "Bluebird" with Donald Campbell and passenger (thought to be Villiers) painted in 1929, watercolour and gouache, 9½in.x14¾in., was auctioned Sotheby's (Sussex) 1989. In 1914, Ford joined the Royal Naval Air Service as a pilot on the outbreak of the 1st World War and continued to produce sketches for the Admiralty until a serious crash, which ultimately prevented him from returning to motoring art, put him into hospital.

Forder, E. (op.1864)
A painting entitled "A Full Coach and Four", s.&d. 1864, 16in.x27in., was auctioned Sotheby's (Chester) 1987.

Forel, Eugène François (op.1886)
French artist whose painting of wrestlers, "Lutteurs de Foire" is dated 1886, 31¾in.x39¾in.

Fores, S.W. (op.1770-1840)
Publisher and print seller of caricatures and sporting subjects who founded the firm of Fores in 1783.

Forrest, J. Haughton (Capt.) (1825-1925)
Marine artist whose yachting pictures were purchased by King Edward VII when he was Prince of Wales. Forrest included a number of yacht racing scenes amongst his work but emigrated to Australia and devoted the last years of his life to painting, where his pictures are now highly appreciated.

Forrest, William S. (op.1840-1866)
London painter, mezzotint engraver and lithographer of sporting subjects, after his own and his contemporaries' work. Exh. at SS (1840-1866) portraits of hounds and horses. His lithograph of the racehorse "Gay Lass", ridden by Tom Hills, is presumably after his own work.

Forrester, Alfred Henry
See his pseudonym, Alfred Crowquill.

Forrestier, Amedee (1854-1930)
Belgian-born special artist and illustrator of some sporting scenes who came to London in 1882 to work for "The Illustrated London News". His drawing (1905) of Mary, Queen of Scots playing golf at St. Andrews in 1563 underlines the Edwardian fashion for portraying subjects in historical costume and supports the popularly held tradition that the Queen was an enthusiastic golfer. Forrestier also contributed work to "The Sporting and Dramatic News" in 1899.

Forsberg, Nils (1842-1934)
Swedish figure painter whose genre painting of a particularly revolting little girl holding a battledore entitled "In the Garden", s.&d. 1884, 18in.x14½in. and inscr. "Paris" was auctioned Christie's (London).

Forster, Neil Andrew (b.1939)
Born in India. Won scholarship to the Byam Shaw School of Art and studied art in Segovia, Spain. Exh. at the RA since 1960 and includes equestrian paintings amongst his work.

Forster, Percy, HRSA (op.1828-1858)
Scottish painter of game subjects who lived at Alnwick. Is said to have been the son of a former gamekeeper to the Duke of Northumberland. Forster was elected an Honorary Member of the RSA in 1828 (proposed by the Scottish engraver William Lizars (q.v.)) and exhibited ten paintings there (1828-1831) including "A portrait of an Ox, the property of Adam Boyne, Esq. of Linplum" (1831). "The Leading Hound" was exh. at the RA in 1845, his only exhibit there, and "Minnow Fishing on the Tweed" was exh. at the BI.

Foster, Arthur W. (op.1870s)
Equestrian painter of several fox-hunting scenes in Leicestershire.

Foster, Bell
A watercolour of "Spectators Watching a Cricket Match", 8¾in.x11¾in., was auctioned Phillips, Pilkington Collection 1989.

Foster, Deryck, RSMA (b.1924)
Marine painter in oil. Studied at the Southern School of Art, Bournemouth (1939-1942) and at the Central School of Art (1946-1947). His paintings include a number of yacht racing scenes.

Foster, Myles Birket, RWS (1825-1899)
Distinguished watercolourist, illustrator and wood engraver. Apprenticed to the wood engraver E. Landells, he began his career as a wood engraver of blocks for "The Illustrated London News". He started his own print business in 1846 but from 1859 he concentrated

on painting, often working in collaboration with Lowes Dickinson (q.v.) on large subscription pictures for the publishing company that they formed together. He covered a number of sporting subjects and painted several particularly fine watercolours of fox-hunting and hounds and some fly fishing scenes. His ice skating drawing entitled "January - Recreations on the Ice" pencil and grey wash was engraved for "The Illustrated London Almanac", London Recreations (1853). A tiny watercolour of a "Landscape with a Cricket Match in Progress", 3⅛in.x5½in., was auctioned Sotheby's, 5 April 1973. The batsman has just played a square cut and the ball is shown in mid-air, travelling towards the viewer. Doncaster Museum and AG have "Tattersall's Sale at Doncaster" by Lowes Dickinson (q.v.) and Birket Foster in their collection. Birket Foster, whose great travelling companions on the continent were the artists W.Q. Orchardson (1832-1910) and "Fred" Walker (q.v.), was elected RWS in 1862.

Foster (Forster), Paul (op.1840-1858)
Berwickshire sporting painter who exh. one painting at the RA "The Leading Hound standing over a Dead Fox", signed with inits. and dated 1845 (No. 45).

Foster, Walter H.W. (op.1861-1888)
Landscape painter, particularly of river scenes. Included in this Dictionary for his collaboration with J.S. Noble (q.v.) on their painting "Otter Hunting on the Lowther - Westmoreland" which was exh. at SS in 1873. Foster painted the landscape and Noble the hounds. Foster painted a further canvas "Otter Hunting on the River Lowther" which he exh. at the RA in 1886 (No. 343). He also collaborated with Noble on "Partridge Shooting" 16in.x26in. and on "Wild Duck Shooting" painted in 1886. Exh. at the RA from 1861 and at SS.

Fothergill, George Algernon, MB (1868-1945)
A multi-talented man who was both painter and illustrator of very many sporting sketches, a potter, an author and a doctor. Educated at Uppingham School and Edinburgh University he studied medicine at the Royal College of Surgeons in Edinburgh. Fothergill became the resident clinical assistant in a lunatic asylum until 1901 when he ceased to practise medicine, turning more and more to art and writing. His literary work includes "A Riding Retrospect" (1895), "An Old Raby Hunt Album" (1899), "Notes from a Diary of a Doctor, Sketch Artist and Sportsman" (1901) and "A North Country Album" (1902). Fothergill contributed amusing hunting sketches to Messrs. Fores (1905) entitled "Hunting Types". His patrons included Edward VII, the German Emperor, the Duke of Leeds, the Marquis of Zetland and the Earls of Lonsdale and Rosebery.

Fotheringham, J.F. (op.c.1860)
A set of seven coloured lithographs entitled "Pig Sticking", each 7in.x15½in., by and after this artist were printed by T. Moody c.1860 and exh. by the Parker Gallery for their bicentenary in 1950.

"Fougasse"
The pseudonym used by Kenneth Bird (q.v.), the pen and ink draughtsman and humorist who worked for "Punch". He received severe injuries as a member of the 52nd Division in 1915 at Gallipoli and lived as a semi-invalid in Scotland. Produced "A Gallery of Games" pub. Methuen in 1922. "Fougasse" means literally a "caprice" or "little mime".

Fowler, William (op.1825-1867)
London artist who exh. a number of game paintings at SS (1826-1837). Every sort of game was depicted - hare, pheasants, fish, dead game, and French partridge. Between 1837 and 1857 Fowler confined himself to painting landscapes.

Fowles, Arthur Wellington (c.1850 -aft.1878)
Marine painter from Ryde, Isle of Wight who produced several pictures of fine quality. His many yacht racing scenes include "Foxhound" owned by the 3rd Marquis of Ailsa winning the Queen's Cup off the Royal Yacht Squadron, Cowes (1871), 15½in.x23½in. (Collection The Royal Ocean Racing Club), and the schooner yacht "Cambria" racing off Ryde (1868), 2ft.x3ft.4in.

Fox, Buscall (op.1866-1883)
Equestrian artist from Freckenham, Suffolk, who painted a number of horse and dog portraits. His portrait "A Grey Mare and a Dog in a Stable", s.&d. 1868, 30in.x24in., is particularly attractive, Bonhams 1985.

Fox, Edwin May (op.1830-1870)
Listed in the Birmingham Directory 1845-1870 as an animal painter. His work includes portraits of ponies, hunters, mares and foals, racehorses and greyhounds. His portrait of "A Chestnut Racehorse in a Stable", s.&d. 1866, 24in.x29in., is inscr. "Birmingham", which I take to mean the city, not the horse, since "Birmingham", who won the St. Leger in 1830, was not a chestnut. Fox's attribution of "Tamworth", the inscription given to the portrait of another chestnut racehorse in a loosebox, s.&d. 1833, 28in.x36in., must also refer to the town, since Tamworth is only seventeen miles from Birmingham.

Fox, George (ex.1873-1889)
London figure painter and of some sporting subjects, who exh. at SS (1873-1889). Very apt to cliché his titles, "Coming to the Point", "Hungry as Hunters", "Between Stages" etc. Included in this Dictionary for his paintings entitled "The Winner of the Stakes", 7¾in.x5⅝in., and "Cleaned Out", 8¼in.x8⅝in. Most of his work was painted in a very genre style.

Fox, Henry Charles, RBA (b.1860, op.1879-1928)
London landscape painter in watercolour or gouache who painted a few fox-hunting scenes including "A Huntsman with his Pack" (1927), 10in.x14in. and "After the Hunt" watercolour, s.&d. 1909, 14¾in.x 21¾in., Sotheby's (Chester) 1989. He exh. landscapes at the RA, SS and NWS (1880-1913) and used white heightening quite heavily. Elected RBA (1890).

Fox, Lilla (op.1953)
Contemporary painter whose contribution to sporting art lies in her "Boys Playing Football", drawing, 25in.x17½in. Exh. at the FE in 1953.

Fraiture, Joseph (op.1924-1935)
The artist of a number of pigeon racing scenes, probably French.

Francis, Catharine (op.1842-1857)
A charming pencil and watercolour portrait, "A Young Cricketer at Hampstead", signed, inscr. and dated 1842, 16¼in.x10½in., was auctioned Christie's 1989. Also "Foxhounds in Full Cry", s.&d. 1857, 10in.x18in., Christie's 1991.

Francis, Mike (b.1938)
Contemporary artist and illustrator. Paints a variety of sporting subjects with imagination and flair. Illus. The Lord's Taverners "Fifty Greatest Golfers" with a foreword by HRH The Prince Philip, Duke of Edinburgh. Held first solo exhibition at the Furneaux Gallery, London in 1964.

Francis, W. (op.1822-1824)
This artist exh. two paintings of horses at the BI in 1822 and 1824.

Frankland (Frankland-Russell), Sir Robert (Bt.) (1784-1849)
Amateur painter and etcher of sporting subjects although his work was most competent and often superior to many of his professional contemporaries. Frankland became MP for Thirsk (1815-1834), High Sheriff of Yorkshire (1838) and became Sir Robert Frankland-Russell in 1837. Most of Frankland's work was painted early in his life and later on his art suffered somewhat as his life became dedicated to public work and duties. He used the pseudonym "Amicus RF" (q.v.) on a print of the racehorse "Rosette" pub. by T. Masham, D. Bedale, Yorks. (1811). His "Sketches of Deer Stalking in the Highlands" were engraved in ten plates by himself and pub. in 1839. Frankland's watercolour "The Earl of Darlington's Foxhounds" (The Raby Pack) with hunt servants, 8½in.x11⅞in., is in the Paul Mellon Collection, Upperville, Va, USA. William Harry Vane (1766-1842) 3rd Earl of Darlington (later 1st Duke of Cleveland) was a noted sportsman. Residing at Raby Castle, Co. Durham, he was Master of the Raby Pack (Durham and Yorkshire) extolled by "Nimrod". Darlington with the Raby pack was also painted by J.N. Sartorius (q.v.).

Fraser, Alexander, RSA (1828-1899)
Scottish landscape painter, son of Alexander George Fraser (q.v.). Studied at the Trustees Academy. Exh. at the RA (1869-1885) and at the RSA. Elected RSA (1862). Fraser, a follower of plein air painting, painted several studies of game but his work deteriorated as he became progressively incapacitated by rheumatism.

Fraser, Alexander George, Snr., ARSA (1786-1865)
Scottish still life and game painter who included a few sporting studies of sportsmen and anglers. Fraser was born in Edinburgh and studied art at the Trustees Academy where David Wilkie (q.v.) was a fellow student. In 1813 Fraser moved to London where Wilkie employed him as an assistant, only passing him commissions for which he had no time or interest. As a result, Fraser evolved a life as a shadow of Wilkie and lacked the progressive individuality achieved by his son Alexander Fraser, Jnr. (q.v.). Elected ARSA (1840).

Fraser, Arthur Anderson (1861-1904)
The sixth of seven sons born to Dr. Robert Fraser, six of whom became artists. This landscape painter in watercolour who often featured fishing subjects amongst his work painted in a similar style to his elder brother, Francis (q.v.), but often signed his work Arthur Anderson to avoid confusion. He exh. small landscapes at SS and at the New Water Colour Society but otherwise lived quietly at Holywell, promoting the Jacobite cause of which the members of his family were ardent followers.

Fraser, Eric George (b.1902)
Artist, lithographer and illustrator who drew his impression of "Derby Day" (1926), in pen/ink. Repro. "The Derby" by Michael Wynn Jones, pub. 1979. Fraser studied at Goldsmith's College of Art on a scholarship (1919) and taught lithography there (1923-1924). He is perhaps best known as a graphic artist and has illus. books for many publishers including the Golden Cockerel Press and the Folio Society.

Fraser, Francis Arthur Anderson (1846-1924)
Figure painter and illustrator. The eldest son of Dr. Robert Winchester Fraser and brother of the artists George Gordon (q.v.), Garden William (q.v.), Arthur Anderson (q.v.), Robert Winchester and Gilbert Baird Fraser. Fraser was an excellent draughtsman and a sporadic contributor to both the RA and RBA. His subjects were of country pursuits and his drawings of horsemen and animals, in one predicament or another, must have been based on close observation at first hand. His work is little known, appearing usually with the monogram "FAF" but his paintings and watercolours deserve better recognition for their good draughtsmanship with soft effects.

Fraser, Garden William (1856-1921)
See Garden

Fraser, George Gordon (1859-1895)
Landscape and figure painter, the fifth of the seven sons of Dr. Robert Winchester Fraser, an army surgeon. George Fraser was educated at the Bedford Schools, to which town the family appears to have moved in 1861, where it seems likely that he was taught to draw by Bradford Rudge, a frequent exhibitor in London. Rudge taught art at the Schools (1839-1874), taking private pupils until his death in 1885. George Fraser painted less in watercolour than his brothers but his landscapes were usually enlivened by people and animals. His skill as a draughtsman led to commissions from the currently fashionable magazines and periodicals of the time such as "Strand", "Judy", "Fun" and "The Saturday Journal".

Fraser, H. (op.1886)
"The Polo Players", pastel, s.&d. '86, 20in.x26in. Phillips (Exeter).

Frederick, William (op.c.1810-1825)
Sporting and animal painter, a close friend of Charles Henry Schwanfelder (q.v.) and an exhibitor at the Northern Society for the Encouragement of the Arts, Leeds.

Freelove, William Francis (1846-1920)
This artist is recorded (Mitchell) as the painter of horses and carriages. Many of his vehicle sketches were pub. in "An Assemblage of 19th Century Horses and Carriages" by Perpetua Press (1971).

Freeman, F.C. (op.1855-1861)
A portrait by this artist of "A Gentleman (said to be Thomas Beal), with a Chestnut Mare and Foal in a Landscape", s.&d. 1861, 25in.x30in., was auctioned Christie's 1980.

Freeman, James (1828-1858)
Equestrian artist whose work includes several portraits of horses and dogs, usually signed but rarely dated. His portrait of "Chieftain" a saddled bay hunter and a pointer in a stall, s.&d. 1858, was auctioned Christie's 1972.

Freeman, James Edward (1808-1884)
A portrait of "A Boy with two Ponies and two King Charles Spaniels in a Landscape", s.&d. and inscr. "Fulford" exh. Ackermanns Gallery (1964).

Freeth, Hubert Andrew, RA, PRWS, RP, RE, RBA (1912-1986)
Birmingham-born portrait painter and an etcher. Studied at Birmingham College of Art and the British School at Rome (1936-1939) where he won a scholarship for engraving (1936). Exh. at the RA (from 1936), RE, RP, RBA and RWS. Elected RE (1946), RP (1949), RWS (1955) and RA (1965). His painting "Watford Football Club Dressing Room", 36in.x28in., was exh. at the FE.

Fremond, C.R. (op.1920s)
French painter of trotting races. His painting of sulky racing "A Cracking Pace" was auctioned Bonhams 1986.

French, E.C. (op.1935)
Unrecorded artist whose watercolour "The Hunt", s.&d. '35, 10¾in.x14½in., was auctioned Phillips 1988.

French, Frederick (op.1868-1914)
Sporting artist from Leamington whose work includes a number of portraits of hunters in stables and of foxhounds.

French, P.C. (op.1885)
Exh. one watercolour "Field Sports" at SS in 1885 from a Dublin address. This painting must have been quite highly thought of since it was priced at £42, a high price for a watercolour at that time, compared to the prices of oils at £8-£10.

Frenzeny, Paul (1840-1902)
American artist and illustrator who worked for "The Illustrated London News" (from 1887), acting as special artist in the Spanish American War (1898). A set of four steeplechasing paintings entitled "In the Saddling Enclosure", "Over the Sticks", "Over the Water" and "Leading in the Winner", 15in.x9in., were auctioned Christie's (NY) 1983.

Freyburg, Frank P. (b.1862, op.1893-1903)
Sussex painter of country and fox-hunting scenes, who exh. at the RA (from 1893). Titles include "Jogging Home". Freyburg painted a hunting scene with Ernest Pile Bucknall (q.v.) which was sold for £8,000 at Phillips in 1986, signed by both artists and dated 1898 and entitled "A Refuge in Distress". His painting (1903) of huntsmen and hounds in a moorland landscape "A Check" was auctioned Phillips 1986.

Fried, Pal
20th century Hungarian artist of horseracing scenes.

Friedman, Arnold (1879-1946)
American painter of a baseball game entitled "World Series", 20¼in.x24⅛in. The Phillips Collection, Washington DC. Friedman was a pupil of the Art Students League of New York under Robert Henri.

Friend, Donald Stuart Leslie (b.1914)
Australian topographical and figure artist whose watercolour, pen and ink study "African Boxers", s.&d. '39, 13¾in.x17½in., was sold Christie's (Sth. Ken.) 1986.

Fripp, George Arthur, RWS (1813-1896)
Landscape artist who included a number of estuary and fly fishing scenes amongst his work. A grandson of the marine artist Nicholas Pocock. Exh. RWS from 1841. Elected member in 1845 and served as Secretary (1848-1854). Also exh. at the RA in 1838, 1843, 1844 and 1848.

Fripp, Innes (op.1893-1904)
London artist of genre subjects who painted "The Fishing Party" (1903), 20in.x24in. and "The Golfers" 11in.x9in.

Frith, William Powell, RA, CVO (1819-1909)
Distinguished Yorkshire-born painter of Victorian life. Studied at Sass's Academy and at the RA Schools. Best known perhaps for his "Derby Day" painted between 1856 and 1858, 40in.x88in., although he was helped considerably with the horses by J.F. Herring (q.v.). The painting is now in the collection of the Tate Gallery, London. Frith also painted "The Fair Toxopholites" (1872). The girls depicted in the picture are his three daughters, Alice, Fanny and Louise (Royal Albert Memorial Museum, Queen Street, Exeter). Frith collaborated quite frequently with Richard Ansdell (q.v.) and incidentally painted a portrait of Ansdell's wife. Their painting of a lady with her two spaniels feeding deer outside a house, with park land beyond, was signed by both artists and dated 1860, 35½in.x 27in. This team effort must have been successful for they collaborated again to paint "The Gossips", a man on a grey pony, a game keeper with four game dogs licking up milk from a spilt pail, auctioned Christie's 1982. Frith exh. at the RA from 1840. Sporting works exh. there include "English Archers" (1873) and "Ascot" (1878). He was elected RA 1853 and created a CVO in 1908 in recognition of his long connection with the royal family as a painter of ceremonial events.

Frobisher, Miss Lucy Margaret, R.Cam.A, PS, SWA (op.1915-1937)
Animal and equestrian painter who studied under Lucy Kemp Welch (q.v.) and worked in a very similar style. Exh. at the RA, RSA, RI, ROI, PS, in the provinces

and at the Paris Salon. Elected R.Cam.A. 1937. Head of the Frobisher School of Painting at Bushey, Herts. for many years.

Frohawk, Frederick William (1861-1946)
Norfolk-born animal painter in oil and watercolour, a lithographer and an illustrator. Contributor to the natural history columns of "The Field" from the 1890s onwards and especially prolific during the 1920s. His book "British Birds", pub. posthumously by Ward Lock in 1951, was a fitting memorial to this talented wildlife artist. His work includes studies of merlin and various hawks including falcons.

Frost, Patricia A. (b.1946)
Somerset equestrian artist and illustrator who studied at the West of England College of Art where she took a BA degree. Specialises in paintings of international dressage and show jumping.

Frost, Terry L.G. (b.1915)
Warwickshire-born painter, in both oil and water-colour, who studied art at the Leonard Fuller School of Painting, St. Ives (1946) and at the Camberwell School of Art (1947-1950) under Victor Passmore. An early admirer of the Euston Road Group, Frost turned increasingly to abstract painting. Held his first one-man show at the Leicester Galleries in 1952 and painted his interpretation of a football match, imaginatively entitled "Half Time Lemon Suckers", gouache, signed, 8½in.x 15in., which was exh. at the FE.

Fry, Joseph, Jnr. (op.1828)
Painter of "The Last Red Deer in Epping Forest taken in the garden at Upton 1828 - hunted by Mr. Rounding". The painting was exh. at Norwich in 1950, from the collection of Captain Evelyn Barclay.

Fry, R. Douglas (1872-1911)
Sporting, equestrian and animal painter in oils. Born in Ipswich, Suffolk. Studied art in London and at the Académie Julian in Paris. Became an illustrator for "The Sporting and Dramatic News". His watercolours of the foxhounds "Chisel", "Helpmate", "Smoker" and "Mischief" with "Litchfield", a hunter, were painted in 1894 and inscr., 10¾in.x16in. and auctioned Sotheby's 1985. In 1899 Fry emigrated to Australia where his work is represented in the Sydney Art Gallery. He became an illustrator for the "Sydney Mail" and became friends with Martin Stainforth (q.v.) who greatly encouraged his art career in Australia.

Fry, Roger Eliot, NEAC, LG (1866-1934)
Landscape painter and influential art critic. Studied art at Julians (Paris) and in Italy. Founded the Omega Workshops. Elected NEAC 1893. Member of LG 1918. His painting "A Game of Lawn Bowls" is in Preston H.M. and A.G.

Fryer, Wilfred Moody, RI, SMA (b.1891)
Landscape and marine painter whose "The Barbarians Tour" painted c.1954 qualifies him for inclusion in this Dictionary. Fryer, who studied at Bradford School of Art, exh. at the RA (1922-1930). He was Chairman of

the Langham Sketch Club, President of the Wapping Group and a member of the Croydon Art Society.

Fryer, William (op.c.1850)
"Ten Favourite Hounds, the property of Charles Slingsby, Esq." in which the huntsman is holding up a hare whilst the harriers and riders are galloping across country in the distance, was exh. by Oscar and Peter Johnson in 1969.

Fuchs, Bernard (Bernie) (b.1933)
Born in O'Fallon, Ill., U.S.A. American illustrator for "Sports Illustrated", "Redbook" and others. Artist of the year (1962). Youngest member of the Society of Illustrators, Hall of Fame. Studied at the School of Fine Art at Washington and specialises in sports scenes including golf, horse racing and American football.

Fuller, Edmund G., RBA, RWA (op.1888-1930)
Landscape painter and golf enthusiast who lived for many years in St. Ives, Cornwall. Exh. at the RA (1894-1904). His golfing sketches "The First Drive" and "Entitled to See the Ball" were auctioned Christie's Sth. Ken. A lithograph after the work by this artist of a humorous scene of "Roller Skaters in a Dance Hall" dated 1894, 8¼in.x14in., was auctioned W.H. Lane 1989. Elected RBA (1895).

Fuller, J.T. (op.1866)
"Deer Stalking in the Highlands", s.&d. 1866, was auctioned Sotheby's 1966.

Fuller, Leonard John, ROI, R.Cam.A. (1891-1973)
Portrait, figure and still-life painter who studied at the Clapham School of Art and the RA Schools. National Silver and Bronze Medallist (1912/13). BI scholarship in painting (1913). Art teacher St. John's Wood (1922-1932). Assistant art teacher at Dulwich College (1926-1938). Principal of St. Ives School of Painting (1938). Elected ROI (1933). Elected R.Cam.A. (1939). His painting of "Miss Diana Fishwick, the Lady Golf Champion" (1930), 36in.x28in., was sold Sotheby's (Chester) 1988.

Fulton, David, RSW (1848-1930)
Landscape painter of many fly fishing scenes. Born, worked and died in Glasgow and studied at the Glasgow School of Art. Exh. only once at the RA in 1884. "The Young Angler", s.&d. 1877, 16in.x24in., was auctioned Sotheby's 1980. Elected RSW 1891.

Fulton, Samuel, (1855-1941)
Scottish animal painter, chiefly of dogs. Brother of the landscape artist David Fulton (q.v.). Exh. in Glasgow and Edinburgh and is represented in Glasgow AG by his painting entitled "Foxhounds".

Furness, Robin (Sir Stephen Furness, Bt., MFH) (b.1933)
Talented equestrian artist of hunting and racing scenes, painted in both oils and gouache, who studied part-time at Goldsmith's and Carlisle Art Colleges. Became joint Master of the Bedale Foxhounds in 1979.

Furniss, Harry (1854-1925)
Irish-born talented black and white artist, caricaturist

and author. Studied at the RHA Schools, Dublin and settled in London (1873). Contributed work including sporting subjects for many years to "The Illustrated London News", "The Graphic", "Punch", "The Illustrated Sporting and Dramatic News" and to other magazines. Exh. at the RA from 1925 and FAS from 1894. Included in this Dictionary for the one hundred sketches he made of the cricketer W.G. Grace to mark his centenary which were formed into a small book in 1896 called "How's That". His work also covered hockey, rowing and golf scenes.

Furse, Charles Wellington, ARA, NEAC, IS (1868-1904)
Portrait painter, very often of sporting personalities in sporting scenes, and some animal portraiture. Born in Middlesex, the brother of J.H.M. Furse (q.v.). Studied art at the Slade School, under Legros, and in Paris at the Académie Julian and at the Westminster School of Art, under Professor Fred Brown (q.v.). Exh. at the London galleries from 1888 and was elected NEAC (1892) and ARA (1904). Founder member of the International Society (1898). Exh. at the RA (from 1888) including his portrait of "John Lawrence, Esq. Master of the Llangibby Foxhounds Monmouthshire", (1897). Furse's last painting, exh. posthumously at the RA in 1905, was of the children of the Master of the York and Ainsty, Lycett Green Esq., "Out Cub Hunting". His portrait of Mr. and Mrs. F.S. Oliver, "Angling in Norway" was painted in 1903 although an earlier portrait of Mrs. Oliver fishing solo in Norway is thought to be a preliminary work for the larger painting.

Furse, John Henry Monsell (1860?-1950)
Animal painter and sculptor and brother of Charles Wellington Furse (q.v.). Studied at the Herkomer School at Bushey and the Slade School. Exh. at the RA, Glasgow Institute, Walker AG and Manchester AG (1892-1907) and between 1881 and 1887 he worked at the British Museum. Furse was born a cripple in both legs and had frequent mental breakdowns. Despite this, he overcame his physical handicap and learnt to ride.

"Fusbos"
The pen name used sometimes by the sporting illustrator George Finch Mason (q.v.).

G

"GDG"
Alias George Denholm Armour (q.v.) the sporting artist who produced four cartoons for "Vanity Fair" under this mono.

"GG"
Pseudonym used by H. G. Harper (q.v.), the sporting journalist and artist.

Gaadt, George (b.1941)
Illustrator for advertisements, editorial and children's books born in Eire, Pa., U.S.A. Painted several American football scenes including: "New England Patriots 1979" and "Super Bowl XII" (Game Programme illustration) 1978, both mixed media on illustration board

Gabriel, C. Wallis (op.1882-1894)
Two portraits of racehorses in stables are recorded by Mitchell. Gabriel, who came from Weston, Bath, exh. one painting at the RA in 1882 and one at Manchester in 1885.

Gael, Barent (1620-1703)
Dutch painter of several deer hunting scenes.

"Gaf"
A watercolour entitled "At Ascot", s.&d. 1919 and inscr. and another of a similar racing scene, 19¾in.x 8¼in., were auctioned Phillips 1986.

Gainsborough, Thomas, RA (1727-1788)
Society portrait and landscape painter, often of sporting scenes, and a great rival of Sir Joshua Reynolds (q.v.). Studied art at the St. Martin's Lane Academy, under Hubert Gravelot (q.v.) and later under Francis Hayman (q.v.) who almost certainly influenced him towards an enthusiasm for cricket. He was, therefore, the inevitable choice to paint the portrait of the 3rd Duke of Dorset (1745-1799), the exceptionally keen cricketer and founder member of the MCC. The portrait, 30in.x25in. was painted in 1782 and engraved by J. Scott. Gainsborough, who settled in London in 1774 and was patronised by King George III and Queen Charlotte, also painted the portrait of Colonel St. Leger with his horse which was engraved in 1783 by Gainsborough Dupont (1767-1797), the mezzotint engraver, and the artist's nephew and pupil. Gainsborough's painting of "Partridge Shooting near Sudbury" with Mr. William Humphrey

and a companion drawing a field of corn at the edge of a copse, 32½ in.x44½ in. was auctioned Sotheby's 1966. Mr. Humphrey was Mayor of Sudbury six times between 1722 and 1787. The painting was in the Hutchinson Collection until 20 July 1951.

Gale, Benjamin (1741-1832)
A Hull portrait and landscape painter who only painted cattle to advertise the products of the local breeder improvers, thereby heavily endowing his subjects with fat. Born in Yorkshire, he was a drawing master by profession and he also painted marine subjects. In 1800 he became a friend of J.C. Ibbetson (q.v.) and became resident drawing master in 1803 to the Nettlethorpe family at Scawby Hall, Lincolnshire.

Gall, François (1912-1945)
French artist of several equestrian scenes, particularly racing.

Gallindo, R.E. (op.1881)
This artist painted "An Inter-Regimental Polo Match at Rawalpindi" in 1881.

Gallon, Robert Samuel Ennis (op.1830-1868)
London portrait painter and lithographer whose portrait of "Old Alick" (Alick Brotherton, 1756-1840), the holemaker to the Royal Blackheath Golf Club, painted c.1835, 25½ in.x19¾ in., is in the collection of the Royal Blackheath Golf Club London. Gallon exh. at the RA (1830-1868).

Galloway, Madge (op.1896-1898)
Cheshire artist of some sporting scenes including "Over the Fence" and "Across the Fields", a pair of hunting scenes, 13½ in.x20½ in., Phillips (Midlands) 1988.

Galsworthy, Gordon C. (op.1893-1912)
Exh. two works at SS in 1893 including "Boys Fishing" and exh. at the RA from 1899. His portrait of a chestnut horse grazing at sunset, painted in 1897, was auctioned Sotheby's 1977.

Galsworthy, Jocelyn (b.1942)
Portrait painter whose passion for cricket has encouraged her to paint the game. Galsworthy studied at Winchester Art School and with Peter Loew in Munich. Later she received tuition from Kenneth Green, RBA, RP, in London and with Professor Jean Lefeyre in Paris. Her successful paintings of cricket matches, which she usually paints in pastel, are in many private collections.

Gambado, Geoffrey
Pseudonym used by the English romantic and sporting painter, Henry Bunbury (q.v.).

Gamley, Andrew Archer, RSW (1869-1949)
Scottish landscape painter who studied at the ECA and gained the Carnegie Travelling Scholarship. Lived in Edinburgh in 1896 and exh. at the RSA, RSW and other major exhibitions. His watercolour of the golf course "Muirfield", 5¾ in.x8in., was auctioned Sotheby's (Glasgow). Elected RSW (1924).

Gandy, Walton (op.1893)
Exh. a watercolour view of the golf links at Littlehampton, Sussex, at SS in 1893 from a London address.

Garbutt, Joseph ("Putty") (op.1870-1900)
A glazier by trade, hence the nickname, and a painter of most subjects including equestrian scenes. His painting of a stable interior with lads rubbing down horses, s.&d. 1848 and inscribed "Halifax", 23¾ in.x 29½ in., was auctioned Bonhams 1981. Garbutt lived at South Shields, Co. Durham, and his work is represented in South Shields Museum.

Garden, William Fraser (1856-1921)
This landscape painter, largely in watercolours, was born William Garden Fraser. He was the fourth son of the seven sons born to Dr. Robert Winchester Fraser, a surgeon with the army who retired on half pay in 1856, returning with his family to his native Scotland to settle in Edinburgh. Six of the seven sons became artists so William Garden reversed his name to avoid confusion with his brothers and to retain some original identity. Like his brothers he was educated at the Bedford Schools to which town the family appear to have moved in 1861 and where he came under the influence of Bradford Rudge. Like his brothers, W.G. was obsessed by the River Ouse which flows from Bedford to St. Ives and which he painted in all its moods. He exh. regularly at the RA signing his work W.F. Garden. His fine watercolour "Shooting in the Snow" painted in 1888, 7½ in.x14½ in., was auctioned Sotheby's 1981.

Gardner, Caroline Bromley (b.1950)
Equestrian artist who studied under Signorina Nerina Simi in Florence. Her work has been exh. by Frost and Reed and the Tryon Gallery, London.

Gardner, Daniel (c.1750-1805)
Portrait painter who studied under George Romney before entering the RA Schools in 1770 as one of their first pupils. He won a silver medal in 1771 then for a short time joined the studio of Sir Joshua Reynolds (q.v.). His portrait of the young cricketer, Frederick Francis Baker, painted in gouache and pastel, 20in.x 16in., c.1780 shows one of Gardner's spasmodic flashes of brilliance for after the death of his wife he became difficult and eccentric. The stitching on the undyed cricket ball that young Baker holds in his left hand is of particular historical interest to cricketers. Gardner also introduced cricket into his group portrait "The Rumbold Family", gouache and pastel, 43¾ in.x 31½ in. (private collection).

Gardner, Edwin C. (op.1867-1888)
A London landscape painter in both oil and watercolour who exh. eleven works at SS (1867-1884), and three at the RA (1884-1886), none of them sporting. His very fine watercolour of the first "Eclipse Stakes, Sandown Park", s.&d. 1886 and inscr., 9½ in.x15in., was auctioned Sotheby's 1986. The race was run on 23 July and depicts "Bendigo", the winner, with T. Cannon up, "Candlemas", second, with F. Archer up, and "St. Gatien", third, with C. Wood up. Five other runners of the original twelve are also shown. George Finch Mason (q.v.) also painted this race but the horses and riders are seen from the opposite side of the course.

Gardner, H. (op.1890)
An apparently unrecorded artist whose work includes a watercolour, painted in 1890, entitled "Lawn Tennis at Brighton". Croquet players are featured in the foreground, in a garden setting with the Pavilion building behind, 11¾in.x14in., auctioned Sotheby's 1986.

Gardner, Philip
Contemporary artist of sporting scenes including cricket, rugby and human figures in action. His watercolour of a rugby game entitled "Charging All Blacks", s.&d. 1979, 12¼in.x15¾in., is a powerful representation. Gardner spent thirty years as a copywriter and creative director of an advertising agency before starting a professional career in art. His first exhibition in 1971 brought an almost immediate success.

Garfit, William, RBA (b.1944)
Contemporary artist of angling scenes who lives near Cambridge and was educated at Bradfield. Garfit, who studied at the Cambridge School of Art, the Byam Shaw School and at the RA Schools, is a keen angler himself but he almost never paints anglers or fish, only the stream or river. The cleverness of depicting the landscape makes the viewer think of fishing and illustrates the power of illusion. He shows his work at the Tryon and Moorland Gallery, London. Exh. regularly at the RA, RSBA and NEAC (since 1965). Contributes illustrations to "The Shooting Times".

Garland, Henry (op.1854-1892)
Landscape and animal painter usually with bags of sentiment. Born at Winchester, he was father of the animal painter Valentine Garland (q.v.) and brother of William Garland (q.v.). Exh. at the RA, BI and SS (1854-1890). Sporting titles at SS include "A Pointer","A Study of Italian Partridges" and "The Winner of the Match - Excelsior Cricket Club, Islington". This last painting shows the hero of the match carried shoulder high by his team mates, one of whom raises aloft the flag of the Excelsior Cricket Club. Garland painted the cricket scene, 31in.x53in., in 1864 and exh. it at SS in 1865 where it was bought by a Mr. Saire. Garland lived for some time in Islington so the Excelsior was almost certainly his local cricket club. It was clearly not a commissioned work so we must assume that he painted it either as a cricket enthusiast, although he does not appear to have painted further cricket scenes, or (more likely) because he found the scene appealing. MCC Collection.

Garland, Valentine Thomas (op.1868-d.1914)
Animal painter who lived in Winchester and London, son of Henry Garland (q.v.). Exh. at the RA, BI, SS and NWS from 1868-1894. Sporting titles at SS include "A Sleeping Hound", "Gone Away" and "Two Old Poachers". His kennel scene with hounds and terriers, signed, 12in.x8in., was auctioned Christie's 1976 and his fine fishing scene of a terrier and a collie dog sitting in the boat of a fly fisherman with creel, fishing rods and fish in the bottom of the boat, 11in.x15in., was auctioned Andrew Grant, 1990.

Garland, William (op.1850-d.1882)
Landscape, portrait and genre painter but also of some animal subjects. Brother of Henry (q.v.), he also lived at Winchester. Pavière records a painting of a grey hunter with a greyhound in a stable painted by him in 1872. A bay hunter in a landscape, s.&d. 1850, 20in.x 25in., was auctioned Sotheby's (Chester) 1986. He exh. four paintings at the RA (1857-1873) and ten at SS.

Garnam, A.C. (op.1890s)
Animal artist whose portrait of "Davyson 87th" s.&d. 1895, bred by John Hammond and exh. by HRH the Duke of York in 1895 was auctioned Sotheby's 1978. The subject was also painted by F. Babbage (q.v.).

Garrard, E. (op. 1793)
This London artist exh. a portrait of a horse and a portrait of "Saltram" at the RA in 1793.

Garrard, George, ARA (1760-1826)
Sporting artist who studied at the RA Schools (1778) and became a pupil of Sawrey Gilpin (q.v.) whose daughter, Matilda, he married. Garrard accompanied Colonel Thornton on his sporting tour of Scotland in about 1786 in his role as an artist. His occasional equestrian portraits are of a very high quality and his patrons included the 8th Duke of Hamilton, the Duke of Bedford and the Whitbread family. He painted the portraits of the famous racehorse "Eclipse", foaled in 1764, and "Tandini" c.1780, foaled in 1773, both in the collection of Tattersalls, Newmarket.

Garrard, R.H., Jnr. (op.1814)
Son of George Garrard (q.v.) and grandson of Sawrey Gilpin (q.v.). Exh. at the RA in 1814 "Portrait of a Well Known Hunter bred by N. Worcester, the property of S. Shephard".

Garratt, Samuel (1865-1947)
Landscape painter and of some sporting subjects. Born at Barwell, Leicestershire, the son of a farm labourer. Started life as a boot maker, studying art for fifteen years in the evenings at Leicester School of Art. Exh. at the RA in 1914, "Coursing on the Dorset Downs".

Garraway, Edward (op.1875-1892)
This London artist exh. two watercolours at SS in 1875 and 1876, neither of them remotely connected with sport. His portraits of the chestnut racehorse "Sanfoin" with jockey up, and the racehorse "Memoir" s.&d. 1890, 20in.x24in., were auctioned Banks and Silver 1986. Garraway painted the portraits of several hunters, often in their loose boxes, and usually s.&d. his work.

Garstin, Alethea, RWA (b.1894 op.1910-1970)
Daughter of the artist Norman Garstin (1847-1926) who lost his eye in a hunting accident in Ireland and who taught her to paint. Her fine study of girls at a gymkhana entitled "Waiting Their Turn", 5½in.x 9¾in., was exh. at the Fine Art Society, December 1978-January 1979.

Garston, Gerald (b.1925)
Designer of an American baseball game entitled "Between Innings" dated 1971, silkscreen, 20in.x20in., Collection Philadelphia Museum of Art.

Gaskell, George Arthur (op.1871-1900)
Painted figure and domestic scenes with dollops of genre, such as "See my Little Kitties". Exh. (1871-1900) at the RA and SS, including "A Young Archer", s.&d. 1873, 23½in.x17in., exh. at the RA 1873 No. 572.

Gatehouse, Charles E. (1866-1952)
Somerset based sporting artist and caricaturist. Studied art for two years at the Slade School. He painted a number of solid portraits of hunters and always s.&d. his work.

Gathorne-Hardy, The Hon. Alfred E. (1849-1918)
Sportsman, writer and illustrator. Younger son of the 1st Earl of Cranbrook. A fine fly fisherman who wrote "The Salmon", pub. 1898, and illus. by W. Douglas Adams (q.v.). He was a welcome and frequent visitor with his father and brother, Lord Medway, to Braemore in Scotland and mentioned several remarkable feats in the River Broom on that estate.

Gauci, A.M. (op.1848-1870)
Animal painter though better known as an engraver. He was the son and brother of lithographers, both working in London. He engraved many of the illustrations of the celebrated Shorthorn cattle that appeared in "Coates Herd Book" between 1863 and 1867. He also contributed one plate to "A Comparative View of the English Racer and Saddle Horse" (1836) and engraved "The Age" (of the coach) after the work by C.C. Henderson (q.v.).

Gaudier Brzeska, Henri, LG (1891-1915)
French figure artist who included "The Cyclist", pen, black ink with wash, 10in.x15in. in his work. Henri Gaudier came to London in 1906 on a scholarship and took the name Brzeska after meeting Sophie Brzeska in 1910. He became a founder member of the London Group in 1913. He joined the French army at the outbreak of the 1st World War and was killed at Neuville Saint Vaast on 5 June 1915.

Gauguin, Paul (1848-1903)
French Impressionist painter included in this Dictionary for his billiard painting entitled "At the Café", s.&d. 1888, Pushkin State Museum of Fine Arts, Moscow. Exh. at the Gauguin exhibition at the Grand Palais, Paris 10.1.89-20.4.89. Gauguin was a close friend of Vincent Van Gogh (q.v.). In 1888 the two artists spent a brief, stormy but productive visit to Arles where they both painted the local café with its billiard table. Gauguin considered the figure in his cafe picture "much too neat and stiff" but he made the most of the wreaths of smoke.

Gaunt, John (op.1825)
This Leeds artist exh. a painting of "Spaniels and Woodcock" at the Northern Society for the Encouragement of the Arts in Leeds (1825). The price asked for the work was £4.10s. Charles Henry Schwanfelder's (q.v.) painting of Loch Lomond, hung in the same exhibition, was priced at £63 which might indicate that Gaunt's work was not highly rated.

Gautez, G. (op.1860)
Collaborated with W.L. Walton (q.v.) on the international boxing contest between John C. Heenan and Tom Sayers on 17 April 1860 at Farnborough, which Gautez and Walton produced as a tinted lithograph pub. G. Newbold in November 1860.

Gavarni, Pierre
The pseudonym of Sulpice Guillaume Chevalier, the 19th century caricaturist but the name, nevertheless, that he used to sign his painting "Races at Longchamp" (1874) which shows elegant society members lining the race track, apparently more interested in their own affairs than the finish of the race. Musée Carnavalet.

Gay, Edward, NA (1837-1928)
American landscape painter who was born in Dublin, Ireland. Gay, who went to America in 1848, studied art in Germany under Karl Lessing (1808-1888). He is included in this Dictionary for his painting "Ice Skating in Mount Vernon", s.&d. 1879, 20in.x16in., Christie's (Belfast) 1991. Mount Vernon, NY, the city suburb which was Gay's home, was the subject for many of his paintings. Gay, who received the Metropolitan Prize for the picture "Broad Acres", presented to the Metropolitan Museum of Art, NY, was elected NA in 1907. He occasionally collaborated with a fellow emigré, A.F. Tait (q.v.).

Gay, Walter (1856-1937)
American-born painter who specialised in painting interior scenes. Born Hingham, Mass., USA he lived most of his life in Paris. Exh. three paintings at the RA (1877-1891). His painting "The Gunsmith" s.&d. 1886, 14½in.x10½in., was auctioned Christie's 1964. His painting entitled "The Fencing Lesson", 27in.x42¾in. was exh. at the Paris Solon in 1879 and was Gay's first major painting to be exh. there.

Gaye, Howard C. (op.1880-1891)
His watercolour painting of a view of a Scottish golf links course, 9½in.x13½in., was auctioned Bonhams 1988.

Gear, Joseph (W.) (1768/9-1853)
Marine painter to HRH the Duke of Sussex during the Anglo-French War. His paintings in watercolour include cock-fighting and bull-baiting scenes and his horse-racing scenes show the influence of John Wootton (q.v.). His son was Joseph Gear, Jnr. (op.1800-1860). Aquatinted after his own work two sets of angling, hare-coursing, fox-hunting and shooting prints. Exh. four marine paintings at the RA but no sporting (1811-1821). He also exh. at SS several engravings and watercolours (1824-1845) including a watercolour of Lady Caroline Maxe and her family setting off for a morning ride with their favourite donkey. He emigrated to America in 1824.

Gear, Mabel (Mrs. Ivor Symes), RI, ROI (b.1900)
Animal and bird painter who lived for some time in Hertfordshire. Studied at Colchester School of Art and under Septimus Power (q.v.) at Bushey. Exh. at the RA, RI, ROI, RBA and abroad. Elected ROI (1925) and RI (1927).

Geddes, Andrew, ARA (1783-1844)
Scottish portrait painter and of some sporting personalities including his full-length study of a golfer standing with

a golf club in his right hand, black/red chalk, 10½in.x 7½in. The Paul Mellon Collection, Upperville, Va, USA and the portrait of Charles Knowles Robison skating, exh. Spinks (London) 1991. Geddes exh. at the RA (1806-1845) and the BI (1919-1842). Elected ARA (1832).

Geddes, William, of Blairgowrie (op.1841-1884)

Scottish still life painter, in particular of fish studies, who exh. at the RSA and the Glasgow Institute of Fine Arts (1841-1884). His fish paintings include "Islay Sea Trout, s.&d. 1852 and "Brown Trout with a Creel", s.&d. 1881, auctioned Christie's 1988.

Gee, David (1795-1872)

Coventry portrait painter and of some battle scenes and landscapes. Included in this Dictionary for his fine portrait of a gentleman, his horse and his dog. Warwick Auctions (Coventry) 1991.

Gee, Gilbert (op.1940)

Contemporary painter of equestrian scenes including "The South Stafford Hunt", signed, 17in.x23¾in., Bonhams 1990. Gee exh. at Birmingham from 1940.

Gentle, C.

A portrait of a bay racehorse with Sir Tatton Sykes up, signed and inscr., 7¾in.x10¼in., was auctioned Sotheby's 1972.

Gere, Charles March, RA, RWS, RBSA, NEAC (1869-1957)

Gloucestershire painter of landscapes and figure subjects who studied at the Birmingham School of Art, where he afterwards taught for many years, and in Italy. Worked as an illustrator with William Morris at the Kelmscott Press and later for the Ashdene Press. Exh. at the RA from 1890 and elected a member (1939), NEAC (1911) and RWS (1926). His famous painting entitled "The Tennis Party", 15in.x42in., is in the collection of the Cheltenham Museum & A.G. This painting is said to represent members of the artist's family including his sister Edith, who was married to the stained glass artist, Henry Payne RWS (1868-1940). Gere lived with his sister, the artist Margaret Gere (1878-1965) who accompanied him on his annual sketching trips abroad (1900-1917).

Géricault, Theodore Jean Louis André (1791-1824)

Equestrian painter and lithographer who also painted military subjects. Fellow pupil with Eugène Delacroix in the Pierre Guerin studio (1816) and pupil of Carl Vernet (q.v.). Came to England in 1820. His engraving of "French Post Horses" appeared in "The Sporting Magazine" May 1825. Painted the Derby at Epsom (twice) and a number of military subjects early in his career. A fine lithograph of two boxers in combat (1811) was auctioned Christie's 1985. Géricault was killed as a result of a riding accident at the age of thirty-three.

Gérome, Jean Léon (1824-1901)

French orientalist artist with a deep interest in shooting. Gérome painted several shooting scenes including "The Hunt of the Baron Salomon de Rothschild" featuring portraits of well-known Parisian society figures,

auctioned Christie's 1990 and sold for £350,000. His painting "The Cock Fight" was finished in 1847 and hangs in the Louvre, Paris.

Gerusez, Victor (1840-1906)

Alias "Crafty" (q.v.), the pseudonym by which he is probably better known. French painter and illustrator who contributed to "The Graphic" (1871). His versatility in equestrian drawings are seen to their best advantage in the contributions he made to the "History of Celebrated English and French Thorough-Bred Stallions" (S.F. Touchstone 1890).

Gessner, Johann Conrad (1764-1826)

Zurich-born landscape painter who included many hunting and sporting scenes amongst his work. He studied art in Dresden and Italy before coming to London in 1796 where he stayed for eight years. He learnt lithography from its inventor A. Senefelder and exh. twenty-four paintings at the RA (1797-1803). Titles include "Hunting" (1802) and a "Bear Hunt".

Ghilchik, David Louis, SWE, ROI (1892-1972)

Artist, wood engraver and illustrator who studied at the Manchester College of Art and then at the Slade School in London, under Henry Tonks (q.v.). He continued his studies in Paris before going on to Florence and Venice on a travelling scholarship. Ghilchik became a Punch cartoonist until 1937 but he was also a fine landscape painter and a lover of the arts. Elected President of the London Sketch Club in 1942 and a Member of the Royal Society of Oil Painters. In later life he appeared frequently on television and was known affectionately as "Baldilocks". Exh. widely in the UK (1930-1939) at the RA, ROI, RI, RBA and NEAC. His work included a number of sporting scenes and games, especially golf and lawn tennis. He illus. "The Rubaiyat of a Golfer" (1946) by J. A. Hammerton. Elected SWE 1920, of which Society he was a founder member.

Gibb, Harry Phelan (1870-1948)

Painter of equestrian scenes, some inscr. "Alnwick". Studied art at Newcastle, Paris (under Laurens). Antwerp and Munich. Lived in Paris for twenty-five years and exh. there, in London and New York. His sporting work includes fox-hunting scenes which he often painted in pairs.

Gibb, J. (op.1860)

Unknown Scottish painter of "Curling", 12in.x18in., s.&d. 1860, auctioned Christie's 1986.

Gibb(s), T. H. (op.1830-1890)

Northumberland artist who painted sporting subjects and exh. (1883-1885) at the RSA and RHA. He painted a number of otter hunting scenes including "Marked in his Holt", s.&d. 1890, "Gone Away - "Otter Hunting on the Liddel", s.&d. 1888 and "Otter Hunting on the Esk", s.&d. 1885, auctioned Sotheby's 1964. He collaborated with C.H. Robertson (q.v.) on a major painting entitled "Close Touch", an otter hunting scene featuring the Carlisle Otter Hunt on the river Eden above Armathwaite, 31in.x47in., auctioned Phillips (Edinburgh) 1988.

Gibbon, Benjamin Phelps (op.1828)
Exh. a study of two dogs at SS in 1828, his only exhibit, from a London address.

Gibbons, Ruth (b.1945)
Painter and illustrator who specialises in equestrian subjects particularly of racehorses. Has exh. at the Tryon and Morland Gallery (1985).

Gibbs, F.J. or J.F. (exh.1854-1858)
Animal and sporting painter who exh. at the RA and BI (1854-1858) from a London address. Titles include "Dogs after a Rat" and "Not to be Caught".

Gibbs, Patrick Anthony Sanderson (b.1959)
Studied at the Ruskin School of Fine Art and Drawing and at Goldsmith's College London (1983-1984). A keen sportsman who specialises in large paintings of snooker, often 8ft.x4ft., and often featuring his local snooker club in South West London.

Gibbs, Percy William (op.1894-1937)
Landscape painter who won the Creswick Prize for landscape painting while studying art at the RA Schools, 1894/5. Exh. at the RA and other leading galleries and lived at East Molesey, Surrey. Included in this Dictionary for his painting of "The Croquet Match" signed, 19½in.x32½in., auctioned Sotheby's 1989 and for "The Molesey Regatta" painted c.1925, 2ft.x3ft., auctioned 1989.

Giberne, Edgar (op.1872-1890)
Sporting artist and illustrator who drew Highland and sporting scenes for "The Illustrated London News" (1889-1890). He also illus. children's books and exh. at the RA and RBA (1872-1888).

Gibson, C.W. (op.1889)
The painter of a huntsman and his horse standing at a gate with the hunt beyond, s.&d. 1889, 15½in.x22in., auctioned Christie's 1964.

Gibson, Charles Dana (1867-1944)
American painter and illustrator famous for his sketches of pretty girls immortalised as the "Gibson girls" which filled the pages of contemporary magazines and calendars. Included in this Dictionary for his pen/ink drawing (1913) entitled "Everybody Up - Seventh Inning Stretch" - an integral part of the game of basketball. The drawing, 22in.x24in., is in the New York Public Library.

Gibson, Vincent
Contemporary artist whose painting "The Parade before the Ascot Gold Cup 1896" hangs at Ascot Racecourse.

Gibson, William Alfred (1866-1931)
Scottish-born landscape painter in oil who studied art in Glasgow and included a number of fishing and shooting scenes amongst his work. Exh. at the RA, RSA, GI and abroad and represented in several public collections. "Setting out on a Duck Shoot", 20in.x24in., was auctioned Phillips 1986.

Gifford, John (op.c.1865-1898)
Victorian sporting painter of game and shooting subjects often in Highland settings who usually signed, but rarely dated his work. Titles include "The End of the Day", "Waiting for Master", "A Pony with Three Sporting Dogs and Dead Game", "Gun Dogs and Highland Ponies after the Shoot", "Picking up a Runner", etc. Does not seem to have exh. in London.

Gifford, M.B. (op.1924)
Painter of "The Squire", a chestnut cob in a stable, s.&d. 1924, 19in.x24in., auctioned Sotheby's (Mentmore) 1977.

Gilbert, Arthur (1819-1895)
Prolific landscape artist, particularly of night and moonlight scenes who included a number of shooting and fishing subjects amongst his work. Titles include "Duck Shooting in a Landscape at Sunset", 8½in.x14½in., "Fishing on a Summer Afternoon", s.&d. 1882, "An Angler on a Lake", s.&d. 1893, etc.

Gilbert, Edward (late 19th - early 20th century)
Recorded by Mitchell as the artist of a portrait of "Shotover", winner of the Derby 1882, engraved by E.G. Hester and pub. by G.B. McQueen in 1882, but this painting is more likely to have been by Edward Gilbert Hester (q.v.).

Gilbert, Miss Ellen (op.1863-1891)
Prolific figure painter and of sentimental scenes from Blackheath who surprisingly painted a number of sporting scenes, including "A Young Cricketer", exh. at SS in 1890, "The Lost Game" and "Red to Play".

Gilbert, Frederick (op.1862-1891)
London illustrator and painter from Blackheath, brother of Sir John Gilbert with whom he lived, who contributed a golfing scene entitled "A Match at Blackheath" c.1870 to his illustration output. He also seems to have been responsible for a pair of shooting studies with gundogs entitled "A Good Stand" and "On the Alert" both signed, each 9in.x15in., auctioned Sotheby's 1986.

Gilbert, Joseph Francis (1792-1855)
Landscape painter who also included equestrian paintings amongst his work. His very fine view of Manchester Racecourse, 19in.x39¼in., painted c.1847, was recently auctioned. In a description of the opening meeting "The Illustrated London News" (29 May 1847) commented "This new course allowed to be one of the finest in England lies in Broughton, 2 miles from the Manchester Exchange on land belonging to Mr. Fitzgerald of Irwell Castle immediately below the old course of Kersall Moor. It is almost surrounded by the River Irwell, is nearly on a level and upwards of a mile in length." The foundation of the original stand was laid on 13 March 1847; it held 1,000 people and was completed within two months at a cost of over £8,000. Gilbert's work includes portraits of hunters and spaniels. His paintings of "Priam" winning the Gold Cup and "A View of Goodwood Racecourse" were both engraved by John Heaviside Clark (1771-1863). Gilbert exh. at the RA (1813-1816) and the BI (1823-1824).

Gilbert, Josiah (1814-1892)

Draughtsman and portrait painter in pastel and watercolour. His drawing "The Sportsman", s.&d. 1851, pencil, black chalk and wash, 11½in.x9½in., was auctioned Sotheby's 1986. Josiah Gilbert, the son of the Revd. Joseph Gilbert, studied at the RA Schools and Sass's Academy and exh. at the RA and elsewhere (1837-1865).

Gilbert, Terence (b.1946)

London-born artist, the son of the Warden of the National Gallery where he studied Old Master techniques. He also studied at Camberwell Art School from the age of eleven. He started to paint freelance from 1966 and travelled in Europe, USA and the Middle East. In 1983 his watercolours were included in an Exhibition of British Art, staged by the Royal Academy of Arts which was held in Abu Dhabi and Dubai. Terence Gilbert's paintings are mainly in oil on canvas or gesso board. His work done in the field is in watercolour and conté chalk. His knowledge of anatomy and draughtsmanship, together with his love of colour and talent for painting in any medium, have ensured that his work is represented in collections all over the world. The sports painted by Gilbert include polo, hunting, falconry, coursing and fishing.

Gilbert, W.J. (op.1830-1870)

Suffolk painter of many equestrian and sporting scenes. Of provincial talent, his pictures were nevertheless extremely decorative and he paid great attention to detail. He appears to have exh. only one painting publicly (at the Portland Gallery in 1851) but it was not sporting. His pair "Shooting" and "Hare Coursing" both s.&d. 1856, 12in.x16½in., were auctioned Sotheby's (Chester) 1981. Gilbert usually s.&d. his work.

Gilchrist, Herbert H. (op.1876-1896)

This versatile artist exh. six works at the RA (1880-1896) including "Game of Ninepins in New England". "The Opening Meet at Arundel", signed and inscr., 26¾in.x32in., was auctioned Christie's 1984.

Gilchrist, Miss Joan A. (op.1885-1888)

Landscape and coastal painter who exh. three landscapes at the NWS (1885-1888) from her address in Devon where she also painted "The Mousehole Regatta" 7in.x5in.

Giles, Benjamin (op.1812)

Animal painter in watercolour from Garboldisham, Blo'Norton, Suffolk. His watercolour portrait of a "Suffolk dun polled Ox", s.&d. 1812, 11¾in.x18in., was auctioned Bonhams 1985. At the turn of the century the only existing herd of dun polled oxen was at Old Buckenham, Attleborough, Norfolk and the owner of this herd purchased Giles' painting from the granddaughter of the man who had originally commissioned it and the owner of the ox.

Giles, E. (op.1833)

Painter of "The First Pony", s.&d. 1833, 14in.x12in., auctioned Bonhams 1982.

Giles, Godfrey Douglas (Major) (1857-1941)

Equestrian painter, in particular of racing scenes, and an army officer until he retired in 1884. In 1885 Giles went to Paris to study art under Carolus-Duran (q.v.) exhibiting at the Paris Salon in that year. Exh. at the RA from 1882 and at SS in the same year, giving his address as the Junior Army and Navy Club. He settled in Newmarket which became his home for many years. His sporting work includes "The Finish of the Derby 1893", painted for Mrs. McAlmont who won the Derby that year with "Isinglass", "The Derby 1901" (won by "Common"), "The Worksop Handicap, Chesterfield 1894". He also painted polo, hunting and pig-sticking scenes. He illus. work for "The Badminton Library", "The Graphic", "Black and White" and "Vanity Fair" and became well known through the prints that were produced after his work.

Giles, James William, RSA (1801-1870)

Aberdeen sporting artist and illustrator, the brother of John West Giles (q.v.) who also specialised in painting Highland scenes. Exh. twenty-one paintings at the Institution for the Encouragement of the Fine Arts in Scotland including "Snipe Shooting" (1829) and at the RSA including "The Rifle and the Rod" (1851) and "Waiting for a Quiet Shot". His painting entitled "A Fox Breaking Cover" has Harrow on the Hill in the background. Giles' watercolour "The Billiard Room" complete with resplendent billiard table, s.&d. 1855, 11¾in.x17¾in., was painted at the old Balmoral Castle. The billiard room there also doubled up as the library and was only 32ft.x17ft. Queen Victoria complained that she and the Duchess of Kent were forever having to get out of their chairs "to be out of the way of the cues". Elected RSA in 1829. Giles illus. "The Anglers Companion to the Rivers and Lochs of Scotland" by Thomas Tod Stoddart, pub. Wm. Blackwood & Sons, London (1837). Elected RSA (1830).

Giles, John West (op.1830-1864)

Aberdeen sporting artist, the brother of James William Giles (q.v.). Exh. at the SS and RA (1832-1864). Titles include "Grouse Shooting - North Wales" which shows that grouse flourished there 150 years ago, and "Hounds at Fault" (RA 1848).

Giles, Norman Edward (op.1930s)

Motor racing draughtsman, who at the age of eighteen won the speed competition which was run for young motor racing artists between 1935 and 1939.

Gilfillan, Tom (op.1932-1953)

Scottish urban and landscape artist who painted the Derby winner "Pinza" with Sir Gordon Richards up. Signed, 28in.x36in. (auctioned Christie's 1983). "Pinza," who won the Derby in 1953, was Sir Gordon Richards' only Derby winner. Gilfillan is also known for his golfing scenes.

Gill, Arthur Eric Rowton, SWE (1882-1940)

Artist, engraver and book illustrator, very often of sporting subjects, who worked as Eric Gill. The son of a clergyman, Gill studied for two years at Chichester Technical and Art School then served a three year apprenticeship with the London architect, Douglas Caroe, while attending evening classes in lettering at the Central School of Arts and Crafts under Edward Johnston, with whom he shared lodgings (1902-1904). Examples of Gill's sporting work includes "Bunkered" signed, watercolour, c.1915, 8½in.x11¾in., Sotheby's (Glasgow) and "The Tennis Player" (wood engraving) c.1924, 4½in.x4⅛in., V & A Museum, London. Gill formed a community of craftsmen (the Guild of St. Dominic) at Ditchling in Sussex. Here he taught engraving to pupils such as David Jones (1895-1974) whose great talent was brief since poor eyesight forced his retirement in 1930. Founder member SWE (1920).

Gill, Edmund (1820-1894)
London landscape artist who included a number of river and some angling scenes in his work. Exh. at SS (1842-1881) and painted in the style of David Cox. His nickname was "Waterfall Gill".

Gill, Edmund Ward (1829-1868)
London painter who exh. at the BI, RA and SS (1843-1855). Despite Gill's reputation as a still life painter he did paint quite excellent live sporting studies and it is particularly interesting to know why he should have inflicted still life studies only on the public at exhibitions. His portrait of James M. Hopton with his gun and dogs at Dulas, painted c.1845, was auctioned Sotheby's 1964.

Gill, Edwyn (op.1809-1831)
The poem "Dick Christian" by "A. Quornite" (Fores 1892) refers to the painting of this extraordinary steeplechase by E. Gill of Northampton which was later engraved. He would also seem to be the painter of "Osirus", a bay hunter in a landscape, s.&d. 1818, 27½in.x34½in., auctioned Sotheby's 1967. Two angling caricatures by Edwyn Gill, dated 1812, were in the Gilbey Collection (1940) and he is probably the same artist as the E. Gill who exh. one rustic scene at the RA in 1810. He is certainly the same Edwyn Gill whose portrait of a fine stallion trotting in a landscape, dated 1829, 25in.x30in., was auctioned Christie's 1987.

Gill, F.T. (op.1847)
Exh. one painting at BI in 1847 entitled "Breaking Cover" from a London address.

Gill, Herbert (op. mid-late 19th century)
Animal and equestrian artist whose work includes studies of hunters in stables and several of cattle.

Gillard, William (b.1812)
Liverpool artist of game dogs and dead game subjects who exh. "A Ride in the Fields" at the RA in 1856.

Giller, William C. (b.1805)
Engraver of sporting subjects, also a watercolour painter. Exh. at SS (1825-1839). His paintings entitled "Dead Game", 24in.x36in., were exh. at HM and AG Preston (1943) "British Sporting Paintings".

Gillet(t), Edward Frank, RI (1874-1927)
East Anglian painter of landscapes and sporting subjects, also a dry point etcher. Worked until 1896 as a clerk for the Committee of Lloyds in the City, after which he became a full-time artist. He worked on "The Daily Graphic" (1898-1908), "Black and White" (1908-1911) and "The Illustrated Sporting and Dramatic News" (1910-1923). He specialised in fox-hunting and hare-coursing scenes including his painting entitled "Beccles - Coursing", 21 February 1914, grisaille watercolour, 9½in.x13¾in., Wingfield Sporting Gallery, London. Exh. at the RA and RI and was elected RI (1909). He also painted a football match, "The Cup Final", Southampton v. Sheffield United, at Crystal Palace in 1902.

Gillett, G. (op.1862-1871)
An artist from Melton Mowbray who is said (Pavière) to have painted sporting subjects and who exh. at BI and SS (1862-1871).

Gilliam, T.H. (op.1893)
Equestrian draughtsman operating at the end of the 19th century.

Gillig, Jacob (1636-1701)
Dutch still life painter of fish subjects including salmon and trout, pike, perch, roach and other freshwater fish. His painting "A Day's Fishing" with Isaac Walton, the angler, beyond, s.&d. 1687, 30in.x23¾in., was auctioned Bonhams 1975.

Gillray, James (1757-1815)
An important draughtsman, etcher, aquatint and stipple engraver of caricatures, very often of sporting subjects. Studied art at the RA Schools and was apprentice to a letter engraver before turning to caricature in about 1780. In 1787 he became a professional caricaturist working for Messrs. Fores and then as chief caricaturist to Mrs. Hannah Humphrey with whom it seems he lived. His "Peep at Christies" or "Tally Ho", 1796, engraved after his own design, 14in.x9¾in., defies imagination. He is included in this Dictionary for his aquatint after his own design of "Mendoza" the boxer, 17½in.x13¾in. pub., presumably, by Mrs. Hannah Humphrey since his last print appeared in 1811, and "The Fencing Match between the Chevalier d'Eon de Beaumont and the Chevalier de St. George", an engraving taken from the original painting by Mather Brown (q.v.).

Gilpin, Sawrey, RA (1733-1807)
Sporting painter and etcher. Born at Carlisle, studied art in 1749 under Samuel Scott, the marine painter, with whom he remained for nine years. Gilpin lived in Newmarket where he studied horse portraiture. The sportsman, Colonel Thornton, was his chief patron for whom he painted "The Death of a Fox" (exh. at the RA 1793, engraved by J. Scott, pub. 1 April 1811) which is said to have influenced Ben Marshall (q.v.) in his decision to become an animal and equestrian painter. His patrons included William Augustus, Duke of Cumberland for whom he painted greyhounds, and the 3rd Earl of Albemarle whom he painted out pheasant shooting at Quidenham, Norfolk, in 1768, and Samuel Whitbread. Gilpin and his son-in-law, George Garrard (q.v.) accompanied Colonel Thornton on his sporting tour of the Highlands, making illustrations of their journey as they travelled. Gilpin exh. at the RA from 1786 and was elected RA 1795. He collaborated with

several artists including Philip Reinagle (q.v.), George Garrard (q.v.), George Romney, George Barret, Snr. (q.v.), Richard Cosway and J.M.W. Turner (q.v.). It was of Sawrey Gilpin that "Anthony Pasquin" (q.v.) alias John Williams, art critic to the "Morning Herald" at the end of the 18th century, wrote in 1794 "Mr. Gilpin is inferior to Mr. Stubbs in anatomical knowledge but is superior to him in grace and genius".

Gilroy, John T. Young, MA (Hon), ARCA, FRSA, (1898-1985)

Portrait painter in oil and watercolour. Born Newcastle upon Tyne, the son of the marine artist John William Gilroy. Won a scholarship to King Edward VII School of Art, Armstrong College, Newcastle, studying under Professor Hatton. Served in 1st World War. Took up a scholarship at the Royal College of Art after the war and won a further travelling scholarship to study in France and Italy. His studies after the Old Masters culminated in the superb draughtsmanship he showed as a mature artist. He returned to England and taught at the Royal College of Art working on the first of many royal portrait commissions. In 1928 Gilroy entered the commercial art world joining the well established Bensons advertising agency. With Dorothy L. Sayers as copywriter, Gilroy commenced a career of twenty-three years in Guinness advertising where he produced some of the most memorable and lasting images in British advertising, such as the "Man with the Girder - Guinness for Strength", and "The Toucan - Guinness is Good for You". Gilroy was a keen fly fisherman and painted many fishing scenes. He also painted a number of golf sketches in both oil and watercolour. Gilroy's painting "Derby Day" (1966) shows fellow members of the Garrick Club enjoying a day out at Epsom, with not a horse to be seen. Nevertheless, the atmosphere, the fun and the thrill of the race meeting are all conveyed, as if they were. Garrick Club.

Gioja, Belisario (1829-1906)

Italian painter of genre and figure subjects whose fine painting of billiards played by ladies and gentlemen in Regency costume was auctioned Phillips 1986.

Girardot, Ernest Gustave (19/20th century)

French painter of "The Polo Player" s.&d. 1902, 13¼in.x9⅜in., Sotheby's (NY) 1988.

Glackens, William J. (1870-1938)

American painter and illustrator of most subjects in oil and watercolour whose illustrations for "Glen Derry", inscr. "New York Herald", ink on paper, were auctioned Sotheby's (NY) 1978.

Glascott, S. (op.1833-1852)

Exh. at SS (1833-1852) from a Brighton address. Titles include "Shooting" in 1843.

Glass, James William (1825-1857)

American military and portrait painter who exh. at the RA (1848-1855) and at the BI and SS. His equestrian portrait of the Duke of Wellington first brought him to recognition in England.

Glass, John James, ARSA (1820-1885)

Scottish animal and sporting painter who studied at the Trustees Academy (1838) and included a number of equestrian portraits amongst his work. Exh. at the RA 1847 and 1859 and at the RSA. Elected ARSA (1849). Glass later emigrated to Australia and gave up painting.

Glaze, G. (op.1845-1862)

Painter of equestrian portraits and game still lifes in both oil and watercolour.

Gleichen, Lady Helena (Countesse) (c.1864-d.1947)

Animal and equestrian painter, the sister of the distinguished artist and sculptor, Lady Theodore Gleichen, RE, and daughter of Prince Victor Hohenlohe-Langenburg. She studied at the Frank Calderon School of Animal Painting under Frank Brangwyn and Arthur Lemon (q.v.). She first exh. at the RA in 1901 including a portrait of Gerald Dudley-Smith, Esq. MFH and Lady Barbara Smith with the Crome Hounds. Other titles include "Gone Away" (1902) and "Davis, the Huntsman" (1911).

Glendening, Alfred Augustus (op.1861-1903)

Prolific landscape artist in oil, very often of river and angling scenes. Exh. at the RA, BI and SS (1864-1903). Worked extensively in Sussex, Scotland and Wales. His son and pupil was the genre and landscape painter Arthur Glendening, Jnr. (1861-1907).

Glindoni, Henry Gillard, RBA, ARWS (1852-1913)

London painter of historical and figure subjects. Worked for various photographers including Blanchards, colouring prints and painting on porcelain. His watercolour "A Duel", s.&d. 1881, 31in.x21½in., was auctioned Sotheby's (Chester) 1986.

Glover, John, OWS, RBA (1767-1849)

Animal and landscape artist who exh. at SS (1824-1833). All his exh. works were landscapes except two of cattle and one in 1829 entitled "Spearing Bay Trout by Torchlight". Glover joined the Society of Painters in Watercolours in 1804 and was elected President in 1815. He painted enormous canvases of "great big cows" which were not always well received. Roget reports (in the "History of the Old Watercolour Society") that a cattleman who called at an exhibition with a bulldog had great difficulty in restraining his dog from attacking a bull in one of Glover's large canvases. Elected RBA in 1824. Emigrated to Tasmania with his family in 1831.

Goddard, Charles (op.1853)

This artist from Hastings, Sussex exh. two pictures at the SS in 1853. A watercolour portrait of a hunter and hounds in a yard is recorded (Mitchell).

Goddard, George Bouverie (1832-1886)

A self-taught animal painter in both oil and watercolour who came to London in 1849 and spent two years sketching at the Zoological Gardens. He worked for "Punch" and "The Illustrated London News" for whom he painted the Waterloo Cup 1876 which was used in the February 1877 issue. Exh. at the RA (1856-1886) including "Gone to Ground" in 1869, and "Lord Wolverton's Bloodhounds" in 1875, a vast canvas at

14ft. A report on the Summer Exhibition at Burlington House, recorded in Baily's Magazine Vol. 27, June 1875, reads "Lord Wolverton's Bloodhounds is perhaps the most striking hunting subject there. How correct it is we cannot say. The flung up heads of one or two of the hounds look true and you can almost hear their deep tongued bay. Mr. Goddard has painted his picture "con amour" we should imagine and has caught inspiration from his theme. To look at it makes you long to see the famous Ralston pack." Goddard painted a number of equestrian portraits of racehorses and hunters as well as otter hounds and greyhound coursing.

Godwin, Miss Mary, LG (1887-1960)
Figure painter in oil and watercolour who studied art at King's College under Byam Shaw (1908-1911), under Sickert (1911-1914), and Gillman (1915). Also at the Westminster Polytechnic. Exh. at the RA, NEAC, LG and PS, the provinces and abroad. Her painting "The Shooting Gallery", 23½in.x19½in., features rifle shooting and was auctioned Sotheby's 1982.

Goff, Frederick E.J. (1855-1931)
London topographical painter mostly in watercolour whose view of Epsom racecourse and grandstand in pen, ink, pencil and watercolour, 4in.x5½in., drawn in great detail and inscr. "Epsom" was auctioned Christie's (Sth. Ken.) 1986.

Goings, Ralph (b.1928)
Painter of an American baseball still life entitled, unimaginatively, "Baseball", watercolour on foam core, 5¼in.x5¼in. The Gladstone Collection of Baseball Art.

Gold
An artist by this surname exh. two paintings, one of dogs and one of horses, at FS in 1782 from a London address.

Golden, Miss Grace, ARCA (Lond.) (b.1904)
Figure and landscape painter. Studied at Chelsea School of Art under J.D. Revel (1884-1967) and the RCA under Sir William Rothenstein (1872-1945). Exh. at the RA (1936-1940) and became a war artist (1939-45). Contributed a painting of "The Derby" for "Everywoman" which was repro. in 1939, watercolour and pencil.

Goldschmidt, Anthony
Contemporary British painter of "The Ice Hockey Players", signed watercolour and bodycolour, 27in.x 19¼in., Bonhams 1990.

Goldsmith, Callander (op.1878-1910)
Sussex artist, presumably from Newhaven since many of his paintings are so inscr. Painted small pictures of horses, mostly hunters, and hunting scenes.

Goldsmith, Walter H. (op.1880-1926)
Landscape painter who lived at Maidenhead. He exh. at SS (1880-1892). All local scenes including his painting "Regatta Day" at Bray in 1884.

Goltzius, Hendrick (1558-1616)
Dutch artist who came from a long line of painters. A pupil of Philipp Galle (1537-1612) Goltzius is probably better known as an engraver than a painter. He produced more than three hundred engravings including several of hawking and falconry.

Gooch, James (op.1789-1837)
Painted landscapes, animals, equestrian and country scenes. Exh. at SS (1824-1837) and BI (1819-1833). "A Retriever with a Partridge", s.&d. 1789, 8¼in.x10¼in., was auctioned Christie's 1965.

Gooch, Miss Matilda (exh.1857-1877)
Exh. at SS (1857-1877) including "The Fatal Shot" in 1868 from a Twickenham address.

Gooch, Thomas (c.1750-1802)
Presumed to be a pupil of Sawrey Gilpin (q.v.) since his exhibition work to the SA (1778-1780) was sent from Gilpin's address in Knightsbridge. Exh. seventy-six paintings at the RA, mostly portraits of horses and dogs. Best known for his series entitled "The Life and Death of a Racehorse" which he exh. at the RA in 1783. He engraved the plates in aquatint each 11¼in.x 3¼in., and pub. them in 1790. This theme was so popular that a number of leading sporting artists copied the idea including Charles Ansell (q.v.), T. Rowlandson (q.v.) (1789), Charles Towne (q.v.), Henry T. Alken (q.v.) (1821), J.F. Herring, Snr. (q.v.) and Edwin Cooper (q.v.). Gooch also painted a number of shooting scenes including "Two Gentlemen going a'Shooting" dated 1787, a painting which was largely inspired by G. Stubbs (q.v.) who had painted a very similar scene in 1768 when he was working for the Duke of Portland. Gooch also worked for George Pitt, created 1st Baron Rivers of Stratfield Saye in 1776, and painted his children, the Hon. Marcia and the Hon. George Pitt (later 2nd Lord Rivers) out riding in 1782, The Paul Mellon Collection, Upperville, Va, USA. See also Agasse (q.v.).

Good(e), John (op.1810-1852)
Oxfordshire sporting artist from Adderbury who exh. at SS in 1835 two paintings of a hunting party and of a fox breaking covert. His portrait of James Hills, huntsman (1835-1865), John Goddard and Thomas Slatter, Whips, with some of the favourite hounds of Lord Redesdale's pack, the Heythrop, was engraved by W.H. Simmonds and repro. in the "Heythrop Hunt" by G.T. Hutchinson, pub. John Murray, London, 1935. Good(e) also painted "The Old Berkshire Hounds" which was mezzotinted by P. Thomas in 1853 and contributed a portrait of "Anthony", a shorthorn bull belonging to a Mr. Lovell of Banbury, c.1835, which was pub. in "Coates Shorthorn Herd Book" - Vol.15.

Good, Thomas Sword, of Berwick, HRSA (1789-1872)
Good started his career as a house painter, painting portraits only as a sideline. Came to London in 1822. Pupil of Sir David Wilkie, RA (q.v.). Good painted a number of angling scenes including "The Salmon Fishers" dated 1818. Exh. at SS a "Study of Dead Snipe" in 1824 and then did not exhibit again until 1831. His painting entitled "Fisherman with a Gun", a rather unsporting sounding combination, was described as "vivid" by "The Tyne Mercury", 7 June 1825 reporting

exhibition held at the Northumberland Institution for the Promotion of Fine Arts Newcastle in 1825, where the painting was hung. Good is said to have inherited a legacy some time in the early 1830s and appears to have given up painting. Elected ARSA (1828).

Good(e), W.E. (op.1845-1865)
Oxfordshire sporting artist, clearly closely related to John Good(e) (q.v.) since both exh. from the same address. Exh. four paintings at the BI (1854-1866) including "Otter Hunting", "Boys Ferreting Rabbits" and "Otter Hounds". The last painting may have been exh. posthumously. He was possibly William Edward Good(e) whose death is recorded at St. Georges, Hanover Square, London in the last quarter of 1865.

Goodall, John Strickland, RI, RBA (b.1908)
Draughtsman and painter in watercolour who studied with (Sir) Arthur Stockdale Cope, RA (1923), John Watson Nicol, Harold Speed (1924) and at the RA Schools 1925-1929. Exh. at the RA,RI, RBA and in the provinces. Paints Edwardian scenes, very often of sporting subjects including cricket, skating, racing, archery, etc. Exh. Christopher Wood Gallery London, including the exhibition to celebrate his 80th birthday in July 1988.

Goodman, H.M. (op.1877)
The unrecorded painter of "The Croquet Game" s.&d. 1877, Oscar and Peter Johnson, London.

Goodrich, William R.E. (op.1912-1923)
Sheffield artist who exh. one painting at the RA 1912. His watercolour of a whipper-in with his pack on a country lane with a house beyond, s.&d. 1923, 10¼in.x 14¼in., was auctioned Bonhams 1984.

Goodwin, Albert, RWS (1845-1932)
A landscape artist who painted mainly in watercolours. He also painted coastal and hunting scenes. He was a pupil of the artist Ford Madox Brown and a friend of John Ruskin. He was also the uncle of the marine artist Sydney Goodwin (1867-1944). His watercolour "Going to the Meet", s.&d. '69, 11½in.x19in., was auctioned Sotheby's (Sussex) 1987.

Goodwin, Richard le Barre (1840-1910)
American artist of sporting still lifes.

Goodwin, S. (op.1749)
A trompe-d'oeil of a white woodcock with engravings and a copy of the "London Gazette", signed and inscr., 38½in.x22½in., was exh. Hull Fine Art Gallery. The inscription reads "This remarkable bird was shot November 7th by one of the Earl of Gainsborough's servants and painted from the bird itself by S. Goodwin, with the London Gazette and dated 1749".

Gordon, "Jan" (Godfrey Jervis), RBA (1882-1944)
Painter, etcher, lithographer, writer and art critic. Exh. three paintings at the British Sporting Paintings Exhibition at the Preston HM and AG in 1943 entitled "They Still Play Bowls", "Snooker at the Old Savage" and "The Mark".

Gordon, Sir John Watson RA, PRSA (1788-1864)
Leading Scottish portrait painter, after the death of his friend and teacher, Sir Henry Raeburn RA (q.v.), who assumed the name of Gordon in 1826. Became Limner for Scotland to Her Majesty Queen Victoria (1850-1864). Elected RSA (1829), RA (1851) and PRSA (1850-1864). His portrait of John Taylor, Captain of the Honorable Company of Edinburgh Golfers in 1807/8/14/15/23 and 1825, 96in.x60in., hangs in the clubhouse at Muirfield. He also painted the portrait of Douglas H.C.L.A. Robertson, a member of the Royal and Ancient, standing full-length on a fairway by a gate holding a wooden club in his right hand, 65in.x35½in., auctioned Sotheby's 1971. Amongst the several archery portraits painted by Sir John Watson Gordon was the painting of James, Andrew, 1st Marquis of Dalhousie, (1812-1860), President of the Council of the Royal Company of Archers (1848-1860). He is resplendent in livery with bow, arrow and target.

Gore, Spencer Frederick (1878-1914)
An Impressionist painter much influenced by Sickert and the French Impressionists including Camille Pissarro (q.v.). He was one of the founders of the Camden Town Group, formed in 1911, of which he became President. Gore is not an artist normally associated with sporting paintings and indeed his "Cricket Match" is certainly painted in his impressionistic style which makes the details of the game rather difficult to pick out. The match was probably played at or near Hartingfordbury, Hertfordshire, his house at the time, and viewed from over the fence near the boundary. In this painting, dated 1909, there are resemblances to the cricket match that Pissarro painted at Bedford Park in 1897 which is at the Jeu de Paume, Paris. Gore's "Cricket Match", s.&d. 1909, 16in.x18in., is in the collection of the Wakefield City AG.

Gosling, William W., RBA (1824-1883)
London painter of landscape and rural scenes who included some angling watercolours amongst his work. Exh. at SS (1849-1884). Elected Member in 1854. Titles include "A Bit of Poaching in the Backwater" in 1880, and "Flew Netting on the Thames" in 1865.

Gotch, Bernard Cecil (b.1876)
Landscape painter in watercolour whose rugby football painting "Stanleys XV v. Oxford University", 1950, was auctioned Hamptons (Malvern) 1992.

Gotch, Thomas Cooper, NEAC, RBA, RI (1854-1931)
Portrait, landscape and allegorical painter. Studied at Heatherleys School, the Ecole des Beaux Art, the Slade School and in Paris under J.P. Laurens (1880-1883). Included in this Dictionary for his "Game of Croquet" a watercolour, 4in.x7¼in., auctioned David Lane 1985. Gotch was a founder member of the NEAC and President of the Royal British Colonial Society of Artists (1913-1928).

Gotschke, Walter (b.1912)
German painter of motor racing subjects who originally studied as an architect. His first pub. works were a series of pen/ink motor racing subjects for the newspaper "Brunner Tageszeitung" which were to mark the beginning of a career establishing Gotschke as one of the

most respected motoring artists of all time. His deceptively impressionistic painting belies the technical accuracy of his subject matter and his work has appeared in most major motor publications, worldwide.

Goubie, Jean Richard (1842-1899)
French painter of equestrian scenes, usually non-sporting such as "The Morning Ride", but occasionally hunting.

Goulburn, Cecilia (op.1910)
This artist painted a still life watercolour of a perch caught at St. Ives, Bingley, Yorks., 22 August 1910, weight 1lb. 2oz.

Gould, Alexander Carruthers, RBA, RWA (1870-1948)
Landscape and marine artist who painted in both oil and watercolour, the son of Sir Francis Carruthers Gould (q.v.). Exh. at the NEAC (1909-1916) including a portrait of a horse. He also painted a watercolour of "The Exmoor Staghounds" which was auctioned Bonhams 1987 and an oil of the same hounds entitled "Stoke Common, Exmoor", 25in.x30in.

Gould, Sir Francis Carruthers (1844-1925)
Caricaturist and illustrator, born at Barnstaple, the second son of Richard Gould, an architect, and educated in the town. Lived at Porlock, Somerset. A member of the London Stock Exchange for more than twenty years, he also lectured about Parliamentary affairs. Knighted (1906). Political cartoonist and contributor to "Pall Mall Gazette" and later "The Westminster Gazette". He also contributed seven cartoons to "Vanity Fair" (1879-1899) under his initials F.C.G. or C.G. "Sporting Types", a set of eleven watercolours, all signed with inits., each 8in.x5in., were auctioned Sotheby's (Sussex) 1988. Father of the artist Alex Carruthers Gould (q.v.).

Gow, Andrew Carrick, RA, RI (1848-1920)
Painter of historical and military subjects who is also known to have painted fencing scenes. The son of James Gow (q.v.). Andrew Gow studied art at Heatherleys and exh. regularly at the RA from 1869. He was elected RI (1868), RA (1891) and was made Keeper of the RA from 1911.

Gow, James, RBA (1852-1885)
Exh. two paintings of anglers at SS in 1883 and 1885.

Gowdy, W. (op.1898)
"Setters putting up a Grouse", s.&d. '98, 12in.x18in., was auctioned Phillips (Chester) 1987.

Gower, Thomas (1792-1819)
"A Hunting Breakfast in the Olden Times", a large oil painting which measures 2ft.6in.x 2ft. was referred to by "Cuthbert Bede" (q.v.) author of "Verdant Green" in Fores "Sporting Notes and Sketches" 1886/7. It was painted by the author's uncle, his mother's elder brother, who died in 1819 at the age of twenty-seven having exh. pictures at Somerset House and other London galleries. It was the subject of the pair of hunting sketches "Fox Hunters in the Days of Squire Weston" and "Fox Hunters Regaling in the Present Degenerate Days" by John Leech (q.v.) which were

eventually produced in the 23 February issue 1856 of "The Illustrated London News". A duplicate of Gower's painting but signed "Echstein Pin- Rowlandson delin" turned up in a private collection in 1884 but no such subject by Rowlandson has yet been discovered - the "Hunt Dinner" No. 7 of his "Miseries of Social Life" is a different scene.

"Gownsman"
The pseudonym used by Henry Charles Seppings Wright (q.v.).

Gozzoli, Benozzo (1420-1497)
An Italian painter, a pupil of Fra Angelico. He decorated the chapel of the Medici palace in Florence with a fresco, using the theme of the three Kings. This fascinating painting shows not only the enormous hunting retinue which accompanied monarchs at that time but the cheetahs who worked with the falcons for hunting deer and large game. Note the cosy way in which the cheetah is riding pillion with his handler, while the falcon stands guard over the prey.

Grace, A.L. (op.1884)
"A Century for England" and "Visions of a Hat Trick". Prints after these cricket works were auctioned Phillips 1986. A.L. Grace, whose other paintings include "Preparing the Tackle" and a "Fisherman Threading his Hook", rarely dated his work.

Grace, Miss Hariette Edith (1860-1932)
Sussex artist from Brighton who painted portraits, landscapes and nature studies. Exh. at the RA (1881-1900), mostly still lifes and flower paintings. Her watercolour "An Early Form of Cricket at Stoneyhurst College", painted in 1894 is at Brighton Art Gallery.

Grace, James Edward, RBA (1851-1908)
Landscape painter and a book illustrator who is included in this Dictionary for his charming illustrations to the Marquis of Granby's book "The Trout" (1899). He studied art at the Liverpool Institute and at South Kensington and exh. at the RA and elsewhere (1871-1907). Elected RBA (1879).

Graeme, Colin (op.1858-1910)
See also Roe. An interesting artist of muddled identity who signed his work both Colin Graeme and Colin Graeme Roe. One theory (Mitchell) is that Roe, thought to be the son of Robert Henry Roe, fell out with his family and thereby ceased to use the family name signing his second christian name as his surname. Interestingly, Colin Graeme/Roe collaborated with Clarence Roe (q.v.) on at least one painting including "A Portrait of a Pointer", s.&d. by both artists in 1894, which may bear this theory out. Specialised in gundogs and shooting scenes. He also painted portraits of hunters, usually in stables, and otter hunting scenes. Whichever signature he chose to use, he almost always dated his work.

Graham, Madge (op.1910-1936)
Flower, figure and landscape painter who lived in France for many years. Exh. quite prolifically (1910-1936). Her painting entitled "Moon at Noon at

Wimbledon" c.1930 showing a rather unconventional view of tennis on the outside courts at Wimbledon by moonlight, 15¾in.x19¾in., was auctioned Sotheby's (Bel.) 1979.

Grainger, James (b.1956)
Contemporary painter of naïve scenes including his interpretation of real tennis entitled "The King of Tennis", oil on board, 21in.x14in. Exh. regularly in London at the Portal Gallery.

Grainger, Vic (b.1931)
Painter of greyhound racing scenes who cleverly captures the thrill of stadium racing. Born in Mansfield, Nottingham, Grainger became a commercial artist before laying it aside in favour of sporting commissions.

Grandjean, Edmund Georges (1844-1908)
French landscape painter of some equestrian scenes including "The Dressage Practice" and "The Riding School". A fine pair of paintings, 19½in.x16½in., auctioned Sotheby's (NY) 1987.

Grant, A. (op.1786-1789)
A painting by this artist of the "Royal Hunt at Windsor" was engraved by S. Fores in 1786. Grant exh. two landscape paintings at the RA in 1788 and 1789.

Grant, Charles Jameson (op.1831-1837)
Draughtsman, etcher and lithographer of humorous subjects, many printed for the penny "radical" papers. Included in this Dictionary for his lithograph of a cricket match, presumably after his own work, entitled "Bowl'd Out or the K--g and All England Against the Borough Mongers", pub. 1831, 8¾in.x13¾in.

Grant, Donald (b.1942)
Australian artist of several ballooning scenes including "Soaring in the Heavens" s.&d. 1971, 21¾in.x34in. and "The Big Sky", 39½in.x49¼in., Sotheby's (Sussex) 1990.

Grant, Duncan James Corrowr, LG (1885-1978)
An artist not usually associated with painting sports scenes but included in this Dictionary for his studies of "Wrestlers", pen/ink/gouache, 15in.x11in., his superb "County Cricket" scene, painted in watercolour in the mid-1950s, 9in.x13in., and his painting entitled "Football" dated 1911 showing a game of Rugby football. Tate Gallery Collection, London. Studied at the Westminster School of Art, in Italy, in Paris under J.E. Blanch (1906) and then at the Slade School. A member of the Camden Town Group (1911) and of the LG (1919).

Grant, Sir Francis, PRA (1803-1878)
Scottish portrait and sporting painter, the younger son of a Perthshire laird who married as his second wife, after his first wife died in 1827, Isabella, sister of the 4th Duke of Rutland. Grant loved fox-hunting and spent much of his time hunting around Melton Mowbray where he kept a hunting establishment from 1827 until his death in 1878. There he painted his famous sporting work "The Melton Hunt Breakfast" where all the members are identified in "Meltonia" by Tom Markland, pub. Fores 1892. He became a great friend and pupil of John Ferneley, Snr (q.v.) from about 1824, who

painted his portrait on a favourite hunter and exh. it at the RA (1850). Grant himself exh. at the RA, BI and SS (1834-1879). He was elected ARA (1842), RA (1851) and PRA (1866), the only Scot to have held the office, in which year he was also knighted. This was despite a slight reluctance on the part of the Queen who felt that he was not really in the top league as a painter to become PRA "Since he boasts of never having been to Italy or studied the Old Masters". Such was her prejudice even though Grant had painted her portrait riding in Windsor Park with Lord Melbourne (1840) which had established his reputation as a leading society portrait painter. Nevertheless he was one of the very few sporting artists, apart from Sir Alfred Munnings (q.v.) and Abraham Cooper (q.v.), to attain this position. Later, in his established role as PRA, Grant featured prominently in C.W. Cope's painting "Hanging at the RA" painted in 1876 in which work Sir J.E. Millais (q.v.) also features. Amongst the sporting subjects which Grant exh. at the RA was "The Meeting of His Majesty's Staghounds" (1837) with the pack's huntsman, Mr. Charles Davis (q.v.) Exh. SA (1829-1833) including "The First Meeting of the North Berwick Golf Club" with portraits of Robert Oliphant of Coudie (putting), Captain Brown, Colonel Norval, J. Campbell of Saddel, Sir David Baird, Mr. Macdonald of Clanranald, Lord Elcho, G. Wanchope, Mr. Carnegie and Mr. Stewart of Alderson. (Oliphant, Baird and Campbell also feature in "The Golfers" by Charles Lees (q.v.)). Several of the golfers also feature in Grant's hunting scenes for which he became perhaps better known. Exh. RSA (1852-1880) including a portrait of the 1st Duke of Buccleuch (KG), a Captain General of the Royal Company of Archers (The RSA was given its Royal Charter in 1838). Grant also painted John Whyte Melville of Bennochy & Strathkinnes, the 19th century captain of the R & A Golf Club of St. Andrews (1823). The portrait, 96in.x54in., is in the R & A Collection. The National Trust (Shugborough) have Grant's large painting "A Shooting Party at Ranton Abbey" (1840). Grant's studio sale was held at Christie's on 28 March 1879.

Grant, James Ardern, ARE, RP (1885-1973)
Liverpool painter and etcher of game subjects who studied under Fred Burridge in Liverpool, Julians in Paris and the London Central Technical School. Elected ARE (1928) and RP (1931).

Grant, John (op.1836)
A painting of John Walker, huntsman to the Fife Foxhounds with his whips and hounds, s.&d. 1836 is recorded (Mitchell). Francis Grant (q.v.) had an elder brother called John who became Laird of Kilgraston (on the borders of Fife) so it seems possible that he may have been responsible for this painting.

Grant, John (op.1880-1889)
A portrait of the racehorse "Plaisentrie" s.&d. 1886 is recorded (Mitchell). A bay racehorse with jockey up, s.&d. 1889, 16½in.x23in. and a chestnut racehorse with jockey up on a racecourse s.&d. 1880, 16½in.x 21in. are also paintings by this artist who clearly operated at a later date than the earlier John Grant (q.v.).

Grant, Thomas (op.c.1898)
A painting of trout, pike and grayling lying on a bank, 19½ in.x23½ in. auctioned Bearnes 1988.

Grant, William James (1829-1866)
London historical painter who studied at the RA Schools. Exh. at the RA 1847 to 1866 and BI. His hunting painting entitled "The Meet", s.&d. '62, 24in.x 30in. was auctioned Christie's (NY) 1987.

Gravelot, Hubert François Bourguignon (1699-1773)
French-born draughtsman and engraver. A close associate of both William Hogarth (q.v.) and Francis Hayman (q.v.) at the St. Martin's Lane Academy. He came to London in 1732 and stayed until 1745 before returning to Paris where, apart from one final visit to London, he remained. Introduced a rococo style of drawing to England which he used to effect in his "Youth Playing Cricket", one of the designs for a decorative border. Many of these designs were later transfer printed on to china plates, examples of which are in the V & A Museum and the Melbourne Cricket Club (from the collection of Anthony Baer, Esq.). Gravelot ran a studio in London where he taught drawing to, amongst others, Thomas Gainsborough (q.v.). Gravelot's pen/ink and watercolour portrait entitled "The Sporting Lady", 6½ in.x8¾ in., is in the Paul Mellon Collection, Upperville, Va, USA. The lady is shown carrying a cocked gun over her left shoulder and dead game birds over her right shoulder - a man behind her smiles derisively and points at her.

Gravely, Percy (op.1886-1927)
Painter of some equestrian subjects including a portrait of Sir Maryon-Wilson, 10th Bt. on "Toby" in a moorland landscape with two dogs, "Paddy" a bay hunter in a courtyard, s.&d. 1927 and inscr., and "Queen Bess" a pony in a landscape, inscr., s.&d. 1925. Gravely exh. at SS from 1886 from his address in Bushey, Hertfordshire.

Grave(s), Charles (b.1886)
Black and white artist, illustrator, and watercolourist who worked for "Sporting Life", "The Daily Chronicle" and "The Daily Graphic". Several clever pen and ink sketches of cricket in the 1920s were sold by Phillips 1989 from the Pilkington Collection. His work is probably undervalued.

Graves, Frederick (op.1819-1821)
A fine pencil drawing of a "Pointer Retrieving a Pheasant" and a "Whippet chasing a Rabbit", both signed and the first dated 1821, the second on Whatman paper dated 1819, 5in.x7in. were auctioned Christie's (Sth. Ken.) 1984.

Graves, John Woodcock (op.c.1865)
A portrait of John Peel, the huntsman (1770-1854) was painted by Graves from memory in about 1865 whilst he was in Tasmania. He emigrated there in 1833.

Gravet (c.1955)
An artist by this name painted "Motor Car Racing", 24in.x36in., Bonhams 1990.

Gray (op.1783)
Unknown artist from Bedford Row, London who exh. four pictures at the FS in 1783, two of which were horse portraits.

Gray, Cedric (op.1931)
Painter of "The Old Retainers" in 1931. Portraits of three old hounds, 23½ in.x19½ in., auctioned Sotheby's (Chester) 1987.

Gray, D.B. (op.1895-1902)
Black and white artist who specialised in animal drawings, particularly horses, and contributed to the "English Illustrated Magazine" (1895) and "Punch" (1902).

Gray, Douglas Stannus, ROI, RP (1890-1959)
Portrait and landscape painter who painted tennis and cricket scenes including "Cricket on the Green, Southwick" (the artist's house in the background), s.&d. '53. 19¾ in.x30in., and "After a Game of Lawn Tennis" (figures in the evening light), 18⅞ in.x25¼ in. Exh. Spink/Nevil Keeting November 1988. Gray studied art at the Croydon Art School and the RA Schools, winning the Landseer and British Institute Scholarships. Exh. at the leading London galleries and elsewhere (1919-1939). Elected ROI (1927), RP (1934).

Gray, H. Barnard (op.1844-1871)
Landscape and sporting painter who exh. at the BI, the RA, SS and elsewhere. Titles at SS include "Retrieving" (1849) and "A Young Covey" (1858).

Gray, John (op.1885-1904)
Painter of portraits, landscapes and flowers who strayed from his normal subjects to paint a hunt with hounds on a lane scattering young children and their mother, entitled "A Quiet Walk Disturbed", s.&d. '99, 18in.x 22½ in., auctioned Bonhams 1984.

Gray, William (op.1835-1883)
Sculptor and landscape painter who included several equestrian and animal portraits amongst his work. "A Bay Hunter in a Landscape", s.&d. 1861, 18in.x 24½ in., was auctioned Bonhams 1985.

Grayme (op.1776)
A dark bay racehorse with a white blaze and docked tail standing in a wooded landscape, s.&d. 1726, 8in.x9in., was auctioned Sotheby's 1976.

Greaves, Walter (1846-1930)
Painter and etcher of London scenes, particularly the Thames. Son of a Chelsea boat builder and brother of Henry Greaves (1850-1900). Both brothers were friends, assistants and possibly pupils of James Whistler (1834-1903). Greaves' sporting work includes "The Last Chelsea Regatta" which he engraved as his finest plate, 10¼ in.x21¾ in., and a "Hot Air Balloon at the Royal Cremorne Gardens", a watercolour painted with his brother Henry, s.&d. by both artists 1872, 19½ in.x 24½ in., auctioned Christie's 1985.

Green, Alexander (op.1844-1861)
Exh. three paintings at SS (1844-1861) including one entitled "Poachers Selling Game" (1844).

Green, Alfred H. (op.1848)
Painter of equestrian scenes who copied the work of J.F. Herring (q.v.) signing it with his own name. "Feeding the Horse", s.&d. 1848, 46in.x36in., Christie's 1990.

Green, Charles, RI (1840-1898)
Watercolour painter of historical subjects and illustrator. Included in this Dictionary for his watercolours "The Croquet Player" signed with mono. and dated 1867, 6½in.x4½in., exh. at the Maas Gallery, London, and "At the Races" signed with inits. and inscr. "Langham Sketching Club" and dated 1867, 5¼in.x6¼in., auctioned Phillips 1988.

Green, Donald E.
Contemporary artist of Rugby personalities painted in watercolour, including Eddie Butler of Wales and Jim Renwick of Scotland, etc. Artwork for "Rugby World 1981".

Green, Henry (op.1914)
This artist's painting of "The Tetrarch", s.&d. 1914, was auctioned Bonhams 1982. "The Tetrarch", born 1911 and known as "the Spotted Wonder" for the white "splodges" all over his body, was one of the most remarkable two year olds ever seen on the Turf. He only ran as a two year old and was never beaten.

Green, James (1771-1834)
Portrait painter who was apprenticed to Thomas Martyn, a natural history draughtsman of Great Marlborough Street, London. Studied at the RA Schools and first exh. at the RA in 1792. He was the husband of Mary Green (q.v.) and painter of the portrait of John Warde of Squerries, Kent (1752-1838), the itinerant Master of hounds, seated with his favourite hound "Glory" at his knee, a painting which was later engraved by C. Turner. A similar subject was also painted by William Barraud (q.v.).

Green, Mary (1776-1847)
Miniaturist and watercolour artist who was married to the portrait painter James Green (q.v.). She was the daughter of William Byrne, the engraver and a member of the Associated Artists in Watercolour (op.1808-1812). Her painting "The Young Cricketers", s.&d. 1840, and inscr., 10in.x12in., auctioned Sotheby's 1990.

Green, Nathaniel Everett (op.1852-1885 d.1899)
Landscape painter who studied at the RA Schools and exh. from 1854. Painted in Scotland, contributing illustrations to Queen Victoria's "More Leaves from the Journal of Life in the Highlands" (1884). His portraits of "Venom" and "Paggie" s.&d. 1885 and inscr. "Hartham", 16in.x20in., were auctioned Sotheby's 1986.

Green, Roland (1896-1972)
Wildlife artist and gamebird painter who held an exhibition of watercolours and etchings at Ackermanns Gallery in 1931. He was a contemporary of the game-bird painter, J.C. Harrison (q.v.) who held a rival exhibition at the other end of Bond Street. His work includes both pheasants and grouse in flight, and black game. He also painted "Peregrine Falcon" and "An Uneven Contest", a pair of falconry watercolours, both s.&d. 1916 and 1917 respectively, each 10in.x7¾in. Lawrence (Crewkerne) 1989.

Green, Stephen
Contemporary painter who exh. a rowing work entitled "Eights at Putney" at the RA in 1956.

Greene, V. (op.c.1930-1951?)
Unknown painter of a cricket painting entitled "Old Trafford", England v. West Indies with Douglas Jardine (1900-1958) at the wicket, painted c.1932-1933, signed and inscr., watercolour, 18in.x14in., auctioned Honiton Galleries 1991. Greene's portrait of Francis Ouimet (1893-1967), the American amateur golfer, playing at Hoylake, 17in.x11in., is undated but may have been painted at about the time that Ouimet became the first non-British captain of the Royal & Ancient in 1951. Greene also painted the 1933 Ryder Cup and a portrait of Pam Barton (1917-1943), winner of two British Ladies Amateur Championships and the French and American Ladies Championships, playing at Dalmaney Golf Course c.1938.

Greengrass, William Edward (b.1892, exh.1930-1938)
A coloured linocut of athletics by this artist entitled "Hurdlers", s.&d. 1932, is in the collection of the British Museum.

Greenham, Robert Duckworth, RBA, ROI (1906-1976)
London-born painter, etcher, wood engraver and mural decorator. Included in this Dictionary for "A Regatta, Hampton Court", s.&d. 1944, 9½in.x13in., which was auctioned Christie's 1989. Greenham studied at the Byam Shaw School of Art, at the Vicat Cole School (1924) and at the RA Schools (1926-1929), winning the Landseer and British Institute Scholarships and the Creswick Prize. Exh. at the leading London galleries and elsewhere (1925-1940). Elected RBA (1931) and ROI (1933).

Greenup, Joseph, RI (op.1930s, d.c.1946)
London painter who exh. at the RI and RP. Included in this Dictionary for his portrait of "A Skater", signed watercolour, 23½in.x18½in., Bonhams 1987.

Gregory, Charles (op.1830-1850)
Landscape artist of a number of equestrian and sporting scenes including several portraits of hunters in land-scapes. A dark bay harnessed carriage horse with a groom, and a liver and white spaniel in a stable court-yard, s.&d. 1842, were auctioned Bonhams 1983.

Gregory, Edward John, RA, PRI (1850-1909)
Painter of figure subjects, landscapes and town scenes in both oil and watercolour. Studied art at the RCA and at the RA Schools. Worked as a black and white artist for "The Graphic" (1871-1875). Exh. at the RA from 1875. Elected RA and PRI (1898). Included in this Dictionary for "The Skater", watercolour and pencil, signed and inscr., 17¼in.x12½in., a charming picture of a young lady holding her skates and standing on the edge of a frozen river bustling with skaters.

Gregory, George (1849-1938)
Marine artist, usually connected with the 19th century but in fact much more of his work was still being painted in the 1930s. Born in the Isle of Wight where he lived

and died. Painted scenes in the Solent, very often of yachts racing. Son of Charles Gregory (1810-1896) the marine artist, his work is represented in the Royal Thames Yacht Club.

Gresley, Harold, NSA, RWS (b.1892-1967)
Landscape painter in watercolour and oil, the son of the artist Frank Gresley (1855-1936). Studied at Derby Art School (1912) and Nottingham Art School (1919) under Arthur Spooner (q.v.). Exh. at the RA, RI, RWS, etc. Elected NSA (1936), RWS (1945). Occasionally painted fox-hunting scenes including "In Full Cry", signed watercolour, 14in.x20½in., auctioned Christie's 1989.

Grey, Alfred, RHA (op.1869-1924, d.1926)
Irish landscape and cattle painter who included some equestrian scenes amongst his work. His portrait of the mare "Melusine" painted in 1880, 30in.x26in., was auctioned Phillips 1986. Exh. at the principal London galleries from 1873. Elected RHA (1870).

Grey, Charles, RHA (1808-1892)
Scottish portrait painter who worked chiefly in Ireland. Elected RHA in 1846. Portrait examples of his work are in the Ulster Museum and Trinity College, Dublin. His painting entitled "Merry Days in Glensila" depicting a group of the Wingfield family stalking was one of a pair painted for Lord Castlereagh in 1885. The other was destroyed in the Powerscourt fire in 1974, 51in.x86½in. Glensila in Angus, Scotland, was an estate belonging to the Earl of Airlie and was rented by the Castlereaghs for many years. Grey painted a number of equestrian and other portraits for the Wingfield family including his portrait of a bay hunter standing in the grounds at Powerscourt with Sugar Loaf Mountain beyond, 19⅞in.x25⅞in., painted in October 1859, auctioned Christie's 1986.

Grey, Gregor, RHA (op.1873-1911)
Animal and sporting artist whose work includes portraits of game dogs. Exh. at the RHA (1880-1911).

Greyson, W. (op.1822)
A watercolour portrait of a grey horse standing outside a stable in a landscape, signed by this artist and painted in 1822, was auctioned Phillips 1986.

Gribbin, O. (op.c.1920s)
Pigeon racing artist.

Gribble, Paul (b.1938)
Versatile lithographer and a painter of sporting subjects who served an apprenticeship as a graphic designer at a studio in a Bristol printing and packaging company. Born in Bristol, Gribble was fortunate in serving his apprenticeship under Edwin Penny, the famous bird painter. Gribble is probably one of the last artists to have drawn directly on to litho plates for commercial reproduction, and during this period he won many awards for graphics. During the last decade Gribble has become a full-time painter and his work has sold throughout Europe and the USA.

Grierson, Charles MacIver, RI, PS (1864-1939)
Irish-born painter in oil, watercolour and pastel who included a few sporting subjects in his work. "After the Hunt", a watercolour painted in 1920, and "An Interested Audience - A Break in a Tennis Party", a watercolour, 13¾in.x20½in. Studied art under Fred Brown (q.v.) at the Westminster School of Art. Exh. at the main London galleries from 1885. Elected RI (1892) and PS (1904).

Griesedieck, Ellen
A leading contemporary American sports illustrator and painter who was born in St. Louis, Missouri and is a graduate of the University of Colorado. Her watercolour/pastel paintings have been commissioned by a variety of sporting publications including "World Tennis", "Golf", "Sports Illustrated", "Road and Track" and the National Football League Pro magazines. She has illus. two books - "Richard Petty: King of the Road" and "Golf - the Passion and the Challenge". Griesedieck's work is exh. at the annual Auto Art exhibitions.

Griffier, Robert (1688-c.1750)
London painter of river scenes, landscapes, hunting and hawking scenes. The son and pupil of John (Jan) Griffier, the Dutch landscape painter, Robert Griffier spent his time between Amsterdam and London. His painting "Regatta on the Thames" dated 1748 (Collection the Duke of Buccleuch) might well have been influenced by Canaletto.

Griffin-Bernstorff, Ann
Contemporary Irish painter of naïve scenes including "A Real Tennis Match", 18in.x 16in., Portal Gallery Ltd, London. Studied at the National College of Art, Ireland and in Paris.

Griffiths, Alfred (op.1850-1895)
Midlands artist who specialised in studies of racing pigeons, painted for local breeders and owners in the Liverpool and Manchester area. Several of his paintings were of pigeons exh. at the Liverpool Dog, Poultry and Pigeon Show in 1895. He also painted equestrian portraits of hunters.

Griffiths, C.J. (op.1820-1859)
This provincial artist painted a number of equestrian and sporting works between 1820 and 1859 including "Race Day, Ringwood, Hampshire", 8¼in.x11¾in., painted in 1820 and exh. at the Leger Galleries, London. Portraits of hunters (1859) and a study of a liver and white foxhound in a landscape (1843) are other paintings recorded by this artist.

Griffiths, John (1837-1918)
Welsh-born landscape and topographical painter who studied art at the National Art Training School, after which he worked on the decorations at the South Kensington Museums. Appointed the first Principal of the Bombay School of Art (1869-1893). Exh. Indian subjects at the RA including "Black Buck Hunting in India - the Kill" in 1904, the last year that Griffiths exh. there.

Griffiths, Mark
"The Goalie's anxiety at the Penalty Kick", powder paint on paper, 14½in.x11¾in. Bonhams 1988.

Griffiths, P.
Contemporary painter of "The Polo Players", 12in.x 20in., s.&d. 1961. Blackburn Museum and AG.

Griggs, Frank (op.1925-1938)
A portrait of the Derby winner "Bois Roussel" (1938) and a watercolour of the Ascot Stakes (1925) are recorded by this artist.

Grimbaldeston, Walter (op.1711-1738)
This sporting artist, a contemporary of Wootton and Tillemans (qq.v.), was clearly influenced by both artists. His work, whilst echoing the Italian and Flemish influences found in Wootton and Tilleman's work (but not evident in the work of another contemporary, James Seymour), is already distinctive in its interest in local topography and its careful observation of men and animals. His painting "The Kill", 48in.x48in., one of a set of three hunting scenes (private collection) was exh. at the British Sporting Heritage Exhibition, Sotheby's, 1984.

Grimshaw, John Atkinson, (1836-1893)
Distinctive Leeds painter of landscapes, often by moonlight, or sunset, and of town views and dockyards. His early work is signed J.A. Grimshaw but in about 1867 he dropped the "John" and signed himself "Atkinson Grimshaw". His equestrian work includes a portrait of the dun gelding "Pale Ale" painted in 1863 with Henry Palmer in the saddle and "Her Favourite Pony", a young girl out riding, s.&d. 1867, 55½in.x43½in., auctioned Christie's 1975.

Grimstone, Edward (op.1837-1879)
Painter of animals, portraits and some sporting works. Exh. at the RA (1837-1879) including "Return from the Chase" (1841), "The Dying Hound" and a study of pike (1843).

Grineau, Bryan de (1882-1957)
See also de Grineau and Bryan. Examples of de Grineau's sporting work contributed to "The Illustrated London News" include "Bedford School, Students playing Cricket Outside", s.&d. 1952 and inscr., pencil, 18in.x29in., repro. in "The Illustrated London News" 14.6.52; "Students Playing Hockey in front of Welbeck College", signed and inscr., 17in.x26¼in., pencil; "A Lacrosse Match at Wycombe Abbey", s.&d. 1955, 18¾in.x15½in., inscr. and repro. in "The Illustrated London News" 12.2.55; "Girton College, Cambridge", showing the Emily Davis tennis court, s.&d. 1950 and inscr., pencil, repro. in "The Illustrated London News" 22.4.50.

Griset, Ernest Henry (1844-1907)
Talented animal artist, illustrator and caricaturist. Born in France, he studied art under Louis Gallait who may have been responsible for Griset's permanent move to London in the mid-1860s. Became known for his grotesque prehistoric animal paintings but his early work was very French in style with his beautifully delicate pen drawings tinted with soft colouring. His horse and driving sketches are particularly subtle, depicting speed with elegance. He is included in this Dictionary for his charming series of nine sketches of salmon trout fishing entitled "Mr. Lovejoy's Holiday Trip to the Highlands", pen, black ink and watercolour and each inscr., 6⅞in.x5½in., Christie's 1984.

Grooms, Red (b.1937)
Watercolour painter of an American baseball game entitled "Spring Training in West Palm Beach", dated 1985, 14in.x17in., private collection, USA. A rather fey portrait (1979) of the American footballer, Fran Tarkenton, painted in vinyl, was exh. at NAMOS, Indianapolis (1991). Grooms, best known for his sculpture, studied at the Art Institute of Chicago, the Peabody College for Teachers, Nashville Tn, the Hans Hoffmann School, NYC and the New School for Social Research. Collections of his work are at Rutgers University and the Art Institute of Chicago.

Grossmith, Walter Weedon (1854-1919)
Painter, author and actor. Educated at Simpsons School in Hampstead, London. Studied art at the Slade and the RA Schools. He is most widely known for his publication "Diary of a Nobody" which first appeared in "Punch" in 1888. His pen and ink drawing "Jack Fishing" is in the collection of the Piscatorial Society and was contributed by Grossmith to "The Illustrated Sporting and Dramatic News" on 9 January 1884.

Grove, David (op.1961-1987)
Born Washington DC. Portrait painter and an illustrator. President of the Society of Illustrators in San Francisco and a photographer in the early part of his career. Painted the portraits of the American footballers "Joe Federspiel", 1978 and "Jeff Siemon 1978", oil on gesso panel.

Grund, Norbert (1717-1767)
German figure and landscape painter whose study "Skaters on a Frozen Lake", 7½in.x10in., was auctioned Sotheby's (Mount Juliet Kilkenny) 1987.

Grunler, Lois (b.1809)
German portrait painter whose fine oil of the Prince of Rohan's favourite hunter, 21½in.x25½in., was exh. at Colnaghi 1986.

Gryeff, Adriaan de (1670-1715)
See De Gryeff

Guay, Gabriel (op.1876)
French artist whose "Fishing on the Seine", s.&d. 1876, 15¾in.x20¼in., was auctioned Christie's 1983.

Gudgeon, Ralston, RSW (1810-1984)
Scottish animal and bird painter who studied at the Glasgow Art School where he won several competitions. Held his first one-man show at Annans Gallery, Glasgow. In 1933 he won the Torrance Memorial Award at the Glasgow Institute. In 1936 he was elected RSW, at that time the youngest RSW ever created. His paintings can be found in numerous galleries and collections all over the world. He was also a frequent illustrator of the cover of "The Scottish Field". He painted a number of fishing scenes including "Nearly Hooked" and "Trout and Minnows".

Gudin, Herminie (op.1852-1890)
French marine and estuary painter and of watery subjects. A fine painting of rowing "Au Bord de la Rivierè", 17½in.x25¼in., painted 1890, exh. McConnel Mason, London.

Gueldry, Ferdinand Joseph (b.1858)
French artist who painted some magnificent rowing pictures including "Le Repos de l'Equip", 1900, 15½in.x24in., which he exh. at the Paris Salon in 1901. This shows rowers resting after a race. "Eights Racing at Putney", 15in.x21¼in., was auctioned Sotheby's 1986, and "Repairing the Scull", 16in.x18in. and dated 1895, Sotheby's (NY) 1989.

Guest, Miss (c.1880-d.1959)
Hound and terrier painter, much admired by Lionel Edwards (q.v.). She was a Master of Hounds in 1907.

Guest, Alison (Mrs. H. Nesfield) (b.1951)
Contemporary artist of fox-hunting and country scenes who has had two exhibitions in London galleries. Winner of the first prize in 1982 of the competition organized by "Horse and Hound" to celebrate the centenary of the Masters of Foxhounds Association. Her painting "The Four O'Clock Fox" featuring the end of the day's hunting at Long Holcombe, Exmoor in December 1981 shows a traditional scene painted in a traditional style but with flair and an obvious knowledge of the sport.

Guest, Thomas Douglas (1781-after1839)
Portrait artist who specialised in paintings of boxers including a portrait of the Champion of England Tom Cribb (engraved in 1811 by John Young) and portraits of Thomas Belcher (1783-1854) and Molyneux. An engraving of Belcher by Charles Turner after the work by Guest and pub. in 1811 is in the collection of the British Museum.

Guevara, Alvaro, NEAC (1894-1951)
Boxer and bohemian painter of boxing scenes. Born in Chile. Settled in England (1910). Studied at Bradford School of Art and the Slade School of Art (1912-1915). Exh. at Roger Fry's Omega Workshops (1916) and became a close friend of Edith Sitwell. Married the artist Meraud Guinness in 1929. Elected NEAC (1930) and moved to France in the same year. Arrested by the Germans in 1941 and returned to Chile.

Guillonet, Octave Denis Victor (1872-1967)
"Ascot Races", 86in.x142½in., and "Henley Regatta", 85in.x143½in., both auctioned Sotheby's (NY) 1988, are two of his major sporting pictures.

Guinard, Gaston (op.1926)
French painter of equestrian scenes including "The Parade to the Post" auctioned Christie's (NY) 1986.

Gundry, Thomas (op.1891)
This artist exh. a work entitled "In Training" at the RA in 1891 from a London address.

Gunton, William (op.1829)
Animal painter who specialised particularly in dog studies. He exh. three paintings at SS in 1829 and three

at BI including "Dogs with Birds of Sport". A pheasant escaping the clutches of a fox, pencil and watercolour, 7in.x6in., was auctioned Bonhams July 1988 and "Hounds in a Landscape" and "A Spaniel by a Pond" were auctioned Bonhams 1987.

Guria, Ben
Pencil caricatures of famous cricketers including Sir Julian Cahn etc. Phillips (West Two) London.

Gustavson, Leland R. (1896-1966)
Painter and magazine illustrator mainly for the "Saturday Evening Post" and "McCalls". Gustavson painted several golfing scenes depicting moments in U.S. golf history.

Guthrie, Sir James, PRSA, HRA, RSW (1859-1930)
Glasgow landscape and portrait painter whose sporting work includes a portrait of Henry, son of the Revd. Munro Gibson DD painted three-quarter length holding a football and looking to the left, s.&d. 1881. This painting is listed in the catalogue of Guthrie's works, compiled by Sir J.L. Caw in 1932, and taken from Guthrie's own catalogue. The painting was owned at that time (1932) by Dr H.W. Gibson of Hampstead. The game of lawn tennis also featured in a number of paintings by this artist including two listed in the 1932 catalogue. One, 19in.x18in., s.&d. 1891, was owned by Miss A.M. Rankine of Glasgow and the other, 24in.x 18in., s.&d. 1892, was owned by Mrs George Burrell of Paisley. Guthrie studied art in London and Paris and became a leading member of the Glasgow School. He was also a close friend of Joseph Crawhall (q.v.), working with him in Lincolnshire, Brig O'Turk, Dunbar and the Clyde in 1879, 1881, 1882, 1883, 1884 and 1885. Exh. at the leading galleries. Elected President of the Glasgow Art Club (1896-1898), RSA (1892), PRSA (1902-1919). Knighted (1903). Member of NEAC and RSW.

Guy, Robert
Contemporary painter and illustrator who studied at Exeter College of Art and Design. A keen and proficient skier, Guy illus. the "Story of Ski-ing" by Ranulph Rayner, pub. David & Charles.

Guys, Constantin Ernest Adolphe Hyacinthe (1802-1892)
Dutch-born artist of French parentage who worked in England as French tutor to the grandson of Thomas Girtin, the watercolourist. Contributed to "The Illustrated London News" (1843-1860), chiefly as a European correspondent. Worked mostly in pen and ink but sometimes in watercolour. His work, which frequently includes horses, is highly regarded and sought after. His painting of Mat Dawson training on Limekilns, Newmarket, 1890, 13¾in.x10¾in., was auctioned Sotheby's (Sussex) 1988.

Gwathmey, Robert (1903-1988)
American social realist painter of an American baseball game entitled "County Stadium (World Series)" dated 1958, 32½in.x45½in. Collection Terry Dintenfass Gallery.

Gwi(y)n, James (1700-1769)
Draughtsman of forty-seven drawings engraved for Domenico Angelo's "L'Ecole des Armes", London (1763). The principal figure in all the drawings is Domenico Angelo Malevolti Tremamondo (1716-1802) the famous fencing master, whose fencing academy in Soho was patronised by the fashionable members of society. See also T.J. Rawlins. The Earl of Pembroke, the Chevalier d'Eon and John Hamilton Mortimer (q.v.), the artist, all posed as models for Domenico Angelo's fencing partners. Angelo taught fencing to the two sons of George III and employed Gwin to make the drawings which he, Domenico, then presented to the King, after publishing his treatise on the sport.

Gwynn, William (op.1795-1845)
Shropshire animal painter and publisher whose work includes "At the Finishing Post" s.&d. 1827 and inscr. "Ludlow", 17¾in.x23½in., was auctioned Sotheby's (NY) 1987. A print by W. Wright after a portrait of a "Shropshire Pig" c.1795 is at Reading University and a portrait of twin oxen, bred by J. Ackers, Esq. MP for Ludlow, seen standing in a landscape with a King Charles Cavalier spaniel, crows mobbing a hawk in the sky above them, a view of Ludlow Hill beyond, s.&d. 1845 and inscr., were auctioned Bonhams 1981. Other portraits of hunters are inscribed "Ludlow" and variously dated 1836, 1838 and 1820. Gwynn usually appears to have signed, dated and inscribed his work.

H

"HB"
Pseudonym used by the artist John Doyle (q.v.)

"HH"
Pseudonym used by Henry Heath (q.v.) for his work contributed to Messrs. Fores (1831).

Haag, Karl (Carl), RWS (1820-1915)
Landscape and sporting painter. Also a miniature painter in watercolours. Born in Bavaria, studied art in Nuremburg and Munich. Came to England in 1847 and worked on two large paintings of stag shooting at Balmoral for Queen Victoria. Exh. at the RA (1849-1881), SS and OWS. Elected RWS (1882). Colls. V & A Museum and the Bristol Gallery.

Hacker, Arthur, RA, RI (1858-1919)
Portrait painter and illustrator. Born in London, the son of Edward Hacker the line engraver of sporting subjects. Studied art at the RA Schools (1876-1880) and under Bonnat in Paris (1880-1881). He became a popular society portrait painter and exh. prolifically at the RA, RI, and NEAC. Elected RA (1910) and RI (1918). His portrait of the "Fisher Boy with his Rod", 24¾in.x22½in., is enchanting. It was sold originally from the artist's studio sale and again at Sotheby's 1982.

Hackert, Johann Gottlieb (1744-1793)
German landscape painter, one of four artist brothers. Studied art in Berlin, Paris and Rome and came to London in 1772. Exh. a portrait of four hounds "after nature" at the RA (1773).

Hackney, Arthur, VPRWS, RE, ARCA (Lond.) (b.1926)
Yorkshire-born landscape painter and etcher. Studied at Burslem School of Art and at the RCA where he obtained his diploma in 1949 and a travelling scholarship to France and Italy. Brother of the artist Alfred Hackney. Exh. at the RA, RE, NEAC and RWS. Elected RE (1960) and RWS (1957) His painting of football "Spectators returning Home after Port Vale v Accrington Stanley", watercolour, 27in.x14in., was exh. at the FE in 1953.

Haddelsey, Vincent (b.1934)
Grimsby-born, self-taught painter of racing, polo, rodeo riding, hunting and driving scenes painted in a naïve style. His work is represented in many private collections throughout the world, including that of Her Majesty the Queen. Solo exhibition at Usher Gallery, Lincoln, 1985.

Haddon, David W. (exh.1884-1911)
Birmingham painter who exh. at the Royal Society of Artists, Birmingham and the Walker AG Liverpool. His painting "Four of the Eleven" (boys playing cricket) signed and inscr., 7in.x9in., was auctioned Sotheby's 1986.

Hagarty, James (op.1762-1783)
London painter of a wide variety of subjects including sporting scenes and horse portraits. Exh. at the FS (1767-1783).

Hagedorn, Karl, RBA, RSMA, NS, NEAC (1889-1969)
Landscape artist who painted a number of bathing, beach and swimming scenes. Born in Berlin. Educated in Germany. Settled in England (1905) and became

naturalised (1914). Studied art in Manchester, the Slade School and in Paris. Exh. at the International Exhibition of Decorative Art in Paris (1925) and at the RA, RBA and NEAC. Elected RBA (1935).

Haig, Miss Violet (op.1904)
Animal painter who exh. one work at the SWA in 1904. A portrait of "Dido", 11¼in.x6¾in., was auctioned Bonhams 1985.

Haigh, Arthur Grenfell (1870-1963)
Cheshire-born equestrian and animal artist in oil and occasionally watercolour, also a sculptor. His grandfather was David Haigh, a renowned MFH of the Old Surrey Hunt. Settled in Newmarket taking private commissions to paint animals and horses. The Duke of Beaufort was his patron which led to commissions from the Cotswold racing and hunting fraternity. Amongst the racehorses he painted were portraits of "The Tetrarch", "Diomedes", "Airborne", April V" and "Ocean Swell". Tom Walls, the actor, was the owner of "April V" (the 1932 Derby winner) for whom Haigh also painted a number of hunter portraits.

Hailey, Clarence Thomas (1867-1949)
Photographer and equestrian artist, born in Clare, Suffolk (which is why he was called Clarence). Came to London and took a photographic studio in Baker Street. Founded the first Bloodstock Agency in 1909. This became a partnership (1929) and a limited company on the death of Clarence Hailey (1949) renamed Clarence Hailey Ltd. Hailey travelled widely in South America but lived a large part of his life at Aston Rowant where he founded the Aston Park Stud in 1929 for William Barnett to stand his Derby winner "Trigo". A self-taught artist who painted a great deal from his photographs, many of which are to be found in the museum at Newmarket. His paintings tend to be faithfully photographic, not surprisingly, and rather studied. His portraits of "Aboyeur", winner of the Derby (1917) ridden by E. Piper and the racehorse "Aleppo" with jockey up, painted in 1916, 19in.x26in., were sold respectively at Christie's (Sth. Ken.) and Sotheby's (Sussex) 1988/89.

Haines, Miss Agnes Eliza (op.1887/8)
Exh. a painting of a fish in 1887 at the Institute of Oil Painters from a London address.

Haines, William (1778-1848)
Portrait painter in watercolours who exh. at SS (1824-1839) including a watercolour portrait of a Highland sportsman.

Hainsworth, Arthur (op.c.1895)
An unrecorded Victorian artist whose hunting gouache "In Full Cry", 16½in.x13in., was auctioned Sotheby's 1985.

Hair, Thomas H. (op.1838-1856)
Mediocre Northumbrian painter of landscapes, towns and industrial subjects who exh. at the RA (1841-1849), the BI and at the SS. He made, etched and pub. a series of views entitled "Sketches of the Coalmines in Northumberland and Durham" in 1839. His painting of

"Salmon Netting on the Tweed" (1840) was exh. at Christopher Cole, Henley on Thames, 1984 and his fine painting "Otter Hunting on the Tell, Northumberland", s.&d. 1856, 10in.x14in., was sold by Bracketts, Tunbridge Wells 1988.

Haken, William
A painting of the Yarmouth to London coach "Old Blue" passing the London to Norwich coach and vice versa, a pair signed by this artist, 8¾in.x14½in., were auctioned Bearnes 1982.

Hale, Kathleen (Mrs. McClean) (b.1898)
Illustrator, lithographer and animal artist who painted in both oil and watercolour. Creator of "Orlando" the marmalade cat which first appeared in book form in 1938, originally dreamt up for her two small sons. Hale, who was born in Scotland, studied at the Manchester School of Art and the East Anglian School of Painting and Drawing, under Cedric Morris, in 1938. Exh. LG, the NEAC and elsewhere.

Hale, Philip Leslie (1865-1931)
American painter, teacher and writer. Born Boston, the son of the Revd. Edward Everett Hale. Studied art in New York and won many medals. His equestrian painting "Riders on the Beach", 48in.x76¼in., was auctioned Sotheby's (NY) 1978.

Halfpenny, Joseph Samuel (1748-1811)
This painter, etcher and aquatint engraver of only moderate talent was the Clerk of Works during the 19th century restorations of York Minster. Included in this Dictionary for his portrait of Edward Constable and his brother, Francis, of Burton Constable, Yorkshire, boar hunting. Painted in watercolour, exh. Frank Sabin, London. Halfpenny also painted angling subjects.

Hall, Arthur (op.1914-1940)
Equestrian artist of many hunting scenes painted in both oil and watercolour. Hall exh. at the RA and elsewhere (1916-1940).

Hall, Gilbert (op.1858-1875)
Landscape painter and of some fishing scenes including "Ssh, I've got a bite", s.&d. 1869, 29¾in.x45in., auctioned Christie's 1985.

Hall, Harry (1813-1882)
Sporting painter, particularly of equestrian scenes. A faithful portrayer of sportsmen and their animals before the innovation of photography. Although his work covered all aspects of country sports he is best remembered for his portraits of racing personalities and racehorses. He painted no less than forty-three consecutive winners of the Derby. Most of these were painted for engraving for "Baily's Magazine" until he quarrelled with the proprietor over a pay rise, or the lack of it. After the death of J. F. Herring, Snr. (q.v.) Harry Hall could be said to have stepped into his shoes so far as horse racing portraiture was concerned and, living at Newmarket with already a great reputation, it would have been odd if he had not found plenty of commissioned work for his brush. He was by all accounts a most extraordinary looking fellow, being almost as wide as he was tall, with an enormous head covered in woolly hair.

Hall, Henry R. (op.1895-1905)
This painter from Broughton in Furness exh. one painting at the RA in 1902 entitled "Evening Glow". He is included in this Dictionary for his two major paintings of otter hunting, "Otter Hunting on the River Sallock", s.&d. 1905 and inscr. "Hitting the Drag", 40in.x60in., auctioned Bonhams 1984 and "Otter Hunting near Alnwick, Northumbria", signed and inscr., 20in.x 30in., auctioned Christie's 1985.

Hall, Sydney Prior (1842-1922)
Painter and illustrator, born in Newmarket, the son and pupil of Harry Hall (q.v.). Studied at the RA Schools and under A. Hughes. Contributed illustrations to "The Graphic", covering the Prince of Wales's Indian tour and the Franco-Prussian war. An artist of great ability, his sporting output is small but covers hunting and cricket scenes in watercolour. "Eton v Harrow Match at Lords - A Boundary Hit", repro. in "The Graphic", Saturday 22 July 1899.

Halland, C.J.
19th century painter of a set of six humorous sporting sketches, all signed and inscr., each 10½in.x14in., auctioned Sotheby's 1973.

Hallet, J. (19th century)
A painting by this artist entitled "Morning, Salisbury Plain - the Bath to Bristol Royal Mail", signed, 16½in.x27¾in., was auctioned Sotheby's (Sussex) 1990.

Halley, Alexander Hay (op.1916)
Landscape painter and of some equestrian scenes who lived at Guildford, Surrey. He exh. at the ROI in 1916 a painting of a mare and a foal - price £12.12s.

Halley, W.A. (op.1861)
Military and equestrian painter whose work includes portraits of hunters.

Halliday, George D. (op.1953)
Engraver. Included in this Dictionary for his aquatint entitled "Footballers", etched in 1953 and exh. at the RA that year.

Halliday, J. (op.c.1890)
His painting entitled "A Hot Corner at Abel Water", showing HRH The Prince of Wales at a battue, Sandringham, signed watercolour, was auctioned Anderson & Garland (Newcastle), 1985.

Ham, George (op.1900-1953)
The pseudonym used by Georges Hamel (q.v.).

Hambridge, Jay (1867-1924)
American painter and illustrator whose fine work entitled "Crowd at the Polo Grounds" was repro. in "Harper's Weekly" in 1895. The spirited crowd encourages the New York Giants playing to a capacity crowd on their home ground. The four colour proof, 18⅞in.x14in., is in the Museum of the City of New York. The title is misleading because the game being played is not polo but American football.

Hamel, Georges (1900-1972)
French artist of motor racing scenes, famous for his poster work during the 1930s and 1950s. He came to England where he was strongly influenced by Frederick Gordon Crosby (q.v.) and where he became better known as "George Ham". "An Alfa Romeo 8C Tipo 308", an original poster for the Englebert Tyre Company, pencil and red chalk on tissue paper, 15in.x12in., together with the finished poster 9½in.x7½in., were auctioned Christie's (Monaco) 1989.

Hamer, J. (op.1861-1868)
Brixton artist of definitely chilly subjects, most taking place in icy situations. Exh. at SS (1861-1868). Sporting titles include "Quiet Enjoyment in the Highlands - Skating", "Quiet Enjoyment in the Highlands - Fishing". "The Fox Wintering in the Pack Ice", however, is of a yacht, not an animal.

Hamilton, Anton-Ignaz (1696-1770)
Austrian painter working for the Saxe Weimars and then for Augustus III of Poland. His fine painting "Hawking for Kites" shows the work of a team of three kites - the "hausse pied" on the right, the "tombisseur" on the left and the "preneur" in the middle. Collection Österreichische Galerie, Vienna.

Hamilton, Charles (op.1831-1867)
Bedfordshire painter of historical and sporting subjects, often depicted in Eastern settings. Exh. at the RA and SS. Titles include "Persian Sportsmen" (1832), "The Falconer's Boy" (1835) and a portrait of Robert Oldacre, huntsman to R.G.S. Sebright with horses and hounds (1837). A falconer riding on his Arab stallion with his dog running alongside with other equestrian figures in a landscape was auctioned Sotheby's 1972.

Hamilton, Hugh Douglas (1734-1806)
Irish portrait painter. "Charles Powell Leslie at Shuttlecock Play", pastel over pencil, 22in.x15in., auctioned Sotheby's 1988.

Hamilton, John (op.c.1920s)
The painter of a pair of corny, comic, continental billiard scenes, but well painted (c.1920s), oil on board, 10in.x16in.

Hamilton, Letitia Marion, RHA (1879-1964)
Irish landscape painter and enamel plaque artist who included a number of equestrian scenes amongst her work. Studied Dublin Metropolitan School of Art, Chelsea Polytechnic and under Sir William Orpen (q.v.) and Frank Brangwyn ARHA. Won third prize in the Olympic Arts Competition July/August 1948 with her painting entitled "Meath Hunt Point to Point Races". Elected ARHA (1934). "Polo at Phoenix Park, Dublin", 5in.x7in., signed with inits. and dated 1958, oil on board, Anderson of Dublin.

Hamilton, William, RA (1750/1-1801)
History and portrait painter and of some sporting subjects including "The Return from Coursing", pen/ink and watercolour, 7¼in.x9¾in., the Paul Mellon Collection, Upperville, Va, USA. Hamilton studied at the RA Schools (1769) having previously trained as an architectural draughtsman. He later turned to figure painting and exh. at the RA (1771-1801). Elected RA (1789). William Beckford (1759-1844), first cousin to

the famous sportsman Peter Beckford (1740-1811), author of "Thoughts Upon Hare and Fox Hunting" and "Essays of Hunting", commissioned Hamilton to paint several pictures for his gallery at Fonthill Abbey. Four of Hamilton's designs were exh. at the RA (1799/1800) and Joseph Farington (q.v.) records a visit by Hamilton to Fonthill on 13 April 1801.

Hamilton, William E. (op.1874)
This artist exh. a painting of horses at the Dudley Gallery in 1874 from a London address.

Hamilton-Renwick, Lionel (b.1919)
Northumberland-born equestrian painter. Studied at Heatherleys and at the Byam Shaw Schools, pupil of Frederick Whiting (q.v.) and later of Gilbert Scott Wright (q.v.). A keen sportsman, from a family with hunting, racing and coursing interests, Hamilton-Renwick had his first exhibition at Walker's Gallery, Bond Street, in 1953. His intimate knowledge of the sports he paints has led him to be recognised as a leading painter of equestrian scenes.

Hamlyn, E. (op.1894)
"Golf in a Country Landscape", a watercolour showing a group of golfers with hills behind and long horned cattle in front, s.&d. 1894, 17¾in.x23½in., Sotheby's (Bel.).

Hammick, Joseph William (op.1907-1912)
Landscape painter from Tunbridge Wells, Kent who exh. at the RA (1907-1912) including "The Opening Meet of the Devon and Somerset Staghounds" (1908 No. 1508).

Hammond, Arthur Henry Knighton, RI, RSW, ROI (1875-1970)
Born at Arnold in Notts. Studied Nottingham School of Art, under Wilson Foster, Westminster and Paris. Elected RI (1933), ROI (1938) and RSW (1940). Exh. at the RA (1930-1961) including "The Day of the Oaks, Epsom" (1938). Hammond was also a prolific black and white artist and an etcher. He painted a great number of horse racing scenes including "Returning from the Derby" (1901), "Arriving at Ascot" (1901) and "At the Finish", showing the race between "Ard Patrick" and "Risinglass" battling out the Derby in 1902 in weather that was cold and rainy. The famous "Sceptre", an even money favourite, could only manage fourth place that year.

Hammond, Arthur J. (1875-1947)
American artist whose painting entitled "The Last Day of the Season, Prestbury, Cheshire", signed and inscr., watercolour, 9¾in.x14¾in., was auctioned at Bonhams in 1983. Hammond, who was born in Connecticut, was a pupil of Eric Pape, Charles Woodbury and G.L. Noyes. He became a member of the New Haven Pen and Pencil Club and the American Federation of Arts.

Hammond, Gertrude E. Demain (Mrs. McMurdie), RI (1862-1952)
Brixton-born figure painter in watercolour and an illustrator. The sister of the figure artist Miss Christine M. Demain Hammond (op.1886-1893). Studied at the Lambeth School of Art from 1879 and at the RA Schools from 1885. Exh. at the RA and RI from 1886. Elected RI (1896). Bronze medal winner at the Paris Exhibition (1900). Illus. "Pilgrim's Progress" (1904 edn.) and "The Virginians" (1902), "The Fairy Queen" (1909) and "Stories from Shakespeare" (1910). Painted a number of hunting scenes in watercolour including "A Promising Start", "In Full Cry", "The Hunt Assembling", etc.

Hammond, Henry (op.c.1910)
Painter in both oil and watercolour of hunting and shooting scenes, signed Henry Hammond.

Hammond, Horace (ex1902-1939)
Painter of landscapes and of several hunting scenes in watercolour. Pen and wash artist. He exh. at the RA, the Walker AG, Liverpool and the RBSA. His hunting scenes are usually small watercolours, painted in pairs, including "The Chase", "The Kill" and "The Meet".

Hammond, Robert John (op.1881-1914)
Landscape painter who included a number of pheasant shooting scenes amongst his work.

Hammond, William Oxendon (op.1858-1896)
Amateur artist and sportsman whose sketches and watercolours concentrate predominantly on sporting scenes which take place in Scotland and Kent. His sporting work, painted in watercolour, includes "Duck Shooting", signed with inits. and dated 1884, 9¾in.x 14¼in., "The End of the Day", fishermen by a salmon by the edge of a loch, s.&d. 1884, 9¾in.x 12½in., "The Day's Bag", signed with inits. and dated 1853 and inscr., 30½in.x14¾in. and "Falcons with their Handlers on the Moors", 7½in.x20¼in., Bonhams, 1991. Hammond's drawings of hawks and falcons in particular show an intimate knowledge of falconry.

Hancock, Charles (1802-1877)
Sporting and animal painter, born in Marlborough, the son of a cabinet maker. He is thought to have studied art under the Norwich landscape painter James Stark (1794-1859) and went with Stark to Norfolk in 1817 when Stark left London through illness for a period of twelve years. Hancock certainly exh. at the Norwich Society (1818-1820) and painted a portrait of Stark's son some years later. In 1830 Hancock worked in a studio at Tattersalls, Knightsbridge, London where he contributed illustrations to their "English Racehorses" (as did Harry Hall (q.v.)). He exh. twenty-three paintings at the RA (1819-1847), fifty-five at BI and forty-seven at SS until 1867. Titles at SS include a "Study of Ben Burnett, the Wyckham Poacher", a noted Buckinghamshire character, "The Rat Catcher" (1813), "The Poacher Pursued", "The Poacher's Confederate", "Ghillies Returning", "Grouse", "A Highland Ghillie restraining Two Deerhounds until the Wounded Hart Breaks from the Herd", and a "Deer Stalker in his Bothy". He contributed to "The Sporting Review" (1842-1846) and by 1835 was a well established animal painter. Unfortunately Hancock's painting career was interrupted several times by his spectacularly unsuccessful flirtation with business ventures. His horse portraiture is good and he is one of the few artists to paint the subject of ferreting frequently and successfully. Hancock illus. an edn. of "Nimrod".

Hancock, Robert (1730-1817)
Born at Burslem, Staffordshire, Hancock studied engraving under S. Ravenet and first worked in a porcelain manufactory in Battersea. This celebrated draughtsman and line engraver was then employed by the Royal Worcester Porcelain Company (founded in 1751) to engrave plates for the purpose of transfer. Many of the plates and sketches that he made were of very fine quality hunting and sporting scenes. In 1772 Hancock was made a director of the company, resigning this post in 1774.

Hand, Thomas (op.1790-d.1804)
London sporting and landscape artist who painted a number of hunting and shooting scenes. He exh. at the RA (1792-1804) including "The First Shot in September" (1802). Hand was both assistant and devoted friend of the sporting artist George Morland (q.v.). He is unfortunately known to have copied a good deal of Morland's work which has had an adverse effect on the authenticity and sometimes therefore on the value of Morland's work. Thomas Hand died within weeks of George Morland. Examples of his work are to be found at the Tate Gallery London and his portrait of George Morland, on a grey hunter with a couple of foxhounds, s.&d. 1794, 23¾in.x31½in., is in the Paul Mellon Collection, Upperville, Va, USA.

Handley, V.F.
Australian? "Polo", watercolour, signed, 18in.x15in., Miles Carpenter, London.

Hanfstaengl, Franz Seraph (1804-1877)
German lithographer and photo engraver of sporting subjects and portraits. He specialised in golfing, football, cricket, polo, rowing, fishing, fox-hunting and shooting subjects, usually after the work by his British contemporaries.

Hannaford, Charles Arthur, RBA (1887-1972)
Landscape painter in watercolour, son of the artist C.E. Hannaford, RBA. Studied at Plymouth Art School and exh. mainly at the RBA. Lived for many years in Norfolk and painted a number of fly fishing scenes in Scotland.

Hannan, William (?-d.1775)
A topographical artist whose painting of three anglers fishing in a mill pool with the mill behind, 29½in.x 47½in., is a magnificent fishing study. Auctioned Sotheby's 1977.

Hansen, Hans Jacob, RSW (1853-1947)
Scottish born landscape and figure painter in watercolour who studied painting in Edinburgh, under Robert Buchan Nisbet (q.v.) and J. Ross. Exh. at the principal London galleries from 1876 including the RA, RI and RBA. Silver medal winner at the Salzburg International Exhibition. Exh. a painting entitled "Regatta at Richmond" at the London Sketch Club in 1899 which was reported in the Brighton Society's column "In and Out of London" on 11 March 1899 as being in "an impressionist style and an interesting showing of English landscape". His watercolour "Henley Regatta - Night Falls", 9in.x11in., has a wonderful sense of atmosphere and was painted c.1910. David Messum, London.

Hardie, Charles Martin, RSA (1858-1917)
Scottish painter of portraits, landscapes and figurative subjects which occasionally embraced fishing, cricket and curling. He studied at the RSA Life School in Edinburgh and exh. at the RA and the RSA (1885-1903). "The Curling Match between North and South at Carsebreck" (1900) is in the collection of the Royal Caledonian Curling Club. His portrait of a boy playing cricket was painted in 1896 and his superb fishing painting "A Cast During the Midday Break", 20in.x 30in. and painted in 1885, was auctioned Bonhams 1983. Elected RSA (1895).

Harding, Frederick (op.1829)
Portrait painter in watercolour who exh. a painting of J.L. Richards, Esq. and his horse "Cupid" at SS in 1829.

Harding, James Duffield, RWS (1798-1863)
Topographical painter in watercolour, a lithographer and a teacher who studied under Samuel Prout and Charles Pye, the engraver. His portrait of "Charles James Packe Shooting Partridge on Moat Hill, Loughborough, with Charnwood Forest, Leicestershire Beyond", signed watercolour, 28½in.x41½in., was exh. at the BSH Exhibition, Sotheby's, 1984/5. His angling works include "A Highland River in Spate - Trout Fishing". Collection Glasgow AG.

Hardman, John (op.1799-1846)
I have listed this artist's christian name as "John" since this is the name that I have read on the signatures of at least five of his paintings. I am aware however, that he is also listed as James, or perhaps there were brothers? The bulk of the work by this artist that I have personally seen is dated between 1799 and 1817. He exh. two paintings at the RA in 1812, portraits of the horses "Worthy" and "Elizabeth" with her colt foal, the property of the Honourable East India Company. Presumably this was a commissioned work and he also appears to have worked for Lord Tredegar of Ruperra Castle, Newport, Co. Monmouth. His horses are not always "droopy and sleazy" (Mitchell) and his work could certainly bear further investigation.

Hardman, Thomas Hawthorn (op.1885-1895)
Landscape artist who exh. four paintings at the RA (1889-1895) including a hunting scene entitled "Drawing Covert, Hertfordshire" (1895). His other 1895 exhibit at the RA entitled "Rabbiting" was, according to "Bailys Magazine", June 1895 (p.428) "rather loftily situated" — in other words it was hung too high to be seen properly. Apart from that "it was a poor piece of work depicting two guns ferreting a hedgerow, one either side, with the usual poacher and ratcatcher managing the ferrets and terriers".

Hardman, Mrs. Thomas (Emma Louise) (op.1885-c.1935)
Landscape painter, the wife of Thomas Hawthorn Hardman (q.v.) who exh. five paintings at the RA including "Wild Fowl Shooting - an Anxious Moment" (1902).

Hardy, Charles (op.1815)
Drew title page "Trophies of Angling" for "The Anglers Guide" (1815).

Hardy, David (op.1855-1870)
Painter of rustic subjects and some hunting scenes, usually set in a wooded landscape. Brother of Heywood Hardy (q.v.) and James Hardy Jnr. (q.v.) .

Hardy, Dorothy M. (Mrs. Dorothy M. Payne) (op.1885-d.1937)
Very competent painter and illustrator of equestrian subjects, said to be related to Dudley Hardy (q.v.). Contributed to "The Strand Magazine" (1891) and Fores "Sporting Notes and Sketches" (1905). Her painting of "Minoru" winning the 1897 Derby for King Edward VII, 12in.x19¾in., was auctioned Sotheby's 1984. Her drawing entitled "At the Spinning Wheel", (auctioned Sotheby's Chester 1986) is dated 1885.

Hardy, Dudley, RBA, RI, ROI, RMS, PS, RWS (1867-1922)
Painter, illustrator and black and white artist. Born in Sheffield, the son of the marine painter Thomas Bush Hardy (q.v.). He studied art at the age of fifteen at the academy at Dusseldorf and then at Antwerp (1884-1885) and finally in Paris. Exh. his first painting at the RA (1885) and was elected RBA (1889), RI (1897) and ROI (1898). He was a founder member of the London Sketch Club and became President in 1902. He painted a number of equestrian studies, both racing and hunting, which were well executed and painted mostly in grisaille. He became best known, however, for his poster "The Yellow Girl" designed for Jerome K. Jerome's monthly magazine "Today". It took London by storm when it appeared and was supposed to have started the poster craze in Britain. The Derby's return after the war (1919) was announced by another brilliant poster by Hardy showing the world and his wife on the way to the races.

Hardy, Edmund (op.c.1870)
Two paintings signed by this artist but undated entitled "Refreshment for the Hunt at the Pig & Whistle Inn" and "Picking up the Scent", each 20in.x30in., were sold by Lawrence of Crewkerne in 1980.

Hardy, Frederick Daniel (1826-1911)
Painter of genre scenes, particularly those featuring children, as for example "A Game of Shuttlecock", signed, 6½in.x8½in,. Bonhams. Hardy studied art under Thomas Webster (q.v.) and exh. at the RA and BI (1851-1898).

Hardy, Heywood, ARWS, RP, RE, RWA (1842-1933)
Equestrian and animal painter, etcher and illustrator. The youngest son of James Hardy, Snr (q.v.) and brother of David Hardy (q.v.) and James Hardy, Jnr. (q.v.). Studied art in Paris and Antwerp. He shared a studio with the animal painter Briton Riviere (q.v.) in 1870 and tended to paint rather romantic scenes set in the 18th and 19th centuries - a pastime indulged in by many Edwardian painters. He painted "The Cleveland Hounds Exercising by the Sea" in 1891 for the Wharton family and another study of the hounds with Colonel and Mrs. Wharton at Shelton Castle in 1889. His other sporting patrons included Sir Frederick Millbank, Bt. (1820-1890) whom he painted with his loader, Tom Taylor, in a grouse butt in 1891, Colonel Maxwell Rouse of Thirby Hall, Bedale, Master of the Bedale Hunt, Colonel Wyndham Murray, The Marquis of Zetland and the Sitwells of Rennishaw. Heywood Hardy also collaborated with the Hon. John Collier (q.v.) on the portrait of Gerald Heywood Hardy, Master of the Meynell Hunt, painted in 1913 and sold to the USA for £17,000 by Sotheby's in March 1990. Hardy also collaborated with other painters including Frank Walton (q.v.). Hardy exh. at the RA from 1861 and also at the BI, SS and NWCS. Elected RE (1880), RWA (1883), RP (1891), ARWS (1885).

Hardy, James, Snr. (1801-1879)
Father of the equestrian artists Heywood Hardy (q.v.), James Hardy, Jnr. (q.v.) and David Hardy (q.v.). His exhibits at SS (1842-1866) include no sporting paintings but he exh. ten paintings at the RA (1832-1857) including a portrait of "Lord George Lennox on a Favourite Pony". His painting of "Mus" a chestnut racehorse in a landscape, s.&d. 1841, 40½in.x50in., was painted for the 5th Duke of Richmond (for the sum of 25 guineas) and was auctioned Christie's 1976.

Hardy, James, Jnr. RI (1832-1889)
Sporting artist, the son of James Hardy, Snr. and brother of Heywood and David Hardy (qq.v.). Best known for his pictures of dogs and game which were very often set in Highland landscapes. He exh. nine paintings at the RA, all sporting (1862-1886), eight at BI, and forty-five at SS (1853-1871). Almost all of them were sporting but many were of dead game. Auctions of his work were held at Christie's on 9 March 1878, and after his death, on 4 April 1889. Elected RI (1877). "A Successful Day's Shooting", s.&d., 1880, 12in.x16in., was auctioned Sotheby's 1985.

Hardy, Paul (op.1886-1906)
Historical painter and illustrator of a number of sporting scenes including "Summer Sport up the River", monochrome gouache c.1906. He contributed to "The Sporting and Dramatic News" and is probably best known for his illustrations to "The Children of the New Forest" (1892).

Hardy, Thomas Bush, RBA (1842-1897)
Marine painter and watercolourist, the father of the artist Dudley Hardy (q.v.). Hardy's prolific coastal scenes include a number of yacht racing scenes, usually painted in watercolour.

Hardy, W.F.
"Tug of War", a terrier and a girl fighting over a wrap after the girl has been playing shuttlecock, her shuttle and racket on the floor, s.&d. 1891, 9½in.x7½in., Bonhams. The artist was possibly W. Howard Hardy (q.v.).

Hardy, W. Howard (op.1868-1893)
Victorian landscape artist of small merit who nevertheless painted a great number of pleasant game bird and

dog scenes. Exh. several landscapes at SS (1868-1893). Always signed but very rarely dated his work.

Hare, Charles Elam (1893-c.1950)
Illus. "The Language of Field Sports" (1939), revised edn. 1949.

Hargitt, Edward, RI, ROI (1835-1895)
Scottish landscape painter who studied under Horatio McCulloch at the Trustees Academy, Edinburgh. Elected RI (1867) and ROI (1883). A well-known ornithologist, Hargitt painted equestrian portraits and shooting scenes in watercolour.

Hargreaves, Harry
Contemporary cricket cartoonist for "Punch" and "The Cricketer" whose books "Not Out" (pub. Hammond 1960) and "How's That" are drawn by a clever artist whose love of the game, which he played with distinction, is apparent.

Hargreaves, John (op.1834)
A painting of a grey stallion "Essence", a bay hunter "Johnny" and two hounds, "Trap" and "Prompt", with a groom in a wooded landscape, 27in.x35in., s.&d. 1834 was auctioned Christie's 1970. Hargreaves is thought to have worked in the Liverpool area during the first half of the 19th century.

Hargreaves, Mrs. Lucy (op.1888-1914)
Landscape painter in oil, watercolour and pastel who included several equestrian scenes and portraits of hunters in her work. Exh. widely between 1894 and 1914.

Harland, J.S. (op.1852)
An unrecorded artist whose portrait of a grey hunter with sheep and cattle in a landscape with the sea beyond, s.&d. 1852 was auctioned Sotheby's 1981. An aquatint by J. Harris of "The Scarborough Steeplechase" after work by Harland was pub. by Ackermanns.

Harmar, Fairlie (Viscountess Harberton), NEAC (1876-1945)
Portrait, figure and landscape painter in oil and watercolour whose painting "After a Game of Lawn Tennis" was exh. at the NEAC in 1916. Studied art at the Slade School (1894-1897) and exh. at the major London galleries and abroad. Elected NEAC in 1917. Exh. Lefevre Gallery. Married 7th Viscount Harberton (1933).

Harper, Charles G. (1863-1943)
Illustrator and painter who specialised in coaching and driving scenes. Like those of Heywood Hardy (q.v.) these were often set in the 19th century, usually depicting a rather romantic situation. He was also an author, writing books on the English countryside, illus. by himself. His coaching illustrations included those he made for "The Brighton Road" (1892), "The Dover Road" (1895), "The Portsmouth Road" (1895), "The Exeter Road" (1899), "The Bath Road" (1899) and "The Great North Road" (1900). Pub. with Lord Teignmouth "The Smugglers" (1923).

Harper, H.G. ("GG") (b.1851)
Sporting journalist, illustrator and artist who used the pseudonym "GG". He lived a large part of his life at Epsom where he trained and rode his own racehorses. He hunted with the Surrey Foxhounds and wrote several sporting novels and books.

Harper, John (op.1814-1838)
Exh. eleven paintings at the RA (1814-1824), mostly of fish and dead game, from a Staffordshire address. His painting of a "Retriever with Dead Game", dated 1838, 23in.x38in., was auctioned Sotheby's (Sussex) 1986.

Harper, Thomas (op.1817-1843)
Exh. nineteen portraits at the RA including a watercolour of "Joseph Hornsby Fishing". A.N. Gilbey Collection, auctioned Christie's April 1940.

Harrington, Robert, of Carlisle (1800-1882)
A pupil of the sporting artist Abraham Cooper (q.v.), Harrington painted portraits of horses and dead game. He also collaborated with Sam Bough (q.v.) to paint the Carlisle Steeplechase at Broadfield in 1844, 24½in.x 35½in., signed with initials by both artists. His patrons included G. Sharp of Hoddens Castle, Dumfriesshire. Many of his works were engraved by C. Hunt and Thomas Fairland but were pub. by himself.

Harris
A man called "Harris" (according to Mitchell) was an agent operating in the early part of the 20th century who commissioned artists to sign his name instead of their own on horse portraits for his clients. See Walter Herbert Wheeler.

Harris, Albert C. (op.1916/17)
Several paintings of pheasant shooting and retrievers, both on the grouse moor and with dead game, were painted by this artist in oil and watercolour.

Harris, George F. (op.1858-1881)
Portrait painter who exh. at the RA (1858-1881) and SS (1858-1860). Included in this Dictionary for his portrait of "A Sergeant in the Welsh 21st (Breconshire Old Militia Battalion) in dress uniform, winner of the Lord Lieutenant's prize 1880/1881" for competitive rifle shooting. A target range is in the background and at his side is the presumably successful rifle. A good still life study of "Brown Trout with a Creel", 13½in.x16¾in., was auctioned Christie's 1991 proving the versatility of this artist.

Harris, H. (op.c.1910-1946)
A signed portrait of a racehorse entitled "Sussex Martlett" was auctioned at Spencers (Carmarthen), 15 May 1990 and fetched £800. A portrait of "Las Vegas", winner of the Manchester November Handicap 1946, trained by A. Boyd, ridden by Harry Wragg, owned by Sir William Chaytor was auctioned Christie's (Sth. Ken.) 1991.

Harris, Robert (late 19th century)
Portraits of saddled hunters have been seen by this artist.

Harrison, Christopher J. (b.1935)
Contemporary artist of clever still life studies of sporting equipment - fishing, golf and cricket. Harrison is the son of Frederick Clifford Harrison (q.v.) under whom

he studied. He became a freelance commercial artist (1963-1973) specialising in still life and transport illustration after which he specialised in distinctive, extremely high quality trompe-l'oeil paintings. His sporting commissions include those from Gary Lineker, the England and Spurs striker, and his racing work is displayed at Goodwood racecourse. His work was on view at Halcyon Gallery's Exhibition at Selfridges September 1989. Harrison is a regular exhibitor at the RA Summer Exhibition, London, since 1974 and at the RBA.

Harrison, Frederick Clifford (op.1901-1984)
A leading commercial, trompe-l'oeil and still life artist who worked for Shell and BP during the 1920s and depicted a number of motor racing scenes in poster form. Exh. several still lifes at the RA (1967-1970). Father of the sporting still life painter, Christopher Harrison (q.v.).

Harrison, George Lovell (op.1881-1904)
Sporting, figure and domestic artist who contributed hunting scenes to "The Illustrated London News" (1884-1886). Exh. two paintings at SS in 1881/2 and 1883/4, neither sporting. His painting of two nondescript dogs sitting on a rug by a chair entitled "Waiting for Master", dated 1882, was sold Phillips 1986.

Harrison, John Cyril (1898-1985)
Wiltshire-born artist of game birds, usually painted in watercolour. Lived in British Columbia between 1912 and 1915. Studied at the Slade School of Art after demobilisation from the 1st World War. Exh. at Vicars Bros Galleries in Bond Street, London in 1931, an exhibition which was composed almost entirely of British game birds on the wing, painted in watercolour.

Harrison, John F. (op.1837-1865)
An itinerant horse painter who exh. three paintings at the RA (1845-1865). His portrait of Squire Jenkins (1777-1856) of Llanharan House, Glamorgan, with his own private pack of foxhounds, the Llanharan pack, was originally painted as a set of three in 1837, each 24¾in.x36½in. Lane Fine Art. His equestrian paintings include several portraits of horses, usually s.&d., and a fine study of two Dalmatians, painted in 1856, was auctioned Sotheby's 1985.

Harrison, Sammy (op.1937)
Contemporary artist whose boxing portrait of Benny Lynch, the 1937 World Fly Weight Champion, signed, 34in.x22½in., was auctioned Christie's 1986.

Harrowing, Walter (op.1865-1904)
Sporting artist who painted portraits of beagles, hunters, brood mares, coach horses and still lifes of game between these dates. Very little is known of his background.

Hart, Dick (op.1953)
Contemporary painter of the "Football Players" 46½in.x31in. Contributed to the FE.

Hart, T.R. (op.1860)
A portrait by this artist of a "Gentleman Driving a Gig", s.&d. 1860, 19¾in.x29½in. was auctioned Christie's 27.6.80.

Hartley, Thomas C. (op.1820-1860)
Portrait painter whose sole claim to sporting fame seems to lie in the watercolour portrait of J.F. Herring (q.v.) which he exh. at SS in 1837. Much of his work which he exh. at the RA, BI, SS and OWS (1820-1860) was portraits.

Hartman, George (1894-1976)
Painter of an American baseball game in 1966 entitled "The Orioles Win the Series", 14in.x18in. Hartman, who obviously watched and was extremely excited by this match, returned to his studio to paint Brooks Robinson, the Baltimore Orioles' great third batsman, jumping in the air for joy with two team-mates against a background of audience packed stands. Orioles won the World Series that year from the more experienced and better backed Los Angeles Dodgers in four games, holding them scoreless for an unheard of thirty-three innings.

Hartrick, Archibald Standish, OBE, RWS, NEAC, IS (1864-1950)
Painter, lithographer and etcher of numerous genre subjects and landscapes. Born in India he studied art under Alphonse Legros at the Slade School (1884-1885) and in Paris at the Académie Julian, under Boulanger and at the Atelier Cormon (1886-1887). He joined the staff at "The Daily Graphic" in 1890 and contributed to "The Strand Magazine", "The Yellow Book" and other papers. Exh. at the NEAC (1893-1908). Sporting titles include "The Archer", "The Poacher" and "Heavy-weights". Elected NEAC (1893), IS (1906) and RWS (1920). Hartrick taught at the Camberwell and Central Schools of Art and was awarded an OBE.

Hartwell, William (op.c.1953)
Painter of a football scene entitled "In the Goal Mouth", watercolour, 11½in.x16½in., which Hartwell contributed to the FE.

Harvey, Sir George, PRSA (1806-1876)
Scottish landscape and religious painter. Included in this Dictionary for "The Curlers" which he exh. at the RA (1873). The original large painting by Harvey of this subject was exh. at the Royal Society of Artists in 1835. Exh. at the RSA (1827-1880) including "The Bowlers" (1850 No. 452) which is now in the National Gallery of Scotland. He also painted a fine picture of bowls entitled "Village Bowlers" in 1852, depicting the game as played in Victorian times. Elected RSA (1830), PRSA (1864-1876). Knighted (1867).

Harvey, George Wills, AR Canadian A (1846-1910)
Landscape painter who emigrated to Halifax, Canada in about 1882. Elected AR Canadian A (1883). His portrait "The Archer", painted in 1904, 28in.x35½in., was auctioned Christie's (Sth. Ken.) 1986.

Harvey, H.E. (op.1893)
Competent painter in watercolour of a group of ladies playing golf on a seaside course during a stiff breeze. Harvey, who lived in Edinburgh, exh. one painting at the RSA in 1893.

Harvey, Marion Roger Hamilton (b.1886)
Scottish animal painter, born in Ayr. Painter of horses and dogs in pastel, oil and crayons. Exh. Glasgow.

Harvey, R.L. (op.1947)
Equestrian artist who specialised in hunting, racing and coaching scenes, including "The Ladies Race" and a portrait of the horse "Patsy", s.&d. 1947 and inscr., 9in.x12½in., Sotheby's (Sussex) 1988.

Harvey, William (1796-1866)
Wood engraver and illustrator who was apprenticed to Thomas Bewick (q.v.) until 1817. Contributed a drawing of "Ascot Races" to "The Observer" in 1828.

Harwood, Edward (b.1814, op.1844-1872)
Exh. "A Football Match at Rugby School" at the RA in 1859, his only apparent exhibit from a Rugby address. This painting was repro. and discussed in "Country Life", "Letters to the Editor", 10 November 1928.

Haseltine, Herbert (1877-1962)
Distinguished sculptor of equestrian portraits, and a painter. Of American parentage, Haseltine went to Harvard, after which he studied art at the RA Schools, in Munich and then in Paris at the Académie Julian under Aimé Morot. A keen polo player and a hunting man, Haseltine was well qualified to model the many important commissions he received from King Edward VII and other members of the Royal Family.

Hassall, John, RI, RMS (1868-1948)
Illustrator and poster artist who depicted a number of motor racing scenes. Born at Walmer, Kent, the son of Christopher Hassall, RN. He studied art in Antwerp and in Paris, under Bouguereau (1891-1894) after which he embarked on a career in commercial art which was to lead to his becoming the "poster king" of Britain. His illustration work embraced a wide variety of subject matter including sport. In about 1900 Hassall produced several strongly coloured sets of lithographs featuring golf. These include "The Links at St. Andrews" (exceptionally rare and perhaps the best set of golf prints of this era), "Before and After", a set showing a young boy on the tee, and "The Seven Ages of the Golfer". Good sets of golfing prints after Hassall, in unfaded condition, are highly prized, especially when signed in pencil, and original works are seldom sold. He was elected RI (1901), RMS the same year and succeeded Dudley Hardy (q.v.) as President of the London Sketch Club in 1903. His jolly fisherman in the poster "Skegness is so Bracing" became so famous that Skegness wanted to erect a statue to Hassall in the town.

Hassam, Childe (1859-1935)
Distinguished American painter and etcher of landscapes which include "The Golf Course at Easthampton", s.&d. 1926, 9in.x12in., auctioned SPB 1978. Hassam, who was born in Boston, studied in Boston and Paris. Member ANA (1902), NA (1906), AWCS, NYWCC. Boston AC.

Hassell, Edward, RBA (op.1830-d.1852)
Prolific artist of every subject in most mediums. The son of the artist John Hassell (q.v.). He exh. mostly at SS including "Punt Fishing" (1847) and "Stopping to Bait" (1849). He was elected RBA (1841) and became Secretary (1846).

Hassell, John (1767-1825)
Draughtsman and engraver who was a great friend of the sporting artist George Morland (q.v.). He produced numerous guide books, with aquatints after his own drawings, including "Excursions of Pleasure and Sports on the Thames" in 1823.

Hatherell, William, RI, ROI, RWA (1855-1928)
Landscape and figure painter and an illustrator who entered the RA Schools (1877-1879). His fine painting "King Edward's Derby" (1909) was painted for Bovril Ltd. and shows the King's horse "Minoru" winning the Derby by a short head from "Louviers" who was certainly in front of "Minoru" two strides after the post. Beautifully executed gravures of Hatherell's picture were made and sold by Bovril Ltd. at 10s.6d. each, post free. The gravures carried no advertisement matter and could also be obtained in exchange for Bovril coupons. Hatherell was a regular contributor to magazines from about 1889 and joined the staff of "The Graphic" in 1892. He also illus. a number of books including "The Prince and the Pauper" (S.L. Clemens 1923). Exh. at the RA and RWS from 1879. Elected RI (1888), ROI (1898) and RWA (1903). Was a member of the Langham Sketching Club and made an Hon. Member in 1900.

Hatton, Brian (1887-1916)
Brilliant child artist who attracted the attention of Princess Louise and the artist G.F. Watts (q.v.) when he was only twelve years old. Attended George Harcourt's painting school in Arbroath and the Académie Julian in Paris. He became a member of the Chelsea Arts Club but was killed in action during the 1st World War. Hatton painted several very fine equestrian portraits and a retrospective exhibition of his work was held at the Walker Galleries, London, in February 1926.

Haugh, George (1756-1827)
Baptised in Carlisle on 12 March 1756 so could have been born the previous year. Portrait painter of some sporting subjects who entered the RA Schools (1772) for eight years, a contemporary of Samuel Alken, Snr. (q.v.). His fine portrait of the Countess of Effingham with gun and shooting dogs, 17¼in.x15in., dated 1787, is in the Paul Mellon Collection, Upperville, Va, USA. Exh. at the RA and BI (1777-1818). His portrait of "Rover" the Duke of Kingston's Favourite Setting Dog, painted in 1776, was exh. Ackermanns 1975. The portrait of the Countess of Effingham was also exh. at Ackermanns in 1930 as reported in "The Connoisseur" in June of that year.

Haughton, Moses, Snr. (1734-1804)
Portrait and still life painter who trained originally in Birmingham as an enameller. Exh. RA 1788 to 1792. His sporting subjects include a portrait of George Farmer of Witton Manor, Staffs., standing full length with a shot-gun, dogs and a dead duck, 42¼in.x37½in., and "A Sportsman with his Game by a Waterfall", 9⅜in.x12in.

Haughton, Moses, Jnr. (1772-1848)
Portrait painter, nephew of Moses Haughton (q.v.). Studied at the RSA Schools and became a pupil of the sporting artist George Stubbs (q.v.). Exh. at the RA (1800-1848).

Havell, Alfred Charles (1855-1928)
London sporting painter who was born at 41 Sloane Square on 8 March 1855. Son of the sporting painter Edmund Havell, Jnr. (q.v.) who was himself the nephew of William Havell, the landscape painter and one of the founders of the Royal Society of Painters in Watercolour. Grand nephew of the engraver, Robert Havell, whose son Robert Havell, Jnr. (q.v.) was famed for his connection with Audubon's (q.v.) "Birds of America". Alfred Havell worked for many years at Messrs. Fores, as did John Beer (q.v.), Finch Mason (q.v.) and Cuthbert Bradley (q.v.) at their famous shop in Piccadilly "in a room so filled with tobacco smoke that the ordinary mortal could hardly breathe in it". He died of pneumonia at his home in South Hampstead on 13 March 1928. He exh. twice at the RA in 1878 and 1884 but neither were sporting subjects. Havell painted a series "Great Derby Winners" for Messrs. Fores including the portrait of the racehorse "Rock Sand", winner of the 1903 Derby and the Triple Crown with Danny Maher up.

Havell, Charles Richard (1827-1892)
Animal and equestrian painter, the son of Edmund Havell, Snr (q.v.). Like his brother Edmund, Jnr. (q.v.), he taught drawing in Reading and was also headmaster of the School of Art there. Like the other members of his family he was a talented draughtsman, exhibiting in London (1858-1866). He collaborated with William H. Hopkins (q.v.) on a portrait of "A Favourite Horse, the property of S.F. Somers" which Hopkins exh. at the SS in 1858 under his name, but with an acknowledgement to C.R. Havell who painted the figure. The Havell family can claim to be one of the largest artistic families whose work spreads over two centuries but in this Dictionary we are concerned only with those members who are known to have painted sporting scenes.

Havell, Edmund, Snr. (1785-1864)
Portrait painter, sometimes of sporting subjects, father of Edmund Havell, Jnr. (q.v.) and Charles Richard Havell (q.v.) and brother of the landscape painter William Havell. Edmund Havell became a drawing master at Reading School but joined his father, Luke, in the family business in Reading after his elder brother, William, retired. He established a local reputation as an artist and exh. occasionally at the RA (1814-1847).

Havell, Edmund, Jnr. (1819-1894)
Sporting painter and engraver, sometimes of his own work. Part of the complex clan of Havells. Edmund, Jnr. was the son of Edmund, Snr. (q.v.) who was himself the son of Luke (op.c.1740-1750). Edmund Havell became a drawing master at Reading, like his father Edmund Snr., but found time to produce a number of fine quality sporting paintings in both oil and watercolour. He also visited the United States and exh.

in Philadelphia. He became the father of Alfred Charles Havell (q.v.), the London sporting painter. Havell painted the racehorse "Withingate", with jockey up in blue and black silks, with William H. Hopkins (q.v.) with whom he collaborated on a number of sporting paintings including the portrait of "The Glossy Peer" (Lord Hardwicke) and the Royal Buckhounds in Windsor Forest, which was exh. at the RA and regarded by many as one of the finest hunting portraits ever seen. The 5th Earl of Hardwicke (1836-1897) was Master of the Buckhounds (1874-1880). Havell exh. in London (1835-1879) including a portrait of "Bob Ward, huntsman to the Hertfordshire Hounds", at the RA (1878), "River Trout" at SS (1840) and "Thames Trout" (1842).

Havell, George (op.1826-d.1840)
Sporting painter and engraver. Apart from a solitary but famous print of the Blenheim Stage Coach about to leave the Star Hotel at Oxford, pub. by himself, and dated January 1831, but engraved by Frederick James Havell, he seems to have left the printing side of the business to the other members of his large family. George Havell was the brother of William Havell and worked in collaboration with his other brother Frederick James Havell. He exh. four paintings at the RA and his 1833 exhibit was entitled "Foxes Disputing a Prize". "Coursing at Yarnton, Oxon." shows a keeper with two greyhounds and a chestnut hunter in a landscape. Inscr. "Yarnton", it was auctioned at Sotheby's in 1982.

Havell, Robert, Snr. (1769-1832)
Artist and aquatint engraver, very often of sporting subjects, the son of Daniel Havell with whom he often collaborated. They worked from a house in Oxford Street called the Zoological Gallery where they produced many sporting lithographs including the rowing crew of Queen's College, Oxford (1832) and several coaching scenes.

Havell, Robert, Jnr. (1793-1878)
Engraver, printer and sporting painter, he worked with his father Robert, Snr. (q.v.) in the printing business from about 1816 to 1828. He became a close friend of the bird artist J.J. Audubon (q.v.), Audubon becoming a godfather to Robert's second child who died in 1838 at the age of eight. This probably decided Robert Havell to emigrate to the United States with his wife and daughter, Amelia. At first they stayed with the Audubons in New York and then they moved to Brooklyn and in 1841 to Ossining. They moved once more in 1857 to Tarrytown, New York. Robert Havell turned more and more to oil painting but invited his brother, Henry Augustus, to come to New York where they set up a print selling and colouring business. The business failed owing to a severe fire, after which Henry returned to England. Robert Havell engraved and pub. (1830-1838) all but the first ten plates of Audubon's "Birds of America", approximately 426 plates. The order from William Lizars, (q.v.) came about through a strike by the colourists in Lizars' workshop in the summer of 1827. Robert Havell painted pheasant, partridge and duck shooting pictures as well as hunter portraits and a painting of "The Admiral's Regatta, Greenwich". His

engraving after his own work of "The Reading and Telegraph Coaches Meeting near Salt Hill with a distant view of Eton and Windsor" was pub. in 1835, 12½ in.x19¾ in.

Havinden, Ashley, OBE (1903-1973)
Poster artist who worked for BP and depicted many motor racing scenes during the 1930s. Havinden who was born in Kent, trained as a lithographic and a photogravure printer (1920-1922). He joined the advertising agency, W.G. Crawford Ltd. and studied in the evenings at the Central School of Arts and Crafts. Studied drawing under Henry Moore for a few months in 1933. Created an OBE.

Hawken, Joy
Contemporary animal painter and illustrator who studied at the Northampton School of Art for two years and a further three years at Leicester where she won the David Murray Scholarship to the RA Schools. She illus. the Collins edition of "Black Beauty" and Century Hutchinson recently pub. an anthology entitled "The World's Greatest Dog Stories". Her commissions include portraits of the racehorses "Blakeney", "Celtic Shot", "Aldaniti" and "Mtoto" who featured on the 1990 Injured Jockeys Christmas card.

Hawker, Peter (Lt. Col.) (1786-1853)
Artist, soldier and author who wrote and illus. "Instructions to Young Sportsmen" (1814, first edn.). He served in the Peninsular War with the 14th Light Dragoons and advised William IV on the revision of the archaic English game laws in 1831. The new Act (1831) abolished the unfair system of qualification which had been in existence since the Game Act of 1671. See William Hamilton RA.

Hawkes (op.1920s)
A painter of this surname is responsible for "La Jeune Joueuse de Golf", 21in.x32¾in., a fabulous golf oil painting of a lady driving off the tee, with her male partner watching - a caddie behind, 1920s, Stanislas Machoir, Versailles 78000, Hotel des Ventes Rameau, 5 Rue Rameau.

Hawkin, S. (op.1853)
Draughtsman and painter whose work "The Cambridgeshire Stakes" was engraved in four plates by C.N. Smith in 1853. Each 13¾ in.x21in.

Hawkins, Harold Frederick (Fred) Weaver (b.1893-op.1941-1972)
Painter of an oil painting entitled "Football" dated 1952, 23⅜ in.x27½ in., Sotheby's (Mel.) 1989. Hawkins, who was born at Sydenham in 1893, studied at Camberwell and Westminster Schools of Art and at the RCA. Exh. at the RA, NEAC and other leading London galleries.

Hawkins, Henry, RBA (op.1820-1881)
Predominantly a portrait painter in both oil and watercolour. A prolific exhibitor at SS of almost every subject including several sporting and equestrian portraits and one of "The Right Hon. Earl Brownlow's Harriers", painted in 1862. Elected RBA (1824).

Hawkins, Sheila (b.1905)
Animal painter, born Western Australia. Studied at the Australian National Gallery Art School and became a commercial artist. Arrived in London 1931 where she has stayed. Much of her illustration work depicts animals in humorous situations. During the 1930s she worked in the studio of Shell Mex Advertising (the first woman to be employed there).

Hawkins, Waterhouse Benjamin (op.1832-1841)
Animal painter, chiefly of horses, dogs and fish who exh. five paintings at the RA including one of "A Perch" (1833) and "A Wounded Pheasant" (1839). His exhibition work at SS (1833-1840) included "A Useful Dun, the property of Sir B. Hall" (1839), "Spring" a celebrated Welsh greyhound, the property of Sir Charles Morgan, Bt. (1839), "Torey" and "Fortune", two pointers the property of Sir B. Hall, Bt. Llanover, Monmouthshire, and "Adams and Brownies" being portraits of the keeper and kennel of spaniels, the property of Sir Charles Morgan, Bt. of Tredegar, Monmouthshire.

"Hay"
Pseudonym used by a caricaturist, in the style of Pellegrini, contributing to "Vanity Fair" 1886,1888, 1889 and 1893.

Haycock, Frederick (b.1948)
Illustrator and sporting painter from Warwickshire who won second prize in 1984 in the competition organised by "Horse and Hound" with his painting "One Draw More - The Quorn at Ashby Pastures". First prize in this competition for young sporting artists was won by Leesa Sandys-Lumsdaine (q.v.). Haycock paints in a traditional style but with great observation and skill as is shown in another hunting work "The Fernie at Peathing Parva".

Haycock, G.B. (op.1862-1888)
London exhibitor of dead game and still lifes at SS between these dates, from the same address in Regents Park as W. Haycock (q.v.).

Haycock, Washington (op.1862-1864)
London exhibitor of dead game and still lifes at SS between these dates, from the same address in Regents Park as G.B. Haycock (q.v.)

Haydon, Benjamin Robert (1786-1846)
Historical painter of impressive sized canvases who included a few sporting scenes amongst his work, particularly of shooting subjects. He is perhaps best known to sportsmen for his quote in a letter to his friend, the artist Seymour Kirkup (1788-1880) who lived in Florence. "Wherever they (the English) go racing, cricket, trial by jury, foxhunting and portraits are the simple commodities first planned or thought of. Blessed be the name of John Bull!". Haydon, a turbulent and quarrelsome character, committed suicide in 1846, a victim of his own despair and disappointment.

Hayes, Claude, RHA, RI (1852-1922)
Irish-born landscape and portrait painter, son of the marine painter Edwin Hayes (1820-1904). Studied art

at Heatherleys School, at the RA Schools and at Antwerp, under Verlat. Exh. from 1876 at the RA and also at SS, NWS, GG, NG and elsewhere. He painted hunting scenes quite frequently, usually in watercolour. Elected RI (1886).

Hayes, John (1786/7-1866)
Portrait painter who studied art at the RA Schools (1801) aged thirteen years and was a frequent exhibitor at the RA from 1814. His sitters included William Scott, the leading jockey of his day, whose portrait Hayes exh. at the RA in 1835 (No. 61). The portrait of Scott was engraved by William Roffe for "The Sporting Magazine", October 1835. Scott is wearing a black jacket and cap, the racing colours of John Bowes, and the portrait was painted to commemorate Bowes' Derby win of 1835 with "Mundig" whom William Scott rode to victory.

Hayes, Michael Angelo, RHA (1820-1877)
Irish painter of military and equestrian subjects. Son and pupil of Edward Hayes, RHA (1797-1864). Best known in sporting circles for the six plates engraved by John Harris (1811-1865) after Hayes' work entitled "Car Travelling in Southern Ireland", pub. 1836. Pub. "The Delineation of Animals in Rapid Motion" (1876). Elected RHA (1854) and Secretary (1856). Sacked and reinstated (1857 and 1861). Retired (1870).

Hayes, S.H.B. (op.1865)
Two sets of four tiny (6in.x4in.) hunting and steeple-chasing scenes were painted by this artist in 1865 and were exh. by Ackermanns in November 1974.

Hayllar, Edith (1860-1948)
One of the four artist daughters of James Hayllar, (q.v.). She seems to have studied art under her father and lived in a large family house at Wallingford, on the Thames. Her work includes a number of sporting scenes which she painted with considerable talent. These include at least two versions of "The First of October" one dated 1888 and exh. at the RA (No. 885). She exh. at SS (1881-1889) including "The Tennis Players" (1884).

Hayllar, James, RBA (1829-1920)
Sussex-born portrait and landscape painter and of genre subjects. Studied art at the RA Schools and in Italy (1851-1853). Exh. at the RA from 1851 and at SS. Father of Edith and Mary Hayllar (qq.v.). Elected RBA (1876). Included in this Dictionary for his portrait entitled "A Cricketer", MCC Collection, Lords.

Hayllar, Mary (Mrs. H.W. Wells)
(op.1880-1887)
An artist sister of Edith Hayllar (q.v.) who exh. at SS "Marking the Tennis Court" (1882). Her other tennis painting "The Lawn Tennis Season", oil on card, 7⅝in.x9⅝in., s.&d. 1881 is at Southampton AG (No. 241, Chipperfield Bequest 1911).

Hayman, Francis, RA (1708-1776)
Portrait painter and a friend of the artist William Hogarth (q.v.). Painted a number of sporting scenes including a set of twelve sporting subjects, designed to decorate the supper boxes in Vauxhall Gardens, entitled "British Heroes". Unfortunately all the paintings are lost but are known through the engravings by Nathaniel Parr (1723-d.after1751), pub. T. and J. Bowles (1743), British Museum Collection. A delightful story is told about Hayman and the Marquess of Granby. A keen pugilist, the artist was persuaded in later years, against his better judgement, "to put up his fists" in a friendly bout with the Marquess of Granby who had visited his studio for a portrait sitting. A little later the sound of banging brought a terrified Mrs. Hayman up the stairs to find the two distinguished men rolling about the floor "like two enraged bears". "Cricket in Marylebone Fields", 34in.x43in. The MCC Coll. Engraved by Guillaume Phillippe Benoist (1725-1800).

Hayter, Charles (1761-1835)
A pen/ink portrait of "the famous walker on the last 500 yards of twelve miles within two hours which he won by 1½ minutes, June 1st 1801", 9in.x7in., Abbott & Holder, 1992. Hayter, who studied at the RA Schools (1786) was the father of John Hayter and Sir George Hayter (qq.v.). He is best known for his miniatures but he also drew portraits in crayon and, in this case, pen/ink. Unfortunately, Hayter has not inscr. his portrait with a name, but lovers of pedestrian history may be able to recognise the subject – Captain Barclay being perhaps the best known walker at that time. Robert, Barclay Allardice (1779-1845) commonly known as "Captain Barclay" performed a feat of extraordinary athletic endurance at Newmarket Heath between 1 June and 12 July 1809. He walked 1,000 miles in 1,000 hours. His performance, for a wager, led to many similar attempts which led to a great increase in professional athletics generally, as well as encouraging public interest. It also led to an awareness amongst athletes for rigorous and sustained training. Hayter exh. at the RA (1786-1832).

Hayter, Sir George (1792-1871)
Portrait painter, the son of Charles Hayter (q.v.) and brother of John Hayter (q.v.). Studied at the RA Schools and in Italy (1815-1818). In 1837 he was appointed portrait and history painter to Queen Victoria for whom he had painted the State portrait in 1836. He painted a large picture of her Coronation and was knighted in 1842. He exh. at the RA (1809-1838). His pencil and brown wash drawing "A Shooting Party at Woburn Spinneys", signed with inits. and dated 1824, 9in.x7½in., was auctioned Christie's 1985.

Hayter, John (1800-1891)
The younger son of Charles Hayter (q.v.), a portrait and miniature painter in crayon, who was Drawing Master to Princess Charlotte. John was the younger brother of Sir George Hayter (q.v.) but seems to have been completely overshadowed by him. He exh. at the RA and BI (1815-1879) including his portrait of Master Edwin Landseer entitled "The Cricketer" (1815), the only sporting portrait of the 126 he exh. there. The two artists were students at the RA Schools (1815-1818). ("Sir Edwin Landseer" by Richard Ormonde p.5, pub. 1983, Philadelphia Museum of Art.)

Haytley, Richard (op.1746-1769)
Portrait painter of an unknown sportsman with his double barrelled flintlock shot-gun, s.&d. 1752. The Paul Mellon Collection, Upperville, Va, USA.

Haywood, John F. (b.1936)
Painter of wildlife and in particular falconry scenes and portraits. Studied at Coventry College of Art. A keen falconer and ornithologist. Has exh. at the Mathaf Gallery, London, since 1976, including "Sakers and Salukis Resting", gouache, 20in.x28in. and "Second Year Peregrine on a Stone Curlew", gouache, 20in.x 28in. (1987).

Hazlehurst, H. (op.1815)
An engraving entitled "The Adventures of Knutsford Racecourse" by Richard Gilson Reeve (1803-1889) engraved in 1815 apparently when he was twelve years old (perhaps by his father?) is after a painting by this artist and shows a busy and interesting crowd scene taking place around the grandstand. See C. Brooke.

Heade, Reginald C.W. (op.1930s)
Painter in oil, watercolour and chalk who exh. at the RA and RI (1932-3). Included in this Dictionary for his oil "Mary Queen of Scots Playing Golf at Truro".

Headley, S. Tardrew
A painting of the London - Bath Royal Mail drawing up outside the Jenny Diver Inn, signed twice, 19in.x29in., was auctioned Sotheby's 1974.

Heal(e)y, Robert (op.1765-d.1771)
Heal(e)y was an Irish portrait painter who had a short career between 1765, when he was a student, until his death in 1771. He is best known for a series of drawings done for the Connolly family at Castletown in February 1768. His equestrian portrait group "Tom Connolly with his Friends Hunting" was auctioned Christie's 1983.

Heaphy, Thomas, PRBA (1775-1835)
Miniature and portrait painter to HRH The Princess of Wales. Exh. fifty-three works at the RA (1797-1836) including "Heron Shooting" (1812), "Studies of Fish from Nature", trout, grayling, greyfish, etc. (1813), and "The Fisherman's Frolic" (1826). He also exh. "The Game of Putt" at SS (1824). He was elected RBA (1824), and became the first President of this Society.

Heard, Hugh Percy (1866-1940)
Landscape artist who painted mostly in watercolour. Born Bideford, Devon, the brother of the artist Nathaniel Heard (b.1872). Hugh Percy Heard, who exh. at the RBA, LS, DG and the RA (1886-1940), visited Paris with George Belcher (q.v.) returning to Devon in 1911. He was drowned by falling off a bus on Bideford Quay and into the estuary which is sad as he is known to have hated the sea. Ironically, his marine paintings are amongst his finest work. His golfing scene at Westward Ho, a watercolour, 11½in.x19½in., is in a private collection.

Hearne, Thomas, FSA (1744-1817)
Topographical draughtsman, who was apprenticed to the celebrated etcher and line engraver William Woollett (1735-1785). A set of twelve rustic and sporting landscapes including shooting, coursing, angling and fox-hunting, after the work by Hearne were engraved in 1810 by William Byrne, Jnr. with whose father William Byrne (1743-1805) Hearne formed a close collaboration.

Heath, Charles (op.1857-1858)
An equestrian artist who operated at a later date than those given for the line engraver, Charles Heath (1758-1848). His portraits of hunters in their stables, of which two are recorded, are competent studies.

Heath, Henry (op.1824-1850)
Draughtsman, etcher and lithographer, mainly of caricatures after his own designs. He was the brother of W. Heath (q.v.) and worked in a very similar style. He often used the pseudonym "HH" for his work for Messrs. Fores. He is believed to have emigrated to Australia in 1850. His three fishing scenes "Eel Bobbing at Battersea", "Barbel Fishing at Twickenham" and "Roach Fishing at Broxbourne", all signed, are in the collection of the Piscatorial Society. Heath's four caricatures of shooting subjects, each watercolour, 9in.x 6½in. (approx.), are in the Paul Mellon Collection, Upperville, Va, USA.

Heath, R.B. (op.1894)
An unrecorded artist of a small pen and ink sketch entitled "The Meet", s.&d. 1894, 6½in.x9½in., auctioned Sotheby's (Sussex) 1987.

Heath, Thomas Haste (op.1901-1906)
Minor Welsh painter from Cardiff who exh. at the RA from 1901. His main work was undoubtedly "The Steam Powered Navvy working on the Aber Branch of the Rhymney Railway in Glamorgan" which he was commissioned to paint for Davies Middleton & Davies Ltd. of Cardiff. The painting was hung by the RA in 1906 but the reason for Thomas Heath's inclusion in this Dictionary is his painting of the magnificent bay horse called "Charlie" who won first prize at the Cardiff Horse Show but who was subsequently sold to a Bombay construction firm and killed by a train.

Heath, William (1795-1840)
Draughtsman, etcher and lithographer of caricatures and military subjects who worked for a time under the pseudonym of "Paul Pry". He was the brother of Henry Heath (q.v.). Much of his engraved work was after his own designs including "Sporting in the Scottish Isles", a set of four plates pub. in 1835. A coloured aquatint after the work by this artist of the great fight between Broom and Hannan for £1,000, which took place at New Park Farm, Bicester, Oxon. on 26 January 1841 was engraved by C. Hunt and pub. by John Moore in 1841. Print size 17in.x26in. Heath's watercolour "Woodcock Shooting", 9⅝in.x7⅛in., The Paul Mellon Collection, Upperville, Va, USA.

Heathcote, E.S. (op.1880-1905)
Included in this Dictionary for his (or her) painting "Polo Ponies", s.&d. 1898, 13in.x16in., Sotheby's (NY). Conceivably related to J.M. Heathcote (q.v.) who lived with his family at Connington Castle.

Heathcote, John Moyer (1800-1890)
Patron and pupil of Peter de Wint (q.v.) whose style he attempted to copy. Included in this Dictionary for his picture "Ice Racing on Whittlesey Mere" in 1875. Heathcote's son was also John Moyer Heathcote Jnr. (1834-1912) who worked in a similar style. The painting is therefore more likely to be by him.

Heddon, R. (op.1864)
Marine painter of the American yacht "Henrietta", winner of the Atlantic Yacht Race 1864, a watercolour 11in.x17¼in.

Hedges, W.S. (op.1841)
"A Race Meeting at Jacksonville, Alabama", s.&d. 1841, 19¾in.x33¼in., was auctioned Christie's (NY) 1983. A photograph of this painting appeared in "Country Life" 1979 under "Correspondence", its then owner unable to identify the racecourse and asking for suggestions. His request seems to have been answered but he failed to ask, at the same time, for information on the artist. Perhaps he already knew it?

Hedley, Ralph, RBA (1851-1913)
Yorkshire-born genre painter and of animal subjects who studied at Newcastle Art School. His portrait of "Crib" and "Rosa", a bull dog and a bull bitch in a barn, s.&d. '81, 20in.x24in. was auctioned Bonhams 1986. The celebrated "Crib" was owned by Harry Verelst and was by Hall's "Nimble" out of "Rosa". This subject was also allegedly painted by Abraham Cooper (q.v.) and others. Hedley exh. at the RA from 1879 and at the Northumbrian Art Institute where he became President. He was also President of the Bewick Club. Examples of his work are at the Laing AG, Newcastle. Elected RBA (1899).

Heelas, Maud Grant (op.1885-c.1940)
Enterprising and an obviously very sporting artist who painted a fine Rugby football scene entitled "Going for the Line" in 1920, exh. Ackermann & Son Ltd., London, 1989. The significance of the scene is not known nor is it apparent why a respectable maiden lady from the Wokingham area should have chosen this subject to paint, as the only known representation of her work. Her family are thought to have run a department store in Reading.

Helck, Peter, NA (1895-1989)
American motor racing artist and enthusiast who lived in Millerton, New York and who saw his first motor race in 1906. Studied art in Hammersmith, London, under Sir Frank Brangwyn RA as a private pupil between 1920 and 1921. His first professional assignment was designing programme covers for the Brighton Motordrome in 1913 and then for the Super Sheepshead Speedway (1915-1916). Worked for "Autocar" and "Esquire" with eight full colour spreads of motor racing pictures in the latter (1944-1945). Pub. his first book "The Chequered Flag" in 1961 and "Great Auto Races" in 1976.

Helleu, Paul Cesar (1859-1927)
French portrait and figure painter and an etcher whose paintings of "Deauville Regatta" (Les Regattes à Deauville), 23½in.x28¾in., Sotheby's 1989, and "Sailing at Cowes" 1899, 25½in.x31¾in., Sotheby's 1988, are social documentations of an important era. Helleu studied at the Ecole Nationale des Beaux Arts under Gérome (q.v.). Exh. in England at the RE and other leading galleries (1892-1908). Elected RE (1897).

"Helvelyn"
Alias William Lamonby (d.1925), hawking correspondent of "The Field". He was also the son of F.W. Lamonby - see "Skiddaw".

Hemsley, William, RBA (1819-c.1893)
Self-taught landscape and genre painter and of some sporting subjects who started his career as an architect. "The Start of the Race" was auctioned Christie's, 9 October 1964. His portrait group of Mr. and Mrs. William Judd and their family of Curzon Lodge, Old Brompton, dressed quaintly as gentlefolk and gypsies in a park with their dogs, with an old servant kneeling by a pile of dead game, undoubtedly held some significance for the subjects, but this is less apparent today.

Hemy, Charles Napier, RA, RI, RWS ROI (1841-1917)
Marine painter, brother of Thomas Hemy (q.v.). Studied at Newcastle Art School and with Baron Leys in Antwerp. An ardent yachtsman, Hemy turned to marine painting in about 1880 and settled in Falmouth. His work includes many yacht racing scenes and his influence is seen in the work of his pupil J. Montague Dawson (q.v.). He exh. at the RA from 1865. Elected RA (1910), RI (1884), ROI (1885) and RWS (1897).

Hemy, Thomas Marie Madawaska (1852-1937)
North Shields marine painter who studied art at the Newcastle Art School, under W. Cosens Way, and under Verlat in Antwerp. Exh. at the RA from 1873, also at SS, NWS and GG. Painted several scenes of both Rugby and Association Football. Examples of his work are in the FA Collection, London. Hemy was called Marie Madawaska because he was born aboard the "Marie Madawaska" off the Brazilian coast on his parents' way to Australia. "Football at Harrow School", the field with a match in progress, an etching (11in.x23¾in. pub. Dickinson 1888) by W Cox after the work of this artist was exh. at the Parker Gallery No. 457 1950. A further etching of Rugby School, "Big Side Football" by F.G. Stevenson after the work by Hemy was pub. 1890 (21in.x14in.). "Sunderland v Aston Villa", s.&d. 1895, 17¼in.x29in., FA Collection.

Henderson, Charles Cooper (1803-1877)
A leading painter of coaching scenes and of occasional horse portraits in both oil and watercolour. He was also an etcher, producing several sets of prints, one entitled "Road Scrapings", twelve etchings, each 8in.x11¾in. Another set entitled "Coaching Recollections" was pub. 1842/3. Henderson himself drove a yellow mail phaeton with a well-matched pair of greys in Hyde Park during the Season. His mother left him a fortune in 1850 which relieved him of the need to earn a living, after which his best and serious work declined.

Henderson, Fred (op.1852-1860)

Equestrian painter whose racehorse portraits include "Tournament", "Thormanby" and "Hampton". His painting of "Tournament", a chestnut racehorse by "Touchstone" out of "Happy Queen" with jockey George Fordham up, held by his owner James Stoddart-Douglas in Chilston Park, is s.&d. 1857, 27in.x36in., and was auctioned Christie's 1966. "Thormanby" with Henry Custance up won the Derby in 1860. Their portrait by Henderson was exh. at the Gallery of British Sports and Pastimes, Hutchinson House (1949).

Henderson, Joseph Morris, RSA (1863-1936)

Landscape painter, the son of the Scottish water-colourist Joseph Henderson RSW (1832-1908). Henderson's golf painting "The Lighthouse Green, Turnberry", 16in.x20in., was auctioned Sotheby's 1986.

Henderson, William (op.1857-1893)

Yorkshire landscape painter whose sporting scenes include "Hounds Running a Fox to Earth", "Foxhounds in Landscapes", and "Setters in a Highland Landscape". Mitchell records a portrait of a bay hunter in a stable, dated 1857. Exh. at SS (1874-1892).

Hendrie, Robert (op.1867-1868)

This artist exh. one picture at the RA (1867/8) entitled "Cub Hunting - Noon at Lullingstone".

Henley, H.W. (op.1891-1894)

Exh. 1891-1894 at the Royal Society of Artists, Birmingham. "Grouse Shooting in a Highland River Landscape" 20in.x30in. was auctioned Bonhams 1987.

Henning, Archibald Samuel (op.1825-1841)

This artist exh. a painting of a horse's head at the RA in 1828. He also painted a fine scene of "Ladies and Gentlemen at a Race Meeting", s.&d. 1841, 24½in.x 29½in.. His portrait of Johnny Walker, the champion of the boxing lightweights, born at Lambeth 1819, height 5ft.5½in., weight 9st.2 lbs., was engraved as a coloured aquatint by G. Hunt and pub. by S. Noble c.1840. Examples British Museum.

Henrard, Hubert (op.1857)

A portrait "A Dark Bay Hunter in a Landscape", s.&d. 1857, 11¾in.x13¾in., was auctioned Christie's 1981 and "A Study of a Hound" was auctioned Sotheby's (Sussex) 1984.

Henri, Robert (1865-1929)

American painter who studied at the Académie Julian and the Ecole des Beaux Arts. Oddly enough he rejected the widely fashionable plein air and impressionistic movement, favouring a somewhat sombre style. Included in this Dictionary for his amusing pen/ink drawing of George Luks (q.v.) playing baseball (1904), 7in.x4¾in. (Whitney Museum of American Art). Henri's pupil was Keith Sholto Douglas (q.v.).

Henry, Everett (1893-1961)

A coloured lithograph after his "The First Amateur Golf Championship held in America" (1894) was made by E. Currier in 1931 for a series in "Fortune" magazine. Whilst records show that this is not the first U.S. Amateur Championship, nevertheless players drawn by Henry are amongst the earliest champions of the American game. They include: Charles Blair Macdonald, famous not only as a player but also as a course designer in his later years, John Reid the Scottish emigré, influential in the foundation of St. Andrews Golf Club in 1888 and Lawrence Stoddard who beat Macdonald in one of the last invitation matches before the founding of the United States Golf Association.

Henry, Paul, RHA (1876-1958)

Irish portrait and landscape painter who studied at the Belfast School of Art and in Paris under J. P. Laurens at the latter's Academy. He moved to Whistler's newly opened studio later in the same year (1896) Included a few sporting scenes amongst his work. Exh. at the RA, RHA, Paris Salon, Canada, the USA and Australia. Elected RHA (1929).

Henson, S. (op.1794)

Portrait of Henry Denne Esq. (1775-1822) leaning against a fence holding a gun in his left hand with a dead snipe in his right hand with two dogs at his feet and a view of a village beyond, s.&d. 1794, 49in.x39in., was auctioned Christie's 1971. Henry Denne of Felbridge, near Tunbridge Wells, was a great shot. The painting and its subject were discussed in "The Field", 29.9.1937.

Henwood, Thomas (op.1842-1859)

Sussex portrait, equestrian and sporting artist. "The Scorer", a portrait of William Davies, painted in 1842, 14in.x12in., is well known to cricketers. Coll. MCC. Davies was scorer to Lewes Priory Club, Sussex and died in the same year that his portrait was painted. Henwood who supplied the drawings for most of the plates in Horsfield's "History of Sussex", included foxhounds, greyhounds, hunters and racehorses amongst his work. He is recorded in "Kelly's Directory" for 1855 as "Thomas Henwood, Artist, Keene Street, Lewes" and he was at the same address in 1858. His sporting paintings include a portrait of "A Greyhound with Black Markings", s.&d. 1854, 18in.x22in., and "Foxhounds in a Kennel Yard", s.&d. 1842, 20in.x24in., Bonhams 1987.

Hepper G. (op.1856-1868)

Painter of sporting and equestrian subjects whose work is usually clearly s.&d. and inscr. "Doncaster" He exh. three works at the BI (1866-1867) including a portrait of "An Old Coachman". Hepper, whose patrons included Earl Fitzwilliam, may also have been a copyist since a painting of otter hunting, clearly inscr. "after Landseer" (q.v.) and dated 1857 was auctioned Sotheby's (Bel.) 1973. He also painted the portraits of the racehorses "Middleton", "Jerry" and "Cotherstone". The paintings are s.&d. 1856 but all the racehorses were, by that date, dead or long into retirement.

Hepper, W.J. (op.1881)

A portrait of a black hunter standing in a stable, a terrier nearby, s.&d. '81, 19½in.x23½in., Bearnes 1991.

Hepple, Wilson (1854-1937)

Northumberland painter of animal and sporting subjects including "Coursing" and "Over the Fence", a fox-hunting and a coursing scene. Both painted "en grisaille", each 13½in.x10in., both auctioned Christie's 1990. Hepple painted a portrait of the greyhound "Snowflight" winner of the Waterloo Cup (1882) with a hare in an open landscape. A lithograph after this work was pub. by Gibson Brothers, Newcastle. His other hunting scenes include "Huntsmen and Hounds Crossing the Lane", 15in.x19in. and "Drawn Blank - Last Meet of the Season" (1931), 18in.x26in. Hepple, who was a founder member of the Bewick Club was largely self-taught although he did study for a period of time under William Cosens Way as did his contemporaries Thomas Hemy (q.v.) and Ralph Hedley (q.v.).

Hepworth, Charles Hayden (op.1856-1902)
Doncaster equestrian artist who painted the portraits of many notable racehorses including those of "Ladas" and "Beeswing".

Herberte, Edward Benjamin (op.1857-1893)
Warwickshire artist of sporting subjects who painted in both oil and watercolour. A pupil of J.F. Herring (q.v.) his work clearly shows Herring's influence. His subject matter was of predominantly hunting scenes although he also painted "The Grand National at Aintree" in 1880.

Herdman, Robert Inerarity, RSA, RSW (1829-1888)
Scottish painter of genre and historical subjects in both oil and watercolour. Included in this Dictionary for his "Portrait of a little Girl with a Shuttlecock and Racket" - signed with mono. and dated 1866, 45in.x32½in., Lawrence Crewkerne, 1987. Herdman, a classics scholar, studied art under Robert Scott Lauder at the Trustees Academy (1847-1853), winning the Keith Prize in 1854. Exh. at the RSA from 1850. Elected RSA (1863).

"Herge"
Alias Georges Remi. Belgian illustrator and creator of "Tintin" who first appeared in 1929. Remi's early work appeared in "Le Boy-Scout Belge" creating a patrol leader called "Tortor". He later worked for "Le Vingtième Siècle" and during the war in the 1940s for "Le Soir Jeuness". Under the heading "Dog fight" ("The Times" 12.12.1991), "The Saga of Tintin" was to have serious repercussions when "Herge's" widow sought to claim £120,000 (1.2 million francs) from a Belgian artist, who depicted the cartoon hero having sexual relations with his dog, "Snowy".

Herman, Josef, OBE, RA (b.1911)
Leading figure painter and of several sports including tennis, snooker and football. Herman, who was born in Poland and studied at the Warsaw School of Art and Decoration, came to England in 1940, basing himself in Glasgow until 1944. He held a solo exhibition at Lefevre Gallery in 1943 and has exhibited widely since. Awarded an OBE (1981).

Herring, Benjamin, Snr. (1806-1830)
Painter of sporting subjects, the brother of the better known J.F. Herring, Snr. (q.v.). Benjamin Herring's painting "Bay Mares Drawing "The Lord Nelson", London to York Coach, with John Frederick Herring Snr. Driving", 17½in.x30in., was auctioned Christie's

1986. J.F. Herring, Snr. drove part time from 1816, working on part of the Lord Nelson run from York to Leeds, via Wakefield. Around 1819-1820 he joined Mr. George Clark and took over the famous Highflyer coach run from York to London, so the artist may have used a small licence here. Herring's portrait of a dark bay hunter in an extensive landscape, s.&d. 1829, 12½in.x 15½in. was auctioned Christie's (Sth. Ken.) 1986.

Herring, Benjamin, Jnr. (1830-1871)
Sporting artist, the youngest son of John Frederick Herring, Snr. (q.v.). Benjamin Herring, Jnr. collaborated with his father on a number of paintings after his brother Charles' death, but his style was a shadow of his father's, if compared directly. His portrait of the Oaks winner "Hippia" is s.&d. 1867. Exh. at BI and SS (1861-1863). He also painted in collaboration with R.R. Ripley (q.v.) exhibiting "A South Coast Scene", a joint effort, at the RA in 1856/7.

Herring, Charles (1828-1856)
Animal painter who included several portraits of hunters amongst his work. Exh. one animal painting at the SS in 1842. The fourth son of J.F. Herring, Snr. (q.v.). Charles Herring died at the age of twenty-eight from scarlet fever. His work is rare but includes a portrait of a grey hunter with two stable lads, signed with mono. and dated 1842, 8¾in./x11½in., auctioned Christie's 1978, a portrait of heavy horses, and a boy with a hunter, dog and cat in a stable, pencil and grey wash, 4½in.x5½in., signed. Bonhams 1984.

Herring, John Frederick, Snr. (1795-1865)
Sporting painter, born in Surrey of American/Dutch extraction. Herring spent a short but productive time in the studio of Abraham Cooper RA (q.v.), the only art education he appears to have had. He specialised in racing subjects and his few hunting scenes are rare. Herring painted the start of the 1844 Derby which became known as "the dirtiest Derby in history". He sometimes collaborated with his three sons, John Frederick Jnr. (q.v.), Benjamin Jnr. (q.v.) and Charles (q.v.). He also collaborated with James Pollard (q.v.) on a number of racing scenes including "The Doncaster Gold Cup" (1838), "The Emperor of Russia's Cup at Ascot" (1845) and "The Dead Heat for the Doncaster Great St. Leger" (1839). Herring painted thirty-three successive winners of the St. Leger and not surprisingly lived a large part of his life in the Doncaster area before settling in Newmarket in 1830 and then in London in 1835. Herring suffered serious financial difficulties after his move to London which, thanks to a great friend and patron William Taylor Copeland (1797-1868), head of the Spode Porcelain Factory at Stoke on Trent, were resolved. He painted many pictures for the Copeland family, some of which were adapted and used as designs on the Spode china. Herring's first patron and the man who also commissioned him to paint his famous series of St. Leger winners was William Sheardown, proprietor of "The Doncaster Gazette". A number of Herring's works were sold at the dispersal of Sheardown's estate in August 1888. Exh. at the RA (1818-1846). Herring's daughter married the painter William Harrison Weir (q.v.).

Herring, John Frederick, Jnr. (1820-1907)
Eldest surviving son of John Frederick Herring, Snr. (q.v.) Specialised in farmyard scenes but collaborated on a number of paintings with Alexander F. Rolfe (q.v.), not surprisingly since Herring married his sister. She, as K. Herring, painted a number of landscapes in oil often featuring cattle. John Frederick Herring, Jnr. was a very competent artist but another example, as with Lambert Marshall (q.v.) of a son suffering the fate of a famous father in the same field. But for this handicap Herring might have been considered a better artist in his own right. Known to the rest of the family as Fred he signed his earliest work J. Fred Herring, sometimes adding Jnr. to his signature. He did not exh. at the RA until 1863, probably to avoid further conflict with his father, by whom he was much influenced, over the similarity of their styles.

Heseltine, Michael (b.1961)
A painter of equestrian scenes, particularly polo. Son of the artist John Heseltine (b.1923). Studied at the Maidenhead School of Art, leaving in 1983 to devote his time to travel and painting. Has journeyed through Australia, Indonesia, the West Indies and Europe. He has had several one-man shows at the New Academy Gallery, Cadogan Contemporary and Medici Gallery, the London Church Street Gallery, Bath and Sherborne Gallery, Dorset. Has undertaken special commissions for Drinkwater and Sabey, Ocean Transport and Trading and the Westbury Hotel, sponsors of the Westbury Cup for polo at Smith's Lawn, Windsor.

Hesp, Agnes E. (op.1932-1934)
Lancashire animal and equestrian painter who exh. three paintings at the Walker AG, Liverpool (1932-1933). Her pair "Riding to Hounds", dated 1934, were auctioned Sotheby's (Chester) 1987.

Hester, Edward Gilbert (c.1843-1903)
Line, mezzotint and aquatint engraver of sporting and sentimental subjects after the work of his contemporaries and possibly after his own work. An aquatint of the racehorse "Shotover" after E. Gilbert (q.v.) (1882) is more likely to be after his own work. "Shotover" won the 2000 Guineas and the Derby in 1882.

Hester, Robert Wallace (b.1866-op.1885-1904)
London painter and engraver whose set of four hunting paintings, "Picking up the Scent", "Out of the Woods", "The Chase" and "The Kill", each 13½in.x21in., all s.&d. 1885/6, were auctioned Sotheby's (NY) 1989. Hester exh. five works of art at the RA (1897-1904).

Hewison, William, NDD, ATD, MSIA (b.1925)
Painter and illustrator who studied at South Shields Art School (1941-1943) and Regent Street Polytechnic Art School (1947-1949). Art editor "Punch" (1960-1984). His painting of a football scene "Final Whistle", watercolour, 15in.x 19in., was exh. at the FE. Elected NDD (1949), ATD (1950) and MSIA (1954).

Hewitt, Geoffrey (b.1930)
Painter of two football scenes entitled "North-Eastern League", 27½in.x35in., and "Junior Trial Match" (wash) 8in.x6in. Both paintings were shown at the FE

in 1953. Hewitt exh. at the RA (1952-1955) including "Trials at White City" (1952, No.562). Hewitt, who was born in Co. Durham, graduated from the RCA in 1953 where his tutors were Carel Weight (q.v.), John Minton and Ruskin Spear (q.v.). Taught at Sunderland College of Art (1953-1955) and then at the Birmingham College of Art. Has exh. at the RA, the RSA, the LG and the RBA.

Hicks, George Elgar, RBA (1824-1914)
London society portrait painter who also painted scenes of busy Victorian life. Studied art at the RA Schools in 1844. Became a very competent illustrator. Exh. at SS (1847-1890) - no sporting scenes. Elected member (1889). Hicks was a keen croquet player and featured the game several times in his paintings. In 1864 he painted "The Croquet Player", 24in.x16½in., a portrait of Mrs. Creagh Osborne in the act of taking a shot. He also depicted a croquet party at Pennington Cottage, Lymington, Hants., in the same year, with a view across the Solent to the Isle of Wight. The players are again Mrs. Creagh Osborne who partners Miss Crozier. Mrs. Maturin stands behind the post while Mr. Peacock and Mr. Daniel play to her left. Mr. St. Barbe raises his fist behind them while Mr. Joubert, probably a portrait photographer and an engraver, lounges on the lawn in the bottom right. Hicks painted at least one preliminary sketch for the larger oil in the same year and his account book records that a sketch for the "Croquet Party" was sold to Mr. Wallace for £20. Hicks made three oil sketches of archery studies, "Stringing", "Knocking" and "Losing" which he mentions in his notebook of 1863 and which he also sold to Mr. Wallace for £35 each. His portrait "Three Young Cricketers" features the three sons of the Earl of Dudley who commissioned their portraits from Hicks in 1883. Hicks unfortunately only had time to finish a sketch, 11¼in.x8½in. for the painting before the commission was cancelled on the Earl's death. Southampton AG.

Hicks, Miss Mary (op.1890)
This artist from Colchester, Essex exh. one painting of ptarmigan at SS in 1890.

Hicks, Miss Minnie J. (op.1892-3)
This artist from Hendon exh. one painting of partridge at SS in 1892/3.

"Hieover, Harry"
Pseudonym used by the sporting artist Charles Bindley (q.v.).

Hieni-Merre, Franz (1870-1943)
German artist who painted "Trap Racing in St. Moritz", 19in.x25in., Zurich 1986.

Higgins, Charles S. (b.1893)
Painter in oil and watercolour, a caricaturist and an illustrator who worked under the alias of "Pic". His work included several sporting caricatures, mostly done just before and after the 2nd World War. As an author Higgins wrote under the name of "Ian Dall".

Higgs, J. (op.1939)
This artist painted a portrait of King George V shaking the hand of an unknown footballer, dated 1933, 22½in.x 29½in., auctioned Phillips 1989.

Highmore, Joseph (1692-1780)
Distinguished portrait painter and a painter of conversation pieces. Some of his portraits feature sporting personalities and equestrian subjects. Attended the life classes held by John Vanderbank (q.v.) at Sir Godfrey Kneller's Academy in St. Martin's Lane. Highmore was highly influenced by the work and ideas of Hubert Gravelot (q.v.) as was William Hogarth (q.v.), his contemporary. They may well have introduced Highmore to the game of cricket, or to cricket playing patrons. Certainly Highmore painted the portrait of the cricket loving John Duncombe who married Highmore's daughter, Susanna and became one of the six preachers in Canterbury Cathedral in 1766, the same year that Highmore painted his portrait. Duncombe, an undergraduate at Corpus and a fellow of the College from 1751-1758, was the author of the poem "Surrey Triumphant of the Kentish-mens Defeat" (1773) a description of a cricket match between Surrey and Kent, played near Canterbury. Highmore's obituary appeared in "The Gentleman's Magazine" in 1780.

Highton, T. (op.1801-1815)
Animal and equestrian painter who exh. at the RA (1801-1815) from a London address. His patrons, for whom he painted dog portraits, included the Earl of Warwick and Lord Sedley.

Hilditch, George (1803-1857)
London landscape artist who exh. a number of fresh water fish paintings at SS (1824-1854), i.e. "Trout and Salmon Trout", "Perch", "Tench", "Carp" and several of "Pike". He also painted "Hunters by a Stream", with a third hunter standing in the water. Sotheby's 1987.

Hill, Derek (b.1916)
Landscape and portrait painter in oil, stage designer and writer. Studied art in Munich, Vienna and Paris and stage design in Russia, China and Japan. His first one-man exhibition was held in 1943 at the Nicholson Gallery. Hill became Director of Art at the British School in Rome (1953-1955) and (1957-1959). Represented in several public collections. His large canvas (30in.x45½in.) entitled "Hunting in Limerick", painted in greens and browns, was auctioned Christie's 1990.

Hill, Frank (b.1881)
Etcher, engraver and watercolourist. Studied at the Central School of Arts and Crafts. Exh. chiefly in the provinces and also in the USA. His mixed media picture "The Athlete" was auctioned Bonhams 1989.

Hill, F.L. (op.c.1888-1919)
Several equestrian scenes by this artist have come up at auction including a painting of "Aylesbury Races", "A Coaching Scene" and "The Hunt Kennels". This artist is possibly Mme. F.E. de Lannoy Hill who exh. at the SWA and the London Salon.

Hill, G.M. (op.1906)
A portrait of "Mountain Maid", a bay horse in a stable, s.&d. 1906, 12in.x16in. Bonhams 1986.

Hill, J.C. (op.1862)
A chestnut horse standing by a wall, s.&d. 1862, auctioned Christie's, 28 July 1961.

Hill, James John, RBA (1811-1882)
Birmingham-born landscape and portrait painter. Came to London in 1839. Painted several portraits of hunters in landscapes or stable yards. His patroness was Lady Burdett Coutts for whom he painted portraits, animal, dog and equestrian studies. Elected RBA (1842).

Hill, Justus (op.1884-1889)
A watercolour especially painted for the magazine "Fishing" showing Thames barbel was painted by this artist in 1885 and is in the collection of the Piscatorial Society.

Hill, Rowland Henry (1873-1952)
Yorkshire-born landscape, sporting and country genre painter. Also a cartoonist. Born in Halifax and worked there before studying at the Bradford School of Art and at the Herkomer School at Bushey. Worked as a cartoonist under the pseudonym of "Rip". Contributed work to "Black and White", "Truth" and "The Sketch". Travelled on the continent and settled at Hinderwell, Yorks., in 1908. Exh. at the RA. His watercolour of a huntsman with hounds entitled "The Meet", s.&d. 1934, is in a private collection.

Hill, Thomas (1829-1908)
English-born artist who went to the USA in 1840. His painting of a Victorian family croquet match is entitled "Palo Alto Spring", 1878 (Stanford University of Art) and shows that croquet was a game in which the old and young could play together.

Hill, W.H. (op.1873)
A painting of a pony and trap, s.&d. (18)73, 16in.x 24in., Tennants (Yorks.) 1990.

Hillman, R.S. (op.c.1830)
Unrecorded American painter of "The First Trotting Race" painted in a competent, but primitive style, c.1830, Hall of Fame of the Trotter, Goshen, NY.

Hills, Robert, OWS (1769-1844)
A prolific painter and etcher of animals who showed more than 600 works at the OWS of which he was a founder member in 1804. Many of these were studies of deer. His RA exhibit in 1820 was "The Wounded Stag". Born in Islington, Hills received drawing lessons from John Gresse. He lived in Newman Street, a contemporary and neighbour of James Ward (q.v.) who lived at number 6. Agasse (q.v.) lived at the same time at number 4 but there is no evidence that Hills and Ward knew him or were on friendly terms.

Hillyard, J.W. (op.1833-1861)
Landscape and country scene painter who painted several hunting scenes including "On the Scent", "Taking a Fence", "The Meet", etc. Exh. one work at BI in 1833 and at SS (1835-1861).

Hilton, T. (op.1805)
Yorkshire painter whose portrait of the racehorse "Haphazard" is recorded as having been engraved by J. Wessell in 1805. "Haphazard" is chiefly remembered as the sire of "XYZ" and for defeating Lord Strathmore's "Walnut" in a match for 500 guineas. "Haphazard" was also painted by Ben Marshall (q.v.) and appears to have

been engraved twice in 1805, once by W.B. Cook and once by his brother, George Cook, with whom he collaborated on several plates.

Hilton, William, RA (1786-1839)
Lincoln painter of historical and biblical subjects. Taught to paint by his father, the provincial portrait painter William Hilton (op.1777-1797). Exh. at the RA and BI (1803-1839), including "The Caledonian Hunt" at the RA in 1822. A pair of prints entitled "Pike Fishing" and "A Trout Angler" were engraved by H.R. Cook.

Hinckley, Thomas Hewes (1813-1896)
American artist of animal and sporting subjects which include portraits of greyhounds and spaniels with dead game. He modelled his painting style on that of Sir Edwin Landseer (q.v.) whose work he studied, and exh. at the RA (1858).

Hincks, S.C. (op.1858-1867)
Surrey painter of animals and sporting subjects who exh. seven works at the BI (1858-1867). Titles include "At the Covert Side" and "Deer Stalking in the Highlands".

Hind, R.N. (op.1859)
This artist is known solely through the engraving after his work by G. Greatbach of "'Daisy' the Celebrated Trotting Pony belonging to Mr. William Pearce", pub. 1859, 18in.x22in.

Hine, Harry, RI, ROI (1845-1941)
Landscape painter in both oil and watercolour whose four tiny hunting scenes, "Setting Out", "Drawing Covert", "Full Cry" and "The Kill", each 3¼in.x 6¾in., were auctioned at Christie's 1983. Hine was the son of the artist Harry T. Hine and he exh. at the RA, RI, RBA and other London galleries from 1873. Hine is also known to have painted portraits of fighting cocks.

Hines, Theodore (op.1876-1890)
Landscape and river scene painter particularly of the river Thames. Included in this Dictionary for his painting "Henley Regatta", 13½in.x20in., Sotheby's 1989.

"Hippias"
Author of "Country Notes" for the first issues of "Country Life" from January 1897 Vol.I.

Hiscock, David
Contemporary figure painter. One of the six artists chosen worldwide, sponsored by VISA EMR to cover the 1992 Olympic Games in Barcelona.

Hixon, R. (op c.1812)
Draughtsman, aquatint engraver and publisher of sporting and coaching works, presumably after his own designs. His portrait of "Sir John", a racehorse, and "A Tandem and a Barouche", pub. 1812, are known through their engravings.

Hixon, William J. (op.1825-1857)
London artist of equestrian portraits who exh. ten works, mostly of animals at the BI (1825-1857), four works at the RA (1827-1856) and sixteen at SS (1825-

1834) including "Hunters at Grass". Hixon's painting of Lieutenant Horne's Arabian stallion "Humdanick" dated 1832 and inscr., 17¾in.x24in., was auctioned Christie's (NY) 1983. His portrait of a grey hunter in a stable interior with a terrier, painted in 1832, was auctioned Christie's 1980.

Hoad, Norman (b.1923)
Sussex-born equestrian artist who joined the RAF in 1941 and retired with the rank of Air Vice Marshall in 1978. Studied art, part time (1950-1952), at York College of Art. He quickly established himself as an artist specialising in aviation subjects and is a founder member of the Guild of Aviation Artists. Since the early 1970s his work has expanded to include horses and all aspects of equestrian art. He is a founder member of the Society of Equestrian Artists (1979) and his work is in many public and private collections.

Hobart, John R. (op.1829-1859)
Suffolk equestrian and sporting artist from Monks Eleigh near Ipswich. Hobart was the first official Suffolk Horse Society artist. His sporting subject matter includes portraits of hunters, pointers, shire horses but he does not appear to have painted hunting scenes or indeed horses in action. He always seems to have signed and dated his work.

Hobday, William Armfield (1771-1831)
Portrait painter whose portrait of Henry Pierce, the boxer, known as "the Game Chicken", 25¼in.x19¼in., was painted in 1805. Hobday, who studied at the RA Schools and exh. at the RA from 1794, was made bankrupt in 1829 through a gallery speculation.

Hobson, Anthony, Phd, NDD, ATD, FRSA, FSEAD, Hon.FHS (b.1920)
Distinguished contemporary painter of several real tennis paintings in oil. These include portraits of the celebrated Jim Dear, the former real tennis and rackets world champion, and Henry Johns, for many years senior professional to the MCC at Lords. His 8ft.x5ft. canvas, "The Dinner Match at Leamington", with its forty-four portraits was commissioned by the Leamington Tennis Court Club in 1982. Hobson studied at Leicester College of Art, gaining the National Diploma in Design and the Art Teacher's Diploma. Exh. at the RA, and elsewhere.

Hockney, David (b.1937)
Leading 20th century painter and print maker who studied at Bradford School of Art (1953-1957) and at the RCA (1959-1962). Included in this Dictionary solely for the picture that he sent from his Los Angeles home to The 1853 Gallery, outside Bradford, using a fax machine. The picture, spanning 14ft.x10ft., of an undisclosed sporting scene, was put together according to Hockney's previously faxed directions.

Hodge, Thomas (1827-1907)
Born in Truro. Became a brilliant golfing artist, a game he lived for and played all his life. Very little is known about his early life. He must have had some artistic or draughtsman's training for when he was only twenty-four he pub. a book on military fortifications and was

regarded as an authority on the subject. He later opened a boarding school in Scotland to train boys for the Colonial service, which was a very successful enterprise. He drew sketches of Scottish golfing characters between 1860 and 1890 including the legendary Tom Morris and Alan Robertson. In 1891 he illus. Andrew Laing's "Golfing Papers" and Robert Clark's "Golf - A Royal and Ancient Game". His watercolour portrait of George Glennie, the famous amateur golfer, painted in 1880, 8¼in.x6in., hangs in the Royal & Ancient Golf Club at St. Andrews. Hodge, who provided many of the illustrations for the Golf issue of the "Badminton Library Series", was an extremely competent golfer, winning the King William IV Gold Medal three times and the Silver Cross.

Hodges, J. (op.1848)
A portrait of the greyhound "Jenny Lind", the property of Mrs. Titchmarsh of Shepreth, s.&d. 1848 and inscr., was auctioned Bonhams 1985.

Hodges, Walter Parry (1760-1845)
Sporting and equestrian artist from Dorset whose surname was originally Parry. Walter Parry took the name of Hodges at the request of an uncle's will. His many hunting works show sporting scenes from the Blackmore Vale but he was also a frequent visitor to Enderby and Melton Mowbray, becoming a friend of C. Lorraine Smith (q.v.). His watercolour painting of "The Quorn Hunt", inspired by Nimrod's account of a day out with Squire Osbaldeston's hounds, which appeared in "The Quarterly Review" in 1832, is in the Paul Mellon Collection, Upperville, Va, USA. Hodges usually worked in watercolour. He is widely known for the prints after his work. These include "Hare Hunting - Ware Turnips" engraved in aquatint by R.G. Reeve and pub. by Thomas Maclean in 1836, "Chase and Death of the Roebuck" (1834) and "Yellowham Woods and Cocktails Done" engraved by Henry Thomas Alken (q.v.), repro. "The Field", 25.10.1923.

Hodgkinson, Cecil Thomas (1896-1979)
Lincolnshire painter in watercolour of wildfowl, including mallard and tufted duck, shovellers and teal. His rather amateur watercolour study of a salmon being played by an invisible hand, 8in.x10½in., entitled "Caught" was auctioned Sotheby's (Sussex) 1989. Hodgkinson exh. in the provinces and became Chairman of the Lincolnshire Artists Society (1954/5).

Hodgson, Robert (op.1780-1787)
Painter of a portrait of the fighting cock "Old Trodgon", 30in.x25in., which was exh. by Oscar and Peter Johnson, London, previously in the Hutchinson Collection.

Hodgson, W. (op.1838-1841)
Animal painter who exh. two portraits of horses and one of a dog at the RA (1838-1841) from a London address. His fine watercolour "A Hunting Morning", signed and inscr., 15¾in.x24½in., auctioned at Christie's (NY) in 1985.

Hodgson, William J. (op.1878-1903)
Black and white sporting artist who contributed to "Punch" (1892-1897) and who was previously working

in Scarborough (1878) and at Clovelly, Devon (1891). A fine pen and ink draughtsman in the style of Caldecott (q.v.), much of his work was of sporting subjects.

Hoffman, Frank (1888-1958)
American painter and illustrator whose dramatic painting entitled "Safe at Home" represents the vivid action in a game of baseball. This fine motion picture was repro. on the front cover of "Liberty Magazine", 18 April 1925. The original oil on canvas, 34in.x35in., Judy Goffman Fine Art, NY.

Hoffmann, Hans (c.1530-1591/2)
16th century German artist whose only known animal painting "The Hare in the Forest" was originally commissioned by Emperor Rudolph II of Prague, probably the greatest collector and art patron of his age, who paid the enormous sum of 200 guilders for it on 22 October 1585. In 1584 Hoffman worked at the Munich court and in 1585 he was summoned to Rudolph's prestigious court at Prague and was appointed Hofmaler (Court Painter). The subject was inspired by Albrecht Durer's well-known study of a hare in 1502, now in the Albertina, Vienna. "The Hare in the Forest" was probably one of the 764 pictures which Queen Christina had taken to Stockholm as war booty in 1648/9 and it is not known when it came to England. In 1983 it was found in the attic of a Yorkshire farmhouse and the owners brought it to Sotheby's.

Hofland, Thomas Christopher, RBA (1777-1843)
Landscape painter and illustrator, very often of sporting subjects. A pupil of John R. Rathbone. Hofland who wrote and illus. "British Anglers Manual" (1839) also painted "Trout Fishing in Lake Awe" (see also John Hollins for a similar subject, colour plate 169 repro. "Angling in British Art" Shaw Sparrow) and "Grouse Shooting", 40in.x50in., exh. Preston HM and AG "British Sporting Paintings" (1943). Hofland's principal patron was the 3rd Earl of Egremont (1751-1837) but he also made botanical drawings for King George III (1738-1820). Exh. at SS (1824-1843). Elected RBA (1824).

Hogarth, Arthur Paul, ARA (b.1917)
Painter of many sports scenes including American football, show jumping and golf. Contributor to a number of leading American and European periodicals including "Sports Illustrated" and "The Sunday Telegraph Magazine". Hogarth studied at Manchester Art School and in London and Paris. His study of the Old West seen through the eyes of British artists was pub. as "Artists on Horseback" (NY 1972). Hogarth's showjumpers walking the course at the Dublin Horse Show in 1972 are lively inspirations, pencil and watercolour drawing, Abbott and Holder, London.

Hogarth, William (1697-1764)
Important portrait painter and an equally important engraver. Hogarth served an apprenticeship under the silver plate engraver, Elias Gamble, and produced his first print in 1720. He is probably best known for his famous series "A Harlot's Progress" (1732), "A Rake's Progress" (1735) and "Marriage à la Mode" (1745).

The publication of engravings after these series showed Hogarth's radically different approach to the art of print making and reached the widest possible audience to the benefit of both his profit and his fame. The son-in-law of Sir James Thornhill (q.v.), he later successfully took over Thornhill's drawing academy which he had inherited from Sir Godfrey Kneller (q.v.) and which, under his direction, went to pieces. Hogarth was known to have pugnacious and progressive opinions but the St. Martin's Lane school flourished under his directorship. A friend of the artist Francis Hayman RA (q.v.), Hogarth is included in this Dictionary for his portrait of John Broughton (1705-1789), the prize-fighter, and his group portrait "The Pascall Family with Mr. Pascall Fishing" (repro. "Angling in British Art", Shaw Sparrow, colour plate p.200).

Hogg, Arthur H. (op.1901-1907)
Black and white artist specialising in horse subjects. Contributed to "Fun" (1901) and "Punch" (1906-7).

Hogley, Stephen E. (op.1874-1893)
Yorkshire landscape and sporting artist with a depressing palette. Even his fly fishing subjects, which should be fun, are darkly depressing. He painted his otter hunting and fishing scenes in both oil and watercolour and very often painted Highland scenes. Exh. three paintings at the Manchester City AG and two at SS (1874-1893).

Holbein, Hans, the Younger (1497-1543)
German painter and engraver from Augsburg who lived for a long time in England and became official painter to King Henry VIII (1491-1547). His fine portrait of Robert Cheseman, Henry's falconer, painted in 1533, 20in.x24½in., is in the collection of Koninglijk Kabinet can Schilderijen "Mauritshuis", The Hague.

Hold, Abel (op.1836-1903)
Yorkshire painter of game and still lifes who exh. (1850-1871) at the RA, BI and SS. "Partridge Shooting over Pointers", s.&d. 1836, shows a competent but naïve hand, Sotheby's (Sussex) 1990.

Hold, Ben (op.1896-1903)
Brother of the Yorkshire game and still life painter Abel Hold (q.v.), Ben Hold painted similar subjects. His painting of a fisherman in the foreground of a river landscape, 18in.x13in., was auctioned Gorringes 1986.

Hold, Thomas (op.late 19th century)
Painted game birds, not always dead, and foxes, often depicting them as the pursuer not the pursued. Related presumably to the other two Holds, Thomas does not appear to have exh. in any of the major London galleries. "The Day's Bag", s.&d. 1878, 25½in.x42½in., Sotheby's 1990, is an excellent example of Tom Hold's work at its best.

Holding, Henry James G. (1833-1872)
Landscape and marine painter who also painted several equestrian portraits and hawking scenes.

Holiday, Charles Gilbert Joseph (1879-1937)
London-born equestrian painter who studied art at the RA Schools. His style is an impressionistic one and his broad direct strokes enabled him to capture movement and action with success in any medium, but particularly in watercolour and pastel. His draughtsmanship was superbly disciplined so that his impressionistic style was not achieved at its expense. So far as sport is concerned, he probably excelled more than any other artist in portraying polo successfully and was a master at depicting speed. By 1900 Holiday's work appeared in "Black and White", "The Graphic" and "The Strand" magazines and in 1904 he exh. the first of six paintings at the Royal Academy. Holiday died from a combination of a fall with the Woolwich Drag on top of wounds received twenty years earlier with the Gunners. Amongst the sports he painted were tennis, show jumping, polo, hunting, racing, ice hockey and he also painted the posters for the Royal Tournament.

Hollams, Mabel F. (Mrs. Charles Lionel Fox) SWA (1877-1963)
Painter of equestrian portraits who studied at the Calderon School of Animal Painting, Kensington, and at the Atelier Julian in Paris. Exh. four paintings at the RA (1897-1900). Hollams worked with great speed, painting horse and dog portraits to satisfy her many commissions. She is alleged rarely to have discussed money for a painting but her butler always waited to bid farewell to collecting clients with a silver salver, on which they were expected to place £25 in cash. Elected SWA (1902). Her patrons included the Earls of Sefton, Beatty and Lord Cornwallis. Lord Cornwallis was Master of the Linton Beagles (1888-1932) and Mabel Hollams painted him with the beagles.

Holland, James Sylvester (b.1905)
Landscape and figure painter who studied at Rochester School of Art and at the RCA. His contribution to football art lies in his work entitled "Captain, Supporter and Mascot", 29½in.x56½in., exh. at the FE in 1953. Holland exh. at the NEAC and LG.

Holland, John (op.1831-1884)
Nottingham landscape painter whose interesting picture of "Nottingham Races" contains a multitude of figures and horses as does his charcoal and wash drawing entitled "The Regatta", 16½in.x30¼in., auctioned Sotheby's 1986.

Holland, Philip (ex.1850-1886)
London painter of fruit, flowers and game, both alive and dead, who exh. at SS (1850-1886). His exhibition work includes many studies of snipe, pheasant, partridges and hares.

Hollins, John, ARA (1798-1855)
Birmingham-born portrait and landscape painter. He was the son of a glass painter, under whom he is thought to have studied. Included in this Dictionary for his celebrated group portrait "Salmon Fishing on Loch Awe" (see also Hofland for a similar subject) which he painted with F.R. Lee, RA (q.v.) in 1854, and his other famous group portrait "A Consultation Previous to an Airial Voyage from London to Weiburg in Nassau on November 7th 1836" showing many noted people of the day. This was engraved by John Henry Robinson, RA

(1796-1871) in 1843 (8in.x11¾in.). An engraving by G.T. Payne of "Charles Green the Aeronaut", after the work by Hollins, was pub. in 1838.

Hollis, Thomas (1818-1843)
Landscape painter, son of George Hollis (1793-1842), an etcher and topographer. Studied art under H.W. Pickersgill and at the RA Schools. He painted a few equestrian portraits, usually mares and foals.

Holloway, W.H. (op.1919-1925)
A painting entitled "Fast Work at the Net" showing four young men playing a lawn tennis doubles game was included in "Boys Own Annual" 1924/25.

Hollyer, W.P. (op.1878-1899)
Genre painter of Scottish scenes including many of deer and grouse.

Holmes, Edward, RBA (op.1841-1894)
Landscape, marine and portrait painter who exh. a number of genre paintings at SS (1841-1894). Titles include "The Young Angler", "The Keeper's Bag", "The First Ride", "The Afternoon Ride" and "A Fishing Party". Elected RBA (1889).

Holmes, George Augustus, RBA (op.1852-d.1911)
Genre painter who exh. at the RA (1852-1909) and at the BI, GG, Paris Salon and elsewhere. He also exh. at SS (1853-1894), mostly sugary titles but they include "The Morning Ride" (1890). Elected RBA (1863). Holmes was particularly fond of greyhounds and painted pairs of greyhounds many times. He also painted equestrian portraits. His portrait of "A Foxhound", 7½in.x9½in., was auctioned Andrew Grant 1990.

Holt, Edward (op.1884)
Several shooting and fishing scenes by this artist have appeared at auction including "A Midday Rest from the Shoot", s.&d. 1884, Sotheby's (NY) 1983. His work is clearly signed "Edward" and not "Edwin".

Holt, Edwin Frederick (op.1850-1905)
A prolific painter of genre subjects which he exh. at SS (1850-1865), BI (1853-1860) and at the RA (1854-1858). He also painted numerous sporting scenes which he seems to have kept quite separate from his exhibition work. Examples include "The Sportsman's Rendezvous", 27in.x20in., signed and inscr. "Prize med.t RA 1878", "At the Blacksmith", signed and inscr. 1898 "Prize med.t RA 1898". The inscriptions on both these paintings are somewhat baffling in view of Holt's exhibition dates and the sort of work that he is known to have exh. Other sporting work which he usually seems to have s.&d. includes "A Sportsman with a Pointer and a Setter Shooting Pheasants in a Cornfield" (1865) and a "Portrait of the stud stallion "Citadel", the property of the Hon. Earl of Stamford and Warrington", who was awarded first prize of £100 and a silver cup value £25 at the Teddington Show (1864). Holt lived at Venetia Cottage, West Drayton, Middx. at about this time. Holt's most interesting painting is his view of the Coronation celebrations entitled "A Thames Boathouse", s.&d. 9 August 1902, 7¾in.x12in., which not only shows that he was actively painting at this date but is also an interesting historical record. An under-rated artist whose work would reward further research.

Holt, Ellen F. (Mrs) (op.1857-1906)
A very competent painter, the wife of E. F. Holt (q.v.). Her work numbers several sporting scenes including portraits of foxhounds.

Holyoake, Rowland (ex.1880-1907)
Genre painter of portraits and landscapes, the son of the artist William Holyoake (q.v.). His study of the racehorse "Count Schomberg" s.&d. 1898, 24in.x29in., was auctioned Gorringes 1990. Exh. (1880-1907) at RI, NWS, GG and elsewhere including his painting entitled "The Compleat Angler", 20in.x22in., 1901 (No. 717).

Holyoake, William, RBA (1834-1894)
Genre painter and painter of crowd scenes. Included in this Dictionary for his two sporting paintings entitled "Keen Spectators at the Boat Race", 20in.x24in. which shows fashionably dressed women jostling for a good view and "Derby Day", 20in.x24in., auctioned Christie's 1978. Holyoake exh. at the RA (1865-1885), BI (1856-1867) and at SS (1879-1888) but no other painting title is remotely connected with sport. Elected RBA (1879).

Homer, Winslow, NA (1836-1910)
Distinguished American artist whose painting "A Game of Croquet" 1866 is in the Arts Institute at Chicago. Homer, who was born in Boston, started work as a lithographer in 1855. In 1857 he took up painting and illustrating and in 1859 he came to New York where he studied for a short time at the National Academy of Design. He was elected an Associate of the National Academy (1864) and an Academician the following year. Homer painted a series of five major croquet paintings which were amongst the earliest representations of the game to appear in fine art. They were painted between 1865-1869 and show that Homer had a detailed knowledge of the rule book and the conventions of the game. The other paintings are in the Yale University AG, New Haven, The National Academy of Design, New York, The Albright Knox AG, Buffalo NY. The fifth painting "The Croquet Match" is in the Terra Museum of American Art.

Hone, Nathaniel, RA (1718-1784)
Portrait painter of some sportsmen and sporting subjects. Hone, who was born in Dublin into a Presbyterian family of Dutch origin, came to England and started his career as an itinerant painter. He built up an extremely fashionable practice in London as a miniature painter and married a rich wife in 1742. Hone was instrumental in setting up the Incorporated Society of Artists and became a Director in 1766. He gave up miniature painting in the 1760s. Exh. at the RA (1769-1784) becoming a foundation RA.

"Robin Hood"
The sporting writer C.M. Browne whose contributions on coursing matters to "The Field" from 1863-1892 were highly regarded.

Hook, James Clarke, RA, HFRPE (1819-1907)

Land and seascape painter who studied with the portrait painter John Jackson and in 1836 at the RA Schools, where he won a travelling scholarship to France and Italy for three years. Exh. at the RA (1839-1902) including "The Broken Oar" (1886). Other sporting titles include "Salmon Trappers, Norway" (1873), "Fishing by Proxy" (1877), "He Shot a Fine Shoot" (1886) and "Tickling Trout" (1889). "A Wily Angler watching his Red Float" was repro. "Angling in British Art" (Shaw Sparrow, colour plate p.48). Hook was also an etcher who contributed work to the Etching Club. Elected RA (1860).

Hopkins, Arthur, RWS, RBC (1848-1930)

London landscape and genre painter, in watercolour and oil, and an illustrator. Entered the RA Schools (1872) and exh. from that year at the principal London galleries, mainly the RWS and RA. Contributed to "The Graphic", "Punch" and "The Illustrated London News". Elected RWS (1896). Hopkins painted several sporting subjects including "Henley Royal Regatta" (1891), drawn for "The Illustrated London News" of that date, a portrait of H.F. Lawford and W. Renshaw in the fifth round (golf) drawn for "The Graphic" and repro."Fifty Years of Wimbledon" by A. Wallis Myers, "A Lesson in Lawn Bowls" painted 1893, "The "Bluebell" Winning the Schooner Match at the RAYC off Shanklin" (1866), "Witchcraft" (built by S. White) at East Cowes in 1865. His watercolour "Rough Shooting", 14½in.x21in. painted in black and white, was auctioned Sotheby's 1987. Arthur Hopkins was the brother of Gerard Manley Hopkins, poet and entertainer, and of Everard Hopkins (1860-1928), watercolourist and illustrator. "The Last Game of the Season", originally drawn for "The Illustrated London News" (1872), repro."The History of Croquet" by D.M.C. Prichard (pub. Cassells London 1981).

Hopkins, Mrs. Edward (née Frances Ann Beechey) (1838-1919)

Painter of Canadian landscapes including a sketch of a cricket match inscr. "Cricket Ground, Montreal - 26th September 1859. Second day of match between The All England Eleven and Twenty Two Gentlemen of Canada", Phillips 1989. Frances Hopkins exh. at the RA (1861-1902), also at the RBA and Walker AG, Liverpool. She lived in Canada (1858-1870) as the wife of the Secretary to the Governor of the Hudson Bay Company.

Hopkins, Francis Powell (Major) (1830-1913)

Golfing artist and journalist who wrote for "The Field" as early as 1863. He very often used the nom de plume "Shortspoon", a variety of golf club. Hopkins was born in Cambridge, the son of a Fellow of Peterhouse. On his retirement from the army (1866) he went to live at Westward Ho in North Devon where, two years previously, England's oldest links course was founded. A proficient golf player himself, Hopkins discovered a talent far above average for drawing and watercolour painting and at a time before photography was established portrayed golfing scenes with a rare skill and liveliness. His watercolours include scenes not only at Westward

Ho but at Hoylake, St. Andrews, Sandwich and Blackheath. An oil painting, 21¼in.x44½in., "Golf at Blackheath", painted in 1875 shows that Hopkins was also proficient in this medium. The scene shows the first tee with Greenwich Park in the background and the 1874 Captain, James L. Bennet, about to drive and, having his ball teed up, is Colonel Hegan Kennard, MP, who succeeded him in 1875. Amongst those watching is George Glennie whose portrait was also painted by Thomas Hodge, Heywood Hardy and John Ballantyne (qq.v.) Many of Hopkins' golfing paintings have been used to illustrate a recent biography compiled by Stirk and Henderson entitled "Shortspoon". Hopkins also illus. "Fishing Experiences of Half a Century" (1893) and "Sixty Three Years Angling" (1891) by John MacVine.

Hopkins, William H. (op.1853-1890 d.1892)

Sporting and equestrian artist who worked for "Bailys Magazine". Hopkins took over the position that Bailys offered from Harry Hall (q.v.) who had quarrelled with the owner over money, or the lack of it, to produce paintings each year of the Derby winner for engraving. His first commission was a painting of "Shotover", who with Tom Cannon up, had just won the Derby (1882) for the Duke of Westminster. For some unaccountable reason Hopkins made the mare look as unattractive as he could, painting her with her ears laid back. Although the portrait was a good likeness the public were incensed, far preferring Hall's highly coloured photographic work. The outcome was that Mr. Baily's series of Derby winners started and ended in 1882 with "Shotover". Despite this hiccup Hopkins was regarded as a fine equestrian painter, knowledgeable about his subject and his work could be relied on for accuracy of detail as well as being artistic. He exh. at SS (1853-1873) including "The Warrener's Pony" (1856) and "A Favourite Horse", the Property of S.F. Somers, Esq. on which painting Hopkins collaborated with C.R. Havell (q.v.). He also collaborated with Edmund Havell, Jnr. (q.v.) on a number of paintings including the portrait of the "Glossy Peer" (Lord Hardwicke) with the Royal Buckhounds, of which he was Master at the time (1874-1880), in Windsor Forest. The painting was hung at the Royal Academy and was regarded by many as one of the finest hunting portraits ever seen. An interesting but less flattering report on Hopkins' work at the July Exhibition at Burlington House is recorded in "Bailys Magazine" 1875 and reads as follows. "We cannot altogether compliment Mr. Hopkins upon his pair of hunting studies in Gallery No. 5. There is not one atom of character in either men, horses or hounds and they are altogether on too small a scale and too carelessly executed to take rank above the ordinary sporting prints which attract passers by in Regents Street or Piccadilly". The writer possibly remembered the saga of "Shotover".

Hopkinson, John (b.1940)

Cleethorpes painter of figure subjects, many featuring football crowds and supporters. These he paints in a style reminiscent of William Roberts, RA (q.v.)

exaggerating particular features like hands and feet. Has had several one-man exhibitions in both London and the North of England including Fox Fine Arts, London (1978). Paints in most mediums. "Manchester City Football Club Supporters" and "Tottenham Hotspurs Football Supporters", pen, black ink and coloured crayons.

Hoppner, John, RA (1758-1810)
Society portrait painter who entered the RA Schools (1775). Won a Gold Medal (1782) and exh. at the RA (1780-1807). Elected RA (1795). Portrait painter to the Prince of Wales (1789). Included in this Dictionary for his portraits of the champion boxer, Richard "Gentleman" Humphries in 1788 and "Sir Foster Cunliffe with Bow in Hand". Cunliffe was founder of the Royal Society of Bowmen and the portrait was painted, c.1790, before rivalry with the younger Lawrence began to affect Hoppner's work. His pupil was Sir Augustus Wall Callcott, RA (q.v.) and his work is represented in the Tate Gallery, London.

Hoque, Zil, BA.Hons (b.1962)
Figure artist in both oil and watercolour and a lithographer. Born in Bengal, India, he studied at the Central School of Art and Design (1982-1986) where he obtained an Honours Degree in Fine Art. First one-man exhibition in 1987 at the Jablonski Gallery, London. His association with fencing has led him to paint dramatic scenes of the sport and his work in this subject is shown and promoted by the Wingfield Sporting Gallery, London.

Horlor, A. (op.c.1880)
Portrait of a young cricketer, full length, standing on a bench in a wooden garden seat in a wooded landscape holding a cricket bat, 21¼in.x17¼in. Pilkington Collection.

Horlor, George William (op.1849-1891)
Animal and sporting painter who specialised in Highland shooting scenes, painted in a bright, cheerful style. Exh. at SS (1854-1866). Titles include "The Shooting Pony", "Dead Game", "Sport on the Moorland", "Setters and Game", and "The Warrener". Horlor's portrait of Arthur Edwin May, MP, dressed in the hunting livery of the Cheltenham Stag Hounds of which he was Master in 1860, is in the Cheltenham AG.

Horn, George (b.1964)
Contemporary artist of football and other sporting scenes who studied at Glasgow School of Art after leaving Glasgow University. His "Round the World Boat Race", 1974, 24in.x36in., was auctioned Bonhams 1987 and shows "Great Britain II" and "Pen Duick VI" competing.

Horne, Edwin (op.1953)
Painter who contributed a pen and gouache of a football match entitled "Floodlight Incident", 17in.x12½in., to the FE.

Horner, George Christopher (op.1838-1867)
Talented but unrecorded artist whose hunting scene, s.&d. 1852 and inscr. "Liverpool", 28in.x36in., shows members of the Cheshire Hunt with Beeston Castle behind. The Master of the Cheshire Hunt at this date was Captain John White. Horner's portrait of the cow "Yorkshire Rose", dated 1838, is to be found at Reading University.

Horner, Thomas (op.1800-1844)
Landscape and topographical artist who made numerous drawings of tours through the Vale of Neath. An album of twenty-five small finished watercolours in the collection of the British Museum includes a small version of "A Meet at Batchelor's Hall in the Vale of Neath, Wales" (Batchelor's Hall, Rheola, Glamorganshire, was the home of the Edwards-Vaughan family). The larger drawing, pen/ink, blue/brown wash, 9⅞in.x 17⅞in. was in the collection of the Duke of Sutherland from an album in his possession, broken up in 1957. Horner may well have been related to George Christopher Horner (q.v.) since they both operated in the same area.

Horton, Miss Etty (op.1892-1903)
London artist who exh. two works at the RA in 1893 and 1903 and two works at SS in 1892 and 1893 including a cricket painting entitled "Stumped".

Horwood, Charles (op.1969)
Contemporary artist of racing scenes including "Cantering to the Start, Epsom", s.&d. '69, 11½in.x15¼in., auctioned Sotheby's (Sussex) 1987.

"Hotspur"
Alias Mr. Sydney Galtrey of "The Daily Telegraph", who was the original "Hotspur" and who also wrote "Memoirs of a Racing Journalist". Peter Scott is the present "Hotspur" and the racing journalist and author, Bill Curling, was the previous "Hotspur".

Houghton, George (op.1969)
Contemporary artist of golfing scenes including "Autumn Shower, The Sixth Tee, Worthing", watercolour, s.&d. 1969, and "The Thirteenth Tee, Upper Course, Worthing", watercolour, both auctioned Phillips (Scotland) 1986.

Howard, Frank (1805-1866)
Equestrian artist who illus. "The Equestrian", a handbook of horsemanship c.1839. A very attractive watercolour drawing by this artist entitled "The Derby Won", s.&d. 1833, was exh. at Messrs. Ackermanns Galleries in 1930 as reported in "The Connoisseur" of that year (June). Howard's painting of the "Derby" was aquatinted by E. Duncan (q.v.).

Howard, George James, 9th Earl of Carlisle, HRWS (1843-1911)
Landscape painter in oil and watercolour who studied art at the RCA under Legros and Giovanni Costa. Travelled widely and was Chairman of the Trustees of the National Gallery for thirty years. Honorary Member of the Royal Society of Painters in Watercolour. Exh. (1868-1910) at the Grosvenor Gallery and also at the New Gallery. Howard painted a delightful study, 15in.x20in., of his children, Dorothy, Aurea, Charles and Hubert playing croquet.

Howe, B.A. (op.1840-1857)
Painter of sporting scenes, mostly of game dogs and dead game. Exh. three works at SS (1844-1857). "A Fox with a dead Pheasant", s.&d. 1840, 25in.x30in. was auctioned Christie's 1986.

Howe, James (1780-1839)
Scottish equestrian and sporting painter, born in Skirling, Peebleshire, the son of a minister. Howe worked closely with the Highland Society of Scotland in the early 19th century and is represented at Reading University in a bound collection of prints, pub. by Ballentines, Edinburgh, 1832. His paintings include portraits of hunters, racehorses and lurchers. His work is usually signed and dated. His sporting scenes include "Musselburgh Races", "Perth Races" (pen/ink) Perth Museum and AG, "Skirling Fair", "The Horse Fair at the Grass Market, Edinburgh" and "Hawking". His painting of the famous Scottish falconer, Mr. Malcolm Fleming of Barochan Castle near Paisley, Renfrewshire, seated on his horse with his hooded falcon on his fist and his falconers John Anderson (1745-1831) and his assistant George Harvey with the falcons and dogs, hangs in the Scottish National Portrait Gallery in Edinburgh. The painting was engraved in mezzotint by Charles Turner in 1816 (22in.x24½in.). Howe, who went to London in 1806 to paint horses for George III, encouraged by Lord Buchan who was an enthusiastic supporter, also drew wonderfully humorous studies of horses, dogs and gamekeepers. His pupil was William Kidd (q.v.).

Howe, W.
Illustrator to the "Annals of Sporting" of which fourteen plates after Howe's work were engraved by William Lizars (1788-1859).

Howell, Peter (b.1932)
Equestrian artist, discovered and promoted by Ackermanns, London, who gave him several one-man exhibitions and established him internationally. Started his career as a jockey and from 1963 he began to paint as a serious artist. Head studies of "Brigadier Gerard", signed, inscr. and dated '74 were auctioned Christie's (Tattersalls) 1988.

Howie, A.
A portrait of the racehorse "Leda" (1824) by "Filo da Puto" out of "Treasure" was auctioned Tennants (Yorkshire) 1985. The reverse of the painting bears the artist's stamp on the stretcher and canvas. It reads "A Howie. Portrait & animal painter. 29, Princes Street, Edin.". Inscr. on the reverse of canvas only, 1830, 23in.x30in.

Howie, James (op.1822-1839)
Several sporting paintings clearly signed by this artist and dated, overlap with the dates of James Howe (q.v.).

Howitt, Samuel (1756-1823)
Amateur (later professional) sporting artist, illustrator and an etcher. Howitt was the son of a local Essex squire and worked as a drawing master at a private academy (Dr Goodenough's Academy) in Ealing. He would appear to have been self-taught and began to exhibit at the Incorporated Society of Artists in 1783. In 1779 Howitt married a sister of Thomas Rowlandson (q.v.) but they lived apart for much of the marriage. He produced a number of particularly fine and accurate watercolours of oriental field sports, mostly set in India. So far as is known Howitt never went to India but is presumed to have based his incidents on sketches brought home by Captain Thomas Williamson (1759-1817) (q.v.) in 1798. These fifty or so sporting watercolours were in the collection of the Earl of Ducie and were shown at an exhibition at the Leger Galleries in December 1976. His work as an illustrator covered "Miscellaneous Etchings of Animals" (1803), "Oriental Field Sports" (1805/7/8) and "The British Sportsman" (1799/1800) containing seventy-two plates. He also illus. Beckford's "Thoughts on Hunting" and contributed 157 plates to "The Sporting Magazine". Howitt's watercolours covered a great number of sporting subjects including steeplechasing, hunting, otter hunting and beagling.

Howse, George, NWS (op.1830-d.1860)
London landscape painter whose three famous rowing watercolours entitled "The Procession of Boats", "The Start" and "The Race" at Oxford were afterwards lithographed by Vincent Brooks (1814-1885). Howes is better known for his many railway prints.

Howson, Peter (b.1958)
Contemporary Glaswegian artist of sporting scenes. His vibrantly coloured paintings of footballers, boxers and wrestlers, are well illustrated in his "Just Another Bloody Saturday" which captures the physical and visual violence of the game of football played under the glare of arc lights. The National Gallery of Modern Art, Glasgow. Howson, who moved to Glasgow from London in 1962, studied at Glasgow School of Art (1975-1977) and (1979-1981). Exh. at Flowers East, London.

Hoyle, Walter ARCA (b.1922)
Mural painter, designer and print maker who studied at Beckenham School of Art and the RCA. Included in this Dictionary for his painting of a football match entitled "Goal", 35½in.x27½in., exh. at the FE. Examples of his work are at the British Museum and the V & A.

Hoynck, Otto (c.1636-c.1686)
Dutch animal painter who was born at the Hague. He was in the Guild in 1661 and in England in 1676. His portrait of a greyhound, 44in.x56in., s.&d. 1675/6, auctioned Christie's 1956, is interesting as two collars hang in a tree showing that the dog won these as prizes while a tablet underneath the tree elaborates on the hound's achievements. It reads "March 6th 1671. My Lord Shaftesbury's collor [sic] was given Red which he won. March 7th 1671/2. The Duke of Albemarle's collor was given Blue which he won then".

Hubbard, Bennet (1806-1870)
Lincolnshire-born animal and equestrian painter, the son of a hairdresser from Louth. Hubbard studied art under William Etty RA and John Varley. Several of his

horse and cattle portraits were engraved and examples of the "Trusthorpe Ox" (c.1837) and the prize heifer "Flower" (1846) can be seen at Reading University. His portrait of "Cure All" with William George Loft up, winner of the Grand National in 1845, was also engraved. Hubbard exh. seven works at the RA (1839-1864), mostly human portraits and portraits of spaniels and ponies. He also exh. twenty-four pictures at the Louth Art Exhibition (1869).

Hudson, Thomas (1701-1779)
Portrait painter who studied art under Jonathan Richardson (1665-1745) whose daughter Hudson married. He established a good practice painting the portraits of many distinguished patrons including the 3rd Duke of Marlborough and his family, 119¾in.x 193in., c.1754 and "Mrs. Mathew Michell and her Children", 76in.x64in., c.1757, Leicestershire Museum and AG. The inclusion of cricket bats and balls in both portrait groups shows the influence the game had on society at this time. Hudson numbered Reynolds and Wright of Derby (qq.v.) amongst his pupils.

Huggins, William (1820-1884)
Liverpool-born animal artist who exh. at the RA from 1842. His large equestrian portrait group of Mr. Gorton, Master of the Holcombe Hunt (with a leash of hounds) was exh. at the RA in 1854. Most of Huggins' work centred round farmyard life although he painted many wild animal pictures and several portraits of lions. His paintings have an unusual luminous quality, created by painting transparent colours over a white background. This same technique was applied to his horse's coats which gives them a rich velvety look.

Hughes, Edward (1832-1908)
London figure artist who exh. at SS (1864-1879). Titles include "Croquet", "Wild Duck and Teal" and "A Day's Sport in the Sixteenth Century".

Hughes, Talbot, ROI, PS (1869-1942)
Painter of figure and genre subjects. Included in this Dictionary for "The Croquet Player" s.&d. 1905, coloured pencils, 13¾in.x9¾in., Christie's (NY) and "The End of the Game". Hughes exhibited much of his work at the RA (1871-1903). The son of the still life painter, William Hughes, and the brother of Sir Herbert Hughes-Stanton, RA.

Hughes, Trajan (op.1709-1712)
Little known still life and animal painter in a style suggestive of Francis Barlow (q.v.). He gave great attention to the landscapes in which he set his subjects, painting them with fine detail.

Hulk, John Frederick (1855-1913)
Dutch artist who included several sporting scenes amongst his work. "Duck Shooting" was exh. at the RA (No. 221) in 1895. This was, according to "Bailys Magazine", June 1895, " a very inferior painting. Too slatey in colour and an impractical shot." Hulk clearly took the reprimand to heart for in 1910 he painted another version of "Duck Shooting" with better success. "The Beaufort Hounds", 31in.x49½in., signed, was auctioned Sotheby's (NY) 1990.

Hull, Edward (op.1817-1877)
Draughtsman, etcher and lithographer of sporting subjects after his own and his contemporaries' work. His set of six lithographs "Fox Hunting at Melton Mowbray" (1835) and a pair of lithographs "Coursing at Hampton Court Park" are after his own work. Two of the original watercolours, each 10¼in.x14¼in., numbers 5 and 6 of the set of six, "Fox Hunting at Melton Mowbray", are in the Paul Mellon Collection, Upperville, Va, USA.

Hull, Edward (op.1860-1895)
Landscape and figure painter, also an illustrator. He is not the same as Edward Hull (q.v.), the lithographer of sporting subjects, but they may have been related since both painted and engraved "Coursing at Hampton Court Park with Mr. Sawyer, Queen Victoria's Head Keeper on his bay horse 'Spark'".

Hull, John (b.1952)
Contemporary painter in acrylic of an American baseball game entitled "Minor League All Star Game, Clinton" 1988, 24in.x36in. The players are sitting out against an intriguing background of advertising hoardings on which one proclaims "U call we haul".

Hulley, T.
A painting of a bay racehorse, with jockey up, being led by a groom, on a racecourse, other figures in the background, s.&d. 1829, is recorded (Mitchell).

Hum, George (op.1901)
Obscure caricaturist whose name "Geo Hum" may well have been a pseudonym. He contributed one cartoon to "Vanity Fair", in November 1901, the subject of which is the reason for his inclusion in this Dictionary. The Deutsch prize was offered by the Aero Club of France to anyone who could fly from St. Cloud around the Eiffel Tower (completed in 1889) and return in a period of thirty minutes. This feat was seen as a symbol of the beginning of a new century and a new mode of transportation. The Brazilian-born, Alberto Santos Dumont (1873-1932), won the prize in 1901 and with it worldwide fame. After his arrival in Paris in 1892, Santos Dumont trained as an engineer and learned how to make and fly fire balloons and kites. By 1898 he had made his first gasoline powered balloon and over the next three years he constructed and tested five airstrips before winning the Deutsch Prize in 1901.

Humphrey, Mrs. A.A. (née Florence Pash) (op.1890-1904)
This artist exh. at the NEAC (1898-1904) and previously between 1890 and 1898 as Miss Pash. In 1899 her NEAC exhibit was entitled "Croquet".

Humphrey, Ozias, RA (1742-1810)
Distinguished portrait painter who usually painted in watercolour. His brother, William Humphrey, was Steward to the 3rd Duke of Dorset (1745-1799), the famous cricketer. Ozias Humphrey is supposed to be the subject of a fishing painting by Julius Caesar Ibbetson (q.v.) and he in his turn painted the portrait of George Stubbs (q.v.) in 1777 and again in 1794. Humphrey exh. the latter portrait at the RA in the same year.

Humphries, Alan (op.1925)
A set of three watercolours by this artist depicting the 1925 Grand National, each 9in.x15in., were auctioned Dennis Pocock & Dreweatt, Marlborough 1986.

Hunt, Cecil Arthur, VPRWS, RBA (1873-1965)
Landscape painter in oil, tempera and watercolour who was particularly interested in mountain and rock subjects. His painting of the "Great St. Bernard Pass" shows sportsmen ski-ing, pencil and gouache, 9¾in.x 13¾in., inscr., auctioned Sotheby's 1988. Elected RWS (1925) and VPRWS (1930-1933). Represented in many public collections at home and abroad.

Hunt, Charles (1806-1877)
Sporting painter, mostly of coaching subjects and a well-known aquatint engraver after his own work and that of his contemporaries. Engravings after his own work include "The Red Rover, Southampton Coach" and "The Birthday Team" which shows the famous "Quicksilver", Devonport to London Mail Coach passing Windsor Castle. His original paintings include a portrait of "Phosphorus", winner of the Derby in 1837 with Edwards up, "The Young Sportsman" painted in 1872, "Off to the Derby" and "The Return" painted in 1858. He was the father of Charles Hunt, Jnr. (q.v.) and possibly the brother of George Hunt with whom he often collaborated early in his career.

Hunt, Charles, Jnr. (b.1830)
Aquatint engraver of sporting subjects after his own and his contemporaries' work. The son of C. Hunt, Snr. (q.v.) with whom he collaborated on many plates.

Hunt, Edgar (1876-1953)
Painter of animal subjects, the brother of Walter Hunt (q.v.) and son of Charles Hunt, Jnr. (q.v.). Unlike his brother, Walter, Edgar Hunt was not a sporting painter preferring farmyard subjects which he painted in meticulous detail.

Hunt, Edwin Henry (op.1880-1890)
Aquatint engraver of sporting subjects after his own and his contemporaries' work. He was probably related to G. and the two C. Hunts (qq.v.). Edwin Hunt painted a number of greyhound and horse racing pictures, which he engraved himself, for publication by George Rees for whom he worked.

Hunt, Lynn Bogue (1878-1960)
American illustrator and painter of sporting subjects including shooting, salmon fishing, trout fishing, shooting with game dogs and wildfowl.

Hunt, Walter (1861-1941)
Painter of animal subjects, particularly farmyard scenes, but also of sporting subjects. He exh. several paintings of otter hunting at the RA including "Otter Hunting - the Find" (1888), "Breaking Cover" (1901) and "Otter Hounds in Full Cry" (1910). Hunt was the son of Charles Hunt, Jnr. (q.v.) and the brother of Edgar Hunt (q.v.). Both brothers painted in a very similar style and appear to have been taught to paint by their father.

Hunt, William Henry, RWS (1790-1864)
Landscape and still life painter who also included a number of sporting scenes amongst his work. Hunt painted mainly in watercolour and studied art under John Varley and at the RA Schools which he entered in 1808. Hunt's cricket watercolour entitled "Middle Leg" painted in 1856 was auctioned Bearnes 1980. He used the game of cricket in several of his paintings including "The Boy Cricketer" and "The Boy Batsman", both 15½in.x10½in., MCC Collection. A mezzotint by W. Bromley entitled "Done Up" after the work by Hunt, pub. in 1841, shows a boy asleep in a chair with a cricket bat and ball lying on the floor. The Witt Collection have a pair of pen, brown ink drawings of "A Race Meeting with a Grandstand near the Coast", s.&d. 1843. "A Young Archer" was exh. at the Old Water Colour Society 1840 (No. 245) and his "Portrait of a Sporting Gentleman" painted in 1836, watercolour and pencil, was auctioned Sotheby's (NY) 1985. Hunt developed a very individual technique of watercolour painting over a white background which gives his painting an enamel like quality which was much copied by his contemporaries. Hunt was elected RWS (1826) and his studio sale was held by Christie's on 16 May 1864.

Hunt, William Morris (1824-1879)
American painter who worked with the French Barbizon painters, leaving France for his native Boston in 1855. His broad stroke painting of three men in an open field playing stick ball entitled unimaginatively "The Ball Players", 16in.x24in., is in the Detroit Institute of Arts.

Hunter, Colin, ARA, RI, RSW, ROI, RE (1841-1904)
Scottish seascape painter who unwisely exh. his painting "Salmon Fishing on the Dee" at the RA in 1895 (No. 529). This was described by "Bailys Magazine", June 1895, as "having nothing whatsoever to do with fishing from a sporting point of view, being merely a picture of a man in the water with a huge net, scooping for salmon". Hunter, who studied under Milne Donald in Glasgow, nevertheless went on to become one of the leading marine painters of his day. Elected RSW (1879), RE (1881), RI (1882), ROI (1883), ARA (1884).

Hunter, George Sherwood, RBA (op.1855-d.1920)
Scottish painter of landscape and genre subjects but also several sporting scenes. Exh. at SS (1882-1894). Titles include "A Heavy Shot", "Salmon Fishermen Emptying a Fly Net", "A Young Fisherman", "A Close Shave", "Who Wins", "Brittany Peasants Playing Bowls", etc. Elected RBA 1889.

Hunter, Robert (op.1752-1803)
Leading Irish portrait painter in Dublin between 1753 and 1783. Included in this Dictionary for his portrait of "Owen O'Malley (b.1771) of Spencer Park, County Mayo". O'Malley is standing full length holding a shuttlecock and racket, 49in.x39¼in., Sotheby's 1988.

"Hurst" - alias J.W. Hurst Willoughby (d.1925)
The eldest son of Mr. John Cook Willoughby who wrote for "The Field" on poultry matters.

Hussey, Harold (op.1953)
Painter of a football match entitled "The End of the Game" 46in.x26½in., exh. at the FE.

"Hustlebuck"
The pseudonym used by Keith Sholto Douglas (q.v.) for his humorous sketches in collaboration with Lawson Wood (q.v.).

Hutchins, C. (op.1850)
Draughtsman and lithographer whose engraving of "Victoria Bowling Green, Welsh-pool", presumably after his own work, was pub. c.1850.

Hutchinson, Peter C. (1935-1984)
Lincolnshire equestrian artist who painted many horse portraits on commission.

Hutchinson, William Henry Florio (op.1837-1861)
Painted big game hunting scenes including "Buffalo Shooting" and "Sand Grouse Shooting" in 1837. Exh. two paintings at SS in 1859. Worked under the pseudonym "George Trigger" contributing a series of portraits entitled "Sporting Gallery" to "The Bengal Sporting Magazine", a series of twenty volumes which ran from January 1833 to November 1842. This suggests that Hutchinson may have served in the army out in India as a young man, like his contemporaries P.C. Trench, C.W. Smith (qq.v.) and Captain Frederick Parr (see "Junglicus").

Hutchison, Robert Gemmell, RSA, RSW, ROI (1855-1936)
Scottish painter of portraits and genre subjects. Born in Edinburgh he studied at the Board of Manufacturers School of Art. Exh. at the RSA from 1879 and at the RA from 1880. Elected RSW (1895), RSA (1911). Hutchison also painted some sporting scenes including a game of golf entitled "The Lost Ball". His portrait of "Jenny", a chestnut hunter in a loose box, signed and inscr., was auctioned Christie's (Sth. Ken.) 1988.

Hutchison, Sir William Oliphant, Hon. RA, PRSA, VPRP (b.1889-c.1971)
Kirkcaldy-born portrait and landscape painter, who studied at Edinburgh College of Art and in Paris. Exh. RA, RBA, RSA and elsewhere. His painting entitled "Derby Day" was exh. at the RA in 1933. Elected RSA (1943), RP (1948), PRSA (1950). Knighted (1953). VPRP (1960).

Hyland, Benedict (op.1883-1886)
Landscape and animal painter whose sporting work includes studies of thoroughbred horses and foxhounds.

"Hyme"
James Crawford Wood who wrote for "The Field" on hunting subjects in the absence of "Brooksby" who went to the Boer War (1900-1902). Wood was also an excellent polo correspondent and remained with "The Field" until 1919.

Hysing, Hans (1678-1753)
Swedish portrait painter, apprenticed in Stockholm to a goldsmith (1691-1694) and then to David Krafft. Came to London in 1700 where he studied under Michael Dahl (1659?-1743). Set up on his own c.1715. He painted the "Royal Princesses" (1730) and his portrait of "Colonel William Kennedy standing wearing a blue coat and holding a gun with a dog and a brace of partridge by his side", 48½in.x38½in., was auctioned Sotheby's 1984.

I

Ibbetson, Julius Caesar, RA (1759-1817)
Portrait and landscape painter in both oil and watercolour, an illustrator and an etcher. Ibbetson, who was largely self-taught through copying the Old Masters, lived at Masham and was concerned mainly with subjects drawn from the Lake District and his beloved Yorkshire. His style is neat and lively and he was a contemporary and friend of both George Morland (q.v.) and Samuel Howitt (q.v.) with whom he formed the London School. Ibbetson painted a number of sporting scenes including a portrait of the distinguished Royal Academician and friend of George Stubbs (q.v.)

Ozias Humphrey (q.v.) angling on the River Dart, 13in.x18½in., and a portrait of the sportsman, William Danby, Esq. of Swinton, Yorkshire, out shooting with a white pointer, painted in 1817. His portrait of Charles Knowles Robison ice skating in 1813 on Craig Lockhart Skating Pond, Edinburgh, with other skaters beyond, shows that he and his subject had an intimate knowledge of this healthy pursuit.

Icart, Louis (1888-1953)
20th century French painter and etcher in the art deco style who used thoroughbred horses and greyhounds as models for figure movement at speed. He also used

sport, particularly golf, as a subject designed to flatter the female form.

"Idstone"

Alias the Revd. Thomas Pearce who wrote extensively on canine matters in the second half of the 19th century. His son was Frank C.S. Pearce, first editor of the Kennel Stud Book (1873).

Ince, Joseph Murray (1806-1859)

London river and estuary painter in watercolour who studied art under David Cox in 1823 and exh. at SS (1826-1858). Titles include "Trout from Nature" and "Salmon Spearers at Buckland Mill on the Usk by Moonlight". Ince's watercolour of a shooting party in a wood, s.&d. 1850, was auctioned Christie's 1987.

Ingall, Susan (op.1930s-1940s)

Painter of equestrian subjects, mostly portraits of horses. Ingall's work is normally signed and dated.

Ingalton, William (1794-1866)

Surrey figure painter who concentrated much of his work in the Windsor/Eton area. He exh. "The Skittle Players" at the RA in 1817, of which another version, or possibly a sketch for this painting, dated 1816, was exh. by Mr. G. Douglas Thompson at the Palser Gallery, King Street, London W1 in 1932. Ingalton exh. "The Game of Putt" at the BI in 1817.

Ingpen, A.W. (op.1830-1838)

London artist who exh. several horse portraits and sporting scenes at the RA (1832-1838). Ingpen also exh. at SS (1830-1836). Titles include "Portrait of 'Cocktail', the property of William Abbott, Esq.", "Portrait of an Ass", "Portrait of a Shetland Pony", and "A portrait of 'Cydnus', own brother to 'Euphrates'".

Innes, Augusta (Mrs., née Withers) (op.1844)

Victorian artist of game birds.

Innes, Charles (op.1988)

Contemporary artist whose "Croquet" was exh. (No. 355) at the RA Summer Exhibition 1988.

Insall, Frank (op.1930s)

Painter of sporting subjects and an illustrator who contributed a rugger painting entitled "The Try" to "Chums Annual" in 1938. His oil paintings of "Rabbit Shooting", 18¼in.x24¼in., and "Fishing" are definitely painted with above average talent. Wingfield Sporting Art, London.

Inshaw, David (b.1943)

Contemporary printmaker and a painter of sporting scenes particularly cricket. "The Badminton Game" (1972/3) is in the collection of the Tate Gallery, London, and "The Cricket Game", painted in 1974 was exh. at the Waddington Galleries Ltd., London. Inshaw, who was born in Staffordshire, studied at the Beckenham School of Art (1959-1963) and at the RA Schools (1963-1966).

Inskipp, James (1790-1868)

Landscape, portrait and still life painter who drew a series of illustrations for Sir Harry Nicholas's edn. of Isaac Walton's "Compleat Angler" (1833-1836). His painting of Charles Cotton, the author of the second part of "The Compleat Angler", with his fishing house on the banks of the Dub (Beresford Dale, Staffordshire in the background) was exh. in 1834 at SS (No. 495).

"Ionicus"

Alias Joshua Charles Armitage (b.1913) Artist and illustrator of many books including over fifty by P.G. Wodehouse, "Meet Mr. Mulliner" etc. Born in Hoylake, Cheshire, the son of a fisherman. Contributor to "Punch" since 1944. Designer of book jackets for Penguin books since 1968. Has included golf subjects in his work. For example, his portrait of John Ball, Jnr. driving from the 19th tee at St. Andrews in the Amateur 1907, playing against C.A. Palmer. Phillips (Chester) 1991. Ball won the Open in 1890, the first amateur and the first Englishman to do so - see also Morrison for portrait of Ball. Armitage is a long time member of the Royal Liverpool Golf Club at Hoylake, which is the fourth oldest course in England (1869).

Irvin, Albert (b.1922)

Abstract painter who contributed "The Goalkeeper", 30in.x29½in., to the FE. Irvin, who was born in London, studied at the Northampton School of Art (1940-1941) and the Goldsmiths College (1946-1950). Taught at Goldsmiths (1962-1983). Has had several solo exhibitions in London and won the Giles Bequest prize at the Bradford International Print Biennale (1986).

Irving, William (1866-1943)

Portrait and landscape painter who studied in Newcastle upon Tyne, under William Cosens Way, and at the Académie Julian. Became an illustrator to the Newcastle Chronicle. Exh. at the RA from 1898 including "Blaydon Races, a Study from Life", in 1903.

Isenberg, H. (op.1909)

"Berliner Lawn Tennis Club E.V.I. Winturnier", lithograph in colour, s.&d. 1909, 28in.x118¾in. (poster) Christie's (Sth. Ken.)

Isherwood, Travis (op.1953)

Exhibitor of a football painting entitled "The Stand, Maine Road", 24½in.x20in., at the FE.

Isom, Graham (b.1945)

Talented contemporary painter of figure and equestrian subjects in both oil and watercolour. Studied at the Ravensbourne College of Art for four years. Became an art teacher to 'A' level students in 1966 for five years and a professional artist in the early 1970s. His many hunting, polo and racing scenes include "The Prix de l'Arc de Triomphe" (1986), "Dancing Brave" and "Triptych", "The Prince of Wales Cup" and "The Cheltenham Gold Cup" (1989), a painting which won the American Academy of Equine Art Founders Award for Oil Painting in the same year. Graham Isom has become widely known through the many limited edn. prints after his work, pub. Michael Stewart Fine Art Ltd.

Isom, Joe (op.1972)

Contemporary painter of an American football portrait of "Alan Page, the Minnesota Vikings Defensive Tackle", acrylic 1972.

Israels, Isaac (1865-1934)
Dutch portrait and figure painter whose equestrienne painting entitled "An Amazon in Rotten Row, Hyde Park, London", signed and inscr., 17⅞in.x14⅝in., was auctioned Christie's (Amsterdam) 1987.

Ivester-Lloyd, Jack (b.1905)
Author and illustrator of many sporting books including "Beagling" (1944), "Come Hunting" (1952) and "Full Cry" which was illus. by his father, Thomas Ivester-Lloyd (q.v.) in 1939.

Ivester-Lloyd, Thomas (1873-1942)
Liverpool-born sporting painter, best known for beagling and fox-hunting scenes which he painted in both oil and watercolour. Became Master of the Sherrington Foot Beagles and illus. the British section of Sir John Buchanan-Jardine's "Classic Hounds of the World". Father of Jack Ivester-Lloyd (q.v.). He illus. many books and his horse and hound portraiture is of a very high quality.

J

JNP (op.1869-1872)
An unknown amateur painter of a delightful sketch in pen/ink and sepia wash of a game of croquet signed with inits. and dated 1872 found in a sketch book of mainly Sussex scenes dated 1869-1872.

"Jack High"
The nom de plume used by J.A. Manson, author of "The Complete Bowler - the History of the Royal and Ancient Game of Bowls", pub. A.C. Black (1912).

Jack, Richard, RA, RI, RP, ARCA (Lond.) (1866-1952)
Sunderland-born portrait and figure painter whose 1913 portrait of Harold Hilton (1869-1942), 49½in.x39½in., hangs in the Royal Liverpool Golf Club. Hilton won the Open Golf Championship in 1892 as an amateur, the second golfer to achieve the feat and one of only three ever to do so, and he won the Open again in 1897. He was Amateur Champion four times between 1900 and 1913 having been runner up three times in the 1890s and in 1911 he held the British and US titles simultaneously. Richard Jack's formal painting shows Hilton with a golf club under his arm. Jack studied at York School of Art and in 1886 won a National Scholarship to the RCA. He also won a Gold Medal and a Travelling Scholarship which enabled him to study in Paris at the Académie Julian and at the Atelier Colarossi. He exh. twenty-five works at the RA from 1893. Elected RP (1899), RI (1917) and RA (1920). For the last twenty years of his life he worked in Canada and died in Montreal. His work is represented in many public collections.

Jackson, Frederick William, RBA, NEAC (1859-1918)
Lancashire artist of marine subjects and landscapes who painted in both oil and watercolour. Studied at the Oldham School of Art, at the Manchester Academy and in Paris, under Lefèbvre and Boulanger. Exh. at the principal London galleries from 1880, mainly at the RA and SS. "Deck Quoits", signed, 6½in.x9½in., was auctioned Phillips 1986. Elected RBA 1890.

Jackson, George E. (op.1830-1891)
Paintings signed G.Jackson, Jnr. dated 1833, G.E. Jackson and inscr. "Norton" and dated 1891 and George Jackson inscr. "Wadhurst, Kent" have come up at auction and elsewhere between 1830 and 1891. They may be by the same artist but the span of time is long and the signatures various. G. Jackson exh. once at the RA in 1844 and the majority of his work appears to be portraits of hunters accompanied by dogs, either terriers or spaniels. Jackson's portrait "Two Pointers" signed G. Jackson Jun. dated 1833 suggests that he might himself have been a younger son of another George Jackson.

Jackson, Gilbert (op.1622-1640)
Portrait painter whose painting of Master William Hickman with a hawk on his left gloved fist merits his inclusion in this Dictionary. The painting, 49in.x 33½in., s.&d. 1634, is in a private collection and is repro. in "The Dictionary of 16th and 17th Century British Painters", Ellis Waterhouse (1988).

Jackson, John, RA (1778-1831)
Yorkshire-born portrait painter who studied at the RA Schools (1804) where he went at the suggestion of Sir George Beaumont, 6th Bt. (1753-1827), the artist and art patron. Jackson became a close friend of David Wilkie and Benjamin Haydon (qq.v). Jackson's portrait of a gentleman in a wooded river landscape wearing a brown jacket and holding a fishing rod and hat with two dogs nearby, and a building beyond, is typical of the conversation pieces so much in demand by the new aristocracy where the sitters were almost always depicted holding some appendage of sport, such as a

fishing rod or a shot-gun. His portrait of "Tom Cribb, the Celebrated Boxer" (1781-1848) was engraved by George Hunt and pub. by J. Moore in 1842 and is in the collection of the British Museum. Cribb was perhaps the most famous of all heavyweight champion boxers and reigned supreme between 1809 and 1822.

Jacobs, Dennis (op.1953/4)
This print maker is included in the Dictionary for his lithograph entitled "The Football Match", 12in.x18in., exh. at the FE.

Jacobs, John Emmanuel (op.1879-1898)
Exh. at SS (1879-1894). Titles include "Punting", "Over the Brook" and "A Gap in the Hedge". His portrait of "Ormonde" (1883), a bay racehorse by "Bend'Or" out of "Lily Agnes" trained by J. Porter, ridden by Fred Archer and owned by the great Duke of Westminster, 19½in.x24½in., was auctioned Christie's 1972.

Jacobson, Antonio (1850-1921)
Prolific American marine artist whose many yacht racing scenes include "The 'Grayling' Leading a Race", s.&d. 1888 and inscr. "New York", 24in.x42in., "Sailing Ships Tacking during a Regatta in New York Harbour", s.&d. 1886, and "A Racing Cat Boat", s.&d. 1878, Wm. Doyles (NY) 1986.

Jacomb-Hood, George Percy, RP, RBA, RE, ROI, RBC, NEAC (1857-1929)
Portrait painter, illustrator and an etcher who studied art at the Slade School, where he won a travelling scholarship and the Edward Poynter Prize, and in Paris under Laurens. Exh. at the RA from 1878 and was an original member of the RP. Contributed illustrations to "The Graphic" who sent him to Athens in 1896 to attend the Olympic Games and again to India for the tour of the Prince of Wales and the 1911 Durbar. His watercolour "Tent Pegging in India", 10in.x9in., was painted while on tour with King George V when he was a member of his personal staff in 1911. S.&d. 1912, the painting shows a member of Skinners Horse galloping at speed with his lance at the ready to pick up the peg. Jacomb-Hood also contributed to "The Illustrated London News". He was elected RE (1881), RBA (1884) and NEAC (1886). Jacomb-Hood's fine watercolour "A Croquet Match", 8½in.x11¼in., inscr. "Hurlingham" was auctioned Sotheby's (Sussex) 1985.

Jagger, Charles (1770-1827)
Recorded by Pavière as the painter of a watercolour portrait of Thomas Browne Evans shooting with two pointers. Coll. Major E.H. Evans Lombe. Exh. Norwich 1950.

Jagger, David, RP, ROI (c.1892-1958)
A landscape, figure and portrait painter who exh. widely (1917-1940) including at the RA. Brother of the sculptor Charles Jagger and Edith Jagger the landscape painter. Jagger also painted several equestrian portraits and riding scenes. "The Tennis Player", a portrait of Lord Foley aged fourteen standing before a seaside landscape, dressed for a game of lawn tennis and carrying a racket, was painted in 1934, 68½in.x44in.,

Sotheby's 1986. Jagger painted a companion piece entitled "The Sporting Girl", 24in.x18in, Phillips 1987.

Jalland, George Herbert (op.1888-1908)
Author, artist and illustrator, mostly of equestrian subjects, who contributed articles and many illustrations to the "Badminton Magazine of Sports and Pastimes" in the 1890s. These include the clever sketches which accompanied the article "Ladies in the Hunting Field" by Lady Mabel Howard in 1896. The article discussed the teasing question of how long hunting would continue, a question by no means answered nearly one hundred years later. Jalland also contributed to "Punch" from 1888, "The Sporting Magazine", "The Graphic" and to "Fores Sporting Notes and Sketches". He signed his work with a mono. of his three initials followed by his surname in full, and sometimes followed by the date. Jalland drew and painted a wide variety of sporting subjects including polo and hockey as well as hunting, shooting and racing.

James P.F. (op.1930s)
Watercolour portraits of members of the Press Club playing billiards. Burlington Gallery, London

James, Robert (1809-1853)
Nottingham based painter of portraits and genre subjects who exh. at the RA from 1841. His masterly painting "Tossing for Innings" c.1843, 35½in.x57in., MCC Collection, shows a group of ragged chimney-sweeps about to play a game of cricket on an open common. A smaller version of this painting, 25½in.x 19½in., is also in the MCC Collection.

Jamieson, Alexander, ROI, IS (1873-1937)
Glasgow-born painter of landscapes, urban scenes and also some portraits. Studied art at the Haldane Academy, Glasgow, winning a scholarship to Paris in 1898. Elected a member of the IS in 1904 and ROI in 1927. Jamieson's portrait of Walter Andrew Inderwick, painted in 1924, shows Inderwick taking aim with his bow and arrow and the picture was probably painted to celebrate his championship win in 1924. He had previously been archery champion in 1921. He is seen shooting in the grounds of the Royal Toxophilite Society, Bayswater, London.

"Jan"
Alias Godfrey Jervis Gordon (1882-1944). Painter, etcher and lithographer who exh. three paintings at the exhibition of British Sporting Paintings (1943), Preston HM and AG.

Jank, Angelo (1868-1956)
German equestrian painter, particularly of hunting and steeplechasing scenes, who painted in oils.

Jardine, Alexander W. (op.1983-d.1987)
Painter of freshwater fish and an illustrator for the United Kingdom postage stamps (1983) using fish designs.

Jardine, Charles, SWLA (b.1953)
Third generation naturalist and fresh water fish painter. Studied at Canterbury College of Art. Became a game

angling instructor on the Test and Itchin rivers in Hampshire. Jardine has exh. at the Mall Galleries for many years and was made a member of the Society of Wildlife Artists in 1983. He has also illus. several books on fishing and his work is in many private collections throughout the world.

Jardine, Sir William, HRSA (1800-1874)
Born Edinburgh. Naturalist and painter who was elected an Honorary Member of the SA in 1827. Exh. four paintings, two of dead game (1829-1833). Brother-in-law of William Lizars (q.v.) who engraved and pub. ten plates of the "Birds of America" for J.J. Audubon and twelve plates for Jardine's "Illustrations of the British Salmonidae" (1839-1845). Elected HRSA (1827).

Jarvis, George (op.1874-1890)
Painted genre and figurative subjects and exh. at SS between those dates, including a work in 1881/2 with the intriguing title, "Sport".

Jay, Florence (op.1905-1920)
This artist specialised in dog portraiture including those of foxhounds and beagles. "Fancy" and "Trusty", portraits of two beagle bitches, s.&d. 1912, a pair, each 18in.x 24in., were auctioned Bonhams 1986.

Jay, J.A.B. (op.1878-1887)
Almost certainly closely related to Florence Jay (q.v.) whom this artist very much resembles in style. Exh. two paintings at the RA (1878-1880) entitled "Ware Hare, Challenger!" and "On the Way Home". He, or she, painted several hunting oils including a portrait of "Sparkler" a four year old foxhound and "Advocate", another foxhound, painted in 1887, auctioned Bonhams in 1986. Jay's painting "Hare Coursing" shows a single man on a horse (not wearing a pink coat) s.&d. 1884.

Jeanniot, Pierre-Georges (1848-1934)
French painter of "Polo Sketches", signed, black chalk, 10¾in.x16in. Auctioned Sotheby's (Sussex) 1987.

"Jedd"
Alias John Edwards (q.v.), contemporary artist and sporting cartoonist.

Jefferys, William (1723 or 1730-1805)
All-round painter of landscapes, portraits and coach decorating and the father of the highly talented historical painter James Jefferys (1751-1784). "Cricket at the Free School Maidstone", pen and wash (Maidstone Public Library), shows the game being played at one of the important centres of early cricket. Just how early is seen in the passage from "The Life and Death of Thos. Wilson, Minister of Maidstone" (1672): "Maidstone was formerly a very profane town in as much as I have seen Morris-dancing, cudgel playing, stoolball, crickets, and many other sports opening and publicly on the Lord's Day". Evidence, perhaps, that stoolball and cricket were in fact two separate games and not, as is generally thought, one and the same.

Jellicoe, John F. (op.1865-1888)
London illustrator and minor sporting artist who submitted an illustration pub. in "The Illustrated Sporting & Dramatic News" (1890) entitled "Cricket for Ladies", 9½in.x13in.

Jenkins, Arthur Henry (b.1871 exh.1898-1938)
Scottish-born landscape and figure painter in both oil and watercolour. Studied at Edinburgh College of Art and in Paris at Colarossi's. "On the Way to the Bath Races", signed and inscr., 13½in.x17¼in., was auctioned Sotheby's 1984.

Jenkins, Thomas (1722-1798)
Devon-born history and portrait painter who frequently painted sporting personalities, posing his subjects either with rod or gun. Jenkins went to Rome in 1753 where he shared a house with Richard Wilson and he remained in Italy for virtually the rest of his life, becoming an honorary Accademico di St. Luca in Rome in 1761.

Jennings, Chris (b.1942)
Contemporary painter of racehorse portraits including those of "Arkle" and "Red Rum" in the early 1970s. Studied at St. Alban's School of Art, St. Martin's School of Art and the Royal College of Art.

Jennings, Miss E. (op.1837-1854)
London artist who exh. a watercolour study of horses at SS in 1837. Several equestrian portraits signed "Jennings" and dated between 1837 and 1854 are probably attributable to this artist.

Jensen, Arthur
Painter of "A Skier in a Winter Landscape", 30¾in.x 40½in., auctioned Sotheby's (Chester) 1987.

Jerman, R. Henry (op.1908)
Scottish painter of a still life entitled "Trout on a Highland River Bank", s.&d. 1908, 14in.x18in., auctioned Christie's (Sth. Ken.) 1986.

Joel, Charles (op.c.1905)
"The Chase" and "Taking the Fence", a pair of signed oils, 5in.x10½in., were auctioned Christie's 1972.

Johns, W.E. (op.1884-1895)
This artist painted a set of six watercolours depicting "Dog Fights", five signed and inscr. and the first dated 1895, the second October 1884, auctioned Sotheby's 1974.

Johnson, Avery F. (b.1906)
American landscape and sporting artist of hunting, shooting and fishing scenes. His painting of "Ernest Hemingway Deep Sea Fishing off Quay West", signed, watercolour, 14½in.x21¼in., was auctioned Christie's (Sth. Ken.) 1986.

Johnson, Carl (b.1946)
Painter of sporting subjects, including wrestling. His acrylic on canvas, 35¾in.x35¾in., entitled "One Pin Fall" was painted in 1987.

Johnson, Charles Edward, RI, ROI (1832-1913)
Landscape and sporting painter, very often of Scottish subjects. He lived in Edinburgh between 1863 and 1897. Johnson painted fishing, fox-hunting and stalking subjects. His RA exhibit entitled "In the Midlands", showing a pretty landscape with cub hunting playing a secondary role, became the subject of some criticism in "Bailys Magazine" (1886): "Johnson has erred in the matter of detail. Men do not wear pink coats or chimney

pot hats when they go cub hunting". Johnson, who studied at the RA Schools, ran a school of landscape painting in Richmond, Surrey, from 1896. Elected RI (1882) and ROI (1883).

Johnson, Doug (b.1940)
A leading illustrator and a painter of famous American football personalities including "John Gilliam of the Minnesota Vikings" (1960s-1970s), acrylic 1978. Johnson was born in Toronto and studied at the Ontario College of Art for three years. He was an instructor at SVA until 1974 and creative director of "The Chelsea Theatre Center". His work has been exh. at the Art Gallery of Ontario, the Brooklyn Museum and the S of I for which he produced "The Illustrators".

Johnson, Edward Killingworth, RWS (1825-1923)
Self-taught painter in watercolour of genre and equestrian scenes who exh. at SS (1846-1885). Titles include "A Stone in the Shoe", etc. Elected RWS (1876).

Johnson, F. (op.1791-1797)
Equestrian artist from Croydon who exh. three horse portraits at the SA in 1791 including a portrait of the racehorse "Glory". In 1797, as an honorary exhibitor, he exh. at the RA a painting entitled "Snipes".

Johnson, Henry W. (op.1893-1910)
A pair of "Hunting Scenes" s.&d. 1893 presumably by this artist were exh. at Cox & Co., Duke Street, London W1. Johnson, who seems to have practised as an architect in Market Harborough, Leics., also exh. one architectural drawing at the RA in 1910.

Johnson, Herbert (1848-1906)
Landscape and figure painter whose fine painting of "The Prince of Wales Shooting Tiger in the Terai" was exh. at the RA. Johnson was sent by "The Graphic" as a special artist on the royal tour of India in 1875 and to Egypt in 1882. He also exh. at SS (1868-1885). Titles include "The Falconer".

Johnson, J.J. (op.1874-1904)
Several sporting paintings, including portraits of race-horses and hunting scenes, have been seen by this artist dated between 1874 and 1904. (See Jones, Louie Johnson.)

Johnson, J. William (op.1874-1904)
American painter of equestrian scenes and portraits, mostly hunting, who operated between these dates.

Johnson, James (op.c.1940)
"Playing Billiards in the Long Gallery", c.1940. From the collection of Sir William Bromley Davenport, Bt.

Johnson, Sidney Yates (op.1896-1908)
Landscape and sporting artist whose work includes many Scottish sporting scenes, particularly of salmon fishing. Surprisingly little is recorded about this extremely competent painter.

Johnson, T.B. (op.1832-1843)
Author and illustrator of "The Shooter's Companion" and "The Sportsman Encyclopaedia". Johnson was a printer from Liverpool who wrote profusely on field sports and edited a periodical (that failed) called "The Sportsman's Cabinet and Town and Country Magazine" (1832). A bitter denouncer of the work of the sporting artist Henry T. Alken (q.v.) which somewhat dented this artist's reputation at the time. His portrait was painted in watercolour by Miss M. H. Johnson in 1843 and exh. at the RBA.

Johnston, Cyril David (20th century)
Contemporary wildlife and game painter in watercolour and gouache whose "Studies of Partridge" and "Portrait of a Fighting Cock" were painted in 1976 and 1971 respectively.

Johnstone, A. David (20th century)
Contemporary motor racing artist whose watercolour painting of "A Pre-War Mercedes Racing Car", 20in.x28in. was auctioned Dreweatt Neate 1990.

Jonas, John (Johnny) (b.1948)
Portrait and landscape painter. Studied art at the Fine Arts Academy in Florence and lived in France for some years. His social sporting scenes include Ascot, Henley and Lords as well as lawn bowls and polo scenes.

Jonas, Lucien (b.1880)
French landscape and figure painter whose work entitled "The Cyclist", s.&d. 1934, 36½in.x23in., was auctioned Sotheby's 1987.

Jones, Adrian (Captain), MVO, MRCVS (1845-1938)
Sporting and animal painter and a sculptor. Born in Ludlow, educated Ludlow Grammar School and the Royal Veterinary College London where he qualified in 1866. In 1871 Jones was stationed in Ireland as veterinary officer to the Queen's Bays and spent the happiest decade of his life, becoming amateur huntsman of the Regimental harriers. Jones had no formal art training but worked under C.B. Birch ARA, the sculptor, who encouraged him to exhibit a model of his own favourite hunter at the RA in 1884 entitled "One of the Right Sort". Jones left the army in 1891 (after twenty-three years) and established himself in a studio in Chelsea where he became a friend of James McNeil Whistler. He moved in artistic and fashionable circles which provided him with important commissions for both painting and sculpture. He became famous for his large bronze groups of horses. These include "The Quadriga of Peace", completed in 1912 and placed above the arch at Hyde Park Corner, and "Duncan's Horses" at the Veterinary College, London. Undoubtedly Jones' veterinary training and anatomy studies helped him, as it helped Stubbs (q.v.) and Leonardo da Vinci, to portray their subjects with an accuracy often missing in other sporting artists' work. His portrait of the racehorse "Sheen" with F. Webb up, in the colours of Prince D. Soltykoff, 27½in.x35in., was auctioned Phillips 1984. "Sheen" won the Cesarewitch in 1890 with 9st. 2lbs. Jones painted the portraits of many famous racehorses but is probably better known for his sculpture.

Jones, Alexander Charles
See Alexander Charles-Jones

Jones, Charles, RCA, ARSA (1836-1892)
Animal painter, particularly of sheep, who included some Highland sporting scenes amongst his work. Born

in Wales, member of the Royal Cambrian Society. Generally known as "Sheep" Jones, for obvious reasons and to distinguish him from the many other Jones painters. Exh. at SS (1860-1892). Sporting titles include "The Sportsman's Friends", "Setter and Blackcock", "Waiting for the Keeper" and "Disturbing the Grouse". "A Grey Stallion and Groom", s.&d. 1861, 9½in.x 13½in., was auctioned Sotheby's (Sussex) 1988.

Jones, Dave (20th century)
Contemporary painter of a major golf work entitled "Augusta National, The 13th Hole". The Augusta National Golf Club.

Jones, George, RA (1786-1869)
Portrait painter and of military and historical subjects who also painted a number of hunter portraits. Studied at the RA Schools in 1801 but interrupted his artistic career to serve in the army and the Peninsular War. He was a close friend of Sir Francis Chantrey, RA (q.v.) the distinguished sculptor and sportsman, and his portrait sketch of Sir Francis fishing, s.&d. 12 June 1832 is entitled "Blowing" - now called dapping (for method see Chantrey). The sketch is in the collection of the Houghton Fishing Club. In 1849 Jones pub. "Recollections of Sir Francis Chantrey". Examples of Jones' work can be seen in the British Museum who have many of his watercolours and eleven volumes of academical studies bequeathed by him.

Jones, George Smetham (op.1888-1901)
London equestrian artist of steeplechasing and hunting scenes, very often comic, usually painted in watercolour or pen and ink. He exh. a sporting work entitled "Not a Moment to Lose" at the RA in 1888 and "Disaster" at SS in 1888/9. Jones usually s.&d. his work.

Jones, H.F. (op.1860-1866)
Sporting artist whose work is usually signed, but rarely dated, nor is it inscr. He operated at an earlier date than either H.H. or Herbert St. John Jones. "Going to the Derby" (1866) was auctioned Christie's (NY) 1983.

Jones, Herbert H. (op.1896-1904)
Equestrian portrait painter. Jones' portraits of cattle and horses are not inscr. "Nantwich" nor do they depict Cheshire scenes (see Herbert St. John Jones).

Jones, Herbert St. John (op.1905-1923)
Prolific equestrian artist whose sporting works include hunting, coaching, steeplechasing and shooting scenes. Much of his work is inscr. "Nantwich" and those paintings that aren't depict Cheshire scenes including Jones' painting of the Cheshire Hunt before Beeston Castle, dated 1923.

Jones, Miss Louie Johnson (b.1856 op.1880-1922)
Animal and equestrian painter. Studied at the Calderon School of Animal Painting and at St. John's Wood School. She painted a large frieze of horses at Cheadle Royal, Cheshire and exhibitions of her work were held by Colnaghi. She is almost certainly the same artist as J.J. Johnson (q.v.). Her sporting work includes a painting of "Two Setters on the Roam", s.&d. 1903, 16in.x35¾in., exh. at the Queen's Park Art Gallery,

Manchester, 1904 (No. 317), "Outlaw" and "Comet", two favourite horses belonging to Sir Philip Lee Brocklehurst, s.&d. 1910, 27½in.x33¾in., auctioned Christie's 1978 and a portrait of a "Racehorse in a Landscape" s.&d. 1905.

Jones, Miss Martha (Mary) K. (ex.1845-1863)
Flower painter from London who exh. three paintings at SS (1852-1859) one entitled "A Stray Shot" and two paintings of flowers.

Jones, Paul (op.1855-1888)
Sporting artist, very often of game dogs. He was an enthusiastic terrier man, depicting them rabbiting or chasing cats and rats. Included a number of shooting scenes amongst his work. Thought to be a son of S.J.E. Jones (q.v.).

Jones, Richard (1767-1840)
Sporting and equestrian artist who exh. eleven pictures at the RBSA (1832-1835). His portrait of "Lady", the famous Birmingham trotting mare, s.&d. 1836, was auctioned Bonhams 1983. The subject was engraved by C. Hunt (1838). Jones' portrait of Stephen Denstone of Stanwardine Hall on his dark bay hunter raising the halloo with the field to the right and the running fox in the left distance, 34⅞in.x43¾in., was auctioned Bonhams 1980. The subject was engraved by H. Quilley in 1838. Four coursing subjects after the work by Jones were engraved by Charles Turner in 1821 for Ackermanns, repro. "The History of the Greyhound" by Ash. Jones painted "Brocklesby Betty" in 1824 for Lord Yarborough.

Jones, Samuel John Egbert (op.1820-1846)
Painter of equestrian and sporting scenes who exh. at SS (1825-1836). Titles include "A Light Chestnut Horse" and "A Mare and a Foal". Jones' sporting work includes "Pheasant and Woodcock Shooting", "Duck and Pheasant Shooting", "Trout Fishing", etc. His work is usually signed but rarely dated.

Jones, Stanley Robert, ATD (b.1927)
Contemporary painter who exh. a painting of football entitled "The Final Whistle" 19½in.x29in., at the FE. Jones exh. at the RA (1951-1958).

Jones, Thomas (op.1827)
Draughtsman and etcher of boxing prints which were drawn and dated 1827. Pub. by S.W. Fores, 15½in.x 11in., they include portraits of the boxers, "Edward Stockman" and "Reuben Martin".

Jones, W.A. (op.1863)
"Coaches Passing Along a Road" with buildings in the background, s.&d. 1863, 17½in.x29½in., was auctioned 1974.

Jones, William (1798-1860)
Painter of still life and several shooting scenes including "Shooting Snipe" and "Woodcock", "Snipe Shooting", "Partridge Shooting", etc.

Jones, William (op.1830s)
Painter of angling scenes, thought not to be the same artist as William Jones (q.v.). Five angling paintings by Jones were in the collection of A.N. Gilbey, sold

Christie's 25-26 April 1940. A pair entitled "Bottom Fishing" and "Playing a Fish", each 11½in.x15½in., are in the Paul Mellon Collection, Upperville, Va, USA.

Jonniaux, Alfred (b.1882)
Belgian portrait artist whose painting of Captain Wardle, a huntsman of the Fernie, exercising puppies was auctioned by Bonhams 1986.

Josi, Charles, RBA (op.1827-1851)
London painter of animal, sporting and landscape subjects in both oil and watercolour. Exh. at the RA (1827-1851), BI and SS. Titles include "Studies of Horses", "The Reigate Harriers", and "Hard Pressed". Elected RBA 1838. Josi exh. a portrait of "A Favourite Mare" at the BI (No. 482), in 1831, of whom "The New Sporting Magazine" said "At a first glance we were at a loss to determine whether the name "Josi" belonged to the mare or the artist. Favourites however are not always remarkable for beauty as appears by the work before us". Despite this unflattering tribute Josi apparently persevered, for his sporting subjects include fox-hunting, steeplechasing and shooting scenes. Much of his work was painted in watercolour and usually signed and dated.

Jouclard, Adrienne (b.1882)
French artist whose "Rugby Football in Jean-Bouin Stadium" was exh. at the XIVth Olympiad Sport in Art Competition and Exhibition at the V & A Museum, London, 1948 (No.105).

Jowett, Percy Hague, RWS, NEAC, NS, ARCA (Lond.) (1882-1955)
Landscape and interior painter in both oil and watercolour. Studied at Leeds College of Art and at the RCA where he received his diploma (1907) and in Italy. Held one-man shows at St. George's Gallery in 1923, 1925, 1927 and 1929. Exh. at the RA, RWS, RWA, NEAC, the provinces and abroad. He was Principal of the Central School of Arts and Crafts (1930-1935) and of the RCA 1935-1948. His (attrib.) painting of "The Billiard Room with a Player in the act of Taking a Shot", 14in.x10in., was auctioned Christie's (Sth. Ken.) 1988. ("Connoisseur" April 1923 p.245 for comments on his exhibition.)

Joy, Thomas Musgrove (1812-1866)
Painter of portraits, historical, genre and sporting subjects who exh. at SS between 1832 and (posthumously) 1867. Titles include "A Falconer", "F. Ellis, Esq. with Favourite Pony and Dogs" and "A Portrait of the Children of Sir. J.H. Halkett, Bart. with a Favourite Pony and Dog". In 1864 Joy painted "The Meeting of the Subscribers to Tattersalls Before the Races" which hangs in the Tattersalls Room at Newmarket and shows racing personalities at the time when Tattersalls were in their Hyde Park Corner premises. Joy studied art under Samuel Drummond, ARA and exh. from 1831 to 1867 at the RA, BI, SS and NWS. In 1841 he was commissioned by Queen Victoria to paint portraits of the Prince and Princess of Wales. His studio sale was held at Christie's on 18 June 1866. His painting entitled "Shooting Game from a Steady Cob", c.1850, makes this feat look simple. Joy painted "A Cricket Match at Christchurch" from which a print was taken.

Joy, William (1803-1867)
Marine painter, brother of the marine artist John Cantiloe Joy. William Joy occasionally painted river landscapes, with anglers fishing in the foreground, and a painting of this subject, dated 1840, 12in.x16in., was auctioned Sotheby's 1987. Joy exh. at the RA in 1824 and 1832 and at the BI and SS.

Joyner, J. (op.1825-1833)
London landscape painter whose "Partridge Shooting", s.&d. 1832, was exh. Frost & Reed, London. Joyner exh. at the RA, BI and SS, from the same address as M. Joyner (op.1837-1868).

June, John (op.1740-1788)
Line engraver of sporting subjects after his own and his contemporaries' work, including "Death of the Fox", British Museum London.

"Junglicus"
The pseudonym used by the amateur artist Captain Frederick Parr of the 54th Regiment for his pen/ink/ wash sketches contributed to "The Bengal Sporting Magazine", January 1833-November 1842.

Jungnickel, Ludwig Heinrich (1881-1965)
German animal and equestrian artist whose paintings of "Lippizaner Horses at Dressage" are the most sporting of his output which is generally of cats and donkeys. Usually painted in watercolour but his gouache painting in spray technique "The Tennis Player", 18in.x7in., fetched a high price for this artist at auction.

Jury, Julius (1821-d.after 1870)
Figure painter who also painted fish and fishing subjects. His work was repro. in "The Fisherman's Magazine" (1864).

"Jusius"
An anonymous pamphleteer who wrote about the 3rd Duke of Grafton's scandalous private life. The Duke was the most successful bloodstock breeder of his day and owned Euston Hall Stud.

Jutsum, Henry (1816-1869)
Landscape painter who studied under James Stark. Exh. at the RA, BI, SS, NWS and elsewhere (1836-1869). Elected ANWS in 1843 and resigned in 1847. Painted several angling scenes including "Trout Fishing in Berwickshire" and "The Young Sportsman's Rest". His studio sale was held at Christie's April 1882.

K

Kantor, Morris (1896-1974)
American painter whose dramatic work entitled "Baseball at Night", dated 1934, adds a new visual dimension to the tension of the game.

Kate
See Ten Kate

Kaufmann, Wilhelm (b.1895)
Austrian painter of "The Footballers" depicting a goalkeeper attempting to save a goal. This work was contributed to the Art Exhibition held at the V & A Museum, during the Olympic Games in London (1948).

Kay, John (1742-1826)
Scottish draughtsman, miniature painter and etcher of portrait caricatures whose sketch of Alexander McKellar (d.c.1813) the fanatical golfer, entitled "Cock o' the Green", drawn in 1803, was included in Kay's "Edinburgh Portraits" pub. 1838 which Kay started in 1784 and which contained over 900 characters from the Edinburgh area.

Keane, Michael Anthony (b.1907)
Dublin born painter of equestrian subjects, particularly hunting, who worked as a commercial artist before returning to Dublin to study medicine at the Royal College of Surgeons where he qualified with first class honours. He practised as a doctor in England and his daughter is Sally Mitchell, a specialist in sporting art and author of the "Dictionary of British Equestrian Artists", pub. ACC 1985.

Kearsley, Nigel (b.1921)
Painter of country sporting scenes in oils who drew on C.E.M. Lyne (q.v.) for inspiration and guidance. His equestrian portraits are painted for private commissions on both sides of the Atlantic.

Keel, Thomas (op.1908)
"An Otter Hunt" and "Otters with a Salmon", a pair, both signed by this artist, and one dated 1908 were auctioned Christie's (Sth. Ken.) 1982.

Keeling, E.J. (op.1853-1877)
Lancashire based equestrian and sporting artist whose paintings, usually signed and dated, have been recorded between these operating dates. He was almost certainly a close relation of William Knight Keeling, RI (1807-1886), the Manchester portrait painter and watercolourist. His sporting subjects seem to have ranged between hunting portraits, riding horses and shooting subjects with game dogs. His work does not seem to have included racing portraits or racing scenes.

Keene, Charles Samuel (1823-1891)
Black and white artist, illustrator and etcher. An uncle of Aster and Alfred Chantrey Corbould (qq.v.). Keene was articled first to a solicitor, then to an architect. He was then articled to Josiah Wood Whymper, RI (1813-1903), the wood engraver. Keene left Whymper in 1852 to set up on his own as a freelance illustrator and worked for various publishers including "The Illustrated London News" and "Punch". It was with "Punch" that he was to make his name and he contributed work to it until 1891 in which year a memorial exhibition of his work was held at the Fine Art Society (March). He was a friend of the sporting artist Joseph Crawhall (q.v.) on whom he relied heavily, as he did with all his friends, for amusing situations to inspire his drawings. His sporting work includes a portrait of Charles Harbord, the 5th Lord Suffield (1830-1914) dressed for hunting and mounted on his horse.

Keeping, Charles William James (1924-1988)
One of the best and most prolific book illustrators of the 20th century. A lover of horses and an expert on Victorian London, Keeping drew numerous illustrations for children's books during the 1960s and 1970s. Studied art at Regent Street Polytechnic where he later became a visiting lecturer in lithography (1956-1963).

Keiller, Raymond (op.c.1958)
Unknown painter of a golfing scene painted in vibrant colours entitled "The Golf Course", watercolour, 13in.x 18⅞in., signed. Wingfield Sporting Gallery, London.

Keith, A.W. (op.1882)
A painting by this artist entitled "Jumping the Water", s.&d. 1882, 13¾in.x11¾in., was auctioned Sotheby's (Sussex) 1986.

Keith, N.M. Barry (op.1905)
Writer and illustrator of equestrian subjects who contributed work to "Fores Sporting Notes and Sketches" in 1905.

Kell, W.F. (op.1872-1877)
Still life painter of river fish who operated between these dates and who exh. at SS (1875-1877).

Keller, Arthur I. (1866-1924)
Painter and illustrator and a member of the American Watercolor Society and the NY Watercolor Society. His watercolour "A Mixed Foursome" was commissioned for the cover of the March 1900 issue of "The Ladies Home Journal". The original, 15¾in.x11¾in., hangs in the PGA World Golf Hall of Fame in Pinehurst, North Carolina.

Keller, Lou
Contemporary painter of American football personalities whose portrait of "Keith Lincoln, the San Diego Chargers Half Back" (1960s), oil, was painted in 1974.

Kelly, Sir Gerald Festus, PRA, RHA, HRSA (1879-1972)
Distinguished portrait and landscape painter in oil. Studied art in Paris, where he lived for some years. Exh. at the RA from 1909 and was elected NPS (1910), RHA (1914), RA (1930) and PRA (1949-1954). Knighted (1945) and made KCVO (1955). Painted the State portraits of the King and Queen (1945) and is represented in many public collections. He exh. a painting of cricket at the RA in 1957 entitled "Kennington Oval", 6in.x7in.

Kelly, Richard Barrett Talbot, RI (1896-1971)
Painter of birds in watercolour. Son of the artist Robert Talbot Kelly (q.v.) under whom he studied. Served in the Royal Artillery (1915-1929). Exh. at the RA, RI, Paris Salon and in the provinces. Elected RI (1924). Illus. and pub. "The Way of Birds" (1937), "Bird Life and the Painter", and other works. Art master at Rugby School for many years. His watercolour "Greyhounds on a Leash" was painted in 1922.

Kelly, Robert George Talbot, RI, RBA, RBC (1861-1934)
Landscape and figurative painter who specialised in Egyptian and Moroccan scenes. His paintings include hawking and falconry subjects. Exh. at SS (1890-1894). Elected RBA 1893, RI 1907. He was the father of Richard Barrett Talbot Kelly (q.v.) and son of R.G. Kelly, the landscape painter, under whom he studied art.

Kelly, Victor, C., RBSA, ARCA (b.1923)
Contemporary painter of football and rugger scenes, painted in watercolour, including "The Scrum", 12in.x17in. Kelly is Secretary of the RBSA, a member of the Easel Club and Past President of the Birmingham Watercolour Society. He studied at Liverpool College of Art.

Kemp-Welch, Lucy Elizabeth, RI, ROI, RBA, RCamA (1869-1958)
Painter of equestrian and country subjects. Born in Bournemouth and studied under Sir Hubert Herkomer at his school at Bushey from 1891. She took over the Herkomer School (1905-1926). Her great friend was her pupil, Margaret Frobisher (q.v.) who eventually took over the school at Bushey from Kemp-Welch. Kemp-Welch exh. four works at the RA (1895-1904). Her sister was Miss Margaret Kemp-Welch, the painter and engraver. Elected RBA (1902), RI (1907) and R.Cam.A. (1919). Her first solo exhibition was held at the Fine Art Society, Bond Street in 1905. In 1914 she was elected President of the Society of Animal Painters who held their first exhibition at Leicester Galleries. Other members included Alfred Munnings and Lionel Edwards (qq.v).

"Ken"
The pseudonym of an unknown painter of golfing portraits, including that of "Percy Allis playing the Coronation Foursomes at Moor Park" and dated 1937.

Kendrick, Matthew, RHA (c.1797-1874)
Dublin born marine artist who included yacht racing scenes amongst his work. He exh. at the RHA (1827-1872) and was elected RHA (1850).

Kennard, Edward (op.1888)
Black and white artist and illustrator who contributed drawings of sport to "The Graphic" in 1888.

Kennedy, Joseph (ex.1862-1888)
North Devon painter from Barnstaple who exh. at the RA, RHA, RBA and SS (1862-1888) including a portrait of "Three Blue Racing Pigeons". He may have taught art at the Kidderminster Government School of Art, since he painted a view of the school which he exh. at SS in 1867.

Kenney, John Theodore Eardley (1911-1972)
Sporting artist, author and illustrator of many equestrian books who studied at the Leicester School of Art and started his career as a commercial artist. Kenney's main interests were fox-hunting and the Fernie Hunt, which subject he painted many times. In 1952 he retired from his commercial art career to devote himself to painting sporting pictures. A fine fox-hunting artist, he worked mainly in oil but also in watercolour and sometimes in pen and ink. He was influenced by the work of Alfred Munnings (q.v.) and in his turn was a strong influence on the work of Neil Cawthorne (q.v.) whom he helped considerably in the early stages of his career.

Kenrick, G.W. (op.1836)
Watercolour portraits of the racehorses "Bay Middleton" (winner of the Derby 1836) and "Miss Lettie" (winner of the Oaks 1836) in their stables, a pair, each signed, auctioned David Lay (Penzance) 1987.

Kent, William (1685-1748)
Painter, illustrator, landscape gardener and interior decorator, there seems no end to his accomplishments. He is featured in this book for his sketch "Bowls Played at Stowe House", pen, ink and brown wash c.1735. In the background is the temple of ancient virtue (designed by Kent for Lord Cobham in the 1730s) which still stands. (Collection British Museum.) Kent was not an animal painter, indeed his only claim to fame in this field appears to be his illustration of "The Two Owls and the Sparrow" which he provided for the poet John Gay's "Fables" (Thompson and Watts 1727). Kent designed twenty of the plates for this book, John Wootton (q.v.) doing the rest for these fifty fables. Kent concentrated on the human element whilst Wootton, not surprisingly, was at his best portraying the animals and birds. Kent learnt to paint in Italy where he spent ten years, returning to England in 1719, in the train of his newly found patron Lord Burlington. Horace Walpole that wit and eccentric, later the 4th Lord Orford, who had a generally poor opinion of Kent's powers as an illustrator, allowed that "such of the drawings as he designed for Gay's "Fables" have some truth and nature". Kent, who was not a very good engraver of his own work, illustrated by the three very unsatisfactory plates which he designed and engraved for Gay's "Poems on Several Occasions" (Tomson and

Lintot, 1720), later took a Huguenot immigrant engraver, Pierre Fourdinier, to work for him, with the result that their joint illustrations to Pope's translations of the "Odyssey" (pub. by Bernard Lintot in 1726) were a great success. Quite different in character were the thirty-two illustrations he made for the Brindley and Wright edn. of Spenser's "Faerie Queen", not pub. until 1751, three years after Kent's death. Many of these are preserved in the V & A Museum. They remain William Kent's crowning achievement in his least celebrated and undeservedly neglected role, the exact opposite of Horace Walpole's judgement of them as "the most execrable performance you ever beheld".

Kerr, George Cochrane (op.1873-1906)
Marine painter in oil and watercolour, who exh. at the RA, RI and SS from 1873. Titles at SS include "Practising for the Regatta". Kerr's rowing painting "Racing on the Medway at Rochester", 18½in.x35in., was auctioned Christie's 1969.

Kessell, James Everett, RBSA (b.1915)
Coventry portrait and landscape painter, in oil and watercolour, and of some figure subjects. Studied at Coventry School of Art 1928-1934 and 1945-1952. Exh. at the RA, RBA, ROI, RSMA, NS, the Paris Salon and elsewhere. Elected RBSA (1968). His football painting entitled "A Corner of Coventry City Football Ground, Coventry v. Bournemouth, 14th March 1953", 26½in.x 34½in., was exh. at the FE, No. 43.

"Kestler" (op.c.1910)
The pseudonym used by an illustrator who worked for the "Yorkshire Evening Post" in the years around 1910, recording international and first class cricket in a humorous but comprehensive style.

Key, Katherine (Mrs.) (op.1892-1919)
Exh. one painting at SWA (1919). Her pen, brown ink and watercolour drawing of "Sir Tatton Sykes and his Hounds", s.&d. April 1892 and extensively inscr. 13in.x 18½in., was auctioned Christie's (Sth. Ken.) 1988.

Keyl, Friedrich Wilhelm (1823-1871)
Born in Frankfurt, but lived mainly in London, where he died. Pupil under Verboeckhoeven in Brussels. In 1845 he moved to London and became a pupil of Sir Edwin Landseer (q.v.) who introduced him to the Royal Family from whom he had many commissions. Painted animals, landscapes and country subjects. Exh. forty-two works at the RA and thirty-four works, almost all of animals, at the BI. His painting of a saddled horse and game dogs outside a country house, s.&d. 1854, 35½in.x49¼in., Sotheby's (Bel.) 1977.

Khnopff Fernand (1858-1921)
Belgian painter. Born at Grembergen, near Termouche, Khnopff belonged to an old wealthy and distinguished family. He studied law at Brussels University but gave it up to pursue an artistic career. Studied art at the Academy of Brussels, under Xavier Mellery, and then at the Académie Julian, Paris under Gustave Moreau, who greatly influenced his painting. Later Khnopff came to London where he admired the ideas of both Burne Jones and Rossetti. He was an exceptional artist

and his works appear in numerous public and private collections. His obituary appeared in the January 1922 issue of "The Connoisseur". His painting of "Marguerite Khnopff playing Tennis", s.&d. 1889, was auctioned Poulain et Le Fur, Paris, 1989 and his pastel drawing entitled "Tennis Memories" was repro. as a book illustration.

Kidd, William H., RSA (1790-1863)
Prolific Scottish painter who studied under James Howe (q.v.), the animal painter. He exh. at SS (1826-1853). Sporting titles include "The Snared Pheasant", "Dead Game", "The Sportsman's Return", "The Old Fisherman", "The Dying Grouse", "Landing Fish", "The Weary Angler" and "A Sketch of a Horse". Kidd settled in London in 1817. Elected HRSA (1829).

Kilburne, George Goodwin, Snr., RI, ROI (1839-1924)
Painter of sporting and hunting subjects, very often in watercolour. He was also an illustrator and an engraver. Born in Norfolk, Kilburne was apprenticed for five years to the Dalziel brothers, the engravers and illustrators, and married Robert Dalziel's daughter. Later Kilburne turned from engraving to painting specialising in hunting and genre scenes very often, like many of his Edwardian contemporaries, set in the 18th century. A very talented draughtsman, Dalziel records of his apprentice work that it was "so perfect that it was published with the set to which it belonged". He was the father of George Goodwin Kilburne, Jnr. (q.v.), another example of the misleading father/son relationships carrying the same Christian names. Exh. at SS (1862-1885), no sporting titles. He was elected RI (1868) and ROI (1883).

Kilburne, George Goodwin, Jnr., RBA (1863-1938)
Exh. at SS (1882-1894). Sporting titles include "Off to the Meet", "A Blank Day", "A Scratch Meeting", "This Day a Fox will Die". Lived at Horsham, Sussex and Tunbridge Wells from where he exh. his two paintings at the RA in 1906 and 1907. Exh. forty-seven paintings at the RBA. Elected RBA (1889). Painted "The Hunt Cup at Ranelagh", a polo scene after which prints were repro. The painting is referred to in "Bailys Magazine" (1900). Son of George Goodwin Kilburne (q.v.).

Killingbeck, Benjamin (op.1763-1789)
Portrait and sporting painter, usually of equestrian subjects, although his "Sportsmen with their Gundogs Shooting Partridge" was auctioned Sotheby's 1965. An admirer and imitator of George Stubbs (q.v.), Killingbeck is thought to have come from Yorkshire. Exh. FS (1769-1782), SA (1777-1783) and RA (1776-1789). Killingbeck painted racehorses for the Earl of Eglington and the Marquis of Rockingham. He painted Richard Tattersall's famous racehorse "Highflyer" in 1783, a subject that was also painted by Stubbs. He usually painted very large canvases and in 1773 he painted an Arab horse "as large as life" for Harry Verelst. His output also included several portraits and conversation pieces. Killingbeck was a somewhat indifferent etcher,

stipple and mezzotint engraver of portraits and animal subjects after his contemporaries' and his own designs. He may have been a relation of Mr. James Killingbeck, an eminent painter and limner, of Pontefract who married a clergyman's widow in 1769. Indeed Mr. James Killingbeck and Benjamin Killingbeck may have been one and the same artist.

Kinahan, Coralie
Irish 20th century equestrian painter whose racing scene "Laytown Races", 18in.x30in., was auctioned Christie's (Belfast) 1990.

Kinch, Hayter (op.1811-1841)
An equestrian painter from Fareham, Hants. who exh. seventeen pictures at the RA (1811-1824) twelve of which were of horses. The first picture exh. was of a member of the Hambledon Hunt. His painting of "Doxy" a dapple grey hunter, the property of John Bourke, 4th Earl of Mayo, in a landscape, inscr. "Painted at Bangor 1835", 19½in.x25½in., was auctioned Sotheby's 1990. All his paintings seem to be signed and dated and painted in oil on canvas.

Kinch, Henry (op.1881)
Equestrian artist whose several horse portraits were painted in the 1880s.

"King Cob"
Alias Charles Richardson. See "Shotley".

King, Cecil George Charles, RI, ROI, RBA, RSMA (1881-1942)
Marine and landscape painter in oil and watercolours. Studied art at Goldsmiths, Westminster Art School and in Paris. King was official naval artist in the Baltic during the 1st World War. Exh. seven naval pictures at Portsmouth in 1936 and four at Portsmouth in 1938 including "Britannia" leading at Cowes Regatta. At one time King was honorary official marine painter to the RTYC. Twelve of his paintings are in the Imperial War Museum, all of naval subjects. A founder member of the RSMA in 1937.

King, Jeremy C.G. (b.1933)
Born in Oundle. Studied at the Lancaster College of Art and London University Institute of Education. Left teaching in 1967 to take up painting and lithography full time. He is regularly commissioned by CCA to create limited edn. lithographs and has regularly exh. in the UK and the USA. Exh. at the RA from 1961. His paintings of rowing scenes, including "Leander", are colourful representations in his own distinct style.

King, Jessie Marion (Mrs.E.A. Taylor) (1875-1949)
Illustrator, especially of children's books. Married to the artist and furniture designer, Ernest Archibald Taylor (1908). Studied at Glasgow School of Art and taught book decoration at this school in 1902. A member of the Glasgow Lady Artists Club in Blythswood Square, she was considerably influenced by the painter Charles Rennie Mackintosh and his circle. A great dog lover whose spaniel "Pete" was painted by Marion R.H. Harvey (q.v.).

King, John (op.1830-1834)
American portrait painter whose sporting work includes a double portrait of "Two Boys, standing full length holding Bows and Arrows", s.&d. 1834, 36in.x28in., auctioned Bonhams 1986 and "The Prize Fight", s.&d. 1830.

King, John Gregory (b.1929)
Equestrian and sporting artist who specialises in hunting, shooting, fishing, steeplechase and three day eventing scenes. Born at West Tytherley near Salisbury, in the same house in which he now lives. He was strongly influenced by the sporting artist Lionel Edwards (q.v.) and although brought up to farm, he began to draw and paint from an early age. A founder member of the Society of Equestrian Artists, King has had many exhibitions and his hunting and polo pictures have been repro. as prints and as illustrations for numerous books and magazines.

King, Thomas W. (op.1825-1837, d.1845)
Line engraver and painter of sporting scenes including "Study of the Hound 'Spot'", "Waiting for Master", "The Apprentices Fight" and "The Young Stalker". His recorded work is both s.&d. and painted in oil. Described as "a shiftless pupil of Knapton" (q.v.) (Edwards).

King, William Gunning, NEA (1859-1940)
Figure painter, etcher and illustrator who studied art at South Kensington and the RA Schools. Elected NEA (1887). A vigorous illustrator of rural life which he drew in fine quality pen work. Contributed to "The Sporting and Dramatic News" (1896), "Illustrated London News", "The Graphic", "Punch", "The Sketch", "The English Illustrated Magazine" and "Quiver". He exh. at the RA, RBA, RI, ROI, NEA, etc.

Kingwell, Miss Mabel Amber (op.1914-1923)
This painter exh. at the RA and Walker AG (1914-1923). "Shaun Spadah", the winner of the 1920 Grand National and "The Biennial Stakes at Newmarket Heath", a pair of watercolours, 10in.x14½in., were auctioned Sotheby's 1985. Her other sporting subjects include steeplechasing and fox-hunting scenes, although the bulk of her work was indisputably confined to studies of Dartmoor ponies and donkeys. She lived at North Huish and Plymouth in South Devon

Kinnear, James S. (op.1880-1917)
Edinburgh landscape painter of "A Chestnut Racehorse in a Stable", 24in.x36in., auctioned Sotheby's 1986.

Kinsella, E.P. (op.c.1910)
German artist of cricket subjects, at the turn of the century, "The Hope of His Side", "The Boss", etc. watercolours, 13in.x8½in., Christie's.

Kinsey, Anthony (op.1953)
Painter who contributed a football painting entitled "Down at the Valley", 29in.x21½in., to the competition and subsequent FE.

Kirby, Thomas (1775-c.1847)
Painter of portraits and landscapes. Entered the RA Schools 1795. Exh. at the RA (1796-1846) and BI

1808-1847). Kirby's portrait of "Pierce Wynne Yorke (1826-1891) of Erdigg Hall", standing full length in a brown coat and white breeches holding a cricket bat, 51¼ in.x39½ in., was auctioned Christie's 1980.

Kirchner, Ernest Ludwig (1880-1938)
Prolific German landscape and figure artist, often of nudes, whose painting entitled "Hockey Players", which represents a game of ice hockey in progress, is at Marlborough Girson Gallery, New York. Kirchner painted a number of sports including "An Ice Skater", "A Uni-Cyclist" and "A Tennis Player". He normally painted in watercolour and drew in pen and ink or chalk. Usually signed but rarely dated his work.

Kirk, Joel (b.1948)
Surrey born animal and wildlife artist who lives in Dorset. Studied Southend College of Art (1972-1975).

Kirkham, Norman
Contemporary painter in watercolour of a golf scene entitled "this is the Ailsa Course at Turnberry, Ayrshire" (1988), Christie's (Glasgow) 1988.

Kirtley, Dennis C. (b.1924)
Equestrian painter, particularly of racehorses, whose subjects range from portraits of "Crepello" and "St. Paddy" in the 1950s and 1960s to those more recently of the unbeaten Derby winner "Golden Fleece" and the champion European sire "Be My Guest". Kirtley, who was born and has lived all his life in Sunderland, has a passion for racehorses and a flair for portraying them in action. His work has been exh. at many leading northern galleries and he held his first solo exhibition at Sunderland Art Gallery in 1967.

Kitaj, Ronald Brooks (b.1932)
American painter born in Cleveland, Ohio, who studied in London at the RCA (1960-1962). Kitaj played an influential role in an erratic art movement, popular at the time, of portraying everyday objects, often unrelated, with explanatory notes written into the painting, densely filling the canvas. His painting of an American baseball game entitled "Upon Never Having Seen Konfax Pitch" (1967), 14⅛ in.x10in., private collection, is certainly an unusual interpretation of the game. Obviously baseball holds a fascination for him for he painted "Amerika Baseball" in 1983/4.

Kit Cat, Dick
Pseudonym used by the artist Richard Doyle (q.v.).

Kline, Hibberd V.B. (op.1909)
Designer of a colour lithograph entitled "The Last Mile", 1909, showing a rowing race in three parts.

Knapton, George (1698-1778)
Portrait painter in oils and crayons who was apprenticed to Richardson (1715-1722) at the St. Martin's Lane Academy. He also studied in Italy (1725-1732). An early exponent of conversation pieces, his portrait groups include the large study of "The Princess of Wales and her eight children" (1751) which is in the Royal Collection. Many of his portraits were of distinguished sporting personalities including "William Green of Wykin" whom Knapton painted in a grey coat, white stock and black hunting cap, with a hunt in full cry in the background, 29¼ in.x24in., from the Craven Collection. Knapton's pupils included Thomas King (q.v.). Knapton's portrait of "Master Francis Burrell", threequarter length in a brown coat and blue and silver waistcoat holding a battledore, a shuttlecock on the table beside him, Signed and dated 175? (indis.) and inscr., 29⅞ in.x25¼ in.. was auctioned Christie's.

Knell, William Adolphus (c.1805-1875)
Marine painter and engraver in aquatint. His portrait of "The yacht 'Mystery', racing for the Harwich Regatta Cup", (1854), signed and inscr., 13in.x20in., was auctioned Christie's 1976. He was clearly a better painter than he was an engraver and indeed much of his own work was engraved by professionals like J. Harris whose colour aquatint "A Four Oar'd Outrigger" (1851), one of four views by Knell, were repro. by Fores "Sporting Scraps".

Kneller, Sir Godfrey, Bt. (1646-1723)
Distinguished court and society portrait painter who studied under Bol and Rembrandt in the 1660s. He was in Rome and Venice between 1672 and 1675 and settled in England (1676). Became principal painter to William and Mary (1688), jointly with Riley, and on Riley's death in 1691 he continued in that office until his death. Kneller's work includes portraits of several distinguished sportsmen and he is famous for his portrait of "The Members of the Kit Cat Club" (c.1703-1721) and the portrait of the Countess of Mar in her riding habit, painted in 1715. Kneller was knighted in 1692 and made a baronet in 1715.

Knight, A. Roland (op.1879-1921)
Angling artist of freshwater fish including "Brown Trout", "Salmon Fishing", "Pike" and "Perch". Most of his paintings are action fishing scenes but he also painted still lifes of dead fish, artistically arranged on the bank, usually with a rod. Occasionally he painted grouse and game birds and very occasionally coaching subjects. Usually signed but rarely dated his work.

Knight, Charles Neil (1865 op.1899)
Usually painted genre subjects but his painting of his father entitled "Playing Golf off the Fairway", 15in.x 10in. and inscr., is an exception to the rule. Knight studied in Paris at the Académie Julian and exh. two works at SS, the RA and in Liverpool. He lived in Bath and was the secretary of the Bath Society of Artists.

Knight, John Baverstock (1785-1859)
Art connoisseur and amateur landscape artist in both oil and watercolour. He was also an etcher. His brown ink and watercolour drawing, 4¾ in.x6⅜ in., "Sportsmen on the Edge of a Wood with Pointers", s.&d. 1816, was illus. in "Bailys Magazine" (ex. coll. L.G. Duke).

Knight, John William Buxton, RBA, RCA, RE (1843-1908)
Landscape and sporting artist, in both oil and watercolour. Studied at the RA Schools. Elected RBA (1875) and RE (1881). Exh. at the RA (1861-1907). His name occasionally appears as Buxton-Knight. He painted

several fox-hunting scenes including "Hounds Meeting Outside a Village Inn", "Meet of Foxhounds in a Landscape", "Foxhounds drawing a Covert", and a portrait of "A White Saddled Horse" (1888).

Knight, Dame Laura (née Johnson), DBE, RA, RWS, RE, RWA, PSWA (1877-1970)

Distinguished painter of landscape and figure subjects in both oil and watercolour, and an etcher. Studied at Nottingham School of Art, under Wilson Foster, and at the RCA where she was a pupil of distinction. Married the artist Harold Knight (1903) and settled at Newlyn, Cornwall. Her sporting subjects include Ascot racing and boxing scenes. Knight won an Hon. Mention with her "Sketches of Boxers" in the Olympic Arts Competition, held in London at the V & A Museum, July/August 1948. Boxing was a subject she painted many times and several preliminary sketches exist of the oil painting, now in the National Gallery of Canada, Ottawa, "The Canadians Boxing at Whitley Camp" (c.1970).

Knight, S.S. (op.1850-1856)

A pair of fine hare coursing scenes, s.&d. 1850, each 14in.x21in., were auctioned Sotheby's 1981, and "A Racehorse in a Stable", s.&d. 1856, 24in.x29in., was auctioned Joel-Melbourne 1985.

Knight, William Henry (1823-1863)

Painter of genre subjects who gave up a career as a solicitor to become a professional painter. Entered the RA Schools (1845). His major paintings include "Boys Snow Balling" (1853) and "The Young Naturalist" (1857). Much of his work featured children including "The Village Team" showing boys playing cricket, 3½in.x6in. His other sporting work includes "A Huntsman with his Greyhounds", s.&d. 1850, 30in.x 24½in., auctioned Christie's (NY) 1989. A watercolour "A Huntsman by an Oak Tree, signed William Henry Knight, and inscr. "Sherwood", dated 1837, may be a very early work by this artist.

Knip, Henriette (Mrs. Ronner) RI (1821-1909)

Dutch animal painter who painted several sporting subjects including "An English Setter", "Snipe and Woodcock", "On the Point", "A Gamekeeper and his Dog by a Stream", "A Flat Coated Retriever by a Tree" (with a gun and dead game in a basket). Dog carts were obviously a favourite subject as she painted a number of these little carts pulled by dogs. Henriette Knip was born in Amsterdam and studied under her father, J.A. Knip. After her marriage she continued to paint under her maiden name. Exh. widely at the leading London galleries. Elected RI 1894.

Knowles, Frederick J. (b.1874)

Manchester born painter of landscape and figure subjects who studied at the Cavendish School of Art. Exh. in London at the R. Cam. A. Knowles painted in both oil and watercolour and he is the artist of a watercolour showing "A Huntsman leading his Hounds on a Grey Horse across a Heath", 9in.x12in., Abbott and Holder, London.

Knox, Wilfred (op.1920-1950)

Marine artist whose work includes many yacht race scenes.

Knox, William, RBA (op.1919-1947)

Marine artist in both oil and watercolour. His work includes many yacht race scenes. He is supposed to have used the alias "A.D. Bell" (q.v.) for much of his work, though for what reason is obscure.

Knyff, Leonard (1650-1722)

Landscape, still life and animal painter, born in Haarlem, Holland, son of Wouter Knyff, the landscape painter and was probably trained by him. Came to London (1681) and became naturalised (1694). An admirer of Francis Barlow (q.v.), his painting of "Arthur, 3rd Viscount Irwin, with his Gun, Pointer and dead Game", 104in.x108½in. (in the Collection of Temple Newsam House), is painted in a similar style. Knyff probably painted this in 1700 as it is documented as paid for (£35) at that date.

Koch, Ludwig (1866-1943)

Highly talented Austrian equestrian artist of polo and hunting scenes, usually watercolour. "Riding Off", s.&d. 1925, watercolour and gouache, 9½in.x12½in., Sotheby's (Sussex) 1987 and "A Polo Match", s.&d. 1922, 36¼in.x28¼in., Christie's (NY) 1989.

Koehler, Henry (b.1927)

American sporting painter. Born in Louisville, Kentucky, the son of a lumber merchant. Graduated at Yale University and worked with an advertising company for seven years before going freelance. His first sporting commission was from "Sports Illustrated". In 1950 Koehler took up riding and has hunted regularly with many American hunts, including the Litchfield County Hounds in Connecticut. He is also a keen sailor. Since 1961 Henry Koehler has held over forty one-man exhibitions, mainly in America, but also in London at Messrs. Ackermanns, Wildenstein and Partridge Fine Arts Ltd. His paintings can be found in the National Museum of Racing, Newmarket, and in numerous private collections on both sides of the Atlantic. His sporting subjects include polo, cricket and lawn bowls. His work has been described, according to his official handout, as "a visual equivalent of Dick Francis - full of intimate insights into the racing world, predictable, professional and engaging".

Koerner, Henry (b.1915)

Austrian painter who emigrated to the USA in 1939 having previously studied at the Vienna Academy of Design. His painting of a fantasy American baseball game entitled "Rose Arbor" (1947) is seen from a rose trellised garden, through which the viewer can also see a tennis match taking place beyond and in fact, within, the baseball game. The Museum of Modern Art, New York.

Koethe, Wolfgang

Contemporary German artist who has lived and worked in Great Britain for some time. Clearly interested in football since he painted the "England-Germany World Cup Final" (1966).

Kondracki, Henry (b.1953)

Contemporary painter of boxing studies including "Loser", 1990, 60in.x42in. Born in Edinburgh. Studied at the Byam Shaw School of Fine Art (1981-1982) and at the Slade (1982-1986).

Kossak, Jerzy (Jerry) (1890-1963)
Polish equestrian artist who lived and worked in America and whose paintings include several of fox-hunting scenes. "Full Cry", s.&d. 1927, 17½in.x39½in., was auctioned Christie's (NY) 1986.

Kray, Reg (20th century)
A crayon sketch of a boxer inscribed "Venture - a Quitter Never Wins, a Winner Never Quits", signed, 23¼in.x15¼in., was auctioned at Outhwaites in 1986. This artist is better known as the other half of the infamous Kray twins, whose interest in boxing subjects is well known. Another boxing masterpiece by Kray, 23¼in.x28in., was sold at Bonhams, July 1991 for £580, reflecting no doubt the fame of the man rather than the talent of the artist.

Krishna, Mary Elizabeth, ARCA (1909-1968)
Born Mary E. Oldfield in Battersea. Studied at Ealing College of Art (1925-1927) where she gained a scholarship to the Royal College of Art (1927). At the RCA she met the Indian artist, Roop Krishna, whom she married in Lahore in 1936 where they lived for the following ten years. They returned to London in 1946 where an exhibition of their work was held at India House. From 1948 they lived in a basement flat in Thurloe Street, South Kensington, until Mary died in 1968. Two years later Roop took his own life. Her painting of a football match entitled "Chelsea v West Bromwich Albion", 19½in.x23½in., was exh. at the FE.

Kuell, Victor John (op.1953/4)
Contemporary painter of a football match entitled "Offside Dispute", 29½in.x23¾in. which was exh. at the FE.

Kushner, Robert (b.1946)
Contemporary painter of an American baseball game entitled "L.A. Dodgers" (1978), 66¾in.x30⅛in., showing Kushner's interpretation of the players portrayed in vivid colour.

"Kyd"
Pseudonym used by the caricaturist and illustrator Joseph Clayton Clarke (op.1882-1889) who contributed to "The Illustrated London News" (1882).

L

Lacretelle, Jean Edouard (1817-1900)
French painter of historical and mythological subjects who died in Paris but spent a considerable amount of time in England, based in London. Exh. at the Paris Salon (1841-1881) and worked in oil, watercolour and gouache. Exh. at the RA and SS. His portrait of "Trumpeter" with his groom in a paddock, signed and inscr., 18in.x24in., was auctioned Tennants 1985.

Lacroix, Tristan (op.1883-1896)
French equestrian artist whose paintings of polo and racing are usually s.&d. Sometimes known as (de) La Croix. "Les Haras de Suresnes", s.&d. 1893, 21in.x 32in., was auctioned Neumeister, Munich (1989).

Ladbrooke, John Berney (1803-1879)
Norfolk-born landscape, animal and sporting painter, the third son of Robert Ladbrooke, the Norwich school painter of landscapes and portraits. His uncle by marriage was John Crome who was alleged to have taught him to paint but this is unlikely as in about 1811 the Ladbrookes and the Cromes quarrelled and set up rival establishments. Ladbrooke was largely an oil painter but he occasionally painted in watercolour. He exh. at the RA between 1821 and 1872, BI and SS. His painting of a chestnut hunter in a landscape, s.&d. 1863 and inscr. "Lincoln", 24½in.x29½in., was auctioned Christie's 1971.

La Dell, Edwin, ARA, RBA, ARCA (Lond.) (1914-1970)
Landscape and figure painter and a lithographer. Studied art at the RCA and became Senior Tutor there from 1948. Exh. at the principal London galleries and was elected RBA in 1950 and ARA in 1969. He painted several football scenes including "Stamford Bridge, figures outside the turnstile of Chelsea Football Ground", pen, black ink and gouache, 14in.x20½in., and "Stamford Bridge at 2.45pm.", watercolour, 13¾in.x 20½in. and inscr. La Dell's painting of "Lords", 15½in.x22½in., was auctioned Sotheby's (Sussex) 1987.

La Farge, John (1835-1910)
American painter with cosmopolitan interests. Student of William Morris Hunt (q.v.) by whom he was highly influenced. Included in this Dictionary for his somewhat romantic portrayal of baseball in his watercolour "Standing Dance Representing the Game of Ball", 1890/1, 8in.x11½in. Private Collection, USA.

La Fontaine, Thomas Sherwood (b.1915)

Portrait, sporting and equestrian painter who studied art at the Regent Street Polytechnic School (1934-1936), at the City and Guilds, Kennington (1936-1939) and then at the Spenlove School, under Reginald Grenville Eves, RA, RI, ROI, RP (1876-1941), in 1939. His sporting subjects include polo, fox-hunting, steeplechasing and flat racing. His work is much in demand in America.

Lagos, Bruce (op.1880-1881)

Painter of a portrait of a sportsman with a double barrelled shotgun, signed, 36½in.x24½in., auctioned Sotheby's (Glen.) 1985. This is possibly the artist Bruck-Lajos (1846-1910) although a B. Lagos exh. two works at the RHA (1880/1) from an address in Paris.

Laidlay, William James, NEAC (1846-1912)

Landscape painter who studied art in Paris under Carolus Duran and Bouguereau (1879-1885). Founder member of the NEAC where he exh. between 1888 and 1892. His sporting exhibits there include "Duck Shooting on the Broads" (1888) and "After the Shot" (1891). Laidlay exh. at the principal London galleries from 1882 and at the Société des Artists Français in Paris (1880-1912).

Laloin, Cecil

A painting of "Bowls" by this artist is mentioned in "Bowls Encyclopaedia", by John P. Munro, pub. 1951.

Lamb, Jim

20th century painter of American football scenes including a picture of the "Minnesota Vikings 1979". Acrylic on illustration board.

Lamb, Lynton Harold, LG, SWE (b.1907)

Landscape painter, born in India, who contributed "Village Football", 29in.x24½in., to the FE. Lamb, who studied at the Central School of Arts and Crafts (1928-1930) under Meninsky and William Roberts (q.v.), exh. at the leading London galleries and elsewhere and was elected LG (1939). He was on the staff at the Slade School (1950-1971) and also lectured at the RCA. His publications include "The Purpose of Painting" (1936) and "Preparation for Painting" (1954).

Lambdin, George Cochran (1830-1896)

American portrait painter and figure artist whose painting of "The Biddle Children Fishing on the Schuykill", s.&d. 1869 and inscr., 20¼in.x16in., was exh. New York Finch College Museum of Art, December 1973/January 1974.

Lambert, Clement (Clem) (1855-1925)

Landscape painter in both oil and watercolour whose portraits of a golfer addressing the ball and another having played it, a pair, each 23in.x21in., were auctioned Phillips (London) 1989. Lambert came from Brighton and was for many years on the Brighton Fine Art Committee. He exh. at the RA from 1882 and at other leading galleries from 1880.

Lambert, E.F. (c.1790-1846)

Portrait and figure painter, also an etcher, who included sporting and equestrian subjects amongst his work. His portrait of the racehorse "Formosa" was engraved by G. Brown and his billiard scene was drawn and etched in 1827. Lambert also painted coaching scenes including "The London to Maidstone Mail Coach at Kennington Gate" c.1837 and "The Brighton Coach at the Bull and Mouth" (repro. Blew's "Brighton and its Coaches" 1894). Exh. RA and SS between 1823 and 1846.

Lambert, George (1700-1765)

Painter of topographical landscapes, often highly allegorical, who included several deer hunting and duck shooting scenes amongst his work. He was a pupil of the sporting painter John Wootton (q.v.), which explains his interest in sporting subjects, and of Gaspard Poussin, which explains his classical backgrounds. He was the first Chairman of the Society of Artists (1761) and was elected its first President shortly before his death.

Lambert, George Washington, ARA (1873-1930)

Australian painter of figure subjects whose fine painting, dated 1910, and entitled "The Fencing Match" is thought to portray a scene at Osborne House, Isle of Wight. The onlookers include a number of famous Edwardian society figures including Lady Ottoline Morrell, George Bernard Shaw, and Sir Winston Churchill. Exh. David Ker Gallery, London. Lambert, who studied art at the Sydney School of Art (1891), won a three year travelling scholarship to Paris and came to London to teach at the London School of Art in 1910, painting "The Fencing Match" in the same year. Returned to Australia c.1928. Elected ARA 1922. Exh. widely from 1904.

Lambert, J.F. (op.1850)

A painting of Eton boys skulling on the river Thames with Windsor Castle beyond signed J.F. Lambert and dated 1850, 21in.x29in., was auctioned Christie's, 1970.

Lambert, James, Snr. (1725-1788)

Sussex landscape and animal painter, his landscapes always enlivened by cattle or sheep. Probably taught to paint by the Smiths of Chichester (q.v.) to whom he was related. Painted a number of animal portraits including "Mr. Bakewell's Famous Ram" exh. at the RA (1774). Exh. seventeen paintings at the SA, thirty at FS and seven at the RA. There is a self-portrait by him in the Museum at Lewes, Sussex. His painting of a skewbald hare hanging over a table, signed and inscr. "Killed on the South Downs, Nr. Lewes, December 2nd 1771", 30in.x25in., was exh. at Colnaghi June 1986.

Lambert, James, Jnr. (1741-1799)

Nephew and pupil of James Lambert (q.v.) who called himself "a coach and sign painter". He painted several competent Sussex landscapes and he exh. still lifes and flower pieces at the FS and the RA (1769-1778).

Lambert, Joseph W. (op.1822-1851)

Animal and sporting painter who exh. nine paintings at the RA including "The Surrey Foxhounds Breaking Cover" (1836). He exh. four works at the BI including "Shooting Pony and Pointer" (1823) and eleven at SS between 1822 and 1851 from a Carshalton address. Titles at SS include "Portrait of a Spaniel", "The Rabbit Catcher" and a "Lurcher Spaniel".

Lami, Eugène Louis (1800-1890)
French figure painter, equally at home in both France and England. He painted in watercolour, gouache and oil and was also a lithographer. His subjects include English sporting scenes, fox-hunting, racing, cock-fighting and boxing. Lami studied under Horace Vernet and Baron Gros where he met Géricault (q.v.) and Richard Parkes Bonington (1801-1828) who helped him with his watercolour work. In 1826 Lami came to England where he made a series of lithographs entitled "Souvenir de Londres" which included several of his English sporting scenes. His second set of lithographs entitled "Voyage en Angleterre" include English coaching scenes. Lami started his career as a litho-grapher and collaborated with Vernet (1822) with the "Collection of French Army Uniforms 1791-1814". Between 1830 and 1837 Lami made his name as a painter of battle scenes and in 1838 he became official painter at the court of Louis-Philippe. He was a founder of the Société de Aquarellistes in the late 1870s.

La Nave, Francesca (b.1954)
Italian printmaker whose sporting interest comes as a result of her English husband's love of cricket and Sumo wrestling. She frequently features these two sports in her engravings. Born in Florence, La Nave studied at Chelsea Art School (1979-1982). She has exh. widely including the Sport in Print exhibition at Leicester College of Art.

Lance, Eveline (op.1891-1893)
Landscape painter. Her watercolour "Outdoor Play", 8¼in.x6¼in., depicts the game of shuttlecock and was auctioned Christie's 1986. She seems to have painted in watercolour and exh. watercolour landscapes at SS and NWS (1891-1893).

Lance, George (1802-1864)
Painter of still lifes, who studied under B.R. Haydon (q.v.) and exh. at RA, BI, SS and NWS between 1824 and 1864. He also exh. at the Liverpool Academy of which he was an honorary member. His best known pupil was William Duffield (q.v.). Although more commonly known as a painter of still lifes, Lance nevertheless touched on sporting subjects as his example "The Young Falconer", exh. at BI in 1842, shows. In 1856 a correspondent of the "Art Journal" wrote of the artist "How is it that Lance is not in the Academy, not even an Associate?. These are matters which the world outside the Temple of Art in Trafalgar Square cannot understand. We find his pictures occupying honourable positions in the public galleries, side by side with those men who are entitled to have cabbalistic letters after their names and we know also that his pictures are coveted and possessed by the most enlightened art patrons of the kingdom who value them as highly as any work which academician or associate ever painted". Lance, who was incidentally the brother-in-law of J.W. Archer (q.v.), was himself painted by William Fisk who exh. the portrait at SS in 1834.

Landells, Ebenezer (1808-1860)
Engraver and illustrator who studied under Thomas Bewick (q.v.). Came to London (1829) and for a time ran the Fine Art Department of Branston and Vizetelly. He contributed sporting work to "The Sporting Review" (1842-1846) before he became involved as a projector of newspapers and founder of "Punch". The Dalziel brothers became his pupils. Landells' particular claim to fame is in his role as special artist accompanying Queen Victoria's first tour of Scotland. The drawings were for "The Illustrated London News Special" but the Queen later bought the drawings, the first of their kind to be made for a newspaper on the spot. Landells was not a particularly good artist and was probably a better engraver.

Lander, Benjamin (op.c.1910)
"Huntsmen taking a Ditch with Hounds", c.1910, 16in.x20in. Michael Newman, 1990.

Lander, Edgar Longley (b.1883 op.1902-1936)
Black and white artist who regularly exh. watercolours and etchings at the RA and RSA (1920-1936). His pencil drawing of a very pretty girl with her golf bag and sticks entitled "The Idol of the Links" was repro. in "The Bystander" May 1910.

Landseer, Charles, RA (1799-1878)
Historical painter of some sporting subjects, the elder brother of Edwin Landseer (q.v.) and brother and son of the engravers Thomas and John Landseer ARA. Studied with his father and with B.R. Haydon (q.v.) and at the RA Schools. Exh. at the RA, BI and SS (1828-1879). Elected RA (1845) and Keeper of the RA from 1851 to 1873. His studio sale took place at Christie's on 14 April 1880. Sporting titles of his exh. work include "The Tired Huntsman" (1840), "The Tyrolese Hunter" (1828) and "A Highlander seized by a Bloodhound" (1838). His portrait of "A Sportsman standing in the Hall of a Mansion holding a Gun with two Dogs", 30in.x25in., was auctioned Christie's 1967. Illus. "Days of Deerstalking" (William Scrope 1883) and "Days and Nights of Salmon Fishing" (1898).

Landseer, Sir Edwin Henry, RA (1802-1873)
Distinguished Victorian animal painter and sculptor. Son and pupil of the engraver, John Landseer, ARA and pupil of Benjamin Haydon (q.v.). His elder brother, Thomas (1795-1880) was also an engraver and an RA. As a sculptor Edwin Landseer is widely known for his lions at Trafalgar Square. Made his debut at the RA at the age of thirteen and exhibited forty-three paintings there including "Prosperity" (1865). The painting shows a gentleman standing in a beautiful garden with a croquet set beside him, holding a horse and surrounded by dogs and by all the trappings of wealth. Landseer was undoubtedly talented as a young man but although he became the most popular painter of his day, he was greatly influenced by fashion and by commissioned work. He was a particularly favourite painter of Queen Victoria for whom he painted a fine portrait of Prince Albert which shows him surrounded by "the trophies of his skill, the grouse, the ptarmigan

and the stag". Landseer's several paintings of field sports include otter hunting and his large canvas entitled "The Otter Speared" but known less emotively as "The Otter Hunt" was painted in 1844 and shows the 4th Earl of Aberdeen's otter hounds hunting the banks of the river near Haddo House, Lord Aberdeen's seat in Aberdeenshire. An enthusiastic sportsman, in 1868 he stayed at Braemore, the estate of his old friend Sir John Fowler in whose game book he drew charming sketches of deer and not so charming sketches of fellow guests. His only portrait of a racehorse "Voltigeur" was painted for the Earl of Zetland in 1870 and he is known to have had very great trouble with this commission. An interesting report on the 1875 Summer Exhibition at Burlington House is recorded in "Bailys Magazine". It reminds its readers of the disastrous portrait of "Voltigeur" and reads as follows: "For after Sir Edwin's great "Voltigeur" fiasco his noble owner will be in no hurry to repeat the experiment among our Royal Academicians". Landseer fell hopelessly in love with the Duchess of Bedford and became a virtual alcoholic. His pen and ink sketch entitled "The Snooker Player", drawn obviously before 1873, shows that snooker was played considerably earlier than had been first thought. Landseer, whatever society made him later in his life, was a fine draughtsman and some of his early drawings are amongst his best. "The Great Pigeon Match at Chillingham", pen and black ink on H. Whatman paper (1833), 9⅜in.x14⅝in., s.&d. 1836, depicts Viscount Charles Augustus Bennett Ossulston (1810-1899), later the 6th Earl of Tankerville, Mr. W.M. Stanley and little Barnes, the keeper's son. Ossulston and Landseer met in the 1830s and became lifelong friends. Elected RA in 1831, Landseer was knighted in 1850 and in 1865 he refused the Presidency of the Royal Academy.

Lane, Albert (op.1856-1872)
Landscape painter who lived in North Devon and usually confined his subject matter to that part of the country. Exh. at the RA, BI and SS between 1856 and 1866. His "Landscape with Cricketers", one of a pair, entitles him to a Dictionary entry although the cricketers are secondary to the landscape.

Lane, George (op.1940-1955)
Motor racing artist who worked for "Motor" Magazine during the 1940s and 1950s. He usually painted in grisaille, covering racing events at Le Mans and Brooklands. Famous for his ability to depict speed and his accuracy in technical details.

Lane, Samuel (1780-1859)
Suffolk portrait painter who studied under Joseph Farington (q.v.) and under Sir Thomas Lawrence who employed him as his chief assistant. Lane over came his deafness and partial dumbness to build up a most successful practice. His portrait of Lord George Bentinck (1802-1848), one of the ablest administrators in the history of horse racing, painted in 1836, 50⅜in.x 39⅞in., hangs in the National Portrait Gallery London.

Lane, Theodore (1800-1828)
Painter in oil and watercolour of several sporting subjects including the celebrated dog "Billy" killing 100 rats at the Westminster Pit (etched and pub. Knight and

Lacey 1825). Dogs were backed to kill a given number of rats within a set time, the dogs being weighed, since weight in relation to performance was crucial, and timed by a stop watch. The sport is said to persist today in the "Black Country". Lane, who was apprenticed to the topographer, Joseph Charles Barrow, exh. seven paintings at the RA including a portrait of a dog in 1816, seven at BI and three at SS between 1800 and 1828. His portrait entitled "A Gouty Angler", s.&d. 1828 is in the Tate Gallery Collection. He also collaborated with the sporting journalist Pierce Egan on "The Life of an Actor, Peregrine Proteus" (1825) which had twenty-seven colour plates and many woodcuts, and illus. "Anecdotes of the Turf" (1827). Lane, who was also an engraver, produced a number of humorous prints including "A Trip to Ascot Races" (1827) and his drawing of "The Game of Rackets" was etched in aquatint by G. Hunt. He died tragically at the age of twenty-eight by falling through a skylight in Gray's Inn Road and was so badly mutilated that he was only recognisable by his card case. The RA ran a subscription for his widow.

Lange, Janet (op.1855-1865)
French illustrator who, despite his name, was male and who according to Vizetelly (see Ebenezer Landells) was an artist "whose reputation stood high as a delineator of military episodes, court pageants and the like". His painting depicting "Napoleon III Shooting at Compiègne" (1865), 37in.x74in., is a particularly fine work and was auctioned at the Mentmore sale in 1977 by Sotheby's. Lange was also a painter of hawking scenes, in the romantic style. His "Lady of the Manor", an oil painting of which the artist himself made a print, shows a lady riding side-saddle, a hawk returning (unusually) to her gloved right fist. Collection Bibliotèque Nationale, Paris.

Langlois, J. (op.c.1890-1895)
Painter, almost exclusively of pictures of terriers which he very often painted in pairs. Langlois, who usually signed but very rarely dated his work, appears to have operated at the end of the 19th century and may have been of French extraction.

Laning, Edward (1908-1981)
American modernist who studied at the Art Institute Chicago and under Max Weber at the Art Students League in New York (1926). He was highly influenced by John Sloan (q.v.) and Kenneth Hayes Miller and became an ardent Realist. His urban scapes include a fine baseball scene entitled "Saturday Afternoon at Sportsman's Park" which Laning painted in 1939, 36in.x32in., the Gladstone Collection of Baseball Art. Laning worked for "Life" magazine during the war years (1943/4).

Lanqueville, E.
See Longueville, E.

Lanyon, Ellen (b.1926)
American figure artist whose portrait of "A Tennis Player", 72in.x48in., was auctioned in Chicago in 1986.

Laporte, George Henry (1799-1873)
Animal painter to HRH the Duke of Cumberland and the King of Hanover. The Hanover Museum hangs his

"Cheval et Piqueur". He contributed forty-three plates to the old "Sporting Magazine" and exh. at SS between 1825 and 1838. Sporting titles include "Dead Game", "Yorick and his Steed", "Study of a Brood Mare" and "A Race - A Sketch". He was a founder member of the Royal Institute and he first exh. at the BI in 1818. Laporte specialised in equestrian paintings of fox-hunting, racing, coaching and shooting subjects. He worked in both oil and watercolour and was presumably taught to draw by his father, the draughtsman and etcher, John Laporte (1761-1839), who was drawing master at Addiscombe Military Academy. An interesting painting dated 1847 shows an early painting of "A Horse Show" with a horse being examined in a tent. His painting of Captain Becher riding "The Bantam", s.&d. 1831, pencil and watercolour, was auctioned Neale & Son, Nottingham, 1988. Engravings after Laporte's sporting work include "Lords Cricket Ground", 5in.x 7½in., by Ebenezer Stalker and "Coursing and Racing" (1860) by Henry A. Papprill (b.1816).

Laroon (Lauron), Marcellus II (1648/9-1701/2)
Portrait painter, draughtsman and engraver, the second son of Marcellus Laroon I, a French artist who settled in the Hague in the early years of the 17th century. Laroon II came to England as a young man and became studio assistant to Godfrey Kneller (q.v.). He is included in this Dictionary for his twenty-four fencing drawings which were engraved by William Elder and others and pub. as "The Art of Defence" in two issues (1699). Collection British Museum and The Paul Mellon Collection, Upperville, Va, USA.

Laroon (Lauron), Marcellus, III (1679-1772)
Although not normally an artist of sporting subjects his painting in the Tate Gallery "A Hunting Party" merits this artist's inclusion in the Dictionary. Born in Chiswick, son of Marcellus Laroon II (q.v.). Laroon became a soldier, retiring with the rank of Captain in 1732, although his painting career seems to have started some time before his retirement. He seems to have settled in Oxford where he died.

Laserstein, Lotte (b.1898)
German-born artist who has lived in Kalmar, Sweden since 1937. Studied art for six years (1919-1925) at the Berlin Academy, under Erich Wolfsfeld. Her interesting painting entitled "The Tennis Player" was exh. at the Belgrave Gallery, London in November 1987. Tennis was always Laserstein's game and probably her only real relaxation from work. She used to play with Erich Wolfsfeld, a fellow enthusiast, and they were both coached by Laserstein's athletic model, Traute Rose. Laserstein paints in a powerfully realistic style. Her first pupil was Gottfried Meyer (q.v.) (1931) whose work she undoubtedly influenced ("The Fencer" 1934).

Laskowski, François (1869-1952)
Born in Poland, studied art in Strasburg and Paris. He painted several sports scenes in watercolour, including "A Crafty Fox", "Jumping a Fence" and "The Bicyclist", but he is best remembered for his poster designs which were widely compared with those of Forain, de Feure, Valloton and Ibels. Laskowski rarely

exh. in his lifetime and much of his best work was produced in Europe, where he worked for the publisher and impresario, Riccordi, in Milan. Laskowski lived in England for some time and died at Minehead in 1952. He is relatively little known in England but, in the exchange of artistic ideals between pre-1st World War Paris and Milan, his work assumes a significant importance in the development of "belle epoque" poster design.

"Latakia"
The nom de plume used by the croquet contributor to "The Field", Walter Whitmore Jones (1831-1872). He wrote the "field" rules of croquet which were pub. in "The Field" in 1866.

Latham, Molly M. (op.1920-1938)
Equestrian artist, wife of the watercolour painter Harold Latham, RI. Lived in Sussex for some years painting Sussex hunting scenes with a very competent hand. "The South Down Hunt at Ditchling Potteries", s.&d. 1936, and "The Leaconfield Hunt" near Plaistow, with Lady Leaconfield in the foreground, s.&d. '34, are two good examples of this artist's work. Molly Latham exh. at Ackermanns in 1938.

La Thangue, Henry Herbert, RA (1859-1929)
Distinguished "plein air" painter of landscapes who studied at South Kensington, Lambeth and the RA Schools (1874-1877) where he was a Gold Medallist. He also studied at the Ecole des Beaux Arts under Gérome. He is included in this Dictionary for "Resting after the Game", s.&d. 1888, exh. Spinks, London. This painting shows the artist's wife resting after a game of lawn tennis and may well have been inspired by Lavery's (q.v.) "Tennis Party".

Latoix, Gaspard (op.1882-1909)
Painter of equestrian scenes and very often of Indians riding their ponies. Exh. widely at the leading London galleries.

Lauder, Charles James, RSW, RGI (1841-1920)
Portrait painter and of architectural subjects, son of James Thompson Lauder who was also a portrait painter. Studied art at Glasgow School of Design, under Heath Wilson. Exh. at the principal London Galleries from 1890. His portrait of Sir John Aird in hunting costume, painted in 1874, 15½in.x19½in., was auctioned Christie's 1975. Elected RSW (1885). Resigned (1913).

Laurence, Frank (op.1879)
A pair of equestrian paintings, "Jumping a Dry Stone Wall" and "The Refusal", s.&d. 1879, 28½in.x26½in., were auctioned Bonhams 1985.

Laurent, Alfred Joseph (b.1922)
Belgian-born portrait and landscape painter and an illustrator. Studied under the Dutch painter Paul Daemen. Escaped to England from Belgium in 1940 and married an English girl. Commissioned by International Artists to paint "The Amateur Golf Championship" held at Formby, Lancashire (1958) for the Wiggins Teape Group.

Laurie, Robert (c.1755-1836)
London-born portrait painter and mezzotint engraver of portraits, caricatures and sporting subjects. Laurie

invented a method of printing mezzotints in colour for which he received a premium from the Society of Arts in 1776. "Woodcock Shooting" shows the Laurie family with their friends, the Bosanquets, s.&d. 1824, 25½in.x 29in., auctioned Sotheby's 1982.

Lavery, Sir John, RA, RSA, RHA, PRP, HROI, NPS, NS, IS (1856-1941)

Belfast-born portrait, figure and landscape painter in both oil and watercolour. Studied art at the Haldane Academy in Glasgow, Heatherleys School in London and at the Académie Julian and the Atelier Colarossi in Paris. Highly influenced by the "plein air" artist, Jules Bastien Lepage (1848-1884). The "plein air" movement was totally unacceptable in England at the time when genre paintings were all the rage. Lavery returned to Glasgow in 1881 and exh. at the RSA. Exh. at the Paris Salon from 1883 and at the RA from 1886. Settled in London (1897). He turned increasingly to portraiture and after his move to London spent the winters in Tangier where he kept a studio. Elected RSA (1896), RHA (1906), NPS (1910), RA (1921), NS (1930) and PRP (1932). He was knighted in 1918. Lavery painted many social sporting scenes including his impression of "The Maidenhead Regatta" which he exh. at the ROI (1932) and which "The Connoisseur" described as "being on the verge of prismatic". He is probably best known for his painting "The Tennis Party" which he exh. at the RA (1886) and which is now in Aberdeen AG. Several sketches for the final work are known and his watercolour "A Rally" showing a mixed double at lawn tennis is in the Glasgow AG. Golf was also a sport that Lavery painted several times including "The Golf Course at North Berwick", "Nancy, Lady Astor playing golf at North Berwick" (1920) and a large and handsome oil of "North Berwick Golf Course from the Ladies Tee" (1918). He painted this scene again in 1922 when he was staying with Sir Patrick Ford. His painting of the "Jockey's Dressing room at Ascot" is in the National Gallery and two further racing paintings "A View of the Royal Enclosure during the Ascot Gold Cup", painted in 1922, 16in.x30in., and "The Derby", 2ft.x2ft.6in., painted in the same year, were auctioned Christie's 1991. The former painting sold to a private collector at £56,000.

Law, Ernest George (1862-1929)

Landscape painter, mostly in watercolour, who exh. at SS between 1891 and 1893. Titles include "The Game-keeper".

Lawrence, Jacob (b.1917)

American painter of narrative, urban scenes who used the game of baseball to define the essence of living in the ghettos of New York's Harlem where Lawrence was brought up. He studied at the Harlem Art Workshop which was sponsored by the Works Progress Administration's Federal Art Project. Lawrence was the first black artist to have a retrospective exhibition at the Museum of Modern Art. Lawrence painted "Strike" (depicting a fast game of baseball) in 1949. This was two years after Jackie Rodgers joined the Brooklyn Dodgers and one year after the Cleveland Indians added the great Negro superstar and pitcher, Satchell Page, to their team.

Lawrence, Joshua (op.1840-1842)

Exh. two watercolour portraits at SS in 1842 from a London address. His portrait "A Chestnut Hunter held by a Groom", s.&d. 1840, 17in.x23in., was auctioned Christie's 1972.

Lawrence, Richard (op.1793-1816)

Animal painter and sculptor, and a veterinary surgeon in Birmingham. He exh. five paintings at the RA between 1793 and 1814 including "Portraits of two Horses at the Veterinary College" (1793), "A Stag Swimming" (1807), "A portrait of the celebrated Durham Ox" and "A portrait of a Hunter, the property of Lord Middleton" (1814).

Leader, Benjamin Williams, RA (1831-1923)

Landscape painter from Worcester. Included in this Dictionary for his enchanting croquet scene entitled "The Croquet Party", 9in.x12in., painted in 1871, auctioned Christie's 1991. "The Croquet Party" shows the Malvern hills in the distance, a Worcestershire background which Leader used several times in his landscapes. Leader, who was born Benjamin Williams but changed his surname to distinguish himself from all the other artist Williams to whom he was not related, exh. at the RA (1857-1922). Elected RA (1898).

Leakey, James (1775-1865)

Exeter landscape painter who exh. twelve paintings at the RA, mostly views in the West Country but also portraits and figure subjects. His busy painting of the Red Lion Inn entitled "Good Entertainment for Man and Horse", s.&d. 1823, 23½in.x17in., was auctioned Phillips 1979.

Lear, Edward (1812-1888)

Fine topographical watercolourist. The son of a stock-broker and the youngest of twenty-one children. Lear worked for the 13th Earl of Derby at Knowsley between 1831 and 1836, producing meticulously detailed drawings of birds and animals for Lord Derby's "Knowsley Menagerie" (1856). The collection of prints and drawings that he built up formed the nucleus of the collection of the City of Liverpool Museums, now the Merseyside County Museums. His watercolour "A Still Life with Pheasants and other Game Birds", 7in.x9in., was auctioned Sotheby's 1981.

Leatham, Ruth M. (op.1908)

A watercolour entitled "Better Luck Next Time - A Hunting Accident", s.&d. 1908, 9½in.x15in., was auctioned Bonhams 1987.

Leavers, Lucy A. (op.1881-1905)

Figure, animal and domestic painter from Nottingham.

Lee, Bruce

Contemporary painter of the American football star, Joe Ehrmann, Baltimore Colts defensive tackle, water-colour, 1980.

Lee, Frederick Richard, RA (1798-1879)

Landscape artist from Devon who painted many river fishing scenes and fish still lifes. Entered the RA Schools (1818), exh. RA (1824 to 1870). Elected RA (1838). He sometimes collaborated with the animal painter T.S. Cooper (q.v.) and with Edwin Landseer (q.v.). His still life painting "Pike and Perch on a Bank with Fishing Tackle" painted in 1858 was exh. Sheffield City AG (Victorian Paintings 1968 No. 201). His paintings of angling subjects include "Fishing a Highland River", s.&d. 1851, 28½in.x36½in., Sotheby's 1982, "English River Fish on a River Bank with a Creel", s.&d. 1834, 29in.x40in., Sotheby's (NY) 1987 and "The Angler" s.&d. 1839, 12in.x17in., Sotheby's (Sussex) 1983. A painting of a Percheron mare and foal, s.&d. 1863, 16in.x24¼in., and inscr. "First Prize Royal Show at Exeter Meeting, 1863" was auct. Christie's (NY) 1987.

Lee, Rupert (attrib.)

"Lords Test Match", 8½in.x4in., exh. the Leicester Galleries "Works by Artists of Fame and Promise" No. 41, auctioned Christie's (Sth. Ken.) 1989.

Leech, John (1817-1864)

Sporting artist and an even more talented illustrator. The son of a coffee house keeper at Ludgate Hill. Educated at Charterhouse, with the novelist William Thackeray, a fellow student who became a lifelong friend. Leech started his career as a medical student at St. Bartholomews Hospital but abandoned this in 1838 to pursue an artistic career. Leech was virtually self-taught but took a crash course in etching from George Cruikshank (q.v.) and one in wood engraving from John Orrin Smith (1799-1843). He became a regular contributor to "Punch" from its first issues, eventually sharing about a third of the work with "Dicky" Doyle (q.v.). He is responsible for creating the famous pictorial characters of "Handley Cross" (1854). A keen huntsman, Leech hunted with the Puckeridge so that his numerous hunting sketches usually have Hertfordshire backgrounds. He became a close friend of the artist Sir John Everett Millais (q.v.) with whom he went fishing and shooting in Scotland where he found the perfect scenery for the salmon fishing, deer stalking and grouse shooting exploits of his comic character, Mr. Briggs. Millais was also responsible for persuading Leech to paint in oils, a medium in which Leech was never totally happy - viz. his "Difficult Going with the Devon and Somerset Staghounds". Some twenty-five marvellous original angling sketches were presented to the Piscatorial Society in 1871 by a new member of the Society, Mr. T.H. Parker, as a reproach to the Society for not being more welcoming to new members "so that they might have something amusing to look at". Leech contributed work to "The Illustrated London News" including "Humours of the Road" and his charming croquet sketch to "Punch" entitled "A Nice Game for Two or More". This was pub. as a chromolithograph by Agnew and Son in 1865. British Museum, London.

Lee-Hankey, William, RWS, RI, ROI, RE, NS (1869-1952)

Landscape painter in oil and an etcher who is included in this Dictionary for his illustrations to "The Compleat Angler" (Walton), 1913.

Leemans, Antonius (1631-1673)

Dutch painter of hunting scenes. The elder brother of Johannes Leemans (q.v.) with whom he sometimes collaborated.

Leemans, Johannes (1633-1688)

Dutch painter of hunting still lifes and trompe-l'oeils. He occasionally collaborated with his elder brother Antonius Leemans (q.v.).

Lees, Caroline

Contemporary painter of hunting, shooting and fishing still lifes in watercolour. Born in Shropshire, she received training under Ralph Nuttal Smith at the Colchester School of Art. She extended her studies in drawing and watercolour painting under Lesley Exton and Brockie Stevenson at the Corcoran School of Art in Washington DC. Elected member of the Washington Water Color Association.

Lees, Charles, RSA (1800-1880)

Scottish portrait painter with a keen interest in sporting subjects. Pupil of Sir Henry Raeburn, RA (q.v.). Lees painted "The Golfers, St Andrews" in 1847. It shows a match at St Andrews, played in 1841, between Sir David Baird and Sir Ralph Anstruther on one side, and Major Playfair and John Campbell of Saddell on the other. Three of the four players are also featured in the painting by Sir Francis Grant (q.v.) "First Meeting of the North Berwick Golf Club". Lee's painting was engraved (in black and white) by Charles E. Wagstaff and pub. in Edinburgh by Hill in 1850 (Scottish National Portrait Gallery and the R&A Collection). The crowded scene is on the fifteenth green of the Old Course. (Note the little girl offering refreshments in the form of lemonade on the right of the picture.) The original painting , measuring 4ft.3in.x7ft., is privately owned by a descendant of one of the spectators. Lees ranks high amongst golfing artists since he also painted "A Golf Match" (1847) and "Summer Evening at Musselburgh" (1859). "The Grand Curling Match of the Royal Caledonian Curling Club at Linlithgow", 1853, 59⅛in.x96½in., by courtesy of The Royal Caledonian Curling Club. An engraving by John Le Conte after this work (1858), 22½in.x37¼in., is recorded. "Curling on Duddingston Loch" painted in 1866. Private collection. Elected RSA (1830).

Lees, Derwent, NEAC (1885-1931)

Australian-born landscape painter in both oil and watercolour who was lame from an early age, due to a fall from a horse. He studied art in London at the Slade School, under Fred Brown and Henry Tonks, (qq.v) and taught at the School (1908-1918). Exh. at the NEAC and was elected a member in 1911. Held his first one-man show at the Chenil Galleries in 1914, the same year that he painted "The Billiard Hall", 16in.x24in., Sotheby's. He travelled widely but had a particular affection for the South of France where he spent some time. His portrait together with that of his wife, was painted by A.A. McEvoy (1878-1927) who exh. the painting at the NEAC in 1915. Lees was stricken by an incurable mental disease by 1930 when he gave his last exhibition at the Redfern Gallery, London W1.

Lees, F.J. (op.1865-1895)

London landscape and portrait painter in both oil and watercolour who specialised in angling subjects. His portraits of two young men fishing and counting their catch, a pair both s.&d. 1869, each 15in.x24in., were auctioned Christie's (Sth. Ken.) 1985. A historically fascinating, but repulsive watercolour study of a pike attempting to swallow a barbel, s.&d. 1895, 8¾in.x 13¾in., is in the collection of the Wingfield Sporting Gallery, London. The inscription reads "An amazing incident showing a Jack Pike of 6lbs. attempting to swallow a Barbel of 13/3lbs. - found on Monkey Island 1895". Lees exh. one portrait at the RA in 1866 and one elsewhere.

Leeson, Lawrence Joseph, ATD (b.1930)

This artist contributed "Football Jerseys", 25in.x30in., to the FE.

Leffel, David

Contemporary painter of the American football star, O.J. Simpson, Buffalo Bill's running back, oil (1974). Collection National Football League, New York.

Leftwich, George Robert (op.1875-1911)

Listed (Wood) as a painter of domestic subjects to which one must add equestrian subjects, particularly horse racing. His very fine racing painting, 29in.x43½in., of Fred Archer up at the St. Leger passing the crowded grandstand poses the question, which St. Leger, since Archer won six between 1877-1886? Similarly "Charles Wood up at the Derby", since Wood won three Derbys between 1883-1897. Neither jockey won their Derby or St. Leger in the same year as each other. Leftwich exh. at the London Salon, the Dudley Gallery and the Manchester City Gallery until 1911.

Leigh, Conrad Heighton (b.1883)

Brighton landscape painter and illustrator whose interesting golfing scene showing players putting on the tenth green at East Brighton c.1940 shows the village of Ovingdean and the St. Dunstan's building in the background, 15½in.x20½in. Leigh contributed work to "The Sketch", "Woman" and other magazines. His fine action watercolour, 14in.x18in., of a hunting scene entitled "At the Gallop" is repro. (plate 305) in Grant's "Dictionary of British Artists" (1900-1950). Leigh studied art in Brighton, under William H. Bond, at the Slade School and at the Académie Julian in Paris. He was a member of the Brighton Arts Club.

Leigh, William Robinson (1866-1955)

American painter, illustrator and writer who won the Corcoran Prize for art at the age of twelve and subsequently studied at the Royal Academy in Munich. In 1906 he visited the American West and returned annually to paint the land and its people. His painting "Western Sports", 24in.x18in., is amongst Leigh's most successful representation of the Indian world and depicts a competition in which each contestant, riding at top speed, had to lower himself alongside his horse and, without breaking pace, pick up the marker and cross the finishing line before a large crowd of enthusiastic spectators. (Thos. Gilcrease.)

Leigh-Pemberton, John, ROI, NS (b.1911)

Natural history painter and of some sporting subjects including "The Meet", s.&d. 1951, 40in.x50in., a romantic conception of the sport designed for a panel in the first class lounge of SS "Uganda", set in an 18th century background. "The Huntsman" and three other hunting paintings were auctioned Phillips 1987. Leigh-Pemberton studied art in London (1928-1931) and exh. at the RA, ROI and other leading London and provincial galleries and abroad. Elected ROI (1936).

Leighton, Clare (1901-1989)

Artist and wood engraver of country, animal and some sporting subjects. Born London, daughter of the author Robert Leighton. Studied at the Brighton School of Art and then at the Slade School. Became a member of the Society of Wood Engravers (1928). Left England (1939) and became an American citizen (1945). Publications include "The Farmers Year", "Country Matters" and "Sometimes Never".

Leighton, Nicolas Winfield Scott (1849-1898)

American equestrian artist, particularly of trotting scenes including "Hunting on a Grey", "Mrs. Abbott of Keane in her Hackney Chaise", "Mounted Gentleman with Dogs Admiring the View", "Lady Foxy" with her owner, Dudley Pinkham Rogers, a portrait of the thoroughbred "La Martine" and Leighton's fine portrait of "St. Julien" the trotting hero who held the world record in 1880. Leighton, who came from Maine, established a studio in Boston, working for Currier and Ives who produced more than 650 prints of racing trotters in the fifty years up to 1895. Certainly Leighton's most dramatic painting of a trotting race is "The Sealskin Brigade" which he painted for A.W. Richmond, who is seen in the centre of the picture driving the grey trotter "Hopeful". "St. Julien" is squeezed into the background.

Leit, C.H. (op.1875)

"After the Hunt", a grey hunter and four foxhounds, s.&d. 1875, 26in.x33in., auctioned Bonhams 1987.

Leitch, William Leighton, RI (1804-1883)

Glasgow born landscape painter in watercolour who moved to London in 1830. Included in this Dictionary for his watercolour study of Izaak Walton standing on the bank of a river, with his fishing tackle, tying a fly. Inscr. "Piscatoribus Sacrum" on a label on the frame, 6⅜in.x4¼in. Auctioned Christie's 1990. Leitch, who taught drawing and painting to the members of the royal family for twenty-two years, was elected RI in 1862.

Lek, Karel, RCA, ATD (b.1929)

Dutch-born painter who studied at Liverpool College of Art. He contributed a wood engraving, 8in.x6in., entitled "Off to the Match" to the FE.

Leland, John B. (op.1833-1834)

Painter and sculptor who exh. a group of "English Greyhounds from Nature" at RBA (1834). His portrait of "Brown Arrow", a greyhound in a landscape, painted in 1833, 10in.x14in., was auctioned Woolley and Wallis 1987.

Leman, Alicia J. (op.1891)
Exh. one sporting painting at the RA entitled "Spotting a Winner" in 1891 from a Putney address.

Lemoine, P. (18th century)
French painter of balloon subjects including a hot air balloon rising from its platform surrounded by spectators, signed, 18½in.x15½in., and a pair entitled "The Ballooning Exhibition", 26in.x35in., auctioned Sotheby's 1972.

Lemon, Arthur (1850-1912)
Painter of genre pastoral scenes and of some hunting studies, including his portrait of an "Irish Huntswoman Riding Sidesaddle", 19in.x17½in., Phillips 1985. Lemon, who spent ten years of his early youth as a cowboy in California, was an excellent equestrian painter. Unfortunately for sporting art it was not a subject that he widely pursued after his return to Europe and his art studies in Paris under Carolus Duran. Lemon was highly influenced by the Italian Classicists and spent a large part of his life in Italy. Exh. widely from 1878.

Lendon, Warwick William, SGA (b.1883)
Early 20th century illustrator who contributed to "Punch", "The Sketch" and "Tatler". Exh. at the ROI, RP, SGA, NEAC and in the provinces between 1918 and 1921 and was elected SGA 1925. An amusing pair of golfing cartoons were auctioned by Hamptons (Godalming), 25 April 1990, showing an irate colonel in plus fours shaking his fist as his golf ball disappears over a cliff.

Lenkewicz, Robert
Eccentric 20th century Plymouth artist who paints in the "Grand Design" series - one to two hundred paintings in each series - as for example his "Observations of Education". Has tended lately towards paintings of the sexually explicit and he has been called "the 20th century Van Gogh" by the BBC who featured his work in a programme. His portrait entitled "The Young Boxer", 40in.x30in., auctioned Michael Newman 1989, is part of a sports series.

Lens, Peter Paul (op.18th century)
London-born miniature painter, the son of Bernard Lens III (1682-1740) and brother of Andrew Benjamin Lens. Sketches of racehorses were exh. by the British Sporting Art Trust at the Tate Gallery in 1980 (Halifax Collection).

Le Roy, F. (op.1843)
A watercolour painting of jockeys mounting their racehorses, s.&d. 1843, 10in.x11½in., was auctioned Sotheby's (Sussex) 1987.

Leslie, Charles Robert, RA (1794-1859)
Painter of historical genre, the father of George Dunlop Leslie (q.v.). His portrait of a fencer entitled "Le Bourgeois Gentilhomme" (1841) (V & A Museum).

Leslie, George Dunlop, RA (1835-1921)
Landscape and figure painter whose portrait of "Bessie Andrew holding a Tennis Racket" and in tennis attire, s.&d. 1888, was exh. Mallams, Cheltenham 1984. Leslie studied at the RA Schools in 1856 where he exh. and was elected an RA in 1876. Son of the Royal Academician, Charles Leslie (q.v.).

Leslie, Sir John (1st Bt.) (1822-1916)
A good amateur portrait and figure painter who studied art under K.F. Sohn in Dusseldorf. "A Fast Forty Minutes in the Vale of Belvoir" was painted in 1853 as a fresco for his friend Lord Bradford, then Lord Newport. Hunting celebrities of the day included in the painting are Sir Richard Sutton, The Duke of Rutland, The Earl Wilton, Lord Forrester and Mr. Gilmore. Leslie was a great sportsman and an excellent shot. A patron of the prize ring, he watched the Sayers/Heenan fight, painted by John Brown and Rowbotham (qq.v.), and won a Grand Military on his own horse. He hunted at Melton Mowbray and played cricket for Oxford (1843). He was also an original member of I. Zingari and a good fencer but above all he was an artist who was the friend of such as Landseer, Millais, Watts, Holman Hunt, Grant, Marochetti and Lord Leighton. He exh. at the RA between 1853 and 1883, BI and SS and was created a baronet in 1876. His obituary appeared in "Bailys" magazine 1916.

Lessells, J. (op.1905)
A pen and ink drawing of the golfing professional "Old" Tom Morris, dated 1905 is recorded.

Lessore, Jules, RI, RBA (1849-1898)
Sussex artist who exh. at SS between 1880 and 1892. Sporting titles include "Hounds at Old Shoreham". Lessore was born in Paris and studied under his father, the artist Emile Aubert Lessore (1805-1876) and F.J. Barrias. Exh. widely from 1879 in England and from 1864 at the Paris Salon. Elected RI (1888).

L'Estrange, Rowland (1869-1919)
Alias "Armadillo" or "Ao". He produced nine cartoons for "Vanity Fair", all after 1900.

Levack, John (op.1856-1857)
Scottish painter of a fine painting "Curling at Rawyards, Loch Airdrie, Lanarkshire" (1857) with the Blue Doo Colliery in the Background, 5ft.x10ft. (Monklands District Council). Levack exh. two pictures at SS (1856-1857).

Levine, David (b.1926)
American painter whose striking oil painting of the dejected crowd at a baseball game entitled "Crowd at Ebbets Field" c.1960 anticipates Brooklyn Dodgers' loss. The artist cleverly portrays the total empathy of the fans with the players on the field. Levine was also a caustic caricaturist and used his skills to portray Leo "the Lip" Durocher, the Dodgers' aggressive short stop, in a brilliant pen and ink study in 1973.

Lewis, Charles George (1808-1880)
Leading engraver of sporting, animal and historical genre after his contemporaries' work. Born in Enfield, he was the son and pupil of F.C. Lewis Snr. (q.v.) and the brother of J.F. Lewis (q.v.). His plates included sporting work after F. Grant (q.v.), W. Evans (q.v.) and H. Calvert (q.v.). Lewis died in Sussex.

Lewis, Charles James, RI (1830-1892)

Landscape painter and of many angling scenes including "Waiting for a Catch", s.&d. 1863, and "Fishing Below a Mill", s.&d. 1864. The artist's studio sale was held by Christie's on 4 March 1893. Elected RI (1882).

Lewis, Frederick (op.1882-1903)

Exh. between 1882 and 1899 at the Walker AG, Liverpool. "A Ceremonial Carriage", s.&d. 1903 is a very fine watercolour and his watercolour "Taking the Fence", s.&d. 1890, 6½in.x11in., was auctioned Sotheby's 1985.

Lewis, Frederick Christian (1779-1856)

Brother of George R. Lewis (q.v.) and father of John F. Lewis (q.v.), F.C. Lewis, Jnr. (q.v.) and C.G. Lewis (q.v.). Landscape painter, etcher and stipple engraver of sporting subjects and landscapes after his own and his contemporaries' work. Studied at the RA Schools and became a pupil of the engraver J.C. Stadler. Engraved a number of sporting scenes including a portrait of "Mundig", winner of the Derby (1835) after C. Hancock (q.v.) and similar racehorse portraits.

Lewis, Frederick Christian "Indian", Jnr. (1813-1875)

Youngest son of F.C. Lewis (q.v.). A pupil of Sir Thomas Lawrence and a mezzotint engraver.

Lewis, George Robert (1782-1871)

Landscape, portrait and figure painter, the younger brother of F.C. Lewis (q.v.). Studied at the RA Schools, under Fuseli and worked with his brother in aquatint. Exh. at the RA (1805-1817), BI, SS, NWS and elsewhere between 1820 and 1859. His portrait of a gentleman standing full length, holding a shot gun with his dogs and dead game in the foreground, s.&d. 1828, 29½in.x24½in., was auctioned Sotheby's 1987.

Lewis, J. (op.1902)

A portrait by this artist of "Messum's Boat House", s.&d. 1902, was exh. at Orleans House Gallery at Twickenham. The artist is possibly Miss Janet Lewis (ex.1891-1894), the Chelsea landscape painter.

Lewis, John Frederick, RA (1805-1876)

Animal and sporting painter who worked almost exclusively in watercolour except in extreme youth and in the last eighteen years of his life. The son of Frederick Christian Lewis (q.v.), the engraver, who wanted his son to follow him in his career but made a curious bargain that if John Frederick could sell a painting in a London exhibition he would allow him to study art. Lewis succeeded in selling a painting entitled "Morning - Ploughing" in 1820 at an exhibition held at the BI. He was not quite fifteen. The bargain struck, he studied art under the portrait painter Sir Thomas Lawrence (1820/1821). He exh. fourteen paintings at the RA between 1821 and 1827; eight of these were of dogs but his main exhibit "Buck Shooting in Windsor Great Park with portraits of His Majesty's deer keepers" (1825) now hangs in the Tate Gallery. From 1824 George IV employed him to paint the royal animals and sporting subjects, a commission which probably lasted until he went abroad in 1826, where he was to live for a large part of his life. After 1827 Lewis' animal paintings began to give way to topography and he painted a great deal in Europe and the Middle East. He was a childhood friend of Sir Edwin Landseer (q.v.) with whom he studied and drew animals at Exeter and whom he depicted in a watercolour entitled "Change in the Strand, Fishing". This was exh. at the OWS in 1830 (No. 95) under the title of "Piscator" with Izaac Walton's quotation "Look you, now you see him plain". The painting was auctioned Christie's (Gilbey sale) April 1940. "Spaniels Hunting", s.&d. September 1822, was exh. at the BI 1832 (No. 209) and "Ferreting in Ampthill Park", 31½in.x42½in., s.&d. 1825 was exh. at the BI, (No. 353).

Lewis, Judith (op.1750-1760)

A pair of interesting hunting scenes entitled "A Family Hunting Party", both s.&d. 1755/6, 24in.x40in., were exh. by Ackermanns at the Grosvenor House Antiques Fair and repro. in "Country Life" (5.6.86). The paintings were previously auctioned by Christie's in 1960.

Lewis, Michael (b.1943)

Studied Plymouth College of Art (1962-1965) and Hornsey College of Art (1965-1966). Taught art for two years in London before moving back to Devon where he taught until 1972. Solo exhibition at Crane Arts, London 1973. "The Cricket Match" (1978), 20in.x22in. (repro. "British Sporting Art in the 20th Century" by Stella Walker, pub. 1989).

Lewis, Thomas (ex.1837-1845)

Portrait painter who exh. at SS between 1837 and 1845 including a portrait of "- - - Scoles, the Celebrated Shot".

Lewsey, Tom (op.1946-1964)

Marine painter in oils very often of yachting and racing scenes. An original exhibitor at the first RSMA exhibition in 1946 with his "'Joyce' Winning at Cowes in a Force 7 Gale". He was a regular exhibitor thereafter, until 1964.

Leyendecker, Joseph Christian (1874-1951)

American painter and sought after magazine illustrator who studied at the Art Institute of Chicago and the Académie Julian in Paris. His painting "Baseball Scene of Batter, Catcher and Umpire" was repro. on the front cover of "Colliers" on 9 October 1915, 31in.x22in.

L'hote, André (1885-1962)

Prolific French portrait and figure painter whose fine Rugby football painting "Le Joue de Rugby", 58¼in.x 17½in., painted c.1917, was auctioned Sotheby's 1988. Lhote painted a number of football and rugby scenes and "Les Footballeurs", 18in.x22in., auctioned in 1989 made £29,630.

"Lib"

Alias Liberio Prosperi (q.v.).

Lichtenstein, Roy (b.1923)

American painter and comic strip artist whose large portrait entitled "Baseball Manager" (1963) is clearly derivative of a newspaper picture. Oil and magna on canvas, 68in.x58in. Blum Helman Gallery, New York.

Lie, Jonas (1880-1940)
American landscape painter who exh. at the National Academy of Design in 1924. His portrait entitled "The Hunter" was auctioned Sotheby's (NY) 1985.

Liebermann, Max (1847-1935)
German painter and illustrator of equestrian scenes, including polo. He worked in pen/black ink and brush with great effect.

Liedeaux, Michael (1881-1923)
"Mich". French poster artist of motoring subjects who usually signed his work "Mich".

Lier, Adolf Heinrich (1826-1882)
German landscape painter who included rustic and hunting scenes amongst his work. "Full Cry", a fox-hunting scene, 9½in.x 16½in., was auctioned Christie's 1983.

Liljefors, Bruno (1860-1939)
Swedish wildlife artist who painted fine and accurate studies of hawks and falcons.

Lindner, Daphne, ARE (b.1912)
Painter and etcher. Studied Cheltenham School of Art and the Royal College of Art where she gained a scholarship, the Robert Austin Prize and a silver medal. Elected ARE (1935). Exh. (1934-1937). Her etching entitled "All In Wrestling", s.&d. 1936, is in the collection of the British Museum.

Lindsay, Sir Ernest Daryl, ARWS (b.1889)
Australian-born landscape painter in oil and water-colour. Brother of the artists (Sir) Lionel Lindsay (1874-1961) and Norman Lindsay (1879-1969). Studied art at the Slade School (1919) and returned to Australia where he painted full time between 1919 and 1939. Exh. two paintings at the RA (1933), one entitled "The Findon Hunt". He also exh. at other leading London galleries and in Australia. Elected ARWS (1937). Keeper of the Prints, National Gallery of Victoria (1939-1941) and Director (1941-1956). Knighted (1956). Lindsay's wife, Joan, wrote the famous book "Picnic at Hanging Rock". His drawing of "The Melbourne Hounds", in pen, brown ink and brown/blue wash, 8¾in.x12¾in., s.&d. and inscr. "December 1st 1937 to Bobby Jenkins" was auctioned Sotheby's 1988. He signed his work "Daryl Lindsay".

Linklater, Barrie R. (b.1931)
Birmingham-born painter and illustrator who emigrated to Australia in 1957 but returned to London in 1961 when he began to specialise in portraits of people and horses. He studied at the Woolwich Polytechnic School of Art and his many commissions include those for H.R.H. the Duke of Edinburgh.

Linnell, John, Snr. (1792-1882)
Landscape painter, pupil of John Varley, the landscape artist as were William Hunt and William Mulready (qq.v.). Entered RA Schools (1805). Exh. at the RA (1807-1882), BI and OWS. The father-in-law of Samuel Palmer (q.v.). Linnell painted several games of cricket and collaborated with Samuel Palmer, whom he accompanied on his sketching tours, on at least one painting of angling. His work is repro. in the "Compleat Angler", 2 vols. (1893). Linnell first visited Palmer in 1828 at Shoreham, Kent, when he commissioned several nature studies. "The Game of Cricket", s.&d. 1874, 27½in.x38½in., auctioned Christie's 1963.

Lintz, Ernest (op.1875-1891)
London painter of domestic subjects. Exh. at SS between 1875 and 1884 including a painting entitled "Tug of War".

Lipscombe, Guy (1883-)
Motor artist in oil and pastel, illustrator and cartoonist. Joined "The Motor" magazine in about 1903 to take over their art department. Exh. at the RA, ROI and elsewhere between 1908 and 1937. Specialised in motor racing scenes where he featured races at Brooklands and other important European venues.

Livemont, Privat (1861-1936)
French illustrator and poster artist who was responsible for several early Automobile Club de France posters.

Livens, Horace Mann, RBA (1862-1936)
Landscape and poultry painter, etcher and engraver. Studied at Croydon School of Art and in Belgium and France. Exh. widely at the leading London galleries and elsewhere from 1883. Titles at SS include a study of a mare and colt and several of poultry. Elected RBA (1895). Member of Society of Twenty Five Artists. Included in this Dictionary for his painting of football entitled "Wembley Stadium", s.&d. 1923, The Harry Langton Collection, London.

Lizars, William Home (1788-1859)
Scottish painter and etcher of genre and natural history subjects. Included in this Dictionary for the first ten plates he engraved for J.J. Audubon's "Birds of America" (1827-1838) and the illustrations he made for Sir W. Jardine's "British Salmonidae" (1839-1841). Lizars studied at the Trustees Academy in Edinburgh where he was born and collaborated with his father, the line engraver D. Lizars.

Lloyd, Edward (op.1846-d.1891)
Equestrian artist from Ellesmere in Shropshire. Lloyd's work includes sporting dogs but his portraits of horses are usually painted in a landscape. The grey hack and charger "Snowdrop" was a favourite subject for Lloyd and he painted the horse several times, the first dated 1853. Lloyd painted for a number of patrons, including the Watkin Williams-Wynn family. He exh. a painting of sheep at the RA in 1861, apparently his only year to exhibit.

Lloyd, Thomas Ivester
See Ivester-Lloyd

Lloyd, Thomas James, RWS (1849-1910)
Landscape painter who exh. from 1870 at the RA, SS, OWS and elsewhere. A comment in "The Art Journal", August 1877 on his RA exhibits that year, states "This artist is making rapid strides and bids fair to become one of our great landscape painters". Lloyd painted several shooting and angling scenes including "Shooting on the Wild Brooks", (1875), "Man Fishing from a Punt", "Chasing the Grey Geese", etc.

Lloyd, W. Stuart, RBA (op.1875-1929)

Landscape painter in watercolour who lived in Brighton and who is included in this Dictionary for his RA exhibit "Wild Duck Shooting" (1883) and "Salmon Fishing, Christchurch Bay, Dorset" (1894). Lloyd exh. at the RA (1875-1902). Elected RBA (1879).

Lobley, Robert, FRSA (b.1934)

Lobley spent his childhood in the Derbyshire countryside. Studied art and wood engraving at St. Martin's School of Art and was Head of Art at a large independent school. He has written and illus. books on painting and other subjects and his work has been featured in "The Field" and on Channel 4 TV. He has painted a number of sporting scenes including "Cricket at Kew Green" and "An Early Morning Shoot". Articles noting this artist's ability to capture the atmosphere of British sporting life in watercolour have appeared in both "Country Life" and "The Field" written by Nicholas Usherwood.

Lock, Anton (1893-)

Painter, etcher and wood engraver of landscapes, equestrian and animal subjects. Studied at Westminster School of Art, under Walter Sickert (1910-1912) and at the Bolt Court School of Lithography (1912-1914). Exh. at the RA, RBA, ROI, RWS, PS, the provinces and at the Paris Salon (1927-1935). Lock held a one-man exhibition entitled "Horses" at the Leger Galleries in 1932 which was opened by James Pryde (q.v.), on the face of it a curious choice since Pryde was not known to favour horses.

Lock(e), William, of Norbury (1767-1847)

Painter of historical and some sporting subjects, son of William Lock(e) (1732-1810). Pupil of Johann Fuseli (1741-1825) by whom he was highly influenced. Lock(e) was also an enthusiastic sportsman as indicated by Fanny Burney in a letter written to her sister, Mrs. Susan Phillips, from Norbury during the winter of 1806. "William Locke has lately taken an unaccountable fancy to hunting, but all the good that has accrued from this amusement is that it has given rise to a few spirited sketches of hunters and huntsmen". It seems that Lock(e)'s enthusiasm for the sporting life was not confined to the hunting field for two studies of the pugilist Johnson, inscr. in ink "Johnson 1790" and three studies of racehorses approaching the winning post are in the Paul Mellon Collection, Upperville, Va, USA. According to Joseph Farington (Diary, 5 July 1803) Lock(e)'s pictures were terrible but so far as his sporting sketches are concerned, this would seem to be a harsh criticism.

Lockey (Locky), Rowland (c.1565-1616)

Portrait painter and miniaturist who studied c.1581 under the miniature painter, Nicholas Hilliard (1547-1618/9). Lockey's portrait of King James VI of Scotland, later James I of England (1566-1625) was painted for Hardwick Hall between 1608/1610. The painting shows the King with a falcon on his fist about to go hunting - a favourite sport of his - and the date, 1574, is inscr. on the top right-hand corner of the portrait. The date would make the King fourteen years old which seems about correct although the portrait was obviously painted from an earlier work since Lockey himself would only have been about nine years old in 1574. Quite apart from this detective work, Lockey was a known copyist, vis-à-vis his copy of Holbein's "More Family" at Nostell Priory (1592) and the NPG (1593).

Lockwood, Lucy (op.1925-1935)

Lived in Melrose, Scotland. Painter of equestrian subjects, portraits of hunters and some hunting scenes.

Lockyer, Thomas (op.c.1894-1910)

Painter for the Royal Worcester Porcelain Company who included a number of angling scenes in his work. His "jewel like" watercolour "Three Trout in a Stream" shows an imaginative study of an otherwise potentially boring subject.

Loder, Edwin (1827-c.1885)

Animal painter including portraits of hunters, cattle and dogs. The son of James Loder (q.v.). He appears to have served in the army (1846-1866) when he was discharged as unfit for further service and was made an out-pensioner at the Royal Chelsea Hospital. He returned to Bath to paint, but his work was never of the same quality as that of his father.

Loder, James, of Bath (op.1820-1860)

Talented portrait painter of equestrian and animal subjects, including coach and carriage horses and racehorses. His work is usually s.&d. and inscr. "Bath". At his best, Loder's work is of a very high quality which recent prices at auction do not fully reflect.

Lodge, George Edward (1860-1954)

Highly talented bird and wildlife painter who was born (Lincolnshire) in the same year as his friend Archibald Thorburn (q.v.). This coincidence was further confounded since both were the outstanding bird painters of their era. Lodge is included in this Dictionary for his outstanding paintings of birds of prey, especially falcons and falconry, his own favourite sport and the subject on which he became an authority. He lived rather aptly at Hawk House in Camberley, Surrey and Thorburn moved to the same village. Lodge worked in both oil, tempera and watercolour. He studied at the Lincoln College of Art after which he was apprenticed to a wood engraver. He exh. at the principal London galleries from 1881.

Logsdail, William, RP, RBC, NEAC (1859-1944)

Portrait and landscape painter who included a number of angling and fox-hunting scenes amongst his work. Studied at Lincoln School of Art, under E.R. Taylor, and under Verlat at the Antwerp Academy. Won gold medals for oil and watercolour painting at the RCA (1875/6). Exh. at the RA between 1877 and 1926 including a portrait of the "Terrier Man of the South Oxfordshire Hunt" in 1923. Exh. at SS (1877-1882) including a "Study of Fish" and "The Salmon Pool on the Lledyr, North Wales". Elected RP (1913). "Returned from the Hunt" (1925), 36½in.x26in., was auctioned Christie's (NY) 1984.

Lombers, Eric (op.c.1930-c.1939)
Painter and illustrator who worked with Tom Eckersley (q.v.) during the 1930s until the war (1939-1945) broke the partnership up. Contributed work for posters to London Transport during the pre-war period including "The Rugby League Final" (1938).

Long, John, Jnr. (op.1827)
A sporting scene, s.&d. 1827, inscr. on the reverse "Emma Mary Long, given to her by her affectionate father with her pony — shot 1836" was auctioned Sotheby's (1963) (Pavière).

Longbottom, Robert J. (op.1830-1848)
Exh. at SS (1831-1845) and at the RA from 1830. Sporting and animal titles include "Portrait of Favourite Spaniel, the property of a Gentleman", "A Mare and Foal" (two studies) and "Antelope", the property of an officer in the 7th Hussars.

Longe, William Verner (1857-1924)
Talented equestrian and landscape painter in watercolour. Born at Cottenham in Cambridgeshire. Studied at Ipswich School of Art and in Brussels. A member of the Ipswich Art Club, he contributed to "The History of the Grand National". His many fine equestrian scenes include "The Finish of the St. Leger" (1904), "The Grand National" (1896), six watercolours of "The Cottenham Races" (1891), "The Gold Cup, Ascot" (1897) inscr. "Persimmon Comes in Alone", "The Inter Universities Challenge Cup" (November 1895), inscr. "Cottenham", "The Grand National" (1912) and a portrait of the Prince of Wales', later Edward VII's, horse "Diamond Jubilee", winner of the 2000 Guineas, the Derby and the St. Leger 1900.

Longmore, W.S. (op.1875-1879)
An angling artist from Walthamstow who exh. a painting of fly fishing at SS in 1876.

"Long Slip"
The pseudonym of a sporting contributor to "Country Life" (1897).

Longstaff, Capt. Sir John, RP (1862-1941)
Australian portrait painter whose portrait of his fellow countryman, Walter Lindrum, the professional billiard player who became so famous during the 1920s and 30s, 50in.x40in., is in the collection of the Clare-Padmore-Thurston Group of Billiard Manufacturers. Longstaff, who exh. predominantly at the RA and the Paris Salon (1891-1920), was elected RP (1915). He studied at the Melbourne Art Schools, under G.F. Folingsby, and won a scholarship in 1887 to study in Paris. He was knighted in 1928.

Longstaff, William (Will) Francis (1879-1953)
Australian-born landscape painter in watercolour who exh. one painting at the RA (1919) of the Somme Valley, no doubt inspired by his appalling experiences in the 1st World War. He also painted a prettier scene of "A Garden with a Putting Green and Players", 19¾in.x23½in., which was auctioned Sotheby's 1988.

Longueville, E. (op.1905-1931)
A painting of the polo pony "Tzar" belonging to the 7th Hussars, s.&d. 1905, 13½x17in., was auctioned Sotheby's (Sussex) 1988. A portrait of "Ability", a bay racehorse s.&d. 1931 and inscr., 13½in.x17½in. was auctioned Sotheby's (Sussex) 1985. The painting was catalogued as being by E. Lanqueville but they are assumed to be the same artist.

"Loose Rein"
Pseudonym used by John Beer (q.v.) for "Tales for Sportsmen" by "Wanderer" illus. with Georgina Bowers (q.v.) (1885).

Loraine, Nevison Arthur, RBA (op.1889-1903)
Figure painter and of rustic and equine subjects. Exh. mainly at SS and the RA from a Chiswick address. Titles include "The Blacksmith's Bench", etc. His portraits of horses in oil are signed, but rarely dated, and are attractively painted. Elected RBA in 1893 and contributed to "The Illustrated London News" (1895).

Lorette, Thinot (op.1860)
Draughtsman and lithographer of sporting subjects, after his own designs and those of his contemporaries, including "Rifle Practice by the Rifle Volunteers" c.1860 and "A Cricket Match at Lords between the Gentlemen and Players", presumably after his work, 9½in.x13¼in.

Lorimer, John Henry, RWS, ROI, RSA, RSW, RP (1856-1936)
Edinburgh painter who exh. forty-three works at the RA and 123 at the RSA. His portrait of Frederick Guthrie Tait, Amateur Champion 1896-1898, standing receiving a club from his caddie, whilst holding another under his left arm, was painted from photographs after Tait was killed in 1900 leading his company of the Black Watch into action in the Boer War - see also J.W. Ritchie. After Tait died, a letter with the paw mark of his beloved terrier "Nails" was found in one of his pockets. Lorimer therefore painted "Nails" standing beside his master, 120in.x60in. Collection of the Royal and Ancient Golf Club of St Andrews. Lorimer studied at the RSA Schools under McTaggart (q.v.) and George Paul Chalmers (1833-1878) and in Paris under Carolus-Duran (q.v.). Elected RSW (1885), ROI (1890), RP (1892), RSA (1900), RWS (1934).

Lorraine Smith
See Smith Lorraine.

Lousada, Maude (Mrs. Julian) (op.1911-1927)
London figure and landscape painter who exh. presumably a golf painting entitled "The Seventh Hole" at the NEAC in 1911, her only year to exhibit.

Loutherbourg, Philip James
See de Loutherbourg

Love, Horace Beevor (1780-1838)
Norwich portrait painter and miniaturist in watercolour and oil. He founded the Norwich Artists Conversaziones with the landscape artist, John Sell Cotman, whose portrait he painted in 1830. Is known to have painted the portraits in Edwin Cooper's (q.v.) pictures and he painted some equestrian work of his own, in a rather primitive style. He exh. at the RA (1833-1836).

Lovegrove, H. (op.1829-1844)
Landscape painter who exh. at the RA, BI and SS. Titles include "Perch caught in the Thames, near Marlow" (BI 1843).

Lowry, Laurence Stephen, RA, RBA, LG,NS (1887-1976)
Celebrated painter and lithographer of northern, urban subjects and industrial scenes. Born Manchester, studied at the Manchester School of Art. He painted several sporting scenes including his football painting representing his lifelong devotion to the game, entitled "After the Match" auctioned Sotheby's, April 1964, "Rounders", 15in.x20in. (1934), (repro. "Burlington Magazine", November 1973) and "Holcombe Races", painted in 1954, 8in.x6in. Elected RBA (1934), NS (1934), LG (1948), RA (1962). Held his first one-man show in 1939 at the Lefevre Gallery.

Luard, Lowes Dalbiac, RBA (1872-1944)
Equestrian and sporting artist who made a last minute decision to study art at the Slade School (1891) instead of going to Oxford University. He went to Paris in 1904 intending to stay three months to continue his studies but he stayed thirty years. Painted the Percheron horses on the streets and quays of Paris and specialised in drawing and painting these wonderfully muscular horses until they were superseded by the motor car. In 1932 he returned to St. John's Wood, London and studied faster equine subjects at Newmarket where he painted "The Lime Kilns Gallop, Newmarket", 10½in.x15¾in. He pub. books on the horse in action in 1921 and 1935 and produced a steady stream of paintings, drawings and etchings of equestrian subjects.

Lucas, John Seymour, RA, RI (1849-1923)
Historical painter in both oil and watercolour whose subject "The Armada in Sight", depicting the well worn (and mythical) tale of Sir Francis Drake nonchalantly playing bowls while the Armada bowled into sight, might have been invented for him. Lucas, who loved to paint his figures in 17th or 18th century costume, studied at St. Martin's School of Art and at the RA Schools and exh. from 1867. He was elected NWS (1877) and RA (1898).

Lucas, John Templeton (1836-1880)
Landscape and genre painter who exh. between 1859-1879 at the RA, BI, SS and elsewhere. Titles include "An Angler preparing for a Day's Sport" (BI 1860).

Lucas, Ralph W. (op.1821-1862)
Landscape painter who exh. at the RA, SS, NWCS and BI. Titles include "Trout Fishing" (BI 1847).

Lucas, Stephen, ARCA (Lond) (b.1924)
Contemporary painter who contributed a football painting entitled "Centre Forward", 24in.x29in., to the FE (1953).

Lucas Lucas, Henry Frederick (1848-1943)
Born at Louth in Lincolnshire, this artist moved to Rugby in 1878 where he remained for the rest of his life. He is well known for his polo paintings but he also painted hunting scenes, particularly of the Pytchley Hunt. He exh. three paintings at the Royal Birmingham Society of Artists (1885-1887) but much of his work was commissioned. His "Hacking Home" shows a relaxed pair of riders, the man smoking a cigarette and his girl companion riding astride - a sign of the changing times that Lucas lived through during his long life. He worked occasionally for Messrs. Fores who pub. several of his works as prints and he illus. "The Foxhunting Alphabet".

Lucas Lucas, William (op.1924-1945)
Equestrian artist whose portrait of the bay racehorse "Ocean Swell" painted in 1945 was presented by the artist to the Craven Club in the same year. "Ocean Swell" (1941) was bred and owned by the 6th Earl of Rosebery. Trained by Jack (later Sir Jack) Jarvis, he won the Derby in 1944 and the Ascot Gold Cup in 1945. Lucas Lucas, who also painted portraits of dogs and greyhounds, usually s.&d. his work. He was almost certainly related to H.F. Lucas Lucas (q.v.).

Luchishkin, Sergei Alexevitch (b.1902)
Russian landscape and figure artist of several skiing paintings. Luchishkin was a member of the Society of Easel Artists (OST), originally established in 1925. OST ultimately had over thirty members and organised four exhibitions in Moscow (1925-1928) and two travelling exhibitions (1929-1930).

Ludlow, A.J. (op.1874-1909)
Painter of pigeon racing scenes, pigeon portraits and cock-fighting portraits, who operated between these dates. Ludlow is known to have painted a portrait of a fighting cock in 1874 for Herbert Atkinson (q.v.) which was repro. as an illustration to Atkinson's articles in the "Fanciers Gazette" in the same year.

Ludlow, Henry Stephen (Hal) (1861-1903)
Portrait painter and illustrator who studied at Heatherleys and Highgate College of Art. Painted in both oil and watercolour. Exh. at the RA, RI and in the provinces. Contributed to "The Illustrated London News" and "The Sketch". Exh. a painting entitled "Playing a Trout" at the RA in 1901 (No. 733). His portrait of "Evans Baillie Noel" the real tennis player in the act of taking a shot, 23½in.x17in., watercolour, is in a private collection. Evans Baillie Noel won the Amateur Rackets Championship in 1907. He was one of the greatest tennis and rackets historians and the Queen's Club Secretary (1914-1928). He was also the tennis and rackets correspondent to "The Times" before the 2nd World War. He had the distinction of being the only person to win an Olympic gold medal for rackets singles, which he did in 1908 when the Olympic Games were held in London. He wrote two vols. of "A History of Tennis" (1924) and "First Steps to Rackets" (1926).

Ludovici, Albert, Snr., RBA (1820-1894)
Painter of genre and some sporting subjects including his portrait of an unknown bearded cricketer (not W.G. Grace) in 1879. Lived mostly in Paris. He exh. at SS between 1857 and 1894. Sporting titles include "A Morning Ride", "Seaside Acrobats", "A Tiger Hunt", "Country Sports", "Carriage and Pair", "Don't Shoot Me" and "A Sportsman's Rest". He also collaborated with Thomas Earl (q.v.) on "The Pet Pup" (1876). Elected RBA (1867).

Ludovici, Albert, Jnr., RBA (1852-1932)
Figure and landscape painter and an illustrator. Born at Prague, the son of the artist Albert Ludovici, Snr. (q.v.). Studied art in Geneva and worked in London and Paris which inspired his book "An Artist's Life in London and Paris" (1926). Influenced by Whistler. Exh. at SS between 1881 and 1888. Sporting titles include "Waiting for the Carriage" and "Jousting - A Tournament on the River". His other sporting work includes regatta and skating scenes. Elected RBA (1881) and NEA (1891).

Luker, William, Snr. (c.1820-1892)
Painter of most subjects, including animals and equestrian portraits. The father of William Luker, Jnr. (q.v.). Exh. at the RA (1851-1889). Titles include "Deer Stalkers", and "A Portrait of a Gentleman", his son in attendance, with favourite pony and deerhound (1851). Exh. at SS between 1851 and 1892. Sporting titles include "A Shot Within Hearing".

Luker, William, Jnr., RBA (b.1867-c.1948)
Equestrian, animal, portrait and landscape artist. Studied art at the RCA. Born in Kensington, London. Son of William Luker, Snr. (q.v.). Exh. at SS between 1885 and 1892 and at the RA from 1886. He painted a number of equestrian scenes including one of HRH The Prince of Wales on "Cark Courtier" at the Blankney Hunt Steeplechase. Luker illus. many books including "The Children's London", and "Kensington Picturesque and Historical". Elected RBA (1896).

Luks, George (1866-1933)
American painter and illustrator who was highly influenced by Robert Henri (q.v.). Luks worked for the Philadelphia Press and was a devoted baseball enthusiast. His cartoon entitled, rather curiously, "Baseball at Nunkie-Now!! Ah! Ah!!" depicts Dr. Andrew Green Ford playing the game c.1916. His less hysterical attempt - his painting, 30in.x25in., of a solemn boy with a baseball c.1925 - shows his fine talent for painting and the influence of Henri. The Metropolitan Museum of Art. His pupil was Philip Evergood (q.v.).

Lumley, Sir John Savile, KCB (op.c.1910-1950)
A painting entitled "Memory of Foxhunting on Boxing Day", s.&d. 1921, 9⅝in.x7⅝in., was auctioned Fenner & Co., Devon 1988. John Savile Lumley is probably best known for his famous World War I recruitment poster entitled "Daddy, what did YOU do in the Great War?". He contributed illustrations widely during the 1920s and 1930s to children's books, annuals and magazines, working for both boys' and girls' publications. He illus. the 1949 edn. of R.L. Stevenson's "The Black Arrow". Lumley shared a studio with G.L. Stampa (q.v.).

Luscombe, Henry Andrews (b.1820, op.1845-1865)
Plymouth marine painter and watercolourist whose work includes a number of yachting and regatta scenes. He was one of the first artists to paint steam warships and to record the events of Victorian naval history. Exh. eleven paintings at the RA between 1845-1865.

Lutyens, Charles Augustus Henry (1829-1915)
London portrait, animal and equestrian painter who retired from an army career in 1857 to become a professional artist. He worked in both oil and watercolour and for the Duchess of Montrose ("Old Six Mile Bottom") for whom he painted a large portrait group of mares and foals. His other patrons included Lords Bradford and Lonsdale and the Duke of Portland. An interesting report on the exhibition at Burlington House in "Bailys Magazine" (Vol. 27 June 1875) reads as follows: "The best hunting picture in the Academy this year is, to our humble thinking, "The Covert Side" of Mr. Lutyens. Man and horse, boots and breeches are perfection. The elderly dandy, for you can see he is that, sits his horse like a workman, and the whole thing looks like business. Mr. Lutyens must be congratulated. But what is that common looking beast carrying Lord Lonsdale's colours and who is the rough stable boy wearing them. Can that be our friend "King Lud" and is the jockey intended for a caricature of "Cus". Mr. Lutyens has also painted "Aventurière" and "g'ang forward" and he has been more successful with Mr. Crawford's horse than with the others but the high metalled racer is clearly not his forte". Exh. RA (1861-1903), BI, SS and GG. Sporting titles include "Hog Hunting", "Doncaster", "Derby Winner" (1873), "Major Browne and the Northumberland Hounds".

Lutyens, Frederick Mansfield (1860-1924)
Equestrian painter, one of the four children of the eccentric artist and traveller, Charles A.H. Lutyens (q.v.) and taught to draw by him. He was made to view subjects through a piece of glass and outline them in crayon. Brother of Sir Edwin Landseer Lutyens, the famous architect who was named Edwin Landseer after his father's friend Sir Edwin Landseer (q.v.). Frederick seems to have survived entirely through commissioned work, and through family connections, painting the racehorses belonging to the royal family. A very keen hunting man, he hunted three days a week with the Hursley. He collaborated with his father on an illus. book entitled "Mr. Spinks and his Hounds" pub. by Vinton and Co. Ltd. prior to 1896.

Luyt, Aria Martinus (1879-1951)
Dutch artist who studied at the Academy of Fine Arts at the Hague and then at the Académie Julian in Paris, under Professor Laurens. Lived in Belgium, Paris, Cape Town and South Africa. "Polo Players" No.195. Exh. at the XIVth Olympiad Sport in Art Competition & Exhibition at the V & A Museum, London 1948.

Lycett, J. (op.1802)
"A Gentleman standing by his Hunter, his Groom in the middle distance", s.&d. 1802, was exh. at Messrs. Ackermanns Galleries in June 1930 as reported by "The Connoisseur" of that date.

Lydon, Alexander Francis (1836-1913)
Painter of angling and freshwater fish still lifes and of pigeon portraits. Contributed to "Feathered World" (1897-1899) and illus. "British Freshwater Fishes" by the Revd. W. Houghton pub. Wm. Mackenzie, 69

Ludgate Hill, London, 1878. This popular work contained, for the first time, coloured illustrations of several species of the salmon and trout families. In almost all cases these were drawn from specimens of the fish themselves. Exh. RA 1861.

Lyle, James (op.1909)
Painter of fresh water still lifes including "A Still Life with brown Trout, Gaff and Fishing Bag and Rod", s.&d. 1909, 12in.x18in., auctioned Christie's 1988.

Lyle, Thomas Byron (op.1880-1891)
Figure and domestic painter who exh. at the RA, RSA, GI and Walker Art Gallery between 1880 and 1891. "Out for a Shot", showing two men with rifles, possibly poachers, s.&d. 1885, 24in.x18in., was auctioned Christie's 1988.

Lynch, Stanislaus (op.1948)
Irish painter who won an hon. mention in the Olympic Arts Competition July/August 1948 for his epic work "Echoes of the Hunting Horn".

Lyne, Charles Edward Michael (1912-1989)
Sporting artist and writer, the third son of a country parson. He was born at Upton Bishop, Hereford. A great great grandson of the sculptor John Bacon RA (1740-1799). Educated at Rossall and from an early age hunting and art became his two main interests. Largely self-taught except for a brief period at the Cheltenham Art College, under Gerald Gardiner. His first book "Horses, Hounds and Country" was pub. when he was only twenty-six but he illus. many other sporting books including "Rhymes of an Irish Huntsman" (1937), "The Horse in Action" (1954), and "The Hunting Diaries of Stanley Barker" (1981). Lyne's work covers most field sports including racing and steeplechasing.

Lyon, David (op.1758-1774)
Little known artist who exh. two paintings, one of a mare and a foal and one of a pointer "from life" at the FS in 1774.

Lyon, John Howard (d.1921)
Scottish painter of sporting subjects including "Shooting on a Grouse Moor", signed, 16in.x20in., auctioned Bonhams 1985. Exh. RSA, RSW and GI between 1902 and 1914.

Lyttleton, Thomas Hamilton (op.1869)
Australian painter of equestrian scenes including "The Autumn Steeplechase at Ballarat 1868", painted in 1869, 15¾in.x24¼in. Lyttleton was at one time Chief of Police in Victoria and illus. "The Pictorial History of Australian Horseracing", collection Victoria State Library, Australia.

M

"M.R."
Caricaturist of the "Vanity Fair" stable who contributed two cartoons between 1900-1901. One of these was an amusing portrait of H.H. the Maharaja of Patiala GCSI complete with polo stick and ball, which was pub. in the Prince's issue (No. 21) of "Vanity Fair", 4 January 1900.

Macaulay, M.M.
Scottish painter of sporting still lifes. "A Still Life" with a huntsman's coat, hat, whip, horn, with a fox's brush, 17in.x30in., and "A Still Life" of a brace of pheasants, a hare, a cartridge bag, on a stone ledge, etc. were auctioned at Christie's (Glasgow) 1984.

McAuliffe, James J. (1848-1921)
American painter of marine subjects and of some trotting races including "Pair Driving", s.&d. 1895 and "Trotter on a Racecourse".

Macbeth, James (1847-1891)
Glasgow born landscape painter whose large oil painting of the 1880 Oxford v. Cambridge boat race shows the two crews rounding one of the bends, cheered on by crowds on the river banks and being followed by a flotilla of steamers and small boats. In 1880 Oxford won the race but the scene shows the Cambridge crew well ahead of Oxford, which either goes to show where the artist's preference lay or how quickly a situation can change. Sotheby's 1990. Macbeth, who exh. at the leading London galleries between 1872-1884, painted mostly around London and sometimes in the Scottish highlands.

Macbeth, Robert Walker, RA, RI, RE, RWS, ROI (1848-1910)
Scottish landscape and rustic genre painter and a painter of equestrian subjects. He was also an accomplished watercolourist and an etcher. Studied art at the RSA Schools and worked as an illustrator for "The Graphic" from 1870, then in its first year. He was the son of the artist Norman Macbeth, RSA, the brother of Henry

Raeburn Macbeth-Raeburn, RA (q.v.) and related to the Scottish portrait painter Sir Henry Raeburn (q.v.). His "Still Life of a Roach", caught in the Little Ouse at Littleport by W. Farrer on 10 October 1876, weighing 30 oz., signed with inits., inscr. and witnessed by the artist and R. Farrer, 12in.x18in., was auctioned Bonhams 1983. He painted several other sporting subjects including "Lunch at a Coursing Meeting". Macbeth exh. at the RA from 1871 including "Hunting with the Devon and Somerset Staghounds" and "Favourites of the Hunt". Also exh. at the OWS, GG, NG and elsewhere. Elected RE (1880), RWS (1901) and RA (1903). Much influenced by Frederick Walker (q.v.) and G.H. Mason.

Macbeth-Raeburn, Henry Raeburn, RA, RE (1860-1947)
Glasgow-born artist and engraver, son of Norman Macbeth, RSA, brother of Robert Walker Macbeth RA (q.v.) and related to Sir Henry Raeburn (q.v.). He took the name of Raeburn from his ancestor to distinguish himself from his brother. Studied at the RSA Schools and at the Académie Julian, Paris. Exh. at the RA from 1881 and turned to engraving in 1890. He was best known in the 1920s for his engravings after the works of Old Masters especially those of Raeburn. Contributed to "The Illustrated London News" (1894-1896) and exh. at the RA from 1881. Elected RE (1899), RA (1933). His portrait of Mr. Paul Mellon riding "Dublin", painted after A.J. Munnings, RA (q.v.) was exh. at the RA in 1934.

Macbeth-Raeburn, Marjorie May (Mrs.) (1902-1988)
Painter of equestrian scenes, daughter of Henry Macbeth-Raeburn (q.v.) and distantly related to Sir Henry Raeburn (q.v.) from whom the second part of her surname came. Both father and daughter were apt to paint studies after previous artists - George Stubbs (q.v.), Sir Henry Raeburn, J.S. Sargent, RA (q.v.), Sir Joshua Reynolds (q.v.), Frank Salisbury (q.v.) and A.J. Munnings RA. (q.v.). Lived at Dedham, Essex. Painted a number of racehorse portraits and scenes including "A Bay Hunter in a Landscape", "A Racehorse with Jockey Up", "Mares and Foals in a Meadow" and "The Start, Newmarket", Christie's (Sth. Ken.) 1988. Usually signed but rarely dated her work.

Maccabe, Gladys (Mrs.), ROI, RUA (b.1918)
Irish painter in oil and watercolour, daughter of the artist George Chalmers and married to the artist Max Maccabe. Studied fashion, design and sculpture at Belfast College of Art (1934-1938) but self taught as a painter. Exh. at the RSA, ROI, RUA, SWA and abroad. Member of the Watercolour Society of Ireland. Has painted a number of racing scenes including "Before the Race at Phoenix Park" and "Jockeys and Trainers" which she painted in watercolour. Her painting of "Skaters", 14½in.x19in., was auctioned David Lay 1989.

McClymont, John I. (op.1880-1900)
Lived in Edinburgh and exh. twice at the RA, thirty-six times at the RSA between 1880-1898 and at the Glasgow Institute. A portrait of "Old" Tom Morris, s.&d. 1900, 19¼in.x15¼in., Sotheby's (Glasgow) 1989.

McCowan, W. (op.c.1906)
A signed watercolour featuring three racehorses entitled "A Driving Finish", 11½in.x19¼in., was auctioned Christie's (Tattersalls) 1989.

McCoy, Miss Margaret H. (op.1926)
Irish painter of equestrian scenes including "Hound Magic" and "Over the Brook". She exh. once at the RHA in 1926.

Macdonald, Richard, RWS, ARCA (Lond.) (b.1919)
Contemporary painter who contributed "The Local Game, Gloucestershire", 67in.x23in., to the FE.

Macdonald, Tom (1914-1985)
Glasgow born painter who contributed "Big Game Up North", pastel, 18in.x14in., to the FE. Macdonald, who trained as a marine engineer, was virtually self taught but was influenced by J.D. Fergusson and spent one year at the GSA (1937-1938).

Macdonnell-Dixon, Clive (op.1907-1911)
Yorkshire artist of equestrian portraits who exh. at the RA and elsewhere between 1907-1911.

McDowall, William (1905-1988)
Ayrshire-born landscape artist who studied under Samuel John Peploe at the Edinburgh College of Art. Retired from Thompson Newspapers in 1969 to East Anglia. Exh. at the RA, RSA, RBA and RI from 1922.

McEwen, R. (op.1822)
A picture entitled "Salmon Fishing" was in the Hutchinson Collection.

McGhie, John (1867-1941)
Scottish landscape painter and etcher whose painting "The Follow Through" is said to be a portrait of the golfer David Rintoul, 24in.x20in., auctioned Christie's (Glasgow) 1983. McGhie studied at the Glasgow School of Art, the RA Schools and at the Académie Julian, Paris. He exh. at the leading London and Scottish galleries between 1891-1940.

McGill, Donald Fraser Gould (1875-1962)
Postcard designer and cartoonist, he made more than 3,000 designs during his career and his seaside postcards were a source of much delight to millions of holiday-makers. His work included many sporting scenes, particularly golf which he depicted in a slapstick way, very popular at the time. Died 13 October at St. James's Hospital, Balham. A typical caption accompanying McGill's work might read - "Isn't it a pity, Mabel still has one feminine trait - she will powder her nose" signed, pencil, watercolour, 8in.x6in., auctioned Christie's 1984.

McGoran, Kieran
Contemporary Irish equestrian artist of both flat and steeplechasing scenes. His steeplechase painting "Over the Hurdle at Cheltenham", 12½in.x15½in., was auctioned Christie's (Belfast) 1990.

Machen, William Henry (1832-1911)
American still life painter whose studies of partridge and game were popular at the time.

McIan, Robert Ranald, ARSA (1803-1856)

Professional actor and painter, also an illustrator. Exh. at the RA from 1836 and elected ARSA in 1852. He specialised in Highland scenes and "Salmon Leistering" was painted c.1840.

McInnes, Jos (op.c.1920s)

"A Snooker Match", oil on linen, 11¾in.x18¾in., Wingfield Sporting Gallery, London. The snooker tables are made by Burroughes & Watts and the metal type pockets became popular after the 2nd World War, although they were around before. The Victorian marking board on the left of the picture has life pool markings. The lamps above the table have Hartley shades which are distinguished by the upturns. These were made after the 2nd World War by the man who pioneered the Hartley head-lamps for cars at Greenfield, North Oldham, Lancs. A pair of golfing sketches in pen/ink dated October 1st '76, possibly by McInnes, were auctioned Bonhams 1988.

McKay, John (op.1841-1860)

Scottish painter of curling scenes including "Curling at New Farm Loch, Kilmarnock", c.1860, oil. The Dick Institute, Kilmarnock. McKay also painted a superb curling scene on a fine 18th century gold presentation snuff box, dated Edinburgh 1841, which is said to represent Duddingston Loch and its octagonal curling house, designed by William Playfair in 1824.

MacKay, William Darling, RSA (1844-1924)

Landscape painter, born at Gifford, East Lothian and lived at Edinburgh having studied at the City's Trustees Academy. Exh. RSA 1864 to 1916 and was Librarian there 1896-1907 and Secretary 1907-1924. Elected RSA 1883. Sporting work includes "Gumping Trout on Gifford Water" (1869), "On Gifford Water" (1870) and "The Firing Range", The Ellis Campbell Collection.

McKelvey, Frank, RHA, RUA (1895-1974)

Belfast-born landscape and figure painter in oil and watercolour who studied at Belfast Municipal School of Art (1912-1917). Exh. in London, Glasgow, Ireland and abroad. Elected RHA (1930). "The Regatta at Holywood", 16in.x20in., was auctioned Sotheby's 1990.

Mackenzie, James Hamilton, ARSA, RSW, ARE (1875-1926)

Painter and etcher who studied at the Glasgow School of Art and in France and Italy. Born and lived in Glasgow, he became President of the Glasgow Art Club. His portrait of a young girl holding a tennis racket, 30in.x18in., was auctioned Christie's 1986.

Mackenzie, William G., ARHA (d.1925)

This artist exh. regularly at the Royal Hibernian Academy until his death in 1925 and is best remembered today for his portraiture. Included in this Dictionary for his portrait of the professional golf champion "Tom Morris" (1821-1908), s.&d. 1904, 33in.x26½in.

MacKinnon, A. (op.1890)

A large, 2ft.6in.x4ft.2in., painting of "The Tarporley Hunt Races" (1890) by this artist was sold for £2,200 at G.A. Property Services, Wolverhampton 1989.

McKivragen, Terence (Terry) (b.1920)

Painter of landscapes, architectural subjects and sporting activities in watercolour and occasionally in acrylic. Studied at Wimbledon Art School and became a graphic artist, specialising in illustration work. He has exh. at the major London galleries since 1980 including the RI, RSBA, RP, RSMA and RWA. Sports covered by McKivragen include cricket, golf, racing and rowing.

MacLeay, Kenneth, ARSA, RSW (1802-1878)

Scottish portrait and figure painter who entered the Trustees Academy in 1822. Brother of MacNeil MacLeay (q.v.). Elected an original ARSA in 1826, resigning and re-elected in 1829. Elected RSW (1878). His pencil and watercolour drawing of a sportsman, s.&d. 1844, 10¼in.x8¼in., was auctioned Christie's (Glasgow) 1983.

MacLeay, MacNeil, ARSA (op.1836-1871)

Scottish landscape painter, brother of the miniaturist Kenneth MacLeay (q.v.). MacLeay's painting of members of the Royal Perth Golfing Society playing on the North Inch in 1866, 17in.x27in., was auctioned Sotheby's 1986. Elected ARSA (1836).

McLennan, (op.c.1833)

"Curling at Curling Hall, Largs", c.1833. John Cairnie is shown delivering a stone from his famous foot-iron; against the garden seat lie a large pair of compasses used for measuring shots. The Royal Caledonian Curling Club, Edinburgh.

Macleod, John (op.1848-1872)

Scottish painter of sporting and equestrian scenes including "A Sportsman with a Pony, A Terrier, and Dead Game" (1848), "A Bay Hunter in a Loose Box with a Terrier" (1870), and "Going to Market", s.&d. 1874. His painting of the Duke of Buccleuch, recorded in the Bowhill catalogue, is amongst his better known pictures. A provincial painter, Macleod usually signed and dated his work. Macleod's painting of "Chanticleer", a grey racehorse belonging to Mr. James Merry of Belladrum, is a good representation of his work. "Chanticleer" who was trained by William and Robert Anson near Edinburgh, won the Doncaster Cup in 1848 ridden by Ned Flatman.

McLeod, Juliet (Mrs. Adrian Thorpe) (b.1917)

Equestrian artist, author and illustrator, born in Buckinghamshire on Christmas Day, the daughter of a distinguished army officer. A keen horseman from the age of three, at sixteen she went to study art at Des Beaux Arts in Paris after which she became a pupil of Lynwood Palmer (q.v.) (1933-1939). Palmer encouraged her to exercise his horses after her studies and taught her to drive a four-in-hand. He also taught her horse anatomy insisting that she study and copy the etchings in George Stubbs' monumental book "The Anatomy of the Horse". She held her first exhibition in 1947 at Messrs. Ackermanns Gallery, London and at Messrs. Fores in 1953 but in 1954 she contracted multiple sclerosis. In 1960 she produced her book of paintings entitled "A Hundred Horses" which had excellent reviews. Her portrait of the Aga Khan leading in

"Blenheim" after winning the 1930 Derby, 14in.x14in., was repro. in the "Sphere" 29.5.1952.

Maclure, Andrew (op.1857-1881)
Landscape painter and a lithographer after his own designs including "The First Shot at Wimbledon" (1860). This is rifle shooting not lawn tennis. Maclure exh. at the RA.

McMacken, Dave (op.1976)
Contemporary painter of American football personalities including the portrait of George Halse, Chicago Bears coach and owner 1920s, acrylic and airbrush, 1976.

MacMaster, James, RSW, RBA (1856-1913)
Scottish landscape painter and watercolourist whose watercolour painting of a golf match at Elie, signed and titled "Simpson v. Kirkaldy", 10in.x14in,, was auctioned Sotheby's 1985. Elected RSW (1885) and RBA (1890).

MacMillan, Ethel (Mrs.) (d.1971)
Studied at the RA Schools. Exh. one painting at RA in 1943 from an address in Edenbridge, Kent. Exh. at the Royal Society of British Artists (1939/40). Her painting of a boxing match entitled "Between Rounds" (c.1940), 15¾in.x11⅜in., was auctioned Phillips 1989.

McNeill, Angus (op.1900-1914)
Painter of two polo sketches entitled "Riding Him Off" and "Out by Himself" which appeared in a national newspaper early in the 20th century.

McPhail, Rodger (b.1953)
Lives in Lancashire, and studied (three years) at Liverpool School of Art. Held first one-man show at Tryon Gallery in 1977, then in 1979, 1982 and 1986. His book "Open Season - An Artist's Sporting Year" (1986) is a pictorial record of the seasons seen through the eyes of an artist and sportsman. He also illus. "The Fishing Season" with text by Colin McKelvie. Painted a series of Spanish partridge shooting commissions in 1975 and visited the USA in 1977 to paint more shooting commissions.

Macpherson, Douglas (1871-?)
Painter and illustrator, the son of the artist John Macpherson. Studied at Westminster School of Art and joined the staff of "The Daily Graphic" (1890-1913). Joined the staff of "The Sphere" (1913) and drew sketches of the 2nd World War for "The Sphere", "The Daily Telegraph" and "The Daily Mail" (1939-1945). Contributed to "Punch" (1906-1909). Exh. one painting at the RA in 1907. A member of the Langham Sketch Club, he contributed a plan of "The Grand National Course at Aintree", s.&d. 1922 to "The Sphere", 25 March issue. The plan shows thirty jumps over 4 miles, 856 yds.

MacQuoid, Percy, RI, ROI (1852-1925)
Artist and illustrator, sometimes of equestrian scenes. Son of the decorative illustrator of "The Illustrated London News", T.R. MacQuoid. Studied art at Heatherleys and at the RA Schools and in France. Worked for "The Graphic" from 1871, at first concentrating on animal subjects. Elected RI (1882) and ROI (1883). He became a well-known authority on

English furniture later in his life, concentrating entirely on this subject and publishing his four vol. "History of English Furniture" in 1905.

McTaggart, M.F. (Lt. Col.) (op.1929)
Wrote and illus. "From Colonel to Subaltern" pub. "Country Life" 1929. His illustrations include many pictures of horses and civilians hunting.

McTaggart, William, RSA, VP, RSW (1835-1910)
Scottish painter of coastal and river scenes in both oil and watercolour. Studied at the RSA Schools, Edinburgh between 1852 and 1859. A contemporary of Orchardson, MacWhirter (q.v.), John Pettie, Tom Graham, G.P. Chalmers, Peter Graham and Hugh Cameron. Exh. at the RSA from 1853 and at the RA from 1866. Elected RSA (1870) and VPRSW from its inception in 1878. His portrait "An Oarsman", 37½in.x29½in., was auctioned Sotheby's (Glasgow) 1987.

MacWhirter, John, RA, RSW, HRSA, RI, RE (1839-1911)
Edinburgh-born landscape painter, the son of a paper mill owner. Apprenticed at the age of thirteen to the publishers, Oliver & Boyd, which was short lived. Under the inspired guidance of the eminent painter Robert Scott Lauder he exh. his first painting at the age of fourteen at the RSA. His contemporaries are still referred to as the Scott Lauder group and include William MacTaggart (q.v.), George Paul Chalmers, John Pettie, William Quiller Orchardson (qq.v.). In 1855 he set off for the continent - the first of many similar trips. In 1870 he moved to London where he had already exh. at the RA from 1865 and where he was to exh. 118 works until 1903. Elected RA (1893) and an honorary member of the RSA (1880). He painted a number of angling scenes in his individual and impressionistic style, including "Home of the Trout" and "A Young Celt Angling in the Isle of Skye".

Madge (op.1907)
A set of four hunting cartoons (well painted in watercolour) s.&d. 1907 with the inscriptions based on billiard terminology, such as "Cannon Off the White" showing a reverend gentleman parting from his grey horse, etc., were auctioned Christie's (Sth. Ken.) 1987.

Madgwick, Clive, MUSA, RBA (b.1934)
Suffolk landscape painter who paints hunting, shooting and fishing scenes in a traditional style. Studied at Epsom College of Art and London University. Painted as an amateur for several years before turning professional in 1973. A regular exhibitor at the RBA and at the Haste Gallery, Ipswich. Has had several one-man shows. His work is found in both public and private collections in the UK, USA and Australia. Represented in the Collection of H.M. The Queen.

Maggs, John Charles (1819-1896)
Bath-born painter of portraits, animals and still lifes but is best remembered for his coaching scenes, many of which feature the Bath or Bristol Mail coaches. His "Bath to Birmingham Mail Coach" and "London to

Bath Mail Coach passing the Hunt in a seven acre forest near Marlborough" painted in 1883 were auctioned Sotheby's 1974. Maggs taught painting in his Bath studio where he held exhibitions of his work. He does not appear to have exh. at the major London galleries. Amongst his patrons were Queen Victoria, The Duke of Beaufort and Joseph Grego for whom he painted a series of eighty metropolitan coaching scenes.

Magill, Miss E. (op.1900-1931)

Animal painter whose portraits of greyhounds and dogs were well painted at the turn of the century. Exh. at the Walker Art Gallery, ROI and SWA.

Magill, Louis (op.1891-1906)

London painter of animal and equestrian subjects who exh. one painting at the RBA in 1891. His fine oil painting of a coaching scene c.1906 was auctioned Hobbs and Chambers April 1990.

Maguire, J. (op.c.1825)

Unknown artist of a painting of "Two Pointers with Gentlemen Shooting in a Field". Arthur Ackermann & Son, London.

"Maida"

Alias David Brown, the sporting contributor to "The Field" on coursing at the end of the 19th century. Started "The Greyhound Stud Book" in 1882 and became its first Keeper until he resigned through ill health in 1892.

Maiden, Joshua (1813-1843)

Equestrian artist, born in Bury, Lancashire, the son of a coachman. He was also the brother of Joe Maiden who was huntsman to the Cheshire Hunt from 1832-1844 during which period he served five Masters. In 1829 on paying a quick visit to the kennels before driving to Litchfield races, huntsman Maiden mounted the copper in which the hounds' feed was on the boil. He lost his footing, fell in and was hideously scalded from top to toe. He twice broke his left leg and had ten pieces of bone removed but he continued to hunt six days a week with one stirrup leather nearly half the length of the other. He is depicted in the foreground of the famous painting of the meet of the Cheshire hunt at Tatton Park, painted by Henry Calvert (q.v.) in 1839. Joshua Maiden is said to have been a pupil of Calvert. Maiden exh. at the Royal Manchester Institute in 1832 and in 1841 when he exh. "The Bury Hunt". His painting of Miss Yates of Bury on a pony in the grounds of a country house was auctioned Sotheby's 1976. Maiden painted in both oil and watercolour as illustrated by his fine watercolour of a bay mare and foal in a landscape, 1838.

Maile, George (op.1808-1824)

London based etcher, stipple, aquatint and mezzotint engraver of sporting subjects after his contemporaries and his own designs.

Maile, J. (op.1824)

This watercolourist and engraver may have been closely related to (or one and the same as) George Maile, the etcher, stipple, aquatint and mezzotint engraver of sporting subjects. He exh. three works at SS in 1824 including a portrait of Izaac Walton, the celebrated angler, a portrait of Charles Cotton, another celebrated angler and an engraving entitled "The Sportsman". This latter title was also engraved by George Maile (q.v.) after B. Marshall and Luke Clennell (qq.v.) in 1824.

Malbon, William (op.1834-1869)

Painter of rural and sporting scenes, working in the Sheffield area. His portrait of a sportsman, his dogs and horse resting, with a boy and dead game in a landscape, signed, inscr. and dated 1848, 28in.x36in., is very typical of his work. Although Malbon was based in Sheffield he also worked in the Derbyshire and Nottingham areas, the latter presumably the inspiration of his painting "The Sherwood Rangers" (1869), Graves AG, Sheffield. A pleasing painter of traditional scenes. Malbon apparently exh. only once in London at SS in 1834.

Malespina, Louis Ferdinand (1874-?)

French painter of equestrian and sporting scenes, including racing and trotting races, at the turn of the century.

Maling, S. (op.1726)

"A Huntsmen and a pack of Harriers, with a village in the distance", s.&d. 1726 was exh. at the Rutland Gallery, London 1960.

Mallard, Jeremy (op.c.1985)

Painted a portrait series of American football players including William Perry "The Fridge" (Chicago Bears), Dan Marino (Miami Dolphins), etc.

Manby, F.H. (op.1880)

A portrait of a rower, watercolour, s.&d. May 1880, 10½in.x7½in., Calton Gallery, Edinburgh.

Manet, Edouard (1832-1883)

French Impressionist painter who was a great horse racing enthusiast and whose frequent companion to the racecourse was Edgar Degas (q.v.). Degas sketched "Manet at the Races" which is in the Metropolitan Museum of Art, New York. Manet's many racing paintings include "At the Races" (1875) and "Races at Longchamp", Art Institute of Chicago. "The Croquet Party" set in the Parisian garden of the painter Alfred Stevens (q.v.), s.&d. 1873, 28½in.x41¾in., Staedelsches Kunstinstitut, Frankfurt.

Mann, Harrington, RP, RE, NEAC, NPS, IS (1864-1937)

Scottish portrait painter in oil. Studied art in Glasgow and at the Slade School under Alphonse Legros (1837-1911) and in Paris under Boulanger and Lefebvre. Exh. at the RA from 1885. Elected RE (1885), RP (1900) and NPS (1911). Spent some time in America painting portraits. His portrait of "Lady Millicent Taylor Dressed for Riding", s.&d. 1922 was auctioned Phillips 1984. Mann's daughter, Cathleen, became Marchioness of Queensberry. He was elected RE (1885), resigned (1891), RP (1900), NPS (1911), NEAC (1891).

Mann, James Scrimgeour, RI, PR. Cam. A (1883-1946)
Marine painter whose work included a number of yacht racing scenes. Studied at Liverpool School of Art, exh. at the RA, RI and in the provinces. Elected RI 1932.

Manning, F. (op.1864-1869)
Painter of animal and equestrian portraits including a portrait of the Derby winner "Pretendre" standing in a loose box, inscr. and dated 25 December 1869, 9¼in.x 23½in. and "Bulldogs Attacking a Badger", s.&d. 1864, 14in.x17in. Bonhams 1987.

Maquinier, J. (op.1870)
A portrait of John Gervaise Howard Marsh (aged eight years and standing on a river bank with a fishing net) dated 1870, was auctioned Bonhams 1988.

March, M.R. (op.1836)
A drawing of "Snipe Shooting", s.&d. 1836, and three other sporting sketches each 3¾in.x5½in. auctioned at Bonhams 1988.

Marchand, André (1877-1950)
French equestrian artist whose painting of the Grand Prix of 1931 with the Boussac and Rothschild horses in the foreground, s.&d. 1932, hangs in the Société d'Encouragement, Paris (French Jockey Club). Marchand was a pupil of Edward Detaille, a nowadays unjustly neglected artist.

Marchetti, Ludovici (1853-1909)
Italian painter of many sporting scenes, particularly racing including "The Races at Longchamp" (1880), "Admiring the New Automobile" (a watercolour unfortunately undated), "Elegante au Courses", etc.

"Marco"
The pseudonym used by Lord Mountbatten of Burma in his articles on the game of polo.

Marczynski, Adam (op.1948)
Polish artist who contributed an ink study of boxers, one of eight sketches depicting movement, to the XIVth Olympiad Sport in Art competition and exhibition held at the V & A Museum, London in 1948 (No.219).

Margetts, J.W. (op.1824-1899)
A painting of a bay hunter, pony and a beagle in a landscape, s.&d. 1824, 27¾in.x36in., painted originally for a Norfolk family and exh. by Messrs. Ackermanns, London. A drawing of a bay hunter in a landscape, s.&d. 1899, pencil and watercolour, 14¾in.x21in., was auctioned Christie's (Sth. Ken.) 1988.

Marin, John (1870-1953)
American watercolour painter of urban scenes whose crayon and pencil drawing entitled "Baseball", showing an elongated figure sliding desperately toward home plate while the umpire stands immobile just beyond, was completed the year he died.

Mark, James (op.1900)
A portrait of a bay hunter in a loose box, s.&d. 1900, 19½in.x23½in., was auctioned Christie's 1976.

Markham, C. (op.1851)
An apparently unrecorded artist of a competent portrait of a chestnut racehorse with jockey up in a landscape, s.&d. 1851, 19in.x23in., auctioned Christie's 1975. The artist is possibly American since the painting was privately owned in the USA until its sale in 1975. The jockey's colours of red/blue are not registered at Weatherbys.

Marks, Henry Stacy, RA, RWS, HRCA, HRPE (1829-1898)
London painter and illustrator. Studied art at J.M. Leigh's School, Newman Street and at the RA Schools (1851). Exh. at the RA from 1853. Elected RA (1878), RSW (1883). Marks was also an etcher and a member of the Junior Etching Club. He is best remembered for his ornithological and genre subjects. Marks was deeply influenced by the pre-Raphaelites largely through his friendship with the artist Sir John Everett Millais, Bt. (q.v.) whom he depicted fishing with a friend. The picture was apparently awful and since Marks was a notorious practical joker, for which Ruskin reproved him, it was probably no accident. It was exh. at the RA in 1895.

"Marlborough"
The pseudonym used by John Lawrence since 1957 for his racing reports to "The Daily Telegraph".

Marquet, Albert (1875-1947)
Prolific French landscape artist who included a number of skiing scenes, usually painted in watercolour, amongst his work.

Marsden, William (op.1871-1890)
Exh. 1889-1890 at the Manchester City AG. He painted a number of sporting and equestrian scenes of which the portrait of the horse "Prince of Wales" standing in a loose box, "The Apprentice Jockey", s.&d. 1871, "Pointers on Guard", "On the Scent", and "A Bloodhound" are examples.

Marshall, Benjamin (Ben) (1767-1834)
Equestrian and sporting artist who was brought up in Leicestershire and was a friend and neighbour of the Ferneley family. John Ferneley Snr. (q.v.) subsequently became Marshall's pupil in London (1801) at the intervention of the Duke of Rutland who had been impressed by the young Ferneley's work. Marshall studied under the portrait painter L.F. Abbott (q.v.) but was said to have been so impressed by Sawrey Gilpin's (q.v.) 1793 Academy picture, "The Death of a Fox", that he turned from human to animal painting. This is not altogether true because he always remained a very good portrait painter. Indeed since Marshall was never a hunting man his hunt groups remain posed, as in portraits, and are rarely shown in action. An exception to this is Marshall's classic painting of the famous race between "Sir Joshua" and "Filho da Puta" on Newmarket Heath in 1816. Ben Marshall was a close friend of Abraham Cooper, RA (q.v.) who also became a pupil of his and to whom he wrote his famous quip "I discover many a man who will pay me 50 guineas for painting his horse who thinks 10 guineas too much for painting his wife". Marshall moved to Newmarket (1812-1825) for this reason. In 1819 he was involved in a coaching accident receiving substantial injuries from

which he never fully recovered. He began to go downhill and his painting with him. He took to sporting journalism in the form of letters written about the turf and pub. by "The Sporting Magazine" under the pseudonym "Observator" and "Breeder of Cocktails", the first appearing in November 1821, and these continued until his death in 1834. His patrons include George III, George IV, Earl St. Vincent, Lord Darlington, Lord Scarborough, Lord Sondes, Mr. Henry Villebois, Mr. Thornhill, Mr. Fulwar Craven and others, like George Osbaldeston, whose portrait entitled "A First Rate Shot" was painted in 1831 and engraved by R. Woodman. This engraving appeared in "The Sporting Magazine" for October 1831. Marshall also painted "Tom Oldaker, the huntsman to the Old Berkeley Foxhounds on his brown mare 'Pickle'" in 1800 for the Master of the Old Berkeley Foxhounds, the Hon. and Revd. William W. Capel.

Marshall, Charles H. (op.1889-1890)

Amateur artist and a solicitor who lived at Retford, Nottinghamshire and who contributed a hunting scene to "Punch" in 1889 and to "Judy" in 1890. His five pen/black ink hunting and racing scenes, each approx. 6in.x5in., depicting various humorous incidents in George II's reign, were seen recently in a London bookshop.

Marshall, Herbert Menzies
RWS, RE, ROI (1841-1913)

Professor of landscape painting at Queens College, London at the turn of the century. "Cricket at Lords", watercolour, is an attractive representation of the game. Marshall, who was a pupil of the French architect Questel, exh. at the leading London galleries and elsewhere between 1871-1893. Elected RE (1881-1891), RWS (1883) and ROI (1901).

Marshall, John (op.1840-1896)

London painter who specialised in sporting scenes when he wasn't churning out popular still lifes for the public galleries. Exh. at SS between 1840 and 1880, titles mostly uninspiring but two studies of terriers with rabbits in 1861 and 1867. Marshall's portrait of horses in 1851 reminds us that this artist was capable of some very competent sporting scenes. He also exh. at the RA but mindful that the Committee never really cared for sporting works was careful to only exh. one in 1848, "The Curate", a portrait of a famous steeplechaser. A decorative coursing scene, painted in 1870, shows Marshall's work at its best. It seems likely that this coursing scene took place in Scotland as the dogs have collars on. These would be collars which they had won at previous meetings when they were often given as prizes. Some very fine coursing collars can be seen in the Leeds Castle Museum.

Marshall, Lambert (1809-1870)

Sporting artist, the youngest son of Ben Marshall (q.v.). He was named after his father's old friend, the celebrated fat man Daniel Lambert whom his father depicted in a now famous portrait. "The Sporting Magazine" pub. his first work, a portrait of his father

in 1826, which was later engraved by William Thomas Fry. This and a companion portrait of his mother are in the Paul Mellon Collection, Upperville, Va, USA. Inevitably Lambert Marshall suffered the fate of his father's fame for any competent work he produced was immediately thought to be heavily guided by his father's hand and considered as a weaker imitation of the great master. An appreciation of his work has possibly suffered accordingly. His human portraits, however, often bear a most uncanny resemblance to many of his father's. His portrait of a bay racehorse with a jockey up on a racecourse, s.&d. 1830, 28in.x36in., auctioned Christie's (NY) 1986, uncannily resembles his father's work.

Marshall, Maude G. (c.1877-1967)

This equestrian artist who was born in County Antrim studied at the Glasgow School of Art, the Frank Calderon School of animal painting in Kensington and in Paris. She was commissioned by the Imperial War Museum to paint horses in wartime and later raised money as director of Glasgow and West of Scotland SPCA to help wounded horses. Her many paintings of horses include "The Future Master of Foxhounds" s.&d. 1953, 20in.x24in., exh. Paisley Art Institute and auctioned Sotheby's 1986.

Marshall, William Elstob (op.1836-1881)

Painter of sporting, equestrian and animal scenes. Exh. at the RBA between 1859 and 1881. Titles include "Seaside Hacks", a subject which he painted many times, "Ferreting Rabbits", and "The Wounded Grouse". His portrait of a black and white Shetland pony, s.&d. 1836, 43in.x54½in., was auctioned Christie's 1968 and his delightful painting "New Brighton Hacks", s.&d. 1881 (horses and dogs by a trough on a beach with lighthouse in the background) is a very fine example of his work, Christie's 1980.

Marshman, J. (op.1876)

Painter and illustrator who contributed sporting subjects to "The Graphic" 1876 and exh. at the DG in the same year a painting of a bullfight.

Marson, Thomas E. (op.1899-1929)

Warwickshire based painter of equestrian subjects whose portraits of hunters include "Pilot", a bay hunter with a groom in a loose box, s.&d. 1909, a saddled chestnut hunter beside a country house in a landscape, Mr. Foster's bay hunter "Comedian" in a loose box, s.&d. 1898 and "Birdseye", a bay cob in a loose box. He exh. 1899-1927 at the RA, ROI, Manchester City AG and RBSA. His portrait of the racehorse "Challenger" in a stable is undated but "Challenger" was born in 1927 and raced as a two year old before being sold to America. Marson lived at Rugby.

Martell, Isaac (op.1780-1789)

London painter of still lifes and game subjects who exh. at the SA 1780 and 1783 and the RA 1781 to 1789. His study of dead game, pheasant, grouse, hare, etc. with a gun, signed, 28in.x38¾in., one of his RA exhibits in 1783, was auctioned Phillips 1985.

Martin, Anson Ambrose (op.1830-1872)
Sporting painter who worked chiefly in Yorkshire and Birmingham where he exh. at the RBSA. He painted fine quality coaching and hunting scenes and presumably collaborated with Charles Cooper Henderson (q.v.) since a coaching painting with the signatures of both artists, dated 1853, is recorded. His portrait of James Taylor Wray (1790-1845) of the Bedale Hunt with his dun hunter, s.&d. 1840, bears witness to his connection with Yorkshire as does "The Arrival of the York/London Royal Mail", signed and inscr. "Allright", 28in.x36in., auctioned Christie's NY 1985. A pair of coloured lithographs, after his painting entitled "The Northern Jockeys", also indicates a connection with Yorkshire.

Martin, Charles John (1820-1906)
London portrait painter, son of John Martin (1789-1854). Exh. at the RA (1836-1896), BI, SS and NWS. Martin also painted several portraits of horses including "Calcutta", a grey hunter with a spaniel in a wooded landscape, s.&d. 1852, and a study of a black cob in a loose box, s.&d. 1871.

Martin, David (1737-1797)
Distinguished Scottish portrait painter, a pupil of Allan Ramsay (q.v.) in London c.1752. Travelled with Ramsay to Italy (1755-1757) and was his chief assistant in the 1760s. He became an active member of the Society of Artists in Great Britain, winning premiums for chalk drawing 1759 and 1761. He became Treasurer in 1772 and Vice President in 1776. Exh. at SA (1765-1778). He settled in Edinburgh c.1783 and in 1785 was appointed portrait painter to the Prince of Wales in Scotland with which title he often signed his paintings. His sporting portraits include those of Sir James Pringle of Stitchill wearing his archer's shooting uniform of the pattern introduced in 1789 (by permission of the Royal Company of Archers) and John Campbell of South Hall, 66½in.x53¾in., s.&d. 1771, dressed in Van Dyke costume but with a cricket bat and ball showing, if nothing else, that the popularity of cricket had reached Scotland by this date.

Martin, Fletcher (1904-1979)
American painter of boxing scenes including his portrait of "A Boxer Seated in the Corner of a Ring", 30¼in.x 34in., and "A Boxer lying on the Boxing Ring Floor", 30in.x40in., a painting which was exh. at the Los Angeles Museum 16th Annual Painting and Sculpture Exhibition in 1934. "The Fleet Fighter" was auctioned Sotheby's (NY) 1989.

Martin, J. Edward B.
Contemporary American artist of equestrian scenes including polo. His oil on board "Polo at Potomack Park, Washington DC", 24¼in.x29¼in., was auctioned Sotheby's (NY) 1990.

Martin, Sylvester (op.1856-1906)
Birmingham based sporting artist, possibly a close relation of Anson Martin (q.v.). He painted hunting and several shooting scenes including "A Quiet Pipe" and "Marking the Covey", s.&d. 1904, each 10⅛in.x

12½in., Christie's 1990 and "Waiting for the Guns" and "The Lads in the Lane" both s.&d. 1902 and 1906 and inscr. His fine painting entitled "Grouse Shooting", s.&d. 1876 and inscr., 18in.x24in., was auctioned Sotheby's (Glasgow) 1986.

Martindale, G. Thomas (op.1820-1832)
Painter of stage and mail coaches, c.1832. His paintings include "The Berkeley Stage" with a stone breaker and his dog in the foreground, "The London to Kettering and Bedford Coach", "The London to Cheltenham Coach" (1830) and "The Aberdeen to Edinburgh Coach".

"Martingale"
Pseudonym for the sporting writer, Mr. Charles White, contributor to "The Doncaster Gazette" and "Sporting Scenes and Country Characters" (1840).

Mason, Frank Henry, RI, RBA, RSMA (1876-1965)
Prolific marine painter in oil and watercolour, also an accomplished etcher. Fifty-six of his watercolours and oils are in the Imperial War Museum. Served in the RNVR as a naval artist in World War I. Many of his paintings include yacht racing scenes in the Firth of Clyde. Exh. at the RA from 1900 onwards, also at the RBA, RHA, RI, etc. and at the RSMA from 1961. "Berwick Salmon", painted in gouache, 8¾in.x21in., was auctioned Sotheby's (Glen.) 1989. "Deepdale Links, Scarborough", watercolour, s.&d. 1910 and inscr., 7½in.x14¾in.

Mason, George Finch (1850-1915)
Sporting artist, author and illustrator, very often depicting humorous studies and caricatures. Educated at Eton (1860-1864) where his father was a master. Mason came from a great sporting family. He refers to his favourite uncle, his mother's younger brother and a bachelor, as having "a passion for the turf" and, as a result presumably of his gambling extravagances, being dubbed "the black sheep of the family". A prolific book illustrator, he wrote and illus. at least fourteen books including "Flowers of the Hunt" (1889), "Heroes and Heroines of the Grand National" (1907) (2nd edn. 1911), "Humours of the Hunting Field" (1886), "The Run of the Season" (1902) and "The White Hart and Other Stories" (1891). He also wrote a series of articles for "Fores Sporting Notes and Sketches" sometimes under the pen name "Fusbos". Nobody who has read his articles can fail to be impressed by the turn of phrase, the humour and the intimate knowledge of both racing and hunting which this author portrays, illustrating his work with talented sketches which are often very funny. Finch Mason wrote several accounts of his early days at Eton for "Fores Sporting Notes and Sketches" in one of which he records seeing the Royal Buckhounds with their huntsman, Charles Davis (q.v.), the brother of R.B. Davis (q.v.) the sporting artist. Finch Mason was "Uncle Toby" of "The Sporting Times" and died at his Chelsea house having been an invalid for a long time. He collaborated with Mr. J. Maunsell Richardson on the work "Gentleman Riders Past and Present" (pub. by Messrs. Vinton and Co.)

where he was described as "a very clever artist and a most charming man". Exh. at the leading London galleries from 1874. His racing watercolours include the "Liverpool Autumn Cup" (1899), "'Refraction' wins the Royal Hunt Cup" (1899), and "The Last Fence at Hurst Park - 'Glenroyal' wins the National Hunt Steeplechase in 1899".

Mason, William (1724-1797)
Draughtsman and painter in watercolour of several horse racing scenes including "A Scene in a Country Town at the Time of the Race" which was engraved by Valentine Green, ARA (1739-1818) in 1783, 17¾in.x 23½in. A pair of similar scenes entitled "Country Race Course with Horses preparing to Start" and "With Horses Running" after the work by this artist, was engraved by J. Jenkins and F. Jukes and published in 1786, 20in.x26¾in. Mason's busy and detailed drawing "The Finishing Line", pencil, pen/ink and watercolour, 14½in.x21in., was auctioned Christie's 1991.

Mason, William (1809-1875)
Print colourer, animal and domestic artist in watercolour and oil. Lived at Kennington for most of his life. A great admirer of Cruikshank (q.v.) through whom he met Charles Dickens and James Hardy (q.v.) whose painting style he followed. By 1851 Mason had four assistants working for him, colouring prints and from 1843 Christmas cards for Henry Cole. He died from a stroke on 3 January 1875. Painted a number of ratting scenes and still lifes of dead game.

Massey, F.E. (op.1871)
"Huntsmen and Hounds", s.&d. 1871, was auctioned Christie's 1928.

Matania, Fortunino, RI (1881-1963)
Historical painter and illustrator, the son of Professor Eduardo Matania. He was trained in his father's studio and illus. his first book at fourteen years old. Matania worked in London for "The Graphic" but returned to Italy (1903) to do his military service. He then settled in London where he joined the staff of "The Sphere" becoming a "special" artist in 1914. Elected RI (1917). Matania's work is somewhat stylised and dated to his own period but he painted several portraits of horses including a study of the Arab horse "Willie", the property of H.B. Musgrave-Clark, painted at Musgrave-Clark's famous Arab stud in Sussex.

Matthews, James (op.c.1875-1905)
Prolific Sussex landscape painter in watercolour, who rarely dated his work, working towards the end of the 19th century in a style similar to Helen Allingham. His painting "A Game of Cricket", s.&d. 1901, 5¾in.x 7½in., was exh. Chris Beetles Ltd., London, and shows local yokels sitting on a bench watching a game of cricket on the village green. His painting output was almost all of Sussex landscapes. He appears not to have exh. in London.

Matthews, John Chester (op.1884-1912)
Painter of equestrian portraits, particularly racing. These include a study of Major Brown's racehorse "The Primate" with Captain Bewicke up in yellow silks, s.&d. 1895, a study of the dark bay racehorse "Omeroid", s.&d. 1892, a study of the racehorse "Field Marshal" with jockey up, s.&d. 1895, and "Louis XIII" in his stable 1900. Matthews exh. a portrait of a horse at SS in 1886/1887 and occasionally contributed to "The Graphic".

Mattinson, Donald (op.1950)
20th century painter whose portrait of the chestnut horse "Kirtling" and a dapple grey horse "Adelecia", s.&d. 1950, were drawn in pen, ink and watercolours, each 13in.x20in., and auctioned at Bonhams 1989.

Maud, W.T. (1865-1903)
Portrait painter and war artist for "The Graphic". Studied at the RA Schools, winning the Landseer Scholarship (1893). Joined "The Daily Graphic" in the same year and succeeded A.S. Hartrick (q.v.) on "The Graphic" (1895) as a "special" (artist). Became a considerably important campaign artist and died during the Somali War in 1903. He illus. "Mr. Facey Romford's Hounds" and "Hawbuck Grange" by R.S. Surtees.

Maurer, Louis (1832-1932)
American painter of equestrian subjects, particularly of trotting races, who was a brilliant rider himself and an excellent exponent of trick riding. His sporting subjects include "Millers Damsel", "George M", "Patch'Em" and "Brown Dick" in their trotting contest for a purse of 500 dollars over the Union Course, 7 July 1859, 30in.x48in., and Alexander Halliday driving his black mare "Neetah" in a brewster buggy, s.&d. 1878, pen, black ink and grey and black wash, 13⅜in.x17½in. Maurer also painted "The Buffalo Hunt", a fine action painting, 16in.x12in., and his dramatic 'Trotters Racing by the Judge's Stand" was auctioned Christie's. Maurer, who was German-born, arrived in New York in 1850 at the age of eighteen and started to work as a lithographer, eventually owning his own printing works. He did not turn to painting until 1872 and enrolled at the Gotham Art School in 1882 when he was fifty, to improve his technique. Maurer lived to be a hundred, mounting a one-man exhibition at the age of ninety-nine. Probably the best known racing painting by this remarkable man is "The First Futurity at Sheepshead Bay" in 1888 which captures the moment when the great "Salvator" was beaten by "Proctor Knott" in this valuable race. The painting is in the collection of the National Museum of Racing and Hall of Fame, Saratoga, NY.

Mauzer, David
Contemporary Latin American painter of "The Football Players", 39⅛in.x27½in., pastel, Sotheby's 1989.

Maxwell-Reekie, William (op.1946)
"An Old Curling Pond, Newtonmore" s.&d. 1946 and inscr., 18in.x24in., Christie's (Scotland).

May, Charles (1847-1932)
Artist and decorator and the elder brother of Phil (Philip William) May (q.v.). Contributed pen and ink sketches to "The English Illustrated Magazine" (1895-1897),

"Pearsons Magazine", "Fun Frolic and Fancy" (1894) and "Madame" (1895). He was also a wallpaper designer. His sketch "One for the Bag" is a portrait of Irwin Cox fishing. Mr. Irwin Cox was Conservative MP for Harrow Division and proprietor of "Law Times" and "The Field".

May, Fred (b.1891, op.1920s)
An illustrator whose sporting sketches include "Hunting Celebrities from the Garth Hunt", The Master (Major L.A. Jackson), Colonel J.S. Talbot, Lord Downshire and Captain R.G. Sturgis, repro. in "The Tatler" April 1922; "Admirals v. Cadets at Cricket, Royal Nautical College, Pangbourne", pen/black ink, 24in.x18½in., Christie's Sth. Ken., repro. in "The Tatler and Bystander"; "The Royal Corps of Signals Golf Tournament", signed, 24in.x18½in., Christie's (Sth. Ken.). May, who studied at Wallasey School of Art and under Seaby at Reading University, contributed illustrations to "The Tatler", "The Weekly Sketch" and "The Graphic".

May, Phil (op.1957)
Contemporary motor artist painting in the style of Bryan de Grineau (q.v.). His motor and aeroplane racing scenes include the Curtis R3C Minus 2 flown by Lt. James H. Doolittle winning the Schneider Trophy over Chesapeake Bay, Ballimari, 1925, 11¾in.x25⅝in., Phillips (Auto) 1985.

May, Philip William (Phil), RI (1864-1903)
Painter, illustrator and black and white artist of many sporting subjects. The son of a Leeds engineer. Educated at St. Georges School, Leeds. After leaving school he became assistant scene painter at Leeds Grand Theatre. Came to London in about 1883 and joined "Society" and "St. Stephen's Review" before leaving for Australia in 1885 to work for "The Sydney Bulletin". In 1888 he returned to Europe to study in Paris. In 1895 he joined "Punch" where he contributed football scenes and was on "The Graphic" staff until 1903 when he died of cirrhosis of the liver. He was an original member of the London Sketch Club (founded in 1898) and the Chelsea Arts Club (founded in the same year) for which his friend, Whistler, proposed him. An excellent horseman which is reflected in his many equestrian sketches. He had a habit of leaving his horse outside his clubs (the Savage was another) and forgetting where he had left him. Elected RI in 1897.

May, S.A. (op.1920s/1930s)
Talented painter and illustrator about whom surprisingly little is known. "Lady Out Shooting with a Spaniel", signed, pastel, 17in.x11in., auctioned Christie's (Sth. Ken.) 1985.

Mayne, C.L. (op.1868)
A piebald hunter in a landscape, s.&d. 1868, 18in.x 24in., was auctioned Bonhams 1985.

Mayor, William Frederick ("Fred") (1865-1916)
Portrait and landscape painter. Included in this Dictionary for his portrait of the cricketer, Tom A. Morris, padded up, 28in.x23in., painted c.1900,

Sotheby's (Sussex). Tom Morris of Timberley Farm, Bury, W. Sussex was a well-known local cricketer who is believed to have played for the Duke of Norfolk's Eleven at Arundel. Mayor probably painted this portrait when he was living close by at Amberley between 1894-1905. He is possibly the artist responsible for a pair of watercolours c.1890s (sold £4,800) of golfing scenes (Hobbs Parker, Ashford) signed Mayor only.

Mays, Douglas Lionel (b.1900)
"Punch" artist and illustrator who studied at Goldsmiths College of Art, under Harold Speed and E.J. Sullivan (1920-1923). Mays, who was a fine lawn tennis player himself, illus. "Tennis Shoes" by Noel Streatfeild, pub. J.M. Dent & Sons Ltd. 1937.

Maze, Paul Lucien (1887-1979)
French-born painter of landscapes, figure scenes and some sporting subjects who was educated in England and joined the British army in 1914. He recorded his experiences in "A Frenchman in Khaki" pub. in 1934. In 1930 Maze gave an exhibition at the Knoedler Galleries (15 Old Bond St. London W1) where his watercolours were described ("Connoisseur" April 1930) as "Sargentesque in their dashing handling and economical statement...since subtlety in the use of colour is not a strong point with Mr. Maze, those drawings in which greyish effects are exploited are the most successful". Maze painted several racecourse scenes including "At the Races", "The Racecourse" and "The Royal Enclosure, Ascot". "Rowing at Oxford", s.&d. 1922, and inscr., 10¾in.x15½in., was auctioned Christie's 1988.

Meacham, Phyllida (b.1938)
Landscape and equestrian painter who studied at Chelsea School of Art and who specialises in polo scenes and portraits of racehorses.

Meade-King, Eric (1911-1987)
Sporting author, painter and illustrator. Educated at Malvern College and studied at the Westminster School of Art, also under Lionel Edwards (q.v.). His first book "The Silent Horn" was pub. by Collins in 1938 and was an instant success, as were two exhibitions he held of his paintings at the Greatorex Galleries in London (1937 and 1938). Eric Meade-King served with the Household Cavalry during the 2nd World War. He includes polo and fox-hunting amongst the sporting work he painted. His fine but somewhat cynically entitled scene "The Plaything of the Devil", showing an impression of the Grand National at Aintree, was painted c.1935 and contributed to "The Sporting and Dramatic Life", Rowles Fine Art, Powys.

Meadows, Edwin L. (op.1854-1881)
London painter of landscapes and equestrian portraits which include "Sambo" a bay hunter, the property of Stanley Vickers, Esq. by a stable in a wooded landscape, painted in 1859, 20in.x30in., "The Midday Break" (with horses), s.&d. '81. Meadows also painted angling scenes including "A River Landscape with an Angler", s.&d. '79. Exh. at the RA (1858-1867), BI and SS.

Meadows, Gordon Arthur (b.1868)
Landscape painter. Son of Arthur Joseph Meadows and nephew of Edwin Meadows (q.v.). His watercolour "Looking Across the Golf Links to St. Mary Magdalene, Ridgway" inscr., s.&d. 1910, 9in.x13½in., was auctioned Phillips (Exeter) 1989.

Meadows, James Edwin (1828-1888)
London landscape painter whose work includes numerous views in Essex, Kent, Sussex and Surrey. His sole claim to sporting fame lies in his farmyard scene with horses, cattle and poultry by a barn, painted in collaboration with John Frederick Herring, Jnr. (q.v.), signed by both artists and dated 1860.

Meagher, William (op.1745)
"A Hunt in Full Cry", s.&d. 23 August 1745, private collection, shows a detailed and interesting view of a hunt taking place beside an unidentified seaside town.

Mearns, A. (op.1855-1872)
Painter of dogs from Kent who exh. four works at the BI between 1855 and 1864 including portraits of pointers and Clumber spaniels and two works at SS. His other sporting paintings include "Spaniels Flushing Ducks" (1866), "The Pheasant Drive" (1872) and "Guarding the Day's Bag" (1868).

Mears, M. (op.1955)
Mitchell records a picture of "The Queen Elizabeth Chase, Hurst Park" (1955) by this artist.

Mease, J. (op.1790-1810)
Painter of equestrian and animal subjects who exh. two horse portraits at the RA 1797 and 1798. He also painted a portrait of a terrier, dated 1790, and one of a gentleman on his hunter, dated 1810.

Meggeson (Miggeson), J.J. (op.1855-1866)
Equestrian painter whose portrait of William Russell on a chestnut hunter with hounds finding the scent, s.&d. 1855, 32½in.x43½in., was auctioned Christie's 1972. He also painted steeplechasing scenes including six horses and riders steeplechasing in open country, s.&d. 1866, 24in.x41½in., Christie's 1972.

Meissonier, Jean Louis Ernest (1815-1891)
French figure painter and sculptor whose sporting work includes portraits of horses and a painting featuring lawn bowls.

Melchers, J. Gari (1860-after 1929)
American painter, born in Detroit, who studied at Dusseldorf Academy (1877-1880) and in Paris, under Lefebvre and Boulanger. Included in this Dictionary for his portrait of Charles Blair Macdonald, one of America's greatest golf pioneers and creator of the National Golf Links in 1910. Macdonald is shown in Melcher's painting pausing during play at the National, his caddy standing beside him. Melchers was elected a member of the NA in 1906.

"Meliora Spero"
Alias Dr. Richard Chandler Alexander Prior (1809-1902), a croquet enthusiast who wrote a letter to "The Field" in 1868 under this pseudonym. Author of "Notes on Croquet and Some Ancient Bat and Ball Games related to It" (1872).

Melling, Henry (op.1829-1854)
Northern painter of marine scenes whose fine painting "The Midnight Race", s.&d. 1854, depicts the start of a race from Liverpool to Douglas, Isle of Man and shows boats both under sail and preparing for the race. Melling was Hon. Sec. of the Royal Mersey Yacht Club and this race is still held annually.

Mellor, Sir John Paget, Bt. KCB - "Quiz" (1862-1929)
Amateur artist and caricaturist, sometimes of sporting subjects including his "Impressions of Alex Herd", pen/ink/grey wash, Christie's (Sth. Ken.) 1991. Alex Herd (Sandy) (1868-1944) was a Scottish professional golfer who won the 1902 Open Championship with the rubber cored ball which was just coming in and which was to take over from the "guttie"; author of "My Golfing Life". Mellor, who exh. at the RA (1906 and 1908) was called to the Bar at the Inner Temple (1886) and served as a barrister and assistant solicitor to the Treasury (1894-1909). He served as a solicitor (1909-1923). Created CB in 1905 and KCB 1911. Mellor's cartoons are usually portraits and signed "Quiz".

Melville, Arthur, ARSA, RSW, RP, RWS (1855-1904)
Scottish-born landscape and figure painter in both oil and watercolour who painted in an impressionistic style which he made his own. Studied at the RSA Schools in Edinburgh and in Paris (1878-1881) at the Académie Julian. Spent two years travelling (1881-1883). Returned to Scotland where he was to have a major influence on the Glasgow School (1883-1889). He first exh. at the RSA in 1875. Came to London in 1889 and made frequent visits to Europe which inspired some of his finest work. A magnificent crowd painter, he died tragically young from typhoid contracted in Spain. "The Lawn Tennis Party at Marcus", watercolour, 29in.x22in., was painted in 1889 and "Skating on Duddingston Loch", 19½in.x26in., is a fine example of his work in watercolour. Elected RSW (1885), RP (1891), ARSA (1886), RWS (1899).

Menasco, Milton
Contemporary American painter of horse racing scenes including "Nashua's Farewell to Keeneland".

Mercer, Edward Stanley, ROI, RP (b.1889)
Portrait and landscape painter. "The Young Cricketer", signed, 72in.x39¼in. The Forbes Magazine Collection. Mercer, who exh. at the leading London galleries and elsewhere between 1913-1932, was elected RP (1920) and ROI (1927).

Mercer, Fletcher J. (1861-1922)
Lincolnshire-born painter of landscapes, flowers and portraits. Studied painting at Whistler's school in Paris and at the Slade. Exh. with the NEAC from 1901. His portrait of E.J. ("Johnny") Jackett, the full back for England in the Rugby International Matches 1905, 1906 and 1907, was exh. at the NEAC in 1907. Jackett's portrait was also painted by H.S. Tuke (q.v.).

Mercier, Philip (b.c.1689-d.1761)
Portrait painter and engraver whose sitters included only two known sporting personalities. Mercier, who

was born in Berlin of French Huguenot parents, studied art in Berlin and Paris. He was greatly influenced by Watteau whose work he etched. He settled in London in 1720, gaining the patronage of Frederick, Prince of Wales. Mercier's portrait of Sir Edward Hales, 5th Bt. (c.1724-1802) dated 1744, shows him standing at the edge of a wood after shooting, holding a single barrelled flintlock gun in his left hand with a brace of game and a dead hare lying on the ground beside his dog, 80in.x51in., The Paul Mellon Collection, Upperville, Va, USA. Mercier's only other known sporting portrait "A Young Man with Gun and Dog" is in the collection of the Balnagowan Estates Co. Ltd., Balnagowan Castle, Ross-shire.

Merian, Matthaus the younger (1621-1687)
Swiss-born portrait painter who depicted "The High Borne Prince James, Duke of York" in the act of playing a shot at real tennis, etching, 7½in.x5in., from the "True Effigies of... King Charles... with the...Royall Progenie"(p.10). The British Museum, London.

Merry, Tom (1852-1902)
Caricaturist and cartoonist whose "The Grand National Favourites" and "Gamblers at Ascot" appeared in "St. Stephens Review" (Presentation Cartoon) 29 March 1884 and 14 June 1884. These were based on political sketches that Merry did for "St. Stephens Review" between 1885 and 1890. All his work appeared as two (or single) page coloured lithographs often wittily taken from famous paintings of the day by John Seymour Lucas (q.v.), Stanley Berkeley (q.v.) or parodies of Hogarth.

Methuen, Paul Ayshford, Lord, RA, RWS, PRWA, RBA, NEAC (1886-1975)
Landscape and figure painter who is included in this Dictionary for his RA exhibit "Badminton Olympic Trials" (1953). Methuen, who studied at the Slade School of Art, under Sir Charles Holmes and subsequently under Walter Sickert in London, had his first solo exh. at the Warren Gallery, London in 1928. Elected RBA (1939), RWS (1952), RA (1959) and PRWA from 1939.

Metz, Conrad Martin (1749-1827)
German-born portrait painter who studied at the RA Schools in 1772 where he won a silver medal in 1780. His portrait of two boys dressed for cricket, one holding a bat in a wooded landscape, 36in.x30in., s.&d. 1776, was auctioned Sotheby's (1985). Metz exh. at the RA (1781-1794) but lived in Rome after 1801.

Mew, Thomas Hillier (op.1850-1875)
Equestrian artist from the Isle of Wight, the brother of Frederick Mew, the architect. His best known portrait of the racehorse "Thormanby" was painted (1860) for Mr. J. Kelleray of Averton, Isle of Wight. The artist was paid £10 for the picture which is 16in.x21in. "Thormanby", who won the Derby in 1860, ridden by Custance, was owned by one of the less attractive· figures on the turf in the 19th century, Mr. James Merry. Merry, netting over £85,000 from his winnings on "Thormanby's" Derby gave £100 to the jockey

Custance with the hope that so large a sum would not turn his head. Mew also painted steeplechase and hunting scenes, very often in multiples and sometimes in watercolour.

Meyer, Emile (op.1889-1891)
19th century French painter of equestrian scenes including "The Show Horse", s.&d. 1891, and "The Riding School".

Meyer, F. John (op.1826-1844)
Painter of portraits and of some sporting subjects. His portrait of the children of Horman Fisher shows the son holding a bow and clearly portrays him as a serious archer, 71in.x52½in., Julian Simon Fine Art, London. Meyer exh. the painting at the RA in 1834 (No.250). An aquatint after the work by Meyer entitled "Equestrian Match Against Time" was engraved by Henry·Hoppner Meyer (q.v.) and exh. by the Parker Gallery, London 1950. Meyer was presumably a close relation of Henry Hoppner Meyer.

Meyer, Gottfried (b.1911)
German-born figure painter and etcher who studied at the Berlin Academy in 1932, under Erich Wolfsfeld, and for the previous year (1931) under Lotte Laserstein (q.v.). Meyer's fine work "The Fencer", 58⅞in.x 36½in., was painted in 1934 and undoubtedly shows Laserstein's influence. His model for the picture was not a sportsman, in fact the young man had a weak heart and was therefore able to pose for Meyer quite frequently. The painting which was exh. in London in 1990 (Agnews) is one of the few pre-war works by Meyer not destroyed by allied bombing and represents, almost certainly, his finest figure painting period, indeed the period during which he won the Prix de Rome for his figure drawings, exh. at the Preussische Akademie der Kunste (1935).

Meyer, Henry Hoppner (1782-1847)
Painter, line, stipple, mezzottint and aquatint engraver. A portrait of a boxer, thought to be "Deaf" Burke standing full length, his fists raised for a fight, 24in.x 20in., and signed H. Meyer was auctioned Christie's 1991. Jem Burke (the Deaf Un) was born in London c.1809. He had his first fight, against Ned Murphy, when he was eighteen. Burke's greatest fight (1833) was against Simon Byrne, a contest which lasted 3 hours 6 minutes. Byrne should have won the contest in the 19th round as the sponge was flung up from Burke's corner but the referee was persuaded to let the fight go on. 80 rounds later on Byrne was taken off in a coma and died three days later and Burke claimed the title.

Meyer, Louis (op.1901-1907)
Painter of sporting subjects and animals including "Sportsmen and their Dog in a wooded Landscape with a Village beyond" and "Lion and Lioness", dated 1901. He exh. one painting at the Royal Society of Artists, Birmingham, in 1907.

Meyer-Wismar, Ferdinand (1833-1917)
Swedish landscape painter and of fresh water angling scenes including "Landing the Fish", signed and inscr., 32in.x21¾in., Christie's 1983.

Meynard, G. (op.1978)
Contemporary painter of a golf scene entitled (unimaginatively) "Golf", s.&d. '78 (1978), acrylic, 51¼in.x35¼in., Stanilas Machoir, Versailles 78000, Hotel des Ventes Rameau, 5 Rue Rameau.

Miartani, P.
Unknown artist of a boxing painting, 21in.x27in., Sotheby's (NY) 8.6.1990

"Mich"
The pseudonym used by Michael Liedeaux (q.v.), the French poster artist.

Midworth, R. (op.19th century)
Mitchell records a portrait of a racehorse by this artist.

Milbanke, Mark Richard (1875-1927)
London portrait painter who exh. a portrait of "Sheffield Neave Esq. late Master of the Essex Stag Hounds" at the RA in 1901 (No.326). He also painted a set of four watercolours depicting soldiers of the Devonshire and Yorkshire regiments and the Dragoon Guards, each 14in.x10in.

Miles, George Francis (1852-1891)
Portrait and marine painter, also of genre scenes into which category his painting of lawn tennis falls, "Pause in the Match", s.&d. 1883, Wimbledon Lawn Tennis Museum. Miles exh. at the RA and GG between 1874-1887 and favoured female portraiture.

Miles, John (op.1811-1840)
Provincial painter of animals and sporting subjects from Northleach, Gloucestershire. Paintings recorded by him are of a Gloucestershire Old Spot Pig, several of prize cows, the famous Garden of Eden (which sold for £9,000 when auctioned by Christie's in 1980) and a portrait of Squire Osbaldeston's "Tom Thumb" winning a wager in a trotting match. The same incident was painted by F.C. Turner (q.v.). He also painted a work with the intriguing title "An Instance Never Known Before" which was s.&d. 1811.

Miles, William (op.1841-1860)
Victorian sporting artist from Exeter, Devon, who exh. one picture at the BI in 1841. In 1860 he published a work entitled "Stables and Stable Fittings". His fine painting of two ladies, two horses and two springer spaniels, painted in 1845 (in a private collection) is a striking example of this artist's work. A portrait of a grey side-saddled pony, 20in.x27¼in., was exh. at "Sport and the Horse", June 1969, Oscar and Peter Johnson, London.

Millais, Sir John Everett Bt., PRA (1829-1896)
This eminent artist, lithographer and etcher spent many weeks on successive seasons at the beautiful 42,000 acre estate Braemore belonging to Sir John Fowler in whose game book he drew stalking, shooting and fishing sketches between 1867 and 1869. In 1868 he appears to have been at Braemore at the same time as Sir Edwin Landseer (q.v.). Millais was an outstanding naturalist and a big game shot. His angling scenes include the fine portrait of Sophie Millais and her eleven salmon which he painted in watercolour in 1891. He borrowed Culra

Hut on Ben Alder from the Pennington Ramsdens in 1919 while recuperating from an illness and spent much of his time painting the interior of the hut which happened to be lined with asbestos. When the hut was returned to its owners the asbestos was carefully removed and the pictures rescued. His "Derby Day", an ink sketch, was drawn in 1894. He became a member of the Etching Club and the Junior Etching Club. He also features prominently in the painting by C.W. Cope entitled "Hanging at the RA" (1876) in which painting Sir Francis Grant (q.v.) sits in the President's chair. Elected RA (1863). Created Baronet (1885). Elected PRA (1896).

Millais, John Guille (1865-1931)
The fourth son of Sir John Everett Millais (q.v.). Widely travelled painter, lithographer and etcher of birds and animals who pub. many natural history books including "British Deer and their Horns" (1897). He also wrote with Archibald Thorburn (q.v.) "The Natural History of British Game Birds" (1909). His many illus. books include "Game Birds and Shooting Sketches" (1892), "Shooting" (1887) (Sir R. Payne Gallwey), "The Encyclopaedia of Sport" (1898) and "American Big Game" (1915).

Millais, Raoul Hesketh (b.1901)
Painter of equestrian and sporting subjects including hunting, racing, coursing and many portraits of distinguished racehorses. Second son of the artist John Guille Millais (q.v.) and therefore a grandson of Sir John Everett Millais (q.v.). Studied for three years at the RA Schools, under Augustus John, where his contemporaries were John Skeaping (q.v.) and the Zinkheisen sisters (qq.v.) and at the Byam Shaw School of Art. Travelled with his father in 1920. A keen fox-hunting man, he hunted with the Beaufort and received many commissions to paint equestrian portraits and classic racehorse winners including "Big Game, "Sun Chariot" and Sir Winston Churchill's "Colonist". His painting of the Queen arriving at Ascot in 1977 is now in the Royal Collection.

Millar, James (c.1735-1805)
The leading portrait painter in Birmingham during the last quarter of the 18th century, Millar also painted a number of sporting subjects. Exh. SA (1771), RA (1784-1790). His portrait of a gentleman out shooting with his dog with an interesting hammer shotgun, s.&d. 1790, 93¾in.x57¾in., was exh. Oscar and Peter Johnson, London. Millar is recorded in the Birmingham Trade Directory (1800-1801).

Miller, Alfred Jacob (1810-1874)
American painter of equestrian and racing scenes in watercolour including "Racing at Fort Laramie", 7in.x12in. Miller, who came from Baltimore, visited Europe in 1833 where he studied art in Paris, Rome and Florence. He is probably best known for his series of sketches made for Sir William Drummond Stewart, the Scottish baronet, whom he accompanied to the Rocky Mountains in 1837.

Miller, George W. (op.1850-1896)
Animal and equestrian painter whose portrait of a horse in a stable, s.&d. 1850, 24in.x29in., was auctioned Sotheby's 1984. He also painted portraits of cattle and horses in landscapes. Exh. at SS and the RA between 1890 and 1896.

Miller, J. (op.1820-1864)
London painter of portraits, animal and equestrian subjects who exh. at the RA and at SS between 1846 and 1864.

Miller, James (op.1773-1791)
Portrait painter and of some equestrian and sporting subjects including coaching scenes. Exh. SA 1773 to 1791 and RA 1781 to 1788. He appears to have been the son of John Miller (see Johann Sebastian Muller).

Miller, John (b.1715-d.1792)
See Johann Sebastian Muller

Miller, John (Jack) Lawrence
Contemporary artist of sporting subjects particularly of horse racing scenes. His watercolour "In the Paddocks, Lingfield - Springtime", s.&d. 1985, 27in.x38½in., was auctioned Christie's (Sth. Ken.) 1990. Miller studied at Goldsmith's Art School, London. His first sporting commission was a study of polo at Cowdray Park for the Maharaja of Jaipur.

Miller, Roy (b.1938)
Manchester painter of equestrian and sporting subjects who studied at Manchester Regional College of Art and at Farnham College of Art. Amongst the classic racehorses he has painted are "Bustino", "Dahlia", "Highclere" and "Brigadier Gerard". His dramatic "Night Racing at Happy Valley" shows the thrill of horse racing at Hong Kong by night, with the track surrounded by hundreds of lit-up apartment blocks towering above it. The painting is in the collection of the Royal Hong Kong Jockey Club.

Millett, Frederick (Fred) (op.1818)
Painter of animals and still lifes who signed his work "Fred Millett".

Millichap, G.T. (op.1837-1846)
"A Covey of Partridges in a Landscape", s.&d. 1837, 12in.x17in., was auctioned Christie's (Sth. Ken.) 1984. Exh. one work at the RA and one at SS between 1845 and 1846.

Millière, Maurice (1871-1946)
French figure artist and sculptor whose "At the Cricket Game" is s.&d. 1906, auctioned Christie's (NY) 1986. Millière also painted motoring scenes in the early 20th century.

Milliken, Robert W. (b.1920)
Wildlife and bird painter, also of shooting scenes, who includes a number of wildfowl and game birds amongst. his work. "A Woodcock in Flight", "Pheasants in Winter", "The Pack Grouse", etc. His watercolour "The Sunken Butt", inscr. with title, 24¾in.x39¾in., was exh. at Calton Gallery, Edinburgh.

Millington, John (op.1985)
Watercolour painter of yachting scenes including his painting of the J Class yacht "Endeavour 1" racing off Cowes, 10in.x14½in., which was auctioned Bonhams 1988.

Million-Guiet
20th century motor racing artist whose portrait of a 5 litre Bugatti, signed number 7140, painted in gouache, 10in.x16in., was auctioned in Paris 1986.

Millner, William (1818-1870)
Lincolnshire animal and equestrian painter and art teacher. Father of William Edward Millner (q.v.).

Millner, William Edward (1849-1895)
Lincolnshire animal and equestrian painter, the son of William Millner (q.v.). His study of a bay hunter in a field under a tree, painted in 1883, was auctioned Henry Spencer and Sons (1985) and his portrait of a dun mare standing in a landscape, s.&d. 1885, was auctioned Bonhams 1985. He also painted a hunting scene entitled "The Look Out" in 1882. Millner who was, like his father, an art teacher, exh. at the leading London galleries and elsewhere between 1869-1896. A number of his paintings can be seen in the Gainsborough Old Hall Museum.

Mills, Reginald (op.1921-1938)
Mitchell records hunting scenes and landscapes in watercolour by this artist.

Milnes, H. (op.1846)
Mitchell records a horse portrait, 16¼in.x22½in., by this artist, s.&d. 1846, auctioned Phillips May 1980.

Miró, Joan (1893-1983)
Spanish surrealist painter who trained at the School of Fine Arts in Barcelona and initially became a follower of Picasso (q.v.) and his cubist movement in 1919. His enthusiasm for sport is reflected in his work with footballers and the game of football.

Mitan, James (1776-1822)
Etcher, line and aquatint engraver of landscapes after the work of his contemporaries. A pupil of G.S. Agar and T. Cheesman. He also studied at the RA Schools. Ten engravings of freshwater fish by Mitan are in the collection of the Piscatorial Society.

Mitchell, E. (op.1885-1890)
Primitive painter of heavy horses including portraits of the prize shire horses "Knight Errant", "Prince of Wales" and "Horse Power".

Mitchell, J.A. (op.1826-1832)
Painter of equestrian subjects which include hunting and steeplechasing scenes. Mitchell seems to have lived at Leamington and most of his hunting scenes depict incidents in this county including his painting of the North Warwickshire Hunt at Stoneleigh Abbey, 44½in.x71in. "Preparing for the Hunt", s.&d. 1826, 50in.x40in., was exh. at HM and AG, Preston, "British Sporting Paintings" (1943). Exh. one painting at the RA in 1832. He also exh. at the RBSA. His portrait of Captain Becher on the steeplechaser "Vivian" was engraved by the Hunts as part of Fores "Celebrated Winners" series.

Mitchell, John Campbell, RSA (1865-1922)
Scottish artist of sea and landscapes painted in both oil and watercolour. Two very early works of Mitchell's entitled "One of the Wrong Sort - Who Goes out with the Hunters Because It Is the Fashion" and "One of the Right Sort - Who Hunts Because He Likes It", a pair, s.&d. 1879 were exh. at the Park Lane Antiques Fair, 1985. Mitchell studied at the RA Schools. Elected RSA (1918).

Mitchell, Winslow W. (op.1850-1852)
Equestrian portrait painter whose study of a bay hunter and a dog in a stable, 11½in.x16in., and his painting of a sportsman resting in a courtyard with horses and dogs, s.&d. 1851, 26in.x36½in., were auctioned at Sotheby's and Christie's respectively in 1985.

Moberl(e)y, Mariquita Jenny
(Mrs. H.G., née Phillips) RI, BWS, NSA, ASWA (b.1855)
Portrait, figure, landscape, flower and miniature painter. Studied art in Germany (under Bertha Froriep) and in Paris (under Carolus Duran). Elected ASWA (1902) and exh. widely (1881-1935). She painted an amateur but interesting watercolour of a lawn tennis mixed doubles match with Crystal Palace in the background which was auctioned Bonhams 1988.

Moerenhout, Joseph (Josef) Jodocus (1801-1875)
Flemish painter of equestrian scenes including his portrait of a horse in a stable, s.&d. 1842, and "Riding Out", auctioned in 1985.

Mogford, John, RI (1821-1885)
Exeter-born painter and a member of a large Devonshire family. His brother, Henry Mogford (op.1837-1846) was a very competent watercolourist. John Mogford painted marine and coastal scenes but also some equestrian portraits including a bay hunter in a landscape, s.&d. 1837 and inscr. "J. Mogford, Exeter", 25in.x30in., which was exh. at Ackermanns in 1978. He studied at the Government School of Design at Somerset House, London and married a daughter of Francis Danby. Exh. at the RA (1846-1881), BI, SS, NWS, GG and elsewhere. Elected RI (1867). His studio sale was held at Christie's, 25 February 1886.

Mogford, Thomas (1809-1868)
Exeter-born painter and a member of a large Devonshire family. Studied art at Exeter, under John Gendall and a Mr. Cole whose daughter he married. Exh. at the RA from 1838. He became a well-known West Country portrait and landscape painter. He also painted a number of equestrian portraits including a chestnut stallion with a dog in a landscape, a dark bay stallion in a landscape, a dapple grey Anglo-Arab in a landscape and a study of a Devon ox.

Moira, Gerald Edward (Geraldo Eduardo Lobo de Moura) PROI, VPRWS, RWA, NPS (1867-1959)
Landscape and portrait painter who studied at the RA Schools (1887-1889), a pupil of J.W. Waterhouse, and in Paris. He himself taught art and became principal of Edinburgh College of Art (1924-1932). Exh. at the RA from 1891. Elected NPS (1911), RWA (1919), RWS (1930), PROI (1945) and VPRWS (1953). Painted in oil and watercolour. His portrait entitled "The Fisherwoman", a charming picture of a lady in petticoats and blue frock with sun hat, fly fishing, was painted in watercolour in 1856. Usually signed his work Edward Moira and was originally called Geraldo Eduardo Lobo de Moura, the son of a Portuguese miniaturist who settled in London.

Moller, Rudolph (b.1881)
German artist whose "Steglitzer Race Track", s.&d. 1911, was auctioned in Munich in 1986.

Monahan, Hugh (1914-1970)
Irish born painter of birds and wildfowl including "Flighting Duck at Dusk", s.&d. 1940 and inscr. "Shovellers flighting Holyhead", 24½in.x29½in., Christie's 1991. Monahan was President of the Wildfowlers Association of Great Britain and Ireland.

Money, Keith (b.1935)
Painter of equestrian scenes including "The Grand National" (1982) and a portrait of the American Triple Crown winner "Secretariat" held by a groom, s.&d. 1974 and inscr., 30in.x36in., auctioned Christie's (Tattersalls) 1989.

Monk, William, RE (1863-1937)
Painter and etcher, mostly of architectural subjects, but very often set against a river background. "Westminster From the River", "The Tower of London" etc. Born in Chester. Studied art at Chester and at the Antwerp Academy. Exh. at the RA between 1894 and 1904 and at many other public galleries. Elected RE (1899). Founded and worked with the London Almanac for thirty-five years. His watercolour "The Boat Race - Kington on the River Arrow, Herefordshire", painted in 1931, signed and inscr., was auctioned at Bonhams. This inscription may be a mistake and perhaps should have been "Kingston", the river Arrow at Kington being thought too small to hold a regatta of this size.

Montague, Alfred, RBA (1832-1883)
Birmingham landscape and coastal painter who included a fine painting of skating on a frozen river amongst his work. Exh. at the RA (1836-1870), BI and SS. Elected RBA 1843.

Montaut, Ernest Edouard (1879-1909)
French lithographer known as "The Father of Automobile Art". Montaut was amongst the first artists to devote his talents to the subject of motoring and is credited with the invention of virtually every artistic technique for the visual rendering of speed. His delicately hand-coloured lithographs were pub. in two sizes: the smaller, 12in.x9in., were often offered in a string bound album entitled "10 Ans de Courses 1897-1907" and the larger, 36in.x18in, were sold individually. After his death the publishing company Mabileau et Cie continued to produce lithographs in the Montaut style affording recognition for many of Montaut's co-workers and followers including "Campion" and "Gamy", the latter thought to have been Montaut's wife, Marguèrite, a successful artist in her own right.

Monument, R. (op.1868)
A primitive portrait of a prize-fighting cock, s.&d. 1868, 20in.x24in., was auctioned Sotheby's 1987.

Moody, Fannie (Mrs. Gilbert King) SWA (b.1861-c.1947)
Animal painter and illustrator who included hound portraiture amongst the sentimental dog subjects she painted. Daughter of T.W. Moody (1824-1886), an art master at the South Kensington Schools. Fannie Moody studied art under J.T. Nettleship (q.v.) and contributed to "The Illustrated London News" 1892 to 1899. Exh. at the RA, RBA, RMS, ROI, SWA and the Birmingham and Liverpool Art Galleries. Her painting "Hounds Coming out of Kennels", 25in.x19in., was auctioned Sotheby's (Bel.) 1978. She also painted ponies and terriers.

Moor, G. (op.1842)
Painter of freshwater still lifes, some posed on a river bank, and one s.&d. 1842, Bonhams (1985).

Moore, Barlow (op.1863-1897)
Shipping and marine painter to the Royal Thames Yacht Club whose work includes many paintings of yacht racing scenes, "A Yacht Racing in Portsmouth Harbour" (1884), "A Yawl of the Royal Dorset Yacht Club Racing in Portsmouth Harbour" (1897) and "A Yacht Racing off the Needles" (1885) etc. He painted in both oil and watercolour. Moore exh. at the RA in 1868 and at the BI in 1863.

Moore, Claude T. Stanfield (1853-1901)
River and coastal scene painter whose work includes a number of rowing and yacht racing scenes, for example "The Thames at Westminster with twenty eights racing towards Westminster Bridge", s.&d. '91, 24in.x44½in., auctioned Sotheby's 1986. Exh. one work entitled "Beating up the Thames" at SS and his work is represented in the Nottingham AG, the town in which he was born.

Moore, Fay
Contemporary equestrian painter, in particular of horse racing scenes in America.

Moore, Miss Gwendolen (op.1896-1939)
Liverpool landscape and flower painter who exh. between 1905 and 1939 at the Walker AG, Liverpool and Birmingham. Her painting "Who's For a Ride", a watercolour of a man and a woman wheeling their bicycles along a road, s.&d. 1896 was auctioned Sotheby's 1979.

Moore, Henry, RA, RBA, RWS (1831-1895)
Yorkshire-born landscape and marine painter. His father was the portrait painter William Moore (q.v.) and his brother was the neo-classical painter Albert Joseph Moore, with whom he went to London in 1853. Moore studied under his father at the York School of Design and at the RA Schools, and exh. at the RA (1835-1895) and elsewhere. The Glasgow AG has his painting "St. Albans Race", which is more sea and sky than yacht racing, and the V & A Museum, London, has "Strath Fillan, Perthshire with a Leaping Salmon" repro. "Angling in British Art", Shaw Sparrow, p.41. Moore was elected RWS (1880) and RA (1893).

Moore, I. (J.) (op.1812)
Painter of equestrian and sporting scenes who operated in the early part of the 19th century. His portrait of a bay racehorse in a landscape, s.&d. 1812, 25in.x30in., was auctioned Christie's 1974 and a fine pair of paintings entitled "Coursing" and "The Chase", both signed, 11¼in.x15¾in., were auctioned Sotheby's 1971.

Moore, R.H. (op.1868-1893)
Animal and sporting illustrator, a sculptor and a black and white artist who depicted many coursing scenes in the 1870s and 1880s which were repro. in "The Book of the Greyhound" (Ash). He also illus. "Sport in Many Lands" by Major Henry Asbury Leveson (1828-1875) (written under his pseudonym "The Old Shekarry") pub. c.1868. He worked extensively for "The Illustrated London News" 1875-1890 and contributed to "The Sporting and Dramatic News" 1890. Exh. NWS, RBA. "Good Companions", s.&d. 1893, was auctioned Bonhams 1989.

Moore, Rubens Arthur, NSA (op.1881-1920)
Nottingham landscape painter whose painting entitled "The Day's Bag", s.&d. 1893, 15½in.x21½in., was auctioned in Nottingham 1990. Elected NSA 1893.

Moore, William (1790-1851)
Yorkshire portrait painter in watercolour, oil and pastel whose watercolour and pencil drawing "The Young Archers", s.&d. 1833, 16¼in.x10¼in., was auctioned Christie's 1988.

Moorhouse, George Mottram (b.1882)
Westmorland figure painter in oil, watercolour and pastel and an etcher. Studied at Lancaster School of Art. Exh. at the RA, RSA, RHA, R.Cam.A and RWA. Painted a picture of the hunt at the edge of the sea, signed, watercolour, 16in.x24in., auctioned Sotheby's 1984.

Morby, Walter J. (op.1875-1898)
London landscape painter who painted a number of fox-hunting scenes including "In Full Cry" (s.&d. '98), "Through the Gate", "The Chase" and "The Kill". He exh. at the RA, RBA, RHA, RI between 1883 and 1890.

Morden, W.G. (op.1957)
Painter of "The FA Cup Final" (1957), "Manchester United Against Aston Villa at Wembley", Wiggins Teape Group.

Moreau, Alain
Contemporary painter of a portrait of the American footballer "Brad Vaylett. NY Grants Line Backer", oil 1978.

Moreau, Albert (op.1948)
French artist who contributed a lithograph of a boxer covering his face with his gloves at the XIVth Olympiad Sport in Art exhibition at the V & A Museum, London in 1948 (No. 240).

Moreland, Arthur (op.1895-1901?)
Draughtsman and cartoonist who contributed work to "The Morning Leader" c.1895. His drawing of a golfer and caddy contemplating their ball which has landed in a cow pat is fairly illustrative of his work, s.&d. 1901, watercolour and pen, Sotheby's Glasgow.

Morgan, Frederick (Fred) ROI (1856-1927)
Animal and portrait painter who exh. from 1865 at the RA, BI, NWS, GG and elsewhere. Elected ROI 1883. "The Badminton Lesson", signed, 29½ in. x19½ in., auctioned Sotheby's 1989. Elected ROI (1883).

Morgan, John, RBA (1823-1886)
Painter of genre subjects, generally featuring children. His paintings entitled "Ginger Beer" and "The Fight in the Country" illustrate his style to perfection. The former, 40in.x27in., exh. at the RA 1860 (No. 572), shows children, one with a cricket bat over his shoulder, stopping their game for refreshments. The second painting, 27in.x41in., also shows a cricket match taking place in the background while two boys fight in the foreground and boy spectators, cricket bats over their shoulders, look on. This painting was exh. at the RA 1869 (No.472) where Morgan exh. from 1852. Elected RBA 1875.

Morgan, William (1826-1900)
American painter, born in London and emigrated to America early in his life. Studied art at the schools of the National Academy of which he became an Associate in 1865. A painting by Morgan of a chestnut and two bay racehorses with jockeys up on a race course, 30⅛ in.x 50in., s.&d. '81 was auctioned Christie's 1987. Morgan painted "The Herefordshire Hunt" in which Sir Veltres Cornwall and Mr. Arkwright as well as the huntsman and hounds are represented "in an easy natural style which augers well for the future of the artist" ("Bailys Magazine" 1861). "As Mr. Morgan purposes to follow this painting up with other paintings of hunts and their Masters, we think he will have no reason to regret his want of patronage. The portraits are lifelike, and the grouping of the hounds free from the old conventional system so much in vogue with painters of the present day".

Morier, David (c.1705-1770)
Swiss painter of battle and equestrian scenes who came to England in 1743. He painted a number of equestrian portraits for distinguished patrons who included the Duke of Cumberland, the Earl of Pembroke and Baron d'Eisenberg. "The Godolphin Arabian" painted for the Duke of Cumberland is the horse portrait for which Morier is perhaps best remembered. It is also the picture that is supposed to have inspired Stubbs (q.v.) and it is possible that they were friends. Morier was a contemporary of the portrait painter Richard Brompton (q.v.) for whom he is supposed to have painted the horses in Brompton's portrait groups. Both artists shared the Earl of Pembroke as a patron, both suffered from debt problems and both painted for the Royal Family.

Morland, George (1763-1804)
Probably the most prolific and naturally talented painter of English country life of his period. Although in later life he was reputedly rarely sober and frequently hiding from his creditors, or in prison, his paintings always retained their freshness and spirited technique. Tremendously popular in his own day, Morland's works remain the most copied and faked of any English painter which has perhaps tended to undermine the value of his genuine work. He was the son of the artist Henry Robert Morland, an example of whose work hangs in the National Gallery, London. Morland married a sister of James and William Ward (qq.v.) while his own sister married James Ward. He painted a great number of sporting subjects including shooting, skating, bathing and hunting scenes. The copious output of his short life often features sympathetically painted, tired old greys and weary old sportsmen - a theme that his brother-in-law, James Ward, was to pursue with such success. Morland was an enthusiastic sportsman, particularly in the hunting field, when he was sober enough to sit on his horse. That he occasionally managed to do so is shown by Thomas Hand (q.v.) whose portrait of Morland on a grey hunter with a couple of foxhounds, s.&d. 1794, 23¾ in.x31½ in., is in the Paul Mellon Collection, Upperville, Va, USA.

Morland, John (b.1930)
Wildlife and landscape artist who won the Gold Medal from the Royal Horticultural Society in 1979 for his botanical drawings. Better known in sporting circles perhaps, for his series of twenty-four famous British Golf Courses and Links.

Morley, George (op.1831-1889)
Painter of equestrian and sporting subjects who operated from Rugby. He exh. at the RA from 1832 to 1863 of which his first exhibit (No. 208) "A Shetland Pony", was the property of and ridden by H.R.H. the Princess Victoria. No less than twelve of his RA works were of animals owned by the Royal Family. He exh. two works at the BI (1843) and (1845) including "The Fox Gone to Earth". Amongst his many other patrons were the Duke of Norfolk and the Earls of Rosebery and Surrey. "The Master of the Craven Hunt, Mr. Dundas on his hunter with a groom", 21in.x27in., s.&d. 1844 and inscr., was auctioned Christie's 1987. Morley moved to Clifton (near Rugby) during the late 1850s. Three of his works were in the Hutchinson Sporting Gallery.

Morley, Robert, RBA (1857-1941)
Painter of animal and historical subjects and of some landscapes. Born in London, son of Professor Henry Morley LLD. Studied at the Slade School, under Poynter and Legros, and afterwards at Munich and Rome. He was a Slade Scholar and a painting medallist. Exh. from 1879 at the RA and from 1884 at SS and elsewhere. After 1888 he turned to animal painting and landscapes. Elected RBA in 1889, Hon. Sec. to RBA in 1890 and subsequently Hon. Treasurer until 1896. In 1921 he exh. at the Society of Animal Painters "Half a dozen anecdotes rendered with his wanted taste for the whimsicalities of animal life!".

Morrell, R.J. (op.1838-1839)
Exhibited "Fuss" a portrait of a Skye terrier at the RA and another study of a dog at SS from a London address. "Taking a Fence", s.&d. 1838, 9½ in.x12in., was auctioned Phillips 1987 and his portrait of "Dr. Syntax", a grey racehorse belonging to James Stoddart-Douglas, Esq. in a loosebox, 25in.x30in., is interesting since the story about this horse is recounted in "Bailys Magazine" (1915).

Morris, Alfred (op.1853-1873)
London painter of landscape and sporting subjects who exh. at the RA, BI, SS between 1853 and 1873. His sporting subjects include "The Day's Bag", painted in 1861, 36in.x50in., "Terriers with a Dead Rabbit", painted in the same year, and "Guarding the Day's Bag", painted in 1860.

Morris, Alice (op.1882-1908)
Officially described as a flower painter but she also painted several animal subjects including "A Study of a Black Cob in a Stable", s.&d. 1894 and "The Day's Bag", a watercolour, s.&d. 1908. Lived in Manchester and Leicester and exh. at BI, Walker AG, Manchester and elsewhere between 1882 and 1900.

Morris, James Charles (op.1851-1863)
Landscape, animal and sporting painter who favoured Scottish Highland scenes. A pupil of T. Sidney Cooper (q.v.), he exh. at the RA, BI, SS and elsewhere between 1851 and 1863. Operated at the same address as William Walker Morris (q.v.). His portrait of a pony, setters and dead grouse in a Highland landscape, 49in.x40in., was auctioned Christie's 1975.

Morris, John (op.1873-1877)
Painter of rustic and some sporting scenes including "The Day's Bag", 36in.x28½in. and "Saving his Brush", a painting of hounds streaming through a gate after a fox. Also "A Garron and Three Setters" in a mountainous landscape with the day's game, and a boy with pony and dogs, feeding the horse. His work, usually signed, but rarely dated is unlike the work of J.W. Morris (q.v.) which is almost always signed and usually dated.

Morris, John W. (op.1866-1900)
Painter of sporting subjects including "The Otter Hunt", "The Wounded Stag" and "The Twelfth of August". He favoured Highland scenes although his three exh. paintings were of genre subjects.

Morris, L. John (b.1906)
Surrey-born equestrian painter who studied art at Kingston and Farnham Schools of Art and who painted in the Australian outback between 1925 and 1933. He lived in Africa between 1942 and 1951 where he played polo. Studied marine painting under John Stobbart, RSMA, exh. regularly with the RSMA at the Guildhall, London and also with the FBA. Has specialised exclusively in equestrian art since 1970 and holds one-man exhibitions regularly at the Sandown race meetings. Three large works commissioned by United Racecourses Ltd. hang permanently in the foyer at Sandown Park, Members Stand. He founded the Society of Equestrian Artists in 1978. His painting of "Juliette Marny with jockey up" (Lester Piggott), s.&d. 1974, 24in.x20in., was auctioned Phillips 1986.

Morris, Philip Richard, ARA (c.1833-1902)
Painter of portraits and animal subjects and some sporting scenes including "A Hunt Fording the Stream", 35½in.x59½in., a very fine painting which Morris exh. at the RA in 1880, (No. 424). Morris studied at the RA Schools (1855) where he won two Silver Medals and in 1858 the Gold Medal for a biblical picture entitled "The Good Samaritan". Awarded a travelling scholarship and visited France and Italy. Exh. at the RA (1858-1901), BI, SS, GG and elsewhere. Resigned as an RA in 1900 and concentrated almost exclusively on portrait painting towards the latter part of his life. Elected ARA 1877, RA 1900.

Morris Richard (op. 1830-1844)
Draughtsman, landscape painter and aquatint engraver who exh. at SS, BI and the RA between these dates. He was also the author of "Essays on Landscape Gardening" c.1831. An etching by Morris after his own work of a panoramic view round Regent's Park contained a section devoted to a cricket match. Harrow and Little Primrose Hill can be seen beyond the Park. "The Regents Park", brown wash over etching, 4⅞in.x 18⅞in., dated 1831, pub. by R. Ackermann. Museum of London.

Morris, Robert Cleminson
See Cleminson

Morris, William Walker (op.1849-1886)
Painter of sporting subjects who operated from the same address as J.C. Morris (q.v.). Exh. from 1850 at the RA, BI and SS, mostly genre subjects. His sporting subjects include "The Game Stall", exh. BI 1853 (No. 163), "The Young Lad with his Dogs and Dead Game" painted in 1860, "An Angling Party" painted in 1861, and "Two Ponies with Two Terriers and Sportsmen Beyond, Rabbit Shooting" painted in 1860.

Morrish, William Snell (1844-1917)
Devonshire painter, son of Sydney S. Morrish, the landscape painter. W.S. Morrish painted landscapes in Devon sometimes featuring sporting scenes including "The Start of the Hunt - Bellaford Tor", s.&d. 1884, 16in.x24in., auctioned Christie's (Sth. Ken.) 1991. He exh. Devon landscapes at the RA, RBA, RI between 1880 and 1903.

Morrison, Robert Edward, RCA (1852-1925)
Isle of Man-born portrait painter who lived in Liverpool from 1882. Studied at Liverpool School of Art and in Paris at the Académie Julian under Bouguereau and Tony Fleury. Exh. at the RA from 1884 and painted many notable Lancashire personalities. His portrait of the amateur golf champion John Ball, Jnr., with golf club, s.&d. 1899, 51½in.x37¼in., is in the collection of the Royal Liverpool Golf Club at Hoylake.

Morrow, Noel (b.1915)
Lives at Havant near Chichester, Sussex and has painted marine subjects in watercolours all his life. Exh. at the RSMA and RI. He is an expert on typography and book design. His watercolour "Storm A'Stern" shows a 470 Class racing dinghy running before a strong breeze with thundery grey clouds forming in the background. There are surprisingly few paintings of dinghies sailing or racing although it is an exhilarating sport enjoyed by thousands of people of all ages.

Morrow, Norman (op.1911-1916)

Irish painter and illustrator who contributed drawings to "The Graphic" (1911-1916) and to "The Bystander" (13 July 1910) entitled "Are Prize Fights too Brutal", "The Bystander's" view of how they might be reformed: "We hope that the result of the contest at Reno and the rather unpleasant flavour it leaves in everyone's mouth will not put an end to prize fighting. These fistic battles are quite interesting and there is no reason why they should not be intensely respectable. Our artist (Morrow) puts forward a few suggested sketches of an idyllic combat of the future".

Morshead, Arminell (op.1916-1934)

Devon painter of equestrian subjects, in particular polo, who studied at the Slade School of Art and exh. briefly at the major exhibitions from addresses in Hertfordshire and Surrey. Her sporting subjects include hunting and polo and she was also an etcher.

Mortimer, Alex (op.1885-1888)

A painting of a bay racehorse with jockey up, signed, 9in.x10¾in., was auctioned Bearnes 1982. Mortimer exh. in London and elsewhere between 1885-1888.

Mortimer, John Hamilton, ARA (1740-1779)

Portrait painter sometimes of sporting personalities depicted in sporting scenes. Born at Eastbourne, the son of a well to do mill owner who was the brother of Roger Mortimer, an itinerant painter of religious histories and portraits in East Sussex. John Hamilton Mortimer was a pupil of Thomas Hudson (q.v.) with whom he studied before entering the St. Martin's Lane Academy. An all round sportsman who fished with Benjamin West (q.v.), fenced at Dominico Angelo's fencing academy in Soho, played cricket and shot. Mortimer had many friends amongst playwrights, painters, actors and sportsmen, some of whom helped dissipate his life to an early death at the age of thirty-nine. A painting of a boxer said to be John Bruton (d.1789 aged eighty-five years) painted on paper is attributed to this artist, 23½in.x16½in. and inscr. A self portrait of Mortimer with his elder brother, Charles Smith Mortimer and his father Thomas, standing in a landscape with dogs and game at their feet, painted in the early 1760s in the neighbourhood of Eastbourne where the family lived, was auctioned Bonhams 1984 and is now in the Paul Mellon Collection, Upperville, Va, USA. Mortimer's portrait of Monsieur Masson, the tennis player, holding a racket is in a private collection but the mezzotint after this painting by Richard Brookshaw is in the collection of the British Museum. Mortimer was particularly fond of boxing and painted a number of boxing portraits. The most famous of these was his oil painting depicting the fight between Jack Broughton and George Stevenson ("The Coachman"). The fight took place on 24 April 1741 at Stevenson's gymnasium near the Tottenham Court Road and lasted forty-five minutes with Broughton retaining his title as Heavyweight Champion. Broughton drew up the set of rules upon which those sponsored by the Marquis of Queensberry were based. The painting was in the collection of the Dukes of Hamilton at Hamilton Palace. An engraved version in mezzotint by John Young (1755-1825) was pub. as "The Set To", c.1812. It has been pointed out that the fight between Broughton and Stevenson took place when Mortimer was only one year old. An explanation may lie in Broughton's boxing school in Soho, started by Jackson which shared rooms with Henry Angelo's Fencing Academy and was frequented by Mortimer. See James Gwi(y)n (q.v.) and Charles Turner (q.v.). "The Reverend Charles Everard and two others playing Billiards". Courtesy, National Trust, the Bearsted Collection.

Mortlemans, Edward Eugene (b.1915)

Mural painter and illustrator who studied at the Slade School of Fine Art, under Randolph Schwabe, winning their Diploma Prize in 1949. He painted for many private commissions but turned to book illustration after 1953. He has illustrated books by Ian Fleming, Gerald Durrell, Simone de Beauvoir and Solzhenitsyn. His painting in gouache, 23½in.x18½in., entitled "The Polo Players" shows his skill in portraying figure movement.

Morton, E. (op.1937)

The V & A Museum have a 1937 poster entitled "Road Racing at Brooklands" by this artist.

Moseley, R.S. (op.1862-1902)

Painter of animal and sporting subjects who exh. at the RA, BI, SS and elsewhere from 1862. Specialised in dog portraits, both for commissioned and exhibition work, including "Sandringham Count" painted in 1893 and inscr. "The property of HRH The Prince of Wales", 24in.x18in. "The Ratcatcher's Daughter" shows her appropriately with a dead rat, s.&d. 1888 and inscr. "London", Bonhams (1986).

Moser, H.J. (op.1936-1939)

German-born motor artist, influenced by the style of Georges Hamel (q.v.). Moser designed motor racing works used on the front covers of "Speed" magazine between 1936-1939 after which he returned to Germany before hostilities broke out, in a rather mysterious way, adding fire to rumours that he was a German spy. "BRDC 9th International 500, 18th September 1937". An original poster, 29½in.x19½in., by this artist advertising the event was auctioned Christie's Monaco 1989. In 1937 the length of this race was reduced from 500 miles to 500 kilometres and it was won by Cobb and Bertram at 127.05 mph. It was the fastest long distance race in the world at the time.

Moser, R.J. (op.1934)

Painter of motor racing subjects. "An Amil Car on the Embankment at Brooklands", s.&d. 1934, watercolour, 20¼in.x28in. was auctioned Sotheby's 1983. R.J. and H.J. Moser may well be the same artist.

Moss, Donald (b.1920)

American specialist painter of sporting subjects. Born in Somerville, Maine, USA. Worked for "Sports Illustrated" for over twenty years. Designed US Olympic stamps 1976.

Mote, George William (1832-1909)

Surrey landscape artist who also painted a number of sporting subjects including "A Partridge Shoot",

28in.x36in., "A Tennis Party", 18in.x24in., and "Shooting over Pointers in a Turnip Field", 8¾in.x 13¼in. Interesting self taught artist, Mote worked in both oil and watercolour and started his life as a gardener and caretaker to Sir Thomas Phillips, the great manuscript collector, at Middle Hill near Broadway, Worcestershire.

Mott, J. (op.1844-1854)
Painter of equestrian and animal subjects who exh. one painting each at the RA and at SS in 1854. His study of a prize White Shorthorn heifer, painted in 1844, and his portrait of a racehorse with groom, painted in 1846, shows that Mott was a competent animal and equestrian painter.

Motta, William A. (b.1934)
American painter of motor racing scenes who was born in Santa Maria, California. He studied at the Art Center College of Design in Los Angeles where he graduated with honours in 1957. In 1960 he joined the staff of "Road and Track" magazine and became Art Director in 1978. Motta's professional career gives him the opportunity to study in detail the great racing and touring cars of the world which become the subject matter for his own paintings in acrylic. Motta has won many awards including the National Automotive Art Competition Special Award for 1969 and the Golden Palette Award of the Laguna Beach (California) Festival of the Arts. His work hangs in numerous public and private collections including the Alfa Romeo and the Mercedes Benz museums.

Mount, William Sidney (1807-1868)
American artist whose "Eel Spearing at Setauket" (1843), 29in.x36in., is in the collection of the New York Historical Association, Cooperstown, New York.

Mouron, Adolphe (1901-1968)
"Cassandre". French poster artist who went into business with Charles Loupot and other poster artists in 1930, forming "L'Alliance Graphique", one of whose earliest publications was the famous "Triplex" motor poster in 1931. Signed A.N. Cassandre.

Mower, Martin (b.1870)
American painter of "The Croquet Party" c.1913. Isabella Stewart Gardens Museum.

Muirhead, David Thomson, ARA, ARWS, NEAC, (1867-1930)
Scottish-born landscape painter, the brother of the artist John Muirhead, who trained initially as an architect. Came to London in 1894 and studied at the Westminster School of Art and at the RA Schools. Exh. widely. Elected ARA (1928), ARWS (1924), NEA (1900). "The Cricket Match", s.&d. 1926, 20in.26¾in., was auctioned Phillips (1987).

Muller, J. (op.c.1911)
A pair of paintings entitled "Putting up Game", 21in.x 29½in., were auctioned by Christie's (Sth. Ken.) in 1983.

Muller, Johann Sebastian (b.c.1715-d.1792)
German artist who became better known as John Miller after 1760. Miller was also an engraver of sporting subjects after his own and the work of his contemporaries. He engraved a print of the racehorse "Atlas" after the work by William Shaw (q.v.) in 1761. Muller's (Miller's) four artist sons, including John Frederick, James and Richard Miller, all appear to have lived at the same address and signed their work either Mr. Miller or J. Miller which adds to the complication of disentangling them.

Muller, Rosa (née Branwhite) (op.1861-1867)
German painter of a number of angling scenes some of which took place in Wales, including "Angling on the River Lledr, North Wales". Painted in both oil and watercolour. Usually signed but rarely dated her work. She was married to Edmund Gustavus Muller and lived with him in Bristol. Exh. three works at SS between 1861 and 1867, two of landscapes in North Wales.

Muller, William James (1812-1845)
Painter of a number of minor sporting scenes including "The Gunsmith", "Wooded Landscape with an Angler", etc. Muller was a landscape painter who included a number of angling scenes amongst his work, often featuring Welsh rivers. He was the brother of Edmund Gustavus Muller and therefore brother-in-law of Rosa Muller (q.v.). Studied art under J.B. Pyne. A fine draughtsman who died very young at the age of thirty-three in 1845. The sale of his works was held at Christie's, 1-3 April 1846. Exh. at the RA (1835-1845), BI and SS. Both he and his brother, Edmund Muller, lived in Bristol. He painted in oil, watercolour and drew in pencil. Usually dated his work.

Muller-Cornelius, Ludwig (1864-1943)
German painter of horse and coach scenes. "Horse and Coach outside a Farmhouse", "Mail Coach before a Bavarian Inn"," Post Coach before a Farm", "Mail Coach Halted Outside a Farm House", etc.

Mullins, George (op.1736-1775)
Irish landscape painter whose fine painting of a fishing party is in the Ashmolean Museum, Oxford. It depicts anglers having fished a northern river, grouped around a fishing rod and a still life of a salmon and a brown trout, c.1772. Mullins, who was a pupil of James Mannin in Dublin, c.1756, exh. in Dublin (1765-1769). He came to London in 1770 and exh. at the RA (1770-1775).

Mulready, William, RA (1786-1863)
Irish landscape painter of genre subjects who studied at the RA Schools in 1800. Exh. at the RA from 1804 to 1862, BI and SS. Elected RA 1816. Married to Elizabeth Varley, the sister of John Varley, the landscape painter. He included a number of angling scenes amongst his work usually depicting small boys fishing as exh. at the RA in 1814 (No. 75) and again in 1862, (No. 10). Children featured in many of his paintings including "The Young Pugilists". The picture for which he is probably best known and which is now in the V & A Museum shows a vicar stopping a fight between two boys and is entitled "The Fight Interrupted" which Mulready exh. at the RA in 1816. Perhaps influenced by its success, the young pugilists was a

subject to which Mulready constantly returned. His son William Mulready, Jnr., born in 1805, was a painter of dead game subjects who exh. at the RA, BI, SS between 1835 and 1842.

Muncaster, Claude Grahame, PPRSMA, PRWS, ROI, RBA (1903-1974)

Marine and landscape artist in oil and watercolour, also an etcher and an author. His original name was Grahame Hall and he was the son of the artist Oliver Hall, RA. In November 1945 he changed his name by deed poll to Muncaster, although he had already exh. under that name from 1923, and previously as Grahame Hall. Exh. at the RA from 1919 and held his first one-man show in 1926 at the Fine Art Society. Elected RWS (1936), SMA (1939), RBA (1946), ROI (1948), PRWS (1951-1960) and PSMA (1958). Wrote several books on art and lived in Sussex. He included a number of yacht racing scenes amongst his work.

Mundy, W. (op.1814)

A painting by this artist entitled "Landscape with Hounds", s.&d. 1814, ex Dalton Hall Coll., was exh. Preston HM & AG (1955), illus. in catalogue (No 5).

Munnings, Sir Alfred James, KCVO, PRA, RWS, RP (1878-1959)

Distinguished Suffolk-born landscape and equestrian painter and probably the leading painter of equestrian scenes in the 20th century. Painted in both oil and watercolour, but predominantly in oil. Studied at Norwich School of Art and at Julian's in Paris. Exh. at the RA from 1898. Elected RA (1925), RWS (1929) and PRA (1944-1949). Knighted (1944). KCVO (1947). Munnings was a great draughtsman and spurned the use of photographs. He was also an excellent horseman, hunting regularly with the Norwich Staghounds and the Dunston Harriers. His paintings covered a wide range of equestrian sports but predominantly hunting and racing. Munnings was also an etcher and worked by day (while he studied in the evenings at Norwich School of Art) at Norwich Lithographers (1893-1898) designing wrappers for Kaleys chocolates and calendars for Bullards Brewery. Illus. his own book "An Artist's Life" (1950).

Murdoch, W.G. Burn (op.1882-1919)

Painter, lithographer and an etcher who studied at the Antwerp Academy and under Carolus Duran in Paris, then in Madrid, Florence and Naples. Murdoch illus. "Angling Sketches" for Andrew Lang in 1891 (new edn. 1895).

Murray, David (op.1733)

Described by Waterhouse as "a sort of Scottish Wootton". Murray's painting "The Caledonian Hunt", s.&d. 1773, is at The Binns.

Murray, Sir David, RA, ROI, RWS, PRI, HRSW, HRSA (1849-1933)

Prolific Scottish landscape painter in both oil and watercolour, also of some marine and coastal scenes. His sporting subjects included angling, shooting and cricket and "Waiting for the Guns", 36in.x49in., was auctioned Sotheby's 1986. Murray's "The Angler" was exh. at the RA 1895 (No. 590). The angler, according to "Bailys Magazine", June 1895, was pushed in as an afterthought into one of Murray's landscapes. His "Cricket on the Village Green at Pulborough, Sussex", 12in.x14in., s.&d. '91 (Rutland Gallery London) is an impressionistic and decorative view but one which might not satisfy a cricketer's idea of the game. Elected RSW (1878), ROI (1886), RWS (1886), HRSW (1886), RA (1905), RI (1916), PRI (1917) and HRSA (1919).

Murray, H. (op.1850-1860)

Prolific painter in oil, watercolour and gouache of hunting and coaching scenes, very often painted in pairs or sets of four. He exh. two historical paintings at the BI and SS (1850-1860). Titles of his paintings include "The Meet", "Hounds Moving to Draw", "Mishap in the Field", "The End of a Fast Run", "Clearing a Fence", "Full Cry", "Halt at an Inn", etc.

Murray, Robert (Bob) (op.1954)

Contemporary painter of motor racing scenes including "Le Mans, 1954".

Murray, Thomas (1663-1734)

Scottish born portrait painter whose study in oil of the royal racehorse trainer, Tregonwell Frampton in a dark blue coat and white cravat holding a whip in his right hand, s.&d. 1703, 95in.x58in., was auctioned Christie's 1966.

Murray, W. L. (op.1848)

Unrecorded artist whose watercolour portrait "A Young Cricketer", 7½in.x5½in., s.&d. 1848, was auctioned Phillips (Pilkington Collection) 1989. He is possibly the same artist as William Murray (q.v.).

Murray, William (op.1800-1807)

Obscure Scottish? painter known through his small portraits of hounds including "A Foxhound Outside a Kennel", 6½in.x8in., inscr. "W. Murray Pinxt 1803". The Paul Mellon Collection, Upperville, Va, USA. He is possibly the same artist as W.L. Murray (q.v.).

Myles, William Scott (c.1850-1911)

Scottish painter of still lifes of freshwater fish including "Rainbow and Silver Trout", dated '95, and "Still Life of a Trout". Exh. RSA 1886 to 1889.

Mynors, Stella (op.1920-1945)

Painter and illustrator of equestrian scenes, in particular hunting. Her painting of "The Cottesmore Hounds", the Prince of Wales taking a fence in the foreground, a pastel and coloured wash drawing in 1920, was auctioned Phillips 1987 and her drawing for "The Field" (1937) with two ladies hunting shows an extremely competent hand. Her portrait of the Earl of Londesborough on the polo ground, which she painted in mixed media, 21¼in.x28in., was auctioned Bonhams 1988 and her portrait of the 1945 Derby winner "Dante", the first Northern trained horse to win this classic, is painted in watercolour and inscr., 18in.x 24¾in., Bonhams, 1991.

N

"Nadar"
See Gaspard Félix Tournachon

Nagal, Pat
20th century painter of American football scenes.

Nairn, George, ARHA (1799-1850)
Irish painter of portraits, landscapes, animals and equestrian scenes in oil and a regular exhibitor at the RHA (1826-1849). Married to the landscape painter Cecilia Nairn (1791-1857). "Fez", "Grimalde", "Tidy", and "Carlo" are just a few of the hunter portraits he painted. Two examples are in the National Gallery of Ireland but many of them were painted for private patrons.

Naish, John (b.1771)
Painter of animal and sporting scenes. Entered the RA Schools (1791) and exh. at the RA (1790-1795) including a portrait of a spaniel, s.&d. ?1791 on reverse, Sotheby's 1979.

Nakken, Willem Carel (1835-1926)
Dutch painter of equestrian and coaching scenes including "Groom with Horse and Buggy", "Coachman with a Landau", and "After the Chase". His watercolour of a piebald horse in a stable interior, s.&d. '75, 6¼in.x9½in., was auctioned Bonhams 1984.

Nash, Arthur, MIPA (b.1916)
Painter and typographer who studied art at the London School of Printing and Graphic Arts and Camberwell School of Arts and Crafts. Signs his work "Arthur Nash". "The All England Lawn Tennis Doubles Championship at Wimbledon", signed 1957. Wiggins Teape Group.

Nash, G.R. (op.1849)
A watercolour inscr. "Shanghai Park - Spring Race Meeting", s.&d. April 1849 was auctioned Sotheby's (Bearne) 1985.

Nash, John Northcote, CBE, RA, NEAC, LG, SWE (1893-1977)
Painter and illustrator in oil and watercolour and a wood engraver of landscapes and still lifes. Brother of the better known Paul Nash (q.v.). John Nash developed a very distinctive style of painting and although he had no formal training was enthusiastically encouraged by his elder brother. "A Game of Croquet", pen, ink and watercolour, s.&d. 1913, 8¼in.x11in., is a very good example of his witty interpretation of the game and he uses the same style with effect for his watercolour study entitled "Uncle Herbert Beagling". He took up oil painting in 1914 and held his first one-man show in 1921 at the Goupil Gallery. Taught at the Ruskin School of Art, Oxford (1922-1927) and at the RCA (1934-1940) and again (1945-1957). Illus. a great many books including Gilbert White's "The Natural History of Selborne" (1951, 1972), "Rural Rides" (3 vols.) by William Cobbett (1930) and "The Art of Angling" by Trevor Housby (1965). Founder member LG (1914), NEAC (1919), SWE (1921), RA (1951) and created CBE (1964).

Nash, Joseph, Jnr., RI (op.1859 d.1922)
Painter in watercolour of marine and coastal subjects but also some sporting scenes including "Rabbit Shooting at Crayling near Jedburgh, Roxburghshire", s.&d. 1864, and "The Hawking Party about to Set Off", s.&d. 1873. Exh. in London from 1859 and at the RA from 1877. Elected RI (1886). Son of Joseph Nash, the topographical painter.

Nash, Paul, LG, NEAC, SWE (1889-1946)
Painter, wood engraver, art critic and photographer. Elder brother of John Northcote Nash (q.v.). Studied at Chelsea School of Art (1906-1908), Bolt Court (1908-1910) and the Slade School of Art (1910-1911). Painted "Causey 814", an oil painting exh. by the CEMA in 1943 from which a lithographic poster was made for the Shell petroleum company entitled "Footballers Prefer Shell". The poster itself which is now very rare was exh. at the Redfern Gallery in 1961 as "Goal Posts" and in the V&A Museum in 1975. The design was originally part of "A Shell Guide to Dorset" which was pub. in 1935. Nash, who took a detailed interest in the colour printing of his work, illus. a number of books (1920-1936) and several dust wrappers and bindings. He served in the 1st World War and was appointed official war artist (1917), taught design at the RCA (1924-1925 and 1938-1940). His pupils there included Edward Bawden and Eric Ravilious (qq.v.) and Nash's influence is clearly seen in both artists' work. Member LG (1914), NEAC (1919) and SWE (1922).

Neale, Edward (op.1858-1906)
London landscape and game bird artist, also an illustrator who contributed to "The Illustrated London News" (1899). His sporting work includes "A Fox Eluding the Hunt" (1886), "Ptarmigan on a Moor" (1903), "Ptarmigan in Autumn" (in part white plumage), "The Pheasant Shoot" (1890) and "Ptarmigan and Peregrine Falcon" (1906). Neale painted in both oil

and watercolour and exh. six works at the BI and nine at SS between 1858 and 1881 including "Peregrine Falcon and Mallard" and "Mountain Fox catching Ptarmigan".

Neale, John (op.1846)

Exh. one work only entitled "Dos a Dos?" at the RA but his painting "Salmon Fishing", 15in.x24in., auctioned Sotheby's (Glen.) 1986, merits his entry in this Dictionary.

Neame, Austin (op.1832)

Interesting provincial artist from Canterbury, Kent, who painted portraits of horses and cattle. The Neame family have lived in East Kent for centuries and are descended from a John Neame who was a tanner in St. Mildred's Canterbury around 1450. The name is associated with farmers in the county as well as the brewery firm Shepherd Neame and of course the current High Sheriff, Robert Neame. Austin Neame was a cousin of the Mr. J. Neame of Selling whose fine Durham steer obtained a premium at the Kent and Canterbury fat stock show on 14 December 1832. The steer was painted by Austin Neame, who also painted equestrian and animal portraits for local landowners in the early part of the 19th century.

Neatby, Edward Mossforth, RMS, ARCA (Lond.) (1888-1949)

Leeds-born portrait and landscape painter, son of the miniature painter William James Neatby. Studied at the RCA and Slade School. Elected RMS (1913). Exh. widely including RA, RBA, RI, RMS, RSA. Neatby's painting of a fisherman salmon fishing on the Spey near Newton Moor, 8¼in.x11¼in., was auctioned 1987.

Nedham (Needham), William (op.1823-1849)

Leicestershire painter of equestrian portraits who appears to have been a pupil of J. Ferneley Snr. (q.v.). Amongst the sporting subjects that Nedham painted are portraits of the racehorse "Cannonball" with jockey up, 30in.x34½in., Mr. Robinson of Worcester riding a bay hunter in an extensive landscape (1836), Benjamin Burton on his chestnut hunter with his son Adolphus on a pony in a landscape near Billesdon, Leicestershire, and a gentleman on his horse out shooting with his pointers painted in 1832, 29in.x44in. William Nedham painted in oils, usually signed and inscr. his work "Leicester" and almost always dated it. He painted for Leicestershire patrons but seems not to have exh. any of his work. A portrait of a huntsman on a bay hunter, probably John Tredwell, huntsman to the Quorn, painted in 1841.

Needham, Mrs. Valerie (op.1912-1915)

Portrait and figure painter who exh. three pictures at the RA between these dates, one entitled "Between the Chukkers" which presumably depicts a game of polo.

Neilson, Harry Bingham (1861-1941)

Sporting illustrator and painter who lived in Cheshire and who wrote and illus. "How to Draw in Pen and Ink" (1905) although he was an indifferent draughtsman. He also illus. the book in verse written by Sir Francis Burnald called "The Foxes Frolic" pub. by William Collins at the turn of the century. His painting "Mr. Fox's Hunt Breakfast on Christmas Day" represents five members of the Blankney (Lincs.) Hunt, c.1900.

Neilson, Raymond Perry Rodgers (1881-1964)

American painter who included a number of equestrian portraits amongst his work. His portrait of a bay hunter in a landscape, 25½in.x30¼in., was auctioned Christie's (NY) 1987.

Neiman, Leroy (b.1926)

A leading contemporary painter of many sporting subjects who first came to public notice with a series "A Man at his Leisure" in "Playboy" magazine. Studied at the Art Institute of Chicago. Collections include The Museum of Sport, New York and his awards include Outstanding Sports Artist, Amateur Athletics Union, Sports Artist - New York Jets, major league baseball promotions 1972 and 1976. He lives in New York. His painting of cricket, "Caught and Bowled", signed and inscr. "Lords", June 1961, acrylic on paper, 12¼in.x 25in., was included in his exhibition at the O'Hana Gallery, London in the early 1960s and he has had many one-man exhibitions at leading American galleries. Cricket is a rare subject for him since he is best known for his paintings of horse racing, night clubs, jazz music, casino scenes and golf. His vivid painting entitled "The 18th at Pebble Beach", 24in.x42in., depicts a scene from the 1983 Bing Crosby Pro-Am at that spectacular Californian course. The players are former President Gerald Ford, Jack Nicklaus, Tom Watson, Clint Eastwood and Bob Hope in red plus fours - Neiman is shown sketching.

Nelson, Edmund Hugh (b.1910)

London-born portrait painter in both oil and watercolour, the brother-in-law of E.W. Swanton, the cricketer, whom he depicted in a typically sporting pose, c.1950. He also painted portraits of the author E.M. Forster at King's College, Cambridge and the historian G.M. Trevelyan for Trinity College, Cambridge. Studied at Goldsmith's College of Art (1927-1930) under Clive Gardiner and James Bateman (q.v.). Exh. at the RA, RP, RBA.

Nelson, Paul (op.1953)

Contemporary painter who contributed "Village Football", s.&d. 1953, 19¾in.x29¾in.. to the FE.

Nelson, Phyllis (op.1951-1969)

Contemporary artist of cricket scenes including "Farnham Cricket Ground from the West", s.&d. '51, 6¾in.x7in., and "Cricket at Maidstone, Kent", s.&d. 1969, 25in.x12¾in., auctioned Bonhams 1988.

Neogrady, Antal (1861-1942)

Hungarian painter of a scene entitled "Ladies approaching the Tennis Courts", signed, watercolour, 11¼in.x15¼in., auctioned Sotheby's 1989.

Nesbitt, Charles (op.c.1898)

Unrecorded painter of foxhounds in the snow sitting in their kennel yard, 25in.x30in., auctioned Bonhams 1987.

Nettleship, John Trivett, ROI (1841-1902)
Animal painter who was born at Kettering. Studied art at Heatherleys and at the Slade School. Exh. at the RA from 1874 but exh. only one painting at SS in 1873 entitled "On Guard". Painted a number of big game pictures as the result of a visit to India (1880-1881) at the invitation of the Gaekwar of Baroda for whom he painted a cheetah hunt entitled "The Last Leap but One" which he exh. at the RA 1881 (No. 16) as well as an equestrian portrait. He also painted the portraits of a number of game dogs. He was elected ROI (1894) and pub. "A Life of George Morland" (q.v.) in 1898.

Nev, J. (op.early 19th century)
Primitive painter of cock-fighting scenes, including "Naughty" and "Crafty", portraits of fighting cocks, signed and inscr., 13¾in.x11¾in.

Neville, A.W. (op.c.1867)
A pair of racing scenes entitled "McQueen's Steeple-chasings" after the work by this painter were pub. by J. McQueen of London. They were engraved in aquatint by W. Summers in 1867 and in 1868 and reissued in 1871.

Neville, Louis (op.1887-1914)
Included in this Dictionary for "Kiel Regatta", a watercolour painted in 1912. Neville, who exh. between 1887 and 1914 at RHA, RSA, WG and elsewhere, was a landscape painter in watercolour from Ireland.

Nevin ("Nevinsky"), Patrick (Pat) (op.1930)
Major racing illustrator and cartoonist who worked for "Motor" magazine during the 1930s. This entertaining Ulsterman once signed a drawing "Nevinsky" on the grounds that only foreign artists become famous and found himself stuck with the name. His painting of Branchitsck and Carracciola duelling for a position, 12in.x20½in., and drawn originally for "Motor" magazine is typical of his work, as indeed is his painting "Le Mans 1930", the winning Bentley - Barnato and Kidstone chasing Carracciola's white Mercedes.

Nevinson, Christopher Richard Wynne, ARA, RI, ROI, RBA, NEAC, NS (1889-1946)
Important vorticist painter, etcher and mezzotint engraver and a lithographer of figure subjects, land and urban scapes. Studied at St. John's Wood School of Art and at the Slade School (1908-1912) as well as the Académie Julian, Paris (1912-1913) after which he shared a studio in Paris with Modigliani. He was much influenced in his early works by Cubism. Painted in both oil and watercolour and exh. at the leading London galleries from 1910. Founder member of the LG (1913). Elected NEAC (1929), NS (1930), RBA (1932) and ARA (1939). His major rowing scene at Hampton Court, 24½in.x18in., was auctioned Phillips 1987 and his painting "Derby Day", painted just before his death in 1946 and inscr. in 1947 by his widow, Kathleen Nevinson, 15½in.x19½in., was auctioned Sotheby's 1988. "Any Winter Afternoon in England" (1930), 18¼in.x30in., a painting of a football match, is in the collection of Manchester City AG.

New, Edmund Hort (1871-1931)
Illustrator in black and white, a painter of angling subjects and an architect who studied at the Birmingham Municipal School of Art, under E.R. Taylor and A.J. Gaskin (1886-1895). New taught art and spent much of his working life in Oxford. He was a member of The Art Workers Guild and was elected an Hon ARIBA. He illus. the 1896 edition of "The Compleat Angler" and his illustrations of a trout, carp, salmon trout and pike are repro. in "Angling in British Art", Shaw Sparrow (1923).

Newberry, Angela, ARCA (b.1934)
Contemporary painter, book designer and print maker of interesting wildlife and sporting subjects. Her sports scenes are mostly water related and include yachting and swimming. Angela Newberry studied at Kingston School of Art (1951-1953), Wimbledon School of Art (1953-1954) and the RCA School of Graphic Design (1954-1957). Exh. "Young Contemporaries" 1954/55/56. Contributed "Prints for Schools", Whitechapel AG. Won Vogue Talent Contest (1968). Became joint Editor of "Queen" magazine (with Mark Boxer) (1958-1960). Became scriptwriter for TV and film group and Course Director at the London International Film School (1981-1982). Writer in Residence at the Australian Film and TV School (1982-1983). Returned to full-time print making and built own studio (1984). Exhibitions include: 1987 - America's Cup Exhibition, Perth, Australia, Gillian Jason Gallery, Chicago Arts Fair, Austin Desmond Gallery; 1988 - Royal Society of Painter Etchers, Bankside Gallery, Royal Society of Marine Artists, Mall Galleries and first solo exhibition at the Lyric Theatre, Hammersmith; 1989 - US/UK Print Connection Printmakers Council; 1990 - 222nd RA Summer Exhibition and Rain Forest Art, National History Museum; 1991 - solo exhibitions - Lyric Theatre, Hammersmith and The Ice House, Holland Park. General exhibitions include Japan at Smiths Gallery, Covent Garden and the Bulgarian International Print Biennale, Bulgaria Society of Wildlife Artists, The Mall Galleries, London. Public exhibitions include Manchester City AG, London Borough of Hounslow, St. Thomas's Hospital and St. Mary's Hospital Collection of Contemporary Art.

Newell, Hugh (b.1830)
American painter of genre subjects, born in Belfast, Ireland and died in New Jersey. "Duck Shooting - Susquehanna Flats", s.&d. 1856, 28¼in.x45½in., was auctioned Christie's (NY). This painting was repro. in "Mirror to the American Past" (plate 101, pp.112-113) by Herman, Warner, Williams. Newell was a member of the American Watercolour Society.

Newhouse, Charles B. (c.1805 - d.1877)
Painter of equestrian and sporting subjects, also an illustrator of his own books including "Scenes on the Road, 1834-1835" (with eighteen aquatints) and "Roadsters Album, 1845" (with seventeen aquatints). He painted a great number of coaching scenes including "The London to Birmingham Stage Coach in the Snow" and "The York to London Coach passing another at the

Gallop", watercolour. "A Cocking Cart Going to the Moors" is a particularly outstanding example of this artist's work. The driver drove this two-wheeled turnout standing up, with a passenger beside him and a groom perched behind. His feet were on a level with the horses' heads and the inside of the cart was tall enough to carry gundogs or fighting cocks going to a "main". Many of Newhouse's coaching scenes were engraved by James Baily (Bailey) and Richard Gilson Reeve (q.v.).

Newmarch, G.B. (op.1827-1873)

An extremely competent provincial painter of animals and equestrian subjects including a study of a hunter in a landscape (with a dog) s.&d. 1873. His painting of a prize ox in a landscape is dated 1871 and his portrait of a magnificent bull in a barn is dated 1827. Reading University have a print of Newmarch's work of prize cattle at Birmingham, dated 1849. Newmarch usually seems to have s.&d. his work.

Newton, Alfred Pizzey (Pizzy), RWS (1830-1883)

Self-taught landscape painter who worked mainly in watercolour. His earliest works were painted in the Highlands of Scotland where he obtained the patronage of Queen Victoria when he was painting scenery near Inverlochy Castle. "Stag Hunters crossing a Highland Bridge", s.&d. 1881, 25½in.x22in., was, as the date indicates, a later work.

Newton, Algernon Cecil, RA (1880-1968)

Landscape painter in oils, mostly of London scenes, but he occasionally painted hunting, cricket and racing subjects including his watercolour "The Derby", s.&d. 1920. Born in Hampstead, a grandson of the founder of the famous art colourist firm of Windsor and Newton, Newton studied art at Frank Calderon's (q.v.) School of Animal Painting and the London School of Art, Kensington. A casualty of the 1st World War, in which he served in the army, Newton was invalided out in 1916, and went to Cornwall, where he renewed his earlier acquaintance with the river and landscape painter Lamorna Birch (q.v.) He exh. at the RA from 1903. Elected ARA (1936) and RA (1943). He was the father of the artist Nigel Newton (b.1903). "A Cricket Match at Bournville 1929", 38½in.x 50½in., was painted to celebrate the Jubilee of the firm, Messrs. Cadbury Ltd., and commissioned by a director, William Cadbury.

Newton, C.F. (op.1826-1850)

London artist who exh. one painting at the RA entitled "A Fast Trotting Mare" and a portrait of Lord Zetland's Derby winner (1850) "Voltigeur", dated 1850, is also recorded.

Newton, C.M. (op.1890)

Illustrator of several drawings of rackets for the "Tennis, Lawn Tennis, Rackets and Fives" volume of the Badminton Library of Sports and Pastimes, pub. 1890.

Newton, Ethel (op.1920)

Painter of equestrian and genre subjects whose fox-hunting scene entitled "Breaking Cover", s.&d. 1920, 13in.x17in., was auctioned Tennants (Yorkshire).

Newton, I. or J. (op.1822-1876)

This artist painted portraits of the racehorse "Dr. Syntax" with jockey up, s.&d. 1822, "Traveller" a bay hunter with a dog in a landscape, s.&d. 1828 and a study of a dog sleeping outside his kennel, 1876.

Newton, Richard, Jnr.

American 20th century painter of sporting subjects, particularly coaching and hunting scenes.

Newton Taylor, W.H. (op.1953)

20th century painter who contributed a watercolour "Tomorrow's Professionals", 17½in.x 13½in., to the FE.

Nicholls, George F. (op.1885-1937)

Liverpool watercolour painter of landscape and flower pictures who occasionally painted hunting scenes, one of which he exh. at the RA in 1913.

Nicholls, W. (op.c.1885)

A portrait of a dark bay hunter in a landscape, 25in.x 30in., was auctioned Sotheby's 1986.

Nichols, J. (op.1836-1838)

Angling artist who painted still lifes of fresh water fish. Obligingly he usually signed, dated and inscr. his work "Farnham". He exh. a painting of a trout at the RA from a Farnham address in 1838. Most of his fish studies were posed on the river bank.

Nicholson, Francis (1753-1844)

Yorkshire landscape painter who also painted horses and still lifes. Exh. at the RA (1789-1804), SA (1791). Settled in London after 1804. Predominantly a water-colour painter who unwisely turned to oil painting at the latter end of his life. Nicholson's painting of golf being played beneath Edinburgh Castle on the old Bruntsfield golf course was engraved by J. Walker in 1798. His fine painting "Salmon Fishing" sold as "A Cascade in Wensley Dale", Christie's (1940), was exh. at the RA (1789) (No.333) and is repro. in "Angling in British Art", Shaw Sparrow (1923) p.141.

Nicholson, Richard E. (op.1882-1912)

Yorkshire painter in watercolour who exh. at the RA, RI and the Walker Art Gallery. Titles include "Pigeons and Partridges". His watercolour "Distant Tennis Games", s.&d. 1912, 14½in.x21½in., was auctioned Sotheby's 1986.

Nicholson, Thomas Henry (op.1839-c.1870)

An interesting and imaginative pencil sketch entitled "A Ladies Horse Race" (1839) is in the Virginia Museum of Fine Arts, Richmond, USA. Nicholson was a talented draughtsman and a sculptor who excelled in equestrian subjects. He contributed a number of illustrations to "The Illustrated London News" (1848) and "The Illustrated Times" (1855-1859), although the bulk of his illustrative work appeared in Cassell's "Illustrated Family Paper" (1853-1857). His pupil was Count Alfred d'Orsay (q.v.).

Nicholson, Sir William Newzam Prior, NPS, IS (1872-1949)

Painter, author and illustrator, very often of sporting subjects. Best known for his illustrations to "Memoirs of a Fox Hunting Man" by Siegfried Sassoon (1929). Born at Newark. Studied art at the Herkomer School at Bushey where he met James Pryde's (q.v.) sister who was a fellow student. They married in 1893 and a year later were to become the parents of the abstract artist Ben Nicholson. Nicholson, who later studied at the Académie Julian in Paris, first became known to the public for his illus. work to "An Almanac of Twelve Sports" which was pub. by William Heinemann of London (1898), the text being by Rudyard Kipling. Nicholson was not only an illustrator and an engraver but also a talented portrait painter, as his fine portrait of Marie Tempest bears witness. The two brothers-in-law, Pryde and Nicholson, teamed up in the early 1900s to become the "Beggarstaff Brothers" and together they produced a series of prints and witty books. Nicholson painted in both oil and watercolour and his self portrait "Playing Snooker", 16½in.x8¾in., a watercoloured pencil and ink sketch, is a striking example of the wit that Nicholson was able to find in many of the situations he painted. Nicholson won one of the only two artistic medals awarded to Britons in Olympic history in 1928. The other medal was won by Alfred Thomson (q.v.) in 1948. Nicholson was a founder member of the NPS (1911). Knighted (1936).

Nicol, Erskine, RSA, ARA (1825-1904)
Scottish painter of landscapes and genre scenes. Studied at the Trustees Academy (1838) and went to Dublin, Ireland in 1846 for four years. Settled in London (1862). Exh. in London from 1851 at the RA and BI. His sporting works include "The Donkey Race", 24in.x 29in., "The Rustic Anglers" (painted in 1854), "The First Fishing Lesson" (a watercolour painted in 1863), another "Donkey Race" 34in.x44in. Nicol illus. "Tales of Irish Life and Character" for A.M. Hall, pub. 1909. Elected RSA (1859) and ARA (1866).

Nicol, John Watson, ROI (1856-1926)
Painter of genre subjects and landscapes. Son of Erskine Nicol (q.v.). Exh. at the RA (1876). His portrait of a "Highland Fisherman", s.&d. 1887, 23in.x17½in., was auctioned Holloways 1988.

Niemann, Edmund John, Snr. (1815-1876)
Painter of landscapes and fishing scenes. Son of a German father. His sporting subjects include "A Quiet Shot", "Shooting Grouse on Ilkley Moor", painted in collaboration with Alfred de Prades (q.v.), "A stream in a wood with a sportsman" (painted '66) and "Rainbow Trout on a River Bank" (painted in 1837). Niemann appears to have been self-taught and usually painted very large canvases. Exh. between 1844 and 1872 at the RA, BI, SS and elsewhere. Became a professional painter in 1839, having started his career in Lloyds.

Nieuwerhuys, E.
Exh. two works at the RA, "In for a Shower" and "A Gallop", from a London address.

Nightingale, Basil (1864-1940)
Sporting painter in both oil and watercolour, younger son of Robert Nightingale (q.v.). Worked at Melton Mowbray for some time where he painted his famous portrait of Tom Firr, huntsman to the Quorn on his horse "Whitelegs". In 1902 Nightingale moved to Leamington in Warwickshire. He was an excellent sportsman and a brave rider to hounds. He was undoubtedly a fine artist who painted with humour, always making his subject the most important feature. His backgrounds were usually painted in grey or brown washes to complement his subject but they rarely intrude. He painted Lord Lonsdale, better known as "The Yellow Earl" for his habit of laying on a fleet of yellow carriages to convey guests and hunt servants to his meets at the Quorn and Cottesmore of which he was Master. Nightingale painted Lord Lonsdale leaping a railway track - a daring feat seconded only by the artist's own courageous record. As well as Lord Lonsdale, Nightingale's patrons included the Earl of Warwick, Major Algernon Williams (of Currall Hall, Tenbury Wells) and the Wills family. His painting of the Duke of Westminster's "Ormonde" the Triple Crown winner in 1886, with Fred Archer up, was sold at the Lowther Castle sale (1947) by order of the Earl of Lonsdale.

Nightingale, Robert (1815-1895)
Painter of equestrian and sporting subjects, the father of Basil Nightingale (q.v.). Exh. from 1847 at the RA and SS, none of which was sporting, and his horse portraiture appears to have been confined to private commissions. He was first apprenticed to J. Stannard and later studied at the RA Schools. His portrait of the hound "Guardian" standing near a doorway by a ledge on which there is a pink hunting coat and black hunting cap is a fine example of Robert Nightingale's work. The hound belonged to the first Viscount Chaplin (1840-1923) who commissioned Nightingale to paint many of his hounds and hunters between 1877 and 1892. Nightingale also painted the hunters of W.P. Honeywood, Esq., Marks Hall, Essex, auctioned Christie's (Sth. Ken.) 1990. Father and son collaborated to paint the life size portrait of "Hermit" for Henry Chaplin. A portrait of the race-horse "Wild Georgie" in a stable interior, s.&d. 1881, 25in.x30in., was auctioned Bonhams 1987. "Wild Georgie" was by "Rosicrucian" out of "Belle Esperanza" and was foaled in 1876. He won the Suffolk Yeomanry Cup in 1880 and 1881.

"Nimrod"
Pseudonym used by Charles James Apperley (1788-1843) who wrote a series of essays for "The Quarterly Review" which appeared in book form, such as "The Chase" and "The Road and the Turf".

Nisbet, Robert Buchan, RSA (1857-1942)
Scottish landscape painter in watercolour, whose several golfing scenes include views of St. Andrews, painted from across the Firth of Forth and Gullane, in 1880.

Nixon, John (born c.1750 op.1781 d.1818)
Caricaturist, etcher and amateur painter in watercolour, reminiscent of Thomas Rowlandson (q.v.) whom he knew well. Nixon had close connections with Ireland and visited the island frequently in the 1780s and 1790s. He exh. regularly at the RA. Included in this Dictionary for his pen and brown ink sketches of Ascot

and Enfield races, s.&d. 1791, 5½in.x8¼in., auctioned Phillips 1985 and his watercolour, pen/grey ink drawing of "Harwich, with a Game of Cricket in Progress" s.&d. 1784 and inscr. Nixon visited Holland in 1784 and presumably he saw the match either on the way there, or on the way back, since there is a ship in the background.

Nixon, Kathleen Irene ("Kay") (1895-1988)

Best known as the illustrator of the Enid Blyton stories but Kay Nixon was also an accomplished animal painter in her own right. Studied at the Camden and Birmingham Schools of Art and was an extremely able equestrian artist, particularly in painting portraits of racehorses for their owners. Lived in India between 1927 and 1952 where she painted portraits of the Maharaja's horses for the Bombay Natural History Museum.

Nizzoli, Marcello (1887-1967)

A highly versatile artist, decorator, fabric and fashion designer as well as a skilled poster artist. His poster designs relate mainly to automobile and motorcycle industries and he joined Olivetti as a designer in 1938.

Noble, Charles F. (b.1876 op.1925-1931)

Noble specialised in painting racehorses for their owners amongst whom were "Fair Isle" with T. Weston up, winning the 1000 Guineas in 1930, "Beam" with T. Weston up, winning the Oaks in 1927, "Adam's Apple" with Jack Leach up, winning the 2000 Guineas in 1927, 13¼in.x23in., "Cameronian" ridden by Freddy Fox, winning the 1931 Derby, 13½in.x23½in., which Noble painted for the jockey, "Cloudbank" with Steve Donaghue up, winning the 1925 Goodwood Cup and "Cloudbank" winning the Queen's Prize at Kempton Park in 1925.

Noble, Edwin John, RBA (1876-1941)

Animal painter and illustrator, the son of John Sargent Noble, RBA (q.v.). Studied art at The Slade, Lambeth and the RA Schools. Contributed to "The Studio" (Vol. 14 1898). Exh. at the RA, RSA, RI, RBA and at the Rome International and taught at Calderon's School of Animal Painting (1906-1912) and at the Central and Camberwell School of Arts and Crafts (1914-1921). Exh. three works at the RA (1899-1904) including "The Old Black Mare". He also included racing amongst the sporting subjects he painted. Elected RBA (1907).

Noble, John Rushton (op.1953)

Painter who contributed a football watercolour entitled "Red Heigh Park, Gateshead", 19in.x14in., to the FE.

Noble, John Sargent, RBA (op.1847-1898)

Painter of sporting and equestrian subjects who studied at the RA Schools and became a pupil of Sir Edwin Landseer (q.v.). He exh. at the RA between 1871 and 1895. Elected RBA (1872). He painted several scenes of otter hunting and collaborated with Walter H.W. Foster (q.v.) on a fine painting "Otter Hunting on the river Lowther, Westmoreland" (dogs by Noble and landscape by Foster) which was exh. at SS in 1873 (No.476). The collaboration was so successful that they

worked again on "Partridge Shooting", on "Wild Duck Shooting", painted in 1886, and on "The Forager's Return" which was exh. (1876) at the RBA. Noble also collaborated with J.C. Waite on the painting entitled "Half Way to Market", exh. RBA (1885), and on "Friendly Trading" which was exh. in the same year. Noble painted at least five otter hunting scenes. He tended to paint large canvases and exh. a large canvas of otter hounds at the RA (1876).

Noble, W.R. (op.1846)

Two paintings linked with hare hunting were painted by this artist in 1846. Noble's portrait of two prize greyhounds in a landscape, 16½in.x20½in., were auctioned Sotheby's 1989 and "The Hare's Revenge of the Hunters", a series of four pictures, two signed and one dated 1846, 16½in.x20½in., were auctioned Christie's 1986.

Noble, William Bonneau (1780-1831)

This topographical painter's view of Hall Place School near Bexley Kent with twin cricket matches in progress was one of the engravings made by Samuel Alken (q.v.). Noble exh. at the RA from 1809 but he took his rejected work too seriously which led to depression and his attempted suicide in 1825. Noble exh. at the RA from 1809.

Nockolds, Roy Anthony (1911-1979)

Brilliant motor racing artist. A contemporary of Frederick Crosby (q.v.) and Bryan de Grineau (q.v.) he worked in the 1930s and 1940s for "Motor Sport", "Motor", "Auto Car" and "Speed" which flourished (1935-1939) when it was absorbed by "Motor Sport". Early examples of Nockolds' motor racing work are now collectors' pieces and a major collection of his work hangs at the RAC Club in Pall Mall, London. He also painted landscapes and fly fishing scenes in both oil and watercolour. His painting "Miss England" on Lake Locarno achieving the world water speed record, s.&d. 1933, 26in.x20in., was auctioned Lawrence Crewkerne 1989. Nockolds was born in London and was self-taught in art, apart from some figure drawing lessons. During World War II he worked for the Ministry of Information and served in the RAF. He was ultimately a war artist. He exh. at the RA and at other leading London galleries. He also exh. in New York (1960) at an exhibition of British Motoring Achievements. Became Chairman of the Guild of Aviation Artists (1975) and was a founder member of the Society of Equestrian Artists (1978). His painting of the "International Nine Hour Race at Goodwood" was depicted in poster form, 30in.x20in. The race was held between 1952 and 1954 and Aston Martin won all three races. His painting of the famous racing driver, Fangio, at Reims in 1951 was exh. by Christopher Cole and his fine painting "Salmon Fishing on the River Dee", 24in.x36in., was auctioned Christie's 1988. "Grouse Shooting", 21½in.x17½in., was auctioned Sotheby's (Sussex) 1989.

Nodder, Richard Polydore (op.1793-1820

Painter of sporting pictures and natural history which he exh. at the RA between 1793 and 1820. He was the son of Frederick P. Nodder (d.1800), the painter and line engraver of botanical subjects who was appointed botanical painter to Queen Charlotte in 1780. Nodder painted hunting and racing scenes and equestrian portraits, including "Riding School Exercise" (1816), "Shooting Pony with Pointers" (1820) and "Death of a Fox".

Noel, John Bates (1870-1927)
Worcestershire landscape painter and of some sporting and animal subjects. Born at Malvern, son of the artist David Bates (q.v.). JBN used his second Christian name, Noel, as his surname in order to avoid confusion with his father. It is interesting to note that both father and son painted "The Gamekeeper's Gibbet", John Bates Noel painting his later version in 1908. He exh. at the RA (1894-1907) and at the RBSA (1892-1919). Noel's sporting subjects include "The Ledbury Pack", "Through the Wood", "Cub Hunting on a Misty Morning, Cowleigh Park, Malvern" and "The Hunt at Storridge".

Norman, F.M. (op.1907-1913)
Painter of equestrian portraits, usually hunters posed in their stables, for example "A Chestnut Hunter in a Stable", s.&d. 1907, 20in.x24in., auctioned Phillips 1985.

Norman, Philip, FSA (b.c.1843-1931)
"Football at the Wall", sepia, Eton Loan Collection 1891. The artist was a member of a well-known old Etonian family and was in the Wall Game eleven (1859/1860). The drawing is one of a set which was done for "The English Illustrated Magazine" (1890-1892).

Norris, L. (op.1953)
Contemporary painter of a football match entitled "The Local Team", 48in.x35in., which he contributed to the FE.

North, Brownlow (c.1760-1829)
Gifted amateur artist, the younger brother of the 6th Earl of Guildford. Friend of James Gillray (q.v.) who engraved a set of hunting scenes after his work. He was the son of Brownlow North, Bishop of Winchester.

Northcote, James, RA (1746-1831)
Portrait and history painter and of occasional animal and sporting subjects. Born in Plymouth, the son of a watch maker whose trade he was apprenticed to. A rather pedestrian disciple of Sir Joshua Reynolds (q.v.) whose assistant he became from (1771-1775). Northcote's contact with the Reynolds circle may have ensured his fame, rather than his paintings, since he wrote a valuable book on the life of Sir Joshua Reynolds (1813). He is also remembered for his dull memoirs and the more entertaining "Conversations with James Ward" (q.v.) taken from scripts and notebooks of James Ward which were compiled by Ernest Fletcher (1901). Hazlitt's "Conversations with Northcote" were pub. in book form (1830). Northcote's portrait of his brother, Samuel Northcote, with a falcon, 33in.x28in., was painted for the 3rd Duke of Dorset in 1789. It was originally three-quarters length and included two dogs on the left but some time between 1820 and 1871 it was cut down to its present size. His portrait of his close friend "William Elford (1749-1837) Heron Shooting in Devon", 39¼in.x 49¼in., is in the Paul Mellon Collection, Upperville, Va, USA.

Norton, Benjamin Cam (1835-1900)
Painter of equestrian subjects from the Sheffield area. His portraits of racehorses include "St. Gatien", with jockey Charles Wood up, at Newmarket with a densely packed grandstand to the left (painted in 1885), and several other portraits of unknown racehorses and jockeys at Newmarket. His very large portrait of a St. Bernard dog carrying a terrier in a pocket handkerchief, 50½in.x78in., was auctioned Sotheby's 1977. He exh. "The Random Shot" at BI in 1862, one of his only two London exhibits from a Sheffield address. Apart from this reference to Sheffield he appears to have lived, worked and died in the Newmarket area.

Norton, J.E. (op.1898)
A pair of paintings by this artist of two spaniels and three foxhounds, each 8in.x10in., signed, were auctioned Woolley and Wallis (Salisbury) 1986.

Novice, William (op.1809-1833)
A painting of Tom Oldacre, huntsman of the Old Berkeley Hunt riding with hounds, s.&d. 1813, 27in.x 35in., was auctioned Sotheby's 1972. Novice exh. five pictures at the RA between 1809 and 1833 but none of them was sporting. Exh. at SS in 1827, 1828 and 1829.

Nowell, Arthur Trevethin, RI, RP (1862-1940)
Welsh-born painter of portraits, landscapes and some sporting subjects including his painting of horses, dogs and a dead hare, grouse and a basket in a Highland setting, 7½in.x12½in., auctioned Christie's 1971. Nowell studied at Manchester School of Arts and the RA Schools where he won gold medals for his landscape and historical painting. Exh. from 1881 at the RA, NWS, NG, RP and elsewhere. Elected RI (1913). Travelled widely on the continent, visiting Italy, Spain, Germany, France and Holland. Painted in both oil and watercolour.

Noyes, Henry James (op.1873-1887)
Shrewsbury artist who exh. a picture at the RA giving his address as Shrewsbury School of Art, where presumably he taught art. His painting of two horses looking over a stable door entitled "Stable Friends", 24in.x21½in., was auctioned Sotheby's (Chester) 1981.

Noyes, Robert (c.1780-1843)
A lithograph entitled "Wolverhampton Racecourse", 15in.x24in., after the drawing by Noyes, pub. by Thomas Mann Baynes (1794-1854) is in the Paul Mellon Collection, Upperville, Va, USA. Noyes, who was a drawing master at Wolverhampton School (1822-1831) was also a lithographer. He seems to have been a banker before becoming an artist.

Nunes (Nunez), E.F.
Portuguese-born artist and illustrator who drew many golfing sketches and illustrations. "Golfing Amazons", auctioned Bloomsbury Book Auctions, 1985.

Nutter, Matthew Ellis (1795-1862)
Competent Carlisle painter of animals, landscapes and portraits who became a drawing master at the Carlisle Academy of Arts (founded 1822) and its Secretary. Exh. at the Carlisle Academy from 1822 until 1833 when exhibitions ceased through lack of patronage. Examples of his work are in the Carlisle Art Gallery collection.

O

Oakley, Harold Lawrence (b.1882 exh.1935)
Yorkshire-born painter who studied at the RCA and exh. four works at the Arlington Gallery (1935). Oakley was also a most competent silhouettist and a silhouette of polo at Ranelagh is recorded in the Witt Library.

"Observator"
The nom de plume used by the sporting artist Ben Marshall (q.v.) after his coaching accident when he wrote for "The Sporting Magazine" in the 1820s.

Ocean, Humphrey (b.1951)
Portrait painter. Studied at Tunbridge Wells, Brighton and Canterbury Art Schools (1967-1973). Winner of the Imperial Tobacco Portrait Award in 1982. Has taught at Oxford Polytechnic and the Art Colleges of Canterbury and City and Guilds, London. Has painted portrait commissions from the National Portrait Gallery (Philip Larkin and A.J. Ayer) and has had several one-man exhibitions. His portrait of the black boxer, "Harry Smith and Two other Geezers" dated 1985/6, 77½in.x57in. was exh. at the Camden Art Centre 1986/7 (no.23)

Oden, Dick (op.1982)
Contemporary painter of American football players including a portrait of "John Hannah - New England Patriots Guard", watercolour 1982.

O'Donnell, Hugh (op.1978-1985)
Contemporary American painter of sporting subjects, including boxing, painted in acrylic or oil. "The Run to Earth", presumably depicting a hunting scene, s.&d. 1985 was auctioned Christie's (NY) 1989.

"O'Galop"
Pseudonym used by Maurice Roussillon (q.v.).

Ogram, H.W.R. (op.1925)
A painting of a skating party by this artist, s.&d. 1925, pen, ink and watercolour, 15½in.x24in., was auctioned Sotheby's (Sussex) 1984.

"Old Blue"
Sir Theodore Andrea Cook. Rowing blue at Oxford (1889) and sporting contributor to "The Daily Telegraph" under that nom de plume. Editor of "The Field" (1910-1928). Sporting art enthusiast responsible for the series on the subject which appeared in "The Field" (1926-1928).

"Old Shekarry"
The pseudonym used for the sporting illustrator R.H. Moore (q.v.).

"Old Shikari"
The pseudonym used by the sporting author G.A.B. Dawson, "Nilgiri Sporting Reminiscences", Madras (1880).

Oldenburg, Claes Thure (b.1929)
American pop artist and sculptor who originally worked in magazine illustration and design. His monumental public sculpture "Bat Column", installed in Chicago, exemplifies that city's devotion to its baseball heritage. Oldenburg was also a lithographer and featured baseball in this medium. His lithograph "Bats Spinning at the Speed of Light" (1975) is a theme on the "Bat Column" idea. "The Billiard Table" drawn 1967, and signed, coloured felt marker, 14½in.x17¾in., auctioned Christie's.

Oldfield, John (b.1918)
Sporting painter, particularly of hunting, racing, polo and stalking subjects. Studied art under Arthur Norvis at Repton. Commissioned into the Green Howards, after Sandhurst, in 1938 and retired as a Brigadier in 1969. A regular exhibitor in London and elsewhere he is a member of the Society of Equestrian Artists. He has illus. a number of books on hunting and other horse related subjects. "Pony Lines - Rhinefield", watercolour, painted in 1986, 12¼in.x9in., Tryon and Morland Gallery, London.

Oldmeadow, F.A. (op.1840-1856)
Portrait painter of human and equestrian subjects who exh. four horse portraits at the RA between 1840 and 1847, three of which were commissioned by the Duke of Westminster for whom he worked at Moor Park. His portrait of "Lottery" who won the Grand National in 1839 out of seventeen starters, ridden by J. Mason, s.&d. 1842, was auctioned Bearnes 1987 and his portrait of a gentleman in hunting pink, s.&d. 1842, 36in.x 30in., was auctioned Sotheby's 1977. Other famous racehorses painted by Oldmeadow include "Brunette", "Touchstone", "Banker" and "Maid of Honour".

O'Neil(l), Henry Nelson, ARA (1817-1880)
Historical and genre painter who studied at the RA Schools from 1836 and exh. there from 1838. He was described by T.S. Cooper (q.v.) as the "great unwashed" which implies that he was somewhat Bohemian. On the other hand he had several distinguished clients including Henry Pelham Clinton, 4th Duke of Newcastle. His painting of the "Billiard Room of the Garrick Club", with members playing billiards, 37½in.x61in., shows

the portraits of forty-three famous members including the artists Sir John Everett Millais PRA (q.v.), William Powell Frith RA (q.v.), Thomas Creswick RA (q.v.) and Sir John Gilbert RA. The painting includes a self-portrait of the artist which implies that O'Neil(l) was also a member. He was elected an ARA (1860).

O'Neil, William Sandison (op.1940s)
20th century marine artist who lived at Richmond, Surrey, and whose paintings of yacht racing in pastel were exh. at the Society of Marine Artists (founded in 1946).

Opie, Alfred (op.1864-1869)
Animal painter whose portraits of a retriever and a spaniel are dated 1864 and 1869.

Opie, John, RA (1761-1807)
Cornish-born portrait painter, a great uncle of Alfred Opie (q.v.) and Edward Opie, the genre painter. John Opie studied art under William Wolcot. His sporting portraiture includes a portrait of George Simmons with Richard Plommer hunting a fox on foot with two greyhounds, 41in.x52in., auctioned Christie's 1990. Simmons was the brother of John Simmons of Tresamble in Gwennap. Opie exh. at the RA from 1782, provoking the remark, since his subject matter involving ordinary people was his main forte, "Could people in vulgar life afford to pay for pictures, then Opie would be their man". He was elected RA in 1788, having been able to elevate his subject matter, and became Professor of painting at the RA in 1805, teaching, amongst others, William Chamberlain (q.v.).

Oppenheimer, Joseph, RP (b.1876)
Portrait painter who studied in Munich and exh. (1903-1939) at the RA, RP and on the continent. Won a gold medal at the Munich International Exhibition (1910) and an Hon. Mention at the Carnegie Institute, Pittsburg (1916). His painting of fox-hunting entitled "The Meet near Hurstmonceaux, Sussex", signed, 6¾in.x9¾in., was auctioned Phillips 1985.

Orchardson, Charles M. Quiller, ROI (op.1896 d.1917)
Son of Sir William Quiller Orchardson (q.v.). Portrait painter in oils who exh. fifteen works at the RA (1896-1904). His full length portrait of a young man in hunting pink, a riding crop under his arm, inscr. and dated 1904 was auctioned Bonhams 1984 and his portrait entitled "The Huntsman", s.&d. 1903 was auctioned Sotheby's 1983. He died (of wounds) on 26 April 1917.

Orchardson, Sir William Quiller, RA, HRSA, HRMS, RP (1832-1910)
Scottish genre painter, a regular follower of the Essex Hounds for some years after which he became a trout fisherman of some reputation and painted several fly fishing scenes, ("Baily's", June 1895). He studied art at the Trustees Academy in 1850 (under R.S. Lauder) and came to London (1863). Exh. at the RA from 1963. Elected RA (1877), HRSA (1871), HRMS (1900) RP (1897). Knighted (1907).

Organ, Bryan (Harold), RA (b.1935)
Portrait and figure painter who studied art at Loughborough College of Art (1952-1955) and the RA Schools (1955-1959) Known to have painted golf personalities.

Orme, Ernest (op.1801-1808)
Architectural draughtsman who illus. "A Collection of British Field Sports" (1807-1808). Brother of Edward Orme, the publisher and William Orme, the landscape artist and illustrator. Orme exh. portraits at the RA (1801-1803).

Orpen, Sir William Newenham Montague, RA, RWS, RHA, RI, NEAC (1878-1931)
Distinguished portrait painter in both oil and watercolour who was born in Ireland and studied at the Dublin Metropolitan School of Art (1890-1897) and in London at the Slade School (1897-1899). Exh. at the RA from 1908. Elected NEAC (1900), RHA (1908), NPS (1911), PIS (1921), RA (1920), knighted (1918). In 1923 Sir William Orpen painted a portrait of "Sergeant Murphy", the winner of the Scottish Grand National (1922) and the Grand National (1923). He exh. the painting at the RA in 1924 (No. 655) and again in 1933 (No. 88) It was later exh. at the Commemorative Exhibition of works by late members at the Dublin National Gallery of Ireland (1978) (No. 124). Orpen apparently wanted to show that he could paint horses as well as Alfred Munnings (q.v.). Munnings, who had a painting of a grey horse in the Royal Academy Exhibition of 1923, as well as Orpen, was in America when he read an account saying that "the Irishman's picture was better than mine..." Orpen was the brother of Richard Caulfield Orpen (1863-1938), the architect and watercolourist and Guardian of the National Gallery of Ireland. William Orpen's portrait of the Prince of Wales, later the Duke of Windsor, as Captain of the Royal West Norfolk Golf Club was completed in 1927, 80in.x40in., and commissioned by the Royal and Ancient Golf Club of St. Andrews, Fife, Scotland.

Orr, Jack (1868-1934)
Scottish painter of some sporting subjects including lawn bowls. His painting of this subject entitled "A Good Delivery", s.&d. 1919, 17⅛in.x23in., was auctioned Phillips 1989 while his coaching painting "Happy Reunions at the Inn", 15½in.x21in., was auctioned Giles Hayward 1984. Orr, like many artists of his generation favoured the Edwardian fashion for painting their subjects in an earlier period of history and his coaching scene is no exception, set in an 18th century background. Orr exh. at GI, RA, RSA and RSW between 1909 and 1940.

Orrock, James, RI (1829-1913)
Edinburgh born landscape painter, predominantly in watercolour, who qualified and practised initially as a dentist in Nottingham. Studied under James Ferguson, John Burgess and Stewart Smith and with William Leitch after he came to London in 1866. Included in this Dictionary for his watercolour "A Shoot on the Moors", s.&d. 1881, 19½in.x29½in., Sotheby's (Sussex) 1989. Elected RI (1875).

Osborne, Walter Frederick, RHA, ROI (1859-1903)
Irish portrait painter and illustrator who contributed to
"Black and White" in 1891. He studied at the RHA
Schools (1876) and then at Antwerp (1881-1883). He
travelled widely on the continent. Elected RHA (1886)
and ROI (1891). Osborne was an extremely competent
animal and equestrian painter, a rare example of a son
exceeding his father in talent (see William Osborne).
His portrait "A Bay Racehorse in a Stable", inscr.,
19¾in.x25½in., was auctioned Sotheby's 1984. Examples
of his work are in the National Gallery, Ireland and the
British Museum.

Osborne, William, RHA (1823-1901)
Irish portrait, animal and equestrian painter who
studied at the RHA in Dublin from 1845. Father of
Walter Frederick Osborne (q.v.), the landscape and
portrait painter. He was elected RHA in 1868. He was
an extremely competent equestrian and animal painter
in oils whose work (and that of his son) is becoming
popular and much sought after. He usually signed his
work with a mono. "The Ward Hunt", s.&d. 1873,
109in.x184in. and "A Mare and a Foal" are both in the
National Gallery of Ireland.

O'Shea, Miss G.P. (op 1891-1903)
Irish animal and equestrian painter who exh. (1891-
1899) at the RHA, NG, and at Birmingham, Manchester
and Liverpool AGs. Her portrait of the terrier "Sunday"
s.&d. 1903 was auctioned in 1986 and her pencil drawing
"Crossing the Stream with Hounds", s.&d. 1898, 11in.x
15½in., was auctioned Christie's (NY) 1986.

Osslund, Helmer (1866-1938)
Swedish landscape painter of some fly fishing scenes
particularly of salmon fishing. "Salmon Fishing at Faxelven"
(on the Fax river) was auctioned in Stockholm in 1985.

Osswald, Eugene (op.1879)
German figure painter and of some equestrian subjects
whose painting "Horse Racing in Daglfing" was
auctioned Neales (Nottingham) in 1988.

Ostade, Adriaen Van (1610-1684)
Dutch painter of tavern and peasant scenes. In many of
his scenes peasants are playing bowls.

Osthaus, Edmund Henry (1858-1928)
American painter of game dog portraits who painted in
both oil and watercolour. His portrait "A Pointer and
an English Setter", signed, watercolour, 25⅜in.x35⅞in.,
was auctioned Christie's (NY) 1985.

"Otter"
Alias Henry Jervis Alfred (q.v.) who wrote on fishing
topics for the "Modern Angler" in 1864. He also ran a
tackle shop in Moorgate Street, London and painted
fish subjects quite beautifully.

Oudry, Jean Baptiste (1686-1755)
French court portrait painter and of many sporting
scenes including "La Chasse au Loupe", 50¾in.x76in.
It is thought that this painting was done by Oudry for
the tapestry workshop at Beauvais in 1726, for the
"Chasse Nouvelle" series of six tapestries. The contract
was for six paintings to represent a wolf, stag, fox, boar
and deer hunt. A scene with bloodhounds makes the
sixth painting. These designs were sold by the Beauvais
workshops in 1761. Oudry was responsible with
Desportes (q.v.) for painting the royal hunting scenes in
France. Oudry's painting "A Gentleman with two
Hounds and a dead Deer in a Landscape", 18in.x
15½in., was sold for 68 guineas at the Lowther Castle
sale in 1947, by order of the Earl of Lonsdale.

Ought, William (1753-1778)
Portrait painter in both oil and crayon who entered the
RA Schools in 1771. From 1768-1769 he became a pupil
of Daniel Dodd and exh. at FS (1768-1778). Ought's
portrait of a sportsman standing in a landscape with two
retrievers, holding his gun in his left hand, s.&d. 1778,
was auctioned Sotheby's 1974.

Ouless, Philip John (1817-1885)
Born in Jersey, the father of W.W. Ouless (q.v.).
Studied painting in Paris after which he established
himself in Jersey as a painter of many subjects and also
a teacher. Ouless pub. albums of local views and illus.
volumes of local history. His sketch books are in the
possession of the Société Jersiaise while the Barreau
Gallery has his large oil painting "The Jersey Races on
Goury Racecourse", s.&d. 1850, 33in.x50in. This painting
was lithographed by H. Walter (q.v.). "The Jersey
Races" seems to have been Ouless's only contribution to
sporting art but it was of sufficient quality to establish his
reputation in this field. His "Scenic Beauties of the Island
of Jersey" pub. in 1840 with twenty-five lithographic
prints currently sells in excess of £500.

Ouless, Walter William, RA (1848-1933)
Prolific and successful society portrait painter. Born in
St. Helier, Jersey, the son of Philip Ouless (q.v.).
Commissioned by the MCC to paint Sir Henry
Ponsonby-Fane who had been Club Treasurer and built
up its collection of pictures. Portrait of A.N. Hornby,
Esq., Captain of the Lancashire Eleven, 56in.x41in.,
painted in 1900, Lancashire Country Cricket Club.
Albert Neilson Hornby (1847-1925) played for
Lancashire and England and is immortalised in the
poem "At Lords" by Francis Thompson who watched
him score his century at Old Trafford in 1878 - see also
The Hon. John Collier (q.v.).

"Out Post"
Unknown contributor to "Country Life" 1897.

Ovenden, T. (op.1817-1832)
London painter of fish still lifes, who exh. at the RA.
"Group of Fresh Water Fish" (1817), "A Group of
Fresh Water Fish" (1830) and "A Chub, Trout, Pike
and Gudgeon" (1832).

Overend, William Heysham, ROI (1851-1898)
Yorkshire-born painter and illustrator who worked for
"The Illustrated London News" (1872-1896), "The
Boys Own Paper", "Chums" and "The English
Illustrated Magazine". Originally a marine artist,
Overend contributed a number of such works to the
illustrated papers. He also painted football scenes
including his fine work "England - v-Scotland", dated
1889 and painted with Lionel Percy Smythe (q.v.).
Overend exh. at the RA (1872-1898), SS and elsewhere
and was elected ROI (1886). A painting of the racehorse
"Dandy Jim" at Doncaster signed William Overend is
recorded by Mitchell.

Owen, Sam (op.c.1815)
"Fishing at the Willows", the seat of the late Townley
Ward, Esq. A print engraved and pub. by W.B. Cooke
on 1 July 1815 is in the collection of the Piscatorial Society.

P

Pace, Percy Currall (op.1897-1927)
Surrey-born painter of landscapes and portraits who studied art at the Antwerp Academy School. Exh. at the RA (1897-1903) and at the Paris Salon. His pen and ink drawing of the Super Marine S5 prototype on a test run on the Hamble river in 1926, preparing for the Schneider Trophy, is signed and dated 1927 and inscr., 12½in.x15½in., Sotheby's (Sussex) 1986.

Padday, Charles Murray, RI, ROI (op.1890-1940)
A great yachting artist in both oil and watercolour who depicted the sport of sailing in all its many forms. Lived on the south coast, from 1895, at Bosham, Folkestone and Haling Island and exh. at the RA, RI, ROI and RBA. Elected ROI (1906) and RI (1929). The Walker AG have seven of his paintings and others can be found at the National Maritime Museum. Padday was a leading illustrator of shipping for "The Illustrated London News" from 1896 until about 1916. His work included many yacht racing scenes, although a number of them were painted in monochrome.

Padley, Robert Wilkinson (c.1775-d.1835)
Wildfowl and game bird painter who exh. once only in London at the BI in 1815. Padley was the brother of the well-known Nottingham sportsman, Squire Padley of Bulwell. His work includes many paintings of hawks including "Hobby Hawk and Prey, Shot at Buxton 1812", 19¼in.x15in. Padley also painted the portrait of "A French Partridge" which was auctioned Phillips (Exeter) 1986, Padley's name miscatalogued as "Pidley". None of Padley's known paintings are conventionally signed but most are inscr., s.&d., either on the reverse of the canvas or on the stretcher.

Page, Henry Maurice (op.1878-1890)
Landscape, animal and sporting painter who exh. at the RA and SS from 1878. Titles at the RA include "Sport from Loch and Moor", "Winged" and "On the Flight", while titles at SS include "Highland Sport" (1880), "The Angler's Nook" (1881), "Where the Pike Lie" (1883), and "A Hunting Morn - Merstham, Surrey" (1892). Page lived at Croydon, Surrey, close to the Old Surrey and Burstow hunting country.

Page, Robert (op.1880-1890)
Painter of rustic and equestrian subjects from Great Clacton, Essex. Exh. at the RA, SS and elsewhere (1881-1889). His portrait of a black hunter, s.&d. 1880, 25½in.x30in., was auctioned Sotheby's 1973. An interesting painting by Page of a young poacher avoiding a gamekeeper, with his dogs on the alert and his ferret with a dead rabbit, was painted in 1890.

Page, William (1794-1872)
Landscape and equestrian portrait painter, although he exh. mostly topographical views at the RA. His portrait of a saddled grey hunter and a bay hunter held by a groom, signed, 9in.x10½in., were auctioned Christie's 1967.

Paget, Henry Marriott, RBA (1856-1936)
Painter and illustrator included in this Dictionary for his RA exhibit "A Boxing Contest" (1894). Paget studied at the RA Schools from 1874 and worked as an illustrator for "The Sphere", covering the Balkan War (1912-1913) as their special artist. Exh. at the RA from 1879. Elected RA (1889). Illus. many famous books including "The Black Arrow" by R.L. Stevenson (c.1913).

Paice, George (1854-1925)
Sporting and animal painter who lived at Croydon. Exh. at the RA (1881-1897), SS and elsewhere. Although many of his paintings were equestrian portraits he did paint a number of sporting scenes including "Stag Hunting in the Quantock Hills" (1903) and "The Sprot Cup, the Royal Scots Greys Steeplechase", a set of four, each 7in.x13in., painted in 1913. This was a subject that Paice painted several times, once for the Officers Mess of the Royal Scots Greys. The Sprot Trophy, which is not a cup but a silver heron, was donated by Major Mark Sprot of Riddel in 1902. The steeplechase has been run every year ever since and takes place wherever the Royal Scots Greys are stationed. Paice painted a large number of private commissions, usually in oils, but his landscapes are sometimes watercolour. His portrait of "Marsh Mallow", a bay polo pony by a polo ground, 8in.x12in., is in the collection of the Walker AG, Liverpool.

Paillou, Peter (op.1745-1780)
Game and wildfowl painter who included a number of portraits of falcons, pheasants, ptarmigan, partridge, duck amongst his work. He worked for many years for Thomas Pennant (Waterhouse).

Paisley, John Anderson (op.1844)
A painter whose landscape featuring a groom holding a coach horse with a dog at heel and the coach behind, s.&d. 1844, 18in.x24in., was auctioned Bonhams 1984.

Palfrey, Penry Powell (1830-1902)
A Welsh painter of equestrian and sporting subjects, Palfrey was brought up in London and initially worked on heraldic paintings and stained glass windows. The Duke of Westminster encouraged his horse painting and after 1884 he became a full time equestrian artist. He

apparently received a commission from Queen Victoria and usually painted in watercolour. He illus. a number of books including those written by Sir Walter Gilbey, his friend and patron. A portrait of "Plaisanterie", the mare belonging to Sir Tatton Sykes at Sledmere, painted in 1892 and inscr., was engraved by F. Babbage (q.v.) and repro. in "Bailys Magazine" 1891/3. Palfrey's portraits of the grey hunter "Buthca" saddled in a stable and "Blackberry" were painted for Sir Guy Gilbey of Essex in 1899.

Palmer, Albert (op.1953)
A portrait by this artist of the football professional Willie Hall, 19½in.x23½in. Exh. FE.

Palmer, James (op.1953)
An interesting painting of football played against an industrial background of belching smoke entitled "Players on Cinders", 35in.x27½in. Exh. FE.

Palmer, James Lynwood (1868-1941)
Sporting and equestrian painter, the third son of a Lincolnshire clergyman who became Canon of Rochester Cathedral. Palmer ran away to Canada as a young man to avoid family pressure to become a lawyer or a diplomat. There he had charge of the horses in the Royal Canadian Mounted Police and became a great expert in horses' feet. Without any artistic training and with the help of General Field he earned a living as an artist for some time in New York. He returned to England in 1899 and with the patronage of the Countess of Warwick, a great horsewoman herself, secured commissions to paint all the Duke of Portland's stallions and the racehorses of many other famous patrons, including Edward VII for whom he painted "Minoru" and George V for whom he painted "Scuttle". He collaborated with Claude Prescott (q.v.) on a painting (in grisaille) entitled "The Old Polo Ground", s.&d. May '92, and with Algernon Talmage (q.v.) on a portrait of Edward E. Marshall of Pennsylvania on his bay hunter "Canada", s.&d. 1927 by both artists. Palmer had great personal charm and an uncanny knowledge of a horse. He thus became adviser to the Earl of Derby's stud, a commission which he undertook with thorough professionalism in an age where important owners vied to produce the best and finest bloodstock. It was said that he trained a Grand National winner, first in a harrow and then as a wheeler in his coach, doing ten miles a day. Towards the end of his life the equestrian painter Juliet McLeod (q.v.) became his assistant and her work reflects his influence.

Palmer, Samuel, RWS (1805-1881)
A landscape painter, an illustrator and an etcher who was much influenced by the work of William Blake (1757-1827). Painted "The Young Angler" with John Linnell (q.v.) on Linnell's visit to Palmer at Shoreham, Kent in the late 1820s. Palmer married Linnell's daughter, Hannah, who was a good landscape painter herself.

Palmer, W. (op.c.1825/6)
Painter of equestrian portraits including "Thorney", a saddled chestnut racehorse in a landscape, 20½in.x28in.,

auctioned Sotheby's 1988. "Thorney" by "Seagrave" out of "Primrose" was bred in 1822 by Mr. G. Platel and raced on the flat under the ownership of J. Longdon.

Pannett, Juliet, PS, SGA, FRSA (b.1911)
Painter in both oil and watercolour and an illustrator. Studied at Brighton College of Art. Special artist to "The Illustrated London News" (1958-1964). Her portrait of the cricketer, Colin Cowdrey, s.&d. 1968, charcoal and coloured chalks, 15¾in.x11⅜in. was auctioned Phillips 1989.

"Pantaloon"
Pseudonym sometimes used by the equestrian artist, Isaac Cullin (q.v.).

Pardon, James (op.1800-1850)
Portrait painter and a miniaturist whose portraits include a number of sporting personalities. His portrait of Mr. Bryce on a grey hunter raising his hat, with his hounds and huntsman to the right, 37½in.x51¼in., was auctioned Christie's 1974 entitled "Gone Away - The View Halloo". His portrait of a gentleman on a grey hunter, accompanied by his son on a pony with two pointers, was painted in 1848 and a portrait of a gentleman on a chestnut hunter in a dark green coat, his top hat in his hand, was painted in 1843, 34in.x44in. In this painting the huntsman has dismounted and the hounds are resting. Pardon's portrait of Rice Wynne, Esq. on his hunter, 38in.52in., was exh. at the Preston AG and Museum "British Sporting Paintings" (1943).

Park, Carton Moore, RBA (1877-1956)
Animal painter and illustrator who also painted portraits and some decorative subjects. Studied at the Glasgow School of Art (under Francis Newbery) and pub. his first illustrations in the "Glasgow Weekly Citizen" and "St. Mungo". He painted animals in a strong, unsentimental way, derived from Japanese prints. He was elected RBA (1899) and resigned in 1905 but continued to exhibit in the UK until his emigration to America in 1910.

Park, Harry Morl(e)y (op.1872-1895)
Bristol painter who painted Highland and game shooting subjects in both oil and watercolour. His sporting work includes a portrait of "A Ghillie with his Pony, Dogs and Dead Game", "Rough Shooting on the Moors" and "After the Chase" - a painting depicting two Dandie Dinmonts with two dead rabbits. He favoured dog subjects, particularly those of greyhounds and pointers, and painted them in both oil and watercolour.

Park, Henry (1816-1871)
Painter of animals and equestrian portraits, also of figure subjects including his painting of children racing donkeys in a village. His portrait of a bay horse and a foal in a park landscape, s.&d. 1850, 21in.x29in., was auctioned Henry Duke & Son 1990 and "Tying the Day's Bag", ghillies, a pony and dogs, s.&d. 1860, 13½in.x19in., was auctioned Sotheby's (Glen.) 1980. He exh. four paintings of cattle and sheep at the RA and three paintings at SS.

Park, James Chalmers (b.1858)
Yorkshire painter of British game birds who studied at Leeds School of Art. Park was also an accomplished etcher. His sporting subjects include studies of grouse and partridge, which he painted in watercolour. He exh. in London and Yorkshire until 1930.

Parker, Charles H. (1858-1930)
"The Football Association Cup Final at Crystal Palace", a hand coloured engraving with key. The Harry Langton Collection.

Parker, Henry Perlee, HRSA (1795-1873)
This Newcastle based sporting and animal artist was accused, like Schwanfelder (q.v.), of being a "Jack of all trades". He painted every subject from Northumbrian and Scottish landscapes to the many coastal scenes which earned him the nickname of "Smuggler" Parker. He also painted sporting subjects with considerable talent. Born in Devon he was taught to paint by his father who was a teacher of marine and mechanical drawing in Devonport. Parker moved to Newcastle in 1816 where he established himself and was commissioned to paint large portrait groups such as "The North-umberland Hunt" and the Newcastle festivities to mark the coronation of George IV, a picture bought by the Newcastle Corporation. Parker was a prolific artist and, like Schwanfelder in Leeds, could be relied upon to provide the backbone in the form of thirty or so paintings for each Northumberland institution exhibition. Indeed, with the painter T.M. Richardson, he purchased a plot of land in Blackett Street for £113.10s. and commissioned a building, from John Dobson and Richard Grainger, to found the Northern Academy of Arts. This was largely financed by subscriptions and opened with the first exhibition on 11 June 1828. In 1841 Parker moved to Sheffield where he became drawing master at Wesley College. Parker came to London in about 1845 and exh. at the RA, BI, SS and NWCS. His portrait of the Duke of Rutland's hounds in a wooded landscape with Belvoir Castle in the distance, painted in 1828, and his work entitled "The Disputed Shot" mark his talent in the field of sporting subjects.

Parker, W. (op.1922)
A pair of watercolour studies of a country house with hounds in a lane s.&d. 1922 were auctioned at Phillips (Exeter) 1986.

Parkes, Joanna (Mrs. Daniell) (b.1948)
Painter of equestrian subjects who studied fine art at Stourbridge College of Art. She designed the first day cover for the 200th Derby Day stamps for the Post Office in June 1979. Member of the Society of Equestrian Artists. She hunts with the Ledbury and rides frequently in point-to-points and in cross country events.

Parr, Frederick (Capt.) (op.1833-1843)
See "Junglicus"

Parrocel, Charles (1688-1752)
French battle scene draughtsman, a pupil of his father who also specialised in battle scenes. Parrocel's chalk drawing of a mounted huntsman, black and white on buff paper, presumably a study for an oil painting, sold at auction (Christie's Old Master Drawings 1984) for £11,880. Parrocel's work is represented in the British Museum, London.

Parrott, William (1813-1869)
Painter of several sporting scenes including "Derby Day", s.&d. 1864, auctioned Christie's (1940), "Fishing Hampstead" and "Henley Regatta", exh. Hutchinson Sporting Gallery (Pavière).

Parry, Joseph (1744-1826)
Manchester painter whose work"The Jackass Race at the Eccles Wakes, Manchester" (1821) shows one of several sporting events which took place during the Eccles Wakes, an annual three day fair held in early September. Parry painted a series of these fair scenes, four of which are in the collection of the Manchester City AG.

Parry, Leigh, PPS, FBA (b.1919)
Draughtsman and painter of equestrian subjects, particularly those of eventing and hunting. A descendant of Walter Parry Hodges (q.v.). Parry studied at the St. Martin's School of Art and at Heatherleys. A keen rider to hounds, Parry has hunted with the Burghley and the Fitzwilliam hounds, painting the latter at their opening meet in 1979. He paints in watercolour and pastel. Elected a member of the PS (1966) and became a council member (1974-1978) and President (1983). Elected FBA (1971) and elected to the council of the Society of Equestrian Artists (1983).

Parry, William, ARA (1742-1791)
London-born portrait painter and a skilled copyist of old masters. Patronised by Sir Watkin Williams Wynn, the famous MFH. Parry painted him with his hounds in 1770 before going to Rome where he stayed until 1775. He studied art at several of the London academies, entering the RA Schools in 1769 where he presumably stayed for a year before setting off on his travels.

Parsons, Miss Beatrice E. (1870-1931)
Flower and garden painter who studied at the RA Schools and exh. there (1889-1899). She is included in this Dictionary for her watercolour painting of her nephews and nieces in the garden of Norfolk Lodge, Crowborough, Sussex, s.&d. 1922, 16½ in.x22½ in., Phillips (Chester) 1990. The four children are grouped around the eldest boy who leans on a cricket bat.

Parsons, Elizabeth (b.1953)
Studied in Florence under Signorina Simi. Paints horses, landscapes and portraits. Has exh. at the RP, NEAC and the Society of Equestrian Artists. Also at the Richmond Gallery, Cork Street and the Wingfield Sporting Gallery, London.

Partington, Peter (b.1941)
Contemporary painter of game birds and wildfowl scenes including partridge, snipe, plover, grouse and lapwing.

Parton, George (op.1886-1893)
Birmingham painter who exh. four paintings at the Birmingham AG (1886-1893). His "Still Life of a Roach on a River Bank", s.&d. 1887, 12in.x17⅞ in., was auctioned Bonhams 1985.

Partridge, Alfred A. (op.1885-1893)
Painter of animal and equestrian portraits including "A Bay Hunter in a Stable" and "A Chestnut Hunter in a Stable" s.&d. 1893. A portrait of "The Waif", s.&d. 1888, 16in.x22in., auctioned Christie's (Sth. Ken.) 1984 and a study of a bay hunter in a loose box, with a terrier, s.&d. 1885, 18in.x24in., Heathcote Ball (Leicester) 1984.

Partridge, Henry T. (op.1890-1891)
Painter of animal and equestrian portraits including two of hunters in a stable (1891) and a further study of a horse in a stable, s.&d. 1890. Auctioned Pearsons (Hants.) 1986.

Partridge, J.C. (op.1874-1881)
A painting of a horse and a gig, clearly s.&d. 1881, 18in.x24in., was auctioned Sotheby's (Sussex) 1989. Three portraits of hunters, one s.&d. 1874, were auctioned Russell, Baldwin and Bright 1992.

Pascoe, William E.W. (op.1855-1869)
Animal and equestrian painter whose work includes a portrait of a Devonshire bull, painted 29 December 1855, a study of a blue and white greyhound with a hare, painted 1863, "Hippia" and a bay filly in a stable inscribed "Newmarket" (painted July 1867), and J.D. Wragg's "Favourites", signed and inscr. "Newmarket" (painted 1869). Pascoe lived in the Cambridge area and at one time in Chesterton Road, Cambridge.

Pash, Florence (Mrs. A.A. Humphrey) (ex.1886-1924)
Portrait and figure painter whose painting entitled "Croquet" was exh. at the NEAC in 1899.

Pasmore, John F. (op.1838-1866)
Painter of animal, equestrian, sporting and rustic scenes including "The Sportsman's Lunch", "A Fine Kill", "A Gentleman with Ghillies and Dogs in the Highlands", s.&d. 1838, "A Gentleman with Terrier, Pony and Donkey in a Shed", "A Mastiff Ratting", etc. Pasmore exh. at the RA (1842-1862), BI, SS and elsewhere.

Pasquin, Anthony
Alias John Williams art critic to "The Morning Herald" at the end of the 18th century. It was Pasquin who wrote in 1794 "Mr. (Sawrey) Gilpin is inferior to Mr. (George) Stubbs in anatomical knowledge, but is superior to him in grace and genius".

Patalano, Enrico (op.1890)
An interesting portrait of a fisherman, 84in.x48in., was auctioned Sotheby's (Glen.) 1987. Patalano exh. a portrait at the RA in 1890.

Patch, Thomas (1725-1782)
A topographical artist from Exeter who went to Rome and eventually settled in Florence. Landscape and portrait painter, etcher, line and aquatint engraver, he is included in this Dictionary for his many caricatures of sporting personalities. A friend (in Florence) of Sir Horace Mann who introduced him to Horace Walpole (q.v.), of coursing fame. Patch was also a friend of Sir Joshua Reynolds (q.v.). He is probably best known for his satirical conversation pieces in which the leading English residents or visitors to Florence appear. His son, John Patch, became a surgeon at Exeter Hospital and was painted by William Gandy (d.1729), the portrait painter, son of the more accomplished artist James Gandy (born Exeter 1619). Patch's caricature of an Englishman and his horse, with a view of Florence behind, painted in 1769, 16in.x11¾in., was auctioned Christie's 1983.

Paterson, George M. (op.1880-1906)
Scottish painter of some sporting subjects including his watercolour "A Rough Shoot in the Cornfield at Sunset", s.&d. 1880, 9¼in.x21in., auctioned Sotheby's 1984. Paterson exh. two works at the RA (1881-1886).

Paterson, James, ARCA, NRD, AMGP (1916-1986)
Edinburgh born watercolour painter and a designer of stained glass. He is included in this Dictionary for his watercolour painting "Salmon Fishing, Bideford", s.&d. (19)83 and inscr., 10in.x14in. Exh. J. Collins & Son, Bideford 1990, and "A Cricket Match at Taunton", watercolour, private coll. Paterson won a scholarship to the RCA in 1936 but only took it up after the war (1939-1945) which he spent with the RAF. He joined Bideford School of Art, in 1948, teaching stained glass and became Principal in 1955, a role which he held until 1985. Paterson was a prolific painter of watercolours, many of which are in private collections in England, Europe and the USA. He exh. at the Mall Galleries London and at the RSA and was an Associate of both the RCA and the GP.

Paterson, Mary Viola (b.1899)
Oil painter and lithographer who studied at the Life School, Glasgow School of Art under Maurice Greiffenhagen, RA (1917-1921), also in Paris at the Académie de la Grande Chaumière and the Académie L'hote (André L'hote) (q.v.). She was the daughter of Alexander Nisbet Paterson, ARSA (1862-1947). Mary Paterson exh. at the RA, RSA, SSA and GI. She lived at Helensburgh for some years. She used sporting subjects quite frequently in her work including her coloured wood cut, c.1935, "The Highland Games" which is in the collection of the British Museum. Her horse racing scene "In the Paddock, Malta" showing jockeys mounting their horses at a race meeting in Malta was auctioned Christie's (Glasgow) 1990. Her watercolour of gondoliers racing and her painting entitled "The Start of the Race, the Enterprise Class at Helensburgh Regatta", s.&d. '61, 28½in.x18in., was auctioned Christie's (Sth. Ken.) 1988.

Paton, Frank (1856-1909)
Animal painter, engraver and genre illustrator working in London and Gravesend. Exh. at the RA between 1878 and 1890 when he had a dispute with the organisers which prevented him exhibiting thereafter. Paton's work includes a series of sporting etchings printed in sepia, including the well-known "Royal and Ancient" (St. Andrew's 1794) pub. by Leggatt Brothers, Cheapside, London 1894. This small print, 6in.x4in., shows four golfers in imaginary 18th century costume playing a hole at St. Andrews while four caddies look on with bundles of clubs under their arms. Paton also engraved a series for C.E. Brock (q.v.). He is responsible

for one cartoon of a horse contributed to "Vanity Fair" in 1910. He painted a large part of the presentation work to Lord Willoughby de Broke on his retirement as Master of the Warwickshire hunt which features horse, hounds and landscape. Cecil Cutler (q.v.) painted the portrait of Lord Willoughby de Broke. This work was exh. at Mr. Carter Baird's gallery at 61 Jermyn Street in July 1900. Paton engraved a number of sporting and genre subjects after his own designs and those of his contemporaries. His other sporting works include "The Portsmouth Coach", s.&d. 1897, a watercolour, 9in.x 13½in., auctioned Sotheby's 1989; "The Arrival and the Departure from the Chequers Inn", a pair, s.&d. 1893, watercolours, each 6in.x8in., Christie's (Sth. Ken.) 1989; and "The Manchester Royal Mail", dated 1889. Paton used the hare a great deal in much of his work including the hares which were used to convey New Year's greetings by Edward VII in 1902, a painting which hangs at Goodwood House, Sussex. Paton contributed one equestrian cartoon to "Vanity Fair" in 1910 which appeared posthumously since he died of a heart attack at the age of fifty-three in November 1909.

Paton, W. Hubert (op.1882-1932)
Scottish landscape and figure painter, probably the son of the artist Waller Hugh Paton (1828-1895) and nephew of Sir Joseph Noel Paton (1821-1901). Included in this Dictionary for his watercolour of figures playing lawn tennis in a woodland setting, s.&d. 1882, 15in.x 21in., auctioned Christie's (Glasgow) 1988. Paton exh. at the RSA and elsewhere (1885-1932).

Patrick, James (exh.1880-1905)
Scottish figure painter from Kirkaldy who painted a portrait in watercolour c.1890 of the professional golf champion, Tom Morris (1821-1908) with the Royal and Ancient clubhouse behind him. He also painted "The Links Fair, Kirkaldy", 29in.x50in., s.&d. 1894, Sotheby's (London). Patrick, who lived at the same address as the artists John and John Rutherford Patrick, exh. at the RSA and GI (1880-1905).

Patrick, James McIntosh, RSA, ROI, ARE (b.1907)
Scottish painter and etcher who studied at the Life School at Glasgow School of Art (under Maurice Greiffenhagen, RA) and in Paris. Patrick includes a number of sporting scenes amongst his work and many of his engraved subjects are taken from the Highlands of Scotland. His "Hunt Setting Out from an Exmoor Farm in the Snow" is at the Ferens Art Gallery, Hull. Patrick exh. at the RE, RA, RBA and elsewhere and at the RSA from 1926. He received the Guthrie Award in 1935. Elected ARE (1932), ROI (1949), and RSA (1957). Exh. Fine Art Society Ltd., London.

Patterson, Janet (b.1941)
Figure artist who studied at the Slade School of Art (1960-1964) and won a French Government scholarship to Aix en Provence (1964-1965). Her painting of football entitled "The Playing Field", painted in 1983, was exh. at the RA 1985.

Patterson, Tom (op.1922)
"The Tennis Match", s.&d. 1922, 12¼in.x18¾in., auctioned Christie's (Glasgow).

Paul, John (op.1867-1886)
Painter of equestrian portraits and sporting subjects, the son of the Norwich landscape artist Joseph Paul (1804-1887). John Paul's horse portraits include "A Coach Horse" dated 1886, "A Hunter" dated 1867, "Dunboyne" and "Burgundy" a pair of horses in stable backgrounds, dated 1873, and "A Water Spaniel", with a duck and hunters beyond, in a river setting, dated 1882. His painting of a smart turn-out depicting two horses pulling a vehicle described as a dog cart, s.&d. 1875, was auctioned Sotheby's 1966.

Paul, Sir John Dean, Bt. (1802-1868)
Amateur sporting painter particularly of horses, author and illustrator of books including "The Country Doctor's Horse", written by his father, Sir J.D. Paul (1847) and "The ABC of Fox Hunting" pub. posthumously in 1871. Paul was educated at Westminster and Eton before joining the family bank of Snow, Paul and Paul from 1828. He succeeded his father as 2nd baronet in 1852. In 1855 the bank went bankrupt and the partners were tried for fraud and sentenced to fourteen years transportation although Paul died in St. Albans in 1868.

Paul, Peter (op.1859-1860)
Landscape and sporting painter who painted several sporting scenes including "Return from the Hunt", showing a father and, presumably, his son with their ponies, dogs and the day's bag, dated 1860, 9½in.x 26½in., auctioned Sotheby's 1977. Paul exh. one painting at the RA in 1859 entitled "On the Grass".

Paull, A.B. (Mrs.) (op.1880)
A pair of pencil hunting scenes s.&d. 1880. Exh. SAG AG, London 1985. These are well executed and attractive drawings by a talented but presumably amateur artist.

Pawley, James (op.1836-1869)
Extremely competent provincial painter of animal, equestrian and sporting subjects. His painting of a fine black bull with a herdsman in a landscape dated 1836 and inscr. "Grazed by Mr. Potter of Fakenham, 100 wt.", 16¼in.x23in., was auctioned Christie's 1979 and his fine portrait of William Long, huntsman to the Beaufort on his grey hunter "Bertha" accompanied by the hounds, 42in.x44in., was auctioned Sotheby's 1990. Will Long, successor to Philip Payne as huntsman to the 5th Duke of Beaufort, was described as "small, wiry and very quick". He was a great hound breeder improving the Badminton hounds with sires from the Belvoir, Fitzwilliam and Brocklesby packs. He worked with the Beaufort until 1855 when he retired after a dispute with the 8th Duke. James Pawley exh. a painting of the Tedworth hunt at the RA and two studies from life at the BI and SS (1854-1869). His painting of Lord Hardinge's Arabian horse "Meenee", 17in.x21in., dated 1849 was exh. by Messrs. Ackermanns, London.

Paxton, W.A. (op.c.1909)
American painter, a member of the Californian Art Club in 1926 at which date he was living in Los Angeles, Calif. "Portrait of a Young Archer" painted in water and bodycolour, 12½in.x9⅜in., auctioned Phillips 1985.

Paxton, William McGregor (1896-1941)

American painter and teacher who studied at the Ecole des Beaux Arts in Paris, under Gérome (q.v.) and Dennis M. Bunker in Boston. Included in this Dictionary for "The Croquet Players", 1898. T.W.J. Valsam Collection.

Paye, Richard Morton (op.1773-1821)

Painter of portraits and miniatures. Best known for the engravings after his attractive genre scenes with children. These include "Boy Playing at Marbles" and "Boys Playing at Pegtop" (1780). Both subjects were engraved by Robert Pollard (q.v.). Paye painted in a style similar to that of Joseph Wright of Derby (q.v.). His health and fortune faded in his later years and in 1812 he was helped by the RA fund.

Payne, Arthur Frederick (1831-1910)

Accomplished amateur painter and etcher who exh. at the RA (1858-1873). He and his twin brother, Alfred, both won cricket blues at Oxford and then went on to play for Leicestershire. Payne's watercolour "A Cricket Match at Cowley, Oxford", 5½in.x7½in. was painted in June 1857 (private collection). Cowley Marsh was the venue for the continuous series of annual matches between Oxford and Cambridge which began in 1838 and continued until the move to the Parks in 1881. Arthur Payne, although a useful cricketer, eventually devoted more time to art than cricket and spent long periods in Paris. An exhibition of his work was held in 1982 at Covent Garden Art Gallery.

Payne, C.N. (op.1906)

Contributed motoring sketches to "Punch" in 1906.

Payne, Charles Johnson ("Snaffles") (1884-1967)

Sporting painter and sketch artist, author and illustrator of several books including "A Half Century of Memories" (1949), "'Osses and Obstacles" (1935) and "Four Legged Friends and Acquaintances" (1951). Born at Leamington Spa, Warwickshire, the fourth son of eight children of a boot maker, Payne was accepted by the army in 1901 or 1902. He became a gunner with the Royal Garrison Artillery but left in 1906 due to an illness. His first recorded works date from his army period, mainly full-length, semi-caricature portraits and about this time he began hunting in the Aldershot area. In 1908 Messrs. Fores became his agent and in 1912 Payne moved to Oakham, Rutland and began to hunt in the shires. This inspired his most widely known work, "The Finest View in Europe". During the 1st World War he joined "The Graphic" as a European correspondent and later joined the RNAS as a mechanic. In 1917 he became a lieutenant in the RNVR in the camouflage department where "dazzle painting" had been invented by Norman Wilkinson (q.v.) This inspired Payne's naval paintings. After the war he was a frequent contributor to "The Sporting and Dramatic News" until 1932. During the 2nd World War he worked for a time on aerodrome camouflage and then joined the Home Guard. His last days were spent in Wiltshire where he died. Payne's work was pub. in limited edns., for almost half a century, and has always had a universal appeal.

The early prints were pub. in black and white, then hand coloured and the later prints were photographic colour prints. Many of his prints have a humorous inscription and most are signed in pencil. A large number of the print borders carry an impress mark of two interlocking snaffle bits. Payne used the pseudonym "Snaffles" and signed his paintings both as "Snaffles" and Harry Payne. His sporting subjects include hunting, polo and steeplechasing.

Payne, David (op.1882-1891)

Landscape painter from the Derbyshire area. Included in this Dictionary for his paintings of cricket including "Cricket in Abberley Valley", s.&d. 1890, 28in.x42in., Sotheby's (Chester) and "A Village Cricket Match", signed, 28in.x42in., Sotheby's (1988).

Payne, Dorothy M.

See Dorothy M. Hardy

Payne, Harry

See Charles Johnson Payne

Payne, Wilfrid (op.1953)

Contemporary painter from Nottingham of a football match entitled "Our National Game", exh. FE. Payne exh. one painting at the RA in 1952.

Payne, William (c.1760-1831)

Painter of human and equestrian portraits whose study of a chestnut hunter in a stable, dated 1831, 24¾in.x 29¼in., was auctioned Sotheby's 1981. Payne usually signed but rarely dated his work. He was also a landscape painter, usually in watercolour, and a fine draughtsman.

Peake, Robert (the Elder) (c.1551-1619)

Fashionable portrait painter included in this Dictionary for his portrait of Francis, 4th Earl of Bedford, with an unhooded hawk on his gloved fist, the hood in his right, ungloved hand. The portrait was painted c.1600 since the young Earl is newly breeched, an event which took place when a young boy was seven years old (Woburn Abbey Coll.).

Pearce, Stephen (1819-1904)

Painter of equestrian subjects who was brought up in the Royal Mews, the son of a clerk in the department of the Master of the Horse. As a result many of his subjects were royal horses. He studied at Sass's Academy and the RA Schools and became a pupil of Sir Martin Archer Shee, the portrait painter. His fine painting "Coursing at Ashdown Park", 47¼in.x118in., was presented to the Earl of Craven by the coursers of the United Kingdom at a cost of £1,200 and is probably Pearce's most important work. The painting shows sixty equestrian portraits and was engraved by Charles Mottram (1806-1876) in 1872. (A discourse on this picture is given by Mr. W.G. Borron, who took a principal part in the promotion of the Ashdown Park coursing picture, in his biographical sketch, pp.22-23, Colnaghi cat. 1986). While this painting might have received rave reviews, his portrait of Mr. C. Radclyffe, Master of the South Dorset Hunt, received a less enthusiastic review in "Bailys Magazine", vol. 21, June

1875: "Mr. Pearce's portrait of Mr. C. J. Radclyffe, Master of the South Dorset is like some dozen or so of the same subjects that have been produced from Mr. Pearce's prolific easel. Thoroughly good honest works with little or no imagination in them, we confess they pall upon us." Pearce painted many sporting personalities including W.R. Stretton on a bay hunter, Arthur Brook with the Bexhill Harriers, Freeman Thomas, Master of the Southdown Hounds, a painting that was engraved by J. Scott and pub. by Messrs. Fores in 1904 and an equestrian portrait of George William, 9th Earl of Coventry with hounds and huntsmen in the background painted in 1870, 69½ in.x55¼ in., Christie's 1991.

Pears, Charles, ROI, PPRSMA (1873-1958)
Marine painter, illustrator, lithographer and poster artist of considerable ability who became the first President of the RSMA in 1939. Educated at Hardwick College and served in the RN in the 1st World War. Became official war artist to the Admiralty (1915-1918) and again in 1940. He was also the inventor of naval camouflage. He was a regular magazine illustrator in the 1890s and 1900s. Elected ROI in 1913. Wrote extensively on sailing and yachting including "Two Years Before the Mast". His painting of "The 1934 America's Cup" with Sir Thomas Sopwith's "Endeavour", 40in.x50in., was auctioned Bonhams 1986. Pears painted a number of other yacht racing scenes including the "Island Sailing Club at Cowes".

Pears, Dion (op.1950-1968)
20th century motor racing artist whose prolific work includes "Jaguar XK120s at Crystal Palace", a fine piece which showed one of the last historic races held at Crystal Palace when Jackie Stewart driving Eric Brown's special aluminium bodied XK120 Roadster led Dick Protheroe in his special XK120 Coupé. Pears was one of the few artists to paint motor racing at the shortlived Goodwood race circuit. The 9th Duke of Richmond founded the motor race circuit using the perimeter track of the Westhampnett Airfield. Motor car racing flourished at Goodwood from 1948 to 1966.

Pearson, J. (op.c.1857)
"The Horse Race", 11½ in.x15⅜ in., was auctioned W.H. Lane 1988. Pearson's portrait of "The Flying Dutchman" with Marlow up, 18in.x22in., is s.&d. 1857, the year before the horse was sold for £4,000 to France.

Pearson, Kathleen Margaret, ARWA (1894-1961)
Cheshire portrait and equestrian painter who studied art at the Slade School (1920) and the RA Schools (1921-1926). Elected ARWA (1939). "Winter Sports", 16in.x24in., was auctioned Sotheby's (Sussex) 1988.

Pearson, Robert (op.1892-1909)
Scarborough painter whose painting "A Day's Shooting", s.&d. '93, 16x19½ in., was auctioned Sotheby's (Chester) 1985. He exh. at the RA, RHA and BI (1892-1909).

Peart, Herbert (op.1907)
This artist exh. a study of fishes at the NEAC in 1907.

Peat, Thomas (op.1791-1830)
Portrait and miniature painter who exh. at the RA (1791-1805) and included a number of horse portraits amongst his work which he exh. from the Bath, Leamington and Bristol areas.

Pechaubes, Eugène (1890-1967)
French painter of equestrian subjects particularly French and English racing scenes including "The Chippenham Stakes at Newmarket" (1936) and many racing scenes at both St. Cloud and Longchamp including the Prix de l'Arc de Triomphe in 1931. Pechaubes also painted a number of trotting races, a sport more popular in France than in England, and polo.

Peel, James, RBA (1811-1906)
A prolific landscape painter who operated mostly in the north western counties, the Lake District and North Wales and who worked in a style similar to Benjamin Leader (q.v.). He exh. mostly at SS but also at the RA (1843-1888), BI and elsewhere. His fine fly fishing painting "Casting Up Stream", 12in.x18in., was auctioned Bonhams 1983. Peel painted several other angling scenes including "Fishing by a River Bank", "The Trout Stream, Wensleydale near Matlock", and "An Angler by the River in Duddon Valley, Cumbria."

Peers, M. (op.1828)
Animal and sporting artist of whom "The Manchester Courier" wrote on 2 August 1828 à propos a painting of greyhounds "There is, we should think, a very good opening in Manchester for a tolerable animal painter and we think MP would soon fill up the vacant place if he would exert himself". Unfortunately MP appears not to have been able to exert himself sufficiently for very little more was heard of him.

Pegram, Frederick, RI (1870-1937)
Figure painter and illustrator, first cousin of the Brock brothers C.E., H.M. and R.H. (qq.v.), who numbered cycling, ballooning and cricket amongst the sports he painted. He joined the staff of "Queen" and "The Pall Mall Gazette" in 1886. Contributed to "Punch" (1894-1917) and illus. many books including "Masterman Ready" (1897), "Midshipman Easy" (1896) and "The Bride of Lammermoor" (1898). Elected RI (1921). His painting of the Royal Crescent and Lansdown Crescent, Bath, with a cricket match in progress, 31½ in.x45½ in., was auctioned Sotheby's 1986. He also painted "The English Ladies -v- the Irish Ladies Hockey Match at Richmond" in 1901.

Peile, Edith M. (Miss) (op.1906-1919)
Sporting painter who exh. "The Meet of the Essex Hounds" at the NEAC in 1911. Peile also exh. at the RA (1907-1919), the ROI, SWA and Goupil Gallery.

Peirson, Louis V. (1870-1950)
American middle west painter and engraver who was born and died in St. Pauls. "Lawn Tennis at the Burtons", dated 1905, 26in.x30in., was auctioned Sotheby's 1986. This men's lawn tennis match is believed to have taken place at "The Burtons", St. Pauls, Minnesota, one of America's early courts.

Pell, Catherine M., FRSA
20th century landscape painter who has included hunting and shooting scenes amongst her work. Pell studied at the Burton School of Art and lives in Derbyshire. She is a member of the Staffordshire Society of Artists and many of her hunting studies are made with the Meynell, the South Notts. and the Derbyshire Beagles.

Pellegrini, Carlo (1839-1889)
Aristocratic portrait painter and caricaturist who, known as "Ape" contributed to "Vanity Fair" from January 1869 to April 1889. Pellegrini, who was born in Italy, came to England in November 1864 and included sporting personalities amongst his caricatures for "Vanity Fair". Mr. Herbert Praed, MP, for example, was featured by "Ape" on roller skates (18.7.1874, No. 179).

Pemberton, Richard (op.1840)
A painting of two racehorses, with jockeys up, on a race course, s.&d. 1840, 14in.x18½in., Sotheby's 1979.

Pembery, J.
Painter of rowing scenes including a rowing crew at the Ship Inn on the Thames near Mortlake, 16¼in.x14⅜in., and a crew rowing past the Queen's Head, Mortlake, 16⅛in.x14in., Christie's 1988.

Penfield, Edward (1866-1925)
American painter and illustrator, also a fine etcher. Pupil of the Art Student's League of New York. Member of the Society of Illustrators (1901). His speciality was posters and cover designs and he was the author and illustrator of "Holland Sketches" and "Spanish Sketches". Editor of "Harpers" (1890-1901) and instructor at the ASL. Had a profound impact on American illustration. He is included in this Dictionary for "The Stroke Oar" (1904), lithograph, pub. by F.P. Collier, 13¼in.x10in., and for his watercolour entitled "Steeplechase", 13½in.x 12in. which was repro. on the front cover of "Collier's" Magazine 16 May 1903.

Penny, Edward, RA (1714-1791)
Portrait painter who studied under Thomas Hudson (q.v.) and in Rome. He returned to Cheshire, his birth place, in 1743 but shortly afterwards came to London where he specialised in small scale, full length portraits. Exh. at the SA (1762-1768), becoming Vice President (1765) and was a foundation member of the RA becoming Professor of Painting (1769-1783). Exh. at the RA (1769-1782). He painted the portraits of many distinguished personalities, some of whom were sportsmen. His portrait of the cricket playing Sir William Benett of Fareham, 20in.x14in., whom he has shown standing beside an old type wicket with two forked sticks and a single bail lying between the forks, but for some unaccountable reason without a bat, was painted c.1743/4. (The double wicket was superseded by the introduction of the third stump and the second bail in 1776.) Penny also exh. "Return from the Chase" at the RA and "The Blacksmith's Shop" in 1767.

Pepper, Frank (1910-1988)
Born at Ilford, Essex. Educated Ilford County High School. Creator of such schoolboy heroes as "Roy of the Rovers", one of Britain's most enduring comic strip characters, and "The Boxing Ring". Pepper made his debut in the 1930s with his work for boy's comic papers such as Amalgamated Press's "Triumph" and "Champion", for whom he created "Danny of the Dazzlers", the adventures of a humble orphan boy who becomes a star footballer of North London United. This was written under one of Pepper's many pseudonyms "John Marshall". In the course of a long career - he started as an office boy at the age of fifteen with "The Childrens Newspaper" and "Encyclopaedia" - he contributed to "The Daily Telegraph", "Pearsons Weekly", "The Daily Herald", "The Daily Express", "Tit Bits", "John Bull" and "The News Chronicle".

Perboyre, Paul Emile Leon (b.1826)
French painter of military, equestrian and sporting scenes including his fine painting "Rendezvous de Chasse", 15in.x18in., Sotheby's (NY) 1988.

Percy, Herbert Sidney (op.1880-1900)
Landscape painter from Sutton Scotney who included a number of fishing scenes amongst his work and exh. eight works at SS (1880-1900) including "A Kill from a Mountain Tarn". Also painted a few hunting scenes. His angling scene "Relaxed Fishing", 14in.x10in., was auctioned Bonhams 1983.

Percy, Sidney Richard (1821-1886)
Landscape painter, very often of fishing scenes, fifth son of Edward "Old" Williams (1782-1855) Changed his name to Percy to avoid confusion with other members of the family. Father of two artist children (Percy). His paintings "Fishing the Llendyr, North Wales" and "Fishing the River Orbro" are just two examples.

"Peregrine"
The Revd. Gage Earl Freeman who wrote articles for "The Field" on falconry for many years.

Peri, Peter L. (1899-1967)
A social realist, sculptor and etcher. Born Budapest, Hungary. Lived in Berlin from 1920 to 1933 when he moved to London. Pioneered the use of concrete figurative sculpture. Represented in the Tate Gallery and the British Museum, London. "The Village Game", etching, 20in.x10½in. Exh. FE.

Perling, Robert F. (op.1865)
Perling painted equestrian portraits almost exclusively for the Royal Worcester Porcelain Company.

Pernel, Jean (op.1945)
French 20th century painter of equestrian scenes including "Les Trotteurs", a painting of a trotting race, dated 1945, auctioned Christie's 1989.

Perrett, S. (op.1837)
A primitive portrait of a huntsman with his gun and dogs seated beneath a tree, dated 1837, 32¾in.x27¼in., was auctioned Sotheby's (Sussex) 1989.

Perrin, William F. (op.c.1892)
A portrait of the racehorse "Mahdia", 13¾in.x18in., was auctioned Bonhams 1988.

Perry, G. (op.1831)
A portrait of a chestnut racehorse on a racecourse with jockey up in a green jacket with gold braid and gold cap, dated 1831, 22in.x29in., was auctioned Christie's 1974 having previously been auctioned in 1969.

Perry, Roy, RI (b.1935)
Urban and landscape painter, usually in gouache. Well known for his series of famous cricket grounds painted for the clubs from which prints were commissioned. Roy Perry, who was born in Liverpool, read Economics at Southampton University. He entered the business world but became a full time painter in 1971. In 1978 he won the Gold Medal at the RI and became a full Council Member in 1979. He has twice been a finalist in the Hunting Group painting competition, in 1981 and 1984, and a prizewinner in the Laing Competition (1983). He specialises in painting cricket and golf subjects.

Pethick, Maxwell Nath (1893-1973)
A talented watercolour artist, designer and card illustrator specialising in birds and flowers. Born in Bude, Cornwall, Pethick trained as a commercial artist joining a Leicester firm of dyers and finishers after the 1st World War (in which he fought but was invalided out of the army). After this firm's bankruptcy in 1929 he and the son of the owner set up their own fabric printing business which they split into two in 1937, making one a yarn company and the other a textile printing company with Pethick responsible for all the designs. After the 2nd World War, Pethick found wider scope for his artistic talent producing a large number of designs for Raphael Tuck which were used for greetings cards. He was largely responsible for the semi-humorous pop up cards which were so fashionable in the 1950s and 1960s. A studio sale was held after his widow's death in 1982 and many of his original designs and watercolours came on to the market for the first time, including his pictures of game birds.

Petit-Gerard, Pierre (b.1852)
French painter of equestrian scenes, particularly hunting.

Petley (Lieutenant) (op.1837)
An engraving by Thomas J. Rawlins (q.v.) of "The Cadets Race, Royal Military College, Sandhurst" after the work by this artist was pub. 1837, 11½in.x16½in.

Peto, John Frederick (1854-1907)
A virtually self taught painter with only one year at PAFA (1878). Moved to New Jersey (1889) from Philadelphia where he was born. Visited the West twice but never travelled to Europe. With the exception of one exhibit at Pennsylvania Academy, this artist had no major shows until the 1950s. He painted trompe-l'oeil still lifes characterised by using everyday objects such as string, tin cups, tattered books, umbrellas, torn postcards, etc. His use of light and colour are said to be reminiscent of Vermeer. "For the Track", s.&d. '95, 43½in.x29⅞in., was auctioned Christie's (NY) 1984.

Peto, Ralph (Mrs.) (op.1914-1916)
Exh. "A Study of the Stables at Belvoir" at the NEAC in 1914, her only exhibit there, but she also exh. four paintings at the London Society between 1914 and 1916.

Petrie, George, HRHA (1790-1866)
Irish landscape painter who studied at the Dublin Society School and exh. at the RHA from 1826, the year of its opening. He also exh. once at the RA. He travelled extensively in Ireland, painting Irish landscapes and angling scenes. Elected RHA in 1828 and became Librarian there in 1829. He also became a member of the RIA and was elected to the council in 1830. Elected PRHA in 1856 but resigned in 1859 and was made an honorary member. His watercolour portrait "An Angler in Connemara", 17in.x24in., was auctioned Sotheby's (Chester) 1986.

Pettafor, Charles R. (op.1862-1900)
Landscape painter who exh. at the RA, RBA, RI, and ROI (1862-1900). His watercolour "Golfers on a Links Course in a Coastal Landscape", 49¼in.x29½in., was auctioned Phillips (Scotland) 1986.

Pettie, John, HRSA, RA (1839-1893)
Scottish historical and landscape painter, also of angling scenes including his fine "Trout Fishing in the Highlands", signed, 32½in.x55½in., exh. at the RA 1881 No. 186. Pettie studied at Trustees Academy, Edinburgh, 1856 under R.S. Lauder, where his fellow students were W. MacTaggart (q.v.), a lifelong friend, Tom Graham, John MacWhirter and W.Q. Orchardson (qq.v.), with whom he later shared a studio in London. He exh. at the RA from 1860. Elected HRSA (1871) and RA (1873). He moved to London in 1862 and worked initially as an illustrator for "Good Words", a magazine which first appeared in Edinburgh but which moved to London in 1862. After 1870 he turned more to portrait painting, often depicting his sitters in historical costume, a fashion of his time.

Pettitt, Charles (op.1855-1862)
Yorkshire landscape artist whose "An Otter Hunt on a Mountain Stream", s.&d. 1861 and inscr., 48in.x72in., was auctioned Sotheby's (Scotland) 1986. Pettitt exh. at the BI, SS and elsewhere (1855-1859).

Pettitt, Edwin Alfred (1840-1912)
North Country landscape painter who exh. at the RA from 1858, but mainly at SS. Included in this Dictionary for his fine painting of a golf match at North Berwick, showing the Marine Hotel in its heyday at the turn of the century. Reproductions after his work can be seen at the Burlington Gallery, London.

Petty, William
Contemporary Argentinian artist whose polo painting "Clash of Tacos", 20in.x27in., was exh. at Shillay and Reks Inc. NY.

Peyton, A. (op.1904)
Illustrator of sporting comic strips to "The Graphic" 1904.

Phelps, Julia (op.1988)
Contemporary painter of sporting scenes including "Henley - Two Lengths Ahead" exh. at the RA 1988 and SWA 1988, "A Close Race - Henley Royal Regatta", "A Good Lead - Henley Royal Regatta" and "A Day Out at Henley Royal Regatta".

"Philemon" (op.1932-1980)
Contemporary motor racing artist in gouache and watercolour.

Philips, Charles (1708-1747)
Fashionable portrait painter, the son of the painter Richard Philips who probably taught him art. He painted for the royal family including full size, full length pictures of the Prince and Princess of Wales (1737) and a pair of portraits of Frederick, Prince of Wales with his horse and groom and a portrait of Augusta, Princess of Wales, in a green riding habit with her horse and groom, both s.&d. 1739, 18½in.x23½in., auctioned Christie's 1976. A very fine painting by Philips of the Earl of Scarborough with a hunting party at Rufford Abbey, 46in.x65in., has appeared at auction many times, 1976, 1984, 1985 and 1986.

Phillips, Bert Greer (1868-1956)
American painter, illustrator and teacher. Studied art in New York and in Paris under Constant and Laurens. Painted many Indian subjects; indeed from the time of his arrival in New Mexico in 1898 until his death in 1956, he enjoyed the friendship and confidence of the Pueblo people he painted hunting and playing sports.

Phillips, Douglas (b.1925)
Born Dundee, Scotland. Initially started his career in an office, then served with the Royal Army Service Corps in India and Ceylon (1945-1948) Joined the studio of D.C. Thomson, Dundee and for eighteen years illus. boys' adventure magazines including "The Runners" (1974), "Great Moments in Boxing" (1974), "My Favourite Mountaineering Stories" (1978) and "Adam and the Football Mystery" (1979). Since 1966 Phillips has worked as a freelance children's book illustrator. He specialises in action subjects, often depicting horses, and paints in a loose, free style, sometimes with blotted shading or colour washes.

Phillips, Frank Albert (op.1869-1899)
Portrait painter and painter of sporting subjects particularly shooting, who exh. at the RA (1869-1877). His very fine "The Nizam of Hyderabad, Tiger Shooting" painted in 1891/2 and inscr., was auctioned Sotheby's 1975. "An Ungainly Descent" also shows a shooting scene, dated 1875, 7in.x9¾in., auctioned Sotheby's 1985. His shooting portrait of the Prince of Wales, later Edward VII, attending a batteau with three loaders and a dog handler, s.&d. 1899, is a very fine work indeed.

"Phiz"
Pseudonym used by the sporting artist and illustrator Hablot Knight Browne (q.v.) originally for his illustrations in the serialisation of "Pickwick Papers" by "Boz" (Charles Dickens).

"Pic"
Alias the caricaturist and illustrator Charles Higgins (q.v.) who operated c.1945.

Pic, Marcel (op.1892-1895)
Painter of sporting portraits and caricatures, very often in pastel or coloured crayons. His portrait of "Colonel H.S. Follett, Master of the Norwich Staghounds at the Gallop", s.&d. 1895, 19in.x12½in., coloured crayons, was exh. in 1985 and his pastel entitled "Tally Ho", dated 1894, was auctioned Bonhams 1985. "A Caricature of a Billiards Player", s.&d. 1893, coloured chalks, 18¾in.x12in., auctioned Phillips (West 2) London.

Picasso, Pablo (1881-1974)
Spanish painter and a superb draughtsman and etcher who became leader of the Ecole de Paris. Gained entry into this sporting Dictionary with his charming early work "A Race Meeting at Longchamp" painted in 1901 when he was twenty, which latterly formed part of the Spingold Collection, auctioned Sotheby's November 1976.

Pichat, Oliver (1820-1912)
French painter of equestrian scenes.

Pickard, John (op.c.1901)
Primitive painter of fighting cocks.

Picola Y Lopez, Emanuel (1850?-1892?)
Spanish painter of equestrian scenes, particularly fox-hunting.

Pienne, Arnold (op.1975)
20th century painter whose portrait of Lyon "Punch" Bertrand (1897-1980), the last member of a dynasty that ushered British fencing into the 20th century, hangs in the de Beaumont Centre, London. Bertrand was the son of Felix Bertrand whose portrait was painted by W. Howard Robinson (q.v.).

Pigg, J.W.
Unknown early 20th century painter of prize racing pigeons, usually painted in pairs. Bonhams 1983.

Pignoux (late 19th century)
Elegant figures playing croquet on a beach, s.&d. 1877, 13¾in.x25½in.,Christie's.

Pigott, William Henry (c.1810-1901)
Sheffield landscape painter in oil who painted a number of sporting subjects including "Huntsman and Hounds", "Beagling in Autumn" and "Fly Fishing near Malvern" dated '97. Exh. at the RA and SS from 1869. Examples of his work can be found in Sheffield AG and Museum.

Pike, Sidney (op.1880-1901)
Landscape painter and painter of small hunting scenes, very often set in Sussex and very often painted in pairs or sets of three or four. Exh. at the principal London galleries from 1880.

Pilcher, L.
Unknown painter of a racing pigeon, inscribed "Audrey Studio", auctioned Bonhams 1988.

Pimm, William E. (op.1890-1910)
London landscape painter who exh. at the RA (1890-1910). "Putting on the Sixth Green", 16in.x24in., shows a golf match, and is thought to depict Dr. W. Laidlaw Purves, MD (1843-1918), a Scottish stalwart of the Royal Wimbledon Club wearing his traditional red jacket and Arthur Molesworth who is not wearing a red

jacket. The wearing of red jackets was obligatory at the Royal Wimbledon Club until 1907 as a warning safeguard to the public since the golf course was played over the public common.

Pine, Robert Edge (b.c.1722 op.1742-1788)
London-born portrait and history painter, son of the engraver John Pine (1690-1756). Pine gained the premium of the Society for the Encouragement of Arts for the best historical design in 1760 and again in 1763. Exh. at the FS, RA and SA (1760-1784). He emigrated to America in 1783 where he established himself in Philadelphia and painted "The Congress Voting Independence" to which Edward Savage later made additions. Pine's portrait of the Revd. Robert Waugh (1767-1810) standing full length with a cricket bat and ball in a landscape, 51in.x40½in., was auctioned Christie's 1978. His portrait of a "Young Sportsman" holding a gun in his left hand with two hounds beside him was auctioned Sotheby's 1965.

Pipeshank, George
Alias John Wallace (1841-1905) (q.v.) the artist who painted a series of miniature golfing cartoons for the British Tobacco Co., Cope Bros & Co. Ltd., over a period of years in the 1890s.

Pirie, Sir George, PRSA, HRSW, HRA (1863-1946)
Scottish painter of animals and birds who studied at the Académie Julian, Paris under Boulanger and Lefebvre. Exh. four works at the RA from 1888 and exh. at the RSA from 1887. Elected RSA (1923), PRSA (1933-1944), HRA (1933), HRSW (1934). Knighted (1937). Pirie painted a number of fox-hunting scenes including "After the Hunt", "Hounds Asleep", "A Study of a Hound in a Kennel", "Guarding his Bone", "Saddled Horses", etc.

Pissarro, Camille (1830-1903)
French Impressionist painter and a great lover of English ways. Studied at the Ecole des Beaux Arts in Paris in 1855 and under the guidance of Corot. Exh. at all eight Impressionist exhibitions (1874-1886) and at the Salon and the Salon des Refuses. Pissarro made many trips to London painting two cricket scenes, "Cricket on Hampton Court Green" 21½in.x29in., s.&d. 1890 (The Ailsa Mellon Bruce Collection, National Gallery of Art, Washington) and "Cricket at Bedford Park", 21in.x26in., s.&d. 1897 (Jeu de Paume, Paris). Pissarro does not seem to have been a cricketer but painted his pictures presumably to evoke typically traditional English scenes.

Pitchforth, Roland Vivian, RA, RWS, LG, ARCA (Lond.) (1895-1982)
London landscape artist and wood engraver, brother of the artist Gerald Pitchforth. Born Wakefield, Yorks. Studied Wakefield School of Art (1912-1914) and Leeds College (1914-1915 and 1919-1920) and at the RCA under Sir William Rothenstein and Leon Underwood (1921-1925). Taught at Camberwell School of Art and at Clapham College of Art until 1939. Held first one-man show at the London Artist's Association in 1928. Shared a two-man exhibition at Leger Galleries with Robert Buhler (q.v.) in the 1930s. Pitchforth was fond of painting water scenes in watercolour, in the best English tradition, although some of his early work was also painted in oils. Became a member of the LG (1929). Exh. at the RA from 1941, elected RA (1953). Examples of his work are in the Tate Gallery. He was quite fond of painting fly fishing scenes but his work in sporting subjects is rare. "Salmon Fishing on the River Lune", signed, watercolour, 17in.x23½in., was auctioned Christie's 1989. "Findhorn", depicting a water skier crossing the bay, watercolour, signed and inscr., 5¾in.x 8½in., was auctioned at his studio sale, Bonhams 1990.

Pitman, A.B. (op.1909)
Illustrator whose pen and watercolour sketch of "Kitty", a chestnut mare, the property of a lady, inscr. "Very Fast - Lot 1", s.&d. '09, 5½in.x9in., was auctioned Christie's (Sth. Ken.) 1984.

Pitman, John (op.1810-1846)
Worcestershire painter of equestrian and cattle portraits and some sporting subjects. Pitman was also a draughtsman and a lithographer after his own work including his lithograph of "Nimrod" a racehorse, 16in.x20in., and the "Madresfield Heifer". Some of Pitman's sporting work was engraved by Joseph Gleadah including his work painted in collaboration with J. Clements (q.v.) "The Great Contest (Boxing) between Spring and Langan" (1824). His still life of a hare, partridge, and a pheasant in a landscape, s.&d. 1810, 26½in.x35⅛in., was auctioned Christie's 1988 and his portrait of "Forester", the favourite hunter of John Ward, huntsman to the Cambridgeshire Hounds, showing the horse in a stable, 25in.x30½in., dated 1843, was exh. at the Parker Gallery, London (1950). "Common Snipe" was painted for Henry Clifton on 25 April 1818, "A Phaeton preparing to leave a Country Mansion" was painted in 1846, as was "Horses, Dogs and a Phaeton outside a Gothic Country House" attended by a groom, a gentleman mounted on his skewbald hunter to the right. Pitman's three paintings of greyhounds, "Blast" with "Bijou", "Blackbird" and "Bridesmaid", all signed, inscr. and dated 1823, each 18¼in.x25in., were exh. at Sotheby's, the British Sporting Heritage (1984/5). "Blast" and "Blackbird" won the Amesbury Cup and "Bridesmaid" won the Oaks at Deptford (Wilts.).

Plachte, Erna (1893-1986)
Painter and illustrator, born in Berlin of Jewish parents. Studied at the Berlin Academy of Arts and employed in the 1920s by a number of newspapers to sketch many of the world's leading political figures at the League of Nations. Included in this Dictionary for her sketches of events at the 1928 Olympic Games. She lived for short periods in Paris and Moscow finally settling in England where she died in 1986.

"Plantagenet"
The nom de plume used by the sporting writer and hunting correspondent, E.H. Pearce, contributor to "The Field" in the early 1900s. He had the extraordinary experience of being shut up in Ladysmith with one of his sons while another son came to their relief (1900).

Platt, John (Capt.) (op.1814)
A set of four staghunting scenes were pub. after the work by this artist. A portrait was exh. at the RA 1814 by an A.J. Platt.

Platt, John Edgar, ARCA (Lond.) (1886-1967)
Colour woodcut artist of landscapes, animal and figure subjects including his colour woodcut entitled "The Scrum", 10in.x15¼in. Platt studied at the RCA (1905-1908) and was President of the Society of Graver Printers in Colour (1939-1953). Exh. at the RA from 1913 and at the NEAC and IS from 1917. He was also Principal of Leicester School of Art (1923-1929). Official war artist (1939-1945).

Platt, John Gerald, ARE, ARCA (Lond.) (b.1892)
Painter, etcher and wood engraver of landscapes and figure subjects, who studied art at King Edward VII's School of Art, Armstrong College, Newcastle upon Tyne and at Leicester College of Art (1919-1920) as well as the RCA (1920-1924). Became Principal of Harrow Technical and Art School from 1930 to 1947 and Principal of Hornsey School of Arts and Crafts in 1947. Elected ARE (1924). His colour woodcut of Rugby football entitled "The Scrum" was exh. at the 7th Annual Exhibition of the Society of Graver Printers in Colour held at Messrs. Bromhead Cutts and Co. Gallery in Cork Street, London, March 1922. A review of this print from "The Studio Magazine", 15 March 1922, records "In selecting as the theme for his colour woodcut one of the most exciting incidents in the strenuous game of rugger Mr. John Platt possibly had in mind a suggestion etc......." Inspired by his subject Platt undertook a further colour print of rugger which he exh. at the XIVth Olympiad Sport in Art Exhibition, No. 253, shown at the V & A Museum in London 1948.

Pleissner, Ogden Minton (1905-1983)
American painter of sporting subjects particularly fly fishing and hunting. Pupil of F.J. Boston, George Bridgman, Frank V. DuMond. Member ASL of New York. His watercolour "An Anxious Moment Salmon Fishing, Canada" was auctioned Christie's (NY) 1986. His pencil and watercolour painting "Salmon Fishing", 23¾in.x28¼in., was auctioned Christie's (NY) 1983.

Plessis, H. E. du, LG (b.1894)
Landscape and figure painter in both oil and water-colour who contributed a painting of football entitled "Saturday Afternoon on Blackheath Common", 29½in.x20in., to the FE. Du Plessis, who was born and educated in South Africa, had no formal art training. He began painting in about 1927 and exh. at the LG and other London galleries. Lived in London for some years.

Pochtenny, Alexei Petrovich (1889-1942)
Russian figure painter whose "Athletic Meeting" was painted in the early 1930s, 37½in.x49½in. Pochtenny was a member of the Four Arts Society, founded in 1925 with Pavel Kuznetsov as Chairman. Exhibitions were held in Moscow in 1925, 1926 and 1929 and in 1928 in Leningrad.

Pocock, Innes (op.1852)
London painter who exh. a portrait of hounds at the RA (1852).

Pocock, J. (op.1850-1860)
London painter who exh. three works at SS including one entitled "Foxhunting".

Pohl, May (c.1920s)
Possibly American painter of a lady playing golf entitled "A Fine Swing", signed watercolour, 15in.x11in. Auctioned Phillips (West 2).

Poingdestre, Charles H. (op.1849-d.1905)
Landscape painter particularly of Italian landscapes and genre. He also painted a number of hunter portraits and still lifes of game of which his earliest recorded work, "Still Life of Game on a Larder Shelf", is dated 1850. His study "A Light Bay Hunter Standing in a Coastal Landscape", dated 1881, was auctioned at Bonhams 1982 and "A grey Hunter in a Stable", dated 1889, 11½in.x15in., was auctioned Christie's 1981. Exh. at the RA (1850-1901), also at the BI, SS, NWS, GG, NG and elsewhere. Almost all his exhibition work was of Italian landscapes and he was for many years the President of the British Academy in Rome. Examples of his work are in the V & A Museum.

Pollard, A. Read (op.1884-1885)
A Sussex landscape with huntsman and hounds in the foreground and a view of a windmill in the distance is recorded. Pollard exh. two genre subjects at the ROI in 1884/5.

Pollard, James (1797-1859)
London sporting artist. He was the son of Robert Pollard (q.v.) who ran a print and publishing business. Best known for his many coaching scenes and widely known for the prints made after his work. He also painted fishing scenes and appears to have been at his happiest when he himself was fishing, in particular on the River Lee at Waltham Abbey. His many superb angling paintings show an expert knowledge of the sport. After his wife died in 1840 his work and his fortunes declined and his chief source of income came from painting omnibuses for local Islington proprietors. Pollard was one of the few artists who painted coarse fishing scenes which were pictorially attractive and technically accurate. He also featured cricket in his paintings, viz. "A Cricket Match at Copenhagen House, Islington", oil on panel, 9¼in.x11¾in., present whereabouts unknown. There is also a smaller version of this subject in which a ball has just been bowled and the batsman raises his bat expectantly. An engraving of "A Cricket Match" by and after James Pollard was pub. in 1824.

Pollard, Robert (1755-1838)
A painter and engraver, very often of fishing and shooting subjects. Born at Newcastle upon Tyne. Father of James Pollard (q.v.). Lifelong friend of Thomas Bewick (q.v.) from their apprenticeship days together under Ralph Beilby (1767-1774). Pollard came to London (1774), studied painting and drawing under

Richard Wilson RA and practised for a time as a landscape and marine painter. He then turned to engraving and studied under Isaac Taylor in Holborn. He founded his print and publishing business in Islington in 1781 which he named R. Pollard & Sons. Elected Fellow of the Incorporated Society of Watercolourists (1788).

Pollard, Samuel (op.c.1850)
A watercolour of a driving incident was exh. by Oscar and Peter Johnson 1969.

Pollentine, R.J. (op.1852-1862)
Landscape and animal painter whose still life of trout and tackle on a riverbank "The Day's Catch", 19½in.x 29½in., s.&d. 1857, was exh. Malcolm Innes, London, 1991. Pollentine exh. three works at the RA including a Northumberland landscape. He also exh. at the BI and SS.

Pollett(ott), J. (op.1847-1848)
Four paintings by this artist are recorded between 1847 and 1848, including a portrait of a chestnut hunter, with a pointer carrying a partridge in an extensive landscape, s.&d. 1848, 17in.x22in., the bulldog "Mars" the property of Captain Bethune, s.&d. 1848, 18in.x14in., Bonhams 1986, a horse and gundog in a landscape, s.&d. 1848, 21in.x15in. and a King Charles spaniel, s.&d. 1847, 16in.x21in. Almost certainly this artist exists only in the imagination of past auction cataloguers and the paintings should be ascribed to James Pollard (q.v.).

Pollock, Maurice R. (op.1882-1905)
Painter of landscapes and still life fish, usually arranged on a river bank. His still life with hen and cock salmon, a brace and a half of brown trout and pheasants arranged on a river bank, was painted in 1897, and his still life of fish, again arranged on a river bank, in 1905. He exh. one New Forest landscape at the RA and another at SS (1882-1897). He also exh. at the GG and NG, from a London address.

Ponsonby, Sarah (b.1943)
Equestrian artist. Born in Ireland. Studied at the Accademia del Belle Arti in Florence (1960-1961) and at the Brera Milan (1963). In 1961 she won an award from the Elizabeth T. Greenshield Memorial Foundation, Montreal. She exh. at the Tryon Gallery in 1965 and again with her equestrian bronzes in 1970. Has had many commissions on both sides of the Atlantic.

Ponsonby, William (op.1942)
Contemporary painter whose watercolour "The Polo Match", dated 1942, was auctioned Phillips 1985.

Ponsonby Staples, Sir Robert (12th Bt.) (1853-1943)
See Staples

Poole, Samuel (b.1870)
Landscape painter and illuminator who studied art at Heatherleys and became a designer for twenty-five years with Cedric Chivers Ltd., Bath. Brother of the artist Henry Poole. Exh. at the RA, RBA, RI and ROI from 1892. Lived in Bath and became a member of the Bath Society of Artists. His racing painting "The Finish", signed oil on canvas, 14½in.x18in., was auctioned Sotheby's (Sussex) 1987. Poole painted in both oil and watercolour.

Pope, Alexander (1849-1924)
American artist of angling subjects including "Jumping, Small Mouthed Bass", signed 16in.x20in., auctioned Sotheby's (NY) 1990.

Pope, George F. (op.1856-1879)
"Teal on a River Bank", dated 1879, 17in.x20in., was auctioned Sotheby's (Sussex) 1985 and is obviously a skilled work. He exh. one other painting at SS in 1856.

Pope, Hilda Chancellor (Mrs. Scott) (b.1913)
Landscape painter and a mural decorator whose watercolour of football entitled "After the Game", 22in.x 16½in., was ex. at the FE. Miss Pope studied at the RCA (1932-1935) under Sir William Rothenstein (1872-1945). His son John Rothenstein was one of the panel of judges for the national competition and subsequent exhibition of football art organised by the Arts Council in conjunction with the Football Association in 1953. Hilda Pope has exh. at the RA, RI and NEAC.

Potter, Michael (b.1951)
Contemporary artist of a number of silk screen golfing prints. Born London. Studied in Florence (1969) followed by a photography diploma at Ealing School of Art. Worked as a fashion photographer and then studied silk screen printing. His prints have been used by London Transport and the Holiday Inn Group, also Christie's Contemporary Art in London.

Potts, John Laslett, RBA (1837-1898)
A painter mentioned by Herbert Atkinson (q.v.) as having painted good game cock portraits or cockfighting scenes, "Cock Fighting and Game Fowl" (1977). Potts is better known for his historical scenes, many of which he exh. at the RA and SS (1860-1897). Elected RBA (1890).

Powell, E.R. (op.1924-1929)
Painter of game birds and wildfowl in both oil and watercolour.

Powell, F. (Major)
See Francis Powell Hopkins

Powell, R. (op.1880-1896)
Painter of equestrian subjects whose "Dead Heat for the Derby" was engraved by Edwin Henry Hunt and pub. by George Rees in 1884. The work features the dead heat winners of the 1884 Derby "St. Gatien" and "Harvester" who ran a desperate race on a bitterly cold afternoon. A number of Powell's greyhound portraits were also engraved by the Hunt team. In 1896 Powell pub. one of his own portraits of the racehorse "Persimmon", bred and owned by the Prince of Wales (later King Edward VII) and winner of the Derby and St. Leger in 1896.

Powell, William (op.1856-1878)
Painter of equestrian portraits including "A Dappled Roan in a Landscape", s.&d. 1856, Bonhams 1985 and "A Bay Hunter in a Loose Box", s.&d. 1878, Bonhams 1986.

Powell, William E. (1878-c.1955)
Painter of landscapes, game birds, wildfowl and angling subjects in watercolour for the Royal Worcester Porcelain

Factory in the early years of this century. He does not appear to have exh. in London but many of his paintings appear at auction and are exquisitely painted with fine attention to detail.

Power, Cyril L. (b.1872)

Architect and important linocut artist who specialised in portraying movement. His colour linocut "The Eight" shows a rowing crew in pastel shades of blues and yellow and illustrates his skill in portraying figures in action. Power shared a studio in Hammersmith with Sybil Andrews (q.v.). Together they helped Iain McNab and W.C. Flight set up the New Grosvenor School of Modern Art. After 1929 they extended their collaboration to poster design, primarily for the London Underground.

Power, Harold Septimus, ROI, RI (1878-1951)

Australian painter in both oil and watercolour of animal and equestrian subjects who studied in Melbourne and at the Académie Julian in Paris. Exh. at the RA, RI, ROI, RWA and in Australia. Elected RI (1925), ROI (1916). His sporting work includes "Fox Hunting in North Somerset", "Fox Hunting in the Midlands" (1912) and "Stag Hunting" (1911). Usually signed but rarely dated his work.

Poynter, Sir Edward John (Bt.) PRA, RWS, (1836-1919)

Painter, usually of neo-classical subjects, and an illustrator. Born in Paris, the son of the architect, painter and illustrator Ambrose Poynter (1796-1886). Studied art under Gleyre (1856-1859) having previously attended the RA Schools in London. On a student visit to Italy in 1853 he had met Frederick Leighton who was to have so much influence on his neo-classical ideas. Poynter returned to London in 1860 and exh. at the RA from 1861. "The Earl of Warncliffe out Shooting" signed with inits. and dated '81, 87½in.x52½in., was auctioned Sotheby's 1986.

Prades, de

See de Prades

Prater, Ernest (op.1894-1914)

Black and white artist and illustrator who worked in London and at his home at Westcliffe on Sea. Prater was originally on the staff of "Black and White" acting as special artist for the publication in the Sino Japanese war of 1894. He illus. "The Castle of the White Flag" (1904) and contributed to "Chums", "Pearsons", "The Graphic" (1905-1910), "The Boys Own Paper" and "The Ludgate Monthly". Prater exh. four works at the RA (1897-1904) including his painting of a Rugby football match "A Dash from the Scrimmage". A further football painting in pencil, water and body-colour, "The Football Match", 10¾in.x18in., which was probably used for illustration purposes and bears the stamp of a Leeds agent, Alfred Cook Ltd., dated 31 March 1913, was auctioned Bonhams 1986.

Pratere, Joseph Edmund de la (1826-1888)

Belgian painter of equestrian scenes, particularly hunting.

Pratt, Hilton J(onathan) (c.1845-1895)

Painter of cock-fighting portraits and scenes including a black breasted red cock dressed for the pit, 12½in.x 9½in., and portraits of fighting cocks, a pair signed with mono., 12½in.x15¼in. Pratt very often painted his fighting cocks in pairs and usually signed his work, often with a mono., but rarely dated it. His son was the landscape artist Hilton L. Pratt, Jnr. (op.1867-1873).

Pratt, William M. (1854-1936)

Landscape and marine painter in both oil and watercolour. Born in Glasgow. Studied at Glasgow School of Art and at the Académie Julian in Paris. Exh. at the RA from 1880 including "The Salmon Fishers". These are clearly signed William Pratt but may have been by an unrecorded William Pratt at a slightly earlier date. The MCC had, for example, a painting of a cricket match played at Kenfield, Nr. Canterbury, Kent, s.&d. 1760 by a William Pratt which was discussed and repro. "County Life" (14.12.78). Pratt also exh. at the RSA and widely abroad. A pair of very fine cock-fighting portraits, the cocks ready spurred, both signed, each 20¼in.x16¼in., were auctioned Sotheby's 1987.

Prebble, C. (op.1822)

A good quality hunting scene, 7¾in.x58in., s.&d. 1822 and set into a mirror is recorded by Ackermann.

Prescott, Claude B. (1870-1932)

Painter and illustrator who collaborated with Lynwood Palmer (q.v.) on "The Old Polo Ground", s.&d. May '92, painted in grisaille, 18in.x24in., Christie's (NY) 1985.

Preston, Cloe (op.1920)

A watercolour painting c.1920 entitled "Our Amazons" depicting rather aggressive little girls playing polo was exh. Burlington Gallery, London, 1985.

Preston, M. (op.1841)

A painting of "Coronation", the Derby winner of 1841, is recorded by this artist.

Pretty, Edward (1792-1865)

"Rugby School as it appeared in the year 1809" showing the boys playing cricket, a hand coloured etching by Pretty aquatinted by R. Reeve, was pub. at Rugby by E. Pretty, June 1811, 10¼in.x18¼in., Christie's (Sth. Ken.). Pretty, who was the drawing master at Rugby School until 1855, also exh. two watercolours "Firelight" and "Moonlight" at SS and contributed to "The Gentleman's Magazine" (1985).

Price, Frank Corbyn, RBA, BWS (b.1862-c.1933)

Sussex based landscape painter who exh. at the RA, SS and NWS from 1888. Elected RBA (1895), BWS (1923). "A Day's Shooting", signed, 8¼in.x11¾in., was auctioned Phillips 1986.

Price, Tom (op.1906)

A pair of angling scenes entitled "Fishing from the River Bank", one s.&d. 1906, each 11½in.x8¾in., were auctioned David Lay 1985.

Price, William Lake, AOWS (1810-1891)

Landscape painter in watercolour and a lithographer, mostly after his own works, although the engraving of the Prince of Wales on the Moors in 1885, after the work by Price, was actually engraved by Richard Lane and J.H. Lynch.

Pride, John (b.1877-c.1933)
Painter, black and white artist and illustrator, etcher and engraver. Studied at Liverpool School of Art and exh. between 1903 and 1932. "Out for a Ride", s.&d. 1933, 20in.x30in., was auctioned Bonhams 1986.

Priest, Alfred (1810-1850)
Norwich School painter and etcher of landscapes and marine subjects, after his own designs and those of his contemporaries. A pupil of H. Ninham and J. Stark. Priest moved to London and lived there until 1848 when he returned to Norwich a sick man. Many of his landscapes included studies of game dogs.

Priest, Alfred, RP (1874-1929)
Portrait painter who probably deserves to be better known than he is. His portrait of Sir Max Pemberton (1863-1950), author of "The Amateur Motorist" (1907) and editor of "Vanity Fair", standing behind his Hochkiss motor car is a fine piece and motoring portraits of this date are very rare. Priest studied at the RA Schools (1892-1897), won the Turner Gold Medal and a travelling scholarship to the Académie Julian, Paris (1898). Exh. at the RA, RI, ROI and elsewhere from 1898. On the staff of "The Daily Chronicle" (1904-1905). Elected RP (1917).

Pringle, J. B. (c.1740?)
A study of the dark bay racehorse "Flying Childers" with his groom, in a river landscape, signed and inscr., 28in.x36¼in., was auctioned Bonhams 1981.

Pringle, William J. (c.1805-1860)
This exceptionally talented sporting artist exh. twelve paintings at the Royal Birmingham Society of Artists (1834-1843) including three portraits of named horses. He is listed in the Birmingham Directories (1841-1845). His equestrian studies include "A Chestnut Horse in a Stable," dated 1860, "Chance" a bay racehorse in a landscape with a jockey up, dated 1843, "A White Racehorse" dated 1840, Mr. William Foster's hunter in a stable with a miniature dog sitting on the cornbin beside him, s.&d. 1845, 27½in.x35in., and "A Favourite Gundog", dated 1833. Pringle worked in the Stourbridge and Birmingham areas and "The Stourbridge - Birmingham Mail Coach passing Quinton Toll Gate" is in the collection of the Birmingham AG.

Prinsep, Thomas (op.c.1869)
Thought to be the painter of an unsigned watercolour of a cricket match taking place in front of a Palladian house, in an Indian setting, 10in.x22in., auctioned Walters (Lincoln) 1990, since the Prinsep family are known to have lived in Calcutta at the corresponding time.

Prinsep, Valentine Cameron (Val), RA (1838-1904)
Portrait painter, particularly of classical subjects, who studied in Paris (1859) under Gleyre and went to Rome with Burne Jones (1859-1860). Exh. at the RA from 1862 and was elected RA (1894). Not an artist normally associated with sporting paintings but he exh. one at the RA in 1874 entitled "Newmarket Heath on the Morning of a Race", in which he exercised his vivid imagination and extended his artistic licence to the full, filling the famous heath with all the fun of the fair usually associated with Epsom on Derby Day.

Prior, Melton (1845-1910)
Special artist and illustrator, son of the artist W.H. Prior (1812-1882) under whom he studied. Became war correspondent of "The Illustrated London News" from about 1873 and served in numerous campaigns. Painted a number of equestrian scenes in both battle and in sport. "The Sphere", 4 February 1922, recorded "Never again is a special artist likely to find himself in the uncomfortable position in which the late Melton Prior found himself on the battleground in the Franco-Prussian War. His horse having been killed under him, he had tied his saddle, an even more precious possession than his horse, round his waist and was seen pluckily holding on to this one treasure at the end of the battle".

Prior, W. (op. 1899)
A watercolour painting of a hunting scene - horsemen breaking cover - s.&d. 1899 was auctioned Holloways (Banbury) 1987.

Pritchett, Robert Taylor, FSA (1828-1907)
Painter of landscapes and rustic genre, also of some hunting scenes. He was an intimate friend of John Leech, Charles Keene and Birket Foster (qq.v.). Exh. at the RA and SS. Contributed to leading magazines including "Punch" (1863-1869), "Good Words" (1864-1880) and "The Graphic" (1887). Pritchett was also a gunmaker, becoming a partner in the family business and was the originator of the Enfield rifle. He invented, with W.E. Metford, the Pritchett bullet in 1853 and the three grooved rifle in 1854.

Procter, P.
Victorian watercolour portraits of fighting cocks, a set of four, each 12in.x8½in., were auctioned Sotheby's (Chester) 1986.

Prosperi, Liberio (op.1885-1903)
Italian artist and illustrator who used the pseudonym "Lib" for his caricatures contributed to "Vanity Fair" including his portrait of John Ball in 1892 who in that year won the third of his eight amateur golf championships. "Lib" contributed fifty-five cartoons to "Vanity Fair" (1885-1894 and 1902-1903), many of them of sporting personalities. He exh. two works at the Walker AG, Liverpool in 1891.

Proudfoot, James, RP, ROI, NS (1908-1971)
Portrait painter and black and white artist, born in Perth and educated at Perth Academy. Studied art at Heatherleys, Goldsmiths College and in Paris. Exh. at the RA, PR, RBA, ROI, RSA and the NEAC and in the provinces. Elected member of NS (1932), ROI (1937), UA (1946) and RP (1947). "The Football Match", 27in.x25in., was exh. at the FE and his pen and ink sketch of a young woman playing golf, signed with mono., 6in.x4in., is in a private collection.

Prout, Millicent Margaret (Mrs., née Margaret Fisher), ARA, RWS, ROI, RWA, NEAC, WIAC (1875-1963)

Only daughter of the artist Mark Fisher, RA (1841-1923). Entered the Slade School (1894-1897) and studied under Fred Brown (q.v.). Taught at the Hammersmith School of Art. Elected NEAC (1925) having exh. there since 1906. Elected RWS (1938) and ARA (1948). Settled in Hastings, Sussex (1957) after the death of her husband whom she married in 1908. Included equestrian studies amongst her work, exh. several at NEAC (1909-1916) including "The Roan Mare", "The Kick", "Mare and Foal", "Horses Feeding" and "A Study of a Horse".

Prowett, James Christie (op.1908-d.1946)

Scottish painter who studied at the Paris School of Art where he was a prize winner and a medallist. Lived in Stirling and was a member of the Stirling Fine Art Association and the Glasgow Art Club. His painting of a grilse or young salmon, 9½in.x13½in., was auctioned Sotheby's (Chester) 1981.

Pry, Paul

The pseudonym used by the caricaturist William Heath (q.v.).

Pryce, George Willis (1856-1926)

Painter of a game of golf entitled "Chipping on the Green", 8in.x12in., Christie's (Chester) 1991.

Pryde, James Ferrier (1866-1941)

Black and white artist and illustrator. Born in Edinburgh, the only son in a family of six children belonging to a distinguished doctor of literature. Pryde became a student of the Royal Scottish Academy Schools before he went to Paris and like John Hassall (q.v.) studied under Bouguereau. He returned to London and shared lodgings with his sister who was a student at Bushey. After her first term she became engaged to William Nicholson (q.v.) a fellow student. They married in 1893 and a year later became the parents of the abstract artist Ben Nicholson. The two brothers-in-law teamed up to become the "Beggarstaff Brothers" and were to revolutionise pictorial advertising. In later years, however, they grew apart, perhaps because of Pryde's jealousy of Nicholson's establishment success. He died a disillusioned man after an unsuccessful acting career started in the 1890s. His great patron was Annie, Lady Cowdray, who had married Sir Weetman Pearson, later to become first Viscount Cowdray. For her Pryde painted eighteen large canvases between 1911 and 1922 which hang in the library at Dunecht House, the Scottish home of the Cowdray family built in the 1850s by the 3rd Earl of Crawford and Balcarres. Pearson bought it eventually after Crawford's death in 1908 and immediately gave it to Annie, his wife. Pryde's work is powerful and the result perhaps of a deep and visionary mind. It reflects the artist's own strange melancholic nature which lay beneath the debonair charm displayed to casual acquaintances. Pryde was given a retrospective exhibition at the Leicester Galleries in 1933, but was not well enough to attend it.

Purvis, Tom (1888-1959)

The supreme master of British poster art between the wars. Several of his sporting prints were commissioned by the LNER (London and North Eastern Railway Company). Many of his posters showed sportsmen, including "Golfers at Cruden Bay", etc. and "Modern Days and Modern Ways", showing lady tennis players, a poster done for the Shell Oil and Petrol Company. Many of the Austin Reid posters designed by Purvis also include tennis scenes.

Pybourne, Thomas (b.1708 op.1840)

The life of this painter of racehorses is obscure and examples of his work are rare. There is some well-backed suggestion that he was a pupil of John Wootton (q.v.). Amongst his equestrian portraits is "Milkman, a Galloway of Mr. Leathes"; the horse is standing by the corner of a stable with numerous other horses and riders in the distance. The painting is inscr., 39in.x46in., and was in the collection of Mrs. Isabel de Mussenden-Leathes, a kinsman of Mr. Leathes. A portrait of "Tom Thumb", a Galloway also belonging to Mr. Leathes, s.&d. 1734 and inscr., 39⅛in.x46½in., is now in the Paul Mellon Collection, Upperville, Va, USA, but was previously in the collection of Mrs. Isabel de Mussenden-Leathes. In this painting the bay racehorse stands facing right, seen in profile, and his reins are held by a jockey in a grey jacket, blue cap and breeches, his back turned to the spectator, a racecourse with numerous racehorses and a carriage in the background, a hilly landscape beyond. Galloway was a term used to describe a horse of 14 hands and under. The final race for Galloways in Yorkshire was in 1739. Mr. Leathes seems to have run several horses in the 1730s including "Brocklesby", a winner at Peterborough in 1730, and "White Stockings", a winner at Leicester in 1733. He may well have commissioned Thomas Pybourne to paint more than the two examples here.

Pyne, Charles (b.1842 op.1861-1902)

Landscape painter who exh. at SS and once at the RA in 1864. "Sunday Afternoon Tennis", watercolour, s.&d. 1902, 17in.x29½in., was auctioned Christie's (Sth. Ken.) 1990.

Pyne, William Henry (1769-1843)

Landscape painter and writer on the arts. Pyne studied with H. Pars and exh. at the RA from 1790. He was an active founder member of the OWS, although he retired in 1809. Pyne was a good draughtsman and his figure work was excellent. Engravings of his paintings of whist and billiards are in the British Museum but the actual painting of billiards came to auction at Sotheby's (Sussex) in 1986. Much of Pyne's work was etched by himself including his angling studies which were repro. "Angling in British Art", Shaw Sparrow, illus. p.105.

Q

Quadal, Martin Ferdinand (1736-1808)
Czechoslovakian-born painter who came to London (1772) and entered the RA Schools (1773). Exh. at the RA (1772, 1773, 1779 and 1793). He was in Yorkshire between 1777 and 1779 when he went to Dublin and he died in St. Petersburg in 1808 having gone there to teach art at the Academy. His sporting work includes a military equestrian portrait of the Duke of Buccleuch. He also painted life-size portraits of dogs including "Perico", a dog belonging to George, Duke of Montague, standing in an open landscape, dated 1779. "A Dog Flushing a Duck", dated 1778, 26¾in.x30in., was auctioned Christie's 1974.

Quarrie, Henry S.
Animal and landscape painter whose study of a liver and white spaniel, 18½in.x14½in., was auctioned Christie's 1987. His other sporting works include "Out for a Canter", a study of the fox terrier "Quayside Robinson Lad" and an unnamed white West Highland terrier.

Quigley, Daniel (op.1750-1778)
Quigley appears to have been an Irish painter of equestrian subjects whose work includes "The Chaise Match" run by the Earl of March and Eglinton on Newmarket Heath (29.8.1750). This painting is based on the original by James Seymour (q.v.) of which there are four known versions. Mr. Quigley, a primitive painter who worked in the Seymour tradition, is the only Irish sporting painter so far recorded as working in the mid-18th century. Strickland records him painting as late as 1773 but his portrait of "Irish Hero", a bay racehorse foaled in 1764 by "Coalition", with jockey up, inscr. and quite clearly dated 1778, would indicate that he was working at a later date. "Irish Hero" was bred and owned by Mr. Murphy and he only raced in Ireland where he won a number of matches and plates. He was bought by Lord Clanwilliam in 1773. Other paintings by Quigley include "Flyer", a grey racehorse bred by the Earl of Drogheda out of a "Bannister" mare by "Hero" in 1772, signed and inscr., 25¾in.x29¾in., auctioned Sotheby's 1985, and "Sportsman" ridden by his groom in an open landscape, inscribed "Sportsman, a noted hunter, the property of Thomas Trotter, Esq. taken from the life", dated 1773. Quigley also seems to have been patronised by Windham Quin of Adare (1717-1789) since a set of five paintings by Quigley feature racehorses and jockeys in Quin's colours and standing on the Curragh.

Quintin, H.J. (op.1844-1888)
Prolific equestrian and animal painter whose sporting work includes a portrait of "Governor" a prize Hereford bull bred by Mr. John Hewer of Hampton Lodge, Herefordshire, dated 1848, 24½in.x29¼in. A portrait of a prize Hereford standing in a landscape inscr. "Bred by Mr. Hewer, out of "Old Conqueror" sold to Mr. William Cook in 1845" dated 1845. "A Point to Point Meeting", s.&d. 1844, 24in.x29in. A portrait of the famous prize winning Hereford bull, "Lord Wilton", and another of "Regulator" s.&d. 1874. Stable scenes with hunters and terriers, dated 1888 (a pair). "Benedict" in a stall, 25in.x30in., and a study of racehorses, a pair of portraits of racehorses, each 18in.x24in., and a hunter with rider up, the hunt beyond, s.&d. 1873.

Quinton, Alfred Robert (b.1853)
Landscape painter in watercolour and a black and white artist who studied art at Heatherleys and exh. at the principal London galleries from 1874, including SS, RA and RI. Lived at Finchley for many years and illus. books about topography. His painting (after Alken), s.&d. 1879 and inscr. "A Sale at Old Tattersalls", 18in.x24in., was auctioned Christie's 1972.

"Quiz"
The pseudonym used by Sir John P. Mellor, Bt. (q.v.).

R

Rabinovitch, Samuel (Sam Rabin) (1903-1991)
Brilliant painter of sports, in particular of boxing and wrestling. The son of a hat seller, a Jewish Russian exile from Vitebsk, Rabinovitch lived his early life in Manchester and joined the Slade School of Art in London (1921-1924). Encouraged by Henry Tonks, Rabinovitch kept up his early wrestling interest coached by the great George Mckenzie who was to represent Britain in the Olympic wrestling team from 1908-1928. After Rabinovitch's success in winning a medal at Amsterdam in the 1928 Olympics he turned to professional wrestling to find the money to further his art studies. As Sam Radnor, the wrestler, he became very popular, even appearing in a pre-war film to wrestle against Charles Laughton as Henry VIII in that monarch's private life produced by Alexander Korda and in the following year in Korda's "Scarlet Pimpernel". A sculptor as well as a painter, one example of Rabinovitch's work can be seen in the two massive faces of "Past and Future" carved directly into the stone which crowns "The Daily Telegraph" building in Fleet Street. Rabinovitch became an art teacher at Goldsmith's College in London numbering Bridget Riley and Tom Keating amongst his pupils. Has been described as the English Degas and one of England's most distinguished art teachers and draughtsmen. Exhibitions of his work were held at the Dulwich Gallery and Goldsmith's College Exhibitions 1985/6. His pastel, crayon and pencil boxing sketch entitled "Cautioned", 10¾in.x8½in., was auctioned Christie's 1990.

Rackham, Arthur, RWS (1867-1939)
Illustrator and watercolourist who studied art at Lambeth School where he was influenced by his fellow student Charles de Sousy Ricketts (1866-1931). Rackham joined the staff of the "Westminster Budget" in 1892 and from then onwards concentrated on the illustration of books, establishing himself as one of the foremost Edwardian illustrators. He exh. widely and was elected RWS in 1902. He also became a member of the Langham Sketch Club. He is included in this Dictionary for his self-portrait "Playing Lawn Tennis", signed (mono.), pen, black ink and watercolour, 10½in.x6in. and "Putting", signed, pen/black ink, 6in.x8in., Chris Beetles Ltd. London. Rackham also illus. the 1931 edition of "The Compleat Angler" by Izaak Walton. The original pen/watercolour of Walton reclining against a fence is in the V & A Museum, London.

Raeburn, Sir Henry, RA (1756-1823)
Leading Scottish portrait painter who was born and died in Edinburgh. Exh. at the RA (1792-1823). Elected RA (1815). Knighted (1822). He became President of the Society of Scottish Painters (1812) and King's Painter for Scotland (1823). A keen golfer on the Leith links he painted portraits of two well-known golfers of that era, John Grey and James Balfour. Treasurer until 1795 of the Honorable Company of Edinburgh Golfers (the painting is at Muirfield). Raeburn was also a keen fisherman and an archer and his portrait of Dr. Nathanial Spens in the act of drawing his bow, painted in 1791, shows that he had an intimate knowledge of this sport. Dr. Spens, an Edinburgh worthy, is dressed in the splendid uniform of the Royal Company of Archers against a background of rustling trees and flickering lights. This painting was shown at the Tate Gallery exhibition "Painting in Scotland 1707-1843", November 1986. One of the artist's great qualities lay in his ability to relax his sitters and to depict them doing something they enjoyed rather than posing them formally. Another archery painting by Raeburn is the portrait of Sir Ronald and Robert Ferguson of Raith, 1789. The youth in the foreground is drawing (pulling back) his bow while his brother is holding his bow diagonally at rest facing the artist. Raeburn's portrait of Lt. Col. Bryce McMurdo with his fishing rod is in the collection of the National Gallery, London. Charles Lees, RSA (q.v.) and John Gordon Watson RA (see Gordon, John Watson) were Raeburn's pupils.

Rafter, H. (op.1856)
Sporting artist and illustrator who was working in Coventry in 1856 and contributed to Wyatt's "Industrial Arts of the 19th Century".

Ragell, R. (op.1901)
A portrait of Master Bob Podmore MH, s.&d. 1901 and inscr. "Podmore's Harriers Xmas 1901", 19in.x23in., was auctioned Sotheby's (Sussex) 1984.

Rainey, William H., HROI, RI (1852-1936)
Artist and illustrator who studied art at South Kensington and at the RA Schools before starting a career as a book illustrator. Tended, as did many of his contemporaries, to set his subjects in 18th century costume which includes "A Regency Skating Party" s.&d. 1891, grey wash and body colour. Rainey was elected RI (1891) and ROI (1892), becoming HROI (1930).

Ralston, William (1848-1911)
Scottish author and illustrator whose drawing of a Scots golfer making his drive was part of an advertisement for Scott Adie Ltd., pen/ink, signed, 6in.x5in., Abbott and Holder 1989. Ralston contributed to "Punch" (1870-1886) and to "The Sporting and Dramatic News" (1895).

Ramel, Jacques (op.1950s-1960s)
French poster artist responsible for several of the Monaco Grand Prix posters of the 1950s and 1960s.

Ramos, Adrian (Tod) (b.1956)
Contemporary painter of equestrian scenes including steeplechasing and racing. His painting of the open ditch at the Cheltenham Gold Cup 1985, 36in.x48in., was auctioned Sotheby's (NY) 1988. Son of the portrait painter, Theodore Ramos, Tod Ramos studied at the Brighton School of Art and then at the Gloucester College of Art and Design, Cheltenham. He then studied for three years at the RA Schools. His first London exhibition was held at the Richmond Gallery in 1985 and subsequent exhibitions under the title "The Racing Year" in 1986 and 1988. A racing enthusiast, Ramos worked for the trainer Gordon Smythe, while at the Brighton School of Art and later rode out for "Frenchie" Nicholson.

Ramos, Mel (op.1964-1980)
American painter of graphic art whose portrait of Ezra Johnson, Green Bay Packers Defensive End, watercolour, 1980, shows America's national game represented in Ramos' unique style.

Ramsay, Allan (1713-1784)
Fashionable Scottish portrait painter who featured cricket scenes in some of his portrait groups. Son of the poet of the same name. His pupils were David Martin (q.v.) and (Sir) George Chalmers (q.v.). He studied for some months with Hans Hysing (q.v.) in London in 1734 and went to Italy between 1736 and 1738 where he studied under Francesco Imperiali in Rome and drew at the French Academy there. In Italy he learnt how to draw hands and devise graceful postures which he put to use when he returned to London in 1738 to paint portraits.

Ramsbottom, A.R. (op.c.1910)
A pen and ink drawing of the professional golf champion "Old" Tom Morris c.1910, two years after Morris's death, was drawn by this artist.

Randel, Friedrich (Frederick) (1808-1888)
German painter of equestrian portraits including "Grooming the Horses", dated 1842 and "A Study of a Grey Hunter" which was auctioned Christie's 1983.

Rankin, Andrew Scott (1868-1942)
Scottish animal painter and illustrator who studied at the Manufacturers School, Royal Institute and the Life School, Edinburgh. His subjects painted in both oil and watercolour include Jack Russell terriers and deerhounds. He exh. one work entitled "The Crofter's Cow" at the RA (1892).

Rankin, George (op.1900-1921)
Animal and equestrian painter also of birds and wildfowl which he painted in watercolour. Sporting work includes "On the Scent", grisaille, s.&d. '01, "Blackcocks" dated 1918, "Blackcocks and Greyhen" 1921, "Pheasant in a Wood", 10in.x7in., "Waiting for the Rise", 11in.x18in., watercolour and "Coming to the Butts", 11in.x18in., watercolour.

Ranter, W.B.E. (op.1917)
A boxing portrait of Georges Carpentier, s.&d. 1917, crayon and watercolour was exh. at the Faculty of Arts Gallery of Contemporary Art, Wembley. Georges Carpentier (b.1894), a French boxer who won the world light-heavyweight title, was European champion at four divisions and boxed in every one of the eight professional weights. He was, however, unsuccessful in his bid for the World Heavyweight title against Jack Dempsey in 1921.

Rasmussen, Peter Augustave, RWA, PS (b.1927)
Portrait, animal and equestrian painter, especially of racehorses, a subject in which he was encouraged by the famous trainer, Fred Rimell. Rasmussen studied at Brighton College of Art (1943-1948) and then taught at Chesterfield College of Art (1949-1964) becoming Head of Fine Art. He has painted hunting pictures of the Cottesmore, Ledbury, Berkeley and Beaufort hunts and is particularly interested in capturing the movement of horses. He has had several one-man exhibitions.

Rattray, Alexander Wellwood, RSW, ARSA, NEAC (1849-1902)
Scottish landscape painter and watercolourist who painted a number of fly fishing scenes, very often set in the Highlands of Scotland. His painting "The Salmon Pool, Perthshire", s.&d. '84, 61in.x91½in. was auctioned Sotheby's 1987. Rattray exh. at the RA, GG, RSA, RSW and elsewhere (1883-1898). Elected RSW (1885), NEAC (1887) and ARSA (1896).

Raven, Samuel (1775-1847)
Birmingham animal and sporting artist listed in the trade directories as living in Birmingham between 1814 and 1847. His sporting work includes a white spotted greyhound coursing a hare entitled "The Kill" (a pair), "Terriers with a dead Rabbit in a Landscape", Three bull terriers with a man looking over a fence, "A Resting Ghillie with his Loaded Pony and Dogs", "Black Game Shooting" and "Hounds Breaking Covert". Raven tended to paint small pictures, usually on panel, and sometimes in pairs. He also painted very beautiful pictures on the lids of papier mâché boxes.

Raven-Hill, Leonard, RWA (1867-1942)
Black and white artist, cartoonist and illustrator who worked for "Punch" between 1896 and 1935 and drew many sporting subjects including football. Raven-Hill studied art at Lambeth and then in Paris under Bouguereau and Aimé Morot, and exh. at the Salon from 1887. Besides "Punch" his black and white career included work for magazines such as "Judy" (1889), "Pick Me Up" (1890), "The Daily Graphic" (1890), "Black and White" (1891) and his own publication "The Unicorn" founded in 1895 but which had a short run. He is probably most widely known for his illustrations to Rudyard Kipling's "Stalky & Co." which first appeared

in a Windsor magazine. A great admirer of Charles Keene (q.v.) he numbered amongst his friends many of the leading illustrators of his day such as George Stampa (q.v.) and George Denholm Armour (q.v.) who is known to have collaborated at least once on a horse drawing for "Punch".

Raverat, Gwendolen Mary, SWE, RE (1885-1957)
Wood engraver of landscapes and figure subjects and an illustrator who studied at the Slade School of Fine Art (c.1908-1910). Her style was influenced by Eric Gill (q.v.) as can be seen in "The Bowl Players", wood engraving, 4in.x6⅛in., s.&d. 1922. British Museum. Founder member SWE (1920). Elected RE (1934).

Ravilious, Eric William (1903-1943)
Watercolour painter, wood engraver and an illustrator. Born in London but bought up in Sussex where his father had an antiques shop. Studied at Eastbourne School of Art (1919-1922) and at the RCA Design School. Won a travelling scholarship to Italy (1926). Formed close friendship with the artist Edward Bawden (q.v.) and worked for Wedgwood in 1936 designing pottery and china. Was killed in an aeroplane accident in 1943. Tennis door panels, painted for the Music Room in Geoffrey Fry's Portman Court Flat, 1930. The City of Bristol Museum and AG.

Rawling, Brian
Contemporary painter of stalking and shooting scenes in watercolour including "Nothing Worth Shooting this Year", s.&d. 1974 and "Take the Old Stag when I Whistle him Up", s.&d. '74, 30in.x39in., Phillips 1987.

Rawlins, Thomas J. (op.1837-1860)
Portrait and figure painter, who was also employed to illus. works by "Nimrod", Charles James Apperley (q.v.) with H.T. Alken (q.v.). Rawlins was also an etcher - see Petley. He is included in this Dictionary for his watercolour painting of "Henry Angelo's Fencing Academy in St. James Street, London", 4¾in.x7¼in., The Paul Mellon Collection, Upperville, Va, USA. Angelo's Fencing Academy was first established in Soho by Domenico Angelo Malevolti Tremamondo (1716-1802). His son, Henry Angelo (1760-?1839) is probably the best known of this three generation family of London fencing masters, largely through his two volume book "Reminiscences" (1830). He retired (c.1817) in favour of his son Henry Angelo III (1780-1852) who moved the Academy in 1830 to St. James Street, the scene of Rawlins' drawing. See also Thomas Rowlandson for drawing of Henry Angelo fencing, Charles Turner and James Gwin. Rawlins, who exh. one work at the RA in 1840, contributed to the ILN (1858-1860). He visited India in 1837, a contemporary there of Chevenix Trench, C.W. Smith, and Frederick Parr (qq.v.). A drawing from this trip signed Thomas J. Rawlins and dated 1837 is in the British Museum, London.

Ray, Stuart
"The Cambridge Drag", signed and inscr., 15¾in.x 12¼in., was auctioned Phillips 1988.

Read, John (op.1773-1801)
Provincial painter of birds and wildlife who exh. at the SA (1773-1783) as Mr. Read of Bedford. He painted "The Clubmen of the Royal Academy at a Cricket Match of Double Wickets", signed, 19¾in.x24¾in., from a copy of the original painting, said to be by Francis Hayman (q.v.). He also painted a portrait of a terrier standing beside a drawn hare and another of a sheep, a pair of paintings on metal, both s.&d. 1801, each 8¼in.x11in. His painting of assorted dead game upon a table, dated 1785, was auctioned Sotheby's 1982.

Reader, William (op.1672-after 1700)
Portrait painter who was born in Maidstone, Kent. According to Vertue he "was reduced and got into the Charterhouse", c.1700. Be that as it may, he studied art under Gerard Soest (c.1600-1680/1) and is included in this Dictionary for his portrait of a boy with a pointer who is licking the dead game which the hawk on the boy's fist has presumably killed. The painting, 57in.x 41in., was sold Robinson and Fisher (1938) and is repro. in "The Dictionary of 16th and 17th Century British Painters", Waterhouse, pub. ACC (1988).

Record (op.1832)
An artist by this name painted a portrait of the bay racehorse "Cetus" s.&d. 1832, 5½in.x9¾in. auctioned Bearnes 1977.

"Red Spinner"
The nom de plume used by William Senior (1838-1920), fishing correspondent to "The Field" in the 1880s. He was editor from 1899-1909.

Redgate, Arthur W. (op.1886-1901)
Nottingham landscape painter whose canvas 19¾in.x 26½in. of a pheasant shoot entitled "Bagged" was auctioned Sotheby's 1979. He exh. at the RA from 1886 and at SS.

Redworth, William Josiah, PS (1873-1947)
Buckinghamshire-born painter who studied at the Chelsea Art School and exh. at the major London galleries. Painted in oil, watercolour and pastel although his horse portraiture was almost always in oil. His equestrian portraiture includes studies of the racehorses "Rival", "Romance", "The Reel" and "Rosewood" dated 1897, 11¾in.x16in., "Bucephalus" a hunter, dated 1906, 12in.x16in., "Lord Dalmahoy" the grey horse belonging to Walter Waring, Esq., First Life Guards, s.&d. July 1901 and inscr., 12in.x16in. and three companion pieces of "Archdeacon", "Chamois" and "Niger" also belonging to Walter Waring. His four oil portraits of horses inscr. "Lucy", "Commotion", "Sunbeam" and "Seagull", s.&d. 1909, were auctioned Christie's (1966). Redworth very often painted his horse portraits in sets of four, or even six, and often inscr. them "Slough" which is where he lived.

Reed, G. (op.1823)
A painting of Mr. T. Reed and Mr. T. Squires shooting over pointers on Cudham Hills, Kent, s.&d. 1823, 18in.x24in. was exh. at Oscar and Peter Johnson Ltd., London. Thomas Reed, who died in 1849, was a Kent farmer at High Halstow, about twenty miles from Cudham Hills. The artist may have been his son, but is unrecorded. The work is well painted, in a provincial style.

Reed, Joseph Charles, NWS (1822-1877)
Landscape painter, mainly in watercolour, who alsopainted angling scenes. These include "Fishing on the Spey", s.&d. '61, a watercolour, 16½in.x25in. Reed exh. once at the RA (1874), SS and NWS.

Reed, Kenneth, FRSA (b.1941)
Northumberland-born landscape and sporting painter in watercolour whose enthusiasm for golf has led him to paint the courses at Sunningdale, Gleneagles, Muirfield, St. Andrews and the Ailsa Course at Turnberry. In the States he has painted the courses at Pebble Beach, Cypress Point, Spyglass Hill, Del Monte, Augusta National and the Olympic Club, San Francisco. His painting of the No. 5 court at Wimbledon during the All England Championships is therefore a departure from his golfscapes.

Reeve, Richard Gilson (1803-1889)
A member of a family of English animal engravers and painters. Famous between 1811 and 1857 for illustrating many books on sport. A plate entitled "The Fatal Swoop" from the series devoted to the changes of fortune in the sport of falconry is in the collection of the Musée d'Histoire Naturelle, Paris.

Reeve, Russell (op.1889-1917)
Painter of horses in watercolour and oil including his portrait of a hunter in a box, 19¾in.x26½in., which was auctioned Sotheby's 1983.

Reeves, Richard Stone (b.1921)
Leading New York artist of equestrian scenes who specialises particularly in portraits of champion race-horses including those of "Secretariat", "Seattle Slew", "Affirmed" (beating "Spectacular Bid" in the 1979 Jockey Club Gold Cup at Belmont Park), "Dahlia" and "Allez France". His patrons include Nelson Bunker Hunt, Alec Head, Lester Piggott, Vincent O'Brien, Christy Firestone, Paul Getty and Eddie Maple. A few of his paintings are in the National Museum of Racing at Saratoga but the majority are in private collections all over the world. His son owns the Racing Scene Gallery in New York where an occasional Reeves may be found. He studied at Syracuse University School of Fine Art and is a direct descendant of the 19th century portrait painter, Thomas Sully (1783-1872).

Regamy, Frederic (op.1880-1900)
Prolific late 19th century artist, illustrator and engraver who produced many portraits of fencers during the last two decades of the century. Indeed Regamy and F.H. Townsend (q.v.) were the two great fencing illustrators at the turn of the century.

Reichmann, Franz (op.1912)
A mare and a foal in a landscape, s.&d. 1912 and inscr. "Newmarket", 28in.x36in., was auctioned Christie's (NY) 1986. Possibly related to Mrs. Josephine Reichmann (1864-1939), an American painter who studied at the Art Institute of Chicago.

Reid, Sir George, PRSA, HRSW (1841-1913)
Scottish portrait painter and an illustrator who studied in Edinburgh, Utrecht and Paris. Exh. at the RA and RSA from 1877. Elected RSA (1877) and PRSA (1891-1902), RSW (1892) ROI (1898). Knighted (1902). His vivid style established him as Scotland's leading portrait painter. He illus. many books and several on sporting subjects including "Natural History and Sport in Norway" (1882), "The River Tweed" (1884), "The River Clyde" (1886), and "Salmon Fishing on the Ristigouche" (1883). Reid painted the portrait of "Old" Tom Morris at the age of eighty-one, 46in.x34in. (R & A Collection at St. Andrews). A gravure was pub. in 1903.

Reid, John Robertson, RBA, RI, ROI (1851-1926)
Scottish land and seascape artist in both oils and water-colours, a pupil of William McTaggart (q.v.) at the RSA Schools. Lived in Polperro, Cornwall early in the 20th century. Exh. at the RA from 1877, also at the RBA, RHA, ROI, RSA, NEAC, RBSA and GI. Elected RBA (1880), ROI (1883), RI (1891). He painted several scenes of cricket including "A Country Cricket Match" and "County Cricket Match in Sussex", s.&d. '78. Reid's fine portrait of Lord Selborne (1859-1942) fishing the Itchen near Itchen Abbas is repro. in "Angling in British Art", Shaw Sparrow (1923), p.80.

Reid, Patrick (op.1953)
Contemporary printmaker of a football scene entitled "Torquay Supporters", engraving, 8in.x6in. exh. FE.

Reid, Samuel, RSW (1854-1919)
A Scottish landscape painter in watercolour, the younger brother of the artist Sir George Reid (q.v.). Contributed a number of watercolour illustrations to "The History of Curling" by John Kerr, pub. Edinburgh 1890. Elected RSW (1884).

Reinagle, P.A. (op.1804-1811)
Artist son of Philip Reinagle (q.v.) who exh. six paintings at the RA (1804-1805) of which three were horse portraits. He also exh. horse portraits at the BI (1807-1811) including "Young Woodpecker" and "Robin Hood", celebrated horses belonging to J. Claridge.

Reinagle, Philip, RA (1749-1833)
Originally a portrait painter who studied under Allan Ramsay (q.v.) working in his studio producing copies of royal portraits. He later turned to sporting subjects, in particular pictures of birds and animals. Reinagle was also a specialist in blackline etching and produced a fine series of falconry scenes showing the different kinds of hawking which proved of immense historical importance to later students of the sport. He put his own knowledge of falconry to good use again in his portrait of the famous sportsman Colonel Thornton (c.1755-1823) with a hawk on his fist which he painted in collaboration with John Russell, RA (q.v.). Exh. British Sporting Paintings (1650-1850) Hayward Gallery London 1974/5 (No.80). With the exception of the celebrated "Fox Breaking Cover", commissioned by Colonel Thornton. Reinagle rarely painted hunting scenes. He nevertheless collaborated with George Morland (q.v.) to paint "A Meet in Dorsetshire" with the hunting portraits of Mr. and Mrs. Francis Fayne and other members of the hunt. He was however an outstanding painter of dogs and he

painted two celebrated series for "The Sportsman's Cabinet" pub. by J. Cunder or Conder (1803) and for "The Sportsman's Repository" pub. by Sherwood (1820). Ten paintings forming part of a set of twenty-four painted for "The Sportsman's Cabinet" and representing possibly some of this excellent painter's finest work was shown at the exhibition of BSH at Sotheby's 1984/5. These were studies of hounds and dogs at work, including the pointer, the harrier, the setter, the water spaniel, the greyhound, the staghound, the Spanish pointer, the Springer spaniel, the water dog and the fox hound. Reinagle also painted boxing as a subject, including the very famous fight in 1788 between William Warr and William Wood at Navestock, Essex which hangs above the fireplace in the dining room of Broderick Castle. His fine painting "Salmon Fishing", 25in.x30in., was exh. "British Sporting Paintings", HM and AG Preston (1943).

Reinagle, Ramsay Richard, RA (1775-1862)
Painter of portraits, landscapes and sporting pictures in both oil and watercolour. Son and pupil of Philip Reinagle (q.v.) and named after Allan Ramsay (q.v.) under whom Philip Reinagle studied. Richard Reinagle wrote an account of Allan Ramsay's life for Cunningham's "British Painters". Prolific exhibitor at the RA and BI (1788-1854). Elected RA (1822) but demoted (1848) over the scandal that ensued when he offered a painting for exhibition by another artist as his own work. A very competent painter and a skilled copyist. Amongst his sporting works is a portrait of the greyhound "Major" at Carshalton on the day of the 1,000 Guinea wager and a dark bay hunter in an open landscape, dated 1811, auctioned Sotheby's 1981.

Rembrandt
See Van Rijn

Remington, Frederic (1861-1909)
Born in New York State and acclaimed for his pictures of life in the Wild West as well as his steeplechasing scenes. A master painter of action and excitement which is well illus. in his rousing painting of college football entitled "Touchdown", Yale v. Princeton, Thanksgiving Day, 27 November 1890, Yale 32, Princeton 0. Exh. NAMOS, Indianapolis (1991). Remington first travelled to the West in 1880 working as a hired cowboy and sheep rancher and visiting Indian settlements. One of his most famous paintings is "The Coming and Going of the Pony Express", painted in 1900. Although the Pony Express only operated for eighteen months, the fortitude, courage and speed of the riders excited the imagination of generations of American artists. On 3 April 1860 the first riders left St. Joseph, Missouri and Sacramento, California in a dramatic experiment to provide an overland mail service across the plains, desert and Rocky Mountains, a route of 1,966 miles. On 24 October 1861 the last link in the trans-continental telegraph was completed thus marking the end of the Pony Express.

Ren, Chuck (op.1980)
Contemporary painter of American football scenes including "Philadelphia Eagles" 1980, acrylic on illustration board and "Super Bowl XIVth" Theme Art 1980, acrylic on illustration board.

Renard, Stephen (b.1947)
Marine artist and humorous illustrator. Renard studied sciences at Liverpool University leaving to teach biology and science and becoming head of biology at a large Liverpool school. Highly influenced by the marine painter Stephen Dews (q.v.), Renard includes a number of yacht racing scenes amongst his work. He is a keen yachtsman and spent three years restoring a 1922 Harrison Butler design, "Cyclone".

Rennie, George Melvin (1802-1860)
Scottish landscape painter who painted "The Golf Course, Braemar, Deeside", inscr., 18¾in.x28¼in., Christie's (Scotland). He also finished good fly fishing scenes.

Renoir, Pierre Auguste (1841-1919)
French Impressionist painter included in this Dictionary for "Skating in the Bois de Boulogne" painted in 1868. Born in Limoges, Renoir studied under Marc Charles Gabriel Gleyre (1806-1874) in 1862, forming a lasting friendship with his co-students Monet, Sisley and Bazille. With them he painted in the Barbizon district and became a leading member of the group of Impressionists who met at the Café Guerbois. Renoir, who exh. at four of the Impressionist exhibitions (1874-1882), also exh. at the Paris Salon during the same period.

Renwick, Lionel Hamilton (b.1919)
Born in Northumberland, Renwick became a dairy farmer after the war. A weekly commission from a publication called "Rally" to draw a famous horse encouraged him to spend eighteen months at Heatherleys, followed by further studies at the Byam Shaw School of Art, and with Frederick Whiting (q.v.), Philip Lamb and David Birch ROI. Renwick had his first exhibition in 1953 at the Walker Galleries in London from which he received many painting commissions. This led to a successful career painting racehorses for leading owners, including several royal commissions. He exh. at Messrs. Fores and Frost and Reed and then moved to Newmarket where he breeds miniature Shetlands and prize winning dogs. He is also an international show judge. His talented racehorse commissions include the portrait of "Aureole" painted for Her Majesty Queen Elizabeth II.

Reville, Henry Whittaker (op.1881-1903)
Prolific painter of equestrian scenes, particularly steeple-chasing, racing and coaching. His sporting work includes a portrait of the Lord President of the Hackney Horse Society, Earl Spencer, driving a single horse and trap, dated 1893, "Trojan", the winner of the Kildare Hunt Cup, Irish Grand Military 1889, a portrait of "Hard Times", winner of thirteen steeplechases, painted in 1892, "Twelve Miles an Hour - Easy", the rocket coach c.1891, a pair of fighting cocks dated 1883 and "Skip It", a dark bay hunter in a stable interior, 13½in.x17½in.. Exh. two pictures at the RA and two at SS (1899-1903).

Reynolds, Frank, RI (1876-1953)
Black and white artist and illustrator, son of Frank Reynolds, the artist. He studied art at Heatherleys in Newman Street, under Professor John Crompton. He later went into business but drifted back into art and worked on the magazine "Pick Me Up" and "The Sketch". He also contributed to "The Illustrated London News" and joined the staff of "Punch" in 1919 becoming Art Editor (1920-1932). Reynolds was a prolific book illustrator and was responsible for many of the illustrations for "The New Punch Library" series from 1900 that covered comic situations: "Mr. Punch and the Arts", "Mr. Punch with Horse and Hound", "Mr. Punch on the Links" and "Mr. Punch's Sports and Past Times". He loved Dickens and Kipling and produced some of his finest illustrations for "David Copperfield" and "Pickwick Papers". He was born the same year as his very close friend James Thorpe (q.v.) with whom he also studied at Heatherleys and whom he took to Paris in 1904 for a commission by "The Sketch". Thorpe wrote a fascinating account of this trip in which he recalled that Reynolds had been inspired to produce some of his finest work for a series of articles written by John N. Raphael, the well-known correspondent. The excellent series of articles and drawings was pub. in book form in 1908. His golf sketches give a remarkable view of the social impact of the game; originals are now hard to obtain but a few highly finished watercolours of golf exist beside many black and white sketches. Reynolds also painted golf scenes - his early work - on pottery and porcelain and he drew a number of cricket sketches for Cassells magazine (1907). Reynolds was a keen fly fisherman and painted a number of angling scenes. Elected RI (1903), resigned 1933. Exh. (1903-1930).

Reynolds, Sir Joshua (1723-1792)
Portrait and history painter. Born in Devon. Apprenticed to Thomas Hudson (q.v.) (1740-1743). Practised in Devonshire and London (1743-1749) after which he went to Italy to study the great masters. Returned via Florence and settled in London (1753) for the rest of his life. Unlike Hogarth, Reynolds had influence in high places and knew that patronage was vital to a successful career. Many of his portrait groups feature cricket. He became first President of the newly formed Royal Academy (1768). Knighted in 1769 by George III, who didn't particularly like him.

Rhead, Louis John (1857-1926)
Illustrator and angling artist. Portrait and poster painter, lithographer, and black and white artist in watercolour. Born in England but emigrated to America in 1883. Brother of G.W. Rhead and F.A. Rhead, both artists and illustrators. Studied art in Paris and London before his emigration to America, where he lived in Brooklyn and Long Island, New York. He illus. a large number of children's stories for "Harpers" but his figure drawing was generally regarded as poor and his sense of proportion shaky. Much more successful were his fish drawings for the "Speckled Brook Trout" (pub. New York 1902) and his fly fishing scenes in watercolour portray him at his best in a sport he loved. An exhibition of his poster designs was held in London in 1897.

Rhodes, F.R. (op.1841-1843)
Staffordshire landscape painter who exh. five paintings at the RA including "Pheasant Shooting at Haddon Hall, Derbyshire" and one work at SS.

Ribblesdale, Thomas Lister (4th Baron) (b.1854)
Exh. a sporting subject at the NG (1892) from his London address. Lord Ribblesdale was a trustee of the National Gallery and of the National Portrait Gallery. A Lord in Waiting to Queen Victoria (1880-1885), he was also Master of HM's buckhounds (1892-1895). Ribblesdale succeeded his father as 4th Baron in 1876.

Ribbons, Ian (op.1953)
Contemporary painter whose contribution to football art lies in his work entitled "Red Wins", watercolour, 25in.x36in., exh. FE.

Ribera, Pierre (b.1867 op.c.1925)
French painter of "The Tennis Party", signed, oil on board, 8in.x10in., Priory Gallery, Cheltenham.

Richards, Frank, RBA (op.1892-1925)
Painter of landscapes and figurative subjects in watercolour. Lived in Newlyn, Cornwall. "Tea and Tennis", showing a late Victorian tennis party, pen/black ink, 11½in.x8¼in., was auctioned Sotheby's (Bel.).

Richards, John A. (op.1958-1970)
Book illustrator of several boxing scenes for Corgi paperbacks during the 1960s including "The Roar of the Crowd" and "The Bruiser".

Richardson, Daniel (op.1825-1830)
Painter of fresh water fish, a number of which he exh. at SS (1825-1830), including "Trout" (1826), "Trout" again in 1827, also "Chad and Trout", a "Group of Fish" in 1828, "Dead Game" and "Freshwater Fish" in 1829, and in 1830 "Freshwater Fish".

Richardson, H. Hughes (op.c.1890)
Landscape artist in watercolour whose "Duck Shooting in the Marshes, North Wales", 8in.x12in., was auctioned Phillips 1986.

Richardson, Harry Linley, RBA (b.1878, op.1900-1939)
Painter of figure subjects and landscapes, also an etcher, an illustrator and a draughtsman. Studied at Goldsmith's School of Art, Westminster and at Julians in Paris. Exh. (1900-1939). Elected RBA (1905). Exh. three works at the RA, one entitled "Yorick, the Parson on his Old Horse".

Richardson, R. (op.1917)
Motor artist whose watercolour painting of a "Minerva" four seater touring car, s.&d. 1917, 12½in.x20½in., was auctioned Christie's (Sth. Ken.) 1985.

Richardson, Ralph J. (op.1896-1925)
Painter and illustrator in black and white particularly of equestrian subjects. He contributed to "Punch" (1896-1907) and "The Graphic" (1901) and exh. an illustration of Colonel Botcherby, MFH, at the RA (1900). Illus. a number of books including "The Haughtyshire Hunt".

Richardson, Thomas Miles, Jnr., RSA, RWS (1813-1890)

Landscape painter, mostly in watercolour. Son of Thomas Miles Richardson, Snr. (1784-1848) and worked under his father in Newcastle. Exh. at the RA (1837-1848), BI, SS and OWS. Elected RWS (1851). His best works are perhaps his Highland and sporting sketches which include "The End of a Day's Shooting at Bendderagh, River Garioch near Loch Maree, Ross-shire", watercolour, 1887, and "Stalkers in a Highland Landscape", watercolour, 1833, 7½in.x13¾in. Other sporting paintings include "The Day's Spoil", 14in.x13½in., and "Grouse Shooting at Glencoe, Argyllshire".

Richmond, George, RA (1809-1896)

Portrait painter and watercolourist. Son of Thomas Richmond, Snr. and brother of Thomas Richmond, Jnr. Father of Sir William Blake Richmond who was named after his father's idol, William Blake, who greatly influenced George Richmond's work. After Blake's death in 1827 Richmond was forced to turn to portrait painting to make a living and he eventually became a leading portrait painter of his day. His portrait of Lord Dacre (1808-1890), previously Mr Thomas Brand, standing full length, dressed for hunting, was commissioned by the supporters of the Dacre Hounds of Welwyn, Hertfordshire, in 1866 to mark his retirement from the Mastership. The 22nd Lord Dacre bred a marvellous pack of hounds over thirty years, but his successor, the 23rd Lord Dacre, afterwards created 1st Viscount Hampden, did not continue the pack. Richmond studied at the RA Schools where he became a great friend of Samuel Palmer (q.v.). Exh. at the RA (1825-1884), BI and SS. Elected RA (1866). Richmond was a very keen cricketer and a stalwart member of Lords. As a result he introduced cricket accessories into many of his paintings.

Richter, Wilhelm (1824-1892)

Austrian painter of landscapes and equestrian subjects, in particular hunting. His portrait of a lady riding side-saddle out hunting, painted in 1878, 23in.x28¾in., was auctioned at Christie's. "Off to the Paddock" shows a racehorse being led to the paddock, signed, 22in.x 27¼in., auctioned Bonhams 1980.

Rickards, T. (op.1819)

An interesting watercolour painting of a cricket match at School House, Harrow, 8¾in.x12¼in., was auctioned Sotheby's 1987. The painting was engraved by W. Nicholls in 1819 but the engraving does not include the boys playing cricket.

Ricketts, Charles Robert (op.1850-1874)

Marine painter whose "Royal Thames Yacht Club, Ocean Match from Nore to Dover" was engraved by Andrew Maclure. Ricketts exh. seven works at SS and the RA (1868-1874).

Ricketts, Joy Stanley (b.1929)

Painter of equestrian subjects, in particular the Olympic horses and riders. Famous horses and ponies are commissioned mainly from her annual exhibitions held at the Badminton Horse Trials and the Royal Windsor Horse Show. Ricketts studied at the Birmingham College of Art where she gained an art teacher's diploma with the NDD in book illustration.

Rickman, Philip (1891-1982)

Talented bird painter in watercolour who included falconry and portraits of falcons amongst his work. Born at Richmond, Surrey, the son of a naval commander. Educated at Bradfield College, Berks. Studied art under George E. Lodge (q.v.) at his studio in Thurloe Square. Illus. and pub. many books including "The Handbook of British Birds", "A Bird Painter's Sketch Book" and "Notes from a Bird Painter's Journal". His game birds include "Study of Teal" (a small covey painted in 1929), duck studies and many others.

Rideout, Philip H. (op.1886-1912)

Appropriately named painter of equestrian subjects but in particular coaching and hunting scenes. He very often painted these in sets of four or pairs and usually painted in oil on small canvases. He normally signed his work and very often dated it. "The Kill", s.&d. 1882, 22in.x23in. Christie's 1988.

Ridinger, Johann Elias (1698-1767)

German artist who was a pupil of the Augsburg painter Georg Philipp Rugendas (1666-1742). He specialised in wildlife and hunting pictures although many of his paintings remained in Augsburg. Ridinger became well known for his sporting scenes through his engravings which were very popular throughout Europe, but especially in England.

Ridley, Matthew White (1837-1888)

Landscape and portrait painter from Newcastle on Tyne. Studied at the RA Schools. Exh. at the RA (1862-1888), BI, SS and elsewhere. Although Ridley painted predominantly landscapes he also painted occasional scenes of Victorian life in the manner of W.P. Frith (q.v.) including his version of "Derby Day", signed, 27½in.x42in., which was auctioned Sotheby's 1969.

Rigaud, John Francis, RA (1742-1810)

Portrait and history painter. Born in Turin and came to England (1771) having studied art previously in Italy. Member of the Bologna Academy (1766). Exh. at the RA (1772-1810), BI (1806-1810) and posthumously 1812, 1813 and 1815. Elected RA (1784). Included in this Dictionary for his fine painting of ballooning which is in the Yale Center for British Art, Newhaven, USA. The painting was engraved by Francesco Bartolozzi, RA and pub. by E. Wyatt in 1785 and is in the British Museum Collection. The painting depicts the famous balloonist Vincenzo Lunardi (1759-1806), Mrs. Sage and George Biggin. Lunardi had arranged to take Mrs. Letitia Ann Sage, a famous beauty, and George Biggin from St. George's Fields on 19 June 1785 up in the balloon. However the balloon proved incapable of lifting more than two people so Biggin and Mrs. Sage ascended alone. Needless to say the print shows Lunardi also on board.

Rigg, Ernest H. (op.1895-1904)
Painted genre and rustic subjects but also some equestrian portraits including a pair of oils on canvas, 24½in.x29½in., of bay hunters in stable interiors, both s.&d. 1895, Sotheby's 1980.

Riggs, Robert (1896-1970)
Painter of one of the most evocative and powerful pictures of American baseball of all time. "The Impossible Play" painted in 1949, 10¾in.x31⅜in., is in the Estelle and Arnold J. Kaplan Collection. Riggs exh. watercolours at the Penna Academy of Fine Arts, Philadelphia (1925).

Righi, M.
Decorative paintings of Edwardian golfing scenes painted on copper and signed by this artist are thought to be contemporary. M. Righi is unrecorded.

Riley, Harold Francis, RI (b.1934)
Painter of "Lancs -v- Yorks Rugger Match at Headingley, November 7th 1981", 39½in.x48⅜in., presented to the RFU by Lancs. RFC on the occasion of their Centenary, RFU H.Q., Twickenham. Riley won a scholarship to the Slade School of Art (1951-1958), the youngest boy ever to do so, and in 1952 he won First Prize in the British Universities' Painting Competition organised by the "Sunday Times". In 1959 Riley studied for a year in Italy and the following year he won a Travelling Scholarship to Spain. He then returned to live and work in his home town of Salford. Befriended whilst still at school by L.S. Lowry (q.v.) who persuaded the director of Salford City Art Gallery to buy Riley's painting of a local mill when he was eleven years old. The City Art Gallery now have two hundred of Riley's works. Riley has continued Lowry's work to record Salford and Manchester in paintings and drawings covering one hundred years. Lowry had begun this in 1901 and persuaded Riley to become involved in 1948.

Perhaps Riley's greatest contribution to sporting art lies in the foundation of the National Sporting Hall of Fame Archive housed at the University of Salford, to which Riley adds a portrait of a different sportsman each year. The money raised from the annual dinner, attended of course by the painted sportsman, goes towards a Sports Bursary at the University. The painted sportsmen include Sebastian Coe MP, Sir Henry Cotton, Sir Matt Busby, George Best and Bobby Charlton.

Riley's sporting paintings are in the collections of the University of Salford, Manchester United, David Sexton, the Los Angeles Chamber of Commerce, Jack Nicklaus, Sam Sneed, HRH Prince Philip and HRH The Prince of Wales.

Riley, J.W.
Watercolour painter of many small hunting and steeple-chasing scenes.

"Rip"
The pseudonym used by the artist Rowland Hill (q.v.).

Ripley, Aiden Lassell (1896-1969)
American painter of sporting subjects. Pupil of the School of the Museum of Fine Arts, Boston. Member of Boston Guild of Artists and the Boston Watercolour Society. His sporting work includes "A Hunting Scene", watercolour, 6in.x9in., "Grouse in Pine Woods" dated 1937, a "Trout Fisherman by a Waterfall", "Grouse" dated 1934, watercolour, "Casting Downstream", watercolour, 20in.x28½in., and "A Quail Hunting Party", watercolour, 11in.x17in., Christie's (NY) 1986.

Ripley, R.R. (op.1856-1879)
Painter of landscapes and coaching subjects who exh. two works at the RA, one painted in collaboration with Benjamin Herring Jnr., (q.v.), and four at SS (1856-1879). "The Christmas Mail" shows a single horse and gig being driven head on, down a snowy country lane, by a single top-hatted figure, signed and inscr., 19¼in.x15¼in., auctioned Sotheby's 1985.

Ripon, 2nd Marquess (1852-1923)
Eligible in this Dictionary for his remarkable fifty-three illus. game books, written between 1865 and 1923. As Lord Grey, he was arguably the greatest shot in the golden age of the shooting party and he liked to shoot with three guns and two loaders. The books which record his legendary exploits are all delightfully illus. by himself. Pictures of gun dogs, rabbits, boars, beetles, and bugs are all recorded as well as pictures of himself in action. Succeeded his father as 2nd Marquess (1909).

Ritchie, Alec P.F. (Poster Fame Ritchie) (1869-c.1938)
Very talented poster artist who included many sporting activities amongst his work. Known as the artist who first extracted humour from a geometrical treatment of human figures and who also portrayed the curious effect of ordinary subjects when seen from an altitude. Born in Dundee, where he started his career in the ship building industry and then by selling jute. After this false start he came to London to try his hand at sketching which progress was not without its struggles, at one time finding him in Euston as a pavement artist. His fortunes improved enough to enable him to study for two years in Antwerp where he developed a talent for humorous black and white work. On his return to London he received considerable encouragement from the editor of "The Penny Illustrated Paper", John Latey. From then on his career became one of steady progress. He contributed work to many of the best periodicals including "Pall Mall", "St. Paul's" and "The Sketch". Alec Ritchie produced a unique set of cigarette cards for Players entitled "Straight Line Caricatures" depicting sporting personalities, including amongst others Lord Hawke, Jack Hobbs, Steve Donaghue and The Earl of Derby. He contributed fifteen cartoons to "Vanity Fair" between 1911 and 1913 including a cartoon of John Lavery (q.v.) entitled "He paints various Royalties". Ritchie was an excellent artist and produced lively and accurate caricatures of many sporting personalities.

Ritchie, J.W. (op. early 20th century)
Painter of the Amateur Golf Champion, Frederick Guthrie Tait finishing the swing, s.&d. 1904, 16in.x 12in., Christie's (Scotland). Tait was Amateur Champion

in 1896 and 1898. The painting of Tait was painted posthumously since he was killed in 1900 whilst leading his company of the Black Watch in the 2nd Boer War (see also J.H. Lorimer).

Ritchie, John (op.1855-1875)
Edinburgh painter of genre and some sporting subjects who exh. at the RA (1858-1875), BI and SS. Tended to paint his subjects in historical costume. "Village Cricket", 1855 (MCC Collection), 31½in.x49½in., was exh. at the British Sporting Paintings Exhibition at the Hayward Gallery in 1974 and "A Curling Match", possibly depicting the Royal Caledonian Curling Club pond at Carsebreck, Perthshire, 15in.x27in., was auctioned Christie's 1986.

Riviere, Briton, RA, RE (1840-1920)
Primarily an animal painter although occasionally his animals were depicted in sporting situations. He was the son of the portrait painter William Riviere (1806-1876) under whom he studied. He also studied under J. Pettie and Sir William Quiller Orchardson (qq.v.). Riviere, who painted in both oil and watercolour, shared a studio with the equestrian and sporting artist Heywood Hardy (q.v.). Elected RA (1881). Riviere was a good animal painter but an interesting report on the exhibition at Burlington House, recorded in Bailys Magazine, Vol. 27, June 1875, reads: "Mr. Mansell Lewis must have a noble picture gallery in which to put his chestnut mare, his dogs and himself. The canvas takes up nearly half the end of the third room and commands the attention it doubtless deserves. But why such a size Mr. Riviere? A country gentleman with his horse and dogs is no such uncommon a subject that it must be painted in Brobdingnag proportions." In the July issue of the same magazine Mr. Riviere received an even rougher time from the relentless but amusing pen of his tormentor: "But when an animal painter of Mr. Briton Riviere's calibre enters the field as a painter of horses we are entitled to look for something to furnish an exemplar of what such production should be. We are sorry that we fail to find anything of the sort in his portrait of his gentleman pensively standing at his favourite mare's side, by the sad sea waves and with his dogs grouped in repose in the foreground. Anything more unsatisfactory as representing a horse and dogs it would be impossible to conceive. Professors of the veterinary college must stand aghast before such a production and we commend a study of this equine favourite to Messrs. Field and Maver (a well-known firm of vets) who in all their experience could never have looked over an animal so fearfully and wonderfully made".

Riviere, Hugh Goldwin, RP, ROI (1869-1956)
Portrait painter, very often of sporting subjects, the son of Briton Riviere, RA (q.v.). He was born at Bromley, Kent and studied art at the RA Schools. He exh. at the RA from 1892 and at the Paris Salon. Lived in London and later on at Midhurst, Sussex. His portrait of Sir Robert Fellowes on "Grafton", s.&d. 1913, 18in.x72in., was auctioned Sotheby's 1986. Elected RP (1900) and ROI (1907).

Robb, Brian (b.1913)
Painter and illustrator whose interpretation of a football match entitled "Football", 39in.x29½in., was exh. FE. Robb, who studied at the Chelsea School of Art (1930-1934) and the Slade School (1935-1936) has had several one-man shows in London and elsewhere. His work is represented in the Arts Council Collection, in Southampton and Leicester AGs and elsewhere.

Robb, Emma (op.1880-1896)
Glasgow painter who exh. at the RSA and GI (1886-1896). "A Huntsman and Pack", s.&d. '80, 19½in.x 23½in., was auctioned Anderson and Garland 1987.

Roberton, A. (op.1884-1895)
A set of three hunting scenes all s.&d. 1895 were auctioned Sotheby's (Sussex) 1987. This artist is probably Alfred J. Roberton who exh. five works at SS (1884-1886).

Roberts, F. (op.c.1810)
A set of three equestrian paintings, "A Bay Racehorse with Jockey up", "Racing to the Finish" and "Taking the Brook", each 5½in.x8½in., were auctioned Christie's 1972. Roberts was possibly related to James and Henry Roberts (qq.v.) since he operated at a similar time and painted similar subjects.

Roberts, Henry (op.1741-d.1790)
Etcher and line engraver of sporting subjects after his own designs and those of his contemporaries. His engraving "An Exact Representation of the Game of Cricket", presumably after his own work, was pub. in 1743. He also engraved twelve plates entitled "High Bred Running Horses" after the work by his brother James Roberts (q.v.) with whom he pub. "The Sportsman's Pocket Companion".

Roberts, James (1753-c.1810)
Portrait painter in both oil and watercolour, an etcher and also a painter of miniatures. Entered the RA Schools (1771). Exh. at the RA (1773-1799). Probably best known for his illustrations to the "Sportsman's Pocket Companion" c.1760 and for his series of portraits of actors used as illustrations for Bell's "British Theatre" 1776. He pub. "Introductory Lessons with Familiar Examples in Landscapes" in 1809. Is thought to have taught drawing at Oxford (1784-1794). In about 1795 he was appointed portrait painter to the Duke of Clarence. He was the brother of Henry Roberts (q.v.).

Roberts, James (op.1858-1876)
Yorkshire landscape and equestrian painter who exh. at SS and BI (1858-1876). His fine portrait of the famous trotter "Jack Rossiter", s.&d. 1863, 24in.x36in., was exh. Frost & Reed and repro. "Country Life" 1966.

Roberts, Lunt (op.c.1912-1945)
Keen golfer, artist and illustrator who drew many golfing sketches. Member of the London Sketch Club Golf Team. Roberts became a member of his local golf club at Combe Wood, South London (1936). Each year he completed a portrait of the Club Captain and they line the clubhouse. "Punch" cartoonist.

Roberts, Thomas (b.c.1748-d.1778)

Irish landscape painter. Born in Waterford, the son of John Roberts, the architect. Elder brother of Thomas Sautelle Roberts (q.v.). Trained at the Dublin Society of Artists School and later under the Irish landscape artists, John Butts and George Mullins. Exh. at the Dublin Society (1766-1777). "Foxhunting in Co. Fermanagh, Ireland with a view of Lough Erne" painted c.1770/1771, 22½in.x36in., is in the Paul Mellon Collection, Upperville, Va, USA. Ireland in the 18th century was still full of private packs of foxhounds of which this painting presumably depicts one, possibly that of Colonel Madden from whose property at Castle Walter Roberts painted one of his landscape views of Lough Erne. Horses and sometimes hunts frequently feature in Roberts' landscapes.

Roberts, Thomas Sautelle (b.c.1760-1826)

Irish landscape and sporting painter in oil and watercolour. He added his elder brother's Christian name, Thomas (q.v.) to his own Christian name, Sautelle, after his brother's early death in 1778. Studied at the Dublin Society of Artists School and won a medal in 1779. Entered the RA Schools (1791) and remained in London until 1799. Exh. at the RA and BI (1789-1818) and in Dublin (1800-1821). Elected a Foundation member of the RHA (1823). His painting of mares and foals in a wooded landscape, dated 1779, and inscr. "Dublin", 24½in.x28½in., was auctioned Christie's 1985. Roberts committed suicide in 1826.

Roberts, William Patrick, RA, LG (1895-1980)

Painter in oil and watercolour of figure subjects and portraits. Studied at St. Martin's School of Art and at the Slade School (1910-1913). Travelled in France and became very influenced by Pablo Picasso (q.v.). Joined the Vorticist Group (1914) and the LG (1915). Held first one-man show at the Chenil Galleries (1923) and exh. at the RA from 1952. Elected ARA (1958), RA (1966). Roberts painted many sporting portraits featuring brutish and unnamed boxers and footballers. "The Lesson", 35½in.x27½in., was exh. at the FE. His exhibition work includes paintings of snooker, football, boxing, racing and many of swimming - a subject clearly close to his heart. His painting of horse racing "Cantering to the Post" (1949), 24in.x20in., is in the collection of the Tate Gallery, London.

Robertson, C.H. (op.1824-1840)

Scottish painter of sporting subjects including a portrait of "Caddie Willie" on Bruntsfield Links, painted in 1824. "Caddie Willie", William Gunn, was a caddie with the Royal Burgess Society of Edinburgh. Although Willie is shown on the so-called links at Bruntsfield, a subsequent lithograph, pub. by the artist and printed by Robertson and Ballentyne of Edinburgh, was dedicated to the "Clubs of Edinburgh and Leath". The Society bought the painting for £3 in 1845 which had previously hung in the Golf Tavern at Bruntsfield. It seems that Robertson painted two versions of the portrait but both versions and the lithograph all vary, the castle, for example, being in a different position in each case. One version hangs at Blackheath and one at the Royal Burgess Society of Edinburgh. Robertson's further contribution to sporting art includes a portrait of "Kittie Fell" winning the race at Tinwald Downs, Dumfriesshire in 1833, 25½in.x42½in., and another portrait of "Kittie Fell" with her owner Mr. Barry and groom, s.&d. 1833, 19in.x27½in., was auctioned Sotheby's 1990. "Kittie Fell", a grey mare, was owned by Mr. Barry and was the winner of the Sweepstake held at Tinwald Down on 12 September 1833. She beat three other horses, all of whom were owned by local Scottish farmers. Robertson collaborated with T.H. Gibbs (q.v.) on the painting entitled "In Close Touch", a scene of the Carlisle Otter Hunt on the Eden above Armathwaite, 31in.x47in., auctioned Phillips (Edinburgh) 1988. It is possible that C.H. Robertson and J. Robertson (q.v.) were closely related since they operated at a similar time.

Robertson, David T. (b.1880)

Darlington-born landscape and animal painter who settled in Sunderland and exh. at Stansfield Exhibition, Sunderland, 1911. Self taught in art but included a number of equestrian portraits amongst his work.

Robertson, George (1749-1788)

Landscape and history painter in both oil and watercolour. Studied at Shipley's Academy and won prizes (1760-1761). Studied art in Italy and exh. at the RA (1772), SA (1773-1783) and posthumously (1790). He painted several equestrian portraits including "A Hunter in a Landscape", s.&d. 1779, 17¾in.x23½in., auctioned Sotheby's 1986. A stage coach and four dashing through a village on the Bath - London Road, watercolour, 11½in.x16½in., is in the Paul Mellon Collection, Upperville, Va, USA. The painting was engraved with differences by James Fittler as "The Mail Coach" and dedicated to John Palmer (1742-1818), Surveyor and Comptroller General of the Post Office from 1786. The print is not dated but was presumably published c.1786 to celebrate his appointment.

Robertson, J. (op.1838-1850)

Possibly Scottish painter of equestrian portraits who operated at the same time as C.H. Robertson (q.v.). His equestrian work includes a portrait of Mr.J. Bayliss on "Birthday" with his dog "Rush", dated 1850, and inscr., a portrait of a bay hunter in a landscape, dated 1838, portraits of "Job Trotter", a chestnut hunter with "Gary Ship" and "Flora", and a portrait of the stallion "Cupid" with his groom, G. Revely, and the retriever, "Lion", in a coachyard with a view of Warwick Castle behind.

Robertson, Tom, RBA, ROI, RI (1850-1947)

Glasgow born landscape and marine artist in oils, pastel and watercolour who painted a number of yacht racing and regatta scenes. Studied at the Glasgow School of Art and in Paris, under Benjamin Constant. Exh. at the principal London galleries (from 1880) and widely abroad. Elected RBA (1896), ROI (1912) (Hon retd. 1937) and RI (1912).

Robertson Browne, Ethel C.

See Browne

Robineau, Charles Jean (op.1780-1789)
French portrait painter who painted small, full length portraits for, and of, George IV (as Prince of Wales) 1787 and of C.F. Able, 1780 (Kew Palace). He was possibly the father of the portrait painter Auguste Robineau (op.1785-1816). Robineau painted a fencing match between Mademoiselle la Chevalière D'Eon de Beaumont and Monsieur de St. George in 1787. Charles Geneviève D'Eon de Beaumont (1728-1810) qualified as a doctor of law. He acted as a secret agent for Louis XV in Russia in 1755, presenting himself as a woman to the Empress Elizabeth. After a brief but distinguished army career he came to England in 1762 and lived in England from 1785, supporting himself by exhibitions of fencing. There seems to have been some doubt as to his true sex which was dispelled at his post mortem. In the stipple engraving by Victor Marie Picot (cut impression) 1789, in the collection of the British Museum, he is definitely fencing in full female attire. This subject was also engraved by James Gillray (q.v.). Robineau also painted the portrait of the champion boxer, Daniel Mendoza, which was engraved in mezzotint by Henry Kingsbury and pub. in 1789, 22¼in.x17in.

Robinson, Charles F., ARE (op.1874-1915)
Painter and etcher of landscapes including "The Dead Heat", the University Boat Race 1877, 14in.x24in., a lithograph, presumably after his own work. Elected ARE (1890).

Robinson, Frederick (op.1845)
The athlete, William Shephard of Birmingham, starting his run from a signpost marked "Birmingham 3 miles, Wallsall 5 miles", a very rare lithograph pub. by, and after, Robinson in 1845.

Robinson, Gregory (op.1907-1934)
Marine painter who studied at the RA Schools and later served at sea in World War I. He painted a number of yacht racing scenes including "Yachts Racing off Portsmouth", watercolour and gouache, auctioned Sotheby's 1987. Exh. at the RA one painting only entitled "Bound for London" in 1910. Lived near Southampton.

Robinson, Ken (c.1985)
Contemporary artist whose "Torvill and Dean Ice Skating" painted c.1985 was auctioned Phillips (Sherborne) 1989.

Robinson, Thomas (c.1770-1810)
Portrait, historical and landscape painter who was born near Lake Windermere. Often inscr. his work "Robinson of Windermere" although he lived almost entirely in Ireland from 1790 and died in Dublin 1810. Pupil of George Romney (c.1785). President of the Society of Artists in Dublin (1809/10). His portrait of "Paddywack", a bay colt with a gentleman holding him in a landscape, inscr. "belonging to Major Newberry", 60in.x74in., is in the National Gallery of Ireland.

Robinson, William A. (op.1833-1863)
Painter of equestrian, rustic and sporting subjects including "A Shooting Party", dated 1846, 17in.x24in., and a head of a grey horse and hound, dated 1836. Exh. at the RA, SS and RHA (1842-1863) including a painting entitled "The Young Anglers."

Robinson, William Heath (1872-1944)
Cartoonist and book illustrator who developed a passion for imaginative, but scatter-brained machinery ideas. His mad contraptions reflected the mechanical enthusiasms of the "Industrial Age" while some of his less feverishly imaginative work shows an extraordinary visionary talent. He studied at the RA Schools before starting work for the publishers and was the brother of Charles Robinson (1870-1937), the watercolour painter and illustrator. Robinson painted a number of sporting subjects including "A Round of Golf at Dorisdene Mansions, Maida Vale, London", a pen and ink drawing, 15in.x10¾in., and "Some Golfing Novelties for Next Season", pen and wash, was auctioned Sotheby's 1985. Golf was a particularly favourite subject of his and he used it in his "Sports and Hobbies" series such as "A Perfect Golfing Husband", etc. He contributed sporting work to several magazines including "The Sportsman" (USA), "The Humorist" (1931) and "The Illustrated Sporting and Dramatic News".

Robinson, William Howard (op.1902-1930s)
Scottish portrait and figure painter, also of several sporting subjects. These include "An Evening at the National Sporting Club" (boxing), the Ice Gala at Grosvenor House, a portrait of the greyhound "Future Cutlet" trained at Wembley by Arthur Probert, winner of the greyhound Derby 1933 and one of the foundation sires of today's racing greyhounds. Robinson's fine fencing portrait of Captain Alfred Hutton with foil in hand hangs in the de Beaumont Centre, London. Captain Hutton had his first fencing lesson at the age of twelve from Henry Angelo (the younger) and was a member of the London Fencing Club for more than forty years. Robinson also painted the portrait of Felix Bertrand (1871-1930), son of the fencing master to Louis, the Prince Imperial, after the fall of the Second Empire. Studied art at the Slade School and under Sir S.J. Solomon. Exh. at the RA, NEAC and in the provinces (1902-1917).

Robjent, Richard (b.1937)
Contemporary painter of game birds and wildfowl. "Ptarmigan in a Highland Landscape", dated 1983, was auctioned Sotheby's 1987.

Robson, J.W. (op.1852-1883)
A painting of "Footsteps", a bay racehorse outside a stable s.&d. 1883, 8¼in.x10¾in., was auctioned Sotheby's 1972 and a portrait of a young boy in a white gown, a pointer at his side, dated 1852 was auctioned Christie's (Sth. Ken.) 1988.

Robson, R. (op.1829-1840)
"Voltaire", a dark bay racehorse in an extensive landscape by the sea, signed and inscr. "Durham". "Voltaire" won the cup at Doncaster in 1829. He was the sire of "Charles XII" and "Voltigeur" (see also Armstead). Robson also painted a hunting scene and exh. two paintings at the BI in 1832 and 1834.

Rochard, Simon Jacques (1788-1872)

French painter whose watercolour portrait of two young boys, one holding a cricket bat, s.&d. 1839, 14in.x 19¾in., was exh. John Mitchell and Son, Bond Street, London in 1977.

Roche, Christopher J. (b.1940)

Irish painter of sporting and equestrian subjects who used to be a professional jockey. His painting of the "Three Counties Mink Hounds at Monkland, Hereford-shire on the River Arrow", s.&d. 1983, 24in.x20in., features the three joint masters of the pack at the time, Ian S. Coghill, Peter Cooper and C.R. Sellars. A limited edn. of 200 prints of this painting was issued. Roach also paints steeplechasing, point-to-point, fishing and polo scenes. He is completely self-taught and lives in Worcestershire.

Rockwell, Norman (1894-1978)

American painter and perhaps the most sought after illustrator of his generation. Studied at the National Academy of Design and the Art Student's League, under Thomas Fogarty. Painted many sports scenes but particularly baseball, a number of which appeared in and on the covers of the "Saturday Evening Post". These included "The Dugout", 4 September 1948, "The Rookie" and "The Referee", 21 October 1950. His study of a group of three umpires in the foreground of a baseball field, gazing solemnly at a single cloud in an otherwise blue sky, shows his ability to portray humour.

Rodgers, Joseph C. (op.1880-1889)

Nottingham landscape painter in watercolour and oil who lived amongst a colony of artists of the same name in and about the Newark area. He exh. one painting at the RA (1889), three at the RSA and one at the Walker AG, Liverpool. "The Rabbit Trapper", dated 1880, 24½in.x29½in., Sotheby's (Bel.) 1972, is as near to a sporting picture as he got.

Rodgers, Peter Robertson (b.1916)

Motor car artist who was brought up at Yewlands, Banstead, Surrey and was a fanatical follower of motor car racing, sketching all aspects of the sport while still in his early teens. Much of his work covered the period before the 2nd World War. He exh. his collection of motor racing scenes at the Royal Drawing Society in 1931.

Rodgers, Sydney (op.1953)

"The Village Match", wood engraving, 5in.x3in., exh. at the FE.

Rodway, Eric, ARCA (b.1914)

Birmingham-born painter who studied at the Wimbledon School of Art (1933-1937) and at the RCA (1937-1940). His contribution to football art lies with "The Rugby Player", s.&d. 1953 which Rodway contributed to the FE. (Harry Langton Collection). Rodway exh. at the RA, RBA and the NEAC and has taught at Epsom and Ewell School of Art since 1947.

Roe, Clarence Henry (op.1870-d.1909)

Painter of Highland sporting subjects. Born and worked in Cumbria, probably related to Robert Henry Roe (q.v.) who painted similar subjects. Did not exhibit in London but exh. two works at the RHA in 1887.

Roe, Colin Graeme (op.1858-1910)

See also Graeme. Painter of equestrian and sporting subjects who operated from the Sheffield area. Caused some confusion to earlier art historians since he signed his work both Colin Graeme Roe and Colin Graeme. Roe painted in a rather stark style, generously endowing his animals with exaggerated wide eyes. Thought to be the son of Robert Henry Roe (q.v.).

Roe, Frederick (Fred), RI, RBA (1864-1947)

Figure painter - the father of the sporting art writer F. Gordon Roe and son of Robert Henry Roe (q.v.). Roe, who studied at Heatherleys and under J. Seymour Lucas (q.v.), flirted early in his career with equestrian painting but turned instead to figure painting on the advice of J.F. Herring Jnr. (q.v.) who told him "The love of horses is not in you" which is said to have settled the matter for Roe. Roe painted "La Gondola" for the Waugh family at Newmarket. Elected RBA (1895) and RI (1909).

Roe, Robert (1792-1880)

Painter and etcher, father of Robert Henry Roe (q.v.) by his first marriage. Etched a sketch of a white horse by Bryan Duppa (q.v.), his only known equestrian work. He met Edward Fitzgerald and W.M. Thackeray during his Cambridge days and is said to have instructed the latter in etching.

Roe, Robert Henry (1822-1905)

Highland landscape and animal painter, the elder son of Robert Roe (q.v.) by his first marriage. Robert Henry Roe married Emma, a daughter of the sculptor, Edward Hodges Baily RA (1788-1867) whose most important commission was the statue of Nelson on the column in Trafalgar Square. Their son was Frederick Roe (q.v.). Robert Roe lived in Scotland and painted Highland landscapes and animals but later lived in London and Cambridge. He exh. ten works at the RA (1852-1868). His sporting work includes "Otter Hounds and Deer", dated '60, "Duck Shooting" and "Grouse Shooting", and "Stalking Companions in the Highlands", dated 1861.

Roebuck, Thomas (op.1860)

Provincial animal painter whose portrait of "Crib", a sporting dog, is dated 1860. Roebuck also painted a Durham Shorthorn bull with sheep in 1860.

Rogers, Claude Maurice, OBE, PLG, NEAC (1907-1979)

Figure painter, in a naturalistic style, who studied at the Slade School (1925-1928). A founder member of the Euston Road School (1937). Rogers held his first solo exhibition at the Leicester Galleries (1940). Taught at Camberwell School of Art (1945-1948) and at the Slade School (1948-1963). During this period he made his contribution to sporting art with his painting "West Bromwich v. Chelsea", 1952/1953 which was entered for the FE. Rogers became President of the London Group (1952-1955) and was awarded an OBE in 1959. Professor of Fine Art at Reading University (1963-1972).

Rogers, J(ohn), Snr. (op.1838-1864)

London painter and lithographer of rustic, sporting and equestrian subjects who exh. at the SS and RA

(1838-1864). Lithographs after paintings by him include portraits of Colonel Anson's "Atilla", winner of the Derby in 1842, Mr. Orde's "Beeswing", winner of the Gold Cup at Ascot in the same year, "Running Rein" c.1844 and "Sultan", the Arab horse belonging to Sir John Malcolm, inscr. "Deptford". Portraits of the racehorses "Long Waist" and "Rubens" were lithographed by Rogers after his own work. Another lithograph is recorded (Shaw Sparrow) of "Cadland" who ran a dead heat with "The Colonel" for the Derby in 1828. A cricket match at the Pensioner's Hall, Charterhouse, after the work by Thomas Hosmer Shepherd (q.v.) was engraved by Rogers and pub. by Jones & Co. in 1830. His very fine painting of a pony tethered to a fence, 8⅜in.x11⅝in., was auctioned David Lay 1987. Sometimes Rogers signed his work J.R.S. and sometimes J. Rogers, Snr. but his Christian name is thought to have been John.

Rogers, Philip Hutchings (1786-1853)
Marine and landscape painter, born at Plymouth and encouraged to study art by John Bidlake who sent him to study in London at his own expense. He painted the portrait of a hunting dog on a seashore, s.&d. 1812, 17in.x20¾in., auctioned Christie's 1984.

Rogers, W.G. (op.1885-1909)
Irish artist who painted an amusing billiard scene in watercolour, s.&d. '09, Burlington Gallery, London. Rogers also exh. two paintings at the RHA in 1885 from a Dublin address.

Roland, A. Knight (early 20th century)
Painter of angling subjects including "A Jack in the Roach Swim" (1904), "Hooked", "Salmon Fishing", "Wild Duck Shooting", "The Horse Fair", "Just Caught", etc.

Roland, J. Knight (early 20th century)
Painter of angling subjects who does not appear to have exh. anywhere. His painting "The Grayling", signed and inscr., was auctioned Christie's (Sth. Ken.) 1982.

Rolfe, Alexander F. (op.1839-1872)
Painter of angling and sporting subjects and sometimes still lifes. Exh. mostly at SS and BI. His sporting work includes "A Fisherman by a River", dated 1895, "A Shooting Pony with the Day's Bag", dated 1839, "A Portrait of William Davies with his Dogs and Dead Game", dated 1847, "Grouse Shooting in the Highlands", s.&d. 1858, 27in.x43in., "Two Anglers and a Bailiff in a Punt on a river fishing for bream with a landscape beyond", dated 1856, and a portrait of H.L. Rolfe (q.v.) his artist brother, painting an angling picture, dated 1850. This hangs in the Piscatorial Society Collection . He also collaborated with his brother-in-law J.F. Herring, Jnr. (q.v.) on several sporting scenes and he exh. at the RBA (1839-1872).

Rolfe, Alexander F. (Mrs) (op.1842-1875)
Painter of angling subjects. Wife of Alexander F. Rolfe (q.v.). Lived in London and is supposed to have exh. one sporting subject at SS in 1866. A painting of dead pike and trout on a river bank, dated 1842, was auctioned

Christie's 1981 and an angling painting entitled "Not Caught Yet", signed, inscr, and dated 1875 was auctioned Christie's 1980.

Rolfe, Edmund (op.1830-1841)
Painter of angling subjects and still lifes, also a topographical draughtsman and lithographer who engraved eight views of Dover c.1837. Exh. five paintings at SS, six at BI and two at the RA (1830-1841). Mostly dead game subjects. His still life of heron, hare and pheasant, s.&d. 1837, 15½in.x11½in., was auctioned Sotheby's (Bel.) 1978 and his still life of fish and game, s.&d. 1831, was auctioned Phillips (Bath) 1988.

Rolfe, F. (op.1849-1871)
Painter of angling subjects who lived for a time at the same London address as Henry Leonidas Rolfe and Alexander F. Rolfe (qq.v.). Exh. four works at SS (1849-1853) including "The Salmon Pool on the Usk" inscr., "A Good Morning's Sport", "The Anglers Luncheon" and several other river scenes, and two works at the BI. A painting of "Partridge and Chicks" clearly s.&d. 1871, 23in.x33in., was auctioned Brown and Merry 1992. It is possible that he is the same artist as A.F. Rolfe.

Rolfe, Henry Leonidas (op.1847-1881)
A very prolific painter of angling and sporting subjects and an enthusiastic fisherman. He exh. sixteen pictures at the RA (1847-1874), twenty-three at the BI, ninety-two at SS and forty at various other exhibitions. His portrait painted by his brother Alexander F. Rolfe (q.v.) in 1850 entitled "Limner of Scaly Subjects" hangs in the Piscatorial Society Collection. Rolfe joined the Piscatorial Society in 1864 and was elected an Hon. Member on 1 March 1869. He collaborated with Edward and Alfred Hichins Corbould (qq.v.) on several angling paintings including "The Biter Bit", 17½in.x 15in., signed by both Edward and himself, exh. Sotheby's (BSH) 1984/5, and "Fisherman with their Catch Beside a River" signed by both Alfred Corbould and himself and dated 1862, exh. Ackermanns 1982 and repro. "Country Life" (28.7.1983). One of Rolfe's finest works entitled "A Fine Catch" shows a 50lb and 40lb salmon caught by Mr. Haynes on Loch Tay, s.&d. 1880, 36in.x56in. The fish were caught on 11 and 18 February 1880 with a Phantom Winner. The 50 pounder took one and three-quarter hours to land.

Roll, Miss E. (op.c.1800-1830)
This artist exh. one painting of dead game at the RA (1830) from a London address. She is possibly the same artist referred to in Grant's BL Painters as belonging to an old Devonshire family at Bicton and operating in about 1800.

Roller, George Conrad, RPE (RE) (1858-c.1925)
A portrait painter who also painted a number of sporting and equestrian subjects. Born in Surrey, Roller studied at Lambeth Art School and in Paris, under Bouguereau and Fleury. He was not a sporting painter in the accepted sense but his horses are beautifully painted with superb movement. Although he travelled widely he lived in London and Basingstoke when he was in England. He

was a keen hunting man and rode under National Hunt rules, c.1880. He contributed to several publications including "Black and White", "Pick Me Up" and "Pall Mall" and worked as a sporting advertisement designer to Burberry's and as a picture restorer to the RA for twenty years. He was certainly related to the cricketer W.E. Roller, the distinguished batsman who played cricket for Surrey in the latter part of the 19th century. The famous painting by George Roller, 96in.x57½in., in the Surrey County Cricket Club Collection, shows W.E. Roller walking down the pavilion steps at the Oval as he goes out to bat during the second innings of a County match between Surrey and Lancashire, played on 23, 24 and 25 August 1883. W.E. Roller, who was then an undergraduate, was batting when Surrey needed 112 runs to win with only three wickets standing. On the last day 56 runs were still needed and Roller hit the winning run, being not out for 55. Roller exh. at SS (1887-1896) including "Play Up Surrey". He also exh. at the RA (1884-1906) including, in 1904, No. 233, a portrait of Major W.H. Mullens mounted with his squadron of the Middlesex Imperial Yeomanry, 37½in.x51½in., which is a painting of an impressive battle scene in full action. Roller served in the Boer War and World War I becoming a Colonel in the Middlesex Yeomanry. Elected RE (1885).

Rollo, Roger (The Hon.) (1777-1847)
Painter of sporting subjects, particularly fox-hunting. He was the second son of James, 7th Lord Rollo who, after his retirement from the army, lived at Ayr. Rollo painted a portrait of the Master of the Lanark and Renfrewshire Hunt in 1837, Lord Kelburn, with the huntsman Will Smith, in a landscape probably representing North Ayrshire. His pair "Bagging a Fox" and "The Kill" which also represents the Lanark and Renfrewshire Hunt were also painted in 1837, 9⅝in.x 13⅝in., and were exh. at Ackermanns, London in 1979.

Ronner, Henriette
See Knip, Henriette

Roods, Thomas (op.1833-1867)
London painter of portraits, who exh. at the leading galleries (1833-1867). His portrait group "Mr. Thomas Sherwin and Family Returning from Coursing" was exh. at the RA (1844).

Rook, J. (op.1852)
Draughtsman, lithographer and publisher after his own work including "The Whitehaven Races 1852", 12½in.x 16¼in. A smaller lithograph after this work was pub. by Michael and N. Hanhart in 1852, 10½in.x14¾in.

Rooke, Herbert Kerr, RBA (1872-1944)
Marine painter, appropriately born at Greenwich. A nephew of the artist T.M. Rooke, RWS. Studied art at the Royal College of Art, South Kensington and at the Slade School. Exh. at the RA and RBA (1894-1927). Elected RBA (1899). He painted a number of yacht racing scenes including "A View of Cowes with George V's 'J' Class boat 'Britannia' racing in the foreground", 24⅜in.x49¾in., as well as "First Day of the Regatta" showing a scene at Brixham, inscr. and dated 19 August 1932, 10½in.x14in.

Rooker, Michael Angelo, ARA (1747-1801)
Landscape painter, draughtsman, etcher and line engraver, son of the engraver Edward Rooker (c.1712-1774) by whom he was taught engraving. Pupil also of Paul Sandby (q.v.) who taught Rooker drawing and landscape painting. An interesting letter in "The Connoiseur" dated April 1932 clearly indicates that the Rooker family lived at Bideford, North Devon, where a building in nearby Barnstaple is named after them. Rooker is included in this Dictionary for "A Game of Bowls on the Bowling Green, outside The Bunch of Grapes Inn, Hurst, Berkshire", watercolour, 8¾in.x 10¾in. The Paul Mellon Collection, Upperville, Va, USA.

Rooney, Mick (b.1944)
Born Epsom, Surrey. Studied at Sutton School of Art (1959-1962), Wimbledon School of Art (1962-1964) and under Professor Carel Weight (q.v.) at the Royal College of Art (1964-1967). Taught part-time in various art colleges. Artist in Residence at Towner Art Gallery, Eastbourne (1983) where his work is represented. Has had several solo exhibitions in London and Holland since 1965.

Roos, William (1808-1878)
Competent provincial painter from Wales who painted equestrian and sporting subjects. His portrait of a gentleman with his hunters and two dogs in a landscape, 23in.x26in., was exh. by Iona Antiques and his portrait of Robert Lowther of Acton, Salop, engraved by G. Fairland and pub. June 1849 was exh. Ackermanns 1979. He was awarded a prize for "The Death of Owen Glyndwr" at the Llangollen National Eisteddford of 1858.

Rope, George Thomas (1846-1929)
Animal and landscape painter, born at Blaxhall, Suffolk. Studied art under the landscape painter W.J. Webbe and became his pupil. He was particularly skilful with a pencil and his sketches are of a very high quality. Apart from a visit to the continent in 1882 he spent his life in Suffolk, working at Wickham Market. He exh. two paintings at the RA and one at SS (1876-1885) and three at the Walker AG. He also exh. a large number of pictures at the Ipswich Art Society with Alfred Munnings (q.v.) whom he is said to have influenced. Wrote and illus. a number of books on wildlife including "Sketches of Farm Favourites" (1881) and "Country Sights and Sounds" (1915). His sporting work includes "Gone to Ground", a scene of a huntsman digging out a fox with hounds looking on and a terrier man with a terrier on a lead, dated 1888. Died in 1929 after a driving accident with his pony and trap.

Roper, Edward (op.1884)
Painter of "Kangaroo Coursing", dated 1884.

Roper, Richard (op.1749-1765)
London sporting painter who lived in Little St. Martin's Lane and who specialised in painting racehorses, dogs and dead game. He was an exhibitor at the Room in Spring Garden in 1761 and the succeeding year. His ability as an artist was not considerable, according to

Edward Edwards' "Anecdotes of Painters who have resided or been born in England" (1808, reprinted 1970), but "sufficient to satisfy the gentleman of the turf and stable". He exh. three paintings at the SA and nine at the FS (1761-1765). His portrait of a bay mare held by a groom with hounds in a landscape, 47in.x67in., was auctioned Christie's 1986.

Roper, Thomas (op.1762)
Painter of equestrian and sporting subjects who operated at a similar date to Richard Roper (q.v.). His painting of a saddled chestnut horse with a groom, a huntsman and two hounds outside a stable, dated 1762, 51½in.x71½in., auctioned Christie's 1965 shows that this artist painted in a very similar style to R. Roper.

Rose, Gerard de
See De Rose

Rose, Sheila (op.1955-1967)
Contemporary painter and illustrator of "The Show Jumping Secret" by Josephine Pullein-Thompson, pub. Collins 1963. Rose illus. a number of children's pony and dog books during the 1950s and 1960s. She works in a sketching style using pen and brush.

Rosenbaum, Julius (op.1953)
Contemporary printmaker whose contribution to football art lies in "The Tackle", engraving, 9½in.x8in., FE.

Ross, Gordon (op.1853)
Painted the portrait of the sporting writer and founder of "The Field" magazine in 1853, Robert Smith Surtees (1803-1864), who was also the creator of the famous Jorrocks series.

Ross, James, Snr. (c.1700-1750)
Painter of equestrian and sporting subjects whose rare and splendid paintings include "The Trotman family hunting in Oxfordshire" and "The Shuckborough family hunting in Warwickshire". A painting of a race meeting, s.&d. 1718, 32in.x71in., provenance the 8th Earl of Rosebery and Lady Cybil Grant was auctioned Christie's (NY) 1984. The most important known set of paintings by this rare artist are a set of four hare-hunting scenes entitled "The Meet" (1729), "Full Cry", "The Check" (1730) and "The Death" (1730), all signed and three dated. "A Meet of Foxhounds" (1732) is in the Paul Mellon Collection, Upperville, Va, USA.

Ross, James, Jnr. (1745-1821)
Worcester-based draughtsman and line engraver, possibly the son of James Ross, Snr. (q.v.) and a pupil of Robert Hancock (q.v.).

Ross, Martin
The pseudonym used by the sportswoman, sporting writer and illustrator Dr. Edith Oenone Somerville (1858-1949) (q.v.).

Ross, Thomas (op.1730-1757)
Portrait and landscape painter, draughtsman of figures and animal subjects. Included in this Dictionary for his painting of a party of "Sportsmen in a Landscape, Netting Partridges", 7⅞n.x11¾in., signed and inscr. The Paul Mellon Collection, Upperville, Va, USA.

Said (Pavière) to be related to James Ross (Snr.), Thomas Ross painted the portrait of William Shenstone, 30in.x22¼in., s.&d. 1738, which is in the National Portrait Gallery.

Rossi, Alexander M. (op.1870-1905)
Painter of portraits and of genre subjects who exh. (1870-1903) at the RA, SS, NWS and elsewhere. Painted in oil and watercolour and included in this Dictionary for his charming watercolour portrait of a young girl tennis player, dated 1885, 14⅞in.x26in., auctioned Sotheby's 1979 and Phillips 1989.

Rossiter, Charles (b.1827 op.1850-1890)
Painter of genre subjects. Married (1860) to the bird painter in watercolour, Frances Rossiter, (op.1882-1898). Charles Rossiter exh. (1880-1890) at the RA, RBA and Walker AG including "Rival Anglers" and "Brighton and Back 3/6" (Birmingham AG). Also included in this Dictionary for his painting "A Game of Bowls", signed, 9½in.x8in., Sotheby's (Sussex).

Roth, George (op.1810-1815)
London painter of fish subjects who exh. at the RA between these dates.

Rothenstein, Michael, RA, HFRE (b.1908)
Painter and printmaker, the younger son of Sir William Rothenstein (1872-1945). Michael Rothenstein studied at Chelsea School of Art (1923) and the Central School (1924-1927). Held first solo exhibition at Matthiesen Gallery (1938). Pub. several books on printing and paintings. His contribution to football art lies in his "A Moment of Victory", engraving and aquatint, 12in.x 16½in., which he contributed to the FE.

Rothwell, Thomas (1742-1807)
Landscape painter and of sporting subjects including a spaniel retrieving a pheasant in a wooded river landscape, 13¼in.x17in., and a huntsman on a bay hunter with his dog, the hunt in full cry beyond, 27¾in.x36¼in., auctioned Phillips 1986.

Rountree, Harry (1878-1950)
New Zealand-born animal painter, lithographer and one of the most important illustrators of children's books in the 20th century. He also depicted his own great sport, golf, in many of his drawings and watercolours. He trained in New Zealand as a lithographer, graduating to the design of jam and pickle labels before deciding to come to England in 1901 to study under Percival Gaskell at the Regent Street Polytechnic and to seek his fortune. His fortune was hard to find but eventually the editor of "Little Folks", S.H. Hammer, asked Rountree to illustrate a book on animals which was such a success that not only was his future as an illustrator secured but these paintings were to influence illustration to the present day. He was a great friend of Harold Earnshaw (q.v.) who later married Mabel Lucy Atwell and they played golf together before Earnshaw lost his right arm in the 1914-1918 war. Rountree, who became President of the London Sketch Club in 1914, illus. Bernard Darwin's book "British Golf Courses" with a series of watercolours. Many of the originals came on to the market in the 1970s. Rountree retired to live at St. Ives, Cornwall.

Rousse, Charles (op.1882-1885)
Birmingham painter of landscapes in watercolour. Included in this Dictionary for his amateur but pleasant watercolour painting of lawn bowls, 18in.x22in., George Hotel, Sollihull.

Rousseau, Henri (1844-1910)
A retired French Customs collector who without any formal training started to paint in middle age. He first exh. his paintings in 1886 but attracted no attention whatsoever until he was discovered by Picasso (q.v.). Rousseau has been described as a folk artist of genius and Picasso and his contemporaries revered him as the godfather of 20th century painting. He is included in this Dictionary for his famous but romantic concept of the game of football in 1908 which hangs in the Solomon R. Guggenheim Museum in New York, "Le Douanier - Les Joueurs de Football", s.&d. 1908, 39⅜in.x31½in., sold for £37,000 from the collection of Mrs. Henry D. Sharpe of Providence, Rhode Island, USA.

Rousseau, Henri Emilien (1875-1933)
Born in Cairo, this artist was a pupil of Jean Léon Gérome (1824-1904), the leading French Orientalist. Rousseau painted several falconry scenes many of which are repro. in Christian de Chamerlat's book "Falconry and Art" (1987).

Rousseau, Percival Leonard (1859-1937)
American animal painter of English game dogs including portraits of "English Setters", "Setters in a Field", "'Bob' Finds A Covey" and "A Point to the Far River Bank". Rousseau studied in Paris, under Lefebvre, Herman Léon and Robert Fleury and exh. at the Paris Salon.

Roussillon, Maurice ("O'Galop") (1867-1946)
French poster artist who under the pseudonym "O'Galop" was responsible for the original concept of the Michelin Man, Mr. Bibendum, originated in 1896. The design proved so successful with the Michelin Company that it was kept in use until 1920. "O'Galop" was responsible for a number of different Michelin motor posters up to the 1920s.

Rowbotham, J.B. (op.1860)
Painted with John Brown (q.v.) "The Great Contest between Tom Sayers and the American, John Heenan" which took place on 17 April 1860. This famous boxing picture includes portraits of both artists on the right-hand side.

Rowbotham, Thomas Charles Leeson, RI (1823-1875)
Landscape painter in watercolour and an engraver and lithographer. Son of Thomas Leeson Rowbotham (1783-1853), the landscape painter. Pupil of his father. Exh. (1840-1875) at the RA, SS, NWS and elsewhere. Elected RI (1851) and succeeded his father as Professor of Drawing at the Royal Naval School, New Cross. He painted a number of angling scenes including "Anglers Fishing a Rough Stretch of River", dated 1847, watercolour, auctioned Phillips 1986 and "A Punt and Fisherman by Eel Traps" painted 1874, watercolour, 7¾in.x18¾in., auctioned Sotheby's 1974.

Rowden, Thomas (1842-1926)
Landscape and animal painter who was born in Exeter and specialised in views of Devon and Cornwall. An example of his work is in the Exeter Museum. He was predominantly a watercolourist exhibiting twice at the RHA from 1884. He painted a number of sporting subjects including "Terriers and Hounds Rabbiting", "Norwich and Cairn Terriers Rabbiting", "Pointers Rabbiting", and portraits of "Cock and Hen Pheasants".

Rowland, Bertram (op.1902-1908)
Presumably related to Ralph Rowland (q.v.). A pen, ink and watercolour sketch entitled "A Hunting We Will Go", s.&d. 1902, 5½in.x7in., was auctioned Christie's (Sth. Ken.) 1983.

Rowland, Ralph (op.1905)
Presumably related to Bertram Rowland (q.v.). Humorous illustrator who contributed golf sketches to "Punch" (1905).

Rowlandson, George Derville (1861-1930)
Equestrian painter who was born in India. Studied art in Gloucester, Westminster and Paris. Exh. at the RA and BI (1911-1918). Contributed to "The Illustrated London News" (1897-1900) and "The English Illustrated Magazine" (1899-1900). Painted in both oil and watercolour. "Games of Polo", a pair, 41in.x28in., s.&d. 1902, exh. Colnaghi, June 1986.

Rowlandson, Thomas (1756-1827)
Distinguished draughtsman, etcher and aquatint engraver of political and social satires, sporting subjects, landscapes and topographical views. Son of a bankrupt wool merchant. Entered the RA Schools. Went to Paris to study at the Ecole d'Académie Royal, under Pigalle, until 1775. Returned for a further term to the RA where he was awarded a silver medal in 1777. Exh. his first work at the RA in 1775. Employed by Mr. Ackermann to engrave the plates for the famous "Dr. Syntax in Search of the Picturesque". Much of his work was painted in watercolour and he engraved a great many sporting sketches including "Hunting Scenes in Berkshire" (1801), four plates, each 18¼in.x23¼in. He was particularly fascinated by fencing and painted at least five recorded examples of a man and a woman fencing including "Henry Angelo and Madame Cain Fencing", pen/ink/watercolour, 6⅜in.x9⅞in., The Paul Mellon Collection, Upperville, Va, USA. His drawing in 1787 of "Mr. Henry Angelo's Fencing Academy" is in the Cecil Higgins AG and Museum, Bedford - see also Rawlins for later drawing of Angelo's Fencing Academy. Fencing, billiards, ballooning, wrestling, rowing, cricket, boxing and racing were just some of the sports he painted. His brother-in-law was the artist Samuel Howitt (q.v.) who married Rowlandson's sister. The game of cricket featured quite strongly in Rowlandson's work. "Cricket in White Conduit Fields" c.1790 is seen from the west and can be compared with Robert Dighton's (q.v.) painting of a similar view. Rowlandson also painted "Lords Cricket Ground at St. John's Wood" and the famous "Rural Sports - or a Cricket Match Extraordinary" which

featured lady cricketers and could, depending on your interpretation of Rowlandson's intentions, as Marjorie Pollard put it "savour of exploitation".

Rowntree, Kenneth (b.1915)

Painter who studied at the Ruskin School of Drawing, Oxford and the Slade School of Art. Not by the remotest chance a painter of sporting subjects but included in this Dictionary for the collaboration he made with John Skeaping (q.v.) on the portrait of the racehorse "Ballymoss" winning the King George VI and Queen Elizabeth Stakes at Ascot in 1958, signed by both artists. Rowntree exh. (1936-1940) mainly at the NEAC.

Rudge, Bradford (1805-1885)

Draughtsman, landscape painter and lithographer of architectural subjects and one coaching print after his own work, "The Bedford Times", 12¾in.x21¼in. Rudge settled in Bedford in 1837 and the stagecoach was clearly a local attraction.

Ruggiero, Vincent, FRSA (b.1925)

Contemporary painter of portraits and golf subjects which he calls "Sportraits". Lives in Sussex. "A View of the Clubhouse", the Royal and Ancient at St. Andrews, 17¼in.x23¼in., artist's collection.

Ruggles, W.H. (op.1833-1846)

Equestrian artist from Lewisham who exh. two pictures at the RA in 1833 and 1846, one of which was a portrait of a favourite hunting mare. A portrait of a chestnut racehorse with a jockey up, signed, 18½in.x26½in. was auctioned Christie's (1977).

Rungius, Carl Clemens Moritz (1869-1959)

Celebrated big game artist and illustrator. The eldest of nine children he was born near Berlin to a Lutheran minister, the Revd. Heinrich Rungius and his wife Magdalene. His grandfather, a gifted draughtsman and ornithologist, encouraged Carl's enthusiasm for sketching and natural history. He studied art at the Berlin Academy of Fine Arts where he specialised in representing animal form and anatomy. There he met Richard Friese who was fifteen years older than himself, the most brilliant student of his day and destined to become Europe's finest wildlife artist. After a visit to Maine, USA in 1894 Rungius left Germany for good in 1897 to set up as a freelance artist at Green Point, Long Island, USA. He worked first of all as a magazine illustrator to "Everybodies" and "McClures" and contributed sketches to "Recreation" and "Forest and Stream". After his marriage to his first cousin Louise he moved to a studio in New York where he found that regular sales of his American big game paintings earned high prices. He tended to paint large canvases, very often in the field, and sometimes as large as 66in.x82in. He painted one of a series commissioned for the New York Zoo by that great hunter and naturalist, Dr. William T. Hornaday, who was Rungius' first patron. Towards the latter half of his life Rungius became almost single minded in his pursuit of hunting and painting, to the dismay, it is said, of his wife. Distinctions were heaped upon him and his paintings were exh. nationwide but despite accumulated wealth Rungius

lived in almost monastic simplicity. As no other painter before him he captured the spaciousness and vitality of his beloved Rocky Mountains and the nobility of their great wild creatures. He exh. prolifically at the Society of American Artists.

Ruprecht, Ernst

Leading Swiss poster artist who was responsible for the designs of the posters used to advertise the Swiss Grands Prix from 1947 until motor racing was discontinued in Switzerland in 1955 following the tragedy at Le Mans in the same year.

Rush, Stephen (op.1987)

Contemporary painter of gymnastic scenes in water-colour including "Isometric Bars" s.&d. 1987 and "On the Pommel Horse", s.&d. 1987. W.H. Lane 1988.

Rushton, Raymond (op.1913-1932)

Several fine pieces of Royal Worcester porcelain are painted and signed by Raymond Rushton and dated between 1913 and 1932. Rushton painted many sporting scenes on china including "Sailing Yachts Racing", 3½in. diam. porcelain plaque, s.&d. 1913, Sotheby's (Sussex) 1990.

Russell, Charles Marian (1864-1926)

St. Louis-born, self-taught painter and sculptor who painted the world of the American West before white civilisation changed both the face of the land and the lives of the people. He was an experienced cowboy and had a profound knowledge of cattle and horses. Russell's paintings serve as a magnificent tribute to one of the most important rituals of Indian plains life, that of buffalo hunting. He created a large number of paintings and over one hundred bronzes and had twenty-eight one-man shows in New York city. He also wrote several books including "Trails Ploughed Under".

Russell, James A. (op.1869-1887)

Scottish painter who lived near the river Spey. The Russell family, and there appear to have been a number of them, painted angling scenes at the end of the 19th century. Indeed, several paintings are signed by both James and John Russell (q.v.) which indicates that at least two of them collaborated. James seems to have specialised only in still lifes of fresh water fish. Exh. one painting in 1886 at the RHA. He signed his work both J.A. Russell and James A. Russell.

Russell, John, RA (1745-1806)

Portrait painter in oil and in pastel whose sporting portraiture includes "The Rev. John H. Chandler as a Boy", 49in.x39in., painted in 1767, "The Sons of Thomas Pitt", pastel, 30in.x25in., s.&d. 1804 and a "Portrait of a Young Boy holding a Cricket Ball", pastel, 23⅝in.x17¼in., Pilkington Collection. Cricket also featured in Russell's portrait of The Hon. Edward Rice as a young boy, who is holding the top of a cricket bat, identical to the one featured in Russell's portrait of the Pitt brothers. Russell's association with Francis Cotes (q.v.), whose famous oil of Lewis Cage with cricket bat was painted in 1768, may have encouraged his interest in the game. Russell's portrait of HRH The Prince of Wales in the uniform of the Royal Kentish

Bowmen, 1798, is in the collection of Her Majesty the Queen. The Prince of Wales, later George IV (1762-1830) was influential in restoring archery to a prestige it had lacked since the days of Henry VIII. The Royal Kentish Bowmen was formed in 1785 and was one of the most exclusive as well as one of the earliest of the archery societies. The Prince of Wales took a particular interest in the society, even finding time to shoot with its members at Dartford Heath, near London.

Russell, John (Jack) (Revd.), MFH, MOH (1795-1883)

Born at Dartmouth, Russell bred a pack of hounds when he was a boy at Blundells School, Tiverton, before going up to Oxford where he hunted as much as his studies allowed and more. He bought a terrier from a milkman at Oxford from whom he then bred and developed what is now known as the Jack Russell terrier. He used the terrier, which he hunted with his own pack of hounds, to bolt the foxes from their earths. He never docked their tails; in fact he made good use of them to pull the dogs out from the earths. A fine huntsman with enormous stamina, it is said that whenever he used a whip to turn hounds he never lost a fox by a false caste. See also under Tyddesley Davis and H.B. Young.

Russell, John B. (op.1869-1918)

Presumably a close relation of James A. Russell (q.v.) with whom he collaborated on a painting entitled "Otters with a Salmon", signed by both artists. John Russell exh. one painting at the RSA (1880). Both artists specialised in still lifes of freshwater fish, particularly salmon and trout, and worked in the Strathspey area. Many still life paintings of fish have been wrongly attributed to John Russell RA (1745-1806) (q.v.) since John B. Russell sometimes signed his work "John Russell" (although more normally John B. Russell) and rarely dated it.

Russell, Sir Walter Westley, RA, RWS, NEAC (1867-1949)

Portrait and landscape painter of genre and some sporting subjects. Studied at Westminster School of Art, under Fred Brown (q.v.). Exh. at the RA from 1891 and at the NEAC from 1893. Assistant Professor at the Slade School (1895-1927). Keeper of the RA (1927-1942). Painted a number of landscapes in Sussex including "The Golf Links at Littlehampton" which Russell exh. at the NEAC in 1909 (No. 340).

Russell, William (op.c.1880s)

Victorian painter of angling still lifes, possibly related to John B. and James A. Russell (qq.v.).

Rutard, Carl (op.1660-1680)

Painter of hunting subjects, many of them later engraved by L.P. Boitard (q.v.), who lived in London from 1738.

Rutherford, R.H. (op.1883-1897)

Liverpool artist who was better known as a portrait painter. Exh. at the Walker AG (1883-1897). Lived at Bootle, Lancs. Father of the painter Harry Rutherford (b.1903). Painted a great number of golfing sketches including a watercolour showing "Boys Playing Golf on Sand Hills", dated 1893 and "Caddy Boys Practising Golf behind Ainsdale, Lancs.", Phillips (Scotland) 1986.

Ryck, John de

See De Ryck

Ryder, J.T. (op.1913-1925)

Interesting painter of portraits of racing pigeons, usually posed in a landscape and competently painted, dated and inscr.

Ryman, E.V. (19th century)

Pavière records an undated portrait of a bay hunter held by a groom in a landscape by this artist.

Ryot of Newcastle, J.R. (op.1817-1860)

Provincial painter of equestrian and sporting subjects presumably from the Newcastle area since he inscr. many of his paintings "Newcastle". His work includes "Silvertail" a portrait of a palomino racehorse in a wooded river landscape, signed, inscr. "Newcastle" and dated 1823, "Snipe" winner of the Northumberland and Durham Steeplechase, dated 1845 and inscr. Other titles and portraits include the hunter "Sherrif" and the foxhound "Currdew", "Earth Stopping" dated 1844, "The Kill" dated 1828, "A Favourite Friend", dated 1847, "Gentlemen with their Greyhounds and Horses", in an extensive landscape, dated 1817 and "A Gentleman out Riding with his Dogs and his Gamekeeper", dated 1860. Ryot's work which is extremely competent and pleasing is usually signed, dated and inscr.

Rysbrack, Gerrard (1696-1773)

Flemish painter of game still lifes, youngest brother of the sculptor John Michael Rysbrack (1694-1770). Master at Antwerp (1725). Brother of Pieter Andreas Rysbrack (q.v.).

Rysbrack, Pieter Andreas (1690-1748)

Flemish painter of game still lifes and hunting scenes. Born in Paris, the eldest son of Pieter Rysbrack (1665-1729) an Antwerp landscape painter, and brother of Gerrard Rysbrack (q.v.). Master at Antwerp (1710-1711).

S

Sablet, Jacques (1749-1803)
Swiss-born, French trained painter who lived in Rome, the brother of the artist Jean François Sablet (1745-1819). Known as "Le Romain", Sablet painted the portrait of "Thomas Hope of Amsterdam playing Cricket at Rome", 24½in.x19¾in., s.&d. 1792 and inscribed "Roma" (MCC Collection). Thomas Hope (1769-1831) came from a family of Scottish bankers, at one time based in Amsterdam. When he and Sablet met in Rome he was on a Grand Tour. The curved cricket bat, which Hope is holding in the picture, is long and slender and even old fashioned for that date but when in Rome ....! Hope eventually settled in Surrey where he became a great patron, collector and connoisseur of the neo-classical era. Sablet, who became a friend, was retained by Hope to advise on the decorations of his London house in 1800.

"Sabretache"
Author of "Shires and Provinces" pub. Eyre & Spottiswoode Ltd. 1926.

Sadler, Walter Dendy, RBA, ROI (1845-1923)
Painter of genre subjects and of fishing, golfing and bowling scenes, his subjects often dressed in historical costume. Studied art at Heatherleys School in London and with Wilhelm Simmler in Dusseldorf. Exh. at the RA from 1873, also at SS, GG and elsewhere. Sadler painted a number of golf pictures including "Stymied", 22in.x32in., and "A Caddy to the Royal and Ancient", dated 1914, which was repro. as an etching by J. Doby. Many of Sadler's golf paintings were set in Scottish landscapes and some were used as book illustrations. His portrait of an angler on a riverside path shows a plump, ruddy faced gentleman carrying his cased rods over his shoulder. His fine angling scene "The Pegged Down Fishing Match" and his pair "Fishing - A Pleasure" and "Fishing - A Necessity", dated 1874 give some indication of this artist's passion for the sport. "A Game of Bowls", again a costume piece, shows a bowling scene of the old English type for there are neither ditches nor banks. Sadler moved to Hemingford Grey near St. Ives, Huntingdon after 1896 where he spent the rest of his life and where he could indulge his passion for fishing. He had three daughters and two sons. Elected RBA (1880) and ROI (1883).

Sadler, William (op.1765-1788)
Painter of Irish portraits, history and landscapes who very rarely dated his work. "A Stag Hunt at Killarney" was auctioned Sotheby's 1982. Sadler entered the Drawing School at Dublin in 1765. His better known work includes an equestrian portrait of King William III with a battle beyond, 13in.x18in., Sotheby's 1988.

St. John Jones, Herbert
See Jones

Salaman, Michael (b.1911)
Landscape and portrait painter who studied art at the Slade School and in Paris, at the Académie Ranson. Exh. at the RA, LG and the Leicester Galleries. Retrospective exhibition held at Morley Gallery (1975). Visiting tutor at the RA Schools, Chelsea School of Art, Camberwell School of Arts and Crafts. His contribution to sporting art lies in his football painting "Miners Game at Sandown", 30½in.x23¾in., which he contributed to the FE in 1953 and which is in the V & A Museum, London.

Salisbury, Frank. O., RI, ROI, RP (1874-1962)
London painter of portraits and of a number of sporting personalities. Studied art at Heatherleys, under John Crompton, and at the RA Schools where he won the Landseer Scholarship and in Italy, Germany and France. Exh. at the RA from 1899, also at the RP, RI, ROI and at the Paris Salon. His portrait of Sydney Shephard in hunting attire, dated November 1940, was auctioned Sotheby's 1984.

Salkin, Emile (1900-1977)
"Polo wed strijd Frankrijk - Belgie", an original engraving, 9½in.x7¼in., depicting a polo match between France and Belgium which took place on 11 May 1938. Emile Salkin, a Belgian artist, was interested in many different art forms in the 20th century. During the 1930s, his figurative period, many equestrian riders formed an important place in his work - Royal Albert I Library, Brussels.

"Salloon"
The caricaturist who worked for "The Daily Mirror" in the 1950s, drawing motor racing drivers. Many of his portraits were collected and repro. "Motor Racing Drivers Past and Present", pub. by Shell Mex and BP Ltd. in 1956 to mark the sixtieth anniversary of the British motor industry.

Salter, T.F. (op.1825)
Included in this Dictionary for his (since he is described as "Gent") illustrations to "The Anglers Guide on the Art of Angling", pub. Sherwood & Co., London (1825).

Sambourne, Edward Linley (1844-1910)
Black and white artist whose cartoons for "Punch" from 1867 included football scenes. He drew a number of political sketches with a slight sporting reference and his cartoon of Randolph Churchill and Neville Chamberlain boxing is one example. His daughter was Mrs. Messel, the mother of the late Oliver Messel, the designer, and of Anne, Countess of Rosse, the mother of the Earl of Snowdon.

Samuel, George (op.1785-d.1824)
Landscape painter who illus. the 1808 edition of "The Compleat Angler" by Izaak Walton. Poor George Samuel was crushed to death under a wall which fell on him whilst he was sketching.

Samuels, J.
A portrait of a grey hunter and a bay hunter in a wooded landscape, 15½in.x19½in., was auctioned Christie's 1985.

Sandby, Paul, RA (1725-1809)
Important landscape painter, etcher and aquatint engraver who was influenced by the Dutch masters. Born in Nottingham but lived for thirty-seven years at 4, St. George's Row, off Hanover Square from 1772 until his death. Sandby worked for many years with his elder brother, Thomas (q.v.) who was a draughtsman and architect. They were both founder members of the RA in 1768. A favourite with King George III and Queen Charlotte, Sandby gave drawing lessons to many members of the royal family. He was a detailed topographical artist and his watercolours form an accurate account of views and events of his day. His fine view in watercolour of Wakefield Lodge and Park with mares and foals, dated 1767, was painted for the 3rd Duke of Grafton who held regular race meetings on the lawn in the 1770s and 1780s (The Paul Mellon Collection, Upperville, Va, USA). With his brother Thomas he also made drawings of the racehorses "Eclipse", "Spilletta", and "Miss Elliot" the dam of "Gimcrack". Sandby's painting of golfers playing in front of Edinburgh Castle, c.1746/7, 11½in.x18½in., is in the collection of the British Museum. This was clearly painted during the period that Sandby was working in Scotland and is the earliest representation by at least thirty years of golf being played in Scotland. The use of caddies at this date is an unusual feature of the drawing. "Landscape with a Cricket Match", painted in gouache in 1774, is in the MCC Collection. Sandby learnt to etch in Edinburgh. His importance as a print maker lies in his adoption and development of the aquatint process which had been brought to England from France by the Hon. C. Greville. "XII Views in South Wales (1774-1775)" was the first book to be pub. in England with aquatint plates. The original edns. of Sandby's aquatints were printed in sepia or dark brown.

Sandby, Thomas, RA (1721-1798)
Topographical draughtsman and watercolourist, the elder brother of Paul Sandby, RA (q.v.). Sandby, who was a founder member of the RA in 1768, became its first Professor of Architecture. He also became Deputy Ranger of Windsor Great Park, through his friendship

with the Duke of Cumberland, formed when "the butcher" was putting down the Forty Five Rebellion in Scotland. Sandby and his brother were in Scotland at the time, assisting in the survey of the Highlands undertaken by the Government. Sandby also featured cricket in his watercolour of an Old Mansion, 13½in.x 21in., held in the collection of the Nottingham Castle Museum and AG.

Sandby, W. (Major)
A watercolour painting of a shooting party by this artist was auctioned Christie's 1986.

Sanders, Christopher (op.1953)
Contemporary painter whose contribution to sporting art lies with his football painting entitled "The Pitch shall be .....", 30½in.x26½in., exh. at the FE.

Sanders, W. (op.1826-1838)
London painter of game subjects whose work exh. at SS included a painting of a brace of partridge.

Sanderson, Robert (op.1860-1905)
Edinburgh based painter of dog portraits who contributed dog subjects to "Chums" (1903). Exh. (1880-1903) at the RSA, RSW and the Walker AG, Liverpool. Sanderson also painted coastal fishing scenes in both oil and watercolour.

Sanderson-Wells, John, RI, RBA (1872-1955)
Painter of equestrian and sporting subjects. Studied art at the Slade and at the Académie Julian in Paris. Exh. at the RA from 1895 and elected RI (1903) and RBA (1896). Sanderson-Wells specialised in hunting scenes which he painted in both oil and watercolour, in a style not dissimilar to that of George Wright (q.v.). He also painted a number of coaching scenes often in historical costume. His work became widely known through numerous prints. Named hunts which Sanderson-Wells painted include the Devon and Somerset Staghounds, the Whaddon Chase and Berkeley Hunts, and the Beaufort Hunt near Tetbury. His very few racing scenes include the Grand National Steeplechase of 1934 with "Really True" (second in the 1933 Grand National) and "Forbra" (Grand National winner 1932) jumping Valentines.

Sandham, Henry (1842-1912)
Painter of portraits and field sports who was born in Montreal, Canada, but moved to England at the end of the 19th century. Included in this Dictionary for the golfing image he produced in 1899 for use in an advertising campaign for Canadian Club Whisky, Burlington Gallery, London, and for his painting "Lawn Tennis" pub. as a chromolithograph by L. Prang & Co. (1877). Hallmark Historical Coll., Kansas City, Missouri. Sandham exh. at the RA and elsewhere (1905-1908).

Sands, B. (op.1852-1863)
Portraits painted by this artist of a bay hunter in a stable and a pair of grey hunters in a stable, s.&d. 1859 and 1862, 20in.x25in., were auctioned Christie's 1968. Other equestrian portraits, s.&d., are recorded.

Sandys-Lumsdaine, Leesa (1936-1985)

Equestrian and sporting painter who spent her early childhood in India and trained at the Cheltenham School of Art. Held her first exhibition at the Tryon Gallery in 1967 and had her first one-man exhibition there in 1973. Amongst the classic racehorses she painted are "Arkle", "Mill Reef" and "Nijinsky" and her inspired entry "Echoes of the Past" won the Horse and Hound Centenary Art Competition in 1984. Many of her paintings were reproduced as limited edn. prints and among the best known prints after her work are "Summer Silks and Winter Woollies", "Saturday Night and Sunday Morning", "Absolute Heaven and Absolute Hell". Her painting "Match of the Day", showing two teams of pigs playing football with a turnip, show that this artist had a keen sense of humour. A great dog lover, Leesa Sandys-Lumsdaine bred lurchers and greyhounds, one of which, "Luda Hussar", won the coveted Waterloo Cup.

Sanguinetti, Eduardo (ex.1880-1889)

Italian sculptor and portrait painter. Exh. at the RA, RBA, RI, ROI and elsewhere. His portrait of Lord Suffield, Master of the Buckhounds, Lady Julia Follett and Frank Goodall, the whipper-in, entitled "Full Cry", 72in.x52in., was auctioned Christie's 1981.

Sant, James, RA (1820-1916)

Prolific portrait painter who enjoyed the patronage of many noble families, including the royal family. Appointed portrait painter to Queen Victoria (1872). Included in this Dictionary for "Miss Martineau's Garden" (1873), Tate Gallery, London, which shows a game of croquet taking place at the height of this game's fashion amongst society, since it was about the only acceptable game in which male and female players could play together. Sant, who studied art under John Varley and Augustus Callcott, exh. at the RA (1840-1904). Elected RA (1869) but retired (1914).

Sargent, John Singer, RA (1856-1925)

Important painter of portraits, landscapes and several fishing scenes, many painted during his stay at Sunndal, Norway in 1901 with his friend, the collector George McCulloch, who was an ardent fisherman. His portrait of Alec McCulloch entitled "The Young Salmon Fisher" was one of those painted at Sunndal in August 1901, 11¼in.x8⅜in. Sargent, who studied in Rome, Florence and Paris painted in oil but later turned increasingly to watercolour. He exh. at the RA from 1882 and was elected RA 1897.

Sartorius, Francis (1734-1804)

Painter of equestrian and sporting subjects. Son of John Sartorius and father of John Nost and John Francis Sartorius (qq.v.). Probably taught to paint by his father since he exh. at the FS with his father. Exh. on his own account at the SA (1778-1791) and at the RA (1775-1790), mostly portraits of horses and dogs including a pair of "His Majesty's Coach Horses". His obituary appeared in "The Sporting Magazine" 1804 in which it claimed he was "married and cohabited with five successive wives" which, if true, is sporting in itself. His portrait of "Diomed" owned by Sir Charles Bunbury, Bt., winner of the first Derby, 4 May 1780, with his jockey, Sam Arnull, wearing the new black boots with brown tops, a development from the former white stockings and short gaiters, is probably amongst the best known of his equestrian portraits. His horse portraits, often featuring cropped ears, are painted in the naïve style associated with his dates. Sartorius also painted cock-fighting scenes.

Sartorius, G.W. (op.1773-1785)

Exh. at the FS (1773). His painting of a bay hunter tethered to a tree in a landscape, dated 1785, 28in.x 35in., was auctioned Christie's 1968. I am unable to discover how G.W. fits into the Sartorius family unless he was also William Sartorius. If so, then he was better known for his fruit still lifes.

Sartorius, John (1700-c.1780)

Portrait and equestrian painter, born in Nuremburg. Father of Francis Sartorius (q.v.) and the grandfather of John Nost and John Francis Sartorius (qq.v.). Exh. horse portraits, shooting and dog pictures in England at the FS (1768-1780). His patrons included Lords Melbourne and Abergavenny and the Hon. George Henry Nevill. His work is rare and he heads the family of what Waterhouse describes as "four generations of rather dreary and very prolific horse and sporting painters".

Sartorius, John Francis (op.c.1772-1831)

Son of Francis Sartorius and grandson of John Sartorius (qq.v.). He exh. at the RA (1797-1829). His sporting paintings include racing and coursing as well as hunting, shooting and game birds. His portrait of a huntsman in grey livery holding a hare with three greyhounds at Ashdown Park, amongst the trees, dated 1772, was auctioned Sotheby's 1968 (The Craven Collection).

Sartorius, John Nost (Nott) (1759-1828)

Equestrian and sporting painter, son of Francis and grandson of John and brother of John Francis Sartorius (qq.v.). Probably the most prolific of all the Sartorius family. J.N. Sartorius exh. at the FS, the Society of Artists and the RA (1776-1824). Many of his paintings were engraved and several of his works were pub. in "The Sporting Magazine". His patrons included the Prince of Wales, the Earl of Derby and the Earl of Darlington (who was also painted by Ben Marshall (q.v.) and by Robert Frankland (q.v.) with the Raby pack), Lord Foley, Charles James Fox and Christopher Wilson. He seems to have spent a considerable amount of time at an inn in Carshalton, Surrey (Ziltzer) and worked frequently at Newmarket. Ziltzer lists forty-two prints, mainly portraits of racehorses, hunting and racing scenes. An interesting painting by Sartorius of the "Finish of the Oatland Stakes at Ascot Heath" in 1791 shows a distant view of Oatlands Park, near Weybridge, Surrey, the royal hunting property at the time of Queen Elizabeth I. The house can also be seen in the background of the portrait of "Anne of Denmark Beagling" by Paul Van Somer (q.v.).

Sartorius, S.J. (late 18th century)
A pair of paintings of a sportsman shooting with his dogs and loading the saddle bag, clearly signed S.J. Sartorius, were shown to Sotheby's but never came to auction.

Sartorius, William (op.1730)
Painter of fruit still lifes. Was he also G.W. Sartorius (q.v.)? A painting of turkeys and chickens, with two cocks sparring in an evening landscape, s.&d. 1730, 25in.x30in., was auctioned Bonhams 1982.

Sato, Take (op.1920)
Japanese artist whose British début at the Burlington Gallery, Leicester Square in 1920 showed a glimpse of undulating green turf dotted with green flags and tiny moving figures in his painting entitled "Minehead Golf Course", painted on silk ("Connoisseur" March 1920).

Saville, W. (1862-1867)
Landscape painter from Dover, Kent. "The Shooting Party" shows a group of gentlemen taking refreshment with the spoils of the shoot and their dogs around them, s.&d. 1862, 29in.x24in. Exh. six works at BI (1862-1867). Titles include "Kentish Sheep" and "On the Cliffs near Dover".

Sawrey, Hugh (b.1923)
Australian landscape painter who painted a number of horse racing scenes including "Cloncurry Races" and "Between Races". The bulk of his work is of Australian sheep shearing and cattle scenes

Sayce, Harry H., FIAL, NDD
Contemporary painter whose contribution to sporting art lies in his painting "Football by Floodlight", 27½in.x 19½in., contributed to the FE. Sayce, who studied at Hammersmith School of Art, exh. at the RA and RBA. Head of Art Department, Paddington School, Fellow of the International Institute of Arts and Letters.

Sayer, Mary Anne (op.1783-1838?)
A watercolour painting of a black horse, dated 1838, 8½in.x10½in., by this artist was auctioned in 1986. She may well have been the same Sayer who exh. flower pictures at the FS in 1783.

Scaddon, Robert (op.1743-1774)
Portrait painter and miniaturist who may have been a pupil of Thomas Hudson (q.v.). His portrait of the cricket-playing William Rice, 59in.x42½in., s.&d. 1744, holding a bat in his left hand, is in the MCC Collection (previously auctioned Christie's 1933).

Scaife, Thomas (op.1889-1912)
Painter of animal and equestrian subjects, including a bay stallion in a stable, dated 1889, 17in.x19½in. and a wire haired fox terrier in a wood, dated 1912, 20in.x 26in., auctioned Woolley and Wallis 1987.

Scanlan, Richard Robert (op.c.1828 d.1876)
Watercolour painter of Irish origin of equestrian portraits and sporting scenes who exh. at the RA (1837-1859). A large number of his RA exhibits were horse portraits including two of "His Majesty's State Horses" (1837) and a portrait of the racehorse "Lottery"

winner of the first Grand National (1840). A number of Scanlan's works were inscr. "Cork" including a portrait of a young officer with his greyhound, a watercolour painted in 1828, 13½in.x10in. Scanlan's work includes cock and dog fighting scenes, painted in watercolour, hunting and racing scenes.

Scannell, Edith M.S. (op.1870-1921)
Figure and animal painter in oil and watercolour. Illustrator of childrens' books who exh. at the RA (1870-1903) and also at SS. Painted a number of dog portraits including "Jack Russell Terriers". Books illus. include "The Highwaymen" (1888), "Pets and Playmates" (1887), "The Cousin from India" (1919) and "The Child of the Caravan", E.M. Green c.1888.

Schermer, Cornelis Albertus Johannes (1824-1915)
Dutch painter of military and equestrian subjects including "A Day at the Races", signed, watercolour, 16⅜in.x28in. Christie's (NY) 1986.

Scheuerer, Julius (1859-1913)
German painter of domestic scenes particularly poultry. His hunting painting "On the Fox's Heels", 6¼in.x 9½in., was auctioned Sotheby's (Sussex) 1985.

Schleich, Auguste (1814-1865)
German painter of several gun dog and game paintings including "A Sleeping Fox", dated 1850, watercolour, and "A Retriever with Dead Game", dated '49.

Schmitz, Jules Leonard (op.1824)
Early 19th century German painter whose portrait "A Chestnut Hunter", standing in a wooded landscape, dated 1824, 18½in.x36½in., was auctioned Christie's 1988.

Schofield, John (op.1882-d.1931)
An impressive watercolour of the Rochdale hounds entitled "A Meet at Lydgate", 21 November 1885, inscr. "Shaughraun" with Richard Heap clearing the stone wall at 5ft 10in., 20in.x26in., was auctioned Christie's 1988. Schofield exh. from 1882 at Manchester, Birmingham and at the RCA. Lived at Rochdale, Lancs.

Schreyvogel, Charles (1861-1912)
American painter who specialised, like his contemporaries Charles Marian Russell and Frederic Remington (qq.v.), in scenes of the American West including buffalo hunting. Apprenticed first to a die sinker and then to a New York lithographer. Born in New York. Became a member of the National Academy of Design (1901).

Schultz, Hermann (op.1889)
German portrait painter who painted the tennis playing brothers Leonard Reginald King (1878-1923) and Edwin James King (1877-?) in 1889, inscr. "London", 35½in.x27⅝in. The sportsmen are painted wearing striped blazers and holding tennis rackets. The portrait is in a private collection, USA.

Schwanfelder, Charles Henry (1773-1837)
Very talented Leeds sporting and animal painter, the son of a German house painter. He started his career by helping his father who also painted clock faces, snuff

boxes and tea trays for the local gentry in his spare time. He was a great admirer of William Turner (q.v.) and made numerous sketching trips to Scotland, Yorkshire, the Lake District and Wales, painting landscapes. The quality of his animal sketches led him to be appointed official animal painter to the Prince Regent in 1816 for whom he painted at least three horse portraits for the royal collections. In 1821 he was reappointed to George IV. He was an enthusiastic supporter of the Northern Society for the Encouragement of the Arts and exh. twenty-four paintings at the Society's first exhibition. He exh. ten paintings at the RA and six at the BI (1809-1826) including a portrait of an Arab horse, the property of the Prince Regent (1814). Despite his success, he had his critics. "The Leeds Mercury" commenting on his exhibits in the Northern Society's Exhibition of 1810 accused him of being a "Jack of all trades" and suggested that he should keep to animal painting and not attempt human portraits since "he has little talent for portraiture". Nevertheless commissions poured in for portraits and landscapes as well as for hunters, sporting dogs and even dead game. His close friend William Frederick (q.v.) was a specialist in this field. An indication of Schwanfelder's success at the time is apparent from the Leeds Exhibition List of 1825 where his painting "Loch Lomond" could command a price of £63 and his terriers and cat £52.10s. against poor John Gaunt's (q.v.) spaniel and woodcocks at £4.10s. Even the thirty year old J.F. Herring Snr.'s (q.v.) "Asses" was comparatively lowly priced at £10.10s. Schwanfelder travelled regularly to London from Leeds "well muffled up on the box seat of the coach" which incidentally took thirty-two hours from London to Leeds in 1809 and twenty-four hours in 1830. One of his major patrons was George Lane Fox of Bramham Park. His sporting portraiture included a saddled grey racehorse held by a groom on the gallops with other riders beyond, dated 1837, 25in.x30in., auctioned by Christie's in 1990 and the cricket loving William and Charles Chadwick at Burley Lodge, 39⅝in.x33⅝in., s.&d. 1824. (Art Gallery and Temple Newsam House, Leeds.)

Schwartz, Daniel (b.1929)
American illustrator for several national magazines sometimes of American football scenes. Studied at the Rhode Island School of Design and won a scholarship to the Art Students League of New York, studying with Yasuo Kuniyoshi and John Frazier. He pub. his first illustration for Theatre Arts in 1953. Has had numerous one-man shows and won seven gold medals from the Society of Illustrators.

Scianna, Francesco
Fine contemporary motor racing artist who paints in an abstract style. Eight sketches featuring Alfa Romeo, Maserati, E.R.A. Bugatti and others, each 39½in.x 27in. were auctioned Christie's 1989.

Scott, John (1774-1827)
Animal painter and engraver who made illustrations for "The Sporting Magazine". Amongst his best known engravings are the plates which he executed for Daniel's

"Rural Sports" and "The Sportsman's Repository", pub. in 1820 and dedicated to Sir Charles Bunbury, Bt. (1740-1821) the sportsman brother of the amateur artist Henry William Bunbury (q.v.). "The Sportsman's Repository" contained a series of prints by this engraver who also contributed some fine work to two edns. of "The Compleat Angler". A J. Scott exh. a painting of a dead hare and a grouse, along with such distinguished artists as James Ward (q.v.) and John Crome at the Gallery of the Northern Society for the Encouragement of the Fine Arts (Leeds) in 1825.

Scott, John (1802-1885)
Marine painter who studied painting under John Carmichael (1800-1868), the Newcastle marine painter. John Scott was born and remained all his life in the region of Newcastle. His painting "The Ascension Day Regatta on the Tyne", with the Mayor's barge and cheering crowds watching from moored boats, dated 1844, 23½in.x34⅛in., was auctioned Christie's 1987. The first regatta was held in 1834 and rowing teams came from several countries to enter the competitions. The view is looking up the river with the high and low lights of North Shields on the right-hand side.

Scott, Sir Peter Markham, CBE, DSC and Bar, MA, LLD (1909-1989)
Talented bird artist, naturalist and sportsman who held his first exhibition at the Ackermann Galleries, 20 June - 15 July 1933. Son of Captain R.F. Scott, RN, the South Pole voyager, whose death in 1911 is a national legend. His mother was the well-known sculptor, Kathleen Scott (née Edith Agnes Kathleen Bruce), later Lady Kennett. Peter Scott studied at the Art College Munich and at the RA Schools London. Developed the Severn Wildfowl Trust - a public trust for the protection and study of wildlife. Wrote and illus. many books including "Morning Flight" and "Wild Chorus". He was also a portrait painter numbering HRH Princess Margaret, Sir Richard Paget and Sir Malcolm Sargent amongst his distinguished sitters.

Scott, Septimus Edwin, ARBA, RI, ROI (b.1879 d. after 1932)
Draughtsman and landscape painter. Born in Sunderland, studied at the RCA and exh. at the RA (1900-1904). Elected ARBA (1919), RI (1927) and ROI (1920). Contributed to "The Graphic" (1910) and "The Bystander" where a fine double page of a polo match was especially drawn for the May 1910 issue, inscr. "An exciting moment in the "Galloping Game" - Will he score?" A print of his painting of the Prince of Wales, later Edward VII, out hunting, shows the Prince jumping a fence. Scott also painted football scenes including "The Big Match", painted in poster and watercolour. The Harry Langton Collection of Football Art.

Scott, Thomas (Tom), RSA, RSW (1854-1927)
Scottish painter of landscapes and urban scenes in watercolour, also of many angling scenes including "A Fisherman playing a Trout", "The Catch" dated '87, "Fishing the Tweed at Boleside", dated 1908 and "The Last Stand", s.&d. 1897, 11in.x18in. Private collection.

Scott, who was born in Selkirk, entered the RSA Schools in 1877, having previously worked as a tailor with his father. He was nevertheless already a proficient watercolourist having painted since he was a child. Elected RSW (1885) and RSA (1902).

Scott, Thomas Jefferson (op.1863)
American painter, particularly of racehorses, whose portrait of a gentleman out driving, dated 1863, 22in.x 34¼in., was auctioned Christie's (NY) 1986.

Scott-Brown, William G. (1897-1987)
Landscape and figure painter, also a Harley Street specialist, who began to paint seriously in 1950. Great friend of the artist Paul Maze (q.v.) whose influence is clear to see. Scott-Brown painted a number of golf scenes in pastel and watercolour but he painted less freely in oils. Had three one-man exhibitions with Guy Morrison in London in 1972, 1986 and (posthumously) 1988. Included in this Dictionary for his pastel "The Boule Players in the Place de Lices, San Tropez", 15in.x22in. and "Littlestone Golf Course", signed, 15in.x22in.

Scrags, James (op.1816-1828)
Provincial artist from the King's Lynn area in Norfolk who exh. with Ladbrookes Secessionary Norfolk and the Norwich Society of Artists (1816).

Scrags, John (op.1828-1865)
Provincial artist from the King's Lynn area in Norfolk whose portrait of a dark bay hunter in a paddock, a hunt in the distance, dated 1828, 23½in.x29½in., was auctioned Sotheby's 1978. A portrait of a greyhound and a dead hare in a landscape dated 1865 and inscr. "Lynn", 14¾in.x18¾in. was auctioned Christie's 1967.

Scrivens, William (op.1938)
A stable scene with horses in attendance dated 1938, 11½in.x16in., was auctioned Russell, Baldwin and Bright 1986.

Scrope, William (1772-1852)
A keen sportsman and one of the best amateur artists of his time. Exh. occasionally at the RA and often at the BI, of which he was a founder member (1808-1851). Wrote "The Art of Deer Stalking" (1839) and "Days and Nights of Salmon Fishing on the River Tweed" (1843). This work was the result of several visits to Scotland in the early years of the 19th century when Scrope took Lord Somerville's fishing lodge, the Pavilion, at Melrose which had some of the best fishing beats on the Tweed.

Scruton, J. (op.1829)
Draughtsman and lithographer whose sketch of the New Race Stand at Goodwood c.1829 was lithographed, presumably after his own work, 16¼in.x21¾in.

"Scutator"
The pseudonym used by Mr. K.W. Horlock who wrote, amongst other works, "The Life of a Fox" and "Leaves from a Huntsman's Journal". He adopted a rather chauvinistic approach to sporting ladies who hunted, fished or owned racehorses.

Seaby, Allen William (1867-1953)
Well-known bird and animal painter who studied at Reading University where he became a Professor (1920-1933). He exh. at the RWS and the RA (1936-1938). Pub. "British Ponies" (1936).

Seago, Edward Brian, RWS, RBA (1910-1974)
Painter, predominantly of landscapes but also of equestrian and sporting scenes. Son of a coal merchant, Seago had little formal education and very little artistic training. Nevertheless he won the special prize at the Royal Drawing Society at the age of fourteen and was their "star" pupil. He had some lessons in landscape painting from Bernard Priestman RA. He joined Beavin's Travelling Circus at the age of eighteen (1928) and spent several years touring with them throughout the British Isles and on the continent. His first book "Circus Company" pub. in 1933 was illus. by himself with an introduction by the poet John Masefield. He in his turn illus. Masefield's forty-two poems pub. as "The Country Scene". In 1934 Seago pub. "Sons of Sawdust", the sequel to his first book. He illus. many other books for different authors. He worked with John Kenney (q.v.) on illustrations for "There is an Honour Likewise" (1948). Seago had his first exhibition at the Sporting Gallery in 1933 which was opened by Lord Harewood. A keen yachtsman, Seago produced some fine seascapes though few people connect this artist with marine painting. Exh. from c.1930 at the RA, RHA, ROI, RCA, RSA as well as RWS. Among Seago's equestrian works were portraits of "Foxhunter" (winner of the Ascot Gold Cup 1933), "Alcaster", "Over the Sticks" and "Lord Melchett MFH of the Tedworth". Seago also painted a composite picture of six racehorses, "Hyperion", winner of the Derby and St. Leger 1933, "Sansovino", winner of the Derby 1924, "Bosworth", winner of the Ascot Gold Cup, "Fairway", winner of the St. Leger 1928, "Caerlon", winner of the Eclipse Stakes, 1931 and "Bobsleigh", winner of the Newmarket Stakes. Painted in 1939 for the 17th Earl of Derby who bred and owned all the horses, it was exh. HM and AG Preston "British Sporting Paintings" (1943). Elected RBA (1946), RWS (1959).

Sealy, Allen Culpeper (1850-1927)
A landscape painter who turned his hand to sporting and in particular hunting and racing scenes. Exh. at the RA, SS and elsewhere (1873-1886). He apparently ceased exhibiting in 1886 and appears to have concentrated on painting hunting works. Engraved plates after his work include four hunting mezzotints issued by Dickinson and Foster, 4.1.1890, in which Sealy appears to have collaborated with Alexander Hamilton Wardlow (q.v.). Other hunting mezzotints after the work by Sealy included "Gone Away" issued by Messrs. M. Knoedler & Co and pub. on 14.7.1891. On 8.5.1900 C.F. McQueen & Son issued a photo engraving of Sealy's portrait of the racehorse "Flying Fox" (Triple Crown winner 1899). The original painting, signed and inscr. with the artist's address and dated 1884 was auctioned Sotheby's 1989. Sealy also collaborated with Charles Spencelayh (q.v.) who painted the faces in Sealy's series

of groups of hunts. Together they painted a portrait group of the members of the Royal St. George's Golf Club, Sandwich, Kent, in 1892, 29½in.x59½in., which features more than sixty members and two wives. The Royal St. George became the first English golf course to house the Open Championship in 1894. Sealy, no doubt encouraged by his work on the St. George's Club painting, then crossed the Channel to paint the First Club on the Continent - that of Pau in the Bas-Pyrenees, Southern France. Founded in 1856, the Club flourished under the membership of a fashionable British Colony. Sealy's charming scene with both ladies and gentlemen playing golf was painted in 1893, 19¾in.x30in., Pau GC Collection. Although ladies had their own nine hole course at Pau from the 1880s, mixed play was not allowed so the painting is not historically correct. Sealy died at Bournemouth at the age of seventy-seven.

Searle, A.A. (op.1907)
Equestrian draughtsman who contributed to "Punch" in 1907.

Seavey, E. Leone (op.1911)
American painter whose study of a piebald horse in a landscape, s.&d. 1911, was exh. Brian Sinfield, Burford, Oxon.

Sebright, George (op.1848-1860)
Provincial painter of equestrian subjects including portraits of hunters and racehorses. His paintings include a kennel huntsman and hounds outside a dray yard, Lord Eglinton's "Flying Dutchman" and Lord Zetland's "Voltigeur" with jockeys up on a racecourse, dated 1851, a bay hunter in a landscape with a hunt beyond, dated 1860, an Hussar with his charger in a landscape, dated 1848.

Seddon, Andrew John
"A Day's Catch", showing a brace of salmon on the river bank with a Hardy reel and a rod beside them, 19in.x28in., Bonhams 1991.

Sedgley, W. (op.c.1929)
Painted beautiful scenes, very often depicting sporting or animal subjects, for the Royal Worcester Porcelain Company c.1929.

Segrelles, Jose (op.1920s and 1930s)
Worked for "The Illustrated London News" who repro. his paintings superbly in colour (Christmas Number 1930) which were used to illus. "The Arabian Nights", pub. by Salvat Editores, SA Barcelona. His "Boxing Match" painted in grisaille, 9in.x10½in., is in a private collection.

Selby, Prideaux John (1788-1867)
This artist, sportsman, naturalist and scientific student was born at Alnwick in Northumberland. Selby drew and etched with his brother-in-law, Admiral Mitford, nearly 200 illustrations for his "Illustrations of British Ornithology" produced in two volumes and pub. in Edinburgh (1834). Often regarded as the English equivalent of Audubon's celebrated "Birds of America", this was the first attempt to produce a set of life-sized illustrations of British birds and the predecessor of the monographs of Gould and others. Most of the plates were drawn from specimens in Selby's collection at Twizell in Northumberland. Selby was elected a fellow of the Linnean Society and the Royal Society of Edinburgh. He exh. at the RSA.

Selfe, Madelaine (Mrs.)
Painter of equestrian portraits, racing, hunting, coursing scenes and landscapes. Born before the 1st World War, Selfe was bought up in Bedfordshire and hunted with the Oakley. Studied to be a concert pianist and after the war met Sir Alfred Munnings (q.v.) who encouraged her painting. In 1948 Selfe moved to Salisbury where she had painting lessons with the late Henry Lamb, RA. Some of her work has been repro. as prints and she has illus. a number of books including "Horse Talks" written by her uncle, Colonel B.T. Laurence VC, and "Hounds are Home" by Gordon Ferguson. Famous racehorses who have been painted by Madelaine Selfe include "Our Babu" (1956), "Ballymoss", "Nijinsky" and "Arkle". Her painting of the 200th running of the Oaks, presented by the Jockey Club to the Order of St. John in recognition of their services with the St. John Ambulance at racecourses over the years, is one of her finest achievements. The painting shows the start of the 1978 race which was won by the bay filly "Fair Salinia" ridden by Greville Starkey.

Seligman, Edgar (1866-1958)
A distinguished fencer and an artist whose self-portrait, painted in 1920, hangs at the De Beaumont Centre, London. Seligman was one of two men ever to have won the national championship at all three weapons (the other is Bill Hoskins) and was for many years British épée team captain.

Selous, Percy (op.1888)
A portrait by this artist of the bay horse "Joe", s.&d. 1888 was auctioned Phillips 1984. Percy Selous was presumably related to the painter H.C. Selous (1811-1890) and his nephew F.C. Selous (1851-1917) the famous big game hunter. Percy Selous wrote "Travel and Big Game" (1897) which was illus. not by himself but by Charles Whymper (q.v.) who also illus. several books for F.C. Selous.

Seltzer, Olaf C. (1877-1957)
Born in Denmark, Seltzer came to the United States in 1892 and worked in Great Falls, Montana as a machinist for the Great Northern Railway, before devoting himself full time to painting. On his twentieth birthday he was introduced to Charles Russell (q.v.) who became a very good friend and taught Seltzer to paint. Seltzer said in a newspaper interview shortly before his death that he never painted an oil or watercolour before he met Russell. When Seltzer arrived in Montana in 1892 the Blackfeet Indians were living on land granted to them by treaty in 1888 but they still hunted small game even though the big buffalo hunts were finished. In "Prowlers of the Prairie" Seltzer recreated the Indian world of the past and portrayed the pride and majesty of the Indians as they hunted the buffalo in the days before the herds were destroyed.

Sendel(l), John (op.1836)

Minor provincial painter who worked in the Suffolk area as an assistant in the studios of Edwin Cooper (q.v.). He is also thought to have worked with George Fenn and R.W. Folkard (qq.v.). A portrait of a black hunter and a spaniel, dated 1836, 15½in.x21in., was auctioned Christie's 1987.

Serres, John Thomas (1759-1825)

A noted marine painter, son of the Royal Academician, Dominic Serres, and married to Olivia who believed herself to be the daughter of Frederick, Duke of Cumberland, although losing a claim twice in a court of law during her lifetime. Serres, who exh. at the RA, BI and RSBA, painted "A Boat Race on the River Isis, Oxford". The present whereabouts of this painting is unknown but John Whessell (q.v.) painted a copy and pub. an engraving in March 1822. Serres' watercolour "Oarsmen on Virginia Water, Windsor", dated 1825 and inscr., 15in.x30in., was auctioned Sotheby's 1985.

Seton, Ernest Thompson (1860-1946)

Animal painter, illustrator, writer and naturalist. Born at South Shields, Co. Durham. Christened Ernest Evan Thompson which was later changed to Ernest Thompson Seton to carry on the family name from his direct forebear, George Seton, the last Earl of Winton. His family emigrated to Canada in 1865 and young Ernest Seton was educated in Toronto. Later he studied art at the Ontario College of Art, at the RA Schools, London (1879-1881) and in Paris (1891-1896) under Gérome and Bouguereau. His first important oil painting entitled "Awaiting in Vain", which depicted wolves, was exh. at the Chicago World Fair in 1893. This same fair was covered by Harry Furniss (q.v.) for "The Illustrated London News". Seton began to lecture on wild animals in 1899 and was appointed naturalist to the government of Manitoba. He was author of "Wild Animals I Have Known" and numerous other books, many of which he illus. himself. He became very interested in the American Indian and moved to New Mexico, USA, where he founded the College of Indian Wisdom, Santa Fé. Seton was head of the boy scout movement in America until 1915.

Sewell, John (op.1953)

Contemporary artist who contributed a gouache entitled "QPR Entrance", 27in.x19in., to the FE.

Sextie, William A. (op.1848-1888)

Painter of equestrian portraits, particularly those of racehorses and jockeys. Celebrated racehorses that Sextie painted include "St. Blaise" winner of the Derby 1883, Fred Archer on "Cherry" dated 1884, "Glenquoich" dated 1887, "Shotover" winner of the Derby 1882, "Geheimniss" the Oaks winner in 1882, and "Saucebox" painted for J. Parr, Esq. and pub. as a print by R. Ackermann in 1857 as a pair to a picture by A.F. De Prades (q.v.). He exh. a painting of a horse at the RA (1848) entitled "A Favourite Hackney, the property of the Earl of Granville". His portrait of the famous sportsman, Thomas Assheton Smith, was engraved by F.W. Thompson in 1853, 20¾in.x28in.

Seymour, George L. (op.1876-1916)

Animal painter and illustrator who worked in London and contributed to many magazines including "The Graphic" (1886), "The Illustrated London News" (1887-1892), "The Illustrated Magazine" (1888-1897) and "Pall Mall".

Seymour, James (1702-1752)

Equestrian and sporting painter, the son of James Seymour Snr. (1658-1739), a banker and diamond merchant who supplied plate for racing trophies. It may have been through his father's involvement with racing that James Seymour found his patrons and inspiration. He almost certainly met John Wootton and Peter Tillemans (qq.v) through his father's membership of the Virtuosi Society of St. Luke. Amongst the notable paintings by James Seymour are the match between the Duke of Bolton's brown colt "Looby" and Lord Weymouth's "Conqueror" run on 6 October 1735 at Newmarket, 4 miles for 300 guineas, and "Craven Coursing at Ashdown Park", s.&d. 1743. His portrait of Poulet St. John and his family in the grounds of Dogmersfield Park, Hampshire, with huntsmen on their horses with hounds, 49½in.x146in., auctioned Sotheby's 1968, was also painted by Francis Hayman (q.v.).

Seymour, Robert (1798-1836)

Caricaturist of comic sporting scenes and an illustrator who modelled his work on that of George Cruikshank to the extent that he often signed his work "Shortshanks". He was born in Somerset and apprenticed to a London pattern designer before he turned to the more successful caricatures and comic illustration. He was a somewhat inadequate draughtsman but had some success with his series of comic sportsmen from London having adventures in the country. It was his fame in this field that decided the publishers, Chapman and Hall, to commission the text of "Pickwick Papers" from young Charles Dickens as an accompaniment to Seymour's sketches. Unfortunately only two issues were produced before Seymour shot himself at the early age of thirty-eight in London on 20 April 1836. Seymour illus. T.K. Hervey's "Book of Christmas" (1836/7) with the delightful sketch of the Norfolk coach at Christmas, literally heaped with turkeys hanging from every spare part of the coach and pulled by four, as yet, unwearied horses. From an historical account of Norwich it appears that between Saturday morning and the night of Sunday 22 December 1793, 1,700 turkeys weighing 9 tons 2 cwt 2 lbs, value £680 were sent to London from Norwich and two days after half as many more and the supply must have considerably increased by the time that Hervey was writing forty or so years later. "Sketches by Seymour" (c.1840).

Shahn, Ben (1898-1969)

Lithuanian-born painter who came to America when he was eight years old. Painter and graphic designer, muralist and photographer of the poverty ridden cities of the depression. Included in this Dictionary for his watercolour and gouache painting entitled "Vacant Lot" (1939) showing a small boy with a baseball bat wandering along a street, flanked on one side by a high red brick wall, 19in.x23in., the Eller Gallop Sumner and Mary Catlin Sumner Collection.

Shakespeare, Percy (1907-1943)

Sporting artist, born at Dudley and killed in action in 1943. Painted many sporting scenes, a number of which are on permanent loan to the Civil Defence Headquarters at Priory Hall, Priory Road, Dudley. "An Afternoon at the Ice Rink" was exh. at Birmingham in 1939 with eleven studies for this work but he is also included in this Dictionary for "A Game of Billiards Played in the Officers Mess of H.M.S. Vernon", 28in.x36½in., auctioned Sotheby's 1986. H.M.S. Vernon was a land based training college.

Sharp, H.C. (op.1909)

Watercolour painter of equestrian scenes, particularly hunting.

Sharpe, F.J. (op.1893-1904)

A portrait of Melbourne Bros.' horse and cart from Stamford, Lincoln, s.&d. 1904, 15in.x21in. was auctioned Sotheby's (Chester) 1988. "A Family Game of Golf" dated 1893, 9¾in.x14½in., exh. Oscar and Peter Johnson 1978.

Sharpe, Joseph Henry (1859-1953)

American painter of some animal and sporting scenes and paintings of Indians hunting. Pupil of the Royal Academy in Munich and at the Académie Julian in Paris under Laurens and Benjamin Constant.

Sharples, George (op.1787-1849?)

An obviously competent artist of boxiana of whom Pierce Egan said in 1821: "The portraits taken by this artist are not only considered life itself but admired for their softness of touch and brilliancy of colouring. In crayons Mr. Sharples may be said to have no rival. His likeness of Cribb with the silver cup in his hand and also Mr. Jackson's have been decided [sic] in the sporting world as masterpieces." High praise indeed. Tom Cribb (1781-1848) and John Jackson (1769-1845) were boxing champions of England in 1809 and 1795 respectively.

Shaw, Charles E. (op.1897)

Draughtsman and etcher of "The Anchor, Ripley" with a meeting of cyclists, 1897, 8x15½in.

Shaw, Hugh George (op.1873-1895)

Between 1873 and 1895 this artist from Stratford upon Avon exh. at the RA, SS, ROI and in Birmingham, Manchester and Liverpool. Sporting titles include "Found", "Head of 'Restless' - a leading hound in the pack of otterhounds belonging to G.M. Traherne, Esq.", "St. Hilary Kennels, Glamorganshire" and "The Poacher".

Shaw, James (op.1769-1784)

Portrait painter, born at Wolverhampton. Entered the RA Schools (1769) and became a pupil of Edward Penny (q.v.). Exh. at the RA (1776-1784) two portraits, one of the 6th Earl of Stamford (1765-1838) as a boy, painted in 1773.

Shaw, James (op.1883-1902)

Interesting provincial painter of equestrian subjects including "Preparation for the Gold Cup", 37¼in.x 46in., "A Grey Horse in a Field", weathering a storm and the horse "Fast Trotter", 22in.x14in. He may well be the same James Shaw who operated from Edinburgh (1883-1902) and contributed work to "Punch". Exh. RSA and Walker AG, Liverpool.

Shaw, John Byam Liston, RI, ARWS (1872-1919)

Pre-Raphaelite painter in oil and watercolours. Included in this Dictionary for his painting "The Regatta", in the Lady Lever AG Collection, Port Sunlight. Born in Madras, India, Shaw came to England with his family in 1878 at the age of six. Studied at the St. John's Wood School of Art and at the RA Schools from 1889. Exh. at the major London galleries from 1893 and was elected RI (1898). He illus. several books, none of them sporting, and became a partner with Rex Vicat Cole in the Byam Shaw and Vicat Cole School of Art, Kensington.

Shaw, Joshua (of Bath) (1776-1861)

Landscape and sporting painter in both oil and watercolour, who was born at Bellingborough. Lincolnshire. Apprenticed to a country sign writer and later set up a drawing practice in Manchester. Exh. at the BI and RA (1810-1814). Appears to have emigrated to North America in 1817. His portrait "A Harrier Hound in a Hilly Landscape", dated 1823, 26in.x36in. was exh. at Asprey & Co. in 1976.

Shaw, Kendall (op.1964)

American painter included in this Dictionary for his painting "Four at Bat", 1964, which depicts the baseball players Mantle, Maris, Ruth and Gehrig, the superstars of the New York Yankees, their names spelt out in newspaper print at their feet, acrylic on canvas, 68in.x 96in. Artist's Collection.

Shaw, Nevil, ARCA, ARE (b.1915)

Although a painter of mainly topographical subjects in Kent and Sussex, Shaw has completed a number of paintings and studies related to fishing, football and pigeon racing. Exh. at the RA (1938-1968) including a painting entitled "Wind, Rain and Fisherman" in 1964 (No. 618) and "Charlton -v- Blackpool at the Valley" in 1957 (No. 975). Shaw is also a talented aquatinter and an etcher.

Shaw, R. Frederick (op.1873)

The draughtsman of fourteen angling incidents bound into an album, pen and ink, one inscr. and one dated 1873, auctioned Sotheby's 1979.

Shaw, W.R.B. (op.1839-1852)

London landscape and still life artist who exh. four paintings at the RA and one at BI (1839-1846). He painted several still lifes with game.

Shaw, William, FSA (op.1750 - d.1773)

London equestrian painter who exh. twenty-seven paintings at the SA (1760-1772). Many of them included horses in training, racing brood mares and dogs as well as a portrait of Mr. Poynter and Mr. Hardistey with their dogs partridge shooting, 1764. He was elected FSA (1771). He built "a large painting room with conveniences to receive the animals from which he painted". Amongst his patrons were the 3rd Duke of Ancaster, who became Master of the Horse to George III in 1766, Lord Orford and Lord Montford. His equestrian portraits include that sold as "King Herod", a bay stallion with a stable boy in an open landscape and other horses exercising beyond, 30in.x49in., The Paul Mellon Collection, Upperville, Va, USA, and now thought to be a portrait of the racehorse "Blank", belonging to the Duke of Ancaster, walking towards a mare. He also painted a portrait of "Pam", a bay racehorse, the property of Mr. Wilmott, held by a groom, with a jockey standing nearby in a landscape, dated 1763, 35½in.x44in. Shaw usually signed and considerably dated his work.

Shaw, William (op.1826)
A later William Shaw painted a portrait of "Nimrod", a bay hunter in an extensive landscape, s.&d. 1826.

Shayer, Charles Waller (1826-1914)
Landscape, equestrian and sporting painter, son of William Shayer, Snr. (q.v.), younger brother of Henry Thring Shayer, with whom he worked and studied, and half-brother of William Joseph Shayer (qqv). He is supposed to have been the best horse painter of the Shayer family. Sporting paintings include "The Northampton Races", "A Race Meet", "A Country Fair", dated 1875, "The Ploughman", painted with brother Henry and dated '58, and "Ponies and Lurchers beside Dead Deer" and "Pony and Dogs Standing Beside Dead Game", a pair each 20in.x24in. Charles Shayer exh. only once at SS in 1879.

Shayer, Henry Thring (1825-1864)
The eldest son of William Shayer, Snr. (q.v.), brother of Charles Waller Shayer (q.v.) and half-brother of William Joseph Shayer (q.v.). Shayer worked in the studio with his father and brother and collaborated with his brother on many works. Usually he painted the landscapes and Charles the horses, figures or animals. They collaborated on "The Shooting Party", 11in.x 17in., auctioned Christie's and "The Meet" and "Over the Ditch", a pair of hunting scenes, each 26in.x45in., auctioned Christie's 1980.

Shayer, William Snr. RBA (1788-1879)
Landscape, sporting and rustic painter, born in Southampton. Father of William Joseph, Charles Waller and Henry Thring Shayer (qq.v.). Served a long apprenticeship as a coach painter and exh. at the RA, SS and BI (1825-1879).

Shayer, William Joseph (1811-1892)
Sporting, animal and coaching artist, born in Chichester, the eldest son of the landscape and coach painter, William Shayer (q.v.) and half-brother of Henry and Charles Shayer (qq.v.). Taught to paint by his father. Exh. his first painting, "A Portrait of a Mare", at the Hampshire Picture Gallery, Southampton in 1828 at the age of seventeen. The following year he exh. "Foxes After Landseer" at SS. Although much of W.J.'s work was commissioned, he exh. two paintings at the RA, one at the BI and a total of thirteen at SS. By 1830 Shayer was clearly listed in the Southampton Directory as an animal painter and by 1836 he had moved to London where he produced a number of works for Rudolph Ackermann. In the same year he painted "The

Courser", which was engraved by Andrew Duncan and repro. by Rudolph Ackermann in "The New Sporting Magazine" in June 1836. Despite this apparent success he was unable to support his family from painting alone and in 1841 drove a coach to earn a living in Kennington. He was a skilled horseman; both his father and his uncle who ran the independent post coach from the Anchor Inn, Chichester to London, were accomplished coachmen. Shayer's coaching scenes are unsurpassed pictorial records of how coaching journeys really were and not as depicted on the top of chocolate boxes. Generally his early work was painted in a documentary style while his later efforts became more atmospheric. He occasionally collaborated with other members of his family but suffered from his father's reputation to produce work of an outstanding quality so that any weak work was immediately attributed to his son. It is fair to say, though, that the quality of his work in his final days declined as the result of poor eyesight. He died at Twickenham on 5 November 1892. His sporting works include portraits of "Blue Gown" and "Achievement", a pair of mounted racehorses, dated 1868, "The Shooting Pony", dated 1849 and "Pheasant Shooting", a pair, both s.&d. 1859.

Sheldon, Charles Mills (1866-1928)
American-born painter who studied in Paris at the Académie Julian under Constant and Lefebvre (1890-1891). Travelled through the Southern States of America illustrating articles for the Associated Press (1889). Illustrator to "The Pall Mall Budget" (1892-1895) and contributor to "Black and White", "The Ludgate Monthly", "Strand Magazine" and "Chums". His painting of a public school cricket match, grey wash, 12¼in.x8¼in., was auctioned Phillips 1989.

Sheldon (Williams), Alfred
See Williams

Shelley, Samuel (c.1750-1808)
Miniaturist and watercolour painter whose tiny oval miniature of "Two Children with a Curved Cricket Bat", 4in.x3½in., was auctioned Christie's 1977. Shelley was a founder member of the Old Watercolour Society.

Shelton, Harold, ARE (b.1913)
Draughtsman and etcher. Born St. Helen's, Lancashire. Studied at Wallasey School of Art (1934-1936) and at the RCA (1936-1939). His contribution to football art lies in his drawing, 21½in.x14¼in., "Carlisle United v. Bradford City", exh. at the FE. Shelton, who exh. at the RA and RE, was elected ARE 1940. Became Principal of Carlisle School of Art and then of Hornsey College of Art.

Shelton, Sidney (op.1881-1889)
Landscape painter who exh. two paintings at the RA (1881-1889) and two at the RBA. His portrait of a lady with a tennis racket, thought to be Betty Nuttall, pencil and watercolour, 20¼in.x14½in., was auctioned Christie's 1988. Betty Nuthall (Mrs. F.C. Shoemaker) was born in 1911 in Surbiton, Surrey. She was the first overseas player to win the U.S. Women's singles title

(1930) and the doubles in the same year, with Miss Sarah Palfrey. She never achieved her best form at Wimbledon where she only reached the quarter finals in 1927. She was a member of the British Wightman Cup team 1927-1929, 1931-1934 and 1939.

Shepard, Ernest Howard, OBE (1879-1976)
Artist and book illustrator, best known for his illustrations to the A.A. Milne books featuring Winnie-the-Pooh. Born in London, son of an architect, educated at St. Pauls School. Studied art at Heatherleys, under John Crompton (1896-1897) and at the RA Schools (1897-1902) under Herbert and Canty. Took a studio in Glebe Place, Chelsea where he worked until he married in 1904 when they moved to Surrey and rented a cottage in Shamley Green for 2s.3½d. In 1907 he began drawing for "Punch" and remained on the staff for many years. Provoked heated argument (recorded "Country Life" 1968) as a result of Frank Davis' remark "No- one, I imagine, has ever, or ever will claim Shepard as a distinguished draughtsman". Shepard exh. four works at the RA (1901-1904), none of them sporting, and at the Paris Salon. He exh. at the London Sporting Gallery in 1933 and was created an OBE in 1972. His watercolour "The First Shot", a shooting scene, 6in.x9in., was auctioned Sotheby's 1982. He also drew and painted a number of golfing scenes -·"Betty on the Links", etc. A retrospective exhibition of his work was held at Sally Hunter Fine Art, London (1988).

Shepheard, George (c.1770-1842)
Watercolour painter of landscapes, portraits and an engraver. Studied at the RA Schools. Exh. at the RA, BI, SS, OWS and elsewhere (1800-1842). His sporting work includes portraits of E. Trueman of Cruickshanks, gamekeeper to John Elwes of Colesbourne, Gloucestershire, painted in watercolour and dated July 1809 and "Twelve Cricketers in Characteristic Studies", pen and wash, 8in.x10in., c.1795? (MCC Collection). These famous players include portraits of Lord Frederick Beauclerk, Captain the Hon. E. Bligh (later a General and the ancestor of the Hon. Ivo Bligh of "Ashes" fame), David Harris, Thomas Lord, William Beldam, and the Hon. Charles Lennox (afterwards Duke of Richmond).

Shepherd, G.E. (op.1908-1909)
Illustrator of "The Seven Stages of Golf" (1909) and "Bubbles in Birdland" by H. Simpson (1908).

Shepherd, George Sidney, NWS (op.1830-d.1858)
Figure and landscape painter who painted a number of angling scenes including "Salmon Fishing by a Woodland Pool", s.&d. 1843, watercolour, 18in.x25in., Woolley & Wallis (1990). Son of George Shepherd and the brother of Thomas Hosmer Shepherd (q.v.) who painted his landscape and topographical scenes mostly in watercolour in the style of his father. Exh. at the RA (1830-1858), NWS, RI and SS. Founder member of NWS (1831).

Shepherd, Rupert (b.1909)
A painting of three Aston Martin 1.5 litre racing cars, pen and wash, signed, 9½in.x25in., was auctioned

1989. Shepherd exh. at the RA (1943-1970) including two paintings of a point-to-point, one exh. in 1968 and one in 1969. He was also an engraver.

Shepherd, Stanfield (op.1816-1875)
Painter in watercolour of fine angling and sporting scenes, many of which were presented to the Piscatorial Society by Mr. T.H. Parker in 1871. His work includes a portrait of "A Horse and Groom on Hackney Marsh with Anglers in the Foreground", dated 1816, "Fishing at Teddington", "Jack in a Box", a beautifully painted watercolour of a pike being packed in a wooden crate on which is inscr. "From Waterford to London", 12in.x7¾in. and "Lake Fishing from a Rowing Boat", signed, 6½in.x9¾in.

Shepherd, Thomas Hosmer (1793-1864)
London topographical painter in watercolours who was commissioned by Frederick Grace (1779-1859) to paint a record of old buildings in London before they were demolished. Many of these are in the British Museum. The series includes a painting in watercolour and Indian ink of the Royal Tennis Court, established in 1673 in St. James's Street, Leicester Square, as it appeared in 1850. The first court on the site (now Orange Street) was built in about 1634. It closed in 1866. Shepherd's other sporting work includes "A Coach and Horses in a Wooded Lane", signed, 10in.x15in., auctioned in 1989 and "A Game of Single Wicket Cricket at the Pensioners Hall, Charterhouse", brown wash and pencil, 3⅝in.x 5⅝in., c.1830, Museum of London. This cricket scene was engraved by J. Rogers (q.v.) and pub. Jones & Co., 25 September 1830. Shepherd was the son of George Shepherd and the brother of the topographical painter George Sidney Shepherd (q.v.).

Shepherd, William James Affleck (1867-1946)
Humorous animal draughtsman. Born in London and educated at various private schools but had no formal art training. He worked with Alfred Bryan (q.v.) the cartoonist on "Moonshine" (1890-1893). Shepherd was a first class shot and rode to hounds and these attributes undoubtedly contributed to his becoming an animal draughtsman of the highest class. His speciality was humorous drawings in pen and ink of animals and birds in human clothes, with human personalities, and he contributed a series of these drawings to "The Strand Magazine" which became known as "Zig Zags". He joined "Punch" in 1893 and contributed to other publications such as "The Sporting and Dramatic News" (1892), "Judy" (1886-1889) and "Moonshine" (1890-1893), "Good Words" (1894) and "Black and White" (1896). The publications he illus. include "Zig Zag Fables" (1897), "Uncle Remus" (1901), "The Jovial Puppies" (1907), "The Life of a Foxhound" (1910) and "The Bodley Head Natural History" (1913). He lived in Charlwood, Surrey and in Cirencester, Gloucestershire.

Sheppard, Miss Charlotte Lilian (op.1884 d.1925)
Animal painter in watercolour. Lived in Chelsea. Exh. at the RBA from 1884 and exh. a portrait of a dog at SS.

Sheppard, Joseph (1834-1928)
Provincial painter, born near Weston-super-Mare, the son of a farmer and a student of James H. Davies. He was awarded a prize for a watercolour drawing of apples, followed by a certificate from the Council of Education for free-hand drawing. His portraits of prize cattle are interesting examples of Sheppard's naïve style.

Sheppard, R. (op.1825)
Mansfield artist who was a pupil and friend of John Frederick Herring Snr. (q.v.) with whom the latter often lodged. His portrait of the horse "Vanish" by "Phantom" out of "Treasure", s.&d. 1825 and inscr., 17½in.x22½in., was auctioned Tennants 1985. His portrait of a saddled horse by a blasted tree in a landscape, 11in.x13½in., was auctioned Christie's 1964.

Sheppard, Raymond, RI, PS, SGA (1913-1958)
Painter of landscapes and nature subjects in oil, pastel and watercolour. Also a book illustrator. Born in London. Studied art at Bolt Court. Exh. at the major London galleries and was elected SGA (1947), PS (1948) and RI (1949). Illus. many nature and children's books. Lived in Middlesex.

Shepperson, Claude Allin, ARA, ARE, ARWS (1867-1921)
Watercolour painter, pen and ink artist, illustrator and lithographer. Born at Beckenham, Kent. Lived in London. He studied at Heatherleys and in Paris and became a "Punch" artist although he was always keen to work outside, having a strong dislike of studio lighting. His sporting paintings include several of racing, "Royal Ascot", signed watercolour, 14in.x20½in. and an etching entitled "The Racecourse" being two examples.

Sheriff, John, ("Dr Syntax"), ARSA (1816-1844)
Edinburgh caricaturist animal, equestrian and sporting painter whose portrait of George Parker with the celebrated greyhound "Mountain Dew" dated 1839, 19¾in.x17¼in., was exh. at the Fine Art Society, 1969. He also painted "Katie", a dark bay mare in a loose box, s.&d. 1840, 40in.x50in., Christie's (Tattersalls) 1988. A large collection of Sheriff's pen/ink drawings are in Edinburgh City Art Collection. Elected ARSA (1839).

Sherlock, A. Marjorie (Mrs. W.K.T. Barrett) SGA, WIAC (1897-1973)
Landscape painter and an etcher who studied art at the Slade School, Westminster School of Art, under Walter Sickert and Harold Gilman during the 1st World War, the RCA, Osborne (1926) and at the Académie L'Hote in Paris (1938). Exh. at the RA from 1916, also at the NEAC, IS, SGA, RBA, GI and abroad. "Figures in a Trotting Gig on a Racecourse", 20in.x30in., dated 1914, was auctioned Bonhams 1975.

Sherman, C. (op.1857)
Portrait of a chestnut stallion and a grey mare, s.&d. 1857, 11in.x15in., auctioned Sotheby's (Sussex) 1989.

Shields, Henry (op.1880-1891)
Scottish painter of marine subjects whose series of watercolours of famous Clyde yachts (1880-1887) were pub. as thirty-one chromolithographs by J. Meikle in London and Glasgow in 1888.

Shiels, William, RSA (1785-1857)
Scottish painter of animals, equestrian and sporting scenes, also of domestic and country scenes. Shiels painted a series of pictures of different breeds of horses for the Agricultural Museum of the University of Edinburgh and these were used to illus. "The Breeds of the Domestic Animals of the British Islands" by David Lowe. He became a member of the Scottish Academy at its formation in 1826 and exh. in London (1808-1852) at the RA, BI and SS. "A Good Day's Shooting", dated 1827, 21in.x27in., was auctioned Sotheby's 1984. He painted in both oil and watercolour and normally signed and very often dated his work.

Shiffner, Eleanor Barbara Georgina (b.1896)
Yorkshire-born painter of animals, portraits and landscapes who studied at the Byam Shaw School of Art and at the RA Schools. Her work includes portraits of beagles, "Brandy", "Hannibal", "Brewery", "Bumptious" and V.W.H. Cricklade's "Visible" and "Brassing Betsy". Shiffner exh. at the RA, NEAC, in the provinces and abroad.

Shirley-Fox, John, RBA (1860-1939)
Portrait and sporting painter. Studied art in Paris at the Ecole des Beaux Arts, under Gérome. Exh. at the Paris Salon in 1883 and at the RA from 1890. Lived in London and also in Bath. He pub. "Angling Adventures of an Artist" in 1923 and contributed articles to "The Field" as "Brush and Feather".

Short, Arthur Anderson (op.1923-1927)
Painter of sporting subjects including "The Pick Up from Grouse Shooting - Ogden Moors", dated 12 August 1927, and inscr., colour washes, 5½in.x8in., "The Badsworth Hunt - Cowick Park", dated 1923, 7½in.x9in. and "Shooting Duck", signed, pencil and wash, 4½in.x7⅛in. Phillips (Leeds) 1987.

Short, Frederick Golden (op.1882-1908)
Landscape artist who painted a number of hunting scenes, usually set in Hampshire and the New Forest area. He exh. at the RA, SS, NWS and elsewhere (1885-1892).

Short, M. Dudley (op.1923-1938)
Painter and linocut artist who exh. a golfing sketch at the Little Art Rooms, 8 Duke Street, Adelphi WC2 ("Connoisseur" April 1923). Short also exh. at the Abbey Gallery, the Redfern Gallery and the Society of Women Artists (1929-1938).

"Shortshanks"
Pseudonym derived from George Cruikshank's name and sometimes used by Robert Seymour (q.v.).

"Shortspoon"
Pseudonym used by Major Francis Hopkins (q.v.).

"Shotley"
Charles Richardson of "The Field" (1892). Took over the hunting and racing columns of this magazine from W.C.A. Blew on the latter's death. Richardson also wrote under the name of "King Cob" for "Land & Water". Supposed to have been the godson of the sporting

Shrapnell, E.S.

writer and founder of "The Field", Robert Smith Surtees, which he always denied. Wrote "A History of the English Turf", "The Complete Foxhunter" and "Hunting in Many Counties". Claimed to have known the infamous sportsman George Osbaldeston (1786-1866).

Shrapnell, E.S. (op.1860)
A Hampshire artist who exh. one painting at SS of a widgeon and a plover in 1860.

Shrapnell, N.H.S. (op.1849-1850)
This sporting artist from Gosport, Hampshire, specialised in painted game subjects exhibiting three at SS (1849-1850), including a couple of teal from nature and partridges, and two at BI.

Shuttleworth, Arnold Clarke (b.1897)
Painter of equestrian subjects who studied at Salford Art School but who also qualified as a veterinary surgeon in 1924 at Liverpool University where he later became a lecturer and finally retired in 1862 as Reader. He wrote and illus. articles for various veterinary publications and was for many years veterinary surgeon at Aintree and Haydock Park. His favourite subjects were heavy horses and racing and he has also worked in bronze. His work has been repro. in Haydock Park publications.

Shuttleworth, William Thomas (op.1921)
Yorkshire painter of animals who painted a portrait of a Hereford bull standing in a wooded river landscape for James Beckett of Warburton Park. He exh. at the London Salon in 1921.

Siberechts, Jan (1627-c.1700)
Painter of English country houses who is said to have been brought to England from Antwerp by the Duke of Buckingham. This early artist was a member of the Guild of St. Luke, Antwerp (1648-1649). A watercolour of huntsman and hounds in a landscape inscr. "Wootton and Siberechts" indicates that Wootton (q.v.) may have been a student of Siberechts. The view of Wollaton Hall, Nottinghamshire with its gardens and park is dated 1697 and shows a game of bowls being played on a distant lawn, 74½ in.x53¼ in., The Paul Mellon Collection, Upperville, Va, USA.

Sibley, Charles (op.1826-1847)
Still life painter of dead game subjects and some portraits who exh. at the RA, BI and SS (1826-1847) from a London address.

Sickert, Walter Richard, RA, PRBA, NEAC, ARE (1860-1942)
Impressionist painter and etcher not normally associated with sporting subjects. However he painted "Dieppe Races" whilst he was living in France (1899-1905) which is in the collection of the Birmingham AG. He also contributed three cartoons to "Vanity Fair" in 1897 under the pseudonym "Sic".

Siddall, M. (op.1835)
Animal painter whose portrait of a prize grey Shorthorn in a stall, s.&d. 1835, 23½ in.x19¼ in., was auctioned Sotheby's 1984.

Siddall, R. (op.1863)
Provincial animal and landscape painter whose portrait of a sheep in a meadow s.&d. 1863, 19¼ in.x23¼ in. was auctioned Sotheby's 1986.

Sidley, Samuel (1829-1896)
Yorkshire-born portrait painter who studied at the Manchester School of Art and the RA Schools. He collaborated on several conversation pieces with the sporting artists Richard Ansdell and John Charlton (qq.v.) including a portrait of Annie and Ernest, the children of Angus Holden, Esq., with their pony, signed by both Ansdell and Sidley and dated 1877. Christie's 1991.

Sievan, Maurice (1898-1981)
American draughtsman, painter and illustrator whose drawing "News Boy", 1914, depicts a newspaper boy running down a crowded tenement lined street on New York's Lower East Side shouting out the headlines proclaiming "The Giants Win". Two elderly Jewish men he passes are amused that the game of baseball should be so important as to make big newspaper headlines. The drawing, 7⅛ in.x3⅜ in., is in the Jewish Museum where it was presented by Mrs. L. C. Sievan.

Sillem, Charles (op.1883-1891)
London animal and sporting painter who exh. at the RA. Titles include "Rough Terrier and Rats" (1883) and "A Poacher's Bag" (1889). He also exh. at the RI (1883-1889).

Sillett, James (1764-1840)
A miniature painter, often of game, fruit and flower subjects. Born in Norwich. Is supposed to have studied at the RA Schools, a statement largely put about by himself in his many newspaper advertisements for pupils, but his name is not registered there. He began his career as an heraldic and later a scene painter for Drury Lane and Covent Garden theatres but between 1801 and 1804 was back in Norwich practising as a drawing master. Between 1804 and 1810 he seems to have taken up residence at King's Lynn as Professor of painting in oil and watercolours and a drawing master ("Norwich Mercury" 13 January 1808). He returned to Norwich in 1810 (John Cotman anticipating his return removed himself to Yarmouth). In 1815 Sillett became President of the Norwich Society of Artists. He built up a large and successful drawing practice and was joined by his daughter, Emma, in 1817, who was allowed to teach the youngest pupils. He exh. at the RA (1796-1837). His sporting examples include "Hawk and Prey". He held a number of exhibitions in and around Norwich and from 1823 joined John Crome and others in sending pictures further afield, for example to Newcastle. "A Still Life of Game", including a duck, a pheasant and a hare, with a sporting gun, dated 1812, was auctioned Sotheby's 1979. Two in the series of fourteen plates from "British Feathered Game", mezzotinted by Charles Turner (1810-1812) are after Sillett, the rest are after James Barenger (q.v.).

Simkins, Edith A. (op.1911-1925)
Painter of equestrian subjects including "A Hunter", dated 1911, "A Bay Hunter" (1924), "A Mare and Foal by the Sea", dated 1925 and "A Lady Mounted on a Grey Hunter", Bearnes 1987.

Simms, A.G. (op.1859-1873)
London painter of genre and sporting subjects who exh. at the RA, BI, SS and elsewhere (1859-1873).

Simons, Pinky Marcius (op.1891)
"A Memorial to a Fox Hunting Man" - a portrait of a young boy with emblems of the chase - fox-hunting scenes in England and roebuck hunting in South Africa, signed and inscr. to Mrs. J. Mansfield, a watercolour, 13in.x26in., was painted by this artist and auctioned Sotheby's 1977. Simons exh. one painting at the RA in 1891 from a Northampton address.

Simpson, Charles Walter, RBA, RI, ROI, RSMA (1885-1971)
Sporting painter, author and illustrator. Born in Camberley, Surrey, the son of a Major General. Studied art at the Académie Julian in Paris. Won gold medals at the Panama Exposition in San Francisco (1915) and at the Paris Olympia Exhibition (1924). First exh. at the RA (1907). Elected RBA (1914), RI (1914) and ROI (1923). Wrote and illus. "A Pastorale" (1922) which he had pub. in a limited edn. from his home in St. Ives, Cornwall, "The Harborough Country" (1927), "El Rodeo" (1924), "Leicestershire and its Hunts" (1927), "Trencher and Kennel" (1927) and "The Fields of Home" (1948). He illus. many other books including "Manners and Mannerisms" by Crascredo, under the pseudonym of "The Wag" (1929) and "The Fellowship of the Horse" (1930) by S.G. Goldschmidt. Simpson exh. at the RA, NEAC, RBA, RCA, RHA, RI, ROI, RSA and at the inaugural exhibition at the RSMA (1946). His sporting subjects include flat racing, steeple-chasing, hunting, polo, fencing, carriage driving and almost any other sport undertaken on horseback including show jumping, portraits of Pat Smythe with "Tosca" and "Flanagan" and Colonel Harry Llewellyn on "Foxhunter". "A Golf Match at Prestwick", signed monochrome watercolour reputedly showing Jim Barnes (Champion of the 1925 Open) teeing off at the first tee at Prestwick during a competition, 17½in.x 13½in., Sotheby's. "HRH The Duke of Windsor (when Prince of Wales) Playing Polo at Cowdray Park", 21in.x32in., Royal Exchange Art Gallery, London. Also painted "The Final of the Buenos Aires Challenge Cup" (polo) originally repro. in "Country Life" (21.7.1928), 18in.x12½in., signed mono. C.S.

Simpson, F. (Mrs.) (op.1831)
This artist exh. one painting of a horse and a greyhound at the RA in 1831 from a Derby address.

Simpson, H. Hardey (op.1883-1905)
Painter of equestrian and sporting subjects whose exh. work at the RA includes "A Portrait of John Jones, Huntsman to the North Cheshire Hounds" and "Left at Home". He also exh. two works at SS (1885-1888) from a Cheshire address. His other sporting works include portraits of wire haired fox terriers outside a house (1883), ponies beside an estuary (1905) and a bay hunter and fox terriers in a stable, s.&d. 1896, 13in.x 19in., Phillips 1987.

Simpson, J.H. (op.1877-1890)
Exh. one sporting painting at the RA (1877) entitled "Just Caught It".

Simpson, R. (op.1844)
A sporting spaniel in a river landscape, s.&d. 1844, 6½in.x9in., was auctioned Christie's 1970.

Simpson, Tom, RI (op.1887-1926)
Landscape painter in watercolour and oil who exh. at the RA and SS (1887-1891). His attractive watercolour entitled "The Tennis Party", 9in.x13in., shows a family of all ages playing lawn tennis at the turn of the century. Private Collection.

Simpson, W.P. (op.1883-1886)
Painter of animal subjects including a study of a "King Charles Spaniel", dated 1883, and "A Brood Mare in a Landscape", dated 1886, Bonhams 1985.

Sims, J.W. (op.c.1844)
Four fine coursing paintings, one signed, oil on paper laid down on panel, each 5in.x7¼in., were auctioned at Sotheby's (NY) 1988, catalogue provenance Frost and Reed Ltd., London.

Simson, William, RSA (1800-1848)
Scottish painter of landscapes, portraits and sporting subjects including "The End of the Day", William Scrope (q.v.) on a white pony with his keepers and the day's bag, dated 1848, "Salmon Spearing on the Tweed", pen and brown ink, "A Fawn Greyhound in a Landscape" dated 1831, and "A Courtyard Scene with Boy, Horses and Spaniels". Simson, who studied at the Trustees Academy in Edinburgh, was elected RSA (1830) and travelled to Italy to study in the 1830s. His fine painting "The Twelfth of August at Badenoch" (1829) is in the National Gallery of Scotland.

Sinclair, John (op.1872-1922)
A 19th century copyist who specialised in coaching scenes, particularly those after the work of James Pollard (q.v.) and Ben Marshall (q.v.). He seems nevertheless to have been a fair artist in his own right. Examples of his sporting work include "The Newmarket First Spring Meeting" (1786), "A Match Race", signed and inscr. as titled, 24in.x48in., "The Oxford - London Mail outside the Mitre Inn", "The Birmingham Tally Ho Coaches passing the Crown at Holloway", "The Liverpool - London Mail Coach", dated 1835, and a set of four "Coursing Scenes", each 13½in.x18½in. Sinclair worked for Izods, the Regent Street firm of picture restorers (1900-1912). Many of his works were sold as copies of famous paintings and dated accordingly.

Singleton, John (op.c.1815)
A portrait of the racehorse "Orville" and his owner, Earl Fitzwilliam, 9½in.x15½in., by this artist, was auctioned Anderson & Garland 1988.

Skeaping, John Rattenbury, RA (1901-1980)

Animal and equestrian painter and a sculptor. Born in South Woodford, Essex. Studied art at Goldsmith's College School, the Central School of Arts and Crafts (1917-1919) and at the RA Schools (1919-1920). First exh. at the RA in 1922 and in 1924 won the Rome Prize. Painted in oil, watercolour, pastel and gouache and specialised particularly in racing scenes, portraits and sculpture of horses. Held his first one-man show in 1928 with his then wife, Barbara Hepworth, in Glasgow. Author of "Animal Drawing" (1934), "How to Draw Horses" (1941) and "Les Animeaux dans L'Art" (1969). Elected RA (1960). Occasionally collaborated with Kenneth Rowntree (q.v.) as on the portrait of "Ballymoss" and Scobie Breasley winning the King George VI and Queen Elizabeth Stakes, Ascot, in 1958, signed by both artists, 19in.x29in., Sotheby's 1985.

Sketchley, W. (op.1814)

An original edn. of "The Cocker" by this artist, pub. 1814 was in the possession of Mr. James Tabor, his letter to "The Connoisseur" April 1930. Sketchley was possibly the same artist who exh. a flower piece at FS (1783).

"Skiddaw"

Alias F.W. Lamonby, keeper of "The Greyhound Stud Book" (1892-1914) and sporting correspondent to "The Field" under its editor Frederick Toms (1888-1899). Lamonby originally introduced the starting gate for racing, from Australia, when he bought back a model in 1889. He was also the father of William Lamonby - see "Helvelyn".

Slater, Joseph (1750-1805)

London painter of portraits who entered the RA Schools in 1771 and exh. at the FS and RA (1772-1787). His painting of archery, engraved by James Heath (1757-1834) and pub. by the artist in 1789, is in the British Museum Collection. The bowman has been tentatively identified as Thomas Waring who was secretary to Sir Ashton Lever, founder of the Royal Toxophilite Society.

Slater, Richard E. (op.1953/4)

Contemporary painter whose contribution to football art lies in his painting "Entering the Stands", 38in.x 29in., exh. at the FE.

Slattery, John Joseph (op.1857)

Irish portrait painter whose study of Mrs. Keogh and family with greyhound and dead hare and with Powerscourt waterfall and the Wicklow mountains behind, dated 1857, 63in.x95in., was exh. at the Royal Hibernian Academy 1858.

Slaughter, Stephen (1697-1765)

Portrait painter, born in London but spent many years abroad in Flanders and Paris. Frequently visited Ireland, mostly during the 1730s and 1740s. It is in Ireland that he almost certainly painted the equestrian portraits of Sir George and Lady Frances Hampson and their son, George Francis Hampson, s.&d. 1738, 22in.x27in. The painting is particularly interesting since it shows, in profile, the harness of a lady riding side-saddle at this date. He attended Sir Godfrey Kneller's (q.v.) Academy in 1712 where he learnt to paint, as did John Vanderbank (q.v.). Slaughter became Keeper and Surveyor of the King's pictures, from 1744 until his death. Vertue, who probably knew him, remarked that "Mr. Slaughter is always happy in his designs and finishes the whole with his own hands - not common", presumably a dig at copyists like Thomas Spencer and Thomas Butler (qq.v.). Slaughter's portrait "Wyndham Quinn with Gundog and Game", 40⅛in.x50⅝in., previously attributed to George Knapton (q.v.), c.1745, is now in the Paul Mellon Collection, Upperville, Va, USA.

Sloan, John (1871-1951)

American realist painter, best known as a founder of the Ashcan School and for his dramatic settings and humorous innovations of city life. His design for the New Mexico baseball team uniforms (c.1926) painted in watercolour, 10⅞in.x8⅜in., is in the Kraushaar Galleries and depicts a rather impractical and amusing baseball player wearing an amalgam of gaucho costume and regulation uniform. "Croquet" c.1918, 16in.x20in., was formerly also in the Kraushaar Galleries.

Small, William, RI, HRSA (1843-1929)

Painter in watercolour and an illustrator. Studied at the RSA and came to London in 1865. He exh. at the RA, NWS, GG and elsewhere (1869-1900). Sporting works at the RA include a painting of water polo. His portrait of the Prince of Wales driving a sleigh along the embankment in London dated 1881 was exh. at Jeremy Maas, London and his shooting picture entitled "On the Moors" c.1870 was repro. as a double page in "The Graphic". Elected RI (1883) and HRSA (1917).

Smart, G. (op.1829-c.1860)

Provincial, indeed naïve, painter of Mr. Bright the Tunbridge Wells letterman leading his white pony, painted in 1829 and "The Earth Stopper" c.1860, an applied picture worked in coloured velvets and felts, 10in.x14in. Mr. Smart described himself as "an artist in cloth and velvet figures to his Royal Highness, The Duke of Sussex" and operated in the Tunbridge Wells area, painting the portraits of local personalities. Many of the lettermen were so badly paid that they supplemented their wages by following other trades in their spare time. For example, there was a well-known Sussex letterman - not Mr. Bright - who always carried a card on him inscr. "Letters and ladies safely delivered" for during his spare hours he was a midwife.

Smart, John, RSA, RBA, RSW (1838-1899)

Scottish painter of landscapes, pupil of H. McCulloch. Exh. at the RA, SS, NWS, GG, RSA, RSW and elsewhere (1870-1899). He specialised in painting Highland scenes and very often sporting subjects including "The Island Pool on the Orchy with two Fisherman", 1889, "A Lone Angler" and "Rough Shooting". His golf scenes include "This for the Hole, Macrihanish", dated 1889 and inscr., a watercolour which was exh. at the Royal Scottish Watercolour Society (1889 No. 120) and "A View of the Golf Course at Stirling Castle", with figures in the foreground, dated 1890. Also "The Gully Montrose", watercolour, and "A View of North Berwick Golf Links", a picture which was repro. in the "Golf Book of East Lothian" by John Kerr, pub. 1896. Some of Smart's golf views were engraved by George W. Aikman (q.v.) (1893) and pub. in Smart and Aikman's "The Golf Greens of Scotland". Elected RSA (1877), RSW (1878) and RBA (1878).

Smellie, Robert (op.1880-1908)
The Scottish painter of a pair of bay hunters in landscapes, s.&d. 1881, each 16in.x20½in. This artist exh. at the GI and RSA (1880-1908) from an Edinburgh address.

Smetham-Jones, George W. (op.1887-1907)
Figure and equestrian painter, also of sporting subjects, whose work includes "Fallen at the Post" a steeple-chasing scene, watercolour, s.&d. 1901?, a portrait of a horse outside a stable, pen/ink, s.&d. 1891 and "Comedy" and "Tragedy", a pair of watercolours, each s.&d. 1889, 20in.x12½in., Sotheby's (Chester) 1986. Smetham-Jones exh. at the RA, RBA, RI, BI and Walker AG Liverpool (1887-1893).

Smirke, Robert, RA (1752-1845)
Painter and illustrator who was first apprenticed to a London coach painter, named Bromley. He entered the RA Schools (1772) and exh. at the SA and the RA (1775-1800). Elected RA (1793). Specialised in theatrical paintings but collaborated with John Emes (q.v.) on the painting of the meeting of the Society of Royal British Archers in Gwersyllt Park, Denbighshire. The print after this work was engraved by Cornelis Apostool and pub. in 1794 by John Emes. British Museum.

Smith, Anthony (Tony) (b.1932)
Motoring artist, the son of the artist Gordon T. Smith. Graduated with honours from Moseley Art School. His work can be seen at the Driffold Gallery, Sutton Coldfield. "Nurburgring 1935" shows Nuvolari in the P3 Alfa Romeo overtaking the crippled Mercedes of Von Brauchitsch, s.&d. '88, 19in.x29in., painted in acrylic. The same study was also painted by Nicholas Watts (q.v.).

Smith, C. Webb (op.1860)
Painter of "Pheasants in the Park at Broadwater, Worthing", dated 1860, John Francis, Carmarthen, 1985. Smith is almost certainly the same C.W.Smith who was Captain of the Bengal Archers c.1839 and who drew game bird illustrations to the "Bengal Sporting Magazine", a series of twenty vol. dating from January 1833 to November 1842.

Smith, Carlton Alfred, RI, RBA, ROI (1853-1946)
London portrait and genre painter in both oil and watercolour whose painting entitled "A Game of Shuttlecock", dated '96, 10in.x7in., qualifies him for inclusion in this Dictionary. Smith studied art at the Slade School where he won gold and silver medals. He also worked as a lithographer for several years before taking up painting. He exh. at the RA, RBA, RHA, RI, ROI and the Manchester and Walker AG, Liverpool from 1879. Elected RI (1889) and ROI (1890). Visited India (1916-1923).

Smith, Charles Lorraine, MP, JP (1751-1835)
Amateur sporting artist and sportsman based in Leicestershire. He exh. six paintings at the RA, all of hunting and horses. Like his friend, Henry William Bunbury (q.v.) much of his work depicted humorous incidents in the sporting field. Smith was also an MP, a JP, a poet and a fiddler, and Deputy Master of the Quorn. He had a great influence on sporting art and he made his home available to the many sporting artists operating in and around Leicestershire at that time including John Ferneley (q.v.) (Smith was godfather to Ferneley's son Claude Lorraine Ferneley (q.v.)), George Morland and Henry Alken (qq.v.) (both of whom helped CLS with his painting), Sir R. Frankland (q.v.), Dean Paul (q.v.) and W.P. Hodges (q.v.). Smith was depicted with the Cambridge Harriers by John Ferneley in one of that artist's first RA exhibits in 1806 (No. 919), 34in.x42in. The British Museum has a relatively early study by Smith of George III at Cheltenham, dated 1788.

Smith, Dan
Contemporary artist. "London Scottish -v- London Welsh", 7½in.x11½in., exh. Royal Festival Hall 1980 and the Stock Exchange 1981. Smith won the Sports Council prize for the best painting on a sporting topic with this rugby picture.

Smith, Frederick Sheldon (op.1877-1886)
A fine painting of the London - Bristol mail coach on the road and "The Regent", the Bath - London mail coach on the road in winter, both signed and one dated 1880 were auctioned Christie's 1981. Exh. (1885-1886) at the RA, RSA and Walker AG. Lived in London.

Smith, G. Hill (op.1886-1918)
Watercolour painter and a humorous pen and ink sporting artist who exh. (1886-1918) at Walkers Gallery, London from his Herne Hill address.

Smith, Garden Grant, RSW (1860-1913)
Scottish landscape painter who exh. watercolours at SS from his Edinburgh address and who was the editor of "Golf Illustrated" (1895-1913). He also pub. a number of books on golf. His painting entitled "The Tee Shot", a golfing scene depicting a Scottish caddy, became the frontispiece for a book of the same name, 10⅝in.x 7⅛in. Elected RSW (1890)

Smith, Gean (1851-1928)
American painter of sporting scenes, usually of flat racing or trotting. His work includes a portrait of the American trotter "Alice Barnes" dated 1900 and "Carmello" driven by his owner, Louis Kaplan of New York, dated 1900 and inscr., 20in.x30in., Sotheby's (NY) 1980.

Smith, George Armfield (op.1836-1839)
See also George Armfield. The painter of "The Young Warrener" which was engraved by C.N. Smith, the aquatint engraver of sporting subjects, to whom he was presumably closely related. Exh. five works at the RA including "Fox Prowling", portraits of horses and dogs, two works at the BI and one at SS (1836-1839) before he changed his name to Armfield.

Smith, George (of Chichester) (1714-1776)

A rather repetitive landscape painter who was his own etcher. Born in Chichester, the son of a baker and brother of the artists William and John Smith. Painted a number of frozen winter scenes including one in the Paul Mellon Collection, Upperville, Va, USA, entitled "Duck Shooting", 17in.x19½in., and "A Winter Landscape", s.&d. 1752. His exhibits at the SA and FS (1760-1774) include numerous winter landscapes depicting snow and frost. One with a frozen river and a sportsman shooting duck, 15⅞in.x18½in. was auctioned Sotheby's (Glen.) 1970.

Smith, Graham (op.1945-1950)

20th century painter of sporting subjects including foxhunting, racing, salmon fishing and steeplechasing, usually painted in gouache.

Smith, Herbert Luther (1809-1869)

Portrait painter who exh. at the RA (1831-1854) and was employed by Queen Victoria as a copyist. His portrait in watercolour of a fencing master (probably P.G. Hamon, since it carries his inscription) is dated 1856 and hangs at the De Beaumont Centre, London.

Smith, Howard (op.1953/4)

Contemporary painter and print maker who contributed "Fleeting Impression of Jesse Pye", litho mezzotint, 11½in.x9½in., to the FE.

Smith, J.B. (op.1836)

A portrait of a black hunter with a dog in a loose box signed J.B. Smith and dated 1836 was auctioned Christie's (Sth. Ken.) 1989. This artist and J.L. Smith (q.v.) could be one and the same.

Smith, J.L. (op.1832)

An equestrian painter who exh. a portrait of a horse at the RSBA in 1832. This artist and J.B. Smith (q.v.) could be one and the same.

Smith, J. Wells (op.1870-1882)

Painter of rustic genre scenes. Exh. at SS (1870-1875) including children fishing entitled, for example, "A Bite". He usually s.&d. his work.

Smith, Jane Sophia Clarendon (Mrs. H. Clarendon Smith, née Egerton), NWS (op.1858-1877)

Genre painter, usually in watercolour who exh. at the New Watercolour Society (1858-1877). Her portrait "Four Children in a Summer Landscape", one of them with a cricket bat over his shoulder, watercolour, 19in.x 25in., s.&d. September 1869, was auctioned Sotheby's, 23 April 1974 (363).

Smith, John Raphael (1752-1812)

Portrait painter, engraver (to the Prince of Wales, 1784) and print publisher. Son of Thomas Smith of Derby (q.v.). Founded the London School in 1775 with the sporting painter James Ward (q.v.) (whose sister he married). James Ward was also a pupil of his, as was his brother William Ward (q.v.). Fellow members included Thomas Rowlandson (q.v.) and Julius Caesar Ibbetson (q.v.). Sporting prints by Smith, after his own work, include "The Benevolent Sportsman", "The Sportsman's Repast" (1801), and "A Fencer", a portrait of Henry Angelo (1756-1835) the best known fencing master of the 18th century. Engraved in mezzotint by B.F. Scott and pub. by the engraver in 1791. British Museum, London.

Smith, Linda Jane (b.1962)

Born in Quinton, Birmingham. Studied graphic art at Bournville College of Art in 1980. Specialises in sporting cartoons.

Smith, Phil(ip) W. (op.c.1892-1935)

Etcher of landscapes and horses who lived at Chorlton-on-Medlock, Manchester. Included in this Dictionary for his drypoint of Tattersalls, Knightsbridge, London, showing the old horse auction before it moved to Newmarket. Bourne Gallery Reigate, Surrey. Smith's work was pub. by Colnaghi.

Smith, Richard J. (b.c.1955)

Contemporary artist in his mid-thirties who paints wildlife studies. He works for "The Shooting Times", "Sporting Gun", "Angling" and "The Specialist Angler". His detailed and extremely realistic studies of fish have been commissioned in limited edns. and as greetings cards. He started his career as a medical painter at a hospital in Oxford.

Smith, Stan(ley), ARA, PLG, RWS (b.1929)

Painter and a boxing enthusiast who has effectively captured the drama of the sport in his paintings which include his watercolour "Top of the Bill at Bethnal Green" c.1987. Smith, a fellow of Ruskin College of Art, Oxford (Contemporary), studied at St. Albans School of Art (1948-1951) and has exh. at the RA. His publications include "How to Paint and Draw" and "Drawing and Painting the Figure".

Smith, Thomas (of Derby) (b.c.1720-d.c.1767)

Landscape and sporting painter, author, illustrator and engraver of his own work. Father of the engraver John Raphael Smith (q.v.) and the landscape painter Thomas Correggio Smith. Known as Smith of Derby which is where he was born and chiefly lived. One of the earliest professional painters - although he was self taught - of views of country houses and landscapes. He also turned his hand to sporting subjects including a portrait of "Dainty Dove" held by a groom, a river beyond, dated 1758, 44in.x58½in., and Borlase Cockayne as a boy of eleven years old riding "Sultana" dated 1751 and inscr. The Hon. Mr. Borlase Cockayne on "Sultana" by "Blaze" out of "Lady Thigh", 18¾in.x25in., The Paul Mellon Collection, Upperville, Va, USA. Smith was patronised by many of the Derbyshire nobility, including Sir Robert Burdett 4th Bt., and there are pictures by him at both Chatsworth and Lord Townshend's house at Raynham.

Smith, Thomas (1790-1852) (sometimes known as "Gentleman Smith")

MFH of the Hambledon in Hampshire (1825-1829), the Craven (1829-1833), the Pytchley (1840-1844) and then again to the Hambledon (1848-1852). Author and talented illustrator who wrote and illus. two hunting books, "Extracts from the Diary of a Huntsman", pub.

1838, and "The Life of a Fox - Written by Himself", pub. 1843 when he was Master of the Pytchley. "A Portrait of the Hampshire Hunt Moving Off" in 1819 was engraved by Charles Turner (1773-1857).

Smith, Vivian
A watercolour entitled "A Meet of the Devonshire Harriers", signed by this artist, 20¾in.x27¼in. was auctioned Bearnes 1988.

Smith, William (op.1813-1859)
Painter of sporting subjects including "Two Spaniels in a Landscape" dated 1849 and inscr. "Bob", favourite dog belonging to J. Burne, "A Sportsman and his Grey Pony with Dogs and Game", dated 1831, "The Dover Mail", "A Bay Horse held by a Farmer near a Stable", dated 1837, "A Spaniel with a Rabbit in an extensive Landscape", dated 1848, and a superb portrait of "Sir Rowland Hill of Hawkstone, Shropshire with his Otter-hounds" dated 1837. The sitter was born in 1772, the son of John Hill of Hawkstone in Shropshire and his wife Mary. He was created a Viscount in 1842 in recognition of a long and highly distinguished military career as a general under Wellington in Spain and at Waterloo and later as Commander in Chief of the army. He was an enthusiastic sportsman and lived at Hardwick Grange. The painting of Sir Rowland Hill with his otter hounds is mentioned by Frederick Gordon Roe in "The Connoisseur", June 1930. William Smith exh. thirty-two paintings at the RA and fifteen at the BI (1813-1847).

Smith, William A. (1753-c.1793)
Portrait painter who studied at the RA Schools (1772) and exh. miniatures at the RA (1774). Seems to have painted for the Duke of Gordon and is included in this Dictionary for his portrait of a sportsman with his dog and game, 49in.x39½in., s.&d. 1791, auctioned Sotheby's 1963. Smith seems to have worked in the north-east area of Scotland.

Smythe, Edward Robert (1810-1899)
Ipswich landscape and sporting painter who specialised in fox-hunting and coaching scenes including "Curiosity", "The Chase" and "A Coach and Four". Exh. (1850-1861) at the RA, BI and SS.

Smythe, Emily R. (op.1850-1874)
Sister of Edward Robert and Thomas Smythe (qq.v.) and frequently mistaken for her brother with the same initials. She painted landscapes and animal paintings including "A Grey Saddled Pony and a Dog by a Fence". She exh. five paintings at the RA including one entitled "Favourite Hounds" and four at BI including "A Pony and a Boy" and "The Village Blacksmith" (1850-1874). She lived and worked in Suffolk.

Smythe, Ernest (op.1896-1899)
Illustrator and watercolourist who specialised in hunting subjects and contributed to "The Sketch" (1896) and "The Illustrated London News" (1899).

Smythe, Lionel Percy, RA, RWS, RI, ROI (1839-1918)
Landscape painter. Included in this Dictionary for the football scene he painted with William Overend (q.v.),

"England v. Scotland", signed by both artists, and dated 1889. As both artists worked for the "Illustrated London News", it is thought that this work may have been commissioned by the ILN for reproduction. Smythe, who studied art at Heatherleys, lived mainly in France. He exh. at the RA from 1860 and elsewhere from 1863. Elected RI (1880), ROI (1883), RWS (1894) and RA (1911).

Smyth(e), Sidney (op.1836-1844)
Painter of a study of a horse in a landscape, signed and inscr. "Copenhagen", the name of the celebrated charger of the Duke of Wellington, and dated 1836, 15in.x20in. Presumed to be a member of the East Anglian family of painters.

Smythe, Thomas (of Ipswich) (1825-1906)
Landscape and sporting painter based in East Anglia, the brother of Edward Robert Smythe (q.v.). His sporting work includes "A Sportsman with his Dog and Bag", "The End of the Day", "Gun Dogs in a Stable", "The Midday Rest", "Good Friends", "A Bay Hunter with a Dalmatian and a Retriever in a Courtyard", "A Peasant Boy Badger Hunting with his Dogs", "The Woolpit Horsefair" and "The Day's Bag". His work was usually signed but very rarely dated.

"Snaffle"
Author of "Gun, Rifle and Hound". Wrote under this pseudonym for Fores "Sporting Notes and Sketches" 1905. See also Henry Sperling.

"Snaffles"
Pseudonym used by Charles Payne (q.v.).

Snape, J. (op.1849)
The painter of a portrait of a mare in a stable entitled "The Widow", s.&d. 1849 and inscr., 20in.x27in., auctioned Tennants 1985.

Snape, Martin (op.1874-1901)
Hampshire painter of birds, animals and landscapes who exh. (1874-1901) at the RA, SS, GG and elsewhere. Sporting titles include "The Gamekeeper's Museum" (1894).

"The Snark"
Alias Starr Wood (q.v.).

Snow, John Wray (op.1820-1840)
Painter of equestrian subjects, particularly of racing portraits including "The Recorder" (winner of the Great Leamington Stakes) held by his owner Mr. Eddison in a sunlit landscape, s.&d. 1831, "Retriever" a dark bay racehorse with a groom in a landscape, s.&d. 1839, "Harkaway" a chestnut racehorse held by his owner with a Newfoundland dog in a landscape, dated 1830, engraved by W.B. Scott c.1834, "Laurel" a dark bay racehorse with jockey up, by the starting post with his owner and groom, dated 1831, and "Velocipede" dated 1820 and inscr. "Malton". Said to have come from the Newcastle area. Several of Snow's paintings were engraved including "The Meet At Blagdon", (T.G. Lupton 1840). Snow exh. two works at the RBA in 1832 and contributed illustrations to Tattersalls "British Racehorses" (1838) and "The Illustrated London News" (1848).

Snowdon, Florence A. (op.1908)
Several small hunting scenes in pen, ink and water-colour were painted by this artist including "A Hunting We Will Go", a set of three all s.&d. 1908 and "Miss Millie Travers's Account of a Rattling Run", signed and inscr., Sotheby's (Sussex) 1988.

Snyder, W.P. (op.1879-1889)
Unknown illustrator of American life who contributed to "Harpers Weekly" including a work entitled "At A Collegiate Game of Baseball", 1889, showing smart women and fashionable men in relaxed poses watching the game and "The metropolitan Regatta on the Hudson", a woodcut, 26 July 1879, showing rowing races on the Hudson River.

Somers, C. Bettina
Canadian painter of a dramatic ice hockey event depicting the "Toronto Maple Leafs -v- Chicago Black Hawks", line and wash drawing contributed to the XIVth Olympiad "Sport in Art" Exhibition held at the V&A Museum, London, during the Olympic Games (1948).

Somerset, Richard Gay, VPRCA, ROI (1848-1928)
Manchester-born landscape painter, and of several hunting scenes who exh. at the RA, SS, GG, NG, RCA, ROI and the Walker AG, Liverpool (1871-1927). Educated at Liverpool Collegiate School. Elected VP R.Cam.A (1890) and ROI (1897). Member of the Manchester Academy.

Somerville, Edith Anna Oenone (Dr.), MFH (1858-1949)
Illustrator of hunting books and sketches. Born at Drishane, Ireland. Daughter of an army colonel. Studied art in Paris under Colarossi and Delecluse and attended the Westminster School of Art. On returning to Ireland she set up house with her cousin Violet Martin Ross who wrote under the pseudonym of "Martin Ross" and collaborated with her on a number of books on Irish life which were immensely popular. After the death of Violet Martin in 1915, Edith Somerville carried on with the joint authorship for the rest of her books, alleging that the spirit of her late partner helped her just as much as if she were alive. Her books were so exceptional that she was made an honorary doctor of literature of Trinity College, Dublin in 1932. She was a brilliant horsewoman, becoming Master of the West Carbery Foxhounds and in that capacity she found material for her books and sketches. An ardent feminist, she travelled extensively on the continent and in America but lived most of her life in Castletownsend, West Cork, where she eventually died at the age of ninety-one and was buried beside Violet Martin Ross in Castletownsend churchyard. Her books include "The Real Charlotte" (1894), "Clear as Noon Day" (E. Penrose 1894), "The Silver Fox", "Some Experiences of an Irish RM" (1899) (a copy of which incidentally was inexplicably found at the end of the last war in the captured headquarters of a Japanese general and remains for its finder a most treasured possession), "Further Experiences of an Irish RM" (1908), "Dan

Russel, the Fox" (1911) and "In Mr. Knox's Country" (1915). She exh. at the FAS, RHA, SWA and she held one-woman exhibitions at Goupil and Walkers Gallery in 1920 and 1923 where "Sunset, Mist and Mountain" was exh., 12in.x17in., Phillips 1985.

Somville, Roger (b.1927)
Belgian figure painter in pastel and watercolour whose pastel portrait entitled "L'Athlete", 29in.x22in., was auctioned in 1989.

Song, John (op.1819)
A pair of still lifes with dead game in a larder, both s.&d. 1819, 30in.x39¾in., were auctioned Sotheby's 1985.

Soper, George, RE (1870-1942)
Painter, black and white artist and an engraver whose work, usually of rural scenes, also includes several polo scenes drawn in pencil and painted in watercolour. His etching entitled "The Weekend Luggage", 5⅞in.x 7⅞in., depicting a Highland terrier sitting beside a Gladstone bag and a golf bag with clubs, was amongst the works sold from Soper's studio sale Bonhams 1992 as were many of his polo works. Soper's "Ice Hockey" painted for "Boys Own Annual" 1924/1925 (p.155) is an exciting action picture intended to encourage a passion for sport in the young of the day. Soper studied and drew working horses all his life. Many of his drawings were repro. in "George Soper's Horses" pub. H.F. & G. Witherby (1990).

Soper, Thomas James (op.1836-1890)
Landscape painter who exh. at the RA (1836-1882), the BI, SS, NWS and elsewhere. He painted several angling scenes including "Fishing on the Thames" which is in the collection of the Piscatorial Society.

Sotheby-Pitcher, Neville (op.1907-1939)
Sussex landscape and marine artist whose painting "J Class Racers off Rhode Island", signed, 29in.x22in., was auctioned Christie's (Sth. Ken.) 1986.

"Nim South"
Alias Robert Smith Surtees (1803-1864) who contributed to "The Sporting Magazine" under this name. Surtees became a famous sporting writer - creator of the famous Jorrocks series and founder of "The Field" magazine (1853).

Southard, O.W. (op.c.1895)
Unknown American painter of a still life with a baseball bat and ball c.1895, watercolour, 17in.x27in., in the Gladstone Collection of Baseball Art, USA.

Southgate, Frank RBA (1872-1916)
Painter of birds in watercolour, sporting artist and illustrator. Born in Norfolk and worked mainly in the Norfolk area. Ranked as one of the finest bird artists of his time. Tragically killed in action in France during World War I. He illus., with William A. Dutts, "Wildlife in East Anglia" (1906, pub. Methuen and Co.). His painting "The Flight Shooter", showing a man and his dog shooting, was auctioned in Norwich 1987.

Sowerby, John G. (op.1876-1914)
Landscape painter in both oil and watercolour. He painted a number of sporting scenes including "Pigeon Shooting", signed, 33½in.x53¾in., auctioned Christie's 1978. Sowerby exh. at the RA, RI, RSA, BRU, the Walker AG Liverpool and elsewhere (1876-1914).

Spackman, Isaac (op.c.1750-d.1771)
A painter of birds and animals.

Spahn, Victor (b.1949)
Born in Paris of Russian parents. Studied painting in 1970 after working for several years in the field of mosaics. Has travelled widely throughout the world and exh. frequently in the USA and in France. He is also a lithographer and uses sport frequently in his paintings and prints. "Tennis", an original lithograph, 6 plates, 14 colours, printed in Paris in 1986 on Arches paper. Edn. size 250, signed by the artist and numbered. Artists proofs 25. Image size 23in.x18in., pub. 1987 by CCA Galleries and the artist.

Spalding, Charles B. (op.1837-1865)
Equestrian and sporting painter who lived in Reading, Brighton and London. He exh. five pictures at the RA (1840-1849). His patrons included Queen Alexandra, Sir E. Filmer and John Elmore. Spalding's sporting work includes "The Meet of the Hambledon Hounds at Preshaw House, Warnford" (1844), 39½in.x67in. which was engraved (with a key) by Day and Son, "A Gig drawn by a Black Horse" standing outside a stable, dated 1840, "Tally Ho" and "Gone to Earth", a pair, dated 1865, "The End of Day", a shooting scene, dated 1859, numerous portraits of hunters standing by their stables or barns and a portrait of the racehorse "Elis" s.&d. 1838. "Elis" was reputedly the first horse to be taken to race meetings in a horsebox, a subject also painted by T. Whaite (q.v.). Spalding contributed several illustrations to "The New Sporting Magazine" (1843).

Sparrow, Geoffrey, ARA, ARE, MC, TD, FRCS (Lt. Col.) (1887-1969)
Sussex sporting painter and etcher, caricaturist and author. Born in Ivybridge near Plymouth. Educated Kelly College, Tavistock (1900-1904) and Caius College, Cambridge, whom he represented in rowing and rugger. Sparrow won a scholarship to St. Bartholomew's Hospital. Took a distinguished part with the First Brigade at the defence of Antwerp in the 1st World War. Lived most of his life in Sussex, practising his medical profession, which he started in 1919 in Horsham. Hunted for many seasons with the Crawley and Horsham Foxhounds about whom he wrote and illus. his publication "The Crawley and Horsham Foxhounds" (1925). He also wrote and illus. his autobiography "Foxes and Physic" (1962). His hunting and point-to-point scenes are delightful watercolours or coloured etchings.

Spear, Ruskin, CBE, RA (1911-1990)
Probably one of the very best portrait painters of his time. Studied at Hammersmith School of Art and then at the Royal College of Art (1931) under Sir William Rothenstein and Gilbert Spencer. First exh. at the RA from 1932. Elected ARA (1944) although Sir Alfred Munnings (q.v.) viewed his election and those of Rodrigo Moynihan and Robert Buhler (q.v.) with suspicion, as "elements likely to introduce a new modern spirit into the place", suspicion incidentally which was justified. Spear taught at the RCA from 1945 until 1976. His sporting paintings include portraits of Freddie ("Fiery Fred") Trueman, 82in.x26½in., painted 1963, "Footballers", signed, 30in.x20in., auctioned Christie's, and a portrait of Alex Higgins playing a snooker shot, 15in.x18in. Doncaster Museum and AG have a fine snooker painting by Spear of two figures playing, from which it would appear that they are down to the last red ball, 16¼in.x21½in. "The Big Fight", a boxing contest, 12in.x16in. was auctioned Christie's 1991.

Speechley, G.S. (op.1953)
Contemporary painter. Contributed a football painting "The Crowd", 20½in.x26½in. to the FE.

Spence, Percy Frederick Seaton (1868-1933)
Born in Sydney, New South Wales and spent his early career in Australia exhibiting his work at the Art Society of New South Wales. Came to London in 1895 and worked from Kensington, contributing to magazines. A fine figure draughtsman and an equestrian painter in both oils and watercolour. His work includes "Riding the Rebel", dated 1895, "His Majesty's Mail", a watercolour dated 1909, and "Diana the Huntress", a watercolour painted in 1931. His watercolour of the racehorse "Felstead" with jockey up, dated June 1928, 19½in.x13½in., was auctioned Gorringes July 1990. "Felstead" won the Derby in 1928.

Spencelayh, Charles, HRBSA, RMS, VPBWS (1865-1958)
Etcher and painter of portraits, figure and genre subjects, also some sporting scenes including "Going Out" and "Coming Home", a pair of signed hunting scenes, each 20in.x30in., "A Tasty Morsel" showing an angler threading a fishing hook with bait, signed and inscr., 23¼in.x17¼in., "Hooked" 20in.x25½in., "A Snifter from the Hip Flask", dated '96, painted in gouache. "His First Football", signed, 14in.x10in., Christie's (Sth. Ken.) Spencelayh collaborated with A.C. Sealy (q.v.) on Sealy's series of groups of hunts, Spencelayh painting the faces and Sealy the horses. Together they also painted a golfing portrait group of the members of the Royal St. George's Club, Sandwich, Kent in 1892, 29½in.x59½in., which features more than sixty members (and two wives) in the line. The Royal St. George became the first English golf course to host the Open Championship in 1894. Spencelayh was elected RBSA (1928) and RMS (1897).

Spencer, John S. (op.1835-1863)
Figure painter and of some sporting subjects including "The Hunter", a portrait of a man with his dog and gun, s.&d. 1840, 36in.x28in. He exh. six works at the BI and at SS and one work at the RA (1835-1863).

Spencer, Thomas (op.1700-1767)

Equestrian and sporting painter whose career is obscure. He was probably a pupil of James Seymour (q.v.) to whom much of Seymour's unsigned work has been attributed. He may also have been an assistant to Thomas Butler (q.v.). His sporting work includes "A Portrait of Sir Edward Marshall of Surrey, known as 'the Sporting Baronet', on a Chestnut Racehorse", s.&d. 1752 and inscr. with his coat of arms, "A Portrait of 'Martindale Starling'", a grey thoroughbred stallion being exercised by a groom on the downs, 28in.x36in., painted 1750, and "The Famous Running Horses of the Duke of Grafton". Spencer worked for the publisher J. Cherry between 1740 and 1746 as indeed did James Seymour during which time they contributed thirty-three horse portraits which were engraved by H. Roberts and pub. during these years.

Sperling, Diana (1791-1862)

This young lady gains a place in this Dictionary for her quite delightful watercolours of Regency life in the early 19th century depicting sporting scenes - fox-hunting, cricket, stag hunting, fishing and bowls, battledore and shuttlecock, and even a donkey race. Between 1812 and 1823 she filled her sketch books and the paintings show an interesting insight into country life and sport at that time. She painted her horses in a very similar style to the contemporary artist, Vincent Haddelsey (q.v.). She was born at Dines Hall, Halstead, Essex, the second of five children of John Sperling, a local landowner, and his wife. After Diana Sperling's marriage in 1834 no record, despite much searching, has been found of her paintings in either her maiden or married names.

Sperling, Henry (op.1878-1906)

Reference is made to this animal painter by "Snaffles" (q.v.), author of "Gun, Rifle and Hound", in his article on dachshunds, the little badger hounds. In Fores "Sporting Notes and Sketches" (1905) Sperling drew a picture of a dachshund for the Berlin Dachshund Club and another of two dachshunds leashed together in a snowy landscape, dated 1906. Sperling's portrait of "A Dark Bay Norfolk Roadster in a Stable", s.&d. 1878, 20½in.x24¾in., was auctioned Sotheby's 1985.

Sperling, J.W. (op.1845-1848)

Portrait painter, very often depicting his subjects with their horses in sporting settings. He exh. three paintings at the RA (1845-1848) including a portrait of a grey stallion, the property of the King of Württemburg in 1845.

Spicer, Charles (op.1885-1890)

"Going Out for the Seaton Delaval Plate, Newcastle-on-Tyne", s.&d. 1890, 16in.x30in., was auctioned Christie's 1968. Spicer exh. one work at the RA in 1885.

Spilsbury, Edgar Ashe (op.1800-1828)

London animal and equestrian painter. Exh. paintings at the RA and BI (1800-1828), some of which were horse portraits. His portrait of "A Grey Hunter in a Wooded Landscape", s.&d. 1811, was auctioned Christie's 1983. His portrait of a savage looking lion on the prowl, with a mountainous landscape beyond, s.&d. 1820, was auctioned Sotheby's 1979.

Spindler James G.H. (1862-1916)

Scottish landscape painter in both oil and watercolour whose golf painting "St. Andrews" hangs in the Museum and AG of Dundee.

Spode, Samuel (op.1811-1858)

Provincial equestrian and sporting painter of unbalanced ability. His work is sometimes naïve and sometimes extremely attractive. His best known painting, "Coursing at Stonehenge", s.&d. 1845, is in the British Sporting Art Trust Collection. Other sporting works include "Taking the Ditch", inscr. "George Osbaldeston, Esq. on 'Clasher'" (No. 6 Op.12 "Hunting Recollections" painted by Spode 1837), 24in.x29½in., a portrait of "Bryan-o-Lynn" with his owner, 28in.x36in. and "A Portrait of a Gentleman standing in a Landscape by his Mount with Coursing Hounds at Heel". Spode contributed to "The Sporting Magazine" and does not appear to have exh. at any of the main galleries.

Spooner, Arthur, VPNSA, RBA (op.1890-1962)

Landscape and portrait painter who included several sporting subjects amongst his work, usually of springer spaniels or black labradors holding dead game. "The Nottingham Boat Club" (1894), 39½in.x59½in., is a very fine and major work by this artist. The Nottingham Boat Club was founded in 1894 by a breakaway group from the Nottingham Rowing Club and the painting was commissioned to commemorate the formation of the breakaway club and the start of Sunday rowing. The founders, Alderman Alfred Page, afterwards Lord Mayor of Nottingham and his three sons are all represented in the painting. Spooner also painted "The First Test Match - Tea Interval, Trent Bridge", s.&d. 1938, 36½in.x57in. which was exh. at the RA 1941 (No. 565). Exh. at the RA, RBA, Walker AG, Birmingham AG and elsewhere (1890-1940). Elected NSA (1908), VPNSA (1924 and 1938), RBA (1920).

Spring-Smith, Miss Effie, RBA (b.1907)

London based painter and illustrator who studied at the Ipswich School of Art under George Rushton and at the Slade School under Henry Tonks (q.v.) (1925-1929). Exh. at the RA from 1931, in which year the RA hung her "Cricket in 1760". Other sporting paintings by Spring-Smith include "Hare Shooting at Bruern, Oxfordshire" exh. at the RA (1940). Elected RBA (1939).

Spurrier, Steven, RA, ROI, RBA, NS, PS (1878-1961)

London landscape and figure painter, illustrator and poster designer in oil and watercolour. Studied art at Heatherleys and worked for many years as an illustrator to "The Illustrated London News". Included in this Dictionary for his "Croquet Tournament at Wimbledon - a Moment of Suspense", repro. in "Black and White" magazine, June 1903. Spurrier turned more and more to theatre illustration in his later life and away from social realist subjects, exhibiting widely at the RA, RBA, RI, ROI, RSA, RHA and elsewhere. Elected ROI (1912), RBA (1933) and RA (1952).

"Spy"

Pseudonym used by Sir Leslie Ward (q.v.).

Stafford, Henry (op.1828-1840)
Painter of a portrait of "Heartsease", a greyhound in a landscape inscr. "Winner of the Cup" (presumably the Waterloo Cup) in 1829 and a portrait of "Helmet" inscr. "Winner of the Cup at Altcar (1828) but not allowed the Cup", a pair both signed with inits. and dated 1829 and 1828 respectively, 10½in.x13½in. Henry Stafford was the proprietor of Coates "Shorthorn Herdbook" and prints based on examples of his work are to be found at Reading University, including the Castle Howard oxen (c.1840). The original oil painting of the Castle Howard oxen, 25in.x30in., came up at auction at Christie's 1984. Other work includes "The Cottesmore Prize Heifer" (1837) and "The Duke of Northumberland's Shorthorn Bull" (c.1839). Much of his work was engraved by J.W. Giles (q.v.).

Stainforth, Martin (c.1861-1952)
English-born equestrian artist and an engraver who in 1908 went to Australia in his late forties to stay with his brother. He remained for twenty years painting the great Australian thoroughbreds including "Trenton", (champion sire 1902), "Carbine" and "Manfred", the champion three year old of 1925 who won both the Australian Jockey Club Derby and the Victoria Derby. His portrait of the bay thoroughbred "Redfern", signed and inscr. "Randwick (1-17in.)", 21in.x28in., a watercolour, was auctioned by Phillips in 1988. (Redfern is now a suburb of Sydney.)

Stamland, E. (op.1830s)
Painter of prize cows and farmyard animals who operated from an Abingdon address in 1833.

Stampa, George Loraine (1875-1951)
Illustrator, humorist, caricaturist and sporting artist. Born in Constantinople, the son of the architect G.D. Stampa who was then architect to the Sultan. The family returned to England in 1877 and settled in Appleby. GLS studied art at Heatherleys (1892-1895) where he won a scholarship to the RA Schools (1895-1900). His first drawing for "Punch" appeared when he was still a student (March 1894) and his last entitled "Impression of Parliament" was drawn in 1949. For "Punch" he contributed 2,500 drawings over a period of fifty-six years, specialising in everyday London street scenes. He also contributed a great number of sporting sketches to "Cassells Magazine" in the early 1900s. He worked in all mediums - oil, watercolour, pastel, pen, ink and pencil. Charles Keene and Phil May (qq.v.) were his idols and "Punch" and the Savage Club his great loves. His first cousin Willie Heelis married Beatrix Potter. His friends, and there were many, included Frederick Whiting (q.v.), Alfred Munnings (q.v.), G.D. Armour (q.v.) and John Sanderson-Wells (q.v.). His book illustrations included those to Kipling's dog books and "Collected Essays" by E.V. Lucas. Publications include "Easy French Exercises", a book of humorous colour drawings, "Ragamuffins" (1916), "In Praise of Dogs", an illus. anthology. He became a director of Johnson's Sporting Gallery in Covent Garden, A.E. Johnson being agent for both Lionel Edwards and Gilbert Holiday (qq.v.).

Stampa's only son, Arthur, was fortunate to be more friend and companion to his father than strictly filial and had a wealth of anecdotes and memories to share with anybody who sought him out. "Golf", pen & black ink, 8in.x11in., s.&d. with inits. (1925).

Standing, Henry William (op.1894-1931)
Interesting, presumably provincial, painter of equestrian and sporting scenes including steeplechasing, driving, hunting, riding and shire horses. He painted mostly in water and body colour and his work was of an uneven quality which could indicate that he was self-taught. He quite often painted his scenes in pairs or even in sets of four and he normally s.&d. his work. Occasionally he painted in collaboration with Arthur Standing to whom presumably, he was related.

Standish, W. (op.1854-1859)
Painter of equestrian scenes, particularly racing, who exh. a portrait of the winner of the great St. Leger Stakes at Doncaster 1858 at the BI from a London address. Wood names this horse "Standish" but the undistinguished winner of the 1858 St. Leger was "Sunbeam". His portrait of "Voltigeur" ridden by Flatman and the "Flying Dutchman" ridden by Marlow as they came out for the match at York in 1852, signed, inscr. and dated 1854, 21in.x30in., was auctioned Tennants 1985.

Stanfield, William Clarkson, RA (1792-1867)
Marine painter in oil and watercolour. Well known for his straightforward and realistic style of painting and included in this Dictionary for his fine yacht racing scene entitled "Cowes Regatta", signed and inscr., 9½in.x17½in., auctioned Bonhams 1988.

Stanley, B. (op.1879)
A still life painting with pike, rod and reel, landing net and creel, s.&d. 1879, 22in.x30¼in., was auctioned Bonhams 1981.

Stanley, James Mix (1814-1872)
American painter who was appointed official artist to the expedition, under Governor Stevens, to make a railroad survey from the Missouri River across the Rocky Mountains to the Pacific. His fine painting "A Buffalo Hunt", s.&d. 1868, was auctioned by Parke Bernet (NY) 1950. "A Game of Chance" (c.1853), 28½in.x 39½in., is in the Thomas Gilcrease Institute of Art, Tulsa, USA.

Stannard, Emily (1803-1885)
(Mrs. Joseph, née Coppin)
Painter of fruit, flowers and game still lifes in both oil and watercolour. Born Emily Coppin, she married Joseph Stannard (1826) and after his death (1830) she continued to be known as Mrs. Joseph Stannard. Exh. BI (1832-1833). Her work includes a still life with hare, partridge and a pair of green plovers, with a game bag and a gun and game in an alcove, a shotgun nearby (1835).

Stannard, Emily, Jnr. (op.1875-1907)
Painter of fruit, flowers and game still lifes who worked in oil and watercolour. Exh. at the RA (1900-1903).

Stannard, Henry, RBA (1844-1920)
Bedford landscape and sporting artist, son of John Stannard and father of the artists Henry John Sylvester Stannard (q.v.), Alexander M. Stannard, Emily (q.v.), Lilian and Ivy (q.v.) Stannard. Founder of the Bedford Academy of Arts (1887). Exh. at the RA (1902-1915) and at SS.

Stannard, Henry John Sylvester, RBA, RSA (1870-1951)
Prolific Bedford landscape painter of rustic scenes, still lifes, game and sporting subjects including "Partridge Shooting", signed, watercolour, 10½in.x14in., "Grouse in a Winter Landscape", signed, watercolour, dated 1920, "Fishing", signed, watercolour, "Duck Shooting", signed and inscr., watercolour, 13in.x25in. Brother of Emily Stannard and son of Henry Stannard (qq.v.)

Stannard, Ivy (Mrs. Horn) (1881-1968)
Bedford landscape painter, daughter of Henry Stannard (q.v.) Ran the Bedford Academy of Art for many years and exh. twice at the RA in 1912 and 1916. Her watercolour "A Pack of Grouse Flying over a Moor", auctioned Sotheby's 1985, entitles her - just - to a mention in this Dictionary.

Stanton, Richard (op.1909)
A portrait of "Minoru", a bay racehorse with a jockey up in a landscape, signed and inscr., 12in.x16in. "Minoru" by "Cyllene" out of "Mother Siegel" was trained by Richard Marsh. He won the 2000 Guineas and the Derby in 1909 for his owner Edward VII, ridden by Herbert Jones. "Minoru" was also painted by A.C. Havell (q.v.) in 1909 and Lynwood Palmer (q.v.). "Minoru" was sent to Russia in 1911 along with "Louviers", second in "Minoru's" 1909 Derby, where they both disappeared during the Revolution.

Staples, Sir Robert Ponsonby, 12th Bt. (1853-1943)
Dundee-born portrait painter in oil, watercolour and pastels. Studied at the Louvain Academy of Fine Arts (1865-1870), in Dresden (1867), under Portaels in Brussels (1872-1874). Visited Paris (1869) and exh. at the RA from 1875, also at SS, the Grosvenor Gallery, and the RHA. Worked as an illustrator and cartoonist to "The Sketch", "The Illustrated London News" and "The Graphic" and served as art master at the People's Palace, Mile End Road, 1897. Ponsonby Staples became the 12th Bt. in 1933 inheriting the title from his elder brother, and died ten years later. Lived for some years in Ireland. Major sporting works include "The Last Shot for the Queen's Prize at Wimbledon", 1887 which is in the Worthing Municipal Gallery, "England v. Australia at Lords", 58in.x117in., painted in 1886 with George Hamilton Barrable (q.v.), MCC Collection, "The Tennis Match at the Lawn Tennis Club, Newcastle, Co. Down, Ireland", 5½in.x18in., auctioned Phillips 1991 and "Newcastle Co. Down", a view of the golf course with players putting, the Donnard Hotel in the background with the Sliev behind, watercolour, s.&d. 1912, Phillips (Chester) 1991.

Stark, Arthur James (1831-1902)
Landscape painter, mainly in watercolour, who painted a few equestrian portraits and angling scenes. His work includes a study of a chestnut hunter, the property of the Duke of Rutland. Stark, son and pupil of James Stark, also studied art under Edmund Bristow (q.v.) and the RA Schools. In 1874 he studied with F.W. Keyl, animal painter to Queen Victoria. Exh. at the RA (1863). "A Stable Boy on a Pony", watercolour, 5½in.x6⅞in. is in the Paul Mellon Collection, Upperville, Va, USA, and "Two Anglers about to land a Barbel", s.&d. 1848, 9½in.x11¼in., was auctioned Sotheby's 1971.

Stark, J.G. (op.1937)
Painter of the Sixth International British Empire Trophy Race at Donnington (1937), poster, 1937 - No. E121. V&A Museum.

Stearns, Junius Brutus (1810-1885)
American painter of angling and still life fish scenes. Born at Arlington, Vermont. Stearns studied at the National Academy of Design, NY, where he became an Associate in 1848 and an Academician in 1849. Better known as a portrait painter, he also painted genre subjects. "Striped Bass with Rod and Reel", s.&d. 1848, 13½in.x34in., was auctioned Sotheby's (NY) 1990 and "Trout Fishing", dated 1853, 37in.x50¼in., was auctioned Christie's (NY) 1982.

Steel, John Sydney (1863-1932)
Scottish sporting and game painter. Born in Perthshire where he lived all his life. Educated at Perth Academy and Madras College, St. Andrews. Studied art at the Slade School, under Professor Tonks. Whilst in London he shared a studio with a fellow Perthshire sporting artist, Ernest Briggs (q.v.), author of "Angling and Art in Scotland" (1908). Steel was known by his fellow art students as "Stag" on account of his favourite subject matter, or "Tackets" because of the shooting brogues he invariably wore. After his Slade studies he went to Rome to study for a short time. His great friend John Guille Millais (q.v.) considered that his talent for painting deer was second to none and engaged him as co-illustrator of his book "British Deer and Their Horns" (1897). A keen naturalist and sportsman himself he presented his subjects with great accuracy as they really were and not as many romantic Victorian artists depicted them. Steel joined his friends Millais, Archibald Thorburn (q.v.), Lionel Edwards (q.v.) and Frank Wallace (q.v.) in two successful exhibitions in Grafton Street in 1928 and 1931. He exh. six paintings at the RA, the first when he was only twenty. Sporting titles include "Hunting the Irish Elk" and "The Dead Teal", and five paintings at SS, "A Mixed Bag", "On the Banks of the Tay", "A Highland Evening" and two of dead game.

Steell, David George, ARSA (1856-1930)
Edinburgh-born painter of animals and sporting subjects. Son of Gourlay Steell (q.v.), brother of Gourlay Steell Jnr. and nephew of John Steell, the sculptor. Studied at the Edinburgh School of Art and the RSA. Specialised in shooting and hunting scenes usually painted in oils, which include "The Dumfriesshire

Otter Hounds" featured near Hoddon Castle with Mr. Davidson, the Huntsman, s.&d. 1909, 62½in.x89in., "A Saddled Hunter with a Hound in a Stable", 24½in.x 29¼in., s.&d. 1883, "A Pheasant Covert in October", 10in.x14in., dated 1897, "Two Bay Mares", dated 1896, watercolour, "The Waterloo Cup Winners", "Ptarmigan Raided", "The Twelfth of August", and two ponies and a dog in the grounds of a country house, dated 1878. Elected ARSA (1885).

Steell, Gourlay, RSA (1819-1894)
Scottish animal painter, son of John Steell, an Edinburgh engraver, brother of Sir John Steell, the sculptor and father of David Steell (q.v.). Studied at the Trustees Academy and with R.S. Lauder. Exh. at the RA (1865-1880) and the RSA. Elected RSA (1859). Appointed animal painter to the Royal Highland and Agricultural Society of Scotland (1840) when the Society's building at number 3 George IV Bridge was formed. He was also appointed animal painter to HM Queen Victoria in Scotland after the death of Sir Edwin Landseer (q.v.) in 1878. This honour secured him virtually a monopoly of the animal and sporting commissions in Scotland. Sporting paintings by Steell include "A Portrait of a Gentleman on his favourite Bay Hunter with his Terrier" and "The Return from a Day's Grouse Shooting, Glenochrie", which Steell exh. at the RSA in 1849 (No. 340). Appointed Curator NGS (1882-1894).

Steen, Jan (1629-1679)
Dutch painter of figure and some ball game subjects including "Skittles in the Open Air", History of Art Museum, Vienna and "Nine Pin Players", National Gallery, London.

Steer, Philip Wilson, OM, NEAC (1860-1942)
Marine, landscape and figure painter in oil and watercolour. Studied at Gloucester School of Art, under John Kemp and at the Académie Julian, Paris (1882-1884). Exh. at the RA from 1883. A leading British Impressionist, his work was influenced by a number of powerful styles including those of Monet, Whistler, Constable, Turner and Gainsborough. His work in its turn has influenced leading 20th century artists. Founder member of NEAC. Employed as a war artist in the 1st World War. Six of his marine paintings, all scenes of Dover, are in the Imperial War Museum. "Watching Cowes Regatta", 20in.x40in., signed and painted in 1892, is in the Southampton AG.

Steinacker, Alfred (b.1838)
Austrian painter of hunting and steeplechasing scenes, "Over the Hurdle" and "Over the Ditch", a pair, both signed, each 8in.x10in., "The End of the Fox Hunt", 6in.x13in. and several paintings of boar hunting.

Steinberg, Saul (b.1914)
American painter of "The Corrugated Catcher", 1954, showing an unusual interpretation of a baseball player, a theme that was reflected by John Fawsett's (q.v.) "My Favourite Artist - Saul Steinberg". Steinberg's mixed media painting, 30in.x30in., is in a private collection USA while Fawsett's "My Favourite Artist - Steinberg" 1986, collage, 20in.x28½in., is in the Gladstone Collection of Baseball Art, USA.

Stella, Jacques de (1596-1657)
"Les Jeux et Plaisirs de L'Enfants", four engravings after the work of this French artist by the artist's niece Claudine Bouzonnet (1636-1697) were pub. in Paris in 1657. Three of them show naked infants playing early racket and ball games including "La Paume" (real tennis) and are amongst the earliest prints depicting racket games. Image size 5½in.x4¾in., Sotheby's.

Stern, Max (b.1872)
German painter of "A Game of Boule", 32in.x33in., auctioned Doyle (NY) 1986.

Stevens, Alfred (1823-1906)
Belgian artist who worked in both France and England. A friend of both James Jacques Tissot (q.v.) and Edouard Manet (q.v.) who also had croquet lawns in their gardens and were enthusiastic players and portrayers of the game. Manet's painting "Partie de Croquet à Boulogne" 1871 records several of his friends playing the game in Alfred Stevens' garden in Paris in 1873.

Stevens, Chris (b.1956)
Painter of football scenes. Studied at the University of Reading (1974-1978). Arts Council residency at Sunderland Football Club (1984-1985). Awards include George Rowney sponsorship for a series of paintings based on Arsenal Football Club (1986). Stevens exh. regularly in Great Britain and the USA and his work is included in the collections of the Calouste Gulbenkian Foundation, London, and the National Gallery of Wales.

Stevens, George (op.1810-1865)
London animal and still life painter who exh. at the RA, BI and SA (1810-1864). His sporting work includes "A Covey of Partridge in a Landscape", dated 1840, "A Dead Hare and Woodcock on a Dresser", inscr. "G. Gardiner, Esq., -------- Square, London" dated 1816, and "A Hare Lying in a Field", dated 1815. His "Horse in a Landscape", 18½in.x24½in., dated 1822, was auctioned Christie's.

Stevens, John, RSA (of Ayr) (1793-1868)
Scottish genre and portrait painter who studied at the RA Schools where he obtained two silver medals in 1818. Founder member of the RSA. Exh. at the RA (1815-1857), BI and SS. His portrait of "A Cairn Terrier with a Fisherman's Creel", 30in.x24in., was auctioned Sotheby's 1987. Elected RSA (1826). Died as a result of a railway accident in France — an early casualty.

Stevens, Meg J. (c.1925-c.1979)
Equestrian painter in watercolour and a sculptor who studied art at the Slade School and under Lucy Kemp-Welch (q.v.). She specialised in painting Arab horses.

Stevenson, Anthony W. (op.1889-1907)
Scottish animal painter, particularly of dogs, including a pair of black and tan and white greyhounds, dated 1889.

Stevenson, William Grant, RSA (1849-1919)
Scottish sculptor and animal painter who contributed a number of sketches, drawn from photographs, to "The

History of Curling", by John Kerr, pub. Edinburgh 1890. "Golf at St. Andrews", an etching after the work by this artist dated 1892, 14¾in.x24¾in., by the Scottish etcher Charles Oliver Murray RE (1842-1923) was pub. by the Fine Art Society (1892). Stevenson studied at the RSA schools and painted in oils, often portraying his subjects in a humorous vein. Elected RSA (1896).

Stewart, Allan (1865-1951)
Scottish painter of most subjects including portraits, landscapes, historical, military and some sporting scenes. His imaginative "The First International Foursome", painted in Carolean costume (United States Golf Association Golf Museum) gives full rein to his historical leanings. Stewart, who studied at the RSA and in Paris and Spain, exh. at the RA and RSA from 1892 and elsewhere. He was also on the staff of "The Illustrated London News" (c.1895-1908) acting as their Special Artist in South Africa and later when he accompanied King Edward VII on his Mediterranean tours.

Stewart, Charles Edward (op.1890-1930)
Glasgow-born painter of landscape, hunting and sporting subjects. Studied at the RA Schools and at the Académie Julian, Paris. Sporting work includes "Hounds Returning Home after a Hard Day", "The Start of the Day", "A Warm Day Out" and "Missed", hounds chasing a fox who has disappeared up a tree, signed, 44in.x34in., a painting which Stewart exh. at the RA in 1911 (No. 23). Probably best known for his painting "Every Dog Has His Day" which he exh. at the RA.

Stewart, Frank Algernon (1877-1945)
Sporting author, painter and even more talented illustrator who studied art at the Slade School, under Fred Brown (q.v.) and also at the Frank Calderon (q.v.) School of Animal Painting where Lionel Edwards (q.v.) was the star pupil. Painted mainly in watercolour. Principal paintings include "The Old Surrey and Burstow Hunt", "The Braes of Derwent Hunt" and "The Cleveland Hounds", with Colonel Wharton, the Master, on High Peak, Shelton (1934). He wrote and illus. many books including "The Fox that Walked on the Water" by A. Henry Higginson, sometime Master of the Cattistock Hunt, pub. (1939), "Cross Country with Hounds" (1936), "Hark to Hounds" (1937) and "Hunting Countries" (1935). He also contributed illustrations to "The Field" during the 1920s. Stewart became special war artist in South Africa in 1899 covering the Boer War for "The Illustrated Sporting and Dramatic News" and he also contributed to "The Illustrated London News" covering the relief of Ladysmith. Later, in the foreword to his book "Hark to the Hounds", Stewart was to say "The war in South Africa provided me with continuous opportunities for the study, under various conditions, of horses in action". Returning to London, he joined the City of London Imperial Yeomanry and through them was able to continue his horse studies until the outbreak of the 1st World War when he enlisted with the Second King Henry's Horse and went with them to France in early August 1914. After the war he contributed to "The Bystander" and "The Field", attending horse shows and race meetings where his rapid sketches caught the impression of the moment. He held several exhibitions at Messrs. Vicars Bros. Galleries in Bond Street, London, during the 1920s and 1930s portraying famous hunts with truthful accuracy including the Bicester, the Craven, and the Old Berkshire. This satisfied a large public demand for such paintings and combined accurate detail with a general sense of life and movement. A written review of his exhibition at Vicars in 1933 comments "There seems to be no limit to sportsmen's enthusiasm for Mr. F.A. Stewart's watercolours of hunting countries".

Stinton, Harry (op.c.1900-1940)
Brother of James (q.v.) and the better known John Stinton who all painted animal and sporting scenes for the Royal Worcester Porcelain Company between 1900 and 1940. John Stinton lived until he was 102.

Stinton, James (1870-1961)
Specialised in the painting of game birds for porcelain decoration starting at Graingers and then moving to the Royal Worcester Factory. He retired from Royal Worcester in 1926. His sporting work includes "Grouse over a Moor", "Cock Pheasant rising from the Bushes", "Pheasant and Game in a Snowy Landscape".

Stinton-Wolonts, M.
Painter of a portrait of a lady tennis player, signed, 11¾in.x7½in., auctioned Christie's (Sth. Ken.) 1989.

Stirling-Brown, A.E.D.G. (op.1900-1913)
Obscure equestrian painter, probably Scottish, whose really very talented work needs further study. Sporting paintings include a portrait of Major A.W. Foster's "Rouge Croix" dated 1910, R.B. Hunter, Esq.'s "Frank", a dark bay hunter, "Mogeely", a portrait of a bay hunter in a field dated 1912, a study of the polo pony "Princess" dated 1913 and a bay racehorse with jockey up, dated 1911. He usually painted in oil, s.&d. his work and was also an aquatint engraver. Possibly related to Thomas Stirling-Brown who exh. (1902-1915).

Stockdale, W. Colbrooke (op.1852-1867)
Sporting draughtsman who contributed to "The Illustrated London News" in 1852 and exh. at the RA (1860-1867).

Stokes, George Vernon, RBA, RMS (1873-1954)
Sporting and animal painter, often of dogs, in oils, watercolour and pastel. Also an etcher and an illustrator. Born in London and educated privately. Exh. at the RA (from 1907), the RBA, RI and RMS. Elected RBA (1930) and RMS (1896). Principal works include "Winter Sports" and "The Otter Hunt". Contributed black and white dog illustrations to "Punch" (1905), "The Illustrated London News" (1915), "The Graphic" and "The Sphere". Pub. "How to Draw and Paint Dogs". Stokes worked in Carlisle (1911-1914) and its Museum has a collection of his work.

Stolterfoht, Caroline R. (Mrs.) (op.1854-1908)
Liverpool painter who exh. at the Walker AG (1902-1908). Her humorous set of fifteen drawings entitled "Mr. Tickler's Days Fishing", drawn in pen and brown ink, dated 1854 and inscribed extensively, were auctioned Bonhams 1985.

Stone, Robert (op.1873-1900)
Australian equestrian and sporting artist of a great number of fox-hunting scenes usually painted in pairs, sets of four or even six.

Stone, Rudolph (op.1873-1900)
Painter of decorative sets of hunting scenes usually painted in oil and in pairs or sets of four or six. Almost certainly related to Robert Stone (q.v.) and painted in a very similar style.

"Stoneclink"
Polo contributor to "The Field" during the 1890s.

"Stonehenge"
Alias J.H. Walsh (1810-1888) who wrote "British Rural Sports". He also became editor of "The Field" in 1858, a post which he occupied until his death. A very keen shot and an all round sportsman, a founder of the Battersea Dogs Home.

Stonelake, Frank P., RWA (1879-1929)
A very talented equestrian artist in both oil and watercolour, who studied at the Dublin School of Animal Painting and exh. at the RHA (1902). Born in Bristol, the son of a baker, he studied art at Bristol and in London with the intention of becoming an art teacher. The animal artist Briton Riviere (q.v.) was so impressed by Stonelake's sketches, which he submitted for a possible scholarship, that he persuaded him to become a professional animal painter. He became a founder member of the Bristol Savages (1904) and President (1909 and 1924) exhibiting with them until the year of his death. Between 1908 and 1928, he exh. at the RWA, becoming a member of their Hanging Committee.

Storey, Ross Barron (b.1940)
American painter and illustrator of football scenes. Born Dallas, Texas. Illustrator for "Life" and "This Week" magazines and more recently "Time" magazine. Storey studied art at the FAS and SVA, under Robert Weaver, and at the ACD, Los Angeles where he is presently Chairman of the illustration department.

Stoward, F. (op.1844-1861)
Animal and equestrian painter of portraits of a bay hunter in a stable, prize cattle and a prize shorthorn bull, bred and fed by Mr. Josiah Turnbull.

Stradone, Giovanni (b.1911)
Italian painter of "The Cyclist" contributed to the XIVth Olympiad "Sport in Art Exhibition" held during the Olympic Games in London (1948).

Straet, Jan van der (1523-1605)
Flemish painter of hunting scenes including "Quail Hunting with Hawks", chalk and pen wash, "Two Hunters using the Stalking Cow to Shoot Deer", brown ink over black chalk, "Stallion pacing to the Left", chalk heightened with white, and "A Stag Hunt", brown ink and wash.

Strafford, Hector (op.1830)
Animal painter whose portrait of a large white cat in a stable interior sitting beside a stable broom and a bucket on which Strafford's initials are painted, s.&d. 1830 and inscr., was auctioned Sotheby's 1988.

Stratford, Frank (op.1906)
Little known sporting painter of game shooting subjects including "Three Pointers by a Game Bag", "A Spaniel with a Mallard in a river Landscape" and "A Spaniel with a Pheasant", a pair, "Waiting for Master" (a pony, two dogs and a game basket), a pair, and "Gun Dogs Guarding the Game Bag", s.&d. 1906. Stratford appears to have painted in oils, he usually seems to have signed his work, but rarely dated it, and often painted his sporting scenes in pairs.

Stratton, Frederick (op.1898-1938)
Sussex landscape and figure painter in both oil and watercolour. He exh. at the RA, RI, RID, ROI, NEAC and elsewhere (1898-1932). His painting "The Rugger Match" was exh. at Spinks June 1984.

Streatfield, Robert (1786-1852)
Landscape painter, chiefly known for his views in France and Belgium. Included in this Dictionary for his "Cricket at Spa, Belgium", watercolour, 4½in.x8in., c.1840. Collection of William Drummond, Esq.

Strenger, Erich (op.,1950-1986)
Graphic artist of motor and motor racing subjects who worked for Porsche from the early 1950s, commemorating every racing success with a Victory poster which Porsche pub. themselves.

Stretton, Philip Eustace (op.1882-c.1919)
Animal and sporting painter, particularly of hunting scenes in both oil and watercolour. His sporting works include "The Lost Scent", "Lost Direction" (possibly the painting he exh. at the RA 1891, No. 182 entitled "After the Hunt"), "A Grey Pony in a Stable", and "Hunting with the Quorn" (1894). He exh. (1884-1904) at the RA including "The Pet of the Kennel" (1901).

Stringer, Daniel (op.1754-1776)
A Cheshire sporting artist who worked with his father Thomas (q.v.) and his brother Samuel (q.v.). Studied at the RA Schools (1771). Stringer was a good portrait painter but is said to have degenerated into an alcoholic.

Stringer, Francis (op.1760-1778)
Cheshire animal and sporting painter. Stringer's sporting work includes portraits of racehorses and hunters. An interesting angling painting entitled "The Draught of the Trent", 39in.x49in., shows still lifes of every kind of fish to be found in that river. Auctioned Christie's 1985. Stringer's portrait of the Earl of Stamford's "Tinker" held by a groom in landscape is dated 1763, as are his portraits of "Little Fox" and "Orinoco", two bay hunters with their groom in a landscape.

Stringer, Samuel (op.1774-d.c.1784)
Painter of some equestrian subjects. Son of Thomas Stringer (q.v.). Samuel Stringer, who lived at Knutsford, Cheshire, exh. at Liverpool in 1774.

Stringer, Thomas (op.1772-1790)

Cheshire sporting artist who lived and worked in Knutsford and who specialised in equestrian portraits and hunting scenes. He appears to have been employed by, and certainly worked for, the Egertons of Tatton Park, near Knutsford. His portrait of two gentlemen and a chestnut hunter and a dog on a river bank, dated 1776, is a fine work and was auctioned Sotheby's 1981.

Strutt, Alfred William, RCA, RBC, ARE (1856-1924)

Painter of sporting subjects and a talented etcher. Son of the artist William Strutt (1825-1915). Born in New Zealand while his parents were there on a visit. Studied at the Frank Calderon (q.v.) School of Animal Painting, South Kensington. Exh. at the RA (from 1879), SS, NWS and elsewhere. Elected RBA (1888), ARE (1889). Specialised in animal and sporting subjects and was a popular exhibitor at the London galleries. Patronised by King Edward VII and accompanied him on a hunting trip to Scandinavia. He lived in Kent and Sussex. Strutt painted in both oil and watercolour. His fine painting entitled "The Otter's Holt", 22in.x30in., was auctioned Christie's 1979.

Strutt, Arthur John (1819-1888)

English landscape painter, sometimes of sporting subjects, who lived a large part of his life in Rome, painting views and scenes in the Campagna. The son of Jacob George Strutt (1784-1867), the landscape and portrait painter. Exh. one painting only at the RA (1855) entitled "The Grotto of Egenia, near Rome". His fine painting "The Meet of the Rome Foxhounds at the tomb of Cecilia Metella on the Via Appia", dated 1846 and inscr. "Rome", 36in.x54in., was commissioned by John Donnithorne Taylor, formerly of Guilsborough Hall in Northamptonshire, an Englishman who went to live in Rome in 1840 and became Field Master of the Rome Hunt in 1843. Strutt also painted the Rome Hunt again in 1871 which was auctioned Christie's 1970.

Strutt, Rosa Jameson (1861-1938)

Animal and flower painter. The daughter of William Strutt, RBA, (1825-1915) and sister therefore of Alfred William Strutt (q.v.). Included in this Dictionary for "Kittens at Play on a Snooker Table", watercolour 13⅜in.x25⅝in., signed, Phillips.

Stuart, Gilbert (1755-1828)

An American portrait painter who studied in England (1772-1782) under Benjamin West (q.v.), moving to Ireland to escape his creditors before returning to America. He achieved fame for his many portraits of the American President, George Washington. The portrait of "Young Master Day" shown holding a cricket bat with his spaniel lying beside him, is not signed by Stuart and merely attributed. It was auctioned at Christie's in 1985. (Abraham Cooper (q.v.) also painted the later members of the Day family in 1838). To demonstrate that he could paint more than just head and shoulder portraits, Stuart exh. in 1782 "The Skater", a full length portrait of William Grant, 96⅜in.x58⅛in., which is in the National Gallery of Art, Washington DC.

Stuart (Steuart), Sir John James (1779-1849)

Scottish painter and etcher whose pen, brown ink and coloured wash drawing entitled "Out Hunting", 4¾in.x 7in. was auctioned Sotheby's 1988. A pair of sporting oils "Gun Dogs in a Wood" and "On a Moor", each 10in.x29in., also probably by this artist were auctioned Sotheby's (Chester) 1989. Stuart, who was the 5th baronet of Allanbank, Berwickshire, a title he inherited in 1817, pub. through Colnaghi, two sets of etchings in 1821, followed by a further set in 1828 entitled "Gleanings from the Portfolio of an Amateur".

Stubbs, George, ARA (1724-1806)

Extremely important equestrian and sporting painter who considerably influenced later painters of sporting art. Born in Liverpool. He studied anatomy and worked in York where he gave lessons in anatomy drawing to medical students. This led to his illus. essay commissioned by John Burton entitled "Towards a Complete New System of Midwifery" (1751). His fine work "The Anatomy of the Horse" was pub. in 1766, for which Stubbs engraved the plates himself. In 1759 Stubbs moved to London where he painted English sporting scenes for private patrons, including the Lords Rockingham, Grosvenor, Richmond, Bolingbroke, Grafton and Portland. He became a close friend of Josiah Wedgwood who produced tablets for Stubbs to work on in enamel in the early 1770s. In the 1790s Stubbs was commissioned to paint a series of portraits of famous racehorses for "The Turf Review". Only sixteen of the commission were completed. He was the father of George Townley Stubbs (q.v.). His major sporting works include "The Grosvenor Hunt" (1762), portrait of "Whistlejacket" a life-sized study of a horse, a wonderful series of friezes of mares and foals (1762-1768), and a set of four fine pictures entitled "Shooting" (1767-1770), The Yale Center for British Art, The Paul Mellon Collection, New Haven, Connecticut, USA. He exh. at the SA (1762-1774) and was elected President (1773). He also exh. at the RA (1775-1803) and was elected ARA (1780) but refused, like Joseph Wright of Derby (q.v.), to become an academician when he was appointed in 1781 as he declined to deposit the necessary work. He collaborated with Benjamin Killingbeck (q.v.) on a portrait of "Sir Solomon" a bay racehorse with John Singleton up at Newmarket, 24in.x 29in., auctioned Christie's 1988.

Stubbs, George Townley (c.1756-1815)

Artist and engraver of several sporting scenes, the natural son of George Stubbs (q.v.). He engraved thirty-six prints after his father's work (1788-1791) many of which were portraits of racehorses. Exh. a portrait of a hunter at the RA in 1782, his only year to exhibit there, and between 1771 and 1776 he exh. four drawings and a mezzotint after his father's work at the Incorporated Society.

Stubbs, Richard Spencer (op.c.1815)

Early 19th century painter of sporting subjects including a portrait of a groom with a chestnut hunter in a stableyard, signed, 19½in.x23½in. auctioned Sotheby's 1976 and a portrait of a grey racehorse with its jockey who holds a silver cup, signed, auctioned Sotheby's 1972. Stubbs also painted "Gone to Ground", 21in.x 31in., auctioned Sotheby's 1989.

"Stuff"
The pseudonym used by the artist Henry Charles Seppings Wright (q.v.) for the caricatures he contributed to "Vanity Fair" (1891-1900).

Stull, Henry (1851-1913)
Canadian-born painter of equestrian subjects and portraits who had a studio on Broadway, Madison Square, NY City. Indefatigable contributor to "Leslie's Weekly" for more than forty years, conveying to the readers, owners and patrons the thrill of the New York race tracks. Stull was a keen racing man and a friend of Samuel Riddle, the textile tycoon, who owned the champion racehorse "Man O'War". "Swarthmore" one of Riddle's best horses, ran in Stull's colours of white, gold sash and cuffs and black cap. His portrait of August Belmont II's "Margrave", winner of the Belmont Stakes, is dated 1896, and a fine painting of "Queen Charlotte" and "Lionel" racing neck and neck, dated 1890, was auctioned Christie's 1985.

Sturgess, John (op.1864-1903)
Little known sporting painter, illustrator and a lithographer who was principal hunting and racing artist for "The Illustrated London News" for about ten years, from 1875. He also contributed to "The Sporting and Dramatic News" (1890) and "The English Illustrated Magazine" (1884). Exh. (1880-1884) at the RBA and RHA. He was also a lithographer after his own work including his portrait of the 1864 Derby winner "Blair Athol". His further sporting work includes a portrait of Captain Smith on "Heraut d'Armes", winner of the Conyngham and Punch Cup, Punchestown, dated 1872, "The Finish for the 2000 Guineas" and "The Race for the Oaks", a pair of racing scenes in watercolour, a steeplechase with the jockeys Mr. Clayton Lyon, Mr. Mylton Hulford, the Duke of Hamilton, and Prince Soltykoff, dated 1869. Four hunting plates, after the work by Sturgess, were engraved by William Summers and pub. in 1878, each 24¼in.x46in.

Sturgess, William Stanfield (op.1893-1903)
A sporting and equestrian artist, possibly related to John Sturgess (q.v.). His work includes "A Coach and Pair" leaving the gates of a park, painted in watercolour and dated 1903; "The Age of Steam", two horses ridden by a man and a woman looking at a train, watercolour; a painting of football showing a goal being kicked, dated 1893.

Such, William Thomas
Painter of hunting scenes whose "At the Side of the Covert", s.&d. '56, 31in.x47in., was auctioned Sotheby's 1984.

Suhrlandt, Carl (1828-1919)
German animal and sporting painter whose portrait of Lord Francis Horace Pierrepoint Cecil with dogs and dead game on a hill on the Glentanar estate was auctioned Christie's 1989. He exh. "Russian Huntsmen in a Snowstorm" at SS in 1884. "A Day's Grouse Shooting on the Glentanar Estate, Aberdeenshire" dated 1889, 39½in.x 55in., shows Charles Gordon, 11th Marquess of Huntley with Sir William Cunliffe-Brooks, Bt., Lord Francis Horace Pierrepoint Cecil and other guests. To the right of the picture stands the noted ghillie and stalker, Donald MacIntosh. In the dog cart are three couples of English setters.

Sulimo-Samuillo, Vsevolod Angelovitch (1903-1965)
Russian painter of some sporting scenes including his fine "A Skating Rink", pen and ink, 8½in.x6in. The Russian Museum, Leningrad.

Sullivan, Edmund Joseph, RWS (1869-1933)
Watercolour painter and illustrator of the 1895 edn. of "The Compleat Angler". The original illustrations include "An Otter with a Chub", pen/ink, 4in.x7in. Abbott and Holder, London.

Sullivan, Luke (c.1725-1771)
Topographical and miniature painter in watercolour and oils who was also an engraver. Sullivan was a member and a director of the Incorporated Society of Artists and his friend, the engraver, William Woollett, was secretary. As an assistant to William Hogarth (q.v.) Sullivan engraved several important plates after major compositions by Hogarth including "The March to Finchley", pub. December 1750. Sullivan is popularly supposed to have been the son of an Irish groom to the 4th Duke of Beaufort (1709-1756) who, like his brother the 3rd Duke, was a keen patron of the arts and an enthusiast for the picturesque. He employed the services of the sporting artist John Wootton (q.v.) to paint large hunting scenes to decorate the new Great Hall at Badminton by William Kent. An inventory of pictures at Badminton, dated 1775, lists six views of Badminton by Sullivan. Sullivan's portrait of Henry, 5th Duke of Beaufort on horseback with his servant Mr. Capper, is painted in oils, 77½in.x68½in., after the original portrait by Wootton and remains to this day at Badminton.

Sultan, Donald (b.1951)
Interesting contemporary American painter of baseball scenes who emerged from early minimalist influences to experiment with functional modern materials, such as linoleum tiles glued to wood. His "Baseball and Bat" (1981), oil and graphite on tile over wood, 48⅜in.x 48½in. is at the Blum Helman Gallery (NY).

Summers, Gerald
Contemporary painter of ballooning scenes.

Sunderland, Thomas (1744-1823)
North country sportsman and draughtsman of sporting subjects including a pair of hare hunting scenes inscr. verso on one "Myles Sandy's Hounds and Huntsmen", pen/ink/blue wash, each 12in.x17½in., The Paul Mellon Collection, Upperville, Va, USA. Myles Sandys kept a pack of hounds in Furness, near Ulverston, Cumbria and it is probable that Sunderland, who had a town house in Furness, hunted with them. An Ulverston Theatre playbill c.1810 states that the programme is "By Desire of Miss Sunderland, Lady Patroness of the Hunt".

Sutcliffe, John E., ROI (d.1923)
Figure painter and illustrator who contributed to "The Illustrated London News" (1916) and "The Ladies Realm", where his painting of boxing was repro. in the May 1913 issue. Sutcliffe also painted hunting scenes and exh. at the RA, RBA, RI and ROI. Elected ROI (1920) and was married to the painter E. Earnshaw.

Suthers, Leghe (1856-1924)
Figure, animal and equestrian painter whose pair of portraits of hunters standing in a summer landscape, signed, 19½in.x23¼in., were auctioned David Lay 1986. Suthers exh. at the RA, RSA, Birmingham and Walker AGs (1883-1905) and was elected NEA (1887).

Sutton, Jake (b.1947)
Clever left-handed painter of bright, colourful impressions incorporating several sports subjects, most notably horse racing. Winner of the Daily Express National painting competition (1954). Studied Manchester High School of Art (1960) and St. Martin's School of Art (1965). First one-man exhibition at the Nevill Gallery, Bath (1983). Four one-man exhibitions, Francis Kyle Gallery, London (1986-1991). Sutton was commissioned to design the Royal Mail stamps on the theme "Sport" (1988). Examples of his work are in the V & A Museum, London.

Sverchkoff, N.G. (1817-1898)
Russian painter of equestrian scenes, particularly of horse racing. Sverchkoff was an art professor in Moscow who came to Paris in 1863 to exhibit at the Paris exhibition. He then travelled to London where he held a one-man exhibition. His painting "The Racer" shows a single racehorse, fully extended, galloping to the finish.

Swan, Cuthbert Edmund (1870-1931)
Irish-born animal painter especially of lions, tigers and leopards, who started his career as a sailor before taking up painting full time. He painted some sporting scenes including "Over the Fence", 12in.x16in. Exh. at the RA (from 1893) and also at the ROI, RI and the Paris Salon.

Swan, John Macallan, RA, RWS (1847-1910)
Best known as an animal painter, usually associated with lions and tigers.

Swebach, Bernard Edouard (1800-1870)
French painter of hunting and racing scenes in both oil and watercolour. Specialised in paintings of mounted troops. "A Race Meeting", dated 1819, 21in.x28½in., was auctioned Christie's 1984 and "Chasse au Renard", 17in.x26in., dated 1839, was auctioned 1988.

Swebach des Fontaines, Jacques François
See Desfontaines

Swertschkoff, de
See de Swertschkoff

Swinburn, W. (op.1909)
Painter of the foxhound "Vaulter" in a landscape, s.&d. 1909 and inscr., 16in.x22¼in., auctioned Bonhams 1987. "Vaulter" belonged to the Duke of Beaufort and was the champion stud dog at Peterborough in 1899.

Sydenham, Kenneth
Sporting draughtsman of golfing and other scenes in pen and ink, Sotheby's (Chester) 1985.

Syer, John, RI (1815-1885)
Landscape painter, draughtsman and lithographer of marine sketches, son of the painter James Syer. Studied under J. Fisher, the miniaturist, in Bristol. Exh. at the RA (1846-1875), BI, SS, NWS, GG and elsewhere. Painter of several angling scenes including "Trout Fishing", "An Angler in the Highlands", dated '85, "Fishing", dated '54, and "An Angler by a Shady Pool", dated '54. "A Fox Behind a Rock in a Landscape" was auctioned Phillips 1984.

Sykes, Aubrey F., PPRI, PS (op.1929-1984)
Contemporary painter in oil, pastel and watercolour. "The Hockeystick Maker", s.&d. '84. A signed and limited (500) edn. print was repro. after this work, Mercian Sports. Sykes was a member of the London Sketch Club and was elected PRI in the early sixties, having become a member (1940). He exh. at the RA, RBA, RI and ROI (1929-1940).

Sykes, Charles ("Rilette") (1875-1950)
Sculptor and illustrator, Worked in London as a poster designer and a magazine illustrator contributing to "The Sunday Dispatch" and "Woman" under the pseudonym of "Relette". He also designed de Reske cigarette advertisements and, in 1911, the mascot for the Rolls Royce car that is still in use. He was responsible for designing the Ascot race cups from 1926. Exh. RA, RI and the Walker AG, Liverpool (1911-1938).

Symington, J. Ayton (op.1890-1908)
Edinburgh painter and illustrator for Dent and other publishers (1890-1908). Worked in a variety of media including oil, watercolour, pen and ink, and covered all subjects including several paintings of curling. Contributed to "The Sporting and Dramatic News", "Chums" and "The Windsor Magazine".

Sympson (Simpson), Joseph I. (op.early 18th century)
Line engraver of sporting subjects and portraits after his own and his contemporaries' work. Studied at the Artists' Drawing Academy and was employed by Peter Tillemans (q.v.) to engrave his Newmarket subjects.

Syntax, Dr
Pseudonym used by John Sheriff (q.v.).

T

Tadema, Alma
See Alma

Taffs, Charles H. (op.1894-1911)
Black and white artist who worked in Clapham, London and who contributed illustrations to the leading magazines including "The Illustrated London News" (1899) and "The Graphic" (1910-1911). His picture entitled "Lady Archers at Ranelagh" is dated 1908. He exh. at the RA (1896-1905).

Tait, Arthur Fitzwilliam, NA (1819-1905)
Liverpool-born animal and landscape painter, draughtsman and lithographer. Studied at the Manchester Royal Institute and emigrated to America (1850) where he settled in New York. Elected a full Academician at the National Academy of Design (1858). His lithograph entitled "American Winter Sports - Trout Fishing on Chattequay Lake" was pub. by Currier and Ives (1856) and his painting "Ruffed Grouse and their Young" dated 1863, 23½in.x19½in., was auctioned Christie's 1966. Tait occasionally collaborated with his fellow American emigré Edward Gay (q.v.).

Tait, G.W. (op.1797-1810)
Exh. two portraits at the RA (1797) and a drawing of a wolf (1810). His self-portrait seated beside a chestnut horse in a landscape, s.&d. 1797, 22¼in.x17¾in., was auctioned Sotheby's 1972.

Tally Ho, Ben
Pseudonym used by the sporting artist Henry Thomas Alken, Snr. (q.v.).

Talmage, Algernon Mayow, RA, HRBA, HROI (1871-1939
Painter of many subjects including hunting and equestrian scenes who lived a large part of his life in Cornwall, apart from a spell in France (1914-1918) as official war artist for Canada. It was in Canada that he met Lynwood Palmer (q.v.) with whom he collaborated on the painting of Mr. Edward E. Marshall of Pennsylvania on his hunter "Canada", signed by both artists and dated 1927. This painting was exh. at Colnaghi's Gallery in Bond Street, June 1986. Talmage made great use of sunlight in his work and was highly regarded by his contemporaries. He studied art under Sir Hubert Von Herkomer and ran an art school in St. Ives before coming to London in 1907. He was also a talented etcher although he only started etching in the 1920s. He exh. at the RA, RBA, RHA, ROI, NEA and elsewhere. Equestrian paintings exh. at the RA include a portrait

of Miss Diana Eustace-Duckett with Mrs. Kirby's "Bluebird" 25in.x30in. (1934 No. 272). Elected RA (1929), RBA (1903), HRBA (1923), ROI (1908), HROI (1930).

Tanner, C. (of Dublin) (op.1839-1847)
Equestrian painter who usually inscr. his/her work "Dublin". His/her portraits include racehorses and hunters. A portrait of a spaniel inscr. "Dash", s.&d. 1839, was auctioned Christie's 1982.

Tanner, J. (op.c.1800)
One of George Morland's (q.v.) acolytes and a copyist of his works. Morland refered to him as "The Mohawk" on account of his swarthy complexion.

Tappen(den) (G.) (op.c.1814)
An artist catalogued as Tappenden and signed by this surname only painted the portrait of the 9th Duke of Hamilton's "William", winner of the 1814 St. Leger, ridden by John Shepherd (1765-?1815). (The Duke of Hamilton (1740-1819) was fortunate in winning the St. Leger seven times. "William" was his last winner.) The artist is more likely to be G. Tappen or Tapping (q.v.) who exh. as an honorary member a portrait and two pictures of "a more or less sporting type" (Waterhouse) at the RA (1797-1799).

Tapping, G. (op.1797-1799)
Equestrian and animal painter who exh. at the RA a portrait of a nobleman's groom (1797) and a portrait of a setter finding game. See also Tappen(den).

Taquoy, Maurice (op.1905-1926)
Painted "At the Races" s.&d. 1925, 43in.x33in. Exh. Gallerie Georges, London.

Targett, Thomas G. (op.1866-1887)
Painter of angling scenes and fish still lifes including "Trout Rising to a Mayfly", dated 1885, "Study of Pike and Roach" dated 1870, "A Rainbow Trout and a Pike on a River Bank", dated 1879, "The Catch on the River Bank" dated 1887 and "A Still Life of a Hare, a Cock and Hen Pheasant in a Game Larder" dated 1866 and inscr. "Salisbury" which is the address from where he exh. a painting of game at the RA (1869).

Tarrant, Percy (op.1881-1930)
Figure painter and illustrator in both oil and watercolour who contributed to "The Illustrated London News" (1884-1889) and "The Graphic" (1911). He also exh. at the RA, RBA, RI and ROI (1881-1930). He illus. "Tom's Boy", pub. Chambers (1901). Father of

the children's book illustrator, Margaret Winifred Tarrant. He was not a painter of sporting scenes but scrapes into the Dictionary through "Out for a Spin", a painting of two children and a pony and trap going a good deal too fast, 9in.x6in., auctioned Sotheby's 1986.

Tasker, William H. (of Chester) (1808-1852)

Sporting and topographical painter in both oil and watercolour although he was less talented as a watercolourist. Born in Golden Square, London, the son of a cabinet maker who later returned with his family to Chester. He became a pupil of Robert Norris, the drawing master at the Chester Mechanics Institution. Like his brother, Edward, William Tasker also drew Chester topography for the local publishers. Tasker was much influenced by Daniel Clowes (q.v.) and like him he painted racehorses, making Chester races a central feature. His series of race winners of the Chester Tradesman's Cup (started in 1824 and better known now as the Chester Cup) was painted between 1840 and 1846. Tasker's work often features a single gnarled pollarded willow tree, so often seen in the paintings of Daniel Clowes. One of his first important patrons was Robert Grosvenor, 1st Marquis of Westminster, for whom he painted a number of racehorses including a portrait of "Decoy" (1832) (exh. Liverpool Academy). Tasker's productive years were short for he found that free-lance painting did not pay and in 1846 he became the drawing master at his old school the Chester Mechanics Institute. Examples of Tasker's work are to be found at Grosvenor Museum, Chester.

Tatchell-Bullen, C. (op.1889-1893)

Painter of equestrian portraits and scenes, particularly hunting, who usually s.&d. his work. He painted his small equestrian portraits in oils.

Tattersall, George ("Wildrake") (1817-1849)

A great grandson of the founder of the equestrian auctioneers, Tattersalls, he used the pseudonym "Wildrake" to write and edit a great many books. "The Pictorial Gallery of English Racehorses", pub. in 1850 by Henry G. Bohn, is written unusually under his own name. It contains portraits of all the winners of the Derby, Oaks and St. Leger Stakes during the previous twenty years as well as a history of the principal operations of the turf. Many of the pictures in the book were painted by Tattersall himself. He had originally trained as an architect and designed Tattersalls' stables at Willesden. In 1841 he pub. an illus. treatise entitled "Sporting Architecture" dealing with stables and stud farms. He also produced a series entitled "Cracks of the Day", a set of sixty-five plates of famous racehorses, the forerunner of "The Pictorial Gallery of English Racehorses". In 1843 he collaborated with Henry Alken (q.v.) on the illustrations to "The Reminiscences of Nimrod" and R.S. Surtees' "Hillingdon Hall". He also edited "The Sporting Magazine" in the 1840s. Exh. architectural drawings to the RA (1840-1848).

Taubert, Bertoldo (b.1915)

French painter of racing scenes including "Les Course à Longchamp", 21in.x25in.

Tavener, Robert, RE, ATD, NDD (b.1920)

Etcher, lithographer and illustrator who contributed "The Changing Room", a lithograph 6½in.x10½in., to the FE. Tavener studied at Hornsey College of Art (1946-1950) and exh. at the leading London galleries. A member of the Senefelder Group.

Tavernier, Paul (b.1852)

French painter of equestrian scenes, particularly hunting. He exh. one painting at the Walker A.G. Liverpool (1913) from a Paris address. His woodland scene with huntsmen and hounds was auctioned Bonhams 1981.

Tayler, Albert Chevallier, RBA, ROI, NEA (1862-1925)

Predominantly a portrait painter although his output was fairly varied. He features in this Dictionary for "A Young Fly Fisherman and Companion on a River Bank", 22¼in.x14in. The children's fishing rod is lying beside them, as is their dog. A curious picture of four children feeding a large eagle, presumably a pet, but the scene is set in an open landscape with nothing to suggest captivity, is entitled "Feeding the Eagle", dated 1852, 25½in.x36in. Tayler also painted several cricket scenes some of which are in the MCC. A collection of fourteen studies of cricketers, including portraits of J. Rhodes and N. Denholme Davis, were part of a series of forty-eight drawings for Tayler's "The Empire's Cricketers" pub. by the Art Society (1905) in weekly parts with a text by the cricketer and action photographer George W. Beldam, Sotheby's (Sussex). Tayler studied art at Heatherleys and at the RA Schools, also in Paris and exh. at the Paris Salon in 1891. Exh. at the RA, SS and elsewhere from 1884. He lived, as did many other artists of the time, at Newlyn in Cornwall for twelve years before settling in London. His work can be seen at Birmingham, Bristol, Liverpool and Preston AGs and his portraits at the Imperial War Museum and the Guild Hall. Elected NEA (1886), RBA (1908), ROI (1890).

Tayler, John Frederick, PRWS (1802-1889)

Landscape and figure painter, etcher and illustrator of many sporting scenes including "The Shooting Party" dated 1872, "A Hunting Scene" dated 1854, "Otter Hounds" and "A Hawking Party" dated 1863 (V&A Museum). A further watercolour "An Otter Hunt", dated 1871, was auctioned Sotheby's (Glen.) 1987. Tayler was a determined artist who overcame parental opposition to study art at Mr. Sass's Academy on the recommendation of James Northcote (q.v.). Another product of Mr. Sass's Academy was Stephen Pearce (q.v.), Tayler's junior by seventeen years. Tayler was a watercolour artist of sporting subjects who was originally destined for the church. He studied in Paris under Carl Vernet (q.v.) and was much influenced by Theodore Géricault (q.v.) which is evident from the style of his work. In 1855 he was awarded the Legion of Honour for his services to the Great Exhibition in Paris. Elected RWS (1834) and elected President of the Royal Society of Painters in Watercolour (1856). His patrons included Queen Victoria and amongst his friends was Richard Parkes Bonington. He loved Scotland and spent much of his time wandering through the country with knapsack and sketchbook. Many of his best scenes take place there. Another artist admired by the communicative John Ruskin, though Ruskin always tended to eulogise about sentimentality.

Taylor, Alan (op.1971)
Contemporary painter of "The Cricket Match", dated 5/71, 27½in.x39⅜in., auctioned Phillips 1989.

Taylor, Alfred Henry (op.1832-1867 d.1868)
London portrait painter, included in this Dictionary for his portrait of a gentleman seated with a fishing rod, dated 28 February 1852 and inscr., pencil, watercolour and coloured chalk, 17½in.x13½in., auctioned Sotheby's (Sussex) 1989. Taylor exh. at the RA (1832-1863), BI, SS, NWS and elsewhere.

Taylor, C.J. (op.1898)
Unidentified draughtsman of "Hockey on the Ice" 1898, pen and black ink. He may be Charles Taylor Jnr. (q.v.) but Taylor is not known to have produced many drawings and was in any case not a black/white artist.

Taylor, Charles (op.1834-1871)
London painter of marine and historical subjects. Included in this Dictionary for his painting of racehorses being rubbed down in a stable, dated 1834, 10¾in.x 13¾in., auctioned Sotheby's 1987, and his portrait of "Fitzavon", a bay racehorse with a jockey up, auctioned Christie's (Sth. Ken.) 1982. Exh. (1836-1871) at the RA and SS.

Taylor, Charles, Jnr. (op.1841-1898)
London marine painter, son of Charles Taylor (q.v.). Presumably the painter of a dog guarding the day's catch of fish, signed with mono. and dated 1881. Exh. at the RA, BI, SS, NWS and elsewhere (1841-1880).

Taylor, Françoise (op.1953)
Contemporary painter who contributed a painting of football "Burnden Park", watercolour, 25in.x19½in., to the FE.

Taylor, George (op.1846)
Painter of some hunting scenes including "The Stirrup Cup", dated 1846, 35½in.x48½in., Bonhams 1982, and "The New Shoe", signed watercolour, 9¾in.x 14½in. Christie's (Glasgow) 1983.

Taylor, J.W. (op.1813)
Unknown painter of "The Ooty Hunt", s.&d. 1813, 11in.x17in., auctioned Sotheby's 1989. The artist could be J.W. Taylor who lived in Ryde, Isle of Wight and was elected NWS (1834) but dropped from the Society (1837) because rheumatic fever had crippled his right hand. For an alternative artist see W. Taylor.

Taylor, John Whitfield (b.1908)
Punch artist and cartoonist. Son of G.W. Taylor, former headmaster of a school at Stoke on Trent. Educated at Manchester University and studied art at Stoke on Trent Art School. His son David Taylor, formerly a motoring corespondent and profile writer, became Editor of "Punch" in January 1988. John

Whitfield Taylor produced a number of golf cartoons including "A Hole in One", pen and black ink, signed, 7in.x9½in. and "In his Book, He Sinks It", pen and black ink, signed, 7½in.x9¼in. Wingfield Sporting Gallery, London.

Taylor, Joshua (op.1868)
Landscape and marine painter, also a lithographer of marine subjects, many of yacht and barge racing. His lithograph of "Fiona" taking part in the Royal Thames Yacht Club Match, 17 June 1868, is presumably after his own work, 13½in.x23¾in.

Taylor, Liz (b.1940)
Studied at Rochdale College of Art and pursued her studies with encouragement from L.S. Lowry (q.v.) who became a great friend. Exhibitions include her 1981 showing at the Gallery Moulin de la Gallette in Paris and several at the Salford Art Gallery (1975, 1978, 1980 and 1984). She is a champion croquet player and her paintings of croquet show her knowledge of this sport. Examples of her sporting work include "The Hurlingham Tournament", s.&d. 1988, pastel, 9½in.x11¾in., "Hitting the Peg", s.&d. 1988, pastel, 9½in.x11¾in. and "The Racket and Real Tennis Court at Salford", s.&d. '88.

Taylor, Robert (op.1893)
Marine artist whose painting of "Ariel", winner of the Ocean Race 1893, 24in.x36½in., was auctioned Bonhams 1986.

Taylor, Rosemary (op.1970s)
Rhodesian-born contemporary artist of cricket scenes and of large portraits, some 60in.x84in., of tennis players during the 1970s including Virginia Wade, Bjorn Borg and Jimmy Connors. Exh. Frost and Reed.

Taylor, Stephen (op.1817-1840)
Painter of equestrian, sporting and still life subjects who exh. forty-eight pictures at the RA, many of which were of dead game or subjects connected with shooting. His fine painting "The End of a Day's Shoot", dated 1825, 16¼in.x22½in., was auctioned Christie's 1979 and his portrait of "Curnick", a dark bay saddled hunter by a stable door (a horse with a wicked eye and very full of character), s.&d. 1817 and inscr., 25¼in.x32in., was auctioned Christie's 1990. A further painting of a favourite spaniel in a landscape is dated 1840. A still life of hung woodcock was catalogued as dated 1881 which, if accurate, would extend Taylor's dates considerably further than previously thought.

Taylor, W. (op.1809)
A good watercolour showing a landscape with primitive figures of a gentleman shooting partridge over pointers, dated 1809, was auctioned Bearnes 1989. The artist is possibly Weld Taylor who contributed illustrations to Howitt's "Visits to Remarkable Places" (1841). For an alternative artist see J.W. Taylor.

Templar, C.
A pastel drawing of a steeplechasing scene, signed, 14in.x18in., was auctioned Gorringes 1989.

Temple, Sir Alfred George, HRMS (1848-1928)
"Riding to Hounds", watercolour, dated 1898, 33½in.x 24¾in. was auctioned Sotheby's 1986. Temple exh. two works at the RA (1881-1890), neither sporting. He was an honorary member of the Royal Miniature Society (1919).

Temple, J. (op.1878-1902)
Angling illustrator whose painting of Julius Drewe catching a 39lb. salmon on the River Tummel, 1902, pen, black ink, 10½in.x12in., was exh. Malcolm Innes (London) 1990. "The Illustrated Sporting and Dramatic News" printed a great deal of Temple's work from about 1878 and his painting "Pony Racing at the Ranelagh Club" is amongst his best known work.

Temple, Richard
20th century painter of coaching scenes including "A Coach and Four at the Swan Inn", "The Stage Coach Comet outside the George and Dragon", 19½in.x29½in. A steeplechasing scene entitled "Over the Sticks", 15½in.x 19½in., was auctioned Sotheby's (Chester) 1986.

Temple T. (op.1865-1880)
Painter of equestrian scenes, particularly of hunting and portraits of hunters, but also of racing scenes including "The Run In" dated 1865, 44in.x75in., auctioned Christie's 1987. Other sporting works by Temple include "The Meet of the North Warwickshire Hounds at Kenilworth Castle", dated 1871, 47¾in.x77½in., "A Bay Hunter", dated 1880, 14in.x18in., "A Hunter in a Stable Interior", dated 1869, 13½in.x17¼in., "Study of a White Horse", 26½in.x34½in., "A Bay Hunter", dated 1875, 20in.x24in. and "A Greyhound in a Landscape", 17in.x23in. Christie's (Sth. Ken.) 1985.

Temple, W.H. (The Revd.) (op.1858-1874)
Painter of hunting scenes, many of which were exh. at the RBSA (1858-1874). Possibly one and the same as T. Temple (q.v.) but more likely to have been related.

Teniers, David (the Younger) (1610-1690)
The celebrated Flemish painter of peasant scenes including "Peasants playing Skittles", which is a misleading title, since they are clearly playing bowls. University of Edinburgh, Torrie Collection. Teniers, who was elected Master of the Antwerp Guild in 1653, was also created court painter to the Governor of the Netherlands. He was a friend of the Flemish painter, Sir Peter Paul Rubens (1577-1640) and married Anne, daughter of Jan ("Velvet") Breughel (1568-1625). Teniers' painting "Hawking for Heron", with the Archduke Leopold-William's retinue, is in the Musée du Louvre, Paris.

Ten Kate, Johann Marie (1831-1910)
Dutch painter of several bowling scenes.

Tennant, C. Dudley (op.1898-1918)
Marine and sporting painter and an illustrator in full tone, half tone and black/white. He worked in Liverpool and Surrey and contributed to "Punch" (1907-1908) and "The Graphic" (1910). He was the father of the sculptor Trevor Dudley Tennant (b.1906) and he illus. "V.C.s of the Air" (1918) by Gilbert Barnett.

Tennant, John F. (1796-1872)
Landscape painter of occasional sporting scenes including "A Stag Hunting Party at Rest in the Hills", 16in.x29½in. and "The Old Squire", dated October 1838, 35in.x48in., Manchester City AG.

Tenniel, Sir John, RI (NWS) (1820-1914)
Cartoonist and illustrator well known for his animal drawings in the 1840s who studied at the RA Schools and the Clipstone Street Life Academy. Joined "Punch" in 1851. Became principal cartoonist there in 1864. Famous for his illustrations to Lewis Carroll's "Alice in Wonderland" (1865) and "Alice Through the Looking Glass" (1871). Contributed over 2,000 cartoons to "Punch" including his most famous, "The British Lion's Vengeance on the Bengal Tiger", which appeared in 1857 after the Indian Mutiny, a dramatic but direct piece of political allegory showing the artist's fine handling of animal subjects. Included in this Dictionary for his drawings of Alice playing croquet with a flamingo and "Now Gents 'unt in Gorse", 6in.x7in. His "Epsom Marbles", a parody on the Parthenon frieze, with the leading contemporary elder statesmen leading a procession of costermonger carts, urchins and omnibuses down to Epsom, was done for "Punch". He was elected NWS (1874) and knighted (1893).

Tepper, Saul (b.1899)
American figure artist whose painting "The Wrestling Match" featuring "Gorgeous George", 36in.x40in., was auctioned Skinner, Boston, Mass., 1989.

Terpning, Howard A. (b.1927)
American contemporary painter whose "Rocky Mountain Shooting Match", 19in.x28in., dated 1981, on malachite was auctioned Sotheby's (NY) 1988.

Terrot, Susan (op.1930)
Painter of equestrian scenes whose portrait of a racehorse, dated 1930, was auctioned Christie's 1984.

Terry, Herbert Stanley (b.1890)
Illustrator of comic subjects including several sporting. Terry studied at Wolverhampton School of Art and lived at Thorpe Bay, Essex. He contributed to the major magazines from about 1914 including "Punch", "The Bystander", "The Illustrated Sporting and Dramatic News" and "The Windsor Magazine".

Tesson, Louis
Late 19th century French painter of "A Football Player", signed, charcoal/gouache, 24⅜in.x17¾in. Christie's (Amsterdam).

Thackeray, Lance, RBA (b.c.1870 op.1894 d.1916)
Painter, illustrator and writer who specialised in sporting subjects. A contemporary of Phil May (q.v.) and Tom Browne (q.v.) who also worked for "Punch". Thackeray's work includes a set of mixed foursomes playing golf. He also worked as a postcard artist. He held one-man shows at the Leicester Gallery (1908), The Fine Art Society (1910) and Walkers Gallery (1913). Elected RBA (1899). Became well known for his set of billiard room scenes featuring both men and women players at the

turn of the century. A founder member of the London Sketch Club (1898) and a close friend of Cecil Aldin (q.v.) who also lived in Bedford Park and with whom he explored Kent in a donkey and cart.

Thackeray, T. (op.1783)
An unknown painter of two of Sir John Goodrick's horses at Rebstone, s.&d. 1783.

Thelwell, Norman (b.1923)
A leading cartoonist, painter and illustrator. Thelwell's work covers most fields of equestrianism. Well known for his drawings of shaggy ponies ridden by upper class infants. Born Birkenhead, Cheshire, Thelwell studied at Liverpool College of Art (1947-1950) after the 2nd World War. He sent his first cartoon to "Punch" while teaching at Wolverhampton College of Art (c.1952) and began a relationship with that magazine that was to last twenty-five years. He gave up teaching in 1956 to work at illustration full time. His first girl and pony cartoon appeared in 1953. Illus. over thirty books from 1957, beginning with "Angels on Horseback". "Wrestling with a Pencil" a slightly sporting title, was pub. in 1986.

Thiebaud, Wayne (b.1920)
American object painter who started his art life as a Disney studio animator, cartoonist and commercial art director. For his painting of baseball caps, 1988, he used bright primary colours. Some of the caps are decorated with the symbolic crossed bats and ball and painted in rows. Boring subject but brilliantly and imaginatively painted.

Thirtle, John (1777-1839)
Landscape painter in watercolour whose "Wroxham Regatta", 6in.x10¼in., was exh. at Norwich Castle Museum and AG in 1939 (No. 85) for the Thirtle Centenary Exhibition. Thirtle, who only exh. once at the RA (1808), started his career as a frame maker in Norwich. He was a member of the Norwich Society of Artists. His two sketches of huntsmen were exh. at Norwich in 1927 from the collection of W.W. Rex Spelman.

Thomas, Bert, PS (1883-1966)
Black and white artist and illustrator whose pen/black ink drawing of a football match merits his inclusion in this Dictionary. His father was the sculptor Job Thomas. Bert Thomas worked in London for many of the leading magazines including "Fun", "Punch", "The Graphic", and "London Opinion". He drew a number of posters and contributed to "Mr. Punch with Horse and Hound" pub. by the new Punch Library c.1930. He was a close friend of W. Heath Robinson (q.v.) and both were members of the London Sketch Club. Thomas is probably best known for his "Arf a Mo', Kaiser" cartoon drawn to advertise a tobacco fund for soldiers during the 1st World War. It raised £250,000, not bad for the ten minutes it took to draw.

Thomas, Francis Wynne (b.1907)
Kent-born painter who studied at Heatherleys (1930-1934). Exh. (1936-1939) at the RA, RCA, ROI, RSA and elsewhere. "Erwald An Der Zugspitze", 30in.x25in., is a very fine skiing painting, Sotheby's 1990.

Thomas, Robert Kent (1816-1884)
Draughtsman and a lithographer after the work of his contemporaries and his own designs, mainly of marine subjects. These include the rowing match between Eton and Westminster at Putney (after his own work) dated 1843 and his fine architectural lithograph "The Royal Southern Yacht Club House, Southampton". Thomas appears to have worked as a lithographer for Day and Son, a firm of lithographic publishers, and contributed work to "The Etcher" and "The Portfolio".

Thomas, T.G. (op.1869)
An interesting portrait of a sportsman holding a shotgun with a retriever dog standing in deep heather in a moorland setting, s.&d. 1869, 19½in.x17¼in., was auctioned Bonhams 1992.

Thomas, Walter (op.1940s)
Liverpool marine painter and illustrator who also did advertisement designs for the Blue Funnel, Cunard and the Elder Dempster and White Star lines. He painted in both oil and watercolour and included many yacht racing scenes amongst his work.

Thomas, William Luson, RI, NWS (1830-1900)
Wood engraver and watercolourist. Founder of "The Graphic" and first promoter of "The Daily Graphic" (1890) together with his brother G.H. Thomas. Thomas previously worked for "The Illustrated London News" from about 1850 and in 1863 contributed a painting of the Wimbledon Rifle Shooting Club. He exh. at SS and was elected ANWS (1864) and NWS (1875). Thomas may have had connections with Rugby School since he featured several games of football played by the boys including "Football at Rugby" 1870, pen and black ink (Rugby School) and "Rugby Boys at Football", an illustration contributed to "Boys Own" (p. 401 Midsummer 1863).

Thompson, Algernon Alfred Cankerien (1880-1944)
Painter of equestrian scenes in both oil and watercolour but particularly of racehorse portraits. Born in Sussex, the son of the Revd. Oswell Thompson, vicar of Heathfield. Thompson was educated at Eastbourne College and articled to a firm of solicitors in Lewes where he qualified (1903). He did not practise but became an artist, studying anatomy and drawing in London between 1903 and 1910. His watercolour portrait of HH The Aga Khan's "Mahmoud", winner of the Derby (1936), and his watercolour painting of the Derby (1938) were auctioned Phillips 1986.

Thompson, J.E. (Colonel)
See Violet Flint

T(h)ompson, Jacob C. (1806-1879)
Penrith-born sporting artist who came to the notice of the Earl of Lonsdale in 1824 for whom he painted some copies. One of Thompson's copies was sent to the leading portrait painter Sir Thomas Lawrence who advised him to move to London where he studied at the British Museum and the RA Schools. He returned to Westmorland in 1840 and lived in a cottage provided by his first patron. During this period he painted some of his most celebrated works including a portrait of the

Hon. Henry Lowther (d.1867), the second son of Lord Lonsdale. His fine painting "Stalking at Ulswater", dated 1842, 27½in.x35in., is in a private collection. Other sporting works include "A Sportsman and his Dog in a Scottish Landscape", dated 1835, "Hunters and Prey", dated 1876, "A Portrait of a Chestnut Hunter standing in a River Landscape", dated 1845, "Anglers and their Catch above the River Derwent", dated 1827, "Fishing at Haweswater", dated 1867, 33in.x54in., and a still life of three freshly caught salmon on the river bank, dated 1848. An oil of a fox-hunting scene with hounds clambering up a tree in pursuit of the fox, was painted by J. Tompson who also painted a portrait of a black horse with a groom outside a lodge gate, 36in.x38in., and a brown dog by his master's shoes, 43in.x31in. Both of these paintings were auctioned by Maple and Co. on behalf of the Earl of Lonsdale on 19.4.1947 at the Lowther Castle Sale. Although these are signed J. Tompson they are thought to be by Jacob Thompson. Thompson exh. at the RA (1831-1866), BI and SS.

Thomson, Alfred Reginald, RA, RP (b.1894)
Included in this Dictionary for winning first prize at the Olympic Fine Arts Competition held in London in 1948 with his painting "London Amateur Championships" showing the amateur boxing championships at the Albert Hall. Thomson was one of only two Britons to win artistic medals in Olympic history. The other artist was William Nicholson (q.v.) in 1928. Thomson, who was born in Bangalore, India, attended the Royal School for the Deaf and Dumb, Margate. He then studied under John Hassall (q.v.) and C.M.Q. Orchardson (q.v.) at the London Art School, Kensington. He exh. (1920-1940) and was elected ARA (1938), RP (1944) and RA (1945). He exh. at the RA and elsewhere from 1920. Sporting titles include "The Oxford -v- Cambridge Boat Race" dated 1949, exh. RA (1950), "A Winner of Doggetts' Race" (1958) and "Dinner, Pytchley Hunt" dated 1960, exh. RA (1961). Official War Artist to the RAF (1940-1944). Examples of his work are in the Tate Gallery, the Imperial War Museum and Langan's Brasserie, London.

Thomson, Hugh, RI (1860-1920)
Irish-born painter and illustrator in watercolour who studied under the artist and designer John Vinycombe. Best known in sporting circles for the illustrations to his book "Coaching Days and Coaching Ways" which was pub. (1888) and reprinted (1903). His large watercolour "Golfers at the old Third Putting Green, Wimbledon Common", dated '97, was auctioned Sotheby's 1988. Thomson's work was strongly influenced by that of Randolph Caldecott (q.v.) and the novels of Thackeray with the result that his paintings evoke nostalgia - a world of stage coaches and old world gentility. He was, therefore, a fitting illustrator for the novels of Jane Austen and Mrs. Gaskell. Elected RI 1897 (retired 1907).

Thomson, I. Beatrice (op.1921-1936)
Painter of equestrian, animal and sporting subjects whose portrait of "Lanharran Schemer" a foxhound of

the South Hereford Hunt, 12in.x14½in., inscr. "Season 1921-1924" was auctioned Bonhams 1986. A portrait of "Midge" dated 1936 was auctioned Bonhams 1985.

Thomson (Thompson), James (1790-1850)
Northumberland-born stipple and mezzotint engraver of portraits and sporting subjects after his own designs and those of his contemporaries. He became a pupil of Anthony Cardon (1772-1813). Prints after his own work include "Royal Recreation", showing Queen Victoria, Prince Albert and the Court on horseback, pub. presumably posthumously (1851).

Thomson, The Revd. John, HRSA (1778-1840)
A leading Scottish landscape painter who took lessons from the landscape painter Alexander Nasmyth. The fourth son of Thomas Thomson, Minister of Dailly. John Thomson studied at both Edinburgh and Glasgow Universities and took Holy Orders. He succeeded his father in 1800 and became Minister of Duddingston in 1805. In 1809 he became one of the founder members of the Association of Artists and exh. there on a regular basis until its demise in 1816 through lack of support. Thomson, who was a close friend of Sir Henry Raeburn (q.v.) was an Hon. Member of the RSA in 1830. His painting "A River Scene with Falconer and Falcon" is in the collection of the Glasgow A.G.

Thomson, John Murray, RSA, RSW (1885-1974)
Crieff born animal painter who studied at the RSA Schools and won the Carnegie Travelling Scholarship to Paris. Taught at ECA. Exh. (1912-1940) at the RA, RSA, RSW and elsewhere. Elected RSW (1917) and RSA (1940). His painting of foxhounds and a terrier in a kennel, 16in.x30in., was auctioned Sotheby's (NY) 1988.

Thomson, T. or J. (op.1828-1842)
A lithograph signed T. Thomson (but which may be by James Thomson) of "Temperance", a pedestrian, as he appeared in a walking match between Colnbrook and Hounslow on 4 May 1841. The inscription records that "Temperance" was also a runner. The lithograph was pub. by E.T. Drinkwater in 1842.

Thor, Walter (1870-1929)
French artist - a member of the Salon des Artistes Français - who is best known for his humorous and witty automobile posters covering the early years of the 20th century.

Thorburn, Archibald (1860-1935)
A sporting painter, naturalist and illustrator mostly in watercolour. His sporting watercolours include "A Covey of Grouse in a Moorland Landscape", "Partridges Breaking Cover", dated 1907 and "Pheasants and Rabbits Alarmed", dated 1898, black chalk and grey wash. He illus. many books including "Fishing and Shooting" (S. Buxton) (1902), "The Fox" with G.D. Giles (q.v.) (1906), "The Salmon Rivers of Scotland" (Grimble) (1902), and "Autumns in Argyllshire with Rod and Gun" (A.E. Gathorne Hardy) (1901). The son of Robert Thorburn, ARA, a miniaturist to Queen Victoria, Archibald Thorburn was a close friend of John

Guille Millais (q.v.) and collaborated with him on several books including "The Mammals of Great Britain and Ireland" (1904) and "The Natural History of British Game Birds" (1909) (see J.G. Millais). Thorburn spent some time painting at Loch Maree, the Scottish home of his patron, the great industrialist, J.H. Dixon.

Thorley, John (op.1923)
A portrait by this painter of a bay hunter dated 1923, 16in.x21½in., was auctioned Louis Taylor 1984.

"Thormanby" (c.1840-1915)
Pseudonym used by Willmot Dixon whose (written) works include "Kings of the Turf", "Kings of the Ring", "Shooting Recollections". He was also the author of many novels. Educated at King William's College, Isle of Man and graduated at Trinity College, Cambridge, he was a pupil of the boxer Jim Mace and a keen follower of pugilistica.

Thornber(r)y, William A. (op.1883-1906)
See also W.A. Thornbury. Marine painter who exh. at the leading London galleries from 1883. He signed his early works Thornbury and later Thornley, for reasons best known to himself but a practice indulged in by some Victorian painters. Lived at Rochester in Kent. He exh. 1883-1906. His driving painting "On the Open Road, Two in Hand", 12in.x9in., was auctioned Phillips 1986.

Thornbury, W.A.
See William Thornber(r)y. It is now generally thought that this artist W.A. Thornber(r)y and W.A. Thornley are one and the same. Muddled?

Thorne, Diana (op.1928-1936)
Artist and illustrator of equestrian scenes whose several illus. books on polo include "Polo - Tails Up", "Pepito the Polo Pony" and "Roughy", pub. by the Moray Press, Edinburgh and London. Her painting "Huntsman and Hounds", 17in.x33⅓in., was auctioned Christie's (NY) 1981.

Thornely, Hubert (op.c.1886-1906)
A close relation of W.A. Thornley (see Thornber(r)y W.A.) who also painted in a similar style. It is unlikely that W.A. and Hubert Thornley were the same artist since Hubert contributed equestrian illustrations to "The Penny Illustrated Paper", first pub. c.1848.

Thornhill, James (Sir) (1675/6-1734)
The leading British decorative history painter of his age and a portrait painter. Included in this Dictionary for his painting of "Hanbury Hall" (Worcs.) seen from the bowling green, pen and brown ink with a grey wash over a pencil c.1710, British Museum. Hanbury Hall, which featured a ceiling painted by Thornhill, was owned by Thomas Vernon, an eminent lawyer. Thornhill took over Sir Godfrey Kneller's (q.v.) Academy of Drawing and Painting which he started in 1711 but under Thornhill it was suspected of being used for immoral purposes. Later, under John Vanderbank, (q.v.) the school moved to St. Martin's Lane (1720) and went bankrupt. After Thornhill's death, his son-in-law, William Hogarth (q.v.), put the Academy together again and in his hands it flourished.

Thornley, William A.
See William Thornber(r)y.

Thornton, Herbert (op.c.1850-1860)
Unknown painter of equestrian scenes whose work in this field includes "The Meet", "Breaking Cover", "Full Cry" and "The Kill", a set of four, one signed, each 11½in.x9¼in., and "In Full Cry" and "Taking a Fence", a pair, one s.&d. 1860, 11½in.x9½in. A pointer in a landscape with a farm beyond and inscr. "Derry" may point to Ireland for the background of this artist who usually painted in oils, in sets of four or pairs, and rarely dated his work.

Thorpe, James H. (1876-1949)
Author, artist and illustrator, very often of sporting scenes and particularly of his own sport of cricket. An ardent cricketer, he was responsible for forming cricket teams and matches at the London Sketch Club of which he was a founder member. He himself played for the Artists Cricket Club of which Edwin Abbey was the enthusiastic President. He was born in Homerton, North London and was educated at Bancroft School. He studied art at the Lambeth School of Art and at Heatherleys in Newman Street (1897). His first drawings were accepted by "Troubadour", mainly due to Walter Churcher and he moulded his style on that of Phil May (q.v.) whom he very much admired and later wrote about (1932). He was a close friend of Starr Wood and fellow cricket enthusiast Frank Reynolds (qq.v.) and when Reynolds received his commission to go to Paris by the editor of "The Sketch" (1904) he took Thorpe and Wood "to act as escorts". Inevitably with his enthusiasm for cricket he persuaded his friends to play and in one of these matches against the MCC at Lords, G. Hillyard Swinstead made a hundred. Frank Reynolds bowled them out and Thorpe had the pleasure of shying down Conan Doyle's wicket (his fellow London Sketch Club Member playing for the MCC) from deep mid off. Thorpe illus. the (1911) issue of Izaac Walton's "The Compleat Angler" and "A Cricket Bag" (1929).

Thurlby, Frank (op.1912-1925)
Painter of equestrian portraits who appears to have worked for Mr. Beeby of Melton for whom he painted donkeys in 1915. His portrait of Scotty McTavish, 12in.x 18in., is signed, inscr. and dated 1925 and, catalogued as "Thudly". He is almost certainly the painter of a large black sow inscr. "14180 Primley Godiva", s.&d. 1913, 13½in.x19½in.

Thynne, A. (op.1860)
"Rest for Lunch" showing a Scotsman with his pony and dogs in a Highland landscape, dated 1860, 20in.x 24in., was auctioned Sotheby's 1971.

Tickner, John (b.1913)
Sporting painter, author and illustrator. Author of "Tickner's Rough Shooting" (1964), "Tickner's Terriers" (1977) and "To Hounds with John Tickner", etc. Illustrator and cartoonist to "Horse and Hound" and occasionally "The Shooting Times".

Tielmann, George (op.c.1827/8)
German artist who painted a fine watercolour of their Royal Highnesses Prince George and Princess Augusta

as children with a tennis racket and a ball and a shuttlecock. This is the original from which the lithograph was pub. in 1828 by J.G. Schrader of Hanover, 13in.x17¾in. It is certainly an early picture of a strung racket, Sotheby's (Bel.) 1978.

Tiffin, Sheila

Self-taught contemporary artist who lives in St. Ives and paints a wide range of subject matter. "Two Young Boys Playing Football", s.&d. '89, 8in.x10in., W.H. Lane, Penzance.

Tillemans, Peter (1684-1734)

Antwerp-born topographical painter and draughtsman, also a painter of sporting conversation pieces. He came to England in 1708. He was originally employed by John Bridges (1719) making topographical drawings of Oxford and Northamptonshire. Developed a large practice painting country seats for private patrons, which in turn led to commissions for equestrian portraits and racing scenes. Tillemans was a member of the Virtuosi Club of St. Luke to which John Wootton and James Seymour (qq.v.) also belonged and in 1725 became Steward Virtuosi. Wootton and he were close friends and indeed collaborated together. Tillemans is probably best known for his large panoramic view of "George I and his Court on Newmarket Heath", painted in 1722, "The Starting Point of the Beacon Course at Newmarket" and "End of the Beacon Course". His patrons included the Earls of Spencer, Derby and Portmore, the Dukes of Devonshire, Somerset, Kingston, Rutland and Bolton and he became drawing master to the 4th Lord Byron and his children. He was also a talented engraver, engraving plates after his own work including "The Fox Chase" and a view of the Duke of Kingston's house at Thoresby and part of the park, with "His Grace the Duke and Attendants Going a'Setting" (shooting over setters or pointers). A fine engraving by the line engraver Tomson (q.v.) of a beautiful running horse belonging to His Grace the Duke of Bolton, after the work of Peter Tillemans, was pub. 1738. This shows a very unusual spotted horse.

Tinkler, W.A. (op.1839)

A portrait of a bay racehorse by this artist was auctioned Sotheby's 1964. Tinkler exh. one painting at the RA (1839) from an address in Putney.

Tippet, W.V. (op.1864-1881)

Painter of equestrian portraits who exh. two pictures at SS (1866). His painting of a gentleman holding a hunter outside a house, 18in.x24in., and dated 1881, is recorded and his portrait of a horse in a stable, signed, 13¾in.x 20½in., was auctioned Sotheby's (Sussex) 1983.

Tischbein, Johann-Heinrich (the elder) (1722-1789)

German portrait painter and a friend of the German poet, Johann Goethe (1749-1832). Painter at the court of Count Willhelm VIII and Frederick II Von Hesse Kassel (1720-1785) before becoming the protégé of Lord Hamilton. Frederick II, Landgrave of Hesse and an enthusiastic falconer, commissioned Tischbein to paint large canvases of his hawking exploits for his Schloss Fasanerie, Fulda, where the paintings still hang. One of the paintings shows the cadger in the foreground with the exotically hooded gyrfalcons preparing to hunt herons.

Tissot, James Jacques Joseph (1836-1902)

Highly competent French figure painter. Best known, probably, for his portraits of his mistress, Kathleen Newton, and his smart social crowd scenes predominantly featuring pretty women. He painted several sporting scenes including "Henley Royal Regatta", dated 1877, 18¼in.x37¼in., painted during his stay in England (after the Prussian War) for a period of ten years (the Leander Club, Henley on Thames). "Henley Regatta" shows a wide panorama painted in a fluid impressionistic style. Other paintings by Tissot which feature sporting scenes include "At the Rifle Range", painted 1869, 26½in.x18¾in. (Wimpole Hall National Trust), "Skating on the Lac de Lauchan", 1869 and "Croquet" painted in 1878, 35¾in.x20in., Art Gallery of Hamilton. Tissot also contributed sixty-six caricature portraits to "Vanity Fair" (1871-1877).

Titterton, J. (op.1890s)

Illustrator, particularly of angling scenes, who contributed such work to Messrs. Fores "Sporting Notes and Sketches" during the 1890s.

Todd, Robert Clow (op.c.1845)

Canadian painter of equestrian portraits including a portrait of "Corbeau" a trotting horse, dated 1845, and inscr., 20¼in.x25¼in. auctioned Sotheby's 1987. "Corbeau" won trotting races in Quebec, Canada, and he was subsequently sold to Ireland for breeding to John Pollock of Lismany.

Tolley, Edward (op.1848-1885)

Painter of sporting and equestrian scenes including "A Gentleman Leading a Welsh Cob by a Garden Gate", dated 1875, 25⅛in.x35⅛in., auctioned Christie's 1987, "A Grey Hunter in a Loose Box with a Greyhound, Terrier and a Groom", dated 1861, auctioned Christie's 1986, "A Sportsman and his Dog Flushing Mallard", 11in.x13in., auctioned Christie's 1963, and "A Grey Hunter in a Stall", dated '68, 22in.x29in. Tolley exh. several pictures at the RA and the BI (1848-1867), several of which were horse portraits. His portrait "A Mare in a Stall", dated 1885, 19in.x27in., was auctioned Sotheby's (NY) 1989.

Tolley, Nicholas (b.1958)

Painter of sporting subjects, particularly racing, who obtained a BA in Fine Art (1980). He specialises in race crowd scenes evoking the tension and thrill of the people - not the horses. He is a clever caricaturist of racing personalities.

Tomlinson, Maud (b.1859)

Diarist and illustrator, eligible for this book with her enchanting sketches of badminton and shuttlecock. Examples include "Not played Badminton for some time - kept turning my back on the shuttlecock!" repro. "Country Life" (12/12/1985). Tomlinson's diary with her illustrations was pub. as "Maud", Secker and Warburg (1985).

Tompson, J.
See T(h)ompson, Jacob C.

Tomson, Clifton (of Nottingham) (1775-1828)
Nottingham equestrian and animal painter, also a line engraver, working in the early part of the 19th century for private commissions. He had a number of patrons prominent in the sporting world, amongst them Richard Watt, the owner and trainer, Earl Fitzwilliam, for whom he painted "Orville", William Ellis and Lord Byron, he of "Mazeppa" fame. Tomson appears to have been largely self-taught but his first important break-through came in August 1801 when "The Sporting Magazine" pub. an engraving of his portrait of the racehorse "Moorcock". This was followed in October by "Sir Solomon" and these were the first of thirty-five engravings of his work until 1827. Tomson may indeed have been the son or closely related to the line engraver whose print after the work of Peter Tillemans (q.v.) of a beautiful running horse belonging to His Grace, The Duke of Bolton, was pub. in 1738. From time to time Tomson used the pages of the Nottingham Journal to advertise his work. He appeared as a horse painter in Park Street and invited the public to view "his exhibitions of horse paintings". These advertisements were usually placed to coincide with race meetings. It is difficult to see from his work if he was influenced by any one particular sporting artist but perhaps his style is most similar to that of John Boultbee (q.v.), twenty-five years his senior and from his part of the country. Indeed many of Clifton Tomson's patrons patronised both artists. Tomson in his turn influenced the young Thomas Bretland (q.v.) who was to succeed him as the premier Nottingham animal painter. Tomson had a good eye for a horse and could convey the texture of the coat as well or better than most. Perhaps his landscapes let him down a little, for he was not a painter of trees. He almost invariably included some individually painted small stones in the foreground of his paintings. He died at the comparatively early age of fifty-three and was buried where he was baptised at the church of St. Mary, Nottingham. His portrait of "Evendore", a grey stallion in a landscape, dated 1811, 25in.x30in., and "Coriolanus", a bay racehorse with his trainer and jockey, dated 1804, were auctioned Sotheby's 1969. There is a collection of Tomson's work in the Nottingham AG and the Walker AG, Liverpool.

Tonge, Robert (1823-1856)
Painter of sporting subjects whose portrait of "A Huntsman and Pointers in Cheshire" dated 1851 and inscr., 12in.x16¾in., was auctioned Sotheby's (Chester) 1985 and re-auctioned later as "The Keeper and his Dogs". Tonge, who unusually accepted family pressure to become an artist and not a soldier, became a pupil of a portrait painter in Liverpool and exh. there from 1843. In 1853 Tonge went to Egypt to recover his health, unfortunately to no avail since he died in Luxor. He was elected to the Liverpool Academy just before his death.

Tonks, Henry, FRCS (Professor) (1862-1937)
Born in Solihull, Warwickshire. Educated at Clifton College and joined Sussex County hospital at Brighton at the age of eighteen as a pupil. From there he went to the London Hospital where in his third year his talent for drawing became apparent. Became a House Physician and was then appointed a House Surgeon to Sir Frederick Treves. In 1888 he was admitted as a Fellow to the Royal College of Surgeons and became, a little later, Senior Resident Medical Officer at the Royal Free Hospital. He wrote to Fred Brown (q.v.), then Head of Westminster School of Art asking to join the school but Brown was shortly afterwards appointed Slade Professor of Fine Art at the University of London. Brown offered Tonks the post of assistant at the school and in time (1918) Tonks succeeded him as Slade Professor of Fine Art becoming Emeritus Professor in 1930. During the 1st World War he served in a medical and surgical capacity besides acting as a war artist. Many of his drawings from this period (seventy-two) are preserved at the Museum of the Royal College of Surgeons. He was a regular contributor to the NEAC from 1891 onwards. A strict disciplinarian, he raised the standard of the Slade School to the highest pitch of efficiency, carrying on the tradition laid down by his predecessor. His pupils included many sporting artists. He painted "The Cricket Match" dated 1903 (No. 26) and his work is represented at the Tate Gallery.

Toovey, C.W. (op.1953)
Contemporary print maker who contributed a football engraving entitled "Boys Practising", 4in.x5in., to the FE.

Topham, Francis William, RWS (1808-1877)
Genre painter, illustrator and an engraver who was apprenticed to his uncle, a line engraver.

Topham, Francis (Frank) William Warwick, RI, ROI (1838-1924)
Painter of sentimental subjects, whose "The Queen of the Tournament", dated 1885, 60½in.x88in. is a fine study of a jousting tournament set in mediaeval times, a subject to which Topham frequently returned. A pupil of his father, F.W. Topham (q.v.), the RA Schools and the Atelier Gleyre in Paris. He exh. at the RA from 1860 and at other leading galleries. Elected RI (1879).

Topolski, Felix, RA (1907-1989)
Polish-born painter and draughtsman, the son of an actor. Came to Britain to cover the Jubilee celebrations of King George V for a Polish satirical newspaper and became a naturalised citizen in 1947. War artist (1940-1945). Prince Philip was an admirer but Topolski was an independent painter and his style never really found favour with the art establishment. Included in this Dictionary for his painting "Eton -v- Harrow Cricket Match", which was repro. as a limited edn. of three hundred colour lithographs and his pastel/wash drawing of Goodwood, 25-28 July. Collection Tate Gallery.

Torborch, Gerard (1617-1681)
Dutch painter of an ice scene with golf players, ink wash, 5in.x4in., auctioned Sotheby's (Amsterdam) 1985.

Torgerson, William (op.1880)
American 19th century marine painter whose fine oil, 36in.x60in., "The New York Yacht Club Regatta", dated 1880, was auctioned Sotheby's (NY) 1990. The

painting features "Sappho" (NYYC) who teamed up with "Columbia" to win the America's Cup in 1871. The painting was commissioned by the Cunard Steam Ship Company.

Torrome, Francisco (Frank) J. (op.1890-1913)
Landscape, figure and military painter in both oil and watercolour but also of some sporting scenes. He exh. (1890-1908) at the RA and ROI, RBA and RI. His watercolour "A Meet in the High Street, Kimbolton", dated 1913, 14in.x20½in., was auctioned Sotheby's 1985.

Toulouse-Lautrec, Henri (1864-1901)
French Impressionist painter, best known for his pictures of Paris café life, who was born into a well-to-do family and was crippled from birth. Racing was to lure Toulouse-Lautrec into painting "At the Racecourse" (Musée Toulouse-Lautrec) although the one racehorse featured is of secondary importance to the two Parisien racegoers. Toulouse-Lautrec was the son of the eccentric Count Alphonse, a sportsman and in particular a falconer. Toulouse-Lautrec depicted his father in several sketches and paintings dressed in the amazing range of historical outfits that he normally chose to wear, but with his beloved hawks on his fist. An oil painting, 9¼in.x5½in., of the Count on horseback, in Circassian clothes, bird on fist, is in the Musée Toulouse-Lautrec. Henri Toulouse-Lautrec is also responsible for one of the earliest known motoring portraits. Entitled "L'Automobiliste", 1899, the original lithograph shows Lautrec's cousin, Dr. de Celeyran, wearing the motorist's outfit of the period at the tiller of his Panhard motor car.

Tournachon, Gaspard Félix (1820-1910)
French painter of figure subjects and a wood engraver of some sporting and equestrian subjects. His many equestrian portraits are often signed "Nadar", the pseudonym he frequently used for his oil paintings.

"The Tout" (1870-1950)
Pseudonym for P.R.G. Buchanan, the well-known illustrator for sporting magazines. Racing personalities who Buchanan used in his work include Lord Lonsdale, Prince Aly Khan, The Earl of Westmorland, Sir Walter Gilbey, Sir Humphrey de Trafford, Cecil Boyd Rochfort (knighted 1968), Joe Childs, Captain Lionel Montague and, of course, His Majesty King George V. Buchanan's work was mostly painted in watercolour. His favourite subject was racing but he also painted fox-hunting including "The Quorn Gallery" (1901), repro. "Country Life" (2.12.1976).

Towne, Charles (1763-1840)
Highly talented sporting and animal painter who painted his landscapes with a great deal more detail and care than was usual at that time. Born in Wigan, the son of Richard Town, a Liverpool portrait and heraldic painter, he became an assistant to the coach builder John Laytham, who with the local artist, John Rathbone, greatly encouraged his work as an animal painter. He exh. his first painting in Liverpool (1787) and came to London (1799) in which year he also added an "e" to his surname. He exh. twelve paintings at the RA and four at BI (1799-1823), mostly landscapes but some sporting works. In 1810 he returned to Liverpool and was appointed Vice President of the Academy of Arts (1813) having contributed to the first exhibition in 1810. He painted for the many members of the Yeats family from 1794. Both Towne and James Ward (q.v.) painted portraits of "Old Billy" the horse who made equine history by living to the age of sixty-two when he died in 1822. Towne painted "Old Billy" when he was allegedly sixty-two and Ward painted him in 1812 when he was allegedly fifty-two. Towne also painted several pictures of bull baiting, a subject that was not universally popular amongst other leading sporting artists.

Towne, Francis, FSA (1740-1816)
Landscape painter who is said to have painted some equestrian portraits in oil. Towne studied art at Shipleys in the Strand, winning a First Premium at the Society of Arts (1795). A friend of W. Pars, Towne exh. at the RA, SA, FS and BI from 1762.

Townsend, Frederick Henry Linton Jehne, ARE (1868-1920)
Illustrator, black and white artist, etcher and a fencer. Studied at the Lambeth School of Art and contributed figure drawings to "Punch" from 1903. He became the magazine's first Art Editor in 1905. His sporting work includes "Foxhunting on a Bicycle", dated February 1898, and "Try Our Cork Tipped Golf Bag", dated 1908, a set of four golfing watercolours, each 4½in.x 4½in. Townsend was one of the first artists to show how widely golf products were used for advertising purposes, even in 1910, and to show pictorial evidence of early sponsoring with the first sponsored event, "The News of the World Tournament" dating from the same period. His etching of a gyroscopic judge's box for the detection of foul riding (1913) is now a rare print. Elected ARE (1915). Townsend, like his contemporary Frederic Regamy (q.v.), contributed a great many fencing illustrations to "Punch", "The Illustrated London News" and "The Sphere", which moved his fellow cartoonist on "Punch", Bernard Partridge, to describe his fencing sketches as "prodigies of flashing adroitness in the realization of rapid movement, making the best things of Frederic Regamy tame by comparison". Amongst his finest technical work in this field were Townsend's twenty-four meticulous drawings (1900) used as illustrations to C.F. Clay's translation of the Baron de Bazancourt's "Secrets of the Sword". He also covered the first Epée Club Cup in 1901 (held in Temple Gardens) and the Great Britain v. France epée match held at Crystal Palace in 1904. G.P. Jacomb-Hood (q.v.) records that Townsend died suddenly on a golf course ("With Brush & Pencil", 1925).

Townsend, J.R. (op.1983)
Contemporary painter whose very fine portrait of the Lincolnshire sportsman, Sir Joseph Nickerson, at Rothwell, his Lincolnshire seat was painted in 1983. Nickerson is seated on a small hillock in shooting gear sporting his famous white spats, his shotgun over his shoulder. Nickerson was a controversial character earning considerable public disapproval for his partridge

battues and records of large gamebags. He died in 1990 and his funeral took place on Tuesday 13 March. A fanatical sportsman to the end, it was his wish that no one should miss a day's hunting, shooting or fishing to attend his funeral and that those who did should not wear mourning and should be given a good lunch at the Nickerson Arms, Rothwell. Sir Joseph also requested that donations instead of flowers should be sent to the Joseph Nickerson Fund, Gamekeepers Association, Lloyds Bank.

Townshend, Arthur Louis (op.1880-1895)
Painter of rustic, equestrian and sporting subjects who exh. six works at the RA including a work intriguingly titled "A Bit on Newmarket Heath". His portrait of "Tristan" (foaled 1878), 25in.x32in., has a label on the reverse which informs us that it was sold at the Daniel Cooper sale, 29 May '93, by Christie's. Townshend also painted a portrait of "St. Simon" standing in a loosebox dated '85 and inscr. "Newmarket", and "St. Blaize", winner of the Derby (1883). His work was not confined to racehorses for several paintings of hounds are recorded including a very fine work entitled "A Meet of The Burton Hounds". In 1895 Townshend's address is recorded in Paris where it is possible he went to live. His known biography is surprisingly sparse.

Townshend, John (op.1820-1842)
Landscape and figure painter whose "The Royal British Bowmen in the Grounds of Erthig", Denbighshire, the seat of Simon Yorke, Esq., was painted in 1822. It was engraved in 1823 by William James Bennett (1787-1844). The Royal British Bowmen Club was formed in the late 18th century and flourished, except during the Napoleonic War, until 1880. It was also the first society to admit ladies as members. The ladies as well as the men in the painting are in the uniform of dark green.

Toynbee, Lawrence (b.1922)
Figure and landscape painter, the youngest son of the historian Arnold Toynbee and grandson of the classical scholar Gilbert Murray. Educated at Ampleforth and New College, Oxford, he studied art at the Ruskin School of Drawing under Albert Rotherston, interrupted by the outbreak of war. Served in the Coldstream Guards during the 2nd World War but was invalided out (1945) and returned to the Ruskin to finish his studies. He has taught art, since leaving the Ruskin, at the Oxford College of Art, Bradford College of Art, Radley College, St. Edwards and Morley College, London. An early admirer of the Euston Road School, he has never lost his interest in the subtle graduations of tone which he shared with Victor Pasmore, Lawrence Gowing, Claude Rogers (q.v.), Rodrigo Moynihan and others of that school. It is perhaps to the art of figure movement that Toynbee has made his unique and greatest contribution to British art in the 20th century. An enthusiastic sportsman who played cricket for Oxford as an undergraduate, he has always been keen to depict sporting subjects. Early work in 1953 includes "Chelsea -v- Spurs at Stamford Bridge" and "Mid- Week Practice at Stamford Bridge". Both paintings are owned by Langan's Brasserie, London. Other sports which have attracted the brush of this talented painter are boxing, cricket, rugby football, rowing, tennis, squash and, more recently, golf. An admirer of the work of the fine boxing artist George Bellows (q.v.) and of Charles Cundall (q.v.) whose subject "Hastings Cricket Festival" used to delight audiences to the RA Summer Exhibition. The subject — Hastings Cricket Festival — was also painted by Toynbee. "The Cape Bunker, Westward Ho", 24in.x 40in., 1985, and "Mixed Doubles" 1980, 12in.x16in., both exh. at the Fine Art Society London.

Tracy, John M. (b.1844)
American painter of sporting subjects including many shooting scenes, depicting pointers and setters.

Trappes, Francis M. (op.1868-1885)
Landscape and sporting painter whose work exh. at the RA includes "Woodcock Shooting". He is also included in this Dictionary for "The Road to the Moors", a shooting painting on which he collaborated with Basil Bradley (q.v.), signed by both artists and dated 1878.

Trautschold, Carl Friedrich Wilhelm (1815-1877)
German painter whose fine work "After a Day's Beagling", signed 27½in.x35½in., was auctioned Sotheby's 1968.

Travers, Florence (Mrs.) (op.1889-1902)
Painter of rustic and some equestrian subjects whose "Tally Ho, Mr. Fox", 9½in.x13½in., shows a skittish horse jumping out of his paddock to chase the fox. Travers exh. at the RBA, RI and elsewhere (1889-1902).

Travis, Stuart (op.1920s)
Artist who painted motor cars and fox-hunting subjects and contributed to "Art and the Automobile" (D.B. Tubbs c.1920s)

Treen, W. (op.1833-1877)
Portrait painter, also of some equestrian and sporting subjects whose fine painting "A Bay Hunter with a Cat in a Stable", 24in.x29½in., was auctioned from the collection of the Earl of Craven. His portrait of "Cock Robin", a dark bay horse with two dogs in the grounds of Ashdown Park, the house in the background, 24in.x29½in., also came from the same collection. Treen exh. three portraits at SS and one portrait at the RA (1833-1877) from a London address.

Tregear, Gabriel Shire (op.1827-1832)
Artist and publisher. A print of his picture "The Eagle Paris and Dovor (sic) Coach" was engraved by H. Alken and pub. by G. Tregear, 104 St. Martin's Lane, London (1827).

Trench, Philip Chevenix (op.c.1835-1899)
This artist, who exh. one painting at the RHA in 1880 also painted a pair of grouse shooting scenes, one s.&d. 1883, the other signed with inits. and dated 1899, each 18in.x27in. They were auctioned at Sotheby's 1978. Trench may have been the same P. Trench whose set of tiger shooting scenes were engraved by Edmund Walker and pub. in 1846. He was almost certainly the same P.C. Trench who contributed sporting illustrations to "The Bengal Sporting Magazine" - a series of twenty vols. which ran between January 1833 and November 1842 pub. by the Asiatic Lithographic Press, Calcutta.

This suggests that Trench may have served in the army as a young man like his colleagues C.W. Smith (q.v.) and Captain Frederick Parr alias "Junglicus" (q.v.).

Trendall, Edward W. (op.1816-1836)
In 1828 a prospectus inviting public subscriptions to construct the Grandstand at Epsom racecourse was issued. The design for it by Trendall was begun shortly after this date and it may be the drawing that Trendall exh. at the RA in 1835 (1027) "Grandstand on the Race Ground at Epsom", pen/ink/watercolour, 14¾in.x19in, the Paul Mellon Collection, Upperville, Va, USA.

Tresidder, Hereward H. (1883-1950)
Painter from Falmouth, a pupil of Stanhope A. Forbes RA at Newlyn (1906-1908). Friend of H.S. Tuke (q.v.). Tresidder exh. at the RA (1905-1912) including "The Amateurs", a picture of amateur boxers sparring, which he exh. in 1912, No. 728.

Trickett, John (b. c.1952)
Sheffield painter who started his career as a professional footballer, playing for Torquay, after which he turned to full time painting. He paints a variety of sporting and animal scenes and many of his works have been repro. in limited edn. prints.

Trickett, W. Wasdell (op.1911-1939)
Equestrian portrait painter in both oil and pastels. He obtained many private commissions from the cavalry barracks at Tidworth and Aldershot where he charged between £5-£10 for a horse portrait. Amongst the horses he painted are "Richard" a bay hunter, dated 1925, "Sally" a bay hunter, dated 1925, "Beatie" a cavalry horse, dated 1916, "Wild Iris", the cavalry charger "Nicholas", dated 1923, the polo pony "Nell" and a grey horse in a stable, dated 1911. Sotheby's (Sussex) 1989.

Trigger, George
The pseudonym used by William Henry Florio Hutchinson (q.v.).

Trood, William Henry Hamilton (1860-1899)
Animal painter and sculptor, very often of dog subjects and hunting scenes. Usually accompanied by a large dollop of Victorian sentimentality. He exh. at the RA (1879-1898) and also at the SS (1879-1887). The studio sale for his estate took place at the London Hotel, Taunton, on 12 December 1899. Trood's sporting work includes "A Portrait of a Hunt Terrier", dated 1894, "Facing the Brook", "Over the Fence" and "Above Suspicion".

Trova, Ernest (b.1927)
American painter of objects and design who used baseball as the subject for his painting of the same name c.1960.

Trowell, Johnathan (b.1938)
Painter of animal and equestrian subjects — particularly racing. Studied at Sunderland College of art and awarded scholarship to the RA Schools where he won prizes for his drawings. He is a regular exhibitor at the RA Summer Exhibition and has exh. at the Fine Art Society in London and with Richard Stone Reeves in New York. His patrons include the Prince of Wales.

Troye, Edward de (1808-1874)
English animal and equestrian painter, although born in Lausanne, who emigrated to America in 1831. For the next forty years Troye portrayed the American thoroughbred, both on and off the racecourse. His numerous equestrian portraits include "American Eclipse", "Boston", "Lexington", "Pacific" and "Glencoe". In 1867 Troye wrote and illustrated "The Racehorses of America". After 1870 he stopped painting in the mistaken belief that art would die with the advent of photography. Many of Troye's paintings are housed in the National Museum of Racing Inc., Saratoga Springs, USA.

Truman, I. P. (op.1853)
The artist of the two chestnut racehorses "Sittingbourne" and "West Australian" with jockeys up, in a landscape, dated 1853, auctioned Christie's 1981. "West Australian" (1850) was one of the great English racehorses, winning not only the Triple Crown (1853) but the Ascot Gold Cup (1854) as well. The significance of Truman's painting lies in the fact that, good horse though he was, he had a desperate battle in both the 2000 Guineas and the Derby against "Sittingbourne" (1850) who would undoubtedly have won both races had "West Australian" not been the outstanding racehorse he was. See also J. Truman.

Truman, J. (op.1866)
The painter of a chestnut racehorse in a loosebox dated 1866, 20¼in.x26in., auctioned Christie's 1985. This artist, of whom little is recorded, is thought to be the same as I.P. Truman (q.v.) since he paints in an identical style.

Tschaggeny, Charles Philogene (1815-1894)
Belgian painter of equestrian portraits including "The Stable Boy", a grey hunter in a stable dated 1844, and a bay hunter in an extensive landscape, dated 1849.

Tschudi, Lill (b.1911)
Swiss born artist and printmaker who studied in London in 1929/30 and again in 1934. Her colour lino cut depicting "Ice Hockey" is in the British Museum, London.

Tsvetkov, Victor (b.1920)
Russian painter of "The Finish", a striking picture, 39in.x64in., of the end of an international road race that took place in Leningrad in 1947. In the background are the golden domes of St. Isaac's Cathedral, a central landmark of the city. Born in Leningrad, Tsvetkov studied under Rudolf Frenz at the Repin Art Institute. A fine realist painter, "The Finish" is considered to be one of his finest works. Roy Miles Gallery, London.

Tuck, William Henry (op.1874-1882)
Portrait and animal painter who exh. one human portrait at the RA (1874). His watercolour painting "The Royal Staghounds in Windsor Park", dated 1882, is one of three watercolours recorded by him.

Tucker, Edward (1847-1910)
Westmorland landscape and coastal painter who painted a number of sporting subjects including angling and

shooting scenes. Sporting titles include "Fishing on the Dee", 10½in.x18in., "A Shooting Scene on the River Culm, Devon", 8in.x10in., and "Fishing on a Quiet River Estuary". Tucker usually painted in watercolour and sometimes exh. under the name of "Edward Arden".

Tucker, James Walker, ARWA, ARCA (Lond.) (1898-1972)
Painter of several sporting figures including "A Promising Lad", 39½in.x29½in., exh. at the FE. Tucker, a pupil at the RCA (1922-1927) under William Rothenstein, is likely to have been persuaded by John Rothenstein to enter his football painting into the 1953 competition of football art and subsequent exhibition as the best way of ensuring a high standard of entry since Rothenstein was highly involved in the enterprise. Tucker who became Head of Gloucester College of Art (1931-1963) exh. at the RA from 1927, also at the NEAC and RWA. His "The Champion" was the RA picture of the year in 1941.

Tuer, J. (op.c.1840)
A picture of a two horse jogging cart on the Beetham Road is recorded, signed and inscr. on the reverse. Tuer is likely to be miscatalogued in error for J. Tuitt (q.v.).

Tuitt (Tuite), F.J. or J.T. (op.1842-1851)
Unknown painter of sporting subjects including "Woodcock Shooting", a gentleman shooting on the left, his gamekeeper, to the right, spaniels in the foreground, dated 1847, "The Trysting Place", a Scottish sportsman with eight shooting dogs and the day's game, sitting on a rock in a rocky landscape, dated 1842, and "Pheasant Shooting" (twice): one dated 1851, 36in.x 42½in. and 12¾in.x17¾in., Christie's 1987 and 1991. See also J. Tuer.

Tuke, Henry Scott, RA, RBA, RWS, NEAC (1858-1929)
Portrait and figure painter, usually of young men, whose sporting work includes two pencil portraits of W.G. Grace, the famous cricketer, one dated 1905, 10in.x8in., and a watercolour portrait of W.G. posing in Ranjitsinhji's turban, painted in 1908 after a match played at the great Indian batsman's Sussex home, Shillinglea Park. Tuke also painted a portrait of Johnny Jackett, the Rugby full back for Falmouth and England, 8in.x10in. Johnny Jackett played full back for England in the Rugby International matches 1905, 1906 and 1907. Jackett's portrait was also painted by F.J. Mercer (q.v.). A watercolour, "Fishing", dated 1899, 5½in.x 8¼in., portrays the inevitable two boys, Tuke's recurring subject, in a boat. Tuke studied at the Slade School (1875-1879) and in Florence (1880) and Paris under J.P. Laurens (1881-1883). Exh. at the RA, RBA, RI, ROI, RSA, RSW, RWS and elsewhere. Elected NEAC (1886), RA (1914), RBA (1888), RWS (1911).

Tulloch, Maurice (1894-1974)
Sporting painter and illustrator of many books including "Stories of the Saddle" (G. R. Acton) (1938), "Hunting Without Tears" (Lionel Dawson) (1938) and "A History of the Peshawar Vale Hounds". Probably best known for his illustrations to Ralph Payne Gallway's

"Letters to a Young Shooter" (1939). He became hunting correspondent at "The Daily Telegraph" and "Morning Post" and contributed to "The Hog Hunters Annual", 1936 and 1937. Born in India, Tulloch joined the Indian cavalry while still at Cambridge and served in the Poona Horse. He later took command of the 18th Cavalry. He did not study art until his retirement from the army when, under the guidance of Lionel Edwards (q.v.) Tullock began to paint in oils. He painted many famous racehorses for private commissions and wrote and illus. articles for "The Field". His fine watercolour "Pig Sticking - Kadir Heat", 9¾in.x15in., is in a private collection.

Tunnard, John Charles (1873-1960)
The eldest of the five sons of Charles Thomas Tunnard (1843-1926) of Frampton House in the parish of Frampton, South Lincolnshire by his wife Georgiana (d.1901), daughter of Conolly Norman of Fahan House, Co. Donegal, was born at Frampton House in 1873. He married firstly (8 June 1899) Nina Isobel Christian, 4th daughter of Cecil Long of Sherrington Manor, Berwick, Sussex. She died 25 November 1950 and he married secondly (21 April 1954) Irene Sherard (died 10 October 1972), youngest daughter of John Linton DL of Stirtloe House, Buckden, Huntingdonshire. Tunnard died on 26 January 1960 leaving issue by his first wife, an only son, John Samuel Tunnard, ARA (q.v.). John Charles Tunnard's father was the last squire of Frampton. He was a noted authority on horses and on five occasions acted as a judge at the great Dublin Horse Show. J.C. Tunnard himself became a sporting and equestrian painter and in his youth would stay at the houses of his and his family's friends to paint their horses. He is said to have worked for a time in the studio of John Everett Millais (q.v.) and served in the Remount Service (1914-1916) during World War I. His sporting and equestrian paintings include "A Portrait of a Huntsman", dated 1931, "Huntsmen and Hounds", dated 1923 (coloured chalks), "A Gentleman on a Hunter", "Spaniels putting up a Pheasant", "Otter Hounds" (black and white chalk), "The Fisherman" (pastel, dated 1923), a bay and a grey hunter in looseboxes (1892) and "Saddled" and "Ready", a pair, both dated 1918.

Tunnard, John Samuel, ARA, LG (1900-1971)
Painter of abstracts, landscapes and still life. The only son of John Charles Tunnard (q.v.) by his first wife, Nina. Studied at the RCA (1919-1923). Awarded a diploma in textile design (1921). Played jazz semi-professionally and designed textiles during the 1920s. In 1926 married Mary May Robertson, ARCA, daughter of Peter Robertson of Hampton Hill, Middlesex, but died 18 December 1971 without issue. Elected member of the LG (1934). Teacher of design at Penzance School of Art (1948-1964). Contrary to popular belief Tunnard is not known to have painted sporting pictures.

Tunnicliffe, Charles Frederick, OBE, RA, RE (1901-1979)
Distinguished bird artist, etcher and engraver who was born at Langley in Cheshire and studied (1915-1921) at

Macclesfield and Manchester Schools of Art and at the RCA (1921-1925) where he won a Royal Exhibition scholarship. Tunnicliffe was a great pigeon fancier. He worked mainly in watercolour and specialised in superb bird drawings but quite often depicted horses. He illus. Henry Williamson's "Tarka the Otter" (1932) and "Salar the Salmon" (Faber and Faber 1936) and was awarded a gold medal by the RSPB in 1974. Elected RE (1934), RA (1954), awarded the OBE (1978). His work is often seen at the Tryon Gallery in London. Included in this Dictionary for his watercolours of peregrine falcons, horses and fishing.

Tunstall, Eric, RI (b.1897)
Portrait painter in oil and watercolour whose fine portrait of a fighting cock, dated 1932, 23½ in.x19½ in., was auctioned Christie's 1972. Tunstall studied at Stoke, Hanley and Burslem Art Schools. Exh. at the RI and RP. Elected RI (1953). Born at Stoke on Trent where he lived for very many years.

Turck, Eliza (b.1832 op.1880-1909)
Portrait and miniature painter. Included in this Dictionary for her fine pen, ink and wash studies of quail and chicks, pheasant and snipe, ptarmigan, ducks and woodcock. Some drawn with her sister Harriet. She was the daughter of a naturalised German banker. Eliza Turk studied for six months at Francis Cary's School of Art, then under W. Gale and in 1852 entered the figure class of the Female School of Art in Gower Street. Between 1859 and 1860 she studied in Antwerp and exh. (1880-1909) at the RA, RBA, SWA and elsewhere.

Turmeau, John (1777-1846)
A portrait of Thomas Boycott (1771-1856), Master of the Albrighton Hunt (1825-1830), pencil/watercolour, 8¼ in.x6⅝ in. and inscr., is in the Paul Mellon Collection, Upperville, Va, USA.

Turner, Charles, ARA (1773-1857)
Engraver and draughtsman of portraits and figurative subjects. Also animal and sporting subjects. Studied at the RA Schools, possibly a pupil of John Jones. His prolific mezzotint engravings are often after his own designs and sometimes after those of his contemporaries. From 1812 Turner described himself as "mezzotinto engraver in ordinary to his Majesty" and in 1828 he was elected an associate member of the RA. Best known in sporting circles for the print he made of the painting of the interior of the fives court with Jack Randall and Ned Turner sparring (1821) by T. Blake (q.v.). One does wonder if the boxer Turner, featured in the painting, was in fact a relation of the artist. One also wonders whether it is this Charles Turner who features in the painting by Francis Calcraft Turner (q.v.). It seems likely that it is. Charles Turner engraved an extensive view of Oxford races and worked with Jacques Laurent Agasse (q.v.) on a number of sporting compositions. Other sporting scenes drawn by Turner include his portrait of the pugilist John ("Gentleman") Jackson, boxing champion of England (1795-1803). Jackson shared rooms at 13 Bond Street with Henry Angelo II,

the fencing master (see Rawlins, T.J.) where he taught "the art of self-defence". The 6th Lord Byron, the poet, took boxing lessons from the one and fencing lessons from the other and paid tribute to Jackson in "Don Juan" (Canto XI stanza 19). Charles Turner engraved several plates after the work of Joseph Mallord William Turner (q.v.) who was a friend and trustee although not a kinsman, and worked on a number of plates for Turner's "Liber Studorium" (1806-1819), a series of engravings of different landscapes.

Turner, Charles E. (1883-1965)
A very fine marine artist who painted a great number of yacht racing scenes including King George V sailing in "Britannia" in the Big Class Race, 11 August 1934, with HMY "Victoria & Albert", "Britannia", "Astra", RVS "Shamrock", "Velsheda", "Candida", "Westwood" and the marker boat. "Velsheda" was owned by W.L. Stephenson, "Shamrock" by Tom Sopwith CBE in 1933 but C.R. Fairey in 1934. On 7 July 1936 as a mark of respect "Britannia" was towed to a position south of the Needles by the destroyers "Amazon" and "Winchester" and scuttled. The painting was exh. at the Manchester International Fine Art Exhibition.

Turner, Daniel (op.1775-1801)
Engraver and painter of London rivers and bridges. A pupil of the engraver John Jones (c.1745-1797), he often worked in brown wash. He painted a number of yacht racing scenes including "The Regatta at Battersea" (Christie's 1988), showing the patent mill water tower and Battersea church beyond, 17¾ in.x23⅞ in., and "Yachts of the Cumberland Fleet before St. Pauls starting for Vauxhall", 1775, 17½ in.x23½ in. Exh. "Rule Britannia" Sotheby's 2.1.86-29.1.87.

Turner, Edward (op.1858-1869)
Landscape and genre painter who exh. two cottage scenes at the BI and SS (1858-1862). His painting of a lady and two children in an open carriage in the grounds of a country mansion, traditionally said to be a member of the Churchill family at Blenheim, dated 1869, 24½ in.x39½ in., was exh. Sheffield City AG, "Victorian Paintings", September - November 1968 (No. 138).

Turner, Edwin Page (op.1880-1910)
Recorded as a decorative architect but he was also a painter and his study of two children playing croquet in a cottage garden, dated 1910, 24in.x20in., was auctioned 1987. He exh. seven works at the RA (1880-1884) from a London address.

Turner, Elizabeth (b.1955)
Contemporary painter and illustrator of equestrian subjects who studied art at Norwich, graduating in 1978, and then spent a further period studying in Florence.

Turner, Francis Calcraft (c.1782-d.1846)
This little known sporting and equestrian artist from Lambeth painted "The First Grand National" (1839) with a key of the horses running. In a letter to the editor of "The Sporting Magazine" in June 1825 Turner wrote "I have rode to more hounds and have been in at the

death of more foxes than any artist in existence - nay more, my knowledge of racing, shooting, coursing, etc. is alike". From which the reader may gather that the artist was an all-round sportsman if not perhaps a very modest one. He was a regular contributor to "The Sporting Magazine" with no less then seventy-eight works, the last pub. in the year of his death. Turner, who was clearly a member of a very talented family of artists, painted an extremely interesting portrait of Mr. Charles Turner (q.v.) toasting the blood of "Old Caesar" at Kirkletham Hall after a great run of the Haworth Hunt, dated 1822. This work appeared in William Pick's "Authentic Racing Calendar" (1803-1885). Turner's portraits of "Crucifix" and "Little Wonder" are in the Jockey Club Newmarket and he also painted "Miss Lettie", the 1837 Oaks winner. "The Leamington Grand Steeplechase" (1837) and "The Gold Cup at Goodwood" (1838) are fine paintings. The latter was engraved by Charles Hunt (q.v.) in 1853.

Turner, George Archibald (1821-1845)
Sporting and equestrian painter, the son of Francis Calcraft Turner (q.v.). George Turner died very young of consumption. He was a talented engraver in aquatint and a painter of sporting and equestrian subjects. His study of "A Chestnut Mare", dated 1839, was auctioned Sotheby's (Sussex) 1986. Much of George Turner's engraved work was after the work of his father including "Batteau Shooting" (1840), "Refraction", a portrait of a racehorse, and "The Race for the Wolverhampton Stakes" (1839). Exh. at the RA and SS (1836-1841). Titles include "Lance and his Dog 'Crab'" (1836).

Turner, Graham
Contemporary motor racing artist including a painting of "Jim Clark Cornering in the Works Aston Martin Segatto" 1961, painted in gouache, 10in.x13in.

Turner, J. (op.1871-1872)
Equestrian painter who exh. a painting of horses at the RA in 1872. His portrait of a chestnut racehorse with jockey up, in the colours of Ralph T. Walker, dated 1871, 23½in.x35½in., was auctioned Sotheby's 1986. His portrait of an old English black and tan terrier, 25in.x30in., was auctioned 1985 and his portraits of "Chivalry" and "Palmer", a pair of greyhounds, each 12½in.x16½in., were auctioned 1981.

Turner, James (op.1761-1817)
Portrait and animal painter, said to have been Irish. Exh. SA (1761-1783). His fine watercolour portrait of a tabby cat in a landscape was dated 1817.

Turner, Joseph Mallord William, RA (1775-1851)
Important landscape painter and engraver although much of his work was aquatinted by professional engravers including C. Turner (q.v.), F.C. Lewis (q.v.), I.W. Say, T. Lupton and others. Turner painted in oils but predominantly in watercolour. His paintings of sporting scenes are rare but include "Yacht Racing in the Solent", 18¼in.x28½in., painted c.1827 (Tate Gallery Collection) and very fine sporting birds drawn at Farnley in 1810. Turner exh. at the RA from 1790 and was elected RA 1802. Well known for his remark about

Tom Girtin (1775-1802) "If Tom had lived, I should have starved". His watercolour painting of Wells Cathedral with a game of cricket, 16in.x21in., c.1795, shows a game of double wicket cricket being played in front of the cathedral, the players using long, curved bats although these had, in general, been superseded by the straight bat and the three stump wicket by this date (Lady Lever AG). Cricket again featured in his painting of "The Lake at Petworth, Sunset, Bucks Fighting", 24½in.x57in., c.1829 (HM Treasury and National Trust Collection) painted for the 3rd Earl of Egremont with whom Turner stayed frequently at Petworth, his Sussex home, and for whom he painted some of his finest work. Turner, it seems, was a considerable sportsman - see also John R. Wildman - and shot, fished and coursed with another of his patrons, Walter Ramsden Fawkes (d.1825). The collection of Turner's sketches at Fawkes' home, Farnley Hall near Otley, Yorkshire, includes many drawings of gamebirds, most of which Turner is supposed to have shot himself, and several drawings of shooting parties at Hawksworth Moor and Otley Chevin.

Turner, M.F. (of Nottingham) (op.c.1858-1870)
Animal and sporting painter, thought to have been closely related to William Eddowes Turner (q.v.) since they worked for a time from the same address. M.F. Turner's portrait of a hunter with a terrier in a loosebox, extremely well painted, 22½in.x18½in., was auctioned Sotheby's (Chester) 1986.

Turner, Marjorie (op.c.1885-1902)
Animal and equestrian painter whose work includes studies of the New Forest Foxhounds, pastel, 14¼in.x 15in. and "Stable Companions", a portrait of a New-foundland dog with a small Welsh pony and a cocker spaniel, also painted in pastel. Thought to be closely related to Maud Turner (op.1891-1908), the painter of canine subjects.

Turner, Michael (b.1934)
Contemporary painter of motor car racing scenes at a very high level. Born in Harrow, England, Turner is largely self-taught, attending art school for only one year before national service. Worked in commercial studios for three years until 1957, when he became freelance, opening his own studio to produce aviation and motoring paintings. Turner's concern with technical and historical accuracy, together with his natural artistic interpretation, results in compositions of consumed strength and realism. His first one-man exhibition was held in London in 1965, since when his works have illus. numerous books and been pub. as limited edn. reproductions. Turner is President (1991) of the Guild of Aviation Artists, founded in 1971.

Turner, W. (op.1953)
Contemporary painter whose football painting entitled "The Night before Cup Tie", 22½in.x14½in., was exh. at the FE.

Turner, W.H. (op.1849-1852)
An artist with these initials painted "Horses in a Field", signed with inits. and dated 1849, Christie's 1978 and

Turner, W.H.M.

"A Bay Cob Saddled in a Landscape" s.&d. 1852, 11½in.x15½in., Sotheby's (Chester) 1985. He may or may not be the W.A. Turner who exh. a painting of wildfowl at the RA (1844) since a capital 'A' and 'H' are very similar.

Turner, W.H.M. (Horse Fair Turner) (op.1850-1887)

Painter of equestrian, sporting and genre landscapes. Known as "Horse Fair Turner". His work includes "The Horse Fair", dated 1868, "Out to Grass" dated 1860, "An Irish Horse Fair", dated 1860, "A Horse Fair at Lincoln", dated 1858, "A Horse Fair", dated 1859, "A Horse Fair at Barnet, Essex", dated 1863, "Leonora" a portrait of a chestnut mare and her foal in a landscape, dated 1859 and "Coursing" (signed with inits.) and dated '83. He exh. one painting entitled "An Irish Drove" at SS in 1860.

Turner, William H.M. de Lond (op.1822)

Inevitably the work of so many W. Turners has been miscatalogued and misattributed but this Turner, who is likely to be Scottish and therefore unlikely to be "Horse Fair Turner", even they though appear to share the same initials, is thought to be the artist who painted scenes depicting George IV's visit to Edinburgh in 1822. His painting of "Musselborough Races" is probably of the same date.

Turner, William (1789-1862)

Well-known watercolourist from Oxford, and an occasional lithographer, whose "Exeter College Eight on the Isis, Oxford" was engraved in aquatint by W. Stack in 1824, 11¼in.x19¼in. The original watercolour, 11in.x21¼in., is in the Paul Mellon Collection, Upperville, Va, USA. A similar painting in oil by Turner, believed to have been painted for Henry Moresby of Exeter College in 1826, but showing variations in the details of the spectators, was exh. at the Parker Gallery 1974, attrib. to William Havell (1782-1857)

Turner, William Eddowes (b.c.1820)

Nottingham equestrian, animal and sporting painter in oils, thought to have been self-taught and closely related to M.F. Turner (q.v.). He exh. three landscapes at the BI and four works at SS (1858-1862). His horse portraiture includes that of a mare and foal, dated 1889, "Bawler" a dark bay hunter in a stable, dated 1895. Also portraits of "Bismarck", "Barney" and "Mouse" all dated 1896, the hunter "Mermaid" and the hunter "Assiduity", dated 1885. His dog portraiture includes the celebrated prize whippets "Enterprise" and "Zuba" dated 1894. His patrons included the 6th Duchess of Newcastle for whom he painted a study of her terriers with a view of Newstead Abbey beyond. His other portraits include "Ratler" a foxhound from the Quorn Kennels, winner of the first prize at the Harrogate Show of 1873, a bay cob saddled in a landscape, dated 1852. He is thought to have been the same Turner who exh. one landscape in London in 1857.

"Tuss"

Two cartoons entitled "Cannon and Pot" and "Well Screwed", dated 1907, which are billiard scenes, were painted by this unknown artist.

Tyson, Miss Kathleen (Mrs. Mawer), SMA, SWA (b.1898)

Landscape, portrait and miniature painter. Studied Grimsby and Hull Schools of Art and then at Westminster School of Art. Elected SWA (1939). Exh. (1927-1940) at the ROI, RBA, RA, NEA and elsewhere. Her portrait of a young hockey player, signed, 30in.x25in., oil on canvas, is in a private collection.

U

Uchermann, Carl (op.1880)

Norwegian painter of landscapes and shooting scenes including "Spaniel Putting up Mallard", s.&d. 1880.

Ugo, C. Favretti (op.1888)

Italian figure painter whose painting "Russian Skaters" dated 1888, 27½in.x12¾in., Sotheby's 1988, merits his inclusion in this Dictionary.

Uhlman, Fred, LG (b.1901)

German-born painter in oil who practised as a barrister until 1933. Settled in England and exh. widely in London and on the continent. Elected LG (1943). Included in this Dictionary for his painting of football entitled "The Goal", 10⅜in.x15⅜in., which was exh. at the FE. His work is represented in the Musée de Grenoble, the National Gallery, Sydney and the Fitzwilliam Museum, Cambridge.

Underhill, Graham

Contemporary painter whose scene of the sad collapse of a hot air balloon into a tree entitled "Early Flowering", s.&d. 8/75, 20¾in.x14in., was auctioned Christie's (Sth.Ken.) 20.9.90.

Underhill, William (op.1841-1870)
London painter of sporting subjects and coastal scenes. Born at Birmingham. Exh. at the RA from 1848, BI, SS and elsewhere. "The Salmon Trap" was exh. at the RA (1856). "The Meet of the Beaufort Hounds at Badminton", dated 1841, 27in.x34¾in., was auctioned Sotheby's 1987.

Unsworth, Peter (b.1937)
Studied at Middlesbrough School of Art and at the St. Martin's School of Art. Has had fairly regular one-man exhibitions at the Piccadilly Gallery, London since 1963. Taught art at the Sheffield Regional College of Art (1970). His work is represented by the Arts Council of Great Britain, Kettering AG, Towner AG, Eastbourne, Middlesbrough AG, Hill Samuel, Government Art Collection of New Zealand. Sports subjects painted include cricket, lawn bowls, fencing, football, and rugger.

Urquhart, Murray McNeel Caird, RBA (b.1880)
Scottish-born painter in oil and watercolour who studied at Edinburgh School of Art, the Slade School, the West-minster School of Art and at Frank Calderon's (q.v.) School of Animal Painting. He also studied at the Académie Julian in Paris under J.P. Laurens. His equestrian works include "Juley on 'Bess'", dated 1923, 17in.x20in., and "Tubbing a Hunter", 16in.x20¼in., dated 1923, auctioned Bonhams. He also painted a portrait of Sebastian E.F. Snow, half length holding a cricket bat and ball, s.&d. 1939 and inscr., 24in.x20in. Exh. at the RA, RP, RBA, NEAC and elected RBA (1914).

Usher, James Ward (1845-1921)
Lincoln-born painter who was also a businessman, an investor and an art collector. His watercolour painting "The Quorn Hounds" is in the Usher Gallery which was founded by him.

Uspenky (op.c.1911)
A fine hunting scene with "A Yogari of the Tzar's Hunt", s.&d. 1911, 34in.x31in., was auctioned Sotheby's 1988.

Vachell, R. (op.1851)
Unknown painter of a hunting scene entitled "Full Cry" dated 1851, 12¼in.x18¼in., which was auctioned Sotheby's (Sussex) 1984.

Valentine, John (op.1913-1944)
A good painter of equestrian portraits in oil and watercolour, possibly the same J. Valentine who exh. a landscape at the ROI in 1884. Valentine's work includes "The Morning Ride", dated 1913; the chestnut mare "Red Flower" with her foal "Dan Rufus" at Guyzanze Hall, Northumberland, dated 1944; the painting also shows two hounds. "The Winning Look", dated 1915, was auctioned Bonhams 1989. "The Otter Hunt", signed, watercolour and a study of a chestnut racehorse in a landscape, dated 18?44, auctioned Bonhams 1980 may have been miscatalogued and should be 1944.

Valentine-Daines, Sherree, UA, SWA (b.1956)
Painter of landscapes and sporting activities who studied at Epsom College of Art. Her work is widely exh. and she has won many awards. "England v. Australia, Old Trafford 1985" signed, 35in.x18in., the reverse inscr. with twenty-three signatures of the players. "England v. Wales" at Twickenham 1986, signed verso by the players, 34½in.x58½in. Artist's Collection.

Valkers, Karl (op.1897)
A portrait of a racehorse with a jockey up, dated 1897, 32in.x40in., was auctioned Christie's (NY) 1982.

Van Aken, Joseph (circle of) (c.1709-1749)
Dutch school. "The Game of Shuffleboard", 31½in.x 49½in. Collection of the Earl of Wemyss and March. A painting of a sportsman with his servant in the grounds of a country house, 26½in.x45½in., was auctioned Sotheby's 1986.

Van de Velde, Adriaen (1635/6-1672)
Dutch painter of some sporting scenes including "Two Sporting Dogs by a Stream with a Sportsman and his Gun Beyond", 32in.x39¾in., auctioned Christie's 1965. "Golfers on Ice near Haarlem", s.&d. 1668, 12in.x 14¼in. National Gallery, London.

Van de Velde, Esaias (1591-1630)
Dutch painter of icy subjects including "Pleasure on Ice", a skating scene.

Van de Velde, Willem (The Elder) (1611-1693)
Dutch marine artist who came to England in 1674 and was made, with his son Willem the Younger (q.v.), official marine painter to King Charles II. He worked in London for about thirty years with his son with whom

he closely collaborated. Van de Velde was an out-standing draughtsman. His son usually painted the ships he drew but there was no rigid division of labour. Some fine examples of their work may be seen at the National Maritime Museum at Greenwich and the Peabody Museum at Salem, Mass., USA.

Van de Velde, Willem (The Younger) (c.1633-1707)

Dutch marine artist, the son of Willem Van de Velde (q.v.) with whom he worked closely. The influence of these two men on British marine painting was enormous and their classic "Dutch style" was carried on by succeeding generations of artists well into the early part of the 19th century. The work of such artists as Peter Monamy (1670-1749), the John Cleveleys (father c.1712-1777 and son 1747-1786), Francis Swaine (op.1762-1782) and Charles Brooking (1723-1759) all show their influence.

Van de Venne, Adriaen (1589-1662)

Dutch painter of "A Game of Billiards" c.1625, one of the earliest representations of the sport and the oldest depiction known. Adriaen Van de Venne painted the billiard game as one of 102 miniatures which were made into an album, representing a panorama of contemporary life in Holland. It features several games and sports including "Kolf", the early game played by the Dutch and from which the modern game of golf is thought to descend. The album was probably presented in 1626 to the Prince of Orange, Frederick Hendrick, by his nephew, the so-called "Winter King" of Bohemia. Both he and Frederick appear in the album several times and were keen sportsmen. The album came to the British Museum from the collection of the Earls of Spencer at Althorp House in Northamptonshire where it had been since the 18th century. The "Winter King", Frederick V, was married to Elizabeth Stuart, daughter of James I of England (1566-1625) and elder sister of Charles I (1600-1649). The now extinct game of kolf was played with mallets along a straight alley at the end of which stood a vertical post. The two boys in the picture are probably the King's sons, Charles Louis and Frederick Henry, the latter a godson of the Prince of Orange. The album of 102 miniature drawings remains one of Van de Venne's finest works and illustrates his remarkable talents as a draughtsman.

Vanderbank, John (1694-1739)

Portrait painter, sometimes of equestrian subjects and a book illustrator. Born in London. Trained at the Godfrey Kneller (q.v.) Academy as did Stephen Slaughter (q.v.) virtually his contemporary. Started life classes with Louis Cheron (1720) in St. Martin's Lane which were also attended by William Hogarth (q.v.) who later took over the school and other young artists. Vanderbank produced illustrations, mostly equestrian, for "Croxalls Selected Collection of Novels" (2nd edn. 1729) and numerous designs for illustrations to "Don Quixote", some of which were pub. in the edns. of 1738 and 1742. George Vertue, who knew him, considered Vanderbank "in the art of painting and drawing of all men born in this country superior in skill". However he is said to have lived extravagantly and died at the age of forty-five from an aftermath of debauchery. He illus. "Twenty

Five Actions of the Manage(d) Horse" (1729) of which several drawings are in the Paul Mellon Collection, Upperville, Va, USA. The engravings are by Joseph Sympson and the preface of the book states "Mr. J. Vanderbank .... the better to Execute his Ideas, was himself a disciple in our Riding Schools, and purchased a Fine Horse as a Model for his Pencil".

Van der Helst, Bartholomeus (1613-1670)

Dutch portrait painter whose fine portrait of a child playing golf, 44in.x33in., hangs at the Edward James Foundation, Chichester, Sussex. The painting, frequently repro., shows an unknown child addressing the ball with a club on the sea-shore.

Van der Myn (Mijn), Hermann (1684-1741)

Portrait and decorative painter, born in Holland but spent much of his working life in England to which he came in about 1721. Painted for private patrons. Did not exhibit. The father of several artist children, he died in London in November 1741. His painting of an ornamental pheasant, an English partridge and a spaniel standing beside a shooting gun, s.&d. 1734, 29in.x 23½in., is in a private collection and was exh. Sotheby's, "The British Sporting Heritage" 1984/5.

Van der Neer, Aert (1603-1677)

Dutch painter of skating scenes including "Winter Landscape in the Late Afternoon", signed with double mono., 16in.x20½in., Christie's 1988 and "A River Scene in Winter" showing figures skating.

Van der Putten, Daniel (b.1949)

Born in Holland. Inspired by the English countryside and the old Dutch Masters. "A Winter Morning on the Way to Everden", a hunting scene, was exh. at Astley House Fine Art, Moreton in Marsh, Gloucestershire.

Van der Vaart, John (1653-1727)

Portrait painter, very often of sporting personalities and a mezzotint engraver which he abandoned before 1700. Born in Haarlem, he came to England in 1674 and was naturalised in 1708. After 1713 he seems to have specialised in restoration work. He was particularly talented in painting drapery which is always present in some form in his own portraits and he painted them for William Wissing (q.v.) on whose style his own portraits are modelled. His portrait of Master Montague Drake (1673-1698) holding a flintlock fowling piece, his setter dog beside him, 94in.x50in., is in a private collection but was exh. at Sotheby's, "The British Sporting Heritage", 1984/5.

Van der Vinne, Jan (1663-1721)

Dutch painter from Haarlem, a pupil of Jan Wyck (q.v.). He came to England in about 1686 and painted hunting scenes, landscapes and views of London.

Van Diepenbacke

See Diepenbacke, Abraham van

Van Dongen, Kees (1877-1968)

Painter of equestrian scenes, particularly horse racing, whose watercolour "Polo Ponies at Deauville", 19½in.x 25¼in., was auctioned in France 1988. His fine painting "Blue Grass Races" is in the Virginia Museum of Fine Arts, Richmond, USA.

Vandyke, Peter (1729-d.after 1795)
Dutch portrait painter who was originally brought to England by Joshua Reynolds (q.v.) as a drapery painter. His early portraits certainly show Reynolds' influence. He is included in this Dictionary for his full length portrait "The Tennis Player", 76in.x47in., s.&d. 1779, Christie's 15.10.1957. Vandyke seems to have settled in Bristol and his last recorded portrait is dated 1795. National Portrait Gallery, London.

Van Eyck, Jan (1385-1441)
Flemish painter and an enthusiastic falconer as was his brother, Hubert (d.1426) whom Van Eyck depicted in a portrait, with his falcon on his fist. Collection Bibliotèque National, Paris.

Van Gassel, Lucas (1480-1555)
"King David giving Joab his Letter to Uriah", 13in.x 17¾in. Richard Green Gallery, London. This painting by the French artist, Lucas Van Gassel, shows the Old Testament story of King David and Bathsheba. King David, who coveted Uriah's wife, Bathsheba is seen in the painting giving his letter to Joab, in which he orders Uriah to the front to increase his chances of being killed - a plot in which it may be said that the king was wholly successful. For some reason a game of real tennis is being played in an open court to the king's left hand. The game has nothing whatsoever to do with the Old Testament story but interestingly the game also features in another painting showing the same story by an unknown painter, dated 1559. It is more likely that the games are shown being played because in both artist's minds real tennis courts were a feature of many 16th century aristocratic houses - see "Sport and the Artist: Vol. I: Ball Games", pub. ACC, 1988. The story of David and Bathsheba also inspired Rembrandt's famous painting of Bathsheba now to be found in the Louvre, Paris. Lucas Van Gassel was a Flemish painter of religious and historical subjects, who was born Lucas van Gassel Helmont. He is nevertheless better known as Lucas Van Gassel and lived a great part of his life in France.

Van Gogh, Vincent (1853-1890)
Prolific French impressionist painter of brilliant but unbalanced talent who shot himself at the age of thirty-seven believing himself to be a failure both as a man and a painter. He is included in this Dictionary for his painting "The Night Café" which shows a game of billiards being played in the smoky interior. Van Gogh himself wrote of the scene "The interior of the café at Arles where I eat. The painting expresses the violent passions of humanity by means of red and green. The room is blood red and dark yellow with a billiard table in the middle". The painting is in the collection of Yale University Art Gallery, Bequest of Stephen Carlton Clark. Vincent Van Gogh came to England in 1873. He lived in Hackford Street, Lambeth, while he was working for Goupil's Gallery in Southampton Street.

Van Jones (op.1930s-1970s)
Contemporary painter of equestrian scenes including "A Girl with a Horse", 24in.x31in., " A portrait of HM Queen Elizabeth and Prince Philip preparing for Trooping the Colour", 30in.x32in., and "A Girl with Terriers", 54in.x37in. Sotheby's (1989).

Van Ravesteyn, Jan Anthonisz (c.1578-1657)
A leading portrait painter in the Hague. Included in this Dictionary for his portrait of a young boy with a golf club and ball, dated 1626, auctioned Sotheby's 1992.

Van Rijn, Rembrandt (1606-1669)
Dutch portrait painter and etcher whose etching "The Kolven Player", frequently known as "The Golfer", s.&d. 1654, 3¾in.x5¾in. is in the British Museum.

Van Saben, Henri (1825-1913)
Belgian painter of some angling and minor sporting scenes including "The Children's Skating Party" dated 1864, "The End of a Day's Fishing" and "A Youth Leaning Against a Tree Fishing" while a young girl watches on.

Van Somer, Paul (Paulus Van Someren) (c.1577/78-1621)
Dutch portrait painter who came to England in 1616. Quickly established himself as a leading portraitist. Patronised by the royal family and members of the aristocracy including the Devonshires. His portrait of Anne of Denmark, wife of James I of England (1603-1625) standing full length in hunting dress with her beagles at Oatlands Park, s.&d. 1617, 104½in.x 82in., is in the collection of Her Majesty the Queen, Hampton Court Palace. See also John Nost Sartorius for further painting of Oatlands Park.

Van Uden, Lucas (1595-1672)
Flemish painter of hunting and shooting scenes including a portrait of a huntsman shooting duck.

Van Valkenborch, Lucas (c.1580-1622)
"Two Men Playing a Game of Bowls". History of Art Museum, Vienna, No. 7348.

Van Verstalen, Antoni (1594-1641)
Dutch. "An Ice Scene" with skaters playing a golf-like game.

Van Vleit, K. (1841-1917)
Dutch painter of trotters racing, many of which were painted in 1910.

Varley, Cornelius (1781-1873)
Landscape painter, the brother of the landscape painters John Varley and W.F. Varley. His portrait of Colonel Hawker returning to Key Haven after a day's punt gunning in 1838 is repro. in "Old Sporting" pub. 1948 (McCausland). Varley was a founder member of the OWS but resigned in 1820. He exh. at the RA from 1803 although after 1820 scientific interests took up most of his time.

Vaughan, Harry Nyko (op.c.1951)
"Max (Faulkner) Steps Out", watercolour caricature, 13¼in.x9¾in., Sotheby's (Glasgow). Max Faulkner (born 1916) was the English professional golfer who won the 1951 Open Championship. He was also a Ryder Cup player and British Seniors Champion in 1968.

Vaughan, John Keith (1912-1976)
Self-taught painter in both oil and gouache of figure subjects including "The Wrestlers" (a subject which lends itself well to figure painting), gouache, ink, dated 1965, auctioned Phillips 1989. Vaughan, who worked for the advertising agency Lintas (1931-1939), exh. drawings at the Lefevre Gallery, London in 1942 and had a solo exhibition of paintings at the same gallery in 1946. In the same year he shared a flat with the artist John Minton, moving to Belsize Park in 1952. Held a retrospective exhibition at the Royal West of England Academy, Bristol and another at the Whitechapel Gallery, London in 1962.

Veal, George (op.1886-1890)
This painter of equestrian scenes was described as "a young painter of racing and steeplechasing pictures" (Bailys 1886). His painting "A Race for the Home Turn at Kempton" was exh. at Messrs. McQueen's Gallery in Tottenham Court Road in 1886 as was "A False Start", "Taking a Fence", "Taking a Brook" and "Going to the Post". His portrait of "Hardcash" with jockey up is dated 1890. His painting of a hunting scene entitled "Full Cry", dated '90, 40in.x50in., is extremely interesting and his painting "North Country Jockeys" was engraved by C.R. Stock and pub. 1887, 19½in.x36in.

Venables, Bernard (op.1948)
"The Bowling Green at the Cherry Tree Pub, Welwyn Garden City" painted in 1948 is repro. in "Inns of Sport" by J. Wentworth Day, pub. for Whitbread & Co. Ltd. by the Naldrett Press Ltd., London (1949).

Venat, Victor (op.1870s)
His watercolour painting of a steeplechase at Pau which is taking place at the foot of the Pyrennees on 17.1.72 was auctioned Christie's (Scotland) 1986.

Venner, Victor (op.1900-1924)
Illustrator and cartoonist who included golf amongst the subjects he portrayed. Humorous golfing prints after his work were pub. originally in 1904 including "The Lucky Dog" and "Addressing the Ball". His other known golfing work "The Golfers Link" appeared a few years later. Venner contributed to "Punch" and was a member of the London Sketch Club. Reproductions of his work can be seen at the Burlington Gallery, London.

Verboeckhoven, Eugene Joseph (1798-1881)
Very fashionable 19th century animal painter who was born in Brussels and travelled widely in Europe. He exh. in London, Paris and St. Petersburg. He was a prolific painter of horses as well as bulls, cows, donkeys, lambs, sheep and most other farmyard animals.

Vergett, Noel (op.1920)
Painter of a golfing watercolour of a mixed foursomes leaving the last green, s.&d. 1920, 12¼in.x17¼in., auctioned Bonhams 1988.

Vermeylen, Alphonse (1882-1939)
Born in Antwerp where he lived for most of his life and died. His tennis painting "Au Tennis", 28in.x36½in., was auctioned Sotheby's (Sussex) 1986.

Vernet, Carl (1758-1836)
French master of art who taught a great number of students in this Dictionary. He painted several horse studies and portraits including hare hunting, "Chasseur a l'Affut", depicting two horsemen in a landscape with hounds putting up a hare. A print after this work by Jazet was pub. in Paris c.1840. His painting "The Stud Farm", dated 1812, 21¾in.x27¾in, was exh. at the Detroit Institute of Arts, entitled "From David to Courbet", 1 February - 5 March 1950 (No. 17).

Vernet, Horace (1789-1863)
Painter of military scenes, some sporting and equestrian scenes including a stage coach travelling at speed and a portrait of the Duke of Orléans talking to his groom, entitled "Etude de Chevaux", etc.

Vernon, Arthur Langley (op.1871-c.1922)
Genre painter of several hunting scenes including "Return from the Hunt" and "Asking the Way". He exh. at the main London galleries from 1871. His watercolour "The Old Surrey and Burstow Hounds", 17in.x 13in., was auctioned Taylors (Honiton) 1990.

Vernon, Walter
Painter of equestrian portraits including "Common", a chestnut racehorse with jockey up being held by his owner, 14in.x19in., and a bay horse in a stall. He also painted coaching scenes including a coach and four travelling through a park, and a further coaching scene, 28¾in.x23½in., was auctioned Bonhams 1980.

Veron, Alexandre René (1826-1897)
French painter of river and angling scenes including "A Fisherman on a River Bank" and "A Fisherman in a Punt", each 9in.x7in. David Lay (Cornwall) 1989.

Verpilleux, Emile Antoine, RBA (1888-1964)
Portrait and landscape painter, illustrator and engraver who studied at the Académie des Beaux Art, Antwerp. His fine painting "The Kilkenny in Full Cry" s.&d. 1928, and inscr. "To D. McCalmont" 14in.x16in., was auctioned Sotheby's 1987. Exh. at the RA, RBA, RSA, NEA and elsewhere. Elected RBA (1914). Usually signed his work A.E. Verpilleux, switching his Christian names late in life.

Verschuur, Wouter (1812-1874)
Dutch painter of domestic, farmyard and equestrian scenes, not really of sporting scenes. Most of his horses are painted in their stable interiors. A few are depicted out riding. Pupil of P. Van Oss.

Vial de Saint Bel, M. (op.1771)
A drawing of "Eclipse" by this artist of whom no biographical details appear to have been traced was first pub. in 1771 and is illus. in Theodore Cook's "History of the English Turf". The drawing was intended to show the movement of the horse's legs.

Villon, Jacques (1875-1963)
French painter who uncharacteristically painted "Racehorses Exercising at Chantilly" in 1950. Virginia Museum of Fine Arts, Richmond, USA.

Vinall, Joseph William Topham (b.1873)
Landscape, figure and portrait painter, teacher, writer and examiner. Born in Liverpool. Studied at the RCA and the City and Guilds of London Institution. Exh. (1908-1940) at the RA, RSA, ROI, RBA and elsewhere. His painting in oils of a park scene with people playing tennis on three courts, 13in.x10in., dated 1905, is in a private collection USA.

Vincent, George (1796-1831)
Still life painter of game subjects including dead pheasants and partridge. His painting of ducks on a river in a wooded landscape dated 1828, 18½in.x22½in. was auctioned Christie's 1986. Vincent, who was a pupil of John Crome, exh. at the RA, BI, SS and OWCS.

Vincent, René (1879-1936)
French-born motor car painter and enthusiast, often depicting motor racing scenes and rallies. He studied architecture at the Institut des Beaux Art, but soon turned to painting and became one of the finest interpreters of motor cars in a social setting because his drawings of fashionable women were as good as those of his cars. He worked firstly for the Berliet factory and then moved to Peugot in about 1908. He worked for "La Vie Parisien", "L'Illustration" and other magazines and was also responsible for some of the most striking automobile posters created in France including work for Bugatti, Hispano Suiza, Delahaye and Michelin.

Vine, John (of Colchester) (1808/9-1867)
Born deformed, Vine started life as a country fair curiosity. He painted under great physical difficulty but worked in watercolour and oil and was amazingly prolific, despite his infirmities. His portrait of a gentleman driving a Stanhope gig at speed on a country road, dated 1834, 19½in.x23½in., is a superb example of this naturally talented artist. Other work by Vine includes a portrait of a gentleman, small, full length, wearing a grey coat and black cravat, standing by a horse with two dachshunds, s.&d. 1847. A spaniel outside a kennel, "Generella", a portrait of a bay mare with a dog in a stable, dated 1854 and inscr. "G.J. Hoyles Took's old mare and old dog 'Flint', "Hotspur", a portrait of a bay racehorse in a stable, signed and inscr., 18⅛in.x24in. and a fine watercolour painting of a pig repro. in the "Connoisseur" November 1977. Vine's patrons included The Royal Agricultural Society, Lord Weston and Lady Foley and presumably the owners of the animals mentioned above. He is known to have settled in Colchester in about 1830 and to have married but had no children.

"Vixen"
The pseudonym used by the sporting painter Ninetta Butterworth (q.v.).

Volkers, Emile (op.1873-1901)
German painter of equestrian portraits and racing scenes whose sporting paintings include "Offensive", a portrait of a horse in a stable, a man riding one horse and leading another, a bright bay racehorse and a terrier in a stable, dated 1899, a chestnut hunter in a loosebox dated 1901, a bay hunter and a hound in a stable yard dated 1873, another dated 1874, another dated 1901 and a portrait of a jockey and his horse taking morning exercise.

Von Blaas, Julius (1845-1922)
Austrian artist of equestrian scenes including his fine portrait of "Colonel Kuser" in a trotting race, s.&d. 1899, Sotheby's 1990. He also painted "The Chase", a rather unofficial coursing scene with three greyhounds to one hare being chased by a number of mounted riders, dated 1870, Christie's (NY) 1986.

Von Rentzell, Auguste
A gentleman on a bay horse with three greyhounds coursing a hare in a wintry landscape, a groom following, dated 1836, 15in.x19in., by this artist was auctioned Christie's 1969.

Von Wagner, Alexander (1838-1919)
Hungarian painter of the monumental and dramatic "Chariot Race" (1898), Manchester City AG.

Voss, C.J. (op.1854-1855)
Unknown painter of equestrian portraits whose work includes a portrait of a gentleman seated with his mastiff dog in a garden of a country house, dated 1855, and a portrait of "Bourton", winner of the Grand National 1854 which was engraved by C. Hunt.

Voss, Franklin Brooke (1881-1953)
Distinguished American painter of equestrian portraits. A keen sportsman himself he belonged to the Maryland gentry and was brought up amongst the fox-hunting clubs around Baltimore. He hunted in England with the Duke of Beaufort and his patrons numbered the Witneys, the Riddles and the Vanderbilts in Maryland. Voss spent seven years in New York studying at the Art Students League and he became a close friend of Alfred Munnings (q.v.). Amongst the famous racehorses painted by Voss were "Equipoise", 1933, and "Man o'War" with Clarence Kummer up, 1919. Grooms bringing the polo ponies into the field, s.&d. 1941, 26½in.x40½in. Christie's (NY).

Vuillard, Edouard (1868-1940)
French painter who was a founder member, in 1888, of a group of Parisian artists called "the Nabis", derived from the Hebrew word meaning prophets. He is included in this Dictionary for his painting "The Game of Shuttlecock" (c.1892). Vuillard's work might have faded into relative obscurity had it not been for the efforts of his first dealer, Arthur Tooth, during the 1950s and 1960s.

W

Wadham, B.B. (op.1851-1898)
Landscape and portrait painter whose portrait of a young man in rowing clothes, dated 1851 and inscr., 14in.x12in., was exh. at the London Exhibition (1851). Exh. three landscapes at SS and one at the RA (1871-1883). He also exh. at the Walker AG, Liverpool until 1898.

Wadsworth (Wordsworth), C.H. (op.1911)
Painter of pigeon racing portraits including C. Woodall's racing pigeon "Old Red Bonami" dated 1911 and inscr., 12in.x16in. and "Jackie" the Jersey pigeon champion, bred and raced by Sidley Bros., 17½in.x 13¾in., inscr., auctioned Christie's 1988.

Wadsworth, Thomas (op.1820)
Two children with their horse, dated 1820, 24in.x 19½in.. auctioned Sotheby's 1984.

"Wag"
The pseudonym used by Arthur George Witherby (q.v.).

"The Wag"
The pseudonym sometimes used by the equestrian and sporting artist Charles Simpson (q.v.).

Wageman, Thomas Charles, NWS, (c.1787-1863)
Portrait and landscape painter and an illustrator. Founder member of the NWS (1831) and became portrait painter to the King of Holland. He contributed to "The Annals of Sporting" in 1827 and exh. at the BI, NWS, RA and RBA (1816-1848).

Wagner, Alexander Von
See Von Wagner

Wahlbergson, Erik (1808-1865)
Swedish artist whose "Hunting Hares in Summer", dated 1848, 29in.x41in., was auctioned Stockholm in 1985.

Wahlbom, Carl (1810-1858)
Swedish artist of many equestrian scenes, usually of riders on horseback outside a manor house or in a landscape.

Wain, Louis William (1860-1939)
Humorous painter of cats and sometimes dogs, very often portrayed playing a number of sports, including golf, fishing, tennis, football, etc. Wain, who was born in London, studied at the West London School of Art (1877-1880) and taught there (1881-1882). His feline drawings started in 1883. Joined the staff of "The Illustrated Sporting and Dramatic News" (1882) and "The Illustrated London News" (1886). Wain suffered a mental decline in 1918 which eventually led to his confinement in an asylum.

Wainwright, John (op.1849-1870)
Painter of game still lifes and sporting subjects but particularly shooting. His work includes "The Day's Bag" dated 1862, "A Sportsman's Bag" dated 1858, "A Brace of Partridge by a Cornfield" dated 1863, "Still Life" with dead birds and hunting paraphernalia, dated 1860. Does not appear to have exh. unless he is the John Wainewright who exh. four flower pictures at BI and two at SS (1860-1869). Collaborated on at least one painting with John Faulkner, RHA (q.v.).

Waite, Robert Thorne, RWS (1842-1935)
Landscape and marine painter of some yacht racing scenes including a watercolour entitled "Racing Yachts off St. Catherine's Point, near the Needles, Isle of Wight," 13¼in.x20in., Bonhams 1986. Studied art at South Kensington and painted in both oil and watercolour. Elected RWS (1884). An exhibition of works from his studio was held at the Bourne Gallery, Reigate, March 1976.

Wakefield, W. (op.c.1910?)
A painting of Edwardian golfers, 20in.x24in., was auctioned Michael Newman (Plymouth) 1989.

Waldburger, J.B. (b.1924)
Swiss painter of equestrian scenes.

Walenn, Gilbert (20th century)
"Polo Players", pencil and watercolour, s.&d. 1962, 14½in.x21¼in., Bonhams.

Wales, James (1747-1795)
Scottish landscape and portrait painter and an engraver who worked for many years in India and whose daughter, Susanna, married Sir Charles Warre Malet, 1st Bt. (1753-1815) in 1799. He also drew a portrait of Sir Charles' favourite riding horse, a grey stallion presented to him by the Peshwa of the Marathus in 1790 while he was resident minister at Poona. During this time, Malet negotiated an alliance with the Peshwa and the Nizam against Tippoo Sultan. The drawing is in the collection of Sir Edward Malet, Bt. Wales gave Thomas Daniell many of his drawings, twenty-four of which were used for the final volume of "Daniell's Oriental Scenery". Wales studied art in Scotland and exh. at the SA in 1783 and 1791 and at the RA (1788/9). Went to Bombay (1791) and died there (1795).

Walker
An artist of this name who painted for "Chums Annual" 1938 and 1939 two good action paintings of motor cycle racing entitled "Over the Top" and "The Winner". He is possibly W.H. Walker (q.v.).

Walker, Anthony (1726-1765)

Book illustrator and an engraver who studied at the St. Martin's Lane Academy and worked for Boydell. He designed and engraved the eight plates illustrating William Somerville's famous poem "The Chase" pub. in 1767. His drawing of "Gudgeon Fishing" or "He's Fairly Hooked" engraved by T. Wilson was repro. "Angling in British Art" (Shaw Sparrow). His brother William Walker (1729-1793) was also an illustrator and an engraver and worked on Paul Sandby's "Views in England and Wales". Anthony Walker's son was John Walker (op.1792-1802), the topographical illustrator who contributed to "The Copper Plate Magazine" (1792-1802) and who is almost certainly the same John Walker who exh. at the RA (1796-1800).

Walker, Miss Ethel (Dame), ARA, RBA, RP, NEAC, SMP (1867-1951)

Portrait and landscape painter. Born in Edinburgh, she studied at the Ridley School of Art, the Putney School of Art, the Westminster School of Art, and the Slade School of Art, under Henry Tonks (q.v.). She exh. at the RA from 1898 and held her first solo exhibition at the Redfern Gallery in 1827. Elected a member of the NEAC (1900), RBA (1932), RP (1933), and ARA (1940). She was created CBE in 1938 and a DBE in 1948. She lived and worked in Robin Hood's Bay, Yorkshire, but died in London which she visited often. Her small watercolour painting of a golfer with clubs and bag on the golf links road, Colwyn Bay, dated 1908 and inscr. is in the collection of The Wingfield Sporting Gallery, London.

Walker, Frank H. (ex.1886-1907)

Landscape painter and a painter of many river and angling scenes including a watercolour of an angler fishing the Cuckmere at Litlington, near Alfriston, Sussex, dated 1890, 16in.x27in. Walker exh. at the RA, RBA, RI, The Walker AG, Liverpool and Manchester AG (1886-1907).

Walker, Frederick (Fred) ARA, OWS (1840-1875)

Watercolour painter and an illustrator who studied at the RA Schools (1858) and exh. there from 1863. Included in this Dictionary for his angling watercolours. Walker, who was an enthusiastic fisherman, spent some time painting and fishing in the Highlands, where he stayed with Richard Ansdell RA (q.v.). Elected OWS (1866) and ARA (1871). His studio sale was held at Christie's, 17 July 1875.

Walker, Frederick (op.(19)07)

An unrecorded painter of a steeplechase scene, s.&d. '07, 25in.x30in., auctioned Sotheby's 1982.

Walker, Henry (1786-1849)

London painter and teacher of painting who specialised in domestic animals and whose exhibits at the RA, BI and SS include "A Portrait of an Old Hunter" (1822) and "A Study of a Bull" (1833).

Walker, James (1819-1889)

Irish-born painter who emigrated to America in 1877 where he visited California and supported himself by painting scenes of the large ranches. These paintings today are valued as colourful, accurate representations of the skills and costume of the Californian Vaqueros. The working saddles, bridles and bits of the Vaqueros were passed on to the American cowboy. "The Vaqueros Roping Horses in a Corral" dated 1877, 20in.x36in. is in the Thomas Gilcrease Collection, USA.

Walker, James Alexander (1831-1898)

Painter of military and cavalry scenes who also painted some hunting scenes including "Preparing for the Hunt", 13½in.x16in., auctioned Sotheby's (NY) 1987. A charming painting of a horse in a stable with two dogs and a groom appeared in a London gallery in 1980, attrib. to James Alexander Walker.

Walker, John (1747-1812)

"The Back of the Salvadore House Academy, Tooting", aquatint by Francis Jukes after the work of this artist, showing a game of cricket, pub. April 1787. London Borough of Wandsworth Public Library.

Walker, Joseph Francis (John) (1825-1906)

Yorkshire-based artist of equestrian and sporting scenes whose fine painting of a prize-winning four-in-hand, driven by Major T.C. Constable, dated 1858, with a view of Burton Constable Hall, Yorkshire, in the background, 4ft.2in.x8ft.6in. was auctioned Christie's 1987. Walker appears to have painted a number of sporting and equestrian scenes for Major Constable. Other sporting works by Walker recorded from the Burton Constable Hall Collection include a painting of Sir T. Constable's hounds and four similar. Presumably Major T.C. Constable became Sir T. Constable? Walker's pair "Selling a Horse to a Gentleman", ("Clearing a Fence" and "Showing him off at the Trot") were auctioned Christie's (NY) 1984. He also painted rustic scenes including "A Wagon Team of Horses Crossing a Ford", 24in.x35in., repro. "Country Life" 1977.

Walker, Miss Maude (op.1887-1892)

Figure painter who exh. two works at the RA including "A Fencing Master" (1887) from a London address.

Walker, R. Hollands (op.1883-1920)

Warwickshire landscape painter in watercolours who painted several hunting scenes in pairs or sets of four including "The Hunt", "Going to the Meet" and "Into the Covert", "The Meet", "Setting Off", "In Full Cry" and "The Kill", etc. His watercolours were usually 7½in.x12¼in. or thereabouts, always signed but rarely dated. An exception is "Gathering Hay" dated 1883. Walker exh. seven paintings at the Walker AG, Liverpool (1892-1920). He does not appear to have exh. elsewhere.

Walker, William Henry (op.1906-1926)

Watercolour painter and illustrator who illus. "Alice's Adventures in Wonderland" for Messrs. Lane in 1908. He was also a member of the family who ran Walker's Galleries in London. His watercolour painting "Tally Ho", 10in.x7in., was auctioned Christie's 1984. He exh. five paintings at the Walker AG, Liverpool, one at the RA and 377 at the Walker Gallery, London.

Wall, A.J. (op.1891-1897)
Animal and bird illustrator who contributed to "The Sporting and Dramatic News" (1891), "The Boys' Own Paper" and "The English Illustrated Magazine" (1896-1897).

Wallace, Harold Frank (1881-1962)
Scottish based sporting painter, author and illustrator who collaborated with Lionel Edwards (q.v.) in writing and illustrating "Hunting and Stalking the Deer". He painted mainly in watercolour or gouache and his sporting work includes an angling work entitled "The Fall's Pool, Helmsdale", gouache, signed, 14½in.x21in., with a figure fishing, said to be that of the Hon. Mrs. Robin Grosvenor. Wallace became a great friend of John Guille Millais (q.v.). He exh. (1932-1935) at the RSW and RI. Other publications include "Stalks Abroad" (1908), "The Big Game of Central and Western China" (1913) and "Hunting Winds" (1949).

Wallace, James (1872-1911)
Landscape painter who worked in Northumberland and painted many views of angling and scenes of the River Tweed. His watercolour painting "Salmon Fishing on the River Tweed", dated 1908, 14½in.x21¼in., was auctioned The Auction Galleries (Berwick on Tweed) 1990. Wallace exh. at the RA (1899-1904) from his Northumberland address.

Wallace, John (1841-1905)
Alias "George Pipeshank". Wallace made a set of four lithographs which were pub. by the British Tobacco Company, Cope Brothers & Co. Ltd. at the turn of the century. The illustrations, dated at various years during the 1890s, show British parliamentary figures playing golf on the Scottish links with legendary professionals like "old" Tom Morris. They are doubly interesting as they complement an extremely rare set of fifty tobacco cards sent out with their tobacco by Cope Brothers in about 1900 with many of the illustrations by the mysterious "Pipeshank". An interesting artistic note is that the originals are an identical size to the cards which make them unique as golfing miniatures. Paintings and sketches by Wallace, who was an enthusiastic golf player, were repro. in "The Golf Book of East Lothian" by the Revd. John Kerr.

Wallace, William (op.1870-1928)
Exh. one painting at the RA in 1928. His watercolour "The Angler's Polka" c.1870 was repro. in "Country Life".

Waller, Barbara, ARCA (op.1955 - d.c.1975)
Equestrian painter in oils, particularly of racehorses, from Hampshire.

Waller, Jonathan (b.1956)
Contemporary painter of "The Runner" and "The Biker", both painted in 1989 in vibrant colours and exh. at the Angela Flowers Gallery, London. Waller studied at the Lancaster Polytechnic (1980-1983) and Chelsea School of Art (1984-1985). Held Junior Painting Fellowship at Cardiff (1985-1986).

Waller, Lucy (op.1889-1900)
Animal painter, particularly of dogs, who included some mildly sporting subjects such as "Waiting for Master", dated 1889 and "Tartan King" a Dandie Dinmont terrier, dated 1893. She exh. one painting at SS (1891).

Waller, Renz (d.1979)
German animal painter, co-founder and President of the Deutscher Falkenorden. In 1933 he obtained the patronage of Reichsmarschall Goering who created a state falconry centre, the Reichsfalkenhof in Brunswick. Waller's falconry pictures include a portrait of the "Polar Gyrfalcon" belonging to Goering. Ondheidkamer van Jacht in Visserij Breda, Netherlands.

Waller, Samuel Edmund, ROI (1850-1903)
Animal, historical and genre painter in oil. Studied at Gloucester School of Art, under John Kemp and at the RA Schools, from 1869. Exh. at the RA from 1871. Elected ROI 1883. Worked as an illustrator for "The Graphic" from 1873. He was an excellent equestrian painter and painted several fox-hunting scenes including "The Huntsman's Courtship" dated 1899, "An Afternoon Ride" dated 1894, "The Day of Reckoning" and "At the Window" dated 1891 (the latter not a hunting scene but a rather genre interpretation of a lady and gentleman by a window feeding sugar lumps to a horse). He followed the Edwardian fashion for painting his subjects in period costume. Contributed to "The Sporting and Dramatic News" (1899). Pub. ""Six Weeks in the Saddle" and illus. "The Strange Adventures of a Phaeton" (William Black 1874).

Wallis, Henry, RWS (1830-1916)
Landscape painter and writer who studied at Cary's Academy and then in Paris and at the RA Schools. Influenced by the Pre-Raphaelites at an early date. Exh. at the RA, RBA, RWS from 1854. Elected RWS (1880). "A Game of Bowls", 22in.x36in., was exh. at the London International Exhibition (1871).

Wallis, Joseph Haythorne (op.1861-1890)
Animal painter and of some sporting scenes including "Dead Game and a Retriever", dated 1862 and "Making Friends", a watercolour study of a grey hunter and a dog in a yard, dated 1873, 16in.x24¾in., Bonhams 1984. Wallis exh. six paintings at the RA including a portrait of "Mr. John Bagot Scriven's 'Kitty'" and two at the Grosvenor Gallery in 1880. He is sometimes listed erroneously as Joseph Haythorne Wallace.

Walls, William, RSA, RSW (1860-1942)
Scottish-born animal painter in both oil and watercolour whose sporting work includes two still lifes with rod and fish, trout and fly case, dated 1922, "Hare Coursing", and "The Day's Catch" dated 1915. Walls illus. "Rab and his Master" pub. 1918, a ballad by George Hope Tait who was an extremely accomplished artist in his own right, though not usually of sporting subjects. Walls studied art at the RSA Life School, Edinburgh and also at the Antwerp Academy. He was influenced by the work of Joseph Crawhall (q.v.) and Edwin

Alexander (q.v.) who became his brother-in-law. He was elected RSW (1906) and RSA (1914). He taught animal painting at the Edinburgh College of Art.

Walmesley, J.M. (op.1905-1909)
Unknown painter of a portrait of the prize bull "Village Beau", dated 1909 and "Kirkland" with "Titch" Mason up, winner of the Grand National dated 1905, 8in.x 12in., Rowles Fine Art, Powys.

Walrond, Sir John Walrond, Bt. (op.1863-1888)
Landscape painter and of some angling scenes including his watercolour "The Home Pool at Bogen Guuldalen", dated 1863 and inscr. "104 pounds of salmon taken from this pool", 17in.x11in. Auctioned Woolley and Wallis 1989. Walrond exh. at the RI (1879-1888) from a London address. He also exh. one view of a courtyard at Cairo at the RA (1879). Descendant of Sir John Walrond Walrond, Bt., the painter of birds who exh. (1779-1788) and whose original name was John Walrond Dickinson.

Walsh, J.H.
See "Stonehenge", the pseudonym he used.

Walsh(e), Thomas N.H. (op.1876-1906)
Painter of equestrian, particularly hunting scenes, painted in gouache and watercolour, sometimes over black chalk. His sporting work includes "Huntsman and Hounds in a Landscape", dated 1889, watercolour and crayon, 13in.x17½in., "At the Smithy" a hunter and huntsman, painted in gouache, 10½in.x14½in. dated 1876, "A Huntsman in a Snowy Landscape" dated 1906, 9in.x13in., "A Second Wind" and "Homeward Bound", a pair of hunting scenes in watercolour, each 8½in.x13in. Walsh appears to have painted many of his hunting scenes in pairs. His set of four hunting scenes entitled "Dodson's Hunting Incidents" were engraved (1878/9) by Edward Gilbert Hester (c.1843-1903). Walsh also painted a similar set of four coaching scenes entitled "Dodson's Coaching Incidents", and a set of four racing scenes were engraved by C.R. Stock and pub. in 1887. Walsh seems to have worked for the publisher, Dodson, between 1878 and 1887. His watercolour of a blacksmith shoeing a white stallion, 11in.x 15in., dated 1876 was auctioned 1985.

Walter, Henry G. (c.1786-1849)
Animal and sporting painter, mainly of road subjects, and a lithographer whose chief claim to fame lies with the lithograph he made of "The Jersey Races" pub. posthumously in 1850 after the work by the little known artist P.J. Ouless (q.v.) which is a rare and much-valued print. He also engraved two of his own paintings in aquatint, one of a mail coach and the other of an eight horse stage wagon with great broad wheels travelling the Bath to London road. This friend of the poet William Blake and the landscape painter John Linnell was a drawing and painting master operating in London and Sussex, although he lived the latter part of his life in Torquay where he died. He exh. six paintings at the RA including a portrait of an old hunter (1822), a study of a bull (1833) and studies of animals (1846). He also exh. six paintings at the BI, two at SS and three at the

NWCS (1820-1846). He compiled lithograph drawing books for students containing studies of domestic animals which were portrayed with great skill. His portrait of a dark bay pony in a loosebox dated January 1845, 21½in.x27½in., was auctioned Christie's 1986.

Waltman, Harry Franklin (1871-1951)
American painter of a portrait of "Sir Henry Mills in riding dress with a hunter", dated 1902, 69in.x49in., auctioned Christie's 1985. Waltman, who studied art under Constant and Laureus in Paris, was elected ANA 1917.

Walton, Frank, RI (1840-1928)
Landscape, sporting and coastal painter who exh. "Leisure To Go A'Fishing" at Burlington House in 1901 (No. 464.) His racing scenes entitled "Over the Fence" and "At Full Gallop", each 7in.x12½in., were auctioned Christie's 1984. Walton painted "The Lawn at Goodwood" in 1886, 36in.x60in., with Thomas Walter Wilson (q.v.). This painting and its pendant "The Four-in-Hand Club in Hyde Park" (now destroyed) are discussed in "Country Life" 25 July 1947. Walton also collaborated with Heywood Hardy (q.v.) on a number of paintings including "A Steady Shot" and "The Parson's Holiday" both s.&d. 1892 by both artists. He exh. from 1862 at the leading London art galleries and was elected RI (1882) (Hon. Retd. 1923), ROI (1883) and HROI (1898).

Walton, Henry (1746-1813)
Painter of portraits and of conversation pieces. Born in Norfolk, a pupil of Zoffany (q.v.) c.1769-70. Exh. SA (1771-1773) and RA (1777-1779). He made frequent journeys to Paris but retired to Suffolk where he acted as an art consultant to private collectors. His portrait of "A Gentleman with his Saddled Grey Hunter by a Fence in a Landscape", 24¾in.x30in. was auctioned Sotheby's 1987. The horse has the cropped ears fashionable at the time and the picture is extremely well painted. He also painted "A Cricket Scene at Harrow School" dated 1771 (private collection) and a portrait of "Robert Rayner out Shooting", 41in.x33½in., The Paul Mellon Collection, Upperville, Va, USA. Robert Rayner, a Suffolk farmer, married the artist's niece, Fanny Walton, daughter of Walton's elder brother, Samuel, and afterwards Mrs. Edward Bridgman. Henry Walton's portrait of her in a dark brown riding habit while a groom waits with a bay horse, 13⅜in.x 11⅜in., is also in the Paul Mellon Collection, Upperville, Va, USA.

Walton, W.L. (op.1834-1860)
Landscape topographical and sporting lithographer after his own work and that of his contemporaries. He worked in London for the publishers Day and Son, when it was Day and Haghe, c.1832-1845. A rare lithographic aeronautical print after the work by this artist entitled "The First Carriage Aerial" was pub. by Day and Haghe and features an interesting fictitious flying machine. Walton collaborated with G. Gautez on a tinted lithograph of the international boxing contest between Heenan and Sayers at Farnborough on 17 April

Walwyn, Jean (Mrs. Tom Holt)

1860 which was pub. by G. Newbold in November 1860. He exh. three watercolour landscapes at SS and one work at the RA (1834-1855) from a London address.

Walwyn, Jean (Mrs. Tom Holt) (b.1925)
Monmouth-born painter of equestrian scenes, the daughter of the famous horseman, Colonel Taffy Walwyn. Studied part time with the sculptor, Doris Lindner, and won the Topham Prize for sculpture at Liverpool for designing a racing trophy.

Wambill, Sydney (op.1841)
See Sydney R. Wombill(e)

"Wanderer"
The nom de plume used by the sporting writer William Scarth Dixon.

"Wanderer"
The pseudonym for Elim H. D'Avigdor (q.v.), the author of "Across Country" (1882), illus. Georgina Bowers (q.v.).

Wanklyn, Joan (op.1940s-1960s)
Painter of equestrian scenes whose cover design for the programme for the "International Horse Show", 26 July 1949, was drawn in pastel, 20in.x14in. Her portrait of "Locket" a dark bay hunter in a field, dated 1951, and inscr., was painted in gouache and pencil, 10½in.x14¼in. "Smith's Lawn 1967", repro. "The World of Polo, Past and Present" by J.N.P. Watson, pub. The Sportsman's Press, 1986. Joan Wanklyn grew up in Cheltenham where her love of painting horses was encouraged by frequent visits to the racecourse. She studied at the Royal Drawing Society Studios, Chelsea and at the Central Schools of Art until the 2nd World War interrupted her studies.

Wanostrocht, Nicholas ("Felix") (1804-1876)
Artist and illustrator, mostly of cricket subjects in watercolour. Of Flemish extraction, Wanostrocht lived in Brighton and Wimborne and helped to found the Surrey Cricket Club. As President of "The All England XI", founded in 1846 by William Clarke (of Nottingham), Wanostrocht recorded the team journeys in 1851 in a scrap book (now in the collection of the MCC) and illus. with watercolour sketches nearly every cricket ground they played on including "The All England XI Playing at Trentham, Staffordshire in 1851". He was himself a first-class cricketer and the artist G.F. Watts (q.v.) drew him in many cricket poses from life. He used the pseudonym "Felix" and sometimes "N. Felix" in order to protect his gentleman status in his activities as a professional cricketer. In his spare time he was a school master and inherited a school in Camberwell from his father in 1826. He was also a musician and an author for he wrote and illus. "Felix on the Bat" in 1845. One of his watercolours "The Two XIs of the University of Cambridge", dated 1847, 24in.x36in. is in the MCC Collection. The MCC also have a self-portrait of this artist in their collection.

Wanstall, J.G. (op.1864)
The Piscatorial Society have an angling watercolour by this artist, dated 1864, in their collection.

Ward, Cyril H., R.Cam.A (1863-1935)
Landscape painter, chiefly in watercolour. Educated at Denstone College where he was later an assistant master (1885-1888) and at Selwyn College, Cambridge. He painted full-time from 1888 and exh. at the leading London galleries from 1890, mainly at the RA, RBA and RI. His sporting work includes "Grouse Shooting" dated 1891, 11½in.x18½in., "An Angler in Spring", "Rabbit Shooting on a Surrey Common". In 1924 Ward bought a hotel at Holybourne, Hampshire, when he seems to have given up painting.

Ward, Edmund F. (b.1892)
American figure painter whose boxing scene entitled "Between Rounds" 19in.x23in. was auctioned Sotheby's Parke Bernet (NY) 1985.

Ward, Edward Matthew, RA (1816-1879)
Painter of historical genre and included in this Dictionary for his hawking painting "The Fair Falconer", 13¾in.x11½in. and his RA exhibit (1850) "Izaak Walton Angling - A Summer Day on the Banks of the Colne". Ward studied at the RA Schools (1835) and in Rome (1836-1839). He exh. at the RA (1834-1877), BI, SS, NWS and elsewhere. Ward and his wife Henrietta, daughter of George Raphael Ward (q.v.) were the parents of Sir Leslie Matthew Ward (q.v.) alias "Spy".

Ward, George Raphael (1797-1879)
Mezzotint engraver after the work of his contemporaries. Son and pupil of James Ward (q.v.). He was named after his father's friend and tutor, John Raphael Smith (q.v.). Ward engraved several equestrian portraits including that of "Sir Tatton Sykes" after the work by Sir Francis Grant. He was the father of Henrietta Ward who married E.M. Ward (q.v.) (no relation) in 1848.

Ward, James, RA (1769-1859)
A major animal, historical and sporting painter, also a mezzotint engraver. Born in London, the younger brother of William Ward, ARA (q.v.) and father of G.R. Ward (q.v.). Both brothers were apprenticed to the leading engraver John Raphael Smith (q.v.) at about the age of twelve after which James Ward worked in the newly opened studio of his elder brother for two or three years with whom he formed a partnership. Appointed painter and mezzotinter to the Prince of Wales as a result of the prints pub. by T.Simpson of his first pair of paintings shown at the RA in 1790. Studied anatomy drawing at Mr. Brooks's school in Blenheim Street until he received his first commission from Sir. John Sinclair, Lord Somerville and the Agricultural Society for whom he produced no fewer than 200 portraits of representative breeds of cattle, sheep and pigs in Great Britain, pub. by Josiah Boydell. Unfortunately Boydell went bankrupt and the project collapsed (although one cannot help wondering why the commission was never channelled through Ward's own publishing company which was previously founded with Dr. Daw). One of his early patrons, apart from Sir John Sinclair, was Sir John Fleming Leicester, later 1st Baron de Tably, a famous collector of old masters but who also "bought British" which was considered

unfashionable at that time. Leicester was a great friend of English artists. Between 1823 and 1824 Ward lithographed a series of portraits of celebrated horses which are important early examples of artist's lithography. Ward was elected RA in 1811 but in one of those inexplicable quirks of fate he was to lose almost everything he had worked for with his massive painting, 21ft.x35ft., of an allegorical work commemorating the Duke of Wellington's triumph at Waterloo which he started to paint in 1816 and which consumed his entire life and eventually beggared him. By 1847 Ward was forced to apply to the RA for a pension which he was granted at £100 per annum, as did Hablot Knight Browne (q.v.) some years later in 1879. Both Ward and Charles Towne (q.v.) painted the celebrated "Old Billy", the horse who made equine history by living sixty-two years. Billy died in 1822, Ward painted him in 1812 when the old horse was allegedly fifty-two. Ward's paintings "Confidence" and "Depression" depicting four horses starting a race and the same four coming home, a pair, were auctioned Sotheby's 1966.

Ward, John Stanton, RA, RWS, RP, NEAC, ARCA, VPRP (b.1917)

Hereford-born painter and illustrator in oil and watercolour who studied art at the RCA (1936-1939) under Gilbert Spencer, and again in 1946. Exh. at the leading London galleries. Elected NEAC (1950), RWS (1952), RP (1953), RA (1965). Included in this Dictionary for his angling scene "A Break for Lunch", pen, ink and grey wash over pencil, 24in.x21½in., Sotheby's 1989 and "The St. Lawrence Cricket Ground, Canterbury", watercolour, courtesy Kent Cricket Club. His work is represented in the Royal Collection.

Ward, Sir Leslie Matthew ("Spy") (1851-1922)

Illustrator and cartoonist, portrait painter and draughtsman of portrait caricatures. Born in London, he was the eldest son of E.M. Ward, RA (q.v.). He was also the great grandson of the great animal and sporting painter James Ward (q.v.) through his mother Henrietta, who was the daughter of George R. Ward (q.v.) and who married E.M. Ward (q.v.) (no relation) in 1848. He studied architecture under Sydney Smirke, RA and at the RA Schools where he exh. eleven works. Contributed caricatures to "The Graphic" from 1874. Known principally as "Spy", the cartoonist for the London society magazine "Vanity Fair" who between 1869 and 1914 pub. a chromolithograph in colour as a magazine supplement. These portrayed celebrated sportsmen including the golfer J.H. Taylor in 1906. Ward produced a series of cricket celebrities in "Vanity Fair" between 1878 and 1903 including Spofforth, Hirst and the legendary W.G. Grace. Elected RP (1891) and knighted (1918).

Ward, Louis Arthur, RWA, FCSD (b.1913)

Figure painter in oil and gouache who studied as a full-time student at the West of England College of Art, under R.E.J. Bush, and from there joined the studio of a large printing firm. After the war he taught part time at his former art school and then established himself as a freelance illustrator for magazines and books including Hamlyns, Longmans Green, Amalgamated Press, the BBC, British Printing Corporation, the British Tourist Authority, Kellogg Company and The Imperial Tobacco Company. He read theology at Ripon Hall, Oxford. After serving as a parish priest he returned to full-time painting. A friend of Paul Methuen, RA, Ward was able to use Methuen's studio at Corsham Court. Has painted several sporting scenes including "Derby Day", 36in.x48in. and "Football", 16in.x20in, exh. at the 20th Century Gallery, London. Has held successful one-man shows and has exh. at the leading London galleries. Exh. RWA and other galleries in the West Country. Elected RWA (1955).

Ward, Martin Theodore (1799-1874)

Animal and sporting painter, the son of the engraver William Ward (q.v.), and a nephew of James Ward (q.v.). He studied art under Sir Edwin Landseer (q.v.) and worked in London until 1840 when he moved to Yorkshire, dying there in poverty in 1874. He exh. at the RA (1820-1825), BI and SS (1819-1858). Titles at RA include "Returning from Shooting", "A Portrait of a Favourite Hunter", and "Hounds in a Copse" dated 1832, 12¾in.x17in. Contributed to "The Sporting Annals" (1826). His sporting work includes "Gamekeepers Returning from Shooting", dated 1823, 43in.x55½in., exh. at the BI 1824 (No. 78) and also probably at the RA 1823 (No. 985)

Ward, Rowland (1850-1912)

Draughtsman, sculptor, artist and author of animal, big game, sporting and naturalist subjects. Ward left school at fourteen to join his father's (Henry Ward) taxidermy studio where one of his first jobs was to help model the humming birds for the great ornithologist, John Gould. Ward's sporting work includes the life-size silver fox he made for Sir Bache Cunard, which weighed 37½lb., the 2,500 sporting and big game specimens he modelled for the Duke of Orleans from 1889 onwards and the work he did for countless private clients including the big game hunter F.C. Selous (1851-1917). Famous racehorses such as "Hermit" and "Persimmon" were sent to his studio on their deaths. His own books included "An English Angler in Florida" and he pub. "Hunting and Adventures in South East Africa" (1893) and "Sunshine and Sport in Rhodesia" (1896) for F.C. Selous. Ward studied the cross-breeding of pheasants on his Norfolk estate and was one of the first Englishmen to own a Mercedes "horseless carriage".

Ward, Vernon (1905-1985)

An all-round painter of many subjects including animal and sporting scenes. Born in London. Educated at St. Aloysias College, Highgate. Studied at the Slade under Professor Tonks (q.v.), Wilson Steer and Sir Walter Russell. Best known, like Max Pethick (q.v.) for his greetings card work. His sporting paintings include "The Ski Slopes" 13½in.x17¾in. and "Skiers Descending a Slope", 11½in.x13in. Figure and later landscape painter who specialised particularly in paintings of wildfowl and gundogs. His painting entitled "Royal Ascot", 20in.x16in., is a delightfully romantic indulgence set in period costume. Rowles Fine Art, Powys.

Ward, William, ARA (1768-1826)
Sporting painter and engraver. Born in London, the elder brother of James Ward (q.v.). Apprenticed at an early age to the leading engraver of the day, John Raphael Smith (q.v.). In October 1786 he married Maria, the sister of the erratic George Morland (q.v.) who himself married Annie Ward, William's sister, a month before in the same year. Ward painted in watercolour and examples of his work are to be found at Reading University. Mezzotint engraver of sporting subjects after the work of his contemporaries including several after George Morland and James Ward. He was appointed mezzotint engraver to the Duke of York in 1803 and engraver to the Duke of Clarence, later William IV. Elected ARA (1814).

Ward, William H. (op.1850-1882)
Birmingham painter of still lifes, animals and some sporting scenes including "Fishing Tales" dated 1876, 10in.x8in. He exh. 1850 to 1882 at the RA, BI, SS and the RBSA. His still life of dead mallard, pheasant and fruit on a ledge, dated 1852, 8½in.x11½in., was auctioned Christie's 1977 and his portraits of English bulldogs amidst the sand-dunes, 15½in.x11½in., were auctioned Bonhams 1987.

Warden, W. (op.1890)
Painter of "The London to Brighton Coach" dated 1890, 8in.x12½in., auctioned Sotheby's 1977.

Wardle, Arthur, RI, RBC, PS (1864-1949)
A self-taught London artist best known for his paintings of dogs. He exh. at the RA and the NWS (1880-1938) and held his first one-man exhibition at the Fine Art Society in 1931. Wardle worked in all mediums - oil, watercolour and pastel - and became a member of the Pastel Society in 1911 and a member of the RI in 1922. His sporting work includes "Grouse Shooting", "An Otter Hunt on the Moors", dated 1891, and several other paintings of otter hunting including a set of three entitled "Walking Up", "The Kill", "Full Cry". Wardle also painted several studies of deer stalking.

Wardle, C. Francis (op.1882-1948)
Landscape painter who exh. at the RA, RBA, and ROI (1882-1889). His watercolour study of a hunter in a stable, dated 1948, was auctioned Dennis Pocock, Marlborough, 1986. Wardle's book "All Dogs", illus. by himself, was pub. 1935.

Wardleworth, John L. (op.1910-1940)
Painter of dogs, particularly terriers ratting or rabbiting. Tended to copy the work of his contemporaries, for example Edgar Hunt (q.v.).

Wardlow, Alexander Hamilton (ex.1885-1899)
London painter of portraits and miniatures who collaborated with A.C. Sealy (q.v.) on four hunting works, issued as mezzotints and pub. by Messrs. Dickinson and Foster (qq.v.) 4.1.1890. Dickinson and Foster were also the publishers of Wardlow's painting "The Eton Rowing Procession" which they issued as a lithograph on 2 December 1889. Wardlow exh. at the RA, RHA, RI and elsewhere (1885-1899).

Warhol, Andy (1928-1987)
American painter whose contrived images of trite objects found such favour with the public during the 1960s. Warhol understood the art of marketing to perfection and he gave the public what they thought they wanted in a similar monotonous repetitive form representing a chronological narrative history of a unique age of excess. This form is best illus. in his ten portraits of star athletes ranging from Dorothy Hamill to Muhammad Ali (1977). Warhol's silk screen entitled "Baseball" (1962) depicts Roger Marris at bat. The effect simulates an early film reel of a player in action.

Warne-Browne, Alfred J. (op.1884-1900 d.1915)
Landscape and marine painter in both oil and watercolour whose portrait of a Thames roach from a watercolour especially painted for the magazine "Fishing", s.&d. 1886, is in the collection of the Piscatorial Society. Warne-Browne exh. at the RA, from 1884, the Fine Art Society, the Walker AG Liverpool, RI and also at Arthur Tooth and the Dowdswell Galleries.

Warner, J. (op.1829-1840)
This artist's painting of a mail coach "The Exeter - Sherborne - London Stage Coach", 17in.x31in., was auctioned Christie's 1967. He may be the same J. Warner who exh. in London in 1829.

Warner, John (b.1931)
London-born painter and print maker who studied at Willesden School of Art and graduated with a distinction in 1951/1952. Taught drawing at Willesden and then at the London College of Printing where he became Senior Lecturer in print making. He made and wrote a series of documentary films on art and design towards the end of the 1960s. During the making of a film in Japan he became interested in Sumo wrestling and a number of his paintings depict this sport.

Warner, Mark
Contemporary painter of rowing scenes. Exh. at the Thackeray Gallery, London.

Warren, Ferdinand E. (1899-1981)
His fine oil on canvas, 32in.x47in., a dramatic painting of baseball entitled "Night Ball Game", 1946, is in the Georgia Museum of Art at the University of Georgia.

Warren, Henry Clifford (b.1843 op.1860-1889)
Warren, who was a son of the watercolour painter Henry Warren PNWS (1794-1879), exh. at SS, NWS and elsewhere (1860-1885). He was an unsuccessful candidate for the NWS in 1868 but amongst the seventeen paintings he exh. at SS was one entitled "Foxhunting". A watercolour of a stag hunt at Marsh Ash in the New Forest, dated 1889, was auctioned Sotheby's (Bel.) 1975.

Warren, James R. Warren (op.1888)
Watercolour landscape painter who exh. two paintings at the Goupil Gallery in 1888. His painting of fox-hunting entitled "Taking a Fence", 15½in.x19½in., was auctioned Christie's (Sth. Ken.) 1988.

Warwick, K.W. (op.1906)
"Summer Recreations at Eton College - a View from the Playing Fields", s.&d. 1906, 17¼in.x25¼in. Christie's (Sth. Ken.)

Wasdell Trickett
See Trickett

Washington, Georges (1827-1910)
French painter of equestrian scenes, mostly of mounted Arab soldiers painted in both oil and watercolour, and a great lover of horses. Washington, who was a pupil of Jean Claude Picot, a sportsman himself and a portrayer of an occasional sporting scene, lived in the Chateau des Brouillards, Montmartre. Washington's sporting work includes "A Hawking Party", 10in.x13in., "The Start for the Hunt", 24in.x32in., "Partie de Chasse", 26in.x 37in., "A Hunting Party" 28in.x38in., and "The Falconer Casts off his Falcon", exh. Mathaf Gallery, London.

Washington, William (1895-1956)
Cheshire-born painter and line engraver of architectural views, portraits and figure subjects. Washington studied at the RCA, after working as a railwayman and for a firm of lithographic printers. He taught at Southend and Clapham Art Schools and was Head of the Department of Arts and Crafts at Hammersmith. "The Cricket Bat Maker at his Work Bench", etching, 10¾in.x8⅝in. Signed artist's proof dated 1934. Exh. the Parker Gallery, London 1950.

Wasley, Frank (op.1880-1914)
A British post-impressionist artist of considerable ability whose achievements have become increasingly recognised since the 1970s. He painted in both oil and watercolour and in black and white, specialising in marine and river subjects. Although considered to be a North Country artist he moved from Whitby to Weston-super-Mare in 1903, to Littlehampton in 1908 and to Henley-on-Thames in 1914. He exh. at the RA, RI, RBSA. Included in this Dictionary for his watercolour of a regatta at Venice and for his angling scene entitled "Casting a Fly on a River", although the fisherman, the rod and the fly are hard to see.

Waterlow, Sir Ernest Albert, RA, HRMS, ROI, HROI, RSW, ARWS, RWS, PRWS (1850-1919)
Landscape and animal painter in both oil and watercolour whose work includes a watercolour entitled "Duck Shooting before Old Man Mountain" auctioned Phillips 1987. Studied at Heidelberg, Lausanne and the RA Schools (1872). Won the Turner Gold Medal (1873). Exh. at the RA and RWS (1872-1919). Elected RA (1903), HRMS (1898), ROI (1883), HROI (1899), RSW (1900), ARWS (1880), RWS (1894), PRWS (1897), knighted (1902). Influenced by Fred Walker (q.v.), G.H. Mason, and the Barbizon painters. Represented in several public collections.

Watherston, Marjorie Violet (Mrs. Geare), SWA (op.1920-d.1970)
London painter of portraits, figures and landscapes in oil, watercolour and pastel. Studied art in Paris and at the RA Schools. Exh. at the RA, RSA, RI, ROI, RP, in the provinces and at the Paris Salon where she received an honorary mention 1947. She was the sister of the artist Miss Evelyn Watherston (d.1952) Included in this Dictionary for the "1923 Ladies Lawn Tennis Wimbledon Singles Final" between Susanne Lenglen of France and Kitty McKane (Mrs. Godfree) of England. Susanne Lenglen won 6-2, 6-2. According to the match reports of 14 July 1923 this score reflected not indifferent play by Miss McKane but faultless execution by Mademoiselle Lenglen. Kitty McKane went on to win the title in 1924 and 1926 as well as the mixed doubles titles in those years with Gilbert Leslie Godfree (later her husband).

Watkins Pitchford, Denys James, MBE, ARCA (1905-1990)
Northamptonshire-born author and illustrator of rural books, in particular fishing and shooting, many of which were contributed under the pseudonym "BB" after the size of the shot used for shooting wild geese. He also contributed regularly to "The Shooting Times". He was the son of the Rector of Lamport, Northants. Educated privately and studied at the RCA under Sir William Rothenstein after which he studied in Paris. On his return he became an assistant art master at Rugby School, a position he held between 1929 and 1947. In his will he left his £1,500 in 3½% War Loan to Rugby School as an annual prize for a member of the School Natural History Society. His books include "The Fisherman's Bedside Book" written and illus. in 1945, "Wild Lone - The Story of a Pytchley Fox" in 1938, "The Shooting Man's Bedside Book" 1948, and "The Sportsman's Bedside Book". In 1984 he produced his last book (he had written sixty and illus. thirty) which was partly a compilation of his articles to "The Shooting Times". Despite the use of a pseudonym for his written work, Watkins Pitchford's illustrations were usually contributed under his own name.

Watkiss, Christopher
Contemporary painter of several sporting scenes including golf and cricket. Studied at the Hornsey College of Art (1928-1933). Worked as a graphic artist before the 2nd World War. Set up as a freelance illustrator and has featured in many advertising campaigns for Government ministries and has created design and art work in all media for organisations including BSA, BMC, B/L, Shell BP, Esso, Roots (Chrysler), Union Castle Shipping Line and British Rail. He has exh. with the NEAC, RSMA, RI and the RBA.

Watmough, G. (op.1884-1885)
An interesting painting entitled "Off to the Meet", signed G. Watmough, 28½in.x40½in., was auctioned Christie's (NY) 1987. This may be Amos Watmough (op.1884-1885) who painted plough horses and farmyard scenes.

Watson, Charles John, RPE (1846-1927)
Painter and etcher of landscapes, figure and architectural subjects. Included in this Dictionary for his painting of a referee stopping a boxing match, auctioned Sotheby's (Sussex) 1987. Watson exh. at the leading London galleries from 1872 from a Norfolk address.

Watson, G.L. (1851-1904)

Marine artist who painted many regatta scenes. Son of a Glasgow doctor. He started his career under Sir William Pearce in the Lancefield Shipyard, the birthplace of the Cunard Lines, as a draughtsman recording all marine craft for the company. After three years' apprenticeship he joined A. and J. Ingles of the Point House Shipbuilding Yard as a yacht designer and in 1872 he started up on his own. He specialised in designing and building racing yachts which he drew quite superbly.

Watson, George Spencer, RA, ROI, RP (1869-1934)

Portrait and figure painter. Studied at the RA Schools. Exh. at the RA from 1891. Elected RA (1932). Included in this Dictionary for his painting of "Hawking", gouache and watercolour, dated 1912, 13½in.x19½in. which was exh. at the Fine Art Society in 1948.

Watson, Hamilton (op.c.1911-1928)

20th century painter of coaching scenes including "The Hull Mail outside the Falcon Inn at Waltham Cross", 20in.x30in. and "The Royal Mail", 20in.x30in. Both paintings auctioned Doyle (NY) in 1989.

Watson, Harry, RWS, RWA, ROI (1871-1936)

Landscape, figure and a naturalist painter in watercolour and oil whose colour wash painting "Fishing on a Sunny Afternoon" was auctioned Phillips (Leeds) 1987. Watson, who was born in Yorkshire, studied at Scarborough School of Art (1884-1888), at the RCA and the Lambeth School of Art. He won several gold and silver medals and a Travelling Scholarship to Rome. Elected RWS (1915), the Royal Western Academy (1928) and ROI (1932). From 1913 Watson taught at the Regent Street Polytechnic.

Watson, John (op.1953)

Contemporary painter whose football watercolour entitled "Tossing the Coin", 19in.x13½in., was exh. at the FE.

Watson, John Dawson, RWS, RBA (1832-1892)

Painter, watercolourist and illustrator. Studied at the Manchester School of Design (1847) and the RA Schools (1851). Returned to Manchester in 1852 where he exh. at the Institution. Exh. at the RA (1853-1890), BI, SS, OWS and elsewhere. Considerably influenced by the Pre-Raphaelites and by the work of J.E. Millais (q.v.). Became a very popular magazine illustrator from 1861 onwards. Elected RWS (1869) and RBA (1882). Best known for his illustrations to "Pilgrim's Progress" (1861) and "Robinson Crusoe" (1864). Watson painted several sporting scenes including "The Call of the Hunt" dated 1875, and "A Sportsman in a Winter Landscape", dated 1881. His watercolour "With Jockey to the Fair" dated 1888, 25in.x17½in., shows the lady pillion rider making good use of the crupper.

Watson, John Gordon

See Gordon, John Watson

Watson, Maud West

See Maud Earl

Watson, Michael A., FCSD, FRSA (b.1944)

Draughtsman and watercolour painter who specialises in motor art. Watson, who trained in Newcastle as an industrial designer, was born in Leeds and is one of the founder members of the Society of Motor Artists (1986). His work is in private collections throughout the world and has been repro. as greetings cards and limited edn. reproduction prints. "Le Mans 1963" shows the winning Ferrari 250P of Scarfiotti and Baudini, watercolour, 18in.x14in. Christie's (Monaco) (1989).

Watson, William, Jnr. (op.1866-1885 d.1921)

Liverpool animal and landscape painter. Pupil of Edwin Landseer (q.v.) and Rosa Bonheur. Son of William Watson, the miniaturist. Examples of his work are in the Walker AG, Liverpool and the Mappin AG, Sheffield. Included in this Dictionary for his paintings of shooting and game dogs. "A Spaniel with a Mallard", 30in.x23in., dated 1885 and "A Gordon, Red and White and an Irish Setter with a Ghillie and a Shooting Pony in a Moorland Setting", dated 1867.

Watson, William Smellie, RSA (1796-1874)

Scottish portrait and landscape painter who studied at the RA Schools and was a founder member of the RSA (1826). Included in this Dictionary for his portrait of a gentleman, thought to be Prince Albert, seated, small, full-length, in Highland dress holding a gun with grouse and blackcock at his feet, 21in.x16¾in., auctioned Christie's 1987.

Watt, Daniel (op.c.1843)

Painter of a horse in a stable signed and inscr. "Melton, Mrs. Esme Marshall", 18in.x24in., and two others - a portrait of Lord Albemarle's "Bolingbroke" inscr. "Newmarket" standing in a stable with his groom and a portrait of "Crofts Bog" in a stable, inscr. Ipswich, each 18in.x24in.

Watt, James George (op.1883-1886)

Scottish portrait painter whose study of a fighting cock was auctioned Bonhams 1983.

Watts, George Frederick, OM, RA (1817-1904)

Well-known painter and lithographer of cricket subjects including "The Cut", "Play", "The Draw", "Forward" and "Leg Forward", five lithographs c.1837, and "The Three Graces" who were presumably the three cricket playing Grace brothers, painted in grisaille. Watts was primarily a portrait painter and entered the RA schools in 1835. He is said to have been encouraged to draw cricket subjects by Nicholas Wanostrocht (q.v.) whose Latin classes he attended. Several examples of Watts' cricket work are in the MCC Collection. He first exh. at the RA in 1837, "The Wounded Heron". In 1850 he became the permanent guest of Mr. and Mrs. T. Prinsep at Little Holland House, London, where he remained until 1875 when he removed to the Isle of Wight. He was elected RA 1867. He twice refused a baronetcy in 1885 and 1894 but finally accepted the Order of Merit.

Watts, Nicholas (b.1947)

Contemporary motor racing artist whose work includes paintings of "Le Mans 1929" and "Nurburgring 1935". The latter was also painted by Tony Smith (q.v.); the only difference is the size, Nicholas Watts' being 28½in.x41in., gouache, auctioned Christie's (Monaco).

Watts, who was born in Tunbridge Wells, trained initially as an engineering draughtsman, but his interest in painting motor car racing, in which he shows an outstanding talent, has become a full time occupation.

Weake, David Brian (op.1953)
Contemporary painter who contributed a football picture entitled "Five Minutes before Full Time", 26in.x30in., to the FE.

Weatherby, Richard Charles (b.1896-op.1919-1946)
Born in Yorkshire but lived a large part of his working life in Penzance. Exh. (1919-1946). Painter of several sporting scenes including an impressionist painting of a chestnut thoroughbred horse and groom, c.1930, a watercolour of hounds, 10¼in.x18in., and a painting entitled "Hounds Running", 25in.x30in. This was a subject that Weatherby repeated in a set of six prints, each 12in.x15in., showing humorous views of the Western Foxhounds, c.1930.

Weatherston, J.T. (op.1921)
Unknown painter of a lady with a golf bag, dated 1921, 17in.x13in., and a portrait of a man shooting a hare, 7½in.x11½in. auctioned Christie's 1972.

Weaver, Arthur (b.1918)
Predominantly a landscape painter whose work includes a number of sporting subjects. His successful series of major golf courses, issued in very limited edn. reproductions, are now keenly sought after by collectors. Weaver, who studied at Hornsey School of Art (1934-1938) was commissioned by the MCC in 1980 to paint the special cricket match held at Lords between an Australian and an English cricket team to commemorate the centenary of the Test matches between the two countries. The painting now hangs in the Long Gallery at Lords. Examples of Weaver's golf paintings hang in the collection of the United States Golf Association headquarters in Far Hills, New Jersey. Weaver's fine painting of a curling match at Lake Monteith, near Stirling, Scotland, painted in 1981, was repro. in "Sport and the Artist" Volume 1, Ball Games, pub. ACC 1988 (p.157).

Weaver, Robert (b.1924)
Contemporary American painter whose work includes "Ebbets Field" painted in 1981. A concrete and steel structure, Ebbets Field is situated in a densely urban area of Brooklyn, home of the American game of baseball. Brooklyn joined New York in 1898, becoming one of its five boroughs, yet always retained its distinctive character. Ebbets Field was bought in 1913 by Charles Ebbets who successfully converted it from a garbage area to a modern ball park.

Weaver, Thomas (of Shropshire) (1774-1843)
Born in Shropshire, the son and grandson of farmers. Is said to have had some instruction in painting from John Boultbee (q.v.). Set up as a livestock painter and painted for the famous agriculturalist Thomas William Coke, 1st Earl of Leicester (1752-1842), the owner of Holkham Hall. Weaver painted Coke with his bailiff, shepherd and Southdown sheep with Holkham Hall to the right

of the picture and the church to the left. Weaver used artistic licence here since he could not actually have seen both from the painted viewpoint. The picture hangs at Holkham Hall. All the animals painted by Weaver and humans too, for that matter, have marvellous wit and character illustrated by the most expressive glance, stance or posture - a wicked look, a bored stance or pure disdain. His horses are also well painted although always a little short in the leg. He exh. in London (1801-1814) and at Liverpool until 1822. Weaver's other patrons include Viscount Anson whose favourite mare Weaver painted and exh. at the RA in 1808. Anson later secured a job in the Liverpool Post Office for Weaver's youngest son, Henry Edward. Weaver also painted Sir Charles Bunbury's black racehorse "Smolensko", 1822, the Warwickshire Hunt with its Master, John Corbett, 1812, a study of the famous racehorse "Gimcrack" dated 1819 and inscr. "Shrewsbury" as so many of Weaver's paintings were, 18in.x24in. (this painting was probably a copy since "Gimcrack" died in 1771) and a portrait of Captain John Belton's hunter, dated 1795, with Lichfield Cathedral in the background. A number of plates were engraved after Weaver's work, both of cattle and equestrian subjects.

Webb (op.1755-1765)
An artist of this name painted "Match'Em". The painting of a bay racehorse appears to be in the style contemporary with the dates of the famous stallion (1749-1781). He may also be the artist of a painting of two men with pointers shooting pheasant, again signed by his surname only, 24in.x20in. which was auctioned in 1986.

Webb (op.c.1844)
An artist called Webb with apparently no Christian name exh. a portrait of a horse at the RA in c.1844 from a Melton Mowbray address. Possibly George Webb (q.v.).

Webb, Byron (1831-1867)
Painter of animal and equestrian subjects, some sporting. Son of the marine painter Archibald Webb and brother of the marine painter James Webb. He exh. his first work at the RA in 1846 from his home in Chelsea. From 1855 until 1861 he exh. from Tattersalls for whom he presumably worked since he painted several pictures for Edmund Tattersall. His sporting work includes "A Stalking Party Returning Home" dated '65, "A Ghillie", dated '67, "Three Ponies in Harness Standing by a Barn", dated 1848 and an intriguing painting entitled "Reindeer Coursing over the Snow" dated 1863. Webb also painted skating scenes and was particularly enthusiastic about Highland deer in well painted scenery.

Webb, Charles (1830-1895)
A painter of five coaching scenes entitled "Changing Horses", "Crossing the Ford", "Bowling Along", "Outside the Inn" and "Slow Progress in the Winter Snow", dated '79, 4¾in.x6in., auctioned Sotheby's 1976. Webb studied in Amsterdam, Antwerp and Dusseldorf where he died at the age of sixty-five.

Webb, Edward Walter (1810-1851)

Animal, equestrian and sporting painter, the son of William Webb (q.v.). Webb settled in Warwick in 1835 and worked in Leamington between 1838 and 1845, exh. one picture at the Birmingham Society of Artists in 1838. His fine sporting work includes a pair of hunting scenes entitled "On the Scent" and "The Kill", views of the Warwickshire and Vine Hunts, each 29½in.x35½in., a study of a lady's chestnut hunter dated 1846, several portraits of hunters standing in or outside their stables and a pair of spirited greys harnessed to a landau outside a country house. His fine "Barnet Horse Fair", dated 1849, 26in.x36in., shows his work at its best with his mastery of large crowd scenes.

Webb, George (op.1817)

A portrait of a bay hunter in a landscape, dated 1817, 24⅛in.x30⅛in., auctioned Christie's 1988 is possibly by the same artist who painted "Match'Em" and "Shooting Over Pointers", one of the unknown Webbs.

Webb, I.M. (op.1930s)

A portrait of the racehorse "Ubaldini" with jockey up, dated 193?, 16in.x20in., was auctioned Christie's (Sth. Ken.) 1984.

Webb, Octavius (op.1880-1889)

Painter of animals, equestrian and some sporting scenes, particularly hunting, who exh. briefly at the leading London galleries. Titles exh. at the RA include "A Clumber Spaniel", "Guarding the Hostage", "Waiting for the Master".

Webb, William (of Tamworth) (1780-1846)

Animal and equestrian painter and of some sporting subjects, particularly fox-hunting. Webb came from Staffordshire but he later moved to Melton Mowbray and from there to London. He exh. six pictures at the RA (1819-1828) and a further picture in 1844 from Melton Mowbray. He was the father of Edward Walter Webb (q.v.). Webb's portrait of John Mytton (1796-1834) was engraved by W. Giller and pub. in 1841. John Mytton, squire of Halston, near Shrewsbury, was a famous eccentric sportsman whose racehorse "Euphrates", winner of the Gold Cup at Lichfield (1825), was also painted by Webb in the same year. "Euphrates" continued to race for Mytton until he was thirteen years old. Webb's patrons included the Duke of Richmond, F. Lawley, Esq., and Mr. Robert Carey-Elwes.

Weber, Gotlieb Daniel Paul (1823-1916)

German painter of "The Young Footballers", s.&d. 1912, 15in.x20in., auctioned Sotheby's.

Weber, Otto, RE, ROI, ARWS (1832-1888)

German painter of landscapes, figure subjects and some hunting scenes including a portrait of a groom with two hunters and two terriers outside a house, 31in.x42in. and "Cast a Shoe" signed and inscr., 38½in.x62½in. auctioned Christie's 1979. Weber settled in London in 1872 having painted in Rome and Paris, exhibiting frequently at the Paris Salon where he won medals in 1864 and 1869. Weber exh. at the RA and elsewhere between 1874-1888. He painted for Queen Victoria and exh. her dogs at the RA in 1876. Elected RE (1881), ROI (1883) and ARWS (1878).

Weber, Paul (op.1922)

Unknown painter of "The Young Footballer" dated 1922, 15in.x10in., auctioned Sotheby's 1987. The artist is possibly the German draughtsman Andreas Paul Weber (b.1893).

Webster, Colin

Painter of an equestrian subject entitled "Taking a Fence", 15in.x26½in. auctioned Sotheby's (Bel.) 1974.

Webster, Miss E. Amelia (op.1857-1895)

Painter from Buckingham whose portrait of a hunter, dated 1890 and inscr., 17in.x21in., was auctioned Sotheby's 1981. She exh. two works at the RA in 1857, one at the RBSA in 1870 and was possibly the artist who exh. two paintings at the Manchester AG 1894/5.

Webster, Norman, RWS, RE, ARCA (b.1924)

"Shoot", 9½in.x14in. and "Football on the Village Green", etching, 10in.x8in. FE.

Webster, Thomas, RA (1800-1886)

Painter of genre subjects. Studied at the RA Schools and won a gold medal in 1824. Exh. at the RA (1823-1879), BI and SS. Elected RA (1846) (retd.1876). Painted small Dutch style panels and tended to use children as his subjects. In 1856 he moved to Cranbrook in Kent where he became a senior member of the Cranbrook Colony of Artists who lived and worked there every summer. Included in this Dictionary for his "Game of Football" dated 1839, exh. at the RA in 1839 No. 363 and engraved by Henry Lemon, pub. by Moore McQueen & Co. 1864. The print is in the British Museum. The original painting and an oil sketch for the painting are in the Harry Langton Collection. Webster also painted "The Boy with Many Friends", oil on panel, 24½in.x35½in., s.&d. 1841, Corporation Art Gallery, Bury and "Rough and Tumble", oil on panel, 8½in.x18¼in., s.&d. 1854, present whereabouts unknown.

Webster, Tom (1890-1962)

Staffordshire illustrator and cartoonist, often of sporting subjects and leading cartoonist at the "Daily Mail" in the early 1920s. Examples include "The Humours of Sport" (two vols.) 1936, "Tom Webster of the 'Daily Mail' among the Sportsmen", 1920, "Tom Webster's Annual Cartoons from the 'Daily Mail'", 'Evening News' and 'Weekly Dispatch'" 1921, etc. His pen and black ink racing scene "Those Two French Candidates for the Cambridgeshire - 'Stathros' and 'Masked Marvel' have now taken charge of Newmarket" dated 1925, 11¾in.x10¾in., was auctioned Christie's 1988. Webster was the creator of the famous cross-legged racehorse "Tishy".

Webster Lloyd, T.

See T. Ivester-Lloyd

Wedderburn, Jemima (Mrs. Hugh Blackburn) (1823-1909)

Talented watercolourist, the daughter of the Solicitor General for Scotland, who painted accomplished scenes of Victorian life including many of sports (although not usually depicted from a competitive angle), such as curling, skating, fishing, croquet and grouse shooting. The first known picture of a ladies' curling match is a delightful watercolour by Jemima Wedderburn depicting the family of Sir George Clerk of Penicuik (her uncle and cousins) playing on one of the ponds at Penicuik House, Midlothian in 1847. She met, and often worked with, Sir Edwin Landseer (q.v.) at his studio in St. John's Wood and she had lessons from John Frederick Tayler (q.v.) whose drawing she later commented "was not accurate and his style rather sloppy". Her friends and acquaintants, many of whom she painted, included "Dickie" Doyle (q.v.) who was tiny like herself, Sir David Wilkie (1785-1841) the brilliant painter of Scottish Lowland life, Sir Francis Chantrey (1781-1842) the sculptor, Sir John Everett Millais (q.v.) and John Ruskin who spoke of her as "the best artist he knew". Pub. "Scenes from Animal Life and Character" (1858), "Birds Drawn from Nature (1862), "A Few Words About Drawing for Beginners" (1893) and "Birds from Moidart" (1895).

Weedon, Augustus Walford, RI, RBA (1838-1908)
Landscape painter in watercolour who exh. at the leading London galleries from 1859. Elected RBA (1883) and RI (1887). Included in this Dictionary for his watercolour painting of a shooting party on the moors, dated 1881, 17in.x28in., auctioned Bonhams 1990.

Weedon, J.F. (op.1888)
Illustrator of sporting subjects who contributed to "The Graphic" 1888.

Weekes, Henry, Snr. (op.1851 d.c.1910)
Eldest son of the sculptor Henry Weekes, RA, (1807-1877) brother also of (Herbert) William Weekes (q.v.). Father of Henry Weekes Jnr. (q.v.). Animal and genre painter.

Weekes, Henry, Jnr. (op.1849-1888)
Painter of game, animal and country subjects and of some sporting scenes including "Waiting for the Guns", a fine painting dated 1874, 36in.x28in. and "A Study of a Spaniel with a Blackcock" dated 1871. He was the son of Henry Weekes, Snr. (q.v.). Both tended to paint donkey scenes, "Donkeys Waiting for Hire, "Donkeys Racing" etc. Exh. twenty-six works at the RA including "The Earthstopper" and nineteen works at the BI including "A Drive on the Downs" and the usual donkey scene entitled "Waiting for Hire". He also exh. at the SS.

Weekes, Herbert William (op.1856-1909)
Animal and genre painter also an illustrator. Better known as William Weekes. The son of Henry Weekes RA (1807-1877), the sculptor, and brother of Henry Weekes, Snr. (q.v.). Exh. at the ILN 1883. His sporting subjects include "The Young Waltonians" dated 1875, inscr. with title, 30½in.x21¾in., Sotheby's, (Sussex) 1990. He even more than the two Henry Weekes painted donkey scenes and occasionally scenes of donkey racing. Exh. at the leading London galleries and lived in London.

Weenix, Jan (1640-1719)
Dutch painter of game still lifes and some sporting scenes including a sportsman and his dog resting, a study of a greyhound with a hooded hawk, a still life of game in a landscape, dated 1704, a dog guarding game in a landscape and a still life of dead partridge, horn, hawk's lure and hoods in a niche, 22in.x18in., Sotheby's 1988. The son of Jan Baptist Weenix (q.v.)

Weenix, Jan Baptist (1621-1663)
Dutch painter of game still lifes and some sporting scenes including "The Hunting Party", 46in.x34in., auctioned Robinson, Fisher and Harding, 13.10.1932. Father of Jan Weenix (q.v.).

Weigall, Charles Harvey, NWS (1794-1877)
Watercolour painter of landscape, portraits, animal and sporting subjects. Exh. at the leading London galleries from 1810. Titles at RA include portraits of dogs (after Reinagle) and birds, 1826. Weigall pub. "The Art of Figure Drawing" 1852, "A Manual of the First Principles of Drawing with the Rudiments of Perspective" 1853 and "A Guide to Animal Drawing for the use of Landscape Painters" 1862. His watercolour of fighting cocks, inscr. verso "Fighting Cocks by Weigall", 13½in.x 17¾in. was auctioned Sotheby's 1985. Elected NWS (1834) and served as Treasurer (1839-1841).

Weigall, Henry, Jnr. (1829-1925)
Painter of portraits, animals, equestrian and some sporting scenes, also of genre, like the other members of his family. Son of Henry Weigall, the sculptor (d.1883). Exh. from 1846 at the leading London galleries, including royal portraits, presentation portraits and in 1852 and 1853 portraits of the Duke of Wellington. Other portraits were commissioned by The Jockey Club and Merton College, Oxford. Weigall's pastel head and shoulders portrait of the celebrated jockey Stephen "Steve" Donoghue (1884-1945) in the racing silks of James White, Esq., 2ft.6in.x2ft. and enclosed within a gilt frame, was auctioned 1990.

Weight, Carel Victor Morlais (Professor), CBE, RA, RBA, RWA, LG (b.1908)
Painter of many subjects including sport. Weight studied at Hammersmith School of Art (1928-1930) and at Goldsmith's College (1931-1933). He has exh. at the RA since 1931. Weight painted "A Trip to the Moon", a naïve style painting showing a hot air balloon "lifting off" watched by a crowd below. Painted in the early 1940s, 23in.x14in., the painting came from the estate of the artist Betty Swanwick, who was a close friend of Weight's, auctioned Bonhams 1990. The painting was inspired by a film of the same title and was originally shown at Leicester Galleries in 1946. An Association Football enthusiast, Weight has painted the game several times including "The Village Cup Tie", 36in.x 51in., set in Norfolk and painted in 1938, Sotheby's 1986, and "Football at Fulham" exh. at the RA in 1955. He has also painted cricket including "The First Cricket Match of Spring", 16in.x20in., City AG, Manchester, purchased in 1945 for the Rutherston Collection.

Weiler, Milton C.
American 20th century painter of freshwater fish including brook trout, rainbow trout, northern pike, brown trout, etc. Many were commissioned by the

Garzia Corporation in the 1960s to illustrate their fishing annuals. Usually painted in watercolour and gouache.

Weimar, H.W.S. (op.1893)
A pair of racing scenes, "The Start" dated December 1893 and "The Finish" dated 1893, 18½in.x33½in., were auctioned Christie's 1971.

Weinberg, Frederick
Contemporary American draughtsman whose black paint on metal sketch entitled "The Baseball Player" c.1950, 27in.x17½in., depicts the action of the game. The Gladstone Collection of Baseball Art.

Weir, William Harrison, NWS (1824-1906)
Animal painter and illustrator. Born Lewes, Sussex. He studied colour printing under George Baxter but did not like it so turned to painting and gained a great reputation for his accurate studies of birds and animals. However, the great authority on cock-fighting, Herbert Atkinson (q.v.), mentioned in his notes that Weir failed to reproduce "the red colour of the famous Dalston Black - red cock" a picture which appears in "Our Poultry" (1896). Weir was a friend of Darwin, a keen naturalist, a great lover of animals and a champion of their cause. He exh. six paintings at the RA (1843-1880), also at the BI, SS and NWS. Weir was a keen pigeon fancier and interested in cock-fighting. His watercolour portrait of Mr. Cuthbert Rigby's "Cock o'the North", winner of seventeen fights, at Ellen, Cockermouth and Derwent, dated 1875, 9in.x6½in. was auctioned Bonhams 1984. Weir married, as his first wife, Anne, the eldest daughter of J.F. Herring, Snr. (q.v.). He also designed some race cups for Messrs. Garrard. Amongst his less successful ventures were sentimental fancy pictures of cats and dogs which are said to have influenced the work of Louis Wain (q.v.). He illus. many books including "Wild Sports of the World" (J. Greenwood 1862), "Sable and White" (Stables 1894) and "Shireen" (Stables 1894). He also illus. "The Poultry Book" by W.G. Tegetmeier pub. in 1867. Elected NWS (1851) retired (1870).

Weirs, M.
Unknown painter of several equestrian portraits including "A Bay Racehorse with Jockey Up", 17in.x 23in., auctioned Christie's 1980, "A Saddled Chestnut Hunter in a Landscape", 18in.x24in. and a further portrait of a grey hunter, auctioned Christie's 1987.

Welch, Rosemary (b.1943)
Painter of equestrian scenes and an Associate of the Society of Equestrian Painters. Studied at St. Ives School of Painting, under Leonard Fuller and later under Walter Woodington. Daughter of the artist who illus. many of the Enid Blyton books.

Welles, E.F. (op.1826-1856)
This artist exh. two portraits at the RA, one of a Normandy carthorse, imported by Richard Winnall, Esq. of which "The Sporting Magazine" 1828 said "This is well handled and a good likeness of the animal". Welles also painted a portrait of "Castrel", a twenty-five

year old horse the property of Lechmere Charlton, Esq. on which "The Sporting Magazine" commented "As far as we can judge from the height at which this picture hangs, we have no doubt of its being a correct likeness. It appears to be coloured with freedom and effect". Welles exh. at the leading London galleries (1826-1856). His RA exhibits include portraits of racehorses including "Manfred", a racehorse belonging to Lechmere Charlton, 1827, and several of cattle. Welles was also an etcher and his set of twenty-five plates of sheep and cattle, after his own work, were pub. in 1835. He is thought to have been an acquaintance of Thomas Woodward (q.v.).

Wellings, C. (op.1785)
A portrait by this unrecorded artist of William and Thomas Earle, the former holding a curved cricket bat, s.&d. 1785, 14¼in.x17in., was auctioned Phillips 1989, (ex Lords sale, Lot 35). Wellings may have been connected with William Wellings (op.1793-1801).

Wells, George (op.1824)
Painter of "A Pointer with a Pheasant", dated 1824, 11½in.x17in., auctioned Christie's 1967. Wells may also have been the landscape painter George Well(e)s, RCA (op.1842-1888).

Wells, Henry Tanworth, RA (1828-1903)
Portrait painter whose sporting subjects include a full length portrait of Miss Magniac in a red velvet dress standing by a saddled grey horse with a retriever by her side, dated 1869 and inscr., which was exh. at the Paris Universal Exhibition, 1878, and a painting of the Middleton Hounds at Birdsall, 1873, with the 8th Lord Middleton seated on his horse in the middle of the picture and Lady Middleton to the left. "Bailys Magazine" 1875 called it "A large and pretentious hunting subject, a November morning at Birdsall house with portraits of Lord and Lady Middleton and their sons and daughter-in-law catches the eye in the second gallery and certainly Mr. Wells cannot be complimented on his handiwork. His figures are posed like waxwork ones and each face has that painfully conscious look which we see in Madame Tussauds' Collection - Lady Middleton is made to appear as if a photographer had just focused her and her Lord is not much better..." The horses are apparently modelled from that wooden one which carries Mr. Nicholl's huntsman in his Regent Street window and a glance at the pack would drive Mr. Tom Parrington from the flags to the nearest lunatic asylum". Wells, who was a pupil of J.M. Leigh, was ironically a victim of the development of photography which forced him to give up oil painting. He exh. at the leading London galleries from 1846 and was elected RA 1870.

Wells, John Sanderson, RBA, RI (op.1872-1943)
See Sanderson-Wells

Wells, L. (op.1841-1858)
Painter of sporting subjects whose work includes greyhounds with a dead hare in a landscape, dated 1858, portraits of pointers in Worcestershire countryside, dated 1841 and a portrait of a greyhound in an open landscape, dated 1856. J. Collins (Bideford).

Wells, S. (op.1869)

A portrait of a chestnut hunter standing by a thatched barn in a landscape, dated 1869, 22in.x26½in., was auctioned Christie's 1973.

Wells, William Page Atkinson (1872-1923)

Landscape painter. Born in Glasgow where he lived until 1885. He then went to Australia with his parents and lived in Sydney and Melbourne for five years. On his return to England he studied art at the Slade School, under Legros and later went to Paris where he studied under Bouguereau and Ferrier. He exh. at the leading London galleries, in the provinces and abroad. Lived in Glasgow, then in Lancashire and later on in the Isle of Man. He painted several golfing scenes including "The Putting Green" and "Links Golf". His painting of Westward Ho Golf Links with players, 12in.x16in., was auctioned Sotheby's 1986.

Went, Alfred (op.1893)

Yorkshire artist from Ilkley who exh. two paintings at SS in 1893 including his picture of hounds (but no horses) entitled "Full Cry",13½in.x20½in. "Following the Scent", 13½in.x20½in., was auctioned Sotheby's 1985.

Werner, Carl Friedrich Heinrich, RI (1808-1894)

German watercolour artist and lithographer who exh. at the RA and NWS (1860-1878) and was elected a member of the NWS (1860). He was also a landscape painter who very often incorporated accurate scenes of sports and games into his work. Born at Weimar he studied art at Leipzig and Munich. Came to England but he travelled extensively on the continent and visited Egypt, Palestine, Greece and Syria, painting the views as he went, chiefly in watercolour. His "Cricket Match in Progress", the grand cricket match at Rome, Eton v. the world and "A Cricket Party having Lunch in the Grounds at the Pamphili Doria Villa, Rome", 1850, painted in watercolour, each 6⅞in.x10½in., were painted when he was in Italy (1833-1853). The sketches of these two paintings, pencil on tracing paper, with names of some of the players and spectators suggests that the artist attended the match. Werner also painted fine billiard scenes in watercolour; one dated 1861, 9in.x13¼in., is in a private collection.

Wesley, Gordon H. (op.1953)

"Saturday Afternoon", 27in.x18½in., FE.

West, Benjamin, PRA (1738-1822)

Well-known American portrait painter and lithographer who settled in London in 1763 and executed two early lithographs in 1801. His early American works are depressing but his exhibits at the SA (1764-1768) which were mainly historical works were well received and in about 1768 he became George III's favourite painter, a position which he kept even though the King eventually realised the limitations of his scope. He painted a very few sporting scenes including angling, a study of a mare and foal in a landscape, 9in.x13½in., and "Cricket on the Village Green", Thos. Agnew and Sons Ltd. 1962. His most important cricket painting is his conversation piece entitled "The Cricketers" painted in 1763, 38⅔in.x

49in., private collection, England. The painting shows five American students who are studying in England. Their love of cricket is indicated by the curved bats. Ralph Izard is featured in the group. He came to England in the early 1760s and went to Cambridge. His sister, Sarah, married Lord William Campbell, the third son of the 4th Duke of Argyll, in 1763 and the "Gazette" described her as "a young lady esteemed to have one of the most considerable fortunes in the province". The Izards of Charleston were a well-known South Carolina family of considerable wealth. West's son was Raphael Lamar West (1769-1850) with whom he often collaborated and who emigrated to America in 1800 to oversee and improve the lands which his father had purchased two years previously in Pennsylvania and New York State. Raphael West returned to England in 1802. Benjamin West succeeded Sir Joshua Reynolds as PRA in 1782 but interestingly, and perhaps predictably, was one of only two PRAs who did not receive a knighthood. The other was James Wyatt who succeeded West (1805-1806).

West, Douglas

Contemporary painter of sports scenes including golf and bowls. Started life as a carpenter. His work is exh. in Birmingham and promoted by the Washington Green Gallery.

West, Levon (b.1900)

American painter and etcher in both oil and watercolour whose portrait "The Skier", 14½in.x22in., was auctioned Sotheby's (Sussex) 1990. West was a pupil of Joseph Pennell and won the Charles M. Lea Prize, Philadelphia 1928. His work "The Mountain Rangers" is in the Philadelphia Museum.

West, Peter B. (1833-1913)

Born in England, emigrated to the USA. Settled in Cleveland, Ohio in 1878. A fine equestrian painter, he also painted still lifes and genre subjects. An impressive hunting scene with a treed fox, 24in.x42in., s.&d. 1886, and a coaching scene, 20in.x36in., are in a private collection, USA.

West, Waldron (b.1904)

Contemporary painter of racing portraits including that of "Dancing Brave" held by his trainer, Guy Harwood, in a landscape, dated 1988, 28in.x36in., and a portrait of Senior Jockey, D.L. Jones, 50in.x40in., dated 1963. West, who studied at Worcester School of Art and with Sir Frank Brangwyn, RA, specialises in racing portraits and some of fox-hunting personalities including "Major Fanshawe and the North Cotswold Hounds".

Westall, Richard, RA (1765-1836)

Historical and figure painter, also an illustrator. He painted a few sporting scenes including "Strethon and Phyllis" dated 1794, pencil and watercolour, 17½in.x 13⅞in. This painting depicts the subjects fishing with huge perch rods and the method of fishing is still through a painted quill float. The wicker bass on the left is a rare portrayal of this method of carrying the catch - the creel with shoulder strap being the usual form. This painting was engraved by C. Knight in 1799.

Westall also painted a portrait of a sportsman with his dogs and dead game at his feet offering a dead partridge to a young girl with a basket, 29½in.x25½in. which was auctioned Sotheby's 1985. He became a popular and prolific book illustrator chiefly working for publishers of poetry. He was elected RA (1794) and gave lessons in drawing to Princess Victoria.

Westall, T. (op.c.1790)
The painter of a gentleman shooting with three dogs entitled "On the Point", 13in.x18½in., auctioned Christie's (NY) 1984. "A Basket of Pike, Brown Trout and Perch, Roach and Dace", 19in.x24½in., auctioned Bonhams 1982 may be by the same artist.

Westbrook, Elizabeth T. (Mrs.) (op.1861-1886)
Figurative artist. Included in this Dictionary for her painting exh. at the RA entitled "Light Blue Wins" which may (or may not) be of a sporting nature. She exh. a total of twenty paintings at the RA and SS between her operating dates.

Westrup, E. Kate, ASWA (op.1908-1927)
Sporting artist who contributed to "Punch's Book of Hunting 1914". Elected ASWA in 1923 and exh. at the NEA, RA, SWA until 1927.

Westwood, H. (op.1886-1888)
The artist of a pair of paintings of gundogs entitled "Waiting for Master", each 9½in.x12½in., and probably the same artist who exh. as H.R. Westwood three paintings at the RSA (1886-1888).

Whaite, T. (op.1835-1842)
Manchester painter of equestrian portraits, particularly racehorses, presumably a kinsman of the landscape painter Henry Clarence Whaite (1828-1912). Whaite painted the portraits of several notable greyhounds and racehorses including "Elis" dated 1836 ("Elis", 1833, also painted by C.B. Spalding (q.v.), J.F. Herring, Snr. (q.v.), Abraham Cooper (q.v.) and Thomas Wightman (q.v.), was reputedly the first racehorse to be taken to race meetings in a caravan), "The Queen of Trumps" with T. Lye up, winner of the Champagne Stakes (1834) and the first filly to win both the Oaks and the St. Leger (1835), 24½in.x29½in., "Attila" with William Scott up, dated 1842, 24½in.x29in. and the greyhound "Bessie Bedlam" dated 1836, 14in.x16½in. (this hound was trained by John Thorpe of Kensall near Manchester and won the Waterloo Cup three times). A painting of "Blue Bonnet", Lord Eglington's St. Leger winner of 1842 with T. Lye up, signed W.H. Whaite but thought to be by the same artist, was exh. at the National Gallery of British Sports and Pastimes, Hutchinson House, 1949 (repro. BR August 1949).

Whaley, F. (op.1888)
The painter of a portrait of a saddled chestnut hunter in a stable, dated 1888 and inscr. "Doncaster" 18in.x 24in., auctioned Tennants 1990. He, or she, was possibly part of the large clan of Whaley artists working in Yorkshire at the turn of the century.

Wharam, H. (op.1795-1797)
This painter exh. portraits of a horse and a dog at the RA in 1795 and 1797.

Wheatland, Richard (b.1953)
Motor artist of great technical ability who was a founder member of the Guild of Motoring Artists (1986) and is an active member of the Singer Owners Club, the Vintage Sports Car Club and the Brooklands Society.

Wheatley, Francis, FSA, RA (1747-1801)
Painter of portraits and of several equestrian and sporting subjects including a portrait of a bay hunter with a gentleman and a terrier in a wooded landscape and a house beyond, 20in.x24in. and a portrait of Randal William, 6th Earl and Marquess of Antrim with his wife, Letitia, driving a phaeton in the park of Glenarun, Ballymena, Co. Antrim, dated 1782 and inscr., 39¼in.x50½in. Wheatley was in Ireland between 1779 and 1783/4 where he appears to have eloped with Mrs. John Alexander Gresse, the wife of a well-known drawing master. Wheatley was born in London and studied at Shipley's Drawing School and for a time under Richard Wilson. He collaborated with John Hamilton Mortimer (q.v.) and copied much of his work. He exh. at the SA in 1765 and became one of the first students at the RA in 1769. His equestrian portraits include that of Sir Henry Piggott (1769) and Sir Henry Peyton with his horse (1776). "The Return from Shooting" depicts the Duke of Newcastle with Colonel Litchfield on their horses in a wooded landscape with Clumber House, famous for the breed of spaniel, in the distance (1788). Wheatley is probably best known for his series "The Cries of London" engraved by A. Cardon, T. Gaugain and V. Vendramini.

Wheeler, Alfred, Jnr. (1851-1932)
Animal and sporting painter, the second son of John Alfred Wheeler (q.v.), who worked in his father's studio at Hanwell both before and after his father's death using a variety of signatures: A. Wheeler, Jnr., J. Wheeler, Jnr. and after his father's death J.A. Wheeler, as well as his own Christian name, Alfred. He painted almost entirely for private commissions, a large practice which he inherited from his father and to which he added. His sons included the landscape and animal painter W.H. Wheeler and Frederick "Jack" Wheeler, the black and white artist (qq.v.). His portrait of "Ladas", a bay horse foaled in 1891, is in the Charles H. Theriot Collection, NY. This painting is inscr. "Ladas - A. Wheeler". "Ladas" was also painted by the elder Wheeler. Famous racehorses painted by Alfred Wheeler include "Flying Fox", "Persimmon", winner of the Derby 1896, "Merry Hampton" dated 1887 and the match between "The Baird" and "Rosicrucian" on Newmarket Heath with jockeys T. Cannon and George Fordham, dated 1882. His portrait of the 9th Duke of Beaufort on his hunter with his hounds dated 1882 and inscr. "Hanwell", 35½in.x27¾in., was auctioned Christie's 1980.

Wheeler, Amelia (1854-1938)
A painting of the Duke of Beaufort out with the Beaufort Hunt, dated 1880, was exh. at Oscar and Peter Johnson's Gallery, London, June 1974. She also painted a signed portrait of "St. Simon" with Fred Archer up, 17½in.x 24½in. which was exh. at Frost and Reed 1984. "St. Simon" went to stud in 1886 and was rested in 1885.

For Archer to have been riding him it seems likely that the date of the painting is 1884 after "St. Simon's" outstanding win in the Ascot Gold Cup. Amelia Wheeler was a daughter of John Alfred Wheeler (q.v.) and clearly her subject matter follows the family tradition, featuring as it does the Duke of Beaufort and "St. Simon" the property of the Duke of Portland, another of John Alfred Wheeler's wealthy patrons. On the other hand the painting of "St. Simon" is perhaps a copy of the portrait known to have been painted by John Alfred Wheeler although in the senior Wheeler's portrait trainer Mat Dawson stands to the left of Fred Archer who is mounted on the horse. John Alfred Wheeler must have painted his portrait in 1884 for the reasons already given. Amelia's portrait was either painted in the same year or at a later date, copied from the original. In this family several copies of the same subject would not be unusual. "Ormonde" with Fred Archer up was, for example, painted at least seven or eight times by John Alfred Wheeler and his son Alfred.

Wheeler, Edward J. (Edmund) (op.1880-1902)
Domestic painter and a black and white artist. He used an unusual mono. of "a four-wheeler". He illus. "Tristram Shandy" (Smollett 1894) and contributed to "Punch" (1880-1902) and "The Cornhill Magazine" (1883). His watercolour of children flying a kite on a green with a pony and trap and other figures beyond, 7in.x9in., was auctioned Christie's (Glasgow) 1986. Painter of a portrait of a gentleman in a hunting coat and a top hat on a grey hunter in a field, 19½in.x 23½in.

Wheeler, Frederick John ("Jack") (1875-1930)
Eldest son of Alfred Wheeler and therefore grandson of John Alfred Wheeler (qq.v.). Elder brother of Walter Herbert Wheeler (q.v.). Black and white artist and caricaturist who worked in Bristol and Bath. Painted a number of small fox-hunting scenes including "The Fox Hunt - Full Cry" dated 1929, "The Last Moments of a Fox", etc. A caricature by Frederick John Wheeler was pub. in the Western Counties "Graphic" 7 November 1901. He painted hunting scenes in a style not dissimilar to that of John Alfred Wheeler but of an inferior quality.

Wheeler, John Alfred (1821-1903)
Equestrian, animal and sporting painter, born at Andoversford, near Cheltenham, Gloucestershire. Wheeler joined the army with the Queen's Dragoon Guards, the Bays, where he gained a practical knowledge of horses. On his discharge in 1847 he took up painting, a profession which had previously been discouraged by his family. He appears to have been self-taught but made his headquarters in Bath. Although he later came to London to be near the galleries, he always regretted his move from Bath where most of his business continued to be done. He had two sons, the elder James and the younger son Alfred (qq.v.) who worked in his father's studio. He died suddenly at the age of eighty-two in April 1903 at his home appropriately called Bath Villa at Hanwell. His patrons numbered many well-known sporting personalities including the Duke of Beaufort for whom he painted "The Beaufort Hunt",

168in.x90in., and "The Meet of the Coaching Club, London". (The picture, which portrayed twenty four-in-hand teams including that of the Duke of Beaufort, was sent to Paris in order that copies might be made and these retailed in London for fifteen guineas each.) He exh. a painting of huntsman and hounds at SS in 1875.

Wheeler, John (James) Thomas (1849-1888)
Animal painter, born at Cheltenham, the eldest son of John Alfred Wheeler (q.v.). James Thomas Wheeler died at the early age of thirty-nine. He painted mainly cattle scenes but effected an occasional horse or dog study to vary the monotony of his output. His fine set of three large hunting scenes, each 29in.x49in., was auctioned Morphets 1989 and his study of an early Border Terrier, dated 1872, 10in.x14in. was auctioned Bonhams 1983.

Wheeler, Walter Herbert (1878-1960)
This part-time artist, the third son of Alfred Wheeler, Jnr. and grandson of J.A. Wheeler (qq.v.) painted land-scapes, animals and sporting subjects. He was born in Weston, Bath but moved to Hanworth with his family the following year. He did not make a career as a painter, preferring to join the photographic department of the Autotype Company in Ealing, with which firm he stayed until his retirement at the age of seventy, as head of the department. His job undoubtedly influenced his paintings which were repro. faithfully as photographic likenesses and were exactly what his clients wanted. As a contrast, many of his freehand paintings of animals were quite beautiful which showed his natural talent when not working for commissions. An early painting entitled "Hawking" and another "Memories of an Old Roman Sport" were both exh. at the Paris Salon 1954, again in 1955 and posthumously at the RA (1960). In all he exh. eleven paintings at SS, one at the RA, as well as his contributions to the Paris Salon. This artist is said to have worked occasionally for an agent called Harris (q.v.) who commissioned him to sign horse paintings in his name. His watercolour "Fishing on Chew Magna Reservoir" dated 1895 is a delightful early example of an uncommissioned work. Wingfield Sporting Gallery, London.

Wheelwright, Miss Hene P. (op.1871-1903)
Animal painter who exh. at the SS (1871-1885) and one painting at the RA from a Hawkhurst, Kent address.

Wheelwright, J. Hadwen (op.1834-1849)
Painter of some sporting subjects who exh. at the RA, BI, SS between these dates.

Wheelwright, Rowland, RBA (1870-1955)
Sporting painter who also painted historical and classical subjects. Born in Queensland, Australia, he studied art under Sir Hubert Von Herkomer at Bushey, Herts. where he lived for many years, teaching at the School. Amongst his pupils was Alice des Clayes (q.v.). Exh. twelve paintings at the RA (1895-1904), and at the leading London galleries (1893-1938). His sporting work includes a portrait of "Winifred", a bay hunter in a courtyard, dated 1890, "A Hunt Passing a Gypsy Encampment", 28in.x36in., "The Last Fence", "Saddling

Up" and "On the Gallops". Wheelwright often worked in grisaille including the set of fifteen sporting scenes which formed part of the decoration of a room, auctioned Christie's 1968. Wheelwright exh. at the major exhibitions from 1893 and was elected RBA (1906). A pair of coaching scenes were exh. at Oscar and Peter Johnson's "Sport and the Horse" exhibition, June 1969.

Wheelwright, W. (Mrs.) (op.1892-1912)
A portrait of a horse signed W. Wheelwright is thought to be by Mrs. W.H. Wheelwright (née Maud Stroud) who exh. at the RA and SS (1892-1912).

Wheelwright, W.H. (op.1857-1897)
Painter of equestrian and sporting subjects who exh. two unsporting works at the Dudley Gallery, London in 1878 and 1880. His sporting paintings include "A Collarbone" and "Taking a Fence", both hunting watercolours dated 1873, "Taking a Bank" and "Climbing out of a Ditch" dated 1873, "A Horse Fair" dated 1857 and a portrait of "Barcaldine" with Fred Archer up dated 1883 which was exh. at the National Gallery of British Sports and Pastimes at Hutchinson House, 1949. His coaching painting "Preparing the Coach" dated 1872 is recorded by Sydney Pavière, "Dictionary of British Sporting Painters". A sporting screen of twelve paintings by this artist dated between 1886 and 1891 was auctioned Sotheby's (NY) 1989.

Whelfton, G.L. (op.1901)
Catalogued as the painter of a dapple grey hunter in a stable interior inscr. "Zoedoni", dated 1901, 18in.x 24in. Auctioned Phillips 1987.

Whessell, John (1760-1823)
Painter of equestrian portraits and an engraver from Oxford who exh. fourteen works at the RA (1802-1823), six of which were portraits of racehorses. There are prints of eight celebrated running horses by and after Whessell ("Dick Andrews", "Trumpator", "Parasol", "Meleora", "Eleanor", "Penelope", "Bob Tail" and "Violanti") pub. by Edward Orme (1809). Four of the racehorses were painted and exh. at the RA in 1807, "Bob Tail", "Dick Andrews", "Parasol" and "Violanti". Three were in landscapes, one in a stable. Whessell engraved many plates after other sporting artists. "The Boat Race on the River Isis, Oxford", 15¾in.x21in., painted by Whessell after John Thomas Serres (q.v.) is in the Paul Mellon Collection, Upperville, Va, USA. Whessell engraved the painting in March 1822 showing the race between the eights of Brasenose and Jesus with Brasenose a length ahead of Jesus at the winning post.

"Whipster"
The pseudonym sometimes used by the artist Cuthbert Bradley (q.v.) for his journalistic sporting reports.

Whistler, Rex (1905-1944)
Illustrator and cartoonist, mostly of sports cars, also a painter of murals and interiors, some of sporting scenes, many of which he did for society friends and patrons, for example the mural he painted for the Angleseys at Plas Newydd. Brother of Lawrence Whistler, the poet and glass engraver. Rex Whistler was killed in action during the commando raid on Dieppe in the 2nd World War.

Whitby, T.B. (op.1907)
Painter of the portraits of the horses "Amber" and "Rocket", both dated 1907, 15½in.x19¾in., were auctioned Sotheby's (Sussex) 1989.

Whitby, William (op.1772-1791)
Portrait painter who exh. at the SA 1772 and 1791 and the RA (1775-1789). His portrait of the boxing champion, Richard Humphries, was exh. at the RA (1789). Whitby made an engraving of the portrait which he pub. himself.

Whitcombe, Susie, SEA, SWA (b.1957)
Painter of equestrian and some sporting subjects including jumping, dressage, hunting, polo and driven harness racing as well as racehorses. She paints in the traditional style in both oil and watercolour. Studied at Heatherleys School of Fine Art in London. Gained 3rd prize in 1982 with her painting "The Puckeridge and Thurlow, Hatfield Forest, Noon 1981" in the competition to celebrate the centenary of the Masters of Foxhounds Association. Had an exhibition at the Malcolm Innes Gallery, London, 1988. "The Coronation Cup" repro. "The World of Polo, Past and Present" by J.N.P. Watson, pub. The Sportsman's Press 1986.

White, Daniel Thomas (op. c.1860-1890)
London painter of genre subjects and included in this Dictionary for "Garden Games", two little girls playing a game of battledore and shuttlecock. White exh. at the leading London galleries from 1861 to 1890.

White, Ethelbert, RWS, NEAC, LG (1891-1972)
Painter and wood engraver of landscapes and rustic scenes. Born at Isleworth he studied at St. John's Wood School of Art, under Leonard Walker (1911-1912). Painted in both oil and watercolour and included in this Dictionary for "Cricket on the Village Green at Hampstead Heath" dated 1915, 20in.x24in., "Skaters", 25in.x21in. and "Cyclists", 21¼in.x25¼in. White exh. at the leading London galleries including the NEAC and the LG from 1916. Elected member of the LG (1916), NEAC (1921), RWS (1939).

White, Gilbert (op.1897)
An unrecorded painter whose painting entitled "Asking the Way" shows a coach and four and an ostler, 15in.x23in., dated '97, auctioned Sotheby's (Bel.) 1971.

White, Miss Mildred H. Congden (op.1905-1915)
Animal and sporting painter in a rather feeble style. Studied art at the Frank Calderon (q.v.) School of Animal Painting. Received first prize for animal composition with "The End of the Day".

White, Sydney Watts (op.1892-1924)
Portrait and landscape painter who exh. at the RA, RBA, ROI and elsewhere (1892-1917) His portrait of Miss Kitty McKane (Mrs. Leslie Godfree) born 1896, Wimbledon Ladies Lawn Tennis champion in 1924 and 1926 and Britain's outstanding woman player of the twenties, was painted in 1924, signed, oil, private collection, London.

Whitehead, Frederick William Newton (1853-1938)
Landscape painter, born in Leamington Spa, the son of William Whitehead, a carver and gilder and the brother of Elizabeth Whitehead (c.1880-1930), the landscape and still life painter. Whitehead studied art under John Burgess (1814-1874) of Leamington Spa and in Paris at the Académie Julian under M.M. Boulanger and Jules Lefebvre (1880-1883). He exh. annually at the RA (1881-1899) except for the years 1884, 1888, 1891 and 1897. In 1893 he first met Thomas Hardy who was to become a close friend and in the same year he married Beatrice Case with whom he travelled all over Dorset in a caravan called "Rambler", often mistaken for a gypsy. During the 1st World War he made over one thousand crutches for the wounded. He died in London. His painting of the South Dorset Hunt on Eggardon Hill, signed, 48in.x72in., was auctioned by Christie's in 1985.

Whitehead, John (op.1852)
Provincial painter whose portrait of "Nell" the rat-catcher is dated 1852. This artist who painted at least one other version of this subject was probably a licensed victualler at the "Bluebell Inn" in Moston near Failsworth, Lancashire, according to the contemporary Manchester directories. The painting shows "Nell" aged three years and nine months being held by her owner while an assistant holds a rat. The painting is surprisingly well painted so Whitehead obviously had considerable natural talent.

Whitehead, Tom (b.1886)
Yorkshire-born artist included in this Dictionary for his painting entitled "Out for a Ride" dated 1928, 38in.x 46in., auctioned Sotheby's 1986.

Whiteman, V.E. (Mrs. W.) (op.1907)
Painter of landscapes and animals in both oil and watercolours. Exh. twice at the Society of Women Artists in 1907. Lived in the Leominster region. Included in this Dictionary for "The Stable Door" with a confined hunter looking wistfully out, 10in.x8in., exh. J. Collins, Bideford 1987.

Whiteside, Brian
Contemporary painter of equestrian subjects including a portrait of "Sagace" and "Rainbow Quest" in the Prix de l'Arc de Triomphe dated 1986, 14½in.x22in. Studied at the Halifax School of Art and the RCA and exh. (1929-1938) at the RA, RSA and the Royal Society of Portrait Painters. Whiteside has also painted boxing subjects. His study of a boxer, 14½in.x11½in., was auctioned Sotheby's (Sussex) 1990.

Whitford, Richard (op.1839-1887)
Painter of animals, sporting and equestrian subjects who collaborated on at least one occasion with Thomas Woodward (q.v.) and who worked in both oil and watercolour. Lived for some time in Gloucestershire and quite often inscr. his work "Animal painter to the Queen". There may have been several equestrian painters by the name of Whitford at the Northleach address since many paintings recorded are signed T.R. Whitford(e), William Whitford (qq.v.), Robert Whitford. It seems likely that there were two artists,

Robert and Richard, who operated between these dates. They painted very much in the style of John Miles (q.v.), another Northleach artist animal painter who operated at a slightly earlier date. Recorded works by this family of artists include "Young Quicksilver", a bay horse outside a stable by a paddock dated 1861 and inscr. "Young Quicksilver, first prize at RAS show at Leeds 1861, first prize at Lincoln 1862", a prize ram and a ewe in a landscape dated '39, a grey hunter with a groom and a gentleman by a cottage, dated 1856, a prize Herefordshire bull, dated 1860, "Cleveland" and "Shot", a horse and dog outside a stable and many more. Many of the paintings by both Robert and Richard are inscribed "Northleach".

Whitford, Robert
See Richard Whitford

Whitford, William (op.c.1850)
A portrait of a champion middlewhite sow of barrage balloon proportions by this artist, also from Northleach, was auctioned Holloways (Banbury) 1984.

Whitford(e), T.R. (op.1858-1887)
Paintings by this artist, who may or may not be either Richard or Robert, include a portrait of "Young Quicksilver" described as a strawberry roan hunter standing by a building in a landscape. Unlike the one painted by Richard Whitford, this one is dated 1863. Portrait of a bay hunter standing by a trough, dated 1887, and a riding party at Abbey Manor, dated 1858.

Whiting, Frederick (Fred), RSW, RI, RP, NPS (1874-1962)
This artist of many sporting subjects was born in Hampstead and educated at Deal in Kent and St. Mark's College. He studied art at the RA Schools and then at the Académie Julian in Paris. He became war artist for "The Graphic" in China (1900-1901) and again during the Sino Japanese War (1904-1905). He exh. at the Paris Salon where he received an honorary mention in 1914. Whiting exh. at the leading London galleries and was elected RBA (1911), ROI (1915), RI (1918) and RSW (1921). Elected President of the Artists' Society (1919). Whiting, who painted in the style of Alfred Munnings (q.v.), painted many distinguished personalities, some with sporting interests including his very fine painting of the Princesses Elizabeth and Margaret riding at Windsor in 1945 and the three children of Sir John Duthie out riding. Amongst his pupils was Lionel Hamilton-Renwick (q.v.) who paints in a very similar style. He excelled in painting action subjects and his sporting scenes include racing, coursing, riding out, and hunting which he painted in both oil and watercolour.

Whitley, B. (op.c.1888?)
"The Donkey Sweepstakes at the Cock and Bottle Inn", signed and dated 188(8)?, 19¼in.x23¼in., auctioned Sotheby's 1987.

Whitlock, J. (Codner, John) (b.1913)
Also known as John Codner after 1958. "Ray Warren", 27in.x35in. Football Exhibition 1953.

Whitmarsh, Eliza (Mrs. T.H.) (op.1840-1851)
Amateur painter of horses and dogs who exh. at the RA, SS and BI between these dates.

Whitmore, Evelyn Wolnycke (op.1896-1900)
"Study of a Hunter in a Landscape" signed (with inits.) and dated '96, and a portrait of a woman on her grey horse with a terrier at heel in a landscape, signed (with inits.) and dated 1898. Both pictures were auctioned Bonhams 1983.

Whitmore, Olive (op.1930-1950)
Illustrator, very often of sporting subjects. Books illus. include "Echoes of the Hunting Horn" (Lynch) 1946, "From Foal to Tally Ho", 1948, the story of an Irish hunter and "Gone Away" (Houghland) 1949. Whitmore lived in Berryville, Virginia.

Whitney, Kevin (b.1948)
Figure artist who specialises in paintings of athletes and Olympic disciplines. Studied at the Ipswich and Chelsea Schools. Attended the latter (1967-1970). Lecturer Chelsea School of Art (1976-1977). Master of Arts at Chelsea (1977-1978). Appointed Official Artist British Olympic Association 1983. Pub. "Olympic Challenge" (Muller Blond and White 1984). Appointed Official International Artist and Art Director, Visa Olympic Art '92, Barcelona. Eighth one-man exhibition at St. Judes, London 1989. Seventh one-man exhibition at Conduit Galleries, London 1986, entitled "New Olympism" showing many of the watercolours painted during the Olympic Games at Los Angeles in his role as Official Artist to the British Olympic Association. The paintings were also shown at the Garfield Gallery, LA and at UCLA during the Olympic Games 1984. Whitney has appeared on BBC television in documentaries about his work for the BOA.

Whittaker, James William, OWS (1828-1876)
Landscape painter in watercolour. Born Manchester. Apprenticed to an engraver. Exh. from 1862 at the leading London galleries. Elected OWS in 1864. Included in this Dictionary for his several scenes of angling, particularly of salmon fishing. Ironically he was drowned near Bettws-y-Coed by slipping from the rocky side of a steep gorge above the river Llugwy. His fine painting entitled "Playing a Salmon in a rocky Highland River", dated 1861, 27½in.x25½in., was auctioned Sotheby's (Bel.) 1971.

Whittaker Reville
See Reville

Whittenbury, C.H. (c.1840)
This artist, possibly a serving soldier since he clearly travelled with the army in the East, painted a portrait of Colonel F.D. Daley's Arab horse "Piaree" held by an Indian groom. He also painted an English traveller with a native soldier riding a camel, 13¼in.x16¾in., auctioned Sotheby's 1983.

Whittock, Nathaniel (op.1825-1851)
Draughtsman, lithographer and aquatint engraver of landscapes and topographical views after his own designs and those of his contemporaries. Included in

this Dictionary for his lithograph "The Cricket Ground, Harrow", 4¾in.x7in., presumably after his own work. He styled himself "Teacher of drawing and perspective and lithographis to the University of Oxford." Whittock illus. "The Oxford Drawing Book" 1825, and his own "The Microcosm of Oxford" 1830, "The Decorative Painter and Glaziers Guide" 1837 and the "Miniature Painters Manual" 1844. Contributed to Tallis's "Illustrated London" 1851 (frontispiece).

Whydale, Ernest Herbert, ARE (b.1886)
Landscape painter and etcher, very often of equestrian subjects. Born at Elland, Yorkshire. Studied at the Westminster School of Art and at the Central School of Arts and Crafts. Exh. at the leading London galleries from 1910. Elected ARE (1920). Whydale painted many hunting scenes including "Over the Hedge", watercolour, 20in.x26in., "The Meet", watercolour, 13¾in.x17¾in. and a fine horse painting dated 1947, 20in.x16in., was auctioned Taylors, Honiton, 1989. Whydale's etchings include "The Forge", "The Quarry" and "Shoeing".

Whymper, Charles H., RI (1853-1941)
Landscape, animal and angling painter in both oil and watercolour, also an illustrator and an engraver. His painting of game birds included grouse shooting and duck flighting which were exh. at the International Sport Exhibition at Schevening in 1892. Watercolour paintings of stag, grouse in a snow covered landscape. "The Shoot", brown wash, 13¼in.x9¼in., was auctioned Bonhams 1983. Whymper was the son of the landscape painter Josiah Wood Whymper, RI (1813-1903) and he exh. widely at the leading London galleries from 1876 and the RA from 1882. Studied with the animal painter Joseph Wolf (q.v.). His watercolour "Salmon Fishing", 6¾in.x9¾in., was auctioned Sotheby's (Sussex) 1988. Pub. several papers on the pheasantry of England and illus. many books on travel, sport and natural history including "Wild Sports in the Highlands" 1878, "The Gamekeeper at Home" 1880, and "Big Game Shooting" 1895. He also produced etchings of shooting and fishing subjects. Lived at Houghton in Huntingdonshire. He held a one-man show at the Walker Galleries in 1923. Elected RI (1909).

Whymper, Edward J. (1840-1911)
Artist, engraver, explorer, mountaineer and first successful climber of the Matterhorn on 14 July 1865, from the east side. Whymper, who was trained as a wood engraver, first visited the Alps in 1860 when he was commissioned to make a series of sketches of Alpine scenery. He was the son of the landscape painter Josiah Wood Whymper RI (1813-1903) and the brother of Charles Whymper (q.v.). He is included in this Dictionary for his beautiful drawings of mountaineering although his fame really rests on his pioneer work as an alpinist and for the disaster which struck his party during the descent of the Matterhorn in 1865 when three mountaineers including the Revd. Charles Hudson, reckoned to be the best mountaineer of his time, Lord Francis Douglas and one guide fell to their deaths. Whymper who was the leader and fourth member of the

party had a narrow escape. Whymper wrote "Peaks, Passes and Glaciers" (1862) and illus. "Scrambles Among the Alps" (1870), "Travels Among the Great Andes of the Equator" (1892), "Chamonix and Mont Blanc" (1896) and "Zermatt and the Matterhorn" (1897). Not surprisingly, Whymper was a medallist of the RGS.

Wiberg, Harald (b.1908)
Scandinavian painter of animals and birds in both oil and watercolour. His sporting work includes "Goshawk with Blackcock", dated 1949, "Capercaillie in a Landscape", dated 1949, "Ducks in Flight", "Studies of Deer", dated 1981 and "A Winter Landscape with Hounds and Hare", dated 1984.

Wicksteed, C.F. (op.1790-1846)
Painter of fighting cocks who was probably related to James Whicksteed (1719-1791), an engraver and Philip Wicksteed (op.1763-1786), a pupil of Zoffany. Wicksteed's portrait of a fighting cock, trimmed and spurred, 27in.x10in., was exh. at Frost and Reed, London and his portraits of a black and red game cock and hen and a silver duck wing game cock and hen, a pair, 15¼in.x 13¼in., were auctioned Christie's 1982. Wicksteed also painted "The Show Booth" dated 1831, a fine country scene, although nothing to do with sport, which was exh. at the RA in 1831, No. 376. He was a prolific exhibitor at the RA up to 1846 and the other leading London galleries. Wicksteed's interest in cock-fighting may have been inspired by his relationship with Isaac Wickste(a)d, a famous cock feeder at the beginning of the 19th century.

Widdas, John (op.1802-1858)
Portrait, animal and equestrian painter from Hull, the father of R.D. Widdas (q.v.). His interesting painting of fighting stallions, dated 1851 is inscr. "Vede Macbeth, Act II Scene 3" and inscr. on the back "Mr. Widdas, artist, Bradford. Dr. Wood's coach. To be left till called for. Please be careful"; paper laid on canvas, 23in.x30½in. His portrait of James Heywood hangs in Trinity House, Hull and several coaching and inn signs are recorded by him.

Widdas, Richard (op.1878)
A pair of coaching scenes, including the Hull to Beverley Mail Coach caught in a snow storm, both clearly signed "Richard" and not "Robert" (q.v.), and dated 1878, each 22in.x31¼in. were auctioned Christie's (NY) 1985.

Widdas, Robert Dodd (op.1826-1885)
Born Hull, the son of John Widdas (q.v.). Listed in the Hull Directories as a portrait and animal painter and, interestingly, a photographic artist. His sporting work includes hunting, steeplechasing, and coaching scenes. A particularly fine painting, "The Derby 1870", showing Tattenham Corner, 15¾in.x24¼in., was auctioned Sotheby's 1990. (It had previously come to auction Sotheby's 1984.) His painting "The Grand National 1884" was exh. at Frost and Reed and "Racing at York", dated 1839 shows the jockeys wearing the colours of Lord Chesterfield and W. Awdson.

Widgery, Frederick John (1861-1942)
Devon based landscape artist in both oil and watercolours although he covered a wide area of subjects including hunting and coastal scenes. Son of the artist William Widgery (q.v.). He exh. at the leading London galleries. Studied at the Exeter School of Art, under Verlat at Antwerp, and at the Bushey School of Art, under Herkomer. Chairman of Exeter Public Art Gallery and a magistrate of the city. He painted several sporting scenes including James McCausland on his hunter, dated 1884 and inscr., 13in.x17in., Sotheby's (Sussex) 1986.

Widgery, William (1822-1893)
Exeter landscape and animal painter. Member of the well-known West Country family of landscape painters and father of Frederick John Widgery (q.v.). He originally trained as a stone mason and was self-taught as an artist. Copied a great deal of Landseer's (q.v.) work including "The Kill at an Otter Hunt", dated 1855 and made a considerable amount of money by producing copies of Landseer's famous painting, "The Monarch of the Glen". Painted "The Poltimore Hunt", dedicated to Lord Poltimore, a subject which was later engraved by J. Harris and pub. by William Clifford, Exeter, c.1865 and "The End of a Day's Shoot", 52in.x74in., auctioned Sotheby's (Sussex) 1982.

Wierusz-Kowalski, Alfred von (1849-1915)
Polish painter in both oil and watercolour of equestrian and sporting subjects including "On the Way to the Meet", 12in.x21in., "Beaters Resting in a Wood", 29in.x41in., "Horsemen with Hounds in a Landscape", watercolour, 6in.x4in., and "Taking Aim", 19in.x8in., Christie's (NY) 1988.

Wiffen, Alfred Kemp. R. Cam.A (b.1896)
Animal painter in both oil and watercolour, an etcher and an engraver. Studied at Nottingham School of Art (1928) under Joseph Else. Wiffen moved to Liverpool to teach graphic arts at Liverpool School of Art. Retired in 1961 and became President of Deeside Art Group. Exh. at the RA, R.Cam.A. and in Liverpool and is represented in the Walker AG, Liverpool. Included in this Dictionary for his gouache of the Grand National entitled "The Canal Turn" dated 1952, 14½in.x21½in., auctioned Sotheby's (Chester) 1985.

Wigand, Balthazar (1771-1846)
Austrian painter of landscapes and battle scenes whose "At the Races", 6in.x8in., gouache, was auctioned 1986.

Wigger, Brian
Painting of "Duck Shooting in the Reeds", a watercolour, 14in.x20in. auctioned Phillips 1984.

Wiggs, H.T. Brook (op.1933)
Painter of "The Boat Race at Barnes Bridge" inscr. and dated 1933, 8in.x12in. Private collection, London.

Wightman, Thomas (1811-1888)
Painter of racing subjects including his portrait of "Elis", winner of the St. Leger 1836 but almost more famous as the first horse to travel to a major classic race in a horsebox and win. "Elis" was also painted by J.F.

Herring, Snr. (q.v.), Abraham Cooper (q.v.) and T. Whaite (q.v.). Wightman emigrated to America where he died and the painting of "Elis" was for some time in the Charles H. Thieriot Collection, New York.

Wilby, R.J. (op.1890)
Animal painter whose portrait of the prize Shorthorn bull "Maher" in a landscape inscr. and dated 1890, 9½in.x11½in., pencil, crayon and watercolour is a primitive and amateur effort, auctioned Sotheby's 1986.

Wilcox, Leslie Arthur, RI, RSMA (b.1904)
Marine painter in oil and watercolour. Born Fulham. A self-taught artist who was employed in commercial art between 1918-1939, turning to full time marine painting after 1945. Included in this Dictionary for his "Dragons Racing off the Coast", signed, 24½in.x19½in., auctioned Bearnes 1989. Wilcox exh. at the RI, ROI, RSW, RSMA (past Hon. Sec.) and the RBA and in the provinces. His work is represented in the collections of both Her Majesty the Queen and HRH Prince Philip and the National Maritime Museum.

Wild, Frank Percy, RBA (1861-1950)
Leeds-born portrait and landscape painter, very often of waterbased sporting subjects including "A Race", which was one of his principal works and "A Girl Fishing from a Punt with a Dog", signed, 35½in.x 23½in., which Wild exh. in 1901 at the RA (No. 307) and which was illus. in "Academy Notes". Wild trained originally as an engineer and only took up painting in 1884. Studied art at the Antwerp Academy for four years where he won a Silver Medal, also at the Académie Julian in Paris and in Spain. Exh. at the leading London galleries, the provinces and abroad. Elected RBA (1900).

Wild, W. Watkins (op.1891)
A fine painting of the Bramham Moor Hunt Meeting at Bramham Park with huntsman Tom Smith and the whipper-in Ted Short on the left (the field also includes Mr. George Lane-Fox, the Master, and HRH the Duke of Clarence on the Master's right), dated 1891 and inscr., 22½in.x34in., was auctioned Christie's 1971. Hunting prints after the work by Wild fetched £300 a set in 1987.

Wilde, William (1826-1901)
Nottingham landscape and countryside painter and of several angling scenes including "The Angler", a bright and attractive painting in watercolour dated, '69, 6½in.x 9½in. auctioned Phillips 1986.

Wildman, John R. (op.c.1810-1839)
Portrait painter and of some sporting personalities including a portrait of G. Wildman with gun and dogs (H.W. Arthurton's Collection of sporting paintings, sold Christie's 11 November 1960) and "J.M.W. Turner (q.v.) and Walter Fawkes at Farnley Hall after Coursing", 27in.x35in., The Paul Mellon Collection, Upperville, Va, USA. Walter Fawkes was Turner's greatest patron. Turner's first recorded visit to Farnley Hall was in 1810. He was, it seems, a considerable sportsman and fished, shot and coursed with Fawkes

until the latter's death in 1825. How Wildman met either Turner or Fawkes is not clear although he must have visited Farnley Hall to paint his portraits. His portrait of Turner in 1837 carries an anonymous note. Edmund Wildman, who exh. domestic subjects (1829-1847) was clearly a close relation of John Wildman which suggests that Turner originally met the Wildmans when sketching on the Thames ("Connoisseur" Vol. XLII 1915). John Wildman exh. eight paintings at the RA (1823-1839).

"Wildrake"
Pseudonym used by George Tattersall (q.v.).

Wilkie, Sir David, RA (1785-1841)
The third son of a Scottish country minister, Wilkie studied art at the Trustees Academy, Edinburgh (1799-1803). Entered the RA Schools in 1805 and exh. at the RA (1806-1842). Elected RA (1811). He is included in this Dictionary for his pen and ink drawing entitled "Playing Skittles", a sketch for a painting commissioned by the Duke of Wellington. The finished painting entitled "Chelsea Pensioners reading the Waterloo Dispatch" became justifiably Wilkie's most famous painting but it was far from the original scene envisaged by the Duke of a jovial gathering of old cronies playing at skittles in the King's Road, Chelsea. The sketch is in the British Museum and the oil painting is at Apsley House. Wilkie's study of a deerhound, sheepdog with two rabbits, probably painted for and presented to Sir William Knighton, Secretary to King George IV, and one of Wilkie's closest and most influential patrons, was auctioned Christie's 1976.

Wilkins, J. (op.1795-1800)
This artist is said to have exh. a sporting portrait at the RA between 1795 and 1800. An A.J. Wilkins, Jnr. exh. a picture of St. Ethelbert's, Norwich at the RA in 1796. This was probably either John (b.1767) or James (b.1768), sons of Robert Wilkins (c.1740-1799) who had exh. drawings as children at FS in 1776, 1778 and 1779 (John only).

Wilkinson, Clifford (op.1953)
Contemporary printmaker who contributed a lithograph of a football match entitled "Off the Bar", 18½in.x13in. to the FE.

Wilkinson, Gilbert (op.1935-1939)
An engraving after his painting of bowling entitled "Is it an Old Man's Game?" was repro. in "Illustrated" on 13 May 1939.

Wilkinson, Henry, ARE, ARCA (Lond.) (b.1921)
An engraver very often of sporting subjects. Born at Bath in Somerset. Son of the artist H.R. Wilkinson. Studied at the Winchester School of Art and at the RCA, under Osborne and R.S. Austin where he received his diploma in 1945. Exh. at the RA, RE. Elected ARE in 1946. Has taught engraving at the City and Guilds of London Art School since 1949.

Wilkinson, Norman, OBE, PRI, RBA, ROI, RSMA, HRWS (1878-1971)
One of the best known and most outstanding British

twentieth century marine artists who painted in both oil and watercolour and sometimes drew in dry point. Studied art at the Portsmouth and Southsea School of Art where he later taught. He was also an illustrator and a landscape artist and the inventor of the "dazzle painting" during the war, so admired and copied by Harry Payne of "Snaffles" fame (see Charles Johnson Payne) and awarded an OBE for this work in 1918. Among the many fishing books he illus. were "An Angler's Anthology" 1930, "A Fisherman's Angles" 1931, "A Summer on the Test" (Hills, 1st edn., 1924, 4th edn. 1946). Wilkinson was appointed a naval artist in both World Wars and a large collection of his paintings under the title "The War at Sea" is housed at the National Maritime Museum. He was at one time marine painter to the Royal Yacht Squadron. A founder member of the RSMA at whose inaugural exhibition in 1946 he exh. and continued to do so until 1970. He also exh. at the RA, RBA, RI, ROI, RWS, RBSA and GI. Elected RBA (1902), ROI (1908), RI (1906) and PRI (1937). His many outstanding paintings of salmon fishing include "Salmon Fishing in Glengarry", "A Salmon Leaping", "Fly Fishing", "An Angler Landing a Fish in a Highland River" and his many yacht racing scenes include His Majesty's yacht "Britannia" in the Solent in 1832 (an identical version hangs in the Royal Yacht Squadron, Knightsbridge, London), "Racing Yachts passing the Royal Yacht", a pair of watercolours and "The Second International Six Metre Race, Cowes, 1921". Wilkinson's work also includes a painting of SS racing bi-plane N210, dated 1927 and inscr., a watercolour, 16½in.x10½in., which was auctioned Christie's 1985.

Willard, Archibald (1836-1918)
American painter whose pair of hunting scenes entitled "The Chase" and "The Fall", each 24in.x30in., were auctioned Christie's (NY) 1985.

Willard, Frank (op.1886)
Exh. one painting at the ROI in 1886. His pair of hunting scenes entitled "Full Cry" and "Over the Ditch", both signed, were auctioned Christie's 1979.

Willardson, Dave (op.1972)
Contemporary painter of American footballers including his portrait of Bronko Nagurski of the Chicago Bears (1920-1930s), painted with an airbrush and dated 1972.

Willett, Arthur Reginald (b.1868 op.1883-1929)
Brighton landscape painter who exh. (1883-1892) at the leading London galleries and elsewhere. He painted a number of mediocre hunting and sporting scenes, mostly featuring the Southdown Hunt in Sussex; faceless figures and faraway horses acted as minor characters in his landscapes which were always the important subject. Willett may have emigrated to America since his address in 1929 was 15 East 59th Street, New York City. He was a member of the NY Arch. Lg. (1897).

Williams, Miss Ada (op.c.1877-1905)
"A Rugger Match", s.&d. 1905, watercolour, Bill Minns. The artist is possibly Miss A. Florence Williams who exh. country scenes at the RA and SS (1877-1904).

Williams, Alfred Sheldon (Alfred Sheldon) (op.1844-1881, d.c.1886)
This artist started his career as Alfred Sheldon and became Alfred Sheldon Williams some time between 1865 and 1867. He was a sporting and landscape painter, a farmer and an illustrator who lived all his life at Hartley Wintney in Hampshire. He was the father of Inglis Sheldon Williams (q.v.), the military artist, who spent six years in South Africa and became a trooper in the Boer War. Alfred Sheldon Williams illus. "The Book of the Horse" (Cassells 1875) and contributed to "The Graphic". He also illus. "Old and New London" (Cassells, late 1880s) with a drawing of "The Meet of the Four in Hand Club at Hyde Park" on page 391. See also Thomas Walter Wilson for his version of this subject, painted in 1886. Williams exh. at the RA and SS (1867-1879). Titles include "Hounds Leaving Kennels", "A Sketch In Covert" and "Gone Away". Also "Troop Horses returning from Watering". As Alfred Sheldon he exh. at SS in 1864 and 1865 including "View Halloo" and he exh. two country scenes at BI (1844-1865). His portrait of D. J. Irvine, Esq., MFH, with H.E. Cox, his groom, dated 1854, was exh. at Frost and Reed.

Williams, Alfred Walter (1824-1905)
An artist son of E. Williams (q.v.) who painted similar subjects to the rest of the clan, i.e. coastal landscapes and occasional angling and riverside scenes. His paintings include "Gone Fishing", signed, 12in.x21in., and, unusually, "Playing Football outside the Gun Inn" dated 1844, auctioned Christie's 1989 for £24,000.

Williams, Christopher David, RBA (1873-1934)
Welsh landscape, figure and portrait painter. Born in Maesteg. Studied art at the Royal College of Art (1893-1896) and at the Royal Academy (1896-1901) under George Clausen and John Sargent (q.v.) who helped him to win the Landseer Scholarship in 1898. Frederick Leighton influenced him in his early years and this influence can be seen in his painting of "Ladas, the Marathon Runner", entered for the Gold Medal in 1899 and the main reason for Williams' inclusion in this Dictionary. In 1900 he took a studio at 18 Kensington Court Place with Fred Appleyard (q.v.). The two artists influenced each other, not only in painting but Christopher Williams married Appleyard's sister in 1904. He exh. at the RA from 1902 and was arguably one of the most innovative painters of the time although he is probably better known nowadays through his commissioned work which includes a painting of Lloyd George in the National Museum of Wales, a portrait of Queen Mary at Buckingham Palace together with the investiture of the Prince of Wales at Caernarvon in 1911.

Williams, Edward, Snr. (c.1758-1820)
Etcher and stipple engraver of caricatures and decorative subjects after the work of his contemporaries and his own designs. His portrait of George Wilson the pedestrian accomplishing his task of walking 2,000 miles in twenty-two days, was pub. in 1815. Williams married a sister of James Ward (q.v.) and they became the parents of Edward Williams (q.v.).

Williams, Edward, Jnr. (1782-1855)

A landscape and coastal painter who painted several angling scenes. He was the son of Edward Williams (q.v.), an engraver, who married the sister of James Ward (q.v.) under whom the young Edward Williams studied art. He sired a large colony of artist sons, some of whom changed their names (see Henry Boddington, Sidney Richard Percy and Arthur Gilbert) to maintain some sort of independent identity. His hunting painting "Full Cry", 10½in.x13½in., was auctioned Christie's 1986 and his painting "Perch Fishing", 28in.x23in., was repro. in "Angling in British Art" by Shaw Sparrow and exh. by Ackermanns, London. Williams exh. at the RA, BI, SS and elsewhere (1814-1855).

Williams, Edward Charles (1807-1881)

Minor coastal landscape painter, son of Edward Williams, Jnr. (q.v.) who also painted fishing landscapes. He sometimes collaborated with William Shayer Snr. (q.v.) on large rustic group scenes. His pair of paintings entitled "A Man Fishing" and "A Sportsman Firing over Dogs" were auctioned Christie's 25/26 April 1940. A.N. Gilbey Collection. Williams exh. at the RA, BI, SS and elsewhere (1839-1865).

Williams, F.R. (op.1811)

Unknown painter of a set of hunting scenes entitled "Find the Scent", "Drawing Cover", "Full Cry" and "The Kill", three signed and two dated 1811, 27¼in.x 35¼in. auctioned Christie's 1980. These appear to be good quality copies of paintings by John Nott Sartorius (q.v.) painted seven years after the originals.

Williams, George Augustus (1814-1901)

Another of the clan Williams who again painted coastal landscapes with river and angling subjects to vary the menu. "Young Anglers by a Brook", dated 1844 and inscr. "Boddington", auctioned Sotheby's 1981, is interesting because the painting is inscr. "Boddington", his sister-in-law's maiden name and the name which his brother Henry (q.v.) took as his surname (and who can blame him) to avoid confusion with his five painter brothers.

Williams, George Fleming ( )

"Ware Rabbit", hounds chasing a rabbit while a golf player addresses his ball on the putting green, watercolour, signed, 15in.x22½in., Sotheby's (Glasgow).

Williams, Henry (1798-1885)

Painter of Italian genre, also of some sporting subjects including a portrait of "A Pointer in a Landscape", dated 1822 and "Study of a Dead Buck", sold at the artist's studio sale Christies 21.6.1886, Lot 69, one guinea. Williams exh. at the leading London galleries (1822-1869). He was a pupil of the RA Schools but after 1827 he lived mostly in Rome.

Williams, Henry (1807-1886)

A London landscape and animal painter, not apparently connected with the clan Williams, who exh. at the RA and SS (1832-1839). The MCC have a cricket painting by him in their collection.

Williams, Howard (op.1874-1875)

Author, illustrator and artist whose enchanting and very funny line drawings illus. his book "The Diary of a Rowing Tour from Oxford to London" (1875).

Williams, Inglis Sheldon (1871-1940)

Painter and special artist, the son of Alfred Sheldon Williams (q.v.). After the death of his father, Inglis Williams emigrated to Canada where he farmed (1887-1891). He returned for five years to study at the Slade School, the Ecole des Beaux Arts, Paris and with Sir Thomas Brock, after which he returned to Canada (1895-1896). In 1899, after settling for good in London, he was appointed special artist to "The Sphere" to cover the Boer War in South Africa.

Williams, J.M. (op.1834-1849)

London painter of sporting subjects, still lifes and old ruins who exh. at the RA, BI, SS and NWS (1834-1849). Titles include "Ptarmigan and Wood Pigeon" at the RA (1840) and "Wild Ducks" (1841).

Williams, James T. (op.1828-1840)

This artist exh. nine paintings at the RA including one of racehorses in 1831, partridge shooting in 1833 and a study of an Indian attacking a buffalo in 1834. He also exh. ten paintings at SS (1828-1840), most of them landscapes, but one with the intriguing title "Sporting - an Impression from an Intaglio gem".

Williams, W.D. (op.c.1885)

A portrait of a saddled horse in a loosebox with two small dogs, signed, 20in.x27in., was auctioned Banks and Silvers, Worcester 1988.

Williams, Walter Heath (op.1923-1935)

Landscape and country scene painter whose sporting subjects include "Fishing on a River", 14in.x22in. and a portrait of "Papyrus", a bay racehorse with jockey up, signed and inscr., 22in.x26in., Christie's 1972. Williams rarely seems to have dated his work although it was usually signed.

Williams, Warren, ARCA (1863-1918)

Welsh landscape painter who studied art at the Liverpool School of Art, under John Finnie. Exh. at the major galleries (1901-1918) and elected R.Cam.A in 1906. His paintings of sporting subjects include "The Meet" and "Over the Ditch" , "A Fisherman on the River Glaslyn near Aberglaslyn, Wales", watercolour, "A Good Catch" and "Grouse Shooting", 9in.x14½in., Phillips 1986.

Williams, William (b.c.1740-1804)

History portrait and landscape painter whose sporting work includes a portrait of "Mr. William Trow and his Groom setting out with his Harriers", dated 1789, 25½in.x33¾in., "A Gentleman on a Bay Hunter in a Landscape", "A Chestnut Hunter held by a Groom in a Landscape", 1769, "Sixteen Pairs of Hounds in a Hunt on the South Downs" dated 1791, 32½in.x61in. and "A Champion Bull with a Prize Cabbage", dated 1804, 14½in.x32in. Williams' fine portrait of the racehorse "Tortoise" with jockey up, 25in.x30in., dated 1769 was exh. Arthur Ackermann and Son. He exh. at the FS (1763), SA (1766-1780) and RA (1770-1792) including "A Lady in a Riding Dress" (1773). He also pub. an essay entitled "Mechanics of Oil Colours" 1787, where he described himself as a "History, Portrait and Landscape Painter".

Williamson, Harold Sandys, LG (b.1892)
Painter and commercial artist who contributed poster work to the Empire Marketing Board, the GPO, the Council for the Encouragement of Music and the Arts and for London Transport. His fine detailed painting showing greyhounds racing at Harringay Park, 1927, appeared as a poster, collection London Transport Museum. Williamson studied at Leeds School of Art (1911-1914) and at the RA Schools (1914-1915) where he won the Turner Gold Medal. Served in the 1st World War and became headmaster of Chelsea Polytechnic (1930-1958). He exh. at the RA, LG and the NEAC.

Williamson, Thomas (Capt.) (1758-1817)
Talented draughtsman whose sketches of Indian big game hunting as seen through European eyes in the early 19th century were intended as detailed records of the wild sports of the East and of the natural history of the species involved. These drawings formed the basis for plates of exceptional beauty and rarity, pub. in 1807, in a series called "Oriental Field Sports". Captain Williamson's initial sketches were worked up into finished drawings by Samuel Howitt (q.v.). The engravings themselves were the work of Henri Merke under the direction of the King's print seller, Edward Orme.

Williamson, W. (op.1812)
A portrait of a dark bay saddled hunter with a dog standing by a stable with an open landscape beyond, dated 1812, 25in.x30in. was auctioned Bonhams 1983.

Willington, Bernard
Contemporary painter, born in Swansea, South Wales, who started his career as a mechanical engineer committing himself to full-time work in art after 1979. Willington's work in both oil and watercolour includes hunting and equestrian scenes. He lives in Herefordshire.

Willis, Charles (op.c.1910)
A painting of a fox-hunting scene entitled "The Meet in the Valley" signed and inscr. with title, 22in.x30in., was auctioned Sotheby's 1986.

Willis, Edward Aylburton (1808-1899)
American painter but English born and trained who emigrated to the USA in 1851. "The Brooklyn Hunt" dated 1858 was exh. at Ackermanns and repro. in "The Field" in 1885. The Brooklyn Hunt seems to have been established in the outskirts of New York in 1856 by an Englishman named T.C. Carpendale. It was short-lived and collapsed in 1860 at the outbreak of the Civil War. Willis' other sporting work includes "A Pointer in a Landscape", dated 1829 and dark lemon and white foxhounds in a landscape with kennels beyond, dated 1832, Bonhams 1983.

Willoughby G.
A pair of paintings, "Gathering for the Meet" and "Tally Ho", painted in grisaille, 12¼in.x18in., were recently auctioned, signed G. Willoughby. Another pair "Huntsmen and Hounds outside an Inn", each 13¼in.x19½in. and signed G. Willoughby, were auctioned Bearnes 1978.

Willoughby, William (op.1850-1888)
Lincolnshire painter who inscr. much of his work "Boston". His portrait of a prize Shorthorn steer inscr. "Bred by C. Brooks Esq. of Leak, fed by P. Wedd, butcher of Boston 1858. Weight 89stone 8lbs" was auctioned Bonhams 1980. Willoughby also painted several portraits of racehorses including "Bay Middleton" with jockey up in a landscape, inscr. "Boston", "Priam" with Sam Day up inscr. "Boston" and "Filho da Puta". His painting of the Doncaster Gold Cup of 1850 shows "Voltigeur" beating "The Flying Dutchman" at the stands, also inscr. "Boston", 24½in.x28¾in. Willoughby's portraits of fat cattle are numerous and are all inscr. with the names of their owner, feeder and slaughterer. Willoughby's interesting pair of paintings "The Boston Stump from the Market Place" and "Boston Stump from the River Witham", each 18in.x24in. and inscr. verso were auctioned by Christie's in 1989.

Wills, J. Anthony
Contemporary American painter from Houston, Texas, whose portrait of the US Open Golf Champion, Ben Hogan, was painted in 1967, 49½in.x39½in. Collection USA.

Wills, James (the Revd.) (op.1740-1777)
Painter of religious subjects and some conversation pieces including "The Andrews Family", 43¼in.x56⅞in., s.&d. 1749, Fitzwilliam Museum, Cambridge. Joseph Andrews (1691-1753) and his second wife, Elizabeth, are posed with their son, James, who holds a curved cricket bat similar to the one shown in the painting of the Cathcart family by David Allan (q.v.). The significance of the basket turned on its side, lying beside a second bat, is uncertain but it is clearly and deliberately included to complete the scene. Wills, who was a contemporary and close associate of Hogarth, Hayman and Gravelot (qq.v.), all known cricket enthusiasts and painters, at one time assisted in the running of the St. Martin's Lane Academy. He painted a large religious composition for the Foundling Hospital in 1746, as did Hogarth, Hayman and Highmore (q.v.). In later life Wills was ordained, becoming Vicar of Cannons.

Wills, Richard Allin (b.1939)
Painter of Rugby football scenes, with the added advantage of being an outstanding player himself. Wills played centre back for ten years in first class Rugby in Wales with international experience against the New Zealand and Australian touring sides. Wills studied art at Newport and his paintings have been commissioned by the British Steel Corporation, Rank Xerox Ltd., Hazak Japanese Corporation, and the Rugby World Cup. He has exh. at the RA, RWA, RP and RWS.

Willson, John James (1836-1903)
Born in Leeds. Painter of sporting subjects who exh. two sporting subjects in 1880 from a Yorkshire address.

Willson, who was mainly self-taught except for a few lessons from Edwin Moore and the local portrait painter, Richard Waller, exh. at the RA in 1900. Worked at Headingley, Leeds and founded the Leeds Fine Art Club. He was married to the painter E. Dorothy Willson and contributed to "The Graphic" 1875.

Wilson, Alexander (1766-1813)
Paisley-born artist, poet, and engraver of bird subjects, who emigrated to America. He illus. and engraved his own works, most notably "The American Ornithology" pub. in nine vols. (1808-1814). "Ruffed Grouse and Pheasant" is an example of an illustration from "The American Ornithology", all the engravings from which have now been collected into one vol. entitled "American Bird Engravings" pub. Constable. Wilson died in Philadelphia in 1813.

Wilson, Alexander (op.1803-1846)
Born and worked in Manchester. Painted many equestrian and sporting scenes including "Cock Fighting", dated 1820, originally sold Christie's 1891 to Agnews for 22 guineas, "The Finish - Newmarket Heath" dated 1822, "A Friendly Encounter" between two horses over a gate, dated 1823, "A Horse in Platt Fields, Manchester with Platt Hall in the Distance", dated 1822. He exh. four horse pictures at the RMI in 1833 which included two racehorse portraits of "Chorister" and "Birmingham", the winners of the St. Leger in 1831 and 1830. An exhibition of his work was held at Peel Park Museum, Salford in 1857.

Wilson, Cecil (Major) (op.1901-1926)
Surrey painter of equestrian portraits and of some sporting subjects, particularly polo. His portraits of "Sansovino" 1925 and "Coronach" with Joe Childs up, 1926, are in the Jockey Club Collection, Newmarket. "Sansovino" won the Derby (1924) and "Coronach" won the Derby and the St. Leger (1926).

Wilson, Chester (op.1846-1873)
London portrait painter who exh. at the leading London galleries (1846-1853) and whose exhibition work had nothing whatsoever to do with sport. He is included in this Dictionary for his painting "The Old Coach Road from Sheffield to Manchester", dated 1873, 8in.x 13¾in. which was auctioned Sotheby's (Sussex) 1989.

Wilson, F.S. (op.1892-1896)
Landscape painter who exh. at the RBA and ROI (1892-1893). Included in this Dictionary for his illustration "The Ladies' Archery Club, Shillingford", repro. Badminton Magazine (1896, p.728).

Wilson, H.P. (op.1890-1895)
Figure painter in watercolour and an illustrator who contributed to the "Sporting and Dramatic News" in 1890 and "Black and White" in 1891. He also exh. at the RA from a London address.

Wilson, J.F. (op.1838)
A portrait of a bay hunter in a landscape and another with two dogs, a pair, both signed and one dated 1838, each 24in.x30in. were auctioned Sotheby's 1968. It is thought that this artist is probably Thomas Fairbairn Wilson (q.v.).

Wilson, John (b.1766 op.1783-1809)
This artist painted a portrait of a bay racehorse outside a cottage, dated 1809, 25in.x23in. He is thought to have come from the Derby area and is also thought to have been the painter of a pair of short-faced tumblers (pigeons) c.1810. A John Wilson entered the RA Schools in 1782 and exh. a portrait at the RA in 1783.

Wilson, John (op. 1871)
Painter of "The Oxford and Cambridge Boat Race", s.&d. 1871 and inscr., 22in.x31in. auctioned Sotheby's (NY) 1988.

Wilson, Leslie (exh. London 1934)
"Between Sets", a game of lawn tennis c.1934, signed, 22in.x15¼in., watercolour, Sotheby's (Sussex)

Wilson, M. Wharton (op.1858)
A portrait of the chestnut horse "Cardinal" in a stable, dated 1858, was auctioned Bearnes 1985.

Wilson, Matisse (op.1940)
A portrait of "Thistle", a grey hunter, dated 1940 and inscr., 16in.x20in. was auctioned Bonhams 1986.

Wilson, Miss May (op.1910-1955)
One of identical twins who hunted hounds between 1937 and 1955. She painted hunting cartoons brilliantly and exh. (1910-1936) at the leading London galleries. Recorded as a landscape painter, she was born near Sheffield and studied under Sir John Arnesby-Brown (q.v.). Twin of Violet and sister of Winifred Wilson (qq.v.), both painters, who also studied under Arnesby-Brown.

Wilson, Thomas Fairbairn (op.1808-1846)
Known as Wilson of Hull. Provincial painter of animal and equestrian portraits. His oil painting "The White Ox" dated 1810 is at Reading University Museum of English Rural Life. He is known to have exh. in Hull in 1827 and 1829 at the Assembly Rooms, the exhibition headquarters of the newly found Hull and East Riding Institution for the Promotion of the Fine Arts. His animal and equestrian work includes a portrait of "A Foxhound Bitch with Whelps", dated 1809, "A White Bull", signed and inscr. "Newcastle", "Little Tom", a grey cob aged eighteen years in a landscape with a spaniel in the foreground and an abbey in the distance, dated 1812, "Roseden", a bay racehorse standing in a field with a distant view of St. Nicholas's Church, Newcastle upon Tyne beyond, dated 1809, 24in.x 41¼in. ("Roseden" was the winner of the Carlisle Steeplechase in 1806), "St. John" and "Gandy", two shorthorn bulls in a landscape with Mr. Mason's house beyond, dated 1808. A portrait of "Phenomenon", the silver laced bantam, wearing spurs and standing over his victim is one of the most striking portraits of a fighting cock recorded, signed, 29in.x36in., Bonhams 1989. "Phenomenon", bred by Thomas Clark Esq. of Vauxhall, was the winner of the Gold Cup at Westminster (1823) and of seven "Long Mains".

Wilson, Thomas Walter, RI, ROI (1851-1912)
Landscape painter and an illustrator who exh. at the leading London galleries and elsewhere from 1870.

Included in this Dictionary for his collaboration with Frank Walton (q.v.) on the painting "The Lawn at Goodwood 1886", 36in.x60in., which was exh. Agnew London 1961 "Victorian Paintings 1837-1887" (see "Country Life" 1947 where this painting and its pendant the "Four in Hand Club in Hyde Park", now destroyed, are discussed). See also Alfred Sheldon Williams who painted the same subject.

Wilson, Miss Violet (op.1910-1955)

One of identical twins with Miss May Wilson (q.v.) who hunted hounds between 1937-1955. Violet Wilson painted animals and equestrian scenes although she is recorded as flower and landscape painter. Like her sisters, May and Winifred Wilson (qq.v.), she trained under Sir John Arnesby-Brown and exh. at the RA, ROI, SWA and the Walker AG Liverpool between 1910-1930.

Wilson, William (op.1692-1723)

Bird painter in a style similar to that of Francis Barlow (q.v.). Included in this Dictionary for his fine painting entitled "Shooting Partridge", 26in.x26in., in a private collection, Sweden.

Wilson, Winifred, UA, NSA (op.1904-1950)

"Distant Music", three horses in a field, a hunt in the distance, signed, 22in.x30in., Woolley & Wallis (1987). Elder sister of Violet and May Wilson (qq.v.). Studied under Sir John Arnesby-Brown (q.v.). Was bought up at Bowchief Abbey near Sheffield and painted hunting subjects like the rest of her family. She exh. (1904-1927) at the leading London galleries. Member of the Sheffield Society of Artists.

Wiltshire, S. (op.c.1920-1936)

Well-known pigeon artist who operated in the Bristol area between the wars (i.e. 1920s-1930s) painting the portraits of famous racing pigeons.

Wimar, Carl (1828-1862)

Born in Siegburg, Germany, Wimar lived in St. Louis during the 1840s, the then heart of the fur trade. In 1849 he accompanied his art master on a journey by steam boat to the falls of St. Anthony to make sketches for a panorama of the Mississippi River. It was the first of several journeys that he made during the 1850s. He sketched and painted in oil and watercolour and used a camera to document the Indian world. Wimar's daguerreotypes are some of the earliest photographs of Indian life. Many of his paintings recorded buffalo, which were to the Indian a gift from the great spirit. His painting "The Buffalo Hunt" dated 1861, 22in.x33in., is in the Thomas Gilcrease Institute of American History and Art.

Winans, Walter (1852-1920)

Eccentric American millionaire, artist, poet, explorer, soldier and philosopher and owner of the shooting rights over almost a quarter of a million acres of the Scottish Highlands. A brilliant shot who is said to have been able to bring down a galloping stag stone dead at a range of 200 yards or more. He painted a portrait of himself riding up the Glen from Kashakyle to lead a deer hunt (exh. Sotheby's Christmas 1984). An expert on camouflage, he dyed his favourite grey mare black in order to render her inconspicuous to the quarry. Exh. (1894-1920) at the leading London galleries.

Winder, Daniel (op.1880-1920)

Painter of a portrait entitled "His First Pony" dated 1884, 31½in.x43¼in., Sotheby's (Chester) 1986.

Windred, E.H. (op.1894-1938)

Painter of racing pigeons in a competent but naïve style. Seems to have been an itinerant painter, travelling the country and visiting the pigeon lofts of well-known breeders and racers. His work includes portraits of four birds belonging to Messrs. Bailey Bros. who were winners at Doncaster and Northampton between 1927 and 1930. A portrait of "Trousers" one of a pair of Mr. T. Fry's racing pigeons, the other "Tommy", signed and inscr., each 15¾in.x19¾in., Sotheby's 1987. He also painted portraits of gamecock.

Wingate, Sir James Lawton, PRSA (1846-1924)

A leading Scottish landscape painter whose several sporting scenes include "Waiting for the Shot", 10¼in.x 14¼in., Sotheby's 1975, and "The Poachers" dated 1885, 48in.x56in., Christie's 1984. Wingate exh. mainly at the RSA but also at the RA from 1880. Elected RSA (1886) and PRSA (1919-1924).

Winly, C.J. (op.1841-1881?)

Painter of a portrait of a black pony in a landscape, dated 1841, 14in.x16in., Bonhams 1975. He also painted the same, or a different, black pony in a landscape, dated 1881, 12½in.x14½in., Sothebys 1977.

Winter, Alexander T. (b.1887 exh.1938-1952)

Marine and landscape artist who painted in both oil and watercolour. Exh. at RSMA in 1948 including "Brancaster Regatta - Before the Start" and "Brancaster Regatta - The Start", both oil. He exh. at the RSM again in 1952 and at the RSA and the Goupil Gallery.

Winter, Canon (op.1840s)

Amateur painter who drew and engraved a series of prints entitled "The House Sweepstakes at Eton" c.1840. These were boat races on the river for pair oared boats with coxes. The first such event took place in 1840 when the prizes were £1.10s. and 3s., the stakes 1s. 6d., and those who did not start had to subscribe 1s. Nedigate and Morley won it on the first occasion. There were as many as seventeen starters in some years, the various pairs being handicapped and arranged in rows. When the signal was given everyone did his best, without regard to his opponents - a blow from an oar was not infrequent. Some were swamped and others were driven ashore. "Annals of an Eton House" Gambier/Parry. Repro. "Country Life" (11.7.1968).

Winter, Cornelius Jason Walter (1820-1891)

East Anglian painter whose portrait of a chestnut race-horse with jockey up and his trainer in a landscape, dated 1836, 8¾in.x10¼in. was auctioned Christie's 1981.

Winter, George (op.1848)
Etcher and line engraver of architectural views whose painting of the celebrated Oxford Drag in 1848 features W.W. Beech, sometime Master of the Vine. George Winter was an undergraduate at Brasenose College, Oxford, but he later lived and worked in London.

Winter, J.C. (op.c.1910)
A portrait of the professional golf champion "Harry Vardon" (1870-1937), signed, 8in.x5¾in., Bonhams.

Winter, Johann Georg (1707-1770)
German painter of landscapes and hunting scenes.

Winter, William Tatton, RBA (1855-1928)
Painter of landscapes and of some hunting scenes including his watercolour "Huntsman and Hounds on a Moor", 8in.x10in., dated 1913, Christie's 1986. Winter studied in the evenings at the Manchester Academy of Fine Arts and exh. from 1884 at the leading London galleries and elsewhere. "The Connoisseur" noted his exhibition of watercolours at the Museum Galleries, 1923, "his themes are country glades and suburban heaths, wind tossed foliage and placid rivers, rendered with a feeling for atmospheric truth and limpidity of colour". In 1925 "The Connoisseur" again commented on "his attractive atmospheric style and delicate perception of colour, typically French in feeling with a faint suggestion of Watteau and Corot".

Wissing, William (Willem) (1656-1687)
Portrait painter. Born in Amsterdam and trained at the Hague under Willem Doudijns and A. Van Ravesteijn and also in Paris. Came to England by 1676 and became assistant to Sir Peter Lely until the latter's death (1680). Included in this Dictionary for his portrait of the young "Lord Burleigh with his Gun and Dog", considered by Waterhouse to be Wissing's masterpiece ("Painting in Britain" (1530-1790) 1953 p.71 pl.71A.)

Witham, J. (op.1869-1890)
Painter of marine subjects. "The Medway Barge Race" 1869, 24in.x39¾in., Bonhams 1984, merits his inclusion in this Dictionary.

Witherby, Arthur George ("Wag") (op.1894-1919)
Clever caricaturist for "Vanity Fair" 1894-1895 and 1899-1901. Proprietor of "Vanity Fair" late 19th century. Produced a caricature of the Grand Duke Michailovitch of Russia "who always plays up to the net" standing at the tennis net complete with racket in the Prince's issue (No. 15) of "Vanity Fair", 4 January 1894. Witherby was officially classified as a portrait painter and exh. his work both at the London Salon and Walker's Gallery London (1910-1919). He is known to have been a very keen sportsman.

Witherington, William Frederick, RA (1785-1865)
Landscape painter, pupil of the RA Schools. Included in this Dictionary for his watercolour of the archery contest at Sundorne Castle, 16in.x26½in., exh. the Lower Nupend Gallery, Malvern in 1974. Witherington exh. at the RA and elsewhere from 1811 and was elected RA (1840).

Withers, A.H.J. (op.1871)
A good and extremely detailed watercolour painting entitled "The Derby Day 1871", signed, inscr. and dated, Oct. 1871, 12in.x19¼in., was auctioned Christie's (Tattersalls) 1989. The artist is likely to be Miss Annie E.J. Withers who exh. at the RA, RHA, ROI and elsewhere (1890-1908).

Withers, Augusta Innes (Mrs.) (op.1829-1865)
Painter of birds, very often game birds, and flowers who became Flower Painter in Ordinary to the Queen Dowager in 1833. Member of Society of Lady Artists. She exh. at the RA and elsewhere from 1829. Her sporting work includes "Grouse with Chicks in a Moorland Landscape" dated 1862 and "Grouse with their Young Ones", 17in.x27½in., Sotheby's (Glasgow) 1976.

Withoos, Matthias (1627-1703)
Dutch painter of still lifes and landscapes. Included in this Dictionary for his painting of an otter with two fish with herbage and foliage in a landscape, dated 1665, 18in.x20¾in., which was auctioned Christie's 1964.

Wolf, Joseph, RI (1820-1899)
Painter and lithographer of animals and birds, and an illustrator. His many drawings and paintings of both game birds and hounds are outstanding in their quality of draughtsmanship. Born in Germany. Apprenticed for three years to the Becker brothers, lithographers of Coblenz, he subsequently became a lithographer at Darmstadt. Later Wolf went to Antwerp to learn draughtsmanship and from there he went to London in 1848 where he obtained employment at the British Museum. He illus. John Gould's "Birds of Great Britain" and "Birds of Asia" and he drew for the Zoological Society. He is responsible for the series of twelve magnificent hand coloured plates which illus. the Dutch "Traité de Fauconnerie". written between 1844 and 1853 (by Schlegel and Wulverhorst) and illus. by Wolf during his stay in Antwerp. The original watercolours are now in the Musée d'Histoire Naturelle, Paris. Exh. at the RA and elsewhere from 1849. Elected RI (1874). A collection of his drawings of birds and animals are in the V & A Museum.

Wolfe-Murray, David (Colonel)
Worked under the pseudonym of "Fish Hawk". His gouache painting "Pheasants Breaking Cover", 20in.x 14in. was auctioned Bonhams 1987.

Wollaston, John (op.1738-1775)
Portrait painter, the son of the London portraitist John Wollaston (c.1672-1749). John Wollaston lived in America (1749-1767) painting the portraits of the leading members of American social and official life. His painting "Warner and Rebecca Lewis", c.1760, shows the boy holding a cricket bat with a cricket ball lying on the ground by his tricorn hat. Private collection, on loan to the College of William and Mary Williamsburg, Va, USA.

Wollen, William Barnes, RI, ROI, HROI, RBC (1857-1936)
Sporting, military and portrait painter who painted horses with some skill. "The Connoisseur" commenting

on his 1916 exhibits at the RA recorded "Mr. W.B. Wollen gives a spirited presentment of what may be called a 'rough and tumble' battle of the old type with hand to hand bayonet fighting in his 'Defeat of the Prussian Guard, November 11th 1914'". Wollen was particularly interested in Rugby Union football and included one such painting in 1879 at the RA. His painting entitled "A Mawl in Goal" dated 1881 was repro. in "Country Life" in 1976. Wollen studied art at the Slade School and went as special artist for "The Graphic" to South Africa in 1900 where his fine watercolour "A Rider on a Grey Horse on a Dusty Road", 13in.x18in., was probably painted. His series of paintings (1893) entitled "Episodes from the Derby" was done for "The Illustrated London News" to whom he contributed work (1882-1899). He also contributed to "The Boys Own Paper" (1892-1893), "Chums" (1892), "Black and White" (1891) and "The Strand Magazine" (1891-1894). He exh. at the leading London galleries and elsewhere from 1879 and was elected RI (1888), ROI (1897) and HROI (1934). His watercolour of polo, 11¾in.x15in., was auctioned Sotheby's 1988. He drew football illustrations for "Cassells" magazine (1906-1907). "Newport v Cambridge", s.&d. 1879, 41in.x 59½in., RFU H.Q., Twickenham, exh. at the RA in the same year (1879). "Yorkshire v Lancashire", s.&d. 1895, 58¼in.x94¼in., also RFU H.Q., Twickenham, formerly at the Otley Club in Yorkshire, shows the match between Yorkshire and Lancashire at Bradford Park Avenue in November 1893.

Wolstenholme Dean, Snr. (1757-1837)

Yorkshire-born sporting and equestrian painter who seems to have been a keen hunting man. He exh. his first picture at the RA in 1803 and by 1805 had moved to London where he exh. at the RA until 1824. His exhibits include horse and dog portraits as well as hunting and coursing scenes. Much of his work was engraved by his son Charles Dean Wolstenholme, Jnr. (q.v.) who worked with him and painted in a very similar style.

Wolstenholme, (Charles) Dean, Jnr. (1798-1882)

Painter and aquatint engraver of sporting subjects after his own designs and those of his contemporaries. Born in Waltham Abbey the son of Dean Wolstenholme, Snr. (q.v.) under whom he studied painting and drawing as well as at the RA Schools. Much of his early work was the reproduction of his father's paintings and the first set, four plates "Coursing", appeared in 1817. He exh. at the RA and elsewhere from 1818. Wolstenholme was a great pigeon fancier and painted several pigeon paintings including the series pub. by John Eaton (1834-1860) dedicated "to the Gentlemen of the Feather Club". Examples include "An Almond", "A Black Mottle", "A Bald Head", "A Beard", "The Fantail", "Turbit" and "The Barb". The Pigeon Fanciers of England, Scotland and Ireland presented Wolstenholme with a Testimonial of their achievement for his skill in portraying "those birds which it was the aim of the 'Fancy' to produce" (Gilbey Vol. II 1900 pp.257/8). Both Wolstenholmes were known to over-paint their

prints in oil, for example, "Colonel Jollife's Hounds meeting at Chipstead Church" and "Run to Earth at Pope's Pit near Waltham Heath", a pair of coloured aquatints, by and after Wolstenholme, trimmed and mounted to imitate paintings, Sotheby's 1980. Wolstenholme Jnr. retired to North Road, Highgate in 1862 after which he painted a number of angling scenes usually inscr. "Highgate". Wolstenholme Jnr.'s sporting subjects include cock fighting, angling, portraits of racing pigeons, portraits of fighting bulldogs, hunting, and racing. A very fine portrait of "Driver". the trotting Galloway, the property of the Duke of Gordon, mounted by his jockey, presumably Mr. McDonald, dated 1833, and inscr., 20in.x28in., was auctioned Andrew Grant 1989.

Wombile I./T.W. (op.1834-1837)

Painter of animals and equestrian subjects who exh. four works at SS including portraits of hunters and dogs, from a London address. His various signatures make it hard to see whether his initials are I.W. or T.W. Wombile.

Wombill(e), Sydney R. (op.c.1841-1888)

An engraving of the trotting horse "Confidence" by C. Hunt after the work by this artist was pub. 10 April 1841. The portraits of the three racehorses "Ormonde", "Ayrshire" and "Bendigo" painted by Wombill were engraved by S.A. Edwards and pub. in 1888 by George Rees. Wombill's painting of racing entitled "Neck and Neck" dated 1887, 18in.x30in., was auctioned Christie's 1985. Other sporting works also include "Reliance" driven to sulky with Windsor Castle beyond, dated 1847 and inscr., 26½in.x37in., a portrait of "Isinglass" with jockey up, signed and inscr., 11¾in.x15¾in. and "Melton", winner of the Derby Stakes at Epsom, 1885, with Fred Archer up. A print after this work was engraved by S.A. Edwards and pub. by E.H. Hunt, as was the portrait of "Ormonde" ridden by Fred Archer, who won the Derby and the 2000 Guineas in 1886.

Wood, Catherine M. (Mrs. Richard Henry Wright), SWA (op.1880- 1939)

Still life and genre painter who studied at the Royal Female School of Art. Exh. at the leading London galleries and elsewhere. Elected SWA (1893). Her fine angling painting "The Fly Fisherman's Workbench" dated 1910, 14¾in.x17¾in. was auctioned Christie's 1979.

Wood, Charles

"The Amateur Athletics Association Championships - White City" painted c.1954.

Wood, Clarence Lawson (1878-1957)

Illustrator and painter of humorous and animal subjects, chiefly in watercolour. Born at Highgate, the son of Pinhorn Wood, RI, and the grandson of Lewis John Wood, RI (1813-1901). Studied art at the Slade School and at Heatherleys, attending occasional classes at the Frank Calderon School of Animal Painting. He contributed numerous illustrations to magazines both here and abroad including "The Sketch", "The Graphic", "The Illustrated London News" and occasionally

"Punch". In addition to his freelance work he spent six years with Messrs. C. Arthur Pearson Ltd., the magazine publishers, as their chief artist (Arthur Pearson, later Sir Arthur, was his father's friend and publisher). He was an enthusiastic member of the London Sketch Club, formed in 1898, and its influence can be clearly seen in his early work. Joined the Royal Flying Corps for the duration of the 1st World War and was decorated by the French, after Vimy Ridge. After the war he collaborated with his son-in-law, Keith Sholto Douglas (q.v.) on a series of humorous sketches under the joint pseudonym of "Hustlebuck" and became a household name through the prints issued after his work by Messrs. Lawrence Angelico Ltd. Always a very modest man and shy of recognition, he became virtually a recluse for the last thirty years of his life which has undoubtedly contributed to the lack of real recognition for the work of this very brilliant artist. He illus. many books including "The Old Nursery Rhymes" (Nelson) and exh. at the Brook Street AG, Dudley Gallery, London Salon, RA, RI and Walkers Gallery, London. His many illustrations of golf include "The Flight of McCanny with his Golf Bag" signed, watercolour, 11¾in.x14¾in., auctioned Phillips 1985.

Wood, Frank Warren (1862-1953)

Landscape painter born Berwick-on-Tweed, whose golfing scenes include "The 1st Green at Gullane", painted in 1934 and "Luffness", painted in 1933. Wood, who studied at the South Kensington School of Art and in Paris, became second Master at Newcastle School of Art (1883-1889) and Headmaster of Hawick School of Art (1889-1899). He was known particularly for his "wet" watercolours of the Highlands and the borders and for his paintings of sailing and battleships.

Wood, Harold (b.1918)

Contemporary painter whose portrait entitled "The Boxers" dated 1964, 32½in.x29¾in. was auctioned Phillips 1986. Wood, who was born in Preston, Lancashire, only decided to become a painter in 1946 after spending six months drawing strip cartoons in Fleet Street. For three years he worked solely for Wolf Mankowitz (1953-1956) and had his first solo exhibition at the Beaux Arts Gallery, London, 1956.

Wood, Peter MacDonagh, RSMA (b.1914)

Middlesex-born marine and landscape painter who studied at Southend-on-Sea School of Art and the Slade School, gaining his diploma of Fine Art and his Art Teachers' Diploma. His contribution to sporting art, other than his marine work of racing dinghies lies, in his football painting "Going to the Match", 29½in.x23¾in., which he contributed to the FE. Wood, who has exh. at the RA, RI, ROI, RSMA, RWS, RBA and the NEAC, is represented in the National Maritime Museum and the Merseyside Museum.

Wood, Starr (1870-1944)

Caricaturist and black and white artist who founded his own quarterly magazine "The Windmill" and later "Starr Wood's Magazine" which ran between 1910 and 1935. The latter is filled entirely with his own illustrations.

Many of his works appear under the pseudonym of "The Snark". He contributed to "Punch" 1900 to 1902 and again 1908 and 1914, including "Mr. Punch's Patent Caddie Car" complete with trolley upon which sits a golf bag holder and a large whisky and soda holder. His sports painting "A Rugby Match in Progress", 12in.x9in., pencil and grisaille watercolour, was auctioned Christie's (Sth. Ken.) 1989.

Wood, William (1768-1809)

Portrait and miniature painter from Ipswich. A founder member of the Society of Associated Artists. His miniature of George III returning from hunting, s.&d. 1798, is recorded.

Woodhouse, Frederick W., Snr. (1820-1909)

English-born equestrian painter who emigrated to Australia in 1858. His arrival coincided with the great era of Australian racing. The first Champion Stakes and the first Australian St. Leger were run in 1859, the year after he arrived and the first Melbourne Cup was run in 1861. Woodhouse portrayed the Australian thoroughbred champions for the next fifty years throughout the golden age of the Australian turf. Woodhouse's painting of "Archer" and the winners of the first twelve Melbourne Cups, dated 1889, 29in.x49in., shows the two outstanding owners of the time, John Tait and Etienne de Mestre who dominated the event which almost from the beginning captured the imagination of the Australian public. De Mestre owned "Archer" who won the first two cups and five years later he won the event again with "Tom Whiffler" shown standing behind "Archer". John Tait from Sydney owned and trained three winners "Glencoe" (1868) rearing up in the centre of the picture, "The Barb" (1866) and the bay "The Quack" 1872. Tait also trained "The Powell" to win in 1871. Before he left for Australia, Woodhouse illus. "The Representation of the Brigade Field Day in Ware Park", in 1853.

Woodhouse, Frederick, Jnr. (1848-1927)

The son of Frederick Woodhouse, Snr. (q.v.). Painted equestrian subjects in a softer style than his father. His portraits of "Chicago", "Mentor" and "Emmalea" were painted with great care and are appealing equestrian studies. His three brothers, Herbert, Edwin and Clarence were also painters, recording Australian country life and the heroes of the turf for the next seventy years.

Woodhouse, William (1857-1939)

Morecambe, Lancashire-born wildlife and sporting artist who exh. at the RSA and at the RA (1889-1896). His son was the artist R.B.E. Woodhouse (1897-1987). Woodhouse painted animals, particularly game dogs and game but occasionally sporting subjects including "Grouse and Duck Shooting", "Picking up Snipe", "The Tiger Shoot", dated 1912 and a portrait of "A Setter with Dead Game and a Shotgun". He studied at the Lancaster School of Art for a short time and exh. his first picture at the Lancaster Exhibition in 1880. He worked in oil, watercolour and gouache. His friend and an admirer of his work was Sydney Pavière, curator of the Harris Museum and Art Gallery and author of "A

Dictionary of British Sporting Painters" pub. 1965. "A Saddled Polo Pony with Stables Beyond", signed, 15½in.x22½in., was recently auctioned from the Pilkington Collection.

Woods, James B.

The painter of a pair of portraits of a jockey on a horse in a landscape, 15½in.x12in., each signed, auctioned Bonhams 1986.

Woodville, Richard Caton, RI, ROI (1856-1927)

Battle scene painter, special artist and illustrator, the son of R.C. Woodville, Snr. (1825-1856), the American military artist who settled in London in 1852. (R.C. Woodville Snr. was killed in London on 30 September 1856. His son was born eight months earlier on 7 January 1856). Included in this Dictionary for his grisaille painting "Riders in Rotten Row" dated '85, 18½in.x12¾in., "Under Spotlight at Ranelagh", a polo game, dated 1880, "Hunting in Spain", monochrome gouache dated 1904 and "A Companion", dated 1906. Woodville studied art in Düsseldorf, under Kamphussen, after being brought up in St. Petersburg where he worked for "The Illustrated London News". He turned increasingly to oil painting in the 1880s and abandoned black and white work in 1897. Exh. at the leading London galleries and elsewhere. Elected RI (1882) and ROI (1883).

Woodward, George Moutard (1760-1809)

The son of a Derbyshire squire. A prolific artist of uneven quality who died penniless and destitute in a public house. His caricature work often resembles that of Thomas Rowlandson (q.v.) who engraved for him "Horse Accomplishments", a set of twelve plates pub. in 1799. "The Derby Gig" is an illustration of Woodward's work at its best. "The Mark", showing a gentleman archer relaxing, 8in.x6in. was exh. Abbott and Holder, April/May 1988. This was probably drawn after Woodward moved to London in about 1792. His drawing entitled "The Whistler" showing a rider on a wheezing horse inscr. "This is what I call Travelling to Music - one continued wheeze from Hyde Park Corner to Hammersmith", pen/ink/wash, 8⅝in.x10⅝in., is in the Paul Mellon Collection, Upperville, Va, USA.

Woodward, Nathan (op.1769-1770)

Four hunting scenes, clearly signed by this artist, painted on panel and inscr., include "Lively", a fine horse belonging to Sir Bernard Granville Esq., 1769, "Julip", 1770, "A beautiful mare", "Two of His Majesty's Huntsmen with Stag Hounds Looking for Ye Slot of Ye Deer on Windsor Forest", and "Ye Huntsmen and Hounds before a monument to Sir Bevil Grenville (1596-1643) of Kilkhampton, Cornwall" - an ardent Royalist. Sir Bevil's great-grandson was Sir Bernard Granville (1703-1775) of Colwich Abbey, Co. Stratford. All four panels are approxmately 23½in.x36in., Christie's 1992.

Woodward, Thomas (1801-1852)

Worcestershire painter of sporting and equestrian scenes. Apprenticed for a year to Abraham Cooper (q.v.). Exh. at the RA and other leading London galleries and elsewhere from 1821. An admirer and friend of Edwin Landseer (q.v.) and an acquaintance of E.F. Welles (q.v.). Commissioned by Queen Victoria and Prince Albert to paint their horses during the 1840s. Woodward was an enthusiastic hunting man and an artist of very considerable ability. Apart from Queen Victoria and Prince Albert his patrons included the Duke of Montrose, the Duke of Newcastle, Sir Robert Peel and the Earl of Essex. His portrait "The Ratcatcher" is in the Tate Gallery. "The Puckeridge Foxhounds", dated 1845, was auctioned Christie's 1989 for £190,000. Woodward collaborated on at least one painting with Richard Whitford (q.v.).

Woog, J. (op.late 19th century)

A painter of sporting subjects who usually painted his work in pairs or small sets, no larger than 6in.x13in. His work includes "At the Start" and "The Finish", a pair of racing scenes, "Over the Fence", 6¼in.x12½in., "Full Cry" and "The Kill", a pair, both signed, 6½in.x 12in. and "The Foxhunt", 6in.x13in. This painter clearly signs his name Woog and not Wood.

Woolcott, D. (op.1828)

This artist exh. a painting of a horse and a groom at the RA in 1828 on which "The Sporting Magazine" (page 171) commented "The picture has no great claims to commendation".

Woollett, Henry A. (op.1844-1873)

Painter of country scenes and some equestrian and sporting subjects. His fine hunting scene "The Goodwood Hunt going to draw the Trundle", s.&d. 1844, 28½in.x42½in., was auctioned Christie's 1980. Exh. at SS and elsewhere (1857-1873).

Woollett, Henry Charles (op.1851-1894)

Operated at the same time as Henry A. Woollett (q.v.) and painted similar subjects.

Wootton, Frank (b.1914)

Landscape and aviation painter, also a painter of several sporting subjects including racing, rowing and motor car racing. Born at Milford, Hampshire. Studied at the Eastbourne College of Art, under Eric Ravilious (q.v.) and Reeve-Fowkes, winning a graduate scholarship to the Royal College of Art and a gold medal in 1930. Official war artist to the RAF (1939-1945). Lives at Alfriston, Sussex. Wrote "How to Draw Cars" for "The Studio", pub. 1949 and a companion "How to Draw Aircraft" in 1955. Other publications include "The Aviation Art of Frank Wootton" pub. Peacock Press and "At Home in the Sky" 1984. Worked as a visual reporter for the "Motor" magazine for five years, covering the Monte Carlo rally and the twenty-four hour race at Le Mans. Vice President of the Society of Equestrian Artists and President of the Guild of Aviation Artists. Has had many exhibitions in London and the USA. His painting "Henley Regatta", dated 1959, 24¾in.x29⅝in. was originally commissioned by the Rootes Group. This painting was one of a series covering important sporting events. The other paintings were of motor racing, the King's Cup Air Race, yacht racing and horse racing.

Wootton, John (b.1682/3-1764)

Painter of sporting and battle scenes and classical landscapes. Born Warwickshire. Pupil and assistant of Jan Wyck (q.v.) and possibly also of Jan Siberechts (q.v.) since Wootton collaborated on a watercolour signed by both artists. An early association with the Duke of Beaufort, under whose patronage Wootton visited Rome, led to important commissions most notably from Frederick, Prince of Wales who became his leading patron and Edward Harley, later 2nd Earl of Oxford for whom Wootton painted "The Starting Post at Newmarket" in 1716. A bill at Welbeck Abbey shows that the artist was paid £16.2s.6d for the painting. For Harley he also painted "The Bloody Shouldered Arabian" a horse which had been given to Harley by his brother, Nathaniel Harley and sent back from Aleppo in 1719. Wootton became a member of the Society of Virtuosi of St. Luke and in 1770 became a Steward. He was a founder member of the Academy of Painting in 1711. Four hare hunting scenes, "Going Out in the Morning", "The Chase", "The Hounds at Fault" and "The Death of the Hare", each 20in.x30in., were auctioned at Christie's in 1988. This set may possibly be the lost originals from which the engravings by Bernard Baron were taken in 1726. In the sale of Wootton's work, which he sold off not long before his death from his London house in 1764, Lot 101 consisted of four original paintings of "huntings of Lord Oxford's" from whence the prints were engraved. These were presumably painted for Edward Harley and are major compositions which form the basis of many of Wootton's later engravings. Most of the famous racehorses of his time were painted by Wootton including "Flying Childers", "Lamprey" with Sir William Morgan, his owner, the Duke of Hamilton's grey racehorse "Victorious" and the Duke of Rutland's racehorse "Coneyskin" with jockey up. He collaborated with leading portrait painters including Thomas Hudson and William Hogarth (qq.v.). Wootton's paintings are usually large, his portraits often life-size and his hunting scenes followed closely the style of Peter Tillemans (q.v.).

Wordsworth, C. H. (op.c.1911)

See Wadsworth

Worsdale, John R. (b.1939)

Painter of equestrian portraits. Studied Doncaster School of Art (1955-1959). Majored in Fine Art with lithography as his second subject. Gained National Diploma of Design (1959). Exh. RSMA 1970, 1972, 1975, estuary and coastal subjects.

Worsley, John, RSMA (VP since 1979), NS (b.1919)

Portrait and figure painter, also of marine subjects in both oil and watercolour. Included in this Dictionary for "The Boat Race", a view from the Dove Tavern, Hammersmith, painted in 1948. Worsley studied at Goldsmith's College of Art (1934-1937) and has exh. at the RA and other leading galleries. He served as a naval officer during World War II and was taken prisoner in 1943. His paintings of prison life were concealed in Red Cross milk tins and now form the basis of a large collection of his work in the National Maritime Museum, Greenwich. Worsley is a member of the Guild of Aviation Artists founded in 1971.

Worth, Leslie, PRWS, RBA (b.1923)

Painter of equestrian scenes including "Early Morning Riders on the Tan, Epsom" s.&d. 1951, Christie's (Sth. Ken.) 1989. "Epsom Downs", pencil and watercolour, auctioned Lawrence of Crewkerne 1985. Like Hugh Percy Heard (q.v.), Worth was born at Bideford in Devon. He studied at Bideford and Plymouth Schools of Art as well as the RCA. He won the De Laszlo Silver Medal (1983). He is Vice President of the RWS and a Trustee member of the RBA. Worth exh. regularly at the RA and has had a number of solo exhibitions at Agnew's, London.

Worth, Thomas (1834-1917)

American painter of trotting races including a portrait of the celebrated horse "Dexter" driven by George B. Alley in front of the Old Lake House, Islip, Long Island, pencil, pen and ink, and watercolour, and "Coming from the Trot" painted in 1869. Worth, who was a New Yorker from Greenwich, was a great friend of James Ives, the other half of the Currier and Ives publishing partnership, although he was never actually employed by them. They pub. a great deal of his sporting work which was immensely popular and always full of fun - for example, "Copped at a Cockfight", a lithograph pub. by Cartier and Ives in 1884.

Wortham, M. (op.1906)

A portrait of a chestnut hunter and a Jack Russell terrier, a pair, both dated 1906, 24in.x28½in., were auctioned Sotheby's 1985.

Worthington, A.

A pair of partridge and duck shooting scenes, both signed, each 21½in.x29½in., were auctioned Sotheby's (Sussex) 1989.

Wortley, Archibald John Stuart (1849-1905)

Painter of portraits and sporting subjects who had art lessons from Sir John Millais (q.v.) in 1874. Wortley's brother, Charles, later Lord Stuart of Wortley, married Millais' daughter, Alice, as his second wife in 1886. Archie Wortley and Charles Stuart-Wortley were the grandsons of the 1st Earl of Wharncliffe, which explains the title of Wortley's painting "In Wharncliffe Chase - Winter 1874" which he exh. at the RA that year. Wortley's portrait of the legendary cricketer entitled "W.G. Grace at the Wicket", 48in.x34in., s.&d. 1890, is in the MCC Collection.

Wray, A. (op.1879)

A portrait of Mrs. Nichol and her grandchildren driving a carriage through Richmond Park, dated 1879, 13in.x20¼in. was auctioned Christie's 1987. This artist may have been miscatalogued for L. Wray who exh. two genre subjects from a London address in 1875 and 1879.

Wright, George (1860-1942)

A painter of sporting and equestrian subjects. Born near Leeds, the son of a cashier and manager of a carpet factory. He was the brother of Gilbert Scott Wright (q.v.) with whom he often collaborated. He also collaborated with J.W. Brook (q.v.) on a portrait of Lily, daughter of J. Wallace on "Countess", exh. at the RA (1899). In 1901 Wright moved to Rugby and his polo paintings date from this period. Lucas Lucas (q.v.) was also in Rugby at about this time and his polo paintings date from the same period recording the events of the famous polo club there. From 1925 Wright gave one-man exhibitions at Messrs. Ackermanns Galleries. In 1932 he showed "Unkennelling Bramham Old Hounds" and another study "Exercising Hounds" shows a portrait of Frank Freeman, huntsman to the Pytchley. In a review of this exhibition "The Connoisseur" recorded "In some of his passages of handling and colour Mr. George Wright is not unlike Mr. A.J. Munnings". He also gave exhibitions at the Grand Central Galleries. In 1908 Wright was living in Oxford. He exh. at the RA from 1892 and at the Royal Society of Artists. He illus. several books including "'King', the Story of a Dog" (1936), "'Pinto' the Mustang" (1935) and "Wild Horse Silver " (1934). His fine painting "The Shooting Party", 16in.x24in., was auctioned Christie's 1990. A keen huntsman, Wright hunted with the Old Surrey Hounds. His knowledge of sport and the countryside is reflected in his very fine sporting scenes. He is considered one of the best painters of his time. Died at Seaford in Sussex.

Wright, Gerry (b.1931)

Painter of English landscapes and cricket scenes. Born Maidstone, Kent. Studied Maidstone Art School (1951-1953). Exh. from 1955. "Cricket on a Summer's Evening", 24in.x47½in. Wingfield Sporting Gallery, London.

Wright, Gilbert Scott (1880-1958)

Painter of sporting and equestrian subjects. Born at Headingly near Leeds, the younger brother of George Wright (q.v.). He and his brother are thought to have worked together until about 1925, during which time they collaborated on a number of works used for calendars. Gilbert Wright exh. at the RA from 1909 and for a time had L. Hamilton-Renwick (q.v.) as a pupil. His sporting subjects include hunting, racing and polo but his favourite subject was coaching scenes. Wright was a very fine draughtsman and exceptionally talented, particularly since he was virtually self-taught. His portrait of HRH Edward Prince of Wales going out for a drive, dated '96, 19½in.x29¾in. was auctioned Sotheby's 1989.

Wright, Henry Charles Seppings (1850-1937)

Painter and special artist. Son of a Cornish vicar. Studied in Paris and joined the staff of "The Illustrated London News" in about 1888. Is thought to have contributed twenty-three caricatures to "Vanity Fair" under the pseudonyms "Stuff" and "Gownsman" (1891-1900). He also contributed to "The Graphic" (1887), "Black and White" (1891), "Boy's Own Paper" (1892-1893) and "The Sporting and Dramatic News" (1896). This artist's fine painting "Tobogganing on Harrow on the Hill", dated '95, grisaille, 20¼in.x14in. was auctioned Sotheby's (Sussex) 1988. Wright exh. six works at SS (1883- 1888), none of them sporting.

Wright, James Henry (1813-1883)

A print by Currier and Ives after the work by this artist painted in 1865 of "Hambletonian" with his owner, William Rysdyk, was pub. "Hambletonian" (1849-1859) trotted a mile in 2 minutes 48½ seconds as a three year old, and was never trained for racing. James Wright, portrait and landscape painter, had a studio in Broadway, New York City. The NY Historical Society own his painting of Donagham Manor.

Wright, John Masey, OWS (1777-1866)

Scenery painter and illustrator, whose painting "Ascot Heath Races" was exh. Frank T. Sabin, London (1959). Wright, the son of an organ builder and himself originally a piano tuner for Broadwood, ran a teaching practice where his pupils included Lady Craven, the Marquis of Lansdowne and the daughters of Earl de Grey.

Wright, Joseph (of Derby), ARA (1734-1797)

Portrait and landscape painter and of industrial and scientific scenes. Included in this Dictionary for his portrait paintings of various distinguished sporting personalities. His portrait of the Coltmans setting off for a ride made £1.3 million, a record for the artist, at Christie's in 1984. Wright refused, like George Stubbs (q.v.), to become an Academician. His fine painting of Francis and Charles Mundy in the act of pulling a bow string, while their King Charles spaniel holds an arrow in his mouth, was painted in 1782 and exh. at the RA in the same year (No. 165). Wright was born in Derby and died there sixty-three years later. He became a pupil of Thomas Hudson (1751-1753) and again (1756-1757). He exh. at the SA, FS and RA from 1765 and was elected ARA (1781). He was elected RA (1784) but refused it. Two cricket examples include "The Wood Children", 66in.x53in., s.&d. 1789, Derby City Museum and AG and "The Thornhill Children", c.1790, 57in.x 48½in., private collection.

Wright, Joseph Franklin, ISA, SMP, VANS (b.1924)

Leading Canadian marine artist in oils, watercolours and acrylics who gained a Diploma in Fine Art from the famous art school at Westport, Connecticut, USA in 1971. His painting "Salt Bankers Racing off Halifax - 'Blue Nose' and 'Columbia'" shows the schooners racing for the 1922 International Fisherman's Trophy which "Blue Nose" won., 26¼in.x35½in., exh. at the RSMA (1977). Wright exh. at the RSMA from 1971 and the ROI from 1979. His work is represented in the Nova Scotia Marine Museum Collection and he lives at Port Hawksbury in Nova Scotia.

Wright, Liz (b.1950)

Studied at St. Martin's School of Art, London (1968-1969) and the West of England College of Art, Bristol (1969-1972). Her work has been widely pub. as cards, posters, book covers and limited edn.prints and covers sporting subjects, particularly cricket which she paints in a clear, slightly naïve style. Solo exhibitions include one at the Austin Desmond Gallery, Ascot 1987. "Cricket at Bray", signed, 32in.x36in., collection of the artist.

Wright, Michael (b.c.1918)
Motor racing artist in the 1930s who won "The Speed" competition at the age of fifteen.

Wright, Nora (op.1915-1920s)
Known as an oil painter of eastern scenes but included in this Dictionary for her watercolour painting of a fox-hunting scene entitled "On the Scent" dated 1915, 5¼in.x7¾in., auctioned Phillips 1985. Wright exh. at the RA and other leading London galleries and lived at Horncastle in Lincolnshire.

Wright, S.R. (op.1930)
A very decorative painting of mares and foals in a landscape, dated 1930, 31¾in.x39¾in., was exh. at the Oswestry Gallery, Salop.

Wright, T. (op.c.1751)
A painting of Newmarket, dated April 1751 and inscr. in French "La Course de Newmarket, Peint/Par T. Wright, Londres" was exh. at Messrs. Ackermanns Galleries in 1930 as reported in "The Connoisseur" June 1930. Wright also painted a "Son of Childers" held by a groom, with jockey approaching on a grey horse, and a portrait of the racehorse "Brisk".

Wyatt, L. (op.c.1846?)
19th century cricketers standing before a tent and a 19th century cricketer at the wicket, oil on board, signed, a pair, each 12¾in.x7¾in., Christie's (Sth. Ken.)

Wyatt, Robert
Contemporary Canadian artist who studied at Alberta College of Art from 1967, winning the graduate painting prize in 1971. The scholarship enabled him to pursue post-graduate work at Hornsey College of Art in London. He is currently resident in Glasgow where he now concentrates on painting sporting subjects. Exh. 1989 (November) Malcolm Innes Gallery, London.

Wybrand, Simonz de Geest (The Elder) (1592-1659)
"Portrait of a Young Golfer with a Golf Club", 46in.x 26¾in. Sotheby's (London).

Wyck, Jan (Jan van Wijck) (b.c.1645-d.1700)
Very popular battle and sporting artist who operated in the second half of the 17th century and of whom George Vertue later recorded "His hunting pieces are in grate esteem among our country gentry for whom he often drew horses and dogs by the life". Both John Wootton (q.v.) and Francis Burke were his pupils. Wyck's painting "A Huntsman Coursing with a Pack of Hounds above Berkhampstead, Hertfordshire", 39in.x45in. was probably commissioned by the Wethery family whose seat at Ashlin's Hall may be seen beyond the river on the hill to the left of the painting. Wyck was born at Haarlem, the son of the painter Thomas Wyck (1616-1670) and probably taught by him. Both were originally employed by the Lauderdale family to paint the interior of Ham House in the 1670s. Wyck was a member of the Painter-Stainers Company.

Wydeveld, Arnoud (op.1855-1862)
American painter of angling scenes whose still life portrait of a fish with a rod entitled "A Fine Catch", 18in.x32in. was auctioned Sotheby's (NY) 1988.

Wyeth, Andrew (b.1917)
American painter of perhaps the best known 20th century American painting "Christina's World" (1948) (MOMA). Included in this Dictionary for his painting "The Rabbit Hunter" dated 1937, 16in.x25½in., watercolour, auctioned Sotheby's (NY) 1978 and "The Cross Country Skier on Mount Kearsage", watercolour, 20in.x29in., auctioned in 1989. Wyeth studied art under his father, Newell Convers Wyeth (1882-1945), the painter and illustrator of R.L. Stevenson's "Treasure Island" (1911) and "Kidnapped" (1913). Andrew Wyeth has received Hon. DFA from Colby and Horrard (1955) and from Swarthmore, Dickinson, Tufts, Princeton U. Penn., Amherst, and others. Awards from Penn. Academy of Fine Arts (1949). In 1976 Wyeth became the first living American-born painter to receive a retrospective exhibition at the Metropolitan Museum of Art, New York. Represented in numerous public collections in the USA.

Wyllie, Charles William, ROI (1853-1923)
Marine artist, brother of the more famous marine artist William Lionel Wyllie (q.v.). Included in this Dictionary for his watercolour painting "A Regatta on the Medway with the Warship HMS Worcester in the Background". A similar painting by this artist, but in oils, hangs in the National Maritime Museum at Greenwich. Wyllie, who studied at Leigh's School of Art and the RA Schools, exh. at the RA from 1872. Represented in the Tate Gallery.

Wyllie, Harold (1880-1973)
Painter and etcher of marine subjects who painted some yacht racing scenes. Marine painter to the Royal Yacht Squadron in 1934 and became Vice President of the RSMA (1958). Son of William Lionel Wyllie (q.v.).

Wyllie, William Lionel, RA, RI, RE (1851-1931)
Leading British marine artist who painted in oils and watercolours, dry points and etchings. Studied at Heatherleys and the RA Schools where he won the Turner Gold Medal in 1869. He exh. over two hundred works at the RA from 1868 and was elected RA in 1907. He painted many yacht racing scenes which include "The Regatta at Cowes", a dry point etching, and "12 Metre Yachts Racing in the Solent", dated 1922, a watercolour, 14½in.x21½in., Christie's 1988. Appropriately he lived at Tower House at the entrance to Portsmouth Harbour from 1907 until his death in 1931. A collection of his work may be seen at the National Maritime Museum, Greenwich. William Lionel Wyllie was the father of Harold Wyllie and the brother of Charles William Wyllie (qq.v.).

Wyniatt, Captain (op.1840-1841)
A watercolour painting of the meeting of the Garrison Hounds, November 1840, dated 1841, by this artist was auctioned Christie's (Sth. Ken.) 1984.

Wynn Ellis
See Ellis

Wyse, Henry Taylor (1870-1951)
Scottish born landscape painter whose pastel portrait "A Cyclist in an Autumn Landscape", dated 1908, 10¼in.x 14¾in. was auctioned Christie's (Scotland) 1988. Wyse studied at the Dundee School of Art, at Glasgow and in Paris. He lived in Edinburgh and exh. from 1908 at the RSA, GI in London and in the provinces.

Y

Yarwood, Henry
20th century painter of equestrian portraits including "Memnon" the St. Leger winner of 1825, "Harkaway" who won the Goodwood Cup in 1838 and 1839, "Mango" winner of the St. Leger 1837, "Flying Fox" Triple Crown winner 1900 and "Persimmon" Derby winner 1896.

Yates, Fred J. (b.1922)
Manchester-born painter of figure and leisure subjects who contributed a football painting, "Saturday Afternoon", 47½in.x39½in., to the FE. Yates, who studied at the Manchester College of Art (1946-1951) has painted full time since 1969. Held first solo exhibition at the Reynolds Gallery, Plymouth (1976) and again exh. there (1980). Exh. regularly at the RA. Examples of his work are in the collections of Dewsbury City AG, Torquay AG, Leicestershire, Gloucestershire, Sussex and Buckinghamshire County Councils.

Yates, Harold (b.1916)
Figure painter who studied at Portsmouth School of Art (1930-1931) and joined a commercial studio. Held first solo exhibition at Foyles Art Gallery, London (1935). A recent solo exhibition of his work was held at the Belgrave Gallery, London (1989). Included in this Dictionary for his painting "Motor Bicycles in a Line Up", auctioned Bonhams 1988.

Yeames, William Frederick, RA (1835-1918)
Painter of historical and equestrian subjects including a gruesome fox-hunting scene entitled "After the Hunt" dated 1884, auctioned Christie's 1983. Born in Southern Russia, the son of the British consul, he lived in Odessa and Dresden before returning to London in 1848. Studied art under G. Scharf and in Italy (1852-1858). Exh. at the RA from 1859 and other leading galleries. Elected RA (1878), retired (1913).

Yeats, Jack Butler, RHA, LG (1871-1957)
Prolific painter of Irish life and landscapes. Son of John Butler Yeats RHA and brother of the poet William Butler Yeats. Studied at the Westminster School of Art under Fred Brown (q.v.). Exh. at the RHA from 1899. Elected RHA (1915) and LG (1940). His sporting subjects include boxing - a particularly favourite subject - racing, shooting, trotting, swimming and cricket. Yeats worked for the family firm the Cuala Press and began to paint in oils in about 1913. He had one-man exhibitions at the Waddington Gallery and at the Leger Galleries in 1932 where he exh. "The Drumcliffe Races" described in "The Connoisseur" (December 1932) as an "austerely dramatic composition done several years ago". "Going to the Races" was a subject that very much attracted Yeats (his uncle, William Pollexfen, was a horse trainer) and he was to paint several versions of this title in both oil and watercolour. Many of Yeats' paintings create a sense of occasion such as "In the Liffy Swim" which depicts the annual swimming race held in August. Yeats loved "occasions" such as a racecourse finishing post or the last bank and this is probably why he was so attracted to boxing and its action and drama.

Yeomans, Thomas (c.1805-1860)
A Lincolnshire animal and equestrian painter. Yeomans painted a number of "Leicester Long Wools", presumably for local farmers, which were exh. at the Walker Gallery, Bond Street, in 1930 and 1932. His portrait of "Tsarina" and "Ladybird" with another greyhound in a landscape dated 1846 and inscr. "Grantham", 20in.x 25½in., showed that Yeomans had a natural artistic talent if somewhat provincial. He also painted the greyhounds "Rosie", "Rocket" and "Fanny" entitled "Waiting Expectantly" and dated 1825, 21in.x28in. His portrait of a fighting cock was exh. "The British Sporting Paintings Exhibition" at the Haywood Gallery in 1974 and his portrait of a fox terrier with a badger outside its set, dated 1848, 26in.x33in., was auctioned Christie's (NY) 1982.

"Yoi Over"
The pseudonym of an unnamed author and illustrator of "Bells of the Chase" pub. Hutchinson & Co. c.1926.

Yorke, H.T. (op.1867)
A pair of coaching scenes, s.&d. 1867, were auctioned Sotheby's (1964).

Young, H.B. (op.1878)
Sportsman, draughtsman and etcher of the excellent illustrations to "A Memoir of the Rev. John Russell" (q.v.), pub. 1878.

Young, Harold (Harry) (op.1931-1937)
Painter of a golfing scene in the tropics, dated 1931, a watercolour, 10in.x14½in., auctioned Bonhams 1988.

Young, Tobias (op.1780-1824)
Landscape painter and of some sporting scenes including spaniel flushing woodcock in a mountain landscape dated 1816 and springer spaniel putting up a woodcock, each 27in.x39in.

Young, W.H.
Included in this Dictionary for his painting "The Salmon Fisherman", 15½ in.x23¼ in., auctioned Sotheby's (Sussex) 1986.

Young, William Weston (op.1797-1835)
Topographer and Swansea porcelain painter of bird subjects. He also produced a series of drawings of the proposed park at Merthy Mawr House, Mid Glamorgan, some depicting horses and cattle, for Sir John and Lady Nicholls, c.1812 and 1813.

Yule, V.T.B.
Illustrator, whose pen and ink sketch inscr. "Gof, the game Scotchmen knock L' out of", 8¾ in.x7½ in. was auctioned Sotheby's 1986.

Z

Zaefferer, Adrianna
Contemporary Argentinian equestrian painter who is known internationally throughout racing circles for her paintings of many of the world's leading thoroughbreds including "Brigadier Gerard" and "Mill Reef". Has travelled extensively, settling for a time in Newmarket and has had one-man exhibitions in both the USA and London, particularly at Wildenstein & Co.

Zampogna, Dino
Painter of a racing scene entitled "Longchamp Races" inscr., 19½ in.x23½ in., auctioned Christie's 1963.

Zatzka, Hans (b.1859)
Austrian painter of genre subjects whose painting "The Sleigh Ride" depicts three girls tobogganing, 31in.x 22¾ in., auctioned Christie's (NY) 1986.

Zeeman, Rudolph (op.1930s)
Motor racing painter of cars and racing personalities who drew for "Motor" magazine during the 1930s.

Zellenberg, Franz Zeller Von (1805-1876)
Australian painter of equestrian scenes including "The Race from Baden to Vienna" dated 1837, 10in.x12in. and horses in a landscape dated 1865.

Zellinsky, C.L. (op.1887-1891)
American painter of equestrian subjects, particularly racing. His paintings include "Celebrated Winning Racehorses and Jockeys at the American Turf", dated 1888, and "The Racehorse 'His Highness' with Jockey Up", dated 1891 and inscr., 18in.x24in., auctioned Christie's (NY) 1985. His portrait of "'Hanover' with Jockey Up", dated 1887, 28in.x34in., was auctioned Sotheby's (NY) 1986.

Zew, T.E. (op.c.1900)
Watercolour inscr. "Piebald and skewbald geldings having been driven much together. White mare, sound eyes and wind, has won races" was auctioned Phillips (Bath) 1986.

Ziegler, Henry Bryan (1798-1874)
Landscape and portrait painter, also an etcher. His pen, brown ink and watercolour painting of archery practice on the lawn at Cowdray Lodge is dated 1829, 9½ in.x 20¼ in. Cowdray Lodge was built for W.S. Poyntz by Charles Heathcote Tatham, c.1800, and it was rebuilt in 1876. Charles Heathcote Tatham was the father of William Blake's friend Frederick Tatham. Samuel Palmer, Blake, B.R. Haydon and John Linnell (qq.v.) all visited the house before its sale in the 1830s. Ziegler was a pupil of John Varley, the landscape painter, and later became drawing master to Prince George of Cambridge and taught Queen Adelaide drawing. He accompanied the Duke of Rutland on a trip to Norway and was patronised by King William IV. Exh. at the RA from 1814 and other leading London galleries. His "View of Worcester Race Course and Grandstand" was drawn and etched by himself in 1923, 12½ in.x22¾ in., and pub. by Hunt.

Zimmerman, Theodore Franz (1802-1880)
German painter, mainly in pastels, whose racing scene "In the Lead - the Grand National", 8½ in.x6in. was auctioned W.H. Lane 1989.

Zinkeisen, Anna Katrina (Mrs. G.R.N. Heseltine) RP, ROI, NS (1901-1976)
This talented portrait painter was born in Scotland at Kilcreggan. Her sister was the painter Doris Clare Zinkeisen (q.v.). She studied art at Harrow and at the RA Schools where she won a bronze and a silver medal. Exh. at the RA and other leading London and provincial galleries, also abroad (1920-1940). Elected ROI (1929). Vice President of the ROI. Represented in several public collections. Married to Colonel G.R.N. Heseltine and lived in London. Zinkeisen painted a number of sporting subjects, many of which appeared as posters commissioned by London Transport including "Tennis at Wimbledon" and "The Cup Final, April 28th, 1934".

Zinkeisen, Doris Clare (Mrs. Grahame Johnson), ROI (1898-1991)

Portrait and figure painter born in Dunbartonshire. The sister of the artist Anna Zinkeisen (q.v.) Won a scholarship from Harrow School of Art to the RA Schools. Exh. at the RA and other leading London and provincial galleries, also at the Paris Salon. Elected ROI 1928. Her sporting paintings show the knowledge of an expert since she was an excellent sportswoman, hunting with the Pytchley and showing her champion hack at all the major and international shows. She worked as an official war artist during the 1939-1945 war for the Red Cross who sent her abroad to record the liberation of Belsen. These paintings are now in the Imperial War Museum. Zinkeisen exh. many times at the RA and the Royal Society of Portrait Painters and had numerous one-man shows. The Paris Salon awarded her the bronze, silver and gold medals for her work shown there. This talented artist, with a tendency to depict her subjects in romantic Regency settings, painted a great variety of subject matter including many sporting scenes which include duck shooting, hot air ballooning, flat racing, skating and hacking and show jumping. Her painting of Pat Smythe on "Scorchin", 18½in.x24½in., was repro. as a popular print. Recent paintings by Doris Zinkeisen were shown at the King Street Galleries Ltd., London in November 1978.

Zobel, Benjamin (1762-1831)

German animal and landscape painter whose portraits were often painted as sand pictures. His work included a number of number of mildly sporting subjects.

Zoffany, Johann, RA (1733-1810)

Portrait painter, born near Frankfurt, the son of a court cabinet maker. Apprenticed to Martin Speer, a local painter of some repute, who had himself been a pupil of Solimena. Zoffany made his first journey to Rome in 1750 where he studied under the fashionable portrait painter Masucci. In 1760 Zoffany arrived in England and at first painted clock faces for the clock maker Stephen Rimbault who introduced him as a drapery painter to Benjamin Wilson. Garrick became Zoffany's first major patron and although it can be said that he made his reputation for the conversation pieces with which he is mostly associated, it was the patronage of Queen Charlotte, the wife of George III, which made him so fashionable. Zoffany also won the patronage of the sportsman and English administrator to India, Warren Hastings (1732-1818). Hastings was responsible for the commission of one of the finest paintings of cockfighting in the history of the sport and in 1786 commissioned Zoffany to paint the contest (main) between the gamecocks of Colonel Mordaunt (1749-1790) and those of the Nawab Wazir of Oudh Asaf Ud Daula. (The painting, presented to Asaf Ud Daula, was unfortunately lost during the mutiny of 1857, although Zoffany painted at least two other versions. The painting presented to the Nawab was last seen by Mrs Fanny Parkes who made two visits to the palace in December 1827 and January 1831 and wrote "The picture excellent, but fast falling into decay" ("Wanderings of a Pilgrim in search of the Picturesque") (Christie's 10.4.1992). It was engraved in mezzotint by R. Earlom in 1792 and is nowadays known through the engraving, British Museum.) Zoffany returned to London from India via Margate in 1789. Other occasional sporting subjects painted by him include "The Hunt Breakfast at Mr. Palmer's House" (collection John Hay Whitney) and "The 3rd Duke of Richmond out Shooting" (on loan to the Scottish National Portrait Gallery).

Zulawski, Jacek (op.1948)

Polish artist who contributed a coloured mosaic of a football match to the XIVth Olympiad Sport in Art competition and exhibition at the V&A Museum, London in 1948.

Zwecker, Johann Baptiste (1814-1876)

German-born history painter and illustrator, also an etcher. Zwecker came to London in about 1850 and made numerous illustrations for books and magazines, many of them natural history subjects, including "Wild Sports of the World" (1862), "Out on the Pampas" (G.A. Henty, 1871), "The Rifle and the Hound in Ceylon" (S.W. Baker 1892). He contributed animal drawings to "The Illustrated London News" (1860-1866) and "Woods Natural History" (1862). Exh. at the RA and other leading London galleries.

Abbreviations

A	Associate
AAEA	American Academy of Equine Art
AC	Art Club (preceded by place name)
ACC	Antique Collectors' Club
ACD	Art Center College of Design (USA)
AG	Art Gallery
ARA	Associate of the Royal Academy
ARCA	Associate of the Royal Cambrian Academy
ARHA	Asociate of the Royal Hibernian Academy
ARPE	Associate of the Royal Society of Painters & Etchers
ARSA	Associate of the Royal Scottish Academy
ARSW	Associate of the Royal Scottish Watercolour Society
ARWS	Associate of the Royal Watercolour Society
ASL	Art Students' League
ATD	Art Teachers' Diploma
attrib.	attributed (reasonably supposed to be by the artist quoted)
AWCS	Art Workers Club for Women (New York)
b.	born
Bel.	Belgravia
BI	British Institution (1806-1897)
BM	British Museum
BR	*British Racehorse* magazine
BRU	Bruton Galleries
BSH	British Sporting Heritage (Loan Exhibition, Sotheby's 1984/5)
Bt.	Baronet
b/w	black and white
BWS	British Watercolour Society
c.	circa
CBE	Commander of the Order of the British Empire
CCA	Christie's Contemporary Art
CFC	Chelsea Football Club
CL	*Country Life* magazine
Coll.	Collection
CSD	Chartered Society of Designers
CVO	Commander of the Royal Victorian Order
d.	died
DA	Diploma in Art
DBE	Dame Commander of the Order of the British Empire
DD	Doctor of Divinity
DFA	Diploma of Fine Arts
DG	Dudley Gallery
DSC	Distinguished Service Cross
ECA	Edinburgh College of Art
edn.	edition
exh.	exhibition
F	Fellow
FA	Football Association
FAS	Famous Artists School (USA)
FAS	Fine Art Society, London
FE	The Arts Council of Great Britain/ Football Association Exhibition (1953)
FRCS	Fellow of the Royal College of Surgeons
FRGS	Fellow of the Royal Geographical Society
FRS	Fellow of the Royal Society
FRSA	Fellow of the Royal Society of Arts
FS	Free Society of Artists (1761-1783)
FSA	Fellow of the Royal Society of Antiquarians
GAA	Guild of Aviation Artists (founded 1971)
GCSI	Knight Grand Commander of the Order of the Star of India

GG	Grosvenor Gallery
GI	Glasgow Institute of Fine Art
Glen.	Gleneagles
GMA	Guild of Motoring Artists (founded 1986)
GP	Society of Glass Painters
GSA	Glasgow School of Art
H	Honorary
HM	Harris Museum, Preston
HS	Heraldry Society
IAL	International Institute of Arts and Letters
illus.	illustrated
ILN	*Illustrated London News*
indis.	indistinct(ly)
inits.	initials
ins.	inches
inscr.	inscribed
IPG	Independent Painters Group
IS	International Society of Sculptors, Painters and Gravers
Jnr.	Junior
JP	Justice of the Peace
KT	Knight of the Thistle
LA	Liverpool Academy
LG	London Group
LLD	Doctor of Law
LSC	London Sketch Club
MA	Master of Arts
MB	Bachelor of Medicine
MC	Military Cross
MCC	Marylebone Cricket Club
Mel.	Melbourne
MFH	Master of Foxhounds
MG	Mall Galleries
MIPA	Member of the Institute of Practitioners in Advertising
H	Honorary
HM	Harris Museum, Preston
HS	Heraldry Society
IAL	International Institute of Arts and Letters
illus.	illustrated
ILN	*Illustrated London News*
indis.	indistinct(ly)
inits.	initials
ins.	inches
inscr.	inscribed
IPG	Independent Painters Group
IS	International Society of Sculptors, Painters and Gravers
Jnr.	Junior
JP	Justice of the Peace
KT	Knight of the Thistle
LA	Liverpool Academy
LG	London Group
LLD	Doctor of Law
LSC	London Sketch Club
MA	Master of Arts
MB	Bachelor of Medicine
MC	Military Cross
MCC	Marylebone Cricket Club
Mel.	Melbourne
MFH	Master of Foxhounds
MG	Mall Galleries
MIPA	Member of the Institute of Practitioners in Advertising
MMA	Metropolitan Museum of Art, New York

MOH	Master of Otter Hounds	RFU	Rugby Football Union
MOMA	Museum of Modern Art, New York	RGI	Royal Glasgow Institute of Fine Art
mono.	monogram(med)	RGS	Royal Geographical Society
MP	Member of Parliament	RHA	Royal Hibernian Society
MSIA	Member of the Society of Industrial Artists and Designers	RI	Royal Institute of Painters in Watercolours (from 1881)
MVO	Member of the Royal Victorian Order	RIA	Royal Irish Academy
NA	National Academy of Design, New York (Academician)	RIBA	Royal Institute of British Architects
		RID	Ridley Art Club, London (founded 1938)
NAMOS	National Art Museum of Sports, Indianapolis (founded 1991)	RMA	Royal Military Academy
		RMI	Royal Manchester Institute
NDD	National Diploma in Design	RMS	Royal Society of Miniature Painters
NEAC	New English Art Club	RNVR	Royal Naval Volunteer Reserve
NG	New Gallery	ROI	Royal Institute of Oil Painters
NGS	National Galleries of Scotland	RP	Royal Society of Portrait Painters
NPS	National Portrait Society	RPE	Royal Society of Painters and Etchers (later RE)
NPS	National Society of Painters, Sculptors and Print-makers (founded 1911)	RSA	Royal Scottish Academy (founded 1826, Royal 1838)
NRD	National Registered Designer		
NS	National Society of Painters, Sculptors and Gravers	RSMA	Royal Society of Marine Artists - see also SMA
NSA	New Society of Artists	RSW	Royal Scottish Society of Painters in Watercolours
NT	National Trust		
NWS	New Society of Painters in Watercolours (founded 1831, RI from 1881)	RTS	Racecourse Technical Services
		RTYC	Royal Thames Yacht Club
NY	New York	RUA	Royal Ulster Academy
NY Arch.Lg.	New York Architectural League	RWA	Royal West of England Academy
NYWCC	New York Watercolour Club	RWS	Royal Society of Painters in Watercolours
OBE	Officer of the Order of the British Empire	s.&d.	signed and dated
OM	Member of the Order of Merit	SA	Scottish Academy before Royal Charter
op.	operated/worked; denotes the period in which the artist was most active and is used when the dates of birth and death are not known. Dates shown without this prefix (e.g. 1850-1933) are the years of birth and death.	SEA/S.Equ.A.	Society of Equestrian Artists (founded 1979)
		SEAD	Society of Education in Art and Design
		SGA	Society of Graphic Art
		SI (or S of I)	Society of Illustrators (USA)
		SMA	Society of Marine Artists, before it became Royal (founded 1939, Royal Charter granted by Her Majesty the Queen 1966)
OST	Society of Easel Artists (Russia)		
OWS	Old Society of Painters in Watercolours (founded 1804, RWS from 1881)	SMP	Society of Mural Painters
		Snr.	Senior
P	President	SPB	Sotheby Parke Bernet
PAFA	Pennsylvania Academy of Fine Arts, Philadelphia	SPCA	Society for the Prevention of Cruelty to Animals (founded 1824, Royal 1840)
Penn.	Pennsylvania	SS	Society of British Artists, Suffolk Street (RBA from 1887)
PGA	Professional Golfers' Association		
PP	Past President	SVA	Society of Visual Arts (USA)
PRA	President of the Royal Academy	SWA	Society of Women Artists
PS	Pastel Society	SWE	Society of Wood Engravers
pub.	published	SWLA	Society of Wildlife Artists
q.v.	*quod vide* ('which see'); plural qq.v.	TD	Territorial Decoration
RA	Royal Academy, Royal Academician	UA	United Society of Artists
R & A	Royal and Ancient Golf Club, St. Andrews	Univ. or U.	University
RBA	Royal Society of British Artists	USA	United States of America
RBC	Royal British Colonial Society of Artists	V. & A.	Victoria and Albert Museum
RBSA	Royal Birmingham Society of Artists	Va.	Virginia
R.Cam.A.	Royal Cambrian Academy, Manchester	vol.	volume
RCA	Royal College of Art, London	VP	Vice-President
RE	Royal Society of Painter-Etchers and Engravers	WG	Walker's Gallery, London
		WIAC	Women's International Art Club
repro.	reproduced	ZS	Zoological Society

Select Bibliography

General

ADEC Art Price Annual, 1990.

Arlott, John, *The Oxford Companion to Sport and Games,* Oxford University Press, 1975.

Art in 17th Century Holland, National Gallery, 1976.

Ayres, James, *English Naïve Painting 1750-1900,* Thames & Hudson, 1974.

Baigell, Matthew, *Dictionary of American Art,* John Murray, 1980.

Baillie-Grohman, William A., *Sport in Art from the 15th to 18th Century,* Simkin Marshall Hamilton Kent & Co., first published 1925, reprinted 1969.

The British Portrait 1660-1960, introduced by Roy Strong, Antique Collectors' Club, 1991.

British Sporting Paintings 1650-1850, The Arts Council at the Haywood Gallery, 1974.

Brook-Hart, Denys, *British 19th Century Marine Painting,* Antique Collectors' Club, 1974.

Brook-Hart, Denys, *20th Century British Marine Painting,* Antique Collectors' Club, 1981.

Coombs, David, *Sport and the Countryside — English paintings, watercolours and prints,* Phaidon Press Ltd., 1978.

Cuppleditch, David, *The London Sketch Club,* Dilke Press, 1978.

Curtis, R.A. and Miller, Martin, *The Lyle Official Antiques Review 1971-1972,* Lyle, first edn. 1970.

Dictionary of Art and Artists, Thames and Hudson, 1984.

Dighton, Basil, *An Exhibition of Old Sporting Prints,* Arden Press, no date (c.1920).

The Edwardians and After — The RA 1900-1950, Royal Academy of Arts (in association with Weidenfeld & Nicolson), 1988.

Edwards, Lionel, *Sport in War,* Collins, 1936.

Egerton, Judy, *British Sporting and Animal Paintings 1655-1867, The Paul Mellon Collection,* Tate Gallery, 1978.

Egerton, Judy and Snelgrove, Dudley, *British Sporting and Animal Drawings 1500-1850, The Paul Mellon Collection,* Tate Gallery, 1978.

Encyclopedia of Sport Volumes 1, 2 3 and 4, Heinemann, 1911.

Fawcett, Trevor, *The Rise of English Provincial Art,* Clarendon Press, 1974.

Fielding, Mantle, *American Paintings, Sculptures and Engravings,* 1983.

Fox, Caroline and Greenacre, Francis, *Artists of the Newlyn School,* 1979.

France in the 18th Century, Royal Academy of Arts Winter Exhibition, 1968.

Gaunt, William, *British Painting,* Avalon Press and Central Institute of Art and Design, 1945.

Goldman, Paul, *Sporting Life — An Anthology of British Sporting Prints,* British Museum Publications, 1983.

Grant, M.H., *Dictionary of British Landscape Painters from the 16th Century to the early 20th Century,* F. Lewis Publishers Ltd., 1952.

Graves, Algernon, *Dictionary of Artists,* 3rd edn. 1901, reprinted Kingsmead Reprints 1970.

Hardie, William, *Scottish Painting 1837 to the Present,* Studio Vista, 1990.

Harris, Paul and Halsby, Julian, *The Dictionary of Scottish Painters (1600-1960),* Canongate Publishing and Phaidon Press in association with Bourne Fine Art Ltd., 1990.

Herrmann, Luke, *British Landscape Painting of the 18th Century,* first published by Faber and Faber, 1973.

Heyghe, Rene (gen. ed.), *Modern Art from 1800 to the Present Day,* Hamlyn, 1965.

Hill, Ann (gen. ed.), *A Visual Dictionary of Art,* Heinemann Secker and Warburg, 1979.

Hislop, R. (ed.), *Art Sales Index,* 18th edn., 2 vols, 1985/6.

Hislop, R. (ed.), *Art Sales Index,* 20th edn., 2 vols, 1988/9.

Hook, Philip and Poltimore, Mark, *Popular 19th Century Painting — A Dictionary of European Genre Painters,* Antique Collectors' Club, 1986.

Houfe, Simon, *The Dictionary of British Book Illustrators and Caricaturists,* Antique Collectors' Club, 1978.

Jacobs, Michael and Warner, Malcolm, *The Phaidon Companion to Art and the Artists in the British Isles,* Phaidon, 1980.

Johnson, J. and Greutzner, A., *The Dictionary of British Artists 1880-1940,* Antique Collectors' Club, 1976, reprinted 1980.

Kidd, Charles and Williamson, David, (eds.), *Debrett's Peerage and Baronetage 1985,* Macmillan.

Laver, James, *English Sporting Prints,* Cox & Wyman, 1970.

Lipman, Jean, *American Primitive Painting,* Oxford University Press, 1942.

Lucas, S.T., *Bibliography of Water Colour Painting and Painters,* White Lion Publishers Ltd., 1976.

McCausland, Hugh, *Old Sporting,* The Batchworth Press, 1948.

Mackenzie, Ian, *British Prints, Dictionary and Price Guide,* Antique Collectors' Club, 1987.

McQuillan, Melissa, *Impressionist Portraits,* Thames & Hudson, 1986.

Mallalieu, H.L., *The Dictionary of British Watercolour Artists up to 1920,* Antique Collectors' Club, 1976.

Meyer, E., *International Auction Records,* France, 1974.

Mills, John Fitzmaurice, *The Guinness Book of Arts — Fact and Feats,* Guinness Superlatives Ltd., 1978.

Osborne, Harold (ed.), *The Oxford Companion to Art,* Oxford at the Clarendon Press, 1979.

Paget, Guy, *Sporting Pictures of England,* Collins, 1945.

Pavière, Sydney H., *A Dictionary of British Sporting Painters,* F. Lewis Publishers Ltd., 1965.

Pendred, G.L., *An Inventory of British Sporting Art,* Boydell Press, 1987.

Peppin, Brigitte and Micklethwait, Lucy, *Dictionary of British Book Illustrators — The Twentieth Century,* John Murray, 1983.

Peter Biegel's Racing Pictures, Michael Joseph, 1983.

Pilkington, Matthew, *Dictionary of Painters,* Vols. I and II, printed for Thomas Mclean, Haymarket, 1824.

Robinson, Malcolm, *The American Vision — Landscape Paintings of the United States,* Octopus Books, 1988.

Roe, F. Gordon, *Sporting Prints of the 18th and early 19th Centuries,* The Connoisseur Ltd., first edn. 1927.

Rothenstein, Sir John and Hendy, Sir Philip, *Masterpieces of the Tate and National Gallery,* Thames and Hudson, 1964.

Royal Academy Exhibitors 1905-1970, Volumes I to IV, Hilmarton Manor Press, 1987.

Royal Academy Illustrated Catalogue, 1920.

The Royal Institute of Painters in Watercolours, The Studio, 1906.

The Royal Society of British Artists, 1824-1893 and the New English Art Club, Antique Collectors' Club, 1975, reprinted 1984.

Sparrow, Walter Shaw, *A Book of Sporting Painters,* Bodley Head, 1931.

Sparrow, Walter Shaw, *British Sporting Artists,* Spring Books, 1922.

Siltzer, Captain, Frank, *The Story of British Sporting Prints,* Hutchinson & Co., 1974.

Smith, Edward Lucie, Cohen, Caroline and Higgins, Judith, *The New British Painting,* Phaidon, 1988.

Soviet Art 1920s-1930s, Russian Museum, Leningrad, Harris N. Abrams Inc., New York, 1988.

Spalding, Frances and Collins, Judith, *20th Century Painters and Sculptors,* Antique Collectors' Club, 1991.

Sport in Art Exhibition, London, 1948.

Titley, Norah M., *Bibliography of British Sporting Artists,* British Sporting Art Trust, 1984.

Turnbull, Harry, *Yorkshire Artists — A Short Dictionary,* Thornton Gallery, 1976.

Turner, W.J., *Aspects of British Art,* Collins, 1947.

Walker, Stella A., *Sporting Art — England 1700-1900,* Studio Vista, 1972.

Walker, Stella A., *British Sporting Art in the 20th Century,* The Sportsman's Press, 1989.

Waterhouse, Ellis, *The Dictionary of British 18th Century Painters,* Antique Collectors' Club, 1981.

Waterhouse, Ellis, *The Dictionary of 16th and 17th Century British Painters,* Antique Collectors' Club, 1988.

Waters, Grant M., *Dictionary of British Artists working 1900-1950,* Vols. I and II, Eastbourne Fine Art Publications, 1975.

Wilder, F.L., *English Sporting Prints,* Thames and Hudson, 1974.

Wingfield, Mary Ann, *Sport and the Artist Volume I: Ball Games,* Antique Collectors' Club, 1988.

Wood, Christopher, *The Dictionary of Victorian Painters,* Antique Collectors' Club, 2nd edn., 1978.

Wood, Lt. Col. J.C., *A Dictionary of British Animal Painters,* F. Lewis Publishers Ltd., 1973.

Magazines

Badminton Library Magazines.
Baily's Magazines.
Cassell's Magazines.
The Connoisseur Year Books.
Fores' Sporting Notes and Sketches.
New Sporting Magazines.
The Strand Magazines.

Angling

Briggs, Ernest, *Angling and Art in Scotland,* Longmans, 1908.

Shaw, Sparrow, W., *Angling in British Art,* first published by John Lane Bodley Head Ltd., 1923.

Walton, Izaak, *The Compleat Angler,* illus. Arthur Rackham, Harrap, 1931.

Archery

Heath, E.G., *The History of Target Archery,* David and Charles, 1973.

Baseball

Dinhofer, Shelley, *The Art of Baseball,* Harmony Books, New York, 1990.

Billiards and Snooker

Hendrichs, William, *The History of Billiards,* published privately, 1974.

Trelford, Donald, *Snooker,* Faber & Faber, 1986.

Boxing and Wrestling

FitzBarnard, Capt. L., *Fighting Sports,* Odhams, 1923.

Fleischer & André, *A Pictorial History of Boxing,* Spring Books, 1959.

Kent, Graeme, *A Pictorial History of Wrestling,* Spring Books, 1968.

Shepherd, T.B. (comp.), *The Noble Art,* Hollis & Carter, 1950.

Coaching and Driving

Selway, N.C., *The Golden Age of Coaching and Sport,* F. Lewis Publishers Ltd., 1972.

Cock-fighting

Atkinson, Herbert, *Cockfighting and Gamefowl,* Nimrod, 1977.

Scott, George Ryley, *The History of Cockfighting,* privately printed by Charles Skilton Ltd., London, No. 294 of 1,095 numbered copies, no date (c.1925).

Cricket

Altham, H.S. and Swanton, E.W., *A History of Cricket,* George Allen & Unwin Ltd., 1926.

Simon, Robin and Smart, Alistair, *The Art of Cricket,* Martin Secker & Warburg, 1983.

Warner, Sir Pelham, *Lords 1787-1945,* The Sportsman's Book Club, first published 1946.

Croquet

Pritchard, D.M.C., *The History of Croquet,* Cassells, 1981.

Curling

Kerr, John, *The History of Curling,* David Douglas, Edinburgh, 1890.

Smith, David B., *Curling — An Illustrated History,* John Donald Publishers Ltd., 1981.

Golf

Green, Robert, *Golf — An Illustrated History of the Game,* Collins Willow, 1987.

Pilley, Phil (ed.), *Golfing Art,* foreword by Tony Jacklin, Stanley Paul, 1988.

Stirk, David, *Golf — The History of an Obsession,* Phaidon, 1987.

Hawking

de Chamerlat, Christian, *Falconry and Art,* Philip Wilson Ltd., 1987.

Hockey

Miroy, Nevill, *The History of Hockey,* Lifeline Ltd., 1986.

Horses and Field Sports

Baskett, John, *The Horse in Art,* Weidenfield and Nicolson, 1980.

Blew, W.C.A., *A History of Steeplechasing,* John C. Nimmo, 1901.

Brander, Michael (ed.), *The International Encyclopedia of Shooting,* Pelham Books Ltd., 1972.

The Encyclopedia of the Horse, Peerage Books, 1973.

Fairley, John, *Great Racehorses in Art,* Phaidon Press Ltd., 1984.

Fairley, John, *Racing in Art,* John Murray Ltd., 1990.

Livingstone Learmonth, David, *The Horse in Art,* Studio Publications, 1958.

Longrigg, Roger, *The History of Horse Racing,* Macmillan, 1972.

Miles, Henry Downes (ed.), *The Book of Field Sports,* Volume II, Henry Lee & Co., no date (c.1865).

Mitchell, Sally, *The Dictionary of British Equestrian Artists,* Antique Collectors' Club, 1985.

Mortimer, Roger, Onslow, Richard and Willett, Peter, *Biographical Encyclopedia of British Flat Racing,* Macdonald & Janes Ltd., 1978.

Seth Smith, Michael, *The History of Steeplechasing,* Michael Joseph, 1966.

Vandervell, Anthony, *Game and the English Landscape — The influence of the chase on sporting art and scenery,* Debrett's Peerage Ltd., 1980.

Lawn Tennis

Tingay, Lance, *The History of Lawn Tennis in Pictures,* Tom Stacey Ltd., 1973.

Olympic Sports

The British Olympic Association's Official Report of IXth Olympiad, 1928.

Polo

Watson, J.N.P., *The World of Polo Past and Present,* The Sportsman's Press, 1986.

Wildlife

Nerelli, Martina R., *American Wildlife Painting,* published in association with National Collection of Fine Arts, 1975.

Index of Artists by Sports

Westall, Richard
Westall, T.
Wheeler, Walter Herbert
Whittaker, James William
Whymper, Charles H.
Wild, Frank Percy
Wilde, William
Wildman, John R.
Wilkinson, Norman
Williams, Alfred Walter
Williams, Edward, Jnr.
Williams, Edward Charles
Williams, George Augustus
Williams, Walter Heath
Williams, Warren
Withoos, Matthias
Wolstenholme, (Charles)
    Dean, Jnr.
Wood, Catherine M.
Wydeveld, Arnoud
Young, W.H.

ANIMAL STUDIES

Abbott, Richmond
Adam, Benno Rafael
Adamson, Dorothy
Aldin, Cecil
Alexander, Edwin
Alken, George
Alken, Henry
Allen, J.
Archer, James
Archer, John Wykeham
Armfield, Edward
Arnold, George
Atkinson, John
Austen, Winifred
Ayers, R.
Badcock, Kathleen
Bagshaw, William
Bailey, George
Bailey, John
Baird, William
Baker, Arthur
Barber, Charles
Barker, A.
Batt, Arthur J.
Beatty, J. Lucas
Beavis, Richard
Blampied, Edmund
Blazeby, James
Boultbee, Thomas Joseph
Bramley, Frank
Bransom, Paul
Brightwell, Leonard
Brown, Edward
Bulley, Asburnham H.
Bullock, G.G.
Burras, Thomas
Burton, Nancy Jane
Butler, Mildred Anne
Cadogan, Sidney
Calderon, (William) Frank
Callaway, William
Canfield, Birtley
Carlaw, John
Carr, William
Catton, Charles, Jnr.
Chapman, A.M.
Chapman, W.J.
Chapman, W.P.
Cheviot, Lilian
Christmas, Thomas C.
Clark, John
Cole, A.
Coleman, Charles
Collier, F.S.
Colmore, Nina
Cooper, Edwin
Cooper, Thomas Sydney
Co(u)zens, William
Crawhall, Joseph E.
Crowther, Henry
Daglish-Fitch, Eric
Davis, William Henry
Daws, Frederick Thomas
Dawson, Lucy
Dawson, Mabel
Des Clayes, Alice
Doar, M. Wilson
Douglas, Hope
Driscoll, Barry
Dudgeon, James
Earl, Thomas
Edouart, Augustine
Edwards, Edward
Egerton, Daniel
Fairman, Frances
Fare, G.

Ferneley, Sarah
Fraser, Francis
Fraser, George
Fry, R. Douglas
Furse, John Henry
Gale, Benjamin
Garnam, A.C.
Garrard, R.H., Jnr.
Gauci, A.M.
Gear, Mabel
Gibbon, Benjamin
Gibbs, F.J. or J.F.
Giles, Benjamin
Gill, Herbert
Gleichen, Helena
Glover, John
Gooch, James
Good(e), John
Gray, D.B.
Gray, William
Green, Nathaniel
Guest, Miss
Gwynn, William
Hackert, Johann
Haig, Violet
Hale, Kathleen
Harrison, George
Hawken, Joy
Hawkins, Sheila
Hedley, Ralph
Herring, John Frederick,
    Jnr.
Highton, T.
Hills, Robert
Hinckley, Thomas Hewes
Hoffmann, Hans
Hollams, Mabel F.
Holt, Ellen F.
Horner, George Christopher
Hoynck, Otto
Hubbard, Bennet
Huggins, William
Hughes, Trajan
Hunt, Edgar
Hunt, Walter
King, Jessie Marion
Kirk, Joel
Lambert, James, Snr.
Landseer, Edwin Henry
Leavers, Lucy A.
Leighton, Clare
Lewis, Charles George
Lizars, William Home
Lucas Lucas, William
MacQuoid, Percy
Manning, F.
Marshall, Benjamin
Meadows, James Edwin
Miles, John
Miller, George W.
Miller, J.
Millett, Frederick
Moody, Fannie
Morley, Robert
Naish, John
Neame, Austin
Newmarch, G.B.
Noble, Edwin John
Nowell, Arthur
Nutter, Matthew
Osborne, William
Park, Carton Moore
Park, Henry
Pascoe, William E.W.
Quintin, H.J.
Rankin, Andrew Scott
Riviere, Briton
Rodgers, Joseph
Roebuck, Thomas
Rogers, Philip
Rope, George Thomas
Rountree, Harry
Rousseau, Percival Leonard
Rungius, Carl Clemens
    Moritz
Russell, Charles Marian
Sedgley, W.
Seton, Ernest Thompson
Sheppard, Charlotte Lilian
Sheppard, Joseph
Sheppard, Raymond
Shuttleworth, William
    Thomas
Siddall, M.
Siddall, R.
Simpson, F.
Smythe, Thomas (of Ipswich)
Snape, J.
Soper, George

Spackman, Isaac
Stamland, E.
Strafford, Hector
Swan, John Macallan
Tenniel, John
Trowell, Johnathan
Turner, James
Turner, Marjorie
Walmesley, J.M.
Weaver, Thomas (of
    Shropshire)
Weekes, Henry, Snr.
Wheelwright, Hene P.
White, Mildred H. Congden
Whitford, Richard
Whitford, William
Wilby, R.J.
Wilson, Thomas Fairbairn
Wilson, Violet
Wolfe-Murray, David ("Fish
    Hawk")
Yeomans, Thomas
Zwecker, Johann Baptiste

ARCHERY

Andrews, Henry
Archer, Archibald
Brockhurst, Gerald Leslie
Burton, Mungo
Cowen, William
Crane, R.
Crane, Thomas
Cruikshank, Isaac Robert
De Ryck, John
Emes, John
Etty, William
Faed, John
Frith, William Powell
Gaskell, George
Goodall, John Strickland
Grant, Francis
Hartrick, Archibald
Harvey, George Wills
Hoppner, John
Hunt, William Henry
Jamieson, Alexander
King, John
Martin, David
Meyer, F. John
Moore, William
Paxton, W.A.
Raeburn, Henry
Russell, John
Slater, Joseph
Smirke, Robert
Taffs, Charles H.
Townshend, John
Wilson, F.S.
Witherington, William
    Frederick
Woodward, George Moutard
Wright, Joseph (of Derby)

ASSOCIATION FOOTBALL/ FOOTBALL

Allinson, Adrian
Aumonier, James
Ayrton, Michael
Badmin, Stanley
Baumeister, Willi
Baumer, Lewis
Berkeley, Stanley
Bostock, James
Boswell, James E.
Bretherick, Clarence
Brill, Frederick
Brooks, Henry Jamyn
Bruce, John
Buckman, Edwin
Buhler, Robert
Carse, Alexander
Chamberlain, Christopher
Clarke, Richard E.
Colquhoun, Ithell
Critchlow, M.B.
Cruikshank, Isaac
Cruikshank, Isaac Robert
Cundall, Charles
Cuneo, Terence
Deane, Frederick A.
De Maistre, Roy
De Stael, Nicolas
Deykin, Henry
Dighton, Robert
Dunstan, Bernard
Floyd, Gareth
Fox, Lilla

Freeth, Hubert Andrew
Frost, Terry
Gillet(t), Edward Frank
Griffiths, Mark
Guthrie, James
Hackney, Arthur
Halliday, George D.
Hanfstaengl, Franz
Harrison, Christopher
Hart, Dick
Hartwell, William
Hawkins, Harold
Hemy, Thomas
Herman, Josef
Hewison, William
Hewitt, Geoffrey
Higgs, J.
Holland, James
Hopkinson, John
Horn, George
Horne, Edwin
Howson, Peter
Hoyle, Walter
Hussey, Harold
Irvin, Albert
Isherwood, Travis
Jacobs, Dennis
Jones, Stanley Robert
Kaufmann, Wilhelm
Kelly, Victor
Kessell, James Everett
Kinsey, Anthony
Koethe, Wolfgang
Krishna, Mary Elizabeth
Kuell, Victor John
La Dell, Edwin
Lamb, Lynton Harold
Leeson, Lawrence Joseph
Lek, Karel
L'hote, André
Livens, Horace Mann
Lowry, Laurence Stephen
Lucas, Stephen
Macdonald, Richard
Macdonald, Tom
Mauzer, David
Morden, W.G.
Nash, Paul
Nelson, Paul
Nevinson, Christopher
Newton Taylor, W.H.
Noble, John Rushton
Norris, L
Palmer, Albert
Palmer, James
Parker, Charles H.
Patterson, Janet
Payne, Wilfrid
Pepper, Frank
Peri, Peter L.
Phillips, Douglas
Plessis, H.E., du
Pope, Hilda Chancellor
Prater, Ernest
Proudfoot, James
Raven-Hill, Leonard
Reid, Patrick
Ribbons, Ian
Robb, Brian
Roberts, William Patrick
Rodgers, Sydney
Rogers, Claude
Rosenbaum, Julius
Rothenstein, Michael
Rousseau, Henry
Salaman, Michael
Sambourne, Edward Linley
Sanders, Christopher
Sayce, Harry H.
Scott, Septimus Edwin
Sewell, John
Shaw, Nevil
Shelton, Harold
Slater, Richard E.
Smith, Howard
Smythe, Lionel Percy
Spear, Ruskin
Speechley, G.S.
Spencelayh, Charles
Stevens, Chris
Sturgess, William Stanfield
Taverner, Robert
Taylor, Françoise
Tesson, Louis
Thomas, Bert
Tiffin, Sheila
Toovey, C.W.
Toynbee, Lawrence
Tucker, James Walker

Turner, W.
Uhlman, Fred
Unsworth, Peter
Wain, Louis William
Ward, Louis Arthur
Watson, John
Weake, David Brian
Weber, Gotlieb Daniel Paul
Weber, Paul
Webster, Norman
Webster, Thomas
Weight, Carel Victor Morlais
Wesley, Gordon H.
Whitlock, J. (Codner, John)
Wilkinson, Clifford
Williams, Alfred Walter
Wood, Peter MacDonagh
Yates, Fred J.
Zinkeisen, Anna Katrina
Zulawski, Jacek

ATHLETICS

Berkeley, Stanley
Busby, Thomas
Clark, John Cosmo
Copley, John
Dadd, Richard
Greengrass, William
Hayter, Charles
Hewitt, Geoffrey
Hill, Frank
Neiman, Leroy
Phillips, Douglas
Pochtenny, Alexei Petrovich
Robinson, Frederick
Somville, Roger
Tsvetkov, Victor
Waller, Jonathan
Whitney, Kevin
Williams, Christopher David
Williams, Edward, Snr.
Wood, Charles

AVIATION

Bradshaw, Stanley
Carter
Hoad, Norman
Hollins, John
Hum, George
Pace, Percy
Turner, Michael
Walton, W.L.
Wootton, Frank

BADMINTON

Inshaw, David
May, Philip (Phil) William
Morgan, Frederick (Fred)

BALLOONING

Angus, William
Briscoe, Michael J.
Bulham, Henry Robert
Cocks, E.W.
Cooke, Edward William
Grant, Donald
Greaves, Walter
Lemoine, P.
Pegram, Frederick
Rigaud, John
Rowlandson, Thomas
Summers, Gerald
Underhill, Graham
Zinkeisen, Doris Clare

BASEBALL

Africano, Nicholas
Bellows, George
Blythe, David
Boetticher, Otto
Bouché, Louis
Brown, John George
Chapin, James
Cobb, Henry
Crawford, William
Daugherty, James
De Kooning, Elaine
Delaney, Joseph
De Mejo, Oscar
Dinhofer, Lisa
Dobbs, John
Dufy, Raoul
Eakins, Thomas
Evergood, Philip
Fasanella, Ralph
Fawsett, John

Fogarty, Thomas
Friedman, Arnold
Garston, Gerald
Goings, Ralph
Grooms, Red
Gwathmey, Robert
Hartman, George
Henri, Robert
Hoffman, Frank
Hull, John
Kantor, Morris
Kitaj, Ronald Brooks
Koerner, Henry
Kushner, Robert
La Farge, John
Laning, Edward
Lawrence, Jacob
Levine, David
Leyendecker, Joseph
  Christian
Lichtenstein, Roy
Luks, George
Marin, John
Oldenburg, Claes
Ramos, Mel
Riggs, Robert
Rockwell, Norman
Shahn, Ben
Shaw, Kendall
Sievan, Maurice
Sloan, John
Snyder, W.P.
Southard, O.W.
Steinberg, Saul
Sultan, Donald
Thiebaud, Wayne
Trova, Ernest
Warhol, Andy
Warren, Ferdinand E.
Weaver, Robert
Weinberg, Frederick

BASKETBALL

Allen, R.
Gibson, Charles Dana

BEAGLING

Aldin, Cecil
Barker, Kathleen
Caldwell, Edmund G.
Carr, Tom
Cooper, George
Dalby, John
Daniell, Thomas
Dollman, John Charles
Edwards, Lionel
Emms, John
Fairman, Frances
Howitt, Samuel
Ivester-Lloyd, Jack
Ivester-Lloyd, Thomas
Jay, Florence
Lyne, Charles Edward Michael
Nash, John Northcote
Pigott, William Henry
Sartorius, John Nost (Nott)
Shiffner, Eleanor
Trautschold, Carl Friedrich
  Wilhelm
Van Somer, Paul (Paulus
  Van Someren)

BEAR-BAITING

Alken, Samuel Henry
Bellinger
Manning, F.

BICYCLING

Barnard, Mary B.
Bernasconi, A.
Diggelmann, Alex
Feininger, Lyonel
Fischer, Paul
Gaudier Brzeska, Henri
Jonas, Lucien
Kirchner, Ernest Ludwig
Laskowski, François
Moore, Gwendolen
Pegram, Frederick
Shaw, Charles E.
Stradone, Giovanni
Waller, Jonathan
White, Ethelbert
Wyse, Henry Taylor

BIG GAME HUNTING

Crealock, Henry

Daniell, William
Daws, Frederick Thomas
Devis, Arthur William
Griffiths, John
Howitt, Samuel
Hutchinson, William Henry
Johnson, Herbert
Ludovici, Albert, Snr.
Millais, John Guille
Nettleship, John Trivett
Phillips, Frank
Rungius, Carl Clemens
  Moritz
Russell, Charles Marian
Schreyvogel, Charles
Seltzer, Olaf C.
Sharpe, Joseph Henry
Stanley, James Mix
Trench, Philip Chevenix
Ward, Rowland
Whymper, Charles H.
Williamson, Thomas
Wimar, Carl
Zwecker, Johann Baptiste

BILLIARDS/SNOOKER

Béraud, Jean
Boardman, S.R.
Boilly, Louis
Bunbury, Henry William
Cook, Beryl
Crook, P.J.
Cundall, Charles
Davis, Joseph Lucien
Degas, Edgar
Deighan, Peter
Dighton, Richard
Fletcher, Geoffrey
Gauguin, Paul
Gibbs, Patrick
Giles, James William
Gioja, Belisario
Gordon, ("Jan") Godfrey
  Jervis
Hamilton, John
Herman, Josef
James, P.F.
Johnson, James
Jowett, Percy Hague
Lambert, E.F.
Landseer, Edwin Henry
Lees, Derwent
Longstaff, John
Madge
McInnes, Jos
Mortimer, John Hamilton
Nicholson, William
Oldenburg, Claes Thure
O'Neil(l), Henry
Pic, Marcel
Pyne, William Henry
Rogers, W.G.
Rowlandson, Thomas
Shakespeare, Percy
Spear, Ruskin
Strutt, Rosa Jameson
Thackeray, Lance
  "Tuss"
Van Aken, Joseph
Van de Venne, Adriaen
Van Gogh, Vincent
Werner, Carl Friedrich
  Heinrich

BOXING

Alken, Samuel Henry
Allan, W.
Allingham, Charles
Bastin, A.D.
Bateman, James
Beaton, Cecil
Belcher, George
Bellows, George
Berridge, John
Blake, T.
Bragg, Aston
Brock, Henry Matthew
Brown, John
Buchel, Charles A.
Cauldwell, Leslie Giffen
Chandler, John Westbrooke
Chepik, Sergei
Clark, John Cosmo
Clements, James
Clint, George
Cruikshank, George, Snr.
Cruikshank, Isaac
Cruikshank, Isaac Robert

Cuneo, Cyrus
Dearn, T.D.W.
Deighan, Peter
Dighton, Richard
Dighton, Robert
Eakins, Thomas
Easto, A.
Eden, William
Einsle, J.
Forbes, Vivienne
Friend, Donald
Gautez, G.
Géricault, Theodore
Gillray, James
Guest, Thomas
Guevaro, Alvaro
Harrison, Sammy
Heath, William
Henning, Archibald Samuel
Hobday, William Armfield
Hogarth, William
Hoppner, John
Howson, Peter
Jackson, John
Jones, Thomas
King, John
Knight, Laura
Kondracki, Henry
Kray, Reg
Lami, Eugène Louis
Lenkewicz, Robert
Leslie, John
Lock(e), William
MacMillan, Ethel
Marczynski, Adam
Martin, Fletcher
Meyer, Henry Hoppner
Miartani, P.
Moreau, Albert
Morrow, Norman
Mortimer, John Hamilton
Mulready, William
Ocean, Humphrey
O'Donnell, Hugh
Paget, Henry Marriott
Pepper, Frank
Phillips, Douglas
Pitman, John
Rabinovitch, Samuel (Sam
  Rabin)
Ranter, W.B.E.
Reinagle, Philip
Richards, John
Roberts, William Patrick
Robineau, Charles
Rowbotham, J.B.
Rowlandson, Thomas
Sambourne, Edward Linley
Segrelles, Jose
Sharples, George
Smith, Stan(ley)
Sutcliffe, John E.
Thomson, Alfred Reginald
Toynbee, Lawrence
Tresidder, Hereward H.
Turner, Charles
Walton, W.L.
Ward, Edmund F.
Watson, Charles John
Whitby, William
Whiteside, Brian
Wood, Harold
Zinkeisen, Anna Katrina

BULL-BAITING/FIGHTING

Alken, Samuel Henry
Armour, George
Brown, John
Clark, Joseph
Couper, George
Gear, Joseph
Marshman, J.
Towne, Charles

CAT-BAITING

Alken, Samuel Henry

COACHING/DRIVING

Aldin, Cecil
Alken, Henry
Anderson, John
Annison, Edward
Archer, M.B.
Arnold, George
Arnull, George
Ashland, J.
Atkinson, John Augustus

Bacon, Frederick
Badcock, Kathleen
Barry, James
Beale, Shell
Bell, Arthur
Bird, John Harrington
Bishop, Alfred
Bispham, Henry
Bodger, John
Boughton, H.
Brackett, W.M.
Branscombe, C.J.
Bromley, Clough
Broughton, H. or T.
Bruce, J.
Buck, S.
Burnett, C.
Burtenshaw, George R.
Burton, Charles
Butler, Thomas
Butterworth, Ninetta
Byron, Frederick George
Carr, Tom
Cattermole, Charles
Chichester, N.
Churchyard, Thomas
Clark(e), Frederick Albert
Cooper, T.C.
Corbould, Arthur
Cordrey, John
Cottrell, Henry S.
Cowland, R.M.
Davidson, Thomas
De Loutherbourg, Philip James
Deming, Edwin
Desvignes, Herbert
Dickinson, Lowes Cato
Downman, George
Downman, J.T.
Eakins, Thomas
Egerton, M.
Ellison, Alan
Emery, James
Fairlie, Henry
Faulkner, Charles
Fellow(e)s, William M.
Fenn, George
Fitzhenry, S.
Flavell, W.
Forder, E.
Freelove, William
Fremond, C.R.
Géricault, Theodore
Gregory, Charles
Griset, Ernest Henry
Haddelsey, Vincent
Haken, William
Hallet, J.
Harper, Charles
Harper, H.B.
Hart, T.R.
Harvey, R.L.
Havell, George
Havell, Robert, Snr.
Havell, Robert, Jnr.
Hayes, Michael
Headley, S. Tardrew
Henderson, Charles Cooper
Hepper, G.
Herring, Benjamin, Snr.
Hieni-Merre, Franz
Hill, F.L.
Hill, W.H.
Hixon, R.
Hunt, Charles
Jones, Herbert St. John
Jones, W.A.
Lambert, E.F.
Lambert, James, Jnr.
Laporte, George Henry
Lewis, Frederick
Loder, James, of Bath
Ludovici, Albert, Snr.
Ludovici, Albert, Jnr.
McAuliffe, James J.
McLeod, Juliet
Maggs, John Charles
Magill, Louis
Martin, Anson
Martindale, G. Thomas
Miller, James
Muller-Cornelius, Ludwig
Murray, H.
Nakken, William Carel
Newhouse, Charles
Newton, Richard, Jnr.
Orr, Jack
Paisley, John
Partridge, J.C.

Paton, Frank
Paul, John
Pitman, John
Pollard, James
Pollard, Samuel
Pringle, William J.
Quigley, Daniel
Reville, Henry Whittaker
Rideout, Philip H.
Ripley, R.R.
Robertson, George
Rudge, Bradford
Sanderson-Wells, John
Sartorius, Francis
Scott, Thomas Jefferson
Seymour, James
Shayer, William Joseph
Shepherd, Thomas Hosmer
Sherlock, A. Marjorie
Simpson, Charles Walter
Sinclair, John
Smith, Frederick Sheldon
Smith, Gean
Smith, William
Smythe, Edward Robert
Spalding, Charles B.
Spence, Percy Frederick Seaton
Sperling, Henry
Standing, Henry William
Sturgess, William Stanfield
Tarrant, Percy
Temple, Richard
Thomson, Hugh
Thornber(r)y, William A.
Tregear, Gabriel Shire
Tuer, J.
Turner, Edward
Vernet, Horace
Vernon, Walter
Vine, John (of Colchester)
Von Wagner, Alexander
Walker, Joseph Francis (John)
Waller, Samuel Edmund
Walter, Henry G.
Walton, Frank
Warden, W.
Warner, J.
Watson, Hamilton
Webb, Charles
Webb, Edward Walter
West, Peter B.
Wheatley, Francis
Wheeler, Edward J. (Edmund)
Wheeler, John Alfred
Wheelwright, Rowland
Wheelwright, W.H.
Whitcombe, Susie
White, Gilbert
Widdas, John
Widdas, Richard
Widdas, Robert Dodd
Williams, Alfred Sheldon
Wilson, Chester
Wilson, Thomas Walter
Wombill(e), Sydney R.
Woodward, George Moutard
Wray, A.
Wright, Gilbert Scott
Yorke, H.T.
Zew, T.E.

COCK-FIGHTING

Alken, Samuel Henry
Appart/Appert, A.
Atkinson, Herbert
Baird, William
Barenger, James
Best, John
Birley, Oswald
Cane, Herbert Collins
Cooper, Edwin
Dayrell, B.
Dovaston, Margaret
Fielding, Newton
Gear, Joseph
Gérome, Jean Léon
Hine, Harry
Hodgson, Robert
Johnston, Cyril David
Lami, Eugène Louis
Livens, Horace Mann
Ludlow, A.J.
Monument, R.
Nev, J.
Pickard, John
Pratt, Hilton J(onathan)
Pratt, William
Procter, P.
Reville, Henry Whittaker

Sartorius, Francis
Sartorius, William
Scanlan, Richard Robert
Sketchley, W.
Tunstall, Eric
Watt, James George
Weigall, Charles Harvey
Weir, William Harrison
Wicksteed, C.F.
Wilson, Alexander (op.
  1803-1846)
Wilson, Thomas Fairbairn
Wolstenholme, (Charles)
  Dean, Jnr.
Yeomans, Thomas
Zoffany, Johann

COURSING/GREYHOUND
RACING

Adams, W. Douglas
Agasse, Jacques
Ansdell, Richard
Armstrong, James
Ashton, George
Atkinson, John
Barber, Charles
Barenger, James
Barwick, John
Beard, James
Benson, J.
Bigg, William
Bird, John Harrington
Blake, Benjamin
Botheras, B.B.
Branscombe, C.J.
Bretland, Thomas
Breun, John
Brewster, J.
Brown, R.G.
Brownlow, Charles S.
Calderon, (William) Frank
Carter, Henry William
Cassie, James
Chalon, Henry Barnard
Cockburn, R.D.
Cook, Joshua
Cooper, Abraham
Cottrell, Henry S.
Creswick, Thomas
Dadd, Stephen
Davis, Henry William Banks
Davis, Richard Barrett
Davis, William Henry
Day, G.F.
Dent, Rupert Arthur
Denyer, David
Dixon, George H.
Duval, John
Ellis, Alfred
Folkard, R.W.
Garratt, Samuel
Gear, Joseph
Gilbert, Terence
Gilbert, W.J.
Gillet(t), Edward Frank
Gilpin, Sawrey
Goddard, George
Grainger, Vic
Hamilton, William
Hamilton Renwick, Lionel
Havell, George
Hawkins, Waterhouse
  Benjamin
Hearne, Thomas
Henwood, Thomas
Hepple, Wilson
Hodges, J.
Holmes, George Augustus
Hull, Edward (op.1817-1877)
Hull, Edward (op.
  1860-1895)
Hunt, Edwin Henry
Jay, J.A.B.
Jones, Richard
Kelly, Richard Barrett
  Talbot
Knight, S.S.
Laporte, George Henry
Leland, John B.
Macbeth, Robert Walker
Magill, E.
Marshall, John
Millais, Raoul Hesketh
Moore, I. (J.)
Moore, R.H.
Noble, W.R.
Pascoe, William
Pearce, Stephen
Peers, M.

Pitman, John
Raven, Samuel
Reinagle, Ramsay Richard
Robinson, William Howard
Roods, Thomas
Roper, Edward
Ryot of Newcastle, J.R.
Sandys-Lumsdaine, Leesa
Sartorius, John Francis
Scrags, John
Selfe, Madelaine
Seymour, James
Shayer, William Joseph
Sheriff, John ("Dr. Syntax")
Sims, J.W.
Sinclair, John
Skeaping, John Rattenbury
Slattery, John Joseph
Spode, Samuel
Stafford, Henry
Steell, David George
Turner, Francis Calcraft
Turner, J.
Von Blaas, Julius
Von Rentzell, Auguste
Walls, William
Wells, L.
Whaite, T.
Whiting, Frederick (Fred)
Wildman, John R.
Williamson, Harold Sandys
Wolstenholme, Dean, Snr.
Wolstenholme, (Charles)
  Dean, Jnr.
Yeomans, Thomas

CRICKET

Alken, Samuel Henry
Allan, David
Alleyne, Francis
Allinson, Adrian
Almond
Anderson, John Corbet
Appleyard, Joseph
Arnesby-Brown, John
Atkinson, Charles
Aveling, H.J.
Barrable, George
Barraud, Francis Philip
Barraud, Henry
Barron, Hugh
Basebe, Charles
Batson, Frank
Baxter, Thomas
Bayes, Gilbert
Beach, Thomas
Beechey, William
Beerbohm, Max
Bellany, John
Bettesworth, Walter
Bigg, William
Blake, William
Boin, Rene
Boitard, Louis
Bough, Samuel
Bowyer, William
Brabbins, Oliver
Bradley, Edward
Bradley, Helen
Bridges, John
Bromley, Valentine
Brooker, Harry
Brooks, Henry Jamyn
Brooks, Peter
Broomfield, Frances
Brown, Ford Madox
Brown, John
Buck, Adam
Burgess, William
Burney, James
Burr, Alexander
Calderon, Philip
Chalon, Alfred Edward
Childe, James
Coates, W.R.
Coghill, Sarah
Collet, John
Collier, John
Cook
Cooper, Alfred Egerton
Copley, John Singleton
Cotes, Francis
Coverley-Price, Victor
Craig, David
Crombie, Charles E.
Crook, P.J.
Cruikshank, Isaac Robert
Cundall, Charles
Curtis, John Digby

Cutler, Cecil
Dagley, Richard
Dance, Nathaniel
Daniell, Thomas
Daniels, Alfred
Danloux, Henri Pierre
Davies, Marion
Davis, Joseph Lucien
Davis, Richard Barrett
De Wint, Peter
Deykin, Henry
Dickinson, Lowes Cato
Dighton, Robert
Dodd, Joseph
Dorrell, Edmund
Downey, Thomas
Drew, Mary
Drummond, William
Dunstan, Bernard
East, Alfred
Edridge, Henry
Ellis, Clifford and Rosemary
Elmer, William
Evans, William
Eyre, Edward
Fearnley, Alan
Feller, F.
Fisher, William
Floyd, Gareth
Foster, Bell
Foster, Myles Birket
Francis, Catharine
Furniss, Harry
Gainsborough, Thomas
Galsworthy, Jocelyn
Gardner, Daniel
Gardner, Philip
Garland, Henry
Gilbert, Ellen
Goodall, John Strickland
Gore, Spencer Frederick
Grace, A.L.
Grace, Hariette
Grant, Charles
Grant, Duncan
Gravelot, Hubert
Grave(s), Charles
Gray, Douglas Stannus
Green, Mary
Greene, V.
Grineau, Bryan de
Guria, Ben
Haddon, David
Hall, Sydney Prior
Hanfstaengl, Franz
Hardie, Charles Martin
Hargreaves, Harry
Harrison, Christopher
Hallar, James
Hayman, Francis
Hayter, John
Henwood, Thomas
Hicks, George Elgar
Highmore, Joseph
Hopkins, Mrs. Edward
Horlor, A.
Horton, Etty
Hudson, Thomas
Hunt, William Henry
Inshaw, David
James, Robert
Jefferys, William
Jellicoe, John F.
Jonas, John
Joy, Thomas Musgrove
Kelly, Gerald Festus
"Kestler"
Kinsella, E.P.
Kirby, Thomas
Knight, William Henry
Koehler, Henry
La Dell, Edwin
La Nave, Francesca
Lane, Albert
Laporte, George Henry
Lee, Rupert
Lewis, Michael
Linnell, John, Snr.
Lobley, Robert
Lorette, Thinot
Lowry, Laurence Stephen
Ludovici, Albert, Snr.
McKivragen, Terence
Marshall, Herbert
Martin, David
Matthews, James
May, Charles
May, Frerd
Mayor, William

Mercer, Edward
Metz, Conrad
Millière, Maurice
Morgan, John
Morris, Richard
Muirhead, David
Murray, Sir David
Murray, W.L.
Neiman, Leroy
Nelson, Edmund
Nelson, Phyllis
Newton, Algernon
Nixon, John
Noble, William Bonneau
Ouless, Walter
Pannett, Juliet
Parsons, Beatrice
Paterson, James
Payne, Arthur
Payne, David
Pegram, Frederick
Penny, Edward
Perry, Roy
Pine, Robert Edge
Pissarro, Camille
Pollard, James
Pratt, William
Pretty, Edward
Prinsep, Thomas
Ramsay, Allan
Read, John
Reid, John Robertson
Reynolds, Frank
Reynolds, Joshua
Richmond, George
Rickards, T.
Ritchie, John
Roberts, Henry
Rochard, Simon
Rogers, J(ohn), Snr.
Roller, George
Rowlandson, Thomas
Russell, John
Sablet, Jacques
Sandby, Paul
Sandby, Thomas
Scaddon, Robert
Sheldon, Charles Mills
Shelley, Samuel
Shepheard, George
Shepherd, Thomas Hosmer
Smith, Jane Sophia Clarendon
Spear, Ruskin
Sperling, Diana
Spooner, Arthur
Spring-Smith, Effie
Stampa, George Loraine
Staples, Robert Ponsonby
Streatfield, Robert
Stuart, Gilbert
Tayler, Albert Chevallier
Taylor, Alan
Taylor, Rosemary
Thorpe, James H.
Tonks, Henry
Topolski, Felix
Toynbee, Lawrence
Tuke, Henry Scott
Turner, Joseph Mallord
  William
Unsworth, Peter
Urquhart, Murray McNeel
  Caird
Valentine-Daines, Sherree
Walker, John
Walton, Henry
Wanostrocht, Nicholas
  ("Felix")
Ward, John Stanton
Warwick, K.W.
Washington, William
Watkiss, Christopher
Watts, George Frederick
Weaver, Arthur
Weight, Carel Victor Morlais
Wellings, C.
Werner, Carl Friedrich
  Heinrich
West, Benjamin
White, Ethelbert
Whittock, Nathaniel
Williams, Henry (1807-1886)
Wills, James
Wollaston, John
Wortley, Archibald John
  Stuart
Wright, Gerry
Wright, Joseph (of Derby)
Wright, Liz

Wyatt, L.
Yeats, Jack Butler

CROQUET

Arnst, A.
Bache, Otto
Barker, John Joseph
Bland, Emily
Bowkett, Jane
Brownwood Potts, R.
Caffieri, Hector
Calderon, Philip
Couldery, Horatio
Crook, P.J.
Davidson, Thomas
Deykin, Henry
Dulac, Edmund
Du Maurier, George
Fairbairn, Hilda M.
Gardner, H.
Gibbs, Percy William
Goodman, H.M.
Gotch, Thomas Cooper
Green, Charles
Hicks, George Elgar
Hill, Thomas
Homer, Winslow
Hopkins, Arthur
Howard, George
Hughes, Edward
Hughes, Talbot
Humphrey, Mrs. A.A.
Innes, Charles
JNP
Jacomb-Hood, George Percy
Landseer, Edwin Henry
Leader, Benjamin Williams
Leech, John
Manet, Edouard
Mower, Martin
Nash, John Northcote
Pash, Florence
Paxton, William McGregor
Pignoux
Sant, James
Spurrier, Steven
Stevens, Alfred
Taylor, Liz
Tenniel, John
Tissot, James Jacques Joseph
Turner, Edwin Page
Wedderburn, Jemima

CURLING

Allan, David
Anderson, Robert
Browne, Thomas
Brueghel, Pieter
Doyle, Charles
Duncan (Mr.)
"Elf"
Evans, William
Gibb, J.
Hardie, Charles Martin
Harvey, George
Lees, Charles
Levack, John
McKay, John
McLennan
Maxwell-Reekie, William
Reid, Samuel
Ritchie, John
Stevenson, William Grant
Symington, J. Ayton
Weaver, Arthur
Wedderburn, Jemima

DOG-FIGHTING

Alken, Samuel Henry
Bright, J. (op.1858)
Johns, W.E.
Scanlan, Richard Robert
Wolstenholme, (Charles)
  Dean, Jnr.

DONKEY RACING

Burras, Thomas
Nicol, Erskine
Park, Henry
Parry, Joseph
Sperling, Diana
Weekes, Herbert William
Whitley, B.

DRESSAGE

Bird, John Harrington
Diepenbecke, Abraham

Eisenberg, Reis d'
Frost, Patricia
Grandjean, Edmund
Jungnickel, Ludwig Heinrich
Vanderbank, John
Whitcombe, Susie

EQUESTRIAN STUDIES

Agasse, Jacques
Alexander, Robert L.
Alken, George
Alken, Henry
Alken, Sefferien John
Allen, Henry
Allen, Joseph
Anderson, John
Archer, Alexander
Archer, J.S.
Armstrong, W.
Arnald, George
Arnold, George
Arsenius, John
Arsenius, Karl
Ashton, George
Askey, Felicity
Atkinson, J.
Atkinson, John
Austen, Winifred
Avery, Milton
Babbage, F.
Bache, Otto
Backshell, W.
Bailey, Wilfred
Baird, Nathaniel
Baker, John, RA
Baker, John
Baker, Wilfred
Baldock, Charles
Baldock, James
Bale, Charles
Banks, A.
Barclay, William
Barenger, James
Barker, Benjamin
Barker, Kathleen
Barker, Thomas Jones
Barraud, Henry
Barraud, William
Barret, George, Snr.
Bath, W.
Bathgate, Hattie
Batt, Arthur J.
Beale, Shell
Beatty, J. Lucas
Beaty, Allan C.
Beauchamp, W.K.A.
Beavis, Richard
Beecham, W.R.
Beer, John Axel
Bell, John Christopher
Bellard, I.B.G.
Bellinger
Bennett, Frank Moss
Bennett, Thomas
Benson, E.
Benson, J.
Benstead, Joseph
Bentley, Joseph
Beresford, Frank
Berry, John
Best, Thomas
Bevan, Robert
Bewick, Thomas
Bielfield, H.
Biggs, Thomas
Bindley, Charles
Bird, John Harrington
Blackburn, Joseph
Blake, Geraldine
Blake, William (of Newhouse)
Blampied, Edmund
Blanche, Jacques
Blazeby, James
Blyth, E.
Board, John
Bombled, Louis
Bond, William
Booth, James William
Boult, Francis
Boultbee, John, Jnr.
Boultbee, Thomas
Boulton, P
Bourgeois, Peter Francis
Bowden, W.
Bowen, Ralph
Bowers, Georgina
Bowman, Jean

Boyle, Cerise
Boyne, John
Bradley, V.F.
Bradley, William
Brereton, Robert
Bridgehouse, Robert
Briggs, G.
Briggs, H.
Bright, Alfred
Bristow, Edmund
Brocas, William
Brock, Richard Henry
Brompton, Richard
Brooke, John William
Brookes, Lionel
Brooks, Thomas
Brown, Cecil
Brown, E.M.
Brown, Edward
Brown, J.
Brown, John
Brown, John Lewis
Brown, Nathaniel
Brown, R.G.
Brown, W.M.
Browne, Gordon Frederick
Browne, Hablot Knight ("Phiz")
Bryant, Alfred Moginie
Buckley, John E.
Budd, C.F.
Bullen, Anne
Bulley, Ashburnham H.
Bunbury, Henry William
Burnet, Mabel F.
Burras, Thomas
Burton, May
Burton, Nancy Jane
Butler, Bryon T.
Butler, Elizabeth
Butler, Thomas
Byles, William
Caldecott, Randolph
Calvert, Charles
Calvert, Henry
Carlaw, John
Carter, E.
Carter, R.J.
Carter, Samuel, Jnr.
Carter, Samuel John
Cattermole, Leonardo
Cattley, George A.
Cawse, John
Cawthorne, Neil
Chalon, Henry Barnard
Chalon, John James
Chalon, Kingsley S.
Chamberlain, Julian Ingersoll
Chamberlain, William
Chapman, W.J.
Chapman, W.P.
Chappell, R.
Cheviot, Lilian
Chichester, N.
Chinnery, George
Christmas, Thomas C.
Church, C.
Clark, Albert, Jnr.
Clark, Albert, Snr.
Clark, Albert James
Clark, Benton
Clark(e), James, Snr.
Clark, Samuel Joseph
Clark, William Albert
Clarke, Maud
Claude, Jean Maxime
Cleaver, Ralph
Clifton, Frances
Clint, George
Clowes, Henry, Jnr.
Coates, Thomas J. (Tom)
Cocking, W.
Cole, A.
Cole, George
Cole, James William
Collier, Imogen
Collins, John
Colmore, Nina
Conner, Angela
Conor, William
Cook, S.J.
Cooper, Abraham
Cooper, Edwin
Cooper, George
Cooper, S.
Cooper, Thomas Sydney
Corbould, Alfred
Corbould, Alfred Hitchens
Corbould, Edward Henry

Cottrell, Edmund
Co(u)zens, William
Craig, Henry Robertson
Craig, James
Cranch, John
Crane, John
Craven, Edward
Crawford, Susan
Crawhall, Joseph E.
Croome, J.D.
Crosby, John
Crowther, Henry
Crozier, Robert
Cunaeus, Conradyn
Cuneo, Terence
Dadelbeek, D.
Dalby, David, of York
Dalby, John
Dalby, Joshua
Daniel, W.B.
Danson, R.
Darlridge, A.A.
Dartiguenave, Victor
Davis, Heather
Davis, Richard Barrett
de Bree, Anthony
de Dreux, Alfred
De Lattre, Henri
Delion, Maddlle
de Montpezat, H.
De Prades, Alfred
de von Blaas, Julius
Dobie, Beatrix
Dobson, Henry John
d'Orsay, Alfred
Douglas, Edwin
Douglas, Keith Sholto
Doutreleau, Pierre
Downing, Charles Palmer
Drewell, Robert
Drummond, Arthur
Dubois, Simon
Dunsmore, John
Duppa, Bryan Edward
Duval, John
Edouart, Augustine
Ellis, Alfred
Elsley, Arthur
Elsley, J.
Elvery, James
Elwell, Robert
Estall, William
Etty, William
Evans, F.S.
Evans, S.B. Hope
Fellow(e)s, William M.
Ferneley, Claude Lorraine
Fiefield, J.
Fielder, E.H.
Fielding, Thales Henry
Fillams, R.
Finch, Charles
Fischer, Johann
Fitz, William
Flanders, French
Folkard, R.W.
Forain, Jean Louis
Forbes, Alexander
Forster, Neil
Foster, Arthur W.
Fothergill, George
Fox, Buscall
Fox, Edwin
Francis, W.
Freelove, William
Freeman, F.C.
Freeman, James
Freeman, James Edward
French, Frederick
Frobisher, Lucy Margaret
Fry, R. Douglas
Furse, John Henry
Galsworthy, Gordon C.
Garbutt, Joseph
Gardner, Caroline Bromley
Garland, William
Garrard, E.
Garrard, R.H., Jnr.
Garraway, Edward
Gatehouse, Charles E.
Gauci, A.M.
Gee, David
Gee, Gilbert
Géricault, Theodore
Gerusez, Victor
Gifford, M.B.
Gilbert, Edward
Gilbert, Joseph
Giles, E.

Gill, Herbert
Gillard, William
Gilliam, T.H.
Gilpin, Sawrey
Glass, John James
Glaze, G.
Gleichen, Helena
Gold
Goldsmith, Callander
Gooch, James
Gooch, Thomas
Goubie, Jean Richard
Graeme, Colin (Roe)
Grant, Francis
Gravely, Percy
Gray
Gray, D.B.
Gray, William
Green, Alfred H.
Green, Henry
Gregory, Charles
Grey, Alfred
Grey, Charles
Greyson, W.
Gribble, Paul
Grimshaw, John Atkinson
Guinard, Gaston
Hagarty, James
Hale, Philip
Halley, Alexander
Halley, W.A.
Hamilton, Letitia
Hamilton, William E.
Hamilton-Renwick, Lionel
Hancock, Charles
Harding, Frederick
Hardman, John
Hardy, Dorothy M.
Hardy, Dudley
Hardy, James
Hargitt, Edward
Hargreaves, John
Hargreaves, Lucy
Harrington, Robert
Harris
Harris, Robert
Harrison, John F.
Harrowing, Walter
Hartley, Thomas C.
Harvey, Marion Roger Hamilton
Hatton, Brian
Havell, Charles Richard
Havell, Robert, Jnr.
Hawken, Joy
Hayes, Michael
Heath, Charles
Heath, Thomas Haste
Herring, Charles
Herring, John Frederick, Jnr.
Highton, T.
Hilditch, George
Hill, G.M.
Hill, J.C.
Hill, James John
Hills, Robert
Hixon, William
Hoad, Norman
Hobart, John R.
Hogg, Arthur H.
Holding, Henry James
Holiday, Charles Gilbert
Hollams, Mabel F.
Hollis, Thomas
Holmes, Edward
Holmes, George Augustus
Holt, Edwin Frederick
Holt, Ellen F.
Hopkins, William H.
Howard, Frank
Howie, A.
Hubbard, Bennet
Hulley, T.
Hutchinson, Peter C.
Hutchison, Robert Gemmell
Ingall, Susan
Ingpen, A.W.
Israels, Isaac
Jackson, George E.
Jacobs, John Emmanuel
Jagger, David
Jennings, E.
Johnson, Edward Killingworth
Johnson, F.
Johnson, J. William
Jones, Adrian
Jones, Charles

Jones, George
Jones, Herbert H.
Jones, Louie Johnson
Jones, Richard
Jones, Samuel John Egbert
Josi, Charles
Joy, Thomas Musgrove
Kearsley, Nigel
Keeling, E.J.
Keeping, Charles William James
Keith, N.M. Barry
Kemp-Welch, Lucy Elizabeth
Keyl, Friedrich Wilhelm
Kidd, William
Killingbeck, Benjamin
Kinch, Henry
Kingwell, Mabel Amber
Knight, S.S.
Lacretelle, Jean Edouard
Ladbrooke, John Berney
Lambert, E.F.
Lambert, James, Snr.
Landseer, Edwin Henry
Laporte, George Henry
Laskowski, François
Latoix, Gaspard
Lawrence, Joshua
Lawrence, Richard
Leakey, James
Lewis, Charles George
Lewis, Frederick Christian
Linklater, Barrie R.
Livens, Horace Mann
Lloyd, Edward
Lock, Anton
Lock(e), William
Lockwood, Lucy
Loder, Edwin
Loder, James, of Bath
Longbottom, Robert J.
Loraine, Nevison Arthur
Love, Horace Beevor
Luard, Lowes Dalbiac
Lucas Lucas, William
Luker, William, Jnr.
Lutyens, Charles Augustus Henry
Lutyens, Frederick Mansfield
Lycett, J.
Lyon, David
Macbeth-Raeburn, Henry Raeburn
Macbeth-Raeburn, Marjorie May
McCoy, Margaret H.
Macdonnell-Dixon, Clive
Macleod, John
McLeod, Juliet
MacQuoid, Percy
McTaggart, M.F.
Maiden, Joshua
Mann, Harrington
Margetts, J.W.
Mark, James
Marsden, William
Marshall, John
Marshall, Lambert
Marshall, Maude G.
Marshall, William Elstob
Marson, Thomas E.
Martin, Charles
Matania, Fortunino
Matthews, John Chester
Mattinson, Donald
May, Philip (Phil) William
Mayne, C.L.
Meacham, Phyllida
Mease, J.
Meggeson (Miggeson), J.J.
Meissonier, Jean Louis Ernest
Meyer, Emile
Meyer, F. John
Miles, William
Millais, Raoul Hesketh
Miller, George W.
Miller, J.
Miller, James
Millner, William
Millner, William Edward
Mills, Reginald
Milnes, H.
Mitchell, E.
Mitchell, Winslow
Moerenhout, Joseph (Josef)
Mogford, John
Mogford, Thomas
Moody, Fannie

Morier, David
Morley, George
Morris, Alice
Munnings, Alfred James
Mynors, Stella
Nairn, George
Nakken, Willem Carel
Neame, Austin
Neilson, Raymond
Newmarch, G.B.
Nicholson, Francis
Nieuwerhuys, E.
Nodder, Richard
Nowell, Arthur
Noyes, Henry James
Oldmeadow, F.A.
Osborne, Walter
Osborne, William
Page, Robert
Page, William
Palfrey, Penry
Palmer, James Lynwood
Palmer, W.
Park, Henry
Parsons, Elizabeth
Partridge, Alfred A.
Partridge, Henry T.
Paul, John
Pawley, James
Payne, William
Peat, Thomas
Perling, Robert
Pernel, Jean
Petit-Gerard, Pierre
Philips, Charles
Phillips, Douglas
Pichat, Oliver
Picola Y Lopez, Emanuel
Pitman, A.B.
Pitman, John
Poingdestre, Charles
Pollard, James
Pollett(ott), J.
Powell, William
Pratere, Joseph de la
Pride, John
Pringle, William J.
Prior, Melton
Prout, Millicent Margaret
Quadal, Martin Ferdinand
Quarrie, Henry
Quinton, Alfred
Randel, Friedrich (Frederick)
Rasmussen, Peter
Raven-Hill, Leonard
Redworth, William
Reeve, Russell
Reinagle, P.A.
Reinagle, Philip
Renwick, Lionel Hamilton
Reville, Henry Whittaker
Richardson, Harry
Richardson, Ralph
Richter, Wilhelm
Ricketts, Joy Stanley
Rigg, Ernest H.
Ritchie, Alec P.F.
Riviere, Briton
Riviere, Hugh
Roberts, Thomas
Roberts, Thomas Sautelle
Robertson, C.H.
Robertson, David T.
Robertson, George
Robertson, J.
Robinson, Thomas
Robinson, William A.
Roe, Colin Graeme
Roe, Frederick (Fred)
Roe, Robert
Roller, George
Roos, William
Roper, Richard
Roper, Thomas
Ross, James, Snr.
Rowlandson, George Derville
Ruggles, W.H.
Ryman, E.V.
Ryot, of Newcastle, J.R.
Salkin, Emile
Samuels, J.
Sands, B.
Sartorius, G.W.
Sartorius, John
Sayer, Mary Anne
Scaife, Thomas
Scanlan, Richard Robert
Schmitz, Jules Leonard

Schwanfelder, Charles Henry
Scrivens, William
Seago, Edward Brian
Searle, A.A.
Seavey, E. Leone
Sebright, George
Selfe, Madelaine
Selous, Percy
Sendel(l), John
Sextie, William A.
Seymour, James
Shaw, William
Shaw, William (op.1826)
Shayer, William, Snr.
Shayer, William Joseph
Shepherd, Stanfield
Sheppard, R.
Sheriff, John ("Dr. Syntax")
Sherman, C.
Shuttleworth, Arnold Clarke
Sidley, Samuel
Simkins, Edith
Simpson, F.
Simpson, W.P.
Singleton, John
Skeaping, John Rattenbury
Slaughter, Stephen
Smellie, Robert
Smetham-Jones, George W.
Smith, Charles Lorraine
Smith, J.B.
Smith, J.L.
Smith, Phil(ip) W.
Smith, Thomas (of Derby)
Smythe, Emily R.
Smyth(e), Sidney
Snape, J.
Soper, George
Spence, Percy Frederick
  Seaton
Spencer, Thomas
Sperling, Henry
Sperling, J.W.
Spicer, Charles
Spilsbury, Edgar Ashe
Spode, Samuel
Stark, Arthur James
Steell, Gourlay
Stevens, George
Stevens, Meg J.
Stirling-Brown, A.E.D.G.
Stonelake, Frank P.
Stoward, F.
Strafford, Hector
Stretton, Philip Eustace
Stringer, Daniel
Stringer, Francis
Stringer, Samuel
Stringer, Thomas
Strutt, Alfred William
Stubbs, George
Stubbs, George Townley
Stubbs, Richard Spencer
Sullivan, Luke
Suthers, Leghe
Tait, G.W.
Talmage, Algernon Mayow
Tanner, C. (of Dublin)
Tanner, J.
Tapping, G.
Tasker, William H. (of
  Chester)
Tatchell-Bullen, C.
Tattersall, George
  ("Wildrake")
Tayler, John Frederick
Taylor, Stephen
Temple, T.
Terrot, Susan
Thackeray, T.
Thelwell, Norman
T(h)ompson, Jacob C.
Thomson (Thompson), James
Thorley, John
Thornely, Hubert
Thurlby, Frank
Tinkler, W.A.
Tippet, W.V.
Todd, Robert Clow
Tolley, Edward
Tomson, Clifton (of
  Nottingham)
Tournachon, Gaspard Félix
Towne, Charles
Towne, Francis
Treen, R.
Trickett, W. Wasdell
Trowell, Johnathan
Truman, I.P.

Truman, J.
Tschaggeny, Charles
  Philogene
Tulloch, Maurice
Tunnard, John Charles
Tunnicliffe, Charles
  Frederick
Turner, Elizabeth
Turner, J.
Turner, Marjorie
Turner, W.H.
Turner, W.H.M. (Horse
  Fair)
Turner, William Eddowes
Urquhart, Murray McNeel
  Caird
Valentine, John
Valkers, Karl
Vanderbank, John
Van Jones
Verboeckhoven, Eugene
  Joseph
Vernet, Carl
Vernet, Horace
Vernon, Walter
Verschuur, Wouter
Vine, John (of Colchester)
Volkers, Emile
Von Blaas, Julius
Von Wagner, Alexander
Voss, C.J.
Voss, Franklin Brooke
Wadsworth, Thomas
Wahlbom, Carl
Waldburger, J.B.
Wales, James
Walker, Henry
Walker, James
Walker, Joseph Francis
  (John)
Waller, Samuel Edmund
Wallis, Joseph Haythorne
Walmesley, J.M.
Walter, Henry G.
Walton, Henry
Walwyn, Jean
Wanklyn, Joan
Ward, George Raphael
Ward, James
Ward, Martin Theodore
Wardle, C. Francis
Watson, John Dawson
Watt, Daniel
Weatherby, Richard Charles
Weaver, Thomas (of
  Shropshire)
Webb
Webb, Byron
Webb, George
Webb, I.M.
Webb, William (of
  Tamworth)
Weber, Otto
Webster, E. Amelia
Weirs, M.
Welch, Rosemary
Welles, E.F.
Wells, Henry Tanworth
Wells, S.
Whaite, T.
Whaley, F.
Wharam, H.
Wheatley, Francis
Wheeler, Alfred, Jnr.
Wheeler, Amelia
Wheeler, Edward J.
  (Edmund)
Wheeler, John Alfred
Wheeler, John (James)
  Thomas
Wheelwright, Hene P.
Wheelwright, Rowland
Wheelwright, W.
Whelfton, G.L.
Whitby, T.B.
Whitehead, Tom
Whiteman, V.E.
Whitford(e), T.R.
Whitford, Richard
Whiting, Frederick (Fred)
Whitmarsh, Eliza
Whitmore, Evelyn Wolnycke
Whitmore, Olive
Whittenbury, C.H.
Widdas, John
Williams, Alfred Sheldon
Williams, W.D.
Williams, William
Williamson, W.

Willington, Bernard
Willoughby, William
Wilson, J.F.
Wilson, John
Wilson, M. Wharton
Wilson, Matisse
Wilson, Thomas Fairbairn
Wilson, Violet
Winder, Daniel
Winly, C.J.
Winter, Cornelius Jason
  Walter
Wombile, I./T.W.
Woodhouse, Frederick, Jnr.
Woods, James B.
Woodville, Richard Caton
Woodward, George Moutard
Woodward, Thomas
Woolcott, D.
Woollett, Henry A.
Woollett, Henry Charles
Wootton, John
Worsdale, John R.
Worth, Leslie
Worth, Thomas
Wortham, M.
Wright, George
Wright, Joseph (of Derby)
Wright, S.R.
Yarwood, Henry
Yeomans, Thomas
Young, William Weston
Zaefferer, Adrianna
Zellenberg, Franz Zeller Von
Zew, T.E.
Zinkeisen, Doris Clare

ETON WALL GAME

Evans, William
Norman, Philip

FENCING

Avery, Milton
Bromley, Valentine
Brown, Frederick (Fred)
Brown, Mather
Brunery, François
Charlton, Evan
Clark, John Cosmo
Cohen, Isaac Michael
Craig, David (1888-1961)
Evans, Frederick
Fabris, Pietro
Fletcher, Geoffrey
Gillray, James
Glindoni, Henry
Gow, Andrew Carrick
Gwi(y)n, James
Hoque, Zil
Lambert, George Washington
Laroon (Lauron), Marcellus
  II
Laserstein, Lotte
Leslie, Charles Robert
Meyer, Gottfried
Mortimer, John Hamilton
Pienne, Arnold
Rawlins, Thomas J.
Regamy, Frederic
Robineau, Charles
Robinson, William Howard
Rowlandson, Thomas
Seligman, Edgar
Simpson, Charles Walter
Smith, Herbert Luther
Smith, John Raphael
Townsend, Frederick Henry
  Linton Jehne
Unsworth, Peter
Walker, Maude

FERRETING

Barker, W. Bligh
Douglas, Edwin
Good(e), W.E.
Hancock, Charles
Lewis, John Frederick
Marshall, William Elstob

FISHING

See **ANGLING/FLY
  FISHING**

FIVES

Dighton, Robert

FOOTBALL

See **ASSOCIATION
  FOOTBALL**

**FOX/STAG/BOAR
  HUNTING**

Absolon, John
Adam, Albrecht
Adam, Benno
Adam, Benno Rafael
Adams, Henry Clayton
Aitkin, R. Sinclair
Alderson, D.M. and E.M.
Aldin, Cecil
Aldridge, Denis
Aldworth, Ernest W.
Alexander, Robert L.
Alken, George
Alken, Henry
Alken, Samuel
Allen, Henry
Allinson, Garlies
Andrews, Henry
Ansell, Charles
Armfield, George
Armour, George
Arsenius, John
Atkinson, John
Babbage, F.
Baird, Nathaniel
Baker, Arthur
Baker, John, RA
Baker, Wilfred
Baldock, Charles
Baldock, James
Barclay, James
Barclay, William
Barenger, James
Barker, Wright
Barlow, Francis
Barratt, Thomas
Barraud, Henry
Barraud, William
Barry, James
Barwick, John
Bateman, Henry Mayo
Bath, W.
Batsford, Brian
Beauchamp, W.K.A.
Beaufort, C.
Beavis, Richard
Beedlemaker, Adriaaen
Beer, W. Andrew
Begg, Samuel
Bell, A.D.
Bennett, Frank Moss
Bennett, Thomas
Benstead, Joseph
Berkeley, Stanley
Bevan, Robert
Biegel, Peter
Binns, David
Bird, John Harrington
Bishop, Alfred
Blake, Geraldine
Blake, J.
Blanche, Jacques
Blinks, Thomas
Blyth, E.
Boodle, Walter
Booth, J.L.C.
Boult, Francis
Boultbee, Thomas
Bourhill, James
Bowers, Georgina
Bowman, Jean
Boyle, Cerise
Bradley, Basil
Bradley, Cuthbert
Bradley, V.F.
Brakespeare, William
Bramley, Frank
Branscombe, Charles
Breakell, Mary
Bremy, J.R.
Bretland, Thomas
Breun, John
Bridgeman, G.
Briscoe, Arthur
Brock, Richard Henry
Brook, Maria
Brooke, E. Adveno
Brooke, William
Brown, Cecil
Brown, John Lewis
Brown, R.W.
Browne, Hablot Knight
  ("Phiz")

Browne Blair, Nassau
Browne, Philip
Bucknall, Ernest
Bullen, John
Bunbury, Henry William
Burt, Revell N.
Butcher, Laura
Butterworth, Ninetta
Buxton, Robert
Byng, Robert
Calderon, (William) Frank
Calvert, Henry
Cantelo, C.
Carlile, Joan
Carr, Tom
Carter, Hugh
Carter, Samuel John
Cattley, George A.
Catton, Charles, Snr.
Cawthorne, Neil
Chalon, Henry Barnard
Chamberlain, Julian Ingersoll
Chambers, Alfred
Chapeau, E.C.
Chappell, William
Charles-Jones, Alexander
Charlton, John
Choquet, René
Clampitt, W.J.
Clark, Benton
Clark, Christopher
Clark(e), James, Snr.
Clark, W.
Clark, Maud
Cleaver, Reginald
Cleaver, Roland
Clennell, Luke
Clowes, Daniel
Clowes, Frederick
Clowes, Henry, Snr.
Coates, Michael
Cockburn, R.D.
Cole, George
Cole, James William
Coleman, Charles
Collet, John
Collier, H.H.
Collier, Imogen
Collier, John
Cooper, Thomas George
Cooper, W.P.
Corbet, Edward
Corbould, Alfred Chantrey
Corbould, Aster
Crabtree, Percy
Craig, Frank
Crane, R.
Crawhall, Joseph E.
Crealock, Henry
Crooke, Muriel
Croome, C.J.
Croome, J.D.
Crosby, John
Crossman, F.G.
Cruikshank, George, Snr.
Cunliffe, David
Cutler, Cecil
Dadd, Frank
Dalby, David, of York
Dalby, John
Dalby, Joshua
Daniel, T. Llewelyn
Daniell, Thomas
Davidson, A. Murray
Davis, Arthur
Davis, Charles F.
Davis, Heather St. Clair
Davis, Henry William Banks
Davis, Richard Barrett
Davis, Thomas R.
Davis, Tyddesley
Davis, William Henry
Day, T.
Dayrell, B.
de Bree, Anthony
de Dreux, Alfred
de Gryeff, Adriaan
Demoline, A.
Dent, Rupert Arthur
Denyer, David
De Penne, Olivier
De Prades, Alfred
De Prades, Frank
De Wint, Peter
Desportes, Alexandre
Desvignes, Herbert
Dighton, Richard
Dill, Otto
Dingle, Thomas

Dixon, George H.
Dodd, Arthur
Dollman, John Charles
Dollman, Ruth
Donnithorne, Peter
Douglas, Edward
Douglas, Edwin
Douglas, W.
Dovaston, Margaret
Downing, Charles Palmer
Doyle, John ("HB")
Drake, Nathan
Drumach, H.B.
Drummond, E.
Drummond, Norah Hardy
Dubois, Simon
Dudgeon, James
Dudley, Miss
Du Gravier, A.
Duke, Alfred
Dunn, Joseph
Dunthorne, James
Duppa, Bryan Edward
Duval, John
Eakins, Thomas
Earl, Thomas
Earp, Henry, Snr.
East, Adam
Eden, William
Edwards, Charles
Edwards, James
Edwards, Lionel
Edwards, Sydenham
Egerton, Daniel
Eliot, Granville
Ellis, C. Wynn
Ellison, Alan
Elwell, Francis
Emms, John
Emms, John Victor
England, E.S.
Eyres, Emily
Faulkner, Charles
Fenn, George
Ferneley, Claude Lorraine
Ferneley, John, Snr.
Ferneley, John, Jnr.
Ferneley, Sarah
Fisher, Jonathan
Fitch, Fred
Fitzgerald, Claude
Fitzgerald, Florence
Fletcher, Rosamund
Fleury, H.
Forbes, Alexander
Forrest, William S.
Forster, Percy
Foster, Arthur W.
Foster, Myles Birket
Foster (Forster), Paul
Fothergill, George
Fox, Henry
Francis, Catharine
Frankland, Robert
French, E.C.
Freyburg, Frank
Fry, Joseph
Fryer, William
Fulton, Samuel
Furness, Robin
Furse, Charles Wellington
Gael, Barent
Galloway, Madge
Garland, Valentine
Gear, Joseph
Gee, Gilbert
Gérome, Jean Leon
Gessner, Johann
Gibb, Harry Phelan
Gibson, C.W.
Gilbert, Terence
Gilchrist, Herbert H.
Giles, Godfrey
Giles, James William
Giles, John West
Gill, Edwyn
Gill, F.T.
Gillet(t), Edward Frank
Gillray, James
Gilpin, Sawrey
Gleichen, Helena
Goddard, Charles
Goddard, George
Goldsmith, Callander
Good(e), John
Goodrich, William
Goodwin, Albert
Gould, Alexander Carruthers

Gower, Thomas
Grant, A.
Grant, Francis
Grant, John
Grant, William
Graves, John
Gray, Cedric
Gray, John
Green, James
Gresley, Harold
Grierson, Charles
Griffier, Robert
Griffiths, C.J.
Grimbaldeston, Walter
Grimstone, Edward
Grunler, Lois
Gryeff, Adriaan de
Guest, Miss
Guest, Alison
Hackert, Johann
Haddelsey, Vincent
Haigh, Arthur
Hainsworth, Arthur
Halfpenny, Joseph
Hall, Arthur
Hamilton, Charles
Hamilton-Renwick, Lionel
Hammick, Joseph
Hammond, Arthur
Hammond, Gertrude
Hammond, Henry
Hammond, Horace
Hancock, Charles
Hancock, Robert
Hand, Thomas
Hanfstaengl, Franz
Hardman, Thomas
Hardy, David
Hardy, Dorothy M.
Hardy, Dudley
Hardy, Edmund
Hardy, Heywood
Hargreaves, John
Harper, H.G. ("G.G.")
Harrison, George
Harrison, John F.
Harvey, R.L.
Havell, Edmund, Jnr.
Hawkins, Hency
Haycock, Frederick
Haydon, Benjamin
Hayes, Claude
Hayes, S.H.B.
Heal(e)y, Robert
Hearne, Thomas
Heath, R.B.
Henderson, William
Hendrie, Robert
Henrard, Hubert
Henwood, Thomas
Hepple, Wilson
Herberte, Edward Benjamin
Herring, Benjamin, Snr.
Herring, Benjamin, Jnr.
Herring, John Frederick, Snr.
Hesp, Agnes E.
Hester, Robert Wallace
Hill, Derek
Hill, F.L.
Hill, Rowland
Hillyard, J.W.
Hilton, William
Hine, Harry
Hodges, Walter Parry
Hodgson, W.
Holiday, Charles Gilbert
Holt, Ellen F.
Hopkins, William H.
Horlor, George
Horner, George Christopher
Horner, Thomas
Howe, James
Howitt, Samuel
Huggins, William
Hulk, John Frederick
Hull, Edward
Hyland, Benedict
Isom, Graham
Ivester-Lloyd, Jack
Ivester-Lloyd, Thomas
Jalland, George Herbert
Jank, Angelo
Jay, J.A.B.
Joel, Charles
Johnson, Avery F.
Johnson, Charles Edward
Johnson, Henry W.
Johnson, J.J.

Johnson, J. William
Jones, George Smetham
Jones, Herbert St. John
Jonniaux, Alfred
Josi, Charles
June, John
Keane, Michael Anthony
Kearsley, Nigel
Keene, Charles Samuel
Keith, A.W.
Kenney, John Theodore Eardley
Key, Katherine
Kilburne, George Goodwin, Snr.
Kilburne, George Goodwin, Jnr.
Kinch, Hayter
King, John Gregory
Kingwell, Mabel Amber
Knapton, George
Knight, John William Buxton
Knight, William Henry
Knowles, Frederick J.
Koch, Ludwin
Koehler, Henry
Kossak, Jerzy (Jerry)
La Fontaine, Thomas Sherwood
Lambert, Joseph W.
Lami, Eugène Louis
Lander, Benjamin
Laporte, George Henry
Laroon (Lauron), Marcellus III
Latham, Molly M.
Lauder, Charles James
Laurence, Frank
Leakey, James
Leatham, Ruth M.
Leech, John
Leemans, Antonius
Leemans, Johannes
Lees, Caroline
Leigh, Conrad Heighton
Leigh-Pemberton, John
Leighton, Nicolas Winfield S.
Leit, C.H.
Lemon, Arthur
Leslie, John
Lessore, Jules
Lewis, Judith
Lier, Adolf Heinrich
Lindsay, Ernest Daryl
Lock(e), William
Logsdail, William
Longe, William Verner
Lucas Lucas, Henry Frederick
Lumley, John Savile
Lutyens, Charles Augustus Henry
Lutyens, Frederick Mansfield
Lynch, Stanislaus
Lyne, Charles Edward Michael
Macbeth, Robert Walker
McCoy, Margaret H.
McTaggart, M.F.
Madge
Madgwick, Clive
Maiden, Joshua
Maling, S.
Marshall, Benjamin
Marshall, Charles H.
Marshall, Maude G.
Martin, Anson
Martin, Sylvester
Mason, George Finch
Massey, F.E.
Maud, W.T.
May, Charles
May, Fred
Meade-King, Eric
Meadows, Edwin L.
Meagher, William
Mease, J.
Mew, Thomas Hillier
Milbanke, Mark
Millais, Raoul H.
Millner, William Edward
Mills, Reginald
Mitchell, J.A.
Mitchell, John Campbell
Moody, Fannie
Moorhouse, George
Morby, Walter J.
Morgan, William

Morland, George
Morley, George
Morrell, R.J.
Morris, John
Morris, Philip
Morrish, William Snell
Morshead, Arminell
Mundy, W.
Munnings, Alfred J.
Murray, David
Murray, H.
Murray, William (W.L.?)
Mynors, Stella
Neale, Edward
Nedham (Needham), William
Neilson, Harry
Nesbitt, Charles
Newton, Algernon
Newton, Ethel
Newton, I. or J.
Newton, Richard, Jnr.
Nicholls, George F.
Nicholls, W.
Nicholson, William
Nightingale, Basil
Nightingale, Robert
Nodder, Richard
Noel, John Bates
Norman, F.M.
North, Brownlow
Novice, William
O'Donnell, Hugh
Oldfield, John
Oldmeadow, F.A.
Opie, John
Oppenheimer, Joseph
Orchardson, Charles
Orchardson, William
Osborne, William
O'Shea, G.P.
Oudry, Jean Baptiste
Paice, George
Pardon, James
Parker, Henry Perlee
Parker, W.
Parkes, Joanna
Parrocel, Charles
Parry, Leigh
Parry, William
Partridge, Alfred A.
Paton, Frank
Patrick, James McIntosh
Paul, John Dean
Paull, A.B.
Pawley, James
Payne, Charles ("Snaffles")
Pearce, Stephen
Peile, Edith M.
Pell, Catherine M.
Perboyre, Paul
Percy, Herbert Sidney
Petit-Gerard, Pierre
Peto, Ralph
Philips, Charles
Pic, Marcel
Picola Y Lopez, Emanuel
Pigott, William Henry
Pike, Sidney
Pirie, George
Pitman, John
Platt, John
Pocock, Innes
Pocock, J.
Pollard, A. Read
Power, Harold Septimus
Pratere, Joseph de la
Prebble, C.
Prior, W.
Pritchett, Robert Taylor
Quintin, H.J.
Ragell, R.
Rasmussen, Peter
Raven, Samuel
Ray, Stuart
Reinagle, Philip
Reinagle, Ramsay Richard
Richardson, Ralph
Richter, Wilhelm
Rideout, Philip H.
Ridinger, Johann
Riley, J.W.
Ripley, Aiden Lassell
Robb, Emma
Roberton, A.
Roberts, Thomas
Robson, R.
Roche, Christopher
Rollo, Roger
Rope, George Thomas

Ross, Gordon
Ross, James, Snr.
Rothwell, Thomas
Rowland, Bertram
Rowlandson, George Derville
Rungius, Carl Clemens Moritz
Rutard, Carl
Ryot, of Newcastle, J.R.
Rysbrack, Pieter Andreas
Sadler, William
Sanderson-Wells, John
Sandys-Lumsdaine, Leesa
Sanguinetti, Eduardo
Sartorius, Francis
Sartorius, John Francis
Sartorius, John Nost (Nott)
Scanlan, Richard Robert
Scheuerer, Julius
Schofield, John
Scott, Septimus Edwin
Scrags, John
Sealy, Allen Culpeper
Selfe, Madelaine
Seymour, James
Sharp, H.C.
Shaw, Hugh George
Shaw, Joshua (of Bath)
Shayer, Henry Thring
Shayer, William Joseph
Shepherd, William James Affleck
Short, Arthur Anderson
Short, Frederick Golden
Siberechts, Jan
Simons, Pinky Marcius
Simpson, Charles Walter
Simpson, H. Hardey
Smart, G.
Smith, Charles Lorraine
Smith, Graham
Smith, Thomas ("Gentleman Smith")
Smith, Vivian
Smythe, Edward Robert
Smythe, Ernest
Snow, John Wray
Snowdon, Florence A.
Somerset, Richard Gay
Somerville, Edith Anna Oenone
Spalding, Charles B.
Sparrow, Geoffrey
Spencelayh, Charles
Sperling, Diana
Spode, Samuel
Stampa, George Loraine
Standing, Henry William
Steell, David George
Steinacker, Alfred
Stewart, Charles Edward
Stewart, Frank Algernon
Stirling-Brown, A.E.D.G.
Stone, Robert
Stone, Rudolph
Straet, Jan van der
Stretton, Philip Eustace
Stringer, Thomas
Strutt, Arthur John
Stuart (Steuart), John James
Stubbs, George
Stubbs, Richard Spencer
Sturgess, John
Such, William Thomas
Sullivan, Luke
Sunderland, Thomas
Sutcliffe, John E.
Swan, Cuthbert Edmund
Swebach, Bernard Edouard
Swinburn, W.
Tanner, J.
Tatchell-Bullen, C.
Tavernier, Paul
Tayler, John Frederick
Taylor, George
Taylor, J.W.
Temple, Alfred George
Temple, T.
Temple, W.H.
Tennant, John F.
Tenniel, John
Thirtle, John
Thomas, Bert
T(h)ompson, Jacob C.
Thomson, Alfred Reginald
Thomson, I. Beatrice
Thomson, John Murray
Thorne, Diana
Thornton, Herbert

Tickner, John
Tillemans, Peter
Torrome, Francisco (Frank) J.
Townsend, Frederick Henry Linton Jehne
Townshend, Arthur Louis
Travers, Florence
Travis, Stuart
Trood, William Henry Hamilton
Tuck, William Henry
Tulloch, Maurice
Tunnard, John Charles
Turmeau, John
Turner, Francis Calcraft
Turner, M.F. (of Nottingham)
Turner, Marjorie
Underhill, William
Usher, James Ward
Uspensky
Vachell, R.
Van der Putten, Daniel
Van der Vinne, Jan
Van Uden, Lucas
Veal, George
Vernet, Carl
Vernon, Arthur Langley
Verpilleux, Emile Antoine
Volkers, Emile
Voss, Franklin Brooke
Wahlbergson, Erik
Walker, Anthony
Walker, James Alexander
Walker, Joseph Francis (John)
Walker, R. Hollands
Walker, William Henry
Wallace, Harold Frank
Waller, Samuel Edmund
Walsh(e), Thomas N.H.
Waltman, Harry Franklin
Ward, Martin Theodore
Wardlow, Alexander Hamilton
Warren, Henry Clifford
Warren, James R. Warren
Washington, Georges
Watmough, G.
Watson, John Dawson
Weatherby, Richard Charles
Weaver, Thomas (of Shropshire)
Webb, Edward Walter
Webb, Octavius
Webb, William (of Tamworth)
Webster, E. Amelia
Wells, Henry Tanworth
Went, Alfred
West, Peter B.
West, Waldron
Westrup, E. Kate
Wheeler, Amelia
Wheeler, Frederick John ("Jack")
Wheeler, John Alfred
Wheeler, John (James) Thomas
Wheelwright, Rowland
Wheelwright, W.H.
Whitcombe, Susie
Whitehead, Frederick William Newton
Whiting, Frederick (Fred)
Whitmore, Olive
Whydale, Ernest Herbert
Widdas, Robert Dodd
Widgery, Frederick John
Widgery, William
Wierusz-Kowalski, Alfred von
Wild, W. Watkins
Willard, Archibald
Willard, Frank
Willett, Arthur Reginald
Williams, Alfred Sheldon
Williams, Edward, Jnr.
Williams, F.R.
Williams, Warren
Williams, William
Willington, Bernard
Willis, Charles
Willis, Edward Aylburton
Willoughby, G.
Wilson, May
Wilson, Winifred
Winter, George
Winter, Johann Georg

Winter, William Tatton
Wolstenholme, Dean, Snr.
Wolstenholme, (Charles) Dean, Jnr.
Wood, William
Woodville, Richard Caton
Woodward, Nathan
Woodward, Thomas
Woog, J.
Woollett, Henry A.
Woollett, Henry Charles
Wootton, John
Wright, George
Wright, Gilbert Scott
Wright, Nora
Wyck, Jan (Jan van Wijck)
Wyniatt, Captain
Yeames, William Frederick
Young, H.B.
Zoffany, Johann

**GAME BIRDS
DEAD AND ALIVE**

Adams, W. Douglas
Ainslie, Miss
Amoore, E.J.
Arnold, George (1753-1806)
Atkinson, Christopher
Atkinson, E.
Audubon, John
Ausiter, T.
Austen, Winifred
Bacon, D'Arcy
Baily, R.M.
Barker, W. Bligh
Barry, Frederick
Bell, Edward
Benstead, Joseph
Berthoud, Henry
Best, John
Bewick, Robert
Bewick, Thomas
Blake, Benjamin
Bowles, Ian
Bright, Harry
Brown, R.G.
Bullock, G.G.
Cadogan, Sidney
Callaway, William
Campbell-Black, Geoffrey
Carter, Henry William
Chantry, N.
Chapman, Abel
Chapman, John Watkins
Cleminson, Robert
Cocking, Edward
Coleman, Edward
Collet, John
Comber, Mary
de Gryeff, Adriaan
Edwards, Sydenham
Eglington, Samuel
Ehlers, Ernest
Eichel, G.
Elliott, Daniel
Ellis, Edwin
Elmer, William
Fisk, William Henry
Fitz, William
Fowler, William
Fraser, Alexander
Fraser, Alexander George
Frohawk, Frederick
Giller, William C.
Glaze, G.
Goodwin, Richard le Barre
Goodwin, S.
Grant, James
Hardy, W. Howard
Harper, John
Harrington, Robert
Harris, Albert
Harrison, John Cyril
Hawkins, Waterhouse Benjamin
Haycock, G.B.
Haycock, Washington
Hicks, Mary
Hicks, Minnie J.
Hodgkinson, Cecil Thomas
Hold, Abel
Hold, Ben
Hold, Thomas
Holland, Philip
Hollyer, W.P.
Horlor, George
Howe, B.A.
Hughes, Edward
Hunt, Lynn Bogue

Innes, Augusta
Jardine, William
Kelly, Richard Barrett Talbot
Kidd, William
Knip, Henriette
Lear, Edward
Macaulay, M.M.
Machen, William
Martell, Isaac
Mason, William (1809-1875)
Millais, John Guille
Millichap, G.T.
Milliken, Robert
Monahan, Hugh
Morland, John
Morris, Alfred
Morris, Alice
Morris, James Charles
Neale, Edward
Nicholson, Richard E.
Padley, Robert
Paillou, Peter
Park, James Chalmers
Partington, Peter
Pethick, Maxwell
Pitman, John
Poingdestre, Charles
Pollett(ott), J.
Pope, George F.
Potts, John Laslett
Powell, E.R.
Powell, William E.
Rankin, George
Read, John
Richardson, Daniel
Rickman, Philip
Robjent, Richard
Roll, E.
Roper, Richard
Rowden, Thomas
Russell, John B.
Russell, William
Rysbrack, Pieter Andreas
Sanders, W.
Sartorius, John Francis
Scott, Peter Markham
Scrags, John
Seaby, Allen William
Selby, Prideaux John
Shrapnell, E.S.
Shrapnell, N.H.S.
Sibley, Charles
Sillett, James
Smith, C. Webb
Smith, Richard J.
Song, John
Stannard, Emily
Stannard, Emily, Jnr.
Stannard, Henry
Stannard, Ivy
Stevens, George
Stinton, Harry
Stinton, James
Tait, Arthur Fitzwilliam
Taylor, Stephen
Thorburn, Archibald
Tunnicliffe, Charles Frederick
Turck, Eliza
Turner, Joseph Mallord William
Vincent, George
Ward, Vernon
Weenix, Jan
Weenix, Jan Baptist
Weir, William Harrison
Wells, George
Wiberg, Harald
Williams, J.M
Wilson, Alexander
Wingate, James Lawton
Withers, Augusta Innes
Wolf, Joseph
Wolfe-Murray, David ("Fish Hawk")
Woodhouse, William
Young, William Weston

GAME DOGS

Barber, Charles
Binks, Ruben
Bullock, Ralph
Califano, John
Carter, Henry William
Cleminson, Robert
Corbould, Alfred
Crawshaw, J.T.
De Penne, Olivier

Earl, George
Earl, Maud
Edwards, Sydenham
Emms, John
Gillard, William
Gowdy, W.
Graeme, Colin (Roe)
Graves, Frederick
Gray, H. Barnard
Green, Alexander
Grey, Gregor
Gunton, William
Hardy, James, Jnr.
Hardy, W. Howard
Harper, John
Harvey, Marion Roger Hamilton
Hawkins, Waterhouse Benjamin
Hinckley, Thomas Hewes
Horlor, George
Jackson, George E.
Jay, Florence
Jones, Louie Johnson
Jones, Paul
Keyl, Friedrich Wilhelm
King, Jessie Marion
King, Thomas W.
Kingwell, Mabel Amber
Knip, Henriette
Langlois, J.
Lloyd, Edward
Lyon, David
Magill, E.
Marsden, William
Mearns, A.
Morris, Alfred
Morris, James Charles
Morris, John
Morris, William Walker
Moseley, R.S.
Muller, J.
Naish, John
Nettleship, John Trivett
Norton, J.E.
Opie, Alfred
Osthaus, Edmund
Page, Robert
Park, Harry
Pollett(ott), J.
Priest, Alfred
Quadal, Martin Ferdinand
Quarrie, Henry
Rankin, Andrew Scott
Reinagle, Philip
Roebuck, Thomas
Roper, Richard
Rousseau, Percival Leonard
Rungius, Carl Clemens Moritz
Rysbrack, Gerrard
Sanderson, Robert
Sartorius, John
Scannell, Edith M.S.
Schleich, Auguste
Shaw, Hugh George
Shaw, Joshua (of Bath)
Simpson, R.
Slaughter, Stephen
Smith, William
Smythe, Thomas (of Ipswich)
Sperling, Henry
Stevenson, Anthony W.
Stokes, George Vernon
Stratford, Frank
Tanner, C. (of Dublin)
Thomson, I. Beatrice
Thomson, John Murray
Trood, William Henry Hamilton
Turner, W.H.
Turner, William Eddowes
Uchermann, Carl
Wainwright, John
Waller, Lucy
Wallis, Joseph Haythorne
Ward, Vernon
Wardleworth, John L.
Watson, William, Jnr.
Webb, Octavius
Weekes, Henry, Jnr.
Wells, George,
Westall, T.
Westwood, H.
Wiberg, Harald
Williams, Henry
Willis, Edward Aylburton
Woodhouse, William
Young, Tobias

GENERAL SPORT

Alken, Sefferien
Anderson, John
Anderson, Martin
Ashton, George
Askew, Felicity
Ballantyne, R.M.
Banner, Alfred
Barraud, Francis
Bateman, Henry Mayo
Baumer, Lewis
Beauvais, Walter
Beedlemaker, Adriaaen
Bentley, Nicolas
Beuttler, E.G.O.
Bird, Cyril
Boultbee, John, Jnr.
Boultbee, Thomas
Bradley, Edward
Brightwell, Leonard
Browne, Thomas
Bryant, Joshua
Buxton, Dudley
Caldecott, Randolph
Calvert, Charles
Campion, George Bryant
Canchois, Henri
Carlile, Joan
Chalon, Francis
Clater, Thomas
Claude, Jean Maxime
Cleaver, Reginald
Conder, Charles Edward
Corbould, Alfred Chantrey
Corbould, Alfred Hitchens
Corbould, Aster
Craig, Edward Anthony
Currie, R.W.
Dadd, Stephen
Davis, Joseph Lucien
D'Egville, James
Dixon, Henry Hall
Du Maurier, George
Earnshaw, Harold
Elcock, Howard
Emery, W.F.
Essex, William
Farrow, Will
Fellow(e)s, William M.
Ferneley, John E., Snr.
Fores, S.W.
Frederick, William
French, P.C.
Furniss, Harry
Ghilchik, David
Giberne, Edgar
Gilbert, Ellen
Gilbert, Josiah
Gill, Edmund Ward
Gillett, G.
Glackens, William
Gould, Francis Carruthers
Green, Alexander
Griesedieck, Ellen
Gundry, Thomas
Hagarty, James
Haines, William
Halland, C.J.
Hancock, Robert
Hardy, Paul
Hare, Charles
Hartrick, Archibald
Havell, Edmund, Snr.
Hemsley, William
Henry, Paul
Hockney, David
Hodgson, William J.
Hone, Nathaniel
Howe, W.
Howie, James
Hoynck, Otto
Hunt, Charles, Jnr.
Jarvis, George
Kennard, Edward
King, William Gunning
Landells, Ebenezer
Leman, Alicia
Long, John, Jnr.
McDowall, William
McKivragen, Terence
MacLeay, Kenneth
Maile, George
Miró, Joan
Moller, Rudolph
Moore, R.H.
Orme, Ernest
Parry, Joseph
Paterson, Mary Viola

Paye, Richard
Petley (Lieut.)
Peto, John Frederick
Peyton, A.
Phillips, Bert
Pollard, James
Poole, Samuel
Pryde, James
Rafter, H.
Reynolds, Frank
Ribblesdale, Thomas
Ritchie, Alec P.F.
Roberts, James
Robinson, William Heath
Scrags, James
Seymour, George L.
Seymour, Robert
Simms, A.G.
Simpson, J.H.
Smith, G. Hill
Smith, Linda Jane
Stampa, George Loraine
Stinton, Harry
Stockdale, W. Colbrooke
Stokes, George Vernon
Sutton, Jake
Symington, J. Ayton
Tennant, C. Dudley
Terry, Herbert Stanley
Thomson, John
Topham, Francis (Frank)
    William
Trickett, John
Wageman, Thomas Charles
Wall, A.J.
Ward, William
Webster, Tom
Weedon, J.F.
Wheeler, Walter Herbert
Wheelwright, J. Hadwen
Whistler, Rex
Wild, Frank Percy
Wilkins, J.
Wilkinson, Henry
Williams, Inglis Sheldon
Willson, John James
Wilson, H.P.
Wyatt, Robert
Zobel, Benjamin

GOLF

Abbott, Lemuel
Adams, W. Douglas
Addison, V.S.
Aikman, George
Allan, David
Ambrose, Charles
Avercamp, Hendrick
Bannister, Graham
Barlow, Gordon
Barrow, Julian
Bateman, Henry Mayo
Baxter, Graeme
Beauvais, Walter
Bell, James Torrington
Bell, Thomas Blakemore
Benger, Berenger
Bensing, Frank
Berrie, John
Binnie, William
Bird, Cyril
Boin, Rene
Bond, John
Bonnar, John
Bough, Samuel
Bradley, William
Bril, Paul
Brock, Charles Edmund
Brodie, John Lamont
Brown, James Michael
Browne, Thomas
Bruhl, Louis
Buchanan, Fred
Buchanan-Dunlop, A.H.
Cadmus, Paul
Chalmers, George
Chalmers, Hector
Chamberlain, Joseph
Chaulms, T.
Collier, John
Conder, Charles
Craft, Percy
Crawford, Robert Cree
Crombie, Charles E.
Crowther Smith, H.F.
Cundall, Charles
Cuyp, Aelbert
Davidson, Cara
Davison, Jeremiah

De Geest, Wybrand
De Hooch, Pieter
Deykin, Henry
Dollman, John Charles
Donnison, T.E.
Douglas, James
Drummond-Fish, George
Du Maurier, George
Eliott, Harry
Evans, Powys
Ewing, Leckie
Fergusson, William
Fidler, Harry
Fischer, Paul
Fisher, Vernon
Flower, Clement
Forrestier, Amedee
Francis, Mike
Fripp, Innes
Fuchs, Bernard (Bernie)
Fuller, Edmund
Fuller, Leonard
Furniss, Harry
Gallon, Robert
Gamley, Andrew
Gandy, Walton
Gaye, Howard C.
Geddes, Andrew
Ghilchik, David
Gilbert, Frederick
Gill, Arthur Eric
Gilroy, John
Gordon, John Watson
Grant, Francis
Greene, V.
Griesedieck, Ellen
Gustavson, Leland R.
Hamlyn, E.
Hanfstaengl, Franz
Harrison, Christopher
Harvey, H.E.
Hassall, John
Hassam, Childe
Hawkes
Heade, Reginald
Heaphy, Thomas
Heard, Hugh Percy
Henderson, Joseph
Henry, Everett
Hodge, Thomas
Hogarth, Arthur Paul
Hopkins, Arthur
Hopkins, Francis Powell
Houghton, George
Hutchison, Robert Gemmell
Icart, Louis
Jack, Richard
Jones, Dave
Kay, John
Keiller, Raymond
Keller, Arthur I.
"Ken"
Kirkham, Norman
Knight, Charles Neil
Lambert, Clement (Clem)
Lander, Edgar Longley
Laurent, Alfred Joseph
Lavery, John
Lees, Charles
Leigh, Conrad Heighton
Lendon, Warwick William
Lessells, J.
Longstaff, William (Will)
Lorimer, John Henry
Lousada, Maude (Mrs.
    Julian)
McClymont, John I.
McGhie, John
McGill, Donald Fraser
McInnes, Jos
Mackenzie, William
McKivragen, Terence
MacLeay, MacNeil
MacMaster, James
May, Charles
Mayor, William Frederick
Meadows, Gordon Arthur
Melchers, J. Gari
Mellor, John Paget
Meynard, G.
Moreland, Arthur
Morland, John
Morrison, Robert
Neiman, Leroy
Nicholson, Francis
Nisbet, Robert Buchan
Nunes (Nunez), E.F.
Organ, Bryan (Harold)
Orme, Ernest

Orpen, William
Paton, Frank
Patrick, James
Perry, Roy
Pettafor, Charles
Pettit, Edwin Alfred
Pimm, William E.
Pohl, May
Potter, Michael
Proudfoot, James
Pryce, George Willis
Purvis, Tom
Rackham, Arthur
Raeburn, Henry
Ralston, William
Ramsbottom, A.R.
Reed, Kenneth
Reid, George
Rennie, George
Reynolds, Frank
Righi, M.
Ritchie, J.W.
Roberts, Lunt
Robertson, C.H.
Robinson, William Heath
Rountree, Harry
Rowland, Ralph
Ruggiero, Vincent
Russell, Walter Westley
Rutherford, R.H.
Sadler, Walter Dendy
Sandby, Paul
Sandham, Henry
Sato, Take
Scott-Brown, William G.
Sealy, Allen Culpeper
Sharpe, F.J.
Shepard, Ernest Howard
Shepherd, G.E.
Short, M. Dudley
Simpson, Charles Walter
Smart, John
Smith, Garden Grant
Spencelayh, Charles
Spindler, James G.H.
Stampa, George Loraine
Staples, Robert Ponsonby
Stevenson, William Grant
Stewart, Allan
Sydenham, Kenneth
Sykes, Charles ("Rilette")
Taylor, John Whitfield
Thackeray, Lance
Thomson, Hugh
Torborch, Gerard
Townsend, Frederick Henry
    Linton Jehne
Toynbee, Lawrence
Van de Velde, Adriaen
Van de Venne, Adriaen
Van der Helst, Bartholomeus
Van Rijn, Rembrandt
Van Verstalen, Antoni
Vaughan, Harry Nyko
Venner, Victor
Vergett, Noel
Wain, Louis William
Wakefield, W.
Walker, Ethel
Wallace, John ("George
    Pipeshank")
Watkiss, Christopher
Weatherston, J.T.
Weaver, Arthur
Wells, William Page
    Atkinson
West, Douglas
Williams, George Fleming
Wills, J. Anthony
Winter, J.C.
Wood, Clarence Lawson
Wood, Frank Warren
Wood, Starr
Wybrand, Simonz de Geest
Young, Harold (Harry)
Yule, V.T.B.

GYMNASTICS

Rush, Stephen

HAWKING/FALCONRY

Aldin, Cecil
Andrews, Henry
Azars, Imegal de
Barlow, Francis
Biddulph, S.
Birley, Oswald
Brakespeare, William

Bundy, Edgar
Cattermole, George
Chantry, N.
Cook, Joshua
Cottrell, Edmund
Critchley-Salmonson, Mary
Davidson, Thomas
Detti, Cesare
Dighton, Denis
Dobson, Elizabeth
Drake, Nathan
Faulkner, John
Frohawk, Frederick
Gilbert, Terence
Goltzius, Hendrick
Gozzoli, Benozzo
Green, Roland
Griffier, Robert
Hamilton, Anton-Ignaz
Hamilton, Charles
Hammond, William
    Oxendon
Haywood, John
Holbein, Hans
Holding, Henry James
Howe, B.A.
Howe, James
Jackson, Gilbert
Johnson, Herbert
Joy, Thomas Musgrove
Kelly, Robert George Talbot
Lance, George
Lange, Janet
Lewis, John Frederick
Liljefors, Bruno
Lockey (Locky), Rowland
Lodge, George Edward
Nash, Joseph
Northcote, James
Padley, Robert
Peake, Robert (the Elder)
Reader, William
Reeve, Richard Gilson
Reinagle, Philip
Ridinger, Johann
Rousseau, Henri Emilien
Sillett, James
Straet, Jan van der
Tayler, John Frederick
Teniers, David
Thomson, John
Tischbein, Johann-Heinrich
Toulouse-Lautrec, Henri
Tunnicliffe, Charles
    Frederick
Van Eyck, Jan
Waller, Renz
Ward, Edward Matthew
Washington, Georges
Watson, George Spencer
Weenix, Jan
Wheeler, Walter Herbert
Wolf, Joseph

HOCKEY

Barraud, Francis Philip
Cleaver, Ralph
Crowther, T.S.C.
Deykin, Henry
Goldschmidt, Anthony
Grineau, Bryan de
Hunt, William Morris
Jalland, George Herbert
Pegram, Frederick
Sykes, Aubrey F.
Tyson, Kathleen

HORSE RACING - FLAT

Adam, Benno
Adam, Emil
Adam, Victor
Adrion, Lucien
Aldin, Cecil
Alexander, Carolyn
Alken, George
Alken, Henry
Alken, Samuel
Alonso, Anthony
Amiel, Louis
Anderton, S.J.
Anscombe, R.
Ansell, Charles
Appleyard, Joseph
Armour, George
Armstead, Henry Hugh
Arnold, George
Arnull, George
Arsenius, Karl

Ashley, Frank
Astley, P.H.
Atkinson, John
Audy, Jonny
Bacon, H.L.
Bailey, George
Baker, Frances
Barenger, James
Barker, Benjamin
Barker, T.
Barker, Thomas Jones
Barlow, Francis
Barratt, Thomas
Barry, James
Batsford, Brian
Bauer, Carl
Bawden, Edward
Beach, Thomas
Beatty, J. Lucas
Beauvais, Walter
Beer, John
Beer, W. Andrew
Begg, Samuel
Ben, I.
Béraud, Jean
Berrie, John
Best, John
Best, Thomas
Biegel, Peter
Bihan, Peter Le
Bindley, Charles
Bird, John Harrington
Bodger, John
Bombled, Louis
Bone, David
Bonnard, Pierre
Bott, R.T.
Boudin, Eugène
Boult, Francis
Boultbee, John, Snr.
Boyne, John
Brandt, William
Bressin, J.
Bretland, Thomas
Bright, Alfred
Bright, Harry
Bright, J. (op.1883-1920)
Brittan, Charles
Broadhead, W. Smithson
Brocas, William
Brooke, C.
Brown, Elmore J.
Brown, K.C.
Brown, Paul
Brown, William
Browne, Ethel C. Robertson
Browne Blair, Nassau
Bruce, Matt
Bryan, Alfred
Bryan, John
Bryant, Alice
Buchanan, P.R.G.
Bulmer, Thomas
Bunbury, Henry William
Burford, Thomas
Burney, Edward
Burton, Claire Eva
Busson, Georges
Butler, Thomas
Butterworth, Ninetta
Byles, William
Cadell, Francis
Cameron, Mary
Campion, George Bryant
Cantelo, C.
Carr, Tom
Cattermole, Leonardo
Catton, Charles, Jnr.
Cawthorne, Neil
Cemansky
Chalon, Henry Barnard
Chamberlain, William
Charles-Jones, Alexander
Chepik, Sergei
Church, C.
Clark(e), Frederick Albert
Clifford, H.J.
Clostermann, Johann
Clowes, Daniel
Clowes, Henry, Snr.
Clowes, J.
Coates, Michael
Coleman, Roger
Collie, George
Collinson, James
Compard, Emile
Conor, William
Cooper, Alfred Egerton
Cooper, Edwin

Cornish, John
Cotlison, V.J.
Cottrell, Henry S.
Couper, George
Craig, David (b.1948)
Craig, Henry Robertson
Crane, R.
Crane, William H.
Craven, Edward
Crawford, Susan
Crook, P.J.
Crooke, Muriel
Croome, C.J.
Cross, Henry
Cullin, Isaac
Cumberland, George
Cundall, Charles
Curling, Peter
Cutler, Cecil
Dalby, John
Dallison, Ken
Dalton, H.
D'Arcy, Roger
Darley, Matthew
Davies, C.W.
Davis, Heather
Davis, Henry T.
De Crespigny, Cerise (see Boyle)
Degas, Edgar
Deighan, Peter
Delamarre, Henri
Deming, Edwin
Demoline, A.
Denew, Richard
De Prades, Alfred
De Prades, Antonio
Desfontaines, Jacques
Desvignes, Herbert
De Swertschkoff, Georges
de von Blaas, Julius
Dickinson, Lowes Cato
Dighton, Joshua
Dill, Otto
Dobell, William
Dore, Paul
Douglas, Keith Sholto
Doutreleau, Pierre
Doveton, J.F.
Doyle, Charles
Doyle, John
Draper, George
Drewell, Robert
Drummond, Arthur
Dubost, Antoine
Duer, Douglas
Dufy, Jean
Dufy, Raoul
Dupont, Richard
Duppa, Bryan Edward
Duval, John
Earl, Thomas
Earl, Thomas Percy
Earp, George
Edwards, James
Edwards, Lionel
Eerelman, Otto
Egerton, M.
Elim, Frederick (Frank)
Ellis, J.H.
Ellis, Lionel
Ellison, Alan
Elwell, Francis
Emery, James
Eurich, Richard
Evans, John A.
Ewbank, P.
Farley, William
Farmer, J.
Faulkner, Charles
Fenn, George
Fernandez, H.
Finney, Harry
Fisher, Alvan
Fitzgerald, John Anster
Flatman, J.
Fonesca, John Joseph
Forain, Jean Louis
Forrest, William S.
Foster, Myles Birket
Fox, Edwin
Fox, George
Fraser, Eric
Fried, Pal
Frith, William Powell
Fuchs, Bernard (Bernie)
Furness, Robin
Gabriel, C. Wallis

"Gaf"
Gall, François
Gardner, Edwin C.
Garrard, George
Garraway, Edward
Gear, Joseph
Gentle, C.
Gerusez, Victor
Gibbons, Ruth
Gibson, Vincent
Gilbert, Edward
Gilbert, Joseph
Giles, Godfrey
Gilfillan, Tom
Gilroy, John
Goff, Frederick
Golden, Grace
Gooch Thomas
Goodall, John Strickland
Grant, John
Grayme
Green, Charles
Green, Henry
Griffiths, C.J.
Griggs, Frank
Guillonet, Octave
Guinard, Gaston
Guys, Constantin
Gwynn, William
Haddelsey, Vincent
Haigh, Arthur
Hailey, Clarence
Hall, Harry
Hamilton-Renwick, Lionel
Hammond, Arthur Knighton
Hancock, Charles
Hanfstaengl, Franz
Hardy, Dorothy M.
Hardy, Dudley
Hardy, James
Harper, H.G.
Harris, H.
Harrison, Christopher
Harvey, R.L.
Harvey, William
Hatherell, William
Havell, Alfred Charles
Hawkin, S.
Hayes, John
Hazlehurst, H.
Hedges, W.S.
Henderson, Fred
Henning, Archibald Samuel
Henwood, Thomas
Hepper, G.
Hepper, W.J.
Hepple, Wilson
Hepworth, Charles Hayden
Herring, Benjamin, Jnr.
Herring, John Frederick, Snr.
Hester, Edward Gilbert
Hill, F.L.
Hilton, T.
Hixon, R.
Holiday, Charles Gilbert
Holland, John
Holyoake, Rowland
Holyoake, William
Hopkins, William H.
Horwood, Charles
Howard, Frank
Howe, James
Howell, Peter
Hunt, Charles
Hunt, Edwin Henry
Hunt, William Henry
Hutchison William Oliphant
Hyland, Benedict
Irving, William
Isom, Graham
Jacobs, John Emmanuel
Jalland, George Herbert
Jenkins, Arthur Henry
Jennings, Chris
Johnson, J.J.
Jonas, John
Jones, Adrian
Jones, H.F.
Jones, Louie Johnson
Joy, Thomas Musgrove
Kenrick, G.W.
Killingbeck, Benjamin
Kinahan, Coralie
Kingwell, Mabel Amber
Kinnear, James S.
Kirtley, Dennis C.
Knight, Laura
Knight, S.S.

Koehler, Henry
Lacroix, Tristan
La Fontaine, Thomas Sherwood
Lami, Eugène Louis
Lane, Theodore
Laporte, George Henry
Lavery, John
Leftwich, George Robert
Lens, Peter Paul
Le Roy, F.
Lewis, Frederick Christian
Lock(e), William
Loder, James, of Bath
Longe, William Verner
Lowry, Laurence Stephen
Luard, Lowes Dalbiac
Lucas Lucas, William
Lutyens, Charles Augustus Henry
Lyne, Charles Edward Michael
Lyttleton, Thomas Hamilton
Macbeth-Raeburn, Marjorie May
Maccabe, Gladys
McCowan, W.
McKivragen, Terence
Macleod, John
Malespina, Louis Ferdinand
Manet, Edouard
Manning, F.
Marchand, André
Marchetti, Ludovico
Markham, C.
Marsden, William
Marshall, Benjamin
Marshall, Charles
Marshall, Lambert
Marson, Thomas E.
Martin, Anson
Mason, George Finch
Mason, William
Matthews, John Chester
Maurer, Louis
Maze, Paul
Meacham, Phyllida
Menasco, Milton
Merry, Tom
Mew, Thomas Hillier
Meyer, F. John
Midworth, R.
Millais, John Everett
Millais, Raoul H.
Miller, Alfred
Miller, John (Jack) Lawrence
Miller, Roy
Money, Keith
Moore, Fay
Moore, I. (J.)
Morgan, William
Morier, David
Morris, L. John
Mortimer, Alex
Mott, J.
Muller, Johann Sebastian
Munnings, Alfred J.
Murray, Thomas
Mynors, Stella
Nash, G.R.
Nedham (Needham), William
Neiman, Leroy
Nevinson, Christopher
Newton, Algernon
Newton, C.F.
Newton, I. or J.
Nicholson, Thomas
Nightingale, Basil
Nightingale, Robert
Nixon, John
Nixon, Kathleen ("Kay")
Noble, Charles F.
Noble, Edwin John
Nodder, Richard
Norton, Benjamin
Noyes, Robert
Oldmeadow, F.A.
Osborne, Walter
Osswald, Eugene
Ouless, Philip
Overend, William
Palmer, James Lynwood
Palmer, W.
Parkes, Joanna
Parrott, William
Pascoe, William E.W.
Paterson, Mary Viola
Pearson, J.
Pechaubes, Eugène

Pemberton, Richard
Perrin, William F.
Perry, G.
Picasso, Pablo
Pitman, John
Poole, Samuel
Powell, R.
Preston, M.
Pringle, J.B.
Pringle, William J.
Prinsep, Valentine
Pybourne, Thomas
Quigley, Daniel
Quintin, H.J.
Ramos, Adrian (Tod)
Rasmussen, Peter
Record
Redworth, William
Reeves, Richard Stone
Reichmann, Franz
Remington Frederic
Renwick, Lionel Hamilton
Richter, Wilhelm
Ridley, Matthew
Roberts, F.
Roberts, Henry
Roberts, William Patrick
Robson, J.W.
Robson, R.
Rogers, J(ohn), Snr.
Rook, J.
Roper, Richard
Ross, James, Snr.
Rowlandson, Thomas
Rowntree, Kenneth
Sandby, Paul
Sandys-Lumsdaine, Leesa
Sartorius, Francis
Sartorius, John Francis
Sartorius, John Nost (Nott)
Sawrey, Hugh
Scanlan, Richard Robert
Schermer, Cornelis Albertus J.
Schwanfelder, Charles Henry
Scott, Thomas Jefferson
Scruton, J.
Seago, Edward Brian
Sealy, Allen Culpeper
Sebright, George
Selfe, Madelaine
Sextie, William A.
Seymour, James
Shaw, James
Shaw, William
Shayer, Charles Waller
Shepperson, Claude Allin
Shuttleworth, Arnold Clarke
Sickert, Walter Richard
Simpson, Charles Walter
Sinclair, John
Singleton, John
Skeaping, John Rattenbury
Smith, Gean
Smith, Graham
Smith Phil(ip) W.
Smith, Thomas (of Derby)
Snow, John Wray
Spalding, Charles B.
Spence, Percy Frederick Seaton
Spencer, Thomas
Spicer, Charles
Spode, Samuel
Stainforth, Martin
Standish, W.
Stanton, Richard
Stubbs, George
Stubbs, George Townley
Stubbs, Richard Spencer
Stull, Henry
Sturgess, John
Sutton, Jake
Sverchkoff, N.G.
Swebach, Bernard Edouard
Sykes, Charles ("Rilette")
Sympson (Simpson), Joseph I.
Tanner, C. (of Dublin)
Tappen(den), (G.)
Tasker, William H. (of Chester)
Tattersall, George ("Wildrake")
Taubert, Bertoldo
Taylor, Charles
Temple, J.
Temple, T.
Terrot, Susan
Thackeray, T.

Thompson, Algernon, Alfred Cankerien
Tillemans, Peter
Tinkler, W.A.
Tolley, Nicholas
Tomson, Clifton (of Nottingham)
Toulouse-Lautrec, Henri
Townshend, Arthur Louis
Trendall, Edward W.
Troye, Edward de
Truman, I.P.
Truman, J.
Tulloch, Maurice
Turner, Charles
Turner, Francis Calcraft
Turner, George Archibald
Turner, J.
Turner, W.H.M. (Horse Fair)
Valkers, Karl
Van Dongen, Kees
Veal, George
Vial de Saint Bel, M.
Villon, Jacques
Vine, John (of Colchester)
Voss, Franklin Brooke
Waller, Barbara
Walsh(e), Thomas N.H.
Walter, Henry G.
Wanklyn, Joan
Ward, James
Ward, Louis Arthur
Ward, Rowland
Ward, Vernon
Weaver, Thomas (of Shropshire)
Webb, William (of Tamworth)
Webster, Tom
Weigall, Henry, Jnr.
Weimar, H.W.S.
West, Waldron
Whaite, T.
Wheeler, Alfred (Jnr.)
Wheeler, Amelia
Whessell, John
Whitcombe, Susie
Whiteside, Brian
Whiting, Frederick (Fred)
Widdas, Robert Dodd
Wigand, Balthazar
Wightman, Thomas
Williams, James T.
Williams, Walter Heath
Willoughby, William
Wilson, Alexander (op.1803-1846)
Wilson, Cecil
Wilson, Thomas Walter
Withers, A.H.J.
Wollen, William Barnes
Wolstenholme, (Charles) Dean, Jnr.
Wombill(e), Sydney R.
Woodhouse, Frederick W., Snr.
Woodhouse, Frederick, Jnr.
Woog, J.
Wootton, Frank
Wootton, John
Worth, Leslie
Wright, Gilbert Scott
Wright, John Masey
Wright, T.
Yarwood, Henry
Yeats, Jack Butler
Zaefferer, Adrianna
Zampogna, Dino
Zeeman, Rudolph
Zellenberg, Franz Zeller Von
Ziegler, Henry Bryan
Zimmerman, Theodore Franz

HORSE TRIALS See **SHOWJUMPING/HORSE TRIALS**

HUNTING See **BIG GAME HUNTING, FOX/STAG/BOAR-HUNTING, OTTER HUNTING**

HURDLING

Clark, John Cosmo

HURLING

Deighan, Peter

ICE SKATING/ICE HOCKEY

Aldin, Cecil
Atkinson, John Augustus
Baldry, G.W.
Barclay, John Rankine
Boughton, George
Bramatti, G.
Browne, Thomas
"CJG"
Clark, John Cosmo
Colville, Alex
Dadd, Frank
Darwin, Robin
Diggelmann, Alex
Foster, Myles Birket
Gay, Edward
Geddes, Andrew
Goldschmidt, Anthony
Goodall, John Strickland
Greenup, Joseph
Gregory, Edward
Grund, Norbert
Hamer, J.
Heathcote, John Moyer
Ibbetson, Julius Caesar
Kirchner, Ernest Ludwig
Ludovici, Albert, Jnr.
Maccabe, Gladys
Melville, Arthur
Montague, Alfred
Morland, George
Ogram, H.W.R.
Pearson, Kathleen
Rainey, William H.
Renoir, Pierre
Robinson, Ken
Robinson, William Howard
Shakespeare, Percy
Somers, C. Bettina
Soper, George
Stuart, Gilbert
Sulimo-Samuillo, Vsevolod Angelovitch
Taylor, C.J.
Tschudi, Lill
Tissot, James Jacques Joseph
Ugo, C. Favretti
Van der Neer, Aert
Van de Velde, Esaias
Van Verstaen, Antoni
Webb, Byron
Wedderburn, Jemima
Zinkeisen, Doris Clare

JOUSTING

Cook, Joshua
Ludovici, Albert, Jnr.
Topham, Francis (Frank) William

LACROSSE

Belon, J.
Catlin, George
Copley, John
Deas, Charles
Grineau, Bryan de
Soper, George

LAWN BOWLS/BOULES

Bennett, Frank Moss
Blood, Gerry
Chapman, John Watkins
Clements, James
Cox, Frank E.
Dadd, Frank
Deykin, Henry
Dingley, Humphrey J.
Elgood, George
Fenton, Samuel
Ferneley, Sarah
Focardi, Ruggero
Fry, Roger
Gordon, ("Jan") Godfrey Jervis
Harvey, George
Hopkins, Arthur
Jonas, John
Kent, William
Koehler, Henry
Laloin, Cecil
Lucas, John Seymour
Meissonier, John Louis

Orr, Jack
Ostade, Adriaen Van
Raverat, Gwendolen
Rooker, Michael Angelo
Rossiter, Charles
Rousse, Charles
Sadler, Walter Dendy
Siberechts, Jan
Sperling, Diana
Unsworth, Peter
Van Valkenborch, Lucas
Venables, Bernard
Wallis, Henry
West, Douglas
Wilkinson, Gilbert

LAWN/HARD COURT TENNIS

Aldin, Cecil
Ambrose, Charles
Bellows, George
Boin, Rene
Bolton D.C.
Brewtnall, Edward
Bridgman, Frederick
Broders, Roger
Brook, David
Broomfield, Frances
Butterfield, Sarah
Cleaver, Dudley
Copley, John
Cosomati, Aldo
Coulidge, Rosamund
Davies, Marion
Davis, Joseph Lucien
Deykin, Henry
Dowd, James H.
Flouest
Forbes, Elizabeth
Gardner, H.
Gere, Charles March
Ghilchick, David
Gill, Arthur Eric
Graham, Madge
Gray, Douglas Stannus
Grierson, Charles
Griesedieck, Ellen
Grineau, Bryan de
Guthrie, James
Harmar, Fairlie
Hayllar, Edith
Hayllar, Mary
Herman, Josef
Holiday, Charles Gilbert
Holloway, W.H.
Isenberg, H.
Jagger, David
Jungnickel, Ludwig Heinrich
Khnopff, Fernand
Kirchner, Ernest Ludwig
Koerner, Henry
Lanyon, Ellen
Laserstein, Lotte
La Thangue, Henry Herbert
Lavery, John
Leslie, George Dunlop
Mackenzie, James
Mays, Douglas
Melville, Arthur
Miles, George
Moberl(e)y, Mariquita
Mote, George
Nash, Arthur
Neogrady, Antal
Nicholson, Richard E.
Paton, W. Hubert
Patterson, Tom
Peirson, Louis V.
Purvis, Tom
Pyne, Charles
Rackham, Arthur
Ravilious, Eric
Reed, Kenneth
Ribera, Pierre
Richards, Frank
Righi, M.
Rossi, Alexander M.
Schultz, Hermann
Shelton, Sidney
Simpson, Tom
Spahn, Victor
Staples, Robert Ponsonby
Stinton-Wolonts, M.
Taylor, Rosemary
Tielmann, George
Tomlinson, Maud
Toynbee, Lawrence
Vermeylen, Alphonse

Vinall, Joseph William Topham
Wain, Louis William
Watherston, Marjorie Violet
Watkiss, Christopher
White, Sydney Watts
Wilson, Leslie
Zinkeisen, Anna Katrina

MOTOR/BIKE/KART RACING

Appleyard, Frederick
Appleyard, John
Bergandi, Hector
Brockbank, Russell P.
Brown, Dexter
Bryan, John A.
Bull, Rene
Burnham, Patrick
Carter, Frank William
Corson, Richard
Crosby, Frederick
Cuneo, Terence
Dafter, William
Dallinson, Ken
Davies, Roland
Davis, S.C.H.
De Grineau, Bryan
Demand, Carlo
Eliott, Harry
Faivre, Jules Abel
Fearnley, Alan
Ford, Ernest L.
Giles, Norman
Gotschke, Walter
Gravet
Griesedieck, Ellen
Grineau, Bryan de
Hamel, Georges
Harrison, Frederick
Hassall, John
Havinden, Ashley
Helck, Peter
Johnstone, A. David
Lane, George
Liedeaux, Michael ("Mich")
Lipscombe, Guy
Livemont, Privat
May, Phil
Millière, Maurice
Million-Guiet
Montaut, Ernest Edouard
Morton, E.
Moser, H.J.
Moser, R.J.
Motta, William
Mouron, Adolphe
Murray, Robert (Bob)
Nevin ("Nevinsky") Patrick
Nizzoli, Marcello
Nockolds, Roy
Payne, C.N.
Pears, Dion
"Philemon"
Priest, Alfred (1874-1929)
Ramel, Jacques
Richardson, R.
Rodgers, Peter
Roussillon, Maurice ("O'Galop")
Ruprecht, Ernst
"Salloon"
Scianna, Francesco
Shepherd, Rupert
Smith, Anthony (Tony)
Stark, J.G.
Strenger, Erich
Thor, Walter
Toulouse-Lautrec, Henri
Travis, Stuart
Turner, Graham
Turner, Michael
Vincent, René
Walker
Watson, Michael A.
Watts, Nicholas
Wheatland, Richard
Whistler, Rex
Wootton, Frank
Wright, Michael
Yates, Harold
Zeeman, Rudolph

MOUNTAINEERING

Whymper, Edward J.

NATIONAL HUNT

Alderson, D.M. & E.M.

Aldin, Cecil
Alexander, Lady
Alken, Henry
Anquetin, Louis
Armstead, Henry Hugh
Attwood, Thomas
Bailey, Wilfred
Benstead, Joseph
Biegel, Peter
Blunt, Charles
Bough, Samuel
Broadhead, W. Smithson
Brown, Paul
Cantelo, C.
Collinson, James
Collyer, Margaret
Craig, James
Cullin, Isaac
Davey, Randall
Dent, Adrian
Dent, David
Denton, Charles
Dighton, Joshua
d'Orsay, Alfred
Earl, Percy
Earle, T.A.
Earp, George
Edwards, Lionel
Eliot, Granville
Fairlie, Henry
Farley, William
Fernandez, H.
Frenzeny, Paul
Hamilton, Letitia
Harland, J.S.
Harrington, Robert
Hayes, S.H.B.
Herberte, Edward Benjamin
Howitt, Samuel
Hubbard, Bennet
Humphries, Alan
Jacobs, John Emmanuel
Jank, Angelo
Jennings, Chris
Jones, George Smetham
Jones, Herbert St. John
Josi, Charles
Keith, A.W.
King, John Gregory
Kingwell, Mabel Amber
La Fontaine, Thomas Sherwood
Laporte, George Henry
Lewis, Frederick
Longe, William Verner
Luker, William, Jnr.
Lyne, Charles Edward Michael
Lyttleton, Thomas Hamilton
McGoran, Kieran
MacKinnon, A.
Macpherson, Douglas
Marshall, John
Mason, George Finch
Meade-King, Eric
Mears, M.
Meggeson (Miggeson), J.J.
Merry, Tom
Mew, Thomas Hillier
Mitchell, J.A.
Money, Keith
Morrell, R.J.
Neville, A.W.
Oldfield, John
Oldmeadow, F.A.
Orme, Ernest
Orpen, William
Paice, George
Parkes, Joanna
Payne, Charles ("Snaffles")
Quintin, H.J.
Ramos, Adrian (Tod)
Remington, Frederic
Reville, Henry Whittaker
Riley, J.W.
Roberts, F.
Robertson, C.H.
Roche, Christopher
Rowlandson, George Derville
Sanderson-Wells, John
Sandys-Lumsdaine, Leesa
Sawrey, Hugh
Scanlan, Richard Robert
Seago, Edward Brian
Shepherd, Rupert
Smetham-Jones, George W.
Smith, Graham
Sparrow, Geoffrey
Standing, Henry William

Steinacker, Alfred
Sturgess, John
Sutton, Jake
Templar, C.
Temple, Richard
Turner, Francis Calcraft
Venat, Victor
Voss, C.J.
Walker, Frederick
Walmesley, J.M.
Walton, Frank
Webster, Colin
Wheelwright, Rowland
Widdas, Robert Dodd
Wiffen, Alfred Kemp
Woog, J.
Zimmerman, Theodore Franz

OLYMPIC SPORTS

Adrion, Lucien
Andrews, Sybil
Batiss, Walter
Bennett, Frank Moss
Blood, Gerry
Erni, Hans
Hiscock, David
Moss, Donald
Plachte, Erna
Whitney, Kevin

OTTER HUNTING

Alken, Samuel
Alstrop, E.
Armfield, George
Audubon, John
Bentley, Nicolas
Bough, Samuel
Bradley, Basil
Brittan, Charles
Dav(e)y, A.M.
Davis, Arthur
Dudley, Charles
Emms, John
Fitch, Fred
Foster, Walter H.W.
Gibb(s), T.H.
Goddard, George
Good(e), W.E.
Graeme, Colin
Hair, Thomas
Hall, Henry
Hepper, G.
Hogley, Stephen E.
Howitt, Samuel
Hunt, Walter
Keel, Thomas
Landseer, Edwin Henry
Morris, John W.
Noble, John Sargent
Pettitt, Charles
Robertson, C.H.
Roche, Christopher
Roe, Robert Henry
Steell, David George
Stokes, George Vernon
Strutt, Alfred William
Tunnard, John Charles
Valentine, John
Wardle, Arthur
Widgery, William

PIG STICKING

Bird, John Harrington
Carpenter, Percy
Fotheringham, J.F.
Giles, Godfrey
Tulloch, Maurice

POLO

Armour, George
Barker, Wright
Barry, M.
Blampied, Edmund
Board, John
Borein, Edward
Brooks, Henry Jamyn
Brown, Cecil
Brown, Paul
Cattley, George A.
Cawthorne, Neil
Charles-Jones, Alexander
Copley, John
Couper, George
Coverley-Price, Victor
Craig, David (b.1948)
Crawhall, Joseph E.

Cucuel, Edward
Cuneo, Terence
Dadd, Frank
Dadd, Stephen
De la Bere, Stephen
Deykin, Henry
Dickinson, H.B.
Dill, Otto
Dubaut, Pierre
Earl, George
Edwards, Lionel
Farrow, Will
Fraser, H.
Gallindo, R.E.
Gilbert, Terence
Giles, Godfrey
Girardot, Ernest
Gribble, Paul
Griffiths, P.
Haddelsey, Vincent
Hamilton, Letitia
Handley, V.F.
Hanfstaengl, Franz
Haseltine, Herbert
Heathcote, E.S.
Heseltine, Michael
Holiday, Charles Gilbert
Isom, Graham
Jalland, George Herbert
Jeanniot, Pierre-Georges
Jones, John
Kilburne, George Goodwin, Jnr.
King, John Gregory
Koch, Ludwig
Koehler, Henry
Lacroix, Tristan
La Fontaine, Thomas Sherwood
Liebermann, Max
Longueville, E.
Lucas Lucas, Henry Frederick
Luyt (Luyt), Aria Martinus "M.R."
McNeill, Angus
Martin, J. Edward
Meacham, Phyllida
Meade-King, Eric
Miller, John (Jack) Lawrence
Morshead, Arminell
Mortlemans, Edward
Mynors, Stella
Needham, Valerie
Oakley, Harold
Oldfield, John
Paice, George
Payne, Charles ("Snaffles")
Pechaubes, Eugène
Petty, William
Ponsonby, William
Prescott, Claude B.
Preston, Cloe
Roche, Christopher
Rowlandson, George Derville
Salkin, Emile
Scott, Septimus Edwin
Simpson, Charles Walter
Soper, George
Thorne, Diana
Voss, Franklin Brooke
Walenn, Gilbert
Wanklyn, Joan
Whitcombe, Susie
Wollen, William Barnes
Woodhouse, William
Woodville, Richard Caton
Wright, George
Wright, Gilbert Scott

POWER BOAT RACING

Horn, George

QUOITS

Blair, Andrew
Dighton, Robert
Jackson, Frederick William

RACING PIGEONS

Beer, W. Andrew
Browne, J.
Crehays, G.
Fraiture, Joseph
Gribbin, O.
Griffiths, Alfred
Kennedy, Joseph
Ludlow, A.J.

Pigg, J.W.
Pilcher, L.
Ryder, J.T.
Shaw, Nevil
Wadsworth (Wordsworth), C.H.
Wilson, John
Wiltshire, S.
Windred, E.H.
Wolstenholme, (Charles) Dean, Jnr.

RACKETS

Lane, Theodore
Newton, C.M.

RATTING

Alken, Samuel Henry
Lane, Theodore
Mason, William (1809-1875)
Moseley, R.S.
Sillem, Charles
Whitehead, John

REAL TENNIS

Bancroft, Shelley
Boilly, Louis
Clark, Jean
Couder, Louis
David, Jacques Louis
Grainger, James
Griffin-Bernstorff, Ann
Hobson, Anthony
Ludlow, Henry Stephen
Merian, Matthaus
Mortimer, John Hamilton
Shepherd, Thomas Hosmer
Stella, Jacques de
Taylor, Liz
Vandyke, Peter
Van Gassel, Lucas

RIFLE SHOOTING

Bowyer, William
Godwin, Mary
Harris, George
Lorette, Thinot
MacKay, William Darling
Maclure, Andrew
Staples, Robert Ponsonby
Thomas, William Luson
Tissot, James Jacques Joseph

ROLLER SKATING

Baxter, William
Diggelmann, Alex
Fuller, Edmund
Pellegrini, Carlo

ROUNDERS

Lowry, Laurence Stephen

ROWING/REGATTA

Armstrong, John
Beer, John
Blaker, Hugh
Bone, David
Bonnemer, Thomas
Bridges, John
Brooks, Henry Jamyn
Brown, J.
Burney, Edward
Caffieri, Hector
Clark, John Cosmo
Cleaver, Ralph
Cleveley, Robert
Clint, Alfred
Coleridge, Francis
Cooke, Edward William
Cooper, Alfred Egerton
Craig-Wallace, Robert
Daniels, Alfred
Davidson, R.
de Breanski, Alfred
De la Montagne Cary, William
De Prades, Antonio
Drake-Brookshaw, P.
Dufy, Raoul
Eakins, Thomas
Everett, John
Fairclough, Wilfred
Field, Henry
Furniss, Harry
Gibbs, Percy William

Gilchrist, Joan
Giles, Godfrey
Goldsmith, Walter
Greaves, Walter
Green, Stephen
Greenham, Robert
Griffier, Robert
Gudin, Herminie
Gueldry, Ferdinand
Guillonet, Octave
Hansen, Hans
Hardy, Paul
Hassell, John
Havell, Robert, Snr.
Havell, Robert, Jnr.
Helleu, Paul Cesar
Hines, Theodore
Holland, John
Holyoake, William
Hook, James Clarke
Hopkins, Arthur
Howse, George
Jonas, John
Kerr, George Cochrane
King, Jeremy C.G.
Kline, Hibberd V.B.
Knell, William Adolphus
Lambert, E.F.
Lambert, J.F.
Lewis, J.
Ludovici, Albert, Jnr.
Luscombe, Henry Andrews
Macbeth, James
McKelvey, Frank
McKivragen, Terence
McTaggart, William
Manby, F.H.
Maze, Paul
Monk, William
Moore, Claude
Neville, Louis
Nevinson, Christopher
Paterson, Mary Viola
Parrott, William
Pembery, J.
Penfield, Edward
Phelps, Julia
Power, Cyril L.
Robertson, Tom
Robinson, Charles F.
Rowlandson, Thomas
Scott, John (1802-1885)
Serres, John Thomas
Shaw, John Byam Liston
Snyder, W.P.
Spooner, Arthur
Thirtle, John
Thomas, Robert Kent
Thomson, Alfred Reginald
Tissot, James Jacques Joseph
Toynbee, Lawrence
Turner, Daniel
Turner, William
Valentine-Daines, Sherree
Wadham, B.B.
Wardlow, Alexander Hamilton
Warner, Mark
Wasley, Frank
Westbrook, Elizabeth T.
Whessell, John
Wiggs, H.T. Brook
Williams, Howard
Wilson, John (op.1871)
Winter, Alexander T.
Winter, Canon
Wootton, Frank
Worsley, John

RUGBY FOOTBALL

Arnold, Jane
Barnard, George
Breeden, W.L.
Brooks, Henry Jamyn
Broomfield, Frances
Burgess, H.G.
Campbell, George
Carstairs, John
Clark, John Cosmo
Crowther-Smith, H.F.
De Maistre, Roy
Dodson, Tom
Eckersley, Tom
Emmerson, Percy
Foggie, David
Fryer, Wilfred
Gardner, Philip
Gotch, Bernard Cecil
Grant, Duncan

Green, Donald E.
Gribble, Paul
Harwood, Edward
Heelas, Maud Grant
Hemy, Thomas
Insall, Frank
Jouclard, Adrienne
Kelly, Victor
L'hote, André
Lombers, Eric
Mercer, Fletcher
Platt, John Edgar
Platt, John Gerald
Prater, Ernest
Pretty, Edward
Riley, Harold Francis
Rodway, Eric
Smith, Dan
Stampa, George Loraine
Stratton, Frederick
Thomas, William Luson
Toynbee, Lawrence
Tuke, Henry Scott
Unsworth, Peter
Valentine-Daines, Sherree
Williams, Ada
Wills, Richard Allin
Wollen, William Barnes
Wood, Starr

SAILING/YACHTING

Alexander, R.M.
Annison, Edward
Arnesby-Brown, John
Bagnall, R.H.
Bearman, P.J.
Beaton, F.V.
Beddows, Michael
Beechey, Richard
Bell, A.D.
Bennett, Godwin
Bischoff, C.
Bond, Arthur
Briscoe, Arthur
Brown, Hugh Boycott
Burnett, James
Burns, Milton
Carey, Joseph William
Clark, John Cosmo
Clark, William
Cobb, David
Condy, Nicholas
Congreve, Frances
Cozzens, Frederic
Craig-Wallace, Robert
Cumming, R.A. (R.H.) Neville
Dadd, Frank
Davis, William Steeple
Dawson, Frederick
Dawson, J. Montague
de Breanski, Alfred
Dews, John Steven
Dickinson, Lowes Cato
Dixon, Alec
Dixon, Charles Edward
Dobson, Frank
Dodd, Robert
Dowling, Tom B.
Downie, Patrick
Everett, John
Eyre, Edward
Fanner, Alice
Farington, Joseph
Fisher, Rowland
Fitzgerald, Frederick
Forrest, J. Haughton
Foster, Deryck
Fowles, Arthur Wellington
Gregory, George
Hardy, Thomas Bush
Heddon, R.
Helleu, Paul Cesar
Hemy, Charles Napier
Hopkins, Arthur
Jacobson, Antonio
Kendrick, Matthew
King, Cecil George Charles
Knell, William Adolphus
Knox, Wilfred
Knox, William
Lewsey, Tom
Luscombe, Henry Andrews
Mann, James Scrimgeour
Mason, Frank Henry
Melling, Henry
Millington, John
Moore, Barlow
Moore, Claude

Moore, Henry
Morrow, Noel
Muncaster, Claude
Newberry, Angela
O'Neil, William Sandison
Padday, Charles
Paterson, Mary Viola
Pears, Charles
Renard, Stephen
Ricketts, Charles Robert
Robertson, Tom
Robinson, Gregory
Rooke, Herbert Kerr
Rushton, Raymond
Scott, John (1802-1885)
Seago, Edward Brian
Serres, John Thomas
Shields, Henry
Sotheby-Pitcher, Neville
Stanfield, William Clarkson
Steer, Philip Wilson
Taylor, Joshua
Taylor, Robert
Tennant, C. Dudley
Thomas, Robert Kent
Thomas, Walter
Torgerson, William
Turner, Charles E.
Turner, Daniel
Turner, Joseph Mallord
    William
Van de Velde, Willem (The
    Elder)
Van de Velde, Willem (The
    Younger)
Waite, Robert Thorne
Watson, G.L.
Wilcox, Leslie Arthur
Wilkinson, Norman
Winter, Alexander T.
Witham, J.
Wood, Frank Warren
Wood, Peter MacDonagh
Wright, Joseph Franklin
Wyllie, Charles William
Wyllie, Harold
Wyllie, William Lionel

SHOOTING

Adams, W. Douglas
Ader, W.
Aikman, George
Aikman, William
Alexander, George
Alken, Samuel
Allingham, Charles
Allsop, William
Ansdell, Richard
Ansell, Charles
Ansted, William
Armfield, Edward
Armfield, George
Ashford, William
Austen, Alexander
Bacon, D'Arcy
Banner, Joseph
Barclay, James
Barenger, James
Barker, W. Bligh
Barry, Frederick
Bartlett, John
Bateman, G.
Bateman, James
Bates, David
Bayley, Chapman
Beaufort, C.
Ben, I.
Benham, Thomas
Bennett, S.
Benson, Frank Weston
Benson, J. (op.1870-1890)
Bertrand, Guillaume
Blackburne, E.R.
Bland, John
Boddington, Henry
Bonner, Albert E.
Boroughs, J.
Bough, Samuel
Boult, Augustus
Boultbee, John, Snr.
Breach, Edward
Bretland, Thomas
Briscoe, Arthur
Brooke, E. Adveno
Brown, Edward
Brown, G.
Brown, Nathaniel
Brown, Paul
Brown, Robert

Brown, William, Jnr.
Browne, Philip
Browne, Thomas
Bryant, Joshua
Buckley, John E.
Burgess, F.L.
Burras, T.
Burras, Thomas
Burrows, Robert
Burt, Charles
Burt, Revell N.
Buss, Robert William
Caldwell, Edmund G.
Califano, John
Cameron, Angus
Campione, S.
Carmichael, John Wilson
Carter, Samuel John
Casse, S.B.
Cattermole, George
Chalon, Henry Barnard
Chantrey, Francis
Chapman, Abel
Charles, James
Charles-Jones, Alexander
Childe, Elias
Childe, James
Cole, George
Coleman, Edward
Collet, John
Collins, Elizabeth
Cooper, Abraham
Cooper, Alexander
Cooper, Alfred W.
Copper, D.E.
Corbould, Alfred
Corbould, Aster
Couldery, Horatio
Cranch, John
Crowther, Henry
Crowther, John
Dadd, Frank
Dalby, Joshua
Dance, Nathaniel
Dawson, Henry
Deacon, Augustus
de Block, Eugène
de Bree, Anthony
Denning, Stephen Poyntz
De Prades, Alfred
Desportes, Alexandre
Devis, Arthur
De von Blaas, Eugene
De Wint, Peter
Dobson, Frank
Dobson, William
Douglas, Edwin
Douglas, William
Douglas, William Fettes
Doyle, Charles
Doyle, Richard
Drummond, Arthur
Drummond, James
Drummond, John Murray
Drummond, Norah Hardy
Dudley, Charles
Duke, Arthur
Duncan, Edward
Dunnington, Albert
Duval, John
Earl, George
Eichel, G.
Ellison, Thomas
Elmer, Stephen
Elmer, William
Elsley, Arthur
Emmerson, Henry
Fairless, Thomas
Farquharson, David
Farquharson, Joseph
Faulkner, John
Fellow(e)s, William M.
Ferneley, John, Snr.
Ferneley, Sarah
Fielding, Thales Henry
Finnemore, Joseph
Flint, Savile
Foster, Walter H.W.
Fox, George
Gainsborough, Thomas
Garden, William
Gaunt, John
Gay, Walter
Gear, Joseph
Gérome, Jean Léon
Gibson, William Alfred
Gifford, John
Gilbert, Arthur
Gilbert, Frederick

Gilbert, Josiah
Gilbert, W.J.
Giles, James William
Giles, John West
Gilpin, Sawrey
Glascott, S.
Gooch, Matilda
Gooch, Thomas
Graeme, Colin
Grant, Francis
Gravelot, Hubert
Grey, Charles
Halliday, J.
Hammond, Henry
Hammond, Robert
Hammond, William
    Oxendon
Hand, Thomas
Hanfstaengl, Franz
Harding, James Duffield
Hardman, Mrs. Thomas
Hardy, Heywood
Hardy, James, Snr.
Hardy, James, Jnr.
Hargitt, Edward
Harris, Albert
Haugh, George
Haughton, Moses, Snr.
Haughton, Moses, Jnr.
Havell, Robert, Jnr.
Hawker, Peter
Hawkins, Waterhouse
    Benjamin
Haydon, Benjamin
Hayllar, Edith
Hayter, George
Haytley, Richard
Heaphy, Thomas
Hearne, Thomas
Heath, Henry
Heath, William
Henley, H.W.
Henson, S.
Hincks, S.C.
Hodgkinson, Cecil Thomas
Hofland, Thomas
    Christopher
Hold, Abel
Hold, Thomas
Holt, Edward
Holt, Edwin Frederick
Hook, James Clarke
Hopkins, Arthur
Horlor, George
Hulk, John Frederick
Hunt, Lynn Bogue
Hunter, George Sherwood
Hutchinson, William Henry
Hysing, Hans
Ibbetson, Julius Caesar
Ince, Joseph Murray
Insall, Frank
Jackson, John
Jagger, Charles
Jalland, George Herbert
Jenkins, Thomas
Johnson, Avery F.
Johnson, T.B.
Jones, Herbert St. John
Jones, Martha (Mary) K.
Jones, Paul
Jones, Samuel John Egbert
Jones, William (1798-1860)
Josi, Charles
Joy, Thomas Musgrove
Joyner, J.
Keeling, E.J.
Killingbeck, Benjamin
Knight, John Baverstock
Knyff, Leonard
Lagos, Bruce (Bruck-Lajos)
Laidlay, William James
Lambert, George
Lambert, Joseph W.
Landseer, Charles
Landseer, Edwin Henry
Laporte, George Henry
Laurie, Robert
Leech, John
Lees, Caroline
Lewis, George Robert
Lewis, John Frederick
Lewis, Thomas
Lie, Jonas
Lloyd, Thomas James
Lloyd, W. Stuart
Lobley, Robert
Ludovici, Albert, Snr.
Luker, William, Snr.

Lyle, Thomas Byron
Lyon, John Howard
McPhail, Rodger
Madgwick, Clive
Maguire, J.
Malbon, William
March, M.R.
Marshall, Benjamin
Martin, Sylvester
May, S.A.
Mearns, A.
Mercier, Philip
Meyer, Louis
Millais, John Everett
Millais, John Guille
Millar, James
Milliken, Robert
Moore, Rubens Arthur
Morland, George
Morris, Alfred
Morris, James Charles
Morris, John
Morris, John W.
Morris, William Walker
Mote, George
Muller, J.
Murray, Sir David
Nash, Joseph
Neale, Edward
Newell, Hugh
Niemann, Edmund
Noble, John Sargent
Nockolds, Roy
Northcote, James
Norton, Benjamin
Nowell, Arthur
Orrock, James
Ought, William
Page, Henry
Park, Harry
Parker, Henry Perlee
Pasmore, John F.
Paterson, George M.
Paul, Peter
Pearson, Robert
Pell, Catherine M.
Perrett, S.
Phillips, Frank
Pollard, Robert
Poynter, Edward John
Price, Frank Corbyn
Price, William Lake
Rankin, George
Raven, Samuel
Rawling, Brian
Redgate, Arthur W.
Reed, George
Reinagle, Philip
Rhodes, F.R.
Richardson, H. Hughes
Richardson, Thomas Miles,
    Jnr.
Ripley, Aiden Lassell
Ripon, 2nd Marquess
Robinson, William A.
Roe, Clarence
Roe, Robert Henry
Rolfe, Alexander F.
Ross, James, Snr.
Rothwell, Thomas
Sandby, W.
Sartorius, John
Sartorius, John Francis
Sartorius, S.J.
Saville, W.
Shaw, William
Shayer, Charles Waller
Shayer, Henry Thring
Shayer, William Joseph
Shepard, Ernest Howard
Shepherd, William James
    Affleck
Shiels, William
Short, Arthur Anderson
Simson, William
Small, William
Smart, John
Smith, George (of
    Chichester)
Smith, George Armfield
Smith, Richard J
Smith, William
Smith, William A.
Snape, Martin
Southgate, Frank
Sowerby, John G.
Spalding, Charles B.
Spencer, John S.
Spring-Smith, Effie

Stannard, Henry John
    Sylvester
Stannard, Ivy
Steell, David George
Steell, Gourlay
Stevens, George
Straet, Jan van der
Stuart (Steuart), John James
Stubbs, George
Suhrlandt, Carl
Tayler, John Frederick
Taylor, Stephen
Taylor, W.
Terpning, Howard A.
Thomas, T.G.
Thorburn, Archibald
Thynne, A.
Tickner, John
Tillemans, Peter
Tonge, Robert
Townsend, J.R.
Tracy, John M.
Trappes, Francis M.
Trench, Philip Chevenix
Tucker, Edward
Tuitt (Tuite), F.J. or J.T.
Tulloch, Maurice
Turner, Francis Calcraft
Turner, George Archibald
Turner, Joseph Mallord
    William
Uchermann, Carl
Van Aken, Joseph
Van de Velde, Adriaen
Van der Myn (Mijn),
    Hermann
Van der Vaart, John
Van Uden, Lucas
Varley, Cornelius
Wainwright, John
Wallace, Harold Frank
Walton, Frank
Walton, Henry
Ward, Cyril H.
Ward, Martin Theodore
Ward, Vernon
Wardle, Arthur
Waterlow, Ernest Albert
Watkins Pitchford, Denys
    James
Watson, John Dawson
Watson, William, Jnr.
Watson, William Smellie
Weatherston, J.T.
Webb
Webb, Byron
Webb, George
Wedderburn, Jemima
Weedon, Augustus Walford
Weekes, Henry, Jnr.
Westall, T.
Wheatley, Francis
Whymper, Charles H.
Widgery, William
Wierusz-Kowalski, Alfred
    von
Wigger, Brian
Wildman, John R.
Williams, Edward Charles
Williams, James T.
Williams, Warren
Wilson, William
Winans, Walter
Wingate, James Lawton
Wissing, William (Willem)
Woodhouse, William
Worthington, A.
Wright, George
Yeats, Jack Butler
Young, Tobias
Zinkeisen, Doris Clare
Zoffany, Johann

**SHOWJUMPING/HORSE
TRIALS**

Barrington, E.Z.
Biegel, Peter
Burns, William
Duffield, Frank
Flowers, F.H.
Frost, Patricia
Garstin, Alethea
Hogarth, Arthur Paul
Holiday, Charles Gilbert
King, John Gregory
Laporte, George Henry
Methuen, Paul Ayshford
Meyer, Emile
Ricketts, Joy Stanley

Ritchie, Alec P.F.
Rose, Sheila
Simpson, Charles Walter
Wanklyn, Joan
Whitcombe, Susie
Zinkeisen, Doris Clare

SHUTTLECOCK/ BATTLEDORE

"A.T."
Alma Tadema, Laura
Bartlett, Charles
Bouvier, Joseph
Burr, Alexander
Cameron, David
Chardin, Jean Baptiste
Dandridge, Bartholomew
Davis, Louis
Drew, Mary
Forsberg, Nils
Hamilton, Hugh Douglas
Hardy, Frederick
Hardy, W.F.
Herdman, Robert
Hunter, Robert
Knapton, George
Lance, Eveline
Morgan, Fredrick (Fred)
Smith, Carlton Alfred
Sperling, Diana
Tielmann, George
Tomlinson, Maud
Vuillard, Edouard
White, Daniel Thomas

SKIING

Baumer, Lewis
Birch, Samuel
Bolton, D.C.
Burnham, Patrick
Guy, Robert
Hunt, Cecil Arthur
Jensen, Arthur
Luchishkin, Sergei Alexevitch
Marquet, Albert
Pearson, Kathleen
Pitchforth, Roland
Thomas, Francis Wynne
Ward, Vernon
West, Levon
Wright, Henry Charles
   Seppings ("Stuff")
Wyeth, Andrew
Zatzka, Hans

SKITTLES/NINEPINS/ BOWLING

Angellis, Pieter
Barker, Thomas
Baron, Henri

Bough, Samuel
Browning, Robert Barrett
Buckman, Edwin
Ceriez, Theodore
Craig, William Marshall
De Hooch, Pieter
De Momper, Frans
Ferneley, Sarah
Focardi, Ruggero
Gilchrist, Herbert H.
Hunter, George Sherwood
Hutchins, C.
Ingalton, William
Scott-Brown, William G.
Steen, Jan
Stern, Max
Ten Kate, Johann Marie
Teniers, David
Thornhill, James
Wilkie, David

SNOOKER See BILLIARDS/ SNOOKER

SPORTING PORTRAITS

Backshell, W.
Bacon, H.D.
Bailey, George
Beach, Thomas
Beechey, William
Birley, Oswald
Brompton, Richard
Buss, Robert William
Clark, John
Clennell, Luke
Cleyn, Francis
Closterman, Johann
Cole, George
Collier, John
Cornish, John
Co(u)zens, William
Crozier, Robert
Cuneo, Terence
Devis, Arthur
Dighton, Joshua
   (op.1820-1840)
Douglas, William
Douglas, William Fettes
Drummond, Jane
Dyer, Simon
Fawkes, Lionel
Glass, James William
Grant, Francis
Gravely, Percy
Haines, William
Hartley, Thomas C.
Haugh, George
Haughton, Moses, Snr.
Hayes, John
Henson, S.

Higgins, Charles S.
Highmore, Joseph
Hone, Nathaniel
Hudson, Thomas
Humphrey, Ozias
Hysing, Hans
Kneller, Godfrey
Knyff, Leonard
Lane, Samuel
Law, Ernest George
Lewis, Charles George
Orchardson, Charles
Orme, Ernest
Orpen, William
Palmer, James Lynwood
Pardon, James
Patch, Thomas
Pearce, Stephen
Pellegrini, Carlo
Penny, Edward
Philips, Charles
Pic, Marcel
Prosperi, Liberio ("Lib")
Ramsay, Allan
Reynolds, Joshua
Richmond, George
Riley, Harold Francis
Ritchie, Alec P.F.
Riviere, Hugh
Roods, Thomas
Roos, William
Ross, Thomas
Russell, John
Salisbury, Frank
Schwanfelder, Charles Henry
Shaw, James (op.1769-1784)
Ward, Leslie Matthew
Warhol, Andy
Weigall, Henry, Jnr.
Witherby, Arthur George
   ("Wag")
Wright, Henry Charles
   Seppings ("Stuff")

STALKING

Ansdell, Richard
Balfour-Browne, Vincent
Berkeley, Stanley
Bright, Henry
Cleminson, Robert
Duffield, William
Earl, George
Flanders, French
Frankland, Robert
Fuller, J.T.
Haag, Karl (Carl)
Hancock, Charles
Hincks, S.C.
Johnson, Charles Edward
Johnson, Sidney Yates
King, Thomas W.

Landseer, Charles
Landseer, Edwin Henry
Leech, John
Luker, William, Snr.
Millais, John Everett
Newton, Alfred
Pasmore, John F.
Rawling, Brian
Richardson, Thomas Miles,
   Jnr.
Roe, Clarence
Roe, Colin Graeme
Roe, Robert Henry
Scrope, William
Suhrlandt, Carl
T(h)ompson, Jacob C.
Wallace, Harold Frank
Wardle, Arthur
Webb, Byron
Winans, Walter

STILL LIFES

Chantry, N.
Dennis, William
Laporte, George Henry
Leemans, Johannes
Lees, Caroline
Lees, F.J.
Lovegrove, H.
Lydon, Alexander Francis
Lyle, James
Mulready, William
Nicholson, Francis
Shaw, W.R.B.

SWIMMING/WATER SPORTS

Batiss, Walter
Bunny, Rupert
Charlton, George
Conder, Charles
Hagedorn, Karl
Morland, George
Newberry, Angela
Roberts, William Patrick
Small, William
Whitney, Kevin
Yeats, Jack Butler

TENT PEGGING

Jacomb-Hood, George Percy
Leigh, William

TROTTING

Barenger, James
Beltyukov, Boris
Clark(e), Frederick Albert
Cottrell, Henry S.
Cross, Henry

Fellows, William Dorset
Fremond, C.R.
Hillman, R.S.
Hind, R.N.
Jones, Richard
Leighton, Nicolas Winfield S.
McAuliffe, James J.
Malespina, Louis Ferdinand
Maurer, Louis
Miles, John
Newton, C.F.
Pechaubes, Eugène
Pernel, Jean
Pybourne, Thomas
Roberts, James
   (op.1858-1876)
Sherlock, A. Marjorie
Smith, Gean
Todd, Robert Clow
Van Vleit, K.
Von Blaas, Julius
Wolstenholme, (Charles)
   Dean, Jnr.
Wombill(e), Sydney R.
Worth, Thomas
Wright, James Henry
Yeats, Jack Butler

TUG OF WAR

Buckman, Edwin
Lintz, Ernst

WALKING/PEDESTRIAN RACES

Thomson, T. or J.

WILDFOWL

Dixon, Otto Murray
Morland, John

WRESTLING

Blake, Peter
Bomberg, David
Bourgain, Gustave
Buckman, Edwin
Cuming, Frederick
De Rose, Gerard
Forel, Eugène
Grant, Duncan
Howson, Peter
Johnson, Carl
La Nave, Francesca
Lindner, Daphne
Rabinovitch, Samuel (Sam
   Rabin)
Rowlandson, Thomas
Tepper, Saul
Vaughan, John Keith
Warner, John